THE ECONOMY TODAY

FIFTEENTH EDITION

McGraw Hill Education

The McGraw-Hill Series Economics

THE
ECONOMY TODAY

FIFTEENTH EDITION

Bradley R. Schiller

WITH KAREN GEBHARDT

McGraw Hill Education

THE ECONOMY TODAY, FIFTEENTH EDITION

Published by McGraw-Hill Education, 2 Penn Plaza, New York, NY 10121. Copyright © 2019 by McGraw-Hill Education. All rights reserved. Printed in the United States of America. Previous editions © 2016, 2013, and 2010. No part of this publication may be reproduced or distributed in any form or by any means, or stored in a database or retrieval system, without the prior written consent of McGraw-Hill Education, including, but not limited to, in any network or other electronic storage or transmission, or broadcast for distance learning.

Some ancillaries, including electronic and print components, may not be available to customers outside the United States.

This book is printed on acid-free paper.

1 2 3 4 5 6 7 8 9 LWI 21 20 19 18

ISBN   978-1-259-85202-2
MHID   1-259-85202-4

Senior Portfolio Manager: *Katie Hoenicke*
Lead Product Developer: *Kelly Delso*
Product Developer: *Adam Huenecke*
Core Content Project Manager: *Kathryn D. Wright*
Senior Assessment Content Project Manager: *Kristin Bradley*
Media Content Project Manager: *Karen Jozefowicz*
Senior Buyer: *Laura Fuller*
Senior Designer: *Matt Diamond*
Content Licensing Specialist: *Lorraine Buczek*
Cover Image: *©The-Lightwrighter/Getty Images RF*
Compositor: *Aptara®, Inc.*

All credits appearing on page or at the end of the book are considered to be an extension of the copyright page.

Library of Congress Cataloging-in-Publication Data

Names: Schiller, Bradley R., 1943- author. | Gebhardt, Karen, author.
  Title: The economy today / Bradley R. Schiller, American University Emeritus, with Karen Gebhardt,
    Colorado State University.
  Description: Fifteenth edition. | New York, NY : McGraw-Hill Education, [2019]
  Identifiers: LCCN 2017041610 | ISBN 9781259852022 (alk. paper) | ISBN 1259852024 (alk. paper)
  Subjects: LCSH: Economics.
  Classification: LCC HB171.5 .S292 2019 | DDC 330—dc23 LC record available at
    https://lccn.loc.gov/2017041610

The Internet addresses listed in the text were accurate at the time of publication. The inclusion of a website does not indicate an endorsement by the authors or McGraw-Hill Education, and McGraw-Hill Education does not guarantee the accuracy of the information presented at these sites.

Bradley R. Schiller has more than four decades of experience teaching introductory economics at American University, the University of Nevada, the University of California (Berkeley and Santa Cruz), and the University of Maryland. He has given guest lectures at more than 300 colleges ranging from Fresno, California, to Istanbul, Turkey. Dr. Schiller's unique contribution to teaching is his ability to relate basic principles to current socioeconomic problems, institutions, and public policy decisions. This perspective is evident throughout *The Economy Today.*

Dr. Schiller derives this policy focus from his extensive experience as a Washington consultant. He has been a consultant to most major federal agencies, many congressional committees, and political candidates. In addition, he has evaluated scores of government programs and helped design others. His studies of poverty, discrimination, training programs, tax reform, pensions, welfare, Social Security, and lifetime wage patterns have appeared in both professional journals and popular media. Dr. Schiller is also a frequent commentator on economic policy for television and radio, and his commentary has appeared in *The Wall Street Journal, The Washington Post, The New York Times,* and *Los Angeles Times,* among other major newspapers.

Dr. Schiller received his Ph.D. from Harvard and his B.A. degree, with great distinction, from the University of California (Berkeley). His current research focus is on Cuba—its post-revolution collapse and its post-Castro prospects. On his days off, Dr. Schiller is on the tennis courts, the ski slopes, or the crystal-blue waters of Lake Tahoe.

Courtesy of Bradley R. Schiller

Dr. Karen Gebhardt is a faculty member in the Department of Economics at Colorado State University (CSU). Dr. Gebhardt has a passion for teaching economics. She regularly instructs large, introductory courses in macro- and microeconomics; small honors sections of these core principles courses; and upper-division courses in pubic finance, microeconomics, and international trade, as well as a graduate course in teaching methods.

She is an early adopter of technology in the classroom and advocates strongly for it because she sees the difference it makes in student engagement and learning. Dr. Gebhardt has taught online consistently since 2005 and coordinates the online program within the Department of Economics at CSU.

Dr. Gebhardt was the recipient of the Water Pik Excellence in Education Award in 2006 and was awarded the CSU Best Teacher Award in 2015.

Dr. Gebhardt's research interests, publications, and presentations involve the economics of human–wildlife interaction and economics and online education. Before joining CSU, she worked as an economist at the U.S. Department of Agriculture/Animal and Plant Health Inspection Service/Wildlife Services/National Wildlife Research Center, conducting research on the interactions of humans and wildlife, such as the economic effects of vampire bat–transmitted rabies in Mexico, the potential economic damage from introduction of invasive species to the Islands of Hawaii, bioeconomic modeling of the impacts of wildlife-transmitted disease, and others. In her free time, Dr. Gebhardt enjoys learning about new teaching methods that integrate technology and going rock climbing and camping in the Colorado Rockies and beyond.

Courtesy of Karen Gebhardt

The election of Donald Trump not only transformed the political landscape, but also radically altered the economic policy agenda. Trade policy became a front-page story. So did tax cuts, deregulation, and immigration policy. Sure, these issues were always on the political agenda, but they took on a greater priority with the ascension of the Trump administration. These shifting priorities require us econ professors to adapt. Students are always more interested in economics when we relate our theories to the news of the day. That means that we've got to make room in our syllabi for these rejuvenated issues.

Fortunately, *The Economy Today* is exceptionally well suited for this task. From its inception, this text has been motivated by policy issues. The primary goal has been to help students understand the challenges of economic policy and the consequences of specific actions like tariffs, regulation, and tax reform. It has always provided a *balanced* discussion of these issues, allowing students to assess different perspectives on critical issues. For this edition, instructors will particularly appreciate the unique chapters that provide a solid foundation for explaining, illustrating, and assessing major Trump initiatives. Chapter 16, for example, is devoted to supply-side theory, a core foundation of Trumponomics. Students can explore the theoretical basis for tax cuts, deregulation, and immigration reform. Chapter 35 on international trade goes beyond the theory of comparative advantage to explain why and how some market participants seek to erect trade barriers. The unique chapter devoted to deregulation (Chapter 27) examines the rationale for government regulation of industry, the inherent trade-offs, and the consequences of (de)regulation. The same kind of insistence on critical thinking about policy issues is apparent in Chapter 28 on environmental protection.

Budget issues get attention in both macro and micro. In macro, Chapter 11 on fiscal policy examines both the efficacy of tax and spending tools, as well as the distributional issues that accompany all fiscal interventions. The subsequent Chapter 12 on deficits and debt not only reviews the history and sources of our $20-trillion national debt, but also carefully explains and illustrates the real costs of deficit financing. In micro, we have two companion chapters on taxes (Chapter 33) and transfer payments (Chapter 34). The intent of these parallel chapters is to illustrate the equity vs. efficiency trade-offs that are common to both sides of the public budget. It provides a solid foundation for discussing the distributional effects of the Trump tax cuts and proposed reductions in income transfers.

Another chapter that is uniquely suited to the experiences of the Trump administration is the macro capstone Chapter 18 on theory vs. reality. This chapter reviews competing macro theories, surveys our macro performance, then answers the question of why it's so hard to generate perfect economic outcomes. By now, the Trump administration is well acquainted with the data, goal-conflict, congressional deliberations, and political problems that delay and alter the implementation of major policy initiatives. But students will appreciate this final word on why the economy so often fails to live up to the theoretical expectations that we teach in class.

No other text offers comparable, chapter-length coverage of the policy issues that have taken on a new urgency with the Trump administration. This is not a text full of fables and other abstractions; it's a text loaded with real-world applications, including the policy agenda of the Trump administration (which is explained, illustrated, and assessed—but not championed). This text makes it a lot easier for students to see the relevancy of economic principles to the front-page issues that dominate the news and political debates. It also requires critical thinking about these same economic issues and the economic concepts that underlie them. No other text comes close to this policy-driven, real-world approach. Students respond with greater interest, motivation—and even retention. If our goal is to have students understand both core economic concepts and their relevancy to the world around them, this is the text to use.

A feature titled "The Economy Tomorrow" at the end of every chapter illustrates one of the ways core economic concepts are linked to policy issues. This feature challenges students to relate the concepts they have just learned to a real-world policy problem. In the very first chapter, for example, students are forced to consider how the newly introduced concept of opportunity costs alters perspectives on "harnessing the sun," such as building more solar-power infrastructure. In Chapter 3 students are challenged to consider the deadly consequences of prohibiting the use of the market mechanism to allocate human organs.

The emphasis on real-world policy challenges is not confined to The Economy Tomorrow feature. Every chapter has an array of In the News and World View boxes that offer real-world illustrations of basic economic principles. Israel's success with its "Iron Dome" antimissile defense is a great illustration of what economists call a "public good" (Chapter 4 World View "Israel's 'Iron Dome' Frustrates Hamas"). North Korea's latest missile tests are a timely illustration of the "guns vs. butter" trade-off (Chapter 1 World View "World's Largest Armies"). World View "Trading Chickens for Diapers" in Chapter 13 is a superb illustration of why money is so important to market performance. In the News "Californians Vote to Triple Cigarette Tax" in Chapter 20 on California's 2017 cigarette tax hike provides an opportunity to put the concept of price elasticity to work. You get the picture: this *is* the premier policy-driven, real-world focused introduction to economic principles.

DIFFERENTIATING FEATURES

The policy-driven focus of *The Economy Today* clearly differentiates it from other principles texts. Other texts may claim real-world content, but none comes close to the empirical perspectives of this text. Beyond this unique approach, *The Economy Today* offers a combination of features that no other text matches, including the following.

Macro Focus on Short-Run Cycles

Most principles texts moved away from the short-run business cycles to more emphasis on long-run macro dynamics about 10–15 years ago. Many authors even suggested the business cycle was dead. Now they know they missed the boat. The 2008–2009 Great Recession reminded everyone that the business cycle remains a central concern of both economic policy and economic theory. *The Economy Today* is one of the few texts that still puts greater emphasis on short-run cyclicality than on long-run stability.

One-Model Macro

Another pedagogical advantage of *The Economy Today* is its use of a single framework for teaching all macro perspectives. Other principles texts continue to present both the Keynesian cross framework and the aggregate demand/supply (AD/AS) framework. This two-model approach is neither necessary nor efficient. All of the core ideas of Keynesian theory, including the multiplier, can be illustrated in the AD/AS framework. Keynes never drew the "Keynesian" cross and would not use it today, especially in view of the superiority of the AD/AS model in conveying his ideas. And we all know that the Keynesian cross is of no use in illustrating the short-run trade-off between inflation and full employment that bedevils policymakers and even defines our concept of full employment. Why overburden students with a two-model approach that confuses them and eats scarce instruction time? Instructors who adopt this text's one-model approach are invariably impressed with how much more efficient and effective it is.

Markets versus Government Theme

We all know there is no such thing as a pure market-driven economy and that markets operate on the fringe even in the most centralized economics. So "markets versus government" is not an all-or-nothing proposition. It is still a central theme, however, in the real world as President Trump insisted. Should the government assume *more* responsibility for managing the economy—or will *less* intervention generate better macro and micro outcomes? Public opinion is clear: As the accompanying News reveals, the majority of Americans have a negative view of federal intervention. The challenge for economics instructors is to enunciate principles that help define the boundaries of public and private sector activity. When do we expect **market failure** to occur? How and why do we

market failure: An imperfection in the market mechanism that prevents optimal outcomes.

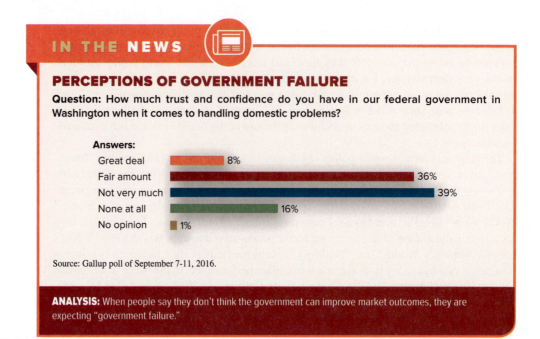

IN THE NEWS

PERCEPTIONS OF GOVERNMENT FAILURE

Question: How much trust and confidence do you have in our federal government in Washington when it comes to handling domestic problems?

Answers:

Great deal	8%
Fair amount	36%
Not very much	39%
None at all	16%
No opinion	1%

Source: Gallup poll of September 7-11, 2016.

ANALYSIS: When people say they don't think the government can improve market outcomes, they are expecting "government failure."

government failure:
Government intervention that fails to improve economic outcomes.

anticipate that government intervention might result in **government failure**? Can we get students to think critically about these central issues? *The Economy Today* certainly tries, aided by scores of real-world illustrations.

Unique Topic Coverage

The staples of introductory economics are fully covered in *The Economy Today*. Beyond the core chapters, however, there is always room for additional coverage. In fact, authors reveal their uniqueness in their choice of such chapters. Those choices tend to be more abstract in competing texts, offering "extra" chapters on public choice, behavioral economics, economics of information, uncertainty, and asymmetric information. All of these are interesting and important, but they entail opportunity costs that are particularly high at the principles level. The menu in *The Economy Today* is more tailored to the dimensions and issues of the world around us. Chapter 2, for example, depicts the dimensions of the U.S. economy in a comparative global framework. Where else are students going to learn that China is *not* the world's largest economy, that U.S. workers are the most productive, or that income inequality is more severe in poor nations than rich ones?

The same empirical foundation is apparent in the chapters on unemployment (6) and inflation (7). We economists take for granted that these are central macroeconomic problems. But students have little personal experience with either problem and even less appreciation of their significance. Chapters 6 and 7 try to bridge this gap by discussing *why* unemployment and inflation are such central concerns—that is, the kinds of socioeconomic harm they inflict. The intent here is to help students understand and embrace our economic goals before we ask them to explore potential solutions.

Chapter 18 on "Theory versus Reality" offers yet another unique perspective on macroeconomics. It confronts the perennial question students ask: "If economic theory is so great, why is the economy so messed up?" Chapter 18 answers this question by reviewing the goal conflicts, measurement problems, design issues, and implementation obstacles that constrain even the best macro policies.

The same emphasis on contemporary policy issues is evident throughout micro. The parallel chapters on taxes (33) and transfers (34) underscore the central conflict between equity and efficiency concerns that impedes easy solutions to important policy questions. The comparison of the Clinton and Pence tax returns in Chapter 33 enlivens the discussion of tax "loopholes."

The extensive coverage of market structure includes *two* chapters on competition. The first (22) presents the standard, static profit maximization model for the perfectly competitive firm. The second chapter (23) adds real-world excitement. Chapter 23 focuses on market dynamics, emphasizing how competitive *forces* alter both market structures and market outcomes. The core case study takes students from the original Apple I (see the photo in Chapter 23) all the way to the iPhone 7 and iWatch. Along the way, the effects of continuous entry, exit, and innovation are highlighted. Students come away with an enhanced appreciation of how competitive markets generate superior outcomes—one of the most important insights of the micro sequence.

Also noteworthy in the micro sequence is the chapter (27) on natural monopoly. We know that natural monopoly presents unique challenges for antitrust and regulatory policy. This chapter first assesses the goal conflicts that complicate government intervention, and then reviews regulatory history and outcomes in the rail, telephone, airline, and cable industries.

"Global perspective," along with "real-world" content, is promised by just about every principles author. *The Economy Today* actually delivers on that promise. This is manifestly evident in the titles of Chapter 2 (global comparisons) and Chapter 37 (global poverty). The global perspective is also easy to discern in the boxed World View features embedded in every chapter. More subtle, but at least as important, is the portrayal of an open economy from the get-go. While some texts start with a closed economy—or worse still, a closed, private economy—and then add international dimensions as an afterthought, *The Economy Today* depicts an open economy from start to finish. These global linkages are a vital part of any coherent explanation of both macro issues (e.g., cyclical instability, monetary control, trade policy) and micro issues (e.g., effective competition, oil prices).

Global Perspective

WHAT'S NEW AND UNIQUE IN THIS 15TH EDITION

Every edition of *The Economy Today* introduces a wealth of new content and pedagogy. This is critical for a text that prides itself on currency of policy issues, institutions, and empirical perspectives. Every page, every example, and all the data have been reviewed for currency and updated where needed. Beyond this general upgrade, this 15th edition offers the following.

Price determination is illustrated in Chapter 3 with NCAA ticket scalping, price cuts on Galaxy 7 phones, and the surge in gasoline prices in the wake of Hurricane Matthew. In macro, there are new CBO estimates of the procyclical state and local spending cut forced by the Great Recession (Chapter 11); the effect of tuition hikes on the inflation rate (Chapter 7); President Trump's hostility to outsourcing (Chapter 6); GAO estimates of the cost of federal regulations (Chapter 16); and Trump's budget proposals (Chapter 11). In micro, the record-breaking Snapchat IPO highlights the role of financial markets in reallocating resources (Chapter 32). Tesla's new "gigafactory" illustrates the advantages of economies of scale (Chapter 27). Those "bikini barristers" in Everett, Washington, emphasize the importance of product differentiation in monopolistic competition (Chapter 26). And the new tariff on Canadian lumber addresses the realities of trade protection (Chapter 35).

36 New In the News Boxes

Israel's deployment of its "Iron Dome" missile defense system offers a great illustration of public goods. Among the new World Views in macro are China's 2016 cut in its reserve requirements (Chapter 14), Venezuela's increasing socialism (Chapter 37), the U.S. 2017 imposition of tariffs on Canadian lumber (Chapter 35), Heritage Foundation's 2017 global rankings on its Index of Economic Freedom (Chapter 1), and the World Bank's perspective on widening global inequality (Chapter 5). In micro, California's 2017 tax hike on cigarettes highlights the importance of price elasticity calculations. The pricing of the iPhone 7 and iWatch highlight the central role of price elasticities (Chapter 20). And the latest OPEC deal illustrates the use of price-fixing to attain monopoly profits (Chapter 25). All In the News and World View boxes are annotated and referred to explicitly in the body of the text.

18 New World View Boxes

As in earlier editions, the 15th edition forges explicit links between the end-of-chapter problems and the content of the chapter. Problems require students to go back into the body of the text and use data from the In the News and World View boxes, as well as from standard tables and texts. This strategy greatly improves the odds of students actually reading the boxed material and comprehending the graphs and tables.

185 New Problems

The discussion questions also require students to make use of material within the In the News boxes and the body of the text. Virtually all of the new Discussion Questions build on such in-chapter content.

In pondering the future, The Economy Tomorrow feature at the end of Chapter 14 asks, "Will crowdfunding displace traditional banks?" (a question that gets a negative answer). In micro, we gaze into the future of climate change and explore the methods of prospect for wider adaptation of electrical vehicles (Chapter 20) and the "War on Coal" (Chapter 28).

CHAPTER-BY-CHAPTER CHANGES: PURPOSE, SCOPE, AND UPDATES

Every page of this text has been subjected to review, revision, and updating. The following list gives a thumbnail sketch of the purpose, scope, and revisions of each chapter.

Chapter 1: Economics: The Core Issues introduces the core issues of What, How, and For Whom and the debate over market reliance or government regulation to resolve them. New global rankings on the extent of market reliance are highlighted. President Trump's call for cuts in space exploration and increases in defense spending highlight the guns vs. butter dilemma (opportunity cost), as does North Korea's continuing food shortage in the midst of an expensive missile program.

Chapter 2: The U.S. Economy: A Global View is intended to give students a sense of how the American economy stacks up to other nations in the world. The completely updated comparisons are organized around the core issues of What, How, and For Whom. The end-of-chapter The Economy Tomorrow feature considers the challenges of the United Nations goal for sustainable global development.

Chapter 3: Supply and Demand introduces the core elements of the market mechanism. Samsung's pricing of the Galaxy S7 illustrate the law of demand. Ticket scalping at the NCAA finals illustrates disequilibrium pricing. Supply/demand shifts are illustrated with gasoline prices in the wake of Hurricane Matthew and oil prices in the wake of Nigerian supply disruptions.

Chapter 4: The Role of Government focuses on the justifications for government intervention (market failures) and the growth of the public sector. Data on tax rates, public opinion about the role of government, state/local bond referenda, and government growth have all been updated. Israel's "Iron Dome" missile defense system is offered as a classic example of a "public good."

Chapter 5: National Income Accounting emphasizes the linkage between aggregate output and income and the utility of their measurement. All the GDP data are updated, as well as the historical comparisons of real and nominal incomes. The World View on standard-of-living inequalities between rich and poor nations has been updated as well. So has the contrast between economic and social measure of well-being.

Chapter 6: Unemployment not only introduces the standard measures of unemployment but also emphasizes the socioeconomic costs of that macro failure. All of the unemployment, labor force participation, and social cost data have been updated.

Chapter 7: Inflation endeavors to explain not only how inflation is measured but also the kinds of socioeconomic costs it imposes. Recent changes in the prices of tuition and other specific goods help illustrate measurement issues. All price and wage series are updated.

Chapter 8: The Business Cycle offers a historical and analytical overview of the nature and origins of cyclical disturbances. The Great Recession of 2008–2009 and its agonizingly slow recovery provide lots of new context. Aggregate supply shifts due to a spate of recent global conflicts are also noted. The core AS/AD model is introduced as a framework for macro analysis.

Chapter 9: Aggregate Demand focuses on the nature and building blocks of the aggregate demand curve. There are six updated In the News features, covering consumer confidence, the Leading Economic Index, cutbacks in private and public investment, and the wealth effect. All data on spending parameters are updated.

Chapter 10: Self-Adjustment or Instability? highlights the core concern of whether laissez-faire macro economies self-adjust or not. The multiplier is introduced and illustrated in the context of the AS/AD model (with sequential, horizontal shifts of the AD curve). New information on the variability of consumption and investment spending is highlighted, as are new CBO perspectives on the causes of the Great Recession.

Chapter 11: Fiscal Policy examines the potential of tax, spending, and income-transfer policies to shift the aggregate-demand curve in desired directions. An explicit, numerical guide for computing the size of an optimal intervention in the context of both output and price variability is introduced (Table 11.3). The broad outlines of President Trump's budget proposals are described and assessed.

Chapter 12: Deficits and Debt not only describes the size and history of U.S. debt, but also emphasizes the critical distinction between cyclical and structural (policy-induced) deficits and the real economic costs and consequences of both deficits and debt. Global comparisons of deficit ratios are provided, along with the latest information on debt ownership. Public anxiety about debt and deficit levels are noted, as well as concerns about Trump budgets. CBO estimates of the size of automatic stabilizers are illustrated.

Chapter 13: Money and Banks focuses on the nature and origins of what we call "money." The virtual collapse of the Venezuelan currency and the resort to barter helps illustrate the critical role money plays in any economy. M1 and M2 statistics are updated, and the nature of T-accounts is clarified. A new table on interest rates helps illustrate the opportunity costs of holding money. The Economy Tomorrow features the (unlikely) potential of bitcoins to replace government-sanctioned fiat money.

Chapter 14: The Federal Reserve System introduces Janet Yellen as the chair of the Fed and assesses the policy tools at her disposal. The experience with three rounds of quantitative easing is reviewed, and the increasing constraints imposed by shadow banking institutions are noted. There is a new World View on China's 2016 cut in reserve requirements and updated depictions of the pile-up of excess reserves in U.S. banks. The Economy Tomorrow feature looks at crowdfunding as a mechanism for sidestepping the traditional bank system.

Chapter 15: Monetary Policy explores both the theoretical potential and actual impact of Fed policy on macro outcomes. The Fed's adoption of employment targeting is highlighted, and the effects of quantitative easing are assessed.

Chapter 16: Supply-Side Policy: Short-Run Options emphasizes that demand-focused policies are not the only game in town—that the aggregate supply curve is important for macro outcomes as well. CBO's latest estimates of the tax elasticity of labor supply are included, along with stats on the Trump administration's expectations for the growth effects of its tax-cut proposals. The impacts of infrastructure spending and deregulation are also discussed.

Chapter 17: Growth and Productivity: Long-Run Possibilities explores the sources, prospects, and limits of economic growth. New global comparisons of productivity, savings, and economic growth are offered.

Chapter 18: Theory versus Reality is the macro capstone chapter that not only reviews macro problems and policy options but also examines the real-world obstacles that preclude perfect macro outcomes. Recent milestones in fiscal, monetary, and supply-side policy are depicted, along with a "report card" on our macroeconomic performance.

Chapter 19: Consumer Choice introduces the notion of consumer choice by first contrasting sociopsychiatric and economic explanations of consumer behavior. Utility theory, consumer surplus, price discrimination, and consumer choice are all discussed and illustrated. The update on LeBron James's endorsements underscores the role of advertising on consumer behavior.

Chapter 20: Elasticity explores price, income, and cross-price elasticities with the iPhone 7 launch, 2017 California tax hike on cigarettes, and consumer responses to higher gasoline prices. The role of prices in charting the future adoption of electric vehicles (EVs) is assessed in The Economy Tomorrow feature. Ten new problems provide practice in computing elasticities.

Chapter 21: The Costs of Production introduces the production function and emphasizes the relationship between productivity and cost measures. Tesla's new "gigafactory" illustrates the nature and sources of economies of scale. There are also new statistics on global competitiveness.

Chapter 22: The Competitive Firm depicts the static equilibrium behavior of the perfectly competitive firm, using the catfish industry as the core example. General Motor's temporary closure of its Detroit factories helps illustrate the differences between shutdown and exit decisions.

Chapter 23: Competitive Markets is a unique assessment of the dynamics of competitive markets—the heart and soul of market economies. The core story focuses on the evolution of the computer market, emphasizing the importance of entry, innovation, and exit to competitive outcomes. Illustrations include the tablet market, India's telecom market, and even long-run equilibrium in the catfish market.

Chapter 24: Monopoly not only examines the unique structural features of monopoly but also offers a unique, step-by-step contrast between competitive and monopoly behavior and outcomes. The American and European antitrust complaints against Google and Microsoft illustrate the nature of entry barriers and monopoly exploitation in the tech world.

Chapter 25: Oligopoly emphasizes how common oligopoly is in familiar product markets and the unique profit opportunities and coordination problems that result. OPEC's explicit price and output agreements illustrate outright price-fixing, while other industries use various entry barriers (e.g., input lockups, shelf-space rentals, distribution control, legal challenges) to thwart competition and increase profits.

Chapter 26: Monopolistic Competition stresses the differences in structure, behavior, and outcomes of this common industry category. The introduction of "Roasteries" at Starbucks and "bikini barristers" in Everett, Washington, illustrate the need for continuous product differentiation. New estimates of the dollar value of specific brands underscores the importance of brand recognition and loyalty.

Chapter 27: Natural Monopolies: (De)Regulation? goes beyond the depiction of this unique industry structure to explore the regulatory dilemmas that result. Quite simply, how can regulators compel natural monopolies to deliver the advantages of economies of scale without stifling innovation and decreasing efficiency? And how much will regulation cost? These questions are illustrated in the trucking, airline, cable, and electricity industries. The willingless of Nevada casinos to pay to escape that state's power monopoly illustrates how oppressive monopoly pricing can be.

Chapter 28: Environmental Protection is one of the world's great challenges, as the 2014 UN Climate Summit emphasized. This chapter explores the role of market incentives in environmental degradation and assesses the various policy options for inducing more eco-friendly behavior. The EPA's "war on coal," the battle over the Indian Point nuclear facility, and proposed "carbon taxes" offer timely illustrations of the theoretical and policy issues in the environmental debates.

Chapter 29: The Farm Problem just won't go away. Low price and income elasticities combine with the vagaries of weather to keep food prices volatile. The Farm Act of 2018 revisits the new price floors and subsidies designed to shelter farmers from market volatility.

Chapter 30: The Labor Market has been roiled in recent years by structural and cyclical forces. This chapter examines the underpinnings of labor demand and supply and then assesses the sources of wage inequalities. Proposals to raise the federal minimum wage are analyzed, as are the sky-high salaries of corporate CEOs.

Chapter 31: Labor Unions have lost ground in the private sector but have gained significant power in the public sector (especially in colleges and secondary schools). The parameters of collective bargaining are spelled out and then illustrated with the 2017–2021 contract for the National Basketball Association players. The 2005–2009 Silicon Valley conspiracy to hold down tech wages offers a vivid example of oligopsony power at work.

Chapter 32: Financial Markets have been front-page news since the onset of the Great Recession. This chapter emphasizes the *economic* role that stock and bond markets play in reallocating resources to new products and processes. Examples range from the financing of Columbus's New World expedition to Snapchat's $3 billion IPO in March 2017. The use of crowdfunding as a source of start-up financing is discussed.

Chapter 33: Taxes: Equity vs. Efficiency continues to be a staple of political debate. Should the "rich" pay more taxes, as President Obama urged? Or should tax rates be reduced to encourage more investment and innovation as President Trump proposed? The nature and terms of the equity/efficiency trade-off are examined, and illustrated with a comparison of the Clinton and Pence tax returns for 2015 (Trump's tax return was not available). New data on global tax rates and tax migrations are provided.

Chapter 34: Transfer Payments: Welfare and Social Security continues the discussion of equity/efficiency trade-offs, emphasizing the work disincentives inherent in all income transfer programs. New data on the redistributive impact of transfers underscores their importance for equity, and the 2017 formula for Social Security benefits highlights the efficiency concern.

Chapter 35: International Trade not only examines the theory of comparative advantage, but also investigates the opposition to free trade and the impact of trade barriers that result. The latest data on trade flows and trade balances (both aggregate and bilateral) are injected. The new U.S. tariff on Chinese steel and Canadian lumber help illustrate the winners and losers from trade barriers.

Chapter 36: International Finance explains how international exchange rates are determined and why they and the 2016–2017 collapse of the Venezuelan bolivar fluctuate. The depreciation of the Ukrainian hryvnia in the wake of Russia's invasion and the 2016–2017 collapse of the Venezuelan bolivar provide new perspectives on currency fluctuations. The loss Serena Williams incurred on her Wimbledon prize money when English voters elected to exit the EU and the pound tumbled is a nice illustration of the distributional effects of currency fluctuations.

Chapter 37: Global Poverty is receding, but billions of people remain desperately poor around the world. This chapter describes the current dimensions of global poverty and the World Bank's new (2017) antipoverty goal. Emphasis is on the importance of productivity advance and the policies that accelerate or restrain that advance. A new World View on Venezuela's economic contraction provides a relevant illustration.

EFFECTIVE PEDAGOGY

Despite the abundance of real-world applications, this is at heart a *principles* text, not a compendium of issues. Good theory and interesting applications are not mutually exclusive. This is a text that wants to *teach economics,* not just increase awareness of policy issues. To that end, *The Economy Today* provides a logically organized and uncluttered theoretical structure for macro, micro, and international theory. What distinguishes this text from others on the market is that it conveys theory in a lively, student-friendly manner.

Clean, Clear Theory

Student comprehension of core theory is facilitated with careful, consistent, and effective pedagogy. This distinctive pedagogy includes the following features:

Concept Reinforcement

Chapter Learning Objectives. Each chapter contains a set of chapter-level learning objectives. Students and professors can be confident that the organization of each chapter surrounds common themes outlined by three to five learning objectives listed on the first page of each chapter. End-of-chapter material, including the chapter summary, discussion questions, and student problem sets, is tagged to these learning objectives, as is the supplementary material, which includes the Test Bank and Instructor's Resource Manual.

Self-Explanatory Graphs and Tables. Graphs are *completely* labeled, colorful, and positioned on background grids. Because students often enter the principles course as graphphobics, graphs are frequently accompanied by synchronized tabular data. Every table is also annotated. This shouldn't be a product-differentiating feature, but sadly, it is. Putting a table in a text without an annotation is akin to writing a cluster of numbers on the board, then leaving the classroom without any explanation.

Reinforced Key Concepts. Key terms are defined when they first appear and, unlike in other texts, redefined as necessary in subsequent chapters. End-of-chapter discussion questions use

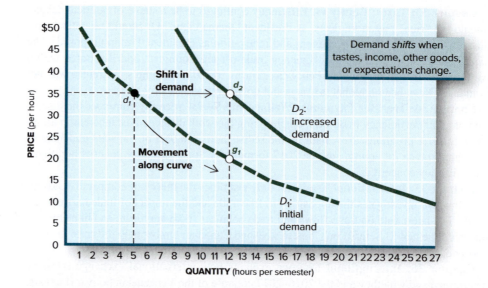

FIGURE 3.3

Shifts vs. Movements

A demand curve shows how a consumer responds to price changes. If the determinants of demand stay constant, the response is a *movement* along the curve to a new quantity demanded. In this case, the quantity demanded increases from 5 (point d_1), to 12 (point g_1), when price falls from \$35 to \$20 per hour.

If the determinants of demand *change,* the entire demand curve *shifts*. In this case, a rise in income increases demand. With more income, Tom is willing to buy 12 hours at the initial price of \$35 (point d_2), not just the 5 hours he demanded before the lottery win.

		Quantity Demanded (Hours per Semester)	
	Price (per Hour)	**Initial Demand**	**After Increase in Income**
A	\$50	1	8
B	45	2	9
C	40	3	10
D	35	5	12
E	30	7	14
F	25	9	16
G	20	12	19
H	15	15	22
I	10	20	27

tables, graphs, and boxed news stories from the text, reinforcing key concepts, and are linked to the chapter's learning objectives.

Boxed and Annotated Applications. In addition to the real-world applications that run through the body of the text, *The Economy Today* intersperses boxed domestic (In the News) and global (World View) case studies intertextually for further understanding and reference. Although nearly every text on the market now offers boxed applications, *The Economy Today*'s presentation is distinctive. First, the sheer number of In the News (97) and World View (58) boxes is unique. Second, and more important, *every* boxed application is referenced in the body of the text. Third, *every* News and World View comes with a brief, self-contained explanation, as the accompanying example illustrates. Fourth, the News and World View boxes are the explicit subject of the end-of-chapter discussion questions and student problem set exercises. In combination, these distinctive features assure that students will actually *read* the boxed applications and discern their economic content. The Test Bank provides subsets of questions tied to the News and World View boxes so that instructors can confirm student use of this feature.

Readability   The one adjective invariably used to describe *The Economy Today* is "readable." Professors often express a bit of shock when they realize that students actually enjoy reading the text. (Well, not as much as a Stephen King novel, but a whole lot better than most texts they've had to plow through.) The writing style is lively and issue-focused. Unlike any other text on the market, every boxed feature, every graph, every table, and every cartoon is ex-

IN THE NEWS

SEAFOOD PRICES RISE AFTER BP OIL SPILL

Oily shrimp? No thank you! The National Oceanic and Atmospheric Administration (NOAA) has closed a third of the Gulf of Mexico in response to the BP oil spill. The explosion of BP's Deepwater Horizon oil rig has spilled nearly 5 million barrels of oil into the Gulf. Whatever their taste, oily fish and shrimp may be a health hazard.

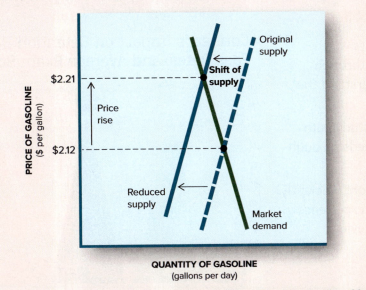

Closure of the Gulf has caused seafood prices to soar. The price of top-quality white shrimp has jumped from $3.50 a pound to $7.50 a pound. Restaurants are jacking up their prices or taking shrimp off the menu.

Source: News reports, June 2010.

ANALYSIS: When factor costs or availability worsen, the supply curve *shifts* to the left. Such leftward supply-curve shifts push prices up the market demand curve.

plained and analyzed. Every feature is also referenced in the text, so students actually learn the material rather than skipping over it. Because readability is ultimately in the eye of the beholder, you might ask a couple of students to read and compare a parallel chapter in *The Economy Today* and in another text. This is a test *The Economy Today* usually wins.

We firmly believe that students must *work* with key concepts in order to really learn them. Weekly homework assignments are *de rigueur* in our own classes. To facilitate homework assignments, we have prepared the student problem set at the end of each chapter. These sets include built-in numerical and graphing problems that build on the tables, graphs, and boxed material that align with each chapter's learning objectives. Grids for drawing graphs are also provided. Students cannot complete all the problems without referring to material in the chapter. This increases the odds of students actually *reading* the chapter, the tables, and the boxed applications.

Student Problem Set

The student problem set at the end of each chapter is reproduced in the online student tutorial software. This really helps students transition between the written material and online supplements. It also means that the online assignments are totally book-specific.

NEW AND IMPROVED SUPPLEMENTS

The following ancillaries are available for quick download and convenient access via the Instructor Resource material available through McGraw-Hill Connect.

 **connect®**

McGraw-Hill Connect® is a highly reliable, easy-to-use homework and learning management solution that utilizes learning science and award-winning adaptive tools to improve student results.

Homework and Adaptive Learning

- Connect's assignments help students contextualize what they've learned through application, so they can better understand the material and think critically.

- Connect will create a personalized study path customized to individual student needs through SmartBook®.

- SmartBook helps students study more efficiently by delivering an interactive reading experience through adaptive highlighting and review.

Connect's Impact on Retention Rates, Pass Rates, and Average Exam Scores

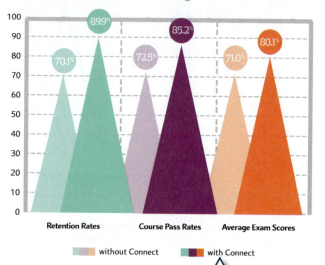

Retention Rates: 70.1% without Connect, 89.9% with Connect
Course Pass Rates: 72.5% without Connect, 85.2% with Connect
Average Exam Scores: 71.0% without Connect, 80.1% with Connect

without Connect | with Connect

Using **Connect** improves retention rates by **19.8%**, passing rates by **12.7%, and** exam scores by **9.1%.**

Over **7 billion questions** have been answered, making McGraw-Hill Education products more intelligent, reliable, and precise.

73% of instructors who use **Connect** require it; instructor satisfaction **increases** by 28% when **Connect** is required.

Quality Content and Learning Resources

- Connect content is authored by the world's best subject matter experts, and is available to your class through a simple and intuitive interface.

- The Connect eBook makes it easy for students to access their reading material on smartphones and tablets. They can study on the go and don't need internet access to use the eBook as a reference, with full functionality.

- Multimedia content such as videos, simulations, and games drive student engagement and critical thinking skills.

Robust Analytics and Reporting

©Hero Images/Getty Images RF

- Connect Insight® generates easy-to-read reports on individual students, the class as a whole, and on specific assignments.

- The Connect Insight dashboard delivers data on performance, study behavior, and effort. Instructors can quickly identify students who struggle and focus on material that the class has yet to master.

- Connect automatically grades assignments and quizzes, providing easy-to-read reports on individual and class performance.

Impact on Final Course Grade Distribution

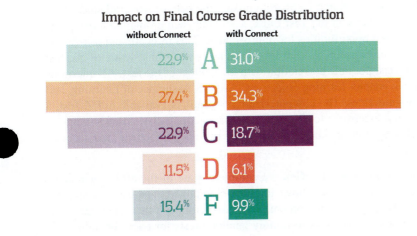

without Connect		with Connect
22.9%	A	31.0%
27.4%	B	34.3%
22.9%	C	18.7%
11.5%	D	6.1%
15.4%	F	9.9%

More students earn **As** and **Bs** when they use **Connect**.

Trusted Service and Support

- Connect integrates with your LMS to provide single sign-on and automatic syncing of grades. Integration with Blackboard®, D2L®, and Canvas also provides automatic syncing of the course calendar and assignment-level linking.

- Connect offers comprehensive service, support, and training throughout every phase of your implementation.

- If you're looking for some guidance on how to use Connect, or want to learn tips and tricks from super users, you can find tutorials as you work. Our Digital Faculty Consultants and Student Ambassadors offer insight into how to achieve the results you want with Connect.

www.mheducation.com/connect

DIGITAL SOLUTIONS

Extensive Algorithmic and Graphing Assessment. Robust, auto-gradable question banks for each chapter now include even more questions that make use of the Connect graphing tool. More questions featuring algorithmic variations have also been added.

Interactive Graphs. This new assignable resource within Connect helps students see the relevance of subject matter by providing visual displays of real data for students to manipulate. All graphs are accompanied by assignable assessment questions and feedback to guide students through the experience of learning to read and interpret graphs and data.

Videos. New to this edition are videos that provide support for key economic topics. These short, engaging explanations are presented at the moment students may be struggling to help them connect the dots and grasp challenging concepts.

Math Preparedness Tutorials. Our math preparedness assignments have been reworked to help students refresh on important prerequisite topics necessary to be successful in economics.

Test Bank. The Test Bank has been rigorously revised for this 15th edition of *The Economy Today*. Digital co-author Karen Gebhardt enlisted the help of her grad students to carefully assess *every* problem in the Test Bank, assigning each problem a letter grade and identifying errors and opportunities for improvement. This in-depth and critical assessment and revision has ensured a high level of quality and consistency of the test questions and the greatest possible correlation with the content of the text. All questions are coded according to chapter learning objectives, AACSB Assurance of Learning, and Bloom's Taxonomy guidelines. The computerized Test Bank is available in EZ Test, a flexible and easy-to-use electronic testing program that accommodates a wide range of question types, including user-created questions. You can access the test bank through McGraw-Hill Connect.

Computerized Test Bank Online. TestGen is a complete, state-of-the-art test generator and editing application software that allows instructors to quickly and easily select test items from McGraw Hill's test bank content. The instructors can then organize, edit, and customize questions and answers to rapidly generate tests for paper or online administration. Questions can include stylized text, symbols, graphics, and equations that are inserted directly into questions using built-in mathematical templates. TestGen's random generator provides the option to display different text or calculated number values each time questions are used with both quick-and-simple test creation and flexible and robust editing tools, TestGen is a complete test generator system for today's educators.

You can use our test bank software, TestGen, or Connect to easily query for learning outcomes and objectives that directly relate to the learning objectives for your course. You can then use the reporting features to aggregate student results in a similar fashion, making the collection and presentation of assurance-of-learning data simple and easy.

Assurance-of- Learning Ready

Many educational institutions today are focused on the notion of *assurance of learning,* an important element of some accreditation standards. *The Economy Today* is designed specifically to support your assurance-of-learning initiatives with a simple yet powerful solution.

Each test bank question for *The Economy Today* maps to a specific chapter learning outcome/objective listed in the text. You can use our test bank software, EZ Test and EZ Test Online, to easily query for learning outcomes/objectives that directly relate to the learning objectives for your course. You can then use the reporting features of EZ Test to aggregate student results in similar fashion, making the collection and presentation of assurance-of-learning data simple and easy.

McGraw-Hill Education is a proud corporate member of AACSB International. Understanding the importance and value of AACSB accreditation, *The Economy Today,* 15th edition, recognizes the curricula guidelines detailed in the AACSB standards for business accreditation by connecting selected questions in the text and the test bank to the six general knowledge and skill guidelines in the AACSB standards.

The statements contained in *The Economy Today,* 15th edition, are provided only as a guide for the users of this text. The AACSB leaves content coverage and assessment within the purview of individual schools, the mission of the school, and the faculty. While *The Economy Today,* 15th edition, and the teaching package make no claim of any specific AACSB qualification or evaluation, we have labeled within *The Economy Today,* 15th edition, labeled selected questions according to the eight general knowledge and skills areas emphasized by AACSB.

PowerPoint Presentations. Developed using Microsoft PowerPoint software, these slides are a step-by-step review of the key points in each of the book's 37 chapters. They are equally useful to the student in the classroom as lecture aids or for personal review at home or the computer lab. The slides use animation to show students how graphs build and shift.

Solutions Manual. Prepared by Karen Gebhardt, this manual provides detailed answers to the end-of-chapter questions.

Built-in Student Problem Set. The built-in student problem set is found at the end of every chapter of *The Economy Today.* Each chapter has 8 to 10 numerical and graphing problems tied to the content of the text.

AACSB Statement

Instructor Aids

Student Aids

ACKNOWLEDGMENTS

This 15th edition of *The Economy Today* represents a continuing commitment to disseminate the core principles of economics to a broad swath of college students. Like earlier editions, it has benefited greatly from the continuing stream of ideas and suggestions from both instructors and students. For all that feedback, I am most grateful. Among those who have contributed feedback to this and earlier editions are the following instructors:

Reviewers

Cynthia E. Abadie
Southwest Tennessee Community College

Mark Abajian
San Diego Mesa College

Steve Abid
Grand Rapids Community College

Ercument G. Aksoy
Los Angeles Valley College

Mauro Cristian Amor
Northwood University

Catalina Amuedo-Dorantes
San Diego State University

Gerald Baumgardner
Penn College

Mack A. Bean
Franklin Pierce University

Adolfo Benavides
Texas A&M University–Corpus Christi

Anoop Bhargava
Finger Lakes Community College

Joerg Bibow
Skidmore College

Eugenie Bietry
Pace University

John Bockino
Suffolk County Community College

Peter Boelman
Norco College

Walter Francis Boyle
Fayetteville Technical Community College

Amber Brown
Grand Valley State University

Don Bumpass
Sam Houston State University

Suparna Chakraborty
Baruch College, CUNY

Stephen J. Conroy
University of San Diego

Sherry L. Creswell
Kent State University

Manabendra Dasgupta
University of Alabama–Birmingham

Antony Davies
Duquesne University

Diane de Freitas
Fresno City College

Diana Denison
Red Rocks Community College

Alexander Deshkovski
North Carolina Central University

John A. Doces
Bucknell University

Ishita Edwards
Oxnard College

Eric R. Eide
Brigham Young University

Yalcin Ertekin
Trine University

Kelley L. Fallon
Owensboro Community & Technical College

Frank Garland
Tri-County Technical College

Leroy Gill
The Ohio State University

Paul Graf
Indiana University

Barnali Gupta
Miami University

Sheila Amin Gutierrez de Pineres
University of Texas–Dallas

Jonatan Jelen
City College of New York

Hyojin Jeong
Lakeland Community College

Barbara Heroy John
University of Dayton

Tim Kochanski
Portland State University

David E. Laurel
South Texas College

Raymond Lawless
Quinsigamond Community College

Richard B. Le
Cosumnes River College

Jim Lee
Texas A&M University–Corpus Christi

Sang H. Lee
Southeastern Louisiana University

Minghua Li
Franklin Pierce University

Yan Li
University of Wisconsin–Eau Claire

Paul Lockard
Black Hawk College

Rotua Lumbantobing
North Carolina State University

Paula Manns
Atlantic Cape Community College

Jeanette Milius
Iowa Western Community College

Norman C. Miller
Miami University

Stanley Robert Mitchell
McLennan Community College

Stephen K. Nodine
Tri-County Technical College

Phacharaphot Nuntramas
San Diego State University

Seth Ari Roberts
Frederick Community College

Michael J. Ryan
Western Michigan University

Craig F. Santicola
Westmoreland County Community College

Rolando A. Santos
Lakeland Community College

Theodore P. Scheinman
Mt. Hood Community College

Marilyn K. Spencer
Texas A&M University–Corpus Christi

Irina Nikolayevna Strelnikova
Red Rocks Community College

Michael Swope
Wayne County Community College

Gary Lee Taylor
South Dakota State University

Deborah L. Thorsen
Palm Beach State College

Ngoc-Bich Tran
San Jacinto College

Markland Tuttle
Sam Houston State University

Kenneth Lewis Weimer
Kellogg Community College

Selin Yalcindag
Mercyhurst College

Erik Zemljic
Kent State University

The text itself and all the accompanying supplements could not make it to the market-place without the prodigious efforts of the production team at McGraw-Hill. In this regard, I want to extend special thanks to Adam Huenecke, who has not only managed the production process, but even tutored me in the use of the digital tools needed to produce a text today. Katie Hoenicke served once again as a valued editor of the entire project. Last but not least, I want to call out Karen Gebhardt, who is the digital co-author for this text. Karen has not only upgraded and synchronized all of the digital dimensions of our text package, but has also motivated me to check and recheck every detail of the text. She is an invaluable partner.

Let me conclude by thanking all the instructors and students who are going to use *The Economy Today* as an introduction to economic principles. I will welcome any reactions (even bad ones) and suggestions you'd like to pass on for future editions.

—**Bradley R. Schiller**

CONTENTS IN BRIEF

CONTENTS

©MOF/Getty Images RF

©REUTERS/Alamy Stock Photo

©Kyodo via AP Images

©Blend Images/Getty Images RF

©Hisham F. Ibrahim/Getty Images RF

THE ECONOMIC CHALLENGE

People around the world want a better life. Whether rich or poor, everyone strives for a higher standard of living. Ultimately, the performance of the economy determines who attains that goal.

These first few chapters examine how the *limits* to output are determined and how the interplay of market forces and government intervention utilize and even expand those limits.

"The Economist in Chief"
©REUTERS/Alamy Stock Photo

1

Economics: The Core Issues

People understand that the president of the United States is the Commander in Chief of the armed forces. The president has the ultimate responsibility to decide when and how America's military forces will be deployed. He issues the orders that military officers must carry out. He is given credit for military successes and blame for military failures. He can't "pass the buck" down the line of command.

Less recognized is the president's role as "Economist in Chief." The president is held responsible not just for the *military* security of the United States, but for its *economic* security as well. Although he doesn't have the command powers in the economic arena that he has in the military arena, people expect him to take charge of the economy. They expect the Economist in Chief to keep the economy growing, to create jobs for everyone who wants one, and to prevent prices from rising too fast. Along the way, they expect the Economist in Chief to protect the environment, assure economic justice for all, and protect America's position in the global economy.

That is a tall order, especially in view of the president's limited constitutional powers to make economic policy decisions. The economy is also buffeted by international and natural forces that no president can control. But no matter. Voters hold the Economist in Chief responsible for economic misfortunes, whether or not he is able to single-handedly prevent them, and give him credit for economic success.

What everyone ultimately wants is a prosperous and growing economy: an economy in which people can find good jobs, enjoy rising living standards and wealth, get the education they desire, and enjoy an array of creature comforts. And we want to enjoy this good life while protecting the environment, caring for the poor, and pursuing world peace.

How are we going to get all this? Is "the economy" some sort of perpetual motion machine that will keep churning out more goods and services every year? Clearly not. During the Great Recession of 2008–2009 the economy churned out less output, eliminated jobs, and reduced living standards and wealth. A lot of college graduates had to move back home when they couldn't find jobs. What went wrong?

Even after the Great Recession ended in June 2009, economic pain persisted. The growth of the economy was agonizingly slow, and unemployment remained high for another 6 years. Was that much distress really necessary? Couldn't the Economist in Chief have fixed these problems? These questions are were debated intensely in the 2016 presidential election. Donald Trump promised "to make America great again" by creating more jobs, building more bridges and roads, strengthening the armed forces, and limiting both illegal immigration and unfair foreign competition. Voters decided to give him the opportunity to serve as Economist in Chief. Like his predecessors, President Trump's challenge has been to convert campaign promises into tangible economic results. To convert campaign promises into desirable economic outcomes requires a knowledge of what makes an economy tick. How are prices, wages, employment, and other economic outcomes actually determined? Does Wall Street run the system? How about selfish, greedy capitalists? The banks? Or maybe foreign nations? Are incompetent bureaucrats and self-serving politicians the root of our occasional woes? Who, in fact, calls the shots?

The goal of this course is to understand how the economy works. To that end, we want to determine how *markets*—the free-wheeling exchange of goods and services—shape economic outcomes—everything from the price of this text to the national unemployment rate. Then we want to examine the role that government can and does play in (re)shaping economic performance. Once we've established this foundation, we'll be in a better position to evaluate what the Economist in Chief *can* do—and what he *should* do. We'll also better understand how we can make better economic decisions for ourselves.

We'll start our inquiry with some harsh realities. In a world of unlimited resources, we could have all the goods we desired. We'd have time to do everything we wanted and enough money to buy everything we desired. We could produce enough to make everyone rich while protecting the environment and exploring the universe. The Economist in Chief could deliver everything voters asked for. Unfortunately, we don't live in that utopia: **we live in a world of limited resources.** Those limits are the root of our economic problems. They force us to make difficult decisions about how *best* to use our time, our money, and our resources. These are *economic* decisions.

In this first chapter we'll examine how the problem of limited resources arises and the kinds of choices it forces us to make. As we'll see, **three core choices confront every nation:**

- **WHAT to produce with our limited resources.**
- **HOW to produce the goods and services we select.**
- **FOR WHOM goods and services are produced—that is, who should get them.**

We also have to decide who should answer these questions. Should people take care of their own health and retirement, or should the government provide a safety net of health care and pensions? Should the government regulate airfares or let the airlines set prices? Should Microsoft decide what features get included in a computer's operating system, or should the government make that decision? Should Facebook decide what personal information is protected, or should the government make that decision? Should interest rates be set by private banks alone, or should the government try to control interest rates? The battle over *who* should answer the core questions is often as contentious as the questions themselves.

THE ECONOMY IS US

To learn how the economy works, let's start with a simple truth: *the economy is us.* "The economy" is simply an abstraction referring to the grand sum of all our production and consumption activities. What we collectively produce is what the economy produces; what we collectively consume is what the economy consumes. In this sense, the concept of "the economy" is no more difficult than the concept of "the family." If someone tells you that the Jones family has an annual income of $42,000, you know that the reference is to the collective earnings of all the Joneses. Likewise, when someone reports that the nation's income is $20 trillion per year—as it now is—we should recognize that the reference is to the grand total of everyone's income. If we work fewer hours or get paid less, both family income *and* national income decline. The "meaningless statistics" often cited in the news are just a summary of our collective market behavior.

The same relationship between individual behavior and aggregate behavior applies to specific outputs. If we as individuals insist on driving cars rather than taking public transportation, the economy will produce millions of cars each year and consume vast quantities of oil. In a slightly different way, the economy produces billions of dollars of military hardware to satisfy our desire for national defense. In each case, the output of the economy reflects the collective behavior of the 340 million individuals who participate in the U.S. economy.

We may not always be happy with the output of the economy. But we can't ignore the link between individual action and collective outcomes. If the highways are clogged and the air is polluted, we can't blame someone else for the transportation choices we made. If we're disturbed by the size of our military arsenal, we must still accept responsibility for our choices (or nonchoices, if we failed to vote). In either case, we continue to have the option of reallocating our resources. We can create a different outcome tomorrow, next month, or next year.

SCARCITY: THE CORE PROBLEM

Although we can change economic outcomes, we can't have everything we want. If you go to the mall with $20 in your pocket, you can buy only so much. The money in your pocket sets a *limit* to your spending.

The output of the entire economy is also limited. The limits in this case are set not by the amount of money in people's pockets, but by the resources available for producing goods and services. Everyone wants more housing, new schools, better transit systems, and a new car. We also want to explore space and bring safe water to the world's poor. But even a country as rich as the United States can't produce everything people want. So, like every other nation, we have to grapple with the core problem of **scarcity**—the fact that **there aren't enough resources available to satisfy all our desires.**

scarcity: Lack of enough resources to satisfy all desired uses of those resources.

Factors of Production

The resources used to produce goods and services are called **factors of production.** *The four basic factors of production are*

factors of production: Resource inputs used to produce goods and services, e.g., land, labor, capital, entrepreneurship.

- *Land.*
- *Labor.*
- *Capital.*
- *Entrepreneurship.*

These are the *inputs* needed to produce desired *outputs.* To produce this text, for example, we needed paper, printing presses, a building, and lots of labor. We also needed people with good ideas who could put it together. To produce the education you're getting in this class, we need not only a text but a classroom, a teacher, a blackboard, and maybe a computer as well. **Without factors of production, we simply can't produce anything.**

Land. The first factor of production, land, refers not just to the ground but to all natural resources. Crude oil, water, air, and minerals are all included in our concept of "land."

Labor. Labor too has several dimensions. It's not simply a question of how many bodies there are. When we speak of labor as a factor of production, we refer to the skills and abilities to produce goods and services. Hence both the quantity and the quality of human resources are included in the "labor" factor.

capital: Final goods produced for use in the production of other goods, such as equipment and structures.

Capital. The third factor of production is capital. In economics the term **capital** refers to final goods produced for use in further production. The residents of fishing villages in southern Thailand, for example, braid huge fishing nets. The sole purpose of these nets is to catch more fish. The nets themselves become a factor of production in obtaining the final goods (fish) that people desire. Thus they're regarded as *capital.* Blast furnaces used to make steel and desks used to equip offices are also capital inputs.

Entrepreneurship. The more land, labor, and capital we have, the more we can produce potential output. A farmer with 10,000 acres, 12 employees, and six tractors can grow more crops than a farmer with half those resources. But there's no guarantee that he will. The farmer with fewer resources may have better ideas about what to plant, when to irrigate, or how to harvest the crops. *It's not just a matter of what resources you have but also of how well you use them.* This is where the fourth factor of production—**entrepreneurship**—comes in. The entrepreneur is the person who sees the opportunity for new or better products and brings together the resources needed for producing them. If it weren't for entrepreneurs, Thai fishers would still be using sticks to catch fish. Without entrepreneurship, farmers would still be milking their cows by hand. If someone hadn't thought of a way to miniaturize electronic circuits, you wouldn't be able to text your friends.

The role of entrepreneurs in economic progress is a key issue in the market versus government debate. The British economist John Maynard Keynes argued that free markets unleash the "animal spirits" of entrepreneurs, propelling innovation, technology, and growth. Critics of government regulation argue that government interference in the marketplace, however well intentioned, tends to stifle those very same animal spirits.

entrepreneurship: The assembling of resources to produce new or improved products and technologies.

Limits to Output

No matter how an economy is organized, there's a limit to how much it can produce. The most evident limit is the amount of resources available for producing goods and services. One reason the United States can produce so much is that it has nearly 4 million square miles of land. Tonga, with less than 300 square miles of land, will never produce as much. The United States also has a population of more than 340 million people. That's a lot less than China (1.4 billion) but far larger than 200 other nations (Tonga has a population of less than 120,000). So an abundance of raw resources gives us the potential to produce a lot of output. But that greater production capacity isn't enough to satisfy all our desires. We're constantly scrambling for additional resources to build more houses, make better movies, and provide more health care. That imbalance between available resources and our wish list is one of the things that makes the job of Economist in Chief so difficult: He can't deliver everything people want.

The science of **economics** helps us frame these choices. In a nutshell, economics is the study of how people use scarce resources. How do you decide how much time to spend studying? How does Google decide how many workers to hire? How does Ford decide whether to use its factories to produce sport utility vehicles or sedans? What share of a nation's resources should be devoted to space exploration, the delivery of health care services, or pollution control? In every instance, **alternative ways of using scarce labor, land, and capital resources are always available, and we have to choose one use over another.**

economics: The study of how best to allocate scarce resources among competing uses.

OPPORTUNITY COSTS

Scientists have long sought to explore every dimension of space. President Kennedy initiated a lunar exploration program that successfully landed men on the moon on July 20, 1969. That only whetted the appetite for further space exploration. President George W. Bush initiated a program to land people on Mars, using the moon as a way station. Scientists believe that the biological, geophysical, and technical knowledge gained from the exploration of Mars will improve life here on Earth. But should we do it? In a world of unlimited resources the answer would be an easy "yes." But we don't live in that world.

Every time we use scarce resources in one way, we give up the opportunity to use them in other ways. If we use more resources to explore space, we have fewer resources available for producing earthly goods. The forgone earthly goods represent the **opportunity costs** of a Mars expedition. *Opportunity cost is what is given up to get*

opportunity cost: The most desired goods or services that are forgone in order to obtain something else.

something else. Even a so-called free lunch has an opportunity cost. The resources used to produce the lunch could have been used to produce something else. A trip to Mars has a much higher opportunity cost. President Obama decided those opportunity costs were too high: he scaled back the Mars programs to make more resources available for Earthly uses (like education, highway construction, and energy development). President Trump agreed. While calling space exploration "wonderful," he observed "Right now, we have bigger problems—we've got to fix our potholes." He reallocated scarce resources from space exploration to domestic infrastructure (roads, bridges, airports).

Your economics class also has an opportunity cost. The building space used for your economics class can't be used to show movies at the same time. Your professor can't lecture (produce education) and repair motorcycles simultaneously. The decision to use these scarce resources (capital, labor) for an economics class implies producing less of other goods.

Even reading this text is costly. That cost is not measured in dollars and cents. The true (economic) cost is, instead, measured in terms of some alternative activity. What would you like to be doing right now? The more time you spend reading this text, the less time you have available for other uses of your time. The opportunity cost of reading this text is the best alternative use of your scarce time. If you are missing your favorite TV show, we'd say that show is the opportunity cost of reading this text. It is what you gave up to do this assignment. Hopefully, the benefits you get from studying will outweigh that cost. Otherwise this wouldn't be the best way to use your scarce time.

Guns vs. Butter

One of the most difficult choices nations must make about resource use entails defense spending. After the September 11, 2001, terrorist attacks on the World Trade Center and Pentagon, American citizens overwhelmingly favored an increase in military spending. Even the unpopularity of the wars in Iraq and Afghanistan didn't quell the desire for more national defense. But national defense, like Mars exploration, requires the use of scarce resources; Americans wanted to feel *safe*. But there is a *cost* to assuring safety: the 1.4 million men and women who serve in the armed forces aren't available to build schools, program computers, or teach economics. Similarly, the land, labor, capital, and entrepreneurship devoted to producing military hardware aren't available for producing civilian goods. An *increase* in national defense implies more sacrifices of civilian goods and services. How many schools, hospitals, or cars are we willing to sacrifice in order to "produce" more national security? This is the "guns versus butter" dilemma that all nations confront.

PRODUCTION POSSIBILITIES

The opportunity costs implied by our every choice can be illustrated easily. Suppose a nation can produce only two goods, trucks and tanks. To keep things simple, assume that labor (workers) is the only factor of production needed to produce either good. Although other factors of production (land, machinery) are also needed in actual production, ignoring them for the moment does no harm. Assume further that we have a total of only 10 workers available per day to produce either trucks or tanks. That's a tiny work force, but it makes the math a lot easier.

Our initial problem is to determine the *limits* of output. How many trucks or tanks *can* be produced in a day with available resources (our 10 workers)?

Before going any further, notice how opportunity costs will affect the answer. If we use all 10 workers to produce trucks, no labor will be available to assemble tanks. In this case, forgone tanks would become the *opportunity cost* of a decision to employ all our resources in truck production.

We still don't know how many trucks could be produced with 10 workers or exactly how many tanks would be forgone by such a decision. To get these answers, we need more details about the production processes involved—specifically, how many workers are required to manufacture either good.

Production Options		
	Output of Trucks per Day	Output of Tanks per Day
A	5	0
B	4	2.0
C	3	3.0
D	2	3.8
E	1	4.5
F	0	5.0

TABLE 1.1

A Production Possibilities Schedule

As long as resources are limited, their use entails an opportunity cost. In this case, resources (labor) used to produce trucks can't be used for tank assembly at the same time. Hence the forgone tanks are the opportunity cost of additional trucks. If all our resources were used to produce trucks (row A), no tanks could be assembled. To produce tanks, we have to reduce truck production.

production possibilities: The alternative combinations of final goods and services that could be produced in a given period with all available resources and technology.

The Production Possibilities Curve

Table 1.1 summarizes the hypothetical choices, or **production possibilities,** that we confront in this case. Suppose we wanted to produce only trucks (i.e., no tanks). Row *A* of the table shows the *maximum* number of trucks we could produce. With 10 workers available and a labor requirement of 2 workers per truck, we can manufacture a maximum of five trucks per day.

Producing five trucks per day leaves no workers available to produce tanks. Our 10 available workers are all being used to produce trucks. On row *A* of Table 1.1 we've got "butter" (trucks) but no "guns" (tanks). If we want tanks, we have to cut back on truck production. The remainder of Table 1.1 illustrates the trade-offs we confront in this simple case. By cutting truck production from five to four trucks per day (row *B*), we reduce labor use in truck production from 10 workers to 8. That leaves 2 workers available for other uses, including the production of tanks.

If we employ these remaining 2 workers to assemble tanks, we can build two tanks a day. We would then end up on row *B* of the table with four trucks and two tanks per day. What's the opportunity cost of these two tanks? It's the one additional truck (the fifth truck) that we could have produced but didn't.

As we proceed down the rows of Table 1.1, the nature of opportunity costs becomes apparent. Each additional tank built implies the loss (opportunity cost) of truck output. Likewise, every truck produced implies the loss of some tank output.

These trade-offs between truck and tank production are illustrated in the production possibilities curve of Figure 1.1. *Each point on the production possibilities curve depicts an alternative mix of output* **that could be produced.** In this case, each point represents a different combination of trucks and tanks that we could produce in a single day using all available resources (10 workers in this case).

Notice in particular how points *A* through *F* in Figure 1.1 represent the choices described in each row of Table 1.1. At point *A*, we're producing five trucks per day and no tanks. As we move down the curve from point *A* we're producing fewer trucks and more tanks. At point *B*, truck production has dropped from five to four vehicles per day while tank assembly has increased from zero to two. In other words, we've given up one truck to get two tanks assembled. The opportunity cost of those tanks is the one truck that is given up. A production possibilities curve, then, is simply a graphic summary of production possibilities, as described in Table 1.1. As such, *the production possibilities curve illustrates two essential principles:*

- *Scarce resources.* There's a limit to the amount of output we can produce in a given time period with available resources and technology.
- *Opportunity costs.* We can obtain additional quantities of any particular good only by reducing the potential production of another good.

These principles help explain why both presidents Obama and Trump chose to devote fewer resources to space exploration. They felt the opportunity costs (reduced education, less infrastructure) were simply too high.

FIGURE 1.1

A Production Possibilities Curve

A production possibilities curve (PPC) describes the various output combinations that could be produced in a given time period with available resources and technology. It represents a menu of output choices an economy confronts.

Point *B* indicates that we could produce a *combination* of four trucks and two tanks per day. Alternatively, we could produce one less truck and a third tank by moving to point *C*.

Points *A, D, E,* and *F* illustrate still other output combinations that *could* be produced. This curve is a graphic illustration of the production possibilities schedule in Table 1.1.

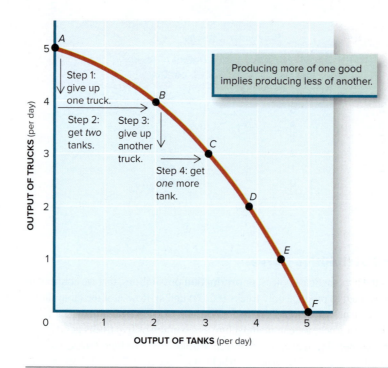

Increasing Opportunity Costs

The shape of the production possibilities curve reflects another limitation on our choices. Notice how opportunity costs increase as we move along the production possibilities curve. When we cut truck output from five to four (step 1, Figure 1.1), we get two tanks (step 2). When we cut truck production further, however (step 3), we get only one tank per truck given up (step 4). The opportunity cost of tank production is increasing. This process of increasing opportunity cost continues. By the time we give up the last truck (row *F*), tank output increases by only 0.5: we get only half a tank for the last truck given up. These increases in opportunity cost are reflected in the outward bend of the production possibilities curve.

Why do opportunity costs increase? Mostly because it's difficult to move resources from one industry to another. It's easy to transform trucks to tanks on a blackboard. In the real world, however, resources don't adapt so easily. Workers who assemble trucks may not have the right skills for tank assembly. As we continue to transfer labor from one industry to the other, we start getting fewer tanks for every truck we give up.

The difficulties entailed in transferring labor skills, capital, and entrepreneurship from one industry to another are so universal that we often speak of the *law of increasing opportunity cost*. This law says that we must give up ever-increasing quantities of other goods and services in order to get more of a particular good. The law isn't based solely on the limited versatility of individual workers. The *mix* of factor inputs makes a difference as well. Truck assembly requires less capital than tank assembly. In a pinch, wheels can be mounted on a truck almost completely by hand, whereas tank treads require more sophisticated machinery. As we move labor from truck assembly to tank assembly, available capital may restrict our output capabilities.

The Cost of North Korea's Military

The production possibilities curve illustrates why the core economic decision about WHAT to produce is so difficult: We can't have everything we want and, worse yet, getting more of one thing implies getting less of something else. We are forced to make difficult choices.

Consider, for example, North Korea's decision to maintain a large military. North Korea is a relatively small country: its population of 25 million ranks fiftieth in the world. Yet

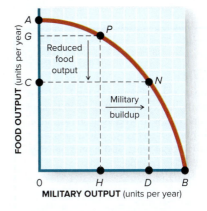

FIGURE 1.2

The Cost of War

North Korea devotes as much as 20 percent of its output to the military. The opportunity cost of this decision is reduced output of food. As the military expands from 0*H* to 0*D*, food output drops from 0*G* to 0*C*.

North Korea maintains the fourth-largest army in the world and continues to develop a nuclear weapons capability. To do so, it allocates as much as 20 percent of all its resources to feeding, clothing, and equipping its military forces. As a consequence, there aren't enough resources available to produce food. Without adequate machinery, seeds, fertilizer, or irrigation, North Korea's farmers can't produce enough food to feed the population (see World View "North Korea's Food Shortage Grows"). As Figure 1.2 illustrates, the opportunity cost of "guns" in Korea is a lot of needed "butter."

WORLD VIEW

WORLD'S LARGEST ARMIES

Rank	Country	Active Military
1	China	2,333,000
2	United States	1,492,200
3	India	1,325,000
4	North Korea	1,190,000
5	Russia	845,000
6	Pakistan	643,800
7	South Korea	630,000
8	Iran	523,000
9	Turkey	510,600
10	Vietnam	482,000

Source: U.S. Central Intelligence Agency 2017.

ANALYSIS: Nations "produce" national defense by employing land, labor, and capital in their armed forces. The opportunity cost of those "guns" are less "butter."

During World War II, the United States confronted a similar trade-off. In 1944 nearly 40 percent of all U.S. output was devoted to the military. Civilian goods were so scarce that they had to be rationed. Staples like butter, sugar, and gasoline were doled out in small quantities. Even golf balls were rationed. In North Korea, golf balls would be a luxury even without a military buildup. As the share of North Korea's output devoted to the military increased, even basic food production became more difficult. (See World View "North Korea's Food Shortage Grows.")

What is the opportunity cost of North Korea's army?

©Ed Jones/AFP/Getty Images

WORLD VIEW

NORTH KOREA'S FOOD SHORTAGE GROWS

North Korea's food shortage has taken another turn for the worse. According to the Food and Agriculture Organization and the World Food Program, food production in 2015–2016 totaled only 4.8 million tons. That's 694,000 tons less than the nation needs to feed itself. In response, the government slashed food rations from 370 grams daily per person to only 360 grams. That allocation is well below the United Nations recommendation of at least 600 grams per day. Widespread starvation continues to plague this nation of 25 million people.

Source: News accounts of 2016–2017.

ROCKET LAUNCH COST ENOUGH TO END NORTH KOREAN FOOD SHORTAGES FOR YEARS

SEOUL—North Korea's latest rocket launches cost an estimated $1.3 billion, according to an official from South Korea's Ministry of Unification. The two launches—one of which failed—cost $600 million. The launch site cost an estimated $400 million and related facilities cost around $300 million. With that much money, North Korea could have purchased 4.6 million tons of corn, a supply of corn that would have eliminated North Korea's food shortages for the next four to five years, according to the Ministry.

Source: Media reports December 2012–January 2013.

ANALYSIS: North Korea's inability to feed itself is partly due to maintaining its large army: resources used for the military aren't available for producing food.

Figure 1.3 illustrates how other nations divide available resources between military and civilian production. The $700 billion the United States now spends on national defense absorbs only 4 percent of total output. This made the opportunity costs of the post-9/11 military buildup and the wars in Iraq and Afghanistan less painful. By contrast, North Korea's commitment to military spending (20 percent) implies a very high opportunity cost.

Percentage of Output Allocated to Military

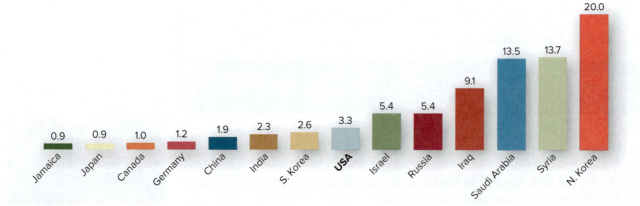

Jamaica	Japan	Canada	Germany	China	India	S. Korea	USA	Israel	Russia	Iraq	Saudi Arabia	Syria	N. Korea
0.9	0.9	1.0	1.2	1.9	2.3	2.6	3.3	5.4	5.4	9.1	13.5	13.7	20.0

FIGURE 1.3

The Military Share of Output

The share of total output allocated to the military indicates the opportunity cost of maintaining an army. North Korea has the highest cost, using one fifth of its resources for military purposes. Although China and the United States have much larger armies, their military *share* of output is much smaller.

Source: Stockholm International Peace Research Institute and U.S. Central Intelligence Agency (2015 data).

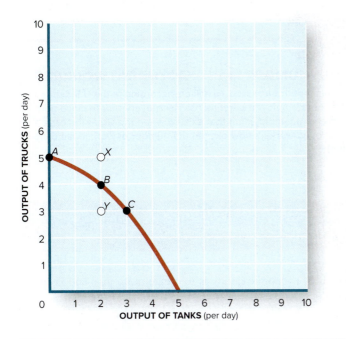

FIGURE 1.4
**Points Inside and Outside
the PPC Curve**

Points outside the production possibilities curve (point *X*) are unattainable with available resources and technology. Points inside the PPC (point *Y*) represent the incomplete use of available resources. Only points on the PPC (*A*, *B*, *C*) represent maximum use of our production capabilities.

Efficiency

Not all of the choices on the production possibilities curve are equally desirable. They are, however, all *efficient*. **Efficiency** means squeezing *maximum* output out of available resources. Every point of the PPC satisfies this condition. Although the *mix* of output changes as we move around the production possibilities curve (Figures 1.1 and 1.2), at every point we are getting as much *total* output as physically possible. Since efficiency in production means simply getting the most from what you've got, **every point on the production possibilities curve is efficient.** At every point on the curve we are using all available resources in the best way we know how.

efficiency: Maximum output of a good from the resources used in production.

Inefficiency

There's no guarantee, of course, that we'll always use resources so efficiently. *A production possibilities curve shows* potential *output, not* actual *output.* If we're inefficient, actual output will be less than that potential. This happens. In the real world, workers sometimes loaf on the job. Or they call in sick and go to a baseball game instead of working. Managers don't always give the clearest directions or stay in touch with advancing technology. Even students sometimes fail to put forth their best effort on homework assignments. This kind of slippage can prevent us from achieving maximum production. When that happens, we end up *inside* the PPC rather than *on* it.

Point *Y* in Figure 1.4 illustrates the consequences of inefficient production. At point *Y*, we're producing only three trucks and two tanks. This is less than our potential. We could assemble a third tank without cutting back truck production (point *C*). Or we could get an extra truck without sacrificing any tank output (point *B*). Instead we're producing *inside* the production possibilities curve at point *Y*. **Whenever we're producing inside the production possibilities curve, we are forgoing the opportunity of producing (and consuming) additional output.**

Unemployment

We can end up inside the production possibilities curve by utilizing resources inefficiently or simply by not using all available resources. This happened repeatedly in the Great Recession of 2008–2009. In October 2009, more than 15 million Americans were unemployed (see In the News "Jobless Workers Outnumber Manufacturing Workers"). These men and women were ready, willing, and available to work, but no one hired them. As a result, we were stuck *inside* the PPC, producing less output than we could have (like point

Y in Figure 1.4). The goal of U.S. economic policy is to create more jobs and keep the United States on its production possibilities curve.

Economic Growth

economic growth: An increase in output (real GDP); an expansion of production possibilities.

The challenge of getting to the production possibilities curve increases with each passing day. People are born every day. As they age, they enter the labor force as new workers. Technology, too, keeps advancing each year. These increases in available labor and technology keep pushing the producing possibilities curve outward. This **economic growth** is a good thing in the sense that it allows us to produce more goods and raise living standards. With economic growth, countries can have more guns *and* more butter (see Figure 1.5). Without economic growth, living standards decline as the population grows. This is the problem that plagues some of the world's poorest nations, where population increases every year but output often doesn't.

THREE BASIC DECISIONS

Production possibilities define the output choices that a nation confronts. From these choices every nation must make some basic decisions. As we noted at the beginning of this chapter, the three core economic questions are

- *WHAT to produce.*
- *HOW to produce.*
- *FOR WHOM to produce.*

FIGURE 1.5

Growth: Increasing Production Possibilities

A production possibilities curve is based on *available* resources and technology. If more resources or better technology becomes available, production possibilities will increase. This economic growth is illustrated by the *shift* from PP_1 to PP_2.

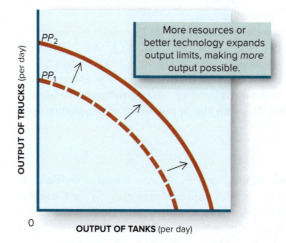

What

There are millions of points along a production possibilities curve, and each one represents a different mix of output. Unfortunately, we can choose only *one* of these points at any time. The point we choose determines what mix of output actually gets produced. That choice determines how many guns are produced, and how much butter—or how many space expeditions and how many sewage treatment facilities get built.

The production possibilities curve itself doesn't tell us which mix of output is best; it just lays out a menu of available choices. It's up to us to pick out the one and only mix of output that will be produced at a given time. This WHAT decision is a fundamental decision every nation must make.

How

Decisions must also be made about HOW to produce. Should we generate electricity by burning coal, smashing atoms, or harnessing solar power? Should we harvest ancient forests even if that destroys endangered owls or other animal species? Should we dump municipal and industrial waste into nearby rivers, or should we dispose of it in some other way? Should we use children to harvest crops and stitch clothes, or should we use only adult labor? There are lots of different ways of producing goods and services, and someone has to make a decision about which production methods to use. The HOW decision is a question not just of efficiency but of social values as well.

For Whom

After we've decided what to produce and how, we must address a third basic question: FOR WHOM? Who is going to get the output produced? Should everyone get an equal share? Should everyone wear the same clothes and drive identical cars? Should some people get to enjoy seven-course banquets while others forage in garbage cans for food scraps? How should the goods and services an economy produces be distributed? Are we satisfied with the way output is now distributed?

THE MECHANISMS OF CHOICE

Answers to the questions of WHAT, HOW, and FOR WHOM largely define an economy. But who formulates the answers? Who actually decides which goods are produced, what technologies are used, or how incomes are distributed?

The Invisible Hand of a Market Economy

Adam Smith had an answer back in 1776. In his classic work *The Wealth of Nations,* the Scottish economist Smith said the "invisible hand" determines what gets produced, how, and for whom. The invisible hand he referred to wasn't a creature from a science fiction movie but, instead, a characterization of the way markets work.

Consider the decision about how many cars to produce in the United States. Who makes that decision? There's no "auto czar" who dictates how many vehicles will be produced this year. Not even General Motors can make such a decision. Instead the *market* decides how many cars to produce. Millions of consumers signal their desire to have a car by browsing the Internet, visiting showrooms, and buying cars. Their purchases flash a green light to producers, who see the potential to earn more profits. To do so, they'll increase auto output. If consumers stop buying cars, profits will disappear. Producers will respond by reducing output, laying off workers, and even closing factories as they did during the recession of 2008–2009.

Notice how the invisible hand moves us along the production possibilities curve. If consumers demand more cars, the mix of output will include more cars and fewer of other goods. If auto production is scaled back, the displaced autoworkers will end up producing other goods and services, changing the mix of output in the opposite direction.

market mechanism: The use of market prices and sales to signal desired outputs (or resource allocations).

How does the market decide who gets this car?

©Samuel Corum/Anadolu Agency/ Getty Images

laissez faire: The doctrine of "leave it alone," of nonintervention by government in the market mechanism.

Adam Smith's invisible hand is now called the **market mechanism.** Notice that it doesn't require any direct contact between consumers and producers. Communication is indirect, transmitted by market prices and sales. Indeed, *the essential feature of the market mechanism is the price signal.* If you want something and have sufficient income, you can buy it. If enough people do the same thing, the total sales of that product will rise, and perhaps its price will as well. Producers, seeing sales and prices rise, will want to exploit this profit potential. To do so, they'll attempt to acquire a larger share of available resources and use it to produce the goods we desire. That's how the "invisible hand" works.

The market mechanism can also answer the HOW question. To maximize their profits, producers seek the lowest-cost method of producing a good. By observing prices in the marketplace, they can identify the cheapest method and adopt it.

The market mechanism can also resolve the FOR WHOM question. A market distributes goods to the highest bidder. Individuals who are willing and able to pay the most for a product tend to get it in a pure market economy. That's why someone else—not you—is driving the new Mercedes Maybach S650.

Adam Smith was so impressed with the ability of the market mechanism to answer the basic WHAT, HOW, and FOR WHOM questions that he urged government to "leave it alone" **(laissez faire). Adam Smith believed the price signals and responses of the marketplace were likely to do a better job of allocating resources than any government could.**

Government Intervention

The laissez-faire policy Adam Smith favored has always had its share of critics. The German economist Karl Marx emphasized how free markets tend to concentrate wealth and power in the hands of the few at the expense of the many. As he saw it, unfettered markets permit the capitalists (those who own the machinery and factories) to enrich themselves while the proletariat (the workers) toil long hours for subsistence wages. **Marx argued that the government not only had to intervene but had to *own* all the means of production**—the factories, the machinery, the land—in order to avoid savage inequalities. In *Das Kapital* (1867) and the revolutionary *Communist Manifesto* (1848), he laid the foundation for a communist state in which the government would be the master of economic outcomes.

The British economist John Maynard Keynes offered a less drastic solution. The market, he conceded, was pretty efficient in organizing production and building better mousetraps. However, individual producers and workers had no control over the broader economy. The cumulative actions of so many economic agents could easily tip the economy in the wrong direction. A completely unregulated market might veer off in one direction and then another as producers all rushed to increase output at the same time or throttled back production in a herdlike manner. The government, Keynes reasoned, could act like a pressure gauge, letting off excess steam or building it up as the economy needed. With the government maintaining overall balance in the economy, the market could live up to its performance expectations. While assuring a stable, full-employment environment, the government might also be able to redress excessive inequalities. **In Keynes's view, government should play an active but not all-inclusive role in managing the economy.**

Continuing Debates

These historical views shed perspective on today's political debates. The core of most debates is some variation of the WHAT, HOW, or FOR WHOM questions. Much of the debate is how these questions should be answered. Conservatives favor Adam Smith's laissez-faire approach, with minimal government interference in the markets. Liberals, by contrast, think government intervention is needed to improve market outcomes. Conservatives resist workplace regulation, price controls, and minimum wages because such interventions might impair market efficiency. Liberals argue that such interventions temper the excesses of the market and promote both equity and efficiency.

World Opinion. The debate over how best to manage the economy is not unique to the United States. **Countries around the world confront the same choice between reliance on the market and reliance on the government.** Public opinion clearly favors the market system, as World View "Market Reliance vs. Government Reliance?" documents. Yet few countries have ever relied exclusively on either the markets or the government to manage their economy.

WORLD VIEW

MARKET RELIANCE VS. GOVERNMENT RELIANCE?

A public opinion poll conducted in countries from around the world found a striking global consensus that the free market economic system is best. In all but one country polled, a majority or plurality agreed with the statement that "the free enterprise system and free market economy is the best system on which to base the future of the world."

Source: GlobeScan Toronto—London—San Francisco 2010.

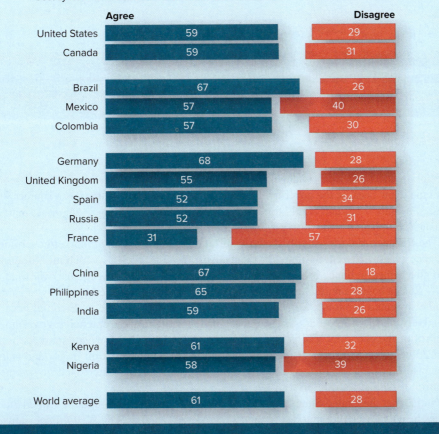

The free enterprise system and free market economy is the best system on which to base the future of the world.

	Agree	Disagree
United States	59	29
Canada	59	31
Brazil	67	26
Mexico	57	40
Colombia	57	30
Germany	68	28
United Kingdom	55	26
Spain	52	34
Russia	52	31
France	31	57
China	67	18
Philippines	65	28
India	59	26
Kenya	61	32
Nigeria	58	39
World average	61	28

ANALYSIS: Most people around the world believe that markets do a good job of answering the core questions of WHAT, HOW, and FOR WHOM.

Degrees of Market Reliance. World View "Index of Economic Freedom" categorizes nations by the extent of their actual market reliance. Hong Kong scores high on this index because its tax rates are relatively low, the public sector is comparatively small, and there

WORLD VIEW

INDEX OF ECONOMIC FREEDOM

Hong Kong ranks number one among the world's nations in economic freedom. It achieves that status with low tax rates, free-trade policies, minimal government regulation, and secure property rights. These and other economic indicators place Hong Kong at the top of the Heritage Foundation's 2017 country rankings by the degree of "economic freedom." The "most free" and the "least free" (repressed) economies on the list of 186 countries are listed here:

Greatest Economic Freedom	Least Economic Freedom
Hong Kong	North Korea
Singapore	Venezuela
New Zealand	Cuba
Switzerland	Congo
Australia	Eritrea
Estonia	Zimbabwe
Canada	Equitorial Guinea
United Arab Emirates	Timor-Leste

Source: *2017 Index of Economic Freedom,* Washington, DC: Heritage Foundation, 2017.

ANALYSIS: Nations differ in how much they rely on market signals or government intervention to shape economic outcomes. Nations that rely the least on government intervention score highest ("most free") on this Index of Economic Freedom.

are few restrictions on private investment or trade. By contrast, North Korea scores extremely low because the government owns all property, directly allocates resources, sets wages, rations food, and limits trade. In other words, Hong Kong is the most market-reliant; North Korea is the most government-reliant.

The Heritage rankings simply *describe* differences in the extent of market/government reliance across different nations. By themselves, they don't tell us which mix of market and government reliance is best. Moreover, the individual rankings change over time. In 1989 Russia began a massive transformation from a state-controlled economy to a more market-oriented economy. Some of the former Soviet republics (e.g., Estonia) became relatively free, while others (e.g., Turkmenistan) still rely on extensive government control of the economy. China has greatly expanded the role of private markets in the last 20 years, and Cuba is grudgingly moving in the same direction in fits and starts. Venezuela has moved in the opposite direction, with sharply increased government control of production and prices.

Notice that the United States is not on the World View list. Although the United States relies heavily on private markets to make WHAT, HOW, and FOR WHOM decisions, it lags behind Hong Kong, Canada, and other nations on the Heritage Index. In 2014, the United States came in 12th, down a few notches from earlier years. That modest decline was due to the increased regulation, higher taxes, and increased government spending that the Obama administration adopted in response to the Great Recession. President Trump's more market-friendly policies have reversed that move. This tug-of-war between more government regulation and more market reliance continues—in both public opinion and the U.S. Congress.

A Mixed Economy

No one advocates *complete* dependence on markets, nor *total* government control of economic resources. Neither Adam Smith's invisible hand nor the governments' very visible hand always works perfectly. As a result, ***the United States, like most nations, uses a combination of market signals and government directives to direct economic outcomes.*** The resulting compromises are called **mixed economies.**

The reluctance of countries around the world to rely exclusively on either market signals or government directives is due to the recognition that both mechanisms can and do fail on occasion. As we've seen, market signals are capable of answering the three core questions of WHAT, HOW, and FOR WHOM. But the answers may not be the best possible ones.

mixed economy: An economy that uses both market signals and government directives to allocate goods and resources.

Market Failure

When market signals don't give the best possible answers to the WHAT, HOW, and FOR WHOM questions, we say that the market mechanism has *failed.* Specifically, **market failure** means that the invisible hand has failed to achieve the best possible outcomes. If the market fails, we end up with the wrong (*sub*optimal) mix of output, too much unemployment, polluted air, or an inequitable distribution of income.

In a market-driven economy, for example, producers will select production methods based on cost. Cost-driven production decisions, however, may encourage a factory to spew pollution into the environment rather than to use cleaner but more expensive methods of production. The resulting pollution may be so bad that society ends up worse off as a result of the extra production. In such a case we may need government intervention to force better answers to the WHAT and HOW questions.

We could also let the market decide who gets to consume cigarettes. Anyone who had enough money to buy a pack of cigarettes would then be entitled to smoke. What if, however, children aren't experienced enough to balance the risks of smoking against the pleasures? What if nonsmokers are harmed by secondhand smoke? In this case as well, the market's answer to the FOR WHOM question might not be optimal.

market failure: An imperfection in the market mechanism that prevents optimal outcomes.

Government Failure

Government intervention might be needed to move us closer to our economic goals. If successful, the resulting mix of market signals and government directives would be an improvement over a purely market-driven economy. But government intervention may fail as well. **Government failure** occurs when government intervention fails to improve market outcomes or actually makes them worse.

Government failure often occurs in unintended ways. For example, the government may intervene to force an industry to clean up its pollution. The government's directives may impose such high costs that the industry closes factories and lays off workers. Some cutbacks in output might be appropriate, but they could also prove excessive. The government might also mandate pollution control technologies that are too expensive or even obsolete. None of this has to happen, but it might. If it does, government failure will have worsened economic outcomes.

The government might also fail if it interferes with the market's answer to the FOR WHOM question. For 50 years, communist China distributed goods by government directive, not market performance. Incomes were more equal, but uniformly low. To increase output and living standards, China turned to market incentives. As entrepreneurs responded to these incentives, living standards rose dramatically—even while inequality increased. That surge in living standards made the vast majority of Chinese believers in the power of free markets (see the World View appearing earlier in this chapter).

Excessive taxes and transfer payments can also worsen economic outcomes. If the government raises taxes on the rich to pay welfare benefits for the poor, neither the rich nor the poor may see much purpose in working. In that case, the attempt to give everybody a "fair"

government failure: Government intervention that fails to improve economic outcomes.

share of the pie might end up shrinking the size of the pie. If that happened, society could end up worse off.

Seeking Balance

None of these failures has to occur. But they might. ***The challenge for any society is to minimize economic failures by selecting the appropriate balance of market signals and government directives.*** This isn't an easy task. It requires that we know how markets work and why they sometimes fail. We also need to know what policy options the government has and how and when they might work.

....

WHAT ECONOMICS IS ALL ABOUT

Understanding how economies function is the basic purpose of studying economics. We seek to know how an economy is organized, how it behaves, and how successfully it achieves its basic objectives. Then, if we're lucky, we can discover better ways of attaining those same objectives.

Ends vs. Means

Economists don't formulate an economy's objectives. Instead they focus on the *means* available for achieving given *goals*. In 1978, for example, the U.S. Congress identified "full employment" as a major economic goal. Congress then directed future presidents (and their economic advisers) to formulate policies that would enable us to achieve full employment. The economist's job is to help design policies that will best achieve this and other economic goals.

The same distinction between ends and means is integral to your own life. Your *goal* (the ends) may be to achieve a specific career. The immediate question is how best to achieve that goal (the means). Should you major in economics? Take computer science? Study art history? Surely, you hope that the course choices you make will best help you attain your career goals. Economists can help select those courses based on studies of other students, their majors, and their career outcomes.

Normative vs. Positive Analysis

The distinction between ends and means is mirrored in the difference between *normative* analysis and *positive* analysis. Normative analysis incorporates subjective judgments about what *ought* to be done. Positive analysis focuses on how things might be done without subjective judgments of what is "best." The Heritage Index of Economic Freedom (World View), for example, constitutes a *positive* analysis to the extent that it objectively describes global differences in the extent of market reliance. That effort entails collecting, sorting, and ranking mountains of data. Heritage slides into *normative* analysis when it suggests that market reliance is tantamount to "economic freedom" and inherently superior to more government intervention—that markets are good and governments are bad.

Debates over the core FOR WHOM question likewise reflect both positive and normative analysis. A positive analysis would observe that the U.S. incomes are very "unequal," with the richest 20 percent of the population getting half of all income (see table in Figure 2.3). That's an observable fact—that is, positive analysis. To characterize that same distribution as "inequitable" or "unfair" is to transform (positive) fact into (normative) judgment. Economists are free, of course, to offer their judgments but must be careful to distinguish positive and normative perspectives.

Macro vs. Micro

macroeconomics: The study of aggregate economic behavior, of the economy as a whole.

The study of economics is typically divided into two parts: macroeconomics and microeconomics. **Macroeconomics** focuses on the behavior of an entire economy—the "big picture." In macroeconomics we worry about such national goals as full employment, control of inflation, and economic growth, without worrying about the well-being or behavior of specific individuals or firms. The essential concern of macroeconomics is to understand and improve the performance of the economy as a whole.

Microeconomics is concerned with the details of this big picture. In microeconomics we focus on the individuals, firms, and government agencies that actually compose the larger economy. Our interest here is in the behavior of individual economic actors. What are their goals? How can they best achieve these goals with their limited resources? How will they respond to various incentives and opportunities?

microeconomics: The study of individual behavior in the economy, of the components of the larger economy.

A primary concern of *macro*economics, for example, is to determine how much money, *in total,* consumers will spend on goods and services. In *micro*economics, the focus is much narrower. In micro, attention is paid to purchases of *specific* goods and services rather than just aggregated totals. Macro likewise concerns itself with the level of *total* business investment, while micro examines how *individual* businesses make their investment decisions.

Although they operate at different levels of abstraction, macro and micro are intrinsically related. Macro (aggregate) outcomes depend on micro behavior, and micro (individual) behavior is affected by macro outcomes. One can't fully understand how an economy works until one understands how all the individual participants behave. But just as you can drive a car without knowing how its engine is constructed, you can observe how an economy runs without completely disassembling it. In macroeconomics we observe that the car goes faster when the accelerator is depressed and that it slows when the brake is applied. That's all we need to know in most situations. At times, however, the car breaks down. When it does, we have to know something more about how the pedals work. This leads us into micro studies. How does each part work? Which ones can or should be fixed?

Our interest in microeconomics is motivated by more than our need to understand how the larger economy works. The "parts" of the economic engine are people. To the extent that we care about the well-being of individuals, we have a fundamental interest in microeconomic behavior and outcomes. In this regard, we examine how individual consumers and business firms seek to achieve specific goals in the marketplace. The goals aren't always related to output. Gary Becker won the 1992 Nobel Prize in Economics for demonstrating how economic principles also affect decisions to marry, to have children, to engage in criminal activities—or even to complete homework assignments in an economics class.

Theory vs. Reality

The economy is much too vast and complex to describe and explain in one course (or one lifetime). We need to simplify it. To do so, we focus on basic relationships, ignoring annoying details. We develop basic principles of economic behavior and then use those principles to predict and explain economic events. This means that we formulate theories, or *models,* of economic behavior and then use those theories to evaluate and design economic policy.

Our model of consumer behavior assumes, for example, that people buy less of a good when its price rises. In reality, however, people *may* buy *more* of a good at increased prices, especially if those high prices create a certain snob appeal or if prices are expected to increase still further. In predicting consumer responses to price increases, we typically ignore such possibilities by *assuming* that the price of the good in question is the *only* thing that changes. This assumption of "other things remaining equal" (unchanged) (in Latin, *ceteris paribus*) allows us to make straightforward predictions. If instead we described consumer responses to increased prices in any and all circumstances (allowing everything to change at once), every prediction would be accompanied by a book full of exceptions and qualifications. We'd look more like lawyers than economists.

ceteris paribus: The assumption of nothing else changing.

Although the assumption of *ceteris paribus* makes it easier to formulate economic theory and policy, it also increases the risk of error. If other things do change in significant ways, our predictions (and policies) may fail. But like weather forecasters, we continue to make predictions, knowing that occasional failure is inevitable. In so doing, we're motivated by the conviction that it's better to be approximately right than to be dead wrong.

Imperfect Knowledge. One last word of warning before you read further. Economics claims to be a science in pursuit of basic truths. We want to understand and explain how the economy works without getting tangled up in subjective value judgments. This may be an impossible task. First, it's not clear where the truth lies. For more than 200 years economists have been arguing about what makes the economy tick. None of the competing theories has performed spectacularly well. Indeed, few economists have successfully predicted major economic events with any consistency. Even annual forecasts of inflation, unemployment, and output are regularly in error. Worse still, never-ending arguments about what caused a major economic event continue long after it occurs. In fact, economists are still arguing over the primary causes of the Great Depression of the 1930s!

In view of all these debates and uncertainties, don't expect to learn everything there is to know about the economy today in this text or course. Our goals are more modest. We want to develop a reasonable perspective on economic behavior, an understanding of basic principles. With this foundation, you should acquire a better view of how the economy works. Daily news reports on economic events should make more sense. Congressional debates on tax and budget policies should take on more meaning. You may even develop some insights that you can apply toward running a business, planning a career, or simply managing your scarce time and money more efficiently.

THE ECONOMY TOMORROW

HARNESSING THE SUN

Powering our homes with solar power is an exciting prospect. Today, more than 50 percent of our electricity is generated from the burning of oil and coal. These fossil fuels pollute the air, damage the land, and, as we saw in the 2010 BP oil spill, damage marine life as well. By contrast, we don't have to burn anything to generate solar power. We just need to harness that power by absorbing it in solar panels that convert solar radiation into electricity. The U.S. Department of the Interior says solar stations built in the deserts of the southwestern states could deliver 2,300 gigawatts of energy, more than double America's entire electricity consumption.

Solar power could also be used to fuel our cars. When automakers peer into the future, they see fleets of electric cars. Those fleets will have to be continuously charged with electricity. Why not solar-powered recharging stations? Just think how much that gasoline-to-solar conversion would help clean up the air we breathe!

Opportunity Costs. It's easy to get excited about a solar-powered future. But before we jump on the solar bandwagon, we have to at least consider the costs involved. Sure, the sun's rays are free. But you need a lot of capital investment to harness that solar power. Solar panels on the roof don't come free. Nor do solar-powered electrical charging stations, solar power plants, or the electrical grids that distribute electricity to users. President Obama committed as much as $200 billion in subsidies and direct spending to accelerate the adoption of solar energy. To develop a nationwide, complete solar power infrastructure would cost *trillions* of dollars.

Remember, economists think in terms of real resources, not money. Paper money doesn't build solar panels; it takes real factors of production—land, labor, capital, and entrepreneurship. Those resources—worth trillions of dollars—could be used to produce

Is solar energy free?
©Darren Baker/Alamy Stock Photo RF

something else. If we invested that many resources in medical technology, we might cure cancer, find an antidote for the AIDS virus, and maybe even eradicate the flu. Investing that many resources in education might make college not only more enjoyable but a lot more productive as well. To invest all those resources in solar development implies that solar development trumps all other social goals. That's a *normative* judgement that not everyone embraces. Many people worry more about their education, their homes, national defense, and the nation's infrastructure than the harm that conventional energy sources inflict on the environment. President Trump himself called President Obama's spending on solar energy a "disaster" and pushed for more development of conventional energy sources, especially natural gas and oil that are much cheaper. While his critics have lambasted President Trump for ignoring the environmental consequences of nonrenewable energy sources, the ongoing debate has highlighted a basic principle of economics: In deciding whether and how intensively to develop solar power, we have to assess opportunity costs—what goods and services we implicitly forsake in order to harness the sun.

SUMMARY

- Scarcity is a basic fact of economic life. Factors of production (land, labor, capital, entrepreneurship) are scarce in relation to our desires for goods and services. **LO1-1**
- All economic activity entails opportunity costs. Factors of production (resources) used to produce one output cannot simultaneously be used to produce something else. When we choose to produce one thing, we forsake the opportunity to produce some other good or service. **LO1-2**
- A production possibilities curve (PPC) illustrates the limits to production—the various combinations of goods and services that could be produced in a given period if all available resources and technology are used efficiently. The PPC also illustrates opportunity costs—what is given up to get more of something else. **LO1-3**
- The bent shape of the PPC reflects the law of increasing opportunity costs: Increasing quantities of any good can be obtained only by sacrificing ever-increasing quantities of other goods. **LO1-3**
- Inefficient or incomplete use of resources will fail to attain production possibilities. Additional resources or better technologies will expand them. This is the essence of economic growth. **LO1-3**
- Every country must decide WHAT to produce, HOW to produce, and FOR WHOM to produce with its limited resources. **LO1-4**
- The study of economics focuses on the broad question of resource allocation. Macroeconomics is concerned with allocating the resources of an entire economy to achieve aggregate economic goals (e.g., full employment). Microeconomics focuses on the behavior and goals of individual market participants. **LO1-4**
- The WHAT, HOW, and FOR WHOM choices can be made by the market mechanism or by government directives. Most nations are mixed economies, using a combination of these two choice mechanisms. **LO1-5**
- Market failure exists when market signals generate suboptimal outcomes. Government failure occurs when government intervention worsens economic outcomes. The challenge for economic theory and policy is to find the mix of market signals and government directives that best fulfills our social and economic goals. **LO1-5**

Key Terms

scarcity
factors of production
capital
entrepreneurship
economics
opportunity cost

production possibilities
efficiency
economic growth
market mechanism
laissez faire
mixed economy

market failure
government failure
macroeconomics
microeconomics
ceteris paribus

Questions for Discussion

1. What opportunity costs did you incur in reading this chapter? If you read another chapter today, would your opportunity cost (per chapter) increase? Explain. **LO1-2**
2. How much time *could* you spend on homework in a day? How much do you spend? How do you decide? **LO1-2**
3. What's the real cost of a "free lunch" as mentioned in the discussion of "Opportunity Costs?" **LO1-2**
4. How might a nation's production possibilities be affected by the following? **LO1-3**
   a. New solar technology.
   b. An increase in immigration.
   c. An increase in military spending.
   d. A natural disaster.
5. What are the opportunity costs of developing wind farms to generate "clean" electricity? Should we make the investment? **LO1-2**
6. Who would go to college in a completely private (market) college system? How does government intervention change this FOR WHOM outcome? **LO1-4**
7. Why do people around the world have so much faith in free markets (World View "Market Reliance vs. Government Reliance?")? **LO1-5**
8. Why did both presidents Obama and Trump reduce spending on America's space exploration program? **LO1-2**
9. What is the connection between North Korea's missile program and its hunger problem? (World View "North Korea's Food Shortage Grows") **LO1-2**
10. Why might more reliance on markets rather than government be desirable? When and how might it be undesirable? **LO1-5**
11. Explain why there are limits to output and how these limits force economies to make tradeoffs. **LO1-1**

APPENDIX

USING GRAPHS

Economists like to draw graphs. In fact, we didn't even make it through the first chapter without a few graphs. This appendix looks more closely at the way graphs are drawn and used. The basic purpose of a graph is to illustrate a relationship between two *variables*. Consider, for example, the relationship between grades and studying. In general, we expect that additional hours of study time will lead to higher grades. Hence we should be able to see a distinct relationship between hours of study time and grade point average.

Suppose that we actually surveyed all the students taking this course with regard to their study time and grade point averages. The resulting information can be compiled in a table such as Table A.1.

According to the table, students who don't study at all can expect an F in this course. To get a C, the average student apparently spends 8 hours a week studying. All those who study 16 hours a week end up with an A in the course.

These relationships between grades and studying can also be illustrated on a graph. Indeed, the whole purpose of a graph is to summarize numerical relationships.

We begin to construct a graph by drawing horizontal and vertical boundaries, as in Figure A.1. These boundaries are called the *axes* of the graph. On the vertical axis (often called the *y*-axis) we measure one of the variables; the other variable is measured on the horizontal axis (the *x*-axis).

In this case, we shall measure the grade point average on the vertical axis. We start at the *origin* (the intersection of the two axes) and count upward, letting the distance between horizontal lines represent half (0.5) a grade point. Each horizontal line is numbered, up to the maximum grade point average of 4.0.

The number of hours each week spent doing homework is measured on the horizontal axis. We begin at the origin again and count to the right. The *scale* (numbering) proceeds in increments of 1 hour, up to 20 hours per week.

TABLE A.1

Hypothetical Relationship of Grades to Study Time

Study Time (Hours per Week)	Grade Point Average
16	4.0 (A)
14	3.5 (B+)
12	3.0 (B)
10	2.5 (C+)
8	2.0 (C)
6	1.5 (D+)
4	1.0 (D)
2	0.5 (F+)
0	0.0 (F)

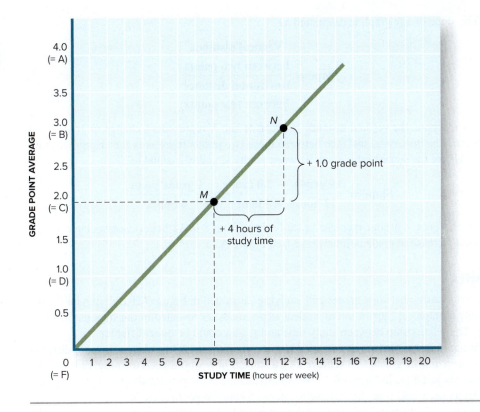

FIGURE A.1
The Relationship of Grades to Study Time

The upward (positive) slope of the curve indicates that additional studying is associated with higher grades. The average student (2.0, or C grade) studies 8 hours per week. This is indicated by point *M* on the graph.

When both axes have been labeled and measured, we can begin illustrating the relationship between study time and grades. Consider the typical student who does 8 hours of homework per week and has a 2.0 (C) grade point average. We illustrate this relationship by first locating 8 hours on the horizontal axis. We then move up from that point a distance of 2.0 grade points, to point *M*. Point *M* tells us that 8 hours of study time per week are typically associated with a 2.0 grade point average.

The rest of the information in Table A.1 is drawn (or *plotted*) on the graph the same way. To illustrate the average grade for people who study 12 hours per week, we move upward from the number 12 on the horizontal axis until we reach the height of 3.0 on the vertical axis. At that intersection, we draw another point (point *N*).

Once we've plotted the various points describing the relationship of study time to grades, we may connect them with a line or curve. This line (curve) is our summary. In this case, the line slopes upward to the right—that is, it has a *positive* slope. This slope indicates that more hours of study time are associated with *higher* grades. Were higher grades associated with *less* study time, the curve in Figure A.1 would have a *negative* slope (downward from left to right).

Slopes

The upward slope of Figure A.1 tells us that higher grades are associated with increased amounts of study time. That same curve also tells us *by how much* grades tend to rise with study time. According to point *M* in Figure A.1, the average student studies 8 hours per week and earns a C (2.0 grade point average). To earn a B (3.0 average), students apparently need to study an average of 12 hours per week (point *N*). Hence an increase of 4 hours of study time per week is associated with a 1-point increase in grade point average. This relationship between *changes* in study time and *changes* in grade point average is expressed by the steepness, or *slope,* of the graph.

The slope of any graph is calculated as

$$\text{Slope} = \frac{\text{Vertical distance between two points}}{\text{Horizontal distance between two points}}$$

In our example, the vertical distance between *M* and *N* represents a change in grade point average. The horizontal distance between these two points represents the change in study time. Hence the slope of the graph between points *M* and *N* is equal to

$$\text{Slope} = \frac{3.0 \text{ grade} - 2.0 \text{ grade}}{12 \text{ hours} - 8 \text{ hours}} = \frac{1 \text{ grade point}}{4 \text{ hours}}$$

In other words, a 4-hour increase in study time (from 8 to 12 hours) is associated with a 1-point increase in grade point average (see Figure A.1).

Shifts

The relationship between grades and studying illustrated in Figure A.1 isn't inevitable. It's simply a graphical illustration of student experiences, as revealed in our hypothetical survey. The relationship between study time and grades could be quite different.

Suppose that the university decided to raise grading standards, making it more difficult to achieve higher grades. To achieve a C, a student now would need to study 12 hours per week, not just 8 (as in Figure A.1). Whereas students could previously get a B by studying 12 hours per week, now they'd have to study 16 hours to get that grade.

Figure A.2 illustrates the new grading standards. Notice that the new curve lies to the right of the earlier curve. We say that the curve has *shifted* to reflect a change in the relationship between study time and grades. Point *R* indicates that 12 hours of study time now "produce" a C, not a B (point *N* on the old curve). Students who now study only

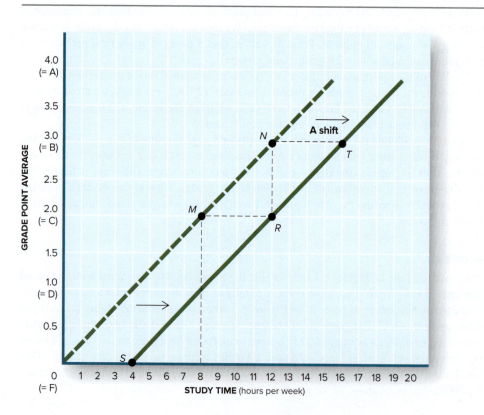

FIGURE A.2

A Shift

When a relationship between two variables changes, the entire curve *shifts*. In this case a tougher grading policy alters the relationship between study time and grades. To get a C, one must now study **12 hours per week (point R)**, not just 8 hours (point M).

GRADE POINT AVERAGE

STUDY TIME (hours per week)

4 hours per week (point *S*) will fail. Under the old grading policy, they could have at least gotten a D. *When a curve shifts, the underlying relationship between the two variables has changed.*

A shift may also change the slope of the curve. In Figure A.2, the new grading curve is parallel to the old one; it therefore has the same slope. Under either the new grading policy or the old one, a 4-hour increase in study time leads to a 1-point increase in grades. Therefore, the slope of both curves in Figure A.2 is

$$\text{Slope} = \frac{\text{Vertical change}}{\text{Horizontal change}} = \frac{1}{4}$$

This too may change, however. Figure A.3 illustrates such a possibility. In this case, zero study time still results in an F. But now the payoff for additional studying is reduced. Now it takes 6 hours of study time to get a D (1.0 grade point), not 4 hours as before. Likewise, another 4 hours of study time (to a total of 10) raise the grade by only two-thirds of a point. It takes 6 hours to raise the grade a full point. The slope of the new line is therefore

$$\text{Slope} = \frac{\text{Vertical change}}{\text{Horizontal change}} = \frac{1}{6}$$

The new curve in Figure A.3 has a smaller slope than the original curve and so lies below it. What all this means is that it now takes a greater effort to improve your grade.

Linear vs. Nonlinear Curves

In Figures A.1–A.3 the relationship between grades and studying is represented by a straight line—that is, a *linear curve*. A distinguishing feature of linear curves is that they have the same (constant) slope throughout. In Figure A.1 it appears that *every* 4-hour

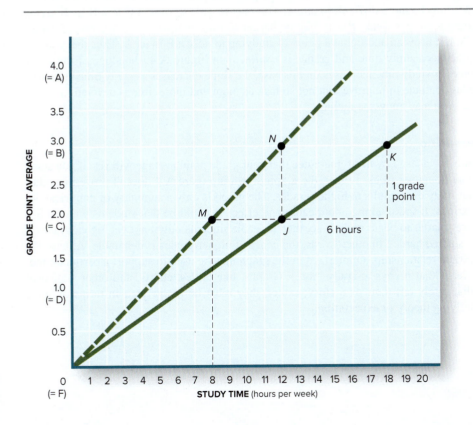

FIGURE A.3

A Change in Slope

When a curve shifts, it may change its slope as well. In this case a new grading policy makes each higher grade more difficult to reach. To raise a C to a B, for example, one must study 6 additional hours (compare points *J* and *K*). Earlier it took only 4 hours to move the grade scale up a full point. The slope of the line has declined from 0.25 (= 1 ÷ 4) to 0.17 (= 1 ÷ 6).

FIGURE A.4

A Nonlinear Relationship

Straight lines have a constant slope, implying a constant relationship between the two variables. But the relationship (and slope) may vary. In this case, it takes 6 extra hours of study to raise a C (point *W*) to a B (point *X*) but 8 extra hours to raise a B to an A (point *Y*). The slope decreases as we move up the curve.

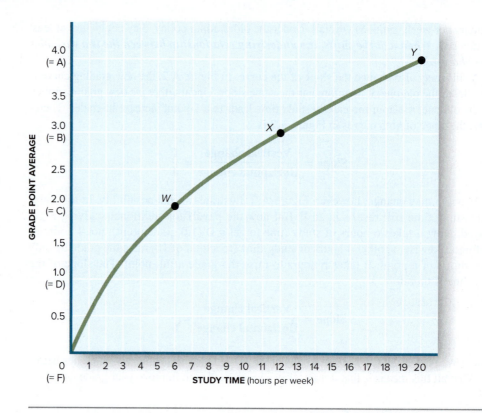

increase in study time is associated with a 1-point increase in average grades. In Figure A.3 it appears that every 6-hour increase in study time leads to a 1-point increase in grades. But the relationship between studying and grades may not be linear. Higher grades may be more difficult to attain. You may be able to raise a C to a B by studying 4 hours more per week. But it may be harder to raise a B to an A. According to Figure A.4, it takes an additional 8 hours of studying to raise a B to an A. Thus the relationship between study time and grades is *nonlinear* in Figure A.4; the slope of the curve changes as study time increases. In this case, the slope decreases as study time increases. Grades continue to improve, but not so fast, as more and more time is devoted to homework. You may know the feeling.

Causation

Figure A.4 doesn't by itself guarantee that your grade point average will rise if you study 4 more hours per week. In fact, the graph drawn in Figure A.4 doesn't prove that additional study ever results in higher grades. The graph is only a summary of empirical observations. It says nothing about cause and effect. It could be that students who study a lot are smarter to begin with. If so, then less able students might not get higher grades if they studied harder. In other words, the *cause* of higher grades is debatable. At best, the empirical relationship summarized in the graph may be used to support a particular theory (e.g., that it pays to study more). Graphs, like tables, charts, and other statistical media, rarely tell their own story; rather, they must be *interpreted* in terms of some underlying theory or expectation.

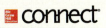

PROBLEMS FOR CHAPTER 1

LO1-2 1. According to Table 1.1 (or Figure 1.1), what is the opportunity cost of the first truck produced?

LO1-3 2. (*a*) Compute the opportunity cost in forgone consumer goods (millions of pounds of butter) for each additional unit of military output (number of planes) produced:

Military output	0	1	2	3	4	5
Consumer goods output	100	90	75	55	30	0
Opportunity cost		___	___	___	___	___

(*b*) As military output increases, are opportunity costs (A) increasing, (B) decreasing, or (C) remaining constant?

LO1-3 3. According to Figure 1.3, how much food production is sacrificed when North Korea moves from point *P* to point *N*?

LO1-2 4. (*a*) If the average North Korean farmer produces 1,800 pounds of food per year, what is the opportunity cost, in pounds of food, of North Korea's army (World View "World's Largest Armies")?

(*b*) If a person needs at least 500 pounds of food per year to survive, how many people could have been fed with the forgone food output?

LO1-2 5. What is the opportunity cost (in civilian output) of a defense buildup that raises military spending from 4.0 to 4.3 percent of a $20 trillion economy?

LO1-4 6. What are the three core economic questions societies must answer?

LO1-3 7. According to the figure (similar to Figure 1.4),

(*a*) At which point(s) is this society producing some of each type of output but producing inefficiently?

(*b*) At which point(s) is this society producing the most output possible with the available resources and technology?

(*c*) At which point(s) is the output combination unattainable with available resources and technology?

(*d*) Show the change that would occur if the resources of this society increased. Label this curve PPC$_2$.

(*e*) Show the change that would occur with a huge natural disaster that destroyed 40 percent of production capacity. Label this curve PPC$_3$.

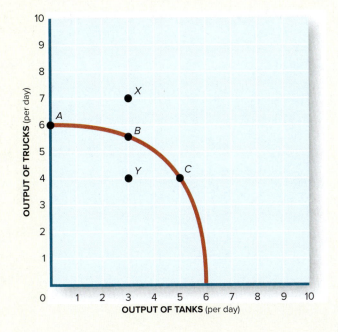

LO1-3 8. You have only 20 hours per week to use for either study time or fun time. Suppose the relationship between study time, fun time, and grades is shown in this table:

Fun time (hours per week)	20	18	14	8	0
Study time (hours per week)	0	2	6	12	20
Grade point average	*0*	*1.0*	*2.0*	*3.0*	*4.0*

(a) Draw the (linear) production possibilities curve on a graph that represents the alternative uses of your time.

(b) On the same graph, show the combination of study time and fun time that would get you a 2.0 grade average.

(c) What is the cost, in lost fun time, of raising your grade point average from 2.0 to 3.0?

LO1-5 9. According to the World View "Market Reliance vs. Government Reliance?" which nation has

(a) The highest level of faith in the market system?

(b) The lowest level of faith in the market system?

LO1-2 10. If a person literally had "nothing else to do,"

(a) What would be the opportunity cost of doing this homework?

(b) What is the likelihood of that?

LO1-1 11. According to the World View "World's Largest Armies," what percent of the total population is serving in the military in

(a) The United States (population = 340 million)?

(b) North Korea (population = 25 million)?

(c) China (population = 1.4 billion)?

LO1-2 12. The Economy Tomorrow: What are the opportunity costs of increasing the number of solar panels in use in the United States?

©Kyodo via AP Images

CHAPTER 2

The U.S. Economy: A Global View

All nations must confront the central economic questions of WHAT to produce, HOW to produce, and FOR WHOM to produce it. However, the nations of the world approach these issues with vastly different production possibilities. China, Canada, the United States, Russia, and Brazil have more than *3 million* square miles of land each. All that land gives them far greater production possibilities than Dominica, Tonga, Malta, or Lichtenstein, each of which has less than 300 square miles of land. The population of China totals more than 1.4 billion people, nearly five times that of the United States, and 25,000 times the population of Greenland. Obviously these nations confront very different output choices.

In addition to vastly uneven production possibilities, the nations of the world use different mechanisms for deciding WHAT, HOW, and FOR WHOM to produce. Belarus, Romania, North Korea, and Cuba still rely heavily on central planning. By contrast, Singapore, New Zealand, Ireland, and the United States permit the market mechanism to play a dominant role in shaping economic outcomes.

With different production possibilities and mechanisms of choice, you'd expect economic outcomes to vary greatly across nations. And they do. This chapter assesses how the U.S. economy stacks up. Specifically,

- **WHAT goods and services does the United States produce?**
- **HOW is that output produced?**
- **FOR WHOM is the output produced?**

In each case, we want to see not only how the United States has answered these questions but also how America's answers compare with those of other nations.

WHAT AMERICA PRODUCES

The United States has less than 5 percent of the world's population and only 12 percent of the world's arable land, yet it produces 20 percent of the world's output.

GDP Comparisons

World View "Comparative Output (GDP)" shows how total U.S. production compares with that of other nations. Every country produces a different mix of output. So, it's impossible to compare output in purely *physical* terms (e.g., so many cars, so many fish, etc.). But we can make

LEARNING OBJECTIVES

After reading this chapter, you should know

LO2-1 The relative size of the U.S. economy.

LO2-2 How the U.S. output mix has changed over time.

LO2-3 How the United States is able to produce so much output.

LO2-4 How incomes are distributed in the United States and elsewhere.

WORLD VIEW

COMPARATIVE OUTPUT (GDP)

The United States is by far the world's largest economy. Its annual output of goods and services is one and a half times larger than China's, three times Japan's, and more than all of the European Union's. The output of Third World countries is only a tiny fraction of U.S. output.

Source: The World Bank (Atlas method).

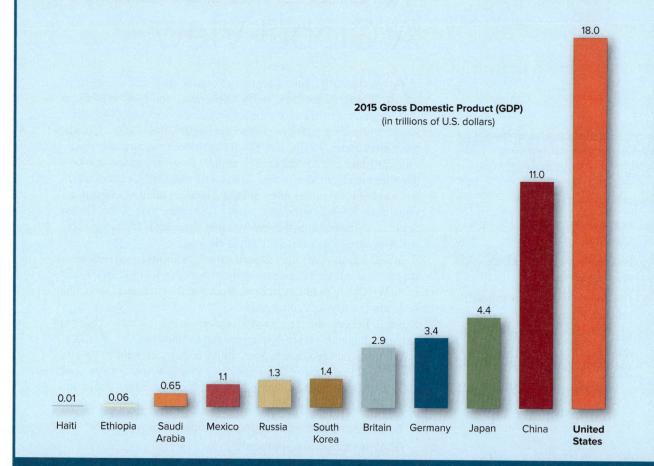

2015 Gross Domestic Product (GDP)
(in trillions of U.S. dollars)

Country	GDP
Haiti	0.01
Ethiopia	0.06
Saudi Arabia	0.65
Mexico	1.1
Russia	1.3
South Korea	1.4
Britain	2.9
Germany	3.4
Japan	4.4
China	11.0
United States	18.0

ANALYSIS: The market value of output (GDP) is a basic measure of an economy's size. The U.S. economy is far larger than any other and accounts for more than one-fifth of the entire world's output of goods and services.

---

gross domestic product (GDP): The total market value of all final goods and services produced within a nation's borders in a given time period.

comparisons based on the *value* of output. We do this by computing the total market value of all the goods and services a nation produces in a year—what we call **gross domestic product (GDP).** In effect, GDP is the "pie" of output we bake each year.

In 2015 the U.S. economy baked a huge pie—one containing more than $18 trillion worth of goods and services. That was far more output than any other nation produced. The second-largest economy, China, produced only two-thirds that much. Japan came in third, with about a third of U.S. output. Cuba, by contrast, produced less than $90 *billion* of output, less than the state of Mississippi. Russia, which was once regarded as a superpower, produced only $1.3 trillion. The entire 27-member European Union produces less output than the United States.

Per Capita GDP. What makes the U.S. share of world output so remarkable is that we do it with so few people. The U.S. population of 340 million amounts to less than 5 percent of the world's total (7.4 billion). Yet we produce more than 20 percent of the world's output.

That means we're producing a lot of output *per person*. China, by contrast, has the opposite ratios: 20 percent of the world's population producing less than 13 percent of the world's output. So China is producing a lot of output but relatively less *per person*.

This people-based measure of economic performance is called **per capita GDP.** Per capita GDP is simply a nation's total output divided by its total population. It doesn't tell us how much any specific person gets. *Per capita GDP is an indicator of how much output the average person would get if all output were divided evenly among the population.* In effect, GDP per capita tells us how large a slice of the GDP pie the average citizen gets.

In 2015 per capita GDP in the United States was roughly $56,000. That means the average U.S. citizen could have consumed $56,000 worth of goods and services. That's a staggering amount by global standards—five times the average for the rest of the world. World View "GDP per Capita around the World" provides a global perspective on just how "rich"

per capita GDP: The dollar value of GDP divided by total population; average GDP.

WORLD VIEW

GDP PER CAPITA AROUND THE WORLD

The American standard of living is nearly five times higher than the average for the rest of the world. People in the poorest nations of the world (e.g., Haiti, Ethiopia) barely survive on per capita incomes that are a tiny fraction of U.S. standards.

Source: The World Bank.

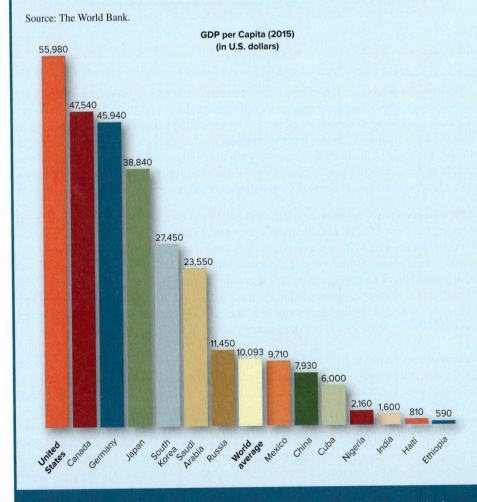

GDP per Capita (2015) (in U.S. dollars)

ANALYSIS: Per capita GDP is a measure of output that reflects average living standards. America's exceptionally high GDP per capita implies access to far more goods and services than people in other nations have.

FIGURE 2.1

U.S. Output and Population Growth since 1900

Over time, the growth of output in the United States has greatly exceeded population growth. As a consequence, GDP per capita has grown tremendously. GDP per capita was five times higher in 2000 than in 1900.

Source: U.S. Department of Labor.

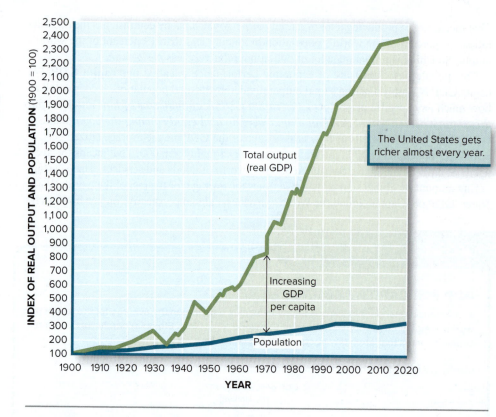

America is. Notice how much more output the average American has than a person in India or, worse yet, Haiti. The gap between U.S. living standards and those in other nations is startling. According to the World Bank, 40 percent of the people on Earth subsist on incomes of less than $3 a day—a level completely unimaginable to the average American. *Homeless* people in the United States enjoy a higher living standard than billions of poor people in other nations (see chapter titled "Global Poverty"). In this context, it's easy to understand why the rest of the world envies (and sometimes resents) America's prosperity.

GDP Growth. What's even more startling about global comparisons is that the GDP gap between the United States and the world's poor nations keeps growing. The reason for that is **economic growth.** With few exceptions, U.S. output increases nearly every year: the pie keeps getting larger. *On average, U.S. output has grown by roughly 3 percent a year, nearly three times faster than population growth (1 percent).* So the U.S. pie is growing faster than the number of people coming to the table. Hence not only does *total* output keep rising, but *per capita* output keeps rising as well (see Figure 2.1). Even the Great Recession of 2008–2009 hardly made a dent in this pattern of ever-rising incomes.

Poor Nations. People in the world's poorest countries aren't so fortunate. China's economy has grown exceptionally fast in the last 20 years, propelling it to second place in the global GDP rankings. But in many other nations total output has actually *declined* year after year, further depressing living standards. Notice in Table 2.1, for example, what's been happening in Zimbabwe. From 2000 to 2015, Zimbabwe's output of goods and services (GDP) *declined* by an average of 1.9 percent a year. As a result, total Zimbabwean output in 2015 was 40 percent *smaller* than in 2000. During those same years, the Zimbabwean population kept growing—by 1.5 percent a year. So the Zimbabwean pie was shrinking every year even as the number of people coming to the table was increasing. As a result, Zimbabwe's per capita GDP fell below $400 a year. That low level of per capita GDP left two-thirds of Zimbabwe's population undernourished.

economic growth: An increase in output (real GDP); an expansion of production possibilities.

	Average Growth Rate (2000–2015) of		
	GDP	Population	Per Capita GDP
High-income countries			
United States	1.6	0.9	0.7
Canada	1.9	1.0	0.9
Japan	0.7	0.0	0.7
France	1.1	0.6	0.5
Low-income countries			
China	10.3	0.5	9.8
Ethiopia	9.6	2.7	6.9
India	7.5	1.5	6.0
Burundi	1.0	1.6	−0.6
Haiti	1.2	1.5	−0.3
Libya	−0.5	1.1	−1.6
Zimbabwe	−1.9	1.5	−3.4

Source: The World Bank, data.worldbank.org

TABLE 2.1

GDP Growth vs. Population Growth

The relationship between GDP growth and population growth is very different in rich and poor countries. The populations of rich countries are growing very slowly, and gains in per capita GDP are easily achieved. In the poorest countries, population is still increasing rapidly, making it difficult to raise living standards. Notice how per capita incomes are *declining* in many poor countries (such as Zimbabwe, Haiti, and Libya).

The Mix of Output

Regardless of how much output a nation produces, the *mix* of output always includes both *goods* (such as cars, big-screen TVs, and potatoes) and *services* (like this economics course, visits to a doctor, or a professional baseball game). A century ago, about two-thirds of U.S. output consisted of farm goods (37 percent), manufactured goods (22 percent), and mining (9 percent). Since then, more than 25 *million* people have left the farms and taken jobs in other sectors. As a result, today's mix of output is completely reversed: ***Eighty percent of U.S. output now consists of services, not goods*** (see Figure 2.2).

The *relative* decline in goods production (manufacturing, farming) doesn't mean that we're producing *fewer* goods today than in earlier decades. Quite the contrary. While some industries such as iron and steel have shrunk, others, such as chemicals, publishing, and telecommunications equipment, have grown tremendously. The result is that manufacturing output has increased fourfold since 1950. The same kind of thing has happened in the farm sector, where output keeps rising even though agriculture's *share* of total output has declined. It's just that our output of *services* has increased so much faster.

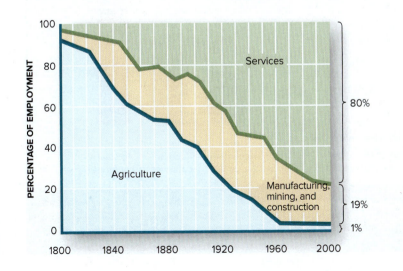

FIGURE 2.2

The Changing Mix of Output

Two hundred years ago, almost all U.S. output came from farms. Today 80 percent of output consists of services, not farm or manufactured goods.

Source: U.S. Department of Commerce.

Development Patterns. The transformation of the United States into a service economy is a reflection of our high incomes. In Ethiopia, where the most urgent concern is to keep people from starving, more than 50 percent of output still comes from the farm sector. Poor people don't have enough income to buy dental services, vacations, or even an education, so the mix of output in poor countries is weighted toward goods, not services.

HOW AMERICA PRODUCES

Regardless of how much output a nation produces, every nation ultimately depends on its resources—its **factors of production**—to produce goods and services. So *differences* in GDP must be explained in part by HOW those resources are used.

Human Capital

We've already observed that America's premier position in global GDP rankings isn't due to the number of humans within our borders. We have far fewer bodies than China or India, yet produce far more output than either of those nations. What counts for production purposes is not just the *number* of workers a nation has, but the *skills* of those workers—what we call **human capital.**

Over time, the United States has invested heavily in human capital. In 1940 only 1 out of 20 young Americans graduated from college; today more than 40 percent of young people are college graduates. High school graduation rates have jumped from 38 percent to more than 85 percent in the same period. In the poorest countries, fewer than half of youth ever *attend* high school, much less graduate (see World View "The Education Gap between Rich and Poor Nations"). As a consequence, the United Nations estimates that 1.2 billion people—a sixth of humanity—are unable to read a book or even write their own names. Without even functional literacy, such workers are doomed to low-productivity jobs. Despite low wages, they are not likely to "steal" many jobs from America's highly educated and trained workforce.

factors of production: Resource inputs used to produce goods and services, e.g., land, labor, capital, entrepreneurship.

human capital: The knowledge and skills possessed by the workforce.

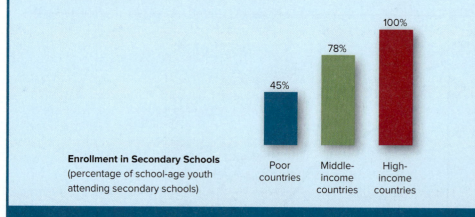

WORLD **VIEW**

THE EDUCATION GAP BETWEEN RICH AND POOR NATIONS

Virtually all Americans attend high school and roughly 85 percent graduate. In poor countries, relatively few workers attend high school and even fewer graduate. Half the workers in the world's poorest nations are illiterate.

Source: The World Bank, WDI2016 Data Set, data.worldbank.org

Enrollment in Secondary Schools
(percentage of school-age youth attending secondary schools)

- Poor countries: 45%
- Middle-income countries: 78%
- High-income countries: 100%

ANALYSIS: The high productivity of the American economy is explained in part by the quality of its labor resources. Workers in poorer, less developed countries get much less education and training.

Analysis: An abundance of capital equipment and advanced technology make American farmers and workers far more productive than workers in poor nations.

(*left*): ©McGraw-Hill Education/Barry Barker, photographer; (*right*): Source: Photo by Jeff Vanuga, USDA Natural Resources Conservation Service

Capital Stock

America has also accumulated a massive stock of capital—more than $80 *trillion* worth of machinery, factories, and buildings. As a result of all this prior investment, U.S. production tends to be very **capital-intensive.** The contrast with *labor-intensive* production in poorer countries is striking. A farmer in India still works mostly with his hands and crude implements, whereas a U.S. farmer works with computers, automated irrigation systems, and mechanized equipment (see the photos above). Russian business managers don't have the computer networks or telecommunications systems that make U.S. business so efficient. In Haiti and Ethiopia, even telephones, indoor plumbing, and dependable sources of power are scarce.

capital-intensive: Production processes that use a high ratio of capital to labor inputs.

High Productivity

When you put educated workers together with sophisticated capital equipment, you tend to get more output. This relationship largely explains why the United States has such a lead in worker **productivity**—the amount of output produced by the average worker. *American households are able to consume so much because American workers produce so much.* It's really that simple.

The huge output of the United States is thus explained not only by a wealth of resources but by their quality as well. *The high productivity of the U.S. economy results from using highly educated workers in capital-intensive production processes.*

productivity: Output per unit of input—for example, output per labor-hour.

Factor Mobility. Our continuing ability to produce the goods and services that consumers demand also depends on our agility in *reallocating* resources from one industry to another. Every year, some industries expand and others contract. Thousands of new firms start up each year, and almost as many others disappear. In the process, land, labor, capital, and entrepreneurship move from one industry to another in response to changing demands and technology. In 1975 Federal Express, Dell Computer, Staples, Oracle, and Amgen didn't exist. Walmart was still a small retailer. Starbucks was selling coffee on Seattle street corners, and the founders of Google, Facebook, and Snapchat weren't even born. Today these companies employ millions of people. These workers came from other firms and industries that weren't growing as fast.

Technological Advance. One of the forces that keeps shifting resources from one industry to another is continuing advances in technology. Advances in technology can be as sophisticated as microscopic miniaturization of electronic circuits or as simple as the

production possibilities: The alternative combinations of final goods and services that could be produced in a given period with all available resources and technology.

reorganization of production processes. Either phenomenon increases the productivity of the workforce and potential output. ***Whenever technology advances, an economy can produce more output with existing resources;*** its **production possibilities** curve shifts outward (see Figure 1.5).

Outsourcing and Trade. The same technological advances that fuel economic growth also facilitate *global* resource use. Telecommunications has become so sophisticated and inexpensive that phone workers in India or Grenada can answer calls directed to U.S. companies. Likewise, programmers in India can work online to write computer code, develop software, or perform accounting chores for U.S. corporations. Although such "outsourcing" is often viewed as a threat to U.S. jobs, it is really another source of increased U.S. output. By outsourcing routine tasks to foreign workers, U.S. workers are able to focus on higher-value jobs. U.S. computer engineers do less routine programming and more systems design. U.S. accountants do less cost tabulation and more cost analysis. By utilizing foreign resources in the production process, U.S. workers are able to pursue their *comparative advantage* in high-skill, capital-intensive jobs. In this way, both productivity and total output increase. Although some U.S. workers suffer temporary job losses in this process, the overall economy gains.

Role of Government

In assessing HOW goods are produced and economies grow, we must also take heed of the role the government plays. As we noted in Chapter 1, the amount of economic freedom varies greatly among the 200-plus nations of the world. Moreover, the Heritage Foundation has documented a positive relationship between the degree of economic freedom and economic growth. Quite simply, when entrepreneurs are unfettered by regulation or high taxes, they are more likely to design and produce better mousetraps. When the government owns the factors of production, imposes high taxes, or tightly regulates output, there is little opportunity or incentive to design better products or pursue new technology. This is one reason why more market-reliant economies grow faster than others.

Recognizing the importance of market incentives doesn't force us to reject all government intervention. No one really advocates the complete abolition of government. On the contrary, the government plays a critical role in establishing a framework in which private businesses can operate. Among its many roles are these:

- *Providing a legal framework.* One of the most basic functions of government is to establish and enforce the rules of the game. In some bygone era maybe a person's word was sufficient to guarantee delivery or payment. Businesses today, however, rely more on written contracts. The government gives legitimacy to contracts by establishing the rules for such pacts and by enforcing their provisions. In the absence of contractual rights, few companies would be willing to ship goods without prepayment (in cash). Even the incentive to write texts would disappear if government copyright laws didn't forbid unauthorized photocopying. By establishing ownership rights, contract rights, and other rules of the game, the government lays the foundation for market transactions.
- *Protecting the environment.* The government also intervenes in the market to protect the environment. The legal contract system is designed to protect the interests of a buyer and a seller who wish to do business. What if, however, the business they contract for harms third parties? How are the interests of persons who *aren't* party to the contract to be protected?

Numerous examples abound of how unregulated production may harm third parties. Earlier in the century, the steel mills around Pittsburgh blocked out the sun with clouds of sulfurous gases that spewed out of their furnaces. Local residents were harmed every time they inhaled. In the absence of government intervention, such side effects would be common. Decisions on how to produce would be based on costs alone, not on how the environment is affected. However, such negative **externalities**—spillover costs imposed on the broader community—affect our collective well-being. To reduce

externalities: Costs (or benefits) of a market activity borne by a third party; the difference between the social and private costs (benefits) of a market activity.

the external costs of production, the government limits air, water, and noise pollution and regulates environmental use.

- *Protecting consumers.* The government also uses its power to protect the interests of consumers. One way to do this is to prevent individual business firms from becoming too powerful. In the extreme case, a single firm might have a **monopoly** on the production of a specific good. As the sole producer of that good, a monopolist could dictate the price, the quality, and the quantity of the product. In such a situation, consumers would likely end up paying too much for too little.

    To protect consumers from monopoly exploitation, the government tries to prevent individual firms from dominating specific markets. Antitrust laws prohibit mergers or acquisitions that would threaten competition. The U.S. Department of Justice and the Federal Trade Commission also regulate pricing practices, advertising claims, and other behavior that might put consumers at an unfair disadvantage in product markets.

    Government also regulates the safety of many products. Consumers don't have enough expertise to assess the safety of various medicines, for example. If they rely on trial and error to determine drug safety, they might not get a second chance. To avoid this calamity, the government requires rigorous testing of new drugs, food additives, and other products.

- *Protecting labor.* The government also regulates how labor resources are used in the production process. In most poor nations, children are forced to start working at very early ages, often for minuscule wages. They often don't get the chance to go to school or to stay healthy. In Africa, 40 percent of children under age 14 work to survive or to help support their families. In the United States, child labor laws and compulsory schooling prevent minor children from being exploited. Government regulations also set standards for workplace safety, minimum wages, fringe benefits, and overtime provisions.

monopoly: A firm that produces the entire market supply of a particular good or service.

Striking a Balance

All these and other government interventions are designed to change the way resources are used. Such interventions reflect the conviction that the market alone might not always select the best possible way of producing goods and services. There's no guarantee, however, that government regulation of HOW goods are produced always makes us better off. Excessive regulation may inhibit production, raise product prices, and limit consumer choices. As noted in Chapter 1, *government* failure might replace *market* failure, leaving us no better off—possibly even worse off. This possibility underscores the importance of striking the right balance between market reliance and government regulation.

FOR WHOM AMERICA PRODUCES

As we've seen, America produces a huge quantity of output, using high-quality labor and capital resources. That leaves one basic question unanswered: FOR WHOM is all this output produced?

How many goods and services one gets largely depends on how much income one has to spend. The U.S. economy uses the market mechanism to distribute most goods and services. Those who receive the most income get the most goods. This goes a long way toward explaining why millionaires live in mansions and homeless people seek shelter in abandoned cars. This is the kind of stark inequality that fueled Karl Marx's denunciation of capitalism. Even today, people wonder how some Americans can be so rich while others are so poor.

U.S. Income Distribution

Figure 2.3 illustrates the actual distribution of income in the United States. For this illustration the entire population is sorted into five groups of equal size, ranked by income. In this depiction, all the rich people are in the top **income quintile;** the poor are in the lowest quintile. To be in the top quintile in 2015, a household needed at least $117,000 of income. All the households in the lowest quintile had incomes under $23,000.

income quintile: One-fifth of the population, rank-ordered by income (e.g., top fifth).

FIGURE 2.3

The U.S. Distribution of Income

The richest fifth of U.S. households gets half of all the income—a huge slice of the income pie. By contrast, the poorest fifth gets only a sliver.

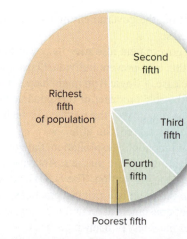

Income Quintile	2015 Income	Average Income	Share of Total Income (%)
Highest fifth	Above $117,000	$202,000	51.1
Second fifth	$72,000–117,000	$ 92,000	23.2
Third fifth	$44,000–72,000	$ 57,000	14.3
Fourth fifth	$23,000–44,000	$ 33,000	8.2
Lowest fifth	$0–23,000	$ 12,500	3.1

Source: U.S. Department of Commerce, Bureau of the Census (averages rounded to thousands of dollars; 2015 data).

The most striking feature of Figure 2.3 is how large a slice of the income pie rich people get: ***The top 20 percent (quintile) of U.S. households get half of all U.S. income.*** By contrast, the poorest 20 percent (quintile) of U.S. households get only a sliver of the income pie—about 3 percent. Those grossly unequal slices explain why nearly half of all Americans believe the nation is divided into "haves" and "have nots."

Analysis: The market distributes income (and, in turn, goods and services) according to the resources an individual owns and how well they are used. If the resulting inequalities are too great, some redistribution via government intervention may be desired.

(*left*): ©Thinkstock/Stockbyte/Getty Images RF; (*right*): ©Natalie Roeth RF

Global Inequality

As unequal as U.S. incomes are, income disparities are actually greater in many other countries. Ironically, income inequalities are often greatest in the poorest countries. The richest *tenth* of U.S. families gets 30 percent of America's income pie. The richest tenth of South Africa's families gets 51 percent of that nation's income (see World View "Income Share of the Rich"). Given the small size of South Africa's pie, the *bottom* tenth of South African families is left with mere crumbs. As we'll see in the chapter titled "Global Poverty," 40 percent of South Africa's population lives in "severe poverty," defined by the World Bank as an income of less than $3 a day.

Comparisons across countries would manifest even greater inequality. As we saw earlier, third world GDP per capita is far below U.S. levels. As a consequence, even **poor** *people in the United States receive far more goods and services than the* **average** *household in most low-income countries.*

WORLD VIEW

INCOME SHARE OF THE RICH

Inequality tends to diminish as a country develops. In poor, developing nations, the richest tenth of the population typically gets 40 to 50 percent of all income. In developed countries, the richest tenth gets 20 to 30 percent of total income.

Source: The World Bank, 2016.

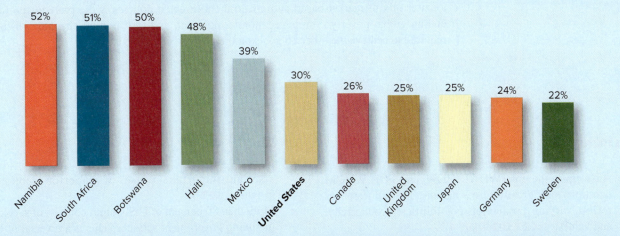

Share of Total Income Received by Top Tenth

Namibia	South Africa	Botswana	Haiti	Mexico	United States	Canada	United Kingdom	Japan	Germany	Sweden
52%	51%	50%	48%	39%	30%	26%	25%	25%	24%	22%

ANALYSIS: The FOR WHOM question is reflected in the distribution of income. Although the U.S. distribution of income is unequal, inequalities are much more severe in most poor nations.

THE ECONOMY TOMORROW

THE UNITED NATIONS AGENDA

Global answers to the basic questions of WHAT, HOW, and FOR WHOM have been shaped by market forces and government intervention. Obviously the answers aren't yet fully satisfactory.

Millions of Americans still struggle to make ends meet. Worse yet, nearly 3 *billion* people around the world live in abject poverty—with incomes of less than $3 a day. More

Continued

than a sixth of the world's population is illiterate, nearly half has no access to sanitation facilities, and a fifth is chronically malnourished.

Then there is a staggering amount of pollution, rampant inequalities, inadequate education, and insufficient health care for billions of people.

The United Nations wants us to fashion better answers for the WHAT, HOW, and FOR WHOM questions. In September 2015 the U.N. adopted a set of 17 specific goals for sustainable development and a 15-year timeline for achieving them. Ending world poverty and eliminating world hunger are the first two on the list. High on the list is also the goal of reducing inequalities across income groups, gender, and race. Protecting the environment and slowing climate change are additional goals.

Can the world meet all these goals? Perhaps. But it will take a lot of resources and even more political will. Consider just the first goal of ending global poverty.

The rich nations of the world have enough resources to wipe out global poverty. But they're not willing to give them up. People in rich nations also have aspirations: they want higher living standards in the economy tomorrow. They already enjoy more comforts than people in poor nations even dream of. But that doesn't stop them from wanting more consumer goods, better schools, improved health care, a cleaner environment, and greater economic security. So the needs of the world's poor typically get lower priority.

How about the poor nations themselves? Couldn't they do a better job of mobilizing and employing their own resources to accelerate economic growth? Governments in many poor nations are notoriously self-serving and corrupt. Private property is often at risk of confiscation and contracts hard to enforce. This discourages the kind of investment poor nations desperately need. The unwillingness of rich nations to open their markets to the exports of poor nations also puts a lid on income growth. In reality, an array of domestic and international policies has perpetuated global poverty. Developing a better mix of market-based and government-directed policies is the prerequisite for ending global poverty. Similar economic, political, and institutional changes will be required to achieve the other 16 goals on the United Nations' wish list.

SUMMARY

- Answers to the core WHAT, HOW, and FOR WHOM questions vary greatly across nations. These differences reflect varying production possibilities, productivity, and values. **LO2-1, LO2-3, LO2-4**

- Gross domestic product (GDP) is the basic measure of how much an economy produces. The United States produces roughly $20 trillion of output per year, more than one-fifth of the world's total. **LO2-1**

- Per capita GDP is a nation's total output divided by its population. It indicates the average standard of living. The U.S. GDP per capita is five times the world average. **LO2-1**

- The high level of U.S. per capita GDP reflects the high productivity of U.S. workers. Abundant capital, education, technology, training, and management all contribute to high productivity. The relatively high degree of U.S. economic freedom (market reliance) is also an important cause of superior economic growth. **LO2-3**

- More than 80 percent of U.S. output consists of services, including government services. This is a reversal of historical ratios and reflects the relatively high incomes in the United States. Poor nations produce much higher proportions of food and manufactured goods. **LO2-2**

- U.S. incomes are distributed very unequally, with households in the highest income class (quintile) receiving more than 10 times more income than low-income households. Incomes are even less equally distributed in most poor nations. **LO2-4**

- The mix of output, production methods, and the income distribution continue to change. The WHAT, HOW, and FOR WHOM answers in tomorrow's economy will depend on the continuing interplay of (changing) market signals and (changing) government policy. **LO2-2, LO2-3, LO2-4**

Key Terms

gross domestic product (GDP)
per capita GDP
economic growth
factors of production

human capital
capital-intensive
productivity
production possibilities

externalities
monopoly
income quintile

Questions for Discussion

1. Americans already enjoy living standards that far exceed world averages. Do we have enough? Should we even try to produce more?   **LO2-1**
2. Why is per capita GDP so much higher in the United States than in Mexico?   **LO2-3**
3. Can we continue to produce more output every year? Is there a limit?   **LO2-3**
4. The U.S. farm population has shrunk by more than 25 million people since 1900. Where did all the people go? Why did they move?   **LO2-2**
5. Is the relative decline in U.S. farming and manufacturing (Figure 2-2) a good thing or a bad thing?   **LO2-2**
6. How many people are employed by your local or state government? What do they produce? What is the opportunity cost of that output?   **LO2-1**
7. Where do growing companies like Google and Facebook get their employees? What were those workers doing before?   **LO2-2**
8. Should the government try to equalize incomes more by raising taxes on the rich and giving more money to the poor? How might such redistribution affect total output and growth?   **LO2-4**
9. Why are incomes so much more unequal in poor nations than in rich ones?   **LO2-4**
10. How might free markets help reduce global poverty? How might they impede that goal?   **LO2-3**

PROBLEMS FOR CHAPTER 2

LO2-1 1. In 2015 the world's total output (real GDP) was roughly $80 trillion. What percent of this total was produced
- (*a*) By the three largest economies (World View "Comparative Output (GDP)")?
- (*b*) By the three smallest economies in that World View?

LO2-1 2. According to the World View "GDP per Capita around the World," how does per capita GDP in the following countries compare against America's (in percentage terms)?
- (*a*) Canada
- (*b*) China
- (*c*) Cuba

LO2-4 3. In 1980, America's GDP per capita was approximately $30,000 (measured in today's dollars). How much higher in percentage terms was America's GDP per capita in 2015 (see World View "GDP per Capita around the World")?

LO2-3 4. (*a*) How much more output does the $20 trillion U.S. economy produce when GDP increases by 1.0 percent?
- (*b*) By how much does this increase per capita income if the population is 340 million?

LO2-1 5. According to Table 2.1, how fast does total output (GDP) have to grow in order to raise per capita GDP in
- (*a*) the United States?
- (*b*) Japan?
- (*c*) Ethiopia?

LO2-3 6. (*a*) If Haiti's per capita GDP of roughly $810 were to DOUBLE every decade (an annual growth rate of 7.2 percent), what would Haiti's per capita GDP be in 50 years?
- (*b*) Compare (a) to the U.S. per capita GDP in 2015 (World View "GDP per Capita around the World)?

LO2-2 7. U.S. real gross domestic product increased from $10 trillion in 2000 to $15 trillion in 2010. During that same decade the share of manufactured goods (e.g., cars, appliances) fell from 16 percent to 12 percent. What was the dollar value of manufactured output
- (*a*) In 2000?
- (*b*) In 2010?
- (*c*) By how much did the dollar value of manufacturing output change?

LO2-4 8. Using the data in Figure 2.3,
- (*a*) Compute the average income of U.S. households.
- (*b*) If all incomes were equalized by government taxes and transfer payments, how much would the average household in each income quintile gain (via transfers) or lose (via taxes)?
  - (*i*) Highest fifth
  - (*ii*) Second fifth
  - (*iii*) Third fifth
  - (*iv*) Fourth fifth
  - (*v*) Lowest fifth
- (*c*) What is the implied tax rate (i.e., tax ÷ average income) on the highest quintile?

LO2-3 9. If 150 million workers produced America's GDP in 2015 (World View "Comparative Output (GDP)"), how much output did the average worker produce?

LO2-1 10. Assuming 2016 per capita GDP growth rate is equal to the average growth rate (2000–2015) provided in Table 2.1, estimate 2016 per capita GDP for each of the following countries using data from World View "GDP per Capita around the World."
- (*a*) China
- (*b*) Canada
- (*c*) Haiti

LO2-2 11. Using the data from the Data Tables, calculate
  (*a*) the federal government's share of total output in 1996, 2006, and 2016.
  (*b*) the state and local government's share of total output in 1996, 2006, and 2016.

LO2-4 12. The Economy Tomorrow: How much more output per year will have to be produced in the world
  just to provide the 3 billion "severely" poor population with $1 more income per day?

3

Supply and Demand

After reading this chapter, you should know

LO3-1 The nature and determinants of market demand.

LO3-2 The nature and determinants of market supply.

LO3-3 How market prices and quantities are established.

LO3-4 What causes market prices to change.

LO3-5 How government price controls affect market outcomes.

Gasoline prices surged in early 2008, rising from $2.99 a gallon in January to $4.05 in July. Consumers were angry every time they filled up their tanks. Popular opinion blamed the "Big Oil" companies and "speculators" for the sky-high prices. They demanded that the government intervene and force prices back down. Congressional hearings were conducted, government investigations were initiated, and "excess profits" taxes on oil companies were proposed.

By the end of 2008, gasoline prices had receded. In early 2009, pump prices were back to less than $2 a gallon. No oil executives or speculators had been arrested. No congressional reports had been completed. No government indictments had been issued. Economists explained this turn of events with "supply and demand." Surging demand and limited supply had caused the price spike; slowing demand and increased supply had pushed pump prices back down. Motorists weren't entirely convinced by this explanation, but they were happy. They filled their tanks and drove off to other economic concerns.

The goal of this chapter is to explain how supply and demand really work. How do *markets* establish the price of gasoline and other products? Why do prices change so often? More broadly, how does the market mechanism decide WHAT to produce, HOW to produce, and FOR WHOM to produce? Specifically,

- **What determines the price of a good or service?**
- **How does the price of a product affect its production and consumption?**
- **Why do prices and production levels often change?**

Once we've seen how unregulated markets work, we'll observe how government intervention may alter market outcomes—for better or worse.

MARKET PARTICIPANTS

A good way to start figuring out how markets work is to see who participates in them. The answer is simple: just about every person and institution on the planet. Domestically, nearly 340 million consumers, about 25 million business firms, and tens of thousands of government agencies participate directly in the U.S. economy. Millions of international buyers and sellers also participate in U.S. markets.

Maximizing Behavior

All these market participants enter the marketplace to pursue specific goals. Consumers, for example, come with a limited amount of income to spend. Their objective is to buy the most desirable goods and services that their limited budgets will permit. We can't afford *everything* we want, so we must make *choices* about how to spend our scarce dollars. Our goal is to *maximize* the utility (satisfaction) we get from our available incomes.

Businesses also try to maximize in the marketplace. In their case, the quest is for maximum *profits*. Business profits are the difference between sales receipts and total costs. To maximize profits, business firms try to use resources efficiently in producing products that consumers desire.

The public sector also has maximizing goals. The economic purpose of government is to use available resources to serve public needs. The resources available for this purpose are limited too. Hence local, state, and federal governments must use scarce resources carefully, striving to maximize the general welfare of society. International consumers and producers pursue these same goals when participating in our markets.

Market participants sometimes lose sight of their respective goals. Consumers sometimes buy impulsively and later wish they'd used their income more wisely. Likewise, a producer may take a two-hour lunch, even at the sacrifice of maximum profits. And elected officials sometimes put their personal interests ahead of the public's interest. In all sectors of the economy, however, ***the basic goals of utility maximization, profit maximization, and welfare maximization explain most market activity.***

Specialization and Exchange

We are driven to buy and sell goods and services in the market by two simple facts. First, most of us are incapable of producing everything we want to consume. Second, even if we *could* produce all our own goods and services, it would still make sense to *specialize,* producing only one product and *trading* it for other desired goods and services.

Suppose you were capable of growing your own food, stitching your own clothes, building your own shelter, and even writing your own economics text. Even in this little utopia, it would still make sense to decide how *best* to expend your limited time and energy, relying on others to fill in the gaps. If you were *most* proficient at growing food, you would be best off spending your time farming. You could then *exchange* some of your food output for the clothes, shelter, and books you wanted. In the end, you'd be able to consume *more* goods than if you'd tried to make everything yourself.

Our economic interactions with others are thus necessitated by two constraints:

1. Our absolute inability as individuals to produce all the things we need or desire.
2. The limited amount of time, energy, and resources we have for producing those things we could make for ourselves.

Together these constraints lead us to *specialize* and interact. Most of the interactions that result take place in the market.

International Trade. The same motivations foster international trade. The United States is *capable* of producing just about everything. But we've learned that it's cheaper to import bananas from Ecuador than to grow them in hothouses in Idaho. So we *specialize* in production, exporting tractors to Ecuador in exchange for imported bananas. Both nations end up consuming more products than they could if they had to produce everything themselves. That's why *global* markets are so vital to economic prosperity.

THE CIRCULAR FLOW

Figure 3.1 summarizes the kinds of interactions that occur among market participants. Note first that the figure identifies four separate groups of participants. Domestically, the rectangle labeled "Consumers" includes all 340 million consumers in the United States. In

FIGURE 3.1

The Circular Flow

- **Business firms** supply goods and services to product markets (point *A*) and purchase factors of production in factor markets (*B*).

- Individual **consumers** supply factors of production such as their own labor (*C*) and purchase final goods and services (*D*).

- Federal, state, and local **governments** acquire resources in factor markets (*E*) and provide services to both consumers and business (*F*).

- International participants also take part by supplying imports, purchasing exports (*G*), and buying and selling factors of production (*H*).

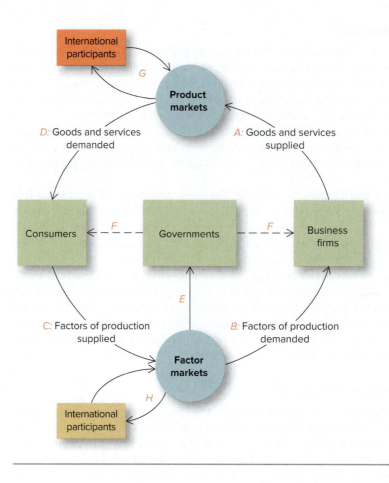

factor market: Any place where factors of production (e.g., land, labor, capital) are bought and sold.

product market: Any place where finished goods and services (products) are bought and sold.

opportunity cost: The most desired goods or services that are forgone in order to obtain something else.

the "Business firms" box are grouped all the domestic business enterprises that buy and sell goods and services. The third participant, "Governments," includes the many separate agencies of the federal government, as well as state and local governments. Figure 3.1 also illustrates the role of global actors.

The Two Markets

The easiest way to keep track of all this activity is to distinguish two basic markets. Figure 3.1 makes this distinction by portraying separate circles for product markets and factor markets. In **factor markets,** factors of production are exchanged. Market participants buy or sell land, labor, or capital that can be used in the production process. When you go looking for work, for example, you're making a factor of production—your labor—available to producers. The producers will hire you—purchase your services in the factor market—if you're offering the skills they need at a price they're willing to pay.

Interactions within factor markets are only half the story. At the end of a hard day's work, consumers go to the grocery store (or to a virtual store online) to buy desired goods and services—that is, to buy *products*. In this context, consumers again interact with business firms, this time purchasing goods and services those firms have produced. These interactions occur in **product markets.** Foreigners also participate in the product market by supplying goods and services (imports) to the United States and buying some of our output (exports).

The government sector also supplies services (e.g., education, national defense, highways). Most government services aren't explicitly sold in product markets, however. Typically, they're delivered "free," without an explicit price (e.g., public elementary schools, highways). This doesn't mean government services are truly free, though. There's still an **opportunity cost** associated with every service the government provides. Consumers and businesses pay that cost indirectly through taxes rather than directly through market prices.

In Figure 3.1, the arrow connecting product markets to consumers (*D*) emphasizes the fact that consumers, by definition, don't supply products. When individuals produce goods and services, they do so within the government or business sector. For instance, a doctor, a dentist, or an economic consultant functions in two sectors. When selling services in the market, this person is regarded as a "business"; when away from the office, he or she is regarded as a "consumer." This distinction is helpful in emphasizing that *the consumer is the final recipient of all goods and services produced.*

Locating Markets. Although we refer repeatedly to two kinds of markets in this text, it would be a little foolish to go off in search of the product and factor markets. Neither market is a single, identifiable structure. The term *market* simply refers to a place or situation where an economic exchange occurs—where a buyer and seller interact. The exchange may take place on the street, in a taxicab, over the phone, by mail, or in cyberspace. In some cases, the market used may in fact be quite distinguishable, as in the case of a Walmart store, the Chicago Commodity Exchange, or a state employment office. But whatever it looks like, *a market exists wherever and whenever an exchange takes place.*

Dollars and Exchange

Figure 3.1 neglects one critical element of market interactions: dollars. Each arrow in the figure actually has two dimensions. Consider again the arrow (*D*) linking consumers to product markets: it's drawn in only one direction because consumers, by definition, don't provide goods and services directly to product markets. But they do provide something: dollars. If you want to obtain something from a product market, you must offer to pay for it (typically with cash, check, debit or credit card). Consumers exchange dollars for goods and services in product markets.

The same kinds of exchange occur in factor markets. When you go to work, you exchange a factor of production (your labor) for income, typically a paycheck. Here again, the path connecting consumers to factor markets (*C*) really goes in two directions: one of real resources, the other of dollars. Consumers receive wages, rent, and interest for the labor, land, and capital they bring to the factor markets. Indeed, nearly *every market transaction involves an exchange of dollars for goods (in product markets) or resources (in factor markets).* Money is thus critical in facilitating market exchanges and the specialization the exchanges permit.

Supply and Demand

In every market transaction there must be a buyer and a seller. The seller is on the **supply** side of the market; the buyer is on the **demand** side. As noted earlier, we *supply* resources to the market when we look for a job—that is, when we offer our labor in exchange for income. We *demand* goods when we shop in a supermarket—that is, when we're prepared to offer dollars in exchange for something to eat. Business firms may *supply* goods and services in product markets at the same time they're *demanding* factors of production in factor markets. Whether one is on the supply side or the demand side of any particular market transaction depends on the nature of the exchange, not on the people or institutions involved.

supply: The ability and willingness to sell (produce) specific quantities of a good at alternative prices in a given time period, *ceteris paribus*.

demand: The willingness and ability to buy specific quantities of a good at alternative prices in a given time period, *ceteris paribus*.

DEMAND

To get a sense of how the demand side of market transactions works, we'll focus first on a single consumer. Then we'll aggregate to illustrate *market* demand.

Individual Demand

We can begin to understand how market forces work by looking more closely at the behavior of a single market participant. Let us start with Tom, a senior at Clearview College.

Tom has majored in everything from art history to government in his five years at Clearview. He didn't connect to any of those fields and is on the brink of academic dismissal. To make matters worse, his parents have threatened to cut him off financially unless he gets serious about his course work. By that, they mean he should enroll in courses that will lead to a job after graduation. Tom thinks he has found the perfect solution: web design. Everything associated with the Internet pays big bucks. Or at least so Tom thinks. And his parents would definitely approve. So Tom has enrolled in web design courses.

Unfortunately for Tom, he never developed computer skills. Until he got to Clearview College, he thought mastering Sony's latest alien-attack video game was the pinnacle of electronic wizardry. Tom didn't have a clue about "cookies," "wireframe," "responsive design," or the other concepts the web design instructor outlined in the first lecture.

Given his circumstances, Tom was desperate to find someone who could tutor him in web design. But desperation is not enough to secure the services of a web architect. In a market-based economy, you must also be willing to *pay* for the things you want. Specifically, **a demand exists only if someone is willing and able to pay for the good**—that is, exchange dollars for a good or service in the marketplace. Is Tom willing and able to *pay* for the web design tutoring he so obviously needs?

Let us assume that Tom has some income and is willing to spend some of it to get a tutor. With these assumptions, we can claim that Tom is a participant in the *market* for web design services; he is a potential consumer.

But how much is Tom willing to pay? Surely Tom is not prepared to exchange *all* his income for help in mastering web design. After all, Tom could use his income to buy more desirable goods and services. If he spent all his income on a web tutor, that help would have an extremely high *opportunity cost*. He would be giving up the opportunity to spend that income on things he really likes. He'd pass his web design class but have little else. It doesn't sound like a good idea.

It seems more likely that there are *limits* to the amount Tom is willing to pay for web design tutoring. These limits will be determined by how much income Tom has to spend and how many other goods and services he must forsake to pay for a tutor.

Tom also knows that his grade in web design will depend in part on how much tutoring service he buys. He can pass the course with only a few hours of design help. If he wants a better grade, however, the cost is going to escalate quickly.

Naturally, Tom wants it all: an A in web design and a ticket to higher-paying jobs. But here again the distinction between *desire* and *demand* is relevant. He may *desire* to master web design, but his actual proficiency will depend on how many hours of tutoring he is willing to *pay* for.

The Demand Schedule

demand schedule: A table showing the quantities of a good a consumer is willing and able to buy at alternative prices in a given time period, *ceteris paribus*.

We assume, then, that when Tom starts looking for a tutor he has some sense of how much money he is willing to spend. He might have in mind some sort of **demand schedule,** like that described in Figure 3.2. According to row *A* of this schedule, Tom is willing and able to buy only 1 hour of tutoring service per semester if he must pay $50 an hour. At such a high price he will learn just enough web design to pass the course.

At lower prices, Tom would behave differently. According to Figure 3.2, Tom would purchase *more* tutoring services if the price per hour were *less*. Indeed, we see from row *I* of the demand schedule that Tom is willing to purchase 20 hours per semester—the whole bag of design tricks—if the price of tutoring gets as low as $10 per hour.

Notice that the demand schedule doesn't tell us anything about *why* this consumer is willing to pay specific prices for various amounts of tutoring. Tom's expressed willingness to pay for web design tutoring may reflect a desperate need to finish a web design course, a lot of income to spend, or a relatively small desire for other goods and services. All the demand schedule tells us is what the consumer is *willing and able* to buy, for whatever reasons.

Also observe that the demand schedule doesn't tell us how many hours of design help the consumer will *actually* buy. Figure 3.2 simply states that Tom is *willing and able* to pay

Tom's Demand Schedule		
	Price of Tutoring (per Hour)	Quantity of Tutoring Demanded (Hours per Semester)
A	$50	1
B	45	2
C	40	3
D	35	5
E	30	7
F	25	9
G	20	12
H	15	15
I	10	20

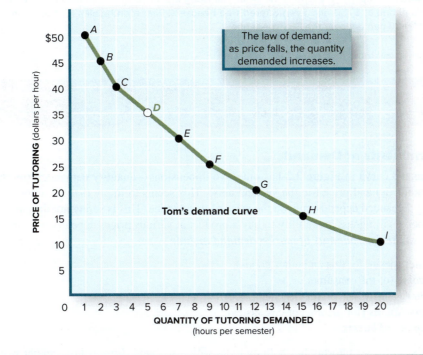

The law of demand: as price falls, the quantity demanded increases.

Tom's demand curve

PRICE OF TUTORING (dollars per hour)

QUANTITY OF TUTORING DEMANDED (hours per semester)

FIGURE 3.2

A Demand Schedule and Curve

A demand schedule indicates the quantities of a good a consumer is able and willing to buy at alternative prices (*ceteris paribus*). The **demand schedule** here indicates that Tom would buy 5 hours of web tutoring per semester if the price were $35 per hour (row *D*). If web tutoring were less expensive (rows *E–I*), Tom would purchase a larger quantity.

A **demand curve** is a graphical illustration of a demand schedule. Each point on the curve refers to a specific quantity that will be demanded at a given price. If, for example, the price of web tutoring were $35 per hour, this curve tells us the consumer would purchase 5 hours per semester (point *D*). If web tutoring cost $30 per hour, 7 hours per semester would be demanded (point *E*). Each point on the curve corresponds to a row in the schedule.

for 1 hour of tutoring per semester at $50 per hour, for 2 hours at $45 each, and so on. How much tutoring he purchases will depend on the actual price of such services in the market. Until we know that price, we cannot tell how much service will be purchased. Hence *"demand" is an expression of consumer buying intentions, of a willingness to buy, not a statement of actual purchases.*

The Demand Curve

A convenient summary of buying intentions is the **demand curve,** a graphical illustration of the demand schedule. The demand curve in Figure 3.2 tells us again that this consumer is willing to pay for only 1 hour of tutoring per semester if the price is $50 per hour (point *A*), for 2 if the price is $45 (point *B*), for 3 at $40 an hour (point *C*), and so on. Once we know what the market price of tutoring actually is, a glance at the demand curve tells us how much service this consumer will buy.

What the notion of *demand* emphasizes is that *the amount we buy of a good depends on its price.* We seldom if ever decide to buy only a certain quantity of a good at whatever price is charged. Instead we enter markets with a set of desires and a limited amount of money to spend. How much we actually buy of any particular good will depend on its price.

demand curve: A curve describing the quantities of a good a consumer is willing and able to buy at alternative prices in a given time period, *ceteris paribus.*

law of demand: The quantity of a good demanded in a given time period increases as its price falls, *ceteris paribus.*

A common feature of demand curves is their downward slope. *As the price of a good falls, people purchase more of it.* In Figure 3.2 the quantity of tutoring demanded increases (moves rightward along the horizontal axis) as the price per hour decreases (moves down the vertical axis). This inverse relationship between price and quantity is so common that we refer to it as the **law of demand.** Samsung used this law to increase sales of the Samsung Galaxy S7 in early 2016 (see In the News "Pricing the Galaxy S7").

IN THE NEWS

PRICING THE GALAXY S7

Samsung lost ground to Apple in the last round of smartphone updates. The South Korean company was determined not to let that happen again. When the Galaxy S6 was launched in April 2015, it carried a base price tag of $850. Only 10 million phones were sold in the first month, below company projections. So when Samsung launched the S7 in March 2016, it priced its phone at $750 and even offered free headsets. First-month sales for the S7 increased by 20 percent over the S6 experience.

Source: Samsung sales history.

ANALYSIS: The law of demand assured Samsung that it could increase smartphone sales by offering the phones at a lower price. That is exactly what happened.

Determinants of Demand

The demand curve in Figure 3.2 has only two dimensions—quantity demanded (on the horizontal axis) and price (on the vertical axis). This seems to imply that the amount of tutoring demanded depends only on the price of that service. This is surely not the case. A consumer's willingness and ability to buy a product at various prices depend on a variety of forces. *The determinants of market demand include*

- *Tastes* (desire for this and other goods).
- *Income* (of the consumer).
- *Other goods* (their availability and price).
- *Expectations* (for income, prices, tastes).
- *Number of buyers.*

Tom's "taste" for tutoring has nothing to do with taste buds. *Taste* is just another word for desire. In this case Tom's taste for web design services is clearly acquired. If he didn't have to pass a web design course, he would have no desire for related services and thus no demand. If he had no income, he couldn't *demand* any web design tutoring either, no matter how much he might *desire* it.

substitute goods: Goods that substitute for each other; when the price of good *x* rises, the demand for good *y* increases, *ceteris paribus.*

Other goods also affect the demand for tutoring services. Their effect depends on whether they're *substitute* goods or *complementary* goods. A **substitute good** is one that might be purchased instead of tutoring services. In Tom's simple world, pizza is a substitute for tutoring. If the price of pizza fell, Tom would use his limited income to buy more pizzas and cut back on his purchases of web tutoring. When the price of a substitute good falls, the demand for tutoring services declines.

complementary goods: Goods frequently consumed in combination; when the price of good *x* rises, the demand for good *y* falls, *ceteris paribus.*

A **complementary good** is one that's typically consumed with, rather than instead of, tutoring. If text prices or tuition rates increase, Tom might take fewer classes and demand *less* web design assistance. In this case, a price increase for a complementary good causes the demand for tutoring to decline. When Samsung cut the price of the Galaxy S7 phones (see In the News "Pricing the Galaxy S7"), it knew that the demand for Walmart wireless service (a complementary good) would increase.

Expectations also play a role in consumer decisions. If Tom expected to flunk his web design course anyway, he probably wouldn't waste any money getting tutorial help; his demand for such services would disappear. On the other hand, if he expects a web tutor to determine his college fate, he might be more willing to buy such services.

Ceteris Paribus

If demand is in fact such a multidimensional decision, how can we reduce it to only the two dimensions of price and quantity? In Chapter 1 we first encountered this *ceteris paribus* trick. To simplify their models of the world, economists focus on only one or two forces at a time and *assume* nothing else changes. We know a consumer's tastes, income, other goods, and expectations all affect the decision to hire a tutor. But we want to focus on the relationship between quantity demanded and price. That is, we want to know what *independent* influence price has on consumption decisions. To find out, we must isolate that one influence, price, and assume that the determinants of demand remain unchanged.

ceteris paribus: The assumption of nothing else changing.

The *ceteris paribus* assumption is not as farfetched as it may seem. People's tastes, income, and expectations do not change quickly. Also, the prices and availability of other goods don't change all that fast. Hence a change in the *price* of a product may be the only factor that prompts an immediate change in quantity demanded.

The ability to predict consumer responses to a price change is important. What would happen, for example, to enrollment at your school if tuition doubled? Must we guess? Or can we use demand curves to predict how the quantity of applications will change as the price of college goes up? ***Demand curves show us how changes in market prices alter consumer behavior.*** We used the demand curve in Figure 3.2 to predict how Tom's web design ability would change at different tutorial prices. Samsung used its knowledge of consumer demand to cut Galaxy S7 prices by $100 (see In the News "Pricing the Galaxy S7").

Shifts in Demand

Although demand curves are useful in predicting consumer responses to market signals, they aren't infallible. The problem is that ***the determinants of demand can and do change.*** When they do, a specific demand curve may become obsolete. A ***demand curve (schedule) is valid only so long as the underlying determinants of demand remain constant.*** If the *ceteris paribus* assumption is violated—if tastes, income, other goods, or expectations change—the ability or willingness to buy will change. When this happens, the demand curve will **shift** to a new position.

shift in demand: A change in the quantity demanded at any (every) price.

Suppose, for example, that Tom won $1,000 in the state lottery. This windfall would increase his ability to pay for tutoring services. Figure 3.3 shows the effect on Tom's demand. The old demand curve, D_1, is no longer relevant. Tom's lottery winnings enable him to buy *more* tutoring at any price, as illustrated by the new demand curve, D_2. According to this new curve, lucky Tom is now willing and able to buy 12 hours per semester at the price of $35 per hour (point d_2). This is a large increase in demand; previously (before winning the lottery) he demanded only 5 hours at that price (point d_1).

With his higher income, Tom can buy more tutoring services at every price. Thus ***the entire demand curve shifts to the right when income goes up.*** Figure 3.3 illustrates both the old (pre-lottery) and the new (post-lottery) demand curves.

Income is only one of the basic determinants of demand. Changes in any of the other determinants of demand would also cause the demand curve to shift. Tom's taste for web tutoring might increase dramatically, for example, if his parents promised to buy him a new car for passing web design. In that case, he might be willing to forgo other goods and spend more of his income on tutors. ***An increase in taste (desire) also shifts the demand curve to the right.***

Pizza and Politics. A similar demand shift occurs at the White House when a political crisis erupts. On an average day, White House staffers order about $300 worth of pizza from the nearby Domino's. When a crisis hits, however, staffers work well into the night and their demand for pizza soars. On the evening of the November 2016 presidential elections, White House staffers ordered more than $1,000 worth of pizza! Political analysts now use pizza deliveries to predict major White House announcements.

FIGURE 3.3

Shifts vs. Movements

A demand curve shows how a consumer responds to price changes. If the determinants of demand stay constant, the response is a *movement* along the curve to a new quantity demanded. In this case, when price falls from $35 to $20 per hour, the quantity demanded increases from 5 (point d_1), to 12 (point g_1).

If the determinants of demand *change*, the entire demand curve *shifts*. In this case, a rise in income increases demand. With more income, Tom is willing to buy 12 hours at the initial price of $35 (point d_2), not just the 5 hours he demanded before the lottery win (point d_1).

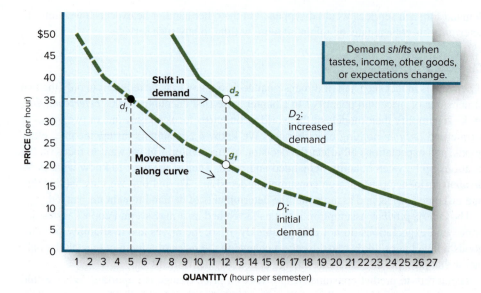

Demand *shifts* when tastes, income, other goods, or expectations change.

	Quantity Demanded (Hours per Semester)		
	Price (per Hour)	Initial Demand	After Increase in Income
A	$50	1	8
B	45	2	9
C	40	3	10
D	35	5	12
E	30	7	14
F	25	9	16
G	20	12	19
H	15	15	22
I	10	20	27

Movements vs. Shifts

It's important to distinguish shifts of the demand curve from movements along the demand curve. ***Movements along a demand curve are a response to price changes for that good.*** Such movements assume that determinants of demand are unchanged. By contrast, ***shifts of the demand curve occur when the determinants of demand change.*** When tastes, income, other goods, or expectations are altered, the basic relationship between price and quantity demanded is changed (shifts).

For convenience, movements along a demand curve and shifts of the demand curve have their own labels. Specifically, take care to distinguish

- ***Changes in quantity demanded:*** movements along a given demand curve in response to price changes of that good.
- ***Changes in demand:*** shifts of the demand curve due to changes in tastes, income, other goods, or expectations.

Tom's behavior in the web tutoring market will change if either the price of tutoring changes (a movement) or the underlying determinants of his demand are altered (a shift). Notice in Figure 3.3 that he ends up buying 12 hours of web tutoring if either the price of tutoring falls (to $20 per hour, leading him to point d_1) or his income increases (leading him to point d_2). Demand curves help us predict those market responses.

Market Demand

Whatever we say about demand for web design tutoring on the part of one wannabe web master, we can also say about every student at Clearview College (or, for that matter, about all consumers). Some students have no interest in web design and aren't willing to pay for related services: they don't participate in the web tutoring market. Other students want such services but don't have enough income to pay for them: they too are excluded from the web tutoring market. A large number of students, however, not only have a need (or desire) for web tutoring but also are willing and able to purchase such services.

What we start with in product markets, then, is many individual demand curves. Fortunately, it's possible to combine all the individual demand curves into a single **market demand.** The aggregation process is no more difficult than simple arithmetic. Suppose you would be willing to buy 1 hour of tutoring per semester at a price of $80 per hour. George, who is also desperate to learn web design, would buy 2 at that price; and I would buy none, since my publisher (McGraw-Hill) creates a web page for my book. What would our combined (market) demand for hours of tutoring be at that price? Collectively, we would be willing to buy a total of 3 hours of tutoring per semester if the price were $80 per hour. Our combined willingness to buy—our collective market demand—is nothing more than the sum of our individual demands. The same kind of aggregation can be performed for all consumers, leading to a summary of the total *market* demand for a specific good or service. Thus, *market demand is determined by the number of potential buyers and their respective tastes, incomes, other goods, and expectations.*

The Market Demand Curve

Figure 3.4 provides the basic market demand schedule for a situation in which only three consumers participate in the market. It illustrates the same market situation with demand curves. The three individuals who participate in the market demand for web tutoring at Clearview College obviously differ greatly, as suggested by their respective demand schedules. Tom's demand schedule is portrayed in the first column of the table (and is identical to the one we examined in Figure 3.2). George is also desperate to acquire some job skills and is willing to pay relatively high prices for web design tutoring. His demand is summarized in the second column under Quantity Demanded in the table.

The third consumer in this market is Lisa. Lisa already knows the nuts and bolts of web design, so she isn't so desperate for tutorial services. She would like to upgrade her skills, however, especially in animation and e-commerce applications. But her limited budget precludes paying a lot for help. She will hire a tutor only if the price falls to $30 per hour. Should tutors cost less, she'd even buy quite a few hours of web design tutoring.

The differing circumstances of Tom, George, and Lisa are expressed in their individual demand schedules (Figure 3.4). To determine the *market* demand for tutoring from this information, we simply add these three separate demands. The end result of this aggregation is, first, a *market* demand schedule (last column in the table) and, second, the resultant *market* demand curve (Figure 3.4*d*). These market summaries describe the various quantities of tutoring that Clearview College students are *willing and able* to purchase each semester at various prices.

How much web tutoring will be purchased each semester? Knowing how much help Tom, George, and Lisa are willing to buy at various prices doesn't tell you how much they're *actually* going to purchase. To determine the actual consumption of web tutoring, we have to know something about prices and supplies. Which of the many different prices illustrated in Figures 3.3 and 3.4 will actually prevail? How will that price be determined?

SUPPLY

To understand how the price of web tutoring is established, we must also look at the other side of the market: the *supply* side. We need to know how many hours of tutoring services people are willing and able to *sell* at various prices—that is, the **market supply.** As on the

market demand: The total quantities of a good or service people are willing and able to buy at alternative prices in a given time period; the sum of individual demands.

market supply: The total quantities of a good that sellers are willing and able to sell at alternative prices in a given time period, *ceteris paribus.*

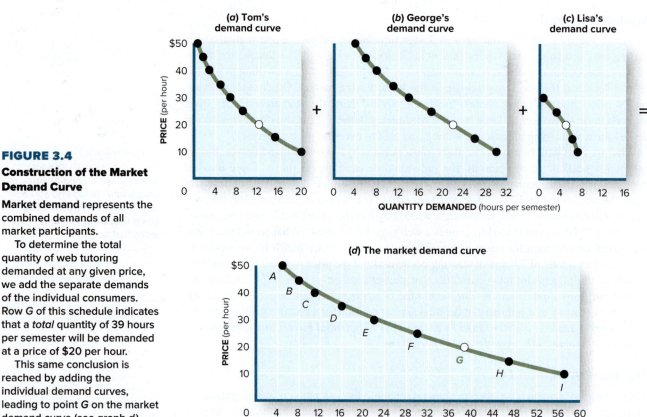

FIGURE 3.4

Construction of the Market Demand Curve

Market demand represents the combined demands of all market participants.

To determine the total quantity of web tutoring demanded at any given price, we add the separate demands of the individual consumers. Row *G* of this schedule indicates that a *total* quantity of 39 hours per semester will be demanded at a price of $20 per hour.

This same conclusion is reached by adding the individual demand curves, leading to point *G* on the market demand curve (see graph *d*).

	Price (per Hour)	Tom	+	George	+	Lisa	=	Market Demand
				Quantity of Tutoring Demanded (Hours per Semester)				
A	$50	1		4		0		5
B	45	2		6		0		8
C	40	3		8		0		11
D	35	5		11		0		16
E	30	7		14		1		22
F	25	9		18		3		30
G	20	12		22		5		39
H	15	15		26		6		47
I	10	20		30		7		57

demand side, the *market supply* depends on the behavior of all the individuals willing and able to supply web tutoring at some price.

Determinants of Supply

Let's return to the Clearview campus for a moment. What we need to know now is how much tutorial help people are willing and able to provide. Generally speaking, web design can be fun, but it can also be drudge work, especially when you're doing it for someone else. Hosting services like Weebly, Squarespace, and GoDaddy have made setting up a website easier and more creative. And the cloud and Wi-Fi access have made the job more convenient. But teaching someone else to design web pages is still work. So why does anyone do it? Easy answer: for the money. People offer (supply) tutoring services to earn income that they, in turn, can spend on the goods and services *they* desire.

How much money must be offered to induce web designers to do a little tutoring depends on a variety of things. The ***determinants of market supply include***

- ***Technology.***
- ***Factor costs.***
- ***Other goods.***
- ***Taxes and subsidies.***
- ***Expectations.***
- ***Number of sellers.***

The technology of web design, for example, is always getting easier and more creative. With a program like Weebly, for example, it's very easy to create a bread-and-butter web page. A continuous stream of new software programs (e.g., Wordpress, DreamWeaver) keeps stretching the possibilities for graphics, animation, interactivity, and content. These technological advances mean that web design services can be supplied more quickly and cheaply. They also make *teaching* web design easier. As a result, they induce people to supply *more* tutoring services at every price.

How much web design service is offered at any given price also depends on the cost of factors of production. If the software programs needed to create web pages are cheap (or, better yet, free), web designers can afford to charge lower prices. If the required software inputs are expensive, however, they will have to charge more for their services.

Other goods can also affect the willingness to supply web design services. If you can make more income waiting tables than you can tutoring lazy students, why would you even boot up the computer? As the prices paid for other goods and services change, they will influence people's decision about whether to offer web services.

In the real world, the decision to supply goods and services is also influenced by the long arm of Uncle Sam. Federal, state, and local governments impose taxes on income earned in the marketplace. When tax rates are high, people get to keep less of the income they earn. Once taxes start biting into paychecks, some people may conclude that tutoring is no longer worth the hassle and withdraw from the market.

Expectations are also important on the supply side of the market. If web designers expect higher prices, lower costs, or reduced taxes, they may be more willing to learn new software programs. On the other hand, if they have poor expectations about the future, they may just find something else to do.

Finally, we note that the number of potential tutors will affect the quantity of service offered for sale at various prices. If there are lots of willing tutors on campus, a lot of tutorial service will be available at reasonable prices.

All these considerations—factor costs, technology, taxes, expectations—affect the decision to offer web services at various prices. In general, we assume that web architects will be willing to provide more tutoring if the per-hour price is high and less if the price is low. In other words, there is a **law of supply** that parallels the law of demand. ***The law of supply says that larger quantities will be offered for sale at higher prices.*** Here again, the laws rest on the *ceteris paribus* assumption: the quantity supplied increases at higher prices *if* the determinants of supply are constant. ***Supply curves are upward-sloping to the right,*** as shown in Figure 3.5. Note how the *quantity supplied* jumps from 39 hours (point *d*) to 130 hours (point *h*) when the price of web service doubles (from $20 to $40 per hour).

law of supply: The quantity of a good supplied in a given time period increases as its price increases, *ceteris paribus.*

Market Supply

Figure 3.5 also illustrates how *market* supply is constructed from the supply decisions of individual sellers. In this case, only three web masters are available. Ann is willing to provide a lot of tutoring at low prices, whereas Bob requires at least $20 an hour. Carlos won't talk to students for less than $30 an hour.

By adding the quantity each tutor is willing to offer at every price, we can construct the market supply curve. Notice in Figure 3.5 how the quantity supplied to the market at $45 (point *i*)

FIGURE 3.5

Market Supply

The market supply curve indicates the *combined* sales intentions of all market participants—that is, the total quantities they are willing and able to sell at various prices.

If the price of tutoring were $45 per hour (point *i*), the *total* quantity of services supplied would be 140 hours per semester. This quantity is determined by adding the supply decisions of all individual producers. In this case, Ann supplies 93 hours, Bob supplies 33, and Carlos supplies the rest.

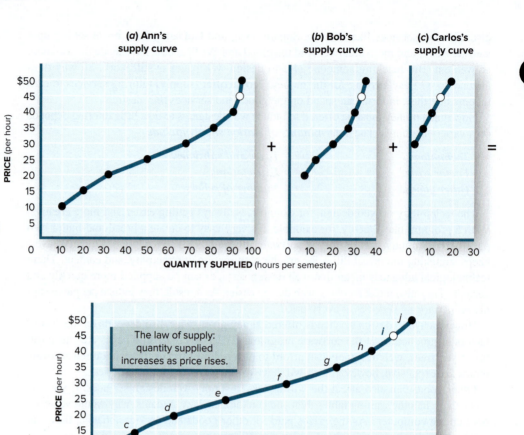

	Price per Hour	Quantity of Tutoring Supplied by					
		Ann	+	Bob	+	Carlos	=	Market
j	$50	94		35		19		148
i	45	93		33		14		140
h	40	90		30		10		130
g	35	81		27		6		114
f	30	68		20		2		90
e	25	50		12		0		62
d	20	32		7		0		39
c	15	20		0		0		20
b	10	10		0		0		10

comes from the individual efforts of Ann (93 hours), Bob (33 hours), and Carlos (14 hours). *The market supply curve is just a summary of the supply intentions of all producers.*

None of the points on the market supply curve (Figure 3.5) tells us how much web tutoring is *actually* being sold on the Clearview campus. *Market supply is an expression of sellers' intentions—an offer to sell—not a statement of actual sales.* My next-door neighbor may be willing to sell his 2004 Honda Civic for $8,000, but most likely he'll never find a buyer at that price. Nevertheless, his *willingness* to sell his car at that price is part of the *market supply* of used cars.

Shifts of Supply

As with demand, there's nothing sacred about any given set of supply intentions. Supply curves *shift* when the underlying determinants of supply change. Thus, *it is important to distinguish*

- *Changes in quantity supplied:* movements along a given supply curve in response to price changes of that good.
- *Changes in supply:* shifts of the supply curve due to changes is technology, factor costs, other goods, taxes and subsidies, or expectations.

Our Latin friend *ceteris paribus* is once again the decisive factor. If the price of a product is the only variable changing, then we can **track changes in quantity supplied along the supply curve.** But if *ceteris paribus* is violated—if technology, factor costs, the profitability of producing other goods, tax rates, expectations, or the number of sellers changes—then **changes in supply are illustrated by shifts of the supply curve.**

In the News "Gas Prices Jump in Matthew's Wake" illustrates how a supply shift pushed up gasoline prices in Florida in October 2016. Damage from Hurricane Matthew made it more difficult and expensive to supply Florida gas stations with fuel. As the market supply curve shifted to the left, the price of gasoline rose.

IN THE NEWS

GAS PRICES JUMP IN MATTHEW'S WAKE

Hurricane Matthew struck the Southeastern United States on October 6, 2016. Winds as high as 140 miles per hour and drenching rains forced thousands of people to evacuate homes in Florida, North Carolina, and Georgia.

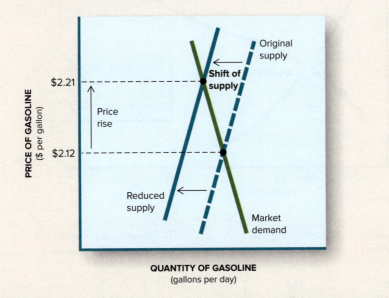

Matthew also drove the price of gasoline higher. Gasoline supplies into Florida come by tanker, then by tanker trucks to gasoline stations. Matthew damaged port facilities, flooded the roads, and destroyed highways. Gas prices rose by 9 cents to $2.21 a gallon due to the resulting leftward shift in market supply.

Source: News reports, October 2016.

ANALYSIS: When factor costs or availability worsen, the supply curve *shifts* to the left. Such leftward supply-curve shifts push prices up the market demand curve.

EQUILIBRIUM

That post-hurricane spike in gasoline prices offers some clues to how the forces of supply and demand set—and change—market prices. For a closer look at how those forces work, we'll return to Clearview College for a moment. How did supply and demand resolve the WHAT, HOW, and FOR WHOM questions in that web tutoring market?

Figure 3.6 helps answer that question by bringing together the market supply and demand curves we've already examined (Figures 3.4 and 3.5). When we put the two curves together, we see that *only one price and quantity combination is compatible with the intentions of both buyers and sellers. This equilibrium occurs at the intersection of the supply and demand curves.* Notice in Figure 3.6 where that intersection occurs—at the price of $20 and the quantity of 39 hours. So $20 is the **equilibrium price:** campus tutors will sell a total of 39 hours of tutoring per semester—the same amount that students wish to buy at that price. Those 39 hours of tutoring service will be part of WHAT is produced in the economy.

equilibrium price: The price at which the quantity of a good demanded in a given time period equals the quantity supplied.

Market Clearing

An equilibrium doesn't imply that everyone is happy with the prevailing price or quantity. Notice in Figure 3.6, for example, that some students who want to buy 60 assistance

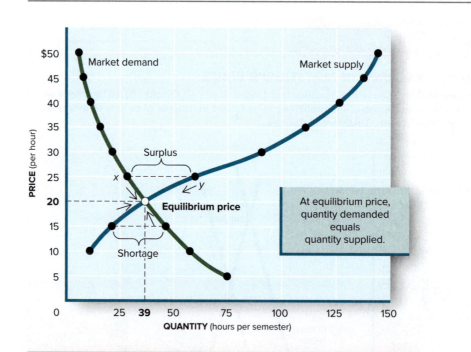

FIGURE 3.6

Equilibrium Price

The intersection of the demand and supply curves establishes the *equilibrium* price and quantity. Only at equilibrium is the quantity demanded equal to the quantity supplied. In this case, the equilibrium price is $20 per hour, and 39 hours is the equilibrium quantity.

At above-equilibrium prices, a market *surplus* exists—the quantity supplied exceeds the quantity demanded. At prices below equilibrium, a market *shortage* exists.

Price (per Hour)	Quantity Supplied (Hours per Semester)		Quantity Demanded (Hours per Semester)	
$50	148		5	
45	140		8	
40	130	Market surplus	11	Nonequilibrium prices create surpluses or shortages.
35	114		16	
30	90		22	
25	62		30	
20	39	Equilibrium	39	
15	20	Market shortage	47	
10	10		57	

services don't get any. These would-be buyers are arrayed along the demand curve *below* the equilibrium. Because the price they're *willing* to pay is less than the equilibrium price of $20, they don't get any web design help. The market's FOR WHOM answer includes only those students willing and able to pay the equilibrium price.

Likewise, some would-be sellers are frustrated by this market outcome. These wannabe tutors are arrayed along the supply curve *above* the equilibrium. Because they insist on being paid *more* than the equilibrium price of $20 per hour, they don't actually sell anything.

Although not everyone finds satisfaction in the market equilibrium, that unique outcome is efficient. ***The equilibrium price and quantity reflect a compromise between buyers and sellers. No other compromise yields a quantity demanded that's exactly equal to the quantity supplied.***

The Invisible Hand. The equilibrium price isn't determined by any single individual. Rather, it's determined by the collective behavior of many buyers and sellers, each acting out his or her own demand or supply schedule. It's this kind of impersonal price determination that gave rise to Adam Smith's characterization of the market mechanism as "the invisible hand." In attempting to explain how the **market mechanism** works, the famed 18th-century economist noted a remarkable feature of market prices. The market behaves as if some unseen force (the invisible hand) were examining each individual's supply or demand schedule and then selecting a price that assured an equilibrium. In practice, the process of price determination isn't so mysterious: it's a simple process of trial and error.

market mechanism: The use of market prices and sales to signal desired outputs (or resource allocations).

Disequilibrium: Surplus and Shortage

Market Surplus. To appreciate the power of the market mechanism, consider interference in its operation. Suppose, for example, that campus tutors banded together and agreed to charge a minimum price of $25 per hour, five dollars more than the equilibrium price. By establishing a **price floor,** a minimum price for their services, the tutors hope to increase their incomes. But they won't be fully satisfied. Figure 3.6 illustrates the consequences of this *dis*equilibrium pricing. At $25 per hour, campus tutors would be offering more than 39 hours of tutoring. How much more? Move up the market supply curve from the equilibrium price until you hit the price of $25. At that price, tutors are prepared to offer the quantity indicated by point *y*. What's wrong with that point? Students in need of tutoring aren't willing to buy that much tutoring at that price. The market demand curve tells us Tom, George, and Lisa are willing to buy only the smaller quantity indicated by point *x* at the price of $25 per hour. We have a discrepancy between the quantity suppliers want to sell and the quantity consumers want to buy. This is a *dis*equilibrium.

price floor: Lower limit set for the price of a good.

In this case, the disequilibrium creates a **market surplus:** more tutoring is being offered for sale than consumers are willing to purchase at the available price. As Figure 3.6 indicates, at a price of $25 per hour, a market surplus of 32 hours per semester exists. Under these circumstances, campus tutors would be spending many idle hours at their keyboards waiting for customers to appear. Their waiting will be in vain because the quantity of web tutoring demanded will not increase until the price of tutoring falls. That is the clear message of the demand curve. As would-be tutors get this message, they'll reduce their prices. This is the response the market mechanism signals.

market surplus: The amount by which the quantity supplied exceeds the quantity demanded at a given price; excess supply.

As sellers' asking prices decline, the quantity demanded will increase. This concept is illustrated in Figure 3.6 by the movement along the demand curve from point *x* to lower prices and greater quantity demanded. As we move down the market demand curve, the *desire* for web design help doesn't change, but the quantity people are *able and willing to buy* increases. When the price falls to $20 per hour, the quantity demanded will finally equal the quantity supplied. This is the *equilibrium* illustrated in Figure 3.6.

Market Shortage. A very different sequence of events would occur if a market shortage existed. Suppose someone were to spread the word that web tutoring services were available at only $15 per hour. Tom, George, and Lisa would be standing in line to get tutorial help, but campus web designers wouldn't be willing to supply the quantity demanded at

market shortage: The amount by which the quantity demanded exceeds the quantity supplied at a given price; excess demand.

that price. As Figure 3.6 confirms, at $15 per hour, the quantity demanded (47 hours per semester) greatly exceeds the quantity supplied (20 hours per semester). In this situation, we speak of a **market shortage**—that is, an excess of quantity demanded over quantity supplied. At a price of $15 an hour, the shortage amounts to 27 hours of tutoring services.

When a market shortage exists, not all consumer demands can be satisfied. Some people who are *willing* to buy web help at the going price ($15) won't be able to do so. To assure themselves of sufficient help, Tom, George, Lisa, or some other consumer may offer to pay a *higher* price, thus initiating a move up the demand curve in Figure 3.6. The higher prices offered will in turn induce other enterprising tutors to tutor more, thus ensuring an upward movement along the market supply curve. Notice, again, that the *desire* to tutor web design hasn't changed; only the quantity supplied has responded to a change in price. As this process continues, the quantity supplied will eventually equal the quantity demanded (39 hours in Figure 3.6).

Self-Adjusting Prices. What we observe, then, is that *whenever the market price is set above or below the equilibrium price, either a market surplus or a market shortage will emerge.* To overcome a surplus or shortage, buyers and sellers will change their behavior. Sellers will have to compete for customers by reducing prices when a market surplus exists. If a shortage exists, buyers will compete for service by offering to pay higher prices. Only at the *equilibrium* price will no further adjustments be required.

Sometimes the market price is slow to adjust, and a disequilibrium persists. This is often the case with tickets to rock concerts, football games, and other one-time events. People initially adjust their behavior by standing in ticket lines for hours, or hopping on the Internet, hoping to buy a ticket at the below-equilibrium price. The tickets are typically resold ("scalped"), however, at prices closer to equilibrium. This is a common occurrence at major college sporting events such as the Final Four basketball championships (see In the News "The Real March Madness: Ticket Prices").

IN THE NEWS

THE REAL MARCH MADNESS: TICKET PRICES

Ticket prices for Monday's NCAA championship game between the Gonzaga Bulldogs and the North Carolina Tar Heels look deceivingly cheap—only $50 according to the NCAA's official website. But don't expect to get into the University of Phoenix stadium for that paltry sum. The 80,000 seats are sold out. Scalpers are charging an average of $4,000 for front-row seats and at least one seat was sold for $18,181.80. Nosebleed seats are going for $375 apiece. It is inevitable that one team will lose on Monday night—but it won't be the scalpers.

Source: Media reports, April 2, 2017.

ANALYSIS: When tickets are sold initially at below-equilibrium prices, a market shortage is created. Scalpers resell tickets at prices closer to equilibrium, reaping a profit in the process.

Business firms can discover equilibrium prices by trial and error. If consumer purchases aren't keeping up with production, a firm may conclude that its price is above the equilibrium price. To get rid of accumulated inventory, the firm will have to lower its price. In the happier situation where consumer purchases are outpacing production, a firm might conclude that its price was a trifle too low and give it a nudge upward. In either case, the equilibrium price can be established after a few trials in the marketplace.

Changes in Equilibrium

No equilibrium price is permanent. The equilibrium price established in the Clearview College tutoring market, for example, was the unique outcome of specific demand and supply schedules. Those schedules themselves were based on our assumption of *ceteris paribus*. We assumed that the "taste" (desire) for web design assistance was given, as were consumers'

incomes, the price and availability of other goods, and expectations. Any of these determinants of demand could change. When one does, the demand curve has to be redrawn. Such a shift of the demand curve will lead to a new equilibrium price and quantity. Indeed, *the equilibrium price will change whenever the supply or demand curve shifts.*

A Demand Shift. We can illustrate how equilibrium prices change by taking one last look at the Clearview College tutoring market. Our original supply and demand curves, together with the resulting equilibrium (point E_1), are depicted in Figure 3.7. Now suppose that all the professors at Clearview begin requiring class-specific web pages from each student. The increased need (desire) for web design ability will affect market demand. Tom, George, and Lisa will be willing to buy more web tutoring at every price than they were before.

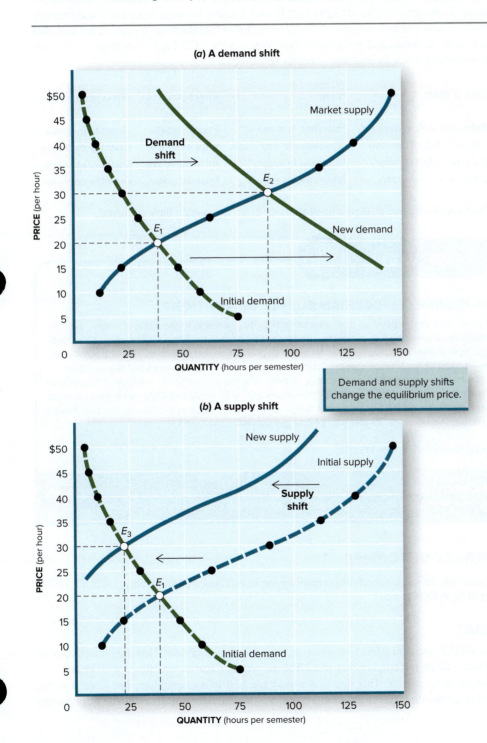

FIGURE 3.7

Changes in Equilibrium

If demand or supply changes (shifts), market equilibrium will change as well.

Demand shift: In (*a*), the rightward shift of the demand curve illustrates an increase in demand. When demand increases, the equilibrium price rises (from E_1 to E_2).

Supply shift: In (*b*), the leftward shift of the supply curve illustrates a decrease in supply. This raises the equilibrium price to E_3.

Demand and supply curves shift only when their underlying determinants change—that is, when *ceteris paribus* is violated.

Demand and supply shifts change the equilibrium price.

That is, the *demand* for web services has increased. We can represent this increased demand by a rightward *shift* of the market demand curve, as illustrated in Figure 3.7a.

Note that the new demand curve intersects the (unchanged) market supply curve at a new price (point E_2); the equilibrium price is now $30 per hour and 90 hours of tutoring is bought. This new equilibrium price will persist until either the demand curve or the supply curve shifts again.

A Supply Shift. Figure 3.7b illustrates a *supply* shift. The decrease (leftward shift) in supply might occur if some on-campus tutors got sick. Or approaching exams might convince would-be tutors that they have no time to spare. ***Whenever supply decreases (shifts left), price tends to rise,*** as in Figure 3.7b.

Lots of Shifts. In the real world, demand and supply curves are constantly shifting. A change in the weather can alter the supply and demand for food, vacations, and baseball games. A new product can change the demand for old products. A foreign crisis can alter the supply, demand, and price of oil (see World View "Oil Higher on Nigerian Supply Disruptions"). Look for and remember these shifts:

Type of Shift	Name	Effect on Price	Effect on Quantity
Rightward shift of demand	"Increase in demand"	Price increase	Quantity increase
Leftward shift of demand	"Decrease in demand"	Price decrease	Quantity decrease
Rightward shift of supply	"Increase in supply"	Price decrease	Quantity increase
Leftward shift of supply	"Decrease in supply"	Price increase	Quantity decrease

When you see a price change, one or more of these shifts must have occurred.

WORLD VIEW

OIL HIGHER ON NIGERIAN SUPPLY DISRUPTIONS

Nigerian militants stepped up their attacks on Nigeria's oil fields. In the last few weeks, the militants have attacked both oil production and export facilities in the Niger Delta region. The resulting supply disruptions have reduced Nigeria's oil production by as much as 750,000 barrels per day—a huge hit for a nation that produced an average of 1.9 million barrels per day in 2015.

The Nigerian supply disruptions have shown up in the price of oil in the United States and Great Britain. Spot prices in the U.S. rose yesterday by 13 cents to $49.12 per barrel for West Texas crude, reflecting tighter global supplies and concerns over continuing supply disruptions. Brent crude rose 35 cents to $47.32 per barrel.

Source: News reports of May 17, 2016.

ANALYSIS: Equilibrium prices change whenever market demand or supply curves shift. In this case, the supply curve is shifting to the left, and the equilibrium price is rising.

MARKET OUTCOMES

Notice how the market mechanism resolves the basic economic questions of WHAT, HOW, and FOR WHOM.

WHAT

The WHAT question refers to the mix of output society produces. How much web tutorial service will be included in that mix? The answer at Clearview College was 39 hours of tutoring per semester. This decision wasn't reached in a referendum, but instead in the market equilibrium (Figure 3.6). In the same way but on a larger scale, millions of consumers and a handful of auto producers decide to include 16 million or so cars and trucks in each year's mix of output. Auto manufacturers use rebates, discounts, and variable interest rates to induce consumers to buy the same quantity that auto manufacturers are producing.

HOW

The market mechanism also determines HOW goods are produced. Profit-seeking producers will strive to produce web designs and automobiles in the most efficient way. They'll use market prices to decide not only WHAT to produce but also what resources to use in the production process. If new software simplifies web design—and is priced low enough—tutors will use it. Likewise, auto manufacturers will use robots rather than humans on the assembly line if robots reduce costs and increase profits.

FOR WHOM

Finally, the invisible hand of the market will determine who gets the goods produced. At Clearview College, who got web tutoring? Only those students who were willing and able to pay $20 per hour for that service. FOR WHOM are all those automobiles produced each year? The answer is the same: those consumers who are willing and able to pay the market price for a new car.

Optimal, Not Perfect

Not everyone is happy with these answers, of course. Tom would like to pay only $10 an hour for a tutor. And some of the Clearview students don't have enough income to buy any tutoring. They think it's unfair that they have to design their own web pages while rich students can have someone else do their design work for them. Students who can't afford cars are even less happy with the market's answer to the FOR WHOM question.

Although the outcomes of the marketplace aren't perfect, they're often optimal. Optimal outcomes are the best possible given our incomes and scarce resources. Sure, we'd like everyone to have access to tutoring and to drive a new car. But there aren't enough resources available to create such a utopia. So we have to ration available tutors and cars. The market mechanism performs this rationing function. People who want to supply tutoring or build cars are free to make that choice. And consumers are free to decide how they want to spend their income. In the process, we expect market participants to make decisions that maximize their own wellbeing. If they do, then we conclude that everyone is doing as well as possible, given their available resources.

THE ECONOMY TOMORROW

DEADLY SHORTAGES: THE ORGAN TRANSPLANT MARKET

As you were reading this chapter, dozens of Americans were dying from failed organs. More than 100,000 Americans are waiting for life-saving kidneys, livers, lungs, and other vital organs. They can't wait long, however. Every day at least 20 of these organ-diseased patients die. The clock is always ticking.

Modern technology can save most of these patients. Vital organs can be transplanted, extending the life of diseased patients. How many people are saved, however, depends on how well the organ "market" works.

The Supply of Organs. The only cure for liver disease and some other organ failures is a replacement organ. More than 50 years ago, doctors discovered that they could transplant an organ from one individual to another. Since then, medical technology has advanced to the point where organ transplants are exceptionally safe and successful. The constraint on this life-saving technique is the *supply* of transplantable organs.

Continued

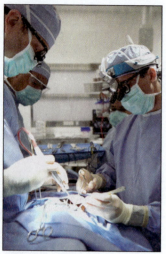

©ERproductions Ltd/Blend Images
LLC RF

Although more than 2 million Americans die each year, most deaths do not create transplantable organs. Only 20,000 or so people die in circumstances—such as brain death after a car crash—that make them suitable donors for life-saving transplants. Additional kidneys can be "harvested" from live donors (we have two kidneys but can function with only one; this is not true for liver, heart, or pancreas).

You don't have to die to supply an organ. Instead you become a donor by agreeing to release your organs after death. The agreement is typically certified on a driver's license and sometimes on a bracelet or "dog tag." This allows emergency doctors to identify potential organ supplies.

People become donors for many reasons. Moral principles, religious convictions, and humanitarianism all play a role in the donation decision. It's the same with blood donations: people give blood (while alive!) because they want to help save other individuals.

Market Incentives. Monetary incentives could also play a role. When blood donations are inadequate, hospitals and medical schools *buy* blood in the marketplace. People who might not donate blood come forth to *sell* blood when a price is offered. In principle, the same incentive might increase the number of *organ* donors. If offered cash now for a postmortem organ, would the willingness to donate increase? The law of supply suggests it would. Offer $1,000 in cash for signing up, and potential donors will start lining up. Offer more, and the quantity supplied will increase further.

Zero Price Ceiling. The government doesn't permit this to happen. In 1984 Congress forbade the purchase or sale of human organs in the United States (the National Organ Transplantation Act). In part, the prohibition was rooted in moral and religious convictions. It was also motivated by equity concerns—the FOR WHOM question. If organs could be bought and sold, then the rich would have a distinct advantage in living.

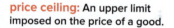

price ceiling: An upper limit imposed on the price of a good.

The prohibition on market sales is effectively a **price ceiling** set at zero. As a consequence, the only available organs are those supplied by altruistic donors—people who are willing to supply organs at a zero price. The quantity supplied can't be increased with (illegal) price incentives. In general, *price ceilings have three predictable effects: they*

- *Increase the quantity demanded.*
- *Decrease the quantity supplied.*
- *Create a market shortage.*

The Deadly Shortage. Figure 3.8 illustrates the consequences of this price ceiling. At a price of zero, only the quantity q_a of "altruistic" organs is available (roughly one-third of

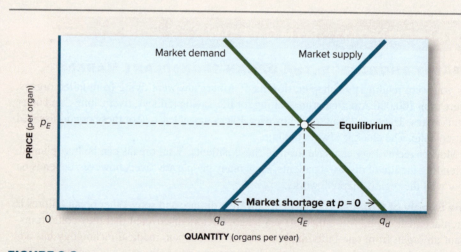

FIGURE 3.8

Organ Transplant Market

A market in human organs would deliver the quantity q_E at a price of p_E. The government-set price ceiling ($p = 0$) reduces the quantity supplied to q_a.

the potential supply). But the quantity q_d is demanded by all the organ-diseased individuals. The market shortage $q_d - q_a$ tells us how many patients will die.

Economists contend that many of these deaths are unnecessary. A University of Pennsylvania study showed that the quantity of organs supplied *doubled* when payment was offered. Without the government-set price ceiling, more organ-diseased patients would live. Figure 3.8 shows that q_E people would get transplants in a market-driven system. In the government-regulated system, only the quantity of q_a of transplants can occur.

Why does the government impose price controls that condemn more people to die? Because it feels the market unfairly distributes available organs. Only people who can afford the price p_E end up living in the market-based system—a feature regulators say is unfair. In the absence of the market mechanism, however, the government must set other rules for who gets the even smaller quantity of organs supplied. That rationing system may be unfair as well.

SUMMARY

- People participate in the marketplace by offering to buy or sell goods and services, or factors of production. Participation is motivated by the desire to maximize utility (consumers), profits (business firms), or the general welfare (government) from the limited resources each participant has. **LO3-1, LO3-2**
- All market transactions involve the exchange of either factors of production or goods and services. Although the actual exchanges can occur anywhere, they take place in product markets or factor markets, depending on what is being exchanged. **LO3-1, LO3-2**
- People willing and able to buy a particular good at some price are part of the market demand for that product. All those willing and able to sell that good at some price are part of the market supply. Total market demand or supply is the sum of individual demands or supplies. **LO3-1, LO3-2**
- Supply and demand curves illustrate how the quantity demanded or supplied changes in response to a change in the price of that good, if nothing else changes (*ceteris paribus*). Demand curves slope downward; supply curves slope upward. **LO3-1, LO3-2**
- Determinants of market demand include the number of potential buyers and their respective tastes (desires), incomes, other goods, and expectations. If any of these

determinants changes, the demand curve shifts. Movements along a demand curve are induced only by a change in the price of that good. **LO3-4**
- Determinants of market supply include factor costs, technology, profitability of other goods, expectations, tax rates, and number of sellers. Supply shifts when these underlying determinants change. **LO3-4**
- The quantity of goods or resources actually exchanged in each market depends on the behavior of all buyers and sellers, as summarized in market supply and demand curves. At the point where the two curves intersect, an equilibrium price—the price at which the quantity demanded equals the quantity supplied—is established. **LO3-3**
- A distinctive feature of the market equilibrium is that it's the only price-quantity combination acceptable to buyers and sellers alike. At higher prices, the quantity supplied is more than buyers are willing to purchase (a market surplus); at lower prices, the amount demanded exceeds the quantity supplied (a market shortage). Only the equilibrium price clears the market. **LO3-3**
- Price ceilings are disequilibrium prices imposed on the marketplace. Such price controls create an imbalance between quantities demanded and supplied, resulting in market shortages. **LO3-5**

Key Terms

factor market	law of demand	law of supply
product market	substitute goods	equilibrium price
opportunity cost	complementary goods	market mechanism
supply	*ceteris paribus*	price floor
demand	shift in demand	market surplus
demand schedule	market demand	market shortage
demand curve	market supply	price ceiling

Questions for Discussion

1. In our story of Tom, the student confronted with a web design assignment, we emphasized the great urgency of his desire for web tutoring. Many people would say that Tom had an "absolute need" for web help and therefore was ready to "pay anything" to get it. If this were true, what shape would his demand curve have? Why isn't this realistic? **LO3-1**

2. Within weeks after Samsung launched its Galaxy Note 7 smartphone in August 2016, the phones started erupting into smoke and flames. How did this affect the demand for Note 7s? What determinants of demand changed? **LO3-1**

3. With respect to the demand for college enrollment, which of the following would cause (1) a movement along the demand curve or (2) a shift of the demand curve? **LO3-4**
   a. An increase in incomes.
   b. Lower tuition.
   c. More student loans.
   d. An increase in textbook prices.

4. Why do militant attacks in Nigeria affect the price of gasoline at U.S. gas stations? (World View "Oil Higher on Nigerian Supply Disruptions") **LO3-5**

5. Why are scalpers able to resell tickets to the Final Four basketball games at such high prices (In the News "The Real March Madness: Ticket Prices")? **LO3-2**

6. In Figure 3.8, why is the organ demand curve downward-sloping rather than vertical? **LO3-1**

7. The shortage in the organ market (Figure 3.8) requires a nonmarket rationing scheme. Who should get the available (q_a) organs? Is this fairer than the market-driven distribution? **LO3-5**

8. What would happen in the apple market if the government set a *minimum* price of $10.00 per apple? What might motivate such a policy? **LO3-5**

9. When Hurricane Matthew struck Florida, Governor Rick Scott signed an emergency declaration outlawing "price gouging," i.e., unjustified price increases. More than 2,700 Floridians filed complaints with the State's Attorney General, most complaining about higher gasoline prices. If fully enforced, how would the governor's action have altered the market outcome depicted in In the News "Gas Prices Jump in Matthew's Wake"? **LO3-5**

10. Is there a shortage of on-campus parking at your school? How might the shortage be resolved? **LO3-3**

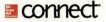

PROBLEMS FOR CHAPTER 3

LO3-1 1. According to Figure 3.3, at what price would Tom buy 12 hours of web tutoring?
    (*a*) Without a lottery win.
    (*b*) With a lottery win.

LO3-3 2. According to Figures 3.5 and 3.6, what would the new equilibrium price of tutoring services be if Ann decided to stop tutoring?

LO3-3 3. According to In the News "The Real March Madness: Ticket Prices"
    (*a*) What was the initial price of a ticket to the NCAA finals?
    (*b*) At that price was there an equilibrium, a shortage, or a surplus?

LO3-3 4. Given the following data on gasoline supply and demand,
    (*a*) What is the equilibrium price?
    (*b*) Suppose the current price is $4. At this price, how much of a shortage or surplus exist?

Price per gallon	$5.00	$4.00	$3.00	$2.00	$1.00		$5.00	$4.00	$3.00	$2.00	$1.00
Quantity demanded (gallons per day)						Quantity supplied (gallons per day)					
Al	1	2	3	4	5	Firm A	3	3	2	2	1
Betsy	0	1	1	1	2	Firm B	7	5	3	3	2
Casey	2	2	3	3	4	Firm C	6	4	3	3	1
Daisy	1	3	4	4	6	Firm D	6	5	3	2	0
Eddie	1	2	2	3	5	Firm E	4	2	2	2	1
Market total	5	10	13	15	22	Market total	26	19	13	16	5

LO3-2 5. Illustrate using a supply and demand graph what happened to gasoline prices in In the News, "Gas Prices Jump in Matthew's Wake."
    (*a*) Which curve shifted?
    (*b*) Which direction did that curve shift (left or right)?
    (*c*) Did price increase or decrease?
    (*d*) Did quantity increase or decrease?

LO3-4 6. Illustrate using a supply and demand graph what happened to oil prices in World View "Oil Higher on Nigerian Supply Disruptions."
    (*a*) Which curve shifted?
    (*b*) Which direction did that curve shift (left or right)?
    (*c*) Did price increase or decrease?
    (*d*) Did quantity increase or decrease?

LO3-1 7. The goal of the price cut described in In the News "Pricing the Galaxy S7," was to
    (*a*) Increase supply.
    (*b*) Increase quantity supplied.
    (*c*) Increase demand.
    (*d*) Increase quantity demanded.

LO3-5 8. Which curve shifts and in which direction when the following events occur in the domestic car market?
    (*a*) The U.S. economy falls into a recession.
    (*b*) U.S. autoworkers go on strike.
    (*c*) Imported cars become more expensive.
    (*d*) The price of gasoline increases.

LO3-5 9. Use the following data to draw supply and demand curves.

Price	$ 8	7	6	5	4	3	2	1
Quantity demanded	2	3	4	5	6	7	8	9
Quantity supplied	10	9	8	7	6	5	4	3

   (a) What is the equilibrium price?
   (b) Suppose the current price is $7,
       (i) What kind of disequilibrium situation results?
       (ii) How large is this surplus or shortage?
   (c) Suppose the current price is $3,
       (i) What disequilibrium situation results?
       (ii) How large is this surplus or shortage?
   Illustrate these answers.

LO3-5 10. In Figure 3.8, when a price ceiling of zero is imposed, does
   (a) The quantity of organs demanded increase?
   (b) The market demand increase?
   (c) The quantity of organs supplied increase?
   (d) The market supply increase?
   (e) The equilibrium price change?

LO3-5 11. The Economy Tomorrow: According to Figure 3.8,
   (a) How many organs are supplied at a zero price?
   (b) How many people die in the government-regulated economy where there is a price
       ceiling = $0?
   (c) How many people die in the market-driven economy?

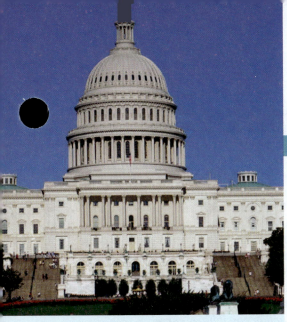

©Hisham F. Ibrahim/Getty Images RF

CHAPTER 4

The Role of Government

The market has a keen ear for private wants, but a deaf ear for public needs.

—**Robert Heilbroner**

Markets do work: the interaction of supply and demand in product markets *does* generate goods and services. Likewise, the interaction of supply and demand in labor markets *does* yield jobs, wages, and a distribution of income. As we've observed, the market is capable of determining WHAT goods to produce, HOW, and FOR WHOM.

But are the market's answers good enough? Is the mix of output produced by unregulated markets the best possible mix? Will producers choose the production process that protects the environment? Will the market-generated distribution of income be fair enough? Will there be enough jobs for everyone who wants one?

In reality, markets don't always give us the best possible outcomes. Markets dominated by a few powerful corporations may charge excessive prices, limit output, provide poor service, or even retard technological advance. In the quest for profits, producers may sacrifice the environment for cost savings. In unfettered markets, some people may not get life-saving health care, basic education, or even adequate nutrition. When markets generate such outcomes, government intervention may be needed to ensure better answers to the WHAT, HOW, and FOR WHOM questions.

This chapter identifies the circumstances under which government intervention is desirable. To this end, we answer the following questions:

- **Under what circumstances do markets fail?**
- **How can government intervention help?**
- **How much government intervention is desirable?**

As we'll see, there's substantial agreement about how and when markets fail to give us the best WHAT, HOW, and FOR WHOM answers. But there's much less agreement about whether government intervention improves the situation. Indeed, an overwhelming majority of Americans are ambivalent about government intervention. They want the government to "fix" the mix of output, protect the environment, and ensure an adequate level of income for everyone. But voters are equally quick to blame government meddling for many of our economic woes.

MARKET FAILURE

We can visualize the potential for government intervention by focusing on the WHAT question. Our goal here is to produce the best possible mix of output with existing resources. We illustrated this goal earlier with production possibilities curves. Figure 4.1 assumes that of all the possible combinations of output we could produce, the unique combination at point X represents the most desirable one. In other words, it's the **optimal mix of output,** the one that maximizes our collective social utility. We haven't yet figured out how to pinpoint that optimal mix; we're simply using the arbitrary point X in Figure 4.1 to represent that best possible outcome.

Ideally, the **market mechanism** would lead us to point X. Price signals in the marketplace are supposed to move factors of production from one industry to another in response to consumer demands. If we demand more health care—offer to buy more at a given price—more resources (labor) will be allocated to health care services. Similarly, a fall in demand will encourage health care practitioners (doctors, nurses, and the like) to find jobs in another industry. *Changes in market prices direct resources from one industry to another, moving us along the perimeter of the production possibilities curve.*

Where will the market mechanism take us? Will it move resources around until we end up at the optimal point X? Or will it leave us at another point on the production possibilities curve with a *sub*optimal mix of output? (If point X is the *optimal,* or best possible, mix, all other output mixes must be *sub*optimal.)

We use the term **market failure** to refer to situations where the market generates imperfect (suboptimal) outcomes. If the invisible hand of the marketplace produces a mix of output that's different from the one society most desires, then it has failed. *Market failure implies that the forces of supply and demand haven't led us to the best point on the production possibilities curve.* Such a failure is illustrated by point M in Figure 4.1. Point M is assumed to be the mix of output generated by market forces. Notice that the market mix (M) doesn't represent the optimal mix, which is assumed to be at point X. We get less health care and more of other goods than are optimal. The market in this case *fails;* we get the wrong answer to the WHAT question.

Market failure opens the door for government intervention. If the market can't do the job, we need some form of *nonmarket* force to get the right answers. In terms of Figure 4.1, we need something to change the mix of output—to move us from point M (the market mix of output) to point X (the optimal mix of output). Accordingly, *market failure establishes a basis for government intervention.* We look to the government to push market outcomes closer to the ideal.

Causes of Market Failure. Because market failure is the justification for government intervention, we need to know how and when market failure occurs. *The four specific sources of market failure are*

- *Public goods.*
- *Externalities.*
- *Market power.*
- *Inequity.*

We will first examine the nature of these problems, then see why government intervention is called for in each case.

optimal mix of output: The most desirable combination of output attainable with existing resources, technology, and social values.

market mechanism: The use of market prices and sales to signal desired outputs (or resource allocations).

market failure: An imperfection in the market mechanism that prevents optimal outcomes.

FIGURE 4.1

Market Failure

We can produce any mix of output on the production possibilities curve. Our goal is to produce the optimal (best possible) mix of output, as represented by point X. Market forces, however, might produce another combination, like point M. In that case, the market fails—it produces a *sub*optimal mix of output.

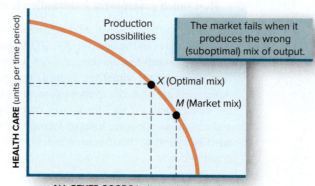

The market fails when it produces the wrong (suboptimal) mix of output.

Public Goods

The market mechanism has the unique capability to signal consumer demands for various goods and services. By offering to pay for goods, we express our preferences about WHAT to produce. However, this mode of communication works efficiently only if the benefits of consuming a particular good are available only to the individuals who purchase that product.

Consider doughnuts, for example. When you eat a doughnut, you alone get the satisfaction from its sweet, greasy taste—that is, you derive a private benefit. No one else benefits from your consumption of a doughnut: The doughnut you purchase in the market is yours alone to consume; it's a **private good.** Accordingly, your decision to purchase the doughnut will be determined only by your anticipated satisfaction, your income, and your opportunity costs.

private good: A good or service whose consumption by one person excludes consumption by others.

No Exclusion. Most of the goods and services produced in the public sector are different from doughnuts—and not just because doughnuts look, taste, and smell different from "star wars" missile shields. When you buy a doughnut, you exclude others from consumption of that product. If Dunkin' Donuts sells you a particular pastry, it can't supply the same pastry to someone else. If you devour it, no one else can. In this sense, the transaction and product are completely private.

The same exclusiveness is not characteristic of national defense. If you buy a missile defense system to thwart enemy attacks, there's no way you can exclude your neighbors from the protection your system provides. Either the missile shield deters would-be attackers—like Israel's "Iron Dome" (see World View "Israel's 'Iron Dome' Frustrates Hamas")—or it doesn't. In the former case, both you and your neighbors survive happily ever after; in the latter case, we're all blown away together. In that sense, you and your neighbors consume the benefits of a missile shield *jointly*. National defense isn't a divisible service. There's no such thing as exclusive consumption here. The consumption of nuclear defenses is a communal feat, no matter who pays for them. Accordingly, national defense is regarded as a **public good** in the sense that *consumption of a public good by one person doesn't preclude consumption of the same good by another person.* By contrast, a doughnut is a private good because if I eat it, no one else can consume it.

public good: A good or service whose consumption by one person does not exclude consumption by others.

WORLD VIEW

ISRAEL'S "IRON DOME" FRUSTRATES HAMAS

The fragile peace between Israel and its Arab neighbors has broken down again. This time, though, Israel has a strategic advantage: its "Iron Dome" air defense system. The Iron Dome intercepts and destroys incoming missiles and mortars. So the hail of missiles Hamas is firing from Gaza into Israel rarely find their targets—they are destroyed in mid-air. The Israeli defense minister claims the Iron Dome is 90 percent effective in shielding population centers. Hamas has no such defense against artillery, bombs, and even ground forces dispatched by Israel into Gaza.

Source: News reports, July 20–28, 2014.

ANALYSIS: An air-defense system is a *public good*, as consumption of its services by one individual does not preclude consumption by others. Nonpayers cannot be excluded from its protection.

The Free-Rider Dilemma. The communal nature of public goods creates a dilemma. If you and I will *both* benefit from nuclear defenses, which one of us should buy the missile shield? I'd prefer that *you* buy it, thereby giving me protection at no direct cost. Hence I may profess no desire for a missile shield, secretly hoping to take a **free ride** on your

free rider: An individual who reaps direct benefits from someone else's purchase (consumption) of a public good.

Flood control is a public good.

Source: NOAA/Department of Commerce

market purchase. Unfortunately, you too have an incentive to conceal your desire for national defenses. As a consequence, neither one of us may step forward to demand a missile shield in the marketplace. We'll both end up defenseless.

Flood control is also a public good. No one in the valley wants to be flooded out. But each landowner knows that a flood control dam will protect *all* the landowners, regardless of who pays. Either the entire valley is protected or no one is. Accordingly, individual farmers and landowners may say they don't want a dam and aren't willing to pay for it. Everyone is waiting and hoping that someone else will pay for flood control. In other words, everyone wants a *free ride.* Thus, if we leave it to market forces, no one will *demand* flood control, and all the property in the valley will be washed away.

The difference between public goods and private goods rests on *technical considerations,* not political philosophy. The central question is whether we have the technical capability to exclude nonpayers. In the case of national defense or flood control, we simply don't have that capability. Even city streets have the characteristics of public goods. Although theoretically we could restrict the use of streets to those who paid to use them, a tollgate on every corner would be exceedingly expensive and impractical. Here again, joint or public consumption appears to be the only feasible alternative. As In the News "Firefighters Watch as Home Burns to the Ground" on local firefighting emphasizes, the technical capability to exclude nonpayers is the key factor in identifying "public goods."

IN THE NEWS

FIREFIGHTERS WATCH AS HOME BURNS TO THE GROUND

OBION COUNTY, Tenn.—Imagine your home catches fire, but the local fire department won't respond, then watches it burn. That's exactly what happened to a local family tonight.

A local neighborhood is furious after firefighters watched as an Obion County, Tennessee, home burned to the ground.

The homeowner, Gene Cranick, said he offered to pay whatever it would take for firefighters to put out the flames but was told it was too late. They wouldn't do anything to stop his house from burning.

©WPSD Local 6/AP Images

Each year, Obion County residents must pay $75 if they want fire protection from the city of South Fulton. But the Cranicks did not pay.

The mayor said if homeowners don't pay, they're out of luck.

This fire went on for hours because garden hoses just wouldn't put it out.

It was only when a neighbor's field caught fire, a neighbor who had paid the county fire service fee, that the department responded. Gene Cranick asked the fire chief to make an exception and save his home; the chief wouldn't.

—Jason Hibbs

©WPSD Local 6, Paducah, KY, September 30, 2010. Used with permission.

ANALYSIS: A product is a "public good" only if nonpayers *cannot* be excluded from its consumption. Firefighters in Tennessee proved that fire protection is not inherently a public good: they let the nonpaying homeowner's house burn down!

To the list of public goods we could add snow removal, the administration of justice (including prisons), the regulation of commerce, the conduct of foreign relations, airport security, and even Fourth of July fireworks. These services—which cost tens of *billions* of dollars and employ thousands of workers—provide benefits to everyone, no matter who pays for them. In each instance it's technically impossible or prohibitively expensive to exclude nonpayers from the services provided.

Underproduction of Public Goods. The free riders associated with public goods upset the customary practice of paying for what you get. If I can get all the national defense, flood control, and laws I want without paying for them, I'm not about to complain. I'm perfectly happy to let you pay for the services while we all consume them. Of course, you may feel the same way. Why should you pay for these services if you can consume just as much of them when your neighbors foot the whole bill? It might seem selfish not to pay your share of the cost of providing public goods. But you'd be better off in a material sense if you spent your income on doughnuts, letting others pick up the tab for public services.

Because the familiar link between paying and consuming is broken, public goods can't be peddled in the supermarket. People are reluctant to buy what they can get free. Hence, *if public goods were marketed like private goods, everyone would wait for someone else to pay.* The end result might be a total lack of public services. This is the kind of dilemma Robert Heilbroner had in mind when he spoke of the market's "deaf ear" (see the quote at the beginning of this chapter).

The production possibilities curve in Figure 4.2 illustrates the dilemma created by public goods. Suppose that point A represents the optimal mix of private and public goods. It's the mix of goods and services we'd select if everyone's preferences were known and reflected in production decisions. The market mechanism won't lead us to point A, however, because the *demand* for public goods will be hidden. If we rely on the market, nearly everyone will withhold demand for public goods, waiting for a free ride to point A. As a result, we'll get a smaller quantity of public goods than we really want. The market mechanism will leave us at point B, with few, if any, public goods. Since point A is assumed to be optimal, point B must be *suboptimal* (inferior to point A). The market fails: we can't rely on the market mechanism to allocate enough resources to the production of public goods, no matter how much they might be desired.

Note that we're using the term "public good" in a peculiar way. To most people, "public good" refers to any good or service the government produces. In economics, however, the meaning is much more restrictive. The term "public good" refers only to those nonexcludable goods and services that must be consumed jointly, both by those who pay for them and by those who don't. Public goods can be produced by either the government or the private sector. Private goods can be produced in either sector as well. The problem is that *the market tends to underproduce public goods and overproduce private goods.* If we want more public goods, we need a *nonmarket* force—government intervention—to get them. The government will have to force people to pay taxes, then use the tax revenues to pay for the production of national defense, flood control, snow removal, and other public goods.

Externalities

The free-rider problem associated with public goods is an important justification for government intervention. It's not the only justification, however. A second justification for

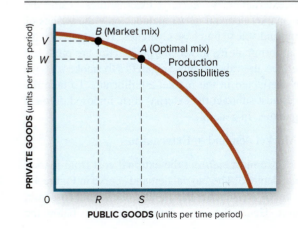

PRIVATE GOODS (units per time period)

PUBLIC GOODS (units per time period)

FIGURE 4.2

Underproduction of Public Goods

Suppose point A represents the optimal mix of output—that is, the mix of private and public goods that maximizes society's welfare. Because consumers won't demand purely public goods in the marketplace, the price mechanism won't allocate so many resources to their production. Instead the market will tend to produce a mix of output like point B, which includes fewer public goods (OR) than are optimal (OS).

intervention arise from the tendency of costs or benefits of some market activities to "spill over" onto third parties.

Consider the case of cigarettes. The price someone is willing to pay for a pack of cigarettes reflects the amount of satisfaction a smoker anticipates from its consumption. If that price is high enough, tobacco companies will produce the cigarettes demanded. That is how market-based price signals are supposed to work. In this case, however, the price paid isn't a satisfactory signal of the product's desirability. The smoker's pleasure is offset in part by nonsmokers' *dis*pleasure. In this case, smoke literally spills over onto other consumers, causing them discomfort, ill health, and even death (see World View "Secondhand Smoke Kills 600,000 People a Year"). Yet their loss isn't reflected in the market price: the harm caused to nonsmokers is *external* to the market price of cigarettes.

WORLD VIEW

SECONDHAND SMOKE KILLS 600,000 PEOPLE A YEAR

Secondhand smoke globally kills more than 600,000 people each year, accounting for 1 percent of all deaths worldwide.

Researchers estimate that annually secondhand smoke causes about 379,000 deaths from heart disease, 165,000 deaths from lower respiratory disease, 36,900 deaths from asthma, and 21,400 deaths from lung cancer.

©Image Source/Getty Images RF

Children account for about 165,000 of the deaths. Forty percent of children and 30 percent of adults regularly breathe in secondhand smoke.

Source: World Health Organization

ANALYSIS: The health risks imposed on nonsmokers via passive smoke represent an external cost. The market price of cigarettes doesn't reflect these costs borne by third parties.

---

externalities: Costs (or benefits) of a market activity borne by a third party; the difference between the social and private costs (benefits) of a market activity.

The term **externalities** refers to all costs or benefits of a market activity borne by a third party—that is, by someone other than the immediate producer or consumer. *Whenever externalities are present, market prices aren't a valid measure of a good's value to society.* As a consequence, the market will fail to produce the right mix of output. Specifically, *the market will underproduce goods that yield external benefits and overproduce those that generate external costs.*

External Costs. Figure 4.3 shows how external costs—*negative* externalitites—cause the market to overproduce cigarettes. The market demand curve includes only the wishes of smokers—that is, people who are willing and able to purchase cigarettes. The forces of market demand and supply result in an equilibrium at E_M in which q_M cigarettes are produced and consumed. The market price P_M reflects the value of those cigarettes to smokers.

The well-being of *non*smokers isn't reflected in the market equilibrium. To take the *non*smokers' interests into account, we must subtract the external costs imposed on *them* from the value that *smokers* put on cigarettes. In general,

$$\text{Social demand} = \text{Market demand} \pm \text{Externalities}$$

In this case, the externality is a *cost,* so we must *subtract* the external cost from market demand to get a full accounting of social demand. The "social demand" curve in Figure 4.3 reflects this computation. To find this curve, we subtract the amount of external cost from every price on the market demand curve. Hence the social demand curve lies below the

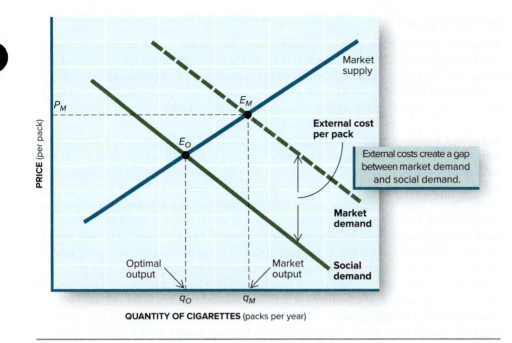

FIGURE 4.3

Externalities

The market responds to consumer demands, not externalities. Smokers demand q_M cigarettes at the equilibrium price P_M. But external costs on nonsmokers imply that the *social* demand for cigarettes is less than (below) *market* demand. The socially optimal level of output is q_O, less than the market output q_M.

market demand curve in this case. What the social demand curve tells us is how much society would be willing and able to pay for cigarettes if the preferences of *both* smokers and nonsmokers were taken into account.

The social demand curve in Figure 4.3 creates a social equilibrium at E_O. At this juncture, we see that the socially *optimal* quantity of cigarettes is q_O, not the larger market-generated level at q_M. In this sense, the market produces too many cigarettes.

Negative externalities also exist in production. A power plant that burns high-sulfur coal damages the surrounding environment. Yet the damage inflicted on neighboring people, vegetation, and buildings is external to the cost calculations of the firm. Because the cost of such pollution is not reflected in the price of electricity, the firm will tend to produce more electricity (and pollution) than is socially desirable. To reduce this imbalance, the government has to step in and change market outcomes.

External Benefits. Externalities can also be beneficial. A product may generate external *benefits* rather than external *costs*. Your college is an example. The students who attend your school benefit directly from the education they receive. That's why they (and you) are willing to pay for tuition, books, and other services. The students in attendance aren't the only beneficiaries of this educational service, however. The research that a university conducts may yield benefits for a much broader community. The values and knowledge students acquire may also be shared with family, friends, and coworkers. These benefits would all be *external* to the market transaction between a paying student and the school. Positive externalities also arise from immunizations against infectious diseases: the person getting immunized obviously benefits, but so do all the people with whom that person comes into contact. Other people (third parties) benefit when you get vaccinated.

If a product yields external benefits, the social demand is greater than the market demand. In this case, the social value of the good *exceeds* the market price (by the amount of external benefit). Accordingly, society wants *more* of the product than the market mechanism alone will produce at any given price. To get that additional output, the government may have to intervene with subsidies or other policies. We conclude then that *the market fails by*

- *Overproducing goods that have external costs.*
- *Underproducing goods that have external benefits.*

If externalities are present, the market won't produce the optimal mix of output. To get that optimal mix, we need government intervention.

Market Power

In the case of both public goods and externalities, the market fails to achieve the optimal mix of output because the price signal is flawed. The price consumers are willing and able to pay for a specific good doesn't reflect all the benefits or cost of producing that good.

The market may fail, however, even when the price signals are accurate. The *response* to price signals, rather than the signals themselves, may be flawed.

monopoly: A firm that produces the entire market supply of a particular good or service.

Restricted Supply. Market power is often the cause of a flawed response. Suppose there were only one airline company in the world. This single seller of airline travel would be a **monopoly**—that is, the only producer in that industry. As a monopolist, the airline could charge extremely high prices without worrying that travelers would flock to a competing airline. At the same time, the high prices paid by consumers would express the importance of that service to society. Ideally, those high prices would act as a signal to producers to build and fly more planes—to change the mix of output. But a monopolist doesn't have to cater to every consumer's whim. It can rake in those high prices without increasing service, thereby obstructing our efforts to achieve an optimal mix of output.

market power: The ability to alter the market price of a good or service.

Monopoly is the most severe form of **market power.** More generally, market power refers to any situation in which a single producer or consumer has the ability to alter the market price of a specific product. If the publisher (McGraw-Hill) charges a high price for this book, you'll have to pay the tab. McGraw-Hill has market power because there are relatively few economics text and your professor has required you to use this one. You don't have power in the textbook market because your decision to buy or not won't alter the market price of this text. You're only one of the million students who are taking an introductory economics course this year.

The market power McGraw-Hill possesses is derived from the copyright on this text. No matter how profitable textbook sales might be, no one else is permitted to produce or sell this particular book. Patents are another common source of market power because they also preclude others from making or selling a specific product. Market power may also result from control of resources, restrictive production agreements, or efficiencies of large-scale production.

Whatever the source of market power, the direct consequence is that one or more producers attain discretionary power over the market's response to price signals. They may use that discretion to enrich themselves rather than to move the economy toward the optimal mix of output. In this case, the market will again fail to deliver the most desired goods and services.

antitrust: Government intervention to alter market structure or prevent abuse of market power.

The mandate for government intervention in this case is to prevent or dismantle concentrations of market power. That's the basic purpose of **antitrust** policy. Another option is to *regulate* market behavior. This was one of the goals of the antitrust case against Microsoft. The government was less interested in breaking Microsoft's near monopoly on operating systems than in changing the way Microsoft behaved.

natural monopoly: An industry in which one firm can achieve economies of scale over the entire range of market supply.

In some cases, it may be economically efficient to have one large firm supply an entire market. Such a situation arises in **natural monopoly,** where a single firm can achieve economies of scale over the entire range of market output. Utility companies, local telephone service, subway systems, and cable all exhibit such scale (size) efficiencies. In these cases, a monopoly *structure* may be economically desirable. The government may have to regulate the *behavior* of a natural monopoly, however, to ensure that consumers get the benefits of that greater efficiency.

Inequity

Public goods, externalities, and market power all cause resource misallocations. Where these phenomena exist, the market mechanism will fail to produce the optimal mix of output in the best possible way.

Beyond the questions of WHAT and HOW to produce, we're also concerned about FOR WHOM output is produced. The market answers this question by distributing a larger share of total output to those with the most income. Although this result may be efficient, it's not necessarily equitable. As we saw in Chapter 2, the market mechanism may enrich some people while leaving others to seek shelter in abandoned cars. If such outcomes violate our vision of equity, we may want the government to change the market-generated distribution of income.

Taxes and Transfers. The tax-and-transfer system is the principal mechanism for redistributing incomes. The idea here is to take some of the income away from those who have "too much" and give it to those whom the market has left with "too little." Taxes are levied to take back some of the income received from the market. Those tax revenues are then redistributed via transfer payments to those deemed needy, such as the poor, the aged, and the unemployed. **transfer payments** are income payments for which no goods or services are exchanged. They're used to bolster the incomes of those for whom the market itself provides too little.

transfer payments: Payments to individuals for which no current goods or services are exchanged, like Social Security, welfare, and unemployment benefits.

Merit Goods. Often our vision of what is "too little" is defined in terms of specific goods and services. There is a widespread consensus in the United States that everyone is entitled to some minimum levels of shelter, food, and health care. These are regarded as **merit good,** in the sense that everyone merits at least some minimum provision of such goods. When the market does not distribute that minimum provision, the government is called on to fill the gaps. In this case, the income transfers take the form of *in-kind* transfers (e.g., food stamps, housing vouchers, Medicaid) rather than *cash* transfers (e.g., welfare checks, Social Security benefits).

merit good: A good or service society deems everyone is entitled to some minimal quantity of.

Some people argue that we don't need the government to help the poor—that private charity alone will suffice. Unfortunately, private charity alone has never been adequate. One reason private charity doesn't suffice is the "free-rider" problem. If I contribute heavily to the poor, you benefit from safer streets (fewer muggers), a better environment (fewer slums and homeless people), and a clearer conscience (knowing that fewer people are starving). In this sense, the relief of misery is a *public* good. Were I the only taxpayer to benefit substantially from the reduction of poverty, then charity would be a private affair. As long as income support substantially benefits the public at large, then income redistribution is a *public* good, for which public funding is appropriate. This is the *economic* rationale for public income redistribution activities. To this rationale one can add such moral arguments as seem appropriate.

Macro Instability

The micro failures of the marketplace imply that we may end up at the wrong point on the production possibilities curve or inequitably distributing the output produced. There's another basic question we've swept under the rug, however. How do we get to the production possibilities curve in the first place? To reach the curve, we must utilize all available resources and technology. Can we be confident that the invisible hand of the marketplace will use all available resources? That confidence was shattered in 2008–2009 when total output contracted and **unemployment** soared. Millions of people who were willing and able to work but unable to find jobs demanded that the government intervene to increase output and create more jobs. The market had failed.

unemployment: The inability of labor force participants to find jobs.

And what about prices? Price signals are a critical feature of the market mechanism. But the validity of those signals depends on some stable measure of value. What good is a doubling of salary when the price of everything you buy doubles as well? Generally, rising prices will enrich people who own property and impoverish people who rent. That's why we strive to avoid **inflation**—a situation in which the *average* price level is increasing.

inflation: An increase in the average level of prices of goods and services.

Historically, the marketplace has been wracked with bouts of both unemployment and inflation. These experiences have prompted calls for government intervention at the macro level. *The goal of macro intervention is to foster economic growth—to get us on the production possibilities curve (full employment), maintain a stable price level (price stability), and increase our capacity to produce (growth).*

GROWTH OF GOVERNMENT

The potential micro and macro failures of the marketplace provide specific justifications for government intervention. We do need government to provide public goods, compensate for externalities, limit the excesses of market power, and redistribute incomes more fairly. We can't rely completely on a private, market-based economy to generate optimal answers to the WHAT, HOW, and FOR WHOM questions.

The question then becomes, "How well does the government respond to these needs?" We'll start answering this question by looking at what the government now does and how it has grown.

Federal Growth

Until the 1930s the federal government's role was largely limited to national defense (a public good), enforcement of a common legal system (also a public good), and provision of postal service (equity). The Great Depression of the 1930s spawned a new range of government activities, including welfare and Social Security programs (equity), minimum wage laws and workplace standards (regulation), and massive public works (public goods and externalities). In the 1950s the federal government also assumed a greater role in maintaining macroeconomic stability (macro failure), protecting the environment (externalities), and safeguarding the public's health (externalities and equity).

These increasing responsibilities have greatly increased the size of the public sector. In 1902 the federal government employed fewer than 350,000 people and spent a mere $650 *million*. Today the federal government employs nearly 4 million people and spends nearly $4 *trillion* a year.

Direct Expenditure. Figure 4.4 summarizes the growth of the public sector since 1930. Let's focus on the federal government, depicted with the orange line. Back in 1930 the federal share of total spending was close to zero. That share grew in the 1930s and sky-rocketed during World War II. Federal purchases of goods and services for the war

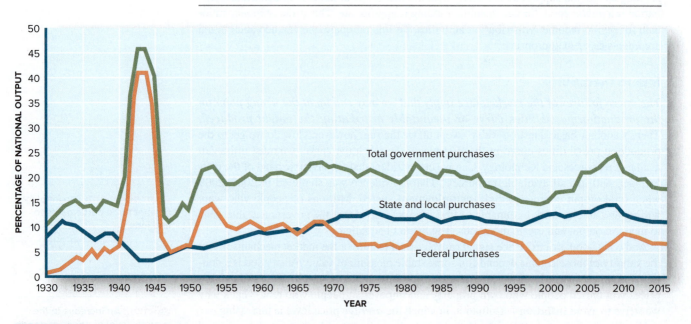

FIGURE 4.4

Government Growth

During World War II the public sector purchased nearly half of total U.S. output. Since the early 1950s the public sector share of total output has been closer to 20 percent. Within the public sector, however, there's been a major shift: state and local claims on resources have grown, while the federal share has declined significantly.

Source: U.S. Bureau of Economic Analysis.

accounted for more than 40 percent of total output during the 1943–1944 period. The federal share of total U.S. output fell abruptly after World War II, rose again during the Korean War (1950–1953), and has declined slightly since then.

The decline in the federal share of total output is somewhat at odds with most people's perception of government growth. This discrepancy is explained by two phenomena. First, people see the *absolute* size of the government growing every year. But we're focusing here on the *relative* size of the public sector. From 1950 until 2008 the public sector grew a bit more slowly than the private sector, slightly reducing its relative size. The trend was interrupted in 2008–2011, when the private sector shrank and the federal government undertook massive stimulus spending. Since then, the federal government's share of total output has hovered around 7 percent. President Trump's stepped-up spending on national defense and infrastructure has increased that share only a couple of decimal points.

Income Transfers. The federal share of output depicted in Figure 4.4 looks small (7 percent) because it doesn't include *all* federal spending. As noted above, Uncle Sam *spends* about $4 trillion a year. But the majority of that spending is for income transfers, not direct expenditure on goods and services. Figure 4.4 only counts direct expenditure on things like national defense, transportation systems, education, and other real goods—the things that are included in the WHAT outcome of the economy. By contrast, income transfers go to people who themselves decide how to spend that money—and thus what gets produced. Hence income transfers don't directly alter the mix of output. Their effect is primarily *distributional* (the FOR WHOM question), not *allocative* (the WHAT question). Were income transfers included, the relative size and growth of the federal government would be larger than Figure 4.4 depicts. This is because ***most of the growth in federal spending has come from increased income transfers, not purchases of goods and services.***

State and Local Growth

State and local spending on goods and services has followed a very different path from federal expenditure. Prior to World War II, state and local governments dominated public sector spending. During the war, however, the share of total output going to state and local governments fell, hitting a low of 3 percent in that period (Figure 4.4).

State and local spending caught up with federal spending in the mid-1960s and has exceeded it ever since. Today ***more than 80,000 state and local government entities buy much more output than Uncle Sam and employ five times as many people.*** Education is a huge expenditure at lower levels of government. Most direct state spending is on colleges; most local spending is for elementary and secondary education. The fastest-growing areas for state expenditure are prisons (public safety) and welfare. At the local level, sewage and trash services are claiming an increasing share of budgets.

TAXATION

Whatever we may think of any specific government expenditure, we must recognize one basic fact of life: we pay for government spending. We pay not just in terms of tax *dollars* but in the more fundamental form of a changed mix of output. Government expenditures on goods and services absorb factors of production that could be used to produce consumer goods. The mix of output changes toward *more* public services and *fewer* private goods and services. Resources used to produce missile shields, operate elementary schools, or journey to Mars aren't available to produce cars, houses, or restaurant meals. In real terms, ***the cost of government spending is measured by the private sector output sacrificed when the government employs scarce factors of production.***

The **opportunity cost** of public spending aren't always apparent. We don't directly hand over factors of production to the government. Instead we give the government part of our income in the form of taxes. Those dollars are then used by government agencies to buy factors of production or goods and services in the marketplace. Thus ***the primary function of taxes is to transfer command over resources (purchasing power) from the private***

opportunity cost: The most desired goods or services that are forgone in order to obtain something else.

sector to the public sector. Although the government also borrows dollars to finance its purchases, taxes are the primary source of government revenues.

Federal Taxes

As recently as 1902, much of the revenue the federal government collected came from taxes imposed on alcoholic beverages. The federal government didn't have authority to collect income taxes. As a consequence, *total* federal revenue in 1902 was only $653 million.

Income Taxes. All that changed, beginning in 1915. The Sixteenth Amendment to the U.S. Constitution, enacted in 1915, granted the federal government authority to collect *income* taxes. The government now collects more than $1.5 *trillion* in that form alone each year. Although the federal government still collects taxes on alcoholic beverages, the individual income tax has become the largest single source of government revenue (see Figure 4.5).

In theory, the federal income tax is designed to be **progressive**—that is, to take a larger *fraction* of high incomes than of low incomes. In 2017, for example, a single person with less than $9,325 of taxable income was taxed at 10 percent. People with incomes of $37,950–$91,900 confronted a 25 percent tax rate on their additional income. The marginal tax rate got as high as 39.6 percent for people earning more than $418,400 in income. Thus *people with high incomes not only pay more taxes but also pay a larger* **fraction** *of their income in taxes.*

Social Security Taxes. The second major source of federal revenue is the Social Security payroll tax. People working now transfer part of their earnings to retired workers by making "contributions" to Social Security. There's nothing voluntary about these "contributions"; they take the form of mandatory payroll deductions. In 2017, each worker paid 7.65 percent of his or her wages to Social Security, and employers contributed an equal amount. As a consequence, the government collected more than $1 trillion from this tax.

At first glance, the Social Security payroll tax looks like a **proportional tax**—that is, a tax that takes the *same* fraction of every taxpayer's income. But this isn't the case. The Social Security (FICA) tax isn't levied on every payroll dollar. Incomes above a certain ceiling ($127,200 in 2017) aren't taxed. As a result, workers with *really* high salaries turn over a smaller fraction of their incomes to Social Security than do low-wage workers. This makes the Social Security payroll tax a **regressive tax.**

Corporate Taxes. The federal government taxes the profits of corporations as well as the incomes of consumers. But there are far fewer corporations (less than 2 million) than consumers (340 million), and their profits are small in comparison to total consumer income. In 2016, the federal government collected less than $350 billion in corporate income taxes, despite the fact that it imposed a top tax rate of 35 percent on corporate profits.

---

progressive tax: A tax system in which tax rates rise as incomes rise.

---

proportional tax: A tax that levies the same rate on every dollar of income.

---

regressive tax: A tax system in which tax rates fall as incomes rise.

FIGURE 4.5

Federal Taxes

Taxes transfer purchasing power from the private sector to the public sector. The largest federal tax is the individual income tax. The second-largest source of federal revenue is the Social Security payroll tax.

Source: Office of Management and Budget, FY2015 data.

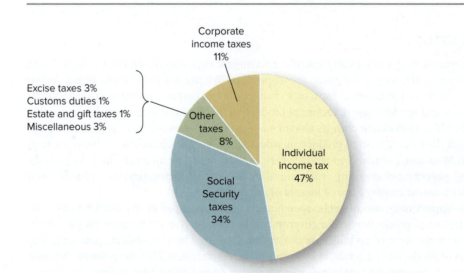

Corporate income taxes 11%

Excise taxes 3%
Customs duties 1%
Estate and gift taxes 1%
Miscellaneous 3%

Other taxes 8%

Individual income tax 47%

Social Security taxes 34%

Excise Taxes. The last major source of federal revenue is excise taxes. Like the early taxes on whiskey, excise taxes are sales taxes imposed on specific goods and services. The federal government taxes not only liquor ($13.50 per gallon) but also gasoline (18.4 cents per gallon), cigarettes ($1.01 per pack), air fares (7.5 percent), firearms (10–11 percent), gambling (0.25 percent), and a variety of other goods and services. Such taxes not only discourage production and consumption of these goods by raising their price and thereby reducing the quantity demanded; they also raise a substantial amount of revenue.

State and Local Revenues

Taxes. State and local governments also levy taxes on consumers and businesses. In general, cities depend heavily on property taxes, and state governments rely heavily on sales taxes. Although nearly all states and many cities also impose income taxes, effective tax rates are so low (averaging less than 2 percent of personal income) that income tax revenues are much less than sales and property tax revenues.

Like the Social Security payroll tax, state and local taxes tend to be *regressive*—that is, they take a larger share of income from the poor than from the rich. Consider a 4 percent sales tax, for example. It might appear that a uniform tax rate like this would affect all consumers equally. But people with lower incomes tend to spend most of their income on goods and services. Thus most of their income is subject to sales taxes. By contrast, a person with a high income can afford to save part of his or her income and thereby shelter it from sales taxes.

Consider a family that earns $40,000 and spends $30,000 of it on taxable goods and services. This family will pay $1,200 in sales taxes when the tax rate is 4 percent. In effect, then, they are handing over 3 percent of their *income* ($1,200 ÷ $40,000) to the state. Now consider a the family that makes only $12,000 and spends $11,500 of it for food, clothing, and shelter. That family will pay $460 in sales taxes in the same state. Their total tax is smaller, but it represents a much larger *share* (3.8 versus 3.0 percent) of their income.

Local property taxes are also regressive because poor people devote a larger portion of their incomes to housing costs. Hence a larger share of a poor family's *income* is subject to property taxes. State lotteries are also regressive for the same reason (see In the News "State Lotteries: A Tax on the Uneducated and the Poor"). Low-income players spend 1.4 percent of their incomes on lottery tickets while upper-income players devote only 0.1 percent of their income to lottery purchases.

IN THE NEWS

STATE LOTTERIES: A TAX ON THE UNEDUCATED AND THE POOR

Americans now spend over $70 billion a year on lottery tickets. That's more than we spend on sporting events, books, video games, movies, and music *combined*. That spending works out to about $640 a household.

Poor people are proportionally the biggest buyers of lottery tickets. Households with less than $25,000 of income spend $1,100 a year on lottery tickets. By contrast, households with more than $50,000 of income buy only $300 of lottery tickets each year.

Education also affects lottery spending: 2.7 percent of high school dropouts are compulsive lottery players, while only 1.1 percent of college grads play compulsively. Since lottery games are a sucker's game to start with—payouts average less than 60 percent of sales—lotteries are effectively a regressive tax on the uneducated and the poor.

Source: Research on lottery sales.

ANALYSIS: Poor people spend a larger percentage of their income on lottery tickets than do rich people. This makes lotteries a regressive source of government revenue.

FIGURE 4.6

Government Failure

When the market produces a suboptimal mix of output like point *M,* the goal of government is to move output to the social optimum (point *X*). A move to *G*$_4$ would be an improvement in the mix of output. But government intervention *may* move the economy to points *G*$_1$, *G*$_2$, or *G*$_3$—all reflecting government failure.

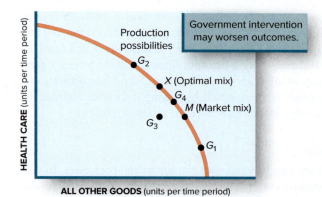

government failure:
Government intervention that fails to improve economic outcomes.

GOVERNMENT FAILURE

Some government intervention in the marketplace is clearly desirable. The market mechanism can fail for a variety of reasons, leaving a laissez-faire economy short of its economic goals. But how much government intervention is desirable? Communist nations once thought that complete government control of production, consumption, and distribution decisions was the surest path to utopia. They learned the hard way that ***not only markets but governments as well can fail.*** In this context, **government failure** means that government intervention fails to move us closer to our economic goals.

Consider again our collective goal of producing the optimal mix of output. In Figure 4.6, this goal is again illustrated by point *X* on the production possibilities curve. Point *M* on the curve reminds us that the market may fail to generate that optimal answer to the WHAT question. This is why we want the government to intervene. We want the government to move the mix of output from point *M* to point *X*.

We have no guarantee that government intervention will yield the desired move. Government intervention might unwittingly move us to point *G*$_1$, making matters worse. Or the government might overreact, sending us to point *G*$_2$. Red tape and onerous regulation might even force us to point *G*$_3$, *inside* the production possibilities curve (with less total output than at point *M*). All those possibilities (*G*$_1$, *G*$_2$, *G*$_3$) represent government failure. **Government intervention is desirable only to the extent that it *improves* market outcomes** (e.g., *G*$_4$).

We face a similar risk when the government intervenes in the HOW and FOR WHOM questions. Regulations imposed on an industry may reduce output with little or no environmental improvements. Taxes and transfers intended to make the distribution of income fairer may actually have the opposite effect. These things won't necessarily happen, but they *could.* Even when outcomes improve, government failure may occur if the costs of government intervention exceed the benefits of an improved output mix, cleaner production methods, or a fairer distribution of income.

Perceptions of Government Failure

Taxpayers seem to have strong opinions about government failure. A 2016 poll asked people how confident they were that the federal government could successfully tackle important problems. As In the News "Perceptions of Government Failure" reveals, 70 percent of Americans don't have such confidence. In other words, they *expect* government failure.

Not surprisingly, people also feel that the federal government *wastes* their tax dollars. The average taxpayer now believes that state governments waste 42 cents out of each dollar, while the federal government wastes 51 cents out of each tax dollar!

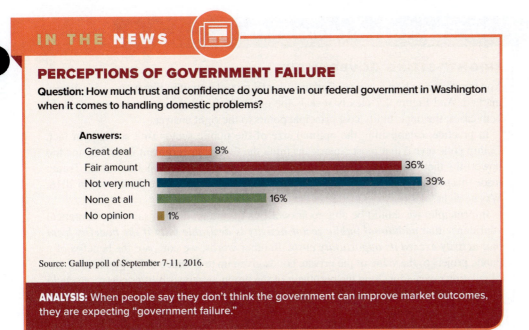

IN THE NEWS

PERCEPTIONS OF GOVERNMENT FAILURE

Question: How much trust and confidence do you have in our federal government in Washington when it comes to handling domestic problems?

Answers:

Great deal	8%
Fair amount	36%
Not very much	39%
None at all	16%
No opinion	1%

Source: Gallup poll of September 7-11, 2016.

ANALYSIS: When people say they don't think the government can improve market outcomes, they are expecting "government failure."

Government "waste" implies that the public sector isn't producing as many services as it could with the resources at its disposal. Such inefficiency implies that we're producing somewhere *inside* our production possibilities curve rather than on it (e.g., point G_3 in Figure 4.6). If the government is wasting resources this way, we can't possibly be producing the optimal mix of output.

Opportunity Cost

Even if the government wasn't wasting resources, it might still be guilty of government failure. Notice in Figure 4.6 that points G_1 and G_2 are on the production possibilities curve. So resources aren't being "wasted." But those points still represent suboptimal outcomes. In reality, *the issue of government failure encompasses two distinct questions:*

- *Efficiency:* Are we getting as much service as we could from the resources we allocate to government?
- *Opportunity cost:* Are we giving up too many private sector goods in order to get those services?

When assessing government's role in the economy, *we must consider not only what governments do but also what we give up to allow them to do it.* The theory of public goods tells us only what activities are appropriate for government, not the proper *level* of such activity. National defense is clearly a proper function of the public sector. Not so clear, however, is how much the government should spend on tanks, aircraft carriers, and missile shields. The same is true of environmental protection or law enforcement.

The concept of opportunity costs puts a new perspective on the whole question of government size. *Everything the government does entails an opportunity cost.* Before we can decide how big is "too big," we must decide what we're willing to give up to support the public sector. A military force of 1.4 million men and women is "too big" from an economic perspective only if we value the forgone private production and consumption more highly than we value the added strength of our defenses. The government has gone "too far" if the highway it builds is less desired than the park and homes it replaced. In these and all cases, the assessment of bigness must come back to a comparison of what is given up with what is received. The assessment of government failure thus comes back to points on the production possibilities curve. Has the government moved us closer to the optimal mix of output (e.g., point G_4 in Figure 4.6) or not?

THE ECONOMY TOMORROW

"RIGHT"-SIZING GOVERNMENT

You don't have to be a genius to find the optimal mix of output in Figure 4.6—it's clearly marked. And Figure 4.2 clearly reveals the optimal size of the government as well. In both cases, the opportunity cost principle points to the right answer.

In practice, establishing the optimal size of the public sector isn't so easy. In fact, Gallup polls reveal that most Americans think the federal government is too big and too powerful—that we are at a point like G_2 rather than point X in Figure 4.6. Donald Trump made this perception a cornerstone of his successful campaign for the presidency in 2016. Was he right?

In principle, we should be able to answer this question. We can say with theoretical confidence that *additional public sector activity is desirable only if the benefits from that activity exceed its opportunity costs.* In other words, we compare the benefits of a public project to the value of the private goods given up to produce it. By performing this calculation repeatedly along the perimeter of the production possibilities curve, we could locate the optimal mix of output—the point at which no further increase in public sector spending activity is desirable.

Valuation Problems. Although the principles of cost–benefit analysis are simple enough, they're deceptive. How are we to measure the potential benefits of improved police services, for example? Should we estimate the number of robberies and murders prevented, calculate the worth of each, and add up the benefits? And how are we supposed to calculate the worth of a saved life? By a person's earnings? Value of assets? Number of friends? And what about the increased sense of security people have when they know the police are patrolling their neighborhood? Should this be included in the benefit calculation? Some people will attach great value to this service; others will attach little. Whose values should be the standard? Should we consult liberals or conservatives on these questions?

When we're dealing with (private) market goods and services, we can gauge the benefits of a product by the amount of money consumers are willing to pay for it. This price signal isn't available for most public services, however, because of externalities and the nonexclusive nature of pure public goods (the free-rider problem). Hence *the value (benefits) of public services must be estimated because they don't have (reliable) market prices.* This opens the door to endless political squabbles about how beneficial any particular government activity is.

The same problems arise in evaluating the government's efforts to redistribute incomes. Government transfer payments now go to retired workers, disabled people, veterans, farmers, sick people, students, pregnant women, unemployed people, poor people, and a long list of other recipients. To pay for all these transfers, the government must raise tax revenues. With so many people paying taxes and receiving transfer payments, the net effects on the distribution of income aren't easy to figure out. Yet we can't determine whether this government intervention is worth it until we know how the FOR WHOM answer was changed and what the tax-and-transfer effort cost us.

Ballot Box Economics. In practice, we rely on political mechanisms, not cost–benefit calculations, to decide what to produce in the public sector and how to redistribute incomes. *Voting mechanisms substitute for the market mechanism in allocating resources to the public sector and deciding how to use them.* Some people have even suggested that the variety and volume of public goods are determined by the most votes, just as the variety and volume of private goods are determined by the most dollars. Thus governments choose the level and mix of output (and related taxation) that seem to command the most votes.

Sometimes the link between the ballot box and output decisions is very clear and direct. State and local governments, for example, are often compelled to get voter approval before building another highway, school, housing project, or sewage plant. *Bond referenda* are direct requests by a government unit for voter approval of specific public spending projects (e.g., roads, schools). In 2016, for example, six state governments sought voter approval for $12 billion of new borrowing to finance public expenditure.

Bond referenda are more the exception than the rule. Bond referenda account for less than 1 percent of state and local expenditures (and no federal expenditures). As a consequence, voter control of public spending is typically much less direct. At best, voters get the opportunity every two years to elect Congressional representatives and every four years a president. Promises about future spending and taxes typically play a major role in those elections. But election campaigns rarely get into the details of government spending and often fail to deliver on campaign promises. So, the ballot box turns out to be a very poor substitute for the market mechanism.

Even if we had the opportunity to vote on every government spending decision, we still might not achieve the optimal mix of output. A democratic vote, for example, might yield a 51 percent majority for approval of new local highways. Should the highways then be built? The answer isn't obvious. After all, a large minority (49 percent) of the voters have stated that they don't want resources used this way. If we proceed to build the highways, we'll make those people worse off. Their loss may be greater than what proponents gain. Hence the basic dilemma is really twofold. ***We don't know what the real demand for public services is, and votes alone don't reflect the intensity of individual demands.*** Moreover, real-world decision making involves so many choices that a stable consensus is impossible.

Public Choice Theory. In the midst of all this complexity and uncertainty, another factor may be decisive—namely self-interest. In principle, government officials are supposed to serve the people. It doesn't take long, however, before officials realize that the public is indecisive about what it wants and takes little interest in government's day-to-day activities. With such latitude, government officials can set their own agendas. Those agendas may give higher priority to personal advancement than to the needs of the public. Agency directors may foster new programs that enlarge their mandate, enhance their visibility, and increase their prestige or income. Members of Congress may likewise pursue legislative favors like tax breaks for supporters more diligently than they pursue the general public interest. In such cases, the probability of attaining the socially optimal mix of output declines.

The theory of **public choice** emphasizes the role of self-interest in public decision making. Public choice theory essentially extends the analysis of market behavior to political behavior. Public officials are assumed to have specific personal goals (for example, power, recognition, wealth) that they'll pursue in office. ***A central tenet of public choice theory is that bureaucrats are just as selfish (utility maximizing) as everyone else.***

public choice: Theory of public sector behavior emphasizing rational self-interest of decision makers and voters.

Public choice theory provides a neat and simple explanation for public sector decision making. But critics argue that the theory provides a woefully narrow view of public servants. Some people do selflessly pursue larger, public goals, such critics argue, and ideas can overwhelm self-interest. Steven Kelman of Harvard, for example, argues that narrow self-interest can't explain the War on Poverty of the 1960s, the tax revolt of the 1970s, or the deregulation movement of the 1980s. These tidal changes in public policy reflect the power of ideas, not simple self-interest. Public choice theory tells us how many decisions about government are made; it doesn't tell us how they should be made. The "right" size of government in the economy tomorrow will depend less on self-interest and more on how much we trust *markets* to generate optimal outcomes or trust government intervention to *improve* on market failures.

SUMMARY

- Government intervention in the marketplace is justified by market failure—that is, suboptimal market outcomes. **LO4-1**
- The micro failures of the market originate in public goods, externalities, market power, and an inequitable distribution of income. These flaws deter the market from achieving the optimal mix of output or distribution of income. **LO4-1**
- Public goods are those that can't be consumed exclusively; they're jointly consumed regardless of who pays. Because everyone seeks a free ride, no one demands public goods in the marketplace. Hence, the market underproduces public goods. **LO4-1**
- Externalities are costs (or benefits) of a market transaction borne by a third party. Externalities create a divergence between social and private costs or benefits, causing suboptimal market outcomes. The market overproduces goods with external costs and underproduces goods with external benefits. **LO4-1**
- Market power enables a producer to thwart market signals and maintain a suboptimal mix of output. Antitrust policy seeks to prevent or restrict market power. The government may also regulate the behavior of powerful firms. **LO4-1**
- The market-generated distribution of income may be unfair. This inequity may prompt the government to intervene with taxes and transfer payments that redistribute incomes. **LO4-1**
- The macro failures of the marketplace are reflected in unemployment and inflation. Government intervention is intended to achieve full employment and price stability. **LO4-1**
- The federal government expanded greatly in the 1930s and World War II, but its share of output has shrunk in recent decades. Recent growth in federal spending has been on income transfers, not output. **LO4-2**
- State and local governments purchase more output (11 percent of GDP) than the federal government (7 percent) and employ five times as many workers. **LO4-2**
- Income and payroll taxes provide most federal revenues. States get most revenue from sales taxes; local governments rely on property taxes. **LO4-3**
- Government failure occurs when intervention doesn't move toward the optimal mix of output (or income). Failure may result from outright waste (operational inefficiency) or from a misallocation of resources. **LO4-4**
- All government activity must be evaluated in terms of its opportunity cost—that is, the *private* goods and services forgone to make resources available to the public sector. **LO4-4**

Key Terms

optimal mix of output	monopoly	inflation
market mechanism	market power	opportunity cost
market failure	antitrust	progressive tax
private good	natural monopoly	proportional tax
public good	transfer payments	regressive tax
free rider	merit good	government failure
externalities	unemployment	public choice

Questions for Discussion

1. Why should taxpayers subsidize public colleges and universities? What external benefits are generated by higher education? **LO4-1**
2. If Israel's "Iron Dome" (World View "Israel's 'Iron Dome' Frustrates Hamas") is so effective, why doesn't a private company produce it and sell its services directly to consumers? **LO4-1**
3. If everyone seeks a free ride, what mix of output will be produced in Figure 4.2? Why would anyone voluntarily contribute to the purchase of public goods like flood control or snow removal? **LO4-1**
4. Should the firefighters have saved the house in In the News "Firefighters Watch as Home Burns to the Ground"? What was the justification for their belated intervention? **LO4-1**
5. Why might Fourth of July fireworks be considered a public good? Who should pay for them? What about airport security? **LO4-1**
6. What is the specific market failure justification for government spending on (*a*) public universities, (*b*) health care, (*c*) trash pickup, (*d*) highways, (*e*) police, and (*f*) solar energy? Would a purely private economy produce any of these services? **LO4-1**

7. If smoking generates external costs, should smoking simply be outlawed? How about cars that pollute?   **LO4-1**

8. The government now spends more than $700 billion a year on Social Security benefits. Why don't we leave it to individuals to save for their own retirement?   **LO4-1**

9. What government actions might cause failures like points G_1, G_2, and G_3 in Figure 4.6? Can you give examples?   **LO4-4**

10. How does Sirius Satellite deter nonsubscribers from listening to its transmissions? Does this make radio programming a private good or a public good?   **LO4-1**

11. Should the government be downsized? Which functions should be cut back? Which ones should be expanded?   **LO4-2**

12. Which taxes hit the poor hardest—those of local, state, or federal governments?   **LO4-3**

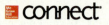

PROBLEMS FOR CHAPTER 4

LO4-1 1. In Figure 4.2, by how much is the market
   (*a*) Overproducing private goods?
   (*b*) Underproducing public goods?

LO4-1 2. (*a*) Use Figure 4.3 to illustrate on the accompanying production possibilities curve the optimal mix of output (*X*).

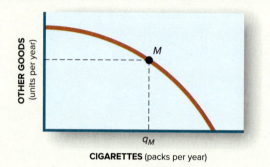

   (*b*) Does the optimal mix include (A) more or (B) fewer "other goods"?

LO4-1 3. Assume that the product depicted below generates external costs in consumption of $3 per unit.
   (*a*) What is the market price (market value) of the product?
   (*b*) Draw the social demand curve.
   (*c*) What is the socially optimal output?
   (*d*) By how much does the market overproduce this good?

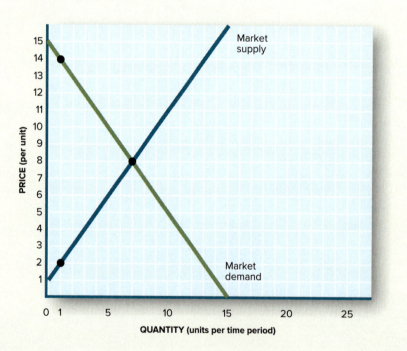

LO4-1 4. Draw market and social demand curves for the consumption of flu shots.

LO4-1 5. If the average working-age adult produces $25,000 of output per year, how much global output is lost as a result of adult deaths from secondhand smoke, according to In the News "Secondhand Smoke Kills 600,000 People a Year?" $ _____

PROBLEMS FOR CHAPTER 4 (cont'd)

LO4-3 6. (*a*) Assuming an 9 percent sales tax is levied on all consumption, complete the following table:

Income	Consumption	Sales Tax	Percentage of Income Paid in Taxes
$10,000	$11,000	_____	_____
20,000	20,000	_____	_____
40,000	36,000	_____	_____
80,000	60,000	_____	_____

(*b*) Is the sales tax (A) progressive or (B) regressive?

LO4-4 7. If a new home can be constructed for $150,000, what is the opportunity cost of federal defense spending, measured in terms of private housing? (Assume a defense budget of $600 billion.)

LO4-1 8. Suppose the following data represent the market demand for college education:

Tuition (per year)	$40,000	$35,000	$30,000	$25,000	$20,000	$15,000	$10,000	$5,000
Enrollment demanded (in millions per year)	1	2	3	4	5	6	7	8

(*a*) If tuition is set at $15,000, how many students will enroll?

Now suppose that society gets an external benefit of $5,000 for every enrolled student.

(*b*) Draw the social and market demand curves for this situation on the graph below.
(*c*) What is the socially optimal level of enrollment at the same tuition price of $15,000?
(*d*) If the government were to intervene and subsidize college education, how large of a subsidy is needed per student each year to achieve this optimal outcome?

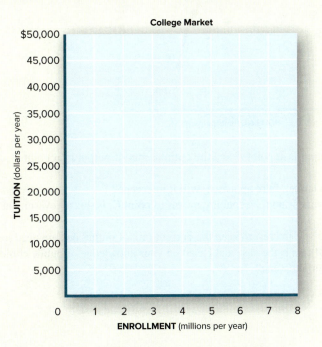

College Market

LO4-1 9. Suppose the market demand for cigarettes is given in the following table.

Price per pack	$10	$9	$8	$7	$6	$5	$4	$3
Quantity demanded (million packs per year)	2	4	6	8	10	12	14	16

Suppose further that smoking creates external costs valued at $2.00 per pack.

Graph the social and market demand curves.

If cigarettes are priced at $6 a pack,
(a) What is the quantity demanded in the market?
(b) What is the socially optimal quantity?
(c) If the government were to intervene and tax cigarettes, how large of a tax is needed per pack to achieve this optimal outcome?

LO4-3 10. According to In the News "State Lotteries: A Tax on the Uneducated and the Poor," what percentage of income is spent on lottery tickets by
(a) A low-income family with income of $20,000 per year?
(b) An middle-income family with income of $60,000 per year?

LO4-3 11. The Economy Tomorrow: The following production possibility curve shows the tradeoff between housing and all other goods.

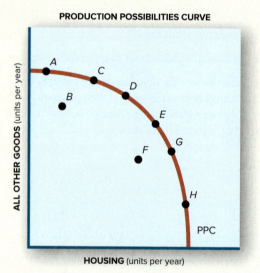

PRODUCTION POSSIBILITIES CURVE

(a) If the current mix of output is at point A and the optimal mix of output is at point D, does a market failure exist?
(b) If the government has a laissez-faire approach, will it intervene?
(c) If the government intervenes and the economy moves to point C, is this a government failure?
(d) Suppose a politician has self interest to keep the current mix of output despite need for more housing in her district. If this is the case and based on your knowledge of public choice theory, will the politician intervene?

©MOF/Getty Images RF

©Monty Rakusen/Cultura/Getty Images RF

©Marcio Jose Sanchez/AP Images

©Brand X Pictures/Getty Images RF

MEASURING MACRO OUTCOMES

Macroeconomics focuses on the performance of the entire economy rather than on the behavior of individual participants (a micro concern). The central concerns of macroeconomics are (1) the short-term business cycle and (2) long-term economic growth. In the long run, the goal is to expand the economy's capacity to produce goods and services, thereby raising future living standards. In the short run, the emphasis is on fully using available capacity, thereby maximizing output and minimizing unemployment. Chapters 5 through 7 focus on the measurement tools used to gauge the nation's macroeconomic performance (both short run and long run). Also examined are the social and economic damage caused by the problems of unemployment and inflation.

©Monty Rakusen/Cultura/Getty Images RF

National Income Accounting

A favorite cliché of policymakers in Washington is that government likes to tackle only those problems it can measure. Politicians need visible results. They want to be able to brag to their constituents about the miles of new highways built, the number of students who graduated, the number of families that left welfare, and the number of unemployed workers who found jobs. To do this, they must be able to measure economic outcomes.

The Great Depression of the 1930s was a lesson in the need for better measures of economic performance. There were plenty of anecdotes about factories closing, farms failing, and people selling apples on the streets. But nobody knew the dimensions of the nation's economic meltdown until millions of workers had lost their jobs. The need for more timely information about the health of the national economy was evident. From that experience a commitment to **national income accounting**—the measurement of aggregate economic activity—emerged. During the 1930s the economist Simon Kuznets (who later received a Nobel Prize for his work) and the U.S. Department of Commerce developed an accounting system to gauge the economy's health. That national accounting system now churns out reams of data that track the economy's performance. They answer such questions as

- **How much output is being produced? What is it being used for?**
- **How much income is being generated in the marketplace?**
- **What's happening to prices and wages?**

It's tempting, of course, to ignore all these measurement questions, especially since they tend to be rather dull. But if we avoid measurement problems, we severely limit our ability to understand how well (or poorly) the economy is performing. We also limit our ability to design policies for improving economic performance.

National income accounting also provides a useful perspective on the way the economy works. It shows how factor markets relate to product markets, how output relates to income, and how consumer spending and business investment relate to production. It also shows how the flow of taxes and government spending affect economic outcomes.

MEASURES OF OUTPUT

The array of goods and services we produce is truly massive, including everything from professional baseball (a service) to guided-missile systems (a good). All these products are part of our total output; the first data challenge is to find a summary measure of all these diverse products.

---

national income accounting: The measurement of aggregate economic activity, particularly national income and its components.

Itemizing the amount of each good or service produced each year won't solve our measurement problem. The resulting list would be so long that it would be both unwieldy and meaningless. We couldn't even add it up because it would contain diverse goods measured in a variety of different units (e.g., miles, packages, pounds, quarts). Nor could we compare one year's output to another's. Suppose that last year we produced 3 billion oranges, 2 million bicycles, and 700 rock concerts, whereas this year we produced 4 billion oranges, 4 million bicycles, and 600 rock concerts. Which year's output was larger? With more of some goods, but less of others, the answer isn't obvious.

Gross Domestic Product

To facilitate our accounting chores, we need some mechanism for organizing annual output data into a more manageable summary. The mechanism we use is price. *Each good and service produced and brought to market has a price. That price serves as a measure of value for calculating total output.* Consider again the problem of determining how much output was produced this year and last. There's no obvious way to answer this question in physical terms alone. But once we know the price of each good, we can calculate the *value* of output produced. The total dollar value of final output produced each year is called the **gross domestic product (GDP).** GDP is simply the sum of all final goods and services produced for the market in a given time period, with each good or service valued at its market price.

Table 5.1 illustrates the use of prices to value total output in two hypothetical years. If oranges were 40 cents each last year and 3 billion oranges were produced, then the *value* of orange production last year was $1,200 million ($0.40 × 3 billion). In the same manner, we can determine that the value of bicycle production was $200 million and the value of rock concerts was $700 million. By adding these figures, we can say that the value of last year's production—last year's GDP—was $2,100 million (Table 5.1*a*).

Now we're in a position to compare one year's output to another's. Table 5.1*b* shows that the use of prices enables us to say that the *value* of this year's output is $2,600 million. Hence *total output* has increased from one year to the next. *The use of prices to value market output allows us to summarize output activity and to compare the output of one period with that of another.*

gross domestic product (GDP): The total market value of all final goods and services produced within a nation's borders in a given time period.

Output	Amount
a. Last Year's Output	
In physical terms:	
Oranges	3 billion
Bicycles	3 million
Rock concerts	700
Total	?
In monetary terms:	
3 billion oranges @ $0.40 each	$1,200 million
2 million bicycles @ $100 each	200 million
700 rock concerts @ $1 million each	700 million
Total	$2,100 million
b. This Year's Output	
In physical terms:	
Oranges	4 billion
Bicycles	4 million
Rock concerts	600
Total	?
In monetary terms:	
4 billion oranges @ $0.40 each	$1,600 million
4 million bicycles @ $100 each	400 million
600 rock concerts @ $1 million each	600 million
Total	$2,600 million

TABLE 5.1

The Measurement of Output

It's impossible to add up all output in *physical* terms. Accordingly, total output is measured in *monetary* terms, with each good or service valued at its market price. GDP refers to the total *market value* of all goods and services *produced* in a given time period.

According to the numbers in this table, the total *value* of the oranges, bicycles, and rock concerts produced "last" year was $2.1 billion and $2.6 billion "this" year. So, we can say that *total output* increased.

GDP vs. GNP. The concept of GDP is of relatively recent use in U.S. national income accounts. Prior to 1992, most U.S. statistics focused on gross *national* product or GNP. Gross *national* product refers to the output produced by American-owned factors of production regardless of where they're located. Gross *domestic* product refers to output produced within America's borders. Thus GNP would include some output from an Apple computer factory in Singapore but exclude some of the output produced by a Honda factory in Ohio. In an increasingly global economy, where factors of production and ownership move easily across international borders, the calculations of GNP became ever more complex. It also became a less dependable measure of the nation's economic health. ***GDP is geographically focused, including all output produced within a nation's borders regardless of whose factors of production are used to produce it.*** Apple's output in Singapore ends up in Singapore's GDP; the cars produced at Honda's Ohio plant are counted in America's GDP.

International Comparisons. The geographic focus of GDP facilitates international comparisons of economic activity. Is China's output as large as that of the United States? How could you tell? China produces a mix of output different from ours, making *quantity*-based comparisons difficult. We can compare the *value* of output produced in each country, however. The World View "Comparative Output" in Chapter 2 shows that the value of America's GDP is much larger than China's.

GDP per Capita. International comparisons of total output are even more vivid in *per capita terms*. **GDP per capita** relates the total value of annual output to the number of people who share that output; it refers to the average GDP per person. In 2017, America's total GDP of $19 trillion was shared by 330 million citizens. Hence our average, or *per capita,* GDP was nearly $58,000. By contrast, the average GDP for the rest of the world's inhabitants was only $11,000. In these terms, America's position as among the richest countries in the world clearly stands out.

> **GDP per capita:** Total GDP divided by total population; average GDP.

Statistical comparisons of GDP across nations are abstract and lifeless. They do, however, convey very real differences in the way people live. World View "Global Inequalities" examines some everyday realities of living in a poor nation, compared with a rich nation. Disparities in per capita GDP mean that people in low-income countries have little access to telephones, televisions, paved roads, or schools. They also die a lot younger than do people in rich countries.

But even the World View fails to fully convey how tough life is for people at the *bottom* of the income distribution in both poor and rich nations. Per capita GDP isn't a measure of what every citizen is getting. In the United States, millions of individuals have access to far more goods and services than our *average* per capita GDP, while millions of others must get by with much less. Although per capita GDP in Kuwait is three times larger than that of Brazil's, we can't conclude that the typical citizen of Kuwait is three times as well off as the typical Brazilian. The only thing these figures tell us is that the average Kuwaiti *could have* almost three times as many goods and services each year as the average Brazilian *if* GDP were distributed in the same way in both countries. ***Measures of per capita GDP tell us nothing about the way GDP is actually distributed or used: they're only a statistical average.*** When countries are quite similar in structure, institutions, and income distribution, however—or when historical comparisons are made within a country—per capita GDP can be viewed as a rough-and-ready measure of relative living standards.

Measurement Problems

Nonmarket Activities. Although the methods for calculating GDP and per capita GDP are straightforward, they do create a few problems. For one thing, ***GDP measures exclude most goods and services that are produced but not sold in the market.*** This may appear to be a trivial point, but it isn't. Vast quantities of output never reach the market. For example, the homemaker who cleans, washes, gardens, shops, and cooks definitely contributes to the output of goods and services. Because she's not paid a market wage for these services, however, her efforts are excluded from the calculation of GDP. At the same time, we do count the efforts of those workers who sell identical homemaking services in

WORLD VIEW

GLOBAL INEQUALITIES

The 600 million residents of the world's low-income nations such as Afghanistan and Malawi have comparatively few goods and services. Their average income (per capita GDP) is only $619 a year, a mere 1.5 percent of the average income of the 1.2 billion residents in high-income nations such as the United States, Japan, and Germany. It's not just a colossal *income* disparity; it's also a disparity in the quality and even the duration of life.

Some examples:

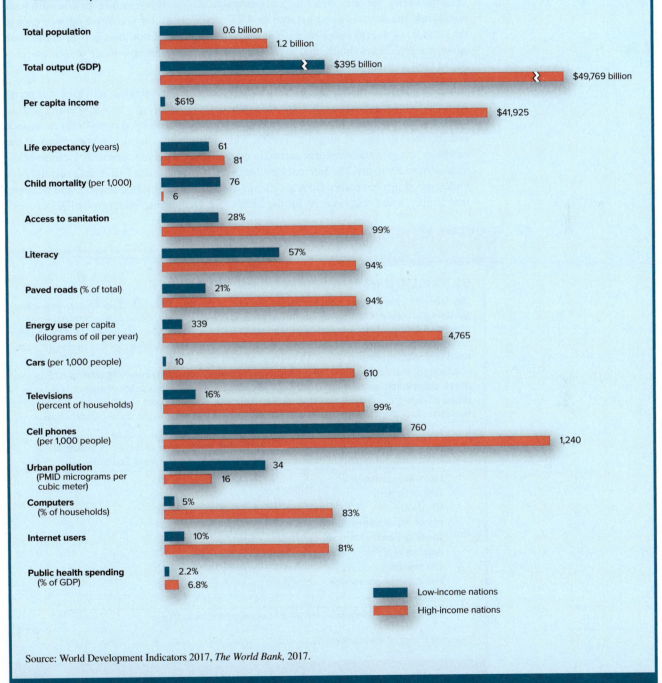

Source: World Development Indicators 2017, *The World Bank,* 2017.

ANALYSIS: Hidden behind dry statistical comparisons of per capita GDP lie very tangible and dramatic differences in the way people live. Low GDP per capita reflects a lot of deprivation.

the marketplace. This seeming contradiction is explained by the fact that a homemaker's services aren't sold in the market and therefore carry no explicit, market-determined value.

The exclusion of homemakers' services from the GDP accounts is particularly troublesome when we want to compare living standards over time or between countries. In the United States, for example, most women now work outside the home. As a result households make greater use of *paid* domestic help (e.g., child care, housecleaning). Accordingly, a lot of housework and child care that were previously excluded from GDP statistics (because they were unpaid family help) are now included (because they're done by paid help). In this respect, our historical GDP figures may exaggerate improvements in our standard of living.

Homemaking services aren't the only output excluded. If a friend helps you with your homework, the services never get into the GDP accounts. But if you hire a tutor or engage the services of a term paper–writing agency, the transaction becomes part of GDP. Here again, the problem is simply that we have no way to determine how much output was produced until it enters the market and is purchased.[1]

Unreported Income. The GDP statistics also fail to capture market activities that aren't reported to tax or census authorities. Many people work "off the books," getting paid in unreported cash. This so-called underground economy is motivated by both tax avoidance and the need to conceal illegal activities. Although illegal activities capture most of the headlines, tax evasion on income earned in otherwise legal pursuits accounts for most of the underground economy. The Internal Revenue Service estimates that more than two-thirds of underground income comes from legitimate wages, salaries, profits, interest, and pensions that simply aren't reported. As In the News "$2 Trillion in 'Underground' Economy"

IN THE NEWS

$2 TRILLION IN "UNDERGROUND" ECONOMY

Day laborers expect to be paid in cash at the end of the day. Babysitters, lawn mowers, and painters also prefer cash payments, most of which never gets reported to the Internal Revenue Service. Lots of renters also pay their rent in cash. None of these "underground" transactions appear in the national income accounts. The IRS estimates the size of this underground economy at $2 trillion—or about 12 percent of total output (GDP).

Although most people think the underground economy consists primarily of criminal activity—drugs, prostitution, gambling, loan sharking—the lion's share of the shadow economy is comprised of legal (noncriminal) activity that is transacted in cash and not reported. A University of Michigan study identified some of the most prominent participants in the underground economy:

	Estimated Percentage of Services Supplied by the Underground Economy
Lawn maintenance	90
Domestic help	83
Child care	49
Home repair/improvements	34
Laundry/sewing services	25
Appliance repair	17
Car repairs	13
Haircuts/beauty service	8
Catering	8

Data from University of Michigan Institute for Social Research, U.S. Department of Labor.

Source: U.S. Internal Revenue Service.

ANALYSIS: GDP statistics include only the value of reported market transactions. Unreported transactions in the underground economy can't be counted and may therefore distort perceptions of economic activity.

[1]The U.S. Commerce Department does, however, *estimate* the value of some nonmarket activities (e.g., food grown by farmers for their own consumption, the rental value of home ownership) and includes such estimates in GDP calculations.

Stages of Production	Value of Transaction	Value Added
1. Farmer grows wheat, sells it to miller.	$0.12	$0.12
2. Miller converts wheat to flour, sells it to baker.	0.28	0.16
3. Baker bakes bagel, sells it to bagel store.	0.60	0.32
4. Bagel store sells bagel to consumer.	0.75	0.15
Total	$1.75	$0.75

TABLE 5.2

Value Added in Various Stages of Production

The value added at each stage of production represents a contribution to total output. Value added equals the market value of a product minus the cost of intermediate goods.

indicates, unreported income is particularly common in the service sector. People who mow lawns, clean houses, paint walls, or provide child care services are apt to get paid in cash that isn't reported. The volume of such mundane transactions greatly exceeds the underground income generated by drug dealers, prostitutes, or illegal gambling.

Value Added

Not every reported market transaction gets included at full value in GDP statistics. If it did, the same output would get counted over and over. The problem here is that the production of goods and services typically involves a series of distinct stages. Consider the production of a bagel, for example. For a bagel to reach Einstein's or some other bagel store, the farmer must grow some wheat, the miller must convert it to flour, and the baker must make bagels with it. Table 5.2 illustrates this chain of production.

Notice that each of the four stages of production depicted in Table 5.2 involves a separate market transaction. The farmer sells to the miller (stage 1), the miller to the baker (stage 2), the baker to the bagel store (stage 3), and, finally, the store to the consumer (stage 4). If we added up the separate value of each market transaction, we'd come to the conclusion that $1.75 of output had been produced. In fact, though, only one bagel has been produced, and it's worth only 75 cents. Hence we should increase GDP—the value of output—only by 75 cents.

To get an accurate measure of GDP we must distinguish between *intermediate* goods and *final* goods. **Intermediate goods** are goods purchased for use as input in further stages of production. Final goods are the goods produced at the end of the production sequence, for use by consumers (or other market participants).

We can compute the value of *final* output in one of two ways. The easiest way would be to count only market transactions entailing final sales (stage 4 in Table 5.2). To do this, however, we'd have to know who purchased each good or service in order to know when we had reached the end of the process. Such a calculation would also exclude any output produced in stages 1, 2, and 3 in Table 5.2 but not yet reflected in stage 4.

Another way to calculate GDP is to count only the **value added** at each stage of production. Consider the miller, for example. He sells 28 cents of flour to the baker, but he doesn't really contribute $0.28 worth of production to total output. His contribution to output is only $0.16. The other $0.12 reflected in the price of his flour represents the contribution of the farmer who grew the wheat.

It's the same story with the baker. He sells a bagel for $0.60. But the baker *adds* only $0.32 to the value of output, as part of his output ($0.28) was purchased from the miller. By considering only the value *added* at each stage of production, we eliminate double counting. We don't count twice the *intermediate* goods and services that producers buy from other producers, which are then used as inputs. As Table 5.2 confirms, we can determine that value of final output by summing up the value added at each stage of production. (Note that $0.75 is also the price of a bagel sold to the final consumer.)

intermediate goods: Goods or services purchased for use as input in the production of final goods or in services.

value added: The increase in the market value of a product that takes place at each stage of the production process.

Real vs. Nominal GDP

Although prices are a convenient measure of market value, they can also distort perceptions of real output. Imagine what would happen to our calculations of GDP if all prices were to double from one year to the next. Suppose that the price of oranges, as shown in Table 5.1 for this year, rose from $0.40 to $0.80, the price of bicycles to $200, and the price of rock concerts to $2 million each. How would such price changes alter measured GDP? Obviously, the price increases would double the dollar *value* of final output. Measured GDP would rise from $2,600 million to $5,200 million.

Unfortunately, the measured increase in GDP is a mirage. There has been no increase in the *quantity* of goods and services available to us. We're still producing the same quantities shown in Table 5.1; only the prices of those goods have changed. Hence **changes in GDP brought about by changes in the price level give us a distorted view of real economic activity.** We wouldn't think that our standard of living had improved just because price increases had raised *measured* GDP from $2,600 million to $5,200 million.

To distinguish increases in the *quantity* of goods and services from increases in their *prices,* we must construct a measure of GDP that takes into account price level changes. We do so by distinguishing between *real* GDP and *nominal* GDP. **Nominal GDP** is the value of final output measured in *current* prices, whereas **real GDP** is the value of output measured in *constant* prices. *To calculate real GDP, we adjust the market value of goods and services for changing prices.*

Note, for example, that in Table 5.1 prices were unchanged from one year to the next: oranges cost $0.40 both last year and this year. When prices in the marketplace are constant, interyear comparisons of output are simple. It's only when prices change that comparisons becomes more complicated. As we just saw, if all prices doubled from last year to this year, this year's *nominal* GDP would rise to $5,200 million. But these price increases wouldn't alter the quantity of goods produced. In other words, *real* GDP, valued at constant prices, would remain at $2,600 million. Thus **the distinction between nominal and real GDP is important whenever the price level changes.**

Because the price level does change every year, both real and nominal GDP are regularly reported. Nominal GDP is computed simply by adding the *current* dollar value of production. Real GDP is computed by making an adjustment for changes in prices from year to year.

Zero Growth. Consider the GDP statistics for 2007 and 2008, as displayed in Table 5.3. The first row shows *nominal* GDP in each year: Nominal GDP increased by $307 billion between 2007 and 2008 (row 2). At first blush, this 2.2 percent increase in GDP looks impressive; that works out to roughly $1,000 more output for every U.S. citizen.

But output didn't really grow that much. Row 3 indicates that *prices* increased by 2.2 percent from year to year. This wiped out the entire increase in the value of output. *Real* GDP actually decreased from 2007 to 2008!

Row 4 in Table 5.3 adjusts the GDP comparison for the change in prices. We represent the price increase as an index, with a base of 100. Thus, a price increase of 2.2 percent raises the base of 100 to 102.2. So the price level change can be expressed as 102.2/100.0, or 1.022.

To convert the *nominal* value of GDP in 2008 to its *real* value, we need only a little division. As row 4 of Table 5.3 shows, we divide the nominal GDP of $14,369 by the indexed price change (1.022) and discover that *real* GDP in 2008 was only $14,060 billion. Hence *real* GDP actually decreased by $2 billion in 2008 (row 5).

Notice in Table 5.3 that in 2007 real and nominal GDP are identical because we're using that year as the basis of comparison. We're comparing performance in 2008 to that of the 2007 **base year.** Real GDP can be expressed in the prices of any particular year; whatever

---

nominal GDP: The value of final output produced in a given period, measured in the prices of that period (current prices).

real GDP: The value of final output produced in a given period, adjusted for changing prices.

base year: The year used for comparative analysis; the basis for indexing price changes.

TABLE 5.3

Computing Real GDP

Real GDP is the inflation-adjusted value of nominal GDP. Between 2007 and 2008, *nominal* GDP increased by $307 billion (row 2). All of this gain was due to rising prices (row 3). After adjusting for inflation, *real* GDP actually decreased by $2 billion (row 5).

	2007	2008
1. Nominal GDP (in billions)	$14,062	$14,369
2. Change in nominal GDP		+$307
Inflation adjustment:		
3. Change in price level, 2007 to 2008		2.2%
4. Real GDP in 2007 dollars $\left(= \dfrac{\text{Nominal GDP}}{\text{Price index}}\right)$	$14,062	$14,060 $\left(= \dfrac{\$14,369}{1.022}\right)$
5. Change in real GDP		−$2

year is selected serves as the base for computing price level and output changes. In Table 5.3 we used 2007 as the base year for computing real GDP in subsequent years. The general formula for computing real GDP is

$$\text{Real GDP in year } t = \frac{\text{Nominal GDP in year } t}{\text{Price index}}$$

This is the formula we used in row 4 of Table 5.3 to compute real GDP in 2008, valued at 2007 base year prices.

The distinction between nominal and real GDP becomes critical when more distant years are compared. In the 70 years between 1933 and 2013, for example, prices rose by an incredible 1,300 percent. But what about real output? Did real output increase that much? Unfortunately not. When we value 2013 output at base year 1933 prices, *real* GDP turns out to be only $1,200 billion, not the *nominal* $16,800 billion as seen in Table 5.4.

Table 5.4 also depicts the divergence between the *nominal* growth of per capita GDP and the real growth. In *nominal* terms, our growth looks spectacular, with per capita

Suppose we want to determine how much better off the average American was in 2013, as measured in terms of new goods and services, than people were during the Great Depression. To do this, we'd compare GDP per capita in 2013 with GDP per capita in 1933. The following data make that comparison.

	Nominal GDP	Population	Nominal per Capita GDP
1933	$ 57 billion	126 million	$ 452
2013	16,800 billion	310 million	54,194

In 1933 the nation's nominal GDP of $57 billion was shared by 126 million Americans, yielding a *per capita* GDP of $452. By contrast, nominal GDP in 2013 was more than 300 times larger, at $16,800 billion. This vastly larger GDP was shared by 310 million people, giving us a per capita GDP of $54,194. Hence it would appear that our standard of living in 2013 was 120 times higher than the standard of 1933.

But this increase in *nominal* GDP vastly exaggerates the gains in our material well-being. The average price of goods and services—the *price level*—increased by 1,300 percent between 1933 and 2013. The goods and services you might have bought for $1 in 1933 cost $14 in 2013. In other words, we needed a lot more dollars in 2013 to buy any given combination of real goods and services.

To compare our *real* GDP in 2013 with the real GDP of 1933, we have to adjust for this tremendous jump in prices (inflation). We do so by measuring both years' output in terms of *constant* prices. Since prices went up, on average, fourteenfold between 1933 and 2013, we simply divide the 2013 *nominal* output by 14. The calculation is

$$\text{Real GDP in 2013 (in 1933 prices)} = \frac{\text{Nominal 2013 GDP}}{\text{Price index}}$$

By arbitrarily setting the level of prices in the base year 1933 at 100 and noting that prices have increased fourteenfold since then, we can calculate

$$\text{Price Index} = \frac{\text{2013 price level}}{\text{1933 price level}} = \frac{1400}{100} = 14.0$$

and therefore,

$$\text{Real GDP in 2013 (1933 prices)} = \frac{\$16,800}{14.0}$$
$$= \$1,200 \text{ billion}$$

With a population of 310 million, this left us with real GDP per capita of $3,870 in 2013—as measured in base year 1933 dollars. This was nearly nine times the *real* per capita GDP of the depression ($452), but not nearly so great an increase as comparisons of *nominal* GDP suggest.

TABLE 5.4

Real vs. Nominal GDP: A Historical View

income a whopping 120 times larger than 1933 levels. In *real* terms, however, the income gain is a much less spectacular 9 times larger.

Figure 5.1 shows how nominal and real GDP have changed just since 2000. Real GDP is calculated here on the basis of the level of prices prevailing in 2009. So 2009 is the *base year* in this case. (Note that real and nominal GDP are identical in that base year.) The dollar value of output produced each year has risen considerably faster than the quantity of output, reflecting persistent increases in the price level—that is, **inflation.**

Notice also how inflation can obscure actual *declines* in real output. Real GDP actually declined in 2008 even though *nominal* GDP rose.

Chain-Weighted Price Adjustments.   Although the distinction between real and nominal GDP is critical in measuring the nation's economic health, the procedure for making inflation adjustments isn't perfect. When we use the prices of a specific year as the base for computing real GDP, we're implicitly freezing *relative* prices as well as *average* prices. Over time, however, relative prices change markedly. Computer prices, for example, have fallen sharply in recent years in both absolute and relative terms. During the same period, unit sales of computers have increased by 20 to 25 percent a year. If we used the higher computer prices of five years ago to compute that sales growth, we'd greatly exaggerate the *value* of today's computer output. If we use today's prices, however, we'll underestimate the value of output produced in the past. To resolve this problem, the U.S. Department of Commerce uses a *chain-weighted* price index to compute real GDP. Instead of using the prices of a *single* base year to compute real GDP, *chain-weighted indexes use a **moving average** of price levels in consecutive years as an inflation adjustment.* When

inflation: An increase in the average level of prices of goods and services.

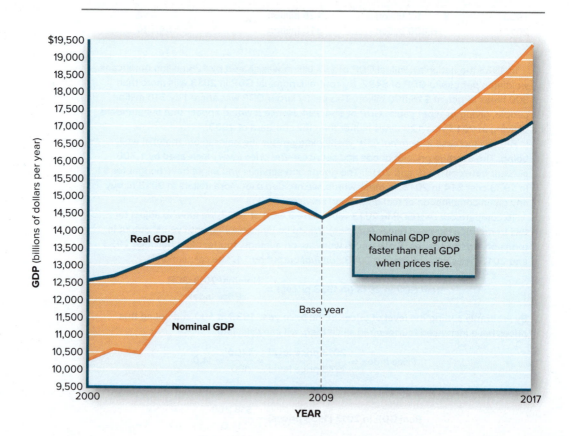

FIGURE 5.1

Changes in GDP: Nominal vs. Real

Increases in *nominal* GDP reflect higher prices as well as more output. Increases in *real* GDP reflect more output only. To measure these real changes, we must value each year's output in terms of common base prices. In this figure the base year is 2009. Nominal GDP rises faster than real GDP as a result of inflation.

Source: U.S. Bureau of Economic Analysis.

chain-weighted price adjustments are made, real GDP still refers to the inflation-adjusted value of GDP but isn't expressed in terms of the prices prevailing in any specific base year.

Net Domestic Product

Changes in real GDP from one year to the next tell us how much the economy's output is growing. Some of that growth, however, may come at the expense of future output. Recall that our **production possibilities** determine how much output we can produce with available factors of production and technology. If we use up some of these resources to produce this year's output, future production possibilities may shrink. *Next year we won't be able to produce as much output unless we replace factors of production we use this year.*

We routinely use up plants and equipment (capital) in the production process. To maintain our production possibilities, therefore, we have to at least replace what we've used. The value of capital used up in producing goods and services is commonly called **depreciation.**[2] In principle, it's the amount of capital worn out by use in a year or made obsolete by advancing technology. In practice, the amount of capital depreciation is estimated by the U.S. Department of Commerce.

By subtracting depreciation from GDP we get **net domestic product (NDP).** This is the amount of output we could consume without reducing our stock of capital and thus next year's production possibilities.

The distinction between GDP and NDP is mirrored in a distinction between *gross* investment and *net* **investment. Gross investment** is positive as long as some new plants and equipment are being produced. But *the stock of capital—the total collection of plants and equipment—won't grow unless gross investment exceeds depreciation.* That is, the *flow* of new capital must exceed depreciation, or our *stock* of capital will decline. Whenever the rate of gross investment exceeds depreciation, **net investment** is positive.

Notice that net investment can be negative as well; in such situations we're wearing out plants and equipment faster than we're replacing them. When net investment is negative, our capital stock is shrinking. This was the situation during the Great Depression. Gross investment fell so sharply in 1932–1934 (see Data Tables at the end of the book) that it wasn't even replacing used-up machinery and structures. As a result, the economy's ability to produce goods and services declined, worsening the Great Depression.

THE USES OF OUTPUT

The role of investment in maintaining or expanding our production possibilities helps focus attention on the uses to which GDP is put. It's not just the total value of annual output that matters; it's also the use that we make of that output. *The GDP accounts also tell us what mix of output we've selected—that is, society's answer to the core issue of WHAT to produce.*

Consumption

The major uses of total output conform to the four sets of market participants we encountered in Chapter 2—namely, consumers, business firms, government, and foreigners. Those goods and services used by households are called *consumption goods* and range all the way from doughnuts to phone services. Included in this category are all goods and services households purchase in product markets. Presently, all this consumer spending claims more than two-thirds of our annual output.

Investment

Investment goods represent another use of GDP. Investment goods are the plants, machinery, and equipment we produce. Net changes in business inventories and expenditures for residential construction are also counted as investment. To produce any of these investment

---

production possibilities: The alternative combinations of final goods and services that could be produced in a given period with all available resources and technology.

depreciation: The consumption of capital in the production process; the wearing out of plant and equipment.

net domestic product (NDP): GDP less depreciation.

investment: Expenditures on (production of) new plants, equipment, and structures (capital) in a given time period, plus changes in business inventories.

gross investment: Total investment expenditure in a given time period.

net investment: Gross investment less depreciation.

---

[2]The terms *depreciation, capital consumption allowance,* and *consumption of fixed capital* are used interchangeably. The depreciation charges firms commonly make, however, are determined in part by income tax regulations and thus may not accurately reflect the amount of capital consumed.

goods, we must use scarce resources that could be used to produce something else. Investment spending claims about one-sixth of our total output.

Government Spending

The third major use of GDP is the *public sector*. Federal, state, and local governments purchase resources to police the streets, teach classes, write laws, and build highways. The resources purchased by the government sector are unavailable for either consumption or investment purposes. At present, government spending on goods and services (*not* income transfers) claims roughly one-fifth of total output.

Net Exports

exports: Goods and services sold to foreign buyers.

Finally, remember that some of the goods and services we produce each year are used abroad rather than at home. That is, we **export** some of our output to other countries, for whatever use they care to make of it. Thus GDP—the value of output produced—will be larger than the sum of our own consumption, investment, and government purchases to the extent that we succeed in exporting goods and services.

imports: Goods and services purchased from international sources.

We **import** goods and services as well. A flight to London on British Air is an imported service; a Jaguar is an imported good. These goods and services aren't part of America's GDP since they weren't produced within our borders. In principle, these imports never enter the GDP accounts. In practice, however, it's difficult to distinguish imports from domestic-made products, especially when goods include value added from both foreign and domestic producers. Even "American-made" cars typically incorporate parts manufactured in Japan, Mexico, Thailand, Britain, Spain, or Germany, with final assembly here in the United States. Should that car be counted as an "American" product or as an import? Rather than try to sort out all these products and parts, the U.S. Commerce Department simply subtracts the value of all imports from the value of total spending. **Thus exports are *added* to GDP and imports are *subtracted*.** The difference between the two expenditure flows is called **net exports.**

net exports: The value of exports minus the value of imports: ($X - M$).

GDP Components

Once we recognize the components of output, we discover a simple method for computing GDP. *The value of GDP can be computed by adding up the expenditures of market participants.* Specifically, we note that

$$GDP = C + I + G + (X - M)$$

where C = consumption expenditure
I = investment expenditure
G = government expenditure
X = exports
M = imports

This approach to GDP accounting emphasizes the fact that *all the output produced in the economy must be claimed by someone.* If we know who's buying our output, we know how much was produced and what uses were made of it. This is the answer to the WHAT question.

MEASURES OF INCOME

There's another way of looking at GDP. Instead of looking at who's *buying* our output, we can look at who's *being paid* to produce it. Like markets themselves. *GDP accounts have two sides: one side focuses on expenditure (the demand side) and the other side focuses on income (the supply side).*

We've already observed (see Figure 3.1) that every market transaction involves an *exchange* of dollars for a good or resource. Moreover, the *value* of each good or resource is measured by the amount of money exchanged for it (its market price). Hence *the total*

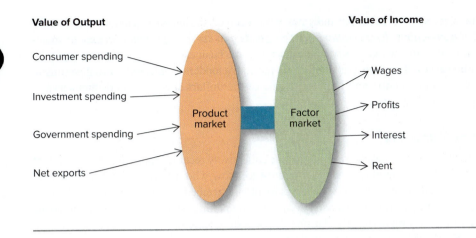

Value of Output

Value of Income

FIGURE 5.2

Output = Income

The spending that establishes the value of output also determines the value of income. With minor exceptions, the market value of income must equal the market value of output.

value of market incomes must equal the total value of final output, or GDP. In other words, one person's expenditure always represents another person's income.

Figure 5.2 illustrates the link between spending on output and incomes. This is a modified version of the circular flow we saw in Chapter 3. The spending that flows into the product market gets funneled into the factor market, where resources are employed to produce the goods people want. The expenditure then flows into the hands of business owners, workers, landlords, and other resource owners. With the exception of sales taxes and depreciation, all spending on output becomes income to factors of production.

The equivalence of output and income isn't dependent on any magical qualities possessed by money. Were we to produce only one product—say, wheat—and pay everyone in bushels and pecks, total income would still equal total output. People couldn't receive in income more wheat than we produced. On the other hand, all the wheat produced would go to *someone.* Hence one could say that the production possibilities of the economy define not only the limits to *output,* but also the limits to real *income.* The amount of income actually generated in any year depends on the production and expenditure decisions of consumers, firms, and government agencies.

Table 5.5 shows the actual flow of output and income in the U.S. economy during 2016. Total output is made up of the four components of GDP: consumption, investment, government goods and services, and net exports. The figures on the left side of Table 5.5 indicate that consumers spent nearly $13 trillion, businesses spent $3 trillion on plant and equipment, governments spent over $3 trillion, and net exports were a *negative* $500 billion (imports exceeded exports). Our total output value (GDP) was thus nearly $18.6 trillion in 2016. That was one-fifth of the *world's* output.

Expenditure		Income	
C: Consumer goods and services	$12,753	Wages and salaries	$10,101
		Corporate profits	2,085
I: Investment in plants,		Proprietors' income	1,418
equipment, and		Rents	705
inventory	3,035	Interest	485
G: Government goods		Taxes on output and	
and services	3,277	imports	1,197
X: Exports	2,233	Depreciation	2,910
M: Imports	(2,733)	Statistical discrepancy	(335)
GDP: Total value of output	$18,566 =	Total value of income	$18,566

Source: U.S. Department of Commerce (2016 data).

TABLE 5.5

The Equivalence of Expenditure and Income (in Billions of Dollars)

The value of total expenditure must equal the value of total income. Why? Because every dollar spent on output becomes a dollar of income for someone.

The right side of Table 5.5 indicates who received the income generated from these market transactions. *Every dollar spent on goods and services provides income to someone.* It may go to a worker (as wage or salary) or to a business firm (as profit and depreciation allowance). It may go to a landlord (as rent), to a lender (as interest), or to government (as taxes on production and imports). None of the dollars spent on goods and services disappears into thin air.

National Income

Although it may be exciting to know that we collectively received more than $18 trillion of income in 2016, it might be of more interest to know who actually got all that income. After all, in addition to the 340 million pairs of outstretched palms among us, millions of businesses and government agencies were also competing for those dollars and the goods and services they represent. By charting the flow of income through the economy, we can see FOR WHOM our output was produced.

Depreciation. The annual income flow originates in product market sales. Purchases of final goods and services create a flow of income to producers and, through them, to factors of production. But a major diversion of sales revenues occurs immediately as a result of depreciation charges made by businesses. As we noted earlier, some of our capital resources are used up in the process of production. For the most part, these resources are owned by business firms that expect to be compensated for such investments. Accordingly, they regard some of the sales revenue generated in product markets as reimbursement for wear and tear on capital plants and equipment. They therefore subtract *depreciation charges* from gross revenues in calculating their incomes. Depreciation charges reduce GDP to the level of *net* domestic product (NDP) before any income is available to current factors of production. As we saw earlier,

$$NDP = GDP - Depreciation$$

Net Foreign Factor Income. Remember that some of the income generated in U.S. product markets belongs to foreigners. Wages, interest, and profits paid to foreigners are not part of U.S. income. So we need to subtract that outflow.

Recall also that U.S. citizens own factors of production employed in other nations (e.g., a Ford plant in Mexico; a McDonald's outlet in Singapore). This creates an *in*flow of income to U.S. households. To connect the value of U.S. output to U.S. incomes, we must add back in the net inflow of foreign factor income.

Once depreciation charges are subtracted from GDP and net foreign factor income added, we're left with **national income (NI),** which is the total income earned by U.S. factors of production. Thus

> **national income (NI):** Total income earned by current factors of production: GDP less depreciation and indirect business taxes, plus net foreign factor income.

$$NI = NDP + Net\ foreign\ factor\ income$$

As Table 5.6 illustrates, our national income in 2016 was $16.1 trillion, nearly 90 percent of GDP.

Personal Income

There are still more revenue diversions as the GDP flow makes its way to consumer households.

Indirect Business Taxes. Another major diversion of the income flow occurs at its point of origin. When goods are sold in the marketplace, their purchase price is typically encumbered with some sort of sales tax. Thus some of the revenue generated in product markets disappears before any factor of production gets a chance to claim it. These taxes on production and imports—often referred to as *indirect business taxes*—must be deducted from national income because they don't represent payment to factors of production. That revenue goes to the government.

Income Flow	Amount (in Billions)
Gross domestic product (GDP)	$18,566
Less depreciation	(2,910)
Net domestic product (NDP)	15,656
Plus net foreign factor income	207
Less statistical discrepancy	267
National income (NI)	16,130
Less indirect business taxes*	(1,197)
Less corporate profits	(2,085)
Less interest and miscellaneous payments	(485)
Less Social Security taxes	(1,250)
Plus transfer payments	2,636
Plus capital income	2,263
Personal income (PI)	16,012
Less personal taxes	(1,966)
Disposable income (DI)	14,046

*Taxes on production and imports.
Source: U.S. Department of Commerce.

TABLE 5.6

The Flow of Income, 2016

The revenue generated from market transactions passes through many hands. Households end up with disposable income equal to about 75 percent of GDP, after depreciation and taxes are taken out and net interest and transfer payments are added back in. Disposable income is either spent (consumption) or saved by households.

Corporate Profits. Theoretically, all the income corporations receive represents income for their owners—the households who hold stock in the corporations. But the flow of income through corporations to stockholders is far from complete. First, corporations have to pay taxes on their profits. Accordingly, a chunk of corporate revenue goes into the public treasury rather than into private bank accounts. Second, corporate managers typically find some urgent need for cash. As a result, another chunk of (after-tax) profits is retained by the corporation rather than passed on to the stockholders in the form of dividends. In Table 5.6 the net result is attained by subtracting all corporate profits from national income, then adding back dividends paid to households in the category "capital income."

Payroll Taxes and Transfers. Still another deduction must be made for *Social Security taxes*. Nearly all people who earn a wage or salary are required by law to pay Social Security contributions. In 2016, the Social Security tax rate for workers was 7.65 percent of the first $118,500 of earnings received in the year. Workers never see this income because it is withheld by employers and sent directly to the U.S. Treasury. Thus the flow of national income is reduced considerably before it becomes **personal income (PI),** the amount of income received by households before payment of personal taxes.

Not all of our adjustments to national income are negative. Households receive income in the form of transfer payments from the public treasury. More than 60 million people receive monthly Social Security checks, for example, and another 14 million receive some form of public welfare. These income transfers represent income for the people who receive them.

personal income (PI): Income received by households before payment of personal taxes.

Capital Income. People also receive interest payments and dividend checks. These forms of capital income provide another source of personal income. Accordingly, our calculation of personal income is as follows:

> *National income* (= income earned by factors of production)
> *less*   indirect business taxes
>   corporate profits
>   interest and miscellaneous payments
>   Social Security taxes
> *plus*   transfer payments
>   capital income
> *equals* ***personal income*** (= income received by households)

FIGURE 5.3

Where Does the Money Go?

Personal income (PI) refers to that portion of the income generated in production that ends up in the hands of private households (after businesses and governments take their shares). But we don't get to keep all that money: households must pay personal taxes on that income. After paying income taxes, households are left with their after-tax **disposable income (DI).** We can then spend our DI on consumer goods and services—or save (not spend) it.

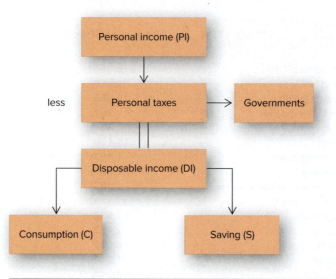

disposable income (DI):
After-tax income of households; personal income less personal taxes.

saving: That part of disposable income not spent on current consumption; disposable income less consumption.

As you can see, **the flow of income generated in production is significantly reduced before it gets into the hands of individual households.** But we haven't yet reached the end of the reduction process. We have to set something aside for personal income taxes. To be sure we don't forget about our obligations, Uncle Sam and his state and local affiliates usually arrange to have their share taken off the top. Personal income taxes are withheld by the employer, who thus acts as a tax collector. Accordingly, to calculate **disposable income (DI),** which is the amount of income consumers may themselves spend (dispose of), we reduce personal income by the amount of personal taxes:

$$\text{Disposable income} = \text{Personal income} - \text{Personal taxes}$$

Disposable income is the end of the accounting line. As Table 5.6 shows, households end up with roughly 75 percent of the revenues generated from final market sales (GDP). Once consumers get this disposable income in their hands, they face two choices. They may choose to *spend* their disposable income on consumer goods and services. Or they may choose to *save* it. These are the only two choices in GDP accounting. **saving,** in this context, simply refers to disposable income that isn't spent on consumption. In the analysis of income and saving flows, we don't care whether savings are hidden under a mattress, deposited in the bank, or otherwise secured. All we want to know is whether disposable income is spent. Thus *all disposable income is, by definition, either consumed or saved; that is,*

$$\text{Disposable income} = \text{Consumption} + \text{Saving}$$

Figure 5.3 summarizes these last steps.

THE FLOW OF INCOME

Figure 5.4 summarizes the broader relationship between expenditure and income. The essential point again is that every dollar spent on goods and services flows into somebody's hands. Thus *the dollar value of output will always equal the dollar value of income.* Specifically, total income (GDP) ends up distributed in the following way:

- To *households* in the form of disposable income.
- To *business* in the form of retained earnings and depreciation allowances.
- To *government* in the form of taxes.

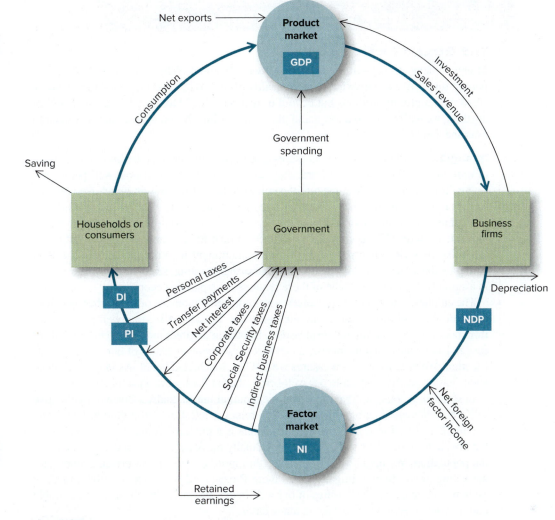

FIGURE 5.4

The Circular Flow of Spending and Income

GDP represents the dollar value of final output sold in the product market. The revenue stream flowing from GDP works its way through NDP, NI, and PI before reaching households in the form of smaller DI. DI is in turn either spent or saved by consumers. This consumption, plus investment, government spending, and net exports, continues the circular flow.

Income and Expenditure

The annual flow of income to households, businesses, and government is part of a continuing process. Households rarely stash their disposable income under the mattress; they spend most of it on consumption. This spending adds to GDP in the next round of activity, thereby helping to keep the flow of income moving.

Business firms also have a lot of purchasing power tied up in retained earnings and depreciation charges. This income, too, may be recycled—returned to the circular flow—in the form of business investment.

Even the income that flows into public treasuries finds its way back into the marketplace as government agencies hire police officers, soldiers, and clerks, or they buy goods and services. Thus *the flow of income that starts with GDP ultimately returns to the market in the form of new consumption (C), investment (I), and government purchases (G).* A new GDP arises, and the flow starts all over. In later chapters we examine in detail these *expenditure* flows, with particular emphasis on their ability to keep the economy producing at its full potential.

THE ECONOMY TOMORROW

THE QUALITY OF LIFE

Money, money, money—it seems that's all we talk about. Why don't we talk about important things like beauty, virtue, or the quality of life? Will the economy of tomorrow be filled with a glut of products but devoid of real meaning? Do the GDP accounts tell us anything we really want to know about the quality of life? If not, why should we bother to examine them?

Intangibles. All the economic measures discussed in this chapter are important indexes of individual and collective welfare; they tell us something about how well people are living. They don't, however, capture the completeness of the way in which we view the world or the totality of what makes our lives satisfying. A clear day, a sense of accomplishment, even a smile can do more for a person's sense of well-being than can favorable movements in the GDP accounts. Or as the economist John Kenneth Galbraith put it, "In a rational lifestyle, some people could find contentment working moderately and then sitting by the street—and talking, thinking, drawing, painting, scribbling, or making love in a suitably discreet way. None of these requires an expanding economy."[3]

The emphasis on economic outcomes arises not from ignorance of life's other meanings but from the visibility of the economic outcomes. We all realize that well-being arises from both material and intangible pleasures. But the intangibles tend to be elusive. It's not easy to gauge individual happiness, much less to ascertain the status of our collective satisfaction. We have to rely on measures we can see, touch, and count. As long as material goods have a positive impact to our well-being, they at least serve a useful purpose.

In some situations, however, more physical output may actually worsen our collective welfare. If increased automobile production raises congestion and pollution levels, the rise in GDP occasioned by those additional cars is a misleading index of society's welfare. In such a case, the rise in GDP might actually mask a *decrease* in the well-being of the population. We might also wonder whether more casinos, more prisons, more telemarketing, more divorce litigation, and more Prozac—all of which contribute to GDP growth—are really valid measures of our well-being. Exclusive emphasis on measurable output would clearly be a mistake in many cases.

Index of Well-Being. Researchers at the Institute for Innovation in Social Policy at Vassar College have devised an alternative index of well-being. Their Index of Social Health includes a few economic parameters (such as unemployment and weekly earnings) but puts more emphasis on sociological behavior (such as child abuse, teen suicides, crime, poverty, and inequality). They claim that this broader view offers a more meaningful guidepost to everyday life than GDP measures of material wealth. According to their calculations, life has gotten worse, not better, as GDP has increased (see In the News "Material Wealth vs. Social Health").

Not everyone would accept the Institute's dour view of our collective social health. Their index, however, does underscore the fact that *social welfare* and *economic welfare* aren't always synonymous. The GDP accounts tell us whether our economic welfare has increased, as measured by the value of goods and services produced. They don't tell us how highly we value additional goods and services relative to nonmarket phenomena. Nor do they even tell us whether important social costs were incurred in the process of production. These judgments must be made outside the market; they're social decisions.

Finally, note that any given level of GDP can encompass many combinations of output. Choosing WHAT to produce is still a critical question, even after the goal of *maximum* production has been established. The quality of life in the economy tomorrow will depend on what specific mix of goods and services we include in GDP.

[3]Cited in Leonard Silk, *Nixonomics,* 2nd ed. (New York: Praeger, 1973), p. 163.

IN THE NEWS

MATERIAL WEALTH VS. SOCIAL HEALTH

National income accounts are regularly reported and widely quoted. They do not, however, adequately reflect the nation's *social* performance. To measure more accurately the country's social health, a Vassar College team of social scientists devised an Index of Social Health with 16 indicators, including infant mortality, drug abuse, health insurance coverage, and poverty among the aged. According to this index, America's social health increased only 6 percent from 1990 to 2011, despite a 34 percent increase in real GDP per capita.

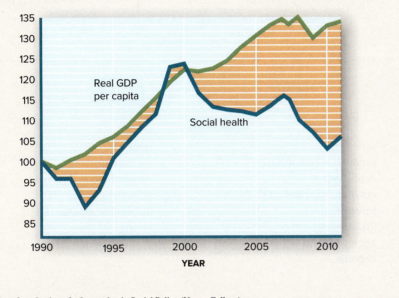

Source: Data from Institute for Innovation in Social Policy (Vassar College).

ANALYSIS: The national income accounts emphasize material well-being. They are an important, but not a complete, gauge of our societal welfare.

SUMMARY

- National income accounting measures annual output and income flows. The national income accounts provide a basis for assessing our economic performance, designing public policy, and understanding how all the parts of the economy interact. **LO5-1**
- The most comprehensive measure of output is gross domestic product (GDP), the total market value of all final goods and services produced within a nation's borders during a given period. **LO5-1**
- In calculating GDP, we include only the value added at each stage of production. This value-added procedure eliminates the double counting that results when business firms buy intermediate goods from other firms and include those costs in their selling price. **LO5-1**
- To distinguish physical changes in output from monetary changes in its value, we compute both nominal and real

GDP. Nominal GDP is the value of output expressed in *current* prices. Real GDP is the value of output expressed in *constant* prices (the prices of some *base year*). **LO5-2**
- Each year some of our capital equipment is worn out in the process of production. Hence GDP is larger than the amount of goods and services we could consume without reducing our production possibilities. The amount of capital used up each year is referred to as *depreciation*. **LO5-4**
- By subtracting depreciation from GDP we derive net domestic product (NDP). The difference between NDP and GDP is also equal to the difference between *gross* investment—the sum of all our current plant and equipment expenditures—and *net* investment—the amount of investment over and above that required to replace worn-out capital. **LO5-4**

- All the income generated in market sales (GDP) is received by someone. Therefore, the value of aggregate output must equal the value of aggregate income.   **LO5-3**
- The sequence of flows involved in this process is
  GDP
  less depreciation
  equals **NDP**
  plus net foreign factor income
  equals national income (**NI**)
  less indirect business taxes,
     corporate profits,
     interest payments, and
     Social Security taxes

  plus transfer payments and
     capital income
  equals personal income (**PI**)
  less personal income taxes
  equals disposable income (**DI**)   **LO5-3**
- The incomes received by households, business firms, and governments provide the purchasing power required to buy the nation's output. As that purchasing power is spent, further GDP is created and the circular flow continues.   **LO5-3**

Key Terms

national income accounting	inflation	imports
gross domestic product (GDP)	production possibilities	net exports
GDP per capita	depreciation	national income (NI)
intermediate goods	net domestic product (NDP)	personal income (PI)
value added	investment	disposable income (DI)
nominal GDP	gross investment	saving
real GDP	net investment	
base year	exports	

Questions for Discussion

1. The manuscript for this text was typed for free by a friend. Had I hired an administrative assistant to do the same job, GDP would have been higher, even though the amount of output would have been identical. Why is this? Does this make sense?   **LO5-1**

2. According to Table 5.3, GDP grew from $14.062 trillion in 2007 to $14.369 trillion in 2008, yet the quantity of output actually decreased. How is this possible?   **LO5-2**

3. If gross investment is not large enough to replace the capital that depreciates in a particular year, is net investment greater or less than zero? What happens to our production possibilities?   **LO5-4**

4. Can we increase consumption in a given year without cutting back on either investment or government services? Under what conditions?   **LO5-4**

5. Why is it important to know how much output is being produced? Who uses such information?   **LO5-1**

6. What jobs are likely part of the underground economy?   **LO5-1**

7. Clear-cutting a forest adds to GDP the value of the timber, but it also destroys the forest. How should we value that loss?   **LO5-1**

8. Is the Index of Social Health, discussed in In the News "Material Wealth vs. Social Health," a better barometer of well-being than GDP? What are its relative advantages or disadvantages?   **LO5-1**

9. More than 4 million websites sell a combined $100 billion of pornography a year. Should these sales be included in (*a*) GDP and (*b*) an index of social welfare?   **LO5-1**

10. Are you better off today than a year ago? How do you measure the change?   **LO5-1**

11. Why must the value of total expenditure equal the value of total income.   **LO5-3**

PROBLEMS FOR CHAPTER 5

LO5-1 1. Suppose that furniture production encompasses the following stages:

Stage 1: Trees are sold to lumber company.	$ 1,000
Stage 2: Lumber is sold to furniture company.	$ 2,500
Stage 3: Furniture company sells furniture to retail store.	$ 6,000
Stage 4: Furniture store sells furniture to consumer.	$12,000

    (*a*) What is the value added at each stage?
    (*b*) How much does this output contribute to GDP?
    (*c*) How would answer (*b*) change if the lumber were imported from Canada?

LO5-2 2. Suppose this year's nominal GDP is $1,000 million and price level is 100. If nominal GDP increases by 2 percent and the price level goes up by 3 percent next year, calculate next year's nominal GDP, price level, and real GDP.

LO5-2 3. What was real per capita GDP in 1933 measured in 2013 prices? (Use the data in Table 5.4 to compute your answer.)

LO5-3 4. If all prices were to double overnight, what would be the
    (*a*) Change in real GDP?
    (*b*) Change in nominal GDP?

LO5-3 5. Based on the following data,

Consumption	$200 billion
Depreciation	20
Retained earnings	12
Gross investment	30
Imports	60
Exports	50
Net foreign factor income	10
Government purchases	80

    (*a*) How much is GDP?
    (*b*) How much is net investment?
    (*c*) How much is national income?

LO5-4 6. Using the data in Table 5.5, what share of U.S. total income in 2016 consisted of
    (*a*) Wages and salaries?
    (*b*) Corporate profits?

LO5-2 7. Nominal GDP was $9,817 billion in 2000 and $18,569 billion in 2016. The chain-weighted price deflator (price index) for GDP was 81.9 in 2000 and 111.4 in 2016.
    (*a*) Calculate real GDP for 2016 using 2000 prices.
    (*b*) By how much did real GDP increase between 2000 and 2016?
    (*c*) By how much did nominal GDP increase between 2000 and 2016?

LO5-4 8. According to Table 5.5, calculate the following as a percentage of GDP for 2016:
    a) Personal consumption expenditures
    b) Gross private investment
    c) Total government purchases
    d) Exports
    e) Imports

LO5-2 9. According to the data in Table 5.3, what is
    (*a*) Real GDP in 2008, at prices of 2007?
    (*b*) Real GDP in 2007, at prices of 2008?

LO5-2   10.   Using the data in the endpapers related to nominal per capita GDP, real per capita GDP, and total population, answer the following for the time period 2000–2010:
      (*a*)   By what percentage did *nominal* per capita GDP increase?
      (*b*)   By what percentage did *real* per capita GDP increase?
      (*c*)   In how many years did *nominal* per capita GDP decline?
      (*d*)   In how many years did *real* per capita GDP decline?

LO5-1   11.   The Economy Tomorrow: According to In the News "Material Wealth vs. Social Health," do per capita GDP data overstate or understate the rise in U.S. well-being since 1990? How do you know?

©Marcio Jose Sanchez/AP Images

CHAPTER **6**

Unemployment

George H. had worked at the General Electric lightbulb factory in Winchester, Virginia, for 18 years. Now he was 46 years old with a wife and three children. With his base salary of $48,200 and the performance bonus he received nearly every year, he was doing pretty well. He had his own home, two cars, company-paid health insurance for the family, and a growing nest egg in the company's pension plan. The H. family wasn't rich, but they were comfortable and secure.

Or so they thought. Overnight the H. family's comfort was shattered. On September 8, 2010, GE announced it was closing the plant permanently. George H., along with 300 fellow workers, was permanently laid off. The weekly paychecks stopped immediately; the pension nest egg was in doubt. Within a few weeks, George H. was on the street looking for a new job—an experience he hadn't had since high school. The unemployment benefits the state and union provided didn't come close to covering the mortgage payment, groceries, insurance, and other necessities. The H. family quickly used up its savings, including the $5,000 set aside for the children's college education.

George H. stayed unemployed for months. His wife found a part-time waitressing job, and his oldest son went to work rather than college. George himself ultimately found a warehousing job that paid only half as much as his previous job.

In the recession of 2008–2009 and its aftermath, more than *8 million* workers lost their jobs as companies "downsized," "restructured," or simply closed. Not all these displaced workers fared as badly as George H. and his family. But the job loss was a painful experience for every one of those displaced workers. That's the human side of an economic downturn.

The pain of joblessness is not confined to those who lose their jobs. In recessions, students discover that jobs are hard to find in the summer. No matter how good their grades are or how nice their résumés look, some graduates just don't get any job offers in a recession. Even people with jobs feel some economic pain: their paychecks shrink when hours or wages are scaled back.

In this chapter we take a closer look at the problem of unemployment, focusing on the following questions:

- **When is a person "unemployed"?**
- **What are the costs of unemployment?**
- **What's an appropriate policy goal for "full employment"?**

As we answer these questions, we'll develop a sense of why full employment is a major goal of macro policy and begin to see some of the obstacles we face in achieving it.

Job Seeker Information

CHAPTER **6**

LEARNING OBJECTIVES

After reading this chapter, you should know

LO6-1 How unemployment is measured.

LO6-2 The socioeconomic costs of unemployment.

LO6-3 The major types of unemployment.

LO6-4 The meaning of "full employment."

THE LABOR FORCE

To assess the dimensions of our unemployment problems, we first need to decide who wants a job. Millions of people are jobless, yet they're not part of our unemployment problem. Full-time students, young children playing with their toys, and older people living in retirement are all jobless. We don't expect them to be working, so we don't regard them as part of the unemployment problem. We're not trying to get *everybody* a job, just those people who are ready and willing to work.

To distinguish those people who want a job from those who don't, we separate the entire population into two distinct groups. One group consists of *labor force participants;* the other group encompasses all *nonparticipants.*

labor force: All persons over age 16 who are either working for pay or actively seeking paid employment.

The **labor force** includes everyone age 16 and older who is actually working plus all those who aren't working but are actively seeking employment. Individuals are also counted as employed in a particular week if their failure to work is due to vacation, illness, labor dispute (strike), or bad weather. All such persons are regarded as "with a job but not at work." Also, unpaid family members working in a family enterprise (farming, for example) are counted as employed. ***Only those people who are either employed or actively seeking work are counted as part of the labor force.*** People who are neither employed *nor* actively looking for a job are referred to as *nonparticipants.* As Figure 6.1 shows, only half the U.S. population participates in the labor force.

Note that our definition of labor force participation excludes most household and volunteer activities. People who choose to devote their energies to household responsibilities or to unpaid charity work aren't counted as part of the labor force, no matter how hard they work. Because they are neither in paid employment nor seeking such employment in the marketplace, they are regarded as outside the labor market (nonparticipants). But if they decide to seek a paid job outside the home, we say that they are "entering the labor force." Students too are typically out of the labor force until they leave school. They *"enter"* the labor force when they go looking for a job, either during the summer or after graduation. People *"exit"* the labor force when they go back to school, return to household activities, go to prison, or retire. These entries and exits keep changing the size and composition of the labor force.

labor force participation rate: The percentage of the working-age population working or seeking employment.

Since 1960, the U.S. labor force has more than doubled in size even though the U.S. population has grown by only 72 percent. The difference is explained by the rapid increase in the **labor force participation rate** of women. Notice in Figure 6.2 that only 1 out of 3 women participated in the labor force in 1950–1960, whereas nearly 6 out of 10 now do so. The labor force participation of men actually declined during the same period, even though it remains higher than that of women.

FIGURE 6.1

The Labor Force, 2016

Only half the total U.S. population participates in the civilian labor force. The rest of the population is too young, in school, at home, retired, or otherwise unavailable.

Unemployment statistics count only those participants who aren't currently working but are actively seeking paid employment. Nonparticipants are neither employed nor actively seeking employment.

Source: U.S. Bureau of Labor Statistics.

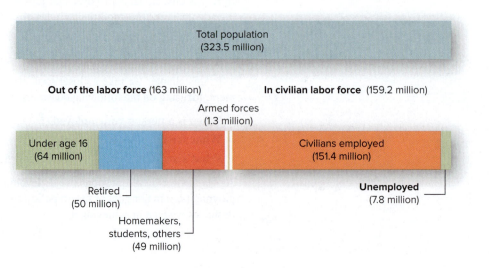

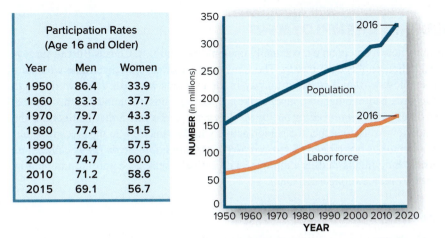

Participation Rates (Age 16 and Older)		
Year	Men	Women
1950	86.4	33.9
1960	83.3	37.7
1970	79.7	43.3
1980	77.4	51.5
1990	76.4	57.5
2000	74.7	60.0
2010	71.2	58.6
2015	69.1	56.7

FIGURE 6.2

A Growing Labor Force

The labor force expands as births and immigration increase. A big increase in the participation rate of women after 1950 also added to labor force growth.

Source: U.S. Bureau of Labor Statistics.

Labor Force Growth

The labor force continues to grow each year along with population increases and continuing immigration. These sources add more than 2 million persons to the labor force every year. This is both good news and bad news. The good news is that labor force growth expands our **production possibilities,** enabling us to produce more output with each passing year. The bad news is that we've got to create at least 2 million *more* jobs every year to ensure that labor force participants can find a job. If we don't, we'll end up *inside* the production possibilities curve, as at point *F* in Figure 6.3.

Unemployment

If we end up inside the production possibilities curve, we are not producing at capacity. We're also not using all available resources, including labor force participants. This gives rise to the problem of **unemployment:** people who are willing and able to work aren't being hired. At point *F* in Figure 6.3 would-be workers are left unemployed; potential output isn't produced. Everybody suffers.

Okun's Law; Lost Output. Arthur Okun quantified the relationship between unemployment and the production possibilities curve. According to the original formulation of **Okun's law,** each additional 1 percent of unemployment translated into a loss of 3 percent in real output. More recent estimates of Okun's law put the ratio at about 1 to 2, largely due to the changing composition of both the labor force (more women and teenagers) and output (more services). Using that 1-to-2 ratio allows us to put a dollar value on the aggregate cost of unemployment. In 2016 the 7.8 milllion workers who couldn't find jobs (see Figure 6.1) could have produced more than $1 *trillion* worth of output. Hence their unemployment implied a loss of $3,000 of goods and services for every American. That's a high cost for macro failure.

production possibilities: The alternative combinations of final goods and services that could be produced in a given period with all available resources and technology.

unemployment: The inability of labor force participants to find jobs.

Okun's law: One percent more unemployment is estimated to equal 2 percent less output.

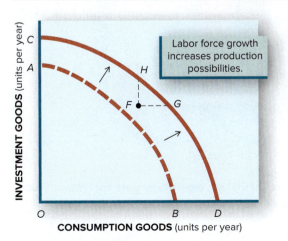

FIGURE 6.3

Labor Force Growth

The amount of labor available for work—the *labor force*—is a prime determinant of a nation's production possibilities. As the labor force grows, so does the capacity to produce. To produce at capacity, however, the labor force must be fully employed. At point *F*, resources are unemployed.

MEASURING UNEMPLOYMENT

To determine how many people are actually unemployed, the U.S. Census Bureau surveys about 60,000 households each month. The Census interviewers first determine whether a person is employed—that is, worked for pay in the previous week (or didn't work due to illness, vacation, bad weather, or a labor strike). If the person is not employed, he or she is classified as either *unemployed* or *out of the labor force*. To make that distinction, the Census interviewers ask whether the person actively looked for work in the preceding four weeks. ***If a person is not employed but is actively seeking a job, he or she is counted as unemployed.*** Individuals neither employed nor actively seeking a job are counted as outside the labor force (nonparticipants).

The Unemployment Rate

unemployment rate: The proportion of the labor force that is unemployed.

In 2016, an average of 7.75 million persons were counted as unemployed in any month. These unemployed individuals accounted for 4.9 percent of our total labor force in that year. Accordingly, the average **unemployment rate** in 2016 was 4.9 percent.

$$\text{Unemployment rate} = \frac{\text{Number of unemployed people}}{\text{Labor force}}$$

$$\text{in 2016} = \frac{7{,}751{,}000}{159{,}187{,}000} = 4.9\%$$

The Census surveys reveal not only the total amount of unemployment in the economy but also which groups are suffering the greatest unemployment. Typically, teenagers just entering the labor market have the greatest difficulty finding (or keeping) jobs. They have no job experience and relatively few marketable skills. Employers are reluctant to hire them, especially if they must pay the a government-set minimum wage. As a consequence, teenage unemployment rates are typically three times higher than adult unemployment rates (see Figure 6.4).

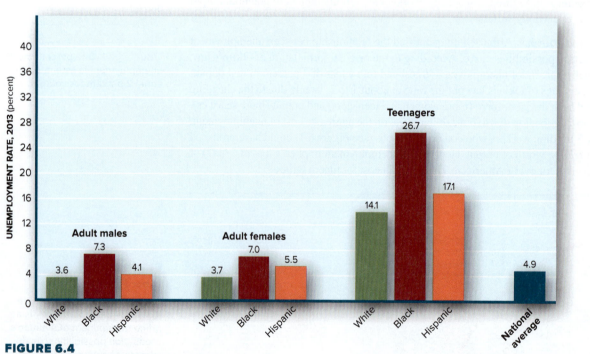

FIGURE 6.4

Unemployment Varies by Race and Sex

Minority groups, teenagers, and less-educated individuals experience higher rates of unemployment. Teenage unemployment rates are particularly high, especially for black and Hispanic youth.

Source: U.S. Department of Labor (2016 data).

Duration	Percentage of Unemployed
Less than 5 weeks	30.5%
5 to 14 weeks	28.7
15 to 26 weeks	14.9
27 weeks or more	25.9
Median duration	10.6 weeks

Source: U.S. Bureau of Labor Statistics (2016 data).

TABLE 6.1

Duration of Unemployment

The severity of unemployment depends on how long the spell of joblessness lasts. About half of unemployed workers return to work quickly, but many others remain unemployed for 6 months or longer.

Minority workers also experience above-average unemployment. Notice in Figure 6.4 that black and Hispanic unemployment rates are much higher than white workers' unemployment rates. In 2016 black teenagers had an extraordinary unemployment rate of 27 percent—five times the national average.

Education. Education also affects the chances of being unemployed. If you graduate from college, your chances of being unemployed drop sharply, regardless of gender or race. Advancing technology and a shift to services from manufacturing have put a premium on better-educated workers. Very few people with master's or doctoral degrees stand in unemployment lines.

The Duration of Unemployment

Although high school dropouts are three times more likely to be unemployed than college graduates, they don't *stay* unemployed. In fact, most people who become unemployed find jobs in 2-3 months. In the fairly robust labor market of 2016, the median spell of unemployment was 10.6 weeks (Table 6.1). Only one out of four unemployed individuals had been jobless for as long as 6 months (27 weeks or longer). People who lose their jobs do find new ones; how fast that happens depends on the state of the economy. *When the economy is growing, both unemployment rates and the average duration of unemployment decline.* Recessions have the opposite effect—raising both the rate and the duration of unemployment.

Reasons for Unemployment

The reason a person becomes unemployed also affects the length of time the person stays jobless. A person just entering the labor market might need more time to identify job openings and develop job contacts. By contrast, an autoworker laid off for a temporary plant closing can expect to return to work quickly. Figure 6.5 depicts these and other reasons for unemployment. In 2016 roughly 1 of every 2 unemployed persons was a job loser (laid off or fired), and only 1 in 9 was a job leaver (quit). The rest were new entrants (primarily teenagers) or reentrants (primarily mothers returning to the workforce). Like the duration of unemployment, the reasons for joblessness are very sensitive to economic conditions. In really bad years like 2008–2010, most of the unemployed are job losers, and they remain out of work a long time.

Discouraged Workers

Unemployment statistics don't tell the complete story about the human costs of a sluggish economy. When unemployment persists, job seekers become increasingly frustrated. After repeated rejections, job seekers often get so discouraged that they give up the search and turn

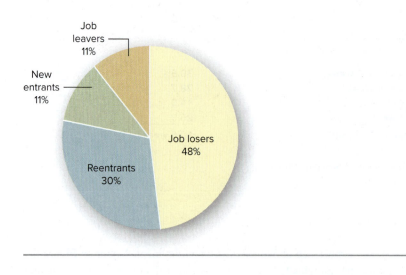

FIGURE 6.5

Reasons for Unemployment

People become unemployed for various reasons. Roughly half of the unemployed in 2016 were job losers. About 40 percent of the unemployed were entering or reentering the labor market in search of a job. In recessions, the proportion of job losers shoots up.

Source: U.S. Labor Department.

discouraged worker: An individual who isn't actively seeking employment but would look for or accept a job if one were available.

underemployment: People seeking full-time paid employment who work only part-time or are employed at jobs below their capability.

to their families, friends, or public welfare for income support. When the Census Bureau interviewer asks whether they're actively seeking employment, such **discouraged workers** are apt to reply no. Yet they'd like to be working, and they'd probably be out looking for work if job prospects were better.

Discouraged workers aren't counted as part of our unemployment problem because they're technically out of the labor force. The Labor Department estimates that nearly 600,000 individuals fell into this uncounted class of discouraged workers in 2016. That's on top of the 7.75 million officially counted as unemployed because they were still actively seeking jobs. In years of lower unemployment, this number declines sharply.

Underemployment

Some people can't afford to be discouraged. Many people who become jobless have family responsibilities and bills to pay: they simply can't afford to drop out of the labor force. Instead they're compelled to take some job—any job—just to keep body and soul together. The resultant job may be part-time or full-time and may pay very little. Nevertheless, any paid employment is sufficient to exclude the person from the count of the unemployed, though not from a condition of **underemployment.**

Underemployed workers represent labor resources that aren't being fully utilized. They're part of our unemployment problem, even if they're not officially counted as *unemployed.* In 2016, nearly 6 million workers were underemployed in the U.S. economy.

The Phantom Unemployed

Although discouraged and underemployed workers aren't counted in official unemployment statistics, some of the people who *are* counted probably shouldn't be. Many people report that they're actively seeking a job even when they have little interest in finding employment. To some extent, public policy actually encourages such behavior. For example, welfare recipients are often required to look for a job, even though some welfare mothers would prefer to spend all their time raising their children. Their resultant job search is likely to be perfunctory at best. Similarly, most states require people receiving unemployment benefits (see In the News "Unemployment Benefits Not for Everyone") to provide evidence that they're looking for a job, even though some recipients may prefer a brief period of joblessness. Here again, reported unemployment may conceal labor force nonparticipation.

IN THE NEWS

UNEMPLOYMENT BENEFITS NOT FOR EVERYONE

In 2016, more than 16 million people collected unemployment benefits averaging $344 per week. But don't rush to the state unemployment office yet—not all unemployed people are eligible.

To qualify for weekly unemployment benefits you must have worked a substantial length of time and earned some minimum amount of wages, both determined by your state. Furthermore, you must have a "good" reason for having lost your last job. Most states will not provide benefits to students (or their professors!) during summer vacations, to professional athletes in the off-season, or to individuals who quit their last jobs.

If you qualify for benefits, the amount of benefits you receive each week will depend on your previous wages. In most states the benefits are equal to about one-half of the previous weekly wage, up to a state-determined maximum. The maximum benefit in 2016 ranged from $235 in Mississippi to a high of $742 in Massachusetts.

Unemployment benefits are financed by a tax on employers and can continue for as long as 26 weeks. During periods of high unemployment, eligibility may be extended another 13 weeks or more by the U.S. Congress. In 2010–2011, benefits were available for up to 99 weeks.

Source: U.S. Employment and Training Administration.

ANALYSIS: Some of the income lost due to unemployment is replaced by unemployment insurance benefits. Not all unemployed persons are eligible, however, and the duration of benefits is limited.

THE HUMAN COSTS

Our measures of unemployment are a valuable index to a serious macro problem. However, they don't adequately convey how devastating unemployment can be for individual workers and their families.

Lost Income. The most visible impact of unemployment on individuals is the loss of income. Even short spells of joblessness can force families to tighten their belts and fall behind on bills (see In the News "The Real Costs of Joblessness"). For workers who've been unemployed for long periods, such losses can spell financial disaster. Typically, an unemployed person must rely on a combination of savings, income from other family members, and government unemployment benefits for financial support. After these sources of support are exhausted, public welfare is often the only legal support left.

Lost Confidence. Not all unemployed people experience such a financial disaster, of course. College students who fail to find summer employment are unlikely to end up on welfare the following semester. Similarly, teenagers and others looking for part-time employment won't suffer great economic losses from unemployment. Nevertheless, the experience of unemployment—of not being able to find a job when you want one—can be painful. This sensation isn't easily forgotten, even after one has finally found employment.

Social Stress. It is difficult to measure all the intangible effects of unemployment on individual workers. Studies have shown, however, that joblessness causes more crime, more health problems, more divorces, and other problems (see In the News "The Real Costs of Joblessness"). Such findings underscore the notion that prolonged unemployment poses a real danger. Like George H., the worker discussed at the beginning of this chapter, many unemployed workers simply can't cope with the resulting stress. Thomas Cottle, a lecturer at Harvard Medical School, stated the case more bluntly: "I'm now convinced that unemployment is *the* killer disease in this country—responsible for wife beating, infertility, and even tooth decay."

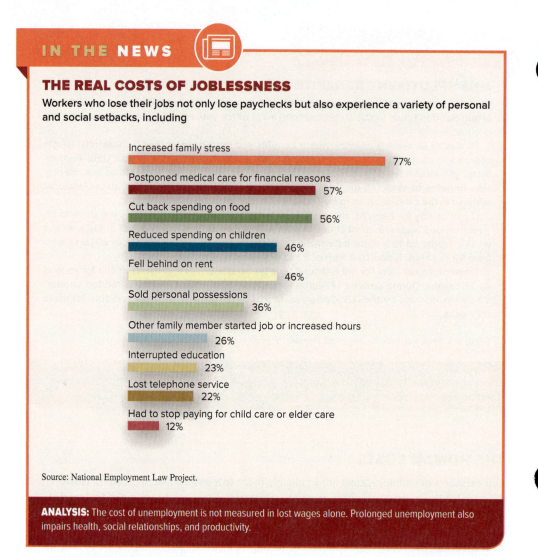

IN THE NEWS

THE REAL COSTS OF JOBLESSNESS

Workers who lose their jobs not only lose paychecks but also experience a variety of personal and social setbacks, including

Increased family stress — 77%

Postponed medical care for financial reasons — 57%

Cut back spending on food — 56%

Reduced spending on children — 46%

Fell behind on rent — 46%

Sold personal possessions — 36%

Other family member started job or increased hours — 26%

Interrupted education — 23%

Lost telephone service — 22%

Had to stop paying for child care or elder care — 12%

Source: National Employment Law Project.

ANALYSIS: The cost of unemployment is not measured in lost wages alone. Prolonged unemployment also impairs health, social relationships, and productivity.

Lost Lives. German psychiatrists have also observed that unemployment can be hazardous to your health. They estimate that the anxieties and other nervous disorders that accompany one year of unemployment can reduce life expectancy by as much as five years. In Japan, the suicide rate jumped by more than 50 percent when the economy plunged into recession. In New Zealand, suicide rates are twice as high for unemployed workers as they are for employed ones. A University of Oxford study estimated that the economic downturn of 2008–2010 triggered more than 10,000 suicides in the United States and Europe.

DEFINING FULL EMPLOYMENT

In view of the economic and social losses associated with unemployment, it's not surprising that *full employment* is one of our basic macroeconomic goals. You may be surprised to learn, however, that *"full" employment isn't the same thing as "zero" unemployment.* There are in fact several reasons for regarding some degree of unemployment as inevitable and even desirable.

Seasonal Unemployment

Some joblessness is virtually inevitable as long as we continue to grow crops, build houses, or go skiing at certain seasons of the year. At the end of each such season, thousands of workers must go searching for new jobs, experiencing some **seasonal unemployment** in the process.

Seasonal fluctuations also arise on the supply side of the labor market. Teenage unemployment rates, for example, rise sharply in the summer as students look for temporary jobs. To avoid such unemployment completely, we'd either have to keep everyone in school or ensure that all students went immediately from the classroom to the workroom. Neither alternative is likely, much less desirable.[1]

seasonal unemployment:
Unemployment due to seasonal changes in employment or labor supply.

Frictional Unemployment

There are other reasons for expecting a certain amount of unemployment. Many workers have sound financial or personal reasons for leaving one job to look for another. In the process of moving from one job to another, a person may well miss a few days or even weeks of work without any serious personal or social consequences. On the contrary, people who spend more time looking for work may find *better* jobs.

The same is true of students first entering the labor market. It's not likely that you'll find a job the moment you leave school. Nor should you necessarily take the first job offered. If you spend some time looking for work, you're more likely to find a job you like. The job search period gives you an opportunity to find out what kinds of jobs are available, what skills they require, and what they pay. Accordingly, a brief period of job search may benefit labor market entrants and the larger economy. The unemployment associated with these kinds of job searches is referred to as **frictional unemployment.**

Three factors distinguish frictional unemployment from other kinds of unemployment. First, enough jobs exist for those who are frictionally unemployed—that is, there's adequate *demand* for labor. Second, individuals who are frictionally unemployed have the skills required for available jobs. Third, the period of job search will be relatively short. Under these conditions, frictional unemployment resembles an unconventional game of musical chairs. There are enough chairs of the right size for everyone, and people dance around them for only a brief period.

No one knows for sure just how much of our unemployment problem is frictional. Most economists agree, however, that friction alone is responsible for an unemployment rate of 2 to 3 percent. Accordingly, our definition of *"full employment"* should allow for at least this much unemployment.

frictional unemployment:
Brief periods of unemployment experienced by people moving between jobs or into the labor market.

Structural Unemployment

For many job seekers, the period between jobs may drag on for months or even years because they don't have the skills that employers require. Imagine, for example, the predicament of steelworkers. During the 1980s, the steel industry contracted as consumers demanded fewer and lighter-weight cars and as construction of highways, bridges, and buildings slowed. In the process, more than 300,000 steelworkers lost their jobs. Most of these workers had a decade or more of experience and substantial skill. But the skills they'd perfected were no longer in demand. They couldn't perform the jobs available in computer software, biotechnology, or other expanding industries. Although there were enough job vacancies in the labor market, the steelworkers couldn't fill them. These workers were victims of **structural unemployment.**

The same kind of structural displacement hit the construction industry from 2007 to 2010. The housing market collapsed, leaving millions of homes unsold and even unfinished. Tens of thousands of carpenters, electricians, and plumbers lost their jobs. These displaced

structural unemployment:
Unemployment caused by a mismatch between the skills (or location) of job seekers and the requirements (or location) of available jobs.

---

[1]Seasonal variations in employment and labor supply not only create some unemployment in the annual averages but also distort monthly comparisons. Unemployment rates are always higher in February (when farming and housing construction come to a virtual standstill) and June (when a mass of students goes looking for summer jobs). The Labor Department adjusts monthly unemployment rates according to this seasonal pattern and reports "seasonally adjusted" unemployment rates for each month. Seasonal adjustments don't alter *annual* averages, however.

workers soon discovered that their highly developed skills were no longer in demand. They couldn't fill job openings in the growing health care, financial, or Internet industries.

Teenagers from urban slums also suffer from structural unemployment. Most poor teenagers have an inadequate education, few job-related skills, and little work experience. For them, almost all decent jobs are "out of reach." As a consequence, they remain unemployed far longer than can be explained by frictional forces.

Structural unemployment violates the second condition for frictional unemployment: that the job seekers can perform the available jobs. Structural unemployment is analogous to a musical chairs game in which there are enough chairs for everyone, but some of them are too small to sit on. It's a more serious concern than frictional unemployment and incompatible with any notion of full employment.

Cyclical Unemployment

cyclical unemployment:
Unemployment attributable to a lack of job vacancies—that is, to an inadequate level of aggregate demand.

The fourth type of unemployment is **cyclical unemployment**—joblessness that occurs when there simply aren't enough jobs to go around. Cyclical unemployment exists when the number of workers demanded falls short of the number of persons supplied (in the labor force). This isn't a case of mobility between jobs (frictional unemployment) or even of job seekers' skills (structural unemployment). Rather, it's simply an inadequate level of demand for goods and services and thus for labor. Cyclical unemployment resembles the most familiar form of musical chairs, in which the number of chairs is always less than the number of players.

The Great Depression is the most striking example of cyclical unemployment. The dramatic increase in unemployment rates that began in 1930 (see Figure 6.6) wasn't due to any increase in friction or sudden decline in workers' skills. Instead the high rates of unemployment that persisted for a *decade* were caused by a sudden decline in the market demand for goods and services. How do we know? Just notice what happened to our unemployment rate when the demand for military goods and services increased in 1941!

Slow Growth. Cyclical unemployment can emerge even when the economy is expanding. Keep in mind that the labor force is always growing due to population growth and continuing immigration. If these additional labor force participants are to find jobs, the economy

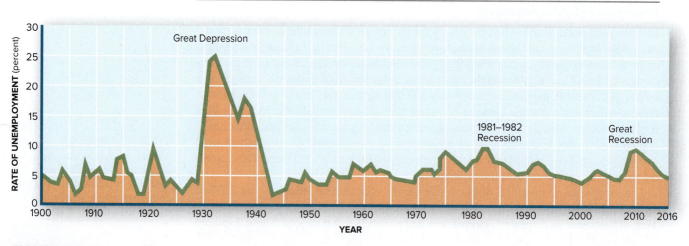

FIGURE 6.6

The Unemployment Record

Unemployment rates reached record heights (25 percent) during the Great Depression. In more recent decades, the unemployment rate has varied from 4 percent in full-employment years to 10 percent in the recession years of 1982 and 2009. Keeping the labor force fully employed is a primary macro policy goal.

Source: U.S. Labor Department.

must grow. Specifically, ***the economy must grow at least as fast as the labor force to avoid cyclical unemployment.*** When economic growth slows below this threshold, unemployment rates start to rise.

The Full-Employment Goal

In later chapters we examine the causes of cyclical unemployment and explore some potential policy responses. At this point, however, we just want to establish a macro policy goal. In the Employment Act of 1946, Congress committed the federal government to pursue a goal of "maximum" employment but didn't specify exactly what that rate was. Presumably, this meant avoiding as much cyclical and structural unemployment as possible while keeping frictional unemployment within reasonable bounds. As guidelines for public policy, these perspectives are a bit vague.

Inflationary Pressures. The first attempt to define *full employment* more precisely was undertaken in the early 1960s. At that time the Council of Economic Advisers (itself created by the Employment Act of 1946) decided that our proximity to full employment could be gauged by watching *prices.* As the economy approached its production possibilities, labor and other resources would become increasingly scarce. As market participants bid for these remaining resources, wages and prices would start to rise. Hence ***rising prices are a signal that employment is nearing capacity.***

After examining the relationship between unemployment and inflation, the Council of Economic Advisers decided to peg full employment at 4 percent unemployment. The unemployment rate could fall below 4 percent. If it did, however, price levels would begin to rise at an accelerating rate. Hence this threshold came to be regarded as an **inflationary flashpoint:** a level of output that would trigger too much inflation. Thus 4 percent unemployment was seen as an acceptable compromise of our employment and price goals.

During the 1970s and early 1980s, this view of our full-employment potential was considered overly optimistic. Unemployment rates stayed far above 4 percent, even when the economy expanded. Moreover, inflation began to accelerate at higher levels of unemployment.

In view of these factors, the Council of Economic Advisers later raised the level of unemployment thought to be compatible with price stability. In 1983 the Reagan administration concluded that the "inflation-threshold" unemployment rate was between 6 and 7 percent.

Changed Labor Force. The quest for low unemployment got easier in the 1990s, largely due to changes in the labor force. The number of teenagers declined by 3 million between 1981 and 1993. The upsurge in women's participation in the labor force also leveled off. High school and college attendance and graduation rates increased. And welfare programs were reformed in ways that encouraged more work. All these structural changes made it easier to reduce unemployment rates without increasing inflation. As a result, the unemployment-rate threshold for **full employment** was set at 4–6 percent. Hence, we recognize that ***full employment entails 4–6 percent unemployment, not zero percent unemployment.***

The "Natural" Rate of Unemployment

The ambiguity about which rate of unemployment might trigger an upsurge in inflation has convinced some analysts to abandon the inflation-based concept of full employment. They prefer to specify a "natural" rate of unemployment that doesn't depend on inflation trends. In this view, the natural rate of unemployment consists of frictional and structural components only. It's the rate of unemployment that will prevail in the long run. In the short run, both the unemployment rate and the inflation rate may go up and down. However, the economy will tend to gravitate toward the long-run **natural rate of unemployment.**

inflationary flashpoint: The rate of output at which inflationary pressures intensify; the point on the AS curve where slope increases sharply.

full employment: The lowest rate of unemployment compatible with price stability, variously estimated at between 4 percent and 6 percent unemployment.

natural rate of unemployment: The long-term rate of unemployment determined by structural forces in labor and product markets.

Although the natural rate concept avoids specifying a short-term inflation trigger, it too is subject to debate. As we've seen, the *structural* determinants of unemployment (e.g., age and composition of the labor force) change over time. When structural forces change, the level of natural unemployment presumably changes as well.

Congressional Targets

Although most economists agree that an unemployment rate of 4–6 percent is consistent with either natural or full employment, Congress has set tougher goals for macro policy. According to the Full Employment and Balanced Growth Act of 1978 (commonly called the Humphrey-Hawkins Act), our national goal is to attain a 4 percent rate of unemployment. The act also requires a goal of 3 percent inflation. There was an escape clause, however. In the event that both goals couldn't be met, the president could set higher, provisional definitions of full employment.

THE HISTORICAL RECORD

Our greatest failure to achieve full employment occurred during the Great Depression. As Figure 6.6 shows, as much as one-fourth of the labor force was unemployed in the 1930s.

Unemployment rates fell dramatically during World War II. In 1944 virtually anyone who was ready and willing to work quickly found a job; the civilian unemployment rate hit a rock-bottom 1.2 percent.

Since 1950 the unemployment rate has fluctuated from a low of 2.8 percent during the Korean War (1953) to a high of 10.8 percent during the 1981–1982 recession. From 1982 to 1989 the unemployment rate receded, but it shot up again in the 1990–1991 recession.

From 1995 to 2007 the unemployment rate stayed in a fairly narrow range and actually dipped below 5 percent in 2007. But the Great Recession of 2008–2009 wiped out that gain, sending the unemployment rate to near-record heights once again (see In the News "Unemployment Rate Hits a 26-Year High"). The unemployment rate started declining as the economy recovered, but the return to full employment was agonizingly slow.

IN THE NEWS

UNEMPLOYMENT RATE HITS A 26-YEAR HIGH

The nation's unemployment rate climbed to 10.2 percent in October, the highest rate since 1983. Nonfarm payrolls dropped another 190,000 last month, adding to 22 consecutive months of job losses. The biggest job losses were in manufacturing, construction, and retail employment.

Since the recession began over 7.3 million jobs have been lost. The unemployment rate has more than doubled from 4.9 percent in December 2007 to its current level of 10.2 percent.

In October, 35.6 percent of unemployed persons were jobless for 27 weeks or more, while 20 percent of the unemployed were jobless for 5 weeks or less.

Among the major worker groups, the unemployment rates for adult men (10.7 percent) and whites (9.5 percent) rose in October. The jobless rates for adult women (8.1 percent), teenagers (27.6 percent), blacks (15.7 percent), and Hispanics (13.1 percent) were little changed over the month.

Source: U.S. Bureau of Labor Statistics, November 10, 2009.

ANALYSIS: When the economy contracts, millions of workers lose jobs, and the unemployment rate rises—sometimes sharply.

THE ECONOMY TOMORROW

OUTSOURCING JOBS

To keep unemployment rates low in the economy tomorrow, job growth in U.S. product markets must exceed labor force growth. As we've observed, this will require at least 2 million *new* jobs every year. Achieving that net job growth is made more difficult when U.S. firms shut down their U.S. operations and relocate production to Mexico, China, and other foreign nations. President Trump vowed to make it more difficult and expensive for American firms to engage in that kind of **outsourcing** (see In the News "Trump Blasts Outsourcing of Jobs").

outsourcing: The relocation of production to foreign countries.

Cheap Labor. Low wages are the primary motivation for all this outsourcing. Telephone operators and clerks in India are paid a tenth as much as are their U.S. counterparts. Indian accountants and paralegals get paid less than half the wages of their U.S. counterparts. Polish workers are even cheaper. With cheap, high-speed telecommunications, that off-shore labor is an attractive substitute for U.S. workers. Over the next 10 years, more than 3 million U.S. jobs are expected to move offshore in response to such wage differentials.

Small Numbers. In the short run, outsourcing clearly worsens the U.S. employment outlook. But there's a lot more to the story. To begin with, the total number of outsourced jobs averages less than 300,000 per year. That amounts to only 0.002 percent of all U.S. jobs and only 3 percent of total U.S. *un*employment. So even in the worst case, outsourcing can't be a major explanation for U.S. unemployment.

Insourcing. We also have to recognize that outsourcing of U.S. jobs has a counterpart in the "insourcing" of foreign production. The German Mercedes Benz company builds cars in Alabama to reduce production and distribution costs. In the process German autoworkers lose some jobs to U.S. autoworkers. In addition to this direct investment, foreign nations and firms hire U.S. workers to design, build, and deliver a wide variety of products. In other words, *trade in both products and labor resources is a two-way street.* Looking at the flow of jobs in only one direction distorts the jobs picture.

Productivity and Growth. Even the gross flow of outsourced jobs is not all bad. The cost savings realized by U.S. firms due to outsourcing increase U.S. profits. Those profits may finance new investment or consumption in U.S. product markets, thereby creating new jobs. more jobs may be gained than lost as a result. Outsourcing routine tasks to foreign workers also raises the productivity of U.S. workers by allowing U.S. workers to focus on more complex and high-value tasks. In other words, outsourcing promotes specialization and higher productivity both here and abroad. *Production possibilities expand, not contract, with outsourcing.*

Consumer Spending. Outsourcing also has an impact on the *demand* side of the market. When outsourcing leads to lower prices for flat-screen TVs, consumers end up spending less on televisions. What do they do with their savings? Typically, they spend the money they saved on their TV purchase by buying something else. So, demand for *other* goods and services increases, leading to more jobs in other industries. That is the nature of a dynamic economy.

Creating Jobs. Workers whose jobs are outsourced won't be consoled by the thought that jobs are being created in other industries. They care about their jobs and income, not what's happening in other industries, much less to the nation's production-possibilities curve. So, they will oppose outsourcing in almost every case. The challenge for economic policy is to keep creating jobs fast enough so that the displaced workers can find new jobs relatively quickly. Stopping the outsourcing of jobs won't achieve our full-employment goal—and may even worsen income and job prospects in the economy tomorrow.

IN THE NEWS

TRUMP BLASTS OUTSOURCING OF JOBS

President-elect Trump launched a Twitter storm at companies that outsource jobs. During the election campaign he vowed to "bring jobs back home" from outsourced factories in Mexico, China, and elsewhere. In a burst of tweets on Sunday morning, Trump threatened that "any business that leaves our country for another country, fires its employees, builds a new factory or plant in the other country, and then thinks it will sell its product back into the U.S. without retribution or consequence, is WRONG! There will be a tax on our soon-to-be-strong border of 35 percent for these companies wanting to sell their products, cars, A.C. units etc., back across the border. This tax will make leaving financially difficult..."

Source: News accounts of December 4, 2016.

©REUTERS/Alamy Stock Photo

ANALYSIS: Outsourcing often causes visible job losses at specific factories and stores. But outsourcing may also create jobs through cost savings, higher productivity, and changing consumption patterns.

SUMMARY

- To understand unemployment, we must distinguish the labor force from the larger population. Only people who are working (employed) or spend some time looking for a job (unemployed) are participants in the labor force. People neither working nor looking for work are outside the labor force.   **LO6-1**
- The labor force grows every year due to population growth and immigration. This growth increases production possibilities but also necessitates continued job creation.   **LO6-1**
- The economy (output) must grow at least as fast as the labor force to keep the unemployment rate from rising. Unemployment implies that we're producing inside the production possibilities curve rather than on it.   **LO6-1**
- The macroeconomic loss imposed by unemployment is reduced output of goods and services. Okun's Law suggests that 1 percentage point in unemployment is equivalent to a 2 percentage point decline in output.   **LO6-2**
- The human cost of unemployment includes not only financial losses but social, physical, and psychological costs as well.   **LO6-2**
- Unemployment is distributed unevenly: minorities, teenagers, and the less educated have much higher rates of

unemployment. Also hurt are discouraged workers—those who've stopped looking for work—and those working at part-time or menial jobs because they can't find full-time jobs equal to their training or potential.   **LO6-1**
- There are four types of unemployment: seasonal, frictional, structural, and cyclical.   **LO6-3**
- Because some seasonal and frictional unemployment is inevitable and even desirable, full employment is not defined as zero unemployment. These considerations, plus fear of inflationary consequences, result in full employment being defined as an unemployment rate of 4–6 percent.   **LO6-4**
- The natural rate of unemployment is based on frictional and structural forces, without reference to short-term price (inflation) pressures.   **LO6-4**
- Unemployment rates got as high as 25 percent in the 1930s. Since 1960 the unemployment rate has ranged from 3.4 to 10.8 percent.   **LO6-1**
- Outsourcing of U.S. production directly reduces domestic employment. But the indirect effects of higher U.S. productivity, profits, and global competitiveness may create even more jobs.   **LO6-3**

Key Terms

labor force
labor force participation rate
production possibilities
unemployment
Okun's law
unemployment rate

discouraged worker
underemployment
seasonal unemployment
frictional unemployment
structural unemployment
cyclical unemployment

inflationary flashpoint
full employment
natural rate of unemployment
outsourcing

Questions for Discussion

1. Is it possible for unemployment rates to increase at the same time that the number of employed persons is increasing? How? **LO6-1**

2. If more teenagers stay in school longer, what happens to (*a*) production possibilities? (*b*) unemployment rates? **LO6-1**

3. When the housing industry implodes, what do construction workers do? **LO6-3**

4. Should the government replace the wages of anyone who is unemployed? How might this affect output and unemployment? **LO6-3**

5. When the GE lightbulb plant in Virginia closed (see Chapter introduction), how was the local economy affected? **LO6-2**

6. Why is frictional unemployment deemed desirable? **LO6-3**

7. Why do people expect inflation to heat up when the unemployment rate approaches 4 percent? **LO6-4**

8. Identify (*a*) two jobs at your school that could be outsourced and (*b*) two jobs that would be hard to outsource. **LO6-4**

9. President Trump suggested that Apple corporation should move its iPhone manufacturing back from China into the United States. Is this a good idea? What impact would it have on employment, wages, and prices? **LO6-4**

10. How can the outsourcing of U.S. computer jobs generate new U.S. jobs in construction or retail trade? (See In the News "Outsourcing May Create U.S. Jobs.") **LO6-4**

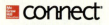

LO6-1 1. According to Figure 6.1,
    (*a*) What percentage of the civilian labor force was employed?
    (*b*) What percentage of the civilian labor force was unemployed?
    (*c*) What percentage of the *population* was employed in civilian jobs?

LO6-1 2. If the unemployment rate in 2016 had been 4.5 percent instead of 4.9 percent (Figure 6.1),
    (*a*) How many more workers would have been employed?
    (*b*) How many fewer would have been unemployed?

LO6-1 3. Between 2000 and 2016 (see Data Tables), by how much did
    (*a*) the labor force change?
    (*b*) unemployment change?
    (*c*) employment change?

LO6-1 4. If the labor force of 160 million people is growing by 1.2 percent this year, how many new jobs have to be created each month to keep unemployment from increasing?

LO6-1 5. Between 1980 and 2015, by how much did the labor force participation rate (Figure 6.2) of
    (*a*) Men change?
    (*b*) Women change?

LO6-2 6. According to Okun's law, how much output (real GDP) was lost in 2009 when the nation's unemployment rate increased from 5.8 percent to 9.8 percent?

LO6-1 7. Suppose the following data describe a nation's population:

	Year 1	Year 2
Population	320 million	330 million
Labor force	150 million	160 million
Unemployment rate	6 percent	6 percent

    (*a*) How many people are unemployed in each year?
    (*b*) How many people are employed in each year?

LO6-1 8. Based on the data in the previous problem, in Year 2, what happens to each of the following when 1 million job seekers become "discouraged workers"?
    (*a*) Number of unemployed persons.
    (*b*) Unemployment rate.
    (*c*) Number of employed persons.

LO6-1 9. According to In the News "Unemployment Rate Hits a 26-Year High," in October 2009
    (*a*) How many people were in the labor force?
    (*b*) How many people were employed?

LO6-1 10. In 2016, how many of the 700,000 black teenagers who participated in the labor market
    (*a*) Were unemployed?
    (*b*) Were employed?
    (*c*) Would have been employed if they had the same unemployment rate as white teenagers?
    (See Figure 6.4 for needed info.)

LO6-4 11. On a graph, illustrate both the unemployment rate and the real GDP growth rate for 2006-2016. (The data required for this exercise can be found in the Data Tables at the end of the book.)
    (*a*) In how many years was "full employment" achieved? (Use the current benchmark.)
    (*b*) Unemployment and growth rates tend to move in opposite directions. Which appears to change direction first?
    (*c*) In how many years does the unemployment rate increase even when output is increasing?

PROBLEMS FOR CHAPTER 6 (cont'd)

LO6-4 12. (*a*) What was the unemployment rate in 2016?

(*b*) How many more jobs were needed to bring the unemployment rate down to the 4 percent low-end of the unemployment threshold?

LO6-3 13. The Economy Tomorrow: For each situation described here, determine the type of unemployment:

(*a*) Steelworkers losing their jobs due to outsourcing.

(*b*) A college graduate waiting to accept a job that allows her to utilize her level of education.

(*c*) The Great Recession of 2008–2009.

(*d*) A homemaker entering the labor force.

©Brand X Pictures/Getty Images RF

Inflation

Germany set a record in 1923 that no other nation wants to beat. In that year, prices in Germany rose a *trillion* times over. Prices rose so fast that workers took "shopping breaks" to spend their twice-a-day paychecks before they became worthless. Menu prices in restaurants rose while people were still eating! Accumulated savings became worthless, as did outstanding loans. People needed sacks of currency to buy bread, butter, and other staples. With prices more than doubling every *day,* no one could afford to save, invest, lend money, or make long-term plans. In the frenzy of escalating prices, production of goods and services came to a halt, unemployment rose tenfold, and the German economy all but collapsed.

Hungary had a similar episode of runaway inflation in 1946, as did Japan. More recently, Venezuela, Russia, Bulgaria, Brazil, Zaire, Yugoslavia, Argentina, and Uruguay have all witnessed at least a tenfold jump in prices in a single year. Zimbabwe came close to breaking Germany's record in 2008, with an inflation rate of *231 million* percent (see World View "Zimbabwe's Trillion-Dollar Currency.")

The United States has never experienced such a price frenzy. During the Revolutionary War, prices did double in one year, but that was a singular event. In the last decade, U.S. prices have risen only 0 to 4 percent a year. Despite this enviable record, Americans still worry a lot about inflation. In response to this anxiety, every president since Franklin Roosevelt has expressed a determination to keep prices from rising. In 1971 the Nixon administration took drastic action to stop inflation. With prices rising an average of only 3 percent, President Nixon imposed price controls on U.S. producers to keep prices from rising any faster. For 90 days all wages and prices were frozen by law—price increases were prohibited. For three more years, wage and price increases were limited by legal rules.

In 1990 U.S. prices were rising at a 6 percent clip—twice the pace that triggered the 1971–1974 wage and price controls. Calling such price increases "unacceptable," Federal Reserve Chairman Alan Greenspan set a goal of *zero* percent inflation. In pursuit of that goal, the Fed slowed economic growth so much that the economy fell into a recession. The Fed did the same thing again in early 2000.

In later chapters we'll examine how the Fed and other policymakers slow the economy down or speed it up. Before looking at the levers of macro policy, however, we need to examine our policy goals. Why is inflation so feared? How much inflation is unacceptable? To get a handle on this basic issue, we'll ask and answer the following questions:

- **What kind of price increases are referred to as *inflation*?**
- **Who is hurt (or helped) by inflation?**
- **What is an appropriate goal for *price stability*?**

As we'll discover, inflation is a serious problem, but not for the reasons most people cite. We'll also see why deflation—falling prices—isn't so welcome either.

WHAT IS INFLATION?

Most people associate **inflation** with price increases for specific goods and services. The economy isn't necessarily experiencing inflation, however, every time the price of a cup of coffee goes up. We must distinguish the phenomenon of inflation from price increases for specific goods. *Inflation is an increase in the average level of prices, not a change in any specific price.*

inflation: An increase in the average level of prices of goods and services.

The Average Price

Suppose you wanted to know the average price of fruit in the supermarket. Surely you wouldn't have much success in seeking out an average fruit—nobody would be quite sure what you had in mind. You might have some success, however, if you sought out the prices of apples, oranges, cherries, and peaches. Knowing the price of each kind of fruit, you could then compute the average price of fruit. The resultant figure wouldn't refer to any particular product but would convey a sense of how much a typical basket of fruit might cost. By repeating these calculations every day, you could then determine whether fruit prices, *on average,* were changing. On occasion, you might even notice that apple prices rose while orange prices fell, leaving the *average* price of fruit unchanged.

The same kinds of calculations are made to measure inflation in the entire economy. We first determine the average price of all output—the average price level—and then look for changes in that average. A rise in the average price level is referred to as inflation.

The average price level may fall as well as rise. A decline in average prices—**deflation**—occurs when price decreases on some goods and services outweigh price increases on all others. This happened in Japan in 1995 and again in 2003. Such deflations are rare, however: The United States has not experienced any general deflation since 1940.

deflation: A decrease in the average level of prices of goods and services.

Relative Prices vs. the Price Level

Because inflation and deflation are measured in terms of average price levels, it's possible for individual prices to rise or fall continuously without changing the average price level. We already noted, for example, that the price of apples can rise without increasing the average price of fruit, so long as the price of some other fruit, such as oranges, falls. In such circumstances, **relative prices** are changing, but not *average* prices. An increase in the *relative* price of apples simply means that apples have become more expensive in comparison with other fruits (or any other goods or services).

relative price: The price of one good in comparison with the price of other goods.

Changes in relative prices may occur in a period of stable average prices, or in periods of inflation or deflation. In fact, in an economy as vast as ours—in which literally millions of goods and services are exchanged in the factor and product markets—*relative prices are always changing.* Indeed, relative price changes are an essential ingredient of the market mechanism. Recall from Chapter 3 what happens when the market price of web design services rises relative to other goods and services. This (relative) price rise alerts web architects (producers) to increase their output, cutting back on other production or leisure activities.

A general inflation—an increase in the *average* price level—doesn't perform this same market function. If all prices rise at the same rate, price increases for specific goods are of little value as market signals. In less extreme cases, when most but not all prices are rising, changes in relative prices do occur but aren't so immediately apparent. Table 7.1 reminds us that some prices fall even during periods of general inflation.

TABLE 7.1

Prices That Have Fallen

Inflation refers to an increase in the *average* price level. It doesn't mean that *all* prices are rising. In fact, many prices fall, even during periods of general inflation.

Item	Early Price	2017 Price
Long-distance telephone call (per minute)	$ 6.90 (1915)	$ 0.02
Pocket electronic calculator	200.00 (1972)	1.99
Digital watch	2,000.00 (1972)	1.99
Pantyhose	2.16 (1967)	1.29
Ballpoint pen	0.89 (1965)	0.29
DVD player	800.00 (1997)	27.88
Laptop computer	3,500.00 (1986)	149.99
Airfare (New York–Paris)	490.00 (1958)	244.50
Microwave oven	400.00 (1972)	35.00
Contact lenses	275.00 (1972)	15.79
Television (19-inch, color)	469.00 (1980)	100.19
Compact disk player	1,000.00 (1985)	4.89
Digital camera	748.00 (1994)	33.96
Digital music player (MP3)	399.00 (2001)	1.51
Cell phone	3,595.00 (1983)	9.99
Smartphone	400.00 (1999)	27.00
E-reader	398.00 (2007)	19.99

REDISTRIBUTIVE EFFECTS OF INFLATION

The distinction between relative and average prices helps us determine who's hurt by inflation—and who's helped. Popular opinion notwithstanding, it's simply not true that everyone is worse off when prices rise. ***Although inflation makes some people worse off, it makes other people better off.*** Some people even get rich when prices rise! The micro consequences of inflation are reflected in redistributions of income and wealth, not general declines in either measure of our economic welfare. These redistributions occur because people buy different combinations of goods and services, own different assets, and sell distinct goods or services (including labor). The impact of inflation on individuals therefore depends on how prices change for the goods and services each person actually buys or sells.

Price Effects

Price changes are the most visible consequence of inflation. If you've been paying tuition, you know how painful a price hike can be. Fifteen years ago the average tuition at public colleges and universities was $1,000 per year. Today the average tuition exceeds $9,600 for in-state residents. At private universities, tuition has increased eightfold in the past 10 years, to more than $33,000 (see In the News "College Tuition Up Again"). You don't need a whole course in economics to figure out the implications of these tuition hikes. To stay in college, you (or your parents) must forgo increasing amounts of other goods and services. You end up being worse off since you can't buy as many goods and services as you could before tuition went up.

IN THE NEWS

COLLEGE TUITION UP AGAIN

College gets more expensive—again. In-state tuition at public four-year colleges rose 2.4 percent in 2016–2017, to an average of $9,650 per year. Out-of-state students paid an average of $24,930 to attend.

Private four-year colleges also saw even bigger price hikes: 3.6 percent—to an average of $33,480. Tuition prices have been outpacing general inflation rates for many years.

Source: The College Board.

ANALYSIS: Tuition increases reduce the real income of students. How much you suffer from inflation depends on what happens to the prices of the products you purchase.

The effect of tuition increases on your economic welfare is reflected in the distinction between nominal income and real income. **Nominal income** is the amount of money you receive in a particular time period; it's measured in current dollars. **Real income,** by contrast, is the purchasing power of that money, as measured by the quantity of goods and services your dollars will buy. If the number of dollars you receive every year is always the same, your *nominal income* doesn't change—but your *real income* will rise or fall with price changes.

Suppose your parents agree to give you $8,000 a year while you're in school. Out of that $8,000 you must pay for your tuition, room and board, books, and everything else. The budget for your first year at school might look like this:

FIRST YEAR'S BUDGET

Nominal income		$8,000
Consumption		
Tuition	$4,000	
Room and board	2,600	
Books	600	
Everything else	800	
Total		$8,000

After paying for all your essential expenses, you have $800 to spend on clothes, entertainment, or anything else you want. That's not exactly living high, but it's not poverty.

Now suppose tuition increases to $4,500 in your second year, while all other prices remain the same. What will happen to your nominal income? Nothing. Unless your parents take pity on you, you'll still be getting $8,000 a year. Your nominal income is unchanged. Your *real* income, however, will suffer. This is evident in the second year's budget:

SECOND YEAR'S BUDGET

Nominal income		$8,000
Consumption		
Tuition	$4,500	
Room and board	2,600	
Books	600	
Everything else	300	
Total		$8,000

You now have to use more of your income to pay tuition. This means you have less income to spend on other things. Since room and board and books still cost $3,200 per year, there's only one place to cut: the category of "everything else." After tuition increases, you can spend only $300 per year on movies, clothes, pizzas, and dates—not $800 as in the "good old days." This $500 reduction in purchasing power represents a *real* income loss. Even though your *nominal* income is still $8,000, you have $500 less of "everything else" in your second year than you had in the first.

Although tuition hikes reduce the real income of students, nonstudents aren't hurt by such price increases. In fact, if tuition *doubled,* nonstudents really wouldn't care. They could continue to buy the same bundle of goods and services they'd been buying all along. Tuition increases reduce the real incomes only of people who go to college.

Two basic lessons about inflation are to be learned from this sad story:

- *Not all prices rise at the same rate during an inflation.* In our example, tuition increased substantially while other prices remained steady. Hence the "average" price increase wasn't representative of any particular good or service. Typically some prices rise rapidly, others rise only modestly, and some actually fall.
- *Not everyone suffers equally from inflation.* This follows from our first observation. Those people who consume the goods and services that are rising faster in price bear a greater burden of inflation; their real incomes fall further. Other consumers bear a lesser burden, or even none at all, depending on how fast the prices rise for the goods they enjoy.

nominal income: The amount of money income received in a given time period, measured in current dollars.

real income: Income in constant dollars; nominal income adjusted for inflation.

TABLE 7.2

Price Changes in 2016

The average rate of inflation conceals substantial differences in the price changes of specific products. The impact of inflation on individuals depends in part on which goods and services are consumed. People who buy goods whose prices are rising fastest lose more real income. In 2016 college students and smokers were particularly hard-hit by inflation.

Prices That Rose (%)		Prices That Fell (%)	
Train fares	+7.4%	Eggs	−21.1%
Apples	+6.8	Televisions	−19.2
Textbooks	+4.7	Gasoline	−11.5
Cable TV	+3.7	Milk	−4.6
Cigarettes	+3.6	Air fares	−3.3
College tuition	+2.7	Coffee	−3.0
Oranges	+0.7	Bananas	−1.0
	Average inflation rate: +1.3%		

Source: U.S. Bureau of Labor Statistics.

Table 7.2 illustrates some of the price changes that occurred in 2016. The average rate of inflation was only 1.3 percent. This was little solace to college students, however, who confronted tuition increases of 2.7 percent and 4.7 percent price hikes on textbooks (sorry!). On the other hand, price reductions on eggs, televisions, and coffee spared consumers of these products from the pain of the *average* inflation rate.

Income Effects

Even if all prices rose at the *same* rate, inflation would still redistribute income. The redistributive effects of inflation originate in not only *expenditure* patterns but also *income* patterns. Some people have fixed incomes that *don't* go up with inflation. Fixed-income groups include retired people who depend primarily on private pensions and workers with multiyear contracts that fix wage rates at preinflation levels. Lenders (like banks) that have lent funds at fixed interest rates also suffer real income losses when price levels rise. They continue to receive interest payments fixed in *nominal* dollars that have increasingly less *real* value. All these market participants experience a declining share of real income (and output) in inflationary periods.

Not all market participants suffer a real income decline when prices rise. Some people's nominal income rises *faster* than average prices, thereby boosting their *real* incomes. Keep in mind that there are two sides to every market transaction. **What looks like a price to a buyer looks like an income to a seller.** Apple growers profited from the 6.8 percent rise in apple prices in 2016. When students pay 2.7 percent higher tuition, the university takes in more income. It is able to buy *more* goods and services (including faculty, buildings, and library books) after a period of inflation than it could before. When the price of this text goes up, my *nominal* income goes up. If the text price rises faster than other prices, my *real* income increases as well. In either case, you lose (sorry!).

Once we recognize that nominal incomes and prices don't all increase at the same rate, it makes no sense to say that "inflation hurts everybody." **If prices are rising, incomes must be rising too.** In fact, on *average,* incomes rise just as fast as prices. Notice in Figure 7.1 that inflation increased *prices* by 82 percent from 1990 to 2016. However, *wages* more than kept pace—at least on average. That fact is of little comfort, however, to those whose wages didn't keep pace; they end up losing real income in the inflation game.

Wealth Effects

Still more winners and losers of the inflation game are selected on the basis of the assets they hold. Suppose you deposit $100 in a savings account on January 1, where it earns 5 percent interest. At the end of the year you'll have more nominal wealth ($105) than you started with ($100). But what if all prices have doubled in the meantime? In that case, your $105 will buy you no more at the end of the year than $52.50 would have bought you at the beginning. Inflation in this case reduces the *real* value of your savings, and you end up worse off than those individuals who spent all their income earlier in the year!

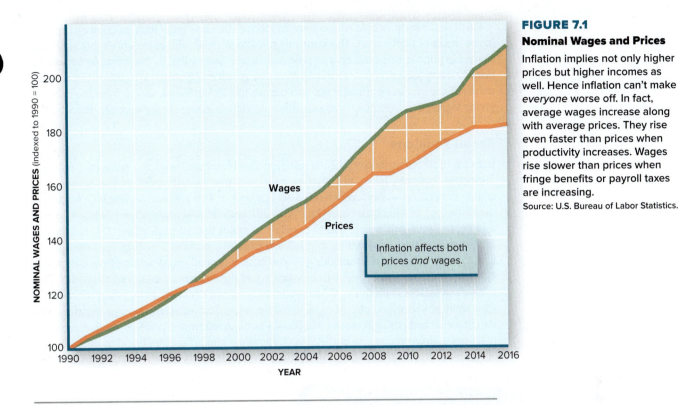

FIGURE 7.1
Nominal Wages and Prices

Inflation implies not only higher prices but higher incomes as well. Hence inflation can't make *everyone* worse off. In fact, average wages increase along with average prices. They rise even faster than prices when productivity increases. Wages rise slower than prices when fringe benefits or payroll taxes are increasing.

Source: U.S. Bureau of Labor Statistics.

Table 7.3 shows how the value of various assets has changed. Between 1991 and 2001, the average price level increased 32 percent. The average value of stocks, diamonds, and homes rose much faster than the price level, increasing the *real* value of those assets. Farmland prices rose too, but just a bit more than average prices. People who owned bonds, silver, and gold weren't so lucky; their *real* wealth declined.

Redistributions

By altering relative prices, incomes, and the real value of wealth, inflation turns out to be a mechanism for redistributing incomes and wealth. ***The redistributive mechanics of inflation include***

- *Price effects.* People who buy products that are increasing in price the fastest end up worse off.
- *Income effects.* People whose nominal incomes rise more slowly than the rate of inflation end up worse off.
- *Wealth effects.* People who own assets that are declining in real value end up worse off.

Asset	Change in Value (%), 1991–2001
Stocks	+250%
Diamonds	+71
Oil	+66
Housing	+56
U.S. farmland	+49
Average price level	+32
Silver	+22
Bonds	+20
Stamps	−9
Gold	−29

TABLE 7.3

The Real Story of Wealth

Households hold their wealth in many different forms. As the value of various assets changes, so does a person's wealth. Between 1991 and 2001, inflation was very good to people who held stocks. By contrast, the real value of bonds, gold, and silver fell.

On the other hand, people whose nominal incomes increase faster than inflation end up with larger shares of total output. The same thing is true of those who enjoy goods that are rising slowest in price or who hold assets whose real value is increasing. In this sense, *inflation acts just like a tax, taking income or wealth from one group and giving it to another.* But we have no assurance that this particular tax will behave like Robin Hood, taking from the rich and giving to the poor. In reality, inflation often redistributes income in the opposite direction.

Social Tensions

Because of its redistributive effects, inflation also increases social and economic tensions. Tensions—between labor and management, between government and the people, and among consumers—may overwhelm a society and its institutions. As Gardner Ackley of the University of Michigan observed, "A significant real cost of inflation is what it does to morale, to social coherence, and to people's attitudes toward each other." "This society," added Arthur Okun, "is built on implicit and explicit contracts. . . . They are linked to the idea that the dollar means something. If you cannot depend on the value of the dollar, this system is undermined. People will constantly feel they've been fooled and cheated."[1] This is how the middle class felt in Germany in 1923 and in China in 1948, when the value of their savings was wiped out by sudden and unanticipated inflation. A surge in prices also stirred social and political tensions in Russia as it moved from a price-controlled economy to a market-driven economy in the 1990s. The same kind of sociopolitical tension arose in Zimbabwe in 2008–2009 (see World View "Zimbabwe's Trillion-Dollar Currency")

WORLD VIEW

ZIMBABWE'S TRILLION-DOLLAR CURRENCY

Imagine the price of coffee *doubling* every day. Or the price of a textbook soaring from $100 to $12,800 in a single week! Sounds unbelievable. But that was the day-to-day reality in Zimbabwe in 2008–2009, when the inflation rate reached an astronomical 231 *million* percent.

The Zimbabwean currency lost so much value that people needed a sackful to buy a loaf of bread. To facilitate commerce, the Zimbabwe central bank printed the world's first $100 *trillion* banknote. Within a week, that $100 trillion note was worth about 33 U.S. dollars—enough to buy six loaves of bread.

©Tsvangirayi Mukwazhi/AP Images

Source: News reports, January 2009.

ANALYSIS: Hyperinflation renders a currency useless for market transactions. The economy contracts, and social tensions rise.

[1] Quoted in *BusinessWeek*, May 22, 1978, p. 118.

and in Venezuela in 2015–2017. On a more personal level, psychotherapists report that "inflation stress" leads to more frequent marital spats, pessimism, diminished self-confidence, and even sexual insecurity. Some people turn to crime as a way of solving the problem.

Money Illusion

Even people whose nominal incomes keep up with inflation often feel oppressed by rising prices. People feel that they *deserve* any increases in wages they receive. When they later discover that their higher (nominal) wages don't buy any additional goods, they feel cheated. They feel worse off, even though they haven't suffered any actual loss of real income. This phenomenon is called **money illusion.** People suffering from money illusion are forever reminding us that they used to pay only $5 to see a movie or $20 for a textbook. What they forget is that nominal *incomes* were also a lot lower in the "good old days" than they are today.

money illusion: The use of nominal dollars rather than real dollars to gauge changes in one's income or wealth.

MACRO CONSEQUENCES

Although microeconomic redistributions of income and wealth are the primary consequences of inflation, inflation has *macroeconomic* effects as well.

Uncertainty

One of the most immediate consequences of inflation is uncertainty. When the average price level is changing significantly in either direction, economic decisions become more difficult. Even something as simple as ordering a restaurant meal is more difficult if menu prices are changing (as they did during Germany's 1923 runaway inflation). In Zimbabwe, postponing bread purchases cost a *billion* Zimbabwean dollars a day (see World View "Zimbabwe's Trillion-Dollar Currency"). The $100 trillion banknote issued in January 2009 was worthless two months later.

Inflation makes longer-term decisions even more difficult. Should you commit yourself to four years of college, for example, if you aren't certain that you or your parents will be able to afford the full costs? In a period of stable prices you can be fairly certain of what a college education will cost. But if prices are rising, you can't be sure how large the bill will be. Under such circumstances, some individuals may decide not to enter college rather than risk the possibility of being driven out later by rising costs.

Price uncertainties affect production decisions as well. Imagine a firm that wants to build a new factory. Typically the construction of a factory takes two years or more, including planning, site selection, and actual construction. If construction costs change rapidly, the firm may find that it's unable to complete the factory or to operate it profitably. Confronted with this added uncertainty, the firm may decide not to build a new plant. This deprives the economy of new investment and expanded production possibilities.

Speculation

Inflation threatens not only to reduce the level of economic activity but to change its very nature. If you really expect prices to rise, it makes sense to buy goods and resources now for resale later. If prices rise fast enough, you can make a handsome profit. These are the kinds of thoughts that motivate people to buy houses, precious metals, commodities, and other assets. But such speculation, if carried too far, can detract from the production process. If speculative profits become too easy, few people will engage in production; instead everyone will be buying and selling existing goods. People may even be encouraged to withhold resources from the production process, hoping to sell them later at higher prices. Such speculation may fuel **hyperinflation** as spending accelerates and production declines. This happened in Germany in the 1920s, in China in 1948–1949, in Russia in the early 1990s, and in Zimbabwe in 2007–2009. No one wanted to hold Zimbabwean dollars

hyperinflation: Inflation rate in excess of 200 percent, lasting at least one year.

or trade for them. Farmers preferred to hold their crops rather than sell them. With the price of a loaf of bread increasing by a billion Zimbabwean dollars a day, why would a baker want to *sell* his bread? Producers chose to hold rather than sell their products. The resulting contraction in supply caused a severe decline in output.

Bracket Creep

Another reason that savings, investment, and work effort decline when prices rise is that taxes go up, too. Federal income tax rates are *progressive;* that is, tax rates are higher for larger incomes. The intent of these progressive rates is to redistribute income from rich to poor. However, inflation tends to increase *everyone's* income. In the process, people are pushed into higher tax brackets and confront higher tax rates. The process is referred to as **bracket creep.** In recent years, bracket creep has been limited by the inflation indexing of personal income tax rates and a reduction in the number of tax brackets. However, Social Security payroll taxes and most state and local taxes aren't indexed.

bracket creep: The movement of taxpayers into higher tax brackets (rates) as nominal incomes grow.

Deflation Dangers

Ironically, a *falling* price level—a deflation—might not make people happy either. In fact, a falling price level can do the same kind of harm as a rising price level. When prices are falling, people on fixed incomes and long-term contracts gain more *real* income. Lenders win and borrowers lose. People who hold cash or bonds win; home owners and stamp collectors lose. Deflation simply reverses the kinds of redistributions caused by inflation.

A falling price level also has similar macro consequences. Time horizons get shorter. Businesses are more reluctant to borrow money or to invest. People lose confidence in themselves and public institutions when declining price levels deflate their incomes and assets.

MEASURING INFLATION

In view of the macro and micro consequences of price level changes, the measurement of inflation serves two purposes: to gauge the average rate of inflation and to identify its principal victims.

Consumer Price Index

Consumer Price Index (CPI): A measure (index) of changes in the average price of consumer goods and services.

The most common measure of inflation is the **Consumer Price Index (CPI).** As its name suggests, the CPI is a mechanism for measuring changes in the average price of consumer goods and services. It's analogous to the fruit price index we discussed earlier. The CPI refers not to the price of any particular good but to the average price of all consumer goods.

By itself, the "average price" of consumer goods isn't a useful number. But once we know the average price of consumer goods, we can observe whether that average rises—that is, whether inflation is occurring. By observing the extent to which prices increase, we can calculate the **inflation rate.**

inflation rate: The annual percentage rate of increase in the average price level; (Price Level$_{Year 2}$ − Price Level$_{Year 1}$)/ Price Level$_{Year 1}$.

We can get a better sense of how inflation is measured by observing how the CPI is constructed. The process begins by identifying a market basket of goods and services the typical consumer buys. For this purpose, the Bureau of Labor Statistics surveys a large sample of families every year to determine what goods and services consumers actually buy. Figure 7.2 summarizes the results of the 2015 survey, which reveal that 32.9 cents out of every consumer dollar is spent on housing (shelter, furnishings, and utilities), 12.5 cents on food, and another 17 cents on transportation. Only 5.1 cents of every consumer dollar is spent on entertainment.

Within these broad categories of expenditure, the Bureau of Labor Statistics itemizes specific goods and services. The details of the expenditure survey show, for example, that private expenditures for reading and education account for only 2.5 percent of the typical consumer's budget, less than is spent on alcoholic beverages, tobacco, and gambling. It also shows that we spend 7 cents out of every dollar on fuel, to drive our cars (3.7 cents) and to heat and cool our houses (3.6 cents).

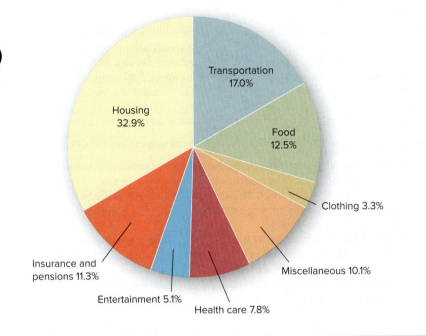

FIGURE 7.2
The Market Basket
To measure changes in average prices, we must first know what goods and services consumers buy. This diagram, based on consumer surveys, shows how the typical urban consumer spends each dollar. Housing, transportation, and food account for more than two-thirds of consumer spending.

Source: U.S. Bureau of Labor Statistics, Consumer Expenditure Survey (2015 data).

Once we know what the typical consumer buys, it's relatively easy to calculate the average price of a market basket. The Bureau of Labor Statistics actually goes shopping in 85 cities across the country, recording the prices of the 184 items that make up the typical market basket. Approximately 19,000 stores are visited, and 60,000 landlords, renters, and home owners are surveyed—every month!

As a result of these massive, ongoing surveys, the Bureau of Labor Statistics can tell us what's happening to consumer prices. Suppose, for example, that the market basket cost $100 last year and that the same basket of goods and services cost $110 this year. On the basis of those two shopping trips, we could conclude that consumer prices had risen by 10 percent in one year.

In practice, the CPI is usually expressed in terms of what the market basket cost in a specific **base year.** The price level in the base year is arbitrarily designated as 100. In the case of the CPI, the average price level for the period 1982–1984 is usually used as the base for computing price changes. Hence the price index for that base year is set at 100. In July 2017, the CPI registered 243. In other words, it cost $243 in 2017 to buy the same market baskets that cost only $100 in the base year. Prices had increased by an average of 143 percent over that period. Each month the Bureau of Labor Statistics updates the CPI, telling us how the current cost of that same basket compares to its cost between 1982 and 1984.

base year: The year used for comparative analysis; the basis for indexing price changes.

Item Weights

Table 7.4 illustrates how changes in the official CPI are computed. Notice that all price changes don't have the same impact on the inflation rate. Rather, *the effect of a specific price change on the inflation rate depends on the product's relative importance in consumer budgets.*

The relative importance of a product in consumer budgets is reflected in its **item weight,** which refers to the percentage of a typical consumer budget spent on the item. Table 7.4 shows the item weights for college tuition and housing. College tuition may loom very large in your personal budget, but only 1.5 percent of *all* consumer expenditures is spent on college tuition. Hence the item weight for college tuition in the *average* consumer budget is only 0.0152.

Housing costs absorb a far larger share of the typical consumer budget. As was first observed in Figure 7.2, the item weight for housing is 0.329. Accordingly, rent increases have

item weight: The percentage of total expenditure spent on a specific product; used to compute inflation indexes.

TABLE 7.4

Computing Changes in the CPI

The impact of any price change on the average price level depends on the importance of an item in the typical consumer budget—its **item weight.**

The Consumer Expenditure Survey of 2015 revealed that the average household spends 1.52 cents of every consumer dollar on college tuition. Households without college students don't pay any tuition, of course. And your family probably devotes *more* than 1.52 cents of each consumer dollar to tuition. On *average,* however, 1.52 cents is the proportion of each dollar spent on tuition. This figure is the *item weight* of tuition in computing the CPI.

The impact on the CPI of a price change for a specific good is calculated as follows:

Item weight × Percentage change in price of item = Percentage change in CPI

Suppose that tuition prices suddenly go up 20 percent. What impact will this single price increase have on the CPI? In this case, where tuition is the only price that increases, the impact on the CPI will be only 0.30 percent (0.0152 × 20) as illustrated below. Thus a very large increase in the price of tuition (20 percent) has a tiny impact (0.30 percent) on the *average* price level.

Housing, on the other hand, accounts for 32.9 percent of consumer expenditures. Thus if housing prices increase 20 percent, and housing is the only price that increases, the impact on the CPI will be 6.58 percent, as shown below.

The relative importance of an item in consumer budgets—its item weight—is a key determinant of its inflationary impact.

Item	Item Weight	×	Price Increase for the Item	=	Impact on the CPI
College tuition	0.0152		20%		0.30%
Housing	0.329		20		6.58

a much larger impact on the CPI than do tuition hikes. Notice in Table 7.4 how a 20 percent hike in tuition has a tiny impact on average inflation, whereas a 20 percent hike in housing prices adds a lot to the CPI.

The Core Rate. Every month the Labor Department reports the results of its monthly price surveys. In its news releases, the department distinguishes changes in the "core" price level from the broader, all-inclusive CPI. The **core inflation rate** excludes changes in food and energy prices, which have a lot of month-to-month variation. A freeze in California or Florida can cause a temporary spike in produce prices; a hurricane in the Gulf can do the same thing to oil prices. These temporary price shocks, however, may not reflect price trends. By excluding volatile food and energy prices from the core rate, we hope to get a more accurate monthly reading of consumer price trends.

core inflation rate: Changes in the CPI, excluding food and energy prices.

Producer Price Indexes

In addition to the Consumer Price Index, there are three Producer Price Indexes (PPIs). The PPIs keep track of average prices received by *producers.* One index includes crude materials, another covers intermediate goods, and the last covers finished goods. The three PPIs don't include all producer prices but primarily those in mining, manufacturing, and agriculture. Like the CPI, changes in the PPIs are identified in monthly surveys.

Over long periods of time, the PPIs and the CPI generally reflect the same rate of inflation. In the short run, however, the PPIs usually increase before the CPI because it takes time for producers' price increases to be reflected in the prices that consumers pay. For this reason, the PPIs are watched closely as a clue to potential changes in consumer prices.

The GDP Deflator

The broadest price index is the GDP deflator. The GDP deflator covers all output, including consumer goods, investment goods, and government services. Unlike the CPI and PPIs, the **GDP deflator** isn't based on a fixed "basket" of goods or services. Rather, it allows the contents of the basket to change with people's consumption and investment patterns. The GDP deflator therefore isn't a pure measure of price change. Its value reflects both price changes and market responses to those price changes, as reflected in new expenditure patterns. Hence the GDP deflator typically registers a lower inflation rate than the CPI.

Real vs. Nominal GDP. The GDP deflator is the price index used to adjust nominal GDP statistics for changing price levels. Recall that **nominal GDP** refers to the *current* dollar value of output, whereas **real GDP** denotes the *inflation-adjusted* value of output. These two measures of output are connected by the GDP deflator:

$$\text{Real GDP} = \frac{\text{Nominal GDP}}{\text{GDP deflator}} \times 100$$

The nominal values of GDP were $10 trillion in 2000 and $15 trillion in 2010. At first blush, this would suggest that output had increased by 50 percent over those 10 years. However, the price level rose by 26 percent between those years. Hence, *real* GDP in 2010 in the base-year prices of 2000 was

$$\frac{\text{2010 real GDP}}{\text{(in 2000 prices)}} = \frac{\text{Nominal GDP}}{\text{Price deflator}} = \frac{\$15 \text{ trillion}}{\frac{126}{100}} = \frac{\$15 \text{ trillion}}{1.26} = \$11.9 \text{ trillion}$$

In reality, then, output increased by only 11.9 percent (from $10 trillion to $11.9 trillion) from 2000 to 2010. **Changes in real GDP are a good measure of how output and living standards are changing. Nominal GDP statistics, by contrast, mix up output and price changes.**

THE GOAL: PRICE STABILITY

In view of the inequities, anxieties, and real losses caused by inflation, it's not surprising that price stability is a major goal of economic policy. As we observed at the beginning of this chapter, every U.S. president since Franklin Roosevelt has decreed price stability to be a foremost policy goal. Unfortunately, few presidents (or their advisers) have stated exactly what they mean by "price stability." Do they mean *no* change in the average price level? Or is some upward creep in the price index acceptable?

A Numerical Goal

An explicit numerical goal for **price stability** was established for the first time in the Full Employment and Balanced Growth Act of 1978. According to that act, the goal of economic policy is to hold the rate of inflation under 3 percent.

Unemployment Concerns

Why did Congress choose 3 percent inflation rather than zero inflation as the benchmark for price stability? One reason was concern about unemployment. To keep prices from rising, the government might have to restrain spending in the economy. Such restraint could lead to cutbacks in production and an increase in joblessness. In other words, **there might be a trade-off between inflation and unemployment.** From this perspective, a little bit of inflation might be the "price" the economy has to pay to keep unemployment rates from rising.

Recall how the same kind of logic was used to define the goal of full employment. The fear there was that price pressures would increase as the economy approached its production possibilities. This suggested that some unemployment might be the "price" the economy has to pay for price stability. Accordingly, the goal of "full employment" was defined as the lowest rate of unemployment *consistent with stable prices*. The same kind of thinking is apparent here. The amount of inflation regarded as tolerable depends in part on the effect of

GDP deflator: A price index that refers to all goods and services included in GDP.

nominal GDP: The value of final output produced in a given period, measured in the prices of that period (current prices).

real GDP: The value of final output produced in a given period, adjusted for changing prices.

price stability: The absence of significant changes in the average price level; officially defined as a rate of inflation of less than 3 percent.

anti-inflation strategies on unemployment rates. After reviewing our experiences with both unemployment and inflation, Congress concluded that 3 percent inflation was a safe target.

Quality Changes

The second argument for setting our price stability goal above zero inflation relates to our measurement capabilities. The Consumer Price Index isn't a perfect measure of inflation. In essence, the CPI simply monitors the price of specific goods over time. Over time, however, the goods themselves change, too. Old products become better as a result of *quality improvements.* A flat-screen TV set costs more today than a TV did in 1955, but today's television also delivers a bigger, clearer picture, in digital sound and color, and with a host of on-screen programming options. Hence increases in the price of TV sets tend to exaggerate the true rate of inflation: Most of the higher price represents more product.

The same is true of automobiles. The best-selling car in 1958 (a Chevrolet Bel Air) had a list price of only $2,618. That makes a 2017 Ford Focus look awfully expensive at $24,775. The quality of today's cars is much better, however. Improvements since 1958 include seat belts, air bags, variable-speed windshield wipers, electronic ignitions, rear-window defrosters, radial tires, antilock brakes, emergency flashers, remote-control mirrors, crash-resistant bodies, a doubling of fuel mileage, a 100-fold decrease in exhaust pollutants, and global positioning systems. As a result, today's higher car prices also buy cars that are safer, cleaner, and more comfortable.

The U.S. Bureau of Labor Statistics does adjust the CPI for quality changes. Such adjustments inevitably entail subjective judgments, however. Critics are quick to complain that the CPI overstates inflation because quality improvements are undervalued.

New Products

The problem of measuring quality improvements is even more difficult in the case of new products. The computers and word processors used today didn't exist when the Census Bureau conducted its 1972–1973 survey of consumer expenditure. The 1982–1984 expenditure survey included those products but not still newer ones such as the cell phone. The omission of cell phones caused the CPI to overstate the rate of inflation. The consumer expenditure survey of 1993–1995 included cell phones but not digital cameras, DVD players, flat-screen TVs, or MP3 players—all of which have had declining prices (Table 7.1). As a result, there's a significant (though unmeasured) element of error in the CPI insofar as it's intended to gauge changes in the average prices paid by consumers. The goal of 3 percent inflation allows for such errors.

THE HISTORICAL RECORD

In the long view of history, the United States has done a good job of maintaining price stability. On closer inspection, however, our inflation performance is very uneven. Table 7.5 summarizes the long view, with data going back to 1800. The base period for

TABLE 7.5

Two Centuries of Price Changes

Before World War II, the average level of prices rose in some years and fell in others. Since 1945, prices have risen continuously. The Consumer Price Index has more than doubled since 1982–1984. It stood at 243 in July 2017.

Year	CPI	Year	CPI	Year	CPI	Year	CPI
1800	17.0	1900	8.3	1950	24.1	1982–1984	100.0
1825	11.3	1920	20.0	1960	29.6	1990	130.5
1850	8.3	1930	16.7	1970	38.8	2000	172.8
1875	11.0	1940	14.0	1980	82.4	2015	237.0

Note: Data from 1915 forward reflect the official all-items Consumer Price Index, which used the pre-1983 measure of shelter costs. Estimated indexes for 1800 through 1900 are drawn from several sources.

Source: U.S. Bureau of Labor Statistics.

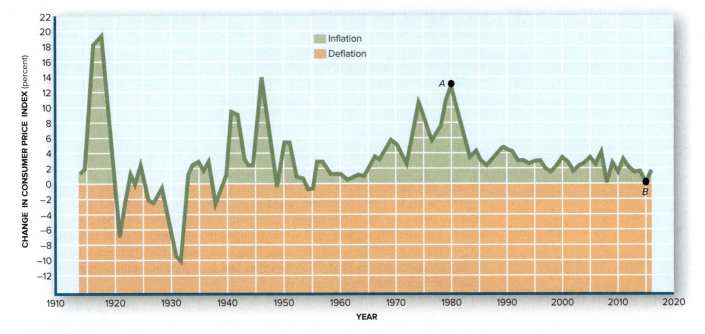

FIGURE 7.3

Annual Inflation Rates

During the 1920s and 1930s, consumer prices fell significantly, causing a general deflation. Since the Great Depression, however, average prices have risen almost every year. But the annual rate of price increases has varied widely: The highest rate of inflation was 13.5 percent in 1980 (point A); the lowest rate (0.1 percent) occurred in 2008 and 2015 (point B).

Source: U.S. Bureau of Labor Statistics.

pricing the market basket of goods is again 1982–1984. Notice that the same market basket cost only $17 in 1800. Consumer prices increased 500 percent in 183 years. But also observe how frequently the price level *fell* in the 1800s and again in the 1930s. These recurrent deflations held down the long-run inflation rate. Because of these periodic deflations, average prices in 1945 were at the same level as in 1800! Since then, however, prices have risen almost every year.

Figure 7.3 provides a closer view of our more recent experience with inflation. In this figure we transform annual changes in the CPI into percentage rates of inflation. The CPI increased from 72.6 to 82.4 during 1980. This 9.8-point jump in the CPI translates into a 13.5 percent rate of inflation (9.8 ÷ 72.6 = 0.135). This inflation rate, represented by point A in Figure 7.3, was the highest in a generation. Since then, prices have continued to increase, but at much slower rates. These low rates of inflation in the United States are far below the pace in most nations.

CAUSES OF INFLATION

The evident variation in year-to-year inflation rates requires explanation. So do the horrifying bouts of hyperinflation that have erupted in other nations at various times. What causes price levels to rise or fall?

In the most general terms, this is an easy question to answer. Recall that all market transactions entail two converging forces, namely *demand* and *supply*. Accordingly, any explanation of changing price levels must be rooted in one of these two market forces.

Demand-Pull Inflation

Excessive pressure on the demand side of the economy is often the cause of inflation. Suppose the economy was already producing at capacity but that consumers were willing and able to buy even more goods. With accumulated savings or easy access to credit, consumers could end up trying to buy more output than the economy was producing. This would be a classic case of "too much money chasing too few goods." As consumers sought to acquire more goods, store shelves (inventory) would begin to empty. Seeing this, producers would begin raising prices. The end result would be a demand-driven rise in average prices, or demand-pull inflation.

Cost-Push Inflation

The pressure on prices could also originate on the supply side. When Hurricanes Katrina and Rita destroyed oil-producing facilities in the Gulf (August 2005), oil prices increased abruptly, raising transportation and production costs in a broad array of industries. To cover these higher costs, producers raised output prices. When a tsunami devastated Sri Lanka in December 2004, it destroyed a huge portion of that country's production capacity, including its vital fishing industry. As market participants scurried for the remaining output, prices rose across the board. The same thing happened in Haiti in January 2010, when an earthquake destroyed production facilities and transportation routes, making goods scarce and increasingly more expensive.

PROTECTIVE MECHANISMS

Whatever the *causes* of inflation, market participants don't want to suffer the consequences. Even at a relatively low rate of inflation, the real value of money declines over time. If prices rise by an average of just 4 percent a year, the real value of $1,000 drops to $822 in 5 years and to only $676 in 10 years (see Table 7.6). *Low rates of inflation don't have the drama of hyperinflation, but they still redistribute real wealth and income.*

Year	Annual Inflation Rate				
	2%	4%	6%	8%	10%
2018	$1,000	$1,000	$1,000	$1,000	$1,000
2019	980	962	943	926	909
2020	961	925	890	857	826
2021	942	889	840	794	751
2022	924	855	792	735	683
2023	906	822	747	681	621
2024	888	790	705	630	564
2025	871	760	665	584	513
2026	853	731	627	540	467
2027	837	703	592	500	424
2028	820	676	558	463	386

TABLE 7.6

Inflation's Impact, 2018–2028

In the past 40 years, the U.S. rate of inflation ranged from a low of 0.1 percent to a high of 13.5 percent. Does a range of 13 percentage points really make much difference? One way to find out is to see how a specific sum of money will shrink in real value in a decade.

Here's what would happen to the real value of $1,000 from January 1, 2018, to January 1, 2028, at different inflation rates. At 2 percent inflation, $1,000 held for 10 years would be worth $820. At 10 percent inflation that same $1,000 would buy only $386 worth of goods in the year 2028.

COLAs

Market participants can protect themselves from inflation by *indexing* their nominal incomes, as is done with Social Security benefits, for example. In any year that the rate of inflation exceeds 3 percent, Social Security benefits go up *automatically* by the same percentage as the inflation rate. This **cost-of-living adjustment (COLA)** ensures that nominal benefits keep pace with the rising prices.

Landlords often protect their real incomes with COLAs as well, by including in their leases provisions that automatically increase rents by the rate of inflation. COLAs are also common in labor union agreements, government transfer programs (like food stamps), and many other contracts. In every such case, *a COLA protects real income from inflation.*

cost-of-living adjustment (COLA): Automatic adjustments of nominal income to the rate of inflation.

ARMs

Cost-of-living adjustments have also become more common in loan agreements. As we observed earlier, debtors win and creditors lose when the price level rises. Suppose a loan requires interest payments equal to 5 percent of the amount (principal) borrowed. If the rate of inflation jumps to 7 percent, prices will be rising faster than interest is accumulating. Hence the **real interest rate**—the inflation-adjusted rate of interest—will actually be negative. The interest payments made in future years will buy fewer goods than can be bought today.

The real rate of interest is calculated as

Real interest rate = Nominal interest rate − Anticipated rate of inflation

In this case, the nominal interest rate is 5 percent and inflation is 7 percent. Hence the *real* rate of interest is *minus* 2 percent.

The distinction between real and nominal interest rates isn't too important if you're lending or borrowing money for just a couple of days. But the distinction is critical for long-term loans like home mortgages. Mortgage loans typically span a period of 25 to 30 years. If the inflation rate stays higher than the nominal interest rate during this period, the lender will end up with less *real* wealth than was initially lent.

To protect against such losses, the banking industry offers home loans with adjustable interest rates. An **adjustable-rate mortgage (ARM)** stipulates an interest rate that changes during the term of the loan. A mortgage paying 5 percent interest in a stable (3 percent inflation) price environment may later require 9 percent interest if the inflation rate jumps to 7 percent. Such an adjustment would keep the real rate of interest at 2 percent. These and other inflation-indexing mechanisms underscore the importance of measuring price changes accurately.

real interest rate: The nominal interest rate minus the anticipated inflation rate.

adjustable-rate mortgage (ARM): A mortgage (home loan) that adjusts the nominal interest rate to changing rates of inflation.

THE ECONOMY TOMORROW

THE VIRTUES OF INFLATION

Despite evidence to the contrary, most people still believe that "inflation hurts everybody." In fact, the distaste for inflation is so strong that sizable majorities say they prefer low inflation and high unemployment to the combination of high inflation and low unemployment. A study by Yale economist Robert Shiller confirmed that *money illusion* contributes to this sentiment: People *feel* worse off when they have to pay higher prices, even if their nominal incomes are keeping pace with (or exceeding) the rate of inflation. Politically, this implies a policy bias toward keeping inflation under control, even at the sacrifice of high unemployment and slower economic growth.

There are times, however, when a little inflation might be a good thing. In the wake of the Great Recession of 2008–2009, the rate of inflation fell to zero. Investors and home

Continued

purchasers could borrow money at unprecedented low rates. Yet market participants were still reluctant to borrow and spend. So the economy was frustratingly slow to recover.

What if, however, people thought prices were going to rise? If prospective home buyers expected housing prices to go up, they'd be more willing to purchase a new home. If investors thought prices were going up, they'd want to get in the game while prices were still low. In other words, *expectations of rising prices can encourage more spending.* A little inflation might actually be a virtue in such circumstances.

The challenge for the economy tomorrow is to find the optimal rate of inflation—the one that's just high enough to encourage more spending, but not so high as to raise the specter of an **inflationary flashpoint.** No one wants to experience a Zimbabwean-type hyperinflation or even a less drastic bout of accelerating inflation. The risk of using a little inflation to motivate buyers is that inflationary expectations may quickly get out of hand.

inflationary flashpoint: The rate of output at which inflationary pressures intensify; the point on the AS curve where slope increases sharply.

SUMMARY

- Inflation is an increase in the average price level. Typically it's measured by changes in a price index such as the Consumer Price Index (CPI). **L07-1**
- At the micro level, inflation redistributes income by altering relative prices, income, and wealth. Because not all prices rise at the same rate and because not all people buy (and sell) the same goods or hold the same assets, inflation doesn't affect everyone equally. Some individuals actually gain from inflation, whereas others suffer a loss of real income or wealth. **L07-2**
- At the macro level, inflation threatens to reduce total output because it increases uncertainties about the future and thereby inhibits consumption and production decisions. Fear of rising prices can also stimulate spending, forcing the government to take restraining action that threatens full employment. Rising prices also encourage speculation and hoarding, which detract from productive activity. **L07-2**
- Fully anticipated inflation reduces the anxieties and real losses associated with rising prices. However, few people can foresee actual price patterns or make all the necessary adjustments in their market activity. **L07-2**
- The U.S. goal of price stability is defined as an inflation rate of less than 3 percent per year. This goal recognizes potential conflicts between zero inflation and full employment as well as the difficulties of measuring quality improvements and new products. **L07-3**
- From 1800 to 1945, prices both rose and fell, leaving the average price level unchanged. Since then, prices have risen nearly every year but at widely different rates. **L07-3**
- Inflation is caused by either excessive demand (demand-pull inflation) or structural changes in supply (cost-push inflation). **L07-4**
- Cost-of-living adjustments (COLAs) and adjustable-rate mortgages (ARMs) help protect real incomes from inflation. Universal indexing, however, wouldn't eliminate inflationary redistributions of income and wealth. **L07-2**

Key Terms

inflation	bracket creep	nominal GDP
deflation	Consumer Price Index (CPI)	real GDP
relative price	inflation rate	price stability
nominal income	base year	cost-of-living adjustment (COLA)
real income	item weight	real interest rate
money illusion	core inflation rate	adjustable-rate mortgage (ARM)
hyperinflation	GDP deflator	inflationary flashpoint

Questions for Discussion

1. Why would farmers rather store their output than sell it during periods of hyperinflation? How does this behavior affect prices? **L07-2**
2. How might rapid inflation affect college enrollments? **L07-2**
3. Who gains and who loses from rising house prices? **L07-2**
4. Who gained and who lost from the price changes in Table 7.2? What happened to the price of breakfast? **L07-2**

5. Whose real wealth (see Table 7.3) declined in the 1990s? Who else might have lost real income or wealth? Who gained as a result of inflation? **LO7-2**

6. If *all* prices increased at the same rate (i.e., no *relative* price changes), would inflation have any redistributive effects? **LO7-2**

7. Would it be advantageous to borrow money if you expected prices to rise? Would you want a fixed-rate loan or one with an adjustable interest rate? **LO7-2**

8. Are people worse off when the price level rises as fast as their income? Why do people often feel worse off in such circumstances? **LO7-2**

9. Prior to December 15, 2016 the largest unit of currency in Venezuela was the 100 bolivar. With inflation running in excess of 500 percent a year, people needed stacks of 100-bolivar notes to buy everyday goods. To buy a pair of 40,000-bolivar jeans a consumer needed at least 400 of the 100-bolivar bills. To alleviate this situation, the Venezuelan government issued 20,000-bolivar notes in December 2016. How did the new notes alter real prices and incomes? **LO7-2**

10. Could demand-pull inflation occur before an economy was producing at capacity? How? **LO7-4**

11. How much do higher gasoline prices contribute to inflation? **LO7-1**

PROBLEMS FOR CHAPTER 7

LO7-1 1. According to World View "Zimbabwe's Trillion-Dollar Currency," what was the price of a loaf
of bread in Zimbabwe, measured in
(*a*) U.S. dollars?
(*b*) Zimbabwe dollars?

LO7-1 2. By how much did the pace of college tuition hikes exceed the 2016 rate of inflation (Table 7.2)?

LO7-1 3. Using the Consumer Price Index (CPI) from the Data Tables at the end of the book

Year	Index
2007	207.3
2008	215.3
2009	214.5
2010	218.1
2011	224.9
2012	229.6
2013	233.0
2014	236.7
2015	237.0
2016	240.0

(*a*) Calculate the inflation rate for 2007–2008, 2008–2009, 2014–2015, and 2015–2016.
(*b*) Which years had inflation?
(*c*) Which years had deflation?

LO7-2 4. If tuition keeps increasing at the same rate as in 2016–2017 (see In the News "College Tuition
Up Again"), how much will it cost to complete a degree at a private college in four years
(2016–2020)?

LO7-1 5. Suppose you'll have an annual nominal income of $40,000 for each of the next three years, and
the inflation rate is 5 percent per year.
(*a*) Find the real value of your $40,000 salary for each of the next three years.
(*b*) If you have a COLA in your contract, and the inflation rate is 5 percent, what is the real
value of your salary for each year?

LO7-2 6. Suppose you borrow $1000 of principal that must be repaid at the end of two years, along with
interest of 5 percent a year. If the annual inflation rate turns out to be 10 percent,
(*a*) What is the real rate of interest on the loan?
(*b*) What is the real value of the principal repayment?
(*c*) Who loses, (A) the debtor or (B) the creditor?

LO7-1 7. If apples, oranges, and bananas are weighted equally in a "fruit price index" and no other fruit
changed prices (see Table 7.2),
(*a*) By how much did fruit prices rise or fall in 2016?
(*b*) Is a consumer better or worse off if they love eating these fruit?

LO7-1 8. To better understand how inflation is measured, pretend that the following table describes the
typical consumer's complete market basket for the year. Compute the item weights for each product.

Item	Quantity	Unit Price	Item Weight
Coffee	20 pounds	$ 7	_____
Tuition	1 year	4,000	_____
Pizza	150 pizzas	10	_____
Cable TV	12 months	30	_____
Vacation	1 week	350	_____
		Total:	_____

PROBLEMS FOR CHAPTER 7 (cont'd)

L07-1 9. To better understand how inflation is measured, suppose the prices listed in the table for Problem 8 changed from one year to the next, as shown here. Use the rest of the table to compute the average inflation rate for this hypothetical complete market basket.

Item	Unit Price		Percentage Change in Price	×	Item Weight (calculated in Problem 8)	=	Inflation Impact
	Last Year	This Year					
Coffee	$ 7	$ 14	_____		_____		_____
Tuition	4,000	4,500	_____		_____		_____
Pizza	10	12	_____		_____		_____
Cable TV	30	36	_____		_____		_____
Vacation	350	300	_____		_____		_____
					Average inflation:		_____

L07-1 10. Use the item weights in Figure 7.2 to determine the percentage change in the CPI that would result from a
  (a) 20 percent increase in entertainment prices.
  (b) 8 percent decrease in transportation costs.
  (c) Doubling of clothing prices.
  (*Note:* Review Table 7.4 for assistance.)

L07-1 11. When Disney's Magic Kingdom in Orlando, Florida opened in 1971 the price of admission was $3.50. In 2017 the ticket price was $105. The CPR index was at 39 in 1971 and 243 in 2017.
  (a) By how much did the nominal price of a Disney ticket increase from 1971 to 2017?
  (b) What was the 1971 price in the dollars of 2017?
  (c) By how much did the real price of a ticket increase between 1971 and 2017?

L07-3 12. On a graph, illustrate both the the inflation rate and the real GDP growth rate for 2006–2016. (The data required for this exercise can be found in the Data Tables at the end of the book.)
  (a) In how many years was the official goal of price stability met?
  (b) In what years were inflation the lowest? The highest?
  (c) Economic growth and inflation rates tend to move in the same direction. Which appears to change direction first?

L07-4 13. The Economy Tomorrow: If home prices are expected to rise in the future, will you be more or less likely to buy a house now?

©MOF/Getty Images RF

©AP Images

©Ariel Skelley/Blend Images RF

©Ingram Publishing RF

CYCLICAL INSTABILITY

One of the central concerns of macroeconomics is the short-run business cycle—recurrent episodes of expansion and contraction of the nation's output. These cycles affect jobs, prices, economic growth, and international trade and financial balances. Chapters 8 through 10 focus on the nature of the business cycle and the underlying market forces that can cause both macroeconomic gain and macroeconomic pain.

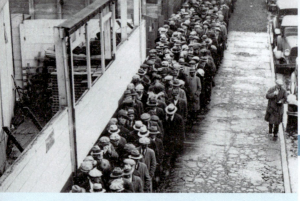

©AP Images

CHAPTER 8

The Business Cycle

In 1929 it looked as though the sun would never set on the U.S. economy. For eight years in a row, the U.S. economy had been expanding rapidly. During the Roaring Twenties, the typical American family drove its first car, bought its first radio, and went to the movies for the first time. With factories running at capacity, virtually anyone who wanted to work found a job readily.

Everyone was optimistic. In his Acceptance Address in November 1928, President-elect Herbert Hoover echoed this optimism by declaring, "We in America today are nearer to the final triumph over poverty than ever before in the history of any land. . . . We shall soon with the help of God be in sight of the day when poverty will be banished from this nation."

The booming stock market seemed to confirm this optimistic outlook. Between 1921 and 1927 the stock market's value more than doubled, adding billions of dollars to the wealth of U.S. households and businesses. The stock market boom accelerated in 1927, causing stock prices to double again in less than two years. The roaring stock market made it look easy to get rich in America.

The party ended abruptly on October 24, 1929. On what came to be known as Black Thursday, the stock market crashed. In a few short hours, the market value of U.S. corporations tumbled in the most frenzied selloff ever seen (see In the News "Market in Panic as Stocks Are Dumped in 12,894,600-Share Day"). The next day President Hoover tried to assure America's stockholders that the economy was "on a sound and prosperous basis." But despite his assurances, the stock market continued to plummet. The following Tuesday (October 29) the pace of selling quickened. By the end of the year, more than $40 billion of wealth had vanished in the Great Crash. Rich men became paupers overnight; ordinary families lost their savings, their homes, and even their lives.

The devastation was not confined to Wall Street. The financial flames engulfed farms, banks, and industry. Between 1930 and 1935, millions of rural families lost their farms. Automobile production fell from 4.5 million cars in 1929 to only 1.1 million in 1932. So many banks were forced to close that newly elected President Roosevelt had to declare a "bank holiday" in March 1933: he closed all of the nation's banks for five days to curtail the outflow of cash to anxious depositors.

Throughout these years, the ranks of the unemployed continued to swell. In October 1929, only 3 percent of the workforce was unemployed. A year later the total was more than 9 percent. Still things got worse. By 1933, more than one-fourth of the labor force was unable to find work. People slept in the streets, scavenged for food, and sold apples on Wall Street.

IN THE NEWS

MARKET IN PANIC AS STOCKS ARE DUMPED IN 12,894,600-SHARE DAY; BANKERS HALT IT

Effect Is Felt on the Curb and throughout Nation—Financial District Goes Wild

The stock markets of the country tottered on the brink of panic yesterday as a prosperous people, gone suddenly hysterical with fear, attempted simultaneously to sell a record-breaking volume of securities for whatever they would bring.

The result was a financial nightmare, comparable to nothing ever before experienced in Wall Street. It rocked the financial district to its foundations, hopelessly overwhelmed its mechanical facilities, chilled its blood with terror.

In a society built largely on confidence, with real wealth expressed more or less inaccurately by pieces of paper, the entire fabric of economic stability threatened to come toppling down.

Into the frantic hands of a thousand brokers on the floor of the New York Stock Exchange poured the selling orders of the world. It was sell, sell, sell—hour after desperate hour until 1:30 p.m.

—Laurence Stern

Source: Stern, Laurence, *The World*, October 25, 1929.

ANALYSIS: Stock markets are a barometer of confidence in the economy. If people have doubts about the economy, they're less willing to hold stocks. The crash of 1929 mirrored and worsened consumer confidence.

The Great Depression seemed to last forever. In 1933 President Roosevelt lamented that one-third of the nation was ill-clothed, ill-housed, and ill-fed. Thousands of unemployed workers marched to the Capitol to demand jobs and aid. In 1938, nine years after Black Thursday, nearly 20 percent of the workforce was still idle.

The Great Depression shook not only the foundations of the world economy but also the self-confidence of the economics profession. No one had predicted the Depression, and few could explain it. The ensuing search for explanations focused on three central questions:

- **How stable is a market-driven economy?**
- **What forces cause instability?**
- **What, if anything, can the government do to promote steady economic growth?**

The basic purpose of **macroeconomics** is to answer these questions—to *explain* how and why economies grow and what causes the recurrent ups and downs of the economy that characterize the **business cycle.** In this chapter we introduce the theoretical model economists use to describe and explain the short-run business cycle. We'll also preview some of the policy options the government might use to dampen those cycles, including the slew of actions taken in 2008–2009 to reverse another macro downturn: the Great Recession of 2008–2009.

macroeconomics: The study of aggregate economic behavior, of the economy as a whole.

business cycle: Alternating periods of economic growth and contraction.

STABLE OR UNSTABLE?

Prior to the 1930s, macro economists thought there could never be a Great Depression. The economic thinkers of the time asserted that a market-driven economy was inherently stable. There was no need for government intervention.

Classical Theory

This **laissez-faire** view of macroeconomics seemed reasonable at the time. During the 19th century and the first 30 years of the 20th, the U.S. economy experienced some bad years in which the nation's output declined and unemployment increased. But most of these episodes were relatively short-lived. The dominant feature of the Industrial Era was *growth:* an expanding economy with more output, more jobs, and higher incomes nearly every year.

laissez faire: The doctrine of "leave it alone," of nonintervention by government in the market mechanism.

A Self-Regulating Economy. In this environment, classical economists, as they later became known, propounded an optimistic view of the macro economy. *According to the classical view, the economy "self-adjusts" to deviations from its long-term growth trend.* Producers might occasionally reduce their output and throw people out of work, but these dislocations would cause little damage. If output declined and people lost their jobs, the internal forces of the marketplace would quickly restore prosperity. *Economic downturns were viewed as temporary setbacks, not permanent problems.*

The cornerstones of classical optimism were flexible prices and flexible wages. If producers couldn't sell all their output at current prices, they had two choices. Either they could (1) reduce the rate of output and throw some people out of work or they could (2) reduce the price of their output, thereby stimulating an increase in the quantity demanded. Classical economists liked the second option. According to the **law of demand,** price reductions cause an increase in unit sales. If prices fall far enough, everything can be sold. Thus flexible prices—prices that would drop when consumer demand slowed—virtually guaranteed that all output could be sold. No one would have to lose a job because of weak consumer demand.

Flexible prices had their counterpart in factor markets. If some workers were temporarily out of work, they'd compete for jobs by offering their services at lower wages. As wage rates declined, producers would find it profitable to hire more workers. Ultimately, flexible wages would ensure that everyone who wanted a job would have a job.

These optimistic views of the macro economy were summarized in Say's law. **Say's law**—named after the 19th-century economist Jean-Baptiste Say—decreed that "supply creates its own demand." Whatever was produced would be sold. All workers who sought employment would be hired. *Unsold goods and unemployed labor could emerge in this classical system, but both would disappear as soon as people had time to adjust prices and wages.* There could be no Great Depression—no protracted macro failure—in this classical view of the world.

Macro Failure. The Great Depression was a stunning blow to classical economists. At the onset of the Depression, classical economists assured everyone that the setbacks in production and employment were temporary and would soon vanish. Andrew Mellon, Secretary of the U.S. Treasury, expressed this optimistic view in January 1930, just a few months after the stock market crash. Assessing the prospects for the year ahead, he said, "I see nothing . . . in the present situation that is either menacing or warrants pessimism. . . . I have every confidence that there will be a revival of activity in the spring and that during the coming year the country will make steady progress."[1] Merrill Lynch, one of the nation's largest brokerage houses, was urging that people should buy stocks. But the Depression deepened. Indeed, unemployment grew and persisted *despite* falling prices and wages (see Figure 8.1). The classical self-adjustment mechanism simply didn't work.

The Keynesian Revolution

The Great Depression effectively destroyed the credibility of classical economic theory. As the British economist John Maynard Keynes pointed out in 1935, classical economists

> were apparently unmoved by the lack of correspondence between the results of their theory and the facts of observation:—a discrepancy which the ordinary man has not failed to observe. . . .
>
> The celebrated optimism of [classical] economic theory . . . is . . . to be traced, I think, to their having neglected to take account of the drag on prosperity which can be exercised by an insufficiency of effective demand. For there would obviously be a natural tendency towards the optimum employment of resources in a Society which was functioning after the manner of the classical postulates. It may well be that the classical theory represents the way in which we should like our Economy to behave. But to assume that it actually does so is to assume our difficulties away.[2]

law of demand: The quantity of a good demanded in a given time period increases as its price falls, *ceteris paribus.*

Say's law: Supply creates its own demand.

[1]David A. Shannon, *The Great Depression* (Englewood Cliffs, NJ: Prentice Hall, 1960), p. 4.
[2]Source: Keynes, John Maynard, *The General Theory of Employment: Interest and Money*, pp 33–34. London, UK: Macmillan, 1936.

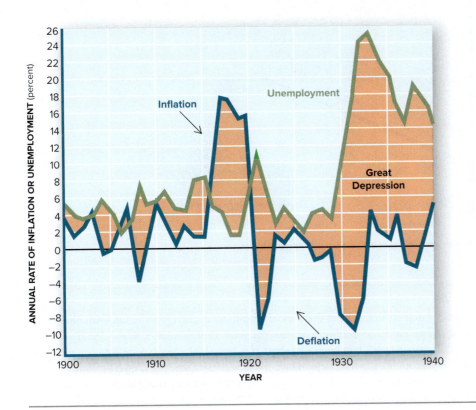

FIGURE 8.1

Inflation and Unemployment, 1900–1940

In the early 1900s, falling price levels (deflation) appeared to limit increases in unemployment. Periods of high unemployment also tended to be brief. These experiences bolstered the confidence of classical economists in the stability of the macro economy. Say's law seemed to work.

In the 1930s, unemployment rates rose to unprecedented heights and stayed high for a decade. Falling wages and prices (deflation) did not restore full employment. This macro failure prompted calls for new theories and policies to control the business cycle.

Source: U.S. Bureau of the Census, The Statistics of the United States, 1957.

Inherent Instability. Keynes went on to develop an alternative view of how the macro economy works. Whereas the classical economists viewed the economy as inherently stable, *Keynes asserted that a market-driven economy is inherently unstable.* Small disturbances in output, prices, or unemployment were likely to be magnified, not muted, by the invisible hand of the marketplace. The Great Depression was not a unique event, Keynes argued, but a calamity that would recur if we relied on the market mechanism to self-adjust.

Government Intervention. In Keynes's view, the inherent instability of the marketplace required government intervention. When the economy falters, we can't afford to wait for some assumed self-adjustment mechanism but must instead intervene to protect jobs and income. The government can do this by "priming the pump": buying more output, employing more people, providing more income transfers, and making more money available. When the economy overheats, the government must cool it down with higher taxes, spending reductions, and less money.

Keynes's denunciation of classical theory didn't end the macroeconomic debate. On the contrary, economists continue to wage fierce debates about the inherent stability of the economy. Those debates—which became intense again in 2008–2014—fill the pages of the next few chapters. But before examining them, let's first take a quick look at the economy's actual performance since the Great Depression.

HISTORICAL CYCLES

The upswings and downturns of the business cycle are gauged in terms of changes in total output. An economic upswing, or expansion, refers to an increase in the volume of goods and services produced. An economic downturn, or contraction, occurs when the total volume of production declines.

FIGURE 8.2

The Business Cycle

The model business cycle resembles a roller coaster. Output first climbs to a peak, then decreases. After hitting a trough, the economy recovers, with real GDP again increasing.

A central concern of macroeconomic theory is to determine whether a recurring business cycle exists and, if so, what forces cause it.

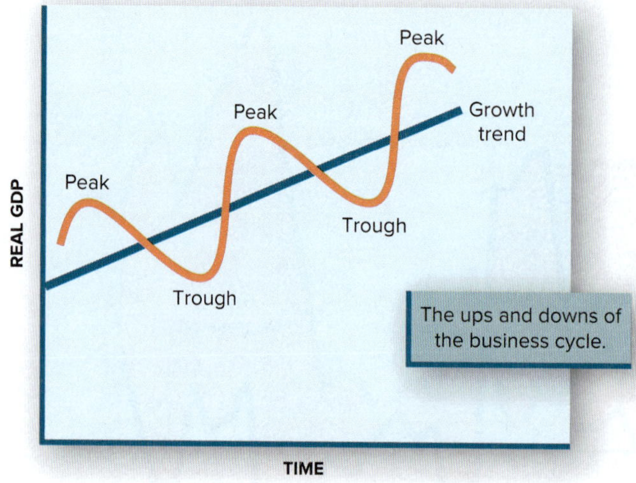

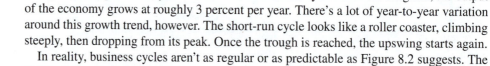

real GDP: The value of final output produced in a given period, adjusted for changing prices.

Figure 8.2 depicts the stylized features of a business cycle. Over the long run, the output of the economy grows at roughly 3 percent per year. There's a lot of year-to-year variation around this growth trend, however. The short-run cycle looks like a roller coaster, climbing steeply, then dropping from its peak. Once the trough is reached, the upswing starts again.

In reality, business cycles aren't as regular or as predictable as Figure 8.2 suggests. The U.S. economy has experienced recurrent upswings and downswings, but of widely varying length, intensity, and frequency.

Figure 8.3 illustrates the actual performance of the U.S. economy since 1929. Changes in total output are measured by changes in **real GDP,** the inflation-adjusted value of all goods and services produced. From a long-run view, the growth of real GDP has been

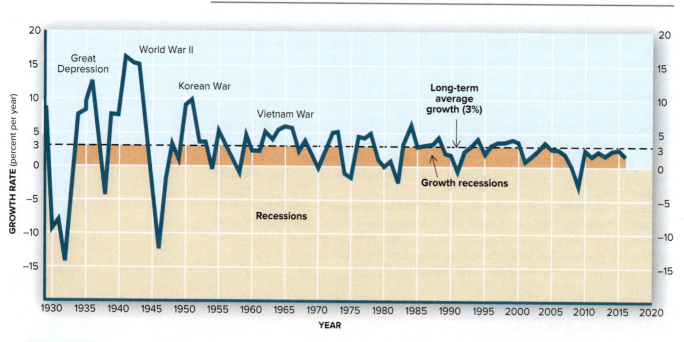

FIGURE 8.3

The Business Cycle in U.S. History

From 1929 to 2017, real GDP increased at an average rate of 3 percent a year. But annual growth rates have departed widely from that average. Years of above-average growth seem to alternate with years of sluggish growth (*growth recessions*) and actual decreases in total output (*recessions*).

Source: U.S. Department of Commerce.

impressive: real GDP today is 15 times larger than it was in 1929. Americans now consume a vastly greater variety of goods and services, and in greater quantities, than earlier generations ever dreamed possible.

Our long-term success in raising living standards is clouded, however, by a spate of short-term macro setbacks. On closer inspection, *the growth path of the U.S. economy isn't a smooth, rising trend but a series of steps, stumbles, and setbacks.* This short-run instability is evident in Figure 8.3. The dashed horizontal line across the middle of the chart represents the long-term *average* growth rate of the U.S. economy. From 1929 through 2017, the U.S. economy expanded at an average rate of 3 percent per year. But Figure 8.3 clearly shows that we didn't grow so nicely every year. There were lots of years when real GDP grew by less than 3 percent. Worse still, there were many years of *negative* growth, with real GDP *declining* from one year to the next. These successive short-run contractions and expansions are the essence of the business cycle.

The Great Depression

The most prolonged departure from our long-term growth path occurred during the Great Depression. Between 1929 and 1933, total U.S. output steadily declined. Notice in Figure 8.3 how the growth rate is negative in each of these years. During these four years of negative growth, real GDP contracted a total of nearly 30 percent. Investments in new plant and equipment virtually ceased. Economies around the world came to a grinding halt (see the World View "Global Depression").

The U.S. economy rebounded in April 1933 and continued to expand for three years (see the positive growth rates in Figure 8.3). By 1937, however, the rate of output was still below that of 1929. Then things got worse again. During 1938 and 1939 output again contracted and more people lost their jobs. **At the end of the 1930s, GDP per capita was lower than it had been in 1929.**

WORLD VIEW

GLOBAL DEPRESSION

The Great Depression wasn't confined to the U.S. economy. Most other countries suffered substantial losses of output and employment over a period of many years. Between 1929 and 1932, industrial production around the world fell 37 percent. The United States and Germany suffered the largest losses, while Spain and the Scandinavian countries lost only modest amounts of output.

Some countries escaped the ravages of the Great Depression altogether. The Soviet Union, largely insulated from Western economic structures, was in the midst of Stalin's forced industrialization drive during the 1930s. China and Japan were also relatively isolated from world trade and finance and so suffered less damage from the Depression.

Country	Decline in Industrial Output
Germany	−47%
United States	−46
France	−31
Chile	−22
Great Britain	−17
Spain	−12
Norway	−7
Japan	−2

ANALYSIS: International trade and financial flows tie nations together. When the U.S. economy tumbled in the 1930s, other nations lost export sales. Such interactions made the Great Depression a worldwide calamity.

World War II

World War II greatly increased the demand for goods and services and ended the Great Depression. During the war years, real GDP grew at unprecedented rates—almost 19 percent in a single year (1942). Virtually everyone was employed, either in the armed forces or in the factories. Throughout the war, America's productive capacity was strained to the limit.

The Postwar Years

recession: A decline in total output (real GDP) for two or more consecutive quarters.

After World War II, the U.S. economy resumed a pattern of alternating growth and contraction. The contracting periods are called *recessions*. Specifically, we use the term **recession** to mean a decline in real GDP that continues for at least two successive quarters. As Table 8.1 indicates, there have been 12 recessions since 1944. The most severe postwar recession occurred immediately after World War II ended. Sudden cutbacks in defense production caused GDP to decline sharply in 1945. That postwar recession was relatively brief, however. Pent-up demand for consumer goods and a surge in investment spending helped restore full employment.

The 1980s and 1990s

growth recession: A period during which real GDP grows but at a rate below the long-term trend of 3 percent.

The 1980s started with two recessions, the second lasting 16 months (July 1981–November 1982). Despite the onset of a second recession at midyear, real GDP actually increased in 1981. But the growth rate was so slow (1.9 percent) that the number of unemployed workers actually rose that year. This kind of experience is called a **growth recession**—the economy grows, but at a slower rate than the long-run (3 percent) average. Thus

- *A growth recession occurs when the economy expands too slowly* (0–2 percent).
- *A recession occurs when real GDP actually contracts.* A depression is an extremely deep and long recession—or when you don't even get socks for Christmas.

In November 1982 the U.S. economy began an economic expansion that lasted more than seven years. During that period, real GDP increased by more than $1 trillion, and nearly 20 million new jobs were created.

In the 20 years from 1986 to 2006 the U.S. economy grew quite well. There was only one year (1991) in which total output contracted (a recession) and only seven years of below 3 percent growth (growth recessions).

TABLE 8.1

Business Slumps

The U.S. economy has experienced 14 business slumps since 1929. In the post–World War II period, these downturns have been much less severe than the Great Depression. The typical recession lasts around 10 months.

Dates	Duration (Months)	Percentage Decline in Real GDP	Peak Unemployment Rate
Aug. 1929–Mar. 1933	43	35.4%	24.9%
May 1937–June 1938	13	9.4	20.0
Feb. 1945–Oct. 1945	8	23.8	4.3
Nov. 1948–Oct. 1949	11	9.9	7.9
July 1953–May 1954	10	10.0	6.1
Aug. 1957–Apr. 1958	8	14.3	7.5
Apr. 1960–Feb. 1961	10	7.2	7.1
Dec. 1969–Nov. 1970	11	8.1	6.1
Nov. 1973–Mar. 1975	16	14.7	9.0
Jan. 1980–July 1980	6	8.7	7.6
July 1981–Nov. 1982	16	12.3	10.8
July 1990–Feb. 1991	8	2.2	6.5
Mar. 2001–Nov. 2001	8	0.6	5.6
Dec. 2007–June 2009	18	4.1	10.0

Great Recession of 2008–2009

That 20-year string of economic growth was broken in 2008. In mid 2007 home prices and stock market prices started falling, sapping consumer wealth and confidence. A credit crisis made loans hard to obtain. Sales of homes, autos, and other big-ticket items plummeted, causing GDP to again contract (see In the News "Sharpest Economic Decline in 26 Years"). The Great Recession of 2008–2009 was the worst since 1981–1982. The unemployment rate peaked at 10 percent when 15 million workers were unable to find jobs.

IN THE NEWS

SHARPEST ECONOMIC DECLINE IN 26 YEARS

It's all bad news on the economic front. The government reported yesterday that the U.S. economy suffered its biggest decline in 26 years in the last quarter of 2008. According to the Department of Commerce, gross domestic product (GDP) fell at an annual rate of 3.8 percent—the largest drop since the first quarter of 1982. Spending was down across the board, especially in the critical area of big-ticket durable goods (down 22 percent). Economists are worried that the plunge in spending will continue, pushing the U.S. economy into another recession.

Source: News reports of January 30, 2009.

ANALYSIS: Everyone agrees that the macro economy can contract on occasion. The debate is whether such contractions self-correct or require government intervention.

Sluggish Recovery. Even after the Great Recession officially ended in June 2009, economic growth was excruciatingly slow. Notice in Figure 8.3 how the economy stayed in the "growth recession" range from 2010 to 2016. The best year of that recovery (2015) exhibited only 2.6 percent growth; the worst year (2011) had a snail's pace of 1.6 percent GDP growth. As a result, unemployment stayed high for five years and receded only when millions of would-be workers stopped looking for work and left the labor force. The appeal of Donald Trump's 2016 campaign promise to "make America great again" was partly the hope that different economic policies would accelerate economic growth.

A MODEL OF THE MACRO ECONOMY

The bumpy growth record of the U.S. economy lends some validity to the notion of a recurring business cycle. Every decade seems to contain at least one boom or bust cycle. But the historical record doesn't really answer our key questions. Are business cycles *inevitable?* Can we do anything to control them? ***Keynes and the classical economists weren't debating whether business cycles occur but whether they are an appropriate target for government intervention.*** That debate continues.

To determine whether and how the government should try to control the business cycle, we first need to understand its origins. What causes the economy to expand or contract? What market forces dampen (self-adjust) or magnify economic swings?

Figure 8.4 sets the stage for answering these questions. This diagram provides a bird's-eye view of how the macro economy works. This basic macro model emphasizes that the performance of the economy depends on a surprisingly small set of determinants.

Macro Outcomes. On the right side of Figure 8.4 the primary measures of macroeconomic performance are arrayed. These basic ***macro outcomes include***

- *Output:* total value of goods and services produced (real GDP).
- *Jobs:* levels of employment and unemployment.

- *Prices:* average price of goods and services (inflation).
- *Growth:* year-to-year expansion in production capacity.
- *International balances:* international value of the dollar; trade and payment balances with other countries.

These macro outcomes define our economic welfare; we measure our economic well-being in terms of the value of output produced, the number of jobs created, price stability, and rate of economic expansion. We also seek to maintain a certain balance in our international trade and financial relations. The economy's performance is rated by the "scores" on these five macro outcomes.

Macro Determinants. On the left side of Figure 8.4 three very broad forces that shape macro outcomes are depicted. These *determinants of macro performance are*

- *Internal market forces:* population growth, spending behavior, invention and innovation, and the like.
- *External shocks:* wars, natural disasters, terrorist attacks, trade disruptions, and so on.
- *Policy levers:* tax policy, government spending, changes in the availability of money, and regulation, for example.

In the absence of external shocks or government policy, an economy would still function: it would still produce output, create jobs, develop prices, and maybe even grow. The U.S. economy operated with minimal government intervention for much of its history. Even today, many less developed countries operate in relative isolation from government or international events. In these situations, macro outcomes depend exclusively on internal market forces.

The crucial macro controversy is whether pure, market-driven economies are inherently stable or unstable. The GDP contraction described in the preceding News wouldn't have surprised classical economists. They knew the economy could sometimes stumble, but they believed the economy would quickly recover from any such setbacks. They saw no need for the box in Figure 8.4 labeled "policy levers." Keynes, by contrast, argued that

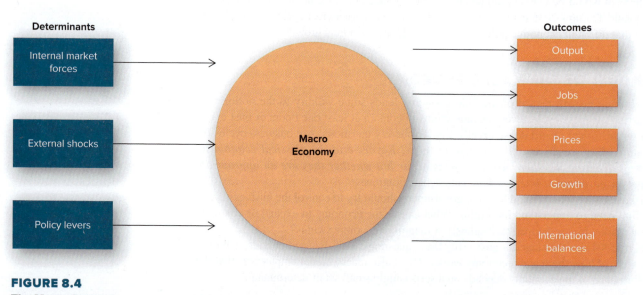

FIGURE 8.4

The Macro Economy

The primary outcomes of the macro economy are output of goods and services (GDP), jobs, prices, economic growth, and international balances (trade, currency). These outcomes result from the interplay of internal market forces such as population growth, innovation, and spending patterns; external shocks such as wars, weather, and trade disruptions; and policy levers such as tax, budget, and regulatory decisions.

policy levers were both effective and necessary. Without such intervention, Keynes believed, the economy was doomed to bouts of repeated macro failure.

Modern economists hesitate to give policy intervention that great a role. Nearly all economists recognize that policy intervention affects macro outcomes. But there are great arguments about just how effective any policy lever is. Some economists even echo the classical notion that policy intervention may be either ineffective or, worse still, inherently *de*stabilizing.

AGGREGATE DEMAND AND SUPPLY

To determine which views of economic performance are valid, we need to examine the inner workings of the macro economy. All Figure 8.4 tells us is that macro outcomes depend on certain identifiable forces. But the figure doesn't reveal *how* the determinants and outcomes are connected. What's in the mysterious circle labeled "Macro Economy" at the center of Figure 8.4?

When economists peer into the mechanics of the macro economy, they see the forces of supply and demand at work. All the macro outcomes depicted in Figure 8.4 are the result of market transactions—an interaction between supply and demand. Hence **any influence on macro outcomes must be transmitted through supply or demand.**

By conceptualizing the inner workings of the macro economy in supply and demand terms, economists have developed a remarkably simple model of how the economy works.

Aggregate Demand

Economists use the term *aggregate demand* to refer to the collective behavior of all buyers in the marketplace. Specifically, **aggregate demand (AD)** refers to the various quantities of output (real GDP) that all people, taken together, are willing and able to buy at alternative price levels in a given period. Our view here encompasses the collective demand for *all* goods and services rather than the demand for any single good.

To understand the concept of aggregate demand better, imagine that everyone is paid on the same day. With their incomes in hand, people then enter the product market. The question becomes, how much output will people buy?

To answer this question, we have to know something about prices. If goods and services are cheap, people will be able to buy more with their available income. On the other hand, high prices will limit both the ability and willingness to purchase goods and services. Note that we're talking here about the *average* price level, not the price of any single good.

Figure 8.5 illustrates this simple relationship between average prices and real spending. The horizontal axis depicts the various quantities of (real) output that might be purchased. The vertical axis shows various price levels that might exist.

The aggregate demand curve illustrates how the real value of purchases varies with the average level of prices. The downward slope of the aggregate demand curve suggests that with a given (constant) level of income, people will buy more goods and services at lower price levels. Why would this be the case? *Three separate reasons explain the downward slope of the aggregate demand curve:*

- *The real balances effect.*
- *The foreign trade effect.*
- *The interest rate effect.*

Real Balances Effect. The most obvious explanation for the downward slope of the aggregate demand curve is that cheaper prices make dollars more valuable. Suppose you had $1,000 in your savings account. How much output could you buy with that savings balance? That depends on the price level. At current prices, you could buy $1,000 worth of output. But what if the price level rose? Then your $1,000 wouldn't stretch as far. *The real value of money is measured by how many goods and services each dollar will buy.* When

aggregate demand (AD): The total quantity of output (real GDP) demanded at alternative price levels in a given time period, *ceteris paribus*.

FIGURE 8.5

Aggregate Demand

Aggregate demand refers to the total output (real GDP) demanded at alternative price levels, *ceteris paribus.* The vertical axis measures the average level of all prices rather than the price of a single good. Likewise, the horizontal axis refers to the real quantity of all goods and services, not the quantity of only one product.

The downward slope of the aggregate demand curve is due to the real balances, foreign trade, and interest rate effects.

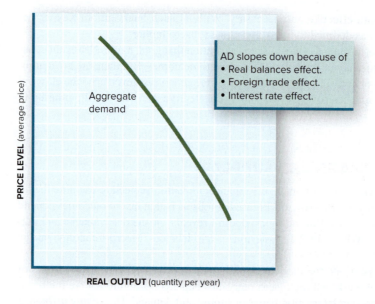

Aggregate demand

AD slopes down because of
• Real balances effect.
• Foreign trade effect.
• Interest rate effect.

PRICE LEVEL (average price)

REAL OUTPUT (quantity per year)

the *real* value of your savings declines, your ability to purchase goods and services declines as well.

Suppose inflation pushes the price level up by 25 percent in a year. What will happen to the real value of your savings balance? At the end of the year, you'll have

$$\begin{array}{c}\textbf{Real value of savings}\\\textbf{at year-end}\end{array} = \frac{\textbf{Savings balance}}{\dfrac{\textbf{Price level at year-end}}{\textbf{Price level at year-start}}}$$

$$= \frac{\$1,000}{\dfrac{125}{100}} = \frac{\$1,000}{1.25}$$

$$= \$800$$

In effect, inflation has wiped out a chunk of your purchasing power. At year's end, you can't buy as many goods and services as you could have at the beginning of the year. The *quantity* of output you demand will decrease. In Figure 8.5 this would be illustrated by a movement up the aggregate demand curve to higher prices and reduced purchases.

A declining price level (deflation) has the opposite effect. Specifically, lower price levels make you "richer": **the cash balances you hold in your pocket, in your bank account, or under your pillow are worth more when the price level falls.** As a result, you can buy *more* goods, even though your *nominal income* hasn't changed.

Lower price levels increase the purchasing power of other dollar-denominated assets as well. Bonds, for example, rise in value when the price level falls. This may tempt consumers to sell some bonds and buy more goods and services. With greater real wealth, consumers might also decide to save less and spend more of their current income. In either case, the quantity of goods and services demanded at any given income level will increase. These real balances effects create an inverse relationship between the price level and the real value of output demanded—that is, *a downward-sloping aggregate demand curve.*

Foreign Trade Effect. The downward slope of the aggregate demand curve is reinforced by changes in imports and exports. Consumers have the option of buying either domestic or foreign goods. A decisive factor in choosing between them is their relative price. If the average price of U.S.-produced goods is rising, Americans may buy more imported goods and fewer domestically produced products. Conversely, falling price levels in the United States may convince consumers to buy more "made in the USA" output and fewer imports.

International consumers are also swayed by relative price levels. When U.S. price levels decline, overseas tourists flock to Disney World. Global consumers also buy more U.S. wheat, airplanes, and computers when our price levels decline. Conversely, a rise in the relative price of U.S. products deters foreign buyers. These changes in import and export flows contribute to the downward slope of the aggregate demand curve.

Interest Rate Effect. Changes in the price level also affect the amount of money people need to borrow. At lower price levels, consumer borrowing needs are smaller. As the demand for loans diminishes, interest rates tend to decline as well. This "cheaper" money stimulates more borrowing and loan-financed purchases. These interest rate effects reinforce the downward slope of the aggregate demand curve, as illustrated in Figure 8.5.

Aggregate Supply

Although lower price levels tend to increase the volume of output *demanded,* they have the opposite effect on the aggregate quantity *supplied.* As we observed, our production possibilities are defined by available resources and technology. Within those limits, however, producers must decide how much output they're *willing* to supply. Their **supply decisions are influenced by changes in the price level.**

Profit Effect. The primary motivation for supplying goods and services is the chance to earn a profit. Producers can earn a profit so long as the prices they receive for their output exceed the costs they pay in production. Hence **changing price levels will affect the profitability of supplying goods.**

If the price level declines, profits tend to drop. In the short run, producers are saddled with some relatively constant costs like rent, interest payments, negotiated wages, and inputs already contracted for. If output prices fall, producers will be hard-pressed to pay these fixed costs, much less earn a profit. Their response will be to reduce the rate of output.

Higher output prices have the opposite effect. Because many costs are relatively constant in the short run, higher prices for goods and services tend to widen profit margins. As profit margins widen, producers will want to produce and sell more goods. Thus **we expect the rate of output to increase when the price level rises.** This expectation is reflected in the upward slope of the aggregate supply curve in Figure 8.6. **Aggregate supply (AS)** reflects the various quantities of real output that firms are willing and able to produce at alternative price levels in a given time period.

aggregate supply (AS): The total quantity of output (real GDP) producers are willing and able to supply at alternative price levels in a given time period, *ceteris paribus.*

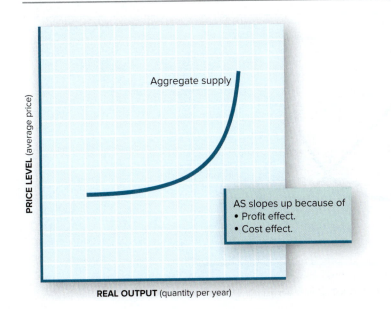

PRICE LEVEL (average price)

Aggregate supply

AS slopes up because of
• Profit effect.
• Cost effect.

REAL OUTPUT (quantity per year)

FIGURE 8.6

Aggregate Supply

Aggregate supply is the real value of output (real GDP) producers are willing and able to bring to the market at alternative price levels, *ceteris paribus.* The upward slope of the aggregate supply curve reflects both profit effects (the lure of widening profit margins) and cost effects (increasing cost pressures).

Cost Effect. The upward slope of the aggregate supply curve is also explained by rising costs. The profit effect depends on some costs remaining constant when the average price level rises. Not all costs will remain constant, however. Producers may have to pay overtime wages, for example, to increase output, even if *base* wages are constant. Tight supplies of other inputs may also unleash cost increases. Such cost pressures tend to multiply as the rate of output increases. As time passes, even costs that initially stayed constant may start creeping upward.

All these cost pressures will make producing output more expensive. Producers will be willing to supply additional output only if prices rise at least as fast as costs.

The upward slope of the aggregate supply curve in Figure 8.6 illustrates this cost effect. Notice how the aggregate supply curve is practically horizontal at low rates of aggregate output and then gets increasingly steeper. At high output levels the aggregate supply curve almost turns straight up. This changing slope reflects the fact that *cost pressures are minimal at low rates of output but intense as the economy approaches capacity.*

Macro Equilibrium

When all is said and done, what we end up with here is two rather conventional-looking supply and demand curves. But these particular curves have special significance. Instead of describing the behavior of buyers and sellers in a single product market, *aggregate supply and demand curves summarize the market activity of the whole (macro) economy.* These curves tell us what *total* amount of goods and services will be supplied or demanded at various price levels.

These graphic summaries of buyer and seller behavior provide some important clues about the economy's performance. The most important clue is point E in Figure 8.7, where the aggregate demand and supply curves intersect. This is the only point at which the behavior of buyers and sellers is compatible. We know from the aggregate demand curve that people are willing and able to buy the quantity Q_E when the price level is at P_E. From the aggregate supply curve we know that businesses are prepared to sell quantity Q_E at the price level P_E. Hence buyers and sellers are willing to trade exactly the same quantity (Q_E) at that price level. We call this situation **macro equilibrium**—the unique combination of prices and output compatible with *both* buyers' and sellers' intentions.

equilibrium (macro): The combination of price level and real output that is compatible with both aggregate demand and aggregate supply.

Disequilibrium. To appreciate the significance of macro equilibrium, suppose that another price or output level existed. Imagine, for example, that prices were higher, at the level P_1 in Figure 8.7. How much output would people want to buy at that price level? How much would business want to produce and sell?

FIGURE 8.7

Macro Equilibrium

The aggregate demand and supply curves intersect at only one point (*E*). At that point, the price level (*P_E*) and output (*Q_E*) combination is compatible with both buyers' and sellers' intentions. The economy will gravitate to those equilibrium price (*P_E*) and output (*Q_E*) levels. At any other price level (e.g., *P_1*), the behavior of buyers and sellers is incompatible.

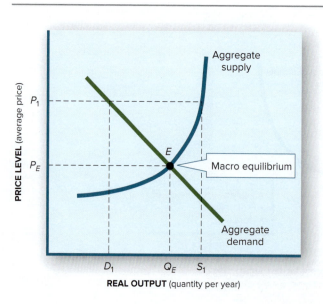

The aggregate demand curve tells us that people would want to buy only the quantity D_1 at the higher price level P_1. In contrast, business firms would want to sell a larger quantity, S_1. This is a *dis*equilibrium situation in which the intentions of buyers and sellers are incompatible. The aggregate *quantity supplied* (S_1) exceeds the aggregate *quantity demanded* (D_1). Accordingly, a lot of goods will remain unsold at price level P_1.

To sell these goods, producers will have to reduce their prices. As prices drop, producers will decrease the volume of goods sent to market. At the same time, the quantities that consumers seek to purchase will increase. This adjustment process will continue until point E is reached and the quantities demanded and supplied are equal. At that point, the lower price level P_E will prevail.

The same kind of adjustment process would occur if a lower price level first existed. At lower prices, the aggregate quantity demanded would exceed the aggregate quantity supplied. The resulting shortages would permit sellers to raise their prices. As they did so, the aggregate quantity demanded would decrease, and the aggregate quantity supplied would increase. Eventually we would return to point E, where the aggregate quantities demanded and supplied are equal.

Equilibrium is unique; it's the only price level–output combination that is mutually compatible with aggregate supply and demand. In terms of graphs, it's the only place where the aggregate supply and demand curves intersect. At point E there's no reason for the level of output or prices to change. The behavior of buyers and sellers is compatible. By contrast, any other level of output or prices creates a *dis*equilibrium that requires market adjustments. All other price and output combinations, therefore, are unstable. They won't last. Eventually the economy will return to point E.

Macro Failures

There are two potential problems with the macro equilibrium depicted in Figure 8.7. The *two potential problems with macro equilibrium are*

- *Undesirability:* The equilibrium price or output level may not satisfy our macroeconomic goals.
- *Instability:* Even if the designated macro equilibrium is optimal, it may not last long.

Undesirability. The macro equilibrium depicted in Figure 8.7 is simply the intersection of two curves. All we know for sure is that people want to buy the same quantity of output that businesses want to sell at the price level P_E. This quantity (Q_E) may be more or less than our full-employment capacity. This contingency is illustrated in Figure 8.8. The output level Q_F represents our **full-employment GDP** potential. It is the rate of output that would be produced if we were fully employed. In Figure 8.8, however, we are producing only the smaller quantity Q_E. In this case, the equilibrium rate of output (Q_E) falls far short of capacity production Q_F. We've failed to achieve our goal of full employment.

full-employment GDP: The value of total market output (real GDP) produced at full employment.

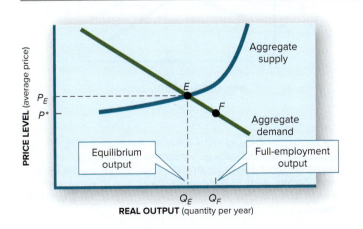

FIGURE 8.8

An Undesired Equilibrium

Equilibrium establishes only the level of prices and output compatible with both buyers' and sellers' intentions. These outcomes may not satisfy our policy goals. In this case, the equilibrium price level (P_E) is too high (above P^*), and the equilibrium output rate (Q_E) falls short of full employment (Q_F).

inflation: An increase in the average level of prices of goods and services.

Similar problems may arise from the equilibrium price level. Suppose that P^* represents the most desired price level. In Figure 8.8, we see that the equilibrium price level P_E exceeds P^*. If market behavior determines prices, the price level will rise above the desired level. The resulting increase in the average level of prices is what we call **inflation.**

It could be argued, of course, that our apparent macro failures are simply an artifact. We could have drawn the aggregate supply and demand curves to intersect at point F in Figure 8.8. At that intersection we'd have both price stability and full employment. Why didn't we draw them there, instead of intersecting at point E?

market failure: An imperfection in the market mechanism that prevents optimal outcomes.

On the graph we can draw curves anywhere we want. In the real world, however, *only one set of aggregate supply and demand curves will correctly express buyers' and sellers' behavior.* We must emphasize here that these real-world curves may *not* intersect at point F, thus denying us price stability or full employment, or both. That is the kind of **market failure** illustrated in Figure 8.8.

Instability. Figure 8.8 is only the beginning of our macro worries. Suppose that the real-world AS and AD curves actually intersected in the perfect spot (point F). That is, imagine that macro equilibrium yielded the optimal levels of both employment and prices. If this happened, could we stop fretting about the state of the economy?

Unhappily, even a "perfect" macro equilibrium doesn't ensure a happy ending. Real-world AS and AD curves aren't permanently locked into their respective positions. They can *shift*—and they will whenever the behavior of buyers and sellers changes.

AS Shifts. Suppose another conflict erupts in oil-producing regions of the Middle East or Nigeria, as happened in 2016 (see Chapter 3 World View "Oil Higher on Nigerian Supply Disruptions"). The price of oil quickly rises. These oil price hikes directly increase the cost of production in a wide range of U.S. industries, making producers less willing and able to supply goods at prevailing prices. Thus the aggregate supply curve *shifts to the left,* as in Figure 8.9a.

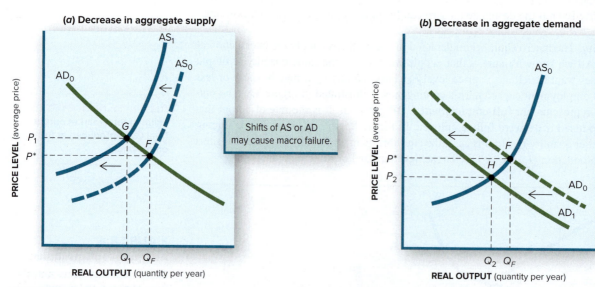

Shifts of AS or AD may cause macro failure.

FIGURE 8.9

Macro Disturbances

(a) **Aggregate supply shifts** A decrease (leftward shift) of the aggregate supply curve reduces real GDP and raises average prices. When supply shifts from AS_0 to AS_1, the equilibrium moves from F to G. At G, output is lower and prices are higher than at F. Such a supply shift may result from higher import prices, natural disasters, changes in tax policy, or other events.

(b) **Aggregate demand shifts** A decrease (leftward shift) in aggregate demand reduces output and price levels. When demand shifts from AD_0 to AD_1, both real output and the price level decline. A fall in demand may be caused by decreased export demand, changes in expectations, higher taxes, or other events.

The September 11, 2001, terrorist strikes against the World Trade Center and Pentagon also caused a leftward shift of aggregate supply. Physical destruction and fear of further terrorism kept some producers out of the market. Intensified security of transportation systems and buildings also increased the costs of supplying goods and services to the market.

The impact of a leftward AS shift on the economy is evident in Figure 8.9. Whereas macro equilibrium was originally located at the optimal point *F,* the new equilibrium is located at point *G.* At point *G,* less output is produced and prices are higher. Full employment and price stability have vanished before our eyes. This is the kind of shift that contributed to the 2001 recession (Table 8.1).

AD Shifts. A shift of the aggregate demand curve could do similar damage. In the fall of 2008, the stock and credit markets took a real beating. Home prices were also falling rapidly. Consumers were seeing some of their wealth vanish before their eyes. As they became increasingly anxious about their future, they cut back on their spending. They were willing to buy *less* output at any given price level; the AD curve shifted to the left, as in Figure 8.9*b.* This AD shift led to lower output and falling prices. The Great Recession of 2008–2009 picked up downward speed (see In the News "Sharpest Economic Decline in 26 Years").

Multiple Shifts. The situation gets even crazier when the aggregate supply and demand curves shift repeatedly in different directions. A leftward shift of the AD curve can cause a recession, as the rate of output falls. A later rightward shift of the AD curve can cause a recovery, with real GDP (and employment) again increasing. Shifts of the aggregate supply curve can cause similar upswings and downswings. Thus *business cycles are likely to result from recurrent shifts of the aggregate supply and demand curves.*

COMPETING THEORIES OF SHORT-RUN INSTABILITY

Figures 8.8 and 8.9 hardly inspire optimism about the macro economy. Figure 8.8 suggests that the odds of the market generating an equilibrium at full employment and price stability are about the same as finding a needle in a haystack. Figure 8.9 suggests that if we're lucky enough to find the needle, we'll probably drop it again.

The classical economists had no such worries. As we saw earlier, they believed that the economy would gravitate toward full employment. Keynes, on the other hand, worried that the macro equilibrium might start out badly and get worse in the absence of government intervention.

The AS/AD model doesn't really settle this controversy. It does, however, provide a convenient framework for comparing these and other theories about how the economy works. Essentially, *macro controversies focus on the shape of aggregate supply and demand curves and the potential to shift them.* With the right shape—or the correct shift—any desired equilibrium could be attained. As we'll see, there are differing views as to whether and how this happy outcome might come about. These differing views can be classified as demand-side explanations, supply-side explanations, or some combination of the two.

Demand-Side Theories

Keynesian Theory. Keynesian theory is the most prominent of the demand-side theories. Keynes argued that a deficiency of spending would tend to depress an economy. This deficiency might originate in consumer saving, inadequate business investment, or insufficient government spending. Whatever its origins, the lack of spending would leave goods unsold and production capacity unused. This contingency is illustrated in In the News "Sharpest Economic Decline in 26 Years" and here by point E_1 in Figure 8.10*a.* Notice that the equilibrium at E_1 leaves the economy at Q_1, below its full-employment potential (Q_F). Thus *Keynes concluded that inadequate aggregate demand would cause persistently high unemployment.*

FIGURE 8.10

Demand-Side Theories

Inadequate demand may cause unemployment. In part (*a*), the demand AD_1 creates an equilibrium at E_1. The resulting output Q_1 falls short of full employment Q_F.

In part (*b*), excessive aggregate demand causes inflation. The price level rises from P_0 to P_2 when aggregate demand expands to AD_2. Demand-side theories emphasize how inadequate or excessive AD can cause macro failures.

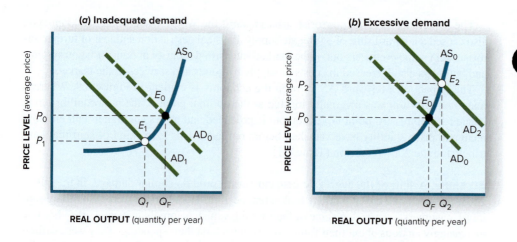

Keynes developed his theory during the Great Depression, when the economy seemed to be stuck at a very low level of equilibrium output, far below full-employment GDP. The only way to end the Depression, he argued, was for someone to start demanding more goods. He advocated a big hike in government spending—a rightward AD shift—to start the economy moving toward full employment. At the time his advice was largely ignored. When the United States mobilized for World War II, however, the sudden surge in government spending shifted the aggregate demand curve sharply to the right, restoring full employment (e.g., a reverse shift from AD_1 to AD_0 in Figure 8.10*a*). In times of peace, Keynes also advocated changing government taxes and spending to shift the aggregate demand curve in whatever direction is desired.

Monetary Theories. Another demand-side theory emphasizes the role of money in financing aggregate demand. Money and credit affect the ability and willingness of people to buy goods and services. If credit isn't available or is too expensive, consumers won't be able to buy as many cars, homes, or other expensive products. "Tight" money might also curtail business investment. In these circumstances, aggregate demand might prove to be inadequate, as illustrated in Figure 8.10*a*. In this case, an increase in the money supply and/or lower interest rates might help shift the AD curve into the desired position.

Both the Keynesian and monetarist theories also regard aggregate demand as a prime suspect for inflationary problems. In Figure 8.10*b*, the curve AD_2 leads to an equilibrium at E_2. At first blush, that equilibrium looks desirable, as it offers more output (Q_2) than the full-employment threshold (Q_F). Notice, however, what's happening to prices: the price level rises from P_0 to P_2. Hence *excessive aggregate demand may cause inflation.*

The more extreme monetary theories attribute all our macro successes and failures to management of the money supply. According to these *monetarist* theories, the economy will tend to stabilize at something like full-employment GDP. Thus only the price level will be affected by changes in the money supply and resulting shifts of aggregate demand. We'll examine the basis for this view in a moment. At this juncture we simply note that *both Keynesian and monetarist theories emphasize the potential of aggregate-demand shifts to alter macro outcomes.*

Supply-Side Theories

Figure 8.11 illustrates an entirely different explanation of the business cycle. Notice that the aggregate *supply* curve is on the move in Figure 8.11. The initial equilibrium is again at point E_0. This time, however, aggregate demand remains stationary, while aggregate supply shifts. The resulting decline of aggregate supply causes output and employment to decline (to Q_3 from Q_F).

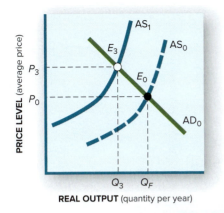

FIGURE 8.11

Supply-Side Theories

Inadequate supply can keep the economy below its full-employment potential and cause prices to rise as well. AS_1 leads to equilibrium output Q_3 and increases the price level from P_0 to P_3. Supply-side theories emphasize how AS shifts can worsen or improve macro outcomes.

Figure 8.11 tells us that aggregate supply may be responsible for downturns as well. Our failure to achieve full employment may result from the unwillingness of producers to provide more goods at existing prices. That unwillingness may originate in simple greed, in rising costs, in resource shortages, or in government taxes and regulation. Inadequate investment in infrastructure (e.g., roads, sewer systems) or skill training may also limit supply potential. Whatever the cause, if the aggregate supply curve is AS_1 rather than AS_0, full employment will not be achieved with the demand AD_0.

The inadequate supply illustrated in Figure 8.11 causes not only unemployment but inflation as well. At the equilibrium E_3, the price level has risen from P_0 to P_3. Hence a decrease in aggregate supply can cause multiple macro problems. On the other hand, an increase—a rightward shift—in aggregate supply can move us closer to both our price-stability and full-employment goals. Chapter 16 examines the many ways of inducing such a shift.

Eclectic Explanations

Not everyone blames either the demand side or the supply side exclusively. *The various macro theories tell us that either AS or AD can cause us to achieve or miss our policy goals.* These theories also demonstrate how various shifts of the aggregate supply and demand curves can achieve any specific output or price level. One could also shift *both* the AS and AD curves to explain unemployment, inflation, or recurring business cycles. Such eclectic explanations of macro failure draw from both sides of the market.

LONG-RUN SELF-ADJUSTMENT

Some economists argue that these various theories of short-run instability aren't only confusing but also pointless. As they see it, what really matters is the *long*-run trend of the economy, not *short*-run fluctuations around those trends. In their view, month-to-month or quarter-to-quarter fluctuations in real output or prices are just statistical noise. The *long*-term path of output and prices is determined by more fundamental factors.

This emphasis on long-term outcomes is reminiscent of the classical theory: the view that the economy will self-adjust. A decrease in aggregate demand is only a *temporary* problem. Once producers and workers make the required price and wage adjustments, the economy will return to its long-run equilibrium growth path.

The monetarist theory we encountered a moment ago has a similar view of long-run stability. According to the monetarist theory, the supply of goods and services is determined by institutional factors such as the size of the labor force and technology. These factors determine a "natural" rate of output that's relatively immune to short-run fluctuations in aggregate demand. If this argument is valid, the long-run aggregate supply curve is vertical, not sloped.

FIGURE 8.12

The "Natural" Rate of Output

Monetarists and neoclassical theorists assert that the level of output is fixed at the natural rate Q_N by the size of the labor force, technology, and other institutional factors. As a result, fluctuations in aggregate demand affect the price level but not real output.

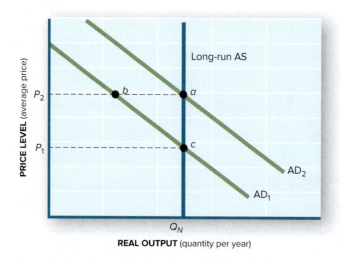

Figure 8.12 illustrates the classical/monetarist view of long-run stability. The vertical long-run AS curve is anchored at the natural rate of output Q_N. The natural rate Q_N is itself determined by demographics, technology, market structure, and the institutional infrastructure of the economy.

If the long-run AS curve is really vertical, as the classical and monetarist theories assert, some startling conclusions follow. The most startling implication is that *shifts of the aggregate demand curve affect prices but not output in the long run.* Notice in Figure 8.12 how the shift from AD_1 to AD_2 raises the price level (from P_1 to P_2) but leaves output anchored at Q_N.

What has happened here? Didn't we suggest earlier that an increase in aggregate demand would spur producers to increase output? And aren't rising prices an extra incentive for doing so?

Monetarists concede that *short-run* price increases tend to widen profit margins. This profit effect is an incentive to increase the rate of output. In the *long run,* however, costs are likely to catch up with rising prices. Workers will demand higher wages, landlords will increase rents, and banks will charge higher interest rates as the price level rises. Hence a rising price level has only a *temporary* profit effect on supply behavior. In the *long run,* cost effects will dominate. In the *long run,* a rising price level will be accompanied by rising costs, giving producers no special incentive to supply more output. Accordingly, output will revert to its natural rate Q_N.

Classical economists use the vertical AS curve to explain also how the economy self-adjusts to temporary setbacks. If AD declines from AD_2 to AD_1 in Figure 8.12, the economy may move from point *a* to point *b*, leaving a lot of unsold output. As producers respond with price cuts, however, the volume of output demanded increases as the economy moves from point *b* to point *c*. At point *c*, full employment is restored. Thus flexible prices (and wages) enable the economy to maintain the natural rate of output Q_N.

Short- vs. Long-Run Perspectives

All this may well be true. But as Keynes pointed out, it's also true that "in the long run we are all dead." How long are we willing to wait for the promised "self-adjustment"? In the Great Depression, people waited for 10 years—and still saw no self-adjustment.

Whatever the long run may hold, it's in the short run that we must consume, invest, and find a job. However stable and predictable the long run might be, short-run variations in macro outcomes will determine how well we fare in any year. Moreover, *the short-run aggregate supply curve is likely to be upward-sloping,* as shown in our earlier graphs. This implies that both aggregate supply and aggregate demand influence short-run macro outcomes.

By distinguishing between short-run and long-run aggregate supply curves, competing economic theories achieve a standoff. Theories that highlight the necessity of policy intervention emphasize the importance of short-run macro outcomes. People *care* about short-run changes in job prospects and prices. If inflation or unemployment is too high, voters insist that "Washington" fix the problem—now.

Theories that emphasize the "natural" stability of the market point to the predictability of long-run outcomes. They prefer to let the economy self-adjust rather than risk government intervention that might worsen macro outcomes. Even if these theories are true, however, the duration of acceptable "short-" and "long-" run periods remains controversial.

THE ECONOMY TOMORROW

COPING WITH RECESSION: 2008–2014

The AS/AD model is a convenient summary of how the macro economy works. A market-driven economy will gravitate to an equilibrium that is compatible with the behavior of both buyers (AD) and sellers (AS). As we've observed, however, that short-run macro equilibrium may not be consistent with our economic goals. That was certainly the case in the Great Recession of 2008–2009, when the equilibrium rate of output was less than full-employment output. People expected newly elected President Obama—the new Economist in Chief—to do something about it. What *could* he do?

Policy Strategies. The beauty of the AS/AD model is that it highlights the strategic options for coping with a recession. In the AS/AD framework, there are really only *three strategy options for macro policy:*

- *Shift the aggregate demand curve to the right.* Find and use policy tools that will stimulate total spending.
- *Shift the aggregate supply curve to the right.* Find and implement policy levers that reduce the cost of production or otherwise stimulate more output at every price level.
- *Laissez faire.* Don't interfere with the market; let markets self-adjust.

The first two strategies assume some form of government intervention is needed to end a recession. The third strategy places more faith in the market's ability to self-adjust.

Policy Tools. There are a host of different policy tools available for implementing any given AS/AD strategy, as President Obama discovered.

- *Classical Laissez Faire.* The laissez-faire strategy advocated by classical economists requires no tools, of course. Classical economists count on the self-adjustment mechanisms of the market—flexible prices and wages—to bring a quick end to recessions. Falling home prices would ultimately spur more sales; declining wages would encourage more hiring. In this view, AS and AD curves "naturally" shift back into an optimal position, where full employment (Q_F) prevails.
- *Fiscal Policy.* Keynes rejected this hands-off approach. He advocated using the federal budget as a policy tool. The government can shift the AD curve to the right by spending more money. Or it can cut taxes, leaving consumers with more income to spend. These budgetary tools are the hallmark of fiscal policy. Specifically, **fiscal policy** is the use of government tax and spending powers to alter economic outcomes.
- *Monetary Policy.* The budget isn't the only tool in the interventionist toolbox. Interest rates and the money supply can also shift the AD curve. Lower interest rates encourage consumers to buy more big-ticket items like cars, homes, and appliances—purchases typically financed with loans. Businesses also take advantage of lower interest rates to buy more loan-financed plant and equipment. **Monetary policy** refers to the use of money and credit controls to alter economic outcomes.

fiscal policy: The use of government taxes and spending to alter macroeconomic outcomes.

monetary policy: The use of money and credit controls to influence macroeconomic outcomes.

Continued

supply-side policy: The use of tax incentives, (de)regulation, and other mechanisms to increase the ability and willingness to produce goods and services.

- *Supply-Side Policy.* Fiscal and monetary tools are used to fix the AD side of the macro economy. **Supply-side policy** pursues a different strategy: it uses tools that shift the aggregate supply curve. Tax incentives that encourage more work, saving, or investment are in the supply-side toolbox. So are deregulation actions that make it easier or cheaper to supply products.
- *Trade Policy.* International trade and money flows offer yet another option for shifting aggregate supply and demand. A reduction in trade barriers makes imports cheaper and more available. This shifts the aggregate supply to the right, reducing price pressures at every output level. Reducing the international value (exchange rate) of the dollar lowers the relative price of U.S.-made goods, thereby encouraging foreigners to buy more U.S. exports. Hence trade policy is another tool in the macroeconomic toolbox.

Taking Action. President Obama never really considered following the do-nothing-and-wait classical approach. He had been elected in November 2008 on the promise of change for the better. In his view, that meant using the available array of activist policy tools to get the economy moving again. His first major intervention was a massive fiscal policy package of increased government spending and tax cuts—the kind of policy Keynes advocated. Over the next five years, President Obama, Congress, and the Federal Reserve used additional policy tools to push the economy out of the Great Recession. Some worked; some didn't. In subsequent chapters we'll examine which tools worked, which didn't, and why.

SUMMARY

- The long-term growth rate of the U.S. economy is approximately 3 percent a year. But output doesn't increase 3 percent every year. In some years real GDP grows much faster; in other years growth is slower. Sometimes GDP actually declines (recession). **LO8-1**
- These short-run variations in GDP growth are a central focus of macroeconomics. Macro theory tries to explain the alternating periods of growth and contraction that characterize the business cycle; macro policy attempts to control the cycle. **LO8-1**
- Classical economists thought the economy would self-adjust, eliminating the need for government intervention. Keynes said the market economy was inherently unstable, necessitating government intervention to attain full employment. **LO8-2**
- The primary outcomes of the macro economy are output, prices, jobs, and international balances. The outcomes result from the interplay of internal market forces, external shocks, and policy levers. **LO8-3**
- All the influences on macro outcomes are transmitted through aggregate supply or aggregate demand. Aggregate demand refers to the rates of output people are willing to purchase at various price levels. Aggregate supply is the rate of output producers are willing to supply at various price levels. **LO8-4**

- Aggregate supply and demand determine the equilibrium rate of output and prices. The economy will gravitate to that unique combination of output and price levels. **LO8-4**
- The market-driven macro equilibrium may not satisfy our employment or price goals. Macro failure occurs when the economy's equilibrium isn't optimal. **LO8-4**
- Macro equilibrium may be disturbed by changes in aggregate supply (AS) or aggregate demand (AD). Such changes are illustrated by shifts of the AS and AD curves, and they lead to a new equilibrium. **LO8-5**
- Competing economic theories try to explain the shape and shifts of the aggregate supply and demand curves, thereby explaining the business cycle. Specific theories tend to emphasize demand or supply influences. **LO8-2**
- In the long run the AS curve tends to be vertical, implying that changes in aggregate demand affect prices but not output. In the short run, however, the AS curve is sloped, making macro outcomes sensitive to both supply and demand. **LO8-4**
- Macro policy options range from laissez faire (the classical approach) to various strategies for shifting either the aggregate demand curve or the aggregate supply curve. **LO8-5**

Key Terms

macroeconomics	recession	inflation
business cycle	growth recession	market failure
laissez faire	aggregate demand (AD)	fiscal policy
law of demand	aggregate supply (AS)	monetary policy
Say's law	equilibrium (macro)	supply-side policy
real GDP	full-employment GDP	

Questions for Discussion

1. If business cycles were really inevitable, what purpose would macro policy serve? **LO8-2**
2. What events might prompt consumers to demand fewer goods at current prices? **LO8-4**
3. If equilibrium is compatible with both buyers' and sellers' intentions, how can it be undesirable? **LO8-4**
4. How did the decline in U.S. home prices in 2006–2008 affect aggregate demand? **LO8-4**
5. What exactly did Say mean when he said that "supply creates its own demand"? **LO8-2**
6. What's wrong with the classical theory of self-adjustment? Why didn't sales and employment increase in 1929–1933 in response to declining prices and wages (see Figure 8.1)? **LO8-2**
7. What might have caused real GDP to decline so dramatically in (*a*) 1929 and (*b*) 1946 (see Figure 8.3)? What caused output to increase again in each case? **LO8-5**
8. How would a sudden jump in U.S. prices affect (*a*) imports from Mexico, (*b*) exports to Mexico, and (*c*) U.S. aggregate demand? **LO8-5**
9. Why might rising prices stimulate short-run production but have no effect on long-run production? **LO8-4**
10. President Trump sought to increase economic growth by cutting taxes and reducing regulation of production. How did these two initiatives affect the AS and AD curves? **LO8-4**

LO8-4 1. In Figure 8.7,
   (a) How much output is unsold at the price level P1?
   (b) At what price level is all output produced sold?

LO8-4 2. In Figure 8.8, what price level will induce people to buy all the output produced at full
LO8-3   employment?

LO8-4 3. Suppose you have $6,000 in savings when the price level index is at 100.
   (a) If inflation pushes the price level up by 10 percent, what will be the real value of your
       savings?
   (b) What is the real value of your savings if the price level *declines* by 5 percent?

LO8-4 4. Use the following information to draw aggregate demand (AD) and aggregate supply (AS)
   curves on the following graph. Both curves are assumed to be straight lines.

Price Level	Output Demanded	Output Supplied
800	0	$800
100	$700	100

   (a) At what rate of real output does equilibrium occur?
   (b) What curve (AD or AS) would have shifted if a new equilibrium were to occur at an output
       level of 600 and a price level of $600?
   (c) What curve would have shifted if a new equilibrium were to occur at an output level of 600
       and a price level of $200?

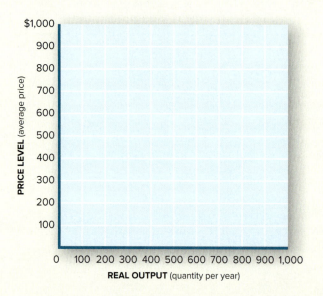

LO8-1 5. According to In the News "Sharpest Economic Decline in 26 Years,"
   (a) By what percentage did GDP decline in the fourth quarter of 2008?
   (b) At that rate, how much output would have been lost in the $14 trillion economy of 2008?
   (c) How much income did this represent for each of the 300 million U.S. citizens?

LO8-1 6. According to Table 8.1,
   (a) What was the largest percentage GDP decline in a post–Great Depression U.S. recession?
   (b) What was
      (i) The longest post–World War II recession?
      (ii) The shortest post–World War II recession?

LO8-5 7. If the AS curve shifts to the left, what happens to
    (a) The equilibrium rate of output?
    (b) The equilibrium price level?

LO8-5 8. If the AD curve shifts to the left, what happens to
    (a) The equilibrium rate of output?
    (b) The equilibrium price level?

LO8-5 9. Assume that the accompanying graph depicts aggregate supply and demand conditions in an economy. Full employment occurs when $5 trillion of real output is produced.
    (a) What is the equilibrium rate of output?
    (b) How far short of full employment is the equilibrium rate of output?
    (c) Illustrate a shift of aggregate demand that would change the equilibrium rate of output to $5 trillion. Label the new curve AD_2.
    (d) What is the price level at this full-employment equilibrium?

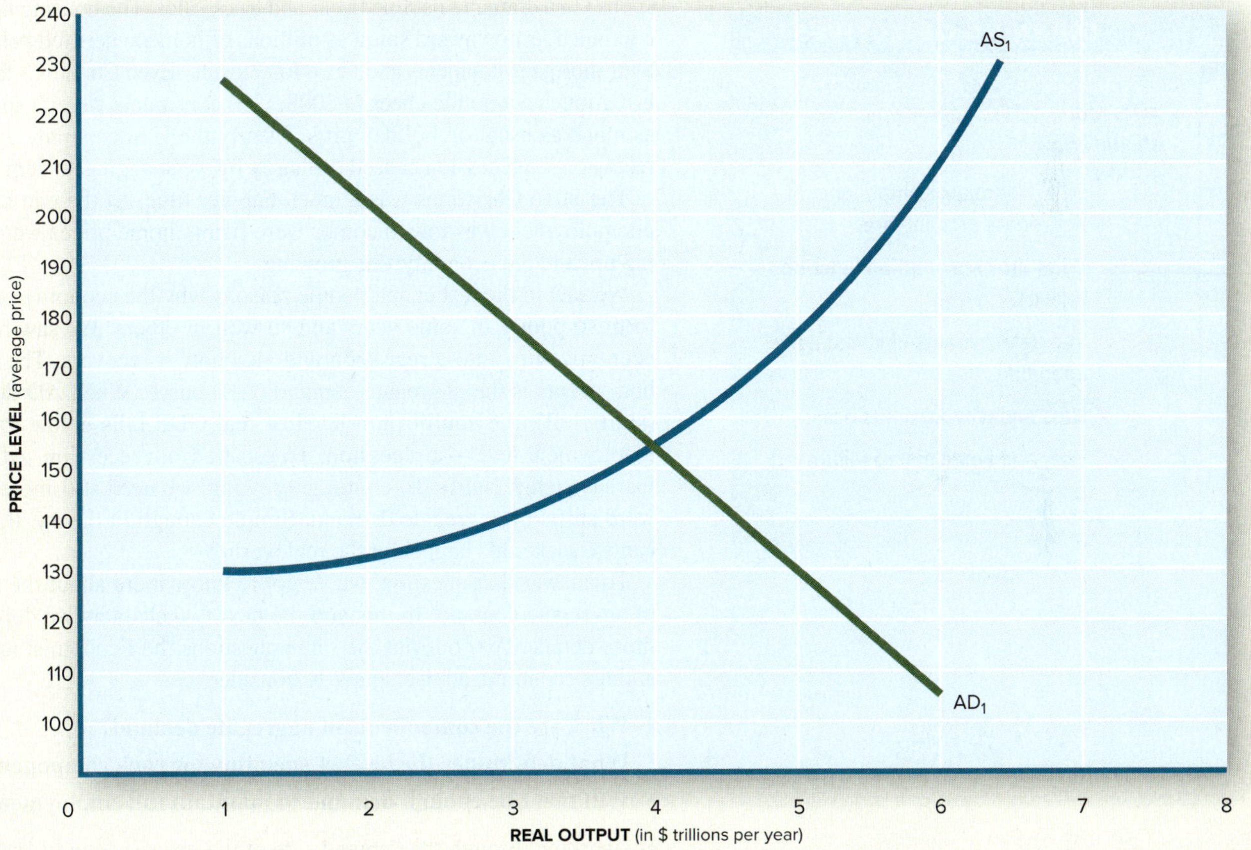

LO8-4 10. How would the objectives of President Trump's tax cuts and deregulation policies shift:
    (a) The aggregate demand curve?
    (b) The aggregate supply curve?

LO8-2 11. The Economy Tomorrow: Graphically show an economy in a recession. What is the
    (a) Classical strategy option for macro policy?
    (b) Keynesian strategy option for macro policy?
    (c) Supply-side strategy option for macro policy?

©Ariel Skelley/Blend Images RF

Aggregate Demand

The last quarter of 2008 was a terrible one for the U.S. economy. Between Labor Day and New Year's Eve, nearly *2 million* workers lost their jobs. A dozen auto plants closed in response to a dramatic decline in car and truck sales. The housing industry continued its downward spiral as millions of homeowners fell behind on their mortgage payments and faced foreclosure. Even Christmas failed to bring much economic cheer in 2008; U.S. consumers weren't spending as much as usual on holiday gifts. Clearly the U.S. economy was in a recession—a recession caused primarily by weak aggregate demand.

The 2016 Christmas was a much happier time. At the end of 2016 unemployment was low, incomes were rising, home prices were moving up, and the economy was growing.

We saw in the last chapter some reasons why the economy can preform so poorly in some years and so well in others. We saw how an economy slips into a recession and also how it recovers. The key to both events is the aggregate demand (AD) curve. When AD declines (shifts left), the equilibrium level of real GDP falls below the full-employment level—a recession. To escape from recession, AD must increase (shift right). To continue growing, we need still more rightward shifts of aggregate demand. Simple enough in theory. But how can we make this happen in the real world?

To answer that question, we've got to know more about the details of aggregate demand. In this and the next two chapters we delve into those details. We confront the same questions the Economist in Chief and his economic advisers have to consider:

- **What are the components of aggregate demand?**
- **What determines the level of spending for each component?**
- **Will there be enough demand to maintain full employment?**

By working through the demand side of the macro economy, we'll get a better view of what might cause business cycles and what might cure them. Later on we'll examine the aggregate supply side more closely as well.

MACRO EQUILIBRIUM

In Chapter 8 we got a bird's-eye view of how macro equilibrium is established. Producers have some notion of how much output they're willing and able to produce at various price levels. Likewise, consumers, businesses, governments, and foreign buyers have some notion of

LEARNING OBJECTIVES

After reading this chapter, you should know

LO9-1 What the major components of aggregate demand are.

LO9-2 What the consumption function tells us.

LO9-3 The determinants of investment spending.

LO9-4 How and why AD shifts occur.

LO9-5 How and when macro failure occurs.

how much output they're willing and able to buy at different price levels. These forces of **aggregate demand** and **aggregate supply** confront each other in the marketplace. Eventually, sellers and buyers discover that only one price level and output combination is acceptable to *both* sides. This is the price–output combination we designate as **(macro) equilibrium.** At equilibrium, the rate of output equals the rate of spending. Producers have no reason to change production levels. In the absence of macro disturbances, the economy will gravitate toward that equilibrium.

The Desired Adjustment

Figure 9.1 illustrates again this general view of macro equilibrium. In the figure, aggregate supply (AS) and demand (AD$_1$) establish an equilibrium at E_1. At this particular equilibrium, the value of real output is Q_E. Notice in the graph that the equilibrium output Q_E is significantly short of the economy's full-employment potential at Q_F. Accordingly, the economy depicted in Figure 9.1 is producing below capacity and thus is saddled with excessive unemployment. This is the kind of situation the U.S. economy confronted in 2008–2009.

All economists recognize that such a *short-run* macro failure is possible. We also realize that the unemployment problem depicted in Figure 9.1 would disappear if either the AD or AS curve shifted rightward. A central macro debate is over whether the curves *will* shift on their own (self-adjust). If not, the government might have to step in and do some heavy shifting.

Components of Aggregate Demand

To assess the possibilities for self-adjustment, we need to examine the nature of aggregate demand more closely. Who's buying the output of the economy? What factors influence their purchase decisions? Why aren't people buying more output?

We can best understand the nature of aggregate demand by breaking it down into its various components. *The four components of aggregate demand are*

- *Consumption (C).*
- *Investment (I).*
- *Government spending (G).*
- *Net exports (X − M).*

Each of these components represents a stream of spending that contributes to aggregate demand. What we want to determine is how these various spending decisions are made. We also want to know what factors might *change* the level of spending, thereby *shifting* aggregate demand.

aggregate demand (AD): The total quantity of output (real GDP) demanded at alternative price levels in a given time period, *ceteris paribus.*

aggregate supply (AS): The total quantity of output (real GDP) producers are willing and able to supply at alternative price levels in a given time period, *ceteris paribus.*

equilibrium (macro): The combination of price level and real output that is compatible with both aggregate demand and aggregate supply.

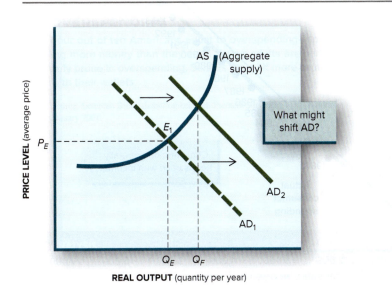

FIGURE 9.1

Escaping a Recession

Aggregate demand (AD) might be insufficient to ensure full employment (Q_F), as illustrated by the intersection of AD$_1$ and the aggregate supply curve. The question is whether and how AD will increase—that is, *shift* rightward—say, to AD$_2$. To answer these questions, we must examine the components of aggregate demand.

dissaving: Consumption expenditure in excess of disposable income; a negative saving flow.

begged, borrowed, or withdrawn from savings. Without peering further into Justin's personal finances, we simply say that he's **dissaving** $25 per week. *Dissaving occurs whenever current consumption exceeds current income.* As In the News "Overspending" revealed, dissaving is common in the United States, especially among younger people who are "livin' large."

If Justin's income contin ues to rise, he'll stop dissaving at some point. Perhaps he'll even start saving enough to pay back all the people who have sustained him through these difficult months. Figure 9.4 shows just how and when this will occur.

The 45-Degree Line. The green line in Figure 9.4, with a 45-degree angle, represents all points where consumption and income are exactly equal ($C = Y_D$). Recall that Justin currently has an income of $100 per week. By moving up from the horizontal axis at $Y_D = \$100$, we see all his consumption choices. Were he to spend exactly $100 on consumption, he'd end up on the 45-degree line at point G. But we already know he doesn't stop there. Instead he proceeds further to point B. At point B the consumption function lies *above* the 45-degree line, so Justin's spending exceeds his income; dissaving is occurring.

Observe, however, what happens when his disposable income rises to $200 per week (row C in the table in Figure 9.4). The upward slope of the consumption function (see graph) tells us that consumption spending will rise with income. In fact, *the slope of the consumption function equals the marginal propensity to consume.* In this case, we see that when income increases from $100 to $200, consumption rises from $125 (point B) to $200 (point C). Thus the change in consumption ($75) equals three-fourths of the change in income. The MPC is still 0.75.

Point C has further significance. At an income of $200 per week Justin is no longer dissaving. At point C his spending exactly equals his income. As a result, he is neither saving nor dissaving; he is breaking even. That is, disposable income equals consumption, so saving equals zero. Notice that point C lies *on* the 45-degree line, where current consumption equals current income.

What would happen to spending if income increased still further? According to Figure 9.4, Justin will start *saving* once income exceeds $200 per week. To the right of point C, the consumption function always lies below the 45-degree line. If spending is less than income, saving must be positive.

The Aggregate Consumption Function

Repeated studies of consumers suggest that there's nothing remarkable about Justin. The consumption function we've constructed for him can be used to depict all consumers simply by changing the numbers involved. Instead of dealing in hundreds of dollars per week, we now play with trillions of dollars per year. But the basic relationship is the same. As we observed earlier in Figure 9.2, we can predict consumer spending if we know how much income consumers have. That's why there are no surprises in In the News "Disposable Income and Outlays: February 2017," which confirms that when disposable income increased in February 2017, people increased both their consumption spending and their saving. (What was the MPC? The MPS?)

IN THE NEWS

DISPOSABLE INCOME AND OUTLAYS: FEBRUARY 2017

Disposable income increased **$44 billion**, or 0.31 percent, in February, according to the Bureau of Economic Analysis. Personal spending increased **$7 billion**.

(in $ billions)	January 2017	February 2017
Disposable income.	14,358	14,402
Personal outlays.	13,587	13,594
Personal savings.	771	808

Source: U.S. Bureau of Economic Analysis.

ANALYSIS: When household incomes increase, consumer spending increases as well. The marginal propensity to consume summarizes this relationship.

Shifts of the Consumption Function

Although the consumption function is a handy device for predicting consumer behavior, it's not infallible. People change their behavior. Neither autonomous consumption (the *a* in the consumption function) nor the marginal propensity to consume (the *b* in $C = a + bY_D$) is set in stone. Whenever one of these parameters changes, the entire consumption function moves. *A change in "a"* **shifts** *the consumption function up or down; a change in "b"* **alters the** **slope** *of the function.*

Consider first the value for *a*. We noted earlier that autonomous consumption depends on wealth, credit, expectations, taxes, and price levels. If any of these nonincome determinants changes, the value of the *a* in the consumption function will change as well.

The plunge in consumer confidence that occurred in December 2008 illustrates how consumer behavior can change abruptly. The continued decline in home prices, mounting job losses, and a declining stock market all weighed heavily on consumer confidence. As In the News "Consumer Confidence Index at Record Low" relates, one out of three consumers expected the economy to worsen further in 2009. With such dismal expectations, they became more cautious about spending their income. That caution caused autonomous consumption to decline from a_1 to a_2 in Figure 9.5, *shifting* the consumer function downward.

IN THE NEWS

CONSUMER CONFIDENCE INDEX AT RECORD LOW

The Conference Board reported yesterday that consumer confidence has plunged. The Board's closely watched Consumer Confidence Index fell to 38 in December—an all-time low. Just 16 months ago the Index stood at 111.

The deteriorating job market appeared to be the main culprit for the loss of confidence. Nearly 2 million jobs were lost this year, and unemployment is spreading. On top of that worry is the plunging stock market that is decimating household savings. Nearly one in three Americans expects business conditions to worsen further in 2009.

Source: News reports, December 2008.

ANALYSIS: When consumer confidence declines, autonomous spending drops and the consumption function shifts downward (as in Figure 9.5). This causes a leftward shift of the AD curve (as in Figure 9.6).

The Consumption function reversed direction in 2016. In November 2016 only 1 out of 10 Americans expected business conditions to worsen in the following six months. That was a dramatic change from 2009 expectations (see In the News "Consumer Confidence Index at Record Low"). The Consumer Confidence index jumped by 6.3 points in November and another 6.6 points in December of 2016 to a level of 113.7. This surge in

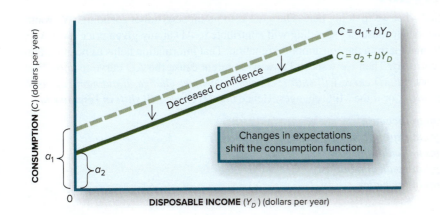

FIGURE 9.5

A Shift in the Consumption Function

Consumers' willingness to spend current income is affected by their confidence in the future. If consumers become more worried or pessimistic, autonomous consumption may decrease from a_1 to a_2. This change will shift the entire consumption function downward.

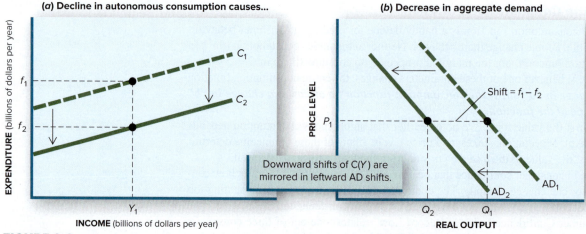

FIGURE 9.6

AD Effects of Consumption Shifts

A downward shift of the consumption function implies that households want to spend less of their income. Here consumption at the income level Y_1 decreases from f_1 to f_2. This decreased expenditure is reflected in a leftward shift of the aggregate demand curve. At the initial price level P_1 consumers demanded Q_1 output. At that same price level, consumers now demand less output, $Q_2 = [Q_1 - (f_1 - f_2)]$.

---

confidence shifted autonomous consumption up from a_2 to a_1 in Figure 9.5 and sent consumers rushing to the malls and showrooms once again.

Shifts of Aggregate Demand. Shifts of the consumption function are reflected in shifts of the aggregate demand curve. Consider again the December 2008 downward shift of the consumption function. A decrease in consumer spending at any given income level implies a decrease in aggregate demand as well. Recall that the aggregate demand curve depicts how much real output will be demanded at various price levels, *with income held constant.* When the consumption function shifts downward, households spend less of their income. Hence, less real output is demanded at any given price level. To summarize,

- *A downward shift of the consumption function implies a leftward shift of the aggregate demand curve.*
- *An upward shift of the consumption function implies an increase (a rightward shift) in aggregate demand.*

These relationships are illustrated in Figure 9.6.

Notice in the graph on the left how the downward shift of the consumption function reduces consumer spending from f_1 to f_2 at the unchanged income Y_1. That decrease in consumption $(f_1 - f_2)$ is reflected in an equivalent decline in aggregate demand, as illustrated by the leftward shift of the AD curve in the graph on the right.

AD Shift Factors

Keep in mind what we're doing here. Our goal is to predict consumer spending. We want to know how much consumer spending will contribute to AD at any given price level. We get that information from the consumption function. That information helps us position the AD curve correctly. Then we want to know what might cause the AD curve to *shift.* We now know that *the AD curve will shift if consumer incomes change, if autonomous consumption changes,* or if the MPC changes. Hence **the AD curve will shift in response to**

- *Changes in income.*
- *Changes in expectations* (consumer confidence).
- *Changes in wealth.*
- *Changes in credit conditions.*
- *Changes in tax policy.*

As we've seen, a recession can change incomes quickly. Consumer confidence can change even more abruptly. A decline in home prices can reduce household wealth enormously. Between 2006 and 2008 home equity declined by roughly $2 trillion. The stock market decline of 2008 further eroded consumer wealth. All these forces combined to shift the AD curve to the left. The end result was the Great Recession of 2008–2009.

The wealth effect reversed in 2014. Rising home and stock-market prices greatly improved the financial situation of U.S. households. They responded with an *upward* shift of the consumption function and a *rightward* shift of the aggregate demand curve (see In the News "Wealth Effect Boosts Spending").

IN THE NEWS

WEALTH EFFECT BOOSTS SPENDING

Rising home prices are bringing smiles to America's retailers. Retail sales climbed 0.2 percent in July, marking the fourth consecutive month of increased sales, according to the U.S. Commerce Department. Analysts credit rising home prices and a surging stock market for the resurgent spending. Home prices are up 19.1 percent so far this year, and the Dow Jones Industrial Average is up 17.9 percent. As household wealth has risen, consumers have been more willing to open their wallets.

Source: U.S. Commerce Department, August 2014.

Shifts and Cycles

Clearly shifts of aggregate demand can be a cause of macro instability. As we first observed in Chapter 8, recurrent shifts of aggregate demand may cause real output to alternately expand and contract, thereby giving rise to short-run business cycles. What we've observed here is that those aggregate demand shifts may originate in consumer behavior. Changes in consumer confidence, in wealth, or in credit conditions alter the rate of consumer spending. If consumer spending increases abruptly, demand-pull inflation may follow. If consumer spending slows abruptly, a recession may occur.

Knowing that consumer behavior *might* cause macro problems is a bit worrisome. But it's also a source of policy power. What if we *want* AD to increase in order to achieve full employment? Our knowledge of consumer-based AD shift factors gives us huge clues about which macro policy tools to look for.

INVESTMENT

Consumption is only one of four AD components. To determine where AD is and whether it might shift, we need to examine the other components of spending as well.

Determinants of Investment

As we observed in Chapter 5, investment spending accounts for roughly 15 percent of total output. That spending includes not only expenditures on new plant, equipment, and business software (all referred to as *fixed investment*) but also spending on inventories (called *inventory investment*). Residential construction is also counted in investment statistics because houses and apartment buildings continue to produce housing services for decades. All these forms of **investment** represent a demand for output; they are part of aggregate demand.

investment: Expenditures on (production of) new plants, equipment, and structures (capital) in a given time period, plus changes in business inventories.

Expectations. Expectations play a critical role in investment decisions. No firm wants to purchase a new plant or equipment unless it is convinced people will later buy the output produced by that plant and that equipment. Nor do producers want to accumulate inventories of goods unless they expect consumers to eventually buy them. Thus *favorable expectations of future sales are a necessary condition for investment spending.*

FIGURE 9.7

Investment Demand

The rate of desired investment depends on expectations, the rate of interest, and innovation. A *change* in expectations will *shift* the investment demand curve. A change in the rate of interest will lead to *movements* along the existing investment demand curve. In this case, an increase in investment beyond the initial $150 billion per year (point *A*) may be triggered by lower interest rates (point *B*) or improved expectations (point *C*).

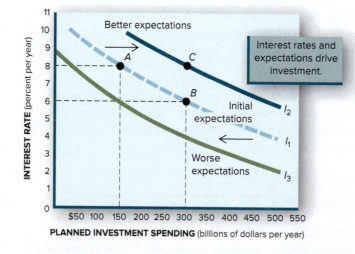

PLANNED INVESTMENT SPENDING (billions of dollars per year)

Interest Rates. A second determinant of investment spending is the rate of interest. Business firms typically borrow money to purchase plants and equipment. The higher the rate of interest, the costlier it is to invest. Accordingly, *we anticipate a lower rate of investment spending when interest rates are high, and more investment at lower rates,* ceteris paribus.

Technology and Innovation. A third determinant of investment is changes in technology and innovation. When scientists learned how to miniaturize electronic circuitry, an entire new industry of electronic calculators, watches, and other goods sprang to life. In this case, the demand for investment goods shifted to the right as a result of improved miniaturized circuits and imaginative innovation (the use of the new technology in pocket calculators). More recently, technological advances and cost reductions in cloud infrastructure have stimulated an investment spree in data storage centers, mobile devices, and fiber optic networks.

The Investment Function. The curve I_1 in Figure 9.7 depicts the general shape of the investment function. To find the rate of investment spending in this figure, we first have to know the rate of interest. At an interest rate of 8 percent, for example, we expect to see $150 billion of investment (point *A* in Figure 9.7). At 6 percent interest, we'd expect $300 billion of investment (point *B*).

Shifts of Investment

As was the case with consumer spending, predicting investment spending isn't quite as easy as it first appears. Any specific investment function (like I_2 in Figure 9.7) is based on a specific set of investor expectations about future sales and profits. Those expectations can change, however.

Altered Expectations. Business expectations are essentially a question of confidence in future sales. An upsurge in current consumer spending could raise investor expectations for future sales, shifting the investment function rightward (to I_2). New business software might induce a similar response. New business tax breaks might have the same effect. If any of these things happened, businesses would be more eager to invest. They'd borrow more money at any given interest rate (e.g., point *C* in Figure 9.7) and use it to buy more plants, equipment, and inventory.

Business expectations could worsen as well. Imagine you were the CEO of a company contemplating a major expansion. Then you read a story about plunging consumer confidence, as In the News "Consumer Confidence Index at Record Low." Would you rethink your plans? Probably. That's what Panasonic's president did in January 2009 (see World View "Panasonic Cuts Spending"). When *business* expectations worsen, investments get postponed or canceled. Suddenly there's less investment spending at any given interest rate. This investment shift is illustrated by the curve I_3 in Figure 9.7.

AD Shifts. As was the case with consumer behavior, we are looking at investor behavior to help us understand aggregate demand. From Figure 9.7 we see that knowledge of investor

WORLD VIEW

PANASONIC CUTS SPENDING

Panasonic Corporation yesterday announced it is slashing planned investment in two Japanese factories that make flat-screen TVs. With consumer spending declining in all its major markets, Panasonic decided to cut its investment by 23 percent over the next three years. The company now plans to invest only 445 billion yen, down from its earlier target of 580 billion yen—a cut of about $1.5 billion.

Source: News reports, January 8–10, 2009.

ANALYSIS: Business investment is based more on expected future sales than on current sales and income. When expectations for future sales growth diminish, investment spending on plants, equipment, and inventory drops.

expectations and interest rates will tell us how much investment will be included in aggregate demand at the current price level. We also see that a change in expectations will alter investment behavior and thereby *shift* the AD curve. ***When investment spending declines, the aggregate demand curve shifts to the left.***

Empirical Instability. Figure 9.8 shows that unstable investment is more than just a theoretical threat to macro stability. What is depicted here are the quarter-to-quarter changes in both

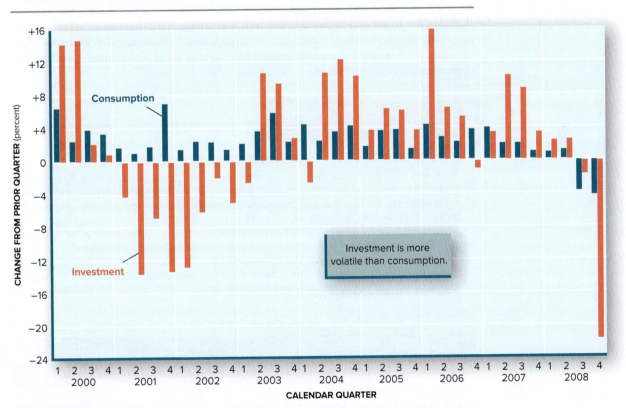

FIGURE 9.8

Volatile Investment Spending

Investment spending fluctuates more than consumption. Shown here are the quarter-to-quarter changes in the real rate of spending for fixed investment (excluding residential construction and inventory changes) and total consumption. Notice the sharp drops in investment spending just prior to the March 2001 recession and the plunge in investment that occurred in 2008. Consumption spending is far less volatile.

Source: *U.S. Bureau of Economic Analysis* (quarterly data seasonally adjusted).

consumer spending and investor spending for the years 2000–2008. Quarterly changes in *consumer* spending never exceeded 6.5 percent and only became negative twice. By contrast, *investment* spending plummeted by 13.3 percent in the post-9/11 quarter and jumped by more than 14 percent in three other quarters. Those abrupt changes in investment (and related AD shifts) were a major cause of the 2001 recession as well as the Great Recession of 2008–2009.

GOVERNMENT AND NET EXPORT SPENDING

The apparent volatility of investment spending heightens rather than soothes anxiety about short-run macro instability. Together, consumption and investment account for more than 80 percent of total output. As we have seen, the investment component of aggregate demand can be both uncertain and unstable. The consumption component of aggregate demand may shift abruptly as well. Such shifts can sow the seeds of macro failure. Will the other components of aggregate demand improve the odds of macro success? What determines the level of government and net export spending? How stable are they?

Government Spending

At present, the government sector (federal, state, and local) spends more than $3 trillion on goods and services, all of which is part of aggregate demand (unlike income transfers, which are not).

Pro-Cyclical State/Local Spending. As we observed in Chapter 5, about two-thirds of all government spending occurs at the state and local levels. That nonfederal spending is limited by tax receipts because state and local governments can't deficit-spend. As a consequence, state and local spending is slightly pro-cyclical, with expenditure rising as the economy (and tax receipts) expands and declining when the economy (and tax receipts) slumps. (See In the News "State/Local Belt Tightening Hurts Economy.") This doesn't augur well for macro stability, much less "self-adjustment." *If consumption and investment spending decline, the subsequent decline in state and local government spending will aggravate rather than offset the leftward shift of the AD curve.*

IN THE NEWS

STATE/LOCAL BELT TIGHTENING HURTS ECONOMY

State and local governments have cut spending at the worst possible time. They had no choice: state and local governments can't finance their expenditures with debt; their spending is limited by tax receipts. And those receipts nosedived when the economy plunged into recession. State sales tax revenues fell by 17 percent in 2009 and income tax receipts fell by 27 percent. Falling home prices cut deeply into the property tax base that cities and countries depend on. So, they had no choice but to cut spending and lay off workers.

State and local governments laid off nearly 600,000 workers from 2008 through 2011. 34 states cut spending on K-12 education, 43 states cut college budgets, and 31 reduced spending on health programs. All these cutbacks deepened the economy's downturn.

Source: Brookings Institution.

ANALYSIS: A recession reduces tax revenues, forcing state and local governments to cut spending. This deepens the recession.

Countercyclical Federal Spending. Federal spending on goods and services isn't so constrained by tax receipts. Uncle Sam can *borrow* money, thereby allowing federal spending to exceed tax receipts. In fact, the federal government typically operates "in the red," with large annual budget deficits. This gives the federal government a unique *counter*cyclical power. If private sector spending and incomes decline, federal tax revenues will fall in response. Unlike state and local governments, however, the federal government can *increase* its spending despite declining tax revenues. In other words, Uncle Sam can help reverse AD shifts by changing its own spending. This is exactly the kind of government action that Keynes advocated and President Obama pursued in 2009–2011. We will examine its potential to stabilize the economy more closely in Chapter 11.

Net Exports

The fourth and final source of aggregate demand is net exports. Our gross exports depend on the spending behavior of foreign consumers and businesses. If foreign consumers and investors behave like Americans, their demand for U.S. products will be subject to changes in *their* income, expectations, wealth, and other factors. In the Asian currency crisis of 1997–1999, this was alarmingly evident: once incomes in Asia began falling, U.S. exports to Asia of rice, corn, lumber, computers, and other goods and services fell sharply. So did the number of Asian students applying to U.S. colleges (a demand for U.S.-produced educational services). This decline in export spending represented a leftward shift of U.S. aggregate demand. Strong GDP growth in India and China has had the opposite effect in recent years.

Imports, too, can be unstable, and for the same reasons. Most U.S. imports are consumer goods and services. Imports, therefore, get caught up in the ebb and flow of consumer spending. When consumer confidence slips or the stock market dips, import spending declines along with the rest of consumption (and investment). As a consequence, *net* exports can be both uncertain and unstable, creating further shifts of aggregate demand.

The AD Curve Revisited

Figure 9.9 illustrates how the four components of spending come together to determine aggregate demand. From the consumption function we determine how much output consumers will demand at the prevailing price level P_O. In this case, they demand Q_C of output as illustrated on the horizontal axis of the graph.

Once we know how much output consumers want to purchase (Q_G), we add investment demand Q_I, as revealed in Figure 9.7 and investor surveys. Local, state, and federal budgets will tell us how much output (Q_G) the government intends to buy. Net exports complete the computation. When we add them all up, we see that output Q_O will be demanded at the prevailing price level P_O. The result of this calculation is illustrated by point d on the demand curve: market participants will demand the quantity Q_O at the price level of P_O.

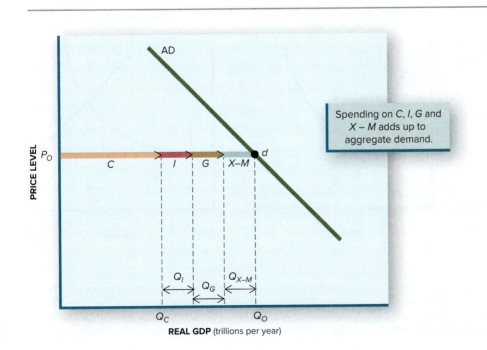

Spending on *C*, *I*, *G* and *X* − *M* adds up to aggregate demand.

FIGURE 9.9

Building an AD Curve

The quantity of output demanded at the prevailing price level originates in the spending decisions of consumers (*C*), investors (*I*), government (*G*), and net exports (*X* − *M*). By adding up the intended spending of these market participants we can see how much output (Q_O) will be demanded at the current price level (P_O). Thus point *d* is the first building block in the construction of the AD curve.

The slope of the AD curve above and below point *d* is based on the responses of real balances, interest rates, and foreign trade to changing price levels (see Chapter 8).

We now know that the AD curve must go through point *d*. But how much output will be demanded at other price levels? The rest of the AD curve reflects how the quantity of output demanded will change if the price level rises or falls (i.e., the real balances, interest rate, and foreign trade effects discussed in Chapter 8).

MACRO FAILURE

In principle, the construction of the AD curve is simple. In practice, it requires an enormous amount of information about the intentions and behavior of market participants. Let's assume for the moment, however, that we have all that information and can therefore accurately depict the AD curve. What then?

Once we know the shape and position of the AD curve, we can put it together with the AS curve and locate macro equilibrium. Here's where our macro problems may emerge. As we noted earlier, *there are two chief concerns about macro equilibrium:*

1. *Undesirability: The market's macro equilibrium might not give us full employment or price stability.*
2. *Instability: Even if the market's macro equilibrium were perfectly positioned (i.e., with full employment and price stability), it might not last.*

Undesired Equilibrium

Figure 9.10*a* depicts the perfect macro equilibrium that everyone hopes for. Aggregate demand and aggregate supply intersect at E_1. At that macro equilibrium we get both full employment (Q_F) and price stability (P^*)—an ideal situation.

Keynes didn't think such a perfect outcome was likely. Why should aggregate demand intersect with aggregate supply exactly at point E_1? As we've observed, consumers, investors, government, and foreigners make independent spending decisions, based on many influences. Why should all these decisions add up to just the right amount of aggregate demand? Keynes didn't think they would. *Because market participants make independent spending decisions, there's no reason to expect that the sum of their expenditures will generate exactly the right amount of aggregate demand.* Instead, there's a high likelihood that we'll confront an imbalance between desired spending and full-employment output levels—that is, too much or too little aggregate demand.

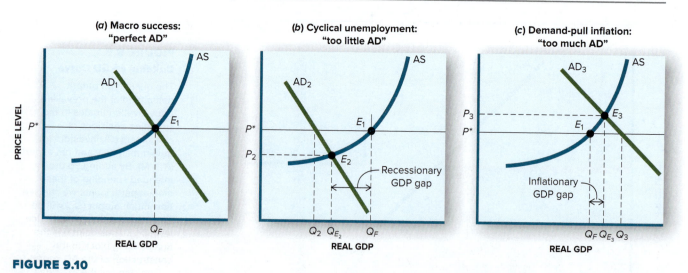

FIGURE 9.10

Macro Failures

Keynesian theory emphasizes that the combined spending decisions of consumers, investors, governments, and net exporters may not be compatible with the desired full employment (Q_F)–price stability (P^*) equilibrium (as they are in panel *a*). Aggregate demand may be too small (panel *b*) or too great (panel *c*), causing cyclical unemployment (*b*) or demand-pull inflation (*c*). Worse yet, even a desirable macro equilibrium (*a*) may be upset by abrupt shifts of aggregate demand.

Recessionary GDP Gap. Figure 9.10*b* illustrates one of the undesired equilibriums that Keynes worried about. **Full-employment GDP** is still at Q_F and stable prices are at the level P^*. In this case, however, the rate of output demanded at price level P^* is only Q_2, far short of full-employment GDP (Q_F). How could this happen? Quite simple: the spending plans of consumers, investors, government, and export buyers don't generate enough aggregate demand at current (P^*) prices.

The economy depicted in Figure 9.10*b* is in trouble. At full employment, a lot more output would be produced than market participants would be willing to buy. As unsold inventories rose, production would get cut back, workers would get laid off, and prices would decline. Eventually, the economy would settle at E_2, where AD_2 and AS intersect. **Equilibrium GDP** would be equal to Q_{E_2} and the equilibrium price level would be at P_2.

E_2 is clearly not a happy equilibrium. What particularly concerned Keynes was the **recessionary GDP gap,** the amount by which equilibrium GDP falls short of full-employment GDP. In Figure 9.10*b*, the recessionary GDP gap equals Q_F minus Q_{E_2}. This gap represents unused productive capacity: lost GDP and unemployed workers. It is the breeding ground of **cyclical unemployment,** the kind of situation President Obama confronted in 2009.

Figure 9.11 illustrates this dilemma with more numerical details on aggregate demand. The table depicts the demand for GDP at different price levels by consumers, investors, government,

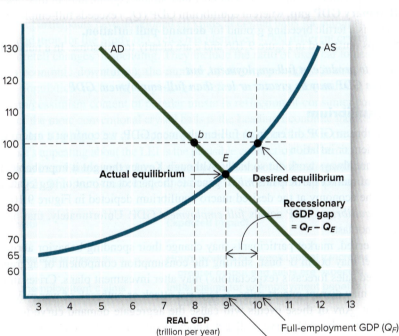

Price Level	Consumers +	Investors +	Government +	Net Exports =	Aggregate Demand	Aggregate Supply
130	3.0	0.25	1.5	0.25	5.0	12.0
120	3.5	0.50	1.5	0.50	6.0	11.5
110	4.0	0.75	1.5	0.75	7.0	11.0
100	4.5	1.0	1.5	1.0	8.0	10.0
90	5.0	1.25	1.5	1.25	9.0	9.0
80	5.5	1.50	1.5	1.50	10.0	7.0
70	6.0	1.75	1.5	1.75	11.0	5.0
60	6.5	2.0	1.5	2.0	12.0	3.0

Real GDP Demanded (in $ trillions) by:

FIGURE 9.11

A Recessionary GDP Gap

The level of aggregate demand depends on the spending behavior of market participants. In this case, the level of GDP demanded at current ($P = 100$) prices ($8 trillion) is less than full-employment GDP ($10 trillion). More output is being produced (point *a*) than purchased (point *b*) at prevailing prices. This results in a lower *equilibrium* GDP ($9 trillion).

The resulting recessionary GDP gap of $1 trillion ($= Q_F - Q_E$) causes unemployment. The price level also declines from 100 to 90.

plan to buy it. The same is true of building permits (indicator 6); people obtain permits only if they plan to build something. Hence both indicators appear to be dependable signs of future investment. That's why an uptick in the LEI is viewed as good news for the economy (see In the News "U.S. Leading Indicators Signal Continuing Recovery").

Unfortunately, the leading indicators aren't a perfect crystal ball. Equipment orders are often canceled. Building plans get delayed or abandoned. Hence shifts of aggregate demand still occur without warning. No crystal ball could predict a terrorist strike or the timing and magnitude of a natural disaster. Compared to other crystal balls, however, the LEI has a pretty good track record—and a very big audience. It helps investors and policymakers foresee what aggregate demand in the economy tomorrow might look like.

IN THE NEWS

U.S. LEADING INDICATORS SIGNAL CONTINUING RECOVERY

The Conference Board Leading Economic Index (LEI) for the United States increased 0.6 percent in February to 126.2 (2010 = 100), the highest level in over a decade. The February uptick in the index follows a 0.6 percent increase in January and a 0.6 increase in December. Widespread gains across a majority of the leading indicators point to an improving economic outlook for the remainder of 2017.

Source: Conference Board, March 17, 2017.

ANALYSIS: Market participants try to predict the economic outlook with measurable indicators like new orders and building permits.

SUMMARY

- Macro failure occurs when the economy fails to achieve full employment and price stability.   **LO9-5**
- Too much or too little aggregate demand can cause macro failure. Too little aggregate demand causes cyclical unemployment; too much aggregate demand causes demand-pull inflation.   **LO9-5**
- Aggregate demand reflects the spending plans of consumers (C), investors (I), government (G), and foreign buyers (net exports = $X - M$).   **LO9-1**
- Consumer spending is affected by nonincome (autonomous) factors and current income, as summarized in the consumption function: $C = a + bY_D$.   **LO9-2**
- Autonomous consumption (a) depends on wealth, expectations, taxes, credit, and price levels. Income-dependent consumption depends on the marginal propensity to consume (MPC), the b in the consumption function.   **LO9-2**

- Consumer saving is the difference between disposable income and consumption (that is, $S = Y_D - C$). All disposable income is either spent (C) or saved (S).   **LO9-1**
- The consumption function shifts up or down when autonomous influences such as wealth and expectations change.   **LO9-2**
- The AD curve shifts left or right whenever the consumption function shifts up or down.   **LO9-4**
- Investment spending depends on interest rates, expectations for future sales, and innovation. *Changes* in investment spending will also shift the AD curve.   **LO9-3**
- Government spending and net exports are influenced by a variety of cyclical and noncyclical factors and may also change abruptly.   **LO9-1**
- Even a "perfect" macro equilibrium may be upset by abrupt shifts of spending behavior. Recurrent shifts of the AD curve may cause a business cycle.   **LO9-5**

Key Terms

aggregate demand
aggregate supply
equilibrium (macro)

consumption
disposable income (DI)
saving

average propensity to consume (APC)
marginal propensity to consume (MPC)
marginal propensity to save (MPS)

wealth effect
autonomous consumption
consumption function
dissaving

investment
full-employment GDP
equilibrium GDP
recessionary GDP gap

cyclical unemployment
inflationary GDP gap
demand-pull inflation
business cycle

Questions for Discussion

1. What percentage of last month's income did you spend? How much more would you spend if you won a $1,000 lottery prize? Why might your average and marginal propensities to consume differ? **LO9-2**

2. Why do rich people have a higher marginal propensity to save than poor people? **LO9-2**

3. How do households dissave? Where do they get the money to finance their extra consumption? Can everyone dissave at the same time? **LO9-2**

4. Why would an *employed* consumer cut spending when other workers were being laid off (see In the News "Consumer Confidence Index at Record Low")? **LO9-2**

5. According to the World View "Panasonic Cuts Spending," why did Panasonic cut investment spending in 2009? Was this a rational response? **LO9-3**

6. Why might a surge in consumer confidence *not* result in increased aggregate demand and an expanding economy? **LO9-4**

7. Why are declining housing permits considered a negative leading indicator? (See In the News "U.S. Leading Indicators Signal Continuing Recovery.") **LO9-5**

8. Why wouldn't market participants always want to buy all the output produced? **LO9-5**

9. If an inflationary GDP gap exists, what will happen to business inventories. How will producers respond? **LO9-5**

10. How might a "perfect" macro equilibrium (Figure 9.10a) be affected by (a) a stock market crash, (b) rising home prices, (c) a recession in Canada, and (d) a spike in oil prices? **LO9-1, LO9-5**

APPENDIX

THE KEYNESIAN CROSS

The Keynesian view of the macro economy emphasizes the potential instability of the private sector and the undependability of a market-driven self-adjustment. We have illustrated this theory with shifts of the AD curve and resulting real GDP gaps. The advantage of the AS/AD model is that it illustrates how both real output and the price level are simultaneously affected by AD shifts. At the time Keynes developed his theory of instability, however, inflation was not a threat. In the Great Depression prices were *falling*. With unemployment rates reaching as high as 25 percent, no one worried that increased aggregate demand would push price levels up. The only concern was to get back to full employment.

Because inflation was not seen as an immediate threat, early depictions of Keynesian theory didn't use the AS/AD model. Instead they used a different graph called the "Keynesian cross." **The Keynesian cross focuses on the relationship of total spending to the value of total output, without an explicit distinction between price levels and real output.** As we'll see, the Keynesian cross doesn't change any conclusions we've come to about macro instability. It simply offers an alternative, and historically important, framework for explaining macro outcomes.

Focus on Aggregate Expenditure

Keynes said that in a really depressed economy we could focus exclusively on the rate of *spending* in the economy without distinguishing between real output and price levels. All he worried about was whether **aggregate expenditure**—the sum of consumer, investor, government, and net export buyers' spending plans—would be compatible with the dollar value of full-employment output.

For Keynes, the critical question was how much each group of market participants would spend at different levels of nominal *income*. As we saw earlier, Keynes showed that consumer spending directly varies with the level of income. That's why the consumption function in Figure 9.4 had *spending* on the vertical axis and nominal *income* on the horizontal axis.

aggregate expenditure: The rate of total expenditure desired at alternative levels of income, *ceteris paribus*.

FIGURE 9A.1

The Consumption Shortfall

To determine how much output consumers will demand at full-employment output (Y_F), we refer to the consumption function. First locate full-employment output on the horizontal axis (at Y_F). Then move up until you reach the consumption function. In this case, the amount C_F (equal to $2,350 billion per year) will be demanded at full-employment output ($3,000 billion per year). This leaves $650 billion of output not purchased by consumers.

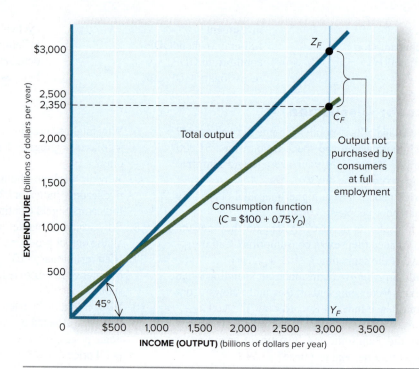

Figure 9A.1 puts the consumption function into the larger context of the macro economy. In this figure, the focus is exclusively on *nominal* incomes and spending. Y_F indicates the dollar value of full-employment output at current prices. In this figure, $3,000 billion is assumed to be the value of Y_F. The 45-degree line shows all points where total spending equals total income.

The consumption function in Figure 9A.1 is the same one we used before, namely

$$C = \$100 + 0.75(Y_D)$$

Notice again that consumers *dissave* at lower income levels but *save* at higher income levels.

The Consumption Shortfall

What particularly worried Keynes was the level of intended consumption at full employment. At full employment, $3 trillion of income (output) is generated. But consumers plan to spend only

$$C = \$100 + 0.75(\$3,000 \text{ billion}) = \$2,350 \text{ billion}$$

and save the rest ($650 billion).[1] Were product market sales totally dependent on consumers, this economy would be in trouble: consumer spending falls short of full-employment output. In Figure 9A.1, this consumption shortfall is the vertical difference between points Z_F and C_F.

Nonconsumer Spending

The evident shortfall in consumer spending need not doom the economy to macro failure. There are other market participants, and their spending will add to aggregate expenditure. Keynes, however, emphasized that the spending decisions of investors, governments, and net export buyers are made independently. They *might* add up to just the right amount—or they might not.

[1] In principle, we first have to determine how much *disposable* income is generated by any given level of *total income*, then use the consumption function to determine how much consumption occurs. If Y_D is a constant percentage of Y, this two-step computation boils down to

$$Y_D = dY$$

where d = the share of total income received as disposable income, and

$$\begin{aligned} C &= a + b(dY) \\ &= a + (b \times d)Y \end{aligned}$$

The term $(b \times d)$ is the marginal propensity to consume out of *total* income.

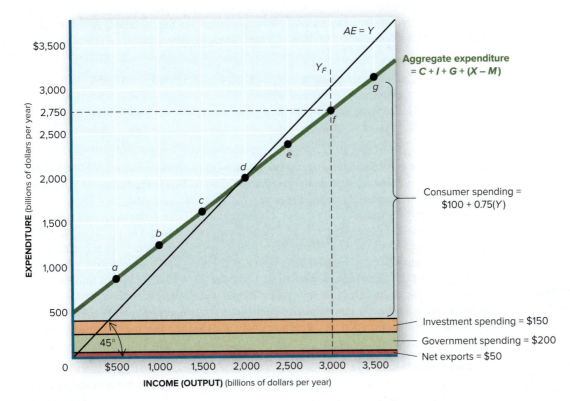

FIGURE 9A.2

Aggregate Expenditure

The aggregate expenditure curve depicts the desired spending of market participants at various income (output) levels. In this case, I, G, and $(X - M)$ don't vary with income, but C does. Adding these four components gives us total desired spending. If total income were $1,000 billion, desired spending would total $1,250 billion, as shown in row b in the table and by point b in the graph.

	At Income (Output) of	Consumers Desire to Spend	+	Investors Desire to Spend	+	Governments Desire to Spend	+	Net Export Spending	=	Aggregate Expenditure
a	$ 500	$ 475		$150		$200		$50		$ 875
b	1,000	850		150		200		50		1,250
c	1,500	1,225		150		200		50		1,625
d	2,000	1,600		150		200		50		2,000
e	2,500	1,975		150		200		50		2,375
f	3,000	2,350		150		200		50		2,750
g	3,500	2,725		150		200		50		3,125

To determine how much other market participants might spend, we'd have to examine their behavior. Suppose we did so and ended up with the information in Figure 9A.2. The data in that figure reveal how many dollars will be spent at various income levels. By vertically stacking these expenditure components, we can draw an *aggregate* (total) expenditure curve as in Figure 9A.2. The aggregate expenditure curve shows how *total* spending varies with income.

A Recessionary Gap

Keynes used the aggregate expenditure curve to assess the potential for macro failure. He was particularly interested in determining how much market participants would spend if the economy were producing at full-employment capacity.

With the information in Figure 9A.2, it is easy to answer that question. At full employment (Y_F), total income is $3,000 billion. From the table, we see that total spending at that income level is

Consumer spending at	$Y_F = \$100 + 0.75(\$3,000)$	$= \$2,350$
Investment spending at	Y_F	$= 150$
Government spending at	Y_F	$= 200$
Net export spending at	Y_F	$= \underline{\quad 50}$
Aggregate spending at	Y_F	$= \$2,750$

In this case, we end up with less aggregate expenditure in product markets ($2,750 billion) than the value of full-employment output ($3,000 billion). This is illustrated in Figure 9A.2 by point f on the graph and row f in the table.

The economy illustrated in Figure 9A.2 is in trouble. If full employment were achieved, it wouldn't last. At full employment, $3,000 billion of output would be produced. But only $2,750 of output would be sold. There isn't enough aggregate expenditure at current price levels to sustain full employment. As a result, $250 billion of unsold output piles up in warehouses and on store shelves. That unwanted inventory is a harbinger of trouble.

The difference between full-employment output and desired spending at full employment is called a **recessionary gap.** Not enough output is willingly purchased at full employment to sustain the economy. Producers may react to the spending shortfall by cutting back on production and laying off workers.

A Single Equilibrium. You might wonder whether the planned spending of market participants would ever be exactly equal to the value of output. It will, but not necessarily at the rate of output we seek.

Figure 9A.3 illustrates where this **expenditure equilibrium** exists. Recall the significance of the 45-degree line in that figure. The 45-degree line represents all points where

---

recessionary gap: The amount by which aggregate spending at full employment falls short of full-employment output.

---

expenditure equilibrium: The rate of output at which desired spending equals the value of output.

FIGURE 9A.3

Expenditure Equilibrium

There's only one rate of output at which desired expenditure equals the value of output. This expenditure equilibrium occurs at point E, where the aggregate expenditure and 45-degree lines intersect. At this equilibrium, $2,000 billion of output is produced and willingly purchased.

At full-employment output ($Y_F = \$3,000$), aggregate expenditure is only $2,750 billion. This spending shortfall leaves $250 billion of output unsold. The difference between full-employment output (point h) and desired spending at full employment (point f) is called the recessionary gap.

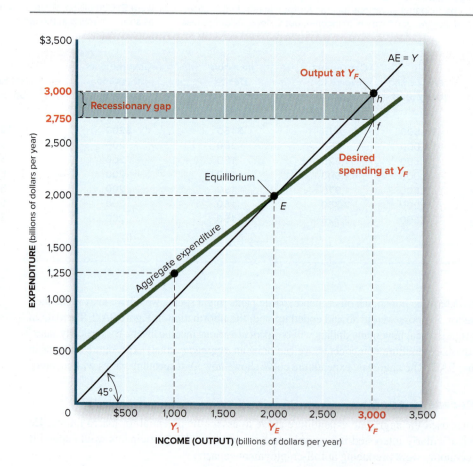

expenditure *equals* income. At any point on this line there would be no difference between total spending and the value of output.

The juxtaposition of the aggregate expenditure function with the 45-degree line is called the Keynesian cross. *The Keynesian cross relates aggregate expenditure to total income (output) without explicit consideration of (changing) price levels.* As is evident in Figure 9A.3, the aggregate expenditure curve crosses the 45-degree line only once, at point *E*. At that point, therefore, desired spending is *exactly* equal to the value of output. In Figure 9A.3 this equilibrium occurs at an output rate of $2,000 billion. Notice in the accompanying table how much market participants desire to spend at that rate of output. We have

$$
\begin{array}{lll}
\text{Consumer spending at} & Y_E = \$100 + 0.75(\$2,000) & = \$1,600 \\
\text{Investment spending at} & Y_E & = 150 \\
\text{Government spending at} & Y_E & = 200 \\
\text{Net export spending at} & Y_E & = \underline{50} \\
\text{Aggregate spending at} & Y_E & = \$2,000 \\
\end{array}
$$

At Y_E we have spending behavior that's completely compatible with the rate of production. At this equilibrium rate of output, no goods remain unsold. At that one rate of output where desired spending and the value of output are exactly equal, an expenditure equilibrium exists. *At macro equilibrium producers have no incentive to change the rate of output because they're selling everything they produce.*

Macro Failure

Unfortunately, the equilibrium depicted in Figure 9A.3 isn't the one we hoped to achieve. At Y_E the economy is well short of its full-employment goal (Y_F).

The expenditure equilibrium won't always fall short of the economy's productive capacity. Indeed, market participants' spending desires could also *exceed* the economy's full-employment potential. This might happen if investors, the government, or foreigners wanted to buy more output or if the consumption function shifted upward. In such circumstances an **inflationary gap** would exist. An inflationary gap arises when market participants want to buy more output than can be produced at full employment. The resulting scramble for goods may start a bidding war that pushes price levels even higher. This would be another symptom of macro failure.

inflationary gap: The amount by which aggregate spending at full employment exceeds full-employment output.

Two Paths to the Same Conclusion

The Keynesian analysis of aggregate *expenditure* looks remarkably similar to the Keynesian analysis of aggregate *demand*. In fact, it is: both approaches lead to the same conclusions about macro instability. The key difference between the "old" (expenditure) analysis and the "new" (AD) analysis is the level of detail about macro outcomes. In the old aggregate expenditure analysis, the focus was simply on total spending, the product of output and prices. *In the newer AD analysis, the separate effects of macro instability on prices and real output are distinguished.*[2] In a world where changes in both real output and price levels are important, the AD/AS framework is more useful.

Key Terms

aggregate expenditure   expenditure equilibrium   inflationary gap
recessionary gap

---

[2]This distinction is reflected in the differing definitions for the traditional *recessionary gap* (the *spending* shortfall at full-employment income) and the newer *recessionary real GDP gap* (the real output gap between full-employment GDP and equilibrium GDP).

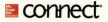

LO9-2 1. If the proportion of the total disposable income spend on consumer goods and services is 94.1 percent and if consumers spend 80 percent of each additional dollar, what is
   (a) The APC?
   (b) The APS?
   (c) The MPC?
   (d) The MPS?

LO9-2 2. According to In the News "Disposable Income and Outlays: February 2017," between January and February by how much did
   (a) Disposable income increase?
   (b) Consumption increase?
   (c) Savings increase?
   (d) What was the MPC?
   (e) What was the MPS?
   (f) What was the APC for February?

LO9-2
LO9-4 3. On the accompanying graph, draw the consumption function $C = \$300$ billion $+ 0.50Y_D$.
   (a) At what level of income do households begin to save? Designate that point on the graph with the letter A.
   (b) By how much does consumption increase when income rises $100 billion beyond point A? Designate this new level of consumption with point B.
   (c) Illustrate the impact on consumption of the change in consumer confidence described in In the News "Consumer Confidence Index at Record Low."

LO9-4 4. Illustrate on the following two graphs the impact of decreased consumer confidence.

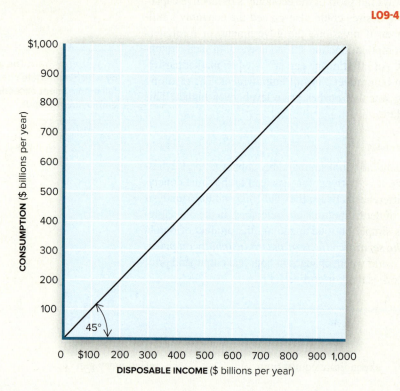

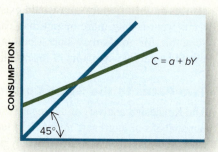

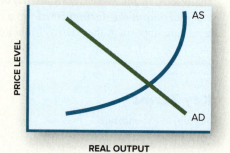

What direction did
(a) The consumption function shift?
(b) AD shift?

LO9-4 5. If every $1,000 increase in the real price of homes adds 6 cents to annual consumer spending (the "wealth effect"),
    (*a*) By how much did consumption *decline* when home prices fell by $2 trillion in 2006–2008?
    (*b*) In which direction did the consumption function shift?
    (*c*) In which direction did the AD curve shift?

LO9-3 6. Illustrate on the following graphs the impact of Panasonic's changed investment plans (World View "Panasonic Cuts Spending").

LO9-4 7. What was the range, in absolute percentage points, of the variation in quarterly growth rates between 2005 and 2008 of
    (*a*) Consumer spending?
    (*b*) Investment spending?
    (*c*) Which is more volatile?
    (*Note:* See Figure 9.8 for data.)

LO9-5 8. Complete the following table:

Price Level	Real Output Demanded (in $ billions) by						
	Consumers	+ Investors	+ Government	+ Net Exports	= Aggregate Demand	Aggregate Supply
120	80	15	20	10	____	320
110	92	16	20	12	____	260
100	104	17	20	14	____	215
90	116	18	20	16	____	200
80	128	19	20	18	____	185
70	140	20	20	20	____	175
60	154	21	20	22	____	170

    (*a*) What is the level of equilibrium GDP?
    (*b*) What is the equilibrium price level?
    (*c*) If full employment occurs at real GDP = $200 billion, what kind of GDP gap exists?
    (*d*) How large is that gap?
    (*e*) Which macro problem exists here (unemployment or inflation)?

LO9-1
LO9-5 9. On the graph on the next page, draw the AD and AS curves with these data that lead to a full-employment equilibrium:

Price level	140	130	120	110	100	90	80	70	60	50
Real output										
Demanded	600	700	800	900	1,000	1,100	1,200	1,300	1,400	1,500
Supplied	1,200	1,150	1,100	1,050	1,000	950	900	800	600	400

    (*a*) What is the full-employment equilibrium
        (*i*) Real output level?
        (*ii*) Price level?

Suppose net exports decline by $150 at all price levels, but all other components of aggregate demand remain constant.

(*b*) Draw the new AD curve.

(*c*) What is the new equilibrium

    (*i*)   Output level?

    (*ii*) Price level?

(*d*) What macro problem has arisen in this economy: unemployment or inflation?

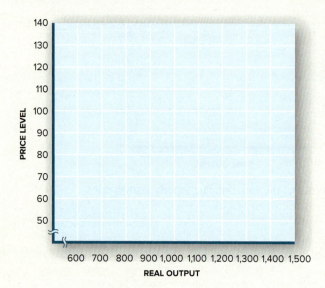

LO9-2 10. Given C = $1000 + 0.80Y$_D$,

    (*a*) How much is saved if Y_D is $40,000?

    (*b*) How much does consumption increase if Y_D increases by $1,000?

LO9-4 11. If the labor force averaged 237 million in 2009–2011, by how much in percentage terms did the state and local layoffs described in In the News "State/Local Belt Tightening Hurts Economy" add to the national unemployment rate, assuming all laid-off workers were actively seeking work?

LO9-4 12. The Economy Tomorrow: Predict the impact on aggregate demand if

    (*a*) The average workweek increased.

    (*b*) Consumer confidence lags.

    (*c*) Retailers are placing larger orders than in the past.

Self-Adjustment or Instability?

John Maynard Keynes took a dim view of a market-driven macro economy. He emphasized that (1) macro failure is likely to occur in such an economy and, worse yet, (2) macro failure isn't likely to go away. As noted earlier, the first prediction wasn't all that controversial. The classical economists had conceded the possibility of occasional recession or inflation. In their view, however, the economy would quickly self-adjust, restoring full employment and price stability. Keynes's second proposition challenged this view. The most distinctive, and frightening, proposition of Keynes's theory was that there would be no automatic self-adjustment; the economy could stagnate in *persistent* unemployment or be subjected to *continuing* inflation.

President Herbert Hoover was a believer in the market's ability to self-adjust. So was President George H.W. Bush. As Hoover and Bush Sr. waited for the economy to self-adjust, however, they both lost their reelection bids. President George W. Bush wasn't willing to take that chance. As soon as he was elected, he pushed tax cuts through Congress that boosted consumer disposable incomes and helped bolster a sagging economy. After the terrorist attacks of September 11, 2001, he called for even greater government intervention. Yet when the economy slowed down in his final year, he seemed willing to await the self-correcting forces of the marketplace.

President Obama embraced the Keynesian perspective from day 1. He explicitly rejected the "worn-out dogma" of classical theory and insisted that only dramatic government intervention could keep a bad economic situation from getting worse. He advocated massive spending programs to jump-start the recession-bound economy of 2008–2009.

President Trump also adopted the Keynesian approach. To accelerate economic growth and "make America great again," he pushed tax cuts for consumers and also tax cuts for businesses. Like Keynes, Trump believed tax cuts that put more disposable income in people's hands would lead to more spending, shifting the aggregate demand curve to the right.

These different presidential experiences don't resolve the self-adjustment debate; rather, they emphasize how important the debate is. In this chapter we'll focus on the *adjustment process*—that is, how markets *respond* to an undesirable equilibrium. We're especially concerned with the following questions:

- **Why does anyone think the market might self-adjust (returning to a desired equilibrium)?**
- **Why might markets *not* self-adjust?**
- **Could market responses actually *worsen* macro outcomes?**

LEAKAGES AND INJECTIONS

Chapter 9 demonstrated how the economy could end up at the wrong macro equilibrium—with too much or too little aggregate demand. Such an undesirable outcome might result from an initial imbalance between **aggregate demand** at the current price level and full-employment GDP. Or the economy could fall into trouble from a *shift* in aggregate demand that pushes the economy out of a desirable full-employment–price-stability equilibrium. Whatever the sequence of events might be, the bottom line is the same: total spending doesn't match total output at the desired full-employment–price-stability level.

The Circular Flow. The circular flow of income illustrates how such an undesirable outcome comes about. Recall that all income originates in product markets, where goods and services are sold. If the economy were producing at **full-employment GDP,** then enough income would be available to buy everything a fully employed economy produces. As we've seen, however, aggregate demand isn't so certain. It could happen that market participants choose *not* to spend all their income, leaving some goods unsold. Alternatively, they might try to buy *more* than full-employment output, pushing prices up.

To see how such imbalances might arise, Keynes distinguished *leakages* from the circular flow and *injections* into that flow, as illustrated in Figure 10.1.

Consumer Saving

As we observed in Chapter 9, consumers typically don't spend *all* the income they earn in product markets; they *save* some fraction of it. This is the first leak in the circular flow. Some income earned in product markets isn't being instantly converted into spending. This circular flow **leakage** creates the potential for a spending shortfall.

Suppose the economy were producing at full employment, with $3,000 billion of output at the current price level, indexed at $P = 100$. This initial output rate is marked by point F

aggregate demand (AD): The total quantity of output (real GDP) demanded at alternative price levels in a given time period, *ceteris paribus*.

full-employment GDP: The value of total market output (real GDP) produced at full employment.

leakage: Income not spent directly on domestic output but instead diverted from the circular flow—for example, saving, imports, taxes.

FIGURE 10.1

Leakages and Injections

The income generated in production doesn't return completely to product markets in the form of consumer spending. Consumer saving, imports, taxes, and business saving all leak from the circular flow, *reducing* potential aggregate demand. If this leakage isn't offset, some of the output produced will remain unsold.

Business investment, government purchases of goods and services, and exports inject spending into the circular flow, *adding* to aggregate demand. The focus of macro concern is whether injections will offset leakage at full employment.

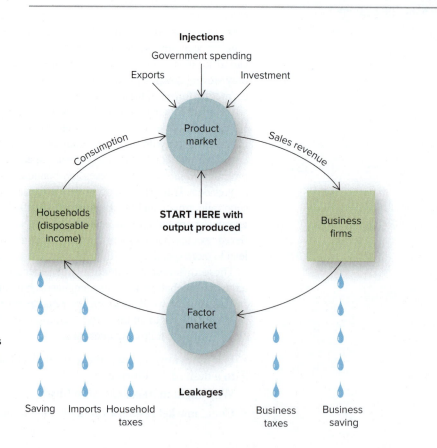

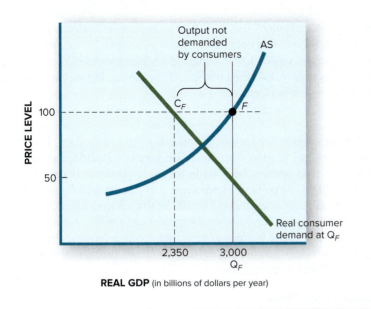

FIGURE 10.2

Leakage and AD

The disposable income consumers receive is only about 70 percent of total income (GDP) due to taxes and income held by businesses. Consumers also tend to save some of their disposable income and buy imported products. As a result of these leakages, consumers will demand less output at the current price level ($P = 100$) than the economy produces at full-employment GDP (Q_F). In this case, $3,000 billion of output (income) is produced (point F), but consumers demand only $2,350 billion of output at the price level $P = 100$ (point C_F).

in Figure 10.2. Suppose further that *all* of the income generated in product markets went directly to consumers (i.e., no taxes, no business retained earnings, etc.). This assumption puts consumers in an all-powerful position: their spending decisions will determine whether the economy stays at full-employment (Q_F). The question then is whether consumers will *spend* enough to *maintain* full employment?

We already observed in Chapter 9 that such an outcome is unlikely. Typically, consumers *save* a small fraction of their incomes.

If the consumption function were $C_F = \$100$ billion $+ 0.75Y$, consumers will spend only

$$C_F = \$100 \text{ billion} + 0.75(\$3,000 \text{ billion})$$
$$= \$2,350 \text{ billion}$$

at the current price level. This consumption behavior is illustrated in Figure 10.2 by the point C_F.

Consumers would demand *more* real output with their current income if prices were to fall (due to the real balances, foreign trade, and interest rate effects, discussed in Chapter 8). Hence the consumption component of aggregate demand slopes downward from point C_F. Our immediate concern, however, focuses on how much (real) output consumers will purchase at the *current* price level. At the price level $P = 100$ consumers choose to save $650 billion, leaving consumption ($2,350 billion) far short of full-employment GDP ($3,000 billion).

The decision to save some fraction of household income isn't necessarily bad, but it does present a potential problem. Unless other market participants, such as business, government, and foreigners, buy this unsold output, goods will pile up on producers' shelves. As undesired inventory accumulates, producers will reduce the rate of output and unemployment will rise.

Imports and Taxes

Saving isn't the only source of leakage. *Imports also represent leakage from the circular flow.* When consumers buy imported goods, their spending leaves (that is, leaks out of) the domestic circular flow and goes to foreign producers. As a consequence, income spent on imported goods is not part of domestic aggregate demand.

In the real world, *taxes are a form of leakage as well.* A lot of revenue generated in market sales gets diverted into federal, state, and local government coffers. Sales taxes are taken out of the circular flow in product markets. Then payroll taxes and income taxes are taken out of paychecks. Households never get the chance to spend any of that income. They

disposable income (DI): After-tax income of households; personal income less personal taxes.

start with **disposable income,** which is much less than the total income generated in product markets. In 2016, disposable income was only $14.1 trillion while total income (GDP) was $18.5 trillion. Hence consumers couldn't have bought everything produced that year with their current incomes even if they had saved nothing. Their disposable income was $4.4 trillion less than the value of output produced.

Business Saving

The business sector also keeps some of the income generated in product markets. Businesses set aside some of their revenue to cover the costs of maintaining, repairing, and replacing plants and equipment. The revenue held aside for these purposes is called a *depreciation allowance*. In addition, corporations keep some part of total profit (retained earnings) for continuing business uses rather than paying all profits out to stockholders in the form of dividends. The total value of depreciation allowances and retained earnings is called **gross business saving.** The income businesses hold back in these forms represents further leakage from the circular flow—income that consumers never see and that doesn't automatically flow directly back into product markets.

gross business saving: Depreciation allowances and retained earnings.

Injections into the Circular Flow

Although leakage from the circular flow is a potential source of unemployment problems, we shouldn't conclude that the economy will sink as soon as consumers start saving some of their income, buy a few imports, or pay their taxes. Consumers aren't the only source of aggregate demand; business firms and government agencies also contribute to total spending. So do international consumers who buy our exports. So before we run out into the streets and scream, "The circular flow is leaking!" we need to look at what other market participants are doing.

The top half of Figure 10.1 completes the picture of the circular flow by depicting **injections** of new spending. When businesses buy plant and equipment, they add to the dollar value of product market sales. Government purchases and exports also inject spending into the product market. These *injections of investment, government, and export spending help offset leakage from saving, imports, and taxes.* As a result, there may be enough aggregate demand to maintain full employment at the current price level, even if consumers aren't spending every dollar of income.

injection: An addition of spending to the circular flow of income.

The critical issue for macro stability is whether spending injections will actually equal spending leakage at full employment. *Injections must equal leakages if all the output supplied is to equal the output demanded* (macro equilibrium). Ideally, the economy will satisfy this condition at full employment and we can stop worrying about short-run macro problems. If not, we've still got some work to do.

Self-Adjustment?

As we noted earlier, classical economists had no worries. They assumed that spending injections would always equal spending leakage. That was the foundation of their belief in the market's self-adjustment. The mechanism they counted on for equalizing leakages and injections was the interest rate.

Flexible Interest Rates. Ignore all other injections and leakages for the moment and focus on just consumer saving and business investment (Figure 10.3). If consumer saving (a leakage) exceeds business investment (an injection), unspent income must be piling up somewhere (in bank accounts, for example). These unspent funds will be a tempting lure for business investors. Businesses are always looking for funds to finance expansion or modernization. So they aren't likely to leave a pile of consumer savings sitting idle. Moreover, the banks and other institutions that are holding consumer savings will be eager to lend more funds as consumer savings pile up. To make more loans, they can lower the interest rate. As we observed in Chapter 9 (Figure 9.7), lower interest rates prompt businesses to borrow and invest more. Hence *classical economists concluded that if interest rates fell far enough, business investment (injections) would equal consumer saving (leakage).*

Leakages	Injections
Consumer saving	**Investment**
Business saving	Government spending
Taxes	Exports
Imports	

FIGURE 10.3

Leakages and Injections

Macro equilibrium occurs only when leakages equal injections. Consumer saving and business investment are the primary flows in and out of the circular flow in a wholly private and closed economy. Hence the relationship between saving and investment reveals whether a market-driven economy will self-adjust to a full-employment equilibrium.

From this classical perspective, any spending shortfall in the macro economy would soon be closed by this self-adjustment of leakage and injection flows. If saving leakage increased, interest rates would drop, prompting an offsetting rise in investment injections. Aggregate demand would be maintained at full-employment GDP because investment spending would soak up all consumer saving. The *content* of AD would change (less *C*, more *I*), but the *level* would remain at full-employment GDP.

Changing Expectations. Keynes argued that classical economists ignored the role of expectations. As Figure 9.7 illustrated, the level of investment *is* sensitive to interest rates. But the whole investment function *shifts* when business expectations change. Keynes thought it preposterous that investment spending would *increase* in response to *declining* consumer sales. A decline in investment is more likely, Keynes argued.

Flexible Prices. The classical economists said self-adjustment was possible even without flexible interest rates. Flexible *prices* would do the trick. Look at Figure 10.2 again. It says consumers will demand only $2,350 billion of output *at the current price level*. But what if prices *fell?* Then consumers would buy more output. In fact, if prices fell far enough, consumers might buy *all* the output produced at full employment. In Figure 10.2, the price level $P = 50$ elicits such a response. (Notice how much output is demanded at the $P = 50$ price level.)

Expectations (Again). Keynes again chided the classical economists for their naïveté. Sure, a nationwide sale might prompt consumers to buy more goods and services. But how would businesses react? They had planned on selling Q_F amount of output at the price level $P = 100$. If prices must be cut in half to move their merchandise, businesses are likely to rethink their production and investment plans. Keynes argued that declining (retail) prices would prompt businesses to invest *less,* not more. This was a real fear in 2008–2009, as In the News "Everything Is on Sale and That's Not Good" suggests.

IN THE NEWS

EVERYTHING IS ON SALE AND THAT'S NOT GOOD

The Bureau of Labor Statistics reported that consumer prices fell in October at their fastest pace in more than 60 years. Prices were down across the board—for cars, clothes, gasoline, and electronics. Housing prices also continued to drop.

Consumers might like the short-term rewards of a nationwide fire sale. But declining prices can eventually hurt. Declining prices squeeze the profit margins of producers, causing them to cut back production and lay off workers. Retailers become more hesitant to restock inventory. A kind of downward spiral may emerge that pushes both prices and production down. This is the kind of deflationary spiral that made the Great Depression of the 1930s so painful.

Source: U.S. Bureau of Labor Statistics and news accounts of December 2008.

ANALYSIS: Deflation does make products cheaper for consumers. But declining prices also reduce business revenues, profits, and sales expectations.

THE MULTIPLIER PROCESS

Keynes not only rejected the classical notion of self-adjustment; he also argued that things were likely to get *worse,* not better, once a spending shortfall emerged. This was the scariest part of Keynes's theory.

To understand Keynes's fears, imagine that the economy is initially at the desired full-employment GDP equilibrium, as represented again by point *F* in Figure 10.4. Included in that full-employment equilibrium GDP is

Consumption	=	$2,350 billion
Investment	=	400 billion
Government	=	150 billion
Net exports	=	100 billion
Aggregate demand at current price level	=	$3,000 billion

Everything looks good in this macro economy. This is pretty much how the U.S. economy looked in 2006–2007: we had full employment and price stability.

The 2007 Q4 Investment Decline

In the fourth quarter of 2007, the U.S. economy took a turn for the worse. The problem began in the housing industry. Housing prices had risen dramatically from 1998 to 2006. This surge in home prices had increased household wealth by trillions of dollars and prompted home builders to construct more new homes every year. These injections of investment spending helped keep GDP growing for a decade. But the party ended in July 2006 when home prices stopped rising. That made home builders rethink their construction plans. When home prices actually began falling in 2007, many home builders called it quits. In the fourth quarter of 2007, residential investment (home construction) declined by a staggering 29 percent (see In the News "Housing Starts Fall to 10-Year Low"), dragging total U.S. investment down by more than $50 billion. The die was cast: a recession was sure to follow.

FIGURE 10.4

AD Shift

When investment spending drops, aggregate demand shifts to the left. In the short run, this causes output and the price level to fall. The initial full-employment equilibrium at *F* is pushed to a new and lower equilibrium at point *b.*

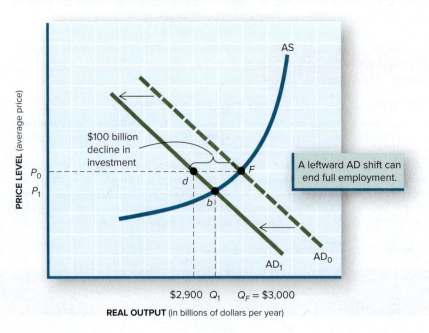

IN THE **NEWS**

HOUSING STARTS FALL TO 10-YEAR LOW

Builders are scaling back. The Commerce Department reported yesterday that housing starts fell to a seasonally adjusted rate of 1.381 million homes, down from 1.471 million in June. This is the fewest number of new homes being built in more than 10 years. Housing permits were down as well, to a seasonally adjusted rate of only 1.373 million. All in all, the data points to a "pretty gloomy" outlook for the housing industry, according to a senior Wells Fargo economist.

Source: U.S. Department of Commerce and news reports of August 2007.

ANALYSIS: A drop in residential construction (investment) in 2007 shifted the AD curve to the left, as in Figure 10.4, throwing thousands of construction employees out of work. This started a series of consumption-based AD shifts in a sequence called the *multiplier process*.

Undesired Inventory. The plunge in residential construction was accompanied by a surge in the number of unsold new homes. Buyers were fleeing the housing market even faster than builders. So inventories of unsold new homes were rising despite the slowdown in construction.

Ironically, this additional inventory is counted as part of investment spending. (Recall that our definition of investment spending includes changes in business inventories.) This additional inventory was clearly undesired, however, as builders had planned on selling these homes.

To keep track of these unwanted changes in investment, we ***distinguish* desired *(or planned) investment from** **actual *investment*.** *Desired* investment represents purchases of new plants and equipment plus any *desired* changes in business inventories. By contrast, *actual* investment represents purchases of new plants and equipment plus *actual* changes in business inventories, desired or otherwise. In other words,

$$\frac{\text{Actual}}{\text{investment}} = \frac{\text{Desired}}{\text{investment}} + \frac{\text{Undesired}}{\text{investment}}$$

Falling Output and Prices. How are business firms likely to react when they see undesired inventory piling up in new housing developments, on car lots, or on store shelves? They could regard the inventory pileup as a brief aberration and continue producing at full-employment levels. But the inventory pileup might also set off sales alarms, causing businesses to alter their pricing, production, and investment plans. If that happens, they're likely to start cutting prices in an attempt to increase the rate of sales. Producers are also likely to reduce the rate of new output.

Figure 10.4 illustrates these two responses. Assume that investment spending declines by \$100 billion at the existing price level P_0. This shifts the aggregate demand curve leftward from AD_0 to AD_1 and immediately moves the economy from point F to point d. At d, however, excess inventories prompt firms to reduce prices. As prices fall, the economy gravitates toward a new **equilibrium GDP** at point b. At point b, the rate of output (Q_1) is less than the full-employment level (Q_F), and the price level has fallen from P_0 to P_1. This economy is now in a recession, and the unemployment rate is rising.

equilibrium GDP: The value of total output (real GDP) produced at macro equilibrium (AS = AD).

Household Incomes

The decline in GDP depicted in Figure 10.4 isn't pretty. But Keynes warned that the picture would get uglier when *consumers* start feeling the impact of the production cutbacks. This is the scary part of the story.

So far we've treated the production cutbacks that accompany a GDP gap as a rather abstract problem. But the reality is that when production is cut back, people suffer. When producers decrease the rate of output, workers lose their jobs or face pay cuts, or both. Cutbacks in investment spending in 2007–2008 led to layoffs among home builders, mortgage companies, banks, equipment manufacturers, auto companies, and even hi-tech companies like Hewlett-Packard, IBM, Yahoo!, and Google. A decline in travel caused layoffs at airlines and aircraft manufacturers. As workers get laid off or have their wages cut, household incomes decline. Thus *a reduction in investment spending implies a reduction in household incomes.*

Income-Dependent Consumption

We saw in Chapter 9 the kind of threat a reduction in household income poses. Those consumers who end up with less income won't be able to purchase as many goods and services as they did before. As a consequence, aggregate demand will fall further, leading to still larger stocks of unsold goods, more job layoffs, and further reductions in income. It's this sequence of events—called the *multiplier process*—that makes a sudden decline in aggregate demand so frightening. *What starts off as a relatively small spending shortfall quickly snowballs into a much larger problem.*

We can see the multiplier process at work by watching what happens to a $100 billion decline in investment spending as it makes its way around the circular flow. The process starts at step 1 in Figure 10.5, when investment is cut back by $100 billion. At first (step 2), the only thing that happens is that unsold goods appear (in the form of undesired inventories). Producers adjust to this problem by cutting back on production and laying off workers or reducing wages and prices (step 3). In either case, consumer income falls $100 billion per year shortly after the investment cutbacks occur (step 4).

How will consumers respond to this drop in disposable income? *If disposable income falls, we expect consumer spending to drop as well.* In fact, the consumption function tells us just how much spending will drop. The **marginal propensity to consume (MPC)** is the critical variable in this process. Since we've specified that $C = \$100$ billion $+ 0.75Y$, we expect consumers to reduce their spending by $0.75 for every $1.00 of lost income. In the present example, the loss of $100 billion of annual income will induce consumers to reduce their rate of spending by $75 billion per year ($0.75 \times \$100$ billion). This drop in spending is illustrated by step 5 in Figure 10.5.

marginal propensity to consume (MPC): The fraction of each additional (marginal) dollar of disposable income spent on consumption; the change in consumption divided by the change in disposable income.

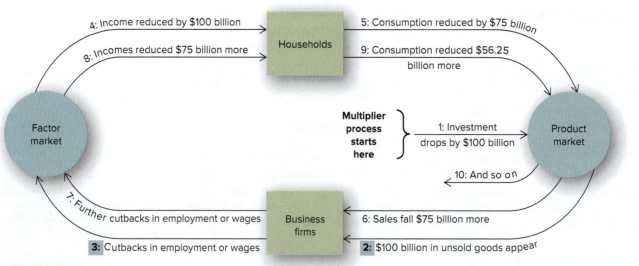

FIGURE 10.5

The Multiplier Process

A decline in investment (step 1) will leave output unsold (step 2) and may lead to a cutback in production and income (step 3). A reduction in total income (step 4) will in turn lead to a reduction in consumer spending (step 5). These additional cuts in spending cause a further decrease in income, leading to additional spending reductions, and so on. This sequence of adjustments is referred to as the *multiplier process.*

The multiplier process doesn't stop here. A reduction in consumer spending quickly translates into more unsold output (step 6). As additional goods pile up on producers' shelves, we anticipate further cutbacks in production, employment, and disposable income (step 7).

As disposable incomes are further reduced by job layoffs and wage cuts (step 8), more reductions in consumer spending are sure to follow (step 9). Again the marginal propensity to consume (MPC) tells us how large such reductions will be. With an MPC of 0.75, we may expect spending to fall by another $56.25 billion per year (0.75 × $75 billion) in step 9. This is exactly what was happening in 2008, as In the News "US GDP Down 3.8% in Q4, Biggest Drop Since 1982" reports.

The Multiplier

The multiplier process continues to work until the reductions in income and sales become so small that no one's market behavior is significantly affected. We don't have to examine each step along the way. As you may have noticed, all the steps begin to look alike once we've gone around the circular flow a few times. Instead of examining each step, we can look ahead to see where they are taking us. Each time the multiplier process works its way around the circular flow, the reduction in spending equals the previous drop in income multiplied by the MPC. Accordingly, by pressing a few keys on a calculator, we can produce a sequence of events like that depicted in Table 10.1.

The impact of the multiplier is devastating. The ultimate reduction in real spending resulting from the initial drop in investment isn't $100 billion per year but $400 billion! Even if one is accustomed to thinking in terms of billions and trillions, this is a huge drop in demand. What the multiplier process demonstrates is that the dimensions of an initial spending gap greatly understate the severity of the economic dislocations that will follow in its wake. *The eventual decline in spending will be much larger than the initial (autonomous) decrease in aggregate demand.* This was evident in the recession of 2008–2009, when layoffs snowballed from industry to industry (see In the News "Unemployment Spreading Fast across U.S. Industries"), ultimately leaving millions of people unemployed.

The Multiplier Cycles

The circular flow of income implies that an initial drop in spending will lead to cumulative changes in consumer spending and income. Here, an initial decline in investment spending of $100 billion (first cycle) causes a cutback in consumer spending in the amount of $75 billion (second cycle). At each subsequent cycle, consumer spending drops by the amount MPC × prior change in income. Ultimately, total spending (and income) falls by $400 billion, or $1/(1 - MPC) \times$ initial change in spending.

Spending Cycles	Change in This Cycle's Spending and Income (Billions per Year)	Cumulative Decrease in Spending and Income (Billions per Year)
First cycle: investment declines.	$100.00	$100.00 } ΔI
Second cycle: consumption drops by MPC × $100.	75.00	175.00
Third cycle: consumption drops by MPC × $75.	56.25	231.25
Fourth cycle: consumption drops by MPC × $56.25.	42.19	273.44
Fifth cycle: consumption drops by MPC × $42.19.	31.64	305.08 } ΔC
Sixth cycle: consumption drops by MPC × $31.64.	23.73	328.81
Seventh cycle: consumption drops by MPC × $23.73.	17.80	346.61
Eighth cycle: consumption drops by MPC × $17.80.	13.35	359.95
⋮	⋮	⋮
nth cycle and beyond		400.00

IN THE NEWS

UNEMPLOYMENT SPREADING FAST ACROSS U.S. INDUSTRIES

The collapse of the housing industry has sent ripple effects across U.S. industries. The surge in construction unemployment is spilling over into other sectors of the economy at an alarming rate. In data released Friday, the Bureau of Labor Statistics reported that the unemployment rate has jumped by more than 2 percentage points over last year in 12 states. Job losses have spread beyond construction to a host of industries, including tourism and professional services. Economists now predict that the national unemployment rate, presently at 6.5 percent, will top 8 percent in the coming months.

Source: U.S. Bureau of Labor Statistics and news accounts, November 2008.

ANALYSIS: Cutbacks in production cause employee layoffs. The newly unemployed workers curtail *their* spending, causing sequential layoffs in other industries. These ripple effects give rise to the multiplier.

multiplier: The multiple by which an initial change in aggregate spending will alter total expenditure after an infinite number of spending cycles; 1/(1 − MPC).

The ultimate impact of an AD shift on total spending can be determined by computing the change in income and consumption at each cycle of the circular flow. This is the approach summarized in Table 10.1, with each row representing a spending cycle. The entire computation can be simplified considerably by using a single figure, the multiplier. The **multiplier** tells us the extent to which the rate of total spending will change in response to an initial change in the flow of expenditure. The multiplier summarizes the sequence of steps described in Table 10.1.[1] In its simplest form, the multiplier can be computed as

$$\text{Multiplier} = \frac{1}{1 - \text{MPC}}$$

[1]The multiplier summarizes the geometric progression $1 + \text{MPC} + \text{MPC}^2 + \text{MPC}^3 + \ldots + \text{MPC}^n$, which equals $1/(1 - \text{MPC})$ when n becomes infinite.

In our example, the initial change in aggregate demand occurs when investment drops by $100 billion per year at full-employment output ($3,000 billion per year). Table 10.1 indicates that this investment drop-off will lead to a $400 billion reduction in the rate of total spending at the current price level. Using the multiplier, we arrive at the same conclusion by observing that

$$\text{Total change in spending} = \text{Multiplier} \times \text{Initial change in aggregate spending}$$

$$= \frac{1}{1 - \text{MPC}} \times \$100 \text{ billion per year}$$

$$= \frac{1}{1 - 0.75} \times \$100 \text{ billion per year}$$

$$= 4 \qquad \times \$100 \text{ billion per year}$$

$$= \$400 \text{ billion per year}$$

In other words, ***the cumulative decrease in total spending ($400 billion per year) resulting from an abrupt decline in aggregate demand at full employment is equal to the initial decline ($100 billion per year) multiplied by the multiplier (4).***

Notice how the size of the multiplier depends on the value of the MPC: the larger the fraction (MPC) of income respent in each round of the circular flow, the greater the impact of any autonomous change in spending on cumulative aggregate demand. The cumulative process of spending adjustments can also have worldwide effects. As World View "Asian Economies Hurt by U.S. Recession" illustrates, Asia's economic growth slowed when the U.S. economy slumped in 2008–2009.

WORLD VIEW

ASIAN ECONOMIES HURT BY U.S. RECESSION

China, Japan, and South Korea are all feeling the pain of the U.S. recession. Japanese exports are down 35 percent in December, compared to last year. Companies like Sony and Toyota report especially heavy declines in U.S. sales. China's export growth has also slowed abruptly, cutting its GDP growth rate to 9 percent in 2008, down from 13 percent in 2007. South Korea has fallen into a recession of its own, with GDP down 3 to 4 percent from last year. The sharp contraction in the U.S. economy has rippled across the global economy, hitting export-dependent Asian nations particularly hard.

Source: News accounts, January 2009.

ANALYSIS: Multiplier effects can spill over national borders. The 2008–2009 recession in the United States reduced U.S. demand for Asian exports, setting off a sequence of spending cuts in Japan, Korea, China, and other Asian nations.

MACRO EQUILIBRIUM REVISITED

The key features of the Keynesian adjustment process are

- ***Producers cut output and employment when output exceeds aggregate demand at the current price level (leakage exceeds injections).***
- ***The resulting loss of income causes a decline in consumer spending.***
- ***Declines in consumer spending lead to further production cutbacks, more lost income, and still less consumption.***

FIGURE 10.6

Multiplier Effects

A decline in investment spending reduces household income, setting off negative multiplier effects. Hence the *initial* shift of AD₀ to AD₁ is followed by a series of aftershocks that ultimately ends up at AD₂. The shift from AD₁ to AD₂ represents reduced consumption.

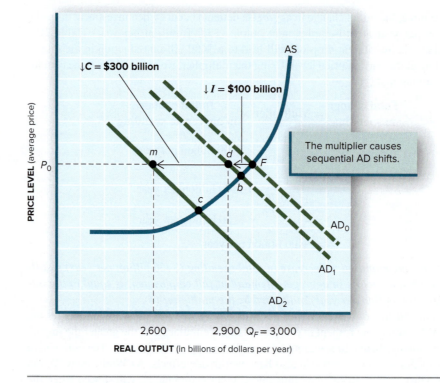

Sequential AD Shifts

Figure 10.6 illustrates the ultimate impact of the multiplier process. Notice that the AD curve shifts *twice*. The first shift—from AD_0 to AD_1—represents the $100 billion drop in investment spending. As we saw earlier in Figure 10.4, this initial shift of aggregate demand will start the economy moving toward a new equilibrium at point *b*.

Along the way, however, the multiplier kicks in and things get worse. ***The decline in household income caused by investment cutbacks sets off the multiplier process, causing sequential shifts of the AD curve.*** We measure these multiplier effects at the initial price level of P_0. With a marginal propensity to consume of 0.75, we've seen that induced consumption ultimately declines by $300 billion when autonomous investment declines by $100 billion. In Figure 10.6 this is illustrated by the *second* shift of the aggregate demand curve, from AD_1 to AD_2. Notice that the horizontal distance between AD_1 and AD_2 is $300 billion. That represents the *cumulative* decline in consumer spending that results from repeated steps in the multiplier process. When added to the initial decline in investment spending ($100 billion), we get a $400 billion shift in AD.

Price and Output Effects

recessionary GDP gap: The amount by which equilibrium GDP falls short of full-employment GDP.

Although aggregate demand has fallen (shifted) by $400 billion, real output doesn't necessarily drop that much. ***The impact of a shift in aggregate demand is reflected in both output and price changes.*** This is evident in Figure 10.7, which is a close-up view of Figure 10.6. When AD shifts from AD_0 to AD_2 the macro equilibrium moves down the sloped AS curve to point *c*. At point *c* the new equilibrium output is Q_E and the new price level is P_E.

cyclical unemployment: Unemployment attributable to a lack of job vacancies—that is, to an inadequate level of aggregate demand.

Recessionary GDP Gap. As long as the aggregate supply curve is upward-sloping, the shock of any AD shift will be spread across output and prices. In Figure 10.7 the net effect on real output is shown as the real GDP gap. ***The recessionary GDP gap equals the difference between equilibrium real GDP (Q_E) and full-employment real GDP (Q_F)*** It represents the amount by which the economy is underproducing during a recession. As we noted in Chapter 9, this is a classic case of **cyclical unemployment.**

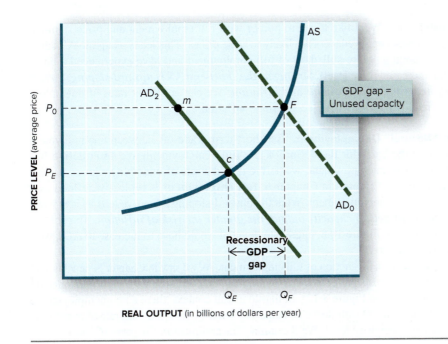

FIGURE 10.7
Recessionary GDP Gap

The real GDP gap is the difference between equilibrium GDP (Q_E) and full-employment GDP (Q_F). It represents the lost output due to a recession.

Short-Run Inflation–Unemployment Trade-Offs

Figure 10.7 not only illustrates how much output declines when AD falls but also provides an important clue about the difficulty of restoring full employment. Suppose the recessionary GDP gap were $200 billion, as illustrated in Figure 10.8. How much more AD would we need to get back to full employment?

Upward-Sloping AS. Suppose aggregate demand at the equilibrium price level (P_E) were to increase by exactly $200 billion (including multiplier effects), as illustrated by the shift to AD$_3$. Would that get us back to full-employment output? Not according to Figure 10.8. ***When AD increases, both output and prices go up.*** Because the AS curve is upward-sloping, the $200 billion shift from AD$_2$ to AD$_3$ moves the new macro equilibrium to point

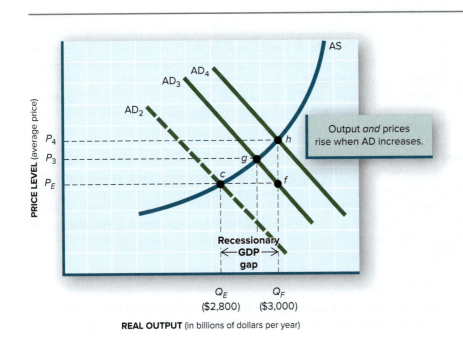

FIGURE 10.8
The Unemployment–Inflation Trade-Off

If the short-run AS curve is upward-sloping, an AD increase will raise output *and* prices. If AD increases by the amount of the recessionary GDP gap only (AD$_2$ to AD$_3$), full employment (Q_F) won't be reached. Macro equilibrium moves to point *g*, not point *f*.

g rather than point *f*. We'd like to get to point *f* with full employment and price stability. But as demand picks up, producers are likely to raise prices. This leads us up the AS curve to point *g*. At point *g*, we're still short of full employment and have experienced a bit of inflation (an increased price level). *So long as the short-run AS is upward-sloping, there's a trade-off between unemployment and inflation.* We can get lower rates of unemployment (more real output) only if we accept some inflation.

"Full" vs. "Natural" Unemployment. The short-term trade-off between unemployment and inflation is the basis for the definition of "full" employment. We don't define full employment as *zero* unemployment; we define it as the rate of unemployment *consistent with price stability.* As noted in Chapter 6, **full employment** is typically defined as a 4 to 6 percent rate of unemployment. What the upward-sloping AS curve tells us is that *the closer the economy gets to capacity output, the greater the risk of inflation.* To get back to full employment in Figure 10.8, aggregate demand would have to increase to AD_4, with the price level rising to P_4.

Not everyone accepts this notion of full employment. As we saw in Chapter 8, neoclassical and monetarist economists prefer to focus on *long*-run outcomes. In their view, the long-run AS curve is vertical (see Figure 8.12). In that long-run context, there's no unemployment–inflation trade-off: An AD shift doesn't change the "natural" (institutional) rate of unemployment but does alter the price level. We'll examine this argument in Chapters 16 and 17.

> **full employment:** The lowest rate of unemployment compatible with price stability, variously estimated at between 4 percent and 6 percent unemployment.

ADJUSTMENT TO AN INFLATIONARY GDP GAP

As we've observed, *a sudden shift in aggregate demand can have a cumulative effect on macro outcomes* that's larger than the initial imbalance. This multiplier process works both ways. Just as a *decrease* in investment (or any other AD component) can send the economy into a recessionary tailspin, an *increase* in investment might initiate an inflationary spiral.

Figure 10.9 illustrates the consequences of a sudden jump in investment spending. We start out again in the happy equilibrium (point *F*), where full employment (Q_F) and price stability (P_0) prevail. Initial spending consists of

$$C = \$2,350 \text{ billion} \qquad G = \$150 \text{ billion}$$

$$I = \$400 \text{ billion} \qquad X - M = \$100 \text{ billion}$$

Increased Investment

Then investors suddenly decide to step up the rate of investment. Perhaps their expectations for future sales have risen. Maybe new technology has become available that compels firms to modernize their facilities. Maybe they want to take advantage of President Trump's tax cuts and investment incentives. Whatever the reason, investors decide to raise the level of investment from $400 billion to $500 billion at the current price level (P_0). This change in investment spending shifts the aggregate demand curve from AD_0 to AD_5 (a horizontal shift of $100 billion).

Inventory Depletion. One of the first things you'll notice when AD shifts like this is that available inventories shrink. Investors can step up their *spending* more quickly than firms can increase their *production*. A lot of the increased investment demand will have to be satisfied from existing inventory. The decline in inventory is a signal to producers that it might be a good time to raise prices a bit. Thus *inventory depletion is a warning sign of potential inflation.* As the economy moves up from point *F* to point *r* in Figure 10.9, that inflation starts to become visible.

Household Incomes

Whether or not prices start rising quickly, household incomes will get a boost from the increased investment. Producers will step up the rate of output to rebuild inventories and

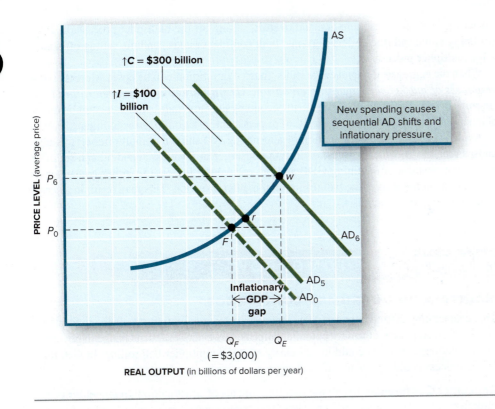

FIGURE 10.9
Demand-Pull Inflation

An increase in investment or other autonomous spending sets off multiplier effects shifting AD to the right. AD shifts to the right *twice*, first (AD$_0$ to AD$_5$) because of increased investment and then (AD$_5$ to AD$_6$) because of increased consumption. The increased AD moves the economy up the short-run AS curve, causing some inflation. How much inflation results depends on the slope of the AS curve.

supply more investment goods (equipment and structures). To do so, they'll hire more workers or extend working hours. The end result for workers will be fatter paychecks.

Induced Consumption

What will households do with these heftier paychecks? By now, you know what the consumer response will be. The marginal propensity to consume prompts an increase in consumer spending. Eventually, consumer spending increases by a *multiple* of the initial income change. In this case, the consumption increase is $300 billion (see Table 10.1).

Figure 10.9 illustrates the results of the sequential AD shifts caused by multiplier-induced consumption. Notice how the AD curve ultimately shifts, from AD$_5$ to AD$_6$.

A New Equilibrium

The ultimate impact of the investment surge is reflected in the new equilibrium at point *w*. As before, the shift of AD has affected both real output and prices. Real output does increase beyond the full-employment level, but it does so only at the expense of accelerating inflation. This is a classic case of **demand-pull inflation.** The initial increase in investment was enough to kindle a little inflation. The multiplier effect worsened the problem by forcing the economy further along the ever-steeper AS curve. The **inflationary GDP gap** ends up as $Q_E - Q_F$.

Booms and Busts

The Keynesian analysis of leakages, injections, and the multiplier paints a fairly grim picture of the prospects for macro stability. *The basic conclusion of the Keynesian analysis is that the economy is vulnerable to abrupt changes in spending behavior and won't self-adjust to a desired macro equilibrium.* A shift in aggregate demand can come from almost anywhere. The September 2001 terrorist attacks on the World Trade Center and Pentagon shook both consumer and investor confidence. Businesses started cutting back production even *before* inventories started piling up. Worsened *expectations* rather than rising

demand-pull inflation: An increase in the price level initiated by excessive aggregate demand.

inflationary GDP gap: The amount by which equilibrium GDP exceeds full-employment GDP.

inventories caused investment demand to shift, setting off the multiplier process. In 2008 declining home and stock prices curtailed both confidence and spending, setting off a negative multiplier process.

When the aggregate demand curve shifts, macro equilibrium will be upset. Moreover, ***the responses of market participants to an abrupt AD shift are likely to worsen rather than improve market outcomes.*** As a result, the economy may gravitate toward an equilibrium of stagnant recession (point *c* in Figure 10.6) or persistent inflation (point *w* in Figure 10.9).

As Keynes saw it, the combination of alternating AD shifts and multiplier effects also causes recurring business cycles. A drop in consumer or business spending can set off a recessionary spiral of declining GDP and prices. A later increase in either consumer or business spending can set the ball rolling in the other direction. This may result in a series of economic booms and busts.

THE ECONOMY TOMORROW

MAINTAINING CONSUMER CONFIDENCE

This chapter emphasized how a sudden change in investment might set off the multiplier process. Investors aren't the only potential culprits, however. A sudden change in government spending or exports could just as easily start the multiplier ball rolling. In fact, the whole process could originate with a change in *consumer* spending.

Consumer Confidence. Recall the two components of consumption: *autonomous* consumption and *induced* consumption. These two components may be expressed as

$$C = a + bY$$

We've seen that autonomous consumption (*a* in the equation) is influenced by *non*income factors, including consumer confidence. As we first observed in Chapter 8, *changes* in consumer confidence can therefore be an AD shift factor: a force that changes the value of autonomous consumption and thus shifts the AD curve to the right or left. A change in consumer confidence can change the marginal propensity to consume (*b* in the equation) as well, further shifting the AD curve.

These AD shifts can be substantial. According to the World Bank, every 1 percent change in consumer confidence alters autonomous consumption by $1.1 billion. That makes the 2007–2008 plunge in consumer confidence particularly scary. As Figure 10.10 illustrates, consumer confidence declined by more than 40 percent from the beginning of 2007 to the end of 2008. That loss of confidence caused consumer spending to drop even further than the cutbacks induced by falling incomes.

Ironically, when consumers try to cope with recession by cutting their spending and saving more of their incomes, they actually make matters worse (see In the News "The Paradox of Thrift"). This "paradox of thrift" recognizes that what might make sense for an *individual* consumer doesn't necessarily make sense for *aggregate* demand.

The Official View: Always a Rosy Outlook. Because consumer spending vastly outweighs any other component of aggregate demand, the threat of abrupt changes in consumer behavior is serious. Recognizing this, public officials strive to maintain consumer confidence in the economy tomorrow, even when such confidence might not be warranted. That's why President Hoover, bank officials, and major brokerage houses tried to assure the public in 1929 that the outlook was still rosy. (Look back at the first few pages of Chapter 8.) The "rosy outlook" is still the official perspective on the economy tomorrow. The White House is always upbeat about prospects for the economy. If it weren't—if it were even to hint at the possibility of a recession—consumer and investor confidence might wilt. Then the economy might quickly turn ugly.

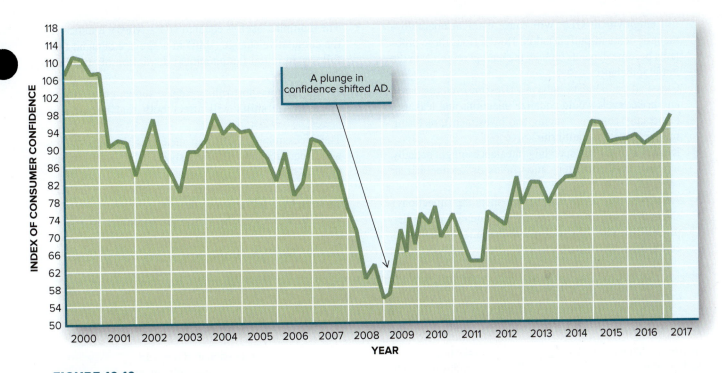

FIGURE 10.10

Consumer Confidence

Consumer confidence is affected by various financial, political, and international events. Changes in consumer confidence affect consumer behavior and thereby shift the AD curve right or left. The steep loss of confidence in 2007–2009 deepened and lengthened the Great Recession.

Source: University of Michigan.

IN THE NEWS

THE PARADOX OF THRIFT

With incomes falling and more job layoffs announced daily, American families are getting thrifty. They are cutting back on spending, reducing credit card debt, and even setting aside a little more money for the proverbial rainy day. This might be a sound financial strategy for individual households. But such thriftiness can drive the economy deeper into recession. It's what economists call the "paradox of thrift": saving more money in a recession pulls the reins on spending just when the economy needs it the most.

Source: News accounts, January 2009.

ANALYSIS: When consumers become more pessimistic about their economy, they start saving more and spending less. This shifts AD leftward and deepens a recession.

SUMMARY

- The circular flow of income has offsetting leakages (consumer saving, taxes, business saving, imports) and injections (autonomous consumption, investment, government spending, exports). **LO10-1**

- When desired injections equal leakage, the economy is in equilibrium (output demanded = output supplied at prevailing price level). **LO10-3**
- An imbalance of injections and leakages will cause the economy to expand or contract. An imbalance at

full-employment GDP will cause cyclical unemployment or demand-pull inflation. How serious these problems become depends on how the market responds to the initial imbalance. **LO10-3**

- Classical economists believed (flexible) interest rates and price levels would equalize injections and leakages (especially consumer saving and investment), restoring full-employment equilibrium. **LO10-3**

- Keynes showed that spending imbalances might actually *worsen* if consumer and investor expectations changed. **LO10-2**

- An abrupt change in autonomous spending (injections) shifts the AD curve, setting off a sequential multiplier process (further AD shifts) that magnifies changes in equilibrium GDP. **LO10-2**

- The multiplier itself is equal to $1/(1 - MPC)$. It indicates the cumulative change (shift) in aggregate demand that follows an initial (autonomous) disruption of spending flows. **LO10-2**

- As long as the short-run aggregate supply curve slopes upward, AD shifts will affect both real output and prices. **LO10-2**

- The recessionary GDP gap measures the amount by which equilibrium GDP falls short of full-employment GDP. **LO10-3**

- Sudden changes in consumer confidence shift the AD curve right or left and may destabilize the economy. To avoid this, policymakers always maintain a rosy outlook. **LO10-3**

Key Terms

aggregate demand (AD)	injection	recessionary GDP gap
full-employment GDP	equilibrium GDP	cyclical unemployment
leakage	marginal propensity to consume	full employment
disposable income (DI)	(MPC)	demand-pull inflation
gross business saving	multiplier	inflationary GDP gap

Questions for Discussion

1. How might declining prices affect a firm's decision to borrow and invest? (See In the News "Housing Starts Fall to 10-Year Low".) **LO10-3**

2. Why wouldn't investment and saving flows at full employment always be equal? **LO10-1**

3. When unwanted inventories pile up in retail stores, how is production affected? What are the steps in this process? **LO10-3**

4. How can equilibrium output exceed full-employment output (as in Figure 10.9)? **LO10-3**

5. How might construction industry job losses affect incomes in the clothing and travel industries? **LO10-2**

6. What forces might turn an economic bust into an economic boom? What forces might put an end to the boom? **LO10-3**

7. Why might "belt-tightening" by consumers in a recession be unwelcome? (See In the News "The Paradox of Thrift.") **LO10-3**

8. What is the "ripple effect" in In the News "Unemployment Spreading Fast across U.S. Industries?" **LO10-2**

9. Will the price level always rise when AD increases? Why or why not? **LO10-3**

10. How did consumer confidence change after the 2016 presidential election (Figure 10.10)? What might have caused this change? **LO10-3**

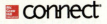

PROBLEMS FOR CHAPTER 10

LO10-3 1. From 2007 to 2009, calculate the percentage change in
  (a) Real consumption.
  (b) Real investment.
  (c) Real government spending.
  (See Data Tables at the end of the book.)

LO10-1 2. If the consumption function is $C = \$600$ billion $+ 0.9Y$,
  (a) What is the MPC?
  (b) How large is autonomous C?
  (c) How much do consumers spend with incomes of $4 trillion?
  (d) How much do they save?

LO10-2 3. If the marginal propensity to consume is 0.95,
  (a) What is the value of the multiplier?
  (b) What is the marginal propensity to save?

LO10-2 4. Suppose that investment demand increases by $200 billion and no leakages occur except household saving. Assume further that households have a marginal propensity to consume of 75 percent.
  (a) Compute four rounds of multiplier effects:

	Changes in This Cycle's Spending	Cumulative Change in Spending
First cycle	_____	_____
Second cycle	_____	_____
Third cycle	_____	_____
Fourth cycle	_____	_____

  (b) What will be the final cumulative impact on spending?

LO10-3 5. Illustrate in the following graph the impact of a sudden decline in consumer confidence that reduces autonomous consumption by $200 billion at the price level P_F. Assume $MPC = 0.5$.
  (a) What is the new equilibrium level of real output? (Don't forget the multiplier.)
  (b) How large is the real GDP gap?
  (c) Did average prices increase or decrease?

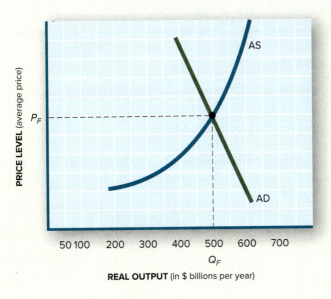

LO10-1 6. By how much did annualized consumption decline in November 2008 when GDP was $14 trillion? (See In the News "US GDP Down 3.8% in Q4, Biggest Drop Since 1982.")

LO10-2 7. If United States exports to Mexico decline by $15 billion by how much will U.S. spending drop if our MPC is 0.75?

LO10-3 8. How large is the inflationary GDP gap in Figure 10.9?

LO10-2
LO10-3 9. The accompanying graph depicts a macro equilibrium. Answer the questions based on the information in the graph.
    (*a*) What is the equilibrium rate of GDP?
    (*b*) If full-employment real GDP is $800, what problem does this economy have?
    (*c*) How large is the real GDP gap?

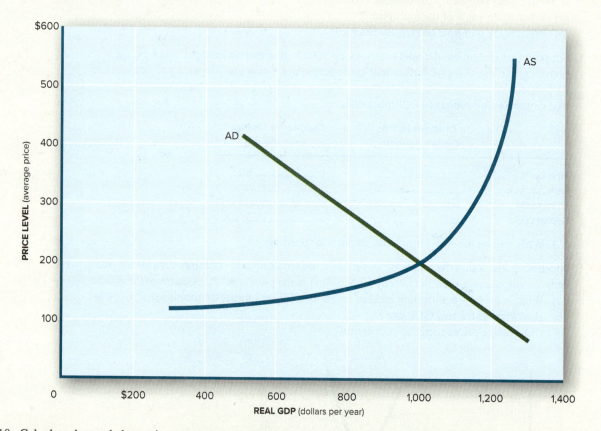

LO10-2 10. Calculate the total change in aggregate spending if investment increases by $200 billion and the marginal propensity to consume is 0.8.

LO10-2 11. The accompanying graph depicts a full-employment macro equilibrium. On the following graph,
    (*a*) Identify this full-employment equilibrium
    (*b*) Show the initial change in aggregate demand when consumer spending falls by $50 billion.
    (*c*) Show the total impact on aggregate demand once multiplier effects are taken into account. Assume the marginal propensity to consume = 0.6.

LO10-3 12. The Economy Tomorrow: Refer to Figure 10.10 to describe the impact of changing consumer confidence on aggregate demand for the following years:
    (*a*) 2002.
    (*b*) 2007–2008.
    (*c*) 2014.

©MOF/Getty Images RF

©Photodisc/Getty Images RF

©NoDerog/iStock/Getty Images RF

FISCAL POLICY TOOLS

The government's tax and spending activities influence economic outcomes. Keynesian theory emphasizes the market's lack of self-adjustment, particularly in recessions. If the market doesn't self-adjust, the government may have to intervene. Specifically, the government may have to use its tax and spending power (fiscal policy) to stabilize the macro economy at its full-employment equilibrium. Chapters 11 and 12 look closely at the policy goals, strategies, and tools of fiscal policy.

11

Fiscal Policy

The Keynesian theory of macro instability is practically a mandate for government intervention. From a Keynesian perspective, too little aggregate demand causes unemployment; too much aggregate demand causes inflation. Since the market itself won't correct these imbalances, the federal government must. Keynes concluded that the government must intervene to manage the level of aggregate demand. This implies increasing aggregate demand when it's deficient and decreasing aggregate demand when it's excessive.

President Obama adopted the Keynesian prescription for ending a recession. Even before taking office, he developed a spending and tax cut package designed to stimulate aggregate demand and "get the country moving again." President Trump wasn't saddled with a recession when he took office but also adopted Keynesian policies to accelerate economic growth. In this chapter we'll examine the fiscal policy tools an Economist in Chief has available, how they work, and what impact they are expected to have. The basic questions we address are

- **Can government spending and tax policies ensure full employment?**
- **What policy actions will help fight inflation?**
- **What are the risks of government intervention?**

As we'll see, the government's tax and spending activities affect not only the *level* of output and prices but the *mix* of output as well.

TAXES AND SPENDING

Article I of the U.S. Constitution empowers Congress "to lay and collect taxes, duties, imposts and excises, to pay the debts and provide for the common defense and general welfare of the United States." Up until 1915, however, the federal government collected few taxes and spent little. In 1902 the federal government employed fewer than 350,000 people and spent a mere $650 million. Today the federal government employs more than 4 million people and spends nearly $4 trillion a year.

Government Revenue

The tremendous expansion of the federal government started with the Sixteenth Amendment to the U.S. Constitution (1913), which extended the government's taxing power to *incomes*. Prior to that, most government revenue came from taxes on imports, whiskey, and tobacco. Once the federal government got the power to tax incomes, it had the revenue base to finance increased expenditure.

Today the federal government collects nearly $4 trillion a year in tax revenues. About half of that revenue comes from individual income taxes (see Figure 4.5). Social Security payroll taxes are the second-largest revenue source, followed at a distance by corporate income taxes. The customs, whiskey, and tobacco taxes on which the federal government depended in 1902 now count for very little.

Government Expenditure

In 1902 federal government expenditures mirrored tax revenues: both were small. Today things are different. The federal government now spends all of its much larger tax revenues—and more. Uncle Sam even borrows additional funds to pay for federal spending. In Chapter 12 we look at the implications of the budget deficits that help finance federal spending. In this chapter we focus on how government spending *directly* affects **aggregate demand.**

Purchases vs. Transfers. To understand how government spending affects aggregate demand, we must again distinguish between government *purchases* and *income transfers.* Government spending on defense, highways, and health care entails the purchase of real goods and services in product markets; they're part of aggregate demand. By contrast, the government doesn't buy anything when it mails out Social Security checks. Those checks simply transfer income from taxpayers to retired workers. **Income transfers** don't become part of aggregate demand until the transfer recipients decide to spend that income.

As we observed in Chapter 4, less than half of all federal government spending entails the purchase of goods and services. The rest of federal spending is either an income transfer or an interest payment on the national debt.

Fiscal Policy

The federal government's tax and spending powers give it a great deal of influence over aggregate demand. *The government can alter aggregate demand by*

- *Purchasing more or fewer goods and services.*
- *Raising or lowering taxes.*
- *Changing the level of income transfers.*

Fiscal policy entails the use of these three budget tools to influence macroeconomic outcomes. *From a macro perspective, the federal budget is a tool that can shift aggregate demand and thereby alter macroeconomic outcomes.* Figure 11.1 puts this tool into the framework of the basic AS/AD model.

aggregate demand (AD): The total quantity of output (real GDP) demanded at alternative price levels in a given time period, *ceteris paribus.*

income transfers: Payments to individuals for which no current goods or services are exchanged, such as Social Security, welfare, and unemployment benefits.

fiscal policy: The use of government taxes and spending to alter macroeconomic outcomes.

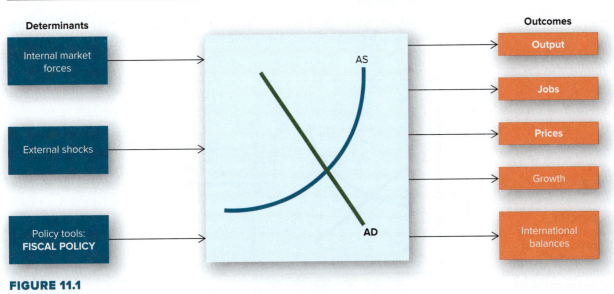

FIGURE 11.1

Fiscal Policy

Fiscal policy refers to the use of the government's tax and spending powers to alter macro outcomes. Fiscal policy works principally through shifts of the aggregate demand curve.

Although fiscal policy can be used to pursue any of our economic goals, we begin our study by exploring its potential to ensure full employment. We then look at its potential to maintain price stability. Along the way we also observe the potential of fiscal policy to alter the mix of output and the distribution of income.

FISCAL STIMULUS

equilibrium (macro): The combination of price level and real output that is compatible with both aggregate demand and aggregate supply.

The basic premise of fiscal policy is that the market's short-run macro equilibrium may not be a desirable one. This is clearly the case in Figure 11.2. **Macro equilibrium** occurs at Q_E, where $5.6 trillion of output is being produced. Full-employment GDP occurs at Q_F, where the real value of output is $6 trillion. Accordingly, the economy depicted in Figure 11.2 confronts a **recessionary GDP gap** of $400 billion. Unless something else happens, unemployment is sure to rise as the economy contracts from Q_F to Q_E.

recessionary GDP gap: The amount by which equilibrium GDP falls short of full-employment GDP.

Keynesian Strategy

The Keynesian model of the adjustment process helps us not only understand how an economy can get into such trouble but also see how it might get out. Keynes emphasized how the aggregate demand curve *shifts* with changes in spending behavior. He also emphasized how new injections of spending into the circular flow multiply into much larger changes in total spending via the multiplier process. *From a Keynesian perspective, the way out of recession is obvious: get someone to spend more on goods and services.* Should desired spending increase, the aggregate demand curve would *shift* to the right, leading the economy out of recession. That additional spending could come from increased government purchases or from tax cuts that induce increased consumer or business spending. Any such **fiscal stimulus** could propel the economy out of recession.

fiscal stimulus: Tax cuts or spending hikes intended to increase (shift) aggregate demand.

Although the general strategy for Keynesian fiscal policy is clear, the scope of desired intervention isn't so evident. Two strategic policy questions must be addressed:

- By how much do we want to shift the AD curve to the right?
- How can we induce the desired shift?

The AD Shortfall

At first glance, the size of the desired AD shift might seem obvious. If the real GDP gap is $400 billion, why not just increase aggregate demand by that amount?

FIGURE 11.2

The Policy Goal

If the economy is in a recessionary equilibrium like point *a*, the policy goal is to increase output to full employment (Q_F). Keynes urged the government to use its tax and spending powers to shift the AD curve rightward.

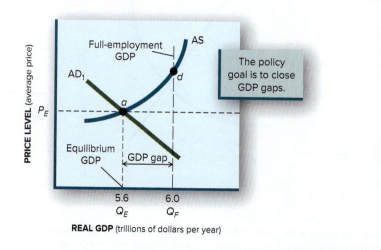

How Large a Shift?. Keynes thought that policy might just work. But it's not quite that simple, as Figure 11.3 illustrates. The intent of expansionary fiscal policy is to achieve full employment. In Figure 11.3, this goal would be attained at point *b*. So it looks like we could restore full employment simply by shifting AD to the right by $400 billion, as the curve AD_2 illustrates. The AD_2 curve does in fact pass through point *b*. That tells us that people would actually demand the full-employment output Q_F at the price level P_E.

But where is the **aggregate supply (AS)** curve? We won't get an *equilibrium* at full employment unless the AD curve intersects with the AS curve at point *b*. What we see in Figure 11.3 is that the AD curve passes thru point *b* but the AS curve is nowhere close. So, the economy can't move point b, as we would like.

So, where will this economy move to? The answer, as always, is to the intersection of the AD and AS curves. in this case, that *equilibrium* occurs at point *c*. At point *c* the new AD_2 curve intersects with the unchanged AS curve.

What's wrong with this new equilibrium? Simple: the *equilibrium* output associated with AD_2 is less than Q_F. Hence **a rightward AD shift equal to the real GDP gap will leave the economy short of full employment** (at the equilibrium point *c* rather than the desired point *b*).

Price Level Changes. The failure of the AD_2 curve to restore full employment results from the upward slope of the AS curve. **When the AD curve shifts to the right, the economy moves up the aggregate supply (AS) curve, not horizontally to the right. As a result both real output and the price level change.**

Figure 11.3 illustrates the consequences of the upward-sloping aggregate supply curve. When the aggregate demand curve shifts from AD_1 to AD_2, we expect cost pressures to increase, pushing the price level up the upward-sloping AS curve. At point *c*, the AS and AD_2 curves intersect, establishing a new equilibrium. At that equilibrium, the price level is higher than it was initially (P_E). Real output is higher as well. But at point *c* we are still short of the full-employment target (Q_F).

The Naïve Keynesian Model: Constant Prices. Under special circumstances the job of restoring full employment wouldn't be that difficult. If there was no cost-push pressure as the

aggregate supply (AS): The total quantity of output (real GDP) producers are willing and able to supply at alternative price levels in a given time period, *ceteris paribus*.

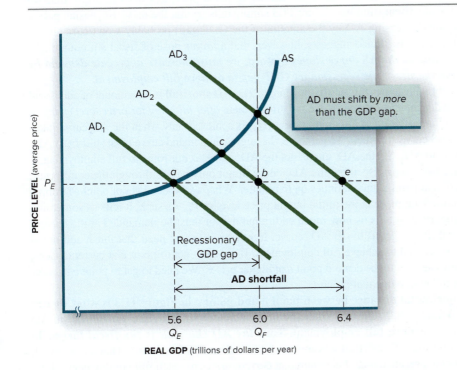

FIGURE 11.3

The AD Shortfall

If aggregate demand increased by the amount of the recessionary GDP gap, we would get a shift from AD_1 to AD_2. The resulting equilibrium would occur at point *c*, leaving the economy short of full employment (Q_F). (Some of the increased demand pushes up prices instead of output.)

To reach full-employment equilibrium (point *d*), the AD curve must shift to AD_3, thereby eliminating the entire AD shortfall. The AD shortfall—the horizontal distance between point *a* and point *e*—is the fiscal policy target for achieving full employment.

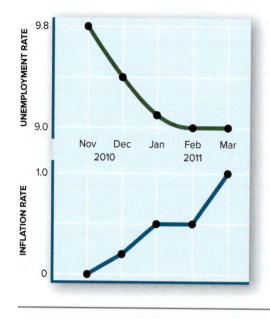

economy expanded, the price level wouldn't rise when AD increased. In such an "inflation-free" environment the AS curve would be *horizontal* rather than upward-sloping. With a horizontal AS curve, rightward shifts of the AD curve would not cause prices to rise. Keynes thought this was the case during the Great Depression, when prices were actually *falling* (see Figure 8.1). So he proposed shifting the AD curve by the amount of the recessionary GDP gap.

The assumption of a horizontal AS curve seems naïve in today's world. Although not every AD shift will raise prices, inflationary pressures do increase as AD expands. This kind of price pressure surfaced in 2011, long before full employment was achieved. Although unemployment was still at 9 percent, the monthly rate of inflation spiked up from 0 to 0.2 to 0.5 to 1.0 percent (Figure 11.4). The short-run AS curve appeared to be sloping upward, raising inflationary fears.

The AD Shortfall. The likelihood of increasing price pressures doesn't imply that we should forsake fiscal stimulus. Figure 11.3 simply tells us that the naïve Keynesian policy prescription (increasing AD by the amount of the GDP gap) probably won't cure all our unemployment ills. It also suggests, however, that a *larger* dose of fiscal stimulus might work. *So long as the AS curve slopes upward, we must increase aggregate demand by more than the size of the recessionary GDP gap to achieve full employment.*

AD shortfall: The amount of additional aggregate demand needed to achieve full employment after allowing for price-level changes.

Figure 11.3 illustrates this new policy target. The **AD shortfall** is the amount of additional aggregate demand needed to achieve full employment *after allowing for price level changes.* Notice in Figure 11.3 that full employment (Q_F) is achieved only when the AD curve intersects the AS curve at point *d*. To get there, the aggregate demand curve must shift from AD_1 all the way to AD_3. So, the AD_3 curve, not the AD_2 curve, is our route to full employment.

Notice something else about the AD_3 curve. It not only passes through the equilibrium intersection at point *d* but continues on to point *e*. What's so special about point *e*? Point *e* is on a horizontal plane at the initial output price level of P_E. As such, it tells us something really important: it tells us how much additional output must be demanded at the *current* price level (P_E) to get us to the AD_3 curve. In other words, we need that much additional aggregate demand to achieve full employment. If we can't get to point *e* at current prices, we simply can't get to the desired point *d* at higher prices. We need to get to point *e* in order to reach full employment at point *d*.

The horizontal distance between point *a* and point *e* in Figure 11.3 is what we call "the AD shortfall." Aggregate demand must increase (shift) by the amount of the AD shortfall to achieve full employment. Thus *the AD shortfall is the fiscal target.* In Figure 11.3 the AD shortfall amounts to $800 billion ($0.8 trillion). That's how much *additional* aggregate demand is required at current prices to reach full employment (Q_F).

Were we to increase AD by enough to attain full employment, it's apparent in Figure 11.3 that prices would increase as well. We'll examine this dilemma later; for the time being we focus on the policy options for increasing aggregate demand by the desired amount.

More Government Spending

The simplest way to shift aggregate demand is to increase government spending. If the government were to step up its purchases of tanks, highways, schools, and other goods, the increased spending would add directly to aggregate demand. This would shift the AD curve rightward, moving us closer to full employment. Hence *increased government spending is a form of fiscal stimulus.*

Multiplier Effects. It isn't necessary for the government to make up the entire shortfall in aggregate demand. Suppose that the fiscal target was to increase aggregate demand by $800 billion, the AD shortfall illustrated in Figure 11.3, by the distance between point *e* ($6.4 billion) and point *a* ($5.6 billion). At first blush, that much stimulus looks perfect for restoring full employment. But life is never that simple.

Were government spending to increase by $800 billion, the AD curve would actually shift *beyond* point *e* in Figure 11.3. In that case we'd quickly move from a situation of *in-adequate* aggregate demand (point *a*) to a situation of *excessive* aggregate demand.

The origins of this apparent riddle lie in the circular flow of income. When the government buys more goods and services, it creates additional income for market participants. The recipients of this income will in turn spend it. Hence each dollar gets spent and respent many times. This is the multiplier adjustment process we encountered in Chapter 10. As a result of this process, *every dollar of new government spending has a multiplied impact on aggregate demand.*

How much "bang" the economy gets for each government "buck" depends on the value of the **multiplier.** Specifically,

$$\frac{\text{Total change}}{\text{in spending}} = \text{Mutiplier} \times \text{New spending injection}$$

The multiplier adds a lot of punch to fiscal policy. Suppose that households have a **marginal propensity to consume** equal to 0.75. In this case, the multiplier would have a value of 4, and each dollar of new government expenditure would increase aggregate demand by $4.

Sequential Shifts. Figure 11.5 illustrates that leveraged impact of government spending. Aggregate demand shifts from AD_1 to AD_2 when the government buys an additional $200 billion of output.

multiplier: The multiple by which an initial change in aggregate spending will alter total expenditure after an infinite number of spending cycles; 1/(1 – MPC).

marginal propensity to consume (MPC): The fraction of each additional (marginal) dollar of disposable income spent on consumption; the change in consumption divided by the change in disposable income.

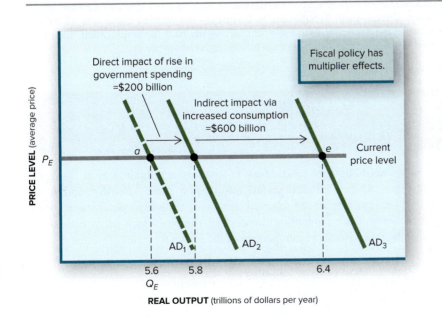

FIGURE 11.5

Multiplier Effects

Fiscal stimulus will set off the multiplier process. As a result of this, aggregate demand will increase (shift) in two distinct steps: (1) the initial fiscal stimulus (AD_1 to AD_2) and (2) induced changes in consumption (AD_2 to AD_3). In this case, a $200 billion increase in government spending causes an $800 billion increase in aggregate demand at the *existing* price level.

Multiplier effects then increase consumption spending by $600 billion more. This additional consumption shifts aggregate demand repeatedly, ultimately reaching AD_3. Thus *the impact of fiscal stimulus on aggregate demand includes both the new government spending and all subsequent increases in consumer spending triggered by multiplier effects.* In Figure 11.5, the shift from AD_1 to AD_3 includes

AD_1 to AD_2: Shift due to $200 billion injection of new government spending.
AD_2 to AD_3: Shift due to multiplier-induced increases in consumption ($600 billion).

As a result of these initial and multiplier-induced shifts, aggregate demand at the current price level (P_E) increases by $800 billion. Thus

$$\begin{matrix} \text{Cumulative increase} \\ \text{(horizontal shift) in AD} \end{matrix} = \begin{matrix} \text{New spending} \\ \text{injection} \\ \text{(fiscal stimulus)} \end{matrix} + \begin{matrix} \text{Induced increase} \\ \text{in consumption} \end{matrix}$$

$$= \text{Multiplier} \times \text{Fiscal stimulus}$$
$$\text{(new spending injection)}$$

The second equation is identical to the first but is expressed in the terminology of fiscal policy. The "fiscal stimulus" is the "new spending injection" that sets the multiplier process in motion. The multiplier carries the ball from there.

The Desired Stimulus. Multiplier effects make changes in government spending a powerful policy lever. The multiplier also increases the risk of error, however. Just as too little fiscal stimulus may leave the economy in a recession, too much can rapidly lead to excessive spending and inflation. This was the dilemma President Trump confronted in his first year. He wanted a massive increase in infrastructure spending and a huge increase in military spending. With the economy virtually at full employment already, there was heightened concern that President Trump's spending plans would shift the AD curve so far to the right that it would accelerate price increases—i.e. move the economy up the ever-steeper AS curve (see In the News "Trump's Spending Proposals Stir Inflation Worries").

IN THE NEWS

TRUMP'S SPENDING PROPOSALS STIR INFLATION WORRIES

Washington, DC. President Trump has said he wants a trillion-dollar program to repair America's road, bridges, railroads, and airports. In addition to this step-up in infrastructure spending, he wants a multibillion dollar increase in defense spending and expanded services for military veterans. Critics—even Republicans in Congress—are worried about how all this spending will affect the economy. With the economy already near full employment, such a massive increase in federal spending could put a lot of pressure on prices.

Source: Media Reports, March 2017.

ANALYSIS: President Trump's initial budget proposals called for substantial increases in spending—spending that would shift the AD curve to the right. Critics worried that the intended AD shift was too great and might push price levels too high.

Policy decisions would be a lot easier if we knew the exact dimensions of aggregate demand, as in Figure 11.3. With such perfect information about AD, AS, and the AD shortfall, we could easily calculate the required increase in the rate of government spending. The general formula for computing the *desired* stimulus (such as an increase in government spending) is a simple rearrangement of the earlier formula:

$$\text{Desired fiscal stimulus} = \frac{\text{AD shortfall}}{\text{Multiplier}}$$

In the economy depicted in Figure 11.3, we assumed the policy goal was to increase aggregate demand by the amount of the AD shortfall ($800 billion). We also assumed an MPC of 0.75 and therefore a multiplier of 4. Accordingly, we conclude that

$$\text{Desired fiscal stimulus} = \frac{\$800 \text{ billion}}{4}$$

$$= \$200 \text{ billion}$$

In other words, a $200 billion increase in government spending at the current price level would be enough fiscal stimulus to close the $800 billion AD shortfall and achieve full employment.

In practice, we rarely know the exact size of the shortfall in aggregate demand. The multiplier is also harder to calculate when taxes and imports enter the picture. Nevertheless, the foregoing formula does provide a useful rule of thumb for determining how much fiscal stimulus is needed to achieve any desired increase in aggregate demand.

Tax Cuts

There is no doubt that increased government spending can shift the AD curve to the right, helping to close a GDP gap. But increased government spending isn't the only way to get there. The increased demand required to raise output and employment levels from Q_E to Q_F could emerge from increases in autonomous consumption or investment as well as from increased government spending. An AD shift could also originate overseas, in the form of increased demand for our exports. In other words, any "big spender" would help, whether from the public sector or the private sector. Of course the reason we're initially at Q_E instead of Q_F in Figure 11.3 is that consumers, investors, and export buyers have chosen *not* to spend as much as required for full employment.

Consumer and investor decisions are subject to change. Moreover, fiscal policy can encourage such changes. Congress not only buys goods and services but also levies taxes. By lowering taxes, the government increases the **disposable income** of the private sector. This was the objective of the 2008 Bush tax cuts, which gave all taxpayers a rebate of $300–600 in the summer of 2008. By putting $168 billion more after-tax income into the hands of consumers, Congress hoped to stimulate (shift) the consumption component of aggregate demand. President Obama used the tax cut tool as part of his 2009 stimulus package and again in 2011.

disposable income (DI): After-tax income of households; personal income less personal taxes.

Taxes and Consumption. An income tax cut directly increases the disposable income of consumers. The question here, however, is how a tax cut affects *spending*. By how much will consumption increase for every dollar of tax cuts?

The answer lies in the marginal propensity to consume. Consumers won't spend every dollar of tax cuts; they'll *save* some of the cut and spend the rest. The MPC tells us how the tax cut dollar will be split between saving and spending. If the MPC is 0.75, consumers will spend $0.75 out of every tax cut $1.00. In other words,

Initial increase in consumption = MPC × Tax cut

If taxes were cut by $200 billion, the resulting shopping spree would amount to

$$\text{Initial increase in consumption} = 0.75 \times \$200 \text{ billion}$$

$$= \$150 \text{ billion}$$

Hence *a tax cut that increases disposable incomes stimulates consumer spending.* A tax cut therefore shifts the aggregate demand curve to the right.

Multiplier Effects. The initial shopping spree induced by a tax cut is only the beginning of the story. Remember the multiplier! The new consumer spending creates additional income for producers and workers, who will then use *their* additional income to increase their own consumption. This will propel us along the multiplier path already depicted in Figure 11.5. The cumulative change in total spending will be

$$\begin{matrix} \textbf{Cumulative change} \\ \textbf{in spending} \end{matrix} = \textbf{Multiplier} \times \begin{matrix} \textbf{Initial change} \\ \textbf{in consumption} \end{matrix}$$

In this case, the cumulative change is

$$\begin{aligned}
\text{Cumulative change} \atop \text{in spending} &= \frac{1}{1 - \text{MPC}} \times \$150 \text{ billion}\\
&= 4 \times \$150 \text{ billion}\\
&= \$600 \text{ billion}
\end{aligned}$$

Here again we see that the multiplier increases the impact on aggregate demand of a fiscal policy stimulus. There's an important difference here, though. When we increased government spending by $200 billion, aggregate demand increased by $800 billion. When we cut taxes by $200 billion, however, aggregate demand increases by only $600 billion. Hence *a tax cut contains less fiscal stimulus than an increase in government spending of the same size.*

The lesser stimulative power of tax cuts is explained by consumer saving. Only part of a tax cut gets spent. Consumers save the rest. This is evident in Figure 11.6, which illustrates the successive rounds of the multiplier process. Notice that the tax cut is used to increase both consumption and saving, according to the MPC. Only that part of the tax cut that's used for consumption enters the circular flow as a spending injection. Hence *the initial spending injection is less than the size of the tax cuts.* By contrast, every dollar of government purchases goes directly into the circular flow. Accordingly, tax cuts are less powerful than government purchases because the initial *spending* injection is smaller.

This doesn't mean we can't close the AD shortfall with a tax cut. It simply means that the desired tax cut must be larger than the required stimulus. It remains true that

$$\textbf{Desired fiscal stimulus} = \frac{\textbf{AD shortfall}}{\textbf{Multiplier}}$$

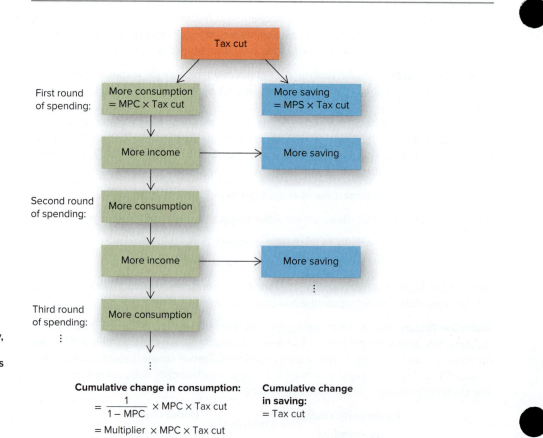

FIGURE 11.6

The Tax Cut Multiplier

Only part of a tax cut is used to increase consumption; the remainder is saved. Accordingly, the initial *spending* injection is less than the tax cut. This makes tax cuts less stimulative than government purchases of the same size. The multiplier still goes to work on that new consumer spending, however.

But now we're using a consumption shift as the fiscal stimulus rather than increased government spending. Hence we have to allow for the fact that the initial surge in consumption (the fiscal stimulus) will be *less* than the tax cut. Specifically,

$$\textbf{Initial consumption injection} = \textbf{MPC} \times \textbf{Tax cut}$$

The fact that consumers will save some fraction of their tax cut forces us to perform one more calculation. We know how to compute the desired fiscal stimulus. Now we want to know how large of a tax cut will deliver that much stimulus. The answer lies in the following equation:

$$\textbf{Desired tax cut} = \frac{\textbf{Desired fiscal stimulus}}{\textbf{MPC}}$$

In the economy in Figure 11.3, we assumed that the desired stimulus is $200 billion and the MPC equals 0.75. Hence the desired tax cut is

$$\text{Desired tax cut} = \frac{\$200 \text{ billion}}{0.75} = \$267 \text{ billion}$$

By cutting taxes $267 billion, we directly increase disposable income by the same amount. Consumers then increase their rate of spending by $200 billion (0.75 × $267 billion); they save the remaining $67 billion. As the added spending enters the circular flow, it starts the multiplier process, ultimately increasing aggregate demand by $800 billion per year.

This comparison of government purchases and tax cuts clearly reveals their respective power. What we've demonstrated is that ***a dollar of tax cuts is less stimulative than a dollar of government purchases.*** This doesn't mean that tax cuts are undesirable, just that they need to be larger than the desired injection of spending. In the News "Just How Stimulating Are Those Checks?" shows that the 2008 tax cut boosted consumer spending by 3.5 percent, thereby shifting AD to the right and accelerating real GDP growth.

IN THE NEWS

JUST HOW STIMULATING ARE THOSE CHECKS?

To get an idea of how much those government rebate checks have spurred spending—and who's benefiting from the buying—business school professors Jonathan Parker (Northwestern) and Christian Broda (University of Chicago) analyzed the spending of 30,000 rebate-receiving households. Using data provided by AC-Nielsen's Homescan, whose participants scan the barcodes on their purchases into a database, the researchers found the rebates "clearly have increased household spending," Parker says. Lower-income households boosted consumption most—spending 6 percent more, compared with a 3.5 percent rise across all households.

—Tara Kalwarski

THE 2008 REBATE BOOST
Additional dollars spent due to stimulus checks*

Appliances, electronics, and furniture — $91

Entertainment and personal services — $87

Food, health, beauty, and household products — $60

Clothing, shoes, and accessories — $32

*Average per rebate-receiving household.

Source: Christian Broda, University of Chicago; Jonathan Parker, Northwestern University. Used with permission.

Source: Kalwarski, Tara. "Just How Stimulating Are Those Checks?" *Businessweek*, September 8, 2008, p. 14. Copyright (c)2015. All rights reserved. Used with permission of Bloomberg L.P.

ANALYSIS: The 2008 tax cuts were a form of fiscal stimulus that boosted consumption (personal spending), increased real GDP growth, and reduced unemployment.

Many taxpayers and politicians demand that any new government spending be balanced with new taxes. Such balancing at the margin, it's asserted, will keep the budget deficit from rising, while avoiding further economic stimulus.

However, changes in government spending (G) are more powerful than changes in taxes (T) or transfers. This implies that an increase in G seemingly "offset" with an equal rise in T will actually increase aggregate demand.

To see how this curious result comes about, suppose that the government decided to spend $50 billion per year on a new fleet of space shuttles and to pay for them by raising income taxes by the same amount. Thus

$$\text{Change in } G = +\$50 \text{ billion per year}$$
$$\text{Change in } T = +\$50 \text{ billion per year}$$
$$\text{Change in budget balance} = 0$$

How will this pay-as-you-go (balanced) budget initiative affect total spending?

The increase in the rate of government spending represents a new injection of $50 billion. But the higher taxes don't increase leakage by the same amount. Households will pay taxes by reducing *both* consumption and saving. The initial reduction in annual consumer spending equals only MPC × $50 billion.

The reduction in consumption is therefore less than the increase in government spending, implying a net increase in *aggregate* spending. The *initial* change in aggregate demand brought about by this balanced budget expenditure is

$$\text{Initial increase in government spending} = \$50 \text{ billion}$$
$$\text{less Initial reduction in consumer spending} = \text{MPC} \times \$50 \text{ billion}$$
$$\overline{\text{Net initial change in total spending} = (1 - \text{MPC}) \$50 \text{ billion}}$$

Like any other changes in the rate of spending, this initial increase in aggregate spending will start a multiplier process in motion. The *cumulative* change in expenditure will be much larger, as indicated by the multiplier. In this case, the cumulative (ultimate) change in total spending is

$$\text{Multiplier} \times \frac{\text{Initial change}}{\text{in spending per year}} = \frac{\text{Cumulative change}}{\text{in total spending}}$$
$$\frac{1}{1 - \text{MPC}} \times (1 - \text{MPC}) \$50 \text{ billion} = \$50 \text{ billion}$$

Thus the balanced budget multiplier is equal to 1. In this case, a $50 billion increase in annual government expenditure combined with an equivalent increase in taxes increases aggregate demand by $50 billion per year.

The different effects of tax cuts and increased government spending have an important implication for government budgets. Because some of the power of a tax cut "leaks" into saving, tax increases don't "offset" government spending of equal value. This unexpected result is described in Table 11.1.

Taxes and Investment. A tax cut may also be an effective mechanism for increasing *investment* spending. As we observed in Chapter 9, investment decisions are guided by expectations of future profit. If a cut in corporate taxes raises potential after-tax profits, it should encourage additional investment. Once additional investment spending enters the circular flow, it too has a multiplier effect.

In 1981 President Reagan convinced Congress not only to cut personal taxes $250 billion over a three-year period but also to cut business taxes another $70 billion. The resulting increase in both consumer spending and investment helped push the economy out of the 1981–1982 recession. President Clinton also embraced the notion of tax incentives for investment. He favored a tax credit for new investments in plants and equipment to increase the level of investment and set off multiplier effects for many years.

President George W. Bush pulled out all the tax cut stops. Immediately upon taking office in 2001, he convinced Congress to pass a $1.35 trillion tax cut for consumers, spread over several years. He followed that up with business tax cuts in 2002 and 2003. The cumulative impact of these tax cuts shifted AD significantly to the right and accelerated recovery from the 2001 recession. President Trump followed the same strategy, on an even grander scale. He urged Congress to reduce the tax rate on corporations from 35 percent to 15 percent. That sharp decline in corporate taxes would not only leave corporations with more profits to reinvest, but also increase the incentive for doing so.

Increased Transfers

A third fiscal policy option for stimulating the economy is to increase transfer payments. If Social Security recipients, welfare recipients, unemployment insurance beneficiaries, and veterans get larger benefit checks, they'll have more disposable income to spend. The resulting increase in consumption will boost aggregate demand. Thus increases in unemployment benefits like those Congress approved in 2008–2010 not only help jobless workers but also boost the macro economy.

Increased transfer payments don't, however, increase injections dollar-for-dollar. Here again, we have to recognize that consumers will save some of their additional transfer payments; only part (MPC) of the additional income will be injected into the spending stream. Hence *the initial fiscal stimulus (AD shift) of increased transfer payments is*

Initial fiscal stimulus (injection) = MPC × Increase in transfer payments

This initial stimulus sets the multiplier in motion, shifting the aggregate demand curve repeatedly to the right.

Impact of the 2009 Fiscal Stimulus

When President Obama took office, the U.S. economy was already deep into recession. The economy was in dire need of some serious fiscal stimulus. it got it in a massive, $787 billion package that included increased government spending, tax cuts, and increased income transfers. That fiscal stimulus, combined with subsequent multiplier effects, was intended to give a significant boost to aggregate demand. According to the Congressional Budget Office, that's exactly what happened.

As Table 11.2 shows, real GDP growth was somewhere between 0.4 and 1.8 percentage points higher in 2009 than it would have been without the fiscal stimulus. With faster growth came 200,000 to 900,000 new jobs. Although both GDP and employment *fell* in 2009, the CBO numbers imply that these declines would have been worse without the fiscal stimulus.

Notice how the impact of the fiscal stimulus continued into further years. The GDP and job gains are actually larger in the second year (2010) than the first (2009). That's because it took time for the new spending and tax cuts to get into the circular flow. The impact of the stimulus continued into 2011–2013, in ever smaller increments, as the multiplier process would predict.

	2009	2010	2011	2012	2013
Real GDP acceleration (%)					
Low estimate	0.4	0.7	0.4	0.1	0.1
High estimate	1.8	4.1	2.3	0.8	0.4
Increase in employment (million jobs)					
Low estimate	0.2	0.7	0.5	0.2	0.1
High estimate	0.9	3.3	2.6	1.1	0.5

Source: Congressional Budget Office (February 2014).

TABLE 11.2

Jobs Impact of the Stimulus

The success of a stimulus program can be measured by the number of jobs created in its wake. The Congressional Budget Office (CBO) estimated the number of jobs created in the years following the February 2009 fiscal stimulus.

FISCAL RESTRAINT

The objective of fiscal policy isn't always to increase aggregate demand. At times the economy may be expanding too fast, and **fiscal restraint** is more appropriate. In these overheated circumstances, policymakers will be more concerned about inflation than unemployment. Their objective will be to *reduce* aggregate demand, not to stimulate it.

The means available to the federal government for restraining aggregate demand emerge again from both sides of the budget. The difference here is that we use the budget tools in reverse. We now want to *reduce* government spending, *increase* taxes, or *decrease* transfer payments.

The AD Excess

As before, our first task is to determine how much we want aggregate demand to fall. To determine this, we must consult Figure 11.7. The initial equilibrium in this case occurs at point E_1, where the AS and AD_1 curves intersect. At that equilibrium the unemployment rate falls below the rate consistent with full employment (Q_F) and we produce the output Q_1. The resulting strains on production push the price level to P_E, higher than we're willing to accept. Our goal is to maintain the price level at P_F, which is consistent with our notion of full employment *and* price stability.

In this case, we have an **inflationary GDP gap**—that is an equilibrium GDP that exceeds full-employment GDP. In Figure 11.7, the size of the inflationary GDP is $Q_1 - Q_F$, which amounts to $200 billion (= $6.2 trillion − $6.0 trillion on the graph). If we want to restore price stability (P_F), however, we need to reduce aggregate demand by *more* than this GDP gap.

The **AD excess**—like its counterpart, the AD shortfall—takes into account potential changes in the price level.

When we shift AD_1 curve to the left (our policy goal), we can't assume prices will be unchanged. On the contrary, the sloped AS curve tells us that the price level will *fall* as aggregate demand declines. So, fiscal restraint, if properly designed, will move us from E_1 to E_2. At the equilibrium E_2, we have reined in the economy to its full-employment potential (Q_F).

How much fiscal restraint do we need to achieve this desired outcome? Notice that the AD_2 curve that passes through the E_2 intersection also passes through point *f*. Therefore, the

FIGURE 11.7

Excess Aggregate Demand

Too much aggregate demand (AD_1) causes the price level to rise (P_E) above its desired level (P_F). To restore price stability, the AD curve must shift leftward by *more* than the inflationary GDP gap: it must shift by the entire amount of the AD excess (here shown as $Q_1 - Q_2$). In this case, the AD excess amounts to $400 billion. If AD shifts by that much (from AD_1 to AD_2), the AD excess is eliminated and equilibrium moves from E_1 to E_2.

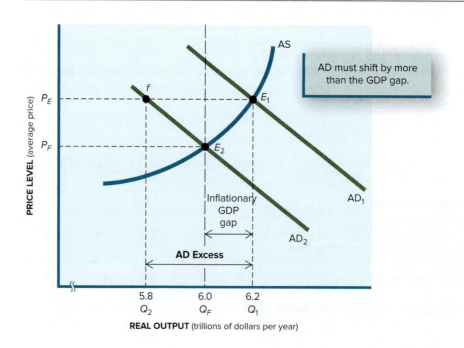

initial AD₁ curve must be shifted far enough to the left to pass through point *f*. If it does, it will also pass through point E_2 and the economy will achieve the desired equilibrium.

The horizontal distance between the initial equilibrium at point E_1 and point *f* is our measure of the AD excess. It represents the amount by which aggregate demand must be reduced at the current price level in order to restrain inflation.

Observe that ***the AD excess exceeds the inflationary GDP gap.*** In Figure 11.7, the AD excess equals the horizontal distance from E_1 to point *f*, which amounts to $400 billion (= $6.2 trillion − $5.8 trillion). This excess aggregate demand is our fiscal policy target. To restore price stability, we must shift the AD curve leftward until it passes through point *f*. The AD₂ curve does this. The shift to AD₂ moves the economy to a new equilibrium at E_2. At E_2 we have less output but also a lower price level (less inflation).

Knowing how large the AD excess is allows us to plot a strategy for fiscal restraint. We once again call on the multiplier to help us. We need the multiplier because every dollar of fiscal restraint will set off a chain reaction of belt-tightening and associated AD shifts. Taking this multiplier process into account, we can compute the desired fiscal restraint as

$$\frac{\text{Desired}}{\text{fiscal restraint}} = \frac{\text{AD excess}}{\text{Multiplier}}$$

Notice the two distinct steps in this policy process. First we determine how far we want to shift the AD curve to the left—that is, the size of the AD excess. Then we compute how much government spending or taxes must be changed to achieve the desired shift, taking into account multiplier effects.

Budget Cuts

The first option to consider is budget cuts. By how much should we reduce government expenditure on goods and services? The answer is simple in this case: we first calculate the desired fiscal restraint with the equation just given. Then we cut government expenditure by that amount.

The AD Excess Target. The GDP gap in Figure 11.7 amounts to $200 billion (= $Q_1 - Q_F$). If aggregate demand is reduced by that amount, however, some of the restraint will be dissipated in price level reductions. To bring *equilibrium* GDP down to the full-employment (Q_F) level, even more of a spending reduction is needed. In this case, the AD excess amounts to $400 billion.

The Multiplier. We don't have to cut government spending by the full amount of the AD excess. Here again, the multiplier will come to our aid. If we assume a marginal propensity to consume of 0.75, the multiplier equals 4. In these circumstances, the desired fiscal restraint is

$$\frac{\text{Desired}}{\text{fiscal restraint}} = \frac{\text{AD excess}}{\text{Multiplier}}$$
$$= \frac{\$400 \text{ billion}}{4}$$
$$= \$100 \text{ billion}$$

What would happen to aggregate demand if the federal government cut that much spending out of, say, the defense budget? Such a military cutback would throw a lot of aerospace employees out of work. Thousands of workers would get smaller paychecks, or perhaps none at all. These workers would be forced to cut back on their own spending, thereby reducing the consumption component of aggregate demand. Hence aggregate demand would take two hits: first a cut in government spending, then induced cutbacks in consumer spending. In the News "Defense Cuts Kill Jobs" highlights the impact of this negative multiplier process.

DEFENSE CUTS KILL JOBS

Cuts in defense spending are making it more difficult to restore full employment. Defense spending was slashed from $837 billion in 2011 to only $770 billion in 2013, following the mandates of the Budget Control Act of 2011 and President Obama's budget decisions. Hardware procurement, Department of Defense civilian employment, and active-duty forces have all been cut. As these defense cuts ripple through the economy, jobs are lost in an array of industries. The National Association of Manufacturers says the resulting loss of jobs and output is substantial: 261,000 fewer jobs in 2014 and 0.2 percentage point shaved off GDP.

Source: National Association of Manufacturers.

ANALYSIS: Reductions in governmental spending on goods and services directly decrease aggregate demand. Multiplier effects induce additional cutbacks in consumption, further reducing aggregate demand.

The marginal propensity to consume again reveals the power of the multiplier process. If the MPC is 0.75, the consumption of aerospace workers will drop by $75 billion when the government cutbacks reduce their income by $100 billion. (The rest of the income loss will be covered by a reduction in saving.)

From this point on the story should sound familiar. The $100 billion government cutback will ultimately reduce consumer spending by $300 billion. The total drop in spending is thus $400 billion. Like their mirror image, *budget cuts have a multiplied effect on aggregate demand.* The total impact is equal to

$$\text{Cumulative reduction in spending} = \text{Multiplier} \times \text{Initial budget cut (fiscal restraint)}$$

This cumulative reduction in spending would eliminate excess aggregate demand. We conclude, then, that *the budget cuts should equal the size of the desired fiscal restraint.*

Tax Hikes

Cuts in government spending aren't the only tool for restraining aggregate demand. Tax increases can also be used to shift the AD curve to the left. The direct effect of a tax increase is a reduction in disposable income. People will pay the higher taxes by reducing their consumption *and* saving less. Only the reduced consumption results in less aggregate demand. As consumers tighten their belts, they set off the multiplier process, leading again to a much larger, cumulative shift of aggregate demand.

Because people pay higher tax bills by reducing both consumption and saving (by MPC and MPS, respectively), *taxes must be increased more than a dollar to get a dollar of fiscal restraint.* This leads us to the following guideline:

$$\text{Desired increase in taxes} = \frac{\text{Desired fiscal restraint}}{\text{MPC}}$$

In other words, changes in taxes must always be larger than the desired change in leakages or injections. How much larger depends on the marginal propensity to consume. In this case

$$\text{Desired fiscal restraint} = \frac{\text{AD excess}}{\text{Multiplier}}$$

Using the numbers from Figure 11.7 as an example, we see that

$$\text{Desired fiscal restraint} = \frac{\$400 \text{ billion}}{4}$$

$$= \$100 \text{ billion}$$

Therefore, the appropriate tax increase is

$$\frac{\textbf{Desired}}{\textbf{tax hike}} = \frac{\textbf{Desired fiscal restraint}}{\textbf{MPC}}$$

$$= \frac{\$100\ \text{billion}}{\text{MPC}}$$

$$= \frac{\$100\ \text{billion}}{0.75}$$

$$= \$133\ \text{billion}$$

Were taxes increased by this amount, consumers would reduce their consumption by $100 billion (= 0.75 × $133 billion). This cutback in consumption would set off the multiplier, leading to a cumulative reduction in spending of $400 billion. In Figure 11.7, aggregate demand would shift from AD_1 to AD_2.

Tax increases have been used to "cool" the economy on several occasions. In 1968, for example, the economy was rapidly approaching full employment, and Vietnam War expenditures were helping to drive up prices. Congress responded by imposing a 10 percent surtax (temporary additional tax) on income, which took more than $10 billion in purchasing power away from consumers. Resultant multiplier effects reduced spending in 1969 more than $20 billion and thus helped restrain price pressures.

In 1982 there was great concern that the 1981 tax cuts had been excessive and that inflation was emerging. To reduce that inflationary pressure, Congress withdrew some of its earlier tax cuts, especially those designed to increase investment spending. The net effect of the Tax Equity and Fiscal Responsibility Act of 1982 was to increase taxes roughly $90 billion for the years 1983 to 1985. This shifted aggregate demand leftward, thus reducing price level pressures.

Reduced Transfers

The third option for fiscal restraint is to reduce transfer payments. *A cut in transfer payments works like a tax hike, reducing the disposable income of transfer recipients.* With less income, consumers spend less, as reflected in the MPC. The appropriate size of the transfer cut can be computed exactly as the desired tax increase in the preceding formula.

Although transfer cuts have the same fiscal impact as a tax hike, they're seldom used. An outright cut in transfer payments has a direct and very visible impact on recipients, including the aged, the poor, the unemployed, and the disabled. Hence this policy option smacks of "balancing the budget on the backs of the poor." In practice, *absolute* cuts in transfer payments are rarely proposed. Instead this lever is sometimes used to reduce the rate of increase in transfer benefits. Then only *future* benefits are reduced, and not so visibly.

FISCAL GUIDELINES

The essence of fiscal policy entails deliberate shifting of the aggregate demand curve.

A Primer: Simple Rules

The steps required to formulate fiscal policy are straightforward:

- *Specify the amount of the desired AD shift* (AD excess or AD shortfall).
- *Select the policy tools needed to induce the desired shift.*

As we've seen, the fiscal policy toolbox contains a variety of tools for managing aggregate demand. When the economy is in a slump, the government can stimulate the economy with more government purchases, tax cuts, or an increase in transfer payments. When the economy is overheated, the government can reduce inflationary pressures by reducing government purchases, raising taxes, and cutting transfer payments. Table 11.3 summarizes

The war was a sharp lesson in Keynesism. Orthodoxy could not stand up any longer. Government accepted the responsibility to maintain a high and stable level of employment. Then economists took over Keynes and erected the new orthodoxy. Once the point had been established the question should have changed. Now that we all agree that government expenditure can maintain employment, we should argue about what the expenditure should be for. Keynes did not *want* anyone to dig holes and fill them.[1]

The alternatives to paying people for digging and filling holes in the ground are virtually endless. With nearly $4 trillion to spend each year, the federal government has great influence not only on short-run prices and employment but also on the mix of output, the distribution of income, and the prospects for long-run growth. In other words, fiscal policy helps shape the dimensions of the economy tomorrow.

Public vs. Private Spending. One of the most debated issues in fiscal policy is the balance between the public and private sectors. Critics of Keynesian theory object to its apparent endorsement of government growth. They fear that using government spending to stabilize the economy will lead to an ever-larger public sector. They attribute the growth of the government's GDP share (from 10 percent in 1930 to 19 percent today) to the big-government bias of Keynesian fiscal policy.

In principle, this big-government bias doesn't exist. Keynes never said government spending was the only lever of fiscal policy. Even in 1934 he advised President Roosevelt to pursue only *temporary* increases in government spending. As we've seen, tax policy can be used to alter consumer and investor spending as well. Hence fiscal policy can just as easily focus on changing the level of *private* sector spending as on changing *public* sector spending.

Output Mixes within Each Sector. In addition to choosing whether to increase public or private spending, fiscal policy must also consider the specific content of spending within each sector. Suppose we determine that stimulation of the private sector is preferable to additional government spending as a means of promoting full employment. We still have many choices. We could, for example, cut corporate taxes, cut individual taxes, reduce excise taxes, or increase Social Security benefits. Each alternative implies a different mix of consumption and investment and a different distribution of income.

The same choices exist when we decide to stimulate AD with more government spending. Do we increase highway construction, bridge repair, military procurement, cancer research, or space exploration? Here again, the content of spending has a profound effect on the shape of the economy tomorrow.

[1]Source: Robinson, Joan. "The Second Crisis of Economic Theory" *American Economic Review,* May, 1972, pg. 6.

SUMMARY

- The economy's short-run macro equilibrium may not co-incide with full employment and price stability. Keynes advocated government intervention to shift the AD curve to a more desirable equilibrium. **LO11-1**
- Fiscal policy refers to the use of the government's tax and spending powers to achieve desired macro outcomes. The tools of fiscal stimulus include increasing government purchases, reducing taxes, and raising income transfers. **LO11-2**

- Fiscal restraint may originate in reductions in government purchases, increases in taxes, or cuts in income transfers. **LO11-4**
- Government purchases add directly to aggregate demand; taxes and transfers have an indirect effect by inducing changes in consumption and investment. This makes changes in government spending more powerful per dollar than changes in taxes or transfers. **LO11-5**

- Fiscal policy initiatives have a multiplied impact on total spending and output. An increase in government spending, for example, will result in more disposable income, which will be used to finance further consumer spending. **LO11-5**
- The objective of fiscal policy is to close GDP gaps. To do this, the aggregate demand curve must shift by *more* than the size of the GDP gap to compensate for changing price levels. The desired shift is equal to the AD shortfall (or AD excess). **LO11-3**

- Because of multiplier effects, the desired fiscal stimulus or restraint is always less than the size of the AD shortfall or AD excess. **LO11-5**
- Time lags in the design, authorization, and implementation of fiscal policy reduce its effectiveness. **LO11-5**
- Changes in government spending and taxes alter the content of GDP and thus influence what to produce. Fiscal policy affects the relative size of the public and private sectors as well as the mix of output in each sector. **LO11-5**

Key Terms

aggregate demand
income transfers
fiscal policy
equilibrium (macro)
recessionary GDP gap
fiscal stimulus

aggregate supply
AD shortfall
multiplier
marginal propensity to consume (MPC)
disposable income

fiscal restraint
inflationary GDP gap
AD excess
crowding out

Questions for Discussion

1. How can you tell if the economy is in equilibrium? How could you estimate the real GDP gap? **LO11-1**
2. How did consumers spend their 2008 tax cut (In the News, "Just How Stimulating Are Those Checks?")? Does it matter what they spend it on? Explain. **LO11-2**
3. What happens to aggregate demand when transfer payments and the taxes to pay them both rise by the same amount? **LO11-2**
4. Why are the AD shortfall and AD excess larger than their respective GDP gaps? Are they ever the same size as the GDP gap? **LO11-3**
5. Will consumers always spend the same percentage of any tax cut? Why might they spend more or less than usual? **LO11-2**
6. How does the slope of the AS curve affect the size of the AD shortfall? If the AS curve were horizontal, how large would the AD shortfall be in Figure 11.3? **LO11-1**

7. In Figure 11.4, why did inflation accelerate when the economy was still so far short of full employment? **LO11-2**
8. How quickly should Congress act to remedy an AD excess or AD shortfall? What are the risks of quick fiscal policy responses? **LO11-5**
9. Why do critics charge that fiscal policy has a "big-government bias"? **LO11-2**
10. When Barack Obama was campaigning for president in 2008, he proposed more government spending paid for with higher taxes on "the rich." What impact would those options have on macro equilibrium? **LO11-2**
11. How did the 2009 fiscal stimulus create more jobs in 2013? (See Table 11.2.) **LO11-5**
12. If fiscal stimulus can close a GDP gap, why not do so immediately? **LO11-5**

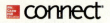
LO11-2 1. Suppose the consumption function is

$$C = \$800 \text{ billion} + 0.8Y$$

and the government wants to stimulate the economy. By how much will aggregate demand at current prices shift initially (before multiplier effects) with
   (a) A $50 billion increase in government purchases?
   (b) A $50 billion tax cut?
   (c) A $50 billion increase in income transfers?

What will the cumulative AD shift be for
   (d) The increased *G?*
   (e) The tax cut?
   (f) The increased transfers?

LO11-2 2. Suppose the government decides to increase taxes by $40 billion to increase Social Security benefits by the same amount. By how much will this combined tax transfer policy affect aggregate demand at current prices if the MPC is 0.9?

LO11-3 3. On the accompanying graph, identify and label
   (a) Macro equilibrium.
   (b) The real GDP gap.
   (c) The AD excess or AD shortfall.
   (d) The new equilibrium that would occur with appropriate fiscal policy.

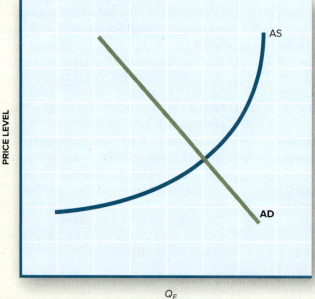

LO11-2 4. If the AD shortfall is $700 billion and the MPC is 0.95,
   (a) How large is the desired fiscal stimulus?
   (b) How large an income tax cut is needed?
   (c) Alternatively, how much more government spending would achieve the target?

LO11-4 5. If the AD excess is $360 billion and the MPC is 0.75,
   (a) How much fiscal restraint is desired?
   (b) By how much do income taxes have to be increased to get that restraint?
   (c) Alternatively, how much should government reduce its spending to achieve the target?

LO11-2 6. (a) According to In the News "Just How Stimulating Are Those Checks?" how much more did the average household spend on appliances, electronics, and furniture when it received the 2008 tax rebate?
  (b) If all 110 million households did so, how much did aggregate consumption increase?
  (c) If the MPC was 0.9, how much would cumulative spending increase as a result?

LO11-5 7. According to the CBO's low estimates (Table 11.2), how many jobs were created by the 2009 fiscal stimulus package for each year 2009–2013?

LO11-4 8. According to In the News "Trump's Spending Proposals Stir Inflation Worries," how much of a cumulative impact on spending could be expected from President Trump's proposed $1 trillion infrastructure spending, assuming an MPC of 0.8?

LO11-2 9. Suppose that an increase in income transfers rather than government spending was the preferred policy for stimulating the economy depicted in Figure 11.5. By how much would transfers have to increase to attain the desired shift of AD?

LO11-4 10. If the marginal propensity to consume was 0.9, how large would each of the following need to be in order to restore a full-employment equilibrium in Figure 11.7?
  (a) A tax increase.
  (b) A government spending cut.
  (c) A cut in income transfers.

LO11-1 11. Use the following data to answer the following questions:

Price level	10	20	30	40	50	60	70	80	90	100
Real GDP supplied	$500	600	680	750	800	880	910	940	960	970
Real GDP demanded	$960	920	880	840	800	760	720	680	640	600

  (a) What is the rate of equilibrium GDP?
  (b) If full employment occurs at a real output rate of $910, how large is the real GDP gap?
  (c) If AD increases enough to restore full employment, what will the price level be?

LO11-2 12. The Economy Tomorrow: The figure depicts an economy's production possibilities. Assume the economy is currently at point a. How would the mix of output change if the economy was stimulated through increased highway construction?

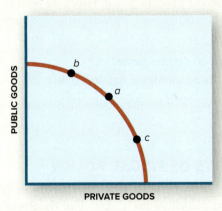

©NoDerog/iStock/Getty Images RF

Deficits and Debt

President Obama's massive 2009 stimulus package was designed to jump-start the recession-bound economy. Critics argued about both the content and size of that package. But the most controversial critique of Obama's fiscal stimulus was that it would ultimately do more harm than good. Those critics argued that the massive deficits generated by Obama's "American Recovery and Reinvestment Act" would undermine America's financial stability. To pay those deficits off, the government would later be forced to *raise* taxes and *cut* spending, taking the wind out of the economy's sails. Whatever short-term boost the economy got from the fiscal stimulus would be reversed in later years.

President Trump's tax cuts and infrastructure spending plans were subjected to the same critique (see In the News "Critics Decry Trump's 'Mountain of Debt'"). Those levers of fiscal stimulus might well boost short-term economic growth. But they would also increase the government's budget deficit and debt. How would that increased indebtedness affect longer-term growth? Would we be trading short-term gains for long-run losses?

Why do these questions arise? Didn't we just show how tax cuts shift aggregate demand rightward, propelling the economy toward full employment? Why would anyone have misgivings about such beneficial intervention?

The core critique of fiscal stimulus focuses on the *budget* consequences of government pump priming. Fiscal stimulus entails either tax cuts or increased government spending. Either option can increase the size of the government's budget deficit. Hence we need to understand how fiscal stimulus is *financed*. We start with these questions:

- **How do deficits arise?**
- **What harm, if any, do deficits cause?**
- **Who will pay off the accumulated national debt?**

As you'll see, the answers to these questions add an essential dimension to fiscal policy debates.

BUDGET EFFECTS OF FISCAL POLICY

fiscal policy: The use of government taxes and spending to alter macroeconomic outcomes.

Keynesian theory highlights the potential of **fiscal policy** to solve our macro problems. The guidelines are simple. Use fiscal stimulus—stepped-up government spending, tax cuts, increased transfers—to eliminate unemployment. Use fiscal restraint—less spending, tax hikes, reduced transfers—to keep inflation under control. From this perspective, the federal budget is a key policy tool for controlling the economy.

IN THE NEWS

CRITICS DECRY TRUMP'S "MOUNTAIN OF DEBT"

During the 2016 election campaign, candidate Trump accused President Obama of burdening the economy with a "mountain of debt." Now the tables are turned. President Trump's budget proposals call for a massive tax cut—"the biggest ever"—and increased spending on infrastructure, border security, national defense, and veterans' services. According to the conservative-leaning Tax Foundation, the tax cuts alone would add $4–6 trillion to the national debt over the next decade.

Source: Media reports, April 2017.

ANALYSIS: President Trump's initial budget proposals entailed significant fiscal stimulus. Critics worried, though, that the tax cuts and spending plans would add significantly to the national debt, causing future economic problems.

Budget Surpluses and Deficits

Use of the budget to stabilize the economy implies that federal expenditures and receipts won't always be equal. In a recession, for example, the government has sound reasons both to cut taxes and to increase its own spending. By reducing tax revenues and increasing expenditures simultaneously, however, the federal government will throw its budget out of balance. This practice is called **deficit spending,** a situation in which the government borrows funds to pay for spending that exceeds tax revenues. The size of the resulting **budget deficit** is equal to the difference between expenditures and receipts:

deficit spending: The use of borrowed funds to finance government expenditures that exceed tax revenues.

$$\text{Budget deficit} = \text{Government spending} - \text{Tax revenues} > 0$$

Budget deficits are a staple of government behavior, as Table 12.1 illustrates. Notice that federal outlays (spending) exceeded federal revenues every year.

Looking closer at Table 12.1 gives us a first clue as to how these annual deficits arise. Notice that the federal government had a relatively small budget deficit ($161 billion) in 2007. But that deficit nearly *tripled* in 2008 and then almost *tripled* again in 2009. As a result, the 2009 deficit was nearly 9 times larger than the 2007 deficit!

Figure 12.1 illustrates how far out of line with prior experience these deficits were. While budget deficits arise nearly every year, prior deficits were small fractions of the 2009–2012 deficits. There were even a few years (1998–2001) in which the federal government managed a **budget surplus**—that is, it brought in more tax revenue than it spent.

The surge in the size of the budget deficit in 2009–2011 caused a lot of anxiety. In early 2011 opinion polls revealed that these huge deficits were the number one economic worry

budget deficit: The amount by which government spending exceeds government revenue in a given time period.

budget surplus: An excess of government revenues over government expenditures in a given time period.

Budget Total (in Billions of Dollars)	2006	2007	2008	2009	2010	2011	2012	2013	2014	2015	2016
Revenues	2,407	2,568	2,524	2,105	2,162	2,303	2,450	2,775	3,022	3,250	3,267
Outlays	−2,655	−2,729	−2,983	−3,518	−3,456	−3,603	−3,537	−3,455	−3,506	−3,688	−3,854
Surplus (deficit)	(248)	(161)	(459)	(1,413)	(1,294)	(1,300)	(1,087)	(680)	(484)	(438)	(587)

Source: Congressional Budget Office.

TABLE 12.1

Budget Deficits and Surpluses

Budget deficits arise when government outlays (spending) exceed revenues (receipts). When revenues exceed outlays, a budget surplus exists.

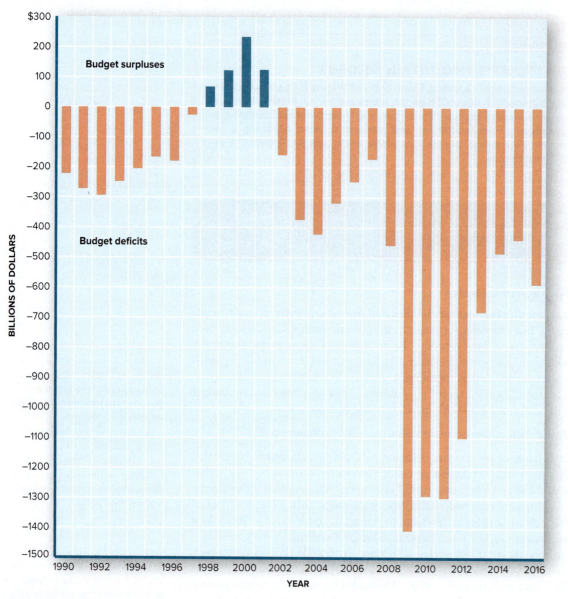

FIGURE 12.1

A String of Deficits

Budget deficits are the rule, not the exception. A budget surplus was achieved in only four years (1998–2001) since 1970. Deficits result from both cyclical slowdowns and discretionary policies. Both forces contributed to the massive deficits of 2009–2011.

Source: Congressional Budget Office.

---

fiscal stimulus: Tax cuts or spending hikes intended to increase (shift) aggregate demand.

fiscal restraint: Tax hikes or spending cuts intended to reduce (shift) aggregate demand.

of Americans. In 2016—after sizable drops in the deficit (Figure 12.1)—the federal deficit was still near the top of Americans' concerns (see In the News "What Worries Americans").

Keynesian View. John Maynard Keynes wouldn't have been so worried. As far as he was concerned, budget deficits and surpluses are just a routine by-product of countercyclical fiscal policy. Deficits can easily arise when the government uses **fiscal stimulus** to increase aggregate demand, just as **fiscal restraint** (tax hikes, spending cuts) may cause a budget surplus. As Keynes saw it, *the goal of macro policy is not to balance the budget but to balance the economy (at full employment)*. If a budget deficit or surplus is needed to shift aggregate demand to the desired equilibrium, then so be it. In Keynes's view, a balanced budget would be appropriate only if all other injections and leakages were in

IN THE NEWS

WHAT WORRIES AMERICANS

When asked, "What are the most important problems facing America today?" Americans cited the following problems in October 2016:

Problem	Percentage of Respondents
Economy in general	17%
Unemployment/jobs	6
Federal deficits/debt	4
Health care	4
Environment/pollution	3
Crime and violence	3
Inequality	2
Hunger/homelessness	2
Education	2
Situation in Iraq/ISIS	1

Source: Gallup poll of October 5–9, 2016.

ANALYSIS: People worry about the government's budget deficits than they do about many social issues. This makes deficits/debt an important political issue as well as an economic issue.

balance and the economy was in full-employment equilibrium. As World View "Budget Imbalances Common" confirms, other nations evidently subscribe to that conclusion as well; budget deficits are common practice.

WORLD VIEW

BUDGET IMBALANCES COMMON

Although U.S. budget deficits receive the most attention, budget imbalances are a common feature of fiscal policy, as these figures reveal.

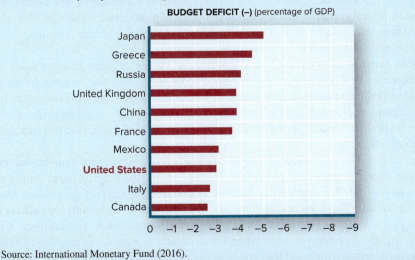

BUDGET DEFICIT (−) (percentage of GDP)

Source: International Monetary Fund (2016).

ANALYSIS: To compare U.S. budget balances to those of other industrialized countries, we must adjust for differences in economic size by computing the *ratio* of deficits or surpluses to GDP. By this measure, U.S. budget imbalances were about average in recent years.

Discretionary vs. Automatic Spending

Theory aside, budget analysts tell us that Congress couldn't balance the federal budget every year even if it wanted to. Congress doesn't have as much control over spending and revenues as people assume. To understand the limits of budget management, we have to take a closer look at how budget outlays and receipts are actually determined.

At the beginning of each year, the president and Congress put together a budget blueprint for the next **fiscal year (FY)**. They don't start from scratch, however. Most budget line items reflect commitments made in earlier years. In FY 2017, for example, the federal budget included $800 billion in Social Security benefits. The FY 2017 budget also provided for $108 billion in veterans benefits, $270 billion for interest payments on the national debt, and many billions more for completion of projects begun in previous years. These expenditures are baked into the budget. Does anyone expect that Congress will just reduce Social Security benefits being paid to retired workers or refuse to pay the interest due on the accumulated debt? Or that it even has the legal authority to do so?

Short of repudiating all prior commitments, there's little that Congress or the president can do to alter these expenditures in any given year. *To a large extent, current revenues and expenditures are the result of decisions made in prior years.* In this sense, much of each year's budget is considered "uncontrollable."

At present, uncontrollables account for roughly 80 percent of the federal budget. This leaves only 20 percent for **discretionary fiscal spending**—that is, spending decisions not "locked in" by prior legislative commitments. In recent years, rising interest payments and increasing entitlements (Social Security, Medicare, civil service pensions, etc.) have reduced the discretionary share of the budget even further. This doesn't mean that discretionary fiscal policy is no longer important; it simply means that the potential for *changing* budget outlays in any year is much smaller than it might first appear.

Automatic Stabilizers. Most of the uncontrollable line items in the federal budget have another characteristic that directly affects budget deficits: their value *changes* with economic conditions. Consider unemployment insurance benefits. The unemployment insurance program, established in 1935, provides that persons who lose their jobs will receive some income (an average of $300 per week) from the government. The law establishes the *entitlement* to unemployment benefits but not the amount to be spent in any year. Each year's expenditure depends on how many workers lose their jobs and qualify for benefits. In 2009, for example, outlays for unemployment benefits increased by $82 billion. That increase in federal spending was due to the 2008–2009 recession: the millions of workers who lost their jobs became eligible for unemployment benefits. The spending increase was *automatic*, not *discretionary*.

Welfare benefits also increased by $70 billion in 2009. This increase in spending also occurred automatically in response to worsened economic conditions. As more people lost jobs and used up their savings, they turned to welfare for help. They were *entitled* to food stamps, housing assistance, and cash welfare benefits according to eligibility rules already written; no new congressional or executive action was required to approve this increase in government spending.

Notice that *outlays for unemployment compensation and welfare benefits increase when the economy goes into recession.* This is exactly the kind of fiscal policy that Keynes advocated. The increase in **income transfers** helps offset the income losses due to recession. These increased transfers therefore act as **automatic stabilizers**—injecting new spending into the circular flow during economic contractions. Conversely, transfer payments *decline* when the economy is *expanding* and fewer people qualify for unemployment or welfare benefits. Hence no one has to pull the fiscal policy lever to inject more or less entitlement spending into the circular flow; much of it happens automatically.

Automatic stabilizers also exist on the revenue side of the federal budget. Income taxes are an important stabilizer because they move up and down with the value of spending and

fiscal year (FY): The 12-month period used for accounting purposes; begins October 1 for the federal government.

discretionary fiscal spending: Those elements of the federal budget not determined by past legislative or executive commitments.

income transfers: Payments to individuals for which no current goods or services are exchanged, such as Social Security, welfare, and unemployment benefits.

automatic stabilizer: Federal expenditure or revenue item that automatically responds countercyclically to changes in national income, like unemployment benefits and income taxes.

- **Changes in Real GDP Growth**
- **When the GDP growth rate decreases by one percentage point**

1. Government spending (*G*) automatically increases for
     Unemployment insurance benefits.
     Food stamps.
     Welfare benefits.
     Social Security benefits.
     Medicaid.
2. Government tax revenues (*T*) automatically decline for
     Individual income taxes.
     Corporate income taxes.
     Social Security payroll taxes.
3. **The deficit increases by $62 billion.**

- **Changes in Inflation**
- **When the inflation rate increases by one percentage point**

1. Government spending (*G*) automatically increases for
     Indexed retirement and Social Security benefits.
     Higher interest payments.
2. Government tax revenues (*T*) automatically increase for
     Corporate income taxes.
     Social Security payroll taxes.
3. **The deficit increases by $31 billion.**

Source: Congressional Budget Office (first-year effects only).

TABLE 12.2

The Budget Impact of Cyclical Forces (in 2016 dollars)

Changes in economic conditions alter federal revenue and spending. When GDP growth slows, tax revenues decline and income transfers increase. This widens the budget deficit.

Higher rates of inflation increase both outlays and revenues, but not equally.

The cyclical balance reflects the budget impacts of changing economic circumstances.

output. As we've observed, if household incomes increase, a jump in consumer spending is likely to follow. The resultant multiplier effects might create some demand-pull inflation. The tax code lessens this inflationary pressure. When you get more income, you have to pay more taxes. Hence income taxes siphon off some of the increased purchasing power that might have found its way to product markets. Progressive income taxes are particularly effective stabilizers because they siphon off increasing proportions of purchasing power when incomes are rising and decreasing proportions when aggregate demand and output are falling.

Cyclical Deficits

Automatic stabilizers imply that policymakers don't have total control of each year's budget. In reality, *the size of the federal budget deficit or surplus is sensitive to expansion and contraction of the macro economy.*

Effects of GDP Growth. Table 12.2 shows just how sensitive the budget is to cyclical forces. When the GDP growth rate slows, tax revenues decline. As the economy slows, more people turn to the government for income support: unemployment benefits and other transfer payments increase. As a consequence, the budget deficit increases. This is exactly what happened in FY 2009: the recession increased the budget deficit by $350 billion *automatically* (see Table 12.3).

Effects of Inflation. Inflation also affects the budget. Because Social Security benefits are automatically adjusted to inflation, federal outlays increase as the price level rises. Interest rates also rise with inflation, forcing the government to pay more for debt services. Tax revenues also rise with inflation, but not as fast as expenditures. Table 12.2 shows that a

TABLE 12.3

Cyclical vs. Structural Budget Balances (in billions of dollars)

The budget balance includes both cyclical and structural components. Changes in the structural component result from policy changes; changes in the cyclical component result from changes in the economy. In 2007 the cyclical surplus increased by $6 billion (from +11 billion to +17 billion) due to faster GDP growth. In 2009 the opposite occurred: the recession widened the cyclical deficit by $225 billion (from −26 to −251 billion).

Fiscal Year	Budget Balance	=	Cyclical Component	+	Structural Component
2000	+236		+58		+178
2001	+128		−1		+129
2002	−158		−83		−75
2003	−378		−107		−271
2004	−413		−58		−355
2005	−318		−20		−298
2006	−248		+11		−259
2007	−161		+17		−178
2008	−459		−26		−433
2009	−1,413		−251		−1,162
2010	−1,294		−300		−994
2011	−1,300		−254		−1,046
2012	−1,087		−191		−896
2013	−680		−189		−491
2014	−484		−146		−338
2015	−438		−79		−359
2016	−587		−69		−518

Source: Congressional Budget Office (March 2017).

one-point increase in the inflation rate *increases* the budget deficit by $31 billion in the first year (and more over time).

The most important implication of Table 12.2 is that neither the president nor the Congress has complete control of the federal deficit. ***Actual budget deficits and surpluses may arise from economic conditions as well as policy.*** Perhaps no one learned this better than President Reagan. In 1980 he campaigned on a promise to balance the budget. The 1981–1982 recession, however, caused the actual deficit to soar. The president later had to admit that actual deficits aren't solely the product of big spenders in Washington.

President Clinton had more luck with the deficit. Although he increased discretionary spending in his first two years, the annual budget deficit *shrank* by more than $90 billion between 1993 and 1995. Most of the deficit reduction was due to automatic stabilizers that kicked in as GDP growth accelerated and the unemployment rate fell. As the economy continued to grow sharply, the unemployment rate fell to 4 percent. That surge in the economy increased tax revenues, reduced income transfers, and propelled the 1998 budget into surplus. It was primarily the economy, not the president or the Congress, that produced the first budget surplus in a generation.

President George W. Bush also benefited from GDP growth. From 2003–2007, economic growth raised both incomes and tax payments. Notice in Table 12.1 how tax revenue jumped from $2,407 billion in 2006 to $2,568 billion in 2007. Tax *rates* weren't increased during those years; people were simply earning more money. The *automatic* increase in revenues helped shrink the deficit from $248 billion in 2006 to $161 billion in 2007.

The recession of 2008–2009 reversed these favorable trends. Even before President Obama convinced Congress to cut taxes and increase government spending, the federal deficit was increasing. Tax receipts were declining as more and more workers lost paychecks. Federal spending was increasing as more workers sought unemployment benefits, welfare, and medical assistance.

That part of the federal deficit attributable to cyclical disturbances (unemployment and inflation) is referred to as the **cyclical deficit.** As we've observed,

cyclical deficit: That portion of the budget deficit attributable to unemployment or inflation.

- *The cyclical deficit widens when GDP growth slows or inflation increases.*
- *The cyclical deficit shrinks when GDP growth accelerates or inflation decreases.*

All of these cyclical changes in the budget occur automatically. Hence, we can't blame (or credit!) Congress or the President for every change in federal deficits. To assess the effect of *policy* decisions on the budget, we need another measure of budget dynamics.

Structural Deficits

To isolate the effects of fiscal policy, economists break down the actual budget balance into *cyclical* and *structural* components:

$$\frac{\text{Total budget}}{\text{balance}} = \frac{\text{Cyclical}}{\text{balance}} + \frac{\text{Structural}}{\text{balance}}$$

The cyclical portion of the budget balance reflects the impact of the business cycle on federal tax revenues and spending—the *automatic* changes we've discussed. The **structural deficit** reflects fiscal policy decisions. Rather than comparing actual outlays to actual receipts, the structural deficit compares the outlays and receipts that would occur if the economy were at full employment.[1] This technique eliminates budget distortions caused by cyclical conditions. Any remaining changes in spending or outlays must be due to policy decisions. Hence, *part of the deficit arises from cyclical changes in the economy; the rest is the result of discretionary fiscal policy.*

Table 12.3 shows how the total, cyclical, and structural balances have behaved in recent years. Consider what happened to the federal budget in 2000–2001. In 2000 the federal surplus was $236 billion. In 2001 the surplus shrank to $128 billion. The shrinking surplus suggests that the government was trying to stimulate economic activity with expansionary fiscal policies (tax cuts, spending hikes). But this wasn't the case. The primary reason for the smaller 2001 surplus was an abrupt halt in GDP growth. As the economy slipped into recession, the *cyclical* component shifted from a *surplus* of $58 billion in 2000 to −$1 billion in 2001. This $59 billion swing in the cyclical budget accounted for most of the decrease in the total budget surplus. By contrast, the *structural* surplus shrank by only $49 billion, reflecting the absence of significant *discretionary* fiscal stimulus.

The distinction between the structural and cyclical components of the budget allows us to figure out who's to "blame" for deficit increases. This was a hot topic when the deficit soared in 2009–2011. According to CBO (Table 12.3), the trillion-dollar *increase* in the 2009 budget deficit was due in part to the economic downturn ($225 billion, i.e., the *change* in the cyclical component from −26 to −251) and the rest to discretionary fiscal policy ($729 billion). So, *policy decisions*, not cyclical changes in the economy did most of the budget damage.

This CBO conclusion reflects the fact that both automatic stabilizers and policy initiatives affect the budget at the same time. To isolate the impact of policy decisions, we must focus on changes in the *structural* deficit, not the *total* deficit. Specifically,

- *Fiscal stimulus is measured by an increase in the structural deficit* (or shrinkage in the structural surplus).
- *Fiscal restraint is gauged by a decrease in the structural deficit* (or increase in the structural surplus).

According to this measure, fiscal policy was actually restrictive during the Great Depression, when fiscal stimulus was desperately needed (see In the News "Fiscal Policy in the Great Depression"). Both Presidents Hoover and Roosevelt thought the government should rein in its spending when tax revenues declined so as to keep the federal budget balanced. It took years of economic devastation before the fiscal policy lever was reversed.

structural deficit: Federal revenues at full employment minus expenditures at full employment under prevailing fiscal policy.

---

[1]The structural deficit is also referred to as the "full-employment," "high-employment," or "standardized" deficit.

IN THE NEWS

FISCAL POLICY IN THE GREAT DEPRESSION

In 1931 President Herbert Hoover observed, "Business depressions have been recurrent in the life of our country and are but transitory." Rather than proposing fiscal stimulus, Hoover complained that expansion of public works programs had unbalanced the federal budget. In 1932 he proposed *cutbacks* in government spending and *higher* taxes. In his view, the "unquestioned balancing of the federal budget . . . is the first necessity of national stability and is the foundation of further recovery."

Franklin Roosevelt shared this view of fiscal policy. He criticized Hoover for not balancing the budget and in 1933 warned Congress that "all public works must be considered from the point of view of the ability of the government treasury to pay for them."

As the accompanying figure shows, the budget deficit persisted throughout the Great Depression. But these deficits were the result of a declining economy, not stimulative fiscal policy. The structural deficit actually *decreased* from 1931 to 1933 (see figure), when fiscal *restraint* was pursued. This restraint reduced aggregate spending at a time when producers were desperate for increasing sales. Only when the structural deficit was expanded tremendously by spending during World War II did fiscal policy have a decidedly positive effect. Federal defense expenditures jumped from $2.2 billion in 1940 to $87.4 billion in 1944!

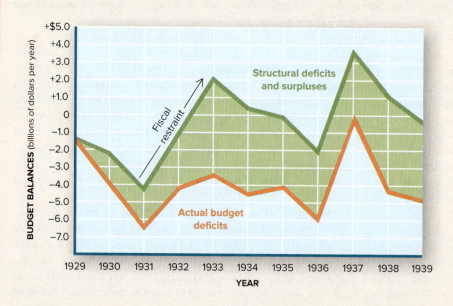

Source: Brown, E. Carey, "Fiscal Policy in the Thirties: A Reappraisal," *American Economic Review*, December 1956. Table 1, The American Economic Association, 1956.

ANALYSIS: From 1931 to 1933, the structural deficit decreased from $4.5 billion to a $2 billion *surplus*. This fiscal restraint reduced aggregate demand and deepened the Great Depression.

ECONOMIC EFFECTS OF DEFICITS

No matter what the origins of budget deficits, most people are alarmed by them. Should they be? What are the *consequences* of budget deficits?

Crowding Out

crowding out: A reduction in private sector borrowing (and spending) caused by increased government borrowing.

We've already encountered one potential consequence of deficit financing: *If the government borrows funds to finance deficits, the availability of funds for private sector spending may be reduced.* This is the **crowding-out** problem first noted in Chapter 11. If

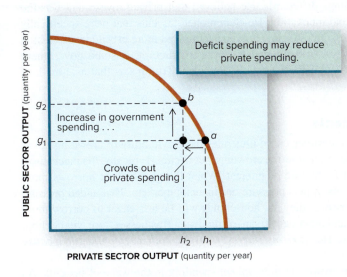

FIGURE 12.2
Crowding Out

If the economy is fully employed, an increase in public sector expenditure (output) will reduce private sector expenditure (output). In this case a deficit-financed increase in government expenditure moves the economy from point *a* to point *b*. In the process the quantity $h_1 - h_2$ of private sector output is crowded out to make room for the increase in public sector output (from g_1 to g_2). If the economy started at point *c*, however, with unemployed resources, crowding out need not occur.

crowding out occurs, the increase in government expenditure will be at least partially offset by reductions in consumption and investment.

If the economy were operating at full employment, crowding out would be inevitable. At full employment, we'd be on the production possibilities curve, using all available resources. As Figure 12.2 reminds us, additional government purchases can occur only if private sector purchases are reduced. In real terms, ***crowding out implies less private sector output.***

Crowding out is complete only if the economy is at full employment. If the economy is in recession, it's possible to get more public sector output (like highways, schools, defense) without cutbacks in private sector output. This possibility is illustrated by the move from point *c* to point *b* in Figure 12.2.

Tax cuts have crowding-out effects as well. The purpose of the 2001 tax cuts was to stimulate consumer spending. As the economy approaches full employment, however, how can more consumer output be produced? At the production possibilities limit, the added consumption will force cutbacks in either investment or government services.

What Figure 12.2 emphasizes is that ***the risk of crowding out is greater the closer the economy is to full employment.*** This implies that deficits are less appropriate at high levels of employment but more appropriate at low levels of employment.

Opportunity Cost

Even if crowding out does occur, that doesn't mean that deficits are necessarily too big. Crowding out simply reminds us that there's an **opportunity cost** to government spending. We still have to decide whether the private sector output crowded out by government expenditure is more or less desirable than the increased public sector output.

President Clinton defended government expenditure on education, training, and infrastructure as public "investment." He believed that any resulting crowding out of private sector expenditure wasn't necessarily an unwelcome trade-off. Public investments in education, health care, and transportation systems might even accelerate long-term economic growth.

President George W. Bush saw things differently. He preferred a mix of output that included less public sector output and more private sector output. Accordingly, he didn't regard any crowding out of government spending that occurred as a result of tax cuts as a real loss.

For his part, President Obama believed that government must play a leading role in education, health care, infrastructure, and the development of alternative energy sources. He viewed a shift of resources from the private sector to the public sector as a necessity to promote both short-run stimulus and long-term growth. Crowding out, if it occurred, wasn't a bad thing from his perspective.

opportunity cost: The most desired goods or services that are forgone in order to obtain something else.

President Trump saw things differently. He believed that private investment was the premier source of growth and innovation. He championed tax cuts that were specifically tailored to encourage business investment. He even encouraged more private investment in public projects like highways, bridges, and airport construction. If some government spending was crowded out by business tax cuts, President Trump saw that as a mark of success.

Interest Rate Movements

Although the production possibilities curve illustrates the inevitability of crowding out at full employment, it doesn't explain *how* the crowding out occurs. Typically, the mechanism that enforces crowding out is the rate of interest. When the government borrows more funds to finance larger deficits, it puts pressure on financial markets. That added pressure may cause interest rates to rise. If they do, households will be less eager to borrow more money to buy cars, houses, and other debt-financed products. Businesses, too, will be more hesitant to borrow and invest. Hence *rising interest rates are both a symptom and a cause of crowding out.*

Rising interests may also crowd out *government* spending in the wake of tax cuts. As interest rates rise, government borrowing costs rise as well. According to the Congressional Budget Office, a one-point rise in interest rates increases Uncle Sam's debt expenses by more than $100 billion over four years. These higher interest costs leave less room in government budgets for financing new projects.

How much interest rates rise again depends on how close the economy is to its productive capacity. If there is a lot of excess capacity, interest rate-induced crowding out isn't very likely. This was the case in early 2009. Interest rates stayed low despite a run-up in government spending and new tax cuts. There was enough excess capacity in the economy to accommodate fiscal stimulus without crowding out. As capacity is approached, however, interest rates and crowding out are both likely to increase.

ECONOMIC EFFECTS OF SURPLUSES

Although budget deficits are clearly the norm, we might at least ponder the economic effects of budget *surpluses*. Essentially, they are the mirror image of those for deficits.

Crowding In

When the government takes in more revenue than it spends, it adds to leakage in the circular flow. But Uncle Sam doesn't hide the surplus under a mattress. And the sums involved (such as $236 billion in FY 2000) are too large to put in a bank. Were the government to buy corporate stock with the budget surplus, it would effectively be nationalizing private enterprises. So where does the surplus go?

There are really only four potential uses for a budget surplus:

- *Spend it on goods and services.*
- *Cut taxes.*
- *Increase income transfers.*
- *Pay off old debt ("save it").*

The first three options effectively wipe out the surplus by changing budget outlays or receipts. There are important differences here, though. The first option—increased government spending—not only reduces the surplus but enlarges the public sector. Cutting taxes or increasing income transfers, by contrast, puts the money into the hands of consumers and enlarges the private sector.

The fourth budget option is to use the surplus to pay off some of the debt accumulated from earlier deficits. This has a similar but less direct **crowding-in** effect. If Uncle Sam pays off some of his accumulated debt, households that were holding that debt (government

crowding in: An increase in private sector borrowing (and spending) caused by decreased government borrowing.

bonds) will end up with more money. If they use that money to buy goods and services, then private sector output will expand.

Even people who haven't lent any money to Uncle Sam will benefit from the debt reduction. When the government reduces its level of borrowing, it takes pressure off market interest rates. As interest rates drop, consumers will be more willing and able to purchase big-ticket items such as cars, appliances, and houses, thus changing the mix of output in favor of private sector production.

Cyclical Sensitivity

Like crowding out, the extent of crowding in depends on the state of the economy. In a recession, a surplus-induced decline in interest rates isn't likely to stimulate much spending. If consumer and investor confidence are low, even a surplus-financed tax cut might not lift private sector spending much.

THE ACCUMULATION OF DEBT

Because the U.S. government has had many more years of budget deficits than budget surpluses, Uncle Sam has accumulated a large **national debt.** In fact, the United States started out in debt. The Continental Congress needed to borrow money in 1777 to continue fighting the Revolutionary War. The Congress tried to raise tax revenues and even printed new money (the Continental dollar) to buy needed food, tents, guns, and ammunition. But by the winter of 1777, these mechanisms for financing the war were failing. To acquire needed supplies, the Continental Congress plunged the new nation into debt. The United States borrowed more than $8 million from France and $250,000 from Spain to help finance the Revolutionary War.

national debt: Accumulated debt of the federal government.

Debt Creation/Bonds

At the time it borrowed money from France and Spain, the Continental Congress promised to repay the loans at a later date. In effect, it gave France and Spain IOUs that contained those promises. We call those IOUs "bonds." Bonds spell out the amount to be repaid, when repayment will occur, and the interest rate that will be paid for the loan.

Today, the U.S. Treasury does the same thing. As the fiscal agent of the U.S. government, the Treasury collects tax revenues, signs checks for federal spending, and—when necessary—borrows funds to cover budget deficits. When the Treasury borrows funds, it issues **Treasury bonds;** these are IOUs of the federal government. As was the case with the Continental Congress, the Treasury's bonds spell out the amount borrowed and the terms of repayment (date, interest rate). People buy those bonds—lend money to the U.S. Treasury—because bonds pay interest and are a very safe haven for idle funds.

Treasury bonds: Promissory notes (IOUs) issued by the U.S. Treasury.

The total stock of all outstanding bonds represents the national debt. It's equal to the sum total of our accumulated deficits, less any repayments in those years when a budget surplus existed. In other words, *the national debt is a stock of IOUs created by annual deficit flows.* Whenever there's a budget deficit, the national debt increases. In years when a budget surplus exists, the national debt can be pared down.

Early History, 1790–1900

During the period 1790–1812, the United States often incurred debt but typically repaid it quickly. The War of 1812, however, caused a massive increase in the national debt. With neither a standing army nor an adequate source of tax revenues to acquire one, the U.S. government had to borrow money to repel the British. By 1816 the national debt was more than $129 million. Although that figure seems tiny by today's standards, it amounted to 13 percent of national income in 1816.

1835–1836: Debt-Free. After the War of 1812, the US. government used recurrent budget surpluses to repay its debt. These surpluses were so frequent that the U.S. government was completely out of debt by 1835. In 1835 and again in 1836, the government had neither national debt nor a budget deficit. The dilemma in those years was how to use the budget *surplus!* Since there was no accumulated debt, the option of using the surplus to reduce the debt didn't exist. In the end, Congress decided simply to distribute the surplus funds to the states. That was the last time the U.S. government was completely out of debt.

The Mexican-American War (1846–1848) necessitated a sudden increase in federal spending. The deficits incurred to fight that war caused a fourfold increase in the debt. That debt was pared down the following decade. Then the Civil War (1861–1865) broke out, and both sides needed debt financing. By the end of the Civil War, the North owed more than $2.6 billion, or approximately half its national income. The South depended more heavily on newly printed Confederate currency to finance its side of the Civil War, relying on bond issues for only one-third of its financial needs. When the South lost, however, neither Confederate currency nor Confederate bonds had any value.[2]

Twentieth Century

The Spanish-American War (1898) also increased the national debt. But all prior debt was dwarfed by World War I, which increased the national debt from 3 percent of national income in 1917 to 41 percent at the war's end.

The national debt declined during the 1920s because the federal government was consistently spending less revenue than it took in. Budget surpluses disappeared quickly when the economy fell into the Great Depression, however, and the cyclical deficit widened (see In the News "Fiscal Policy in the Great Depression").

World War II. The most explosive jump in the national debt occurred during World War II, when the government had to mobilize all available resources. Rather than raise taxes to the fullest, the U.S. government restricted the availability of consumer goods. With consumer goods rationed, consumers had little choice but to increase their saving. Uncle Sam encouraged people to lend their idle funds to the U.S. Treasury by buying U.S. war bonds. The resulting bond purchases raised the national debt from 45 percent of GDP in 1940 to more than 125 percent of GDP in 1946 (see Figure 12.3).

The 1980s. During the 1980s, the national debt jumped again—by nearly $2 *trillion*. This 10-year increase in the debt exceeded all the net debt accumulation since the country was founded. This time, however, the debt increase wasn't war-related. Instead the debt explosion of the 1980s originated in recessions (1980–1981 and 1981–1982), massive tax cuts (1981–1984), and increased defense spending. The recessions caused big jumps in the cyclical deficit while the Reagan tax cuts and military buildup caused the structural deficit to jump fourfold in only four years (1982–1986).

The 1990s. The early 1990s continued the same trend. Discretionary federal spending increased sharply in the first two years of the George H. Bush administration. The federal government was also forced to bail out hundreds of failed savings and loan associations. Although taxes were raised a bit and military spending was cut back, the structural deficit was little changed. Then the recession of 1990–1991 killed any chance of achieving smaller deficits. In only four years (1988–1992) the national debt increased by another $1 trillion.

In 1993 the Clinton administration persuaded Congress to raise taxes, thereby reducing the structural deficit. Continuing recovery from the 1990–1991 recession also reduced the cyclical deficit. Nevertheless, the budget deficits of 1993–1996 pushed the national debt to more than $5 trillion.

Recent Years

Bush Tax Cuts, Defense Spending. After a couple of years of budget surplus, the accumulated debt still exceeded $5.6 trillion in 2002. Then the Bush tax cuts and the defense

---

[2]In anticipation of this situation, European leaders had forced the South to guarantee most of its loans with cotton. When the South was unable to repay its debts, these creditors could sell the cotton they had held as collateral. But most holders of Confederate bonds or currency received nothing.

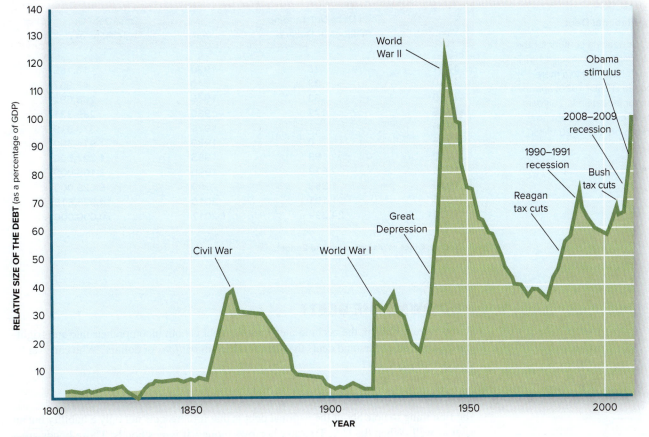

FIGURE 12.3

Historical View of the Debt/GDP Ratio

From 1790 to 1917, the national debt exceeded 10 percent of GDP during the Civil War years only. After 1917, however, the debt ratio grew sharply. World War I, the Great Depression, and World War II all caused major increases in the debt ratio. The tax cuts of 1981–1984 and 2001–2005 and the recessions of 1990–1991, 2001, and 2008–2009 caused further increases in the debt/GDP ratio. The Obama fiscal stimulus pushed the debt ratio still higher.

Source: Office of Management and Budget.

buildup kicked in, increasing the structural deficit by nearly $300 billion in only three years (FY 2002–2004) (Table 12.4). As a consequence, the national debt surged again. By January 2009—*before* the Obama stimulus plan was enacted—the debt exceeded $10 trillion.

Recession and Obama Stimulus. The Great Recession and the Obama fiscal stimulus caused a further surge in the national debt. The trillion-dollar-plus deficits of 2009–2012 (Table 12.1) increased the national debt to almost $20 trillion by the end of 2016. That works out to more than $61,000 of debt for every U.S. citizen. The thought of owing so much money is what worries people so much (see In the News "What Worries Americans").

Trump Stimulus. During the 2016 presidential campaign, Donald Trump railed against the $19 trillion national debt. If elected, he promised that "we're gonna bring it down big league and quickly." To do so, we vowed that "We're gonna stop our deficits." He envisioned eliminating budget deficits and ultimately reducing the national debt largely by shrinking or eliminating some government agencies like the Environmental Protection Agency and the Department of Education. Once he took office, though, he realized that reducing the deficit wasn't so easy. Indeed, the tax cuts and infrastructure spending he wanted actually *increased* the budget deficit, adding to the national debt.

TABLE 12.4

The National Debt

It took nearly a century for the national debt to reach $1 trillion. The debt tripled in a mere decade (1980–1990) and then quintupled again in 20 years. The accumulated debt now totals more than $20 trillion.

Year	Total Debt Outstanding (Millions of Dollars)	Year	Total Debt Outstanding (Millions of Dollars)
1791	75	1930	16,185
1800	83	1940	42,967
1810	53	1945	258,682
1816	127	1960	286,331
1820	91	1970	370,919
1835	0	1980	914,300
1850	63	1985	1,827,500
1865	2,678	1990	3,163,000
1900	1,263	2000	5,629,000
1915	1,191	2010	14,025,615
1920	24,299	2017	20,000,000

Source: Office of Management and Budget.

WHO OWNS THE DEBT?

To the average citizen, the accumulated national debt is both incomprehensible and frightening. Who can understand debts that are measured in *trillions* of dollars? Who can ever be expected to pay them?

Liabilities = Assets

The first thing to note about the national debt is that it represents not only a liability but an asset as well. When the U.S. Treasury borrows money, it issues bonds. Those bonds are a **liability** for the federal government because it must later repay the borrowed funds. But those same bonds are an **asset** to the people who hold them. Bondholders have a claim to future repayment. They can even convert that claim into cash by selling their bonds in the bond market. Therefore, *national debt creates as much wealth (for bondholders) as liabilities (for the U.S. Treasury).* Neither money nor any other form of wealth disappears when the government borrows money.

The fact that total bond assets equal total bond liabilities is of little consolation to taxpayers confronted with $20 trillion of national debt and worried about when, if ever, they'll be able to repay it. The fear that either the U.S. government or its taxpayers will be "bankrupted" by the national debt always lurks in the shadows. How legitimate is that fear?

Ownership of the Debt

Figure 12.4 shows who owns the bonds the U.S. Treasury has issued. The largest bondholder is the U.S. government itself: *federal agencies hold more than 40 percent of all outstanding Treasury bonds.* The Federal Reserve System, an independent agency of the U.S. government, acquires Treasury bonds in its conduct of monetary policy (see Chapters 14 and 15). Other agencies of the U.S. government also purchase bonds. The Social Security Administration, for example, maintains a trust fund balance to cover any shortfall between monthly payroll tax receipts and the retirement benefits it must pay out. Most of that balance is held in the form of interest-bearing Treasury bonds. Thus one arm of the federal government (the U.S. Treasury) owes another arm (the U.S. Social Security Administration) a significant part of the national debt.

State and local governments hold another 3 percent of the national debt. This debt, too, arises when state and local governments use their own budget surpluses to purchase interest-bearing Treasury bonds.

The private sector in the United States owns about a fifth of the national debt. This private wealth is in the form of familiar U.S. savings bonds or other types of Treasury bonds.

liability: An obligation to make future payment; debt.

asset: Anything having exchange value in the marketplace; wealth.

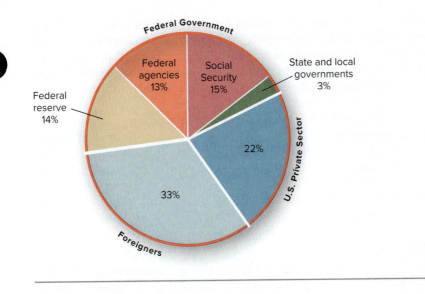

FIGURE 12.4
Debt Ownership

The bonds that create the national debt represent wealth that's owned by bondholders. Almost half of that wealth is held by the U.S. government itself. The private sector in the United States holds only 22 percent of the debt, and foreigners own 33 percent.

Source: U.S. Treasury Department (2014 data).

Much of this private wealth is held *indirectly* by banks, insurance companies, money market funds, corporations, and other institutions. All this private wealth is ultimately owned by the people who have deposits at the bank or in money market funds, who own stock in corporations, or who are insured by companies that hold Treasury bonds. Thus *U.S. households hold about one-fifth of the national debt, either directly or indirectly.*

All the debt held by U.S. households, institutions, and government entities is referred to as **internal debt.** As Figure 12.4 illustrates, two-thirds of the national debt is internal. In other words, *we owe most of the national debt to ourselves.*

The remaining third of the national debt is held by foreign banks, corporations, households, and governments. U.S. Treasury bonds are attractive to global participants because of their relative security, the interest they pay, and the general acceptability of dollar-denominated assets in world trade. Bonds held by foreign households and institutions are referred to as **external debt.**

> **internal debt:** U.S. government debt (Treasury bonds) held by U.S. households and institutions.

> **external debt:** U.S. government debt (Treasury bonds) held by foreign households and institutions.

BURDEN OF THE DEBT

It may be comforting to know that most of our national debt is owned internally, and much of it by the government itself. Figure 12.4 won't still the fears of most taxpayers, however, especially those who don't hold any Treasury bonds. From their perspective, the total debt still looks frightening.

Refinancing

How much of a "burden" the debt really represents isn't so evident. For nearly 30 years (1970–1997), the federal government kept piling up more debt without apparent economic damage. The few years that the government had a budget surplus (1998–2001) weren't markedly different from the deficit years. As we saw earlier (Figure 12.3), deficits and debt stretched out over even longer periods in earlier decades without apparent economic damage.

How was the government able to pile debt upon debt? Quite simple: as debts have become due, the federal government has simply borrowed new funds to pay them off. New bonds have been issued to replace old bonds. This **refinancing** of the debt is a routine feature of the U.S. Treasury's debt management.

The ability of the U.S. Treasury to refinance its debt raises an intriguing question. What if the debt could be eternally refinanced? What if no one *ever* demanded to be paid off more than others were willing to lend Uncle Sam? Then the national debt would truly grow forever.

> **refinancing:** The issuance of new debt in payment of debt issued earlier.

Two things are worrisome about this scenario. First, eternal refinancing seems like a chain letter that promises to make everyone rich. In this case, the chain requires that people hold ever-larger portions of their wealth in the form of Treasury bonds. People worry that the chain will be broken and that they'll be forced to repay all the outstanding debt. Parents worry that the scheme might break down in the next generation, unfairly burdening their own children or grandchildren (see the accompanying cartoon).

Aside from its seeming implausibility, the notion of eternal refinancing seems to defy a basic maxim of economics—namely that "there ain't no free lunch." Eternal refinancing makes it look as though government borrowing has no cost, as though federal spending financed by the national debt is really a free lunch.

There are two flaws in this way of thinking. The first relates to the interest charges that accompany debt. The second, and more important, oversight relates to the real economic costs of government activity.

Debt Service

debt service: The interest required to be paid each year on outstanding debt.

With more than $20 trillion in accumulated debt, the U.S. government must make enormous interest payments every year. **Debt service** refers to these annual interest payments. In FY 2017, the U.S. Treasury paid more than $270 billion in interest charges. These interest payments force the government to reduce outlays for other purposes or to finance a larger budget each year. In this respect, *interest payments restrict the government's ability to balance the budget or fund other public sector activities.*

Although the debt servicing requirements may pinch Uncle Sam's spending purse, the real economic consequences of interest payments are less evident. Who gets the interest payments? What economic resources are absorbed by those payments?

As noted, most of the nation's outstanding debt is internal—that is, owned by domestic households and institutions. Therefore, most interest payments are made to people and institutions within the United States. *Most debt servicing is simply a redistribution of income from taxpayers to bondholders.* In many cases, the taxpayer and bondholder are the same person. In all cases, however, the income that leaks from the circular flow in the form of taxes to pay for debt servicing returns to the circular flow as interest payments. Total income is unchanged. Thus debt servicing may not have any direct effect on the level of aggregate demand.

Debt servicing also has little impact on the real resources of the economy. The collection of additional taxes and the processing of interest payments require the use of some land, labor, and capital. But the value of the resources used for the processing of debt service is trivial—a tiny fraction of the interest payments themselves. This means that *interest payments themselves have virtually no direct opportunity cost for the economy as a whole.* The amount of goods and services available for other purposes is virtually unchanged as a result of debt servicing.

Opportunity Costs

If debt servicing absorbs few economic resources, can we conclude that the national debt really does represent a free lunch? Unfortunately not. But the concept of opportunity cost provides a major clue about the true burden of the debt and who bears it.

Opportunity costs are incurred only when real resources (factors of production) are used. The amount of that cost is measured by the other goods and services that could have been produced with those resources, but weren't. As noted earlier, the *process* of debt servicing absorbs few resources and so has negligible opportunity cost. To understand the true burden of the national debt, we have to look at what that debt financed. *The true burden of the debt is the opportunity cost of the activities financed by the debt.* To assess that burden, we need to ask what the government did with the borrowed funds.

Government Purchases. Suppose Congress decides to upgrade our naval forces and borrows $10 billion for that purpose. What's the opportunity cost of that decision? The economic cost of the fleet upgrade is measured by the goods and services forgone in order to build more ships. The labor, land, and capital used to upgrade the fleet can't be used to produce something else. We give up the opportunity to produce another $10 billion worth of private goods and services when Congress upgrades the fleet.

The economic cost of the naval buildup is unaffected by the method of government finance. Whether the government borrows $10 billion or increases taxes by that amount, the forgone civilian output will still be $10 billion. ***The opportunity cost of government purchases is the true burden of government activity, however financed.*** The decision to finance such activity with debt rather than taxes doesn't materially alter that cost.

The Real Trade-Offs

Although the national debt poses no special burden to the economy, the transactions it finances have a substantial impact on the basic questions of WHAT, HOW, and FOR WHOM to produce. The mix of output is influenced by how much deficit spending the government undertakes. The funds obtained by borrowing allow the federal government to bid for scarce resources. Private investors and consumers will have less access to lendable funds and be less able to acquire incomes or goods. The larger the deficit, the more the private sector gets crowded out. Hence deficit financing allows the government to obtain more resources and change the mix of output. In general, ***deficit financing changes the mix of output in the direction of more public sector goods.***

As noted earlier, the deficits of the 1980s helped finance a substantial military buildup. The same result could have been financed with higher taxes. Taxes are more visible and always unpopular, however. By borrowing rather than taxing, the federal government's claim on scarce resources is less apparent. Either financing method allows the public sector to expand at the expense of the private sector. This resource reallocation reveals the true burden of the debt: ***the burden of the debt is really the opportunity cost (crowding out) of deficit-financed government activity.*** How large that burden is depends on how many unemployed resources are available and the behavioral responses of consumers and investors to increased government activity.

Timing of Burden. Notice also *when* that cost is incurred. If the military is upgraded this year, then the opportunity cost is incurred this year. It's only while resources are actually being used by the military that we give up the opportunity to use them elsewhere. Opportunity costs are incurred at the time a government activity takes place, not when the resultant debt is paid. In other words, ***the primary burden of the debt is incurred when the debt-financed activity takes place.***

If the entire military buildup is completed this year, what costs are borne next year? None. The land, labor, and capital available next year can be used for whatever purposes are then desired. Once the military buildup is completed, no further resources are allocated to that purpose. The real costs of government projects can't be postponed until a later year. In other words, the real burden of the debt can't be passed on to future generations. On the contrary, future generations will benefit from the sacrifices made today to build ships, parks, highways, dams, and other public sector projects. Future taxpayers will be able to *use* these projects without incurring the opportunity costs of their construction.

Economic Growth. Although future generations may benefit from current government spending, they may also be adversely affected by today's opportunity costs. Of particular concern is the possibility that government deficits might crowd out private investment. Investment is essential to enlarging our production possibilities and attaining higher living standards in the future. If federal deficits and debt-servicing requirements crowd our private investment, the rate of economic growth will slow, leaving future generations with less productive capacity than they would otherwise have. Thus ***if debt-financed government spending crowds out private investment, future generations will bear some of the debt burden.*** Their burden will take the form of smaller-than-anticipated productive capacity.

There's no certainty that such crowding out will occur. Also, any reduction in private investment may be offset by public works (such as highways, schools, defense systems) that benefit future generations. So future generations may not suffer a net loss in welfare even if the national debt slows private investment and economic growth. From this perspective, ***the whole debate about the burden of the debt is really an argument over the* optimal mix of output.** If we permit more deficit spending, we're promoting more public sector activity. On the other hand, limits on deficit financing curtail growth of the public sector. ***Battles over deficits and debts are a proxy for the more fundamental issue of private versus public spending.***

optimal mix of output: The most desirable combination of output attainable with existing resources, technology, and social values.

Repayment. All this sounds a little too neat. Won't future generations have to pay interest on the debts we incur today? And might they even have to pay off some of the debt?

We've already observed that the collection of taxes and processing of interest payments absorb relatively few resources. Hence the mechanisms of repayment entail little burden.

Notice also who *receives* future interest payments. When we die, we leave behind not only the national debt but also the bonds that represent ownership of that debt. Hence future grandchildren will be both taxpayers *and* bondholders. If interest payments are made 30 years from today, only people who are alive and holding bonds at that time will receive interest payments. ***Future interest payments entail a redistribution of income among taxpayers and bondholders living in the future.***

The same kind of redistribution occurs if and when our grandchildren decide to pay off the debt. Tax revenues will be used to pay off the debt. The debt payments will go to people then holding Treasury bonds. The entire redistribution will occur among people living in the future.

EXTERNAL DEBT

The nature of opportunity costs makes it difficult but not impossible to pass the debt burden on to future generations. The exception is the case of external debt.

No Crowding Out

When we borrow funds from abroad, we increase our ability to consume, invest, and finance government activity. In effect, other nations are lending us the income necessary to *import* more goods. If we can buy imports with borrowed funds (without offsetting exports), our real income will exceed our production possibilities. As Figure 12.5 illustrates, external borrowing allows us to enjoy a mix of output that lies *outside* our production possibilities curve. Specifically, ***external financing allows us to get more public sector goods without cutting***

FIGURE 12.5

External Financing

A closed economy must forsake some private sector output to increase public sector output (see Figure 12.2). External financing temporarily eliminates that opportunity cost. Instead of having to move from *a* to *b*, external borrowing allows us to move from *a* to *d*. At point *d* we have more public output and no less private output.

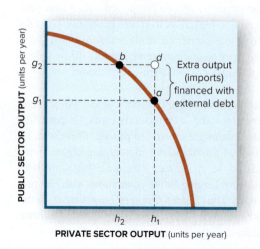

back on private sector production (or vice versa) in the short run. When we use external debt to finance government spending, we move from point *a* to point *d* in Figure 12.5. Imported goods and services eliminate the need to cut back on private sector activity, a cutback that would otherwise force us to point *b*. External financing eliminates this opportunity cost. The move from point *a* to point *d* reflects the additional imports financed by external debt.

The imports needn't be public sector goods. A tax cut at point *b* might increase consumption and imports by $h_1 - h_2$, moving the economy to point *d*. At *d* we have *more* consumption and *no less* government activity.

External financing appears to offer the proverbial free lunch. It would be a free lunch if foreign lenders were willing to accumulate U.S. Treasury bonds forever. They would then own stacks of paper (Treasury bonds), and we'd consume some of their output (our imports) each year. *As long as outsiders are willing to hold U.S. bonds, external financing imposes no real cost.* No goods or services are given up to pay for the additional output received.

Repayment

Foreign investors may not be willing to hold U.S. bonds indefinitely. At some point they'll want to collect their bills. To do this, they'll cash in (sell) their bonds, then use the proceeds to buy U.S. goods and services. When this happens, the United States will be *exporting* goods and services to pay off its debts. Recall that the external debt was used to acquire imported goods and services. Hence *external debt must be repaid with exports of real goods and services.*

....

DEFICIT AND DEBT LIMITS

Although external and internal debts pose very different problems, most policy discussions overlook these distinctions. In policy debates, the aggregate size of the national debt is usually the only concern. The key policy questions are whether and how to limit or reduce the national debt.

Deficit Ceilings

The only way to stop the growth of the national debt is to eliminate the budget deficits that create debt. The first step in debt reduction, therefore, is a balanced annual budget. A balanced budget will at least stop the debt from growing further. **Deficit ceilings** are explicit limitations on the size of the annual budget deficit. A deficit ceiling of zero compels a balanced budget.

deficit ceiling: An explicit, legislated limitation on the size of the budget deficit.

The Balanced Budget and Emergency Deficit Control Act of 1985—popularly referred to as the Gramm-Rudman-Hollings Act—was the first explicit attempt to force the federal budget into balance. The essence of the Gramm-Rudman-Hollings Act was simple:

- First, it set a lower ceiling on each year's deficit until budget balance was achieved.
- Second, it called for automatic cutbacks in spending if Congress failed to keep the deficit below the ceiling.

The original Gramm-Rudman-Hollings law required Congress to pare the deficit from more than $200 billion in FY 1985 to zero (a balanced budget) by 1991. But Congress wasn't willing to cut spending and increase taxes enough to meet those targets. And the Supreme Court declared that the "automatic" mechanism for spending cuts was unconstitutional.

In 1990 President George H. Bush and the Congress developed a new set of rules for reducing the deficit. They first acknowledged that they lacked total control of the deficit. At best, Congress could close the *structural* deficit by limiting discretionary spending or raising taxes. The Budget Enforcement Act (BEA) of 1990 laid out a plan for doing exactly this. The BEA set separate limits on defense spending, discretionary domestic spending, and international spending. It also required that any new spending initiative be offset with increased taxes or cutbacks in other programs—a process called "pay as you go," or simply "paygo."

The Budget Enforcement Act was successful in reducing the structural deficit somewhat. But the political pain associated with spending cuts and higher taxes was too great for elected officials to bear. Since then, recurrent legislated deficit ceilings have proved to be more political ornaments than binding budget mandates.

Debt Ceilings

debt ceiling: An explicit, legislated limit on the amount of outstanding national debt.

Explicit **debt ceilings** are another mechanism for forcing Congress to adopt specific fiscal policies. A debt ceiling can be used either to stop the accumulation of debt or to force the federal government to start *reducing* the accumulated national debt. In effect, debt ceilings are a backdoor approach to deficit reduction. *Like deficit ceilings, debt ceilings are really just political mechanisms for forging compromises on how best to reduce budget deficits.* This was evident in August 2011 when the national debt was again approaching its legislated ceiling ($14.3 trillion). Republicans insisted on cutting federal spending without any tax increases. Democrats insisted that the pain of deficit reduction had to include higher taxes, especially on the wealthy. The prospect of a government shutdown that would accompany a prohibition on federal borrowing forced a budget compromise that included an *increase* in the debt ceiling.

THE ECONOMY TOMORROW

DIPPING INTO SOCIAL SECURITY

The Social Security Trust Fund has been a major source of funding for the federal government for more than 30 years. Since 1985 the Trust Fund has collected more payroll (FICA) taxes each year than it has paid out in retirement benefits. As we noted already, all of those surpluses have been "invested" in Treasury securities, making the Social Security Trust Fund the U.S. Treasury's largest creditor. The Trust Fund now holds $2.8 trillion of Treasury securities (Figure 12.4).

Aging Baby Boomers. The persistent surpluses in the Social Security Trust Fund have largely been the result of aging Baby Boomers. In the 15 years after World War II ended, birthrates soared. These Baby Boomers were in their peak earning years (45–60) between 1990 and 2010 and paying lots of payroll taxes. That kept the Social Security Trust Fund flush with cash.

As we peer into the economy tomorrow, however, the fiscal outlook is not so bright. The Baby Boomers are fast reaching retirement age. As they retire, the *ratio* of workers to retired persons declines. That decline in the ratio of workers to retirees is documented in Table 12.5. That demographic shift implies a reduced inflow of payroll tax revenues and an increased outflow of retirement benefits. As that happens, the annual surplus of Social Security revenues disappears. And with it, the program's ability to continue buying Treasury bonds ends.

Social Security Deficits. As the Trust Fund balance shifts from annual surpluses to annual deficits, Social Security will be able to pay promised benefits only if (1) the U.S. Treasury pays all interest due on bonds held by the Trust Fund and, ultimately, (2) the U.S. Treasury redeems the bonds the Trust Fund will then be holding. This is what scares aging Baby Boomers (and should worry you).

The Baby Boomers wonder where the Treasury is going to get the funds needed to repay the Social Security Trust Fund. There really aren't many options. *To pay back Social Security loans, the Congress will have to raise future taxes significantly, make substantial cuts in other (non–Social Security) programs, or sharply increase budget deficits.* None of these options is attractive. Worse yet, the budget squeeze created by the Social Security payback will severely limit the potential for discretionary fiscal policy.

Year	Workers per Beneficiary	Year	Workers per Beneficiary
1950	16.5	2000	3.4
1960	5.1	2015	2.7
1970	3.7	2030	2.0

Source: U.S. Social Security Administration.

TABLE 12.5

Changing Worker/Retiree Ratios

Sixty years ago there were more than 16 taxpaying workers for every retiree. Today there are only 2.7, and the ratio slips further as Baby Boomers retire. This demographic change will convert Social Security surpluses into deficits, causing future budget problems.

SUMMARY

- Budget deficits result from both discretionary fiscal policy (structural deficits) and cyclical changes in the economy (cyclical deficits).   **LO12-1**
- Fiscal restraint is measured by the reduction in the structural deficit; fiscal stimulus occurs when the structural deficit increases.   **LO12-1**
- Automatic stabilizers increase federal spending and reduce tax revenues during recessions. When the economy expands, they have the reverse effect, thereby shrinking the cyclical deficit.   **LO12-1**
- Deficit financing of government expenditure may crowd out private investment and consumption. The risk of crowding out increases as the economy approaches full employment. If investment becomes the opportunity cost of increased government spending or consumer tax cuts, economic growth may slow.   **LO12-3**
- Crowding in refers to the increase in private sector output made possible by a decline in government borrowing.   **LO12-3**
- Each year's deficit adds to the national debt. The national debt grew sporadically until World War II and then skyrocketed. Tax cuts, recessions, and increased government spending have increased the national debt to more than $18 trillion.   **LO12-2**

- Budget surpluses may be used to finance tax cuts or more government spending, or used to reduce accumulated national debt.   **LO12-1**
- Every dollar of national debt represents a dollar of assets to the people who hold U.S. Treasury bonds. Most U.S. bonds are held by U.S. government agencies, U.S. households, and U.S. banks, insurance companies, and other institutions, and are thus "internal debt."   **LO12-4**
- The real burden of the debt is the opportunity cost of the activities financed by the debt. That cost is borne at the time the deficit-financed activity takes place. The benefits of debt-financed activity may extend into the future.   **LO12-4**
- External debt (bonds held by foreigners) permits the public sector to expand without reducing private sector output. External debt also makes it possible to shift some of the real debt burden on to future generations.   **LO12-4**
- Deficit and debt ceilings are largely symbolic efforts to force consideration of real trade-offs, to restrain government spending, and to change the mix of output.   **LO12-4**
- The retirement of the Baby Boomers (born 1946–1960) is transforming Social Security surpluses into deficits, imposing severe constraints on future fiscal policy.   **LO12-1**

Key Terms

fiscal policy
deficit spending
budget deficit
budget surplus
fiscal restraint
fiscal stimulus
fiscal year (FY)
discretionary fiscal spending
income transfers

automatic stabilizer
cyclical deficit
structural deficit
crowding out
opportunity cost
crowding in
national debt
Treasury bonds
liability

asset
internal debt
external debt
refinancing
debt service
optimal mix of output
deficit ceiling
debt ceiling

Questions for Discussion

1. Why are people worried more about federal budget deficits than environmental protection (In the News "What Worries Americans")?   **LO12-4**

2. Who paid for the Revolutionary War? Did the deficit financing initiated by the Continental Congress pass the cost of the war on to future generations?   **LO12-4**

3. When are larger deficits desirable?   **LO12-1**

4. Can you forecast next year's deficit without knowing how fast GDP will grow?   **LO12-1**

5. In what ways do *future* generations benefit from this generation's deficit spending? Cite three examples.   **LO12-2, LO12-4**

6. If deficit spending "crowds out" some private investment, could future generations be worse off? If external financing eliminates crowding out, are future generations thereby protected?   **LO12-3**

7. A constitutional amendment has been proposed that would require Congress to balance the budget each year. Is it possible to balance the budget each year? Is it desirable?   **LO12-1**

8. What did the surge in defense spending from 1940 to 1944 crowd out?   **LO12-3**

9. What are the "future problems" referred to in In the News "Critics Decry Trump's 'Mountain of Debt'"?   **LO12-4**

10. Which of the following options do you favor for resolving future Social Security deficits? What are the advantages and disadvantages of each option? (a) cutting Social Security benefits, (b) raising payroll taxes, (c) cutting non–Social Security programs, and (d) raising income taxes.   **LO12-1**

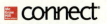

PROBLEMS FOR CHAPTER 12

LO12-2 1. From 2008 to 2010 by how much did each of the following change?
  (*a*) Tax revenue.
  (*b*) Government spending.
  (*c*) Budget deficit.
  (*Note:* See Table 12.1.)

LO12-2 2. Since 1994, in how many years has the federal budget had a surplus? (See Figure 12.1.)

LO12-2 3. What country had the largest budget deficit (as a percentage of GDP) in 2016 (World View "Budget Imbalances Common")?

LO12-1 4. What would happen to the budget deficit if the
  (*a*) GDP growth rate jumped from 2 percent to 4 percent?
  (*b*) Inflation rate increased by two percentage points?
  (*Note:* See Table 12.2 for clues.)

LO12-1 5. Between 2008 and 2016, in how many years was fiscal restraint initiated? (See Table 12.3.)

LO12-1 6. Use Table 12.3 to determine how much fiscal stimulus or restraint occurred between
  (*a*) 2007 and 2008.
  (*b*) 2014 and 2015.

LO12-1 7. According to Table 12.3, the federal deficit fell from $1,300 billion in 2011 to $680 billion in 2013. How much of this $620 billion deficit reduction was due to
  (*a*) The growing economy?
  (*b*) Fiscal restraint?

LO12-4 8. Suppose a government has no debt and a balanced budget. Suddenly it decides to spend $5 trillion while raising only $4.5 trillion worth of taxes.
  (*a*) What will be the government's deficit?
  (*b*) If the government finances the deficit by issuing bonds, what amount of bonds will it issue?
  (*c*) At a 4 percent rate of interest, how much interest will the government pay each year?
  (*d*) Add the interest payment to the government's $5 trillion expenditures for the next year, and assume that tax revenues remain at $4.5 trillion. In the second year, compute the
    (*i*) Deficit.
    (*ii*) Amount of new debt (bonds) issued.
    (*iii*) Total debt at end of year.
    (*iv*) Debt service requirement.

LO12-1 9. According to In the News "Fiscal Policy in the Great Depression,"
  (*a*) How much fiscal restraint occurred between 1931 and 1933?
  (*b*) By how much did this policy reduce aggregate demand if the MPC was 0.80?

LO12-3 10. In Figure 12.5, what is the opportunity cost of increasing government spending from g_1 to g_2 if
  (*a*) No external financing is available?
  (*b*) Complete external financing is available?

LO12-4 11. (*a*) What percentage of U.S. debt do foreigners hold? (See Figure 12.4.)
  (*b*) If the interest rate on U.S. Treasury debt is 4 percent, how much interest do foreigners collect each year from the U.S. Treasury? (Assume a *total* debt of $20 trillion.)

LO12-1 12. Use the data in Table 12.3 to answer questions about *changes* in the structural and total deficits for fiscal years 2008–2015.
  (*a*) In how many years do the two deficits change in *different* directions?
  (*b*) In how many years was the government pursuing fiscal restraint?

L012-2 13. The Economy Tomorrow: Using data in Table 12.5,
- (a) Graph workers per beneficiary since 1960.
- (b) Based on this change in demographics, what is the change in the relationship between payroll taxes and retirement benefits?

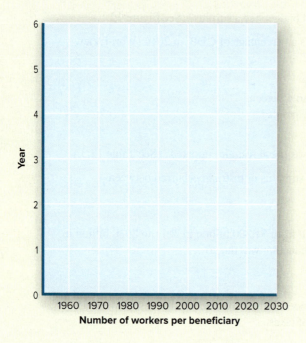

Number of workers per beneficiary

©MOF/Getty Images RF

5

PART

MONETARY POLICY OPTIONS

Monetary policy tries to alter macro outcomes by managing the amount of money available in the economy. By changing the money supply and/or interest rates, monetary policy seeks to shift the aggregate demand curve in the desired direction. Chapters 13 through 15 illustrate how this policy tool works.

©Anatolii Babii/Alamy Stock Photo RF

©Pixtal/age fotostock RF

©Paul J. Richards/AFP/Getty Images

©Anatolii Babii/Alamy Stock Photo RF

CHAPTER 13

Money and Banks

Sophocles, the ancient Greek playwright, had strong opinions about the role of money. As he saw it, "Of evils upon earth, the worst is money. It is money that sacks cities, and drives men forth from hearth and home; warps and seduces native intelligence, and breeds a habit of dishonesty."

In modern times, people may still be seduced by the lure of money and fashion their lives around its pursuit. Nevertheless, it's hard to imagine an economy functioning without money. Money affects not only morals and ideals but also the way an economy works.

This and the following two chapters examine the role of money in the economy today. We begin with a simple question:

- **What is money?**

As we'll discover, money isn't exactly what you might think it is. There's a lot more money in the economy than there is cash. And there's a lot more income out there than money. So money is something quite different from either cash or income.

Once we've established the characteristics of money, we go on to ask,

- **How is money created?**
- **What role do banks play in the circular flow of income and spending?**

In Chapter 14 we look at how the Federal Reserve System controls the amount of money created. In Chapter 15 we look at the implications for monetary policy, another tool in our macro policy toolbox.

LEARNING OBJECTIVES

After reading this chapter, you should know

LO13-1 What money is.

LO13-2 What a bank's assets and liabilities are.

LO13-3 How banks create money.

LO13-4 How the money multiplier works.

WHAT IS "MONEY"?

To appreciate the significance of money for a modern economy, imagine for a moment that there were no such thing as money. How would you get something for breakfast? If you wanted eggs for breakfast, you'd have to tend your own chickens or go see Farmer Brown. But how would you pay Farmer Brown for his eggs? Without money, you'd have to offer him some goods or services that he could use. In other words, you'd have to engage in primitive **barter**—the direct exchange of one good for another—to get eggs for breakfast. You'd get those eggs only if Farmer Brown happened to want the particular goods or services you had to offer.

The use of money greatly simplifies market transactions. It's a lot easier to exchange money for eggs at the supermarket than to go into the country and barter with farmers every time you crave an omelet. Our ability to use money in market transactions, however, depends on the grocer's willingness to accept money as a *medium of exchange*.

barter: The direct exchange of one good for another, without the use of money.

The grocer sells eggs for money only because he can use the same money to pay his help and buy the goods he himself desires. He too can exchange money for goods and services.

Without money, the process of acquiring goods and services would be much more difficult and time-consuming. This was evident when the value of the Venezuelan bolivar plummeted. Trading goods for Farmer Brown's eggs seems simple compared to the complicated barter deals Venezuelan consumers had to negotiate when paper money was no longer accepted (see World View "Trading Chickens for Diapers").

WORLD VIEW

TRADING CHICKENS FOR DIAPERS

Bartering for Survival in Venezuela

Caracas. February 28, 2017—Yeman needs diapers for her 16-month-old baby but can't find them in neighborhood stores. The stores in fact have very few goods to sell and run out of them quickly. So, she uses her smartphone to check the "United Moms" chat group on Facebook. There she discovers that someone has diapers that they are willing to trade for chicken. Luckily, Yeman has some chicken. She contacts the seller and arranges to meet, where she will swap her chicken for three packs of diapers.

Yeman's plight is commonplace in Venezuela these days. The nation's currency—the bolivar—has become worthless. Its market value has plummeted from 6.3 bolivars per U.S. dollar at the beginning of 2016 to 5,000 bolivars per U.S. dollar in early 2017. A bolivar doesn't buy much anymore.

Even if the bolivar were more valuable, there aren't many goods to buy in Venezuela's shrunken economy. People wait for hours in line to buy anything stores have to sell. Then they turn to Facebook, WhatsApp, or Instagram to trade the products they bought for goods they really want. Recent postings on Facebook revealed that a bag of flour could be traded for a bottle of shampoo and that a packet of diapers could be obtained for a kilo of pasta. Staples like sugar, coffee, corn flour, and rice are particularly hard to find.

Source: February 2017 news reports.

ANALYSIS: When the bolivar's value plummeted, its role as a medium of exchange evaporated. Venezuelans had to barter for the few goods that were available, a clumsy and time-consuming process.

THE MONEY SUPPLY

Although markets can't function well without money, they can get along without *dollars*.

Many Types of Money

In the early days of colonial America, there were no U.S. dollars; a lot of business was conducted with Spanish and Portuguese gold coins. Later, people used Indian wampum, then tobacco, grain, fish, and furs as media of exchange. Throughout the colonies, gunpowder and bullets were frequently used for small change. These forms of money weren't as convenient as U.S. dollars, but they did the job.

This historical perspective on money highlights its essential characteristics. ***Anything that serves all the following purposes can be thought of as money:***

- ***Medium of exchange:*** is accepted as payment for goods and services (and debts).
- ***Store of value:*** can be held for future purchases.
- ***Standard of value:*** serves as a yardstick for measuring the prices of goods and services.

All the items used during the colonial days satisfied these conditions and were thus properly regarded as money.

After the colonies became an independent nation, the U.S. Constitution prohibited the federal government from issuing paper money. Money was instead issued by state-chartered banks. Between 1789 and 1865, more than 30,000 different paper bills were issued by 1,600 banks in 34 states. People often preferred to get paid in gold, silver, or other commodities rather than in one of these uncertain currencies.

The first paper money the federal government issued consisted of $10 million worth of "greenbacks," printed in 1861 to finance the Civil War. Soon thereafter, the National Banking Act of 1863 gave the federal government permanent authority to issue money.

Modern Concepts

The "greenbacks" we carry around today aren't the only form of "money" we use. Most people realize this when they offer to pay for goods with a check rather than cash. People do distinguish between "cash" and "money," and for good reason. The "money" you have in a checking account can be used to buy goods and services or to pay debts, or it can be retained for future use. In these respects, your checking account balance is as much a part of your "money" as are the coins and dollars in your pocket or purse. You can access your balance by writing a check or using an ATM or debit card. Checks are more convenient than cash because they eliminate trips to the bank. Checks are also safer: lost or stolen cash is gone forever; checkbooks and debit cards are easily replaced at little or no cost. We might use checks and debit cards even more frequently if everyone accepted them.

money: Anything generally accepted as a medium of exchange.

There's nothing unique about cash, then, insofar as the market is concerned. *Checking accounts can and do perform the same market functions as cash.* Accordingly, we must include checking account balances in our concept of **money.** The essence of money isn't its taste, color, or feel but, rather, its ability to purchase goods and services.

Credit cards are another popular medium of exchange. People use credit cards for about one-third of all purchases greater than $100. This use is not sufficient, however, to qualify credit cards as a form of "money." Credit card balances must be paid by check or cash—that is, with *money*. The same holds true for balances in online electronic credit accounts ("e-cash"). Electronic purchases on the Internet or online services are ultimately paid by withdrawals from a bank account (by check or computer). Online payment mechanisms and credit cards are a payment *service*, not a final form of payment (credit card companies charge fees and interest for this service). The cards themselves are not a store of value, in contrast to cash or bank account balances.

The Diversity of Bank Accounts. To determine how much money is available to purchase goods and services, we need to count not just our coins and currency, but also our bank account balances. This effort is complicated by the variety of bank accounts people have. In addition to simple no-interest checking accounts at full-service banks, people have bank accounts that pay interest, offer automatic transfers, require minimum holding periods, offer overdraft protection, or limit the number of checks that can be written. People also have "bank" accounts in credit unions, brokerage houses, and other nontraditional financial institutions.

Although all bank account balances can be spent, they're not all used the same way. People use regular checking accounts all the time to pay bills or make purchases. But consumers can't write checks on most savings accounts. And few people want to cash in a certificate of deposit just to go to the movies. Hence *some bank accounts are better substitutes for cash than others.*

M1: Cash and Transactions Accounts

Several different measures of money have been developed to accommodate the diversity of bank accounts and other payment mechanisms. The narrowest definition of the **money supply** is designated **M1,** *which includes*

money supply (M1): Currency held by the public, plus balances in transactions accounts.

- *Currency in circulation.*
- *Transactions account balances.*
- *Traveler's checks.*

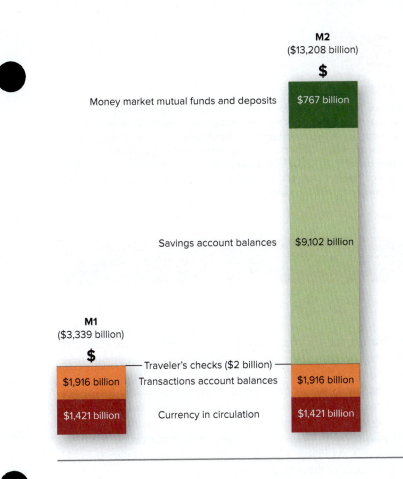

FIGURE 13.1

Composition of the Money Supply

Cash is only a part of the money supply. People also have easy access to transactions account balances by check or debit card. So M1 includes both cash and transactions accounts.

The much larger M2 includes savings accounts, CDs, and other less used bank balances.

Source: Federal Reserve (January 2017 data).

As Figure 13.1 indicates, people hold much more money in **transactions accounts**— bank accounts that are readily accessed by check—than they do in cash. Most people refer to these simply as "checking accounts." The term "transactions account" is broader, however, including NOW accounts, ATS accounts, credit union share drafts, and demand deposits at mutual savings banks. *The distinguishing feature of all transactions accounts is that they permit direct payment to a third party (by check or debit card)* without requiring a trip to the bank to make a special withdrawal. Because of this feature, transactions accounts are the readiest substitutes for cash in market transactions. Traveler's checks issued by nonbank firms such as American Express can also be used directly in market transactions, just like good old-fashioned cash. But few people use traveler's checks these days, as Figure 13.1 confirms.

M2: M1 + Savings Accounts

Transactions accounts aren't the only substitute for cash. People can and do dip into savings accounts on occasion. People sometimes even cash in their certificates of deposit to buy something, despite the interest penalty associated with early withdrawal (see In the News "CDs Not Paying Much"). And banks have made it easy to transfer funds from one type of account to another. Savings accounts can be transformed into transactions accounts with a phone call or computer instruction. As a result, *savings account balances are almost as good a substitute for cash as transactions account balances.*

Another popular way of holding money is to buy shares of money market mutual funds. Deposits into money market mutual funds are pooled and used to purchase interest-bearing securities such as Treasury bills. The interest rates paid on these funds are typically higher than those paid by banks. Moreover, the deposits made into the funds can often be

What do you pay with? Which one is *not* "money"?

©McGraw-Hill Education/Mark A. Dierker, photographer

transactions account: A bank account that permits direct payment to a third party—for example, with a check or debit card.

CDs NOT PAYING MUCH

Stash your money away for five years and you won't reap much of a reward. The highest rate offered by major banks in January 2017 on 5-year certificates of deposit (CDs) was only 1.50 percent. While that's better than the interest paid on checking accounts (0.23 percent), it's not much compensation for five years of thriftiness. Deposit $1,000 in a CD today at that rate and you'll end up with a paltry $1,076.14 in five years. And if you bail out of your CD before the five years are up, you pay an "early withdrawal" penalty that wipes out the little bit of interest earned. Might as well hold onto the cash.

Source: News reports, January 13, 2017.

ANALYSIS: The interest rate paid on a CD account is higher if you promise to keep your money in the bank longer. Because people rarely use CD balances to buy things, CD balances are in M2, but not M1.

---

withdrawn immediately, just like those in transactions accounts. When interest rates are high, deposits move out of regular transactions accounts into money market mutual funds in order to earn a higher return.

Additional measures of the money supply have been constructed to account for the possibility of using savings account balances, money market mutual funds, and various other deposits to finance everyday spending. The most widely watched money measure is **M2,** which includes all of M1 *plus* balances in savings accounts, money market mutual funds, and some CDs ("time deposits"). As Figure 13.1 shows, M2 is four times larger than M1. Table 13.1 summarizes the content of these measures of money.

Our concern about the specific nature of money stems from our broader interest in **aggregate demand.** What we want to know is how much purchasing power consumers have because this affects their ability to purchase goods and services. What we've observed, however, is that money isn't so easily defined. How much spending power people have depends not only on the number of coins in their pockets but also on their willingness to write checks, make trips to the bank, or convert other assets into cash.

In an increasingly complex financial system, the core concept of "money" isn't easy to pin down. Nevertheless, the official measures of the money supply (M1 and M2) are fairly reliable benchmarks for gauging how much purchasing power market participants have.

money supply (M2): M1 plus balances in most savings accounts and money market funds.

aggregate demand (AD): The total quantity of output (real GDP) demanded at alternative price levels in a given time period, *ceteris paribus*.

TABLE 13.1

M1 versus M2

Measures of the money supply are intended to gauge the extent of purchasing power held by consumers. But the extent of purchasing power depends on how accessible assets are and how often people use them.

Measure	Components
M1	Currency in circulation outside bank vaults
	Demand deposits at commercial banks
	NOW and ATS accounts
	Credit union share drafts
	Demand deposits at mutual savings banks
	Traveler's checks (nonbank)
M2	M1 plus
	Savings accounts
	CDs of less than $100,000
	Money market mutual funds

CREATION OF MONEY

Once we've decided what money is, we still have to explain where it comes from. Part of the explanation is simple. Currency must be printed. Some nations use private printers for this purpose, but all U.S. currency is printed by the Bureau of Engraving and Printing in Washington, D.C., or Ft. Worth, Texas. Coins come from the U.S. mints located in Philadelphia and Denver. As we observed in Figure 13.1, however, currency is only a fraction of our total money supply. So we need to look elsewhere for the origins of most money. Specifically, where do all the transactions accounts come from? How do people acquire bank balances? How does the total amount of such deposits—and therefore the money supply of the economy—change?

Deposit Creation

Most people assume that all bank balances come from cash deposits. But this isn't the case. Direct deposits of paychecks, for example, are carried out by computer, not by the movement of cash. Moreover, the employer who issues the paycheck probably didn't make any cash deposits. It's more likely that she covered those paychecks with customers' checks that she deposited or with loans granted by the bank itself.

The ability of banks to lend money opens up a whole new set of possibilities for creating money. *When a bank lends someone money, it simply credits that individual's bank account.* The money appears in an account just as it would with a cash deposit. And the owner of the account is free to spend that money as with any positive balance. Hence, *in making a loan, a bank effectively creates money because transactions account balances are counted as part of the money supply.*

To understand the origins of our money supply, then, we must recognize two basic principles:

- Transactions account balances are a large portion of the money supply.
- Banks can create transactions account balances by making loans.

The following two sections examine this process of **deposit creation** more closely. We will see how banks actually create deposits and what forces might limit the process of deposit creation.

deposit creation: The creation of transactions deposits by bank lending.

Bank Regulation. Banks' deposit creation activities are regulated by the government. The most important agency in this regard is the Federal Reserve System. "The Fed" puts limits on the amount of bank lending, thereby controlling the basic money supply. We'll discuss the structure and functions of the Fed in the next chapter; here we focus on the process of deposit creation itself.

A Monopoly Bank

There are thousands of banks, of various sorts, in the United States. To understand how banks create money, however, we'll make life simple. We'll assume for the moment that there's only one bank in town, University Bank. Imagine also that you've been saving some of your income by putting loose change into a piggy bank. Now, after months of saving, you break the piggy bank and discover that your thrift has yielded $100. You immediately deposit this money in a new checking account at University Bank. How will this deposit affect the money supply?

Your initial deposit will have no immediate effect on the money supply. The coins in your piggy bank were already counted as part of the money supply (M1 and M2) because they represented cash held by the public. *When you deposit cash or coins in a bank, you're only changing the composition of the money supply, not its size.* The public (you) now holds $100 less of coins but $100 more of transactions deposits. Accordingly, no money is created by the demise of your piggy bank (the initial deposit). This transaction will be recorded on the books of the bank.

T-accounts: The accounting ledgers used by banks to track assets and liabilities.

T-Accounts. The "books" the bank uses to record this transaction are called **T-accounts.** On the left side of the T-account, the bank keeps track of all its assets: things of value in its possession. On the right side of the ledger the bank lists its liabilities: what it is obligated to pay to others. When you deposit your coins in the bank, the bank acquires an asset—your coins. It also acquires a liability—the promise to return your $100 when you so demand (your "demand deposit"). These two entries appear in the bank's T-account as shown here:

University Bank		Money Supply	
Assets	Liabilities	Cash held by the public	−$100
+$100 in coins	+$100 in deposits	Transactions deposits at bank	+$100
		Change in M	0

The total money supply is unaffected by your cash deposit because two components of the money supply change in opposite directions (i.e., $100 less cash, $100 more bank deposits). This initial deposit is just the beginning of the money creation process, however. Banks aren't in business for your convenience; they're in business to earn a profit. To earn a profit on your deposit, University Bank will have to put your money to work. This means using your deposit as the basis for making a loan to someone who's willing to pay the bank interest for use of money. If the function of banks was merely to store money, they wouldn't pay interest on their accounts or offer free checking services. Instead you'd have to pay them for these services. Banks pay you interest and offer free (or inexpensive) checking because *banks can use your money to make loans that earn interest.*

The Initial Loan. Typically a bank doesn't have much difficulty finding someone who wants to borrow money. Someone is always eager to borrow money. The question is, How much money can a bank lend? Can it lend your entire deposit? Or must University Bank keep some of your coins in reserve in case you want to withdraw them? The answer will surprise you.

Suppose University Bank decided to lend the entire $100 to Campus Radio. Campus Radio wants to buy a new antenna but doesn't have any money in its own checking account. To acquire the antenna, Campus Radio must take out a loan.

When University Bank agrees to lend Campus Radio $100, it does so by crediting the account of Campus Radio. Instead of giving Campus Radio $100 cash, University Bank simply adds an electronic $100 to Campus Radio's checking account balance. That is, the loan is made with a simple bookkeeping entry as follows:

University Bank		Money Supply	
Assets	Liabilities	Cash held by the public	No change
$100 in coins	$100 your account balance	Transactions deposits at bank	+$100
$100 in loans	$100 Campus Radio account	Change in M	+$100

Notice that the bank's assets have increased. It now has your $100 in coins *plus* an IOU worth $100 from Campus Radio ("loans"). On the right side of the T-account, deposit liabilities now include $100 in your account and $100 in the Campus Radio account.

This simple bookkeeping procedure is the key to creating money. When University Bank lends $100 to the Campus Radio account, it "creates" money. Keep in mind that transactions deposits are counted as part of the money supply. Once the $100 loan is credited to its account, Campus Radio can use this new money to purchase its desired antenna, without worrying that its check will bounce.

Or can it? Once University Bank grants a loan to Campus Radio, both you and Campus Radio have $100 in your checking accounts to spend. But the bank is holding only $100 of **reserves** (your coins). In other words, the increased account balance obtained by Campus Radio doesn't limit *your* ability to write checks. There's been a net *increase* in the value of transactions deposits but no increase in bank reserves.

bank reserves: Assets held by a bank to fulfill its deposit of obligations.

Secondary Deposits. What happens if Campus Radio actually spends the $100 on a new antenna? Won't this "use up all" the reserves held by the bank, endangering your check-writing privileges? The answer is no.

Consider what happens when Atlas Antenna receives the check from Campus Radio. What will Atlas do with the check? Atlas could go to University Bank and exchange the check for $100 of cash (your coins). But Atlas may prefer to deposit the check in its own checking account at University Bank (still the only bank in town). This way, Atlas not only avoids the necessity of going to the bank (it can deposit the check by mail or smartphone) but also keeps its money in a safe place. Should Atlas later want to spend the money, it can simply write a check. In the meantime, the bank continues to hold its entire reserves (your coins), and both you and Atlas have $100 to spend.

Fractional Reserves. Notice what's happened here. The money supply has increased by $100 as a result of deposit creation (the loan to Campus Radio). Moreover, the bank has been able to support $200 of transaction deposits (your account and either the Campus Radio or Atlas account) with only $100 of reserves (your coins). In other words, *bank reserves are only a fraction of total deposits.* In this case, University Bank's reserves (your $100 in coins) are only 50 percent of total deposits. Thus the bank's **reserve ratio** is 50 percent—that is,

$$\frac{\text{Reserve}}{\text{ratio}} = \frac{\text{Bank reserves}}{\text{Total deposits}}$$

reserve ratio: The ratio of a bank's reserves to its total transactions deposits.

The ability of University Bank to hold reserves that are only a fraction of total deposits results from two facts: (1) people use checks and debit cards for most transactions and (2) there's no other bank. Accordingly, reserves are rarely withdrawn from this monopoly bank. In fact, if people *never* withdrew their deposits and *all* transactions accounts were held at University Bank, University Bank wouldn't need *any* reserves. In this most unusual case, University Bank could make as many loans as it wanted. Every loan it made would increase the supply of money.

In reality, many banks are available, and people both withdraw cash from their accounts and write checks to people who have accounts in other banks. In addition, bank lending practices are regulated by the Federal Reserve System. *The Federal Reserve System requires banks to maintain some minimum reserve ratio.* This reserve requirement directly limits banks' ability to grant new loans.

Required Reserves. The potential impact of Federal Reserve requirements on bank lending can be readily seen. Suppose that the Federal Reserve imposed a minimum reserve requirement of 75 percent on University Bank. Such a requirement would prohibit University Bank from lending $100 to Campus Radio. That loan would result in $200 of deposits, supported by only $100 of reserves. The actual ratio of reserves to deposits would be 50 percent ($100 of reserves ÷ $200 of deposits), which would violate the Fed's assumed 75 percent reserve requirement. A 75 percent reserve requirement means that University Bank must hold **required reserves** equal to 75 percent of *total* deposits, including those created through loans.

The bank's dilemma is evident in the following equation:

required reserves: The minimum amount of reserves a bank is required to hold; equal to required reserve ratio times transactions deposits.

$$\frac{\text{Required}}{\text{reserves}} = \frac{\text{Required reserve}}{\text{ratio}} \times \frac{\text{Total}}{\text{deposits}}$$

To support $200 of total deposits, University Bank would need to satisfy this equation:

$$\frac{\text{Required}}{\text{reserves}} = 0.75 \times \$200 = \$150$$

But the bank has only $100 of reserves (your coins) and so would violate the reserve requirement if it increased total deposits to $200 by lending $100 to Campus Radio.

University Bank can still issue a loan to Campus Radio. But the loan must be less than $100 to keep the bank within the limits of the required reserve formula. Thus *a minimum reserve requirement directly limits deposit creation (lending) possibilities.* It's still true, however, as we'll now illustrate, that the banking system, taken as a whole, can create multiple loans (money) from a single deposit.

A Multibank World

Table 13.2 illustrates the process of deposit creation in a multibank world with a required reserve ratio. In this case, we assume that legally required reserves must equal at least 20 percent of transactions deposits. Now when you deposit $100 in your checking account, University Bank must hold at least $20 as required reserves.[1]

excess reserves: Bank reserves in excess of required reserves.

Excess Reserves. The remaining $80 the bank obtains from your deposit is regarded as **excess reserves.** These reserves are "excess" because your bank is *required* to hold in reserve only $20 (equal to 20 percent of your initial $100 deposit):

$$\frac{\text{Excess}}{\text{reserves}} = \frac{\text{Total}}{\text{reserves}} - \frac{\text{Required}}{\text{reserves}}$$

The $80 of excess reserves aren't required and may be used to support additional loans. Hence the bank can now lend $80. In view of the fact that banks earn profits (interest) by making loans, we assume that University Bank will try to use these excess reserves as soon as possible.

To keep track of the changes in reserves, deposit balances, and loans that occur in a multibank world we'll have to do some more bookkeeping. For this purpose we'll again use the same balance sheet, or "T-account," that banks themselves use. Table 13.2 takes us down the accounting path.

Step 1: Cash Deposit. Notice how the balance of University Bank looks immediately after it receives your initial deposit (step 1, Table 13.2). Your deposit of coins is entered on *both* sides of University's balance sheet. On the left side, your deposit is regarded as an asset because your piggy bank's coins have an immediate market value and can be used to pay off the bank's liabilities. The coins now appear as *reserves*. The reserves these coins represent are further divided into required reserves ($20, or 20 percent of your deposit) and excess reserves ($80).

On the right side of the balance sheet, the bank reminds itself that it has an obligation (liability) to return your deposit when you demand. Thus the bank's accounts balance, with assets and liabilities being equal. In fact, *a bank's books must always balance because all the bank's assets must belong to someone (its depositors or the bank's owners).*

Step 2: Bank Loan. University Bank wants to do more than balance its books, however; it wants to earn profits. To do so, it will have to make loans—that is, put its excess reserves to work. Suppose that it lends $80 to Campus Radio.[2] As step 2 in Table 13.2 illustrates, this loan alters both sides of University Bank's balance sheet. On the right side, the bank creates a new transactions deposit for (credits the account of) Campus Radio; this item represents an additional liability (promise to pay). On the left side of the balance sheet, two things happen. First, the bank notes that Campus Radio owes it $80 ("loans"). Second, the bank recognizes that it's now required to hold $36 in *required* reserves, in accordance with its higher level of transactions deposits ($180). (Recall we're assuming that required reserves are 20 percent of total transactions deposits.) Since its total reserves are still $100, $64 is left as *excess* reserves. Note again that *excess reserves are reserves a bank isn't required to hold.*

Changes in the Money Supply. Before examining further changes in the balance sheet of University Bank, consider again what's happened to the economy's money supply during these first two steps. In the first step, you deposited $100 of cash in your checking account. This initial transaction didn't change the value of the money supply. Only the composition

---

[1]The reserves themselves may be held in the form of cash in the bank's vault but are usually held as credits with one of the regional Federal Reserve banks.

[2]Because of the Fed's assumed minimum reserve requirement (20 percent), University Bank can now lend only $80 rather than $100, as before.

Step 1: You deposit cash at University Bank. The deposit creates $100 of reserves, $20 of which are designated as required reserves. This leaves $80 of excess reserves.

University Bank

Assets		Liabilities	
Required reserves	$ 20	Your deposit	$100
Excess reserves	80		
Total	$100		100

Banking System

Change in Transactions Deposits	Change in M
+$100	$0

Step 2: The bank uses its excess reserves ($80) to make a loan to Campus Radio. Total deposits now equal $180. The money supply has increased.

University Bank

Assets		Liabilities	
Required reserves	$ 36	Your account	$100
Excess reserves	64	Campus Radio account	80
Loans	80		
Total	$180	Total	$180

Banking System

Δ Deposits	Δ M
+$80	+$80

Step 3: Campus Radio buys an antenna. This depletes Campus Radio's account but increases Atlas's balance. Eternal Savings gets $80 of reserves when the Campus Radio check clears.

University Bank

Assets		Liabilities	
Required reserves	$ 20	Your account	$100
Excess reserves	0	Campus Radio account	0
Loan	80		
Total	$100	Total	$100

Eternal Savings

Assets		Liabilities	
Required reserves	$16	Atlas Antenna account	$80
Excess reserves	64		
Total	$80	Total	$80

Banking System

Δ Deposits	Δ M
$0	$0

Step 4: Eternal Savings lends money to Herman's Hardware. Deposits, loans, and M all increase by $64.

University Bank

Assets		Liabilities	
Required reserves	$ 20	Your account	$100
Excess reserves	0	Campus Radio account	0
Loan	80		
Total	$100	Total	$100

Eternal Savings

Assets		Liabilities	
Required reserves	$28.80	Atlas Antenna account	$ 80
Excess reserves	51.20	Herman's Hardware account	64
Loans	64		
	$ 144		$144

Banking System

Change in Transaction Deposits	Change in M
+$64	+$64

nth step: Some bank lends $1.00	+1 +1

Cumulative Change in Banking System

Bank Reserves	Transactions Deposits	Money Supply
+$100	+$500	+$400

TABLE 13.2

Deposit Creation

Excess reserves (step 1) are the basis of bank loans. When a bank uses its excess reserves to make a loan, it creates a deposit (step 2). When the loan is spent, a deposit will be made somewhere else (step 3). This new deposit creates additional excess reserves (step 3) that can be used for further loans (step 4, etc.). The process of deposit creation continues until the money supply has increased by a multiple of the initial deposit.

of the money supply (M1) was affected ($100 less cash held by the public, $100 more in transactions accounts).

Not until step 2—when the bank makes a loan—does all the excitement begin. In making a loan, the bank automatically increases the total money supply by $80. Why? Because someone (Campus Radio) now has more money (a transactions deposit) than it did before, *and no one else has any less.* And Campus Radio can use its money to buy goods and services, just like anybody else.

This second step is the heart of money creation. Money effectively appears out of thin air when a bank makes a loan. To understand how this works, you have to keep reminding yourself that money is more than the coins and currency we carry around. Transactions deposits are money too. Hence *the creation of transactions deposits via new loans is the same thing as creating money.*

Step 3: Spending the Loan. Suppose again that Campus Radio actually uses its $80 loan to buy an antenna. The rest of Table 13.2 illustrates how this additional transaction leads to further changes in balance sheets and the money supply.

In step 3, we see that when Campus Radio buys the $80 antenna, the balance in its checking account at University Bank drops to zero because it has spent all its money. As University Bank's liabilities fall (from $180 to $100), so does the level of its required reserves (from $36 to $20). (Note that required reserves are still 20 percent of its remaining transactions deposits.) But University Bank's excess reserves have disappeared completely! This disappearance reflects the fact that Atlas Antenna keeps *its* transactions account at another bank (Eternal Savings). When Atlas deposits the check it received from Campus Radio, Eternal Savings does two things. First, it credits Atlas's account by $80. Second, it goes to University Bank to get the reserves that support the deposit.[3] The reserves later appear on the balance sheet of Eternal Savings as both required ($16) and excess ($64) reserves.

Observe that the money supply hasn't changed during step 3. The increase in the value of Atlas Antenna's transactions account balance exactly offsets the drop in the value of Campus Radio's transactions account. Ownership of the money supply is the only thing that has changed.

Step 4: More Deposit Creation. In step 4, Eternal Savings takes advantage of its newly acquired excess reserves by making a loan to Herman's Hardware. As before, the loan itself has two primary effects. First, it creates a transactions deposit of $64 for Herman's Hardware and thereby increases the money supply by the same amount. Second, it increases the required level of reserves at Eternal Savings. (To how much? Why?)

THE MONEY MULTIPLIER

By now it's perhaps obvious that the process of deposit creation won't come to an end quickly. On the contrary, it can continue indefinitely, just like the income multiplier process in Chapter 10. Indeed, people often refer to deposit creation as the money multiplier process, with the **money multiplier** expressed as the reciprocal of the required reserve ratio. That is,

$$\text{Money multiplier} = \frac{1}{\text{Required reserve ratio}}$$

money multiplier: The number of deposit (loan) dollars that the banking system can create from $1 of excess reserves; equal to 1 ÷ required reserve ratio.

Figure 13.2 illustrates the money multiplier process. When a new deposit enters the banking system, it creates both excess and required reserves. The required reserves represent leakage from the flow of money because they can't be used to create new loans. Excess reserves, on the other hand, can be used for new loans. Once those loans are made, they typically become transactions deposits elsewhere in the banking system. Then some additional leakage into required reserves occurs, and further loans are made. The process continues until all excess reserves have leaked into required reserves. Once excess reserves

[3]In actuality, banks rarely "go" anywhere; such interbank reserve movements are handled by bank clearinghouses and regional Federal Reserve banks. The effect is the same, however. The nature and use of bank reserves are discussed more fully in Chapter 14.

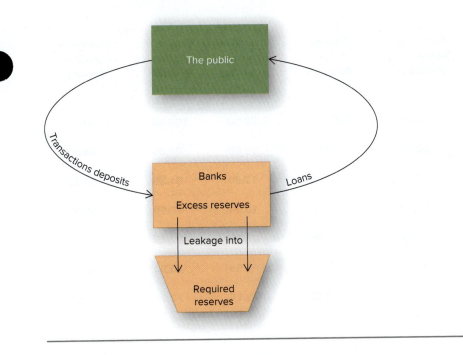

FIGURE 13.2
The Money Multiplier Process

Part of every new bank deposit leaks into required reserves. The rest—excess reserves—can be used to make loans. These loans, in turn, become deposits elsewhere. The process of money creation continues until all available reserves become required reserves.

have completely disappeared, the total value of new loans will equal initial excess reserves multiplied by the money multiplier.

The potential of the money multiplier to create loans is summarized by the equation

$$\begin{matrix} \text{Excess} \\ \text{reserves} \\ \text{of banking} \\ \text{system} \end{matrix} \times \begin{matrix} \text{Money} \\ \text{multiplier} \end{matrix} = \begin{matrix} \text{Potential} \\ \text{deposit creation} \end{matrix}$$

Notice how the money multiplier worked in our previous example. The value of the money multiplier was equal to 5 because we assumed that the required reserve ratio was 0.20. Moreover, the initial level of excess reserves was $80 as a consequence of your original deposit (step 1). According to the money multiplier, then, the deposit creation potential of the banking system was

$$\begin{matrix} \text{Excess reserves} \\ (\$80) \end{matrix} \times \begin{matrix} \text{Money multiplier} \\ (5) \end{matrix} = \begin{matrix} \text{Potential} \\ \text{deposit} \\ \text{creation} (\$400) \end{matrix}$$

When all the banks fully utilized their excess reserves at each step of the money multiplier process, the ultimate increase in the money supply was in fact $400 (see the last row in Table 13.2).

Excess Reserves as Lending Power

While you're struggling through Table 13.2, notice the critical role that excess reserves play in the process of deposit creation. A bank can make additional loans only if it has excess reserves. Without excess reserves, all of a bank's reserves are required, and no further liabilities (transactions deposits) can be created with new loans. On the other hand, a bank with excess reserves can make additional loans. In fact,

- *Each bank may lend an amount equal to its excess reserves and no more.*

As such loans enter the circular flow and become deposits elsewhere, they create new excess reserves and further lending capacity. As a consequence,

- *The entire banking system can increase the volume of loans by the amount of excess reserves multiplied by the money multiplier.*

Required reserves = 0.20	Change in Transactions Deposits	Change in Total Reserves	Change in Required Reserves	Change in Excess Reserves	Change in Lending Capacity
If $100 in cash is deposited in Bank A, Bank A acquires	$100.00	$100.00	$ 20.00	$80.00	$ 80.00
If loan made and deposited elsewhere, Bank B acquires	80.00	80.00	16.00	64.00	64.00
If loan made and deposited elsewhere, Bank C acquires	64.00	64.00	12.80	51.20	51.20
If loan made and deposited elsewhere, Bank D acquires	51.20	51.20	10.24	40.96	40.96
If loan made and deposited elsewhere, Bank E acquires	40.96	40.96	8.19	32.77	32.77
If loan made and deposited elsewhere, Bank F acquires	32.77	32.77	6.55	26.22	26.22
If loan made and deposited elsewhere, Bank G acquires	26.22	26.22	5.24	20.98	20.98
. . .					
If loan made and deposited elsewhere, Bank Z acquires	0.38	0.38	0.08	0.30	0.30
Cumulative, through Bank Z	$498.80	$100.00	$ 99.76	$ 0.24	$398.80
. . .					
And if the process continues indefinitely	$500.00	$100.00	$100.00	$ 0.00	$400.00

Note: A $100 cash deposit creates $400 of new lending capacity when the required reserve ratio is 0.20. Initial excess reserves are $80 (= $100 deposit − $20 required reserves). The money multiplier is 5 (= 1 ÷ 0.20). New lending potential equals $400 (= $80 excess reserves × 5).

TABLE 13.3

The Money Multiplier at Work

The process of deposit creation continues as money passes through different banks in the form of multiple deposits and loans. At each step, excess reserves and new loans are created. The lending capacity of this system equals the money multiplier times excess reserves. In this case, initial excess reserves of $80 create the possibility of $400 of new loans when the reserve ratio is 0.20 (20 percent).

By keeping track of excess reserves, then, we can gauge the lending capacity of any bank or, with the aid of the money multiplier, the entire banking system.

Table 13.3 summarizes the entire money multiplier process. In this case, we assume that all banks are initially "loaned up"—that is, without any excess reserves. The money multiplier process begins when someone deposits $100 in cash into a transactions account at Bank A. If the required reserve ratio is 20 percent, this initial deposit creates $80 of excess reserves at Bank A while adding $100 to total transactions deposits.

If Bank A uses its newly acquired excess reserves to make a loan that ultimately ends up in Bank B, two things happen: Bank B acquires $64 in excess reserves (0.80 × $80) and total transactions deposits increase by $80 as well.

The money multiplier process continues with a series of loans and deposits. When the 26th loan is made (by Bank Z), total loans grow by only $0.30 and transactions deposits by an equal amount. Should the process continue further, the *cumulative* change in loans will ultimately equal $400—that is, the money multiplier times initial excess reserves. The money supply will increase by the same amount.

BANKS AND THE CIRCULAR FLOW

The bookkeeping details of bank deposits and loans are rarely exciting and often confusing. But they demonstrate convincingly that banks can create money. In that capacity, *banks perform two essential functions for the macro economy:*

- *Banks transfer money from savers to spenders by lending funds (reserves) held on deposit.*
- *The banking system creates additional money by making loans in excess of total reserves.*

In performing these two functions, banks change the size of the money supply—that is, the amount of purchasing power available for buying goods and services. Changes in the money supply may in turn alter *spending* behavior and thereby shift the aggregate demand curve.

Figure 13.3 is a simplified perspective on the role of banks in the circular flow. As before, income flows from product markets through business firms to factor markets and returns to consumers in the form of disposable income. Consumers spend most of their income but also save (don't spend) some of it.

Financing Injections

The leakage represented by consumer saving is a potential source of stabilization problems, particularly unemployment. If additional spending by business firms, foreigners, or governments doesn't compensate for consumer saving at full employment, a recessionary GDP gap will emerge, creating unemployment (see Chapters 9 and 10). Our interest here is in the role the banking system can play in encouraging such additional spending.

Suppose for the moment that *all* consumer saving was deposited in piggy banks rather than depository institutions (banks) and that no one used checks. Under these circumstances, banks couldn't transfer money from savers to spenders by holding deposits and making loans.

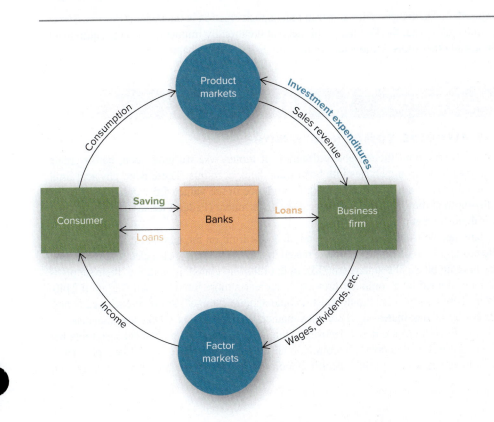

FIGURE 13.3

Banks in the Circular Flow

Banks help transfer income from savers to spenders by using their deposits to make loans to business firms and consumers who want to spend more money than they have. By lending money, banks help maintain any desired rate of aggregate demand.

In reality, a substantial portion of consumer saving *is* deposited in banks. These and other bank deposits can be used as the basis of loans, thereby returning purchasing power to the circular flow. In fact, **the primary economic function of banks isn't to store money but to transfer purchasing power from savers to spenders.** They do so by lending money to businesses for new plants and equipment, to consumers for new homes or cars, and to government entities to build sports stadiums and toll roads. Moreover, because the banking system can make *multiple* loans from available reserves, banks don't have to receive all consumer saving to carry out their function. On the contrary, *the banking system can create any desired level of money supply if allowed to expand or reduce loan activity at will.*

Constraints on Deposit Creation

There are four major constraints on the deposit creation of the banking system.

Deposits. The first constraint is the willingness of consumers and businesses to continue using and accepting checks or debit cards rather than cash in the marketplace. If people preferred to hold cash rather than bank balances, banks wouldn't be able to acquire or maintain the reserves that are the foundation of bank lending activity.

Willingness to Lend. Once banks are holding sufficient reserves, they must be willing to make new loans. In 2009–2010, this condition was violated. Banks had accumulated huge losses on previous mortgage loans. In addition, the economy was sliding into a deepening recession. So banks were reluctant to make new loans that might not get repaid. This put a serious crimp on aggregate demand.

Willingness to Borrow. The third constraint on deposit creation is the willingness of consumers, businesses, and governments to borrow the money that banks make available. The chain of events we've observed in deposit creation depends on the willingness of Campus Radio to borrow $80, of Herman's Hardware to borrow $64, and so on. If no one wanted to borrow any money, deposit creation would never begin. By the same reasoning, if all excess reserves aren't borrowed (lent), deposit creation won't live up to its theoretical potential.

Regulation. The fourth major constraint on deposit creation is the Federal Reserve System. As we've observed, the Fed may limit deposit creation by imposing reserve requirements. These and other tools of monetary policy are discussed in Chapter 14.

THE ECONOMY TOMORROW

ARE BITCOINS TOMORROW'S MONEY?

People worry about the origins and nature of money. As we have seen, banks create money with electronic entries into borrowers' bank accounts. There is no physical limit to the number of such dollars created. Confidence in the value of the dollar is an act of faith—faith in the stability of banks and the government (Federal Reserve) that regulates their deposit creation.

Many people want a more secure and objective limit on the amount of money created. Bitcoins appear to offer such a limit. Created in 2009, bitcoins are also electronic blips. But they have no physical counterparts (like dollar bills and coins). In addition, their supply is allegedly limited by a computer protocol that creates more bitcoins each year until 2140, when 21 million bitcoins would exist. People acquire ("mine") some of each year's new bitcoins by solving increasingly complex mathematical problems. Geeks love the idea.

Every bitcoin has a unique electronic identifier, similar to the physical serial number on a dollar bill. If you own a bitcoin, you have a unique "private key" (like a password) that allows you access to that specific bitcoin. You can transfer bitcoins by giving your "private key" information to someone else. Such electronic transfers enable you to buy and sell goods, making bitcoins an effective medium of exchange.

What distinguishes bitcoin transfers from dollar transfers is their anonymity. Dollar transfers go through banks and other financial institutions. Bitcoin transfers can be made directly without any third-party intermediary, so there is no public record of the transaction. This anonymity made bitcoins an early favorite of drug traffickers, gamblers, and other black marketers. Ordinary citizens also liked the speed and negligible cost of bitcoin transactions.

Bitcoins quickly became a speculative sensation. When first introduced in 2009, a bitcoin was worth 30 cents. In 2011, that value rose to $1. Then the value of bitcoins soared, hitting a peak of $1,147.25 on December 4, 2013. Bitcoins looked more like Zimbabwean dollars or penny stocks than a stable currency. In 2014, the market value of bitcoins tumbled to $400. Bitcoin prices rose for a couple of years after that, hitting another height of $1,230 on January 4, 2017. But the price fell to $776 just a week later.

Will bitcoins be "money" in the economy tomorrow? Not likely. The wild fluctuations in their value make bitcoins a dubious store of value. Those fluctuations and their exclusive electronic nature also constrain their ability to serve as a medium of exchange. As of 2017, only a handful of merchants were accepting bitcoins in payment for real goods and services. The collapse of the major bitcoin exchange (Tokyo-based Mt. Gox) in early 2014—together with the electronic disappearance of millions of bitcoins—undermined their acceptability. The electronic "bank" ("blockchain") that stores bitcoin identifiers is vulnerable to hackers, as are the "private keys" that denote bitcoin ownership. A security breach at a Slovenian bitcoin exchange resulted in a loss of 19,000 bitcoins values at $5.4 million. Another security breach of a competing cryptocurrency (Ethereum) in 2016 led to the theft of $55 million in cyber currency. Last but not least, the Internal Revenue Service ruled in 2014 that bitcoins were deemed *property,* not money. This requires bitcoin users to keep track of the price they pay for bitcoins and the value they get in subsequent transactions. The bitcoin user is then subject to a capital-gains tax on any increase in the value of the bitcoins. This ruling negates the anonymity of bitcoin transactions—or subjects the user to the risk of tax evasion prosecution. Bitcoins aren't going to replace dollars in our concept of money in the economy tomorrow.

SUMMARY

- In a market economy, money serves a critical function in *facilitating exchanges* and specialization, thus permitting increased output. **LO13-1**
- *Money* refers to any medium that's generally accepted in exchange, serves as a store of value, and acts as a standard of value. **LO13-1**
- Because people use bank account balances to buy goods and services (with checks or debit cards), such balances are also regarded as money. The money supply M1 includes cash plus transactions account (checkable) deposits. M2 adds savings account balances and other deposits to form a broader measure of the money supply. **LO13-1**
- The assets a bank holds must always equal its liabilities. **LO13-2**
- Banks have the power to create money by making loans. In making loans, banks create new transactions deposits, which become part of the money supply. **LO13-3**

- A bank's ability to make loans—create money—depends on its reserves. Only if a bank has excess reserves—reserves greater than those required by federal regulation—can it make new loans. **LO13-3**
- As loans are spent, they create deposits elsewhere, making it possible for other banks to make additional loans. The money multiplier (1 ÷ required reserve ratio) indicates the total value of deposits that can be created by the banking system from excess reserves. **LO13-4**
- The role of banks in creating money includes the transfer of money from savers to spenders as well as deposit creation in excess of deposit balances. Taken together, these two functions give banks direct control over the amount of purchasing power available in the marketplace. **LO13-3**
- The deposit creation potential of the banking system is limited by government regulation. It is also limited by the willingness of market participants to hold deposits or borrow money. **LO13-4**

Key Terms

barter
money
money supply (M1)
transactions account
money supply (M2)

aggregate demand
deposit creation
T-accounts
bank reserves
reserve ratio

required reserves
excess reserves
money multiplier

Questions for Discussion

1. Why are checking account balances, but not credit cards, regarded as "money"? **LO13-1**
2. In what respects are modern forms of money superior to the colonial use of wampum as money? **LO13-1**
3. How are an economy's production possibilities affected when barter replaces cash exchanges? (See World View "Trading Chickens for Diapers") **LO13-1**
4. Are digital wallets like ApplePay and GoogleWallet new forms of money? **LO13-1**
5. What percentage of your monthly bills do you pay with (*a*) cash, (*b*) check, (*c*) credit card, and (*d*) automatic transfers? How do you pay off the credit card balance? How does your use of cash compare with the composition of the money supply (Figure 13.1)? **LO13-1**
6. Why must a bank's assets always equal its liabilities? **LO13-2**

7. Does the fact that your bank keeps only a fraction of your account balance in reserve make you uncomfortable? Why don't people rush to the bank and retrieve their money? What would happen if they did? **LO13-3**
8. If people never withdrew cash from banks, how much money could the banking system potentially create? Could this really happen? What might limit deposit creation in this case? **LO13-4**
9. If all banks heeded Shakespeare's admonition "Neither a borrower nor a lender be," what would happen to the circular flow? **LO13-3**
10. What makes bitcoins an unlikely form of money? **LO13-1**

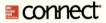

PROBLEMS FOR CHAPTER 13

LO13-1 1. According World View "Trading Chickens for Diapers," how much pasta could a Venezuelan get in barter for one chicken?

LO13-1 2. Of the following three forms of money: cash, checking accounts, savings accounts, which is the largest component of
(*a*) M1?
(*b*) M2?

LO13-2 3. A bank has $1000 in deposits and the required reserve ratio is 10 percent. Based on this information
(*a*) Enter the appropriate values in the T-account.

Assets	Liabilities

(*b*) Calculate the potential total deposit creation of the bank.

LO13-1 4. If you withdraw $100 from your checking account and the required reserve ratio is 10 percent, how much do(es) the bank's
(*a*) Total deposits change?
(*b*) Required reserves change?
(*c*) Excess reserves change?

If you deposit a $300 check in your checking account and the required reserve ratio is 10 percent, how much do(es) the bank's
(*d*) Total deposits change?
(*e*) Required reserves change?
(*f*) Excess reserves change?

LO13-2 5. If a bank has total deposits of $8,000,000 and reserves of $2,000,000
(*a*) What is the current percentage of deposits held in reserve?
(*b*) What percentage of deposits are currently loaned out?

LO13-2 6. Suppose a bank's balance sheet looks as follows:

Assets		Liabilities	
Reserves	$ 700	Deposits	$6,000
Loans	5,300		

and banks are required to hold reserves equal to 10 percent of deposits.
(*a*) How much excess reserves does the bank hold?
(*b*) How much more can this bank lend?

LO13-3 7. Suppose a bank's balance sheet looks like this:

Assets		Liabilities	
Reserves		Deposits	$800
Excess	$140		
Required	40		
Loans	620		
Total	$800	Total	$800

(*a*) What is the required reserve ratio?
(*b*) How much money can this bank still lend?

LO13-4 8. What is the value of the money multiplier when the required reserve ratio is
(*a*) 5 percent?
(*b*) 10 percent?

LO13-3 9. On January 10, 2017, a man in Lebanon, Virginia, frustrated with the DMV bureaucracy, paid his DMV bill with 300,000 pennies that he carted into the DMV office in five wheelbarrows. The DMV had to count all these pennies and deposit them into the DMV bank account. After the DMV deposit and assuming 5 percent reserve requirement, calculate the initial change in
   (a) Money supply.
   (b) Deposits.
   (c) Total reserves.
   (d) Excess reserves.
   (e) Calculate the cumulative change for the banking system in Lending capacity.

LO13-3 10. (a) When the reserve requirement changes, which of the following will change for an individual bank?
       Total deposits
       Total reserves
       Required reserves
       Excess reserves
       Unused lending capacity
   (b) When the reserve requirement changes, which of the following will change in the total banking system?
       Total deposits
       Total reserves
       Required reserves
       Excess reserves
       Unused lending capacity

LO13-3 11. In Table 13.2, how much unused lending capacity does Eternal Savings have at step 4?

LO13-4 12. Suppose that a lottery winner deposits $8 million in cash into her transactions account at the Bank of America (B of A). Assume a reserve requirement of 20 percent and no excess reserves in the banking system prior to this deposit.
   (a) Use step 1 in the following T-accounts to show how her deposit initially affects the balance sheet at B of A.
   (b) Has the money supply been changed by her deposit?
   (c) Use step 2 in the following T-accounts to show the changes at B of A after the bank fully uses its new lending capacity.
   (d) Has the money supply been changed by step 2?
   (e) After the entire banking system uses the lending capacity of the initial ($8 million) deposit, by how much will the following have changed?
       Total reserves
       Total deposits
       Total loans
       The money supply

Step 1: Winnings Deposited
Bank of America

Assets (in Millions)		Liabilities (in Millions)	
Reserves:		Deposits	_____
Required	_____		
Excess	_____		
Loans	_____		
Total assets	_____	Total liabilities	_____

Step 2: Loans Made
Bank of America

Assets (in Millions)		Liabilities (in Millions)	
Reserves:		Deposits	_____
Required	_____		
Excess	_____		
Loans	_____		
Total assets	_____	Total liabilities	_____

LO13-1 13. The Economy Tomorrow: How much does M1 and M2 change in the following situations?

   (*a*) $100 in coins is deposited into a checking account.

   (*b*) $500 is transferred from a savings to a checking account.

   (*c*) $300 is transferred into bitcoin.

The Federal Reserve building in Washington, D.C.
©Pixtal/age fotostock RF

The Federal Reserve System

We've seen how money is created with bank loans. We've also gotten a few clues about how the government limits money creation and thus aggregate demand. This chapter examines the mechanics of government control more closely:

- **Which government agency is responsible for controlling the money supply?**
- **What policy tools are used to control the amount of money in the economy?**
- **How are banks and bond markets affected by the government's policies?**

Most people have a ready answer for the first question. The popular view is that the government controls the amount of money in the economy by printing more or fewer dollar bills. But we've already observed that the concept of "money" isn't so simple. In Chapter 13 we demonstrated that banks, not printing presses, create most of our money. In making loans, banks create transactions deposits that are counted as part of the money supply.

Because bank lending activities are the primary source of money, the *government must regulate bank lending if it wants to control the amount of money in the economy.* That's exactly what the Federal Reserve System does. The Federal Reserve System—the "Fed"—not only limits the volume of loans that the banking system can make from available reserves; it can also alter the amount of reserves banks hold.

The Federal Reserve System's control over the supply of money is the key mechanism of **monetary policy.** The potential of this policy lever to alter macro outcomes (unemployment, inflation, etc.) is examined in Chapter 15. In this chapter, we focus on the *tools* of monetary policy.

STRUCTURE OF THE FED

In the absence of any government regulation, the supply of money would be determined by individual banks. Moreover, individual depositors would bear all the risks of bank failures. In fact, this is the way the banking system operated until 1914. The money supply was subject to abrupt changes, and consumers sometimes lost their savings in recurrent bank failures.

A series of bank failures resulted in a severe financial panic in 1907. Millions of depositors lost their savings, and the economy was thrown

LEARNING OBJECTIVES

After reading this chapter, you should know

LO14-1 How the Federal Reserve is organized.

LO14-2 The Fed's major policy tools.

LO14-3 How open market operations work.

monetary policy: The use of money and credit controls to influence macroeconomic outcomes.

into a tailspin. In the wake of this panic, a National Monetary Commission was established to examine ways of restructuring the banking system. The mandate of the commission was to find ways to prevent recurrent financial crises. After five years of study, the commission recommended the creation of a Federal Reserve System. Congress accepted the commission's recommendations, and President Wilson signed the Federal Reserve Act in December 1913.

Federal Reserve Banks

The core of the Federal Reserve System consists of 12 Federal Reserve banks. Each bank acts as a central banker for the private banks in its region. In this role, the regional Fed banks perform the following services:

- *Clearing checks between private banks.* Suppose the Bank of America in San Francisco receives a deposit from one of its customers in the form of a share draft written on the New York State Employees Credit Union. The Bank of America doesn't have to go to New York to collect the cash or other reserves that support that draft. Instead the Bank of America can deposit the draft (check) at its account with the Federal Reserve Bank of San Francisco. The Fed then collects from the credit union. This vital clearinghouse service saves the Bank of America and other private banks a great deal of time and expense in processing the 10 *billion* checks that are written every year.
- *Holding bank reserves.* Notice that the Fed's clearinghouse service was facilitated by the fact that the Bank of America and the New York Employees Credit Union had their own accounts at the Fed. As we noted in Chapter 13, banks are *required* to hold some minimum fraction of their deposits in reserve. Only a small amount of reserves is held as cash in a bank's vaults. The rest is held in reserve accounts at the regional Federal Reserve banks. These accounts not only provide greater security and convenience for bank reserves but also enable the Fed to monitor the actual level of bank reserves.
- *Providing currency.* Before every major holiday there's a great demand for cash. People want some pocket money during holidays and know that it's difficult to cash checks on weekends or holidays, especially if they're going out of town. So they load up on cash at their bank or ATMs. After the holiday is over, most of this cash is returned to the banks, typically by the stores, gas stations, and restaurants that benefited from holiday spending. Because banks hold little cash in their vaults, they turn to the Fed to meet these sporadic cash demands. A private bank can simply call the regional Federal Reserve bank and order a supply of cash, to be delivered (by armored truck) before a weekend or holiday. The cash will be deducted from the bank's own account at the Fed. When all the cash comes back in after the holiday, the bank can reverse the process, sending the unneeded cash back to the Fed.
- *Providing loans.* The Federal Reserve banks may also lend reserves to private banks. This practice, called "discounting," is examined more closely in a moment.

The Board of Governors

At the top of the Federal Reserve System's organization chart (Figure 14.1) is the Board of Governors, which is responsible for setting monetary policy. The Board, located in Washington, D.C., consists of seven members ("governors"), appointed by the president of the United States and confirmed by the U.S. Senate. Board members are appointed for 14-year terms and can't be reappointed. Their exceptionally long appointments give the Fed governors a measure of political independence. They're not beholden to any elected official and will hold office longer than any president.

The intent of the Fed's independence is to keep control of the nation's money supply beyond the immediate reach of politicians (especially members of Congress, elected for two-year terms). The designers of the Fed system feared that political control of monetary policy would cause wild swings in the money supply and macro instability. Critics argue, however, that the Fed's independence makes it unresponsive to the majority will.

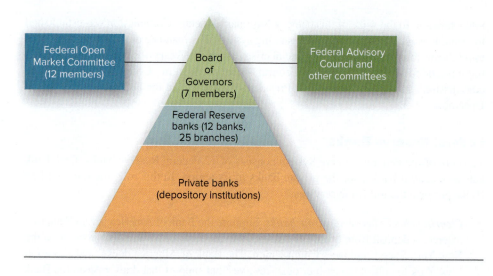

The president selects one of the governors to serve as chair of the Board for four years. The current chair, Jay Powell, was nominated by President Trump in November 2017 to become chair in February 2018. He had been a Fed governor since 2012 and had previously served in the Treasury Department under President George H. Bush. He replaced Janet Yellen, who had been appointed by President Obama in 2014. Chair Powell is the primary spokesperson for Fed policy and reports to Congress every six months on the conduct of monetary policy.

The Federal Open Market Committee (FOMC)

A key arm of the Board is the Federal Open Market Committee (FOMC), which is responsible for the Fed's daily activity in financial markets. The FOMC plays a critical role in setting short-term interest rates and the level of reserves held by private banks. The membership of the FOMC includes all seven governors and 5 of the 12 regional Reserve bank presidents. The FOMC meets in Washington, D.C., every four or five weeks throughout the year to review the economy's performance. It decides whether the economy is growing fast enough (or too fast) and then adjusts monetary policy as needed.

MONETARY TOOLS

money supply (M1): Currency held by the public, plus balances in transactions accounts.

Our immediate interest isn't in the structure of the Federal Reserve but the way the Fed is able to alter the **money supply**. *The Fed's control of the money supply is exercised by use of three policy tools:*

- *Reserve requirements.*
- *Discount rates.*
- *Open market operations.*

Reserve Requirements

required reserves: The minimum amount of reserves a bank is required to hold; equal to required reserve ratio times transactions deposits.

The Fed's first policy tool focuses on reserve requirements. As noted in Chapter 13, the Fed requires private banks to keep some fraction of their deposits "in reserve." These **required reserves** are held either in the form of actual vault cash or, more commonly, as credits (deposits) in the bank's "reserve account" at a regional Federal Reserve bank. *By changing the reserve requirements, the Fed can directly alter the lending capacity of the banking system.*

Recall that the banking system's ability to make additional loans—create deposits—is determined by two factors: (1) the amount of excess reserves banks hold and (2) the money multiplier. Both factors are directly influenced by the Fed's required reserve ratio.

Computing Excess Reserves. Suppose, for example, that banks collectively hold $100 billion of deposits and total reserves of $30 billion. Assume too that the minimum reserve requirement is 20 percent. Under these circumstances, banks are holding more reserves than they have to. Recall that

$$\frac{\text{Required}}{\text{reserves}} = \frac{\text{Required}}{\text{reserve ratio}} \times \frac{\text{Total}}{\text{deposits}}$$

so in this case,

$$\frac{\text{Required}}{\text{reserves}} = 0.20 \times \$100$$

$$= \$20 \text{ billion}$$

Banks are *required* to hold $20 billion in reserve to meet Federal Reserve regulations on their deposit base ($100 billion). We've assumed, however, that they're actually holding $30 billion of reserves. The $10 billion difference between actual and required reserves is **excess reserves**—that is,

$$\frac{\text{Excess}}{\text{reserves}} = \frac{\text{Total}}{\text{reserves}} - \frac{\text{Required}}{\text{reserves}}$$

excess reserves: Bank reserves in excess of required reserves.

Lending Capacity. The existence of excess reserves implies that banks aren't fully utilizing their lending powers. With $10 billion of excess reserves and the help of the **money multiplier,** the banks *could* lend an additional $50 billion.

The potential for additional loans is calculated as

$$\frac{\text{Available lending capacity}}{\text{of banking system}} = \text{Excess reserves} \times \text{Money multiplier}$$

money multiplier: The number of deposit (loan) dollars that the banking system can create from $1 of excess reserves; equal to 1 ÷ required reserve ratio.

or in this case,

$$\$10 \text{ billion} \times \frac{1}{0.20} = \$50 \text{ billion of unused lending capacity}$$

That is, the banking system could create another $50 billion of money (transactions account balances) without any additional reserves.

A simple way to confirm this—and thereby check your arithmetic—is to note what would happen to total deposits if the banks actually made further loans. Total deposits would increase to $150 billion in this case (the initial $100 billion of deposits plus the new loan-created deposits of $50 billion), an amount that could be supported with $30 billion in reserves (20 percent of $150 billion).

Soaking Up Excess Reserves. But what if the Fed doesn't want the money supply to increase this much? Maybe prices are rising and the Fed wants to restrain rather than stimulate total spending in the economy. Under such circumstances, the Fed would want to restrict the availability of credit (loans). Does it have the power to do so? Can the Fed reduce the lending capacity of the banking system?

The answer to both questions is clearly yes. *By raising the required reserve ratio, the Fed can immediately reduce the lending capacity of the banking system.*

Table 14.1 summarizes the impact of an increase in the required reserve ratio. In this case, the required reserve ratio is increased from 20 to 25 percent. Notice that this change in the reserve requirement has no effect on the amount of deposits in the banking system (row 1, Table 14.1) or the amount of total reserves (row 2). They remain at $100 billion and $30 billion, respectively. What the increased reserve requirement does affect is the way those reserves can be used. Before the increase, only $20 billion in reserves were *required,* leaving $10 billion of *excess* reserves. Now, however, banks are required to hold $25 billion (0.25 × $100 billion) in reserves, leaving them with only $5 billion in excess reserves. Thus an increase in the reserve requirement immediately reduces excess reserves, as illustrated in row 4, Table 14.1.

TABLE 14.1

The Impact of an Increased Reserve Requirement

An increase in the required reserve ratio reduces both excess reserves (row 4) and the money multiplier (row 5). As a consequence, changes in the reserve requirement have a substantial impact on the lending capacity of the banking system (row 6).

		Required Reserve Ratio	
		If 20 Percent	If 25 Percent
1.	Total deposits	$100 billion	$100 billion
2.	Total reserves	30 billion	30 billion
3.	Required reserves	20 billion	25 billion
4.	Excess reserves	10 billion	5 billion
5.	Money multiplier	5	4
6.	Unused lending capacity	$ 50 billion	$ 20 billion

There's also a second effect. Notice what happens to the money multiplier (1 ÷ reserve ratio). Previously it was 5 (= 1 ÷ 0.20); now it's only 4 (= 1 ÷ 0.25). Consequently, a higher reserve requirement not only reduces excess reserves but diminishes their lending power as well.

A change in the reserve requirement, therefore, hits banks with a triple whammy. *A change in the reserve requirement causes a change in*

- *Excess reserves.*
- *The money multiplier.*
- *The lending capacity of the banking system.*

These changes sharply reduce bank lending power. Whereas the banking system initially had the power to increase the volume of loans by $50 billion ($10 billion of excess reserves × 5), it now has only $20 billion ($5 million × 4) of unused lending capacity, as noted in the last row in Table 14.1.

Changes in reserve requirements are a powerful tool for altering the lending capacity of the banking system. The Fed uses this tool sparingly so as not to cause abrupt changes in the money supply and severe disruptions of banking activity. From 1970 to 1980, for example, reserve requirements were changed only twice, and then by only half a percentage point each time (e.g., from 12.0 to 12.5 percent). The Fed last cut the reserve requirement from 12 to 10 percent in 1992 to increase bank profits and encourage more lending. In 2016, China did the same thing, hoping to accelerate economic growth (see World View "China Cuts Reserve Requirements").

WORLD VIEW

CHINA CUTS RESERVE REQUIREMENTS

With its vast economy showing signs of slower growth, China has opted to encourage more bank lending. China's central bank, the People's Bank of China, said it is trimming the required reserve ratio for its banks by half a percentage point—to 17 percent, down from 17.5 percent. The lower reserve requirement enables banks to lend more of their reserves. The move is expected to free up about $700 billion yuan ($107 billion) in bank reserves.

Source: News reports, February 29, 2016.

ANALYSIS: A reduction in the reserve requirement transforms some of the banking system's required reserves into excess reserves, thus increasing potential lending activity and profits. It also increases the size of the money multiplier.

The Discount Rate

Banks have a tremendous incentive to maintain their reserves at or close to the minimum established by the Fed. Bank reserves held at the Fed earn lower rates of interest than banks could get from making loans or holding bonds. Hence a profit-maximizing bank seeks to keep its excess reserves as low as possible, preferring to put its reserves to better, more profitable work. In fact, banks have demonstrated an uncanny ability to keep their reserves close to the minimum federal requirement. As Figure 14.2 illustrates, the few times banks held huge excess reserves were in the Great Depression of the 1930s and during the 2008–2009 recession. The banks didn't want to make any more loans and were fearful of loan defaults

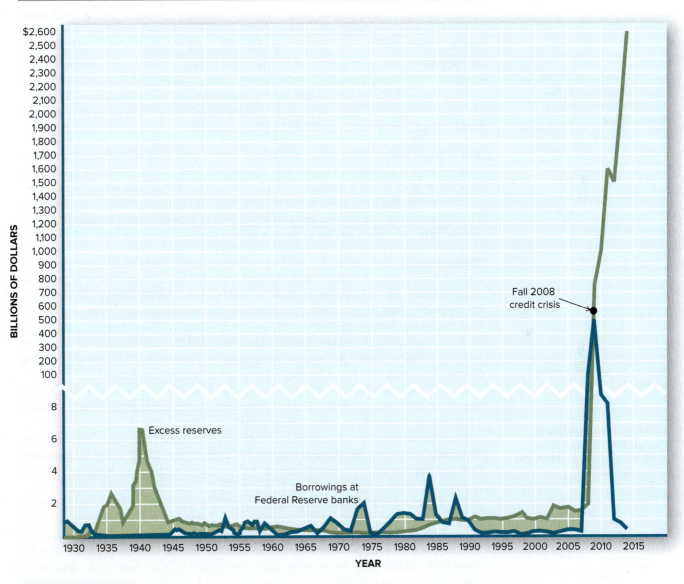

FIGURE 14.2

Excess Reserves and Borrowings

Excess reserves represent unused lending capacity. Hence banks strive to keep excess reserves at a minimum. One exception to this practice occurred during the Great Depression, when banks were hesitant to make any loans. It happened even more dramatically during the Great Recession of 2008–2009, when bank assets lost value and new loans looked risky. By 2014 banks had stockpiled more than $2 trillion in excess reserves. In more normal circumstances, banks try to minimize excess reserves, occasionally falling short of required reserves in the process. At such times they may borrow from other banks (the federal funds market), or they may borrow reserves directly from the Fed. Borrowing from the Fed is called "discounting."

and panicky customers withdrawing their deposits. Notice in Figure 14.2 the enormous jump in excess reserves in 2008–2009 when banks decided to curtail new lending activity.

Because banks continually seek to keep excess reserves at a minimum, they run the risk of falling below reserve requirements. A large borrower may be a little slow in repaying a loan, or the rate of deposit withdrawals and transfers may exceed expectations, or defaults and price declines may reduce the value of assets held by the bank. At such times, a bank may find that it doesn't have enough reserves to satisfy Fed requirements.

Banks could ensure continual compliance with reserve requirements by maintaining large amounts of excess reserves. But that's an unprofitable procedure, and a profit-maximizing bank will seek other alternatives.

The Federal Funds Market. A bank that finds itself short of reserves can turn to other banks for help. If a reserve-poor bank can borrow some reserves from a reserve-rich bank, it may be able to bridge its temporary deficit and satisfy the Fed. *Reserves borrowed by one bank from another are referred to as "federal funds" and are lent for short periods, usually overnight.* Although trips to the federal funds market—via telephone and computer—will usually satisfy Federal Reserve requirements, such trips aren't free. The lending bank will charge interest (the **federal funds rate**) on its interbank loan.[1] The use of the federal funds market to satisfy Federal Reserve requirements also depends on other banks having excess reserves to lend.

Sale of Securities. Another option available to reserve-poor banks is the sale of securities. Banks use some of their excess reserves to buy government bonds, which pay interest. If a bank needs more reserves to satisfy federal regulations, it can sell these securities and deposit the proceeds at a regional Federal Reserve bank. Its reserve position thereby increases. This option also involves distinct costs, however, both in forgone interest-earning opportunities and in the possibility of capital losses when the bond is offered for quick sale.

Discounting. A third option for avoiding a reserve shortage lies in the structure of the Federal Reserve System itself. The Fed not only establishes certain rules of behavior for banks but also functions as a central bank, or banker's bank. Banks maintain accounts with the regional Federal Reserve banks, much the way you and I maintain accounts with a local bank. Individual banks deposit and withdraw "reserve credits" from these accounts, just as we deposit and withdraw dollars. Should a bank find itself short of reserves, it can go to the Fed's "discount window" and borrow some reserves. This process is called **discounting.** *Discounting means the Fed is lending reserves directly to private banks.*[2]

The Fed's discounting operation provides private banks with an important source of reserves, but not without cost. The Fed too charges interest on the reserves it lends to banks, a rate of interest referred to as the **discount rate.**

The discount window is a mechanism for directly influencing the size of bank reserves. *By raising or lowering the discount rate, the Fed changes the cost of money for banks and therewith the incentive to borrow reserves.* At high discount rates, borrowing from the Fed is expensive. High discount rates also signal the Fed's desire to restrain the money supply and an accompanying reluctance to lend reserves. Low discount rates, on the other hand, make it profitable to acquire additional reserves and exploit one's lending capacity to the fullest. Low discount rates also indicate the Fed's willingness to support credit expansion.

In the wake of the 2008 credit crisis, the Fed not only reduced the discount rate but urged banks to borrow more reserves. Notice in Figure 14.2 the spectacular increase in Fed-loaned reserves ("borrowings") in late 2008. The Fed wanted to reassure market participants that the banks had enough reserves to weather the economic storm.

federal funds rate: The interest rate for interbank reserve loans.

discounting: Federal Reserve lending of reserves to private banks.

discount rate: The rate of interest the Federal Reserve charges for lending reserves to private banks.

---

[1] An overnight loan of $1 million at 6 percent interest (per year) costs $165 in interest charges plus any service fees that might be added. Banks make multimillion-dollar loans in the federal funds market.

[2] In the past banks had to present loan notes to the Fed in order to borrow reserves. The Fed "discounted" the notes by lending an amount equal to only a fraction of their face value. Although banks no longer have to present loans as collateral, the term "discounting" endures.

Open Market Operations

Reserve requirements and discount window operations are important tools of monetary policy. But they don't come close to open market operations in day-to-day impact on the money supply. *Open market operations are the principal mechanism for directly altering the reserves of the banking system.* Because reserves are the lifeblood of the banking system, open market operations are of immediate and critical interest to private banks and the larger economy.

Portfolio Decisions. To appreciate the impact of open market operations, you have to think about the alternative uses for idle funds. All of us have some idle funds, even if they amount to just a few dollars in our pocket or a minimal balance in our checking account. Other consumers and corporations have great amounts of idle funds, even millions of dollars at any time. Here we're concerned with what people decide to do with such funds.

People (and corporations) don't hold all their idle funds in transactions accounts or cash. Idle funds are also used to purchase stocks, build up savings account balances, and purchase bonds. These alternative uses of idle funds are attractive because they promise some additional income in the form of interest, dividends, or capital appreciation, such as higher stock prices. Deciding where to place idle funds is referred to as the **portfolio decision.**

portfolio decision: The choice of how (where) to hold idle funds.

Hold Money or Bonds. The Fed's *open market operations focus on one of the portfolio choices people make: whether to deposit idle funds in bank accounts or purchase government bonds.* The Fed attempts to influence this choice by making bonds more or less attractive, as circumstances warrant. The Fed's goal is to encourage people to move funds from banks to bond markets or vice versa. In the process, reserves either enter or leave the banking system, thereby altering the lending capacity of banks.

Figure 14.3 depicts the general nature of the Fed's open market operations. As we first observed in Chapter 13 (Figure 13.2), the process of deposit creation begins when people deposit money in the banking system. But people may also hold their assets in the form of bonds. The fed's objective is to alter this portfolio decision by buying or selling bonds. *When the Fed buys bonds from the public, it increases the flow of deposits (reserves) to the banking system. Bond sales by the Fed reduce the inflow.*

The Bond Market. To understand how open market operations work, let's look more closely at the bond market. Not all of us buy and sell bonds, but a lot of consumers and corporations do: daily volume in bond markets exceeds $1 *trillion.* What's being exchanged in this market, and what factors influence decisions to buy or sell?

In our discussion thus far, we've portrayed banks as intermediaries between savers and spenders. Banks aren't the only mechanism available for transferring purchasing power from nonspenders to spenders. Funds are lent and borrowed in bond markets as well. In this case, a corporation may borrow money directly from consumers or other institutions. When it does so, it issues a bond as proof of its promise to repay the loan. A **bond** is

bond: A certificate acknowledging a debt and the amount of interest to be paid each year until repayment; an IOU.

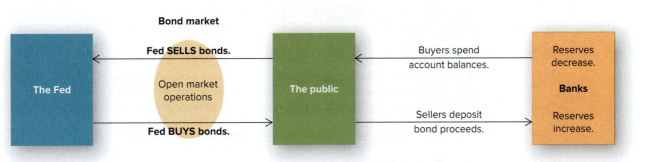

FIGURE 14.3

Open Market Operations

People may hold assets in the form of bank deposits (money) or bonds. When the Fed buys bonds from the public, it increases the flow of deposits (and reserves) to the banks. When the Fed sells bonds, it diminishes the flow of deposits and therewith the banks' capacity to lend (create money).

simply a piece of paper certifying that someone has borrowed money and promises to pay it back at some future date. In other words, *a bond is nothing more than an IOU.* In the case of bond markets, however, the IOU is typically signed by a giant corporation or a government agency rather than a friend. It's therefore more widely accepted by lenders.

Because most corporations and government agencies that borrow money in the bond market are well known and able to repay their debts, their bonds are actively traded. If I lend $1,000 to General Motors on a 10-year bond, for example, I don't have to wait 10 years to get my money back; I can resell the bond to someone else at any time. If I do, that person will collect the face value of the bond (plus interest) from GM when it's due. The actual purchase and sale of bonds take place in the bond market. Although a good deal of the action occurs on Wall Street in New York, the bond market has no unique location. Like other markets we've discussed, the bond market exists whenever and however (electronically) bond buyers and sellers get together.

Bond Yields. People buy bonds because bonds pay interest. If you buy a General Motors bond, GM is obliged to pay you interest during the period of the loan. For example, an 8 percent 2025 GM bond in the amount of $1,000 states that GM will pay the bondholder $80 interest annually (8 percent of $1,000) until 2025. At that point GM will repay the initial $1,000 loan (the "principal").

The current **yield** paid on a bond depends on the promised interest rate (8 percent in this case) and the actual purchase price of the bond. Specifically,

> **yield:** The rate of return on a bond; the annual interest payment divided by the bond's price.

$$\text{Yield} = \frac{\textbf{Annual interest payment}}{\textbf{Price paid for bond}}$$

If you pay $1,000 for the bond, then the current yield is

$$\text{Yield} = \frac{\$80}{\$1,000} = 0.08, \text{ or } 8\%$$

which is the same as the interest rate printed on the face of the bond. But what if you pay only $900 for the bond? In this case, the interest rate paid by GM remains at 8 percent ($80 per year), but the *yield* jumps to

$$\text{Yield} = \frac{\$80}{\$900} = 0.089, \text{ or } 8.9\%$$

Buying a $1,000 bond for only $900 might seem like too good a bargain to be true. But bonds are often bought and sold at prices other than their face value (see In the News "Treasury Prices Fall with Improved Expectations"). In fact, *a principal objective of Federal Reserve open market activity is to alter the price of bonds, and therewith their yields.* By doing so, the Fed makes bonds a more or less attractive alternative to holding money.

IN THE NEWS

TREASURY PRICES FALL WITH IMPROVED EXPECTATIONS

Expectations of accelerated economic growth continue to boost yields on Treasury securities. The price of the Treasury's 2.0 percent 10-year bond fell $17.43 yesterday, from $843.88 to $826.45. The decline in the price of the treasury pushed the yield up from 2.37 percent to 2.42 percent.

The 30-year bond also declined, increasing the yield from 2.96 to 3.00.

Source: Market reports of January 6, 2017.

ANALYSIS: Bond prices and yields move in opposite directions. If the Fed sells bonds, bond prices fall and yields (interest rates) rise.

Open Market Activity. The basic premise of open market activity is that participants in the bond market will respond to changes in bond prices and yields. As we've observed, ***the less you pay for a bond, the higher its yield.*** Accordingly, the Fed can induce people to *buy* bonds by offering to sell them at a lower price (e.g., a $1,000, 8 percent bond for only $900). Similarly, the Fed can induce people to *sell* bonds by offering to buy them at higher prices. In either case, the Fed hopes to move reserves into or out of the banking system. In other words, **open market operations** entail the purchase and sale of government securities (bonds) for the purpose of altering the flow of reserves into and out of the banking system.

Open Market Purchases. Suppose the Fed's goal is to increase the money supply. Its strategy is to provide the banking system with additional reserves. To do so, it must persuade people to deposit a larger share of their financial assets in banks and hold less in other forms, particularly government bonds. The tool for doing this is bond prices. ***If the Fed offers to pay a higher price for bonds ("bids up bonds"), it will effectively lower bond yields and market interest rates.*** The higher prices and lower yields will reduce the attractiveness of holding bonds. If the price offered by the Fed is high enough, people will sell some of their bonds to the Fed. What will they do with the proceeds of those bond sales? Deposit them in their bank accounts, of course. This influx of deposits into bank accounts will directly increase both the money supply and bank reserves—goal achieved.

Figure 14.4 illustrates the dynamics of open market operations in more detail. When the Fed buys a bond from the public, it pays with a check written on itself (step 1 in Figure 14.4). What will the bond seller do with the check? There really aren't any options. If the seller wants to use the proceeds of the bond sale, he or she will have to deposit the Fed check at a bank (step 2 in the figure). The bank, in turn, deposits the check at a regional Federal Reserve bank in exchange for a reserve credit (step 3). The bank's reserves are directly increased by the amount of the check. Thus, ***by buying bonds, the Fed increases bank reserves.*** These reserves can be used to expand the money supply still further as banks put their newly acquired reserves to work making loans.

Quantitative Easing. Federal Reserve open-market purchases were pursued so aggressively in 2009–2011 that they acquired a new name—"quantitative easing," or "QE." The Fed's QE program entailed two important changes in its traditional open market operations. First, it expanded the scope of Fed purchases beyond short-term government bonds to longer-term bonds and other securities (e.g., mortgage-backed securities). Second, the QE program allowed the Fed to purchase bonds directly from commercial banks rather than exclusively through the bond market. This gave the Fed more direct control of bank assets, reserves, and solvency. The Fed used its broadened powers to inject more reserves directly into the banking system and shore up confidence in bank solvency.

open market operations:
Federal Reserve purchases and sales of government bonds for the purpose of altering bank reserves.

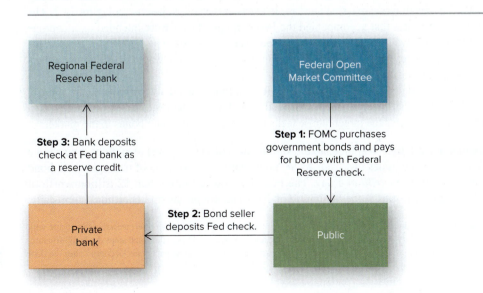

FIGURE 14.4

An Open Market Purchase

The Fed can increase bank reserves by buying bonds from the public. The Fed check used to buy bonds (step 1) gets deposited in a private bank (step 2). The bank returns the check to the Fed (step 3), thereby obtaining additional reserves. To decrease bank reserves, the Fed would sell bonds, thus reversing the flow of reserves.

The first round of quantitative easing (QE1) began in November 2008 and continued through June 2010. During that period, the Fed purchased $1.5 trillion of securities, boosting bank reserves by the same amount (note the spike in excess reserves in Figure 14.2). When economic growth failed to accelerate as hoped, the Fed began a second round of asset purchases in November 2010 that continued to June 2011. A third round (QE3) was initiated in September 2012, with scheduled Fed purchases of $85 billion per month. As excess reserves continued to rise and interest rates fall, the Fed started to reduce its monthly purchases. This "tapering" schedule continued until late in 2014. By the end of the QE programs, the Fed had accumulated more than $2 trillion in bonds and other securities, and bank reserves had risen by a similar amount. These huge bond purchases helped to keep interest rates at historic lows.

Open Market Sales. Should the Fed desire to slow the growth in the money supply, it can reverse the whole process. Instead of offering to *buy* bonds, the Fed in this case will try to *sell* bonds. If the Fed "bids bonds down" (offers to sell them at low prices), bond yields will rise. In response, individuals, corporations, and government agencies will convert some of their transactions deposits into bonds. When they do so, they write a check, paying the Fed for the bonds.[3] The Fed then returns the check to the depositor's bank, taking payment through a reduction in the bank's reserve account. The reserves of the banking system are thereby diminished, as is the capacity to make loans. Thus, ***by selling bonds, the Fed reduces bank reserves.***

The Fed Funds Rate

A market signal of these changing reserve flows is provided by the federal funds rate. Recall that "fed funds" are excess reserves traded among banks. If the Fed pumps more reserves into the banking system (by buying bonds), the interest rate charged for overnight reserve loans—the federal funds rate—will decline. Conversely, if the Fed is reducing bank reserves (by selling bonds), the federal funds rate will increase. Hence ***the federal funds rate is a highly visible signal of Federal Reserve open market operations.*** When Alan Greenspan reduced the federal funds rate *11 times* in 2001, the Fed was underscoring the urgency of monetary stimulus to combat the recession and the aftereffects of the September 11 terrorist attacks.

Beginning in June 2004 the Fed used this same tool to *reduce* lending activity. In fact, the Fed completely reversed course and raised the fed funds rate *17 times* between June 2004 and June 2006.

The Fed changed course yet again in 2007. Between September 2007 and December 2008 the Fed lowered the federal funds rate *10 times* (see In the News "U.S. Federal Reserve Cuts Interest Rates to Historic Low"). The Fed's goal this time was to push bond yields so low that people would prefer to hold their idle funds in banks rather than buy bonds. The result was a massive increase in excess reserves, as we saw in Figure 14.2. The lower interest rates that accompanied the Fed bond purchases were intended to encourage people to borrow and spend these increased excess reserves. The Fed kept interest rates low and excess reserves high in 2010–2016 through successive waves of open market purchases (quantitative easing).

When the Fed announces a change in the federal funds rate, it always refers to the "target" rate. The Fed doesn't actually *set* the fed funds rate. It only establishes a desired "target" rate. When the Fed lowers the target rate, it seeks to hit it by buying more bonds in the market.

Volume of Activity. To appreciate the significance of open market operations, you need a sense of the magnitudes involved. As we noted earlier, the volume of trading in U.S. bond markets exceeds $1 *trillion* a day. The Fed alone owned more than $2 trillion worth of government securities at the beginning of 2017 and bought or sold enormous sums daily.

---

[3]In actuality, the Fed deals directly with only 36 "primary" bond dealers. These intermediaries then trade with each other, "secondary" dealers, financial institutions, and individuals. These additional steps don't significantly alter the flow of funds depicted here. Using electronic transactions rather than paper checks doesn't alter the flow of funds either.

IN THE NEWS

U.S. FEDERAL RESERVE CUTS INTEREST RATES TO HISTORIC LOW

U.S. Central Bank Decision Aimed at Reassuring Market, Stimulating Economy

Washington—The U.S. central bank on December 16 cut interest rates to an all-time low, a move aimed at reassuring financial markets and stimulating banks to lend money.

The Federal Reserve Board lowered the target federal funds rate to a range of 0 percent to 0.25 percent, the lowest level in the history of modern monetary policy. The federal funds rate is the rate at which banks lend to one another. The rate, historically, has an effect on the rates consumers are charged for home mortgage loans and other types of credit. . . .

A cut in the Fed's target rate lowers the interest rates consumers and businesses pay, making it more appealing for them to borrow money. When they spend that lent cash, it boosts the economy by increasing the demand for goods, services, and labor.

—Katherine Lewis

Source: Lewis, Katherine, "U.S. Central Bank Decision Aimed at Reassuring Market, Stimulating Economy," *IIP Digital/U.S.,* December 16, 2008.

ANALYSIS: The Fed uses open market operations to change short-term interest rates. In this case the Fed intended to cut interest rates to nearly zero by aggressively buying Treasury bonds.

Thus open market operations involve tremendous amounts of money and, by implication, potential bank reserves. Each $1 of reserves represents something like $10 of potential lending capacity (via the money multiplier). Thus open market operations can have a profound impact on the money supply.

INCREASING THE MONEY SUPPLY

The three major tools of monetary policy are reserve requirements, discount rates, and open market operations. The Fed can use these tools individually or in combination to change the money supply. This section illustrates the use of each tool to attain a specific policy goal.

Suppose the policy goal is to increase the money supply from an assumed level of $340 billion to $400 billion. In surveying the nation's banks, the Fed discovers the facts shown in Table 14.2. On the basis of the facts presented in Table 14.2, it's evident that

- The banking system is "loaned up." Because excess reserves are zero (see row 5 in Table 14.2), there's no additional lending capacity.
- The required reserve ratio must be equal to 25 percent because this is the current ratio of required reserves ($60 billion) to total deposits ($240 billion).

Item	Amount
1. Cash held by public	$100 billion
2. Transactions deposits	240 billion
3. Total money supply (M1)	$340 billion
4. Required reserves	$ 60 billion
5. Excess reserves	0
6. Total reserves of banks	$ 60 billion
7. U.S. bonds held by public	$460 billion
8. Discount rate	5%

TABLE 14.2

How to Increase the Money Supply

The accompanying data depict a banking system that has $340 billion of money (M1) and no further lending capacity (excess reserves = 0). To enlarge M1 to $400 billion, the Fed can (1) lower the required reserve ratio, (2) reduce the discount rate, or (3) buy bonds held by the public.

Accordingly, if the Fed wants to increase the money supply, it will have to pump additional reserves into the banking system or lower the reserve requirement. *To increase the money supply, the Fed can*

- *Lower reserve requirements.*
- *Reduce the discount rate.*
- *Buy bonds.*

Lowering Reserve Requirements

Lowering the reserve requirements is an expedient way of increasing the lending capacity of the banking system. But by how much should the reserve requirement be reduced?

Recall that the Fed's goal here is to increase the money supply from $340 billion to $400 billion, an increase of $60 billion. If the public isn't willing to hold any additional cash, this entire increase in money supply will have to take the form of added transactions deposits. In other words, total deposits will have to increase from $240 billion to $300 billion. These additional deposits will have to be *created* by the banks in the form of new loans to consumers or business firms.

If the banking system is going to support $300 billion in transactions deposits with its *existing* reserves, the reserve requirement will have to be reduced from 25 percent. We can compute the desired reserve requirement as follows:

$$\frac{\text{Total reserves}}{\text{Desired level of deposits}} = \frac{\$60 \text{ billion}}{\$300 \text{ billion}} = 0.20$$

So the next move is to lower the reserve requirement from 0.25 to 0.20. At the moment the Fed lowers the minimum reserve ratio to 0.20, *total* reserves won't change. The banks' potential lending power will change, however. Required reserves will drop to $48 billion (0.20 × $240 billion), and excess reserves will jump from zero to $12 billion. These new excess reserves imply an additional lending capacity:

$$\underset{(\$12 \text{ billion})}{\textbf{Excess reserves}} \times \underset{(5)}{\textbf{Money multiplier}} = \underset{(\$60 \text{ billion})}{\textbf{Unused lending capacity}}$$

If the banks succeed in putting all this new lending power to work—actually make $60 billion in new loans—the Fed's objective of increasing the money supply will be attained.

Lowering the Discount Rate

The second monetary tool available to the Fed is the discount rate. We assumed it was 5 percent initially (see row 8 in Table 14.2). If the Fed lowers this rate, it will become cheaper for banks to borrow reserves from the Fed. The banks will be more willing to borrow (cheaper) reserves so long as they can make additional loans to their own customers at higher interest rates. The profitability of discounting depends on the *difference* between the discount rate and the interest rate the bank charges its loan customers. The Fed increases this difference when it lowers the discount rate.

There's no way to calculate the appropriate discount rate without more detailed knowledge of the banking system's willingness to borrow reserves from the Fed. Nevertheless, we can determine how much reserves the banks *must* borrow if the Fed's money supply target is to be attained. The Fed's objective is to increase transactions deposits by $60 billion. If these deposits are to be created by the banks—and the reserve requirement is unchanged at 0.25—the banks will have to borrow an additional $15 billion of reserves ($60 billion divided by 4, the money multiplier).

Buying Bonds

The Fed can also get additional reserves into the banking system by buying U.S. bonds in the open market. As row 7 in Table 14.2 indicates, the public holds $460 billion in U.S. bonds, none of which are counted as part of the money supply. If the Fed can persuade people to sell some of these bonds, bank reserves will surely rise.

To achieve its money supply target, the Fed will offer to buy $15 billion of U.S. bonds. It will pay for these bonds with checks written on its own account at the Fed. The people who sell the bonds will deposit these checks in their own transactions accounts. As they do so, they'll directly increase bank deposits and reserves by $15 billion.

Is $15 billion of open market purchases enough? Yes. The $15 billion is a direct addition to transactions deposits, and therefore to the money supply. The additional deposits bring in $15 billion of reserves, only $3.75 billion of which is required (0.25 × $15 billion). Hence the new deposits bring in $11.25 billion of *excess* reserves. These new excess reserves themselves create additional lending capacity:

$$\underset{(\$11.25 \text{ billion})}{\textbf{Excess reserves}} \times \underset{(4)}{\textbf{Money multiplier}} = \underset{(\$45 \text{ billion})}{\textbf{Unused lending capacity}}$$

Thus the $15 billion of open market purchases will eventually lead to a $60 billion increase in M1 as a consequence of both direct deposits ($15 billion) and subsequent loan activity ($45 billion).

Federal Funds Rate. When the Fed starts bidding up bonds, bond yields and market interest rates will start falling. So will the federal funds rate. This will give individual banks an incentive to borrow any excess reserves available, thereby accelerating deposit (loan) creation.

....

DECREASING THE MONEY SUPPLY

All the tools used to increase the money supply can also be used in reverse. ***To reduce the money supply, the Fed can***

- *Raise reserve requirements.*
- *Increase the discount rate.*
- *Sell bonds.*

On a week-to-week basis the Fed does occasionally seek to reduce the total amount of cash and transactions deposits held by the public. These are minor adjustments, however, to broader policies. A growing economy needs a steadily increasing supply of money to finance market exchanges. Hence the Fed rarely seeks an outright reduction in the size of the money supply. What it does is regulate the *rate of growth* in the money supply. When the Fed wants to slow the rate of consumer and investor spending, it restrains the *growth* of money and credit. Although many people talk about "reducing" the money supply, they're really talking about slowing its rate of growth. That was the goal of the Fed when it increased the federal funds rate in December 2016. Fearing that faster economic growth in 2017 might accelerate inflation, the Fed nudged interest rates just a bit higher (see In the News "Fed Raises Key Interest Rate").

IN THE NEWS

FED RAISES KEY INTEREST RATE

Washington D.C— Citing signs of a strengthening economy, the Fed today raised a benchmark federal funds rate from 0.5 percent to 0.75 percent. Noting the low unemployment rate and increased expectations for GDP growth, the Fed said it wanted to prevent the economy from growing too quickly. The improved economic outlook also prompted Fed chair Janet Yellen to project the possibility of three more rate increases in 2017.

Source: Federal Reserve and media, December 14, 2016.

ANALYSIS: The Fed pursues monetary restraint by raising interest rates, increasing reserve requirements, or selling Treasury bonds in the open market.

THE ECONOMY TOMORROW

CROWDFUNDING: BYPASSING THE BANKS

As we have seen, banks play a critical role as intermediaries, moving money from savers to spenders. As such, they help plug leakage holes in the circular flow, keeping aggregate demand at or near its full-employment potential. The Federal Reserve, in turn, helps assure that banks have the right amount of lending capacity to stimulate or restrain aggregate demand, as needed.

Source: www.indiegogo.com, www.gofundme.com, www.crowdrise.com, www.kickstarter.com

The Fed's ability to control bank lending depends on its power to monitor and regulate bank reserves. But what about lending activity that doesn't pass through the banking system? The Internet has created a novel opportunity for savers and spenders to interact *directly,* without the intervention of banking institutions. This kind of peer-to-peer lending is referred to as **crowdfunding.** If someone is rich in ideas, but low on cash, he or she can turn to the Internet for funding. Funds can be solicited by describing the project to be pursued, then asking for individuals to contribute. Typically, hundreds of individuals can contribute, allowing the project to proceed. In April 2013, writer Rob Thomas raised $5.7 million from 91,585 contributors to produce a feature film version of the discontinued *Veronica Mars* TV series. The musician Amanda Palmer raised $1.2 million from 24,833 backers to make a new album and an art book. In January 2017 a group on Kickstarter raised over $12 million from 19,264 backers to fund a board game called "Kingdom Death."

As crowdfunding has become more popular, more than 2,000 Internet sites have been created to serve as platforms for bringing project initiators and potential backers together. Among them are Kickstarter, gofundme, Indiegogo, Crowdrise, and Crowdfunder. Some focus on charitable activities like raising money for accident victims or people with dire health problems. Some, like appbacker, are designed for funding very specific products (new Internet applications). But the largest are intended to facilitate the funding of new business ventures. At these sites, backers (individual contributors) are typically given an equity share in the venture they are helping to fund. In 2016, over $40 billion of projects were crowdfunded.

Crowdfunding bypasses the banks. This alternative conduit of lending/investing potentially weakens the link between the money supply and aggregate demand. It also diminishes the importance of bank reserves as a measure of lending capacity. But the volume of crowdfunding ($40 billion) is so minuscule relative to the size of the money supply (M2 of $13 *trillion*) that traditional banks are still the dominant base for monetary policy.

crowdfunding: The financing of a project through individual contributions from a large number of people, typically via an Internet platform.

SUMMARY

- The Federal Reserve System controls the nation's money supply by regulating the loan activity (deposit creation) of private banks (depository institutions). **LO14-2**
- The core of the Federal Reserve System is the 12 regional Federal Reserve banks, which provide check clearance, reserve deposit, and loan ("discounting") services to individual banks. Private banks are required to maintain minimum reserves on deposit at the regional Federal Reserve banks. **LO14-1**

- The general policies of the Fed are set by its Board of Governors. The Board's chair is selected by the U.S. president and confirmed by the Senate. The chair serves as the chief spokesperson for monetary policy. The Fed's policy strategy is implemented by the Federal Open Market Committee (FOMC), which directs open market sales and purchase of U.S. bonds. **LO14-1**
- The Fed has three basic tools for changing the money supply. By altering the reserve requirement, the Fed can

immediately change both the quantity of excess reserves in the banking system and the money multiplier, which limits banks' lending capacity. By altering discount rates (the rate of interest charged by the Fed for reserve borrowing), the Fed can also influence the amount of reserves maintained by banks. Finally, and most important, the Fed can increase or decrease the reserves of the banking system by buying or selling government bonds—that is, by engaging in open market operations.   **LO14-2**

- When the Fed buys bonds, it causes an increase in bank reserves (and lending capacity). When the Fed sells bonds, it induces a reduction in reserves (and lending capacity).   **LO14-3**
- The federal funds (interest) rate is a market signal of Fed open market activity and intentions.   **LO14-2**
- Crowdfunding is a source of lending and investing that bypasses the banking system, instead relying on direct peer-to-peer funding, typically via the Internet. Although crowdfunding lessens the importance of bank reserves, it is a tiny fraction of loan activity.   **LO14-2**

Key Terms

monetary policy
money supply (M1)
required reserves
excess reserves
money multiplier

federal funds rate
discounting
discount rate
portfolio decision
bond

yield
open market operations
crowdfunding

Questions for Discussion

1. Why do banks want to maintain as little excess reserves as possible? Under what circumstances might banks want to hold excess reserves? (*Hint:* See Figure 14.2.)   **LO14-2**
2. Why do people hold bonds rather than larger savings account or checking account balances? Under what circumstances might they change their portfolios, moving their funds out of bonds and into bank accounts?   **LO14-3**
3. What are the current price and yield of 10-year U.S. Treasury bonds? Of General Motors bonds? (Check the financial section of your daily newspaper.) What accounts for the difference?   **LO14-3**
4. Why did China reduce reserve requirements in 2014? How did they expect consumers and businesses to respond? (See World View "China Cuts Reserve Requirements.")   **LO14-2**
5. Why did the Fed raise the federal funds rate in 2016–2017 (In the News "Fed Raises Key Interest Rate")? What impact would those rate increases have on the economy?   **LO14-1**

6. Why did bond prices decline at the January 2017 auction? (See In the News "Treasury Prices Fall with Improved Expectations.")   **LO14-3**
7. In early 2009, short-term bond yields in the United States fell to less than 0.5 percent. Yet relatively few people moved their assets out of bonds into banks. How might this failure of open market operations be explained?   **LO14-3**
8. In 2008 the Fed reduced both the discount and federal fund rates dramatically. But bank loan volume didn't increase. What considerations might have constrained the market's response to Fed policy?   **LO14-2**
9. If bondholders expect the Fed to raise interest rates, what action might they take? How would this affect the Fed's goal?   **LO14-3**
10. What are the advantages of crowdfunding over traditional bank lending? What are the disadvantages?   **LO14-2**

LO14-1 1. What is the money multiplier when the reserve requirement is
   (a) 0.05?
   (b) 0.10?
   (c) 0.125?
   (d) 0.111?

LO14-2 2. In Table 14.1, what would the following values be if the required reserve ratio fell from 0.20 to 0.10?
   (a) Total deposits
   (b) Total reserves
   (c) Required reserves
   (d) Excess reserves
   (e) Money multiplier
   (f) Unused lending capacity

LO14-2 3. Assume that the following data describe the condition of the banking system:

Total reserves	$100 billion
Transactions deposits	$800 billion
Cash held by public	$400 billion
Reserve requirement	0.10

   (a) How large is the money supply (M1)?
   (b) How large are *required* reserves?
   (c) How large are *excess* reserves?
   (d) What is the money multiplier?
   (e) How much is the unused lending capacity?

LO14-2 4. In Problem 3, suppose the Fed wanted to stop further lending activity. To do this, what reserve requirement should the Fed impose?

LO14-2 5. According to World View "China Cuts Reserve Requirements," what was the money multiplier in China
   (a) Before the rate cut?
   (b) After the rate cut?

LO14-2 6. By how much did the following increase when China cut the reserve requirement (see World View "China Cuts Reserve Requirements"):
   (a) Excess reserves?
   (b) The lending capacity of the banking system?

LO14-2 7. Assume the banking system contains the following amounts:

Total reserves	$90 billion
Transactions deposits	$900 billion
Cash held by public	$100 billion
Reserve requirement	0.10

   (a) Are the banks currently fully utilizing their lending capacity?
   (b) What would happen to the money supply *initially* if the public deposited another $20 billion of cash in transactions accounts?
   (c) What would the lending capacity of the banking system be after this deposit?
   (d) How large would the money supply be if the banks fully utilized their lending capacity?
   (e) What three policy tools could the Fed use to offset that potential growth in M1?

LO14-3 8. According to In the News "Treasury Prices Fall with Improved Expectations," what would the yield be on the Treasury bond if the market price of the bonds were:
   (a) $1,000?
   (b) $800?
   (c) $1,200?

LO14-3 9. Suppose a $1,000 bond pays $40 per year in interest.
  (*a*) What is the contractual interest rate ("coupon rate") on the bond?
  (*b*) If market interest rates rise to 5 percent, what price will the bond sell for?

LO14-3 10. What was the Fed's target for the fed funds rate in December 2016 (In the News "U.S. Fed Reserve Cuts Interest Rates to Historic Low")?

LO14-3 11. Suppose a banking system with the following balance sheet has no excess reserves. Assume that banks will make loans in the full amount of any excess reserves that they acquire.

Assets (in Billions)		Liabilities (in Billions)	
Total reserves	$ 30	Transactions accounts	$400
Securities	190		
Loans	180		
Total	$400	Total	$400

  (*a*) What is the reserve requirement?
  (*b*) Reconstruct the balance sheet of the total banking system if the requirement is changed to 5 percent and all banks have fully utilized their lending capacity.

Assets (in Billions)		Liabilities (in Billions)	
Total reserves	_____	Transactions accounts	_____
Securities	$190		
Loans	_____		
Total	_____	Total	_____

  (*c*) By how much has the money supply changed as a result of the lower reserve requirement (step *b*)?
  (*d*) Suppose the Fed now buys $10 billion of securities directly from the banks. What will the banks' books look like immediately after this purchase?

Assets (in Billions)		Liabilities (in Billions)	
Total reserves	_____	Transactions accounts	_____
Securities	_____		
Loans	_____		
Total	_____	Total	_____

  (*e*) How much excess reserves do the banks have now?
  (*f*) By how much can the money supply now increase due to this open market purchase?

LO12-2 12. The Economy Tomorrow: Suppose a person who is developing an app crowdfunds $40,000 and holds this as cash for future expenses. If this $40,000 comes from donors checking accounts, by how much will the money supply fall if the reserve ratio is 10 percent?

©Paul J. Richards/AFP/Getty Images

Monetary Policy

So what if the Federal Reserve System controls the nation's money supply? Why is this significant? Does it matter how much money is available?

Vladimir Lenin thought so. The first communist leader of the Soviet Union once remarked that the best way to destroy a society is to destroy its money. If a society's money became valueless, it would no longer be accepted in exchange for goods and services in product markets. People would have to resort to barter, and the economy's efficiency would be severely impaired. Adolf Hitler tried unsuccessfully to use this weapon against Great Britain during World War II. His plan was to counterfeit British currency, then drop it from planes flying over England. He believed that the sudden increase in the quantity of money, together with its suspect origins, would render the British pound valueless.

Even in peacetime, the quantity of money in circulation influences its value in the marketplace. Moreover, interest rates and access to credit (bank loans) are basic determinants of spending behavior. As happened in 2008–2009, when credit becomes unavailable, the economy can grind to a halt. Consequently, control over the money supply is a critical policy tool for altering macroeconomic outcomes.

But how much influence does the money supply have on macro performance? Specifically,

- **What's the relationship between the money supply, interest rates, and aggregate demand?**
- **How can the Fed use its control of the money supply or interest rates to alter macro outcomes?**
- **How effective is monetary policy, compared to fiscal policy?**

Economists offer very different answers to these questions. Some argue that changes in the money supply directly affect macro outcomes; others argue that the effects of such changes are indirect and less certain.

Paralleling these arguments about *how* monetary policy works are debates over the relative effectiveness of monetary and fiscal policy. Some economists argue that monetary policy is more effective than fiscal policy; others contend the reverse is true. This chapter examines these different views of money and assesses their implications for macro policy.

LEARNING OBJECTIVES

After reading this chapter, you should know

LO15-1 How interest rates are set in the money market.

LO15-2 How monetary policy affects macro outcomes.

LO15-3 The constraints on monetary policy impact.

LO15-4 The differences between Keynesian and monetarist monetary theories.

monetary policy: The use of money and credit controls to influence macroeconomic outcomes.

THE MONEY MARKET

The best place to learn how **monetary policy** works is the money *market.* You must abandon any mystical notions you may harbor about money and view it like any other commodity that's traded in the marketplace. Like other goods, there's a supply of money and a demand for money. Together they determine the "price" of money, or the **interest rate.**

At first glance, it may appear strange to call interest rates the price of money. But when you borrow money, the "price" you pay is measured by the interest rate you're charged. When interest rates are high, money is "expensive." When interest rates are low, money is "cheap."

Money Balances

Even people who don't borrow must contend with the price of money. People hold cash and maintain positive bank balances as part of the **money supply (M1, M2).** There's an opportunity cost associated with such money balances, however. Money held in transactions accounts earns little or no interest. Money held in savings accounts and money market mutual funds does earn interest but usually at relatively low rates. By contrast, money used to buy bonds or stocks or to make loans is likely to earn a higher rate of return, as Table 15.1 illustrates.

The Price of Money. The nature of the "price" of money should be apparent: People who hold *cash* are forgoing an opportunity to earn interest. So are people who hold money in checking accounts that pay no interest. In either case, *forgone interest is the opportunity cost (price) of money people choose to hold.* How high is that price? It's equal to the market rate of interest.

Money held in interest-paying bank accounts does earn some interest. In this case, the opportunity cost of holding money is the *difference* between the prevailing rate of interest and the rate paid on deposit balances. In Table 15.1 the opportunity cost of holding cash rather than Treasury bonds is 2.36 percent per year.

The Demand for Money

Once we recognize that money does have a price, we can formulate a *demand* for money. When we talk about the "demand" for money, we're not referring to your ceaseless craving for more income. Instead, the **demand for money** refers to the ability and willingness to *hold* money in the form of cash or bank balances. As is the case with all goods, the demand for money is a schedule (or curve) showing the quantity of money demanded at alternative prices (interest rates).

So why would anyone want to "hold" money? The decision to hold (demand) money balances is the kind of **portfolio decision** we examined in Chapter 14. While at first glance it might seem irrational to hold money balances that pay little or no interest, there are many good reasons for doing so.

Transactions Demand. Even people who have mastered the principles of economics hold money. They do so because they want to buy goods and services. To transact business in product or factor markets, we need money in the form of either cash or a positive bank account balance. Debit cards and ATM cards don't work unless there's money in the bank.

interest rate: The price paid for the use of money.

money supply (M1): Currency held by the public, plus balances in transactions accounts.

money supply (M2): M1 plus balances in most savings accounts and money market funds.

demand for money: The quantities of money people are willing and able to hold at alternative interest rates, *ceteris paribus*.

portfolio decision: The choice of how (where) to hold idle funds.

Option	Interest Rate
Cash	0.00%
Checking accounts	0.01
5-month CD	1.20
10-year Treasury bond	2.36
Corporate bond (Aaa)	3.33

Source: Federal Reserve (January 2017 rates).

TABLE 15.1

Portfolio Choices

Idle funds can be held in many forms. Holding funds in cash or checking accounts pays little or no interest. The "price" of holding money is the interest forgone from alternative portfolio choices. When that price is high, people hold (demand) less money.

Payment by e-cash also requires a supporting bank balance. Even when we use credit cards (perhaps via a digital wallet), we're only postponing the date of payment by a few weeks or so. Some merchants won't even accept credit cards, especially for small purchases. Accordingly, we recognize the existence of a basic **transactions demand for money**—that is, money held in cash or bank accounts for everyday purchases.

Precautionary Demand. Another reason people hold money is their fear of the proverbial rainy day. A sudden emergency may require money purchases over and above normal transactions needs. Such needs may arise when the banks are closed or when one is in a community where one's checks aren't accepted. Also, future income is uncertain and may diminish unexpectedly. Therefore, people hold a bit more money (cash or bank account balances) than they anticipate spending. This **precautionary demand for money** is the extra money being held as a safeguard against the unexpected.

Speculative Demand. People also hold money for speculative purposes. Suppose you were interested in buying stocks or bonds but hadn't yet picked the right ones or regarded their present prices as too high. In such circumstances, you might want to hold some money so that you could later buy a "hot" stock or bond at a price you think attractive. Thus you'd be holding money in the hope that a better financial opportunity would later appear. In this sense, you'd be *speculating* with your money balances, forgoing present opportunities to earn interest in the hope of hitting a real jackpot later. These money balances represent a **speculative demand for money.**

The Market Demand Curve. These three motivations for holding money combine to create a *market demand* for money. What shape does this demand curve take? Does the quantity of money demanded decrease sharply as the rate of interest rises? Or do people tend to hold the same amount of money, regardless of its price?

People do cut down on their money balances when interest rates rise. At such times, the opportunity cost of holding money is simply too high. This explains why so many people move their money out of transactions deposits (M1) and into money market mutual funds (M2) when interest rates are extraordinarily high (e.g., in 1980–1982). Corporations are even more careful about managing their money when interest rates rise. Better money management requires watching checking account balances more closely and even making more frequent trips to the bank, but the opportunity costs are worth it.

Figure 15.1 illustrates the total market demand for money. Like nearly all demand curves, the market demand curve for money slopes downward. The downward slope indicates that ***the quantity of money people are willing and able to hold (demand) increases as interest rates fall*** (*ceteris paribus*).

The Money Supply. The money supply curve is assumed to be a vertical line. As we saw in Chapter 13, the Federal Reserve has the power to regulate the money supply through its reserve requirements, discount window, and open market operations. By using these policy tools, the Fed can target a specific quantity for the money supply (M1 or M2).

Equilibrium

Once a money demand curve and a money supply curve are available, the action in money markets is easy to follow. Figure 15.1 summarizes this action. The money demand curve in Figure 15.1 reflects existing demands for holding money. The money supply curve is drawn at an arbitrary level of g_1. In practice, its position depends on Federal Reserve policy (Chapter 14), the lending behavior of private banks, and the willingness of consumers and investors to borrow money.

The intersection of the money demand and money supply curves (E_1) establishes an **equilibrium rate of interest.** Only at this interest rate is the quantity of money supplied equal to the quantity demanded. In this case, we observe that an interest rate of 7 percent equates the desires of suppliers and demanders.

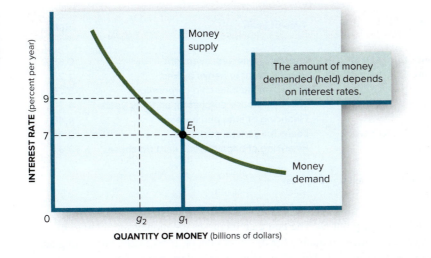

FIGURE 15.1
Money Market Equilibrium

All points on the money demand curve represent the quantity of money people are willing to hold at a specific interest rate. The equilibrium interest rate occurs at the intersection (E_1) of the money supply and money demand curves. At that rate of interest, people are willing to hold as much money as is available. At any other interest rate (e.g., 9 percent), the quantity of money people are *willing* to hold won't equal the quantity available, and people will adjust their portfolios.

At any rate of interest other than 7 percent, the quantity of money demanded wouldn't equal the quantity supplied. Look at the imbalance that exists in Figure 15.1, for example, when the interest rate is 9 percent. At that rate, the quantity of money supplied (g_1 in Figure 15.1) exceeds the quantity demanded (g_2). All the money (g_1) must be held by someone, of course. But the demand curve indicates that people aren't *willing* to hold so much money at that interest rate (9 percent). People will adjust their portfolios by moving money out of cash and bank accounts into bonds or other assets that offer higher returns. This will tend to lower interest rates (recall that buying bonds tends to lower their yields). As interest rates drop, people are willing to hold more money. Ultimately we get to E_1, where the quantity of money demanded equals the quantity supplied. At that equilibrium, people are content with their portfolio choices.

Changing Interest Rates

The equilibrium rate of interest is subject to change. As we saw in Chapter 14, the Federal Reserve System can alter the money supply through changes in reserve requirements, changes in the discount rate, or open market operations. By implication, then, *the Fed can alter the equilibrium rate of interest.*

Figure 15.2 illustrates the potential impact of monetary policy on the equilibrium rate of interest. Assume that the money supply is initially at g_1 and the equilibrium interest rate is

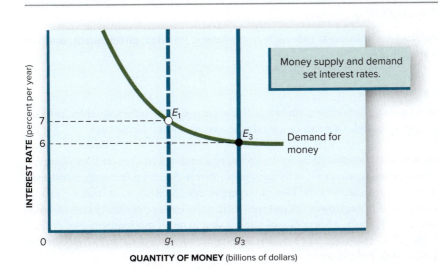

FIGURE 15.2
Changing the Rate of Interest

Changes in the money supply alter the equilibrium rate of interest. In this case, an increase in the money supply (from g_1 to g_3) lowers the equilibrium rate of interest (from 7 percent to 6 percent).

Interest Rate	Type of Loan	Rate
Federal funds rate	Interbank reserves, overnight	0.66%
Discount rate	Reserves lent to banks by Fed	1.25
Prime rate	Bank loans to blue-chip corporations	3.75
Mortgage rate	Loans for house purchases; up to 30 years	4.20
Auto loan	Financing of auto purchases	4.45
Consumer installment credit	Loans for general purposes	9.45
Credit cards	Financing of unpaid credit card purchases	13.61

Source: Federal Reserve (January 2017 rates).

7 percent, as indicated by point E_1. The Fed then increases the money supply to g_3 by lowering the reserve requirement, reducing the discount rate, or, most likely, purchasing additional bonds in the open market. This expansionary monetary policy brings about a new equilibrium at E_3. At this new intersection, the market rate of interest is only 6 percent. Hence *by increasing the money supply, the Fed tends to lower the equilibrium rate of interest.* To put the matter differently, people are *willing* to hold larger money balances only at lower interest rates.

Were the Fed to reverse its policy and *reduce* the money supply, interest rates would rise. You can see this result in Figure 15.2 by observing the change in the rate of interest that occurs when the money supply *shrinks* from g_3 to g_1.

Federal Funds Rate. As we noted in Chapter 14, the most visible market signal of the Fed's activity is the **federal funds rate.** When the Fed injects or withdraws reserves from the banking system (via open market operations), the interest rate on interbank loans is most directly affected. Any change in the federal funds rate, moreover, is likely to affect a whole hierarchy of interest rates (see Table 15.2). *The federal funds rate reflects the cost of funds for banks.* When that cost decreases, banks respond by lowering the interest rates *they* charge to businesses (the prime rate), home buyers (the mortgage rate), and consumers (e.g., auto loans, installment credit, and credit cards).

federal funds rate: The interest rate for interbank reserve loans.

INTEREST RATES AND SPENDING

A change in interest rates isn't the end of this story. The ultimate goal of monetary policy is to alter macroeconomic outcomes: prices, output, employment. Those are the economic outcomes that we really care about. To alter them, the Fed must be able to shift aggregate demand. Hence the next question is

• **How do changes in interest rates affect consumer, investor, government, and net export spending?**

Monetary Stimulus

Consider first a policy of monetary stimulus. The objective of monetary stimulus is to increase **aggregate demand.** One strategy for doing so is to lower interest rates.

aggregate demand (AD): The total quantity of output (real GDP) demanded at alternative price levels in a given time period, *ceteris paribus.*

Investment. Will lower interest rates encourage more spending? In Chapter 9 we observed that investment decisions are sensitive to the rate of interest. Specifically, we demonstrated that lower rates of interest reduce the cost of buying plants and equipment, making capital investment more profitable. Lower interest rates also reduce the opportunity cost of holding inventories. Accordingly, a lower rate of interest should result in a higher rate of desired investment spending. This response is illustrated by the movement down the investment demand curve in step 2 of Figure 15.3.

Step 1: An increase in the money supply lowers the rate of interest.

Step 2: Lower interest rates stimulate investment.

Step 3: More investment increases aggregate demand (including multiplier effects).

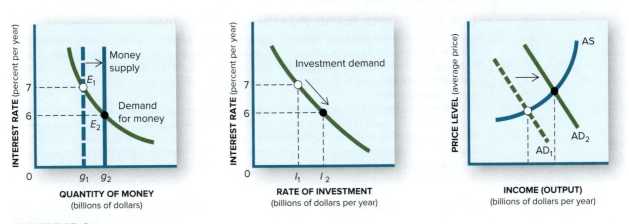

FIGURE 15.3

Monetary Stimulus

An increase in the money supply may reduce interest rates (step 1) and encourage more investment (step 2). The increase in investment will shift AD to the right and trigger multiplier effects that increase aggregate demand by an even larger amount (step 3).

Aggregate Demand. The increased investment brought about by lower interest rates represents an injection of new spending into the circular flow. That jump in spending will kick off multiplier effects and result in an even larger increase in aggregate demand. Step 3 in Figure 15.3 illustrates this increase by the rightward *shift* of the AD curve. Market participants, encouraged by lower interest rates, are now willing to buy more output at the prevailing price level.

Consumers too may change their behavior when interest rates fall. As interest rates fall, mortgage payments decline. Monthly payments on home equity and credit card balances may also decline. These lower interest changes free up billions of consumer dollars. This increased net cash flow and lower interest rates may encourage consumers to buy new cars, appliances, or other big-ticket items. State and local governments may also conclude that lower interest rates increase the desirability of bond-financed public works. All such responses add to aggregate demand.

From this perspective, ***the Fed's goal of stimulating the economy is achieved in three distinct steps:***

- ***An increase in the money supply.***
- ***A reduction in interest rates.***
- ***An increase in aggregate demand.***

This was the intent of the Fed's aggressive open market purchases in 2009 (see In the News "Fed to Expand Bond-Purchase Program"). Note that the Fed announced it was *increasing* its purchases of bonds. As we observed in Chapter 14, increased open-market purchases by the Fed push bond prices *up* and their yields *down*. As bond yield declines so do an array of interest rates (Table 15.2).

Quantitative Impact. Just how much stimulus can monetary policy create? According to former Fed Chairman Ben Bernanke, the impact of monetary policy can be impressive:

$$\text{Bernanke's policy guide:} \quad \frac{\frac{1}{4}\text{ point reduction in}}{\text{long-term interest rate}} = \frac{\$50 \text{ billion}}{\text{fiscal stimulus}}$$

IN THE **NEWS**

FED TO EXPAND BOND-PURCHASE PROGRAM

Information received since the Federal Open Market Committee met in January indicates that the economy continues to contract. Job losses, declining equity and housing wealth, and tight credit conditions have weighed on consumer sentiment and spending. Weaker sales prospects and difficulties in obtaining credit have led businesses to cut back on inventories and fixed investment.

In these circumstances, the Federal Reserve will employ all available tools to promote economic recovery and to preserve price stability. . . . To provide greater support to mortgage lending and housing markets, the Committee decided today to increase the size of the Federal Reserve's balance sheet further by purchasing up to an additional $750 billion of agency mortgage-backed securities, bringing its total purchases of these securities to up to $1.25 trillion this year.

Source: Federal Reserve, March 18, 2009.

ANALYSIS: Lower interest rates encourage market participants to borrow and spend more money. This shifts the AD curve rightward, setting off multiplier effects.

By this rule of thumb, a full-point reduction in long-term interest rates would increase aggregate demand just as much as a $200 billion injection of new government spending.

Monetary Restraint

Like fiscal policy, monetary policy is a two-edged sword, at times seeking to increase aggregate demand and at other times trying to restrain it. When inflation threatens, the goal of monetary policy is to reduce the rate of total spending, which puts the Fed in the position of "leaning against the wind." If successful, the resulting reduction in spending will keep aggregate demand from increasing inflationary pressures.

Higher Interest Rates. The mechanics of monetary policy designed to combat inflation are similar to those used to fight unemployment; only the direction is reversed. In this case, we seek to discourage spending by increasing the rate of interest. The Fed can push interest rates up by *selling* bonds, *increasing* the discount rate, or *raising* the reserve requirement. All these actions reduce the money supply and help establish a new and higher equilibrium rate of interest (e.g., g_3 to g_1 in Figure 15.2).

The ultimate objective of a restrictive monetary policy is to reduce aggregate demand. For monetary restraint to succeed, spending behavior must be responsive to interest rates.

Reduced Aggregate Demand. Figure 15.3 showed the impact of reduced interest rates on investment and aggregate demand. The same figure can be used in reverse. If the interest rate rises from 6 to 7 percent, investment declines from I_2 to I_1 and the AD curve shifts *leftward.* At higher rates of interest, many marginal investments will no longer be profitable. Likewise, many consumers will decide that they can't afford the higher monthly payments associated with increased interest rates; purchases of homes, cars, and household appliances will be postponed. State and local governments may also decide to cancel or postpone bond-financed projects. Thus *monetary restraint is achieved with*

- *A decrease in the money supply.*
- *An increase in interest rates.*
- *A decrease in aggregate demand.*

The resulting leftward shift of the AD curve lessens inflationary pressures.

POLICY CONSTRAINTS

The mechanics of monetary policy are simple enough. They won't always work as well as we might hope, however. Several constraints can limit the Fed's ability to alter the money supply, interest rates, or aggregate demand.

Constraints on Monetary Stimulus

Short- vs. Long-Term Rates. One of the most visible constraints on monetary policy is the distinction between short-term interest rates and long-term interest rates. Bernanke's policy guide (see "Quantitative Impact" in the previous section) focuses on changes in *long-term* rates like mortgages and installment loans. Yet the Fed's open market operations have the most direct effect on *short-term* rates (e.g., the overnight federal funds rate). As a consequence, *the success of Fed intervention depends in part on how well changes in long-term interest rates mirror changes in short-term interest rates.*

In 2001 the Fed reduced the federal funds rate by three full percentage points between January and September, the biggest reduction in short-term rates since 1994. Long-term rates fell much less, however. The interest rate on 30-year mortgages, for example, fell less than half a percentage point in the first few months of monetary stimulus.

The same thing happened when the Fed reversed direction in 2004–2006. The *short*-run fed funds rate was ratcheted up from 1.0 to 5.25 percent during that period—a huge increase. But *long*-term rates (e.g., 10-year Treasury bonds and home mortgages) rose only modestly. Fed Chairman Alan Greenspan characterized these disparate trends as a "conundrum."

The same "conundrum" frustrated Fed Chairman Bernanke in 2008. The Fed was successful in pushing the short-term federal funds rate down from 4.25 percent at the start of 2008 to near zero at year's end, but long-term mortgage and bond rates didn't drop nearly as much. Hence the aggregate demand stimulus was less than hoped for. That was why the Fed started buying longer-term securities through several rounds of "quantitative easing."

Reluctant Lenders. There are several reasons why long-term rates might not closely mirror cuts in short-term rates. The first potential constraint is the willingness of private banks to increase their lending activity. The Fed can reduce the cost of funds to the banking system; the Fed can even reduce reserve requirements. But *the money supply won't increase unless banks lend more money.*

If the banks instead choose to accumulate excess reserves, the money supply won't increase as much as intended. We saw this happen in the Great Depression (Figure 14.2). This happened again in 2008–2014, when the Fed was trying to stimulate the economy. Despite three rounds of quantitative easing (QE1, QE2, and QE3)—massive open market purchases—banks were reluctant to increase their loan activity. Banks were trying to shore up their own equity and were wary of making any new loans that might not get repaid in a weak economy. In such cases, long-term rates stay relatively high even when short-term rates are falling. They were also worried about new banking regulations (Dodd-Frank Act of 2010) that changed both the appropriateness and the profitability of new loans. Rather than making new loans, the banks simply stockpiled their excess reserves (see Figure 14.2). At the beginning of 2015, banks held more than $2 trillion of excess reserves—more than at any other time in history.

Liquidity Trap. There are circumstances in which even *short-term* rates may not fall when the Fed wants them to. The possibility that interest rates may not respond to changes in the money supply is illustrated by the "liquidity trap." When interest rates are low, the opportunity cost of holding money is cheap. At such times people may decide to hold all the money they can get, waiting for income-earning opportunities to improve. Bond prices, for example, may be high and their yields low. Buying bonds at such times entails the risk of capital losses (when bond prices fall) and little reward (since yields are low). Accordingly, market participants may decide just to hold any additional money the Fed supplies in cash

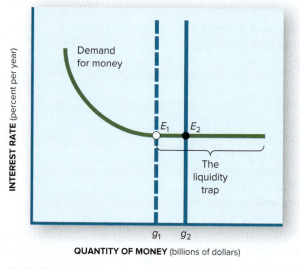

(a) A liquidity trap can stop interest rates from falling.

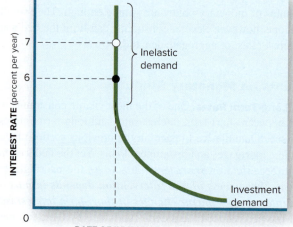

(b) Inelastic investment demand can also impede monetary policy.

FIGURE 15.4

Constraints on Monetary Stimulus

(a) Liquidity Trap   If people are willing to hold unlimited amounts of money (cash and bank balances) at the prevailing interest rate, increases in the money supply won't push interest rates lower. A liquidity trap—the horizontal segment of the money demand curve—prevents interest rates from falling (step 1 in Figure 15.3).

(b) Inelastic Demand   A lower interest rate won't always stimulate investment. If investors have unfavorable expectations for future sales, small reductions in interest rates may not alter their investment decisions. Here the rate of investment remains constant when the interest rate drops from 7 to 6 percent. This kind of situation blocks the second step in the Keynesian approach to monetary policy (step 2 in Figure 15.3).

liquidity trap: The portion of the money demand curve that is horizontal; people are willing to hold unlimited amounts of money at some (low) interest rate.

or bank balances. At this juncture—a phenomenon Keynes called the **liquidity trap**—further expansion of the money supply has no effect on the rate of interest. The horizontal section of the money demand curve in Figure 15.4a portrays this situation.

What happens to interest rates when the initial equilibrium falls into this trap? Nothing at all. Notice that the equilibrium rate of interest doesn't fall when the money supply is increased from g_1 to g_2 (Figure 15.4a). People are willing to hold all that additional money without a reduction in the rate of interest.

Low Expectations. Even if both short- and long-term interest rates do fall, we have no assurance that aggregate demand will increase as expected. Keynes put great emphasis on *expectations*. Recall that **investment decisions are motivated not only by interest rates but by expectations as well.** During a recession—when unemployment is high and the rate of spending is low—corporations have little incentive to expand production capacity. With little expectation of future profit, investors are likely to be unimpressed by "cheap money" (low interest rates) and may decline to use the lending capacity that banks make available.

Investment demand that's slow to respond to the lure of cheap money is said to be *inelastic* because it won't expand. Consumers too are reluctant to borrow when current and future income prospects are uncertain or distinctly unfavorable. Accordingly, even if the Fed is successful in lowering interest rates, there's no assurance that lower interest rates will stimulate borrowing and spending. Such a reluctance to spend was evident in 2008–2014. Although the Fed managed to push interest rates down to historic lows, investors and consumers preferred to pay off old debts rather than incur new ones (see In the News "Consumers Not Responding to Low Interest Rates"). Expectations, not interest rates, dominated spending decisions.

IN THE NEWS

CONSUMERS NOT RESPONDING TO LOW INTEREST RATES

The Federal Reserve has repeated its intention to keep interest rates at historically low levels for at least another year. But consumers aren't taking the bait. Falling home prices, stock-market volatility, and persistent high unemployment have shattered consumer confidence. So, consumers aren't willing to take on more debt to buy new homes, cars, furniture, or other products—no matter how cheap money is. Kansas City Fed president Esther George acknowledged that "record low interest rates are not enough" to induce consumers to take on more debt.

Source: Media reports of 2011–2013.

ANALYSIS: Interest rate cuts are supposed to stimulate investment and consumption. But gloomy expectations may deter people from borrowing and spending.

The vertical portion of the investment demand curve in Figure 15.4b illustrates the possibility that investment spending may not respond to changes in the rate of interest. Notice that a reduction in the rate of interest from 7 percent to 6 percent doesn't increase investment spending. In this case, businesses are simply unwilling to invest any more funds. As a consequence, aggregate spending doesn't rise. The Fed's policy objective remains unfulfilled, even though the Fed has successfully lowered the rate of interest. Recall that the investment demand curve may also *shift* if expectations change. If expectations worsened, the investment demand curve would shift to the left and might result in even *less* investment at 6 percent interest (see Figure 15.4b).

Time Lags. Even when expectations are good, businesses won't respond *instantly* to changes in interest rates. Lower interest rates make investments more profitable. But it still takes time to develop and implement new investments. Hence **there is always a time lag between interest rate changes and investment responses.**

The same is true for consumers. Consumers don't rush out the door to refinance their homes or buy new ones the day the Fed reduces interest rates. They might start *thinking* about new financing, but they aren't likely to *do* anything for a while. It may take 6–12 months before market behavior responds to monetary policy.

Limits on Monetary Restraint

Expectations. Time lags and expectations could also limit the effectiveness of monetary restraint. In pursuit of "tight" money, the Fed can drain bank reserves and force interest rates higher. Yet market participants might continue to borrow and spend if high expectations for rising sales and profits overwhelm high interest rates in investment decisions. Consumers too might believe that future incomes will be sufficient to cover larger debts and higher interest charges. Both groups might foresee accelerating inflation that would make even high interest rates look cheap in the future. This was apparently the case in Britain in 2004, as World View "Rising Rates Haven't Thwarted Consumers" documents.

Global Money. Market participants might also tap global sources of money. If money gets too tight in domestic markets, business may borrow funds from foreign banks or institutions. GM, Disney, ExxonMobil, Netflix, and other multinational corporations can borrow funds from foreign subsidiaries, banks, and even bond markets. As we saw in Chapter 14, market participants can also secure funds from nonbank sources in the United States. These nonbank and global lenders make it harder for the Fed to restrain aggregate demand.

RISING RATES HAVEN'T THWARTED CONSUMERS

The Bank of England continued its tightening of monetary policy on June 10. And with the British economy still expanding at a decent clip, more hikes are on the way.

As expected by most economists, the BOE raised its lending rate by a quarter point, to 4.5 percent. It was the fourth bump up since November 2003. In explaining the move, the BOE's statement pointed to above-trend output growth, strong household, business, and public spending, as well as a labor market that "has tightened further." . . .

The BOE is the first of the world's major central banks to raise rates, but the moves have done little to curb borrowing, especially by consumers. Home buying remains robust. . . .

The easy access to credit and the strong labor markets are boosting consumer spending.

—James C. Cooper and Kathleen Madigan

Cooper, James C., and Kathleen Madigan, "Rising Rates Haven't Thwarted Consumers," *Businessweek*, June 28, 2004, p. 14. Copyright ©2004. All rights reserved. Used with permission.

ANALYSIS: Strong expectations and rising incomes may fuel continued spending even when interest rates are rising.

How Effective? In view of all these constraints on monetary policies, some observers have concluded that monetary policy is an undependable policy lever. Keynes, for example, emphasized that monetary policy wouldn't be very effective in ending a deep recession. He believed that the combination of reluctant bankers, the liquidity trap, and low expectations would render monetary stimulus ineffective. Using monetary policy to stimulate the economy in such circumstances would be akin to "pushing on a string." Alan Greenspan came to much the same conclusion in September 1992 when he said that further Fed stimulus would be ineffective in accelerating a recovery from the 1990–1991 recession. He believed, however, that earlier cuts in interest rates would help stimulate spending once banks, investors, and consumers gained confidence in the economic outlook. The same kind of problem existed in 2001: the Fed's actions to reduce interest rates (11 times in as many months!) weren't enough to propel the economy forward in 2001–2002. Market participants had to recover their confidence in the future before they would start spending "cheap" money. The same lack of confidence limited the effectiveness of monetary stimulus in 2008–2016.

The limitations on monetary restraint aren't considered as serious. The Fed has the power to reduce the money supply. If the money supply shrinks far enough, the rate of spending will have to slow down.

THE MONETARIST PERSPECTIVE

The Keynesian view of money emphasizes the role of interest rates in fulfilling the goals of monetary policy. *In the Keynesian model, changes in the money supply affect macro outcomes primarily through changes in interest rates.* The three-step sequence of (1) money supply change, (2) interest rate movement, and (3) aggregate demand shift makes monetary policy subject to several potential uncertainties. As we've seen, the economy doesn't always respond as expected to Fed policy.

An alternative view of monetary policy seizes on those occasional failures to offer a different explanation of how the money supply affects macro outcomes. The so-called *monetarist* school dismisses changes in short-term interest rates (e.g., the federal funds rate) as unpredictable and ineffective. They don't think real output levels are affected by monetary stimulus. As they see it, only the price level is affected by Fed policy, and then only by changes in the money supply. *Monetarists assert that monetary policy isn't an effective tool for fighting short-run business cycles, but it is a powerful tool for managing inflation.*

The Equation of Exchange

Monetarists emphasize that the potential of monetary policy can be expressed in a simple equation called the **equation of exchange,** written as

$$MV = PQ$$

where M refers to the quantity of money in circulation and V to its **velocity** of circulation. Total spending in the economy is equal to the average price (P) of goods times the quantity (Q) of goods sold in a period. This spending is financed by the supply of money (M) times the velocity of its circulation (V).

Suppose, for example, that only two participants are in the market and that the money supply consists of one crisp $20 bill. What's the limit to total spending in this case? If you answer "$20," you haven't yet grasped the nature of the circular flow.

Suppose I begin the circular flow by spending $20 on eggs, bacon, and a gallon of milk. The money I spend ends up in Farmer Brown's pocket because he is the only other market participant. Once in possession of the money, Farmer Brown may decide to satisfy his long-smoldering desire to learn something about economics and buy one of my books. If he acts on that decision, the $20 will return to me. At that point, both Farmer Brown and I have sold $20 worth of goods. Hence $40 of total spending has been financed with one $20 bill.

As long as we keep using this $20 bill to buy goods and services from each other, we can continue to do business. Moreover, the faster we pass the money from hand to hand during any period of time, the greater the value of sales each of us can register. If the money is passed from hand to hand eight times, then I'll be able to sell $80 worth of textbooks and Farmer Brown will be able to sell $80 worth of produce during that period, for a total nominal output of $160. *The quantity of money in circulation and the velocity with which it travels (changes hands) in product markets will always be equal to the value of total spending and income (nominal GDP).* This relationship is summarized as

$$M \times V = P \times Q$$

In this case, the *equation of exchange* confirms that

$$\$20 \times 8 = \$160$$

The value of total sales for the year is $160.

Monetarists use the equation of exchange to simplify the explanation of how monetary policy works. There's no need, they argue, to follow the effects of changes in M through the money markets to interest rates and further to changes in total spending. The basic consequences of monetary policy are evident in the equation of exchange. The two sides of the equation of exchange must always be in balance. Hence we can be absolutely certain that *if* **M** *increases, prices* (**P**) *or output* (**Q**) *must rise, or* **V** *must fall.*

The equation of exchange is an incontestable statement of how the money supply is related to macro outcomes. The equation itself, however, says nothing about *which* variables will respond to a change in the money supply. The *goal* of monetary policy is to change the macro outcomes on the right side of the equation. It's *possible,* however, that a change in M might be offset with a reverse change in V, leaving P and Q unaffected. Or it could happen that the *wrong* macro outcome is affected. Prices (P) might rise, for example, when we're trying to increase real output (Q).

Stable Velocity

Monetarists add some important assumptions to transform the equation of exchange from a simple identity to a behavioral *model* of macro performance. The first assumption is that the velocity of money (V) is stable. How fast people use their money balances depends on the institutional structure of money markets and people's habits. Neither the structure of

equation of exchange: Money supply (M) times velocity of circulation (V) equals level of aggregate spending ($P \times Q$).

velocity of money (V): The number of times per year, on average, that a dollar is used to purchase final goods and services; $PQ \div M$.

money markets nor people's habits are likely to change in the short run. Accordingly, they say a short-run increase in *M* won't be offset by a reduction in *V*. Instead the impact of an increased money supply will be transmitted to the right side of the equation of exchange, which means that ***total spending must rise if the money supply (M) grows and V is stable.***

Money Supply Focus

From a monetarist perspective, there's no need to trace the impacts of monetary policy through interest rate movements. The focus on interest rates is a uniquely Keynesian perspective. Monetarists claim that interest rate movements are secondary to the major thrust of monetary policy. ***As monetarists see it, changes in the money supply must alter total spending, regardless of how interest rates move.***

A monetarist perspective leads to a whole different strategy for the Fed. Because interest rates aren't part of the monetarist explanation of how monetary policy works, the Fed shouldn't try to manipulate interest rates; instead it should focus on the money supply itself. Monetarists also argue that the Fed can't really control interest rates well because they depend on both the supply of and the demand for money. What the Fed *can* control is the supply of money, and the equation of exchange clearly shows that money matters.

Analysis: If the money supply shrinks (or its growth rate slows), price levels will rise less quickly. The Dropouts—Used by permission of The Estate of Howard Post.

"Natural" Rate of Unemployment

Some monetarists add yet another perspective to the equation of exchange. They assert that not only *V* but *Q* as well is stable. If this is true, then changes in the money supply (*M*) would affect only prices (*P*).

What does it mean for *Q* to be stable? The argument here is that the quantity of goods produced is primarily dependent on production capacity, labor market efficiency, and other "structural" forces. These structural forces establish a **"natural" rate of unemployment** that's fairly immune to short-run policy intervention. This is the *long-run* aggregate supply curve we first encountered in Chapter 8. From this perspective, there's no reason for producers to depart from this "natural" rate of output when the money supply increases. Producers are smart enough to know that both prices and costs will rise when spending increases. Hence rising prices won't create any new profit incentives for increasing output. Firms will just continue producing at the "natural" rate with higher (nominal) prices and costs. As a result, increases in aggregate spending—whether financed by more *M* or faster *V*—aren't likely to alter real output levels. *Q* will stay constant.

If the quantity of real output is in fact stable, then *P* is the only thing that can change. Thus ***the most extreme monetarist perspective concludes that changes in the money supply affect prices only.*** As the "simple economics" in the above cartoon suggests, a decrease in *M* should directly reduce the price level. When *M* increases, total spending rises, but the higher nominal value of spending is completely absorbed by higher prices. In this view, monetary policy affects only the rate of inflation. This is the kind of money-driven inflation that bedeviled George Washington's army (see In the News "'Not Worth a Continental: The U.S. Experience with Hyperinflation'").

natural rate of unemployment: The long-term rate of unemployment determined by structural forces in labor and product markets.

"NOT WORTH A CONTINENTAL": THE U.S. EXPERIENCE WITH HYPERINFLATION

The government of the United States had no means to pay for the Revolutionary War. Specifically, the federal government had no power to levy taxes that might transfer resources from the private sector to the public sector. Instead, it could only request the states to levy taxes of their own and contribute them to the war effort. The states were not very responsive, however: state contributions accounted for only 6 percent of federal revenues during the war years.

To pay for needed weapons and soldiers, the federal government had only two other options: either (1) borrow money or (2) create new money. When loans proved to be inadequate, the Continental Congress started issuing new paper money—the "Continental" dollar—in 1775. By the end of 1779, Congress had authorized issuance of more than $250 million in Continental dollars.

At first the paper money enabled George Washington's troops to acquire needed supplies, ammunition, and volunteers. But soon the flood of paper money inundated product markets. Wholesale prices of key commodities skyrocketed. Commodity prices *doubled* in 1776, in 1777, and again in 1778. Then prices increased *tenfold* in the next two years.

Many farmers and storekeepers refused to sell goods to the army in exchange for Continental dollars. Rapid inflation had taught them that the paper money George Washington's troops offered was nearly worthless. The expression "not worth a Continental" became a popular reference to things of little value.

The states tried price controls and even empowered themselves to seize needed war supplies. But nothing could stop the inflation fueled by the explosive increase in the money supply. Fortunately, the war ended before the economy collapsed. After the war, the U.S. Congress established a new form of money, and in 1787 it empowered the federal government to levy taxes and mint gold and silver coins.

—**Sidney Ratner, James H. Soltow, and Richard Sylla**

ANALYSIS: Rapid expansion of the money supply will push the price level up. As inflation accelerates, money becomes less valuable.

Figure 15.5 illustrates the extreme monetarist argument in the context of aggregate supply and demand. The assertion that real output is fixed at the natural rate of unemployment is reflected in the vertical, long-run aggregate supply curve. With real output stuck at Q^*, any increase in aggregate demand directly raises the price level.

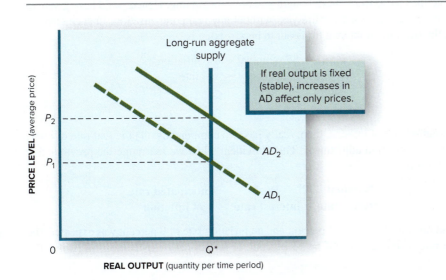

FIGURE 15.5

The Monetarist View

Monetarists argue that the rate of real output is set by structural factors. Furthermore, firms aren't likely to be fooled into producing more just because prices are rising because costs are likely to rise just as much. Hence long-run aggregate supply remains at the "natural" level Q^*. Any monetary-induced increases in aggregate demand, therefore, raise the price level (inflation) but not output.

Monetarist Policies

At first glance, the monetarist argument looks pretty slick. Keynesians worry about how the money supply affects interest rates, how interest rates affect spending, and how spending affects output. By contrast, monetarists point to a simple equation ($MV = PQ$) that produces straightforward responses to monetary policy.

There are fundamental differences between the two schools here, not only about how the economy works but also about how successful macro policy might be. To appreciate those differences, consider monetarist responses to inflationary and recessionary gaps.

Fighting Inflation. Consider again the options for fighting inflation. The policy goal is to reduce aggregate demand. From a Keynesian perspective, the way to achieve this reduction is to shrink the money supply and drive up interest rates. But monetarists argue that nominal interest rates are already likely to be high. Furthermore, if an effective anti-inflation policy is adopted, interest rates will come *down,* not go up. Yes, interest rates will come *down,* not go up, when the money supply is tightened, according to monetarists.

Real vs. Nominal Interest. To understand this monetarist conclusion, we have to distinguish between *nominal* interest rates and *real* ones. Nominal interest rates are the ones we actually see and pay. When a bank pays 5½ percent interest on your bank account, it's quoting (and paying) a nominal rate.

Real interest rates are never actually seen and rarely quoted. These are "inflation-adjusted" rates. Specifically, the **real interest rate** equals the nominal rate *minus* the anticipated rate of inflation; that is,

real interest rate: The nominal interest rate minus the anticipated inflation rate.

$$\begin{array}{ccc} \text{Real} & \text{Nominal} & \text{Anticipated} \\ \text{interest} = & \text{interest} - & \text{inflation} \\ \text{rate} & \text{rate} & \text{rate} \end{array}$$

Recall what inflation does to the purchasing power of the dollar: As inflation continues, each dollar purchases fewer goods and services. As a consequence, dollars borrowed today are of less real value when they're paid back later. The real rate of interest reflects this inflation adjustment.

Suppose you lend someone $100 at the beginning of the year, at 8 percent interest. You expect to get more back at the end of the year than you start with. That "more" you expect refers to *real* goods and services, not just dollar bills. Specifically, you anticipate that when the loan is repaid with interest at the end of the year, you'll be able to buy more goods and services than you could at the beginning. This expectation of a *real* gain is at least part of the reason for making a loan.

Your expected gain won't materialize, however, if all prices rise by 8 percent during the year. If the inflation rate is 8 percent, you'll discover that $108 buys you no more at the end of the year than $100 would have bought you at the beginning. Hence you'd have given up the use of your money for an entire year without any real compensation. In such circumstances, the *real* rate of interest turns out to be zero; that is,

$$\begin{array}{ccc} \text{Real} & \text{8\% nominal} & \text{8\% inflation} \\ \text{interest} = & \text{interest} & - & \text{rate} \\ \text{rate} & \text{rate} \end{array}$$
$$= 0$$

The nominal rate of interest, then, really has two components: (1) the real rate of interest and (2) an inflation adjustment. This is evident when we rearrange the previous formula as follows:

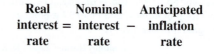

$$\begin{array}{ccc} \textbf{Nominal} & \textbf{Real} & \textbf{Anticipated rate} \\ \textbf{interest rate} = & \textbf{interest rate} + & \textbf{of inflation} \end{array}$$

If the real rate of interest was 4 percent and an inflation rate of 9 percent was expected, the nominal rate of interest would be 13 percent. If inflationary expectations *declined,* the *nominal* interest rate would *fall.* If the real interest rate is 4 percent and anticipated inflation falls from 9 to 6 percent, the nominal interest rate would decline from 13 to 10 percent.

A central assumption of the monetarist perspective is that the real rate of interest is fairly stable. This is a critical point. ***If the real rate of interest is stable, then changes in the nominal interest rate reflect only changes in anticipated inflation.*** From this perspective, high nominal rates of interest are a symptom of inflation, not a cure. Indeed, high nominal rates may even look cheap if inflationary expectations are worsening faster than interest rates are rising. This was the case in Zimbabwe in 2008, when the nominal interest rate rose above 400 percent (see World View "Zimbabwe's Trillion-Dollar Currency," in Chapter 7).

Consider the implications of all this for monetary policy. Suppose we want to close an inflationary GDP gap. Monetarists and Keynesians agree that a reduced money supply (*M*) will deflate total spending. But Keynesians rely on a "quick fix" of *higher* interest rates to slow consumption and investment spending. Monetarists, by contrast, assert that nominal interest rates will *fall* if the Fed tightens the money supply. Once market participants are convinced that the Fed is going to reduce money supply growth, inflationary expectations diminish. When inflationary expectations diminish, nominal interest rates will begin to fall.

Short- vs. Long-Term Rates (Again). The monetarist argument helps resolve the "conundrum" that puzzled former Fed Chairman Alan Greenspan and bedeviled his successor, Ben Bernanke—that is, the contradictory movements of short-term and long-term interest rates. As we observed earlier, short-run rates (like the federal funds rate) are very responsive to Fed intervention. But long-term rates are much slower to respond. This suggests that banks and borrowers look beyond current economic conditions in making long-term financial commitments.

If the Fed is reducing money supply growth, short-term rates may rise quickly. But long-term rates won't increase unless market participants expect inflation to worsen. Given the pivotal role of long-term rates in investment decisions, the Fed may have to stall GDP growth—even spark a recession—to restrain aggregate demand enough to stop prices from rising. Rather than take such risks, ***monetarists advocate steady and predictable changes in the money supply.*** Such a policy, they believe, would reduce uncertainties and thus stabilize both long-term interest rates and GDP growth.

Fighting Unemployment. The link between anticipated inflation and nominal interest rates also constrains monetary stimulus. The Keynesian cure for a recession is to expand *M* and lower interest rates. But monetarists fear that an increase in *M* will lead—via the equation of exchange—to *higher P.* If everyone believed this would happen, then an unexpectedly large increase in *M* would immediately raise people's inflationary expectations. Even if short-term interest rates fell, long-term interest rates might actually rise. This would defeat the purpose of monetary stimulus.

From a monetarist perspective, expansionary monetary policies aren't likely to lead us out of a recession. On the contrary, such policies might heap inflation problems on top of our unemployment woes. All monetary policy should do, say the monetarists, is ensure a stable and predictable rate of growth in the money supply. Then people could concentrate on real production decisions without worrying so much about fluctuating prices.

THE CONCERN FOR CONTENT

Monetary policy, like fiscal policy, can affect more than just the *level* of total spending. We must give some consideration to the impact of Federal Reserve actions on the *content* of the GDP if we're going to be responsive to the "second crisis" of economic theory.[1]

---

[1]See the quotation from Joan Robinson in Chapter 11, calling attention to the exclusive focus of economists on the *level* of economic activity (the "first crisis"), to the neglect of content (the "second crisis").

The Mix of Output

Both Keynesians and monetarists agree that monetary policy will affect nominal interest rates. When interest rates change, not all spending decisions will be affected equally. High interest rates don't deter consumers from buying pizzas, but they do deter purchases of homes, cars, and other big-ticket items typically financed with loans. Hence the housing and auto industries bear a disproportionate burden of restrictive monetary policy. Accordingly, when the Fed pursues a policy of tight money—high interest rates and limited lending capacity—it not only restrains total spending but reduces the share of housing and autos in that spending. Utility industries, public works projects, and state and local finances are also disproportionately impacted by monetary policy.

In addition to altering the content of output, monetary policy affects the competitive structure of the market. When money is tight, banks must ration available credit among loan applicants. Large and powerful corporations aren't likely to run out of credit because banks will be hesitant to incur their displeasure and lose their business. Thus General Motors and Google stand a much better chance of obtaining tight money than does the corner grocery store. Moreover, if bank lending capacity becomes too small, GM and Google can always resort to the bond market and borrow money directly from the public. Small businesses seldom have such an alternative.

Income Redistribution

Monetary policy also affects the distribution of income. When interest rates fall, borrowers pay smaller interest charges. On the other hand, lenders get smaller interest payments. Hence a lower interest rate redistributes income from lenders to borrowers. When interest rates declined sharply in 2008–2009, home owners refinanced their mortgages and saved billions of dollars in interest payments. The decline in interest rates, however, *reduced* the income of retired persons, who depend heavily on interest payments from certificates of deposit, bonds, and other assets. Money supply increases also push up stock and bond prices, disproportionately benefiting higher-income households.

THE ECONOMY TOMORROW

WHICH LEVER TO PULL?

Our success in managing the macro economy of tomorrow depends on pulling the right policy levers at the right time. But which levers should be pulled? Keynesians and monetarists offer very different prescriptions for treating an ailing economy. Can we distill some usable policy guidelines from this discussion for policy decisions in the economy tomorrow?

The Policy Tools. The equation of exchange is a convenient summary of the differences between the Keynesian and monetarist perspectives. There's no disagreement about the equation itself: aggregate spending ($M \times V$) *must* equal the value of total sales ($P \times Q$). *What Keynesians and monetarists argue about is which of the policy tools—M or V— is likely to be effective in altering aggregate spending.*

- *Monetarists* point to changes in the money supply (M) as the principal lever of macroeconomic policy. They assume V is reasonably stable.
- *Keynesian* fiscal policy *must* rely on changes in the velocity of money (V) because tax and expenditure policies have no direct impact on the money supply.

Crowding Out: Constant V. The extreme monetarist position that *only* money matters is based on the assumption that the velocity of money (V) is constant. *If V is constant, changes in total spending can come about only through changes in the money supply.* There are no other policy tools on the left side of the equation of exchange.

Think about an increase in government spending designed to stimulate the economy. How does the government pay for this fiscal policy stimulus? Monetarists argue that there are only two ways to pay for this increased expenditure (*G*): the government must either raise additional taxes or borrow more money. If the government raises taxes, the disposable income of consumers will be reduced, and private spending will fall. On the other hand, if the government *borrows* more money to pay for its expenditures, there will be less money available for loans to private consumers and investors. In either case, more government spending (*G*) implies less private spending (*C* or *I*). Thus *increased G* effectively **"crowds out"** some *C* or *I,* leaving total spending unchanged. From this viewpoint, fiscal policy is ineffective; it can't even shift the aggregate demand curve. At best, fiscal policy can change the composition of demand and thus the mix of output. Only changes in *M* (monetary policy) can shift the aggregate demand curve.

crowding out: A reduction in private sector borrowing (and spending) caused by increased government borrowing.

Milton Friedman, formerly of the University of Chicago, championed the monetarist view with this argument:

> I believe that the state of the government budget matters; matters a great deal—for some things. The state of the government budget determines what fraction of the nation's income is spent through the government and what fraction is spent by individuals privately. The state of the government budget determines what the level of our taxes is, how much of our income we turn over to the government. The state of the government budget has a considerable effect on interest rates. If the federal government runs a large deficit, that means the government has to borrow in the market, which raises the demand for loanable funds and so tends to raise interest rates.
>
> If the government budget shifts to a surplus, that adds to the supply of loanable funds, which tends to lower interest rates. It was no surprise to those of us who stress money that enactment of the surtax was followed by a decline in interest rates. That's precisely what we had predicted and what our analysis leads us to predict. But—and I come to the main point—in my opinion, the state of the budget by itself has no significant effect on the course of nominal income, on inflation, on deflation, or on cyclical fluctuations.[2]

Keynes: *V* Changes. Keynesians reply that the alleged constant velocity of money is a monetarist's pipe dream. Some even argue that the velocity of money is so volatile that changes in *V* can completely offset changes in *M,* leaving us with the proposition that money doesn't matter.

The liquidity trap illustrates the potential for *V* to change. Keynes argued that people tend to accumulate money balances—slow their rate of spending—during recessions. *A slowdown in spending implies a reduction in the velocity of money.* Indeed, in the extreme case of the liquidity trap, the velocity of money falls toward zero. Under these circumstances, changes in *M* (monetary policy) won't influence total spending. The velocity of money falls as rapidly as *M* increases. On the other hand, increased government spending (fiscal policy) can stimulate aggregate spending by putting idle money balances to work (thereby increasing *V*). Changes in fiscal policy will also influence consumer and investor expectations, and thereby further alter the rate of aggregate spending.

How Fiscal Policy Works: Two Views. Tables 15.3 and 15.4 summarize these different perspectives on fiscal and monetary policy. The first table evaluates fiscal policy from both Keynesian and monetarist viewpoints. The central issue is whether and how a change in government spending (*G*) or taxes (*T*) will alter macroeconomic outcomes. Keynesians assert that aggregate demand will be affected as the velocity of money (*V*) changes. Monetarists say no because they anticipate an unchanged *V*.

If aggregate demand isn't affected by a change in *G* or *T,* then fiscal policy won't affect prices (*P*) or real output (*Q*). Thus monetarists conclude that fiscal policy isn't a viable tool for combating either inflation or unemployment. By contrast, Keynesians believe *V will* change and that output and prices will respond accordingly.

Insofar as interest rates are concerned, monetarists recognize that nominal interest rates will be affected (read Friedman's quote again), but *real* rates won't be. Real interest

Continued

---

[2]Source: Friedman, Milton, and Walter H. Heller, *Monetary Vs. Fiscal Policy,* New York, NY: W.W. Norton & Company, 1969, p. 50–51.

Do Changes in G or T Affect	Monetarist View	Keynesian View
1. Aggregate demand?	No (stable *V* causes crowding out)	Yes (*V* changes)
2. Prices?	No (aggregate demand not affected)	Maybe (if at capacity)
3. Real output?	No (aggregate demand not affected)	Yes (output responds to demand)
4. Nominal interest rates?	Yes (crowding out)	Maybe (may alter demand for money)
5. Real interest rates?	No (determined by real growth)	Yes (real growth and expectations may vary)

TABLE 15.3

How Fiscal Policy Matters: Monetarist vs. Keynesian Views

Monetarists and Keynesians have very different views on the impact of fiscal policy. Monetarists assert that changes in government spending (*G*) and taxes (*T*) don't alter the velocity of money (*V*). As a result, fiscal policy alone can't alter total spending. Keynesians reject this view, arguing that *V* is changeable. They claim that tax cuts and increased government spending increase the velocity of money and so alter total spending.

Do Changes in M Affect	Monetarist View	Keynesian View
1. Aggregate demand?	Yes (*V* stable)	Maybe (*V* may change)
2. Prices?	Yes (*V* and *Q* stable)	Maybe (*V* and *Q* may change)
3. Real output?	No (rate of unemployment determined by structural forces)	Maybe (output responds to demand)
4. Nominal interest rates?	Yes (but direction unknown)	Maybe (liquidity trap)
5. Real interest rates?	No (depends on real growth)	Maybe (real growth may vary)

TABLE 15.4

How Money Matters: Monetarist vs. Keynesian Views

Because monetarists believe that *V* is stable, they assert that changes in the money supply (*M*) must alter total spending. But all the monetary impact is reflected in prices and nominal interest rates; *real* output and interest rates are unaffected.

Keynesians think that *V* is variable and thus that changes in *M* might *not* alter total spending. If monetary policy does alter aggregate spending, however, Keynesians expect all outcomes to be affected.

rates depend on real output and growth, both of which are seen as immune to fiscal policy. Keynesians see less impact on nominal interest rates and more on real interest rates.

What all this boils down to is this: fiscal policy, by itself, will be effective only if it can alter the velocity of money. *How well fiscal policy works depends on how much the velocity of money can be changed by government tax and spending decisions.*

How Monetary Policy Works: Two Views. Table 15.4 offers a similar summary of monetary policy. This time the positions of monetarists and Keynesians are reversed, or nearly so. Monetarists say a change in M must alter total spending ($P \times Q$) because V is stable. Keynesians assert that V may vary, so they aren't convinced that monetary policy will always work. The heart of the controversy is again the velocity of money. Monetary policy works as long as V is stable, or at least predictable. *How well monetary policy works depends on how stable or predictable V is.*

Once the central role of velocity is understood, everything else falls into place. Monetarists assert that prices but not output will be directly affected by a change in M because the right side of the equation of exchange contains only two variables (P and Q), and one of them (Q) is assumed to be unaffected by monetary policy. Keynesians, by contrast, aren't so sure that prices will be affected by M or that real output won't be. It all depends on V and the responsiveness of P and Q to changes in aggregate spending.

Finally, monetarists predict that nominal interest rates will respond to changes in M, although they're not sure in what direction. It depends on how inflationary expectations adapt to changes in the money supply. Keynesian economists aren't so sure nominal interest rates will change but are sure about the direction if they do.

Is Velocity Stable? Tables 15.3 and 15.4 highlight the velocity of money as a critical determinant of policy impact. The critical question appears to be whether V is stable. Why hasn't someone answered this simple question and resolved the debate over fiscal versus monetary policy?

Long-Run Stability. The velocity of money (V) turns out, in fact, to be quite stable over long periods of time. Over the past 30 years the velocity of money (M2) has averaged about 1.64, as Figure 15.6 illustrates. Moreover, the range of velocity has been fairly narrow, extending from a low of 1.56 in 1987 to a high of 2.05 in 1997. Monetarists conclude that the historical pattern justifies the assumption of a stable V.

Short-Run Instability. Keynesians reply that monetarists are farsighted and so fail to see significant short-run variations in V. The difference between a velocity of 1.56 and velocity of 2.05 translates into hundreds of billions of dollars in aggregate demand. Moreover, there's a pattern to short-run variations in V: velocity tends to decline in recessions (see Figure 15.6). As the Great Recession of 2008–2009 unfolded, the velocity of money declined steadily from 1.90 in 2008 to a new low of 1.50 in 2015. That was a decline of more than 20 percent in the velocity of money. That magnitude of that decline in V outstripped the Fed's increase in M, rendering monetary policy fairly ineffective. These are precisely the situations in which fiscal stimulus (increasing V) would be appropriate.

Policy Targets. The differing views of monetarists and Keynesians clearly lead to different conclusions about which policy lever to pull.

Monetarist Advice: Target the Money Supply. The monetarists' policy advice to the Fed is straightforward. *Monetarists favor fixed money supply targets.* They believe that V is stable in the long run and unpredictable in the short run. Hence the safest course of action is to focus on M. All the Fed has to do is announce its intention to increase the money supply by some fixed amount (such as 3 percent per year), then use its central banking powers to hit that money growth target.

Continued

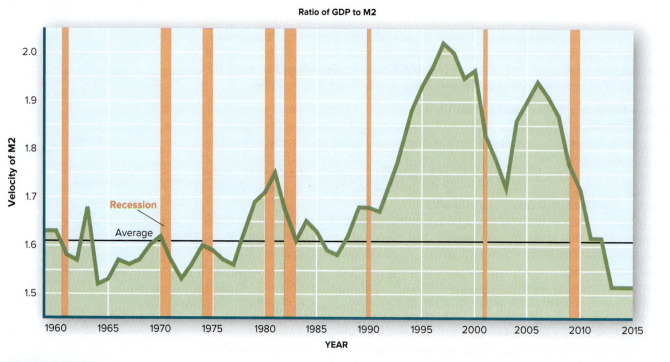

FIGURE 15.6

The Velocity of M2

The velocity of money (the ratio of GDP to M2) averages about 1.64. However, *V* appears to decline in recessions. Keynes urged the use of fiscal stimulus to boost *V*. Monetarists caution that short-run changes in *V* are too unpredictable.

Source: Federal Reserve Bank of St. Louis.

inflation targeting: The use of an inflation ceiling ("target") to signal the need for monetary-policy adjustments.

Interest Rate Targets. Keynesian Advice. *Keynesians reject fixed money supply targets,* favoring more flexibility in control of the money supply. In their view, a fixed money supply target would render monetary policy useless in combating cyclical swings of the economy. Keynesians prefer the risks of occasional policy errors to the straitjacket of a fixed money supply target. *Keynesians advocate targeting interest rates, not the money supply.* Keynesians also advocate liberal use of the fiscal policy lever.

Inflation Targeting. In the past, the Fed has tried both monetarist and Keynesian strategies for managing aggregate demand, depending on the needs of the economy and the convictions of the Fed chairman. The current chair, Janet Yellen, isn't committed to either the monetarist or Keynesian perspective. Instead she tries to walk a thin line between these perspectives. Like her predecessors, Yellen believes that price stability is the Fed's primary goal. The Fed's goal is to keep the inflation rate below the 2–3 percent range. If prices stay below that target, the Fed has typically put monetary policy on auto-pilot without worrying about constant adjustments of its policy tools.

What market participants like about this **inflation targeting** strategy is that it appears to offer greater predictability about whether and how the Fed will act. Critics point out, though, that *future* inflation, not *past* inflation, is the central policy concern. Because today's price movements may or may not be precursors of future inflation, the decision to pull monetary levers is still a judgment call.

Employment Targeting. Further complicating the Fed's task of fighting inflation is a second goal: full employment. It's not enough to keep prices from rising; we also want to create jobs and grow the economy. In the Great Recession of 2008–2009 inflation was a remote worry, but high unemployment was a huge problem. In response, the Fed decided to adopt **employment targeting** as a second component of its policy strategy. In December 2012, the Fed announced that its employment target was a 6.5 percent rate of unemployment. That meant the Fed would continue to inject the economy with monetary stimulus (open market purchases, quantitative easing, low discount rate) until the unemployment rate dropped below 6.5 percent unemployment.

The twin guidelines of inflation targeting and employment targeting appear to simplify monetary policy. If inflation exceeds 2–3 percent, step on the monetary brakes. If unemployment exceeds 6.5 percent, step on the monetary accelerator. In reality, policy decisions aren't that easy. As we have seen (e.g., Figure 11.4), inflation can accelerate long before full employment is reached. So inflation targeting and employment targeting may give conflicting signals about what policy to pursue.

Former Chairman Alan Greenspan recognized this when he said, "The Federal Reserve specializes in precision guesswork." As Fed Chair Yellen peers into the economy tomorrow, she will certainly need that same skill.

employment targeting: The use of an unemployment-rate threshold (6.5 percent) to signal the need for monetary stimulus.

SUMMARY

- The essence of monetary policy lies in the Federal Reserve's control over the money supply. By altering the money supply, the Fed can determine the amount of purchasing power available. **LO15-2**
- There are sharp disagreements about how monetary policy works. Keynesians argue that monetary policy works indirectly through its effects on interest rates and spending. Monetarists assert that monetary policy has more direct and more certain impacts, particularly on price levels. **LO15-4**
- In the Keynesian view, the demand for money is important. This demand reflects desires to hold money (in cash or bank balances) for transactions, precautionary, and speculative purposes. The interaction of money supply and money demand determines the equilibrium rate of interest. **LO15-1**
- From a Keynesian perspective, the impact of monetary policy on the economy occurs in three distinct steps: (1) changes in the money supply alter interest rates; (2) changes in interest rates alter spending plans; and (3) the change in desired spending alters (shifts) aggregate demand. **LO15-2**
- For Keynesian monetary policy to be fully effective, interest rates must be responsive to changes in the money supply, and spending must be responsive to changes in interest rates. Neither condition is assured. In a liquidity trap, people are willing to hold unlimited amounts of money at some low rate of interest. The interest rate won't fall below this level as the money supply increases. Also, investor expectations of sales and profits may override interest rate considerations in investment decisions. **LO15-3**
- Fed policy has the most direct impact on short-term interest rates, particularly the overnight federal funds rate.

Long-term rates are less responsive to open market operations. **LO15-3**
- The monetarist school emphasizes long-term linkages. Using the equation of exchange ($MV = PQ$) as a base, monetarists assert that the velocity of money (V) is stable, so that changes in M must influence ($P \times Q$). Monetarists focus on the money supply; Keynesians, on interest rates. **LO15-4**
- Some monetarists also argue that the level of real output (Q) is set by structural forces, as illustrated by the vertical, long-run aggregate supply curve. Q is therefore insensitive to changes in aggregate spending. If both V and Q are constant, changes in M directly affect P. **LO15-4**
- Monetary policy attempts to influence total expenditure by changing M and will be fully effective only if V is constant. Fiscal policy attempts to influence total expenditure by changing V and will be fully effective only if M doesn't change in the opposite direction. The controversy over the effectiveness of fiscal versus monetary policy depends on whether the velocity of money (V) is stable or instead is subject to policy influence. **LO15-4**
- The velocity of money is more stable over long periods of time than over short periods. Keynesians conclude that this makes fiscal policy more powerful in the short run. Monetarists conclude that the unpredictability of short-run velocity makes any short-run policy risky. **LO15-4**
- Inflation targeting signals monetary restraint when inflation rises above a policy-set ceiling ("target"), currently 2–3 percent. **LO15-2**
- Employment targeting signals the need for monetary stimulus when the unemployment rate is above 6.5 percent. **LO15-2**

Key Terms

monetary policy	speculative demand for money	natural rate of unemployment
interest rate	equilibrium rate of interest	real interest rate
money supply (M1, M2)	federal funds rate	crowding out
demand for money	aggregate demand (AD)	inflation targeting
portfolio decision	liquidity trap	employment targeting
transactions demand for money	equation of exchange	
precautionary demand for money	velocity of money (V)	

Questions for Discussion

1. What proportions of your money balance are held for transactions, precautionary, and speculative purposes? Can you think of any other purposes for holding money? **LO15-1**

2. How would people "adjust their portfolios" in Figure 15.1? **LO15-1**

3. Why do high interest rates so adversely affect the demand for housing and yet have so little influence on the demand for pizzas? **LO15-2**

4. If the Federal Reserve banks mailed everyone a brand-new $100 bill, what would happen to prices, output, and income? Illustrate your answer by using the equation of exchange. **LO15-2**

5. Can there be any inflation without an increase in the money supply? How? **LO15-4**

6. When prices started doubling (see In the News "'Not Worth a Continental': The U.S. Experience with Hyper-inflation"), why didn't the Continental Congress print even *more* money so Washington's army could continue to buy supplies? What brings an end to such "inflation financing"? **LO15-2**

7. Could long-term interest rates rise when short-term rates are falling? What would cause such a pattern? **LO15-3**

8. Why did the stock market "surge" when the Fed announced it intended to buy $1.2 trillion of bonds (see In the News "Fed to Expand Bond-Purchase Program")? **LO15-2**

9. When banks are reluctant to use their lending capacity as in 2012 what do they do with their increased reserves? **LO15-3**

10. If mortgage rates fell to 0 percent ("free money"), why might consumers still hesitate to borrow money to buy a home? **LO15-3**

11. What should the Fed do when prices are rising at a 3.5 percent rate and unemployment is at 7 percent? **LO15-2**

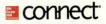

PROBLEMS FOR CHAPTER 15

LO15-1 1. In Table 15.1, what is the implied price of holding money in a checking account rather than investing in Treasury bonds?

LO15-2 2. Suppose home owners owe $8 trillion in mortgage loans.
   (a) If the mortgage interest rate is 5 percent, approximately how much are home owners paying in annual mortgage interest?
   (b) If the interest rate drops to 4 percent, by how much will annual interest payments decline?
   (c) How will this change in the interest rate impact aggregate demand?

LO15-2 3. According to Bernanke's policy guide, what is the fiscal policy equivalent of a 0.5 percent cut in long-term interest rates?

LO15-2 4. Illustrate the effects on investment of
   (a) An interest rate cut (point A).
   (b) An interest rate cut accompanied by decreased sales expectations (point B).

LO15-2 5. How much would the Fed have had to reduce long-term interest rates to get the same stimulus as President Trump's planned $300 billion fiscal stimulus?

LO15-4 6. Suppose that an economy is characterized by

$$M = \$12 \text{ trillion}$$
$$V = 1.8$$
$$P = 1.0$$

   (a) What is the real value of output (Q)?

Now assume that the Fed increases the money supply by 10 percent and velocity remains unchanged.
   (b) If the price level remains constant, by how much will real output increase?
   (c) If, instead, real output is fixed at the natural level of unemployment, by how much will prices rise?
   (d) By how much would V have to fall to offset the increase in M?

LO15-1 7. If the nominal rate of interest is 5 percent and the real rate of interest is 3 percent, what rate of inflation is anticipated?

LO15-2 8. Suppose the Fed decided to purchase $100 billion worth of government securities in the open market. What impact would this action have on the economy? Specifically, answer the following questions:
   (a) How will M1 be affected initially?
   (b) By how much will the banking system's lending capacity increase if the reserve requirement is 20 percent?
   (c) Must interest rates rise or fall to induce investors to utilize this expanded lending capacity?
   (d) By how much will aggregate demand increase if investors borrow and spend all the newly available credit?
   (e) Under what circumstances (A = "recession" or B = "inflation") would the Fed be pursuing such an open market policy?
   (f) To attain those same objectives, what should the Fed do (A = "increase" or B = "decrease") with the
      (i) Discount rate?
      (ii) Reserve requirement?

LO15-3 9. The following data describe market conditions:

Money supply (in billions)	$100	$200	$300	$400	$ 500	$ 600	$ 700
Interest rate	8.0	7.5	7.0	6.5	6.0	5.5	5.5
Rate of investment (in billions)	$ 12	$ 12	$ 15	$ 16	$16.5	$16.5	$16.5

(a) At what rate of interest does the liquidity trap emerge?
(b) At what rate of interest does investment demand become totally inelastic?

LO15-3 10. Use the accompanying graphs to show what happens in the economy when *M* increases from $300 billion to $400 billion.
(a) Show the change in *M* on the first graph.
(b) Identify the change in interest rate on the second graph.
(c) If the multiplier is 1.5, show the cumulative effect of this change in *M* on *AD* in the third graph.

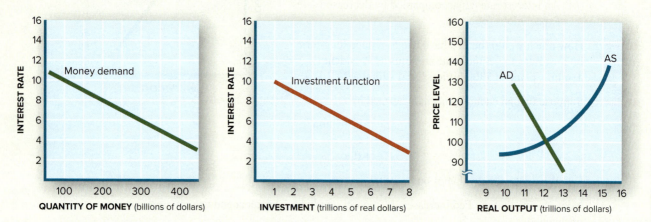

LO15-3 11. According to Figure 15.6, the velocity of money declined from 1.90 in 2008 to 1.50 in 2015. By what percent would *M* have to increase in order to offset fully this decline in *V*?

LO15-4 12. The Economy Tomorrow: Match the statement with either a Monetarist or Keynesian perspective.
(a) The interest rate should be targeted, not the money supply.
(b) A slowdown in spending implies a reduction in the velocity of money.
(c) There should be fixed money supply targets.

PART

©Comstock/Stockbyte/Getty Images RF

©Ingram Publishing RF

SUPPLY-SIDE OPTIONS

Fiscal and monetary policies attempt to alter macro outcomes by managing aggregate demand. Supply-side policies focus instead on possibilities for shifting the aggregate *supply* curve. In the short run, any increase in aggregate supply promotes more output and less inflation. Supply-siders also emphasize how rightward shifts of aggregate supply are critical to long-run economic growth. Chapter 16 focuses on short-run supply-side options; Chapter 17 takes the long-run view.

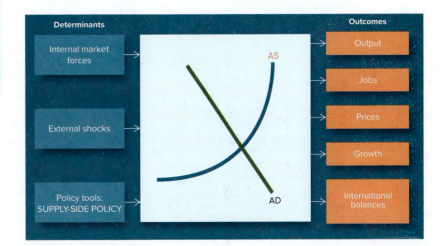

337

©Comstock/Stockbyte/Getty Images RF

16.

Supply-Side Policy: Short-Run Options

Fiscal and monetary policies focus on the *demand* side of the macro economy. The basic premise of both approaches is that macro goals can be achieved by shifting the aggregate demand curve to a desirable macro equilibrium. The aggregate demand curve isn't the only game in town, however; there's an aggregate supply curve as well. Why not focus instead on possibilities for shifting the aggregate *supply* curve?

Any policies that alter the willingness or ability to supply goods at various price levels will shift the aggregate supply curve. This chapter identifies some of those policy options and examines how they affect macro outcomes. The focus is on two questions:

- **How does the aggregate supply curve affect macro outcomes?**
- **How can the aggregate supply curve be shifted?**

As we'll see, the aggregate supply curve plays a critical role in determining how difficult it is to achieve the goals of full employment and price stability.

AGGREGATE SUPPLY

The impetus for examining the supply side of the macro economy sprang up in the stagflation of the 1970s. **Stagflation** occurs when both unemployment *and* inflation increase at the same time. From 1973 to 1974, for example, consumer price inflation surged from 8.7 to 12.3 percent. At the same time, the unemployment rate jumped from 4.9 to 5.6 percent. How could this happen? *No shift of the aggregate demand curve can increase inflation and unemployment at the same time.* If aggregate demand increases (shifts right), the price level may rise, but unemployment should decline with increased output. If aggregate demand decreases (shifts left), inflation should subside, but unemployment should increase. In other words, demand-side theories predict that inflation and unemployment move in *opposite* directions in the short run. When this didn't happen, an alternative explanation was sought. The explanation was found on the supply side of the macro economy. Two critical clues were (1) the shape of the **aggregate supply** curve and (2) potential AS shifts.

LEARNING OBJECTIVES

After reading this chapter, you should know

LO16-1 Why the short-run AS curve slopes upward.

LO16-2 How an unemployment–inflation trade-off arises.

LO16-3 How shifts of the aggregate supply curve affect macro outcomes

LO16-4 The tools of supply-side policy.

stagflation: The simultaneous occurrence of substantial unemployment and inflation.

aggregate supply (AS): The total quantity of output (real GDP) producers are willing and able to supply at alternative price levels in a given time period, *ceteris paribus.*

SHAPE OF THE AS CURVE

As we've seen, the basic short-run objective of fiscal and monetary policy is to attain full employment and price stability. The strategy is to shift the aggregate demand curve to a more favorable position. Now the question turns to the *response* of producers to an aggregate demand shift. Will they increase real output? Raise prices? Or some combination of both?

The answer is reflected in the shape of the aggregate supply curve: ***The response of producers to an AD shift is expressed in the slope and position of the aggregate supply curve.*** Until now we've used a generally upward-sloping AS curve to depict aggregate supply. Now we'll consider a range of different supply responses.

Three Views of AS

Figure 16.1 illustrates three very different supply behaviors.

Keynesian AS. Part (*a*) depicts what we earlier called the "naive" Keynesian view. Recall that Keynes was primarily concerned with the problem of unemployment. He didn't think there was much risk of inflation in the depths of a recession. He expected producers to increase output, not prices, when aggregate demand expanded. This expectation is illustrated by a *horizontal* AS curve. When fiscal or monetary stimulus shifts the AD curve rightward (e.g., AD_1 to AD_2 in Figure 16.1*a*), output (Q) rises but not the price level (P). Only when capacity (Q_*) is reached do prices start rising abruptly (AD_2 to AD_3).

Monetarist AS. The monetarist view of supply behavior is very different. In the most extreme monetarist view, real output remains at its "natural" rate, regardless of fiscal or monetary interventions. Rising prices don't entice producers to increase output because costs are likely to rise just as fast. They instead make output decisions based on more fundamental factors like technology and market size. The monetarist AS curve is *vertical* because output doesn't respond to changing price levels. (This is the long-run AS curve we first encountered in Chapter 8.) With a vertical AS curve, only prices can respond to a shift in aggregate demand. In Figure 16.1*b*, the AS curve is anchored at the natural rate of unemployment Q_N. When aggregate demand increases from AD_4 to AD_5, the price level (P) rises, but output (Q) is unchanged.

Hybrid AS. Figure 16.1*c* blends these Keynesian and monetarist perspectives into a hybrid AS curve. At low rates of output, the curve is nearly horizontal; at high rates of output, the AS curve becomes nearly vertical. In the broad middle of the AS curve, the curve slopes gently upward. In this area, shifts of aggregate demand affect *both* prices and output. The message of this hybrid AS curve is that the outcomes of fiscal and monetary policy depend on how close the economy is to full employment. ***The closer we are to capacity, the greater the risk that fiscal or monetary stimulus will spill over into price inflation.***

The Inflation–Unemployment Trade-Off

Because Figure 16.1*c* allows for varying output and price responses at different levels of economic activity, that hybrid AS curve is regarded as the most realistic for short-run outcomes. The reality it depicts, however, has some disturbing implications. If the AS curve slopes upward, then both prices and output increase when aggregate demand increases. This is not a good thing: the upward slope of the AS curve implies that we can't reduce both unemployment and inflation at the same time—at least not with fiscal and monetary policies. To see why this is the case, consider the simple geometry of policy stimulus and restraint.

Demand Stimulus. Successful monetary and fiscal stimulus will shift the aggregate demand curve rightward. This demand-side effect is illustrated by the AD_6 and AD_7 curves in

The effectiveness of fiscal and monetary policy depends on the shape of the AS curve. Some possibilities include these:

(a) Keynesian AS In the simple Keynesian model, the rate of output responds fully and automatically to increases in demand until full employment (Q^*) is reached. If demand increases from AD_1 to AD_2, equilibrium GDP will expand from Q_1 to Q^*, without any inflation. Inflation becomes a problem only if demand increases beyond capacity—to AD_3, for example.

(b) Monetarist AS Monetarists assert that changes in the money supply affect prices but not output. They regard aggregate supply as a fixed quantum, at the long-run, natural rate of unemployment (here noted as Q_N). Accordingly, a shift of demand (from AD_4 to AD_5) can affect only the price level (from P_4 to P_5).

(c) Hybrid AS The consensus view incorporates Keynesian and monetarist perspectives but emphasizes the upward slope that dominates the middle of the AS curve. When demand increases, both price levels and the rate of output increase. Hence the slope and position of the AS curve limit the effectiveness of fiscal and monetary policies.

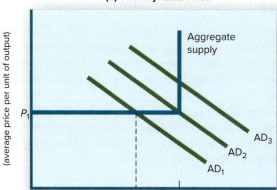

(a) The Keynesian view

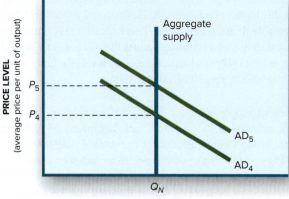

(b) The monetarist view

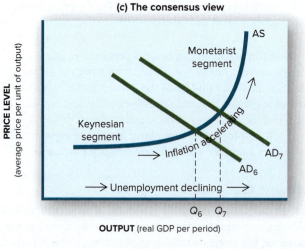

(c) The consensus view

Figure 16.1c. Output increases (from Q_6 to Q_7), but the price level increases as well. This is not what we want. Unfortunately, ***all rightward shifts of the aggregate demand curve increase both prices and output if the aggregate supply curve is upward-sloping.*** This implies that fiscal and monetary efforts to reduce unemployment will also cause some inflation. How much inflation occurs depends on the slope of the AS curve.

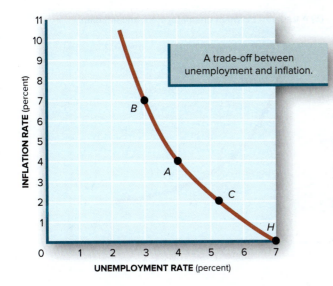

A trade-off between unemployment and inflation.

FIGURE 16.2

The Phillips Curve

The Phillips curve illustrates a trade-off between full employment and price stability. In the 1960s it appeared that efforts to reduce unemployment rates below 5.5 percent (point C) led to increasing rates of inflation (points *A* and *B*). Inflation threatened to reach unacceptable levels long before everyone was employed.

Demand Restraint. We have a similar dilemma with policy restraint. Monetary and fiscal restraint shift the aggregate demand curve leftward. *If the aggregate supply curve is upward-sloping, leftward shifts of the aggregate demand curve cause both prices and output to fall.* Therefore, fiscal and monetary efforts to reduce inflation will also increase unemployment. How much unemployment increases depends again on the slope of the AS curve.

The Phillips Curve. The message of the upward-sloping aggregate supply curve is clear: *Demand-side policies alone can never succeed completely; they'll always cause some unwanted inflation or unemployment.*

Our macro track record provides ample evidence of this dilemma. Consider, for example, our experience with unemployment and inflation during the 1960s, as shown in Figure 16.2. This figure shows a **Phillips curve,** an inverse relationship between inflation and unemployment. Consider point *H* in the graph. At *H*, we have 7 percent unemployment but no inflation. Our goal is to reduce unemployment. As we reduce unemployment from 7 percent to 5 percent, however, prices start rising. We end up at point *C*, with lower unemployment but higher inflation. If we succeed in reducing unemployment further, inflation will accelerate (e.g., points *A* and *B*).

The Phillips curve was developed by a New Zealand economist, Alban W. Phillips, to summarize the relationship between unemployment and inflation in England for the years 1826–1957.[1] The Phillips curve was raised from the status of an obscure graph to that of a policy issue by the discovery that the same kind of relationship apparently existed in other countries and at other times. Paul Samuelson and Robert Solow of the Massachusetts Institute of Technology were among the first to observe that the Phillips curve was a reasonable description of U.S. economic performance for the years 1900–1960. A seesaw kind of relationship existed between inflation and unemployment: when one went up, the other fell.

The trade-off between unemployment and inflation originates in the upward-sloping AS curve. Figure 16.3a illustrates this point. Suppose the economy is initially at equilibrium *A,* with fairly stable prices but low output. When aggregate demand expands to AD_2, prices rise along with output, so we end up at point *B* with higher inflation but less unemployment. This is also shown in Figure 16.3b by the move from point *a* to point *b* on the Phillips curve. The move from point *a* to point *b* indicates a decline in unemployment (more output) but an increase in inflation (higher price level). If demand is increased further, to AD_3, a still lower unemployment rate is achieved but at the cost of higher inflation (point *c*).

Phillips curve: A historical (inverse) relationship between the rate of unemployment and the rate of inflation; commonly expresses a trade-off between the two.

[1]A. W. Phillips. "The Relationship between Unemployment and the Rate of Change of Money Wage Rates in the United Kingdom, 1826–1957," *Economica* (November 1958). Phillips's paper studied the relationship between unemployment and *wage* changes rather than *price* changes; most later formulations (and public policy) focus on prices.

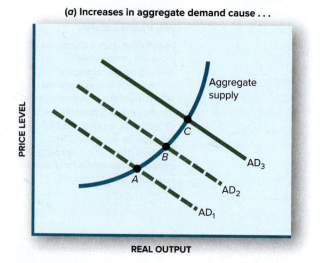

(a) Increases in aggregate demand cause . . .

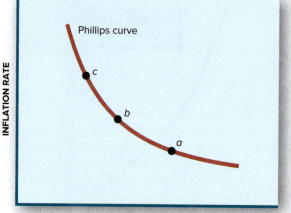

(b) A trade-off between unemployment and inflation.

FIGURE 16.3

The Phillips Curve Trade-off

If the aggregate supply curve slopes upward, increases in aggregate demand always cause both prices and output to rise. Thus higher inflation becomes a cost of achieving lower unemployment. In (*a*), increased demand moves the economy

from point *A* to point *B*. At *B*, unemployment is lower, but prices are higher. This trade-off is illustrated on the Phillips curve in (*b*). Each point on the Phillips curve represents a different AS/AD equilibrium from the graph on the left.

The Inflationary Flashpoint. The Phillips curve reminds us that there is bound to be a trade-off between unemployment and inflation at some point in economic expansions and contractions. But is there a *specific* point at which the trade-off becomes particularly worrisome? With the Keynesian AS curve (Figure 16.1*a*) there is *no* trade-off until full employment (Q^*) is reached, then inflation rockets upwards. Hence the output level Q^* represents the **inflationary flashpoint**—the point at which inflationary pressures intensify—on the Keynesian AS curve.

The hybrid AS curve in Figure 16.1*a* doesn't have such a sharp flashpoint. The slope of the curve seems pretty smooth. In fact, however, inflationary pressures could bubble up as the economy expands. If that were to happen, the AS curve wouldn't be quite so smooth. Instead, at some rate of output, the slope of the AS curve would turn up sharply, as in Figure 16.4. That inflationary flashpoint represents the rate of output at which inflation begins to accelerate significantly. It is a point policymakers want to avoid.

inflationary flashpoint: The rate of output at which inflationary pressures intensify; the point on the AS curve where slope increases sharply.

FIGURE 16.4

The Inflationary Flashpoint

As the economy approaches capacity, inflationary pressures intensify. The point at which inflation noticeably accelerates is the "inflationary flashpoint"—a juncture policymakers want to avoid.

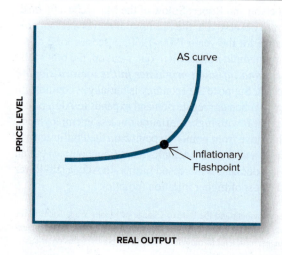

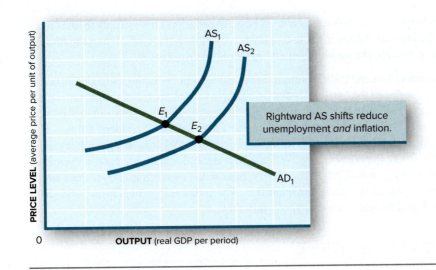

FIGURE 16.5

Shifts of Aggregate Supply

A rightward AS shift (AS_1 to AS_2) reduces both unemployment and inflation. A leftward shift has the opposite effect, creating stagflation.

SHIFTS OF THE AS CURVE

The unemployment–inflation trade-off implied by the upward-sloping AS curve is not etched in stone. Nor is the inflationary flashpoint unmovable. Many economists argue that the economy can attain lower levels of unemployment *without* higher inflation. This certainly appeared to be the case in the 1990s: unemployment rates fell sharply from 1992 to 2000 and again from 2002 to 2008 without any increase in inflation. How could this have happened? There's no AD shift in any part of Figure 16.3 that would reduce both unemployment *and* inflation.

Rightward AS Shifts: All Good News

Only a rightward shift of the AS curve can reduce unemployment and inflation at the same time. When aggregate supply increases from AS_1 to AS_2 in Figure 16.5, macro equilibrium moves from E_1 to E_2. At E_2 real output is higher, so the unemployment rate must be lower. At E_2 the price level is also lower, indicating reduced inflation. Hence a rightward shift of the AS curve offers the best of two worlds—something aggregate *demand* shifts (Figure 16.1) can't do.

Phillips Curve Shift. As we saw in Figure 16.3, the Phillips curve is a direct by-product of the AS curve. Accordingly, *when the AS curve shifts, the Phillips curve shifts as well.* As Figure 16.6 illustrates, the Phillips curve shifts to the left, the opposite of the AS shift in

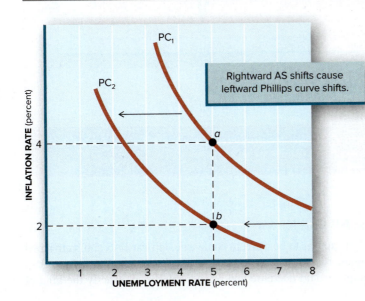

FIGURE 16.6

A Phillips Curve Shift

If the Phillips curve shifts leftward, the short-run unemployment–inflation trade-off eases. With PC_1, 5 percent unemployment ignites 4 percent inflation (point *a*). With PC_2, 5 percent unemployment causes only 2 percent inflation (point *b*).

misery index: The sum of
inflation and unemployment
rates.

Figure 16.5. No new information is conveyed here. The Phillips curve simply focuses more directly on the implied change in the unemployment–inflation trade-off. *When the Phillips curve shifts to the left, the unemployment–inflation trade-off eases.*

The Misery Index. To keep track of simultaneous changes in unemployment and inflation, Arthur Okun developed the "**misery index**"—a simple sum of the inflation and unemployment rates. As In the News "The Misery Index" illustrates, macro misery diminished substantially during the first Reagan administration (1981–1984). President Clinton also benefited from a leftward shift of the Phillips curve through 1998 but saw the misery index climb in 1999–2000. President George W. Bush experienced a sharp increase in the misery index during the recession of 2001. The misery index didn't recede until 2004, when strong output growth reduced the unemployment rate. The index jumped again in 2008–2011 when the high jobless rate made everybody miserable.

IN THE NEWS

THE MISERY INDEX

Unemployment is a problem, and so is inflation. Being burdened with both problems at the same time is real misery.

The late Arthur Okun proposed measuring the extent of misery by adding together the inflation and unemployment rates. He called the sum of the two rates the "discomfort index." Political pundits quickly renamed it the "misery index."

In essence, the misery index is a measure of stagflation—the simultaneous occurrence of inflation and unemployment. In 1980 the misery index peaked at 19.6 percent as a result of high inflation (12.5 percent) as well as high unemployment (7.1 percent). Stagflation—and the misery it causes—has since receded markedly.

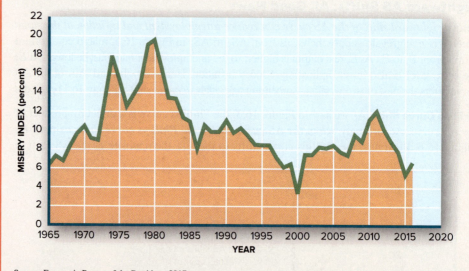

Source: Economic Report of the President, 2017.

ANALYSIS: Stagflation refers to the simultaneous occurrence of inflation and unemployment. The "misery index" combines both problems into a single measure of macro performance.

Leftward AS Shifts: All Bad News

Whereas rightward AS shifts appear to be a dream come true, leftward AS shifts are a real nightmare. Imagine in Figure 16.5 that the AS shift is reversed—that is, from AS_2 to AS_1. What would happen? Output would decrease and prices would rise, exactly the kind of dilemma depicted in the cartoon to the right. In other words, nothing would go in the right direction. This would be rampant stagflation.

A natural disaster can trigger a leftward shift of the AS curve, especially in smaller nations. When a tsunami washed over nations in the Indian Ocean in December 2004, more than 200,000 people were killed. In Sri Lanka, 80 percent of the fishing fleet was destroyed, along with port facilities, railroads, highways, and communications systems. The huge loss of human and physical capital reduced Sri Lanka's production possibilities. This was reflected in a leftward shift of the AS curve. The same kind of devastation hit Japan in 2011, reducing that nation's potential output and intensifying inflationary pressures (see World View "Japan Sees Quake Damage Bill of Up to $309 Billion, Almost Four Katrinas").

WORLD VIEW

JAPAN SEES QUAKE DAMAGE BILL OF UP TO $309 BILLION, ALMOST FOUR KATRINAS

Japan's government estimated the damage from this month's record earthquake and tsunami at as much as 25 trillion yen ($309 billion), an amount almost four times the hit imposed by Hurricane Katrina on the U.S.

The destruction will push down gross domestic product by as much as 2.75 trillion yen for the year starting April 1. The figure, about 0.5 percent of the

©JIJI PRESS/AFP/Getty Images

530 trillion yen economy, reflects a decline in production from supply disruptions and damage to corporate facilities without taking into account the effects of possible power outages.

The figures are the first gauge of the scale of rebuilding Prime Minister Naoto Kan's government will face after the quake killed more than 9,000 people. . .

"The ability to depress economic activity from the supply side is larger than the Great Kobe earthquake and we must bear in mind that these effects could linger for some time," [Bank of Japan board member Ryuzo Miyao] said in a speech in Oita, southern Japan. . . .

—Keiko Ujikrane

Ujikrane, Keiko, "Japan Sees Quake Damage Bill of Up to $309 Billion, Almost Four Katrinas," *Bloomberg News*, March 23, 2011. Copyright ©2011. All rights reserved. Used with permission.

ANALYSIS: A natural disaster destroys production facilities, transportation routes, power sources, and people, causing a leftward shift of the AS curve.

In an economy as large as that of the United States, leftward shifts of aggregate supply are less dramatic. But Mother Nature can still push the AS curve around. Hurricanes Katrina and Rita, for example, destroyed vast amounts of production, transportation, and communications infrastructure in August 2005. Hurricane Mathew did similar damage to the supply side of the economy in October 2016. Hurricane Harvey was even more destructive when it struck Texas in August 2017. Roads were flooded, power supplies were shut down, oil refineries were closed, and all deliveries to the Houston area were suspended. Factories were closed and people had no way to get to work. The resulting delays and cost increases were reflected in another leftward shift of the AS curve.

The September 11, 2001, terrorist attacks on the World Trade Center and Pentagon were another form of external shock. The attacks directly destroyed some production capacity (office space, telecommunications links, and transportation links). But they took an even greater toll on the *willingness* to supply goods and services. In the aftermath of the attacks businesses, perceiving new risks to investment and production, held back from making new commitments. Increased security measures also made transporting goods more expensive. All of these responses shifted the AS curve leftward and the Phillips curve rightward, adding to macro misery.

Policy Tools

From the supply side of macro markets, the appropriate response to negative external shocks is clear: shift the AS curve rightward. As the foregoing graphs have demonstrated, *rightward shifts of the aggregate supply curve always generate desirable macro outcomes.* The next question, of course, is how to shift the aggregate supply curve in the desired (rightward) direction. Supply-side economists look for clues among the forces that influence the supply-side response to changes in demand. Among those forces, the following policy options for shifting the AS curve rightward have been emphasized:

- Tax incentives for saving, investment, and work.
- Human capital investment.
- Deregulation.
- Trade liberalization.
- Infrastructure development.

All these policies have the potential to change supply decisions *independently* of any changes in aggregate demand. If they're effective, they'll result in a rightward shift of the AS curve and an *improved* trade-off between unemployment and inflation.

TAX INCENTIVES

The most renowned supply-side policy option for improving the unemployment–inflation trade-off was the "supply-side" tax cuts of the early 1980s. Tax cuts are of course a staple of Keynesian economics. But tax cuts take on a whole new role on the supply side of the economy. *In Keynesian economics, tax cuts are used to increase aggregate demand.* By putting more disposable income in the hands of consumers, Keynesian economists seek to increase expenditure on goods and services. Output is expected to increase in response. From a Keynesian perspective, the form of the tax cut is not important as long as disposable income increases.

The supply side of the economy encourages a different view of taxes. *Taxes not only alter disposable income but also change incentives to work and produce.* High tax rates destroy incentives to work and produce, so they end up reducing total output. Low tax rates, by contrast, allow people to keep more of what they earn and so stimulate greater output. *The direct effects of taxes on the supply of goods are the concern of supply-side economists.* Figure 16.7 shows the difference between demand-side and supply-side perspectives on tax policy.

Marginal Tax Rates

marginal tax rate: The tax rate imposed on the last (marginal) dollar of income.

Supply-side theory places special emphasis on *marginal* tax rates. The **marginal tax rate** is the tax rate imposed on the last (marginal) dollar of income received. In our progressive income tax system, marginal tax rates increase as more income is received. Uncle Sam takes a larger share out of each additional dollar earned. In 2016, the highest marginal tax rate on personal income was 39.6 percent. That top tax rate was far below the 91 percent rate that existed in 1944, but it was also a lot higher than the 12 percent tax rate imposed in 1914 (see Figure 16.8).

In view of the wild history of tax rates, one might wonder whether the rate selected matters. Specifically, does the marginal tax rate affect supply decisions? Will people work and invest as much when the marginal tax rate is 91 percent as when it is only 12 percent? Doesn't seem likely, does it?

Labor Supply. The marginal tax rate directly changes the financial incentive to *increase* one's work. *If the marginal tax rate is high, there's less incentive to work more*—Uncle Sam will get most of the added income. Confronted with high marginal tax rates, workers may choose to stay home rather than work an extra shift. Families may decide that it doesn't pay to send both parents into the labor market. When marginal tax rates are low, by contrast, those extra work activities generate bigger increases in disposable income.

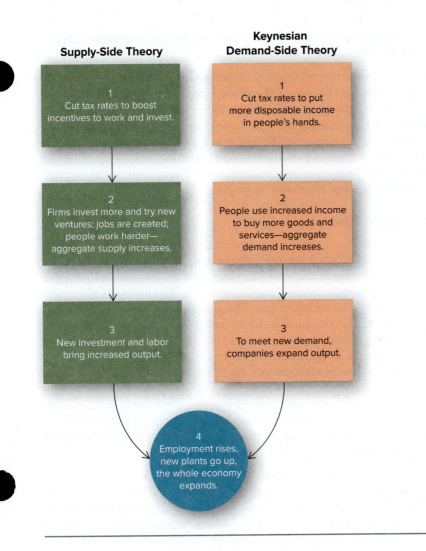

Supply-Side Theory

1
Cut tax rates to boost incentives to work and invest.

2
Firms invest more and try new ventures; jobs are created; people work harder—aggregate supply increases.

3
New investment and labor bring increased output.

Keynesian Demand-Side Theory

1
Cut tax rates to put more disposable income in people's hands.

2
People use increased income to buy more goods and services—aggregate demand increases.

3
To meet new demand, companies expand output.

4
Employment rises, new plants go up, the whole economy expands.

FIGURE 16.7

Two Theories for Getting the Economy Moving

Keynesians and supply-siders both advocate cutting taxes to reduce unemployment. But they have very different views on the kind of tax cuts required and the impact of any cuts enacted.

Entrepreneurship. Marginal tax rates affect not only labor supply decisions but also decisions on whether to start or expand a business. Most small businesses are organized as sole proprietorships or partnerships and are subject to *personal,* not *corporate,* tax rates. Hence a decline in personal tax rates will affect the risk–reward balance for potential entrepreneurs. Columbia Business School professors William Gentry and Glenn Huber have demonstrated that progressive marginal tax rates discourage entry into self-employment. Syracuse professor Douglas Holtz-Eakin and Princeton economist Harvey Rosen have shown that the

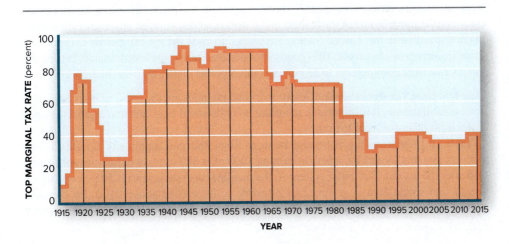

FIGURE 16.8

Changes in Marginal Tax Rates since 1915

The top marginal tax rate on personal income has varied from a low of 12 percent in 1914 to a high of 91 percent in 1944. Supply-side theory emphasizes how these varying tax rates affect work, investment, and production decisions—that is, aggregate supply.

growth rate, investment, and employment of small businesses are also affected by marginal tax rates. As Holtz-Eakin concluded, "Taxes matter."

Investment. Taxes matter for corporations too. Corporate entities account for nearly 90 percent of business output and 84 percent of business assets. Like small proprietorships, corporations, too, are motivated by *after*-tax profits. Hence corporate **investment** decisions will be affected by corporate tax rates. If Uncle Sam imposes a high tax rate on corporate profits, the payoff to investors will be diminished. Potential investors may decide to consume their income or to purchase tax-free bonds rather than invest in plants and equipment. If that happens, total investment will decline and output will suffer. Accordingly, *if high tax rates discourage investment, aggregate supply will be constrained.*

Tax-Induced Supply Shifts

If tax rates affect supply decisions, then *changes* in tax rates will shift aggregate supply. Specifically, supply-siders conclude that *a reduction in marginal tax rates will shift the aggregate supply curve to the right.* The increased supply will come in three forms: more work effort, more entrepreneurship, and more capital investment. This increased willingness to produce will reduce the rate of unemployment. The additional output will also help reduce inflationary pressures. Thus we end up with less unemployment *and* less inflation.

From a supply-side perspective, the form of the tax cut is critical. For example, **tax rebates** are a one-time windfall to consumers and have no effect on marginal tax rates. As a consequence, disposable income rises, but not the incentives for work or production. Rebates directly affect only the demand side of the economy.

To stimulate aggregate *supply,* tax *rates* must be reduced, particularly at the margin. These cuts can take the form of reductions in personal income tax rates or reductions in the marginal tax rates imposed on businesses. In either case, the lower tax rates will give people a greater incentive to work, invest, and produce.

Reagan Tax Cuts. No one understood the supply-side impact of tax rates better than Ronald Reagan. When he was working as an actor during World War II, he had to pay the highest marginal tax rate then in effect—a whopping 91 percent! He vowed that he would cut tax rates dramatically when he became president. And he did: he convinced Congress to cut the top rate on personal taxes from 71 percent in 1981 to a low of 28 percent in 1988. He also cut the top rate on corporate income from 46 percent to 34 percent.

Post-Reagan Rate Changes. The top tax rate on individuals didn't stay at 28 percent for long. President George H.W. Bush agreed with a Democrat-controlled Congress to increase the top rate to 31 percent in 1991. President Clinton raised it even higher—to 39.6 percent in 1993. George W. Bush succeeded in pushing the rate down to 35 percent during his presidency, but President Obama took it back to 39.6 percent in 2012. The top corporate tax rate stayed at 35 percent throughout these years.

Trump Proposals. Donald Trump was convinced that high tax rates on individuals and businesses were a serious drag on U.S. economic growth. He emphasized that the 35 percent corporate tax rate was one of the highest in the world and discouraged businesses from starting or expanding in the United States. He wanted to chop the top tax rate on corporations from 35 percent to 15 percent. His proposal for personal taxes was less dramatic, cutting the top tax rate from 39.6 percent to 33 percent (still 5 points higher than the Reagan low).

How Marginal Tax Rates Work. Clearly, marginal tax rates are the focus of both economic and political debate. It is important, therefore, to understand how cuts in marginal tax rates differ from other forms of tax cuts.

Table 16.1 illustrates the distinction between Keynesian and supply-side tax cuts. Under both tax systems (A and B), a person earning $200 pays $80 in taxes before the tax cut and $60 after the tax cut. But under system A, the marginal tax rate is always 50 percent, which means that Uncle Sam is getting half of every dollar earned above $100. By contrast, system B imposes a marginal tax rate of only 30 percent—$0.30 of every dollar above

investment: Expenditures on (production of) new plants, equipment, and structures (capital) in a given time period, plus changes in business inventories.

tax rebate: A lump-sum refund of taxes paid.

TABLE 16.1

Supply Side: Focus on
Marginal Tax Rates

Initial Alternatives					
Tax System	Initial Tax Schedule	Tax on Income of $200	Tax Rate Average	Tax Rate Marginal	Disposable Income
A	$30 + 50% of income over $100	$80	40%	50%	$120
B	$50 + 30% of income over $100	$80	40%	30%	$120

The same amount of taxes can be raised via two very different systems. Here a person earning $200 pays $80 in taxes under either system (A or B). Thus the *average* tax rate (total tax ÷ total income) is the same in both cases ($80 ÷ $200 = 40%). The *marginal* tax rates are very different, however. System A has a high marginal rate (50%), whereas system B has a low marginal tax rate (30%). System B provides a greater incentive for people to earn over $100.

Alternative Forms of Tax Cut					
Tax System	Initial Tax Schedule	Tax on Income of $200	Tax Rate Average	Tax Rate Marginal	Disposable Income
A	$10 + 50% of income over $100	$60	30%	50%	$140
B	$30 + 30% of income over $100	$60	30%	30%	$140

The average tax rate could be cut to 30 percent under either system. Under both systems, the revised tax would be $60 and disposable income would be increased to $140. Keynesians would be happy with either form of tax cut. But supply-siders would favor system B because the lower marginal tax rate gives people more incentive to earn higher incomes.

$100 goes to the government. Under system B, people have a greater incentive to earn *more* than $100. Although both systems raise the same amount of taxes, system B offers greater incentives to work extra hours and produce more output.

Tax Elasticity of Supply

All economists agree that tax rates influence people's decisions to work, invest, and produce. But the policy-relevant question is, *how much* influence do taxes have? Do reductions in the marginal tax rate shift the aggregate supply curve far to the right? Or are the resultant shifts quite small?

The response of labor and capital to a change in tax rates is summarized by the **tax elasticity of supply.** Like other elasticities, this one measures the proportional response of supplies to a change in price (in this case a tax *rate*). Specifically, the tax elasticity of supply is the percentage change in quantity supplied divided by the percentage in tax rates; that is,

$$\text{Tax elasticity of supply} = \frac{\text{\% change in quantity supplied}}{\text{\% change in tax rate}}$$

Normally we expect quantity supplied to go up when tax rates go down. Elasticity (E) is therefore negative, although it's usually expressed in absolute terms (without the minus sign). The (absolute) value of E must be greater than zero since we expect *some* response to a tax cut. That means that *tax cuts—especially cuts in marginal tax rates—will shift the AS curve to the right.* The policy issue boils down to the question of how large E actually is—how far AS will shift.

If the tax elasticity of supply were large enough, a tax cut might not only shift the AS curve but actually *increase* tax revenues. Suppose the tax elasticity were equal to 1.5. In that case a tax cut of 10 percent would cause output supplied to increase by 15 percent

tax elasticity of supply: The percentage change in quantity supplied divided by the percentage change in tax rates.

(= 1.5 × 10%). Such a large increase in the tax base (income) would result in *more* taxes being paid even though the tax *rate* was reduced. One of President Reagan's economic advisers, Arthur Laffer, actually thought such an outcome was possible. He predicted that tax revenues would *increase* after the Reagan supply-side tax cuts were made. In reality, the tax elasticity of supply turned out to be much smaller (around 0.15), and tax revenues fell substantially. The aggregate supply curve *did* shift to the right, but not very far, when marginal tax rates were cut.

The evidently low tax elasticity of supply helped President Clinton convince Congress to *increase* marginal tax rates in 1993. Although opponents objected that higher tax rates would reduce work and investment, the Clinton administration pointed out that any left-ward shift of aggregate supply was likely to be small. President George W. Bush reversed that shift with the 2001–2004 marginal tax rate cuts. According to a 2006 study by the Congressional Research Service, those tax rate cuts elicited a 0.20 tax elasticity of supply. In 2012, the Congressional Budget Office said the tax elasticity of supply might be higher still—at 0.27. Tax elasticities in that range underscore the significant potential of supply-side tax cuts to shift the aggregate supply curve and alter macroeconomic outcomes.

Savings Incentives

Supply-side economists emphasize the importance of *long-run* responses to changed tax incentives. On the demand side, an increase in income translates very quickly into in-creased spending. On the supply side, things don't happen so fast. It takes time to construct new plants and equipment. People are also slow to respond to new work and investment incentives. Hence the full benefits of supply-side tax cuts—or the damage done by tax hikes—won't be immediately visible.

saving: That part of disposable income not spent on current consumption; disposable income less consumption.

Of particular concern to supply-side economists is the rate of saving in the economy. Demand-side economists emphasize spending and tend to treat **saving** as a leakage prob-lem. Supply-siders, by contrast, emphasize the importance of saving for financing invest-ment and economic growth. At full employment, a greater volume of investment is possible only if the rate of consumption is cut back. In other words, additional investment requires additional saving. Hence *supply-side economists favor tax incentives that encourage saving as well as greater tax incentives for investment.* This kind of perspective contrasts sharply with the Keynesian emphasis on stimulating consumption.

Investment Incentives

capital gains tax: A tax levied on the profit from the sale of property.

An alternative lever for shifting aggregate supply is to offer tax incentives for investment. The 1981 tax cuts focused on *personal* income tax rates. By contrast, President George H. Bush advocated cutting capital gains taxes. A **capital gains tax** is a tax levied on the increase in the value of property, such as land, buildings, and corporate stock, when it's sold. It is different from the *income* taxes levied on the current incomes of individuals and businesses. The capital gains tax applies only when a piece of property (a building, shares of stock, gold, a house, a business, etc.) are sold. If the sales price exceeds the purchase price, then a capital gain exists. That gain is the focus of this tax.

The capital gains tax influences people's decision to start a business, to invest in corpo-rate stocks, or renovate homes, develop land, or make other investments. If the tax rate is low, then the anticipated after-tax profit will be higher. By contrast, higher capital gains tax rates make investment less profitable.

President Clinton's very first proposal for stimulating the economy was a temporary investment tax credit. Shortly thereafter, Congress cut the capital gains tax rate from 28 percent to 20 percent. President George Bush pushed the tax rate still lower, to 15 per-cent in 2003. During the 2008 campaign, Barack Obama vowed to reverse the Bush "tax cuts for the rich" by *raising* marginal income tax rates as well as capital gains and inheri-tance taxes. The Taxpayer Relief Act of 2012 pushed the capital gains tax rate back up to 20 percent while increasing personal and business income tax rates as well. These tax hikes reduced supply-side incentives.

HUMAN CAPITAL INVESTMENT

A nation's ability to supply goods and services depends on its *human* capital as well as its *physical* capital. If the size of the labor force increased, more output could be produced in any given price level. Similarly, if the *quality* of the workforce were to increase, more output could be supplied at any given price level. In other words, increases in **human capital**—the skills and knowledge of the workforce—add to the nation's potential output.

human capital: The knowledge and skills possessed by the workforce.

Structural Unemployment

A mismatch between the skills of the workforce and the requirements of new jobs is a major cause of the unemployment–inflation trade-off. When aggregate demand increases, employers want to hire more workers. But the available (unemployed) workers may not have the skills employers require. This is the essence of **structural unemployment.** The consequence is that employers can't increase output as fast as they'd like to. Prices, rather than output, increase.

The larger the skills gap between unemployed workers and the requirements of emerging jobs, the worse will be the Phillips curve trade-off. To improve the trade-off, the skills gap must be reduced. This is another supply-side imperative. ***Investments in human capital reduce structural unemployment and shift the aggregate supply curve rightward.***

structural unemployment: Unemployment caused by a mismatch between the skills (or location) of job seekers and the requirements (or location) of available jobs.

Worker Training

The tax code is a policy tool for increasing human capital investment as well as physical capital investment. In this case tax credits are made available to employers who offer more worker training. Such credits reduce the employer's after-tax cost of training.

President Clinton proposed even stronger incentives for employer-based training. He wanted to *require* employers to spend at least 1.5 percent of their total payroll costs on training activities. Employers who didn't provide training activities directly would have to pay an equivalent sum into a public training fund. This "play-or-pay" approach would force employers to invest in the human capital of their employees.

Although the "play-or-pay" concept is intriguing, it might actually shift the aggregate supply curve the *wrong* way. The *costs* of employing workers would rise in the short run as employers shelled out more money for training or taxes. Hence the aggregate supply curve would shift *leftward* in the short run, worsening the unemployment–inflation trade-off. Only later might AS shift rightward, and then only to the extent that training actually improved **labor productivity.**

labor productivity: Amount of output produced by a worker in a given period of time; output per hour (or day, etc.).

Education Spending

Another way to increase human capital is to expand and improve the efficacy of the education system. President George H. Bush encouraged local school systems to become more competitive. He suggested they experiment with vouchers that would allow students to attend the school of their choice. Schools would then have to offer services that attracted voucher-carrying students. Schools that didn't compete successfully wouldn't have enough funds (vouchers) to continue.

President Clinton advocated a more conventional approach. He urged Congress to allocate more funds to the school system, particularly programs for preschoolers, like Head Start, and for disadvantaged youth. He acknowledged that vouchers might increase school quality but wanted to limit their use to public schools.

President George W. Bush characterized himself as the "education president." He increased federal spending on education and improved tax incentives for college savings accounts and tuition payments. His No Child Left Behind program also increased school accountability for human capital development. President Obama also emphasized educational improvements as a key to long-run growth. None of these educational tools generate a quick AS curve shift. Rather, any improvements in labor productivity are likely to emerge many years later.

Affirmative Action

Lack of skills and experience aren't the only reasons it's sometimes hard to find the "right" workers. The mismatch between employed workers and jobs is often less a matter of skills than of race, gender, or age. In other words, discrimination can create an artificial barrier between job seekers and available job openings.

If discrimination tends to shift the aggregate supply curve leftward, then reducing discriminatory barriers should shift it to the right. Equal opportunity programs are thus a natural extension of a supply-side approach to macro policy. However, critics are also quick to point out the risks inherent in government regulation of hiring decisions. From a supply-side perspective, laws that forbid discrimination are welcome and should be enforced. But aggressive affirmative action programs that require employers to hire specific numbers or types of workers limit productive capabilities and can lead to excessive costs.

Transfer Payments

transfer payments: Payments to individuals for which no current goods or services are exchanged, like Social Security, welfare, and unemployment benefits.

Welfare programs also discourage workers from taking available jobs. Unemployment and welfare benefits provide a source of income when a person isn't working. Although these **transfer payments** are motivated by humanitarian goals, they also inhibit labor supply. Transfer recipients must give up some or all of their welfare payments when they take a job. That makes working less attractive and therefore reduces the number of available workers. The net result is a leftward shift of the aggregate supply curve.

In 1996 Congress reformed the nation's core welfare program. The supply-side emphasis of that reform was manifest in the very title of the reform legislation: the Personal Responsibility and Work Opportunity Act. Congress set time limits on how long people can draw welfare benefits. The act also required recipients to engage in job-related activities like job search and training while still receiving benefits.

The 1996 reforms had a dramatic effect on recipient behavior. Nationally, more than 5 million adults left welfare between 1996 and 2001. More than half of these ex-welfare recipients entered the labor force, thereby shifting the AS curve rightward.

Recognizing that income transfers reduce aggregate supply doesn't force us to eliminate all welfare programs. Welfare programs are also intended to serve important social needs. The AS/AD framework reminds us, however, that the structure of such programs will affect aggregate supply. With more than 60 million Americans receiving income transfers, the effect on aggregate supply can be significant.

DEREGULATION

Government intervention affects the shape and position of the aggregate supply curve in other ways. The government intervenes directly in supply decisions by *regulating* employment and output behavior. In general, such regulations limit the flexibility of producers to respond to changes in demand. Government regulation also tends to raise production costs. The higher costs result not only from required changes in the production process but also from the expense of monitoring government regulations and filling out government forms. Thomas Hopkins, a Rochester Institute of Technology economist, estimates that the total costs of regulation exceed $700 billion a year. These added costs of production shift the aggregate supply curve to the left.

Factor Markets

Government intervention in factor markets increases the cost of supplying goods and services in many ways.

Minimum Wages. Minimum wage laws are one of the most familiar forms of factor market regulation. The Fair Labor Standards Act of 1938 required employers to pay workers a minimum of 25 cents per hour. Over time, Congress has increased the coverage of that act and the minimum wage itself repeatedly.

The goal of the minimum wage law is to ensure workers a decent standard of living. But the law has other effects as well. By prohibiting employers from using lower-paid workers, it limits the ability of employers to hire additional workers. Teenagers especially may not have enough skills or experience to merit the federal minimum wage. Employers may have to rely on more expensive workers rather than hire unemployed teenagers.

Here again the issue is not whether minimum wage laws serve any social purposes but how they affect macro outcomes. By shifting the aggregate supply curve leftward, minimum wage laws make it more difficult to achieve full employment with stable prices.

Mandatory Benefits. Government-directed fringe benefits have the same kind of effect on aggregate supply. One of the first bills President Clinton signed into law was the Family and Medical Leave Act, which requires all businesses with 50 or more employees to grant leaves of absence for up to 12 weeks. The employer must continue to pay health benefits during such absences and must also incur the costs of recruiting and training temporary replacements. The General Accounting Office estimated these benefits add nearly $700 million per year to payroll costs. These added payroll costs raise the costs of production, making producers less willing to supply output at any given price level. President Obama's sweeping health care reforms (the Affordable Care Act of 2010) reduced incentives for both labor supply and labor demand. One of President Trump's first priorities was to replace the ACA with a less onerous health insurance program.

Occupational Health and Safety. Government regulation of factor markets extends beyond wages and benefits. The government also sets standards for workplace safety and health. The Occupational Safety and Health Administration (OSHA), for example, issued new rules in November 2000 to reduce ergonomic injuries at work. The rules would have required employers to redesign workplaces (assembly lines, computer workstations) to accommodate individual workers. The rules would have also required employers to pay higher health care costs and grant more injury-related leave. OSHA itself estimated that the new regulations would cost employers $4.5 billion a year. Employers said the ergonomics regulations would cost *far* more than that—up to $125 billion a year. Concern over the implied upward shift of aggregate supply prompted Congress to rescind the new ergonomics rules before they took effect.

Product Markets

The government's regulation of factor markets tends to raise production costs and inhibit supply. The same is true of regulations imposed directly on product markets, as the following examples illustrate.

Transportation Costs. At the federal level, various agencies regulate the output and prices of transportation services. In 2013 the Federal Motor Carrier Safety Administration issued new regulations for the trucking industry's drivers. The new regulations specify how many hours a driver can work in a week, how much time must elapse between weeks, how often and for how long drivers must get off the road for a break, and even what hours of the night they must sleep. Although the regulators say the new rules will "ensure that drivers get the rest they need to be alert, safe, and awake," the industry says the new rules cut productivity and raise costs—that is, shift the AS curve to the left.

Similar problems continue to inflate intrastate trucking costs. All but eight states limit the routes, the loads, and the prices of intrastate trucking companies. These regulations promote inefficient transportation and protect producer profits. The net cost to the economy is at least $8 billion, or about $128 a year for a family of four.

Many cities and counties also limit the number of taxicabs and regulate their prices. Some also prohibit or constrain new ride-sharing services like Uber and Lyft that offer cheaper transportation. The net effect of such regulation is to limit competition and drive up the cost of transportation.

Food and Drug Standards. The Food and Drug Administration (FDA) has a broad mandate to protect consumers from dangerous products. In fulfilling this responsibility, the FDA sets health standards for the content of specific foods. The FDA also sets standards for the testing of new drugs and evaluates the test results.

The goal of FDA regulation is to minimize health risks to consumers. Like all regulation, however, the FDA standards entail real costs. The tests required for new drugs are expensive and time-consuming. Getting a new drug approved for sale takes years of effort and requires multimillion-dollar investments. The net results are that (1) fewer new drugs are brought to market and (2) those that reach the market are more expensive. In other words, the aggregate supply of goods is shifted to the left.

Other examples of government regulation are commonplace. The Environmental Protection Agency (EPA) regulates auto emissions, the discharge of industrial wastes, and water pollution. The U.S. Congress restricts foreign imports and raises their prices. The Federal Trade Commission (FTC) limits firms' freedom to increase their output or advertise their products. The Consumer Product Safety Commission regulates toys, mandating expensive tests for the chemical content of materials and paint used in children's toys. Toy manufacturers complain that the required tests are unnecessary and too expensive, especially for the many small businesses that make, sell, or resell children's toys and clothes.

Reducing Costs

Regulation makes toys safer but also more expensive.

©Steve Hix/Corbis/Getty Images RF

Many—perhaps most—of these regulatory activities are beneficial. In fact, all were originally designed to serve specific public purposes. As a result of such regulation, we get safer drugs, cleaner air, and less deceptive advertising. We must also consider the costs involved, however. All regulatory activities impose direct and indirect costs. These costs must be compared to the benefits received. ***The basic contention of supply-side economists is that regulatory costs are now too high.*** To improve our economic performance, they assert, we must *deregulate* the production process, thereby shifting the aggregate supply curve to the right again. President Obama responded to this criticism in January 2011 with an executive order requiring regulatory agencies to "strike the right balance" between regulatory goals and economic growth. He continued, however, to expand the scope of government regulation, as In the News "Obama Regulatory Burden Exceeds $100 Billion a Year" documents.

IN THE NEWS

OBAMA REGULATORY BURDEN EXCEEDS $100 BILLION A YEAR

Washington DC: In its eight-year tenure the Obama administration issued more than 21,000 new rules and regulations, according to the government's own watchdog, the General Accounting Office (GAO). All of these edicts are intended to change market behavior and outcomes in positive ways. But they come at a high cost. By their own calculations, the federal agencies that issue all these rules say those 21,000 new regulations cost $110 billion annually in reduced output and higher production costs. Critics peg the actual cost far higher—some as high as $1 trillion a year. Critics want more cost/benefit analysis and sunset laws that limit the life of federal edicts.

Source: General Accounting Office and Heritage Foundation.

ANALYSIS: Government rules that regulate production, transportation, food safety, financial institutions, and workforce activity can have salutary effects. But they also raise production costs and so shift the aggregate supply curve to the left.

EASING TRADE BARRIERS

Government regulation of international trade also influences the shape and position of aggregate supply. Trade flows affect both factor and product markets.

Factor Markets

In factor markets, U.S. producers buy raw materials, equipment parts, and components from foreign suppliers. Tariffs (taxes on imported goods) make such inputs more expensive, thereby increasing the cost of U.S. production. Regulations or quotas that make foreign inputs less accessible or more expensive similarly constrain the U.S. aggregate supply curve. The quota on imported sugar, for example, increases the cost of U.S.-produced soda, cookies, and candy. Just that one trade barrier has cost U.S. consumers more than $2 billion in higher prices.

Product Markets

The same kind of trade barriers affect product markets directly. With completely unrestricted ("free") trade, foreign producers would be readily available to supply products to U.S. consumers. By increasing the quantity of output available at any given price level, foreign suppliers help flatten out the aggregate supply curve.

Despite the success of the North American Free Trade Agreement (NAFTA) and the World Trade Organization (WTO) in reducing trade barriers, half of all U.S. imports are still subject to tariffs. Nontariff barriers (regulation, quotas, and so forth) also still constrain aggregate supply. This was evident in the multiyear battle over Mexican trucking. Although NAFTA authorized Mexican trucking companies to compete freely in the United States by 2000, U.S. labor unions (Teamsters) and trucking companies vigorously protested their entry, delaying the implied reduction in transportation costs for more than 10 years.

Immigration

Another global supply-side policy lever is immigration policy. Skill shortages in U.S. labor markets can be overcome with education and training. But even faster relief is available in the vast pool of foreign workers. In 2000 Congress increased the quota for software engineers and other high-tech workers by 70 percent, to 195,000 workers. The intent was to relieve the skill shortage in high-tech industries, and with it the cost pressures that were increasing the slope of the aggregate supply curve. Temporary visas for farm workers also help avert cost-push inflation in the farm sector. By regulating the flow of immigrant workers, Congress has the potential to alter the shape and position of the short-run AS curve.

THE ECONOMY TOMORROW

REBUILDING AMERICA

Another way to reduce the costs of supplying goods and services is to improve the nation's **infrastructure**—that is, the transportation, communications, judicial, and other systems that bind the pieces of the economy into a coherent whole. The interstate highway system, for example, enlarged the market for producers looking for new sales opportunities. Improved air traffic controls and larger airports have also made international markets and factors of production readily accessible. Without interstate highways and international airports, the process of supplying goods and services would be more localized and much more expensive.

It's easy to take infrastructure for granted until you have to make do without it. In recent years, U.S. producers have rushed into China, Russia, Eastern Europe, and Cuba looking

infrastructure: The transportation, communications, education, judicial, and other institutional systems that facilitate market exchanges.

Continued

for new profit opportunities. What they discovered is that even simple communication is difficult where Internet access and even telephones are often scarce. Outside the major cities business facilities and accommodations are often equally scarce. There are few established clearinghouses for marketing information, and labor markets are fragmented and localized. Getting started sometimes requires doing everything from scratch.

Although the United States has a highly developed infrastructure, it too could be improved. There are roads and bridges to repair, more airports to be built, faster rail systems to construct, and telecommunications networks to install. As we look to the future, we have to wonder whether that infrastructure will satisfy the needs of the economy tomorrow. If it doesn't, it will become increasingly difficult and costly to increase output.

Declining Infrastructure Investment. The United States has more than $2 trillion worth of public, nonmilitary infrastructure, including highways, bridges, sewage systems, buildings, hospitals, and schools. Like private capital (business plants, equipment, and structures), this *public* capital contributes to our production possibilities.

Investment in public infrastructure slowed down in the 1970s and 1980s. The rate of infrastructure investment peaked at around 3.5 percent of GDP in the mid-1960s. It then declined steadily to a low of about 0.5 percent of GDP in the early 1980s. As a result of this decline in spending, the United States has barely been able to *maintain* existing infrastructure, much less *expand* it. In 2013 the American Society of Civil Engineers said 4,095 of the nation's 85,000 dams were in need of repair. They estimated that the nation's infrastructure—everything from highways to sewers—needed a $3.6 trillion upgrade. Studies by Alan Aschauer and others suggest that *declining infrastructure investment has reduced actual and potential output.* In other words, crumbling infrastructure has shifted the aggregate supply curve leftward.

The Cost of Delay. The U.S. Department of Transportation estimates that people now spend nearly 3.5 billion hours a year in traffic delays. If the nation's highways don't improve, those delays will skyrocket to more than 4 billion hours a year a decade from now. That's a lot of labor resources to leave idle. Moreover, cars stuck on congested highways waste a lot of gasoline—nearly 4 billion gallons a year—and spew enormous amounts of carbon dioxide into our atmosphere.

Delays in air travel impose similar costs. The Federal Aviation Administration says air travel delays increase airline operating costs by more than $2 billion a year and idle more than $3 billion worth of passenger time. That time imposes a high opportunity cost in forgone business transactions and shortened vacations. Ultimately, all these costs are reflected in lower productivity, reduced output, higher prices, and greater environmental damage.

The Rebuilding Process. To alleviate these constraints on aggregate supply, Congress has voted several times to accelerate infrastructure spending. The Transportation Equity Act of 2000 raised federal spending to more than $600 billion in that decade. Among the public investments were the following:

- *Highways:* Highway construction and rehabilitation.
- *Air traffic control:* Modernization of the air traffic control system.
- *Weather service:* Modernization of the weather service (new satellites, a supercomputer).
- *Maglev trains:* Research on magnetically levitated ("maglev") trains that can travel at 300 miles per hour and are environmentally clean.
- *Smart cars and highways:* Research and testing of cars and highways outfitted with radar, monitors, and computers to reduce congestion and accidents.

Other legislation authorized more spending on sewage systems, access to space (e.g., the space shuttle), modernization of the postal service, and construction of

©Justin Sullivan/Getty Images

more hospitals, prisons, and other buildings. To this list President Obama added development of alternative energy sources, expansion of broadband access, an improved electrical grid, and high-speed rail systems. President Trump wanted still more: he proposed to spend $1 trillion on infrastructure development, claiming that level of investment would raise productivity, accelerate economic growth, and create millions of good jobs. What is certain is that infrastructure improvements increase aggregate supply, creating more potential for economic growth without inflation in the economy tomorrow.

SUMMARY

- Fiscal and monetary policies seek to attain full employment and price stability by shifting the aggregate demand curve. Their success depends on microeconomic responses, as reflected in the price and output decisions of market participants. **LO16-1**
- The market's response to shifts in aggregate demand is reflected in the shape and position of the aggregate supply curve. If the AS curve slopes upward, a trade-off between unemployment and inflation exists. The Phillips curve illustrates the trade-off. **LO16-2**
- The inflationary flashpoint is the rate of output where inflation accelerates—where the unemployment–inflation trade-off becomes acute. **LO16-2**
- If the AS curve shifts to the left, the trade-off between unemployment and inflation worsens. Stagflation—a combination of substantial inflation and unemployment—results. This is illustrated by rightward shifts of the Phillips curve. **LO16-2**
- Supply-side policies attempt to alter price and output decisions directly. If successful, they'll shift the aggregate supply curve to the right. A rightward AS shift implies less inflation *and* less unemployment. **LO16-3**

- Marginal tax rates are a major concern of supply-side economists. High tax rates discourage extra work, investment, and saving. A reduction in marginal tax rates should shift aggregate supply to the right. **LO16-3**
- The tax elasticity of supply measures the response of quantity supplied to changes in tax rates. Empirical evidence suggests that tax elasticity is modest but still triggers short-run shifts of the aggregate supply curve. **LO16-3**
- Investments in human capital increase productivity and therefore shift aggregate supply also. Workers' training and education enhancement are policy tools. **LO16-4**
- Government regulation often raises the cost of production and limits output. Deregulation is intended to reduce costly restrictions on price and output behavior, thereby shifting the AS curve to the right. **LO16-4**
- Public infrastructure is part of the economy's capital resources. Investments in infrastructure (such as transportation systems) facilitate market exchanges, expand production possibilities, and reduce environmental impacts. **LO16-4**
- Trade barriers shift the AS curve leftward by raising the cost of imported inputs and the price of imported products. Lowering trade barriers increases aggregate supply. **LO16-4**

Key Terms

stagflation
aggregate supply (AS)
Phillips curve
inflationary flashpoint
misery index
marginal tax rate

investment
tax rebate
tax elasticity of supply
saving
capital gains tax
human capital

structural unemployment
labor productivity
transfer payments
infrastructure

Questions for Discussion

1. Why might prices rise when aggregate demand increases? What factors might influence the extent of price inflation? **LO16-1**

2. How did the 2011 tsunami affect Japan's potential output (World View "Japan Sees Quake Damage Bill of Up to $309 Billion, Almost Four Katrinas")? **LO16-3**

3. Why did President Obama raise the top marginal tax rate to 39.6 percent if higher tax rates reduce aggregate supply? **LO16-4**

4. Which of the following groups are likely to have the highest tax elasticity of labor supply: (*a*) college students, (*b*) single parents, (*c*) primary earners in two-parent families, and (*d*) secondary earners in two-parent families? Why are there differences? **LO16-3**

5. How is the aggregate supply curve affected by (*a*) minimum wage laws, (*b*) Social Security payroll taxes, (*c*) Social Security retirement benefits, and (*d*) tighter border security? **LO16-4**

6. If the government requires power companies to use "clean" energy sources rather than "dirty" ones, how would aggregate supply be affected? **LO16-4**

7. Ride-sharing services like Uber and Lyft offer cheaper transportation than traditional taxicabs, which are regulated by local governments. How do these services affect the AS curve? Should they be regulated? **LO16-4**

8. How does each of the following infrastructure items affect aggregate supply: (*a*) highways, (*b*) schools, (*c*) sewage systems, and (*d*) courts and prisons? **LO16-4**

9. How would the volume and timing of capital investments be affected by (*a*) a permanent cut in the capital gains tax and (*b*) a temporary 10 percent tax credit? **LO16-4**

10. How might the inflationary flashpoint affect policy decisions? How would you represent the flashpoint on the Phillips curve? **LO16-2**

11. Why would anyone object to President Trump's increased infrastructure spending? **LO16-2**

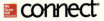

PROBLEMS FOR CHAPTER 16

LO16-1 1. On the following graph, draw the (A) Keynesian, (B) monetarist, and (C) hybrid AS curves, all intersecting AD at point E. If AD shifts rightward, which AS curve (A, B, or C) generates

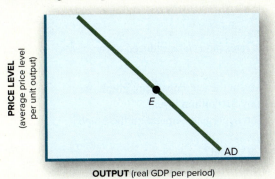

OUTPUT (real GDP per period)

(a) The biggest increase in output?
(b) The biggest increase in prices?

LO16-1 2. Which AS curve (a, b, or c) in Figure 16.1 causes the least unemployment when fiscal or monetary restraint is pursued?

LO16-4 3. Suppose taxpayers are required to pay a base tax of $50 plus 30 percent on any income greater than $100, as in the initial tax system B in Table 16.1. Suppose further that the taxing authority wishes to raise the taxes of people with incomes of $200 by $40.
(a) If marginal tax rates are to remain unchanged, what will the new base tax have to be?
(b) If the base tax of $50 is to remain unchanged, what will the marginal tax rate have to be?

LO16-3 4. Suppose households supply 600 billion hours of labor per year and have a tax elasticity of supply of 0.15. If the tax rate is increased by 10 percent, by how many hours will the supply of labor decline?

LO16-4 5. By how much did the disposable income of rich people decrease as a result of the 2012 hike in the top marginal tax rate from 35 to 39.6 percent? Assume they have $2 trillion of gross income in the highest bracket.

LO16-2 6. According to Figure 16.6, what inflation rate would occur if the unemployment rate rose to 6 percent, with
(a) PC₁?   (b) PC₂?

LO16-3 7. Illustrate the effect of a business tax cut on aggregate supply using the model of the macroeconomy. What happened to the
(a) Equilibrium rate of output?   (c) Unemployment?
(b) Equilibrium price level?

LO16-2 8. On the following graph, plot the unemployment and inflation rates for the years 2005–2015 using Data Tables at the end of the book. Is there any evidence of a Phillips curve trade-off?

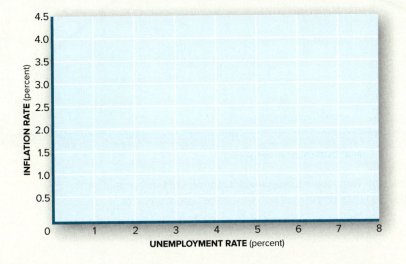

UNEMPLOYMENT RATE (percent)

359

LO16-4   9.   If the tax elasticity of labor supply is 0.20, by what percentage will the quantity of labor supplied increase in response to
     (*a*)   A \$500 per person income tax rebate?
     (*b*)   A 6 percent reduction in marginal tax rates?

LO16-4   10.   If the tax elasticity of supply is 0.27, by how much do tax rates have to be reduced to increase the labor supply by 2 percent?

LO16-3   11.   Suppose an economy is characterized by the AS/AD curves in the accompanying graph. A decision is then made to increase infrastructure spending by \$10 billion a year.
     (*a*)   Illustrate the direct impact of the increased spending on aggregate demand on the graph (ignore multiplier effects).
     (*b*)   If AS is unaffected, what is the new equilibrium rate of output?
     (*c*)   What is the new equilibrium price level?
     (*d*)   Now assume that the infrastructure investments increase aggregate supply by \$20 billion a year (from the initial equilibrium). Illustrate this effect on the graph.
     (*e*)   After both demand and supply adjustments occur, what is the final equilibrium
         (*i*)   Rate of output?
         (*ii*)   Price level?

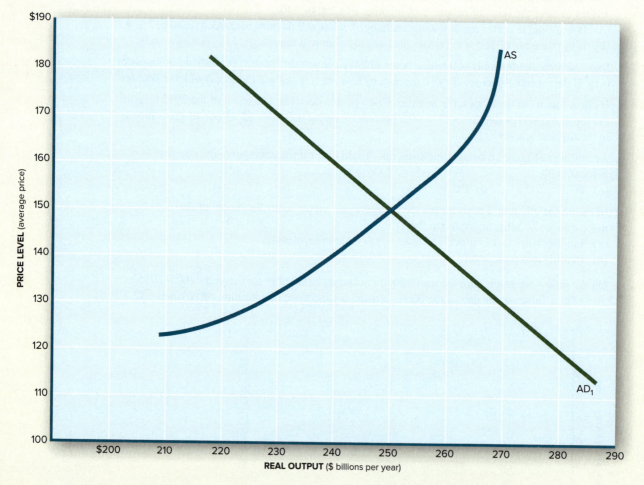

LO16-1   12.   The Economy Tomorrow: The Economy Tomorrow section provides estimates of time spent in traffic delays. If the average worker produces \$110 of output per hour, what is the opportunity cost of
     (*a*)   Current traffic delays?
     (*b*)   Estimated delays in 10 years?

©Ingram Publishing RF

CHAPTER 17

Growth and Productivity:
Long-Run Possibilities

Economic growth is the fundamental determinant of the long-run success of any nation, the basic source of rising living standards, and the key to meeting the needs and desires of the American people.

—*Economic Report of the President, 1992*

Imagine a world with no smartphones, no satellite TV, no social media, and no digital sound. Such a world actually existed—only 40 years ago! At the time, personal computers were still on the drawing board, and laptops weren't even envisioned. Websites were a place where spiders gathered, not locations on the Internet. Home video hadn't been seen, and no one had yet popped any microwave popcorn. Biotechnology hadn't yet produced any blockbuster drugs, and people wore the same pair of athletic shoes for a wide variety of sports.

New products are evidence of economic progress. Over time, we produce not only *more* goods and services but also *new* and *better* goods and services. In the process, we get richer: our material living standards rise.

Rising living standards aren't inevitable, however. According to World Bank estimates, over 2 *billion* people—more than a fourth of the world's population—continue to live in abject poverty with incomes of less than $3 per day. Worse still, living standards in many of the poorest countries have *fallen* in the last decade.

This chapter takes a longer-term view of economic performance. Chapters 8 to 16 were concerned with the business cycle—that is, *short-run* variations in output and prices. This chapter looks at the prospects for *long-run* growth and considers three questions:

- **How important is economic growth?**
- **How does an economy grow?**
- **Is continued economic growth possible? Is it desirable?**

We develop answers to these questions by first examining the nature of economic growth and then examining its sources and potential limits.

THE NATURE OF GROWTH

Economic growth refers to increases in the output of goods and services. But there are two distinct ways in which output increases, and they have different implications for our economic welfare.

FIGURE 17.1

Two Types of Growth

Increases in output result from increased use of existing capacity or from increases in that capacity itself. In part *a* the mix of output at point *A* doesn't make full use of production possibilities. We can get additional output by employing more of our available resources or using them more efficiently. This is illustrated by point *B* (or any other point on the curve).

Once we're on the production possibilities curve, we can get more output only by *increasing* our productive capacity. This is illustrated by the outward *shift* of the production possibilities curve in part *b*.

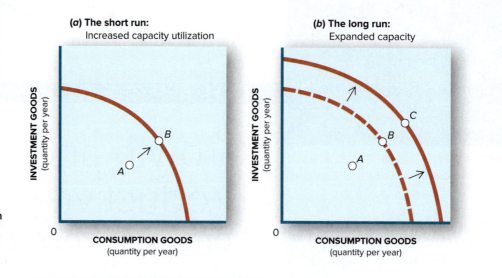

(a) The short run:
Increased capacity utilization

INVESTMENT GOODS (quantity per year)

CONSUMPTION GOODS (quantity per year)

(b) The long run:
Expanded capacity

INVESTMENT GOODS (quantity per year)

CONSUMPTION GOODS (quantity per year)

---

production possibilities: The alternative combinations of final goods and services that could be produced in a given period with all available resources and technology.

economic growth: An increase in output (real GDP); an expansion of production possibilities.

Short-Run Changes in Capacity Utilization

The easiest kind of growth comes from increased use of our productive capabilities. In any given year there's a limit to an economy's potential output. This limit is determined by the quantity of resources available and our technological know-how. We've illustrated these short-run limits with a **production possibilities** curve, as in Figure 17.1*a*. By using all our available resources and our best expertise, we can produce any combination of goods and services on the production possibilities curve.

We don't always take full advantage of our productive capacity. The economy often produces a mix of output that lies *inside* our production possibilities, like point *A* in Figure 17.1*a*. This was our situation in the Great Recession of 2008–2009. When this happens, a major *short-run* goal of macro policy is to achieve full employment—to move us from point *A* to some point on the production possibilities curve (such as point *B*). In the process, we produce more output.

Long-Run Change in Capacity

Once we're fully utilizing our productive capacity, further increases in output are attainable only if we *expand* that capacity. To do so we have to *shift* the production possibilities curve outward as in Figure 17.1*b*. Such shifts imply an increase in *potential* GDP—that is, our productive capacity.

Over time, increases in capacity are critical. Short-run increases in the utilization of existing capacity can generate only modest increases in output. Even high unemployment rates, such as 9 percent, leave little room for increased output. *To achieve large and lasting increases in output we must push our production possibilities outward.* For this reason, economists often define **economic growth** in terms of changes in *potential* GDP.

The unique character of economic growth can also be illustrated with aggregate supply and demand curves. Figure 17.2 depicts both a sloped, *short-run* AS curve and a vertical, *long-run* AS curve. In the short run, macro stabilization policies try to shift the AD curve to a more desirable price–output equilibrium. Such demand-side policies are unlikely to change the country's long-run capacity to produce, however. At best they move the macro equilibrium to a more desirable point on the *short-run* AS curve (e.g., from E_1 to E_2 in Figure 17.2).

Our productive capacity may increase nevertheless. If it does, the "natural" long-run AS curve will also shift. In this framework, *economic growth implies a rightward shift of the long-run aggregate supply curve.* Should that occur, the economy will be able to produce still more output with less inflationary pressure (e.g., as at E_3 in Figure 17.2).

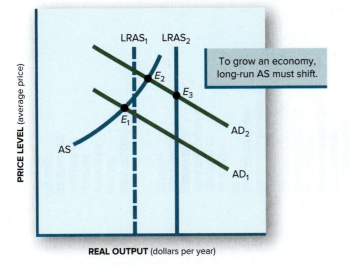

FIGURE 17.2
Shifts of Long-Run Supply

Macro stabilization policies try to shift the aggregate demand curve (e.g., from AD_1 to AD_2) to achieve greater output and employment in the short run.

The vertical long-run AS curve implies that these efforts will have no lasting impact on the natural rate of output, however. To achieve economic growth, the long-run aggregate supply curve must be shifted to the right (e.g., from $LRAS_1$ to $LRAS_2$).

Nominal vs. Real GDP

Notice that we refer to *real* GDP, not *nominal* GDP, in our concept of economic growth. Nominal GDP can rise even when the quantity of goods and services falls, as was the case in 2008. The total quantity of goods and services produced in 2008 was less than the quantity produced in 2007. Nevertheless, prices rose enough in 2008 to keep nominal GDP growing.

Real GDP refers to the actual quantity of goods and services produced. Real GDP avoids the distortions of inflation by adjusting for changing prices. By using 2009 prices as a **base year,** we observe that real GDP fell from $14,874 billion in 2007 to $14,830 billion in 2008 (a drop of $44 billion). Since then real GDP has increased another $2 trillion—evidence of continuing economic growth.

real GDP: The value of final output produced in a given period, adjusted for changing prices.

base year: The year used for comparative analysis; the basis for indexing price changes.

MEASURES OF GROWTH

Typically, changes in real GDP are expressed in percentage terms, as a growth *rate*. The **growth rate** is simply the change in real output between two periods divided by total output in the base period. The percentage decline in real output during 2008 was thus $44 billion ÷ $14,874 billion, or just 0.3 percent. By contrast, real output grew in 2010 by 2.5 percent.

Figure 17.3 illustrates the recent growth experience of the U.S. economy. In the 1960s, real GDP grew by an average of 4.1 percent per year. Economic growth slowed to only 2.8 percent in the 1970s, however, with actual output declines in three years. The steep recession of 1982, as seen in Figure 17.3, reduced GDP growth in the 1980s to an even lower rate: 2.5 percent per year. The 1990s started out even worse, with negligible growth in 1990 and a recession in 1991. The economy performed a lot better after that, however. From 1997 to 2007, real GDP grew by 35 percent—an impressive increase in the quantity of output produced. The Great Recession of 2008–2009, together with an exceptionally slow recovery, put a dent in that record: output grew only 15 percent from 2007 to 2017.

growth rate: Percentage change in real output from one period to another.

The Exponential Process.. Although the consequences of *negative* growth (e.g., job layoffs, unemployment, pay cuts, home foreclosures) merit headlines, variations in *positive* growth rates usually elicit yawns. Indeed, the whole subject of economic growth looks rather dull when you discover that "big" gains in economic growth are measured in fractions of a percent. However, this initial impression isn't fair. First, even one year's "low" growth implies lost output. If we had just *maintained* output in 2008 at its 2007 level—that is, "achieved" a *zero* growth rate rather than an outright decline—we would have had $44 *billion* more worth of goods and services, which works out to nearly $140 worth of goods and services per

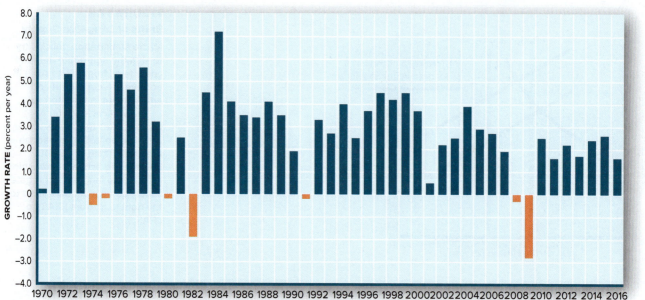

FIGURE 17.3

Recent U.S. Growth Rates

Total output typically increases from one year to another. The focus of policy is on the growth *rate*—that is, how fast real GDP increases from one year to the next. Annual growth rates since 1970 have ranged from a high of 7.2 percent (1984) to a low of *minus* 2.8 percent (2009).

Source: Economic Report of the President, 2017.

person. In today's $20 trillion economy, each 1 percent of GDP growth translates into roughly $600 more output per person. Lots of people would like that extra output.

Second, economic growth is a *continuing* process. Gains made in one year accumulate in future years. It's like interest you earn at the bank: if you leave your money in the bank for several years, you begin to earn interest on your interest. Eventually you accumulate a nice little bankroll.

The process of economic growth works the same way. Each little shift of the production possibilities curve broadens the base for future GDP. As shifts accumulate over many years, the economy's productive capacity is greatly expanded. Ultimately we discover that those "little" differences in annual growth rates generate tremendous gains in GDP.

This cumulative process, whereby interest or growth is compounded from one year to the next, is called an "exponential process." At growth rates of 2.5 percent, GDP doubles in 29 years. With 3.5 percent growth, GDP doubles in only 21 years. In a single generation the *difference* between 2.5 percent growth and 3.5 percent growth amounts to more than $12 trillion of output. That *difference* is roughly 60 percent of this year's total output. From this longer-term perspective, the difference between 2.5 percent and 3.5 percent growth begins to look very meaningful.

GDP per Capita: A Measure of Living Standards

GDP per capita: Total GDP divided by total population; average GDP.

The exponential process looks even more meaningful when we translate it into *per capita* terms. We can do so by looking at GDP *per capita* rather than total GDP. **GDP per capita** is simply total output divided by total population. In 2016, the total output of the U.S. economy was $18.5 trillion. Since there were 320 million of us to share that output, GDP per capita was

$$\text{GDP per capita} \atop (2016) = \frac{\$18.5 \text{ trillion of output}}{320 \text{ million people}} = \$57,813$$

Net Growth Rate (%)		Doubling Time (Years)
0.0%	⟶	Never
0.5	⟶	144 years
1.0	⟶	72
1.5	⟶	48
2.0	⟶	36
2.5	⟶	29
3.0	⟶	24
3.5	⟶	21
4.0	⟶	18

TABLE 17.1

The Rule of 72

Small differences in annual growth rates cumulate into large differences in GDP. Shown here are the number of years it would take to double GDP per capita at various net growth rates. *"Net" growth* refers to the GDP growth rate minus the population growth rate.

Doubling times can be approximated by the "rule of 72." Seventy-two divided by the growth rate equals the number of years it takes to double.

This does not mean that every man, woman, and child in the United States received $57,813 worth of goods and services in 2016; it simply indicates how much output was potentially available to the "average" person. GDP per capita is often used as a basic measure of our standard of living.

Growth in GDP per capita is attained only when the growth of output exceeds population growth. In the United States, this condition is usually achieved. Even when *total* GDP growth slowed in the 1970s and 1980s, *per capita* GDP kept rising because the U.S. population was growing by only 1 percent a year. Hence even relatively slow economic growth of 2.5 percent a year was enough to keep raising living standards.

The developing nations of the Third World aren't so fortunate. Many of these countries exhibit both slower *economic* growth and faster *population* growth. They have a difficult time *maintaining* living standards, much less increasing them. Madagascar, for example, is one of the poorest countries in the world, with GDP per capita of roughly $900. Yet its population continues to grow rapidly (2.8 percent per year), putting constant pressure on living standards. In recent years, Madagascar's GDP grew at a slower rate of only 2.0 percent. As a consequence, GDP per capita *declined* nearly 0.8 percent per year. As we'll see in the chapter titled "Global Poverty" many other poor nations are in similarly dire straits.

By comparison with these countries, the United States has been fortunate. Our GDP per capita has more than doubled since the 1980s, despite several recessions. This means that the average person today has twice as many goods and services as the average person had a generation ago.

What about the future? Will we continue to enjoy substantial gains in living standards? Many Americans harbor great doubts. A 2016 poll revealed that 6 out of 10 adults believe their children's living standards will be no higher than today's. That would happen only if population growth outstrips or equals GDP growth. That seems unlikely. Table 17.1 displays more optimistic scenarios in which GDP continues to grow faster than the population. If GDP *per capita* continues to grow at 2 percent per year—as it did in the 1990s—it will take 36 years to double our standard of living. If GDP per capita grows just half a percent faster, say, by 2.5 percent per year, our standard of living will double in only 29 years. Would you like to have that extra output when you're middle-aged?

GDP per Worker: A Measure of Productivity

The potential increases in living standards depicted in Table 17.1 won't occur automatically. Someone is going to have to produce more output if we want GDP per capita to rise. One reason our living standard rose in the 1980s is that the labor force grew faster than the population. Those in the World War II baby boom had reached maturity and were entering the **labor force** in droves. At the same time, more women took jobs outside the home, a trend that continued into the 1990s (see Figure 6.2). As a consequence, the **employment rate** increased significantly, as Figure 17.4 shows. With the number of workers growing faster than the population, GDP per capita was sure to rise.

labor force: All persons over age 16 who are either working for pay or actively seeking paid employment.

employment rate: The percentage of the adult population that is employed.

Human Capital Investment

Continuing advances in education and skills training have greatly increased the quality of U.S. labor. In 1950 less than 8 percent of all U.S. workers had completed college. Today 35 percent of the workforce has completed four years of college. There has also been a substantial increase in vocational training, both in the public sector and by private firms.

In the 1970s these improvements in the quality of individual workers were offset by a change in the composition of the labor force. As we observed in Chapter 6, the proportion of teenagers and women in the labor force grew tremendously in the 1960s and 1970s. These Baby Boomers and their mothers contributed to higher output. Because teenagers and women (re)entering the labor market generally have less job experience than adult men, however, *average* productivity fell.

This phenomenon reversed itself in the 1990s as the Baby Boomers reached their prime working years. The increased productivity of the workforce is not a reflection of the aging process itself. Rather, the gains in productivity reflect the greater **human capital** investment associated with more schooling and more on-the-job learning.

human capital: The knowledge and skills possessed by the workforce.

Physical Capital Investment

The knowledge and skills a worker brings to the job don't completely determine his or her productivity. A worker with no tools, no computers, and no machinery won't produce much even if she has a PhD. Similarly, a worker with outmoded equipment won't produce as much as an equally capable worker equipped with the newest machines and the best technology. From this perspective, *a primary determinant of labor productivity is the rate of capital investment.* In other words, improvements in output per *worker* depend in large part on increases in the quantity and quality of *capital* equipment (see World View "High Investment = Fast Growth").

WORLD VIEW

HIGH INVESTMENT = FAST GROWTH

Investment in new plants and equipment is essential for economic growth. In general, countries that allocate a larger share of output to investment will grow more rapidly. In recent years, China has had one of the world's fastest GDP growth rates and also one of the highest investment rates.

Country	Gross Investment as Percentage of GDP	Growth Rate of GDP (Average, 2000–2012)
China	51	10.6
India	30	7.7
Vietnam	32	6.6
United States	17	1.7
Greece	10	1.1

Source: The World Bank.

ANALYSIS: Investment increases production possibilities. Countries that devote a larger share of output to investment tend to grow faster.

U.S. workers are outfitted with an exceptional amount of capital equipment. As we first saw in Chapter 2, U.S. productivity is buttressed by huge investments in equipment and technology. The average U.S. worker is supported by more than $100,000 of capital inputs. To *increase* productivity, however, the quality and quantity of capital available to the average worker must continue to increase. That requires capital spending to increase faster than the labor force. With the labor force growing at 1.1 percent a year, that's not a hard standard to beat. How *much* faster capital investment grows is nevertheless a decisive factor in productivity gains.

Saving and Investment Rates. The dependence of productivity gains on capital investment puts a new perspective on consumption and saving. In the short run, the primary concern of macroeconomic policy is to balance aggregate demand and aggregate supply. In this context, savings are a form of leakage that requires offsetting injections of investment or government spending. From the longer-run perspective of economic growth, saving and investment take on added importance. ***Savings aren't just a form of leakage but a basic source of investment financing.*** If we use all our resources to produce consumer, export, and public sector goods, there won't be any investment. In that case, we might not face a short-run stabilization problem—our productive capacity might be fully utilized—but we'd confront a long-run *growth* problem. Indeed, if we consumed our entire output, our productive capacity would actually shrink since we wouldn't even be replacing worn-out plants and equipment. We must have at least enough savings to finance **net investment.**

net investment: Gross investment less depreciation.

Household and Business Saving. Household saving rates in the United States have been notoriously low. In 2000 and again in 2006, U.S. households actually *dis*saved—spending more on consumption than their disposable incomes. In recent years the household saving rate has averaged around 5.5 percent.

Fortunately, household saving is not the only source of investment financing. Businesses themselves generate a lot of cash they can use for further investment. The retained earnings and depreciation allowances that create business savings generated a huge cash flow for investment in the 1990s. The same cash-rich situation emerged in 2012–2016, setting the stage for another investment surge and faster GDP growth.

Foreign investors also continue to pour money into U.S. plants, equipment, software, and financial assets. Maintaining—and growing—these saving flows are essential to financing future investment.

Management Training

The accumulation of more and better capital equipment does not itself guarantee higher productivity or faster GDP growth. The human factor is still critical: how well resources are organized and managed will affect the rate of growth. Hence entrepreneurship and the quality of continuing management are also major determinants of economic growth.

It's difficult to characterize differences in management techniques or to measure their effectiveness. However, much attention has been focused in recent years on the alleged shortsightedness of U.S. managers. U.S. firms, it is said, focus too narrowly on short-run profits, neglecting long-term productivity. There is little evidence of such a failure, however. The spreading use of stock options in management ranks ties executives' compensation to multiyear performance. Moreover, productivity trends in the United States not only have accelerated in recent years but also have consistently surpassed productivity gains in other industrial nations (see World View "U.S. Workers Compete Well"). To maintain that advantage, U.S. corporations spend billions of dollars each year on continuing management training. Accordingly, the charge of shortsightedness is better regarded as a precautionary warning than an established fact.

Research and Development

A fourth and vital source of productivity advance is research and development (R&D), a broad concept that includes scientific research, product development, innovations in production techniques, and the development of management improvements. R&D activity may be a specific, identifiable activity such as in a research lab, or it may be part of the process of learning by doing. In either case, the insights developed from R&D generally lead to new products and cheaper ways of producing them. Over time, R&D is credited with the greatest contributions to economic growth. In his study of U.S. growth during the period 1929–1982, Edward Denison concluded that 26 percent of *total* growth was due to "advances in knowledge." Gordon Moore, the cofounder of Intel, doesn't see an end to research-based productivity advance. His "Moore's Law" predicts a *doubling* of computer power every 18 months.

New Growth Theory. The evident contribution of "advances in knowledge" to economic growth has spawned a new perspective called "new growth theory." "Old growth theory,"

WORLD VIEW

U.S. WORKERS COMPETE WELL

U.S. workers are the most productive in the world, producing more than $100,000 of output per worker annually. In manufacturing, the U.S. productivity lead continues to widen. Among the 19 industrial nations tracked by the Bureau of Labor Statistics, only two have had faster productivity growth than the United States since 2007.

Annual Growth of Manufactured Output per Hour, 2007–2011

Taiwan	5.7
Korea	4.1
United States	3.8
Spain	3.0
United Kingdom	2.2
Japan	2.2
France	1.1
Sweden	0.9
Canada	0.8
Australia	0.5
Italy	0.0
Belgium	−0.2
Germany	−1.9

Source: U.S. Bureau of Labor Statistics.

ANALYSIS: U.S. productivity gains are among the fastest of industrial nations. These gains are fueled by research and development and investment spending.

it is said, emphasized the importance of bricks and mortar—that is, saving and investing in new plants and equipment. By contrast, "new" growth theory emphasizes the importance of investing in ideas. Paul Romer, a Stanford economist, asserts that new ideas and the spread of knowledge are the primary engines of growth. Unfortunately, neither Romer nor anyone else is exactly sure how one spawns new ideas or best disseminates knowledge. The only evident policy lever appears to be the support of research and development, a staple of "old" growth theory.

There's an important link between R&D and capital investment. As noted earlier, part of each year's gross investment compensates for the depreciation of existing plants and equipment. However, new machines are rarely identical to the ones they replace. When you get a new computer, you're not just *replacing* an old one; you're *upgrading* your computing capabilities with more memory, faster speed, and a lot of new features. Indeed, the availability of *better* technology is often the motive for such capital investment. The same kind of motivation spurs businesses to upgrade machines and structures. Hence ***advances in technology and capital investment typically go hand in hand.***

POLICY TOOLS

As we've observed, economic growth depends on rightward shifts of the long-run aggregate supply curve (Figure 17.2). It should not surprise you, then, that growth policy makes liberal use of the tools in the supply-side toolbox (Chapter 16). The challenge for growth policy is to select those tools that will give the economy *long*-run increases in productive capacity.

Increasing Human Capital Investment

Since *workers* are the ultimate source of output and productivity growth, the first place to look for growth-accelerating tools is in the area of human capital development.

Education. Governments at all levels already play a tremendous role in human capital development by building, operating, and subsidizing schools. The quantity and quality of continuing investments in America's schools will have a major effect on future productivity. Government policy also plays an *indirect* role in schooling decisions by offering subsidized loans for college and vocational education.

Immigration. Immigration policy is also a determinant of the nation's stock of human capital. At least 1 million immigrants enter the United States every year. Most of the *legal* immigrants are relatives of people already living in the United States as permanent residents (with green cards) or naturalized citizens. In addition to these *family-based* visas, the United States also grants a much smaller number of *employment-based* visas. The H-1B program offers temporary (three-year) visas to highly skilled foreigners who want to work in U.S. firms. By admitting highly skilled workers, the United States gains valuable human capital and relieves some structural unemployment. Only 65,000 H-1B visas are available each year, however—a tiny percent of the U.S. labor force. Temporary visas for agricultural (H-2A) and other less skilled workers (H-2B) are fewer still. To accelerate our productivity and GDP growth, observers urge us to expand these programs.

Increasing Physical Capital Investment

As in the case of human capital, the possibilities for increasing physical capital investment are also many and diverse.

Investment Incentives. The tax code is a mechanism for stimulating investment. Faster depreciation schedules, tax credits for new investments, and lower business tax rates all encourage increased investment in physical capital. The 2002 and 2003 tax cuts were designed for this purpose. President Obama's 2011 stimulus program also provided increased tax incentives (100 percent expensing) for investment in physical capital. President Trump's proposals for reducing the capital-gains and corporate-income tax rates were explicitly designed to increase domestic investment.

Savings Incentives. In principle, the government can also deepen the savings pool that finances investment. Here again, the tax code offers some policy levers. Tax preferences for individual retirement accounts and other pension savings may increase the marginal propensity to save or at least redirect savings flows to longer-term investments. The Bush 2001 tax package (Chapter 11) included not only a *short-run* fiscal stimulus (e.g., tax rebates) but also enhanced incentives for *long-term* savings (retirement and college savings accounts).

Infrastructure Development. The government also directly affects the level of physical capital through its public works spending. As we observed in Chapter 16, the $2 trillion already invested in bridges, highways, airports, sewer systems, and other infrastructure is an important part of America's capital stock. President Obama's 2009 stimulus program vastly increased spending on roads, bridges, power sources, and educational facilities. President Trump's infrastructure plans are even more ambitious. Investments of that sort reduce transportation costs, increase market efficiency, reduce environmental impact, and expand potential output.

Fiscal Responsibility. In addition to these many supply-side interventions, the government's *macro* policies also affect the rate of investment and growth. Of particular interest in this regard is the federal government's budget balance. As we've seen, budget deficits may be a useful mechanism for attaining short-run macro stability. Those same deficits, however, may have negative long-run effects. If Uncle Sam borrows more funds from the national savings pool, other borrowers may end up with less. As we saw in Chapter 12, there's no guarantee that federal deficits will result in the **crowding out** of private investment. Let's recognize the risk of such an outcome, however. Hence *fiscal and monetary policies must be evaluated in terms of their impact not only on (short-run) aggregate demand but also on long-run aggregate supply.*

Many people fear that the enormous deficits created by the Obama and Trump budgets will ultimately raise interest rates and crowd out private investment (see In the News "Paying for Trump's Infrastructure Spending").

crowding out: A reduction in private sector borrowing (and spending) caused by increased government borrowing.

PAYING FOR TRUMP'S INFRASTRUCTURE SPENDING

Washington D.C.: The conservative Tax Foundation has estimated the economic effects of President Trump's proposed infrastructure spending. They estimate that a $500 billion increase in infrastructure spread out over ten years will indeed create jobs, boost productivity, and increase GDP. But if that spending is funded by deficit borrowing, interest rates will rise and those higher rates will dampen the pro-growth effects of the fiscal stimulus. The net effects will be a modest 0.11 percent increase in the GDP growth rate, an additional 21,400 jobs, $25 billion in productivity gains, and an increase in the government's budget deficit of $21.5–26 billion per year.

Source: Tax Foundation.

ANALYSIS: Any increase in pro-growth government spending must be financed with higher taxes or increased borrowing (deficits). The *net* impact of such spending incorporates both the positive and negative effects of the budget changes.

Maintaining Stable Expectations

The position of the long-run AS curve also depends on a broader assessment of the economic outlook. Expectations are a critical factor in both consumption and investment behavior. People who expect to lose their jobs next year are unlikely to buy a new car or house this year. Likewise, if investors expect interest rates to jump next year, they may be less willing to initiate long-run capital projects.

A sense of political and economic stability is critical to any long-run current trend. Within that context, however, specific perceptions of government policy may also alter investment plans. Investors may look to the Fed for a sense of monetary stability. They may be looking for a greater commitment to long-run price stability than to short-run adjustments of aggregate demand. In the fiscal policy area the same kind of commitment to long-run fiscal discipline rather than to short-run stimulus may be sought. Such possibilities imply that macro policy must be sensitive to long-run expectations.

Institutional Context

Last, but not least, the prospects for economic growth depend on the institutional context of a nation's economy. We first encountered this proposition in Chapter 1. In World View "Index of Economic Freedom," nations were ranked on the basis of an Index of Freedom. Studies have shown how greater economic freedom—secure property rights, open trade, lower taxes, less regulation—typically fosters faster growth. In less regulated economies, there's more scope for entrepreneurship and more opportunity to invest. Recognizing this, nations around the world, from India to China, to Russia, to Latin America, have deregulated industries, privatized state enterprises, and promoted more open trade and investment.

THE ECONOMY TOMORROW

LIMITLESS GROWTH?

Suppose we pulled all the right policy levers and were able to keep the economy on a fast-paced growth track. Could the economy keep growing forever? Wouldn't we use up all available resources and ruin the environment in the process? How much long-term growth is really possible—or even desirable?

The Malthusian Formula for Destruction. The prospect of an eventual limit to economic growth originated in the 18th-century warnings of the Reverend Thomas Malthus. Malthus argued that continued economic growth was impossible because food production couldn't keep pace with population growth. His dire projections earned the economics profession its characterization as the "dismal science."

When Malthus first issued his warnings, in 1798, the population of England (including Wales) was about 9 million. Annual production of barley, oats, and related grains was approximately 162 million bushels, and wheat production was around 50 million bushels, just about enough to feed the English population (a little had to be imported from other countries). Although the relationship between food and population was satisfactory in 1798, Malthus reasoned that starvation was not far off. First of all, he observed that "population, when unchecked, goes on doubling itself every 25 years, or increases in a geometrical ratio."[1] Thus he foresaw the English population increasing to 36 million people by 1850, 144 million by 1900, and more than 1 billion by 1975, unless some social or natural restraints were imposed on population growth.

Limits to Food Production. One natural population check that Malthus foresaw was a scarcity of food. England had only a limited amount of land available for cultivation and was already farming the most fertile tracts. Before long, all available land would be in use, and only improvements in agricultural productivity (output per acre) could increase food supplies. Some productivity increases were possible, Malthus concluded, but "the means of subsistence, under circumstances the most favorable to human industry, could not possibly be made to increase faster than in an arithmetical ratio."[2]

With population increasing at a *geometric* rate and food supplies at an *arithmetic* rate, the eventual outcome is evident. Figure 17.6 illustrates how the difference between a **geometric growth** path and an **arithmetic growth** path ultimately leads to starvation. As Malthus calculated it, per capita wheat output would decline from 5.5 bushels in 1800 to only 1.7 bushels in 1900 (Figure 17.6*b*). This wasn't enough food to feed the English people. According to Malthus's projections, either England died off about 100 years ago, or it has been maintained at the brink of starvation for more than a century only by recurrent plagues, wars, or the kind of "moral restraint" that's commonly associated with Victorian preachments.

Malthus's logic was impeccable. As long as population increased at a geometric rate while output increased at an arithmetic rate, England's doomsday was as certain as two plus two equals four. Malthus's error was not in his logic but in his empirical assumptions. He didn't know how fast output would increase over time, any more than we know whether people will be wearing electronic wings in the year 2203. He had to make an educated guess about future productivity trends. He based his estimates on his own experiences at the very beginning of the Industrial Revolution. As it turned out (fortunately), he had no knowledge of the innovations that would change the world, and he grossly underestimated the rate at which productivity would increase. *Output, including agricultural products, has increased at a geometric rate, not at the much slower arithmetic rate foreseen by Malthus.* As we observed earlier, U.S. output has grown at a long-term rate of roughly 3 percent a year. This *geometric* growth has doubled output every 25 years or so. That rate of economic growth is more than enough to raise living standards for a population growing by only 1 percent a year.

Resource Constraints. As Yale historian Paul Kennedy has suggested, maybe Malthus's doomsday predictions were just premature, not wrong. Maybe growth will come to a screeching halt when we run out of arable land, water, oil, or some other vital resource.

Malthus focused on arable land as the ultimate resource constraint. Other doomsday prophets have focused on the supply of whale oil, coal, oil, potatoes, and other "essential" resources. All such predictions ignore **the role of markets in both promoting more efficient uses of scarce resources and finding substitutes for them.** If, for example, the world were really running out of oil, what would happen to oil prices? Oil

geometric growth: An increase in quantity by a constant proportion each year.

arithmetic growth: An increase in quantity by a constant amount each year.

Continued

[1] Thomas Malthus, *An Essay on the Principle of Population* (1798; reprint ed., Homewood, IL: Richard D. Irwin, 1963), p. 4.
[2] Ibid., p. 5.

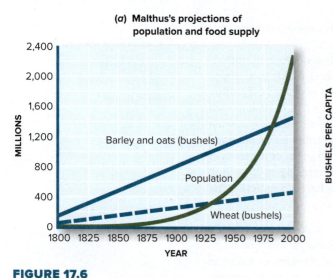

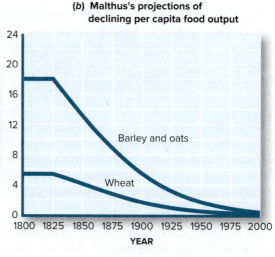

FIGURE 17.6

The Malthusian Doomsday

By projecting the growth rates of population and food output into the future, Malthus foresaw England's doomsday. At that time, the amount of available food per capita would be too small to sustain human life. Fortunately, Malthus overestimated population growth and underestimated productivity growth.

Source: Malthus's arithmetic applied to actual data for 1800.

prices would rise substantially, prompting consumers to use oil more efficiently and prompting producers to develop alternative fuel sources.

If productivity and the availability of substitutes increase fast enough, the price of "scarce" resources might actually fall rather than rise. This possibility prompted a famous "doomsday bet" between University of Maryland business professor Julian Simon and Stanford ecologist Paul Ehrlich. In 1980 Paul Ehrlich identified five metals that he predicted would become so scarce as to slow economic growth. Simon wagered that the price of those metals would actually *decline* over the ensuing decade as productivity and available substitutes increased. In 1990 their prices had fallen, and Ehrlich paid Simon for the bet.

Environmental Destruction. The market's ability to circumvent resource constraints would seem to augur well for our future. Doomsayers warn, though, that other limits to growth will emerge, even in a world of "unlimited" resources and unending productivity advance. The villain this time is pollution. More than 40 years ago, Paul Ehrlich warned about this second problem:

> Attempts to increase food production further will tend to accelerate the deterioration of our environment, which in turn will eventually *reduce* the capacity of the Earth to produce food. It is not clear whether environmental decay has now gone so far as to be essentially irreversible; it is possible that the capacity of the planet to support human life has been permanently impaired. Such technological "successes" as automobiles, pesticides, and inorganic nitrogen fertilizers are major contributors to environmental deterioration.[3]

The "inevitability" of environmental destruction led G. Evelyn Hutchinson to conclude in 1970 that the limits of habitable existence on Earth would be measured "in decades."[4]

It's not difficult for anyone with the basic five senses to comprehend the pollution problem. Pollution is as close these days as the air we breathe. Moreover, we can't fail to observe a distinct tendency for pollution levels to rise along with GDP and population expansion. Scientists are also alarmed by the climate changes that have accompanied

[3]Source: Erhlich, Paul, Anne H. Erhlich, *Population Resources Environment: Issues in Human Ecology,* 2/e, p. 442, San Francisco, CA: W.H. Freeman, 1972.

[4]Evelyn Hutchinson, "The Biosphere," *Scientific American,* September 1970, p. 53; Dennis L. Meadows et al., *The Limits to Growth* (New York: Universe Books, 1972), chapter 4.

population and output growth. If one projects past climate change and pollution trends into the future, things are bound to look pretty ugly.

Although pollution is universally acknowledged to be an important and annoying problem, we can't assume that the *rate* of pollution will continue unabated. On the contrary, the growing awareness of the pollution problem has prompted significant abatement efforts. The Environmental Protection Agency (EPA), for example, is unquestionably a force working for cleaner air and water. Indeed, active policies to curb pollution are as familiar as auto exhaust controls, DDT bans, and tradable CO_2 and SO_2 permits. A computer programmed 10 or 20 years ago to forecast pollution levels wouldn't have foreseen these abatement efforts and would thus have overestimated current pollution levels.

This isn't to say that we have in any final way solved the pollution problem or that we're even doing the best job we possibly can. It simply says that geometric increases in pollution aren't inevitable. There's no compelling reason why we have to continue polluting the environment; if we stop, another doomsday can be averted.

The Possibility of Growth. The misplaced focus on doomsday scenarios has a distinct opportunity cost. As Robert Solow summed up the issue,

> My real complaint about the Doomsday school [is that] it diverts attention from the really important things that can actually be done, step by step, to make things better. The end of the world *is* at hand—the earth, if you take the long view, will fall into the sun in a few billion years anyway, unless some other disaster happens first. In the meantime, I think we'd be better off passing a strong sulfur emissions tax, or getting some Highway Trust Fund money allocated to mass transit, or building a humane and decent floor under family incomes, or overriding President Nixon's veto of a strong Water Quality Act, or reforming the tax system, or fending off starvation in Bengal—instead of worrying about the generalized "predicament of mankind."[5]

Karl Marx expressed these same thoughts nearly a century earlier. Marx chastised "the contemptible Malthus" for turning the attention of the working class away from what he regarded as the immediate problem of capitalist exploitation to some distant and ill-founded anxiety about "natural" disaster.[6]

The Desirability of Growth. Let's concede, then, that continued, perhaps even "limitless," growth is *possible*. Can we also agree that it's *desirable*? Those of us who commute on congested highways, worry about climate change, breathe foul air, and can't find a secluded camping site may raise a loud chorus of nos. But before reaching a conclusion, let's at least determine what it is people don't like about the prospect of continued growth. Is it really economic growth per se that people object to, or instead the specific ways GDP has grown in the past?

First of all, let's distinguish clearly between economic growth and population growth. Congested neighborhoods, dining halls, and highways are the consequence of too many people, not of too many goods and services. Indeed, if we had *more* goods and services— if we had more houses and transit systems—much of the population congestion we now experience might be relieved. Maybe if we had enough resources to meet our existing demands *and* to build a solar-generated "new town" in the middle of Montana, people might move out of the crowded neighborhoods of Chicago and St. Louis. Well, probably not, but at least one thing is certain: with fewer goods and services, more people will have to share any given quantity of output.

This brings us back to the really essential measure of growth: GDP per capita. Are there any serious grounds for desiring *less* GDP per capita, a reduced standard of living? Don't say yes just because you think we already have too many cars on our roads or calories in our bellies. That argument refers to the *mix* of output again and doesn't answer the question of whether we want *any* more goods or services per person. Increasing GDP per capita can take a million forms, including the educational services you're now consuming. The rejection of economic growth per se implies that none of those forms is desirable in the economy tomorrow.

---

[5]Source: Solow, Robert, M., "Is the End of the World at Hand?" *Challenge,* 16(1), p. 50. Armonk, NY: M.E. Sharpe, 1973.
[6]Cited by John Maddox in *The Doomsday Syndrome* (New York: McGraw-Hill, 1972), pp. 40 and 45.

SUMMARY

- Economic growth refers to increases in real GDP. Short-run growth may result from increases in capacity utilization (like less unemployment). In the long run, however, growth requires increases in capacity itself—rightward shifts of the long-run aggregate supply curve. **LO17-1**
- The U.S. economy has grown an average of 3 percent a year, a rate that doubles total output every 24 years. **LO17-1**
- GDP per capita is a basic measure of living standards. GDP per capita will continue to increase as long as output growth exceeds population growth. **LO17-1**
- GDP per worker is a basic measure of productivity. **LO17-1**
- The rate of economic growth is set by the growth rate of the labor force *plus* the growth rate of output per worker (productivity). Over time, increases in productivity have been the primary cause of rising living standards. **LO17-1**
- Productivity gains come from many sources, including better labor quality, increased capital investment, research and development, improved management, and supportive government policies. **LO17-2**

- Supply-side policies increase both the short- and long-run capacity to produce. Monetary and fiscal policies may also affect capital investment and thus the rate of economic growth. **LO17-2**
- Recent U.S. investment growth has been financed primarily with business saving and foreign investment. U.S. households save very little. **LO17-1**
- The argument that there are identifiable and imminent limits to growth—perhaps even a cataclysmic doomsday—are founded on one of two concerns: (1) the depletion of resources and (2) pollution of the ecosystem. **LO17-3**
- The flaw in doomsday arguments is that they regard existing patterns of resource use or pollution as unalterable. They consistently underestimate the possibilities for technological advance or market adaptation. **LO17-3**
- Continued economic growth is desirable as long as it brings a higher standard of living for people and an increased ability to produce and consume socially desirable goods and services. **LO17-3**

Key Terms

production possibilities	GDP per capita	net investment
economic growth	labor force	crowding out
real GDP	employment rate	geometric growth
base year	productivity	arithmetic growth
growth rate	human capital	

Questions for Discussion

1. In what specific ways (if any) does a college education increase a worker's productivity? **LO17-1**
2. How did output per U.S. worker increase so much in 2007–2011 (World View "U.S. Workers Compete Well")? How could German productivity *decline*? **LO17-1**
3. Why don't we consume all our current output instead of sacrificing some present consumption for investment? **LO17-1**
4. How might economic growth be impeded by (*a*) high levels of national debt and/or (*b*) fiscal restraint designed to reduce that national debt? **LO17-2**
5. Should fiscal policy encourage more consumption or more saving? Does it matter? **LO17-2**
6. In 1866 Stanley Jevons predicted that economic growth would come to a halt when England ran out of coal, a doomsday that he reckoned would occur in the mid-

1970s. How did we avert that projection? Will we avert an "oil crisis" in the same way? **LO17-3**
7. Fertility rates in the United States have dropped so low that we're approaching zero population growth, a condition that France has maintained for decades. How will this affect our economic growth? Our standard of living? **LO17-1**
8. Is limitless growth really possible? What forces do you think will be most important in slowing or halting economic growth? **LO17-3**
9. Why do some nations grow and prosper while others stagnate? **LO17-1**
10. Why do economists worry about how pro-growth spending is financed (In the News "Paying for Trump's Infrastructure Spending")? **LO17-2**

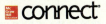

PROBLEMS FOR CHAPTER 17

LO17-1 1. According to the Rule of 72 (Table 17.1), how many years will it take for GDP to double if the economy is growing at
   (*a*) 1 percent a year?
   (*b*) 3 percent a year?

LO17-1 2. According to the Rule of 72 (Table 17.1) and recent growth rates (World View "High Investment = Fast Growth") how long will it be before GDP doubles in
   (*a*) The United States?
   (*b*) India?
   (*c*) Greece?

LO17-1 3. How much *more* output will the average American (U.S. population = 330 million) have a year from now if the $20 trillion GDP grows by
   (*a*) 0 percent?
   (*b*) 1 percent?
   (*c*) 3 percent?

LO17-3 4. According to Figure 17.3, in how many years since 1990 has GDP grown
   (*a*) Faster than the population (1.1 percent growth)?
   (*b*) Slower than the population?

LO17-1 5. If the labor force increases by 1.1 percent each year and productivity increases by 2.8 percent, how fast will output grow?

LO17-1 6. In 2016, 59.7 percent of the adult population (253 million) was employed. If the employment rate increased to 62 percent,
   (*a*) How many more people would be working?
   (*b*) By how much would output increase if per worker GDP were $122,000?

LO17-1 7. If output per worker is now $122,000 per year, how much will the average worker produce next year if productivity improves by
   (*a*) 2.0 percent per year?
   (*b*) 3.0 percent per year?

LO17-1 8. The real (inflation-adjusted) value of U.S. manufacturing output and related manufacturing employment was

	Output	Employment
2000	$1.541 trillion	17,321,000
2016	$2.120 trillion	12,275,000

   (*a*) How many manufacturing jobs were lost between 2000 and 2016?
   (*b*) How much did output increase?
   (*c*) What was average manufacturing productivity (output per worker) in
      (*i*) 2000?
      (*i*) 2016?

LO17-3 9. Suppose that every additional four percentage points in the investment rate ($I \div$ GDP) boost economic growth by one percentage point. Assume also that all investment must be financed with consumer saving. The economy is now assumed to be fully employed at

GDP	$8 trillion
Consumption	6 trillion
Saving	1 trillion
Investment	1 trillion

If the goal is to raise the growth rate by 1 percent,
(*a*) By how much must investment increase?
(*b*) By how much must consumption decline for this to occur?

LO17-1 10. Using Data Tables, graph the real GDP growth rates for 2007–2016.

LO17-1 11. Using Data Tables, calculate nominal GDP per capita for 2007–2016.

LO17-2 12. The Economy Tomorrow: Suppose a country's GDP is 10 billion and the population is 2 million this year.
(*a*) Calculate GDP per capita for this year.
(*b*) Calculate GDP per capita for next year if the population grows by 5 percent and there is no change in output.
(*c*) Calculate GDP per capita for next year if the population grows by 1 percent and output grows by 3 percent.

©MOF/Getty Images RF

©Lars A. Niki RF

POLICY CONSTRAINTS

Macro theories often provide conflicting advice about whether and how the government ought to intervene. To make matters worse, the information needed to make a decision is typically incomplete. Politics muddies the waters too by changing priorities and restricting the use of policy tools. Finally, there's the inescapable reality that everything changes at once—there's no *ceteris paribus* in the real world. Chapter 18 surveys the real-world obstacles to better policy decisions and macro outcomes.

©Lars A. Niki RF

Theory versus Reality

There are no all-powerful, all-knowing superheroes . . . who can rescue . . . the economy all by themselves. You might think that the federal government could revive the economy quickly . . . or that the Fed could fix it. . . . But Washington has far less power over the economy . . . than many people think. We always think there's a person who holds the magic wand. But this society and this economy are far too complex to be susceptible to magic wands.

—**Senator Judd Gregg,** *Fortune,* **November 1, 2010**

Macroeconomic theory is supposed to explain the business cycle and show policymakers how to control it. But something is obviously wrong. Despite our relative prosperity, we haven't consistently achieved the goals of full employment, price stability, and vigorous economic growth. All too often, either unemployment or inflation surges or economic growth slows down. No matter how hard we try to eliminate it, the business cycle seems to persist, as we witnessed again in the last few years.

What accounts for this gap between the promises of economic theory and the reality of economic performance? Are the theories inadequate? Or is sound economic advice being ignored?

Many people blame the economists. They point to the conflicting advice of Keynesians, monetarists, and supply-siders and wonder what theory is supposed to be followed. If economists themselves can't agree, it is asked, why should anyone else listen to them?

Not surprisingly, economists see things a bit differently. First, they point out, the **business cycle** isn't as bad as it used to be. Since World War II, the economy has had many ups and downs, but none as severe as the Great Depression or earlier catastrophes. Second, economists complain that politics often takes precedence over good economic advice. Politicians are reluctant, for example, to raise taxes, cut spending, or slow money growth to control inflation. Their concern is winning the next election, not solving the country's economic problems.

When President Jimmy Carter was in office, he anguished over another problem: the complexity of economic decision making. In the real world, neither theory nor politics can keep up with all our economic goals. As President Carter observed, "We cannot concentrate just on inflation or just on unemployment or just on deficits in the federal budget or our international payments. Nor can we act in isolation from other countries. We must deal with all of these problems simultaneously and on a worldwide basis."

LEARNING OBJECTIVES

After reading this chapter, you should know

LO18-1 The tools of macro policy.

LO18-2 How macro tools should work.

LO18-3 The constraints on policy effectiveness.

business cycle: Alternating periods of economic growth and contraction.

No president learned this lesson faster or more forcefully than George W. Bush. Just as he was putting the final touches on a bipartisan consensus on taxes, spending, and debt reduction, terrorists destroyed the World Trade Center and damaged the Pentagon. In response to those attacks, all major economic policy decisions had to be revised. President Obama also had to revise his economic plans as soon as he took office. An acceleration of the 2008–2009 downturn forced him to abandon promised tax increases on the rich and instead fashion a fiscal stimulus package.

As if the burdens of a continuously changing world weren't enough, the president must also contend with sharply differing economic theories and advice, a slow and frequently hostile Congress, a massive and often unresponsive bureaucracy, and a complete lack of knowledge about the future.

This chapter confronts these and other frustrations of the real world head on. In so doing, we provide answers to the following questions:

- **What's the ideal "package" of macro policies?**
- **How well does our macro performance live up to the promises of that package?**
- **What kinds of obstacles prevent us from doing better?**

The answers to these questions may shed some light on a broader concern that has long troubled students and policymakers alike—namely, "If economists are so smart, why is the economy always in such a mess?"

POLICY TOOLS

Table 18.1 summarizes the macroeconomic tools available to policymakers. Although this list is brief, we hardly need a reminder at this point of how powerful each instrument can be. Every one of these major policy instruments can significantly change our answers to the basic economic questions of WHAT, HOW, and FOR WHOM to produce.

Fiscal Policy

The basic tools of **fiscal policy** are contained in the federal budget. Tax cuts are supposed to increase aggregate demand by putting more income in the hands of consumers and businesses. Tax increases are intended to curtail spending and reduce inflationary pressures. Table 18.2 summarizes some of the major tax changes of recent years.

The expenditure side of the federal budget is another fiscal policy tool. From a Keynesian perspective, increases in government spending raise aggregate demand and so encourage more production. A slowdown in government spending is supposed to restrain aggregate demand and lessen inflationary pressures.

fiscal policy: The use of government taxes and spending to alter macroeconomic outcomes.

Type of Policy	Policy Tools
Fiscal policy	• Tax cuts and increases. • Changes in government spending. • Transfer cuts and increases.
Monetary policy	• Open market operations. • Changes in reserve requirements. • Changes in the discount rate.
Supply-side policy	• Tax incentives for investment and saving. • Deregulation. • Human capital investment. • Infrastructure development. • Free trade. • Changes to immigration policy.

TABLE 18.1

The Policy Tools

Economic policymakers have access to a variety of policy instruments. The challenge is to choose the right tools at the right time.

Fiscal Policy Milestones

Fiscal policy is contained in tax and spending legislation approved by Congress. These are some significant decisions.

Year	Act	Description
1986	Tax Reform Act	Major reduction in tax rates coupled with broadening of tax base.
1990	Budget Enforcement Act	Limits set on discretionary spending; pay-as-you-go financing required.
1993	Clinton "New Direction"	Tax increases and spending cuts to achieve $300 billion deficit reduction.
1994	Contract with America	Republican-led Congress cuts spending, sets seven-year target for balanced budget.
1997	Balanced Budget Act, Taxpayer Relief Act	Package of tax cuts and spending cuts to balance budget by 2002.
2001	Economic Growth and Tax Relief Act	Eight-year, $1.35 trillion in personal tax cuts.
2002	Job Creation and Worker Assistance Act	Business investment tax cuts.
2003	Jobs and Growth Tax Relief Act	Cuts in dividend and capital gains taxes.
2008	Economic Stimulus Act	$168 billion of tax rebates.
2009	American Recovery and Reinvestment Act	$787 billion package of spending and tax cuts.
2010	Continuing Resolution	Extension of tax cuts, unemployment benefits, spending until 2012, plus one-year payroll tax cut.
2011	Deficit Reduction	Package of spending cuts and tax hikes to reduce deficit.
2013	Taxpayer Relief Act	Increased top tax rate on personal income and on capital gains.
2015	Bipartisan Budget Act	Increased discretionary spending by $80 billion for 2016–2017.
2017	Trump Budget Proposals	Increased spending on infrastructure, border security, and defense, combined with huge tax cuts.

automatic stabilizer: Federal expenditure or revenue item that automatically responds countercyclically to changes in national income, like unemployment benefits and income taxes.

structural deficit: Federal revenues at full employment minus expenditures at full employment under prevailing fiscal policy.

fiscal stimulus: Tax cuts or spending hikes intended to increase (shift) aggregate demand.

fiscal restraint: Tax hikes or spending cuts intended to reduce (shift) aggregate demand.

monetary policy: The use of money and credit controls to influence macroeconomic outcomes.

natural rate of unemployment: The long-term rate of unemployment determined by structural forces in labor and product markets.

Who Makes Fiscal Policy? As we first observed in Chapter 11, changes in taxes and government spending originate in both economic events and explicit policy decisions. When the economy slows, tax revenues decline, and government spending increases automatically. Conversely, when real GDP grows, tax revenues automatically rise, and government transfer payments decline. These **automatic stabilizers** are a basic countercyclical feature of the federal budget. They don't represent active fiscal policy. On the contrary, *fiscal policy refers to deliberate changes in tax or spending legislation.* These changes can be made only by the U.S. Congress. Every year the president proposes specific budget and tax changes, negotiates with Congress, then accepts or vetoes specific acts that Congress has passed. The resulting policy decisions represent "discretionary" fiscal policy. Those policy decisions expand or shrink the **structural deficit** and thus give the economy a shot of **fiscal stimulus** or **fiscal restraint**.

Monetary Policy

The policy arsenal in Table 18.1 also contains monetary tools. Tools of **monetary policy** include open market operations, discount rate changes, and reserve requirements.

As we saw in Chapter 15, there are disagreements over how these monetary tools should be used. Keynesians believe that interest rates are the critical policy lever. In their view, the money supply should be expanded or curtailed to achieve whatever interest rate is needed to shift aggregate demand. Monetarists, on the other hand, contend that the money supply itself is the critical policy tool and that it should be expanded at a steady and predictable rate. This policy, they believe, will ensure price stability and a **natural rate of unemployment**.

Who Makes Monetary Policy? Actual monetary policy decisions are made by the Federal Reserve's Board of Governors. Twice a year the Fed provides Congress with a broad overview of the economic outlook and monetary objectives. The Fed's assessment of the

TABLE 18.3

Monetary Policy Milestones

Monetary policy is set by the Federal Reserve Board of Governors.

October 1979	Fed adopts monetarist approach, focusing exclusively on money supply; interest rates soar.
July 1982	Deep into recession, Fed votes to ease monetary restraint.
October 1982	Fed abandons pure monetarist approach and expands money supply rapidly.
May 1983	Fed reverses policy and begins slowing money supply growth.
1985	Fed increases money supply with discount rate cuts and open market purchases.
1987	Fed abandons money supply targets as policy guides; money supply growth decreases; discount rate increases.
1989	Greenspan announces goal of "zero inflation," tightens policy.
1991	Deep in recession, the Fed begins to ease monetary restraint.
1994	Fed slows M2 growth to 1 percent; raises federal funds rate by three percentage points as economy nears full employment.
1995	Greenspan trumpets "soft landing" and eases monetary restraint.
1998	Fed cuts interest rates to cushion United States from Asian crisis.
1999–2000	Fed raises interest rates 6 times.
2001–2003	Fed cuts interest rates 13 times.
2004–2006	Fed raises fed funds rate 17 times.
2007–2008	Fed cuts interest rates 10 times.
2008–2014	Three rounds of "quantitative easing": Fed buys more than $2 trillion of bonds and securities directly from banks.
November 2014	Quantitative easing ends.
December 2016	Fed increases federal funds rate; signals more rate hikes to come.

economy is updated at meetings of the Federal Open Market Committee (FOMC). The FOMC decides which monetary policy levers to pull.

Table 18.3 depicts milestones in recent monetary policy. Of particular interest is the October 1979 decision to adopt a pure monetarist approach. This involved an exclusive focus on the money supply, without regard for interest rates. After interest rates soared and the economy appeared on the brink of a depression, the Fed abandoned the monetarist approach and again began keeping an eye on both interest rates (the Keynesian focus) and the money supply.

Monetarists contend that the Fed never fully embraced their policy. The money supply grew at a very uneven pace in 1980, they argue, not at the steady, predictable rate that they demanded. Nevertheless, the policy shifts of 1979 and 1982 were distinctive and had dramatic effects.

A quick review of Table 18.3 reveals that such monetary policy reversals have been quite frequent. There were U-turns in monetary policy between 1982 and 1983, 1989 and 1991, 1998 and 1999, 2000 and 2001, 2003 and 2004, and again between 2007 and 2008.

In November 2008 the Fed began massive purchases of long-term Treasury bonds and other securities, hoping to bring down long-term interest rates (especially mortgage rates). This first round of "quantitative easing" (QE1) ended in March 2010. When the economic recovery started to look wobbly later that year, the Fed pursued a second round (QE2) of massive ($600 billion) bond purchases from November 2010 to June 2011 and a third round (QE3) from September 2012 to the end of 2014. Monetarists were horrified, fearing that such a huge increase in M would ultimately ignite inflation (P).

The Fed kept interest rates at record low levels for more than six years. When the unemployment rate got very low and prices started to rise the Fed tapped on the brakes a bit. In December 2016 the Fed raised the federal funds target rate slightly (from .50 to .75 percent) and signaled its intention to push rates higher in 2017.

Supply-Side Policy

Supply-side theory offers the third major set of policy tools. The focus of **supply-side policy** is to provide incentives to work, invest, and produce. Of particular concern are high tax rates and regulations that reduce supply incentives. Supply-siders argue that marginal tax rates and government regulation must be reduced to get more output without added inflation.

supply-side policy: The use of tax incentives, (de)regulation, and other mechanisms to increase the ability and willingness to produce goods and services.

In the 1980s tax rates were reduced dramatically. The maximum marginal tax rate on individuals was cut from 70 to 50 percent in 1981, and then still further, to 28 percent, in 1987. The 1980s also witnessed major milestones in the deregulation of airlines, trucking, telephone service, and other industries.

Some of the momentum toward less regulation was reversed during the 1990s (see Table 18.4). New regulatory costs on business were created by the Americans with Disabilities Act, the 1990 amendments to the Clean Air Act, and the Family Leave Act of 1993. All three laws provide important benefits to workers or the environment. At the same time, however, they make supplying goods and services more expensive.

The Obama administration broadened supply-side efforts to include infrastructure development and increased investment in human capital (through education and skill training programs). These activities increase the capacity to produce and so shift the aggregate supply curve rightward. The Obama administration also toughened environmental regulation, however, and introduced new regulations on bank lending (Dodd-Frank) and health care (Affordable Care Act), and paid family leave that shifted the aggregate supply curve leftward. Increases in marginal tax rates on personal income, capital gains, and dividends further diminished incentives to work and invest.

Year	Act	Description
1990	Social Security Act amendments	Increased payroll tax to 7.65 percent.
	Americans with Disabilities Act	Required employers to provide greater access for disabled individuals.
	Immigration Act	Increased immigration, especially for highly skilled workers.
	Clean Air Act amendments	Increased pollution controls.
1993	Rebuild America Program	Increased spending on infrastructure and human capital investment.
	Family Leave Act	Required employers to provide unpaid leaves of absence for workers.
	NAFTA	Lowered North American trade barriers.
1994	GATT renewed	Lowered world trade barriers.
1996	Telecommunications Act	Permitted greater competition in cable and telephone industries.
	Personal Responsibility and Work Opportunity Act	Required more welfare recipients to work.
1997	Taxpayer Relief Act	Created tuition tax credits; cut capital gains tax.
1998	Workforce Investment Act	Increased funds for skills training.
2000	Transportation Equity Act	Provided new funding for highways, rails.
2001	Economic Growth and Tax Relief Act	Increased savings incentives; reduced marginal tax rates.
2002	Job Creation and Worker Assistance Act	Provided more tax incentives for investment.
2003	Jobs and Growth Tax Relief Act	Reduced taxes on capital gains and dividends.
2007	Minimum wage hike	Raised from $5.15 to $7.25 in 2009.
2009	American Recovery and Reinvestment Act	Infrastructure and energy development.
2010	Affordable Care and Dodd-Frank Acts	Raised costs and reduced incentives for labor supply, labor demand, and bank lending.
2013	Taxpayer Relief Act	Raised top marginal tax rate on personal incomes (39.6%), capital gains, and dividends (to 20% from 15%).
2017	Trump tax cuts	Proposed cut in corporate tax rate (35% to 15%) and reduced top marginal tax rate on individuals.

TABLE 18.4

Supply-Side Milestones

Tax and regulatory decisions affect supply decisions.

Who Makes Supply-Side Policy? Because tax rates are a basic tool of supply-side policy, fiscal and supply-side policies are often intertwined. When Congress changes the tax laws, it almost always alters marginal tax rates and thus changes production incentives. Notice, for example, that tax legislation appears in Table 18.4 as well as in Table 18.2. The Taxpayer Relief Act of 2012 not only changed total tax revenues (fiscal policy) but also restructured production and investment incentives (supply-side policy). The 2001–2003 tax cuts also had both demand-side and supply-side provisions.

Supply-side and fiscal policies also interact on the outlay side of the budget. The Transportation Equity Act of 2000, for example, authorized accelerated public works spending (fiscal stimulus) on infrastructure development (increase in supply capacity). The infrastructure and energy development included in President Trump's budget proposals also affect both aggregate demand and aggregate supply. *Deciding whether to increase spending is a fiscal policy decision; deciding how to spend available funds may entail supply-side policy.*

Regulatory policy is also fashioned by Congress. The president and executive agencies play a critical role in this supply-side area in the day-to-day decisions on how to interpret and enforce regulatory policies.

IDEALIZED USES

These fiscal, monetary, and supply-side tools are potentially powerful levers for controlling the economy. In principle, they can cure the excesses of the business cycle and promote faster economic growth. To see how, let's review their use in three distinct macroeconomic settings.

Case 1: Recession

When output and employment levels fall far short of the economy's full-employment potential, the mandate for public policy is clear. Aggregate demand must be increased so that producers can sell more goods, hire more workers, and move the economy toward its productive capacity. At such times the most urgent need is to get people back to work and close the **recessionary GDP gap.**

How can the government end a recession? Keynesians emphasize the need to increase aggregate demand by cutting taxes or boosting government spending. The resulting stimulus will set off a **multiplier** reaction. If the initial stimulus and multiplier are large enough, the recessionary GDP gap can be closed, propelling the economy to full employment.

Modern Keynesians acknowledge that monetary policy might also help. Specifically, increases in the money supply may lower interest rates and thus give investment spending a further boost. To give the economy a really powerful stimulus, we might want to pull all these policy levers at the same time. That's what the government did in early 2001—using tax cuts, lower interest rates, and increased spending to jump-start the economy. The same one-two punch was used again, on a much more massive scale, in 2008–2010.

Monetarists would proceed differently. First, they see no point in toying with the federal budget. In the pure monetarist model, changes in taxes or government spending may alter the mix of output but not its level. So long as the **velocity of money** (*V*) is constant, fiscal policy doesn't matter. In this view, the appropriate policy response to a recession is patience. As sales and output slow, interest rates will decline, and new investment will be stimulated.

Supply-siders emphasize the need to improve production incentives. They urge cuts in marginal tax rates on investment and labor. They also look for ways to reduce government regulation. Finally, they urge that any increase in government spending (fiscal stimulus) focus on long-run capacity expansion such as infrastructure development.

Case 2: Inflation

An overheated economy provides as clear a policy mandate as does a sluggish one. In this case, the immediate goal is to restrain aggregate demand until the rate of total expenditure is compatible with the productive capacity of the economy. This entails shifting the aggregate demand curve to the left to close the **inflationary GDP gap.** Keynesians would do

recessionary GDP gap: The amount by which equilibrium GDP falls short of full-employment GDP.

multiplier: The multiple by which an initial change in aggregate spending will alter total expenditure after an infinite number of spending cycles; $1/(1 - MPC)$.

velocity of money (*V*): The number of times per year, on average, that a dollar is used to purchase final goods and services; $PQ \div M$.

inflationary GDP gap: The amount by which equilibrium GDP exceeds full-employment GDP.

this by raising taxes and cutting government spending. Keynesians would also see the desirability of increasing interest rates to curb investment spending.

Monetarists would simply cut the money supply. In their view, the short-run aggregate supply curve is unknown and unstable. The only predictable response is reflected in the vertical, long-run aggregate supply curve. According to this view, changes in the money supply alter prices, not output. Inflation is seen simply as "too much money chasing too few goods." Monetarists would turn off the money spigot. The Fed's job in this situation isn't only to reduce money supply growth but to convince market participants that a more cautious monetary policy will be continued.

Supply-siders would point out that inflation implies both "too much money" *and* "not enough goods." They'd look at the supply side of the market for ways to expand productive capacity. In a highly inflationary setting, they'd propose more incentives to save. The additional savings would automatically reduce consumption while creating a larger pool of investable funds. Supply-siders would also cut taxes and regulations that raise production costs and lower import barriers that keep out cheaper foreign goods.

Case 3: Stagflation

stagflation: The simultaneous occurrence of substantial unemployment and inflation.

Although serious inflations and recessions provide clear mandates for economic policy, there's a vast gray area between these extremes. Occasionally the economy suffers from both inflation and unemployment at the same time, a condition called **stagflation.** In 1980, for example, the unemployment rate (7.1 percent) and the inflation rate (12.5 percent) were both too high. With an upward-sloping aggregate supply curve, the easy policy options were foreclosed. If aggregate demand were stimulated to reduce unemployment, the resultant pressure on prices might fuel the existing inflation. And if fiscal and monetary restraints were used to reduce inflationary pressures, unemployment might worsen. In such a situation, there are no simple solutions.

Knowing the causes of stagflation will help achieve the desired balance. If prices are rising before full employment is reached, some degree of structural unemployment is likely. An appropriate policy response might include more vocational training in skill shortage areas as well as a redirection of aggregate demand toward labor surplus sectors.

High tax rates or costly regulations might also contribute to stagflation. If either constraint exists, high prices (inflation) may not be a sufficient incentive for increased output. In this case, reductions in tax rates and regulation might help reduce both unemployment and inflation, which is the basic strategy of supply-side policies.

Stagflation may also arise from a temporary contraction of aggregate supply that both reduces output and drives up prices. In this case, neither structural unemployment nor excessive demand is the culprit. Rather, an "external shock" (such as a natural disaster or a terrorist attack) or an abrupt change in world trade (such as a spike in oil prices) is likely to be the cause of the policy dilemma. Accordingly, none of our familiar policy tools is likely to provide a complete "cure." In most cases, the economy simply has to adjust to a temporary setback.

Fine-Tuning

fine-tuning: Adjustments in economic policy designed to counteract small changes in economic outcomes; continuous responses to changing economic conditions.

The apparently inexhaustible potential of public policy to alter the economy's performance has often generated optimistic expectations about the efficacy of fiscal, monetary, and supply-side tools. In the early 1960s such optimism pervaded even the highest levels of government. Those were the days when prices were relatively stable, unemployment rates were falling, the economy was growing rapidly, and preparations were being made for the first trip into space. The potential of economic policy looked great indeed. It was also during the 1960s that a lot of people (mostly economists) spoke of the potential for **fine-tuning,** or altering economic outcomes to fit very exacting specifications. Flexible responses to changing market conditions, it was argued, could ensure fulfillment of our economic goals. The prescription was simple: When unemployment is the problem, simply give the economy a jolt of fiscal or monetary stimulus; when inflation is worrisome, simply tap on the fiscal or monetary brakes. To fulfill our goals for content and distribution, simply pick the right target for stimulus or restraint. With a little attention and experience, the right speed could be found and the economy guided successfully down the road to prosperity. As the economic expansion of the 1990s stretched into the record books, the same kind of economic mastery was claimed. More than a few prominent economists claimed the business cycle was dead.

THE ECONOMIC RECORD

The economy's track record doesn't live up to these high expectations. To be sure, the economy has continued to grow, and we've attained an impressive standard of living. We can't lose sight of the fact that our per capita income greatly exceeds the realities and even the expectations in most other countries of the world. Nevertheless, we must also recognize that our economic history is punctuated by periods of recession, high unemployment, inflation, and recurring concern for the distribution of income and mix of output. The Great Recession of 2008–2009 was our latest lesson in humility.

The graphs in Figure 18.1 provide a quick summary of the gap between the theory and reality of economic policy. The Employment Act of 1946 committed the federal

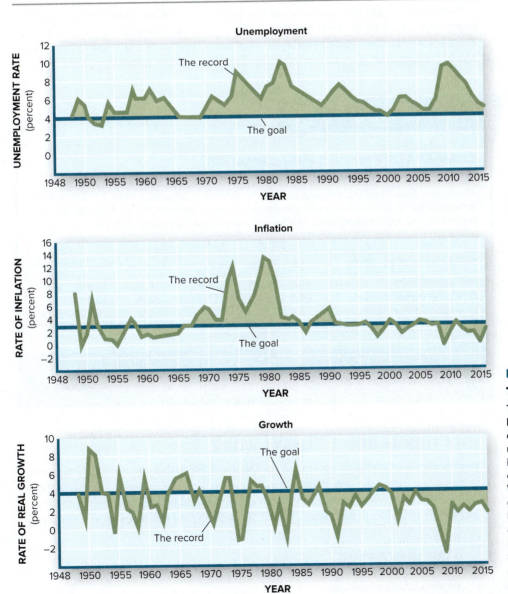

FIGURE 18.1

The Economic Record

The Full Employment and Balanced Growth Act of 1978 established specific goals for unemployment (4 percent), inflation (3 percent), and economic growth (4 percent). We've rarely attained those goals, however, as these graphs illustrate. Measurement, design, and policy implementation problems help explain these shortcomings.

Source: U.S. Bureaus of Labor Statistics and Economic Analysis.

government to macro stability. It's evident that we haven't kept that commitment. In the 1970s we rarely came close. Although we approached all three goals in the mid-1980s, our achievements were short-lived. Economic growth ground to a halt in 1989, and the economy slipped into yet another recession in 1990. Although inflation stayed low, unemployment rates jumped.

The economy performed very well again from 1992 until early 2000. After that, however, growth came to an abrupt halt again. With the economy teetering on recession, the unemployment rate started rising in mid-2000. Some of the people who had proclaimed the business cycle to be dead were out of work. Then the economy was hit by the external shock of a terrorist attack that suspended economic activity and shook investor and consumer confidence. It took two years to get unemployment rates back down into the "full-employment" range (4–6 percent). The cycle began to reverse at the end of 2007, leading to the recession of 2008–2009. Unemployment rose to 10 percent and stayed very high for five years.

Looking back over the entire postwar (1946–) period, the record includes 12 years of outright recession (actual declines in output) and another 20 years of **growth recession** (growth of less than 3 percent). That adds up to a 46 percent macro failure rate. Moreover, the distribution of income in 2016 looked worse than that of 1946, and more than 40 million people were still officially counted as poor in the later year.

Despite many setbacks, recent economic performance of the United States has been better than that of other Western nations. Other economies haven't grown as fast as the United States nor reduced unemployment as much. But as World View "Comparative Macro Performance" shows, some countries did a better job of restraining prices.

growth recession: A period during which real GDP grows but at a rate below the long-term trend of 3 percent.

WORLD VIEW

COMPARATIVE MACRO PERFORMANCE

The performance of the U.S. economy in the 2000s was better than that of most developed economies. Japan had the greatest success in restraining inflation (*minus* 3.5 percent) but suffered from sluggish growth (7.4 percent in an entire decade). The United States grew faster and also experienced less unemployment than most European countries.

Performance, 2000–2010	U.S.	Japan	Germany	United Kingdom	France	Canada
Real growth (10-year increase)	18.0	7.4	8.8	14.9	12.4	20.4
Inflation (10-year change)	26.6	-3.5	17.4	30.0	12.0	22.1
Unemployment (annual average)	6.5	5.2	9.3	6.2	9.8	7.8

Source: *World Economic Outlook*, International Monetary Fund, 2011.

ANALYSIS: Macroeconomic performance varies a lot both over time and across countries. In the 2000s U.S. economic performance was above average on most measures.

WHY THINGS DON'T ALWAYS WORK

There's plenty of blame to go around for the many blemishes on our economic record. Some people blame the president; others blame the Fed or Congress; still others blame China or Mexico. Some forces, however, constrain economic policy even when no one is specifically to blame. In this regard, we can distinguish *four obstacles to policy success:*

- *Goal conflicts.*
- *Measurement problems.*
- *Design problems.*
- *Implementation problems.*

Goal Conflicts

The first factor to take note of is potential conflicts in policy priorities. President Clinton had to confront this problem his first day in office. He had pledged to create new jobs by increasing public infrastructure spending and offering a middle-class tax cut. He had also promised to reduce the deficit, however. This created a clear goal conflict. In the end, President Clinton had to settle for a smaller increase in infrastructure spending and a tax *increase.*

President George W. Bush confronted similar problems. In the 2000 presidential campaign he had promised a big increase in federal spending on education. By the time he took office, however, the federal budget surplus was rapidly shrinking, and the goal of preserving the surplus took precedence. The conflict between spending priorities and budget balancing became much more intense when President Bush decided to attack Iraq. We also noted earlier how President Obama had to set aside some campaign promises (e.g., raising taxes on capital gains, estates, and "the rich") when confronted on day 1 with the urgent need to stimulate aggregate demand. For his part, President Trump had to figure out how to reconcile his ambitious spending plans for infrastructure and the military with his promise to end deficit spending.

These and other goal conflicts have their roots in the short-run trade-off between unemployment and inflation. With aggressive use of fiscal and monetary stimulus, we can surely increase AD and move the economy toward full employment. But we might set off a multiplier process that pushes the economy past its **inflationary flashpoint.** In view of that risk, should we try to cure inflation, unemployment, or just a bit of both? Answers are likely to vary. Unemployed people put the highest priority on attaining full employment. Labor unions press for faster economic growth. Bankers, creditors, and people on fixed incomes demand an end to inflation.

This goal conflict is often institutionalized in the decision-making process. The Fed is traditionally viewed as the guardian of price stability. The president and Congress worry more about people's jobs and government programs, so they are less willing to raise taxes or cut spending.

Distributional goals may also conflict with macro objectives. Anti-inflationary policies may require cutbacks in programs for the poor, the elderly, or needy students. These cutbacks may be politically impossible. Likewise, tight-money policies may be viewed as too great a burden for small businesses, home builders, and auto manufacturers.

Although the policy tools in Table 18.1 are powerful, they can't grant all our wishes. Since we still live in a world of scarce resources, *all policy decisions entail opportunity costs,* which means that we'll always be confronted with trade-offs. The best we can hope for is a set of compromises that yields *optimal* outcomes, not ideal ones.

inflationary flashpoint: The rate of output at which inflationary pressures intensify; the point on the AS curve where slope increases sharply.

Measurement Problems

One reason firefighters are pretty successful in putting out fires before entire cities burn down is that fires are highly visible phenomena. But such visibility isn't characteristic of economic problems. An increase in the unemployment rate from 5 to 6 percent, for example, isn't the kind of thing you notice while crossing the street. Unless you work in the unemployment insurance office or lose your own job, the increase in unemployment isn't likely to attract your attention. The same is true of prices; small increases in product prices aren't likely to ring many alarms. Hence both inflation and unemployment may worsen considerably before anyone takes serious notice. Were we as slow and ill-equipped to notice fires, whole neighborhoods would burn before someone rang the alarm.

Measurement problems are a very basic policy constraint. To formulate appropriate economic policy, we must first determine the nature of our problems. To do so, we must measure employment changes, output changes, price changes, and other macro outcomes. The old adage that governments are willing and able to solve only those problems they can measure is relevant here. Indeed, before the Great Depression, a fundamental constraint on public policy was the lack of statistics on what was happening in the economy. One lasting benefit of that experience is that we now try to keep informed on changing economic conditions. The information at hand, however, is always dated and incomplete. *At best, we know what was happening in the economy last month or last week.* The processes of data collection, assembly, and presentation take time, even in this age of high-speed computers. The average recession lasts about 11 months, but official data generally don't even confirm the existence of a recession until 8 months after a downturn starts! As In the News "Great Recession Officially Ended Last Year" reveals, the 2008–2009 recession ended 15 months before researchers confirmed its demise!

IN THE NEWS

GREAT RECESSION OFFICIALLY ENDED LAST YEAR

CAMBRIDGE September 20, 2010—The Business Cycle Dating Committee of the National Bureau of Economic Research met yesterday by conference call. At its meeting, the committee determined that a trough in business activity occurred in the U.S. economy in June 2009. The trough marks the end of the recession that began in December 2007 and the beginning of an expansion. The recession lasted 18 months, which makes it the longest of any recession since World War II. Previously the longest postwar recessions were those of 1973–75 and 1981–82, both of which lasted 16 months. . . .

A recession is a period of falling economic activity spread across the economy, lasting more than a few months, normally visible in real GDP, real income, employment, industrial production, and wholesale-retail sales. The trough marks the end of the declining phase and the start of the rising phase of the business cycle.

Source: National Bureau of Economic Research, September 20, 2010.

ANALYSIS: In the absence of timely information, today's policy decisions are inevitably based on yesterday's perceptions.

Forecasts. In an ideal world, policymakers wouldn't just *respond* to economic problems but would also *anticipate* their occurrence. If an inflationary GDP gap is emerging, for example, we want to take immediate action to keep aggregate spending from increasing. That is, the successful firefighter not only responds to a fire but also looks for hazards that might start one.

Unfortunately, economic policymakers are again at a disadvantage. Their knowledge of future problems is even worse than their knowledge of current problems. *In designing policy, policymakers must depend on economic forecasts*—that is, informed guesses about what the economy will look like in future periods.

Macro Models. Those guesses are often based on complex computer models of how the economy works. These models—referred to as *econometric macro models*—are mathematical summaries of the economy's performance. The models try to identify the key determinants of macro performance and then show what happens to macro outcomes when they change. The apparent precision of such computer models may disguise inherent guesswork, however.

An economist "feeds" the computer two essential inputs. One is a quantitative model of how the economy allegedly works. A Keynesian model, for example, includes equations that show multiplier spending responses to tax cuts. A monetarist model shows that tax cuts raise interest rates, not total spending ("crowding out"), and a supply-side model stipulates labor supply and production responses. The computer can't tell which theory is right; it just predicts what it's programmed to see. In other words, the computer sees the world through the eyes of its economic master.

The second essential input in a computer forecast is the assumed values for critical variables. A Keynesian model, for example, must specify how large a multiplier to expect. All the computer does is carry out the required mathematical routines, once it's told that the multiplier is relevant and what its value is. It can't discern the true multiplier any better than it can pick the right theory.

Given the dependence of computers on the theories and perceptions of their economic masters, it's not surprising that computer forecasts often differ greatly. It's also not surprising that they're often wrong. Even policymakers who are familiar with both economic theory and computer models can make some pretty bad calls. In January 1990 Fed Chairman Alan Greenspan assured Congress that the risk of a recession was as low as 20 percent. Although he said he "wouldn't bet the ranch" on such a low probability, he was confident that the odds of a recession were below 50 percent. Five months after his testimony, the 1990–1991 recession began. Greenspan's successor, Ben Bernanke, lost the same bet in 2008 (see In the News "Fed Chief Sees No Recession").

IN THE NEWS

FED CHIEF SEES NO RECESSION

WASHINGTON, DC—Fed Chairman Ben Bernanke says fears of a recession are overblown. In his testimony before the Senate Banking Committee yesterday Bernanke acknowledged that rising unemployment, declining home prices, and high energy prices were weighing on consumers. But he sees no recession on the horizon.

"My baseline outlook involves a period of sluggish growth, followed by a somewhat stronger pace of growth starting later this year as the effects of (Fed) and fiscal stimulus begin to be felt," Bernanke told committee members. . . .

—Barbara Hagenbaugh

Source: Media Reports, February 15, 2008.

ANALYSIS: Policy decisions are based on forecasts of economic performance. Bad forecasts can lead to delayed or wrong policy actions.

The Council of Economic Advisers has made similar blunders. The CEA was forecasting 2–3 percent growth just as the economy was falling into the 2001 recession. In early 2008 the Bush White House was predicting a growth pickup later in the year. In fact the downturn *accelerated* in the final months of that year. And in February 2009 Obama's CEA predicted that the unemployment rate would drop from 7.6 percent to 7.0 percent by 2010. Instead it rose to 10 percent.

Leading Indicators. Given the complexity of macro models, many people prefer to use simpler tools for divining the future. One of the most popular is the Leading Economic Index. As noted in Chapter 9 (see Table 9.2), the Leading Indicators are things we can observe today that are logically linked to future production (e.g., orders for new equipment). Unfortunately the logical sequence of events doesn't always unfold as anticipated. All too often, the links in the chain of Leading Indicators are broken by changing expectations and unanticipated events.

Crystal Balls. In view of the fragile foundations and spotty record of computer and index-based forecasts, many people shun them altogether, preferring to use their own "crystal balls." The Foundation for the Study of Cycles has identified 4,000 different crystal balls that people use to gauge the health of the economy, including the ratio of used car to new car sales (it rises in recession); the number of divorce petitions (it rises in bad times); animal population cycles (they peak just before economic downturns); and even the optimism/pessimism content of popular music (a reflection of consumer confidence). Corporate executives claim that such crystal balls are as valuable as professional economic forecasts. In a Gallup survey of CEOs, most respondents said economists' forecasts had little or no influence on company plans or policies. The head of one large company said, "I go out of my way to ignore them." The general public apparently shares this view, giving higher marks to the forecasts of sportswriters and weather forecasters than to those of economists.

Economic forecasters defend themselves in two ways. First, they note that economic policy decisions are inevitably based on anticipated changes in the economy's performance. The decision to stimulate or restrain the economy can't be made by a flip of a coin; *someone* must try to foresee the future course of the economy. Second, forecasters claim that their quantitative approach is the only honest one. Because forecasting models require specific behavioral assumptions and estimates, they force people to spell out their versions of the future. Less rigorous ("gut feeling") approaches are too ambiguous and often inconsistent.

These are valid arguments. Still, one must be careful to distinguish the precision of computers from the inevitable uncertainties of their spoon-fed models. The basic law of the computer is GIGO: garbage in, garbage out. If the underlying models and assumptions are no good, the computer's forecasts won't be any better.

Policy and Forecasts. The task of forecasting the economic future is made still more complex by the interdependence of forecasts, policy decisions, and economic outcomes (see Figure 18.2). First, a forecast is made, based on current economic conditions, likely disturbances to the economy, and anticipated economic policy. These forecasts are then used to project likely budget deficits and other policy variables. Congress and the president react to these projections by revising fiscal, monetary, or supply-side policies. These changes, in turn, alter the basis for the initial forecasts.

This interdependence among forecasts, budget projections, and policy decisions was superbly illustrated in the early months of the George W. Bush presidency. At the beginning of 2001, both the White House and the Congress were forecasting enormous budget surpluses. The central policy debate focused on what to do with those surpluses. The Democrats wanted to spend the surplus; the Republicans wanted to give it back to households with larger tax cuts. As the debate dragged on, however, the weakening economy shrank the surplus. In August 2001 the Congressional Budget Office (CBO) announced that the surplus it had forecast just seven months earlier had vanished. This forced both political parties to change their policy proposals. Protecting the vanishing surplus became the political priority. Spending proposals were scaled back, as were hopes of debt repayment.

President Obama used dire forecasts of the economy to build support for his stimulus proposals. He claimed that the 2008–2009 recession was the worst since the Great Depression and that the economy might *never* recover unless his stimulus package was

FIGURE 18.2

The Interdependance of Forecasts and Policy

Because tax revenues and government spending are sensitive to economic conditions, budget projections *must* rely on economic forecasts. The budget projections may alter policy decisions, however, and so change the basis for the initial forecasts. This interdependence among macro forecasts, budget projections, and policy decisions is inevitable.

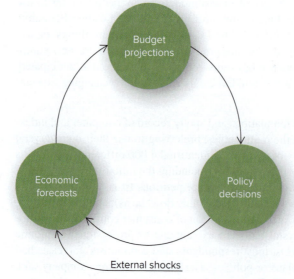

implemented. The resulting fear and uncertainty increased public support for his stimulus plan, which Congress authorized within the first month of his presidency.

External Shocks. Even accurate forecasts can be knocked astray by external shocks. The budget decisions reached in early 2001 didn't anticipate the September 11 terrorist attacks. And budget and economic forecasts made in early 2017 had no way of anticipating the destructive force of Hurricane Harvey on our production capacity. The very nature of external *shocks* is that they are *unanticipated.* Hence, even if we knew enough about the economy to forecast "shockless" outcomes perfectly, an external shock could always disrupt the economy and ruin our forecasts.

As In the News "CBO's Flawed Forecasts" reveals, the CBO's forecasting errors in 2001 and 2005 were not an exception; they were the norm. In January 2016 CBO predicted that the economy would grow at an average rate of 2.2 for the years 2016–2020. Eight months later CBO cut that forecast to 1.9 percent. Worse yet, CBO said there was a one-in-three chance that actual growth would be less than 0.7 percent or greater than 3.2 percent. In other words, *anything* was possible! That's hardly a solid basis for making policy decisions.

IN THE NEWS

CBO'S FLAWED FORECASTS

Every year the Congressional Budget Office (CBO) forecasts the federal budget balance for the next five years. Those forecasts are rarely accurate. The typical CBO forecasting error for the *current* fiscal year amounts to 0.5 percent of GDP, or about $70 billion. Moreover, the errors widen for future years: for the *fifth* year out, CBO's forecasts typically miss the actual budget balance by a startling 3 percent of GDP. This implies that CBO's January 2009 forecast of the 2014 budget balance (a $250 billion deficit) may be off the mark by $500 billion!

Since 1981, CBO has both over- and underestimated federal budget balances. There has been a slightly pessimistic bias, however, especially in the boom years of 1992–2000 and 2003–2007. Forecasts from the president's Office of Management and Budget (OMB) haven't been any better.

Source: *The Budget and Economic Outlook, Fiscal Years 2009–2019,* Congressional Budget Office, January 2009.

ANALYSIS: The economic and budget forecasts that guide policy decisions are often flawed. This reduces the chances of policy success.

Design Problems

Assume for the moment that we somehow are able to get a reliable forecast of where the economy is headed. The outlook, let's suppose, is bad. Now we're in the driver's seat to steer the economy past looming dangers. We need to chart our course—to design an economic plan. What action should we take? Which theory of macro behavior should guide us? How will the marketplace respond to any specific action we take?

Suppose, for example, that we adopt a Keynesian approach to ending a recession. Specifically, we want to use fiscal policy to boost aggregate demand. Should we cut taxes or increase government spending? This was a core decision President Obama confronted as he developed his stimulus program. The choice depends in part on the efficacy of either policy tool. Will tax cuts stimulate aggregate demand? In 1998 Japanese households used their tax cut to increase *savings* rather than consumption. In 2001 U.S. households were also slow to spend their tax rebates. When consumers don't respond as anticipated, the intended fiscal stimulus doesn't materialize. Such behavioral responses frustrate even the best-intentioned policy.

Implementation Problems

Measurement and design problems can break the spirit of even the best policymaker (or the policymaker's economic advisers). Yet measurement and design problems are only part of the story. A good idea is of little value unless someone puts it to use. Accordingly, to understand fully why things go wrong, we must also consider the difficulties of *implementing* a well-designed policy.

Congressional Deliberations. Suppose that the president decides that a tax cut is necessary to stimulate demand for goods and services. Can he simply go ahead and cut tax rates? No, because only Congress can legislate tax changes. Once the president decides on the appropriate policy, he must ask Congress for authority to take the required action, which means a delay in implementing policy or possibly no policy at all. This was particularly frustrating for President Trump, who wanted to do tax, trade, and regulation deals quickly.

At the very least, the president must convince Congress of the wisdom of his proposed policy. The tax proposal must work its way through separate committees of both the House of Representatives and the Senate, get on the congressional calendar, and be approved in each chamber. If there are important differences in Senate and House versions of the tax cut legislation, they must be compromised in a joint conference. The modified proposal must then be returned to each chamber for approval.

The same kind of process applies to the outlay side of the budget. Once the president has submitted his budget proposals (in January), Congress reviews them, then sets its own spending goals. After that, the budget is broken down into 13 different categories, and a separate appropriations bill is written for each one. These bills spell out in detail how much can be spent and for what purposes. Once Congress passes them, they go to the president for acceptance or veto.

Budget legislation requires Congress to finish these deliberations by October 1 (the beginning of the federal fiscal year), but Congress rarely meets this deadline. In most years, the budget debate continues well into the fiscal year. In some years, the budget debate isn't resolved until the fiscal year is nearly over! The final budget legislation is typically more than 1,000 pages long and so complex that few people understand all its dimensions.

Time Lags. This description of congressional activity isn't an outline for a civics course; rather, it's an important explanation of why economic policy isn't fully effective. ***Even if the right policy is formulated to solve an emerging economic problem, there's no assurance that it will be implemented. And if it's implemented, there's no assurance that it will take effect at the right time.*** One of the most frightening prospects for economic policy is that a policy design intended to serve a specific problem will be implemented much later, when economic conditions have changed. This isn't a remote danger. According to economists Christina Romer and Paul Romer, the Fed doesn't pull the monetary stimulus lever until a recession is under way, and Congress is even slower in responding to an economic downturn. Indeed, a U.S. Treasury Department study concluded that almost every postwar fiscal stimulus package was enacted well after the end of the recession it was intended to cure!

Figure 18.3 is a schematic view of why macro policies don't always work as intended. There are always delays between the time a problem emerges and the time it's recognized. There are additional delays between recognition and response design, between design and implementation, and finally between implementation and impact. Not only may mistakes be made at each juncture, but even correct decisions may be overcome by changing economic conditions.

No "Shovel-Ready" Jobs. The lags in implementation were particularly evident in Obama's 2009 fiscal stimulus package. He thought he could kill two birds with one stone by creating short-run jobs with investments in long-term needs like infrastructure and energy development. In his view, there were millions of "shovel-ready" jobs that would fulfill both goals. In fact, though, federal spending doesn't hit the ground that fast. Long delays in federal procurement (bid solicitation, contractor bid preparation, bid review, contract negotiation, environmental impact assessment) create a lag of nearly two years from the time Congress approves funding until a federal shovel actually hits the ground. As a result, most of the stepped-up infrastructure "stimulus" didn't show up until the recession was several years old. Critics said a tax cut would have shifted the AD curve a lot sooner.

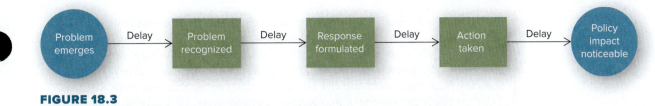

FIGURE 18.3

Policy Response: A Series of Time Lags

Even the best-intentioned economic policy can be frustrated by time lags. It takes time for a problem to be recognized, time to formulate a policy response, and still more time to implement that policy. By the time the policy begins to affect the economy, the underlying problem may have changed.

Politics vs. Economics. Politics often contributes to delayed and ill-designed policy interventions. Especially noteworthy in this regard is the potential conflict of economic policy with political objectives. The president and Congress are always reluctant to impose fiscal restraint (tax increases or budget cutbacks) in election years, regardless of economic circumstances. Fiscal restraint is never popular.

The tendency of Congress to hold fiscal policy hostage to electoral concerns has created a pattern of short-run stops and starts—a kind of policy-induced business cycle. Indeed, some argue that the business cycle has been replaced with the political cycle: the economy is stimulated in the year of an election and then restrained in the postelection year. The conflict between the urgent need to get reelected and the necessity to manage the economy results in a seesaw kind of instability.

Finally, we must recognize that policy design is obstructed by a certain attention deficit. Neither people on the street nor elected public officials focus constantly on economic goals and activities. Even students enrolled in economics courses have a hard time keeping their minds on the economy and its problems. The executive and legislative branches of government, for their part, are likely to focus on economic concerns only when economic problems become serious or voters demand action.

THE ECONOMY TOMORROW

HANDS ON OR HANDS OFF?

In view of the goal conflicts and the measurement, design, and implementation problems that policymakers confront, it's less surprising that things sometimes go wrong than that things ever work out right. The maze of obstacles through which theory must pass before it becomes policy explains many economic disappointments. On this basis alone, we may conclude that *consistent fine-tuning of the economy isn't compatible with either our design capabilities or our decision-making procedures.* We have exhibited a strong capability to avoid or contain major economic disruptions in the last four decades. We haven't, however, been able to make all the minor adjustments necessary to fulfill our goals completely. As Arthur Burns, former chairman of the Fed's Board of Governors, said nearly half a century ago

> There has been much loose talk of "fine tuning" when the state of knowledge permits us to predict only within a fairly broad level the course of economic development and the results of policy actions.[1]

Hands Off. Some critics of economic policy take this argument a few steps further. If fine-tuning isn't really possible, they say, we should abandon discretionary policies altogether and follow fixed rules for fiscal and monetary intervention.

Continued

[1]Source: Burns, Arthur, *Newsweek,* August 27, 1973, pg. 4.

As we saw in Chapter 15, pure monetarism would require the Fed to increase the money supply at a constant rate. Critics of fiscal policy would require the government to maintain balanced budgets, or at least to offset deficits in sluggish years with surpluses in years of high growth. Such rules would prevent policymakers from over- or understimulating the economy. Such rules would also add a dose of certainty to the economic outlook.

Milton Friedman was one of the most persistent advocates of fixed policy rules. With discretionary authority, Friedman argued,

> the wrong decision is likely to be made in a large fraction of cases because the decision makers are examining only a limited area and not taking into account the cumulative consequences of the policy as a whole. On the other hand, if a general rule is adopted for a group of cases as a bundle, the existence of that rule has favorable effects on people's attitudes and beliefs and expectations that would not follow even from the discretionary adoption of precisely the same policy on a series of separate occasions.[2]

The case for a hands-off policy stance is based on practical, not theoretical, arguments. *Everyone agrees that flexible, discretionary policies* could *result in better economic performance. But Friedman and others argue that the practical requirements of monetary and fiscal management are too demanding and thus prone to failure.* Even former Fed Chairman Alan Greenspan, an advocate of hands-on discretion, later admitted he erred 30 percent of the time. Critics of activist policy say that is too high an error rate.

New Classical Economics. Monetarist critiques of discretionary policy are echoed by a new perspective referred to as new classical economics (NCE). Classical economists saw no need for discretionary macro policy. In their view, the private sector is inherently stable, and government intervention serves no purpose. New classical economics reaches the same conclusion. As Robert Barro, a proponent of NCE, put it, "It is best for the government to provide a stable environment, and then mainly stay out of the way."[3] Barro and other NCE economists based this laissez-faire conclusion on the intriguing notion of **rational expectations.** This notion contends that people make decisions on the basis of all available information, including the *future* effects of *current* government policy.

Suppose, for example, that the Fed decided to increase the money supply to boost output. If people had rational expectations, they'd anticipate that this money supply growth will fuel later inflation. To protect themselves, they'd immediately demand higher prices and wages. As a result, the stimulative monetary policy would fail to boost real output.

Discretionary fiscal policy could be equally ineffective. Suppose Congress accelerated government spending in an effort to boost aggregate demand. Monetarists contend that the accompanying increase in the deficit would push interest rates up and crowd out private investment and consumption. New classical economists again reach the same conclusion via a different route. They contend that people with rational expectations would anticipate that a larger deficit now will necessitate tax increases in later years. To prepare for later tax bills, consumers will reduce spending now, thereby saving more. This "rational" reduction in consumption will offset the increased government expenditure, thus rendering fiscal policy ineffective.

If the new classical economists are right, the only policy that works is one that surprises people—one that consumers and investors don't anticipate. But a policy based on surprises isn't practical. Accordingly, new classical economists conclude that minimal policy intervention is best. This conclusion provides yet another guideline for policy decisions. See Table 18.5 for a roster of competing theories.

Hands On. *Proponents of a hands-on policy strategy acknowledge the possibility of occasional blunders. They emphasize, however, the greater risks of doing nothing when the economy is faltering.* Some proponents of the quick fix even turn the new classical

rational expectations: Hypothesis that people's spending decisions are based on all available information, including the anticipated effects of government intervention.

---

[2]Source: Friedman, Milton, *Capitalism and Freedom*. Chicago, IL: University of Chicago Press, p. 53, 1962.
[3]Source: Barro, Robert, "Don't Fool with Money, Cut Taxes," *The Wall Street Journal,* November 21, 1991, p. A14.

Keynesians	Keynesians believe that the private sector is inherently unstable and prone to stagnate at low levels of output and employment. They want the government to manage aggregate demand with changes in taxes and government's spending.
Modern ("neo") Keynesians	Post–World War II followers of Keynes worry about inflation as well as recession. They urge budgetary restraint to cool an overheated economy. They also use monetary policy to change interest rates.
Monetarists	The money supply is their only heavy hitter. By changing the money supply, they can raise or lower the price level. Pure monetarists shun active policy, believing that it destabilizes the otherwise stable private sector. Output and employment gravitate to their natural levels.
Supply-siders	Incentives to work, invest, and produce are the key to their plays. Cuts in marginal tax rates and government regulation are used to expand production capacity, thereby increasing output and reducing inflationary pressures.
New classical economists	They say fine-tuning won't work because once the private sector realizes what the government is doing, it will act to offset it. They also question the credibility of quick-fix promises. They favor steady, predictable policies.

TABLE 18.5

Who's on First? Labeling Economists

It's sometimes hard to tell who's on what side in economic debates. Although some economists are proud to wear the colors of monetarists, Keynesians, or other teams, many economists shun such allegiances. Indeed, economists are often accused of playing on one team one day and on another team the next, making it hard to tell which team is at bat. To simplify matters, this guide may be used for quick identification of the players. Closer observation is advised, however, before choosing up teams.

economics argument on its head. Even the wrong policy, they argue, might be better than doing nothing if enough market participants believe that *change* implied *progress*. They cite the jump in consumer confidence that followed the election of Bill Clinton, who had emphasized the need for a *change* in policy but hadn't spelled out the details of that change. The surge in confidence itself stimulated consumer purchases even before President Clinton took office. The same kind of response occurred after the September 11, 2001, terrorist attacks. Consumers were dazed and insecure. There was a serious risk that they would curtail spending if the government didn't *do something*. Details aside, they just wanted reassurance that someone was taking charge of events. Quick responses by the Fed (increasing the money supply), the Congress (authorizing more spending), and President Bush (mobilizing security and military forces) kept consumer confidence from plunging. President Obama argued that a similar situation existed in early 2009. Claiming that the economy would slide into another Depression if Congress didn't act, he said doing *something*—even if not perfect—was better than doing *nothing*.

Just doing *something* isn't the purpose of a hands-on policy, of course. Policy activists believe that we have enough knowledge about how the economy works to pull the right policy levers most of the time. They also point to the historical record. Our economic track record may not be perfect, but the historical record of prices, employment, and growth has improved since active fiscal and monetary policies were adopted: recessions have gotten shorter and economic expansions longer.

Finally, one must contend with the difficulties inherent in enforcing fixed rules. How is the Fed, for example, supposed to maintain a steady rate of growth in the money supply? As we observed in Chapter 13, people move their funds back and forth between different kinds of "money." Also, the demand for money is subject to unpredictable shifts. Maintaining a steady rate of growth in M2 or any other measure of money would require superhuman foresight and responses.

The same is true of fiscal policy. Government spending and taxes are directly influenced by changes in unemployment, inflation, interest rates, and growth. These automatic stabilizers make it virtually impossible to maintain any fixed rule for budget balancing. Moreover, if we eliminated the automatic stabilizers, we'd risk greater instability.

Continued

PROBLEMS FOR CHAPTER 18

LO18-3 1. If the Congressional Budget Office makes its average error this year, by how much will it underestimate next year's budget deficit? (See In the News "CBO's Flawed Forcasts") (Note: Assume a GDP of $20 trillion.)

LO18-1 2. In 2011 the unemployment rate was 8.9 percent, far above the full-employment threshold (5 percent).
   (a) How many jobs were lost, as a result, in a labor force of 140 million?
   (b) If the average worker produced $100,000 of output, how much output was lost?
   (c) By how much did GDP per capita decline as a result (310 million people)?

LO18-1 3. According to World View "Comparative Macro Performance"
   (a) Which country had the greatest macro misery in the 2000s? (Compute the "misery index" from Chapter 16.)
   (b) Which country had the fastest growth?

LO18-1 4. If infrastructure spending increases by $100 billion and taxes are raised by the same amount, by how much will aggregate demand change if the MPC is .80?

LO18-3 5. The CBO said that it was 66.7 percent confident that the GDP growth rate for 2016-2020 would be between 0.7 and 3.2 percent (In the News "CBO's Flawed Forcasts"). In a $20 trillion economy, what is the implied range of forecasted GDP for a single year?

LO18-3 6. The following table displays Congressional Budget Office forecasts of federal budget balances for the following fiscal year. Compare these forecasts with *actual* surplus and deficits for those same years (see Table 12.3 for data).

Year:	2000	2001	2002	2003	2004	2005	2006	2007	2008	2009
Deficit forecast (in billions of dollars)	+161	+268	+176	−315	−480	−348	−314	−285	−155	−438

   (a) In how many years was the CBO too optimistic (underestimating the deficit or overestimating the surplus)?
   (b) In how many years was the CBO too pessimistic?

LO18-2 7. Complete the following chart by summarizing the policy prescriptions of various economic theories:

	Policy Prescription for	
Policy Approach	**Recession**	**Inflation**
Fiscal		
Classical	_____	_____
Keynesian	_____	_____
Monetarist	_____	_____
Monetary		
Keynesian	_____	_____
Monetarist	_____	_____
Supply side	_____	_____

LO18-2 8. According to In the News "CBO's Flawed Forecasts," what is the implied value of the multiplier for
   (*a*) Increased unemployment benefits?
   (*b*) Infrastructure spending?

LO18-2 9. The Economy Tomorrow: Match the statement with the school of economic thought:

Statement	School of Thought
Money supply should be grown at a steady pace.	Keynesians
Fine-tuning does not work because the private sector will act to offset government policy.	Modern Keynesians (Neo-Keynesians)
Government should manage aggregate demand with changes in taxes and spending.	Monetarists
Inflation is just as much as a concern as recessions.	Supply-siders
Marginal tax rates should be cut to stimulate the economy in times of recession.	New classical economists

8

PART

PRODUCT MARKETS: THE BASICS

The prices and products we see every day emerge from decisions made by millions of individual consumers and firms. A primary objective of microeconomic theory is to explain how those decisions are made. How high a price are consumers willing to pay for the products they want? Which products will consumers actually purchase—and in what quantities? We explore these dimensions of consumer *demand* in Chapters 19 and 20. We move to the *supply* side in Chapter 21, examining the costs that businesses incur in producing the products consumers demand.

©Onoky/SuperStock RF

CHAPTER 19

Consumer Choice

S teve Jobs knew he had a winner with the iPhone. Every time Apple added a feature to the iPod, sales picked up. Now Jobs had a product that combined cell phone services with wireless computing and audio and video download capabilities—all accessible on a touch screen. It was sure to be a hit. The only sticky question was *price*. What price should Apple put on its new iPhone? The company's goal was to sell 10 million iPhones in the first two years of production. If it set the price low enough, it could surely do that. But Apple didn't want to give away the iPhone—it wanted to make a nice profit. Yet if it set the price *too* high, sales would fall short of its sales target. What price should it charge? Apple's pricing committee had to know how many iPhones consumers would buy at different prices. In other words, they had to know the dimensions of *consumer demand*. After considerable deliberation, they set the initial price at $499 for the 4 GB iPhone, launched in January 2007.

Apple's iPhone pricing dilemma underscores the importance of *prices* in determining consumer behavior. Consumers "want," "need," and "just have to have" a vast array of goods and services. When decision time comes, however, product *prices* often dictate what consumers will actually buy. As we observed in Chapter 3, the quantity of a product *demanded* depends on its price.

This chapter takes a closer look at how product prices affect consumer decisions. We focus on three related questions:

- **How do we decide how much of any good to buy?**
- **Why do we feel so good about our purchases?**
- **Why do we buy certain products but not others?**

The law of demand (first encountered in Chapter 3) gives us some clues for answering these questions. But we need to look beyond that law to fashion more complete answers. We need to know what forces give demand curves their downward-sloping shape. We also need to know more about how to *use* demand curves to predict consumer behavior.

DETERMINANTS OF DEMAND

In seeking explanations for consumer behavior, we have to recognize that the field of economics doesn't have all the answers. But it does offer a unique perspective that sets it apart from other fields of study.

The Sociopsychiatric Explanation

Consider first the explanations of consumer behavior offered by other fields of study. Psychiatrists and psychologists have had a virtual field day formulating such explanations. Freud was among the first to describe us humans as bundles of subconscious (and unconscious) fears, complexes, and anxieties. From a Freudian perspective, we strive for ever higher levels of consumption to satisfy basic drives for security, sex, and ego gratifications. Like the most primitive of people, we clothe and adorn ourselves in ways that assert our identity and worth. We eat and smoke too much because we need the oral gratifications and security associated with mother's breast. Oversized homes and cars give us a sense of warmth and security remembered from the womb. On the other hand, we often buy and consume some things we don't really want, just to assert our rebellious feelings against our parents (or parent substitutes). In Freud's view, it's the constant interplay of these id, ego, and superego drives that motivates us to buy, buy, buy.

Sociologists offer additional explanations for our consumption behavior. They observe our yearning to stand above the crowd, to receive recognition from the masses. For people with exceptional talents, such recognition may come easily. But for the ordinary person, recognition may depend on conspicuous consumption. A sleek car, a newer fashion, a more exotic vacation become expressions of identity that provoke recognition, even social acceptance. We strive for ever higher levels of consumption—not just to keep up with the Joneses but to surpass them.

Not *all* consumption is motivated by ego or status concerns. Some food is consumed for the sake of self-preservation, some clothing worn for warmth, and some housing built for shelter. The typical U.S. consumer has more than enough income to satisfy these basic needs, however. In today's economy, most consumers also have *discretionary* income that can be used to satisfy psychological or sociological longings. Single women are able to spend a lot of money on clothes and pets, and men spend freely on entertainment, food, and drink (see In the News "Men vs. Women: How They Spend"). Teenagers show off their affluence in purchases of electronic goods, cars, and clothes (see Figure 19.1).

IN THE NEWS

MEN VS. WOMEN: HOW THEY SPEND

Are men really different from women? If spending habits are any clue, males do differ from females. That's the conclusion one would draw from the latest Bureau of Labor Statistics (BLS) survey of consumer expenditure. Here's what the BLS found out about the spending habits of young (under age 25) men and women who are living on their own:

Common Traits

- Young men have a lot more after-tax income to spend ($15,894 per year) than do young women ($11,826).
- Both sexes spend about $21,000 per year, much more than their income. Education is one of the largest expenditures (around $3,600).
- Neither sex spends much on charity, reading, or health care.

Distinctive Traits

- Men spend twice as much more on alcoholic beverages and smoking.
- Men spend almost twice as much as women do on electronic equipment.
- Young women spend twice as much money on clothing, personal care items, and their pets.

Source: U.S. Bureau of Labor Statistics, 2014–2016, Consumer Expenditure Survey.

ANALYSIS: Consumer patterns vary by gender, age, and other characteristics. Economists try to isolate the common influences on consumer behavior.

FIGURE 19.3

An Individual's Demand Schedule and Curve

Consumers are generally willing to buy larger quantities of a good at lower prices. This demand schedule illustrates the specific quantities demanded at alternative prices. If popcorn sold for 25 cents per ounce, this consumer would buy 12 ounces per show (row *F*). At higher prices, less popcorn would be purchased.

A downward-sloping demand curve expresses the law of demand: the quantity of a good demanded increases as its price falls. Notice that points *A* through *J* on the curve correspond to the rows of the demand schedule.

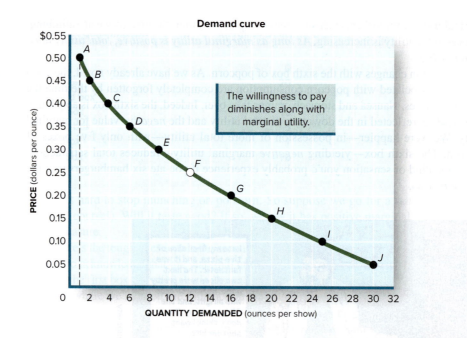

Demand curve

The willingness to pay diminishes along with marginal utility.

Demand Schedule

	Price (per Ounce)	Quantity Demanded (Ounces per Show)
A	$0.50	1
B	0.45	2
C	0.40	4
D	0.35	6
E	0.30	9
F	0.25	12
G	0.20	16
H	0.15	20
I	0.10	25
J	0.05	30

law of demand: The quantity of a good demanded in a given time period increases as its price falls, *ceteris paribus.*

demand curve: A curve describing the quantities of a good a consumer is willing and able to buy at alternative prices in a given time period, *ceteris paribus.*

market demand: The total quantities of a good or service people are willing and able to buy at alternative prices in a given time period; the sum of individual demands.

of buttered popcorn may not be willing to pay so much for a second or third ounce. The same is true for a second pizza, the sixth beer, and so forth. *Because marginal utility declines, people are willing to buy additional quantities of a good only if its price falls.* In other words, as the marginal utility of a good diminishes, so does our willingness to pay. This **law of demand** is illustrated in Figure 19.3 with the downward-sloping **demand curve.**

The law of demand and the law of diminishing marginal utility tell us nothing about why we crave popcorn or why our cravings subside. Those explanations are reserved for psychiatrists, sociologists, and physiologists. The laws of economics simply describe our market behavior.

MARKET DEMAND

Our explanation of an individual's popcorn consumption applies to all products and all consumers. As we saw in Chapter 3, the **market demand** for popcorn is just the sum of all our individual demands for that product. The market demand curve resembles an individual's demand curve but differs in two important respects. First, the units of measurement are larger: the quantities on the horizontal axis are in hundreds, thousands, or possibly millions of units, not single digits. Second, the demand curve expresses the ability and willingness to pay of thousands of consumers, not just one individual.

CONSUMER SURPLUS

The presence of so many individuals on the market demand curve has some interesting implications for both consumers and producers. To see this, let's venture into another market—say, the new car market. Let's focus on a specific car, the Porsche 918 Spyder Hybrid, a sports car with a 608 horsepower V8 engine supplemented by two electrical engines, a top speed of 211 miles per hour, and 71 miles per gallon in all-electric mode.

Lots of people crave this car. But not everyone is willing and able to buy it at the Manufacturer's Suggested Retail Price (MSRP) of $847,975. In fact, most people who *desire* the car aren't prepared to pay anywhere near that much money. Some people are, however. Indeed, some Porsche fans would pay even a *higher* price to get their hands on a 918 Spyder. And it's not just a question of who is rich enough. Remember that there are *four* determinants of an individual's demand: tastes, income, expectations, and other goods (price and availability). So a rich person with little desire for speed might not demand a Spyder at the $847,975 price. On the other hand, a real speed freak with only a modest income might be willing to borrow money, rent out the house, and sell the kids to get behind the wheel of a 918 Spyder.

As individuals work their way through the determinants of demand, they will ultimately decide how much money they are willing to pay for a Porsche 918 Spyder. For those sorry souls who would never think of driving a Spyder, their price would be zero: they would not be part of the market demand for that car. Everyone else, however, would be deciding the *maximum* price they would be willing and able to pay for a new 918 Spyder. That decision will determine where they are positioned on the market demand curve.

Consider the positions depicted in Figure 19.4. Fred is positioned high up on the market demand curve because he is willing to pay as much as $1 million for a Spyder. Michel and Hua are also willing and able to shell out big bucks for the car. Blaise also wants a Spyder but can't or won't spend more than $650,000 to get one.

What we also see on the market demand curve is how many cars the Porsche dealer can sell at the MSRP of $847,975. At that price (point *A* on the graph), four Spyders will be demanded and therefore sold.

Fred will be particularly excited with this deal. We know that Fred would pay as much as $1 million for a 918 Spyder. But he has to pay only the $847,975 price set by the dealer. In his mind, he is getting a real bargain—getting the Spyder for a lot less money than the

You may *desire* a Porsche, but do you *demand* it?

©Sean Gallup/Getty Images

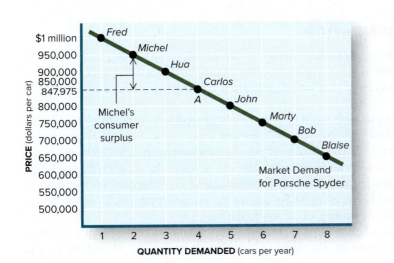

QUANTITY DEMANDED (cars per year)

FIGURE 19.4

Consumer Surplus

A person's position on the market demand curve expresses the maximum price he or she is willing to pay. The difference between that individualized maximum price and the price paid represents "consumer surplus." At the MSRP price of $847,975, Michel would have a consumer surplus of $102,025 (= $950,000 − $847,975).

FIGURE 19.5

Total consumer surplus

Every consumer who buys a product must be willing and able to pay *at least* the prevailing price. Therefore, all consumers buying the good reap some consumer surplus. Their collective consumer surplus is represented by the shaded area in the graph.

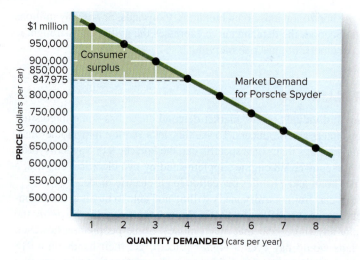

consumer surplus: The difference between the maximum price a person is willing to pay and the price paid.

maximum price he would be willing to pay. We call this "bargain" his **consumer surplus.** Specifically, consumer surplus is the difference between the maximum price a person is willing to pay and the price paid:

$$\frac{\text{Consumer}}{\text{surplus}} = \frac{\text{Maximum price}}{\text{willing to pay}} - \frac{\text{Price actually}}{\text{paid}}$$

In Fred's case, that consumer surplus amounts to $152,025 (= $1 million − $847,975).

Michel enjoys a consumer surplus as well. Notice again in Figure 19.4 where she is on the market demand curve: she is willing to pay as much as $950,000 for a Spyder. So she enjoys a consumer surplus of $102,025 (= $950,000 − $847,975). She cannot wait to tell all her friends what a "bargain" she got.

In fact, everyone who buys a Spyder thinks she or he got a bargain! That is because ***the only people who purchase a product are those whose maximum price equals or exceeds the market price***. In Figure 19.4 only the consumers at or above point *A* drive away in a new Spyder. Anyone *below* point *A* walks; John, Marty, Bob, and Blaise want a Porsche 918 Spyder but are not willing to pay $847,975 to get one.

Now you know why we love to shop. People do not buy things that are priced above their maximum price thresholds. We only buy those things priced at or below our maximum price threshold. So we are always getting some consumer surplus and bragging about the "bargains" we got. This collective consumer surplus is depicted in Figure 19.5.

PRICE DISCRIMINATION

total revenue: The price of a product multiplied by the quantity sold in a given time period: *p* × *q*.

Car dealers are well aware of this consumer surplus phenomenon and determined to profit from it. Consider their options. Figure 19.4 reveals that the dealer can sell four cars at the posted price of $847,975. That would generate **total revenue** (= price × quantity) of $3,391,180.

But he could do better than that if he priced each car separately rather than charging the *same* price for all four cars. Suppose he knew that Fred was willing and able to pay as much as $1 million for a Spyder. Instead of posting a uniform price of $847,975, the dealer could let Fred try to negotiate a price for himself. What is the *most* Fred would pay? $1 million. So the dealer could ask for $1.2 million and let Fred "bargain" his way down to $1 million. Fred would drive off in his Spyder, feeling smug about the "deal" he had struck. And the dealer would be smiling all the way to the bank.

If the dealer handled all the buyers in this way, he would bring in a lot more revenue from the sale of his four cars. He would sell the first car to Fred for $1 million, a car to

Michel for $950,000, a car to Hua for $900,000, and one to Carlos for $850,000. His total revenue would be $3.7 million rather than the $3,391,900 he got with uniform pricing. Pretty nice deal.

What the dealer is doing here is practicing **price discrimination:** charging individual consumers different prices for the same good. In effect, the dealer is picking off consumers from their positions on the market demand curve and charging them the maximum price each is willing to pay. If successful, the dealer will eliminate all consumer surplus and maximize his own revenue.

price discrimination: The sale of an individual good at different prices to different consumers.

There is nothing illegal about this kind of price discrimination. And no one gets harmed. No one paid more for a Spyder than she or he was willing to pay. And the buyers might even feel good about their negotiating skills.

Divide and Conquer. The key to the dealer's success is the ability to negotiate each price individually. There is no transparency here. Car dealers typically conduct negotiations in small cubicles, isolated from other consumers. That way the dealer can probe to discover what maximum price each individual is willing to pay. So long as that price is above the uniform price threshold ($847,975 in this case), the dealer extracts some of that consumer surplus (and increases total revenue).

Price discrimination is rampant in the auto industry, but common in many other markets as well. Next time you are on an airplane, ask your seatmates how much they paid for their tickets. Odds are that it is not the same price you paid. The airlines use a variety of techniques to "divide and conquer" airline passengers. People who must travel on short notice and with uncertain schedules pay high "unrestricted" fares. Travelers who are further down the market demand curve are singled out with advance ticketing, nonrefundable purchases, and minimum-stay restrictions. They end up paying a lower price for the same flight. That is price discrimination.

Even colleges engage in price discrimination. Your school may have a seemingly uniform price for tuition. But schools adjust that price on an individual basis with scholarships and grants. In so doing, they hope to "sell" the school to applicants with exceptional academic or athletic potential who otherwise are not willing and able to pay the posted price.

Price discrimination is most effective when consumers don't have perfect information about market prices and there are few sellers. Price discrimination is also easier to practice in markets where individual consumers make only occasional purchases (e.g., new cars, vacations, college).

CHOOSING AMONG PRODUCTS

Our analysis of demand thus far has focused on the decision to buy a single product at varying prices. Actual consumer behavior is multidimensional, however, and therefore more complex. When we go shopping, our concern isn't limited to how much of one good to buy. Rather, we must decide *which* of many available goods to buy at their respective prices.

The presence of so many goods complicates consumption decisions. Our basic objective remains the same, however: we want to get as much satisfaction as possible from our available income. In striving for that objective, we have to recognize that the purchase of any single good means giving up the opportunity to buy more of other goods. In other words, consuming a Porsche 918 Spyder, popcorn, or any other good entails distinct **opportunity costs.**

opportunity cost: The most desired goods or services that are forgone in order to obtain something else.

Marginal Utility vs. Price

The economic explanation for consumer choice builds on the theory of marginal utility and the law of demand. Suppose you have a $10 gift card for music and video game downloads. The first proposition of consumer choice says you'll prefer the download that gives you the most satisfaction. Hardly a revolutionary proposition.

The second postulate of consumer choice takes into account market prices. Suppose you *prefer* a video game, but music downloads are cheaper. Under these circumstances, your budget may win out over your desires. There's nothing irrational about downloading a song instead of a more desirable video game when you have only a limited amount of income to spend. On the contrary, *rational behavior requires one to compare the anticipated utility of each expenditure with its price.* The smart thing to do, then, is to choose those products that promise to provide the most pleasure for the amount of income available.

Suppose your desire for a video game is *twice* as great as your desire to hear a tune. In economic terms, this means that the marginal utility of the first video game is two times that of the first music download. Which one should you download? Before hitting buttons on your smartphone, you'd better look at relative prices. What if a game costs $3 and a song costs only $1? In this case, you must pay *three* times as much for a video game that gives only *twice* as much pleasure. This isn't a good deal. You could get more utility *per dollar* by downloading music.

The same kind of principle explains why some rich people drive a Ford rather than a shiny new Porsche 918 Spyder. The marginal utility (MU) of driving a Spyder is substantially higher than the MU of driving a Ford. A nice Spyder, however, costs about 30 times as much as a basic Ford. A rich person who drives a Ford must feel that driving a Spyder is not 30 times as satisfying as driving a Ford. For such people, a Ford yields more *marginal utility per dollar spent.*

The key to utility maximization, then, isn't simply to buy the things you like best. Instead you must compare goods on the basis of their marginal utility *and* price. *To maximize utility, the consumer should choose the good that delivers the most marginal utility per dollar.*

Utility Maximization

This basic principle of consumer choice is easily illustrated. Think about spending that $10 gift card on music or game downloads, the only available choices. Your goal, as always, is to get as much pleasure as possible from this limited income. That is, you want to maximize the *total* utility attainable from the expenditure of your income. The question is how to do it. What combination of songs and games will maximize the utility you get from $10?

We've already assumed that the marginal utility (MU) of the first game is two times higher than the MU of the first song. This is reflected in the second row of Table 19.2. The MU of the first video game has been set arbitrarily at 20 utils (units of utility). We don't need to know whether 20 utils is a real thrill or just a bit of amusement. Indeed, the concept of "utils" has little meaning by itself; it's only a useful basis for comparison. In this case,

TABLE 19.2

Maximizing Utility

Q: How can you get the most satisfaction (utility) from $10 if you must choose between downloading songs at $1 apiece or video games at $3 apiece?

A: By playing two games and playing four songs. See the text for explanation.

	Amount of Utility (in Units of Utility, or Utils)				
	From Music Downloads			From Game Downloads	
Quantity Consumed	Total		Marginal	Total		Marginal
0	0		—	0		—
1	10	>	10	20	>	20
2	19	>	9	38	>	18
3	27	>	8	54	>	16
4	33	>	6	66	>	12
5	38	>	5	72	>	6
6	42	>	4	73	>	1
7	45	>	3			
8	47	>	2			
9	48	>	1			
10	48	>	0			

we want to compare the MU of the first game with the MU of the first song. Hence we set the MU of the first game at 20 utils and the MU of the first song at 10 utils. The first game download is twice as satisfying as the first music download:

$$\text{MU game} = 2 \text{ MU song}$$

The remainder of Table 19.2 indicates how marginal utility diminishes with increasing consumption of a product. Look at what happens to the sound of music. The marginal utility of the first song is 10; but the MU of the second song is only 9 utils. The third song generates even less MU (= 8). You started with your favorite song; now you're working down your hits list. By the time you get to a sixth song, music downloads aren't raising your spirits much (MU = 4). By the tenth song, you're tired of music (MU = 0).

Game downloads also conform to the law of diminishing marginal utility. You start with your favorite game (MU = 20), seeking a high score. The second game is fun, too, though not quite as much (MU = 18). As you keep playing, frustration rises and marginal utility diminishes. By the time you play a sixth game your nerves are just about shot; the sixth game gives you only 1 util of marginal utility.

With these psychological insights to guide us, we can now determine how best to spend $10. What we're looking for is the combination of songs and video games that *maximizes* the total utility attainable from an expenditure of $10. We call this combination **optimal consumption**—that is, the mix of goods that yields the most utility for the available income.

We can start looking for the optimal mix of consumer purchases by assessing the utility of spending the entire $10 on video games. At $3 per play, we could buy three games. This would give us *total* utility of 54 utils (see Table 19.2). Plus we'd have enough change to download one song (MU = 10), for a grand utility total of 64 utils.

Alternatively, you could also spend the entire gift card on music downloads. With $10 to spend, you could buy 10 songs. However, this would generate only 48 utils of total utility. Hence, if you were forced to choose between *only* downloading songs or *only* playing video games, you'd pick the games.

Fortunately, we don't have to make such extreme choices. In reality, we can buy a *combination* of songs and video games. This complicates our decision making (with more choices) but permits us to attain higher levels of total satisfaction.

To reach the peak of satisfaction, consider spending your $10 in $3 dollar increments. How should you spend the first $3? If you spend it on one game, you'll get 20 utils of satisfaction. On the other hand, $3 will buy your first three music downloads. The first song has an MU of 10 and the second song adds another 9 utils to your happiness. The third song brings in another 8 utils. Hence, by spending the $3 on songs, you reap 27 utils of total utility. This is superior to the pleasure of a first game, and it's therefore your first purchase.

Having downloaded three songs, you now can spend the second $3. How should it be spent? Your choice now is that first game or a fourth, fifth, and sixth song. That first unplayed game still promises 20 utils of real pleasure. By constrast, the MU of a fourth song is 6 utils. And the MU of a fifth song is only 5 utils. Together, then, the fourth, fifth, and sixth songs will increase your total utility by 15 utils, whereas a first game will give you 20 utils. You should spend the second $3 on a game download.

The decision on how to spend the remaining four dollars is made the same way. The final choice is to purchase either a second game (MU = 18) or the fourth, fifth, and sixth songs (MU = 15). The second game offers more marginal utility and is thus the correct decision.

After working your way through these calculations, you'll end up downloading two games and four songs. Was it worth it? Do you end up with more total utility than you could have gotten from any other combination? The answer is yes. The *total* utility of two games (38 utils) and four songs (33 utils) is 71 units of utility. This is significantly better than the alternatives of spending your $10 on songs alone (total utility = 48) or three games and a song (total utility = 64). In fact, the combination of two games and four songs is the *best* one you can find. Because this combination maximizes the total utility of your income ($10), it represents *optimal consumption.*

optimal consumption: The mix of consumer purchases that maximizes the utility attainable from available income.

Utility-Maximizing Rule

Optimal consumption refers to the mix of products that maximizes total utility for the limited amount of income you have to spend. The basic approach to utility maximization is to purchase the good next that delivers the most *marginal utility per dollar*. Marginal utility per dollar is simply the MU of the good divided by its price: MU ÷ P.

From Table 19.2 we know that a first game has an MU of 20 and a price of $3. It thus delivers a marginal utility per dollar of

$$\frac{MU_{\text{first game}}}{P_{\text{game}}} = \frac{20}{\$3} = 6.67 \text{ utils per dollar}$$

On the other hand, the first song has a marginal utility of 10 and a price of $1. It offers a marginal utility per dollar of

$$\frac{MU_{\text{first song}}}{P_{\text{song}}} = \frac{10}{\$1} = 10 \text{ utils per dollar}$$

From this perspective, the first song is a better deal than the first game and should be purchased.

Optimal consumption implies that the utility-maximizing combination of goods has been found. If this is true, you can't increase your total utility by trading one good for another. All goods included in the optimal consumption mix yield the *same* marginal utility per dollar. We know we've reached maximum utility when we've satisfied the following rule:

$$\text{Utility-maximizing rule: } \frac{MU_x}{P_x} = \frac{MU_y}{P_y}$$

where *x* and *y* represent any two goods included in our consumption.

Rational consumer choice depends on comparisons of marginal utilities and prices. If a dollar spent on product *X* yields more marginal utility than a dollar spent on product *Y*, we should buy product *X*. To use this principle, of course, we have to know the amounts of utility obtainable from various goods and be able to perform a little arithmetic. By doing so, however, we can get the greatest satisfaction from our limited income.

Equilibrium Outcomes

All these graphs and equations make consumer choice look dull and mechanical. Economic theory seems to suggest that consumers walk through shopping malls with marginal utility tables and handheld computers. In reality, no one does this—not even your economics instructor. Yet economic theory is pretty successful in predicting consumer decisions. Consumers don't always buy the optimal mix of goods and services with their limited income. But after some trial and error, consumers adjust their behavior. What economic theory predicts is that the final choices—the *equilibrium* outcomes—will be the predicted optimal ones.

THE ECONOMY TOMORROW

CAVEAT EMPTOR

LeBron James is paid more than $50 million a year to help convince us to drink Sprite and Powerade, eat Big Macs, chew Bubblicious gum, drive a Kia, and buy Samsung TVs. Do these sponsors know something economic theory doesn't? Economists *assume* consumers know what they want and will act rationally to get the most satisfaction they can.

The companies that sponsor basketball star LeBron James don't accept that assumption. They think your tastes will follow LeBron's lead. Your perception of the marginal utility associated with LeBron-endorsed products will increase.

Advertisers now spend more than $200 *billion* per year to change our perceptions. In the United States, this spending works out to more than $600 per consumer, one of the highest per capita advertising rates in the world. Some of this advertising (including product labeling) is intended to provide information about existing products or to bring new products to our attention. A great deal of advertising, however, is also designed to exploit our senses and lack of knowledge. Recognizing that we're guilt-ridden, insecure, and sex-hungry, advertisers promise exoneration, recognition, and love; all we have to do is buy the right products.

A favorite target of advertisers is our sense of insecurity. Thousands of products are marketed in ways that appeal to our need for identity. Thousands of brand images are designed to help the consumer answer the nagging question, Who am I? The answers, of course, vary. *Playboy* magazine says, I'm a virile man of the world; Marlboro cigarettes say, I'm a rugged individualist who enjoys "man-sized flavor." Sprite says, I'll be a winner if I drink the same soda LeBron James does. And I'll be able to jump 8 feet high if I wear Nike Zoom LeBron Soldier 10 shoes.

Are Wants Created? Advertising can't be blamed for all of our foolish consumption. Even members of the most primitive tribes, uncontaminated by the seductions of advertising, adorned themselves with rings, bracelets, and pendants. Furthermore, advertising has grown to massive proportions only in the past 50 years, but consumption spending has been increasing throughout recorded history. Finally, a lot of advertising simply fails to change buying decisions. Accordingly, it's a mistake to attribute the growth or content of consumption entirely to the persuasions of advertisers.

This isn't to say that advertising has necessarily made us happier. The objective of all advertising is to alter the choices we make. Just as product images are used to attract us to particular products, so are pictures of hungry, ill-clothed children used to persuade us to give money to charity. In the same way, public relations gimmicks are employed to sway our votes for public servants. In the case of consumer products, advertising seeks to increase tastes for particular goods and services and therewith our willingness to pay. *A successful advertising campaign is one that increases the perceived marginal utility of a product, thereby* **shifting the demand curve** *for that product to the right* (see Figure 19.6). By influencing our choices in this way, advertising will affect the consumption choices we make in the economy tomorrow. Advertising alone is unlikely to affect the total *level* of consumption, however.

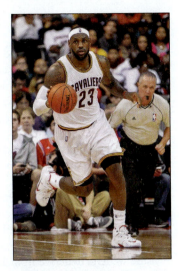

Is this a shoe salesman?!
©Jamie Sabau/Getty Images

shift in demand: A change in the quantity demanded at any (every) price.

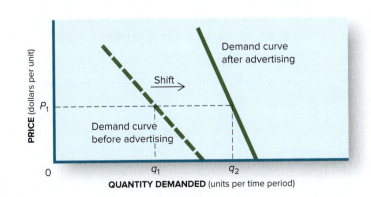

FIGURE 19.6

The Impact of Advertising on a Demand Curve

Advertising seeks to increase our taste for a particular product. If our taste (the product's perceived utility) increases, so will our willingness to buy. The resulting change in demand is reflected in a rightward shift of the demand curve, often accompanied by diminished elasticity.

SUMMARY

- Our desires for goods and services originate in the structure of personality and social dynamics and aren't explained by economic theory. Economic theory focuses on *demand*—that is, our ability and willingness to buy specific quantities of a good at various prices. **LO19-1**
- The determinants of demand include tastes (desires), income, other goods (price and availability), and expectations. **LO19-1**
- Marginal utility measures the additional satisfaction obtained from consuming one more unit of a good. The law of diminishing marginal utility says that the more of a product we consume, the smaller the increments of pleasure we tend to derive from additional units of it. This is a basis for the law of demand. **LO19-1**
- The determinants of demand establish the maximum price a consumer will pay for a good. That maximum price determines where an individual is positioned on the market demand curve. **LO19-1**

- A person will buy a product only if its price is at or below the maximum price that person is willing and able to pay. The difference between that maximum price threshold and the price paid is called "consumer surplus." **LO19-2**
- Producers can extract some or all consumer surplus by charging different prices to individuals, based on their willingness to pay—a practice called "price discrimination." **LO19-3**
- In choosing among alternative goods and services, a consumer compares the prices and anticipated satisfactions that they offer. To maximize utility with one's available income—to achieve an optimal mix of goods and services—one has to get the most utility for every dollar spent. To do so, one must choose those goods promising the most marginal utility per dollar. **LO19-4**
- Advertising seeks to change consumer tastes and thus the willingness to buy. If tastes do change, the demand curve for that product will shift. **LO19-1**

Key Terms

demand
utility
total utility
marginal utility
law of diminishing marginal utility

ceteris paribus
law of demand
demand curve
market demand
consumer surplus

total revenue
price discrimination
opportunity cost
optimal consumption
shift in demand

Questions for Discussion

1. What does the demand for enrollments in your college look like? What is on the axes? How do tuition, enrollment, and total revenue interact? **LO19-1**
2. If the marginal utility of pizza never diminished, how many pizzas would you eat? **LO19-1**
3. How do total and marginal utility change as you spend more time tweeting your friends? **LO19-1**
4. Can you think of any product that violates the law of diminishing marginal utility? **LO19-1**
5. How did Apple decide what price to charge for its 10-year anniversary iPhone in 2017? Could it have charged a higher price? Should it have? **LO19-1**

6. When the producer price discriminates in Figure 19.4, what happens to unit sales? Total revenue? Total profit? **LO19-3**
7. Under what circumstances could a producer extract *the entire* consumer surplus in Figure 19.5? **LO19-2**
8. How does a car dealer determine where a buyer is on the market demand curve? **LO19-3**
9. Why do airlines charge different fares for the same flight? **LO19-3**
10. When you eat out and have $25 to spend, what information do you need to maximize your utility? **LO19-4**

INDIFFERENCE CURVES

A consumer's demand for any specific product is an expression of many forces. As we've observed, the actual quantity of a product demanded by a consumer varies inversely with its price. The price–quantity relationship is determined by

- *Tastes* (desire for this and other goods).
- *Income* (of the consumer).
- *Expectations* (for income, prices, tastes).
- *Other goods* (their availability and price).

Economic theory attempts to show how each of these forces affects consumer demand. Thus far, we've used two-dimensional demand curves to illustrate the basic principles of demand. We saw that, in general, a change in the price of a good causes a movement along the demand curve, whereas a change in tastes, income, expectations, or other goods shifts the entire demand curve to a new position.

We haven't looked closely at the origins of demand curves, however. We assumed that a demand curve could be developed from observations of consumer behavior, such as the number of boxes of popcorn that were purchased at various prices (Figure 19.3).

It's possible, however, to derive a demand curve without actually observing consumer behavior. In theory we can identify consumer *preferences* (tastes), then use those preferences to construct a demand curve. In this case, the demand curve is developed explicitly from known preferences rather than on the basis of market observations. The end result—the demand curve—is the same, at least so long as consumers' behavior in product markets is consistent with their preferences.

Indifference curves are a mechanism for illustrating consumer tastes. We examine their construction and use in this appendix. Indifference curves provide an explicit basis for constructing a demand curve. In addition, they are another way of viewing how consumption is affected by price, tastes, and income. Indifference curves are also a useful tool for explicitly illustrating consumer *choice*—that is, the decision to purchase one good rather than another.

Constructing an Indifference Curve

Suppose you're in an arcade and want to buy some Cokes and play video games but don't have enough money to buy enough of each. The income constraint compels you to make hard decisions. You have to consider the **marginal utility** each additional Coke or video game will provide, compare their respective prices, then make a selection. With careful introspection and good arithmetic you could select the optimal mix of Cokes and video games—that is, the combination that yields the most satisfaction (utility) for the income available. This process of identifying your **optimal consumption** was illustrated in Table 19.2 with downloads of music and video games.

Computing your optimal consumption is difficult because you must assess the marginal utility of each prospective purchase. In Table 19.2 we assumed that the marginal utility of the first music download was 10 utils, while the first game download had a marginal utility of 20. Then we had to specify the marginal utility of every additional music and game download. Can we really be so specific about our tastes?

Indifference curves require a bit less arithmetic. ***Instead of trying to measure the marginal utility of each prospective purchase, we now look for combinations of goods that yield equal satisfaction.*** In the arcade, this entails different combinations of Cokes and games. All we need is to determine that one particular combination of Cokes and video games is as satisfying as another. We don't have to say how many "units of pleasure" both combinations provide—it's sufficient that they're both equally satisfying.

marginal utility: The change in total utility obtained by consuming one additional (marginal) unit of a good or service.

optimal consumption: The mix of consumer purchases that maximizes the utility attainable from available income.

Combination	Cokes	Video Games
A	1	8
B	2	5
C	3	4

TABLE 19A.1

Equally Satisfying Combinations

Different combinations of two goods may be equally satisfying. In this case we assume that the combinations *A*, *B*, and *C* all yield equal total utility. Hence the consumer will be indifferent about which of the three combinations he or she receives.

The initial combination of 1 Coke and 8 video games is designated as combination *A* in Table 19A.1. This combination of goods yields a certain, but unspecified, level of total utility. What we want to do now is to find another combination of Cokes and games that's just as satisfying as combination *A*. Finding other combinations of equal satisfaction isn't easy, but it's at least possible. After a lot of soul searching, we decide that 2 Cokes and 5 video games would be just as satisfying as 1 Coke and 8 games.[1] This combination is designated as *B* in Table 19A.1.

Table 19A.1 also depicts a third combination of Cokes and video games that's as satisfying as the first. Combination *C* includes 3 Cokes and 4 games, a mix of consumption assumed to yield the same total utility as 1 Coke and 8 games (combination *A*).

Notice that we haven't said anything about how much pleasure combinations *A*, *B*, and *C* provide. We're simply asserting that these three combinations are *equally* satisfying.

Figure 19A.1 illustrates the information about tastes that we've assembled. Points *A*, *B*, and *C* represent the three equally satisfying combinations of Cokes and video games we've identified. By connecting these points we create an **indifference curve.** The indifference curve illustrates all combinations of two goods that are equally satisfying. A consumer would be just as happy with any combination represented on the curve, so a choice among them would be a matter of indifference.

indifference curve: A curve depicting alternative combinations of goods that yield equal satisfaction.

An Indifference Map. Not all combinations of Cokes and video games are as satisfying as combination *A*, of course. Surely 2 Cokes and 8 games would be preferred to only 1 Coke and 8 games. Indeed, ***any combination that provided more of one good and no less of the***

FIGURE 19A.1

An Indifference Curve

An indifference curve illustrates the various combinations of two goods that would provide equal satisfaction. The consumer is assumed to be indifferent to a choice between combinations *A*, *B*, and *C* (and all other points on the curve) because they all yield the same total utility.

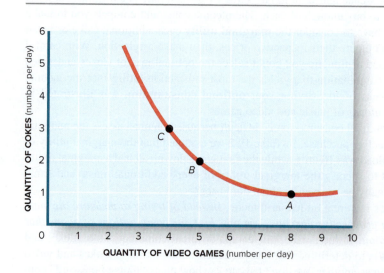

[1]The utility computations used here aren't based on Table 19.2; a different set of tastes is assumed

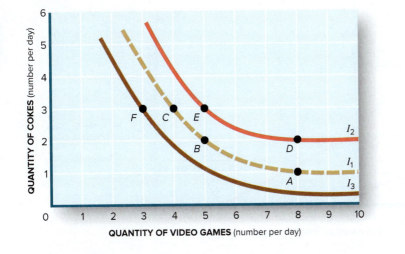

FIGURE 19A.2

An Indifference Map

All combinations of goods depicted on any given indifference curve (e.g., I_1) are equally satisfying. Other combinations are more or less satisfying, however, and thus lie on higher (I_2) or lower (I_3) indifference curves. An indifference map shows all possible levels of total utility (e.g., $I_1, I_2, I_3, \ldots, I_n$) and their respective consumption combinations.

other would be preferred. Point *D* in Figure 19A.2 illustrates just one such combination. Combination *D* must yield more total utility than combination *A* because it includes one more Coke and no fewer games. A consumer wouldn't be indifferent to a choice between *A* and *D*; on the contrary, combination *D* would be preferred.

Combination *D* is also preferred to combinations *B* and *C*. How do we know? Recall that combinations *A*, *B*, and *C* are all equally satisfying. Hence, if combination *D* is better than *A*, it must also be better than *B* and *C*. Given a choice, a consumer would select combination *D* (2 Cokes, 8 games) in preference to *any* combination depicted on indifference curve I_1.

There are also combinations that are as satisfying as *D*, of course. These possibilities are illustrated on indifference curve I_2. All these combinations are equally satisfying and must therefore be preferred to any points on indifference curve I_1. In general, ***the farther the indifference curve is from the origin, the more total utility it yields.***

The curve I_3 illustrates various combinations that are less satisfying. Combination *F*, for example, includes 3 Cokes and 3 games. This is 1 game less than the number available in combination *C*. Therefore, *F* yields less total utility than *C* and isn't preferred: a consumer would rather have combination *C* than *F*. By the same logic we just used, all points on indifference curve I_3 are less satisfying than combinations on curve I_2 or I_1.

Curves 1, 2, and 3 in Figure 19A.2 are the beginnings of an **indifference map**. An indifference map depicts all the combinations of goods that would yield various levels of satisfaction. A single indifference curve, in contrast, illustrates all combinations that provide a single (equal) level of total utility.

indifference map: The set of indifference curves that depicts all possible levels of utility attainable from various combinations of goods.

Utility Maximization

We assume that all consumers strive to maximize their utility. They want as much satisfaction as they can get. In the terminology of indifference curves, this means getting to the indifference curve that's farthest from the origin. The farther one is from the origin, the greater the total utility.

Although the goal of consumers is evident, the means of achieving it isn't so clear. Higher indifference curves aren't only more satisfying, they're also more expensive. We're confronted again with the basic conflict between preferences and prices. With a limited amount of income to spend, we can't attain infinite satisfaction (the farthest indifference curve). We have to settle for less (an indifference curve closer to the origin). The question is, How do we maximize the utility attainable with our limited income?

The Budget Constraint. For starters, we have to determine how much we have to spend. Suppose for the moment that we have only $2 to spend in the arcade and that Cokes and video games are still the only objects of our consumption desires. The price of a Coke is

FIGURE 19A.3

The Budget Constraint

Consumption possibilities are limited by available income. The budget constraint illustrates this limitation. The end points of the budget constraint are equal to income divided by the price of each good. All points on the budget constraint represent affordable combinations of goods.

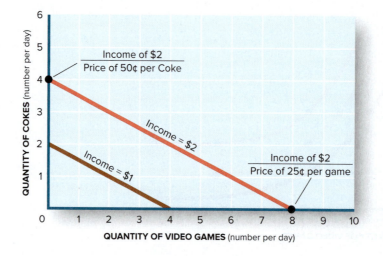

budget constraint: A line depicting all combinations of goods that are affordable with a given income and given prices.

50 cents; the price of a game is 25 cents. Accordingly, the maximum number of Cokes we could buy is 4 if we didn't play any video games. On the other hand, we could play as many as 8 games if we were to forsake Coke.

Figure 19A.3 depicts the limitations placed on our consumption possibilities by a finite income. The **budget constraint** illustrates all combinations of goods affordable with a given income. In this case, the outermost budget line illustrates the combinations of Cokes and video games that can be purchased with $2.

The budget line is easily drawn. The end points of the budget constraint are found by dividing one's income by the price of the good on the corresponding axis. Thus the outermost curve begins at 4 Cokes ($2 ÷ 50 cents) and ends at 8 games ($2 ÷ 25 cents). All the other points on the budget constraint represent other combinations of Cokes and video games that could be purchased with $2.

A smaller income is also illustrated in Figure 19A.3. If we had only $1 to spend, we could afford fewer Cokes and fewer games. Hence a smaller income is represented by a budget constraint that lies closer to the origin.

Optimal Consumption. With a budget constraint looming before us, the limitation on utility maximization is evident. We want to reach the highest indifference curve possible. Our limited income, however, restricts our grasp. We can go only as far as our budget constraint allows. In this context, ***the objective is to reach the highest indifference curve that is compatible with our budget constraint.***

Figure 19A.4 illustrates the process of achieving optimal consumption. We start with an indifference map depicting all utility levels and product combinations. Then we impose a budget line that reflects our income. In this case, we continue to assume that Coke costs 50 cents, video games cost 25 cents, and we have $2 to spend. Hence ***we can afford only those consumption combinations that are on or inside the budget line.***

Which particular combination of Cokes and video games maximizes the utility of our $2? It must be 2 Cokes and 4 video games, as reflected in point *M*. Notice that point *M* isn't only on the budget line but also touches indifference curve I_c. No other point on the budget line touches I_c or any higher indifference curve. Accordingly, I_c represents the most utility we can get for $2 and is attainable only if we consume 2 Cokes and 4 video games. Any other affordable combination yields less total utility—that is, falls on a lower indifference curve. Point *G*, for example, which offers 3 Cokes and 2 video games for $2, lies on the indifference curve I_b. Because I_b lies closer to the origin than I_c, point *G* must be less satisfying than point *M*. We conclude, then, that ***the point of tangency between the budget constraint and an indifference curve represents optimal consumption.*** It's the combination we should buy if we want to maximize the utility of our limited income.

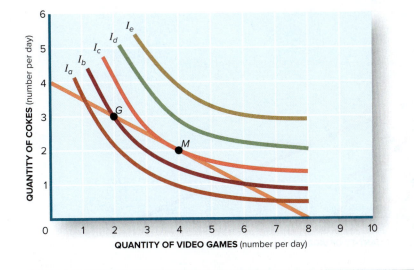

FIGURE 19A.4

Optimal Consumption

The optimal consumption combination—the one that maximizes the utility of spendable income—lies at the point where the budget line is tangent to (just touches) an indifference curve. In this case, point *M* represents the optimal mix of Cokes and video games because no other affordable combination lies on a higher indifference curve than I_c.

Marginal Utility and Price: A Digression. We earlier illustrated the utility-maximizing rule, which required a comparison of the ratios of marginal utilities to prices. Specifically, optimal consumption was represented as that combination of Cokes and video games that yielded

$$\frac{\text{MU Coke}}{\text{P Coke}} = \frac{\text{MU games}}{\text{P games}}$$

Does point *M* in Figure 19A.4 conform to this rule?

To answer this question, first rearrange the preceding equation as follows:

$$\frac{\text{MU Coke}}{\text{MU games}} = \frac{\text{P Coke}}{\text{P games}}$$

In this form, the equation says that the relative marginal utilities of Cokes and video games should equal their relative prices when consumption is optimal. In other words, if a Coke costs twice as much as a video game, then it must yield twice as much marginal utility if the consumer is to be in an optimal state. Otherwise, some substitution of Cokes for video games, or vice versa, would be desirable.

With this foundation, we can show that point *M* conforms to our earlier rule. Consider first the slope of the budget constraint, which is determined by the relative prices of Cokes and video games. In fact, *the (absolute) slope of the budget constraint equals the relative price of the two goods.* In Figure 19A.4 the slope equals the price of video games divided by the price of Cokes (25 cents ÷ 50 cents = ½). It tells us the rate at which video games can be exchanged for Cokes in the market. In this case, one video game is "worth" half a Coke.

The relative marginal utilities of the two goods are reflected in the slope of the indifference curve. Recall that the curve tells at what rate a consumer is willing to substitute one good for another, with no change in total utility. In fact, the slope of the indifference curve is called the **marginal rate of substitution.** It's equal to the relative marginal utilities of the two goods. Presumably one would be indifferent to a choice between 2 Cokes + 5 games and 3 Cokes + 4 games—as suggested in Table 19A.1—only if the third Coke were as satisfying as the fifth video game.

At the point of optimal consumption (*M*) in Figure 19A.4 the budget constraint is tangent to the indifference curve I_c, which means that the two curves must have the same slope at that point. In other words,

marginal rate of substitution: The rate at which a consumer is willing to exchange one good for another; the relative marginal utilities of two goods.

$$\frac{\text{P games}}{\text{P Coke}} = \frac{\text{MU games}}{\text{MU Coke}}$$

FIGURE 19A.5

Changing Prices

When the price of a good changes, the budget constraint shifts, and a new consumption combination must be sought. In this case, the price of video games is changing. When the price of games increases from 25 cents to 50 cents, the budget constraint shifts inward and optimal consumption moves from point *M* to point *N*.

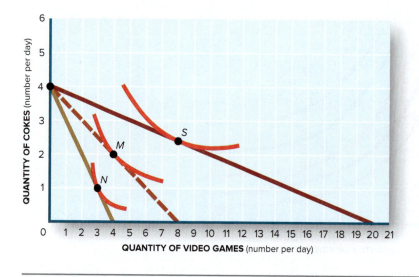

or alternatively,

$$\begin{matrix} \text{Rate of} \\ \text{market exchange} \end{matrix} = \begin{matrix} \text{Marginal rate} \\ \text{of substitution} \end{matrix}$$

Both indifference curves and marginal utility comparisons lead us to the same optimal mix of consumption.

Deriving the Demand Curve

We noted at the beginning of this appendix that indifference curves not only give us an alternative path to optimal consumption but also can be used to derive a demand curve. To do this, we need to consider how the optimal consumption combination changes when the price of one good is altered. We can see what happens in Figure 19A.5.

Figure 19A.5 starts with the optimal consumption attained at point *M*, with income of $2 and prices of 50 cents for a Coke and 25 cents for a video game. Now we're going to change the price of video games and observe how consumption changes.

Suppose that the price of a video game doubles, from 25 cents to 50 cents. This change will shift the budget constraint inward: our income of $2 now buys a maximum of 4 games rather than 8. Hence the lower end point of the budget constraint moves from 8 games to 4 games. ***Whenever the price of a good changes, the budget constraint shifts.***

Only one end of the budget constraint is changed in Figure 19A.5. The budget line still begins at 4 Cokes because the price of Coke is unchanged. If only one price is changed, then only one end of the budget constraint is shifted.

Because the budget constraint has shifted inward, the combination *M* is no longer attainable. Two Cokes (at 50 cents each) and 4 games (at 50 cents each) now cost more than $2. We're now forced to accept a lower level of total utility. According to Figure 19A.5, optimal consumption is now located at point *N*. This is the point of tangency between the new budget constraint and a lower indifference curve. At point *N* we consume 1 Coke and 3 video games.

Consider what has happened here. The price of video games has increased (from 25 cents to 50 cents), and the quantity of games demanded has decreased. This is the kind of relationship that demand curves describe. **Demand curves** indicate how the quantity demanded of a good changes in response to a change in its price, given a fixed income and all other things held constant. Not only does Figure 19A.5 provide the same information, it also conforms to the **law of demand**: as the price of games increases, the quantity demanded falls.

Suppose the price of video games were to fall rather than increase. Specifically, assume that the price of a game fell to 10 cents. This price reduction would shift the budget constraint farther out on the horizontal axis because as many as 20 games could then be

demand curve: A curve describing the quantities of a good a consumer is willing and able to buy at alternative prices in a given time period, *ceteris paribus*.

law of demand: The quantity of a good demanded in a given time period increases as its price falls, *ceteris paribus*.

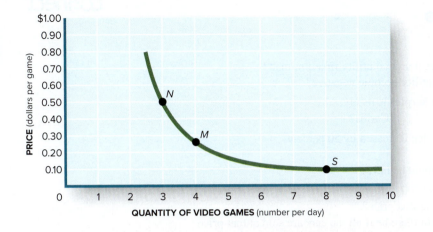

FIGURE 19A.6

The Demand for Video Games

Figure 19A.5 shows how optimal consumption is altered when the price of video games changes. From that figure we can determine the quantity of video games demanded at alternative prices, *ceteris paribus*. That information is summarized here in the demand schedule (below) and the demand curve (above).

Point	Price (per Game)	Quantity Demanded (Games per Day)
N	50 cents	3
M	25	4
S	10	8

purchased with $2. As a result of the price reduction, we can now buy more goods and thus attain a higher level of satisfaction.

Point *S* in Figure 19A.5 indicates the optimal combination of Cokes and video games at the new video game price. At these prices, we consume 8 video games and 2.4 Cokes (we may have to share with a friend). The law of demand is again evident: when the price of video games declines, the quantity demanded increases.

The Demand Schedule and Curve. Figure 19A.6 summarizes the information we've acquired about the demand for video games. The demand schedule depicts the price–quantity relationships prevailing at optimal consumption points *N*, *M*, and *S* (from Figure 19A.5). The demand curve generalizes these observations to encompass other prices. What we end up with is a demand curve explicitly derived from our (assumed) knowledge of consumer tastes.

Key Terms

marginal utility
optimal consumption
indifference curve

indifference map
budget constraint
marginal rate of substitution

demand curve
law of demand

PROBLEMS FOR CHAPTER 19

LO19-1 1. According to Table 19.1,
- (a) With which box of popcorn does marginal utility first diminish?
- (b) With which box does marginal utility become negative?

LO19-2 2. In Figure 19.4, how much consumer surplus is received by
- (a) Fred?   (b) Hua?   (c) Carlos?

LO19-2 3. In Figure 19.4, if Bob's maximum price increased by 50 percent,
- (a) Would he buy a Spyder?
- (b) How much consumer surplus would he have?

LO19-2 4. If the price of a Spyder drops to $700,000 in Figure 19.4 ,
- (a) How many Spyders can be sold at that price?
- (b) How much consumer surplus will there be if all the cars are sold at that price?
- (c) How much revenue will the car dealer get if he sells all the cars at
  - (i) the same price ($700,000)?
  - (ii) the maximum price each buyer is willing to pay?

LO19-3 5. The following data reveal how much each consumer is willing to pay for an Alaskan cruise:

Amy	$ 900	Ed	$2,000
Bob	$1,100	Gigi	$1,300
Carol	$1,500	Hugo	$1,800
Eduardo	$ 400	Isabelle	$1,500

- (a) Draw the market demand for these eight consumers.
- (b) If the cruise costs $1,000, how many passengers will there be?
- (c) If the cruise costs $1,000, how much total revenue will be collected?
- (d) If the cruise costs $1,000, how much consumer surplus will those passengers enjoy?

LO19-4 6. Suppose movie downloads cost $2 apiece and game downloads cost $3. If the marginal utility of movie downloads at the optimal mix of consumption is 10 utils, what is the marginal utility of a game download?

LO19-1 7. Suppose the graph below depicts the demand for football tickets at Grand University.
- (a) If current demand is represented as Demand 2, what is total revenue at the price of $24?
- (b) If the price drops to $12, how many tickets would consumers purchase?
- (c) What is total revenue at that point?
- (d) If the team has a losing streak and the price is still $24, at what point do we end up?
- (e) What is total revenue at that point?

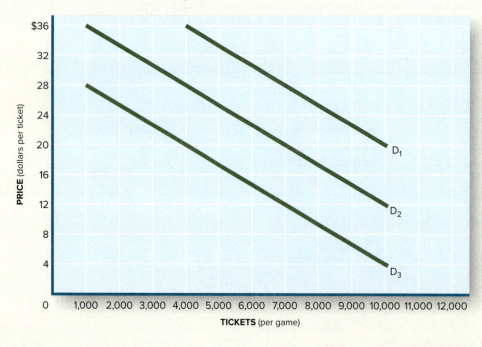

PROBLEMS FOR CHAPTER 19 (cont'd)

LO19-4 8. Suppose the following table reflects the total satisfaction derived from consumption of pizza slices and Pepsis. Assume that pizza costs $1 per slice and a large Pepsi costs $2. With $20 to spend, what consumption mix will maximize satisfaction?

Quantity consumed	1	2	3	4	5	6	7	8	9	10	11	12	13	14
Total units of pleasure from pizza slices	47	92	132	166	196	224	251	271	288	303	313	315	312	300
Total units of pleasure from Pepsis	111	200	272	336	386	426	452	456	444	408	340	217	92	−17

LO19-4 9. A consumer downloads 4 movies and 3 apps per week. Suppose the price is $5 per movie and $3 per app, and the marginal utility is 12 for a movie and 10 for an app.
   (*a*) Calculate marginal utility per dollar.
   (*b*) Is this optimal consumption?
   (*c*) If not, how should they change their consumption to maximize?

LO19-1 10. The Economy Tomorrow: Use the following data to illustrate the relevant demand curve:

Price	$ 10	9	8	7	6	5	4	3	2	1
Quantity	2	4	6	8	10	12	14	16	18	20

   (*a*) If the price increases from $4 to $8, by how much does the quantity demanded decline?
   (*b*) If a successful advertising campaign increases the quantity demanded at every price by 4 units,
      (*i*) Draw the new demand curve D_2.
      (*ii*) How many units are now purchased at $8?

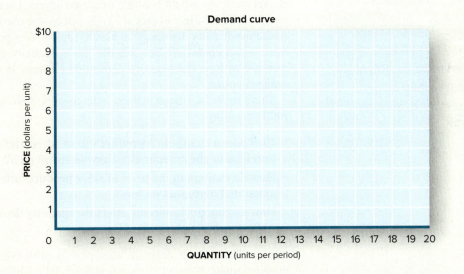

Demand curve

CHAPTER 20

Elasticity

S teve Jobs made a pricing mistake when he launched the 8 GB iPhone in June 2007. He knew all about consumer demand and its many determinants. And he could draw a downward-sloping demand curve just as well as any college economics major (even though he dropped out of Reed College after just one semester). But he overestimated the dimensions of market demand. The demand curve he drew projected that the quantity of iPhones demanded at the price of $599 would be far greater than it turned out to be. This mistake created an instant dilemma. If he kept the price of $599, iPhone sales would come in below publicized projections, and the phone would be deemed a failure. Apple's image of consistent success would be tarnished. Software writers might not develop the library of iPhone apps that would make the iPhone irresistible. So Jobs knew what he had to do: reduce the iPhone's price—fast!

But he couldn't afford to make another mistake. If he reduced the price too little, iPhone sales would still fall short of projections. If he reduced the price too much, sales would soar past production rates and market shortages would frustrate would-be buyers. On the second go-round, Steve Jobs had to pick the right price—the one that would increase the quantity demanded to match Apple's sales projections. The concept that could save him was the "price elasticity of demand"—a measure of how the quantity demanded *changes* in response to a *change* in price.

This chapter focuses on that *elasticity* concept. Among the questions we'll pursue are

- **How does a change in a product's price affect the quantity we purchase or the amount of money we spend on it?**
- **How do changes in the price of *other* products affect the amount of a product we buy?**
- **How do changes in income affect the quantity demanded of various goods and services?**

As we will see, the concept of "elasticity" is part of the answer to all these questions. We w ill also see how Steve Jobs salvaged the original iPhone with the same concept and how Apple used the concept again in 2017 to price the iPhone 8.

LEARNING OBJECTIVES

After reading this chapter, you should know

LO20-1 How to compute price elasticity of demand.

LO20-2 The relationships between price changes, price elasticity, quantity demanded, and total revenue.

LO20-3 What the cross-price elasticity of demand measures.

LO20-4 What the income elasticity of demand tells us.

LO20-5 What the elasticity of supply measures.

PRICE ELASTICITY

What Steve Jobs wanted to know in September 2007 was how much phone sales would *increase* if he *reduced* its price. The same question haunts movie theater owners. They make a big chunk of profit from the sale of popcorn, candy, and soda. People are always complaining about how expensive those snacks are. But will they buy more if prices are reduced? A *lot* more, or just a *little* more?

Like Apple, theater owners know all about the **law of demand** and the downward-sloping **demand curve.** But that law isn't greatly informative; it tells them only that the quantity demanded will increase when the price is reduced. That begs the critical question of *how much.* What the theater owner wants to know is *by how much* the quantity demanded will increase if the price is reduced. Steve Jobs wanted to know the same thing about the demand for iPhones: how many *more* iPhones would be purchased if he reduced its price?

The central question in all these decisions is the response of quantity demanded to a change in price. ***The response of consumers to a change in price is measured by the price elasticity of demand.*** Specifically, the **price elasticity of demand** refers to the *percentage* change in quantity demanded divided by the *percentage* change in price:

$$\text{Price elasticity} \atop (E) = \frac{\text{\% change in quantity demanded}}{\text{\% change in price}}$$

What would the value of price elasticity be if air travel didn't change at all when airfares were cut by 5 percent? In that case the price elasticity of demand would be

$$E = \frac{\% \text{ change in quantity demanded}}{\% \text{ change in price}}$$

$$= \frac{0}{5} = 0$$

But is this realistic? According to the law of demand, the quantity demanded goes up when price goes down. So we'd expect *somebody* to buy more airline tickets if fares fell by 5 percent. In a large market like air travel, we don't expect *everybody* to jump on a plane when airfares are reduced. But if *some* consumers fly more, the percentage change in quantity demanded will be larger than zero. Indeed, ***the law of demand implies that the price elasticity of demand will always be greater than zero.***

Technically, the price elasticity of demand (E) is a negative number since quantity demanded and price always move in opposite directions (law of demand). For simplicity, however, E is typically expressed in absolute terms (without the minus sign). ***The key question, then, is how much greater than zero E actually is.***

Computing Price Elasticity

To get a feel for the dimensions of elasticity, let's return to the popcorn counter at the movies that we first encountered in Chapter 19. We observed there that at a price of 45 cents an ounce the average moviegoer demands 2 ounces of popcorn per show. This is illustrated again in Figure 20.1 at point *B*. At the lower price of 40 cents per ounce (point *C*), the quantity demanded jumps to 4 ounces per show.

Percentage Change in q. We can summarize this response with the price elasticity of demand. To do so, we have to calculate the *percentage* changes in quantity and price. Consider the percentage change in quantity first. In this case, the change in quantity demanded is 4 ounces − 2 ounces = 2 ounces. The *percentage* change in quantity is therefore

$$\% \text{ change in quantity} = \frac{2}{q}$$

law of demand: The quantity of a good demanded in a given time period increases as its price falls, *ceteris paribus.*

demand curve: A curve describing the quantities of a good a consumer is willing and able to buy at alternative prices in a given time period, *ceteris paribus.*

price elasticity of demand: The percentage change in quantity demanded divided by the percentage change in price.

How do prices affect popcorn sales?

©D. Hurst/Alamy Stock Photo RF

FIGURE 20.1

Demand and Elasticity

We know from the Law of Demand that the quantity demanded increases when price is reduced. This demand curve (identical to Figure 19.3) informs us that when the price of popcorn falls from 45 cents per ounce to 25 cents, the quantity demanded increases from 2 (point *B*) to 12 ounces per show (point *F*).

What the price elasticity of demand tells us is how much, *in percentage terms*, the quantity demanded changes in response to various price changes.

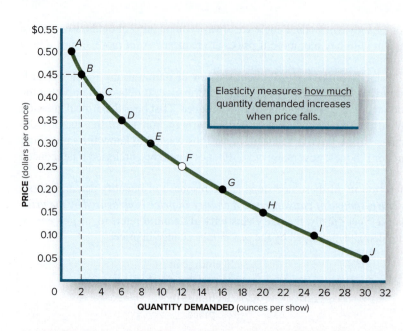

Elasticity measures how much quantity demanded increases when price falls.

	Price (per Ounce)	Quantity Demanded (Ounces per Show)
A	$0.50	1
B	0.45	2
C	0.40	4
D	0.35	6
E	0.30	9
F	0.25	12
G	0.20	16
H	0.15	20
I	0.10	25
J	0.05	30

The computational problem is to transform the denominator *q* into a number. Should we use the quantity of popcorn purchased *before* the price reduction—that is, $q_1 = 2$? Or should we use the quantity purchased *after* the price reduction—that is, $q_2 = 4$? The choice of denominator will have a big impact on the computed percentage change. To ensure consistency, economists prefer to use the *average* quantity in the denominator:[1]

$$\text{\% change in quantity demanded} = \frac{\textbf{Change in quantity}}{\textbf{Average quantity}}$$

Our first task is therefore to compute the **average** quantity: the average of the first (pre–price change) and second (post–price change) quantities. The formula for this calculation is

$$\textbf{Average quantity} = \frac{q_1 + q_2}{2} = \frac{2 + 4}{2} = 3 \text{ ounces}$$

(3 is the average value of 2 and 4).

---

[1]This procedure is referred to as the *arc* (midpoint) elasticity of demand. If a single quantity (price) is used in the denominator, we refer to the *point* elasticity of demand.

We can now complete the calculation of the percentage change in quantity demanded. It is

$$\text{\% change in quantity demanded} = \frac{\text{Change in quantity}}{\text{Average quantity}} = \frac{q_2 - q_1}{\frac{q_1 + q_2}{2}} = \frac{2}{3} = 0.667$$

Popcorn sales increased by an average of 67 percent when the price of popcorn was reduced from 45 cents to 40 cents per ounce.

Percentage Change in p. The computation of the percentage change in price is similar. We first note that the price of popcorn fell by 5 cents ($40¢ − 45¢$) when we move from point B to point C on the demand curve (Figure 20.1). We then compute the *average* price of popcorn in this range of the demand curve as

$$\text{Average price of popcorn} = \frac{p_1 + p_2}{2} = \frac{45¢ + 40¢}{2} = 42.5 \text{ cents}$$

This *average* is the denominator we use in calculating the percentage price change. Using these numbers, we see that the absolute value of the percentage change is

$$\text{\% change in price} = \frac{\text{Change in price}}{\text{Average price}} = \frac{p_2 - p_1}{\frac{p_1 + p_2}{2}} = \frac{5}{42.5} = 0.118$$

The price of popcorn fell by 11.8 percent.

These calculations are a bit cumbersome, but they give us all the information required to compute the price elasticity of demand. In this case,

$$E = \frac{\text{\% change in quantity demanded}}{\text{\% change in price}} = \frac{0.667}{0.118} = 5.65$$

What we get from all these calculations is a very useful number. It says that the consumer response to a price reduction will be extremely large. Specifically, the quantity of popcorn consumed will increase 5.65 times as fast as price falls. A 1 percent reduction in price brings about a 5.65 percent increase in purchases. The theater manager can therefore boost popcorn sales greatly by lowering price a little. Steve Jobs would have been thrilled if the demand for the first iPhones had been that elastic.

Elastic vs. Inelastic Demand. We characterize the demand for various goods in one of three ways: *elastic, inelastic,* or *unitary elastic:*

- *If E is larger than 1, demand is elastic.* Consumer response is large relative to the change in price. This is clearly the case in the popcorn example above ($E = 5.65$).
- *If E is less than 1, demand is **inelastic**.* If demand is inelastic ($E < 1$), consumers aren't very responsive to price changes.
- *If E is equal to 1, demand is **unitary** elastic.* In this case, the percentage change in quantity demanded is exactly equal to the percentage change in price.

Consider the case of smoking. Many smokers claim they'd "pay anything" for a cigarette after they've run out. But would they? Would they continue to smoke just as many cigarettes if prices doubled or tripled? If so, the demand curve would be vertical (as in Figure 20.2b) rather than downward-sloping. Research suggests this is not the case: higher cigarette prices *do* curb smoking. There is at least *some* elasticity in the demand for cigarettes. But the elasticity of demand is low; Table 20.1 indicates that the price elasticity of cigarette demand is only 0.4. Since 0.4 is less than 1.0, we say that cigarette demand is inelastic. But that doesn't mean smokers are completely unresponsive to cigarette prices. If the price goes up, they will buy fewer cigarettes, but not a *lot* fewer.

FIGURE 20.2

Extremes of Elasticity

If demand were perfectly elastic ($E = \infty$), the demand curve would be *horizontal*. In that case, any increase in price (e.g., p_1 to p_2) would cause quantity demanded to fall to zero.

A *vertical* demand curve implies that an increase in price won't affect the quantity demanded. In this situation of perfectly *in*elastic ($E = 0$) demand, consumers are willing to pay *any* price to get the quantity q_1.

In reality, elasticities of demand for goods and services lie between these two extremes (obeying the law of demand).

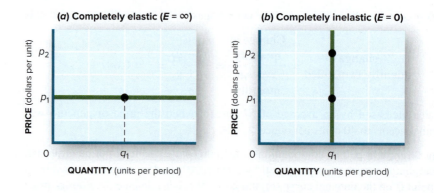

(a) Completely elastic ($E = \infty$)

(b) Completely inelastic ($E = 0$)

Although the average adult smoker is not very responsive to changes in cigarette prices, teen smokers apparently are. Research studies confirm that teen smoking drops by almost 7 percent when cigarette prices increase by 10 percent. Thus the price elasticity of *teen* demand for smoking is

$$E = \frac{\text{Percentage drop in quantity demanded}}{\text{Percentage increase in price}} = \frac{7\%}{10\%} = 0.7$$

Hence higher cigarette prices can be an effective policy tool for curbing teen smoking. The *tripling* of the federal excise tax on cigarettes in 2009 (from 39 cents to $1.01 per pack) raised the price of cigarettes by 13 percent and deterred 250,000 teens from smoking.

According to Table 20.1, the demand for airline travel is much more price-elastic than the demand for cigarettes. Whenever a fare cut is announced, the airlines get swamped with telephone and internet inquiries. If fares are discounted by 25 percent, the number of passengers may increase by as much as 60 percent. As Table 20.1 shows, the elasticity of airline demand is 2.4, meaning that the percentage change in quantity demanded (60 percent) will be 2.4 times larger than the price cut (25 percent).

TABLE 20.1

Elasticity Estimates

Price elasticities vary greatly. When the price of gasoline increases, consumers reduce their consumption only slightly ($E = 0.2$). When the price of fish increases, however, consumers cut back their consumption substantially ($E = 2.2$). These differences reflect the availability of immediate substitutes, the prices of the goods, and the amount of time available for changing behavior.

Product	Price Elasticity
Relatively elastic ($E > 1$)	
Airline travel, long run	2.4
Restaurant meals	2.3
Fresh fish	2.2
New cars, short run	1.2–1.5
Unitary elastic ($E = 1$)	
Private education	1.1
Radios and televisions	1.2
Shoes	0.9
Movies	0.9
Relatively inelastic ($E < 1$)	
Milk	0.6
Cigarettes	0.4
Coffee	0.3
Eggs	0.3
Gasoline, short run	0.2
Electricity (in homes)	0.1

Sources: Houthakker, Hendrick S. and Lester D. Taylor, *Consumer Demand in the United States, 1929–1970*. Cambridge: Harvard University Press, 1966; Bell, F. W., "The Pope and Price of Fish," *American Economic Review,* December 1968; Scarf, Herbert and John Shoven, *Applied General Equilibrium Analysis.* New York: Cambridge University Press, 1984; and Ward, Michael, "Product Substitutability and Competition in Long-Distance Telecommunications," *Economic Inquiry,* October 1999.

Steve Jobs was pleased to discover that the demand for iPhones was even more elastic than that. Two months after launching the 8 GB iPhone in 2007, he reduced its price from $599 to $399. Unit sales not only increased, they soared, as In the News "After iPhone Price Cut, Sales Are Up by 200 Percent" reports. Demand for the iPhone was very elastic.

©McGraw-Hill Education

IN THE NEWS

AFTER IPHONE PRICE CUT, SALES ARE UP BY 200 PERCENT

Piper Gene Munster, the person responsible for a survey dedicated to Apple in which he "found" out an estimated number of iPhones that were sold, has come up with yet another interesting theory.

According to Munster and the past-week Apple announcement about 1 million iPhones sold, the calculations take to the conclusion that after the price cut, the sales increased up to 200 percent. . . .

By Munster's reckoning, Apple and AT&T were selling an average of 9,000 iPhones a day before the price reduction, which would have put their quarterly sales at 594,000 as of September 5.

By the end of the quarter, he believes Apple will have sold a total of 1.28 million iPhones.

Source: Mobilewhack.com, September 11, 2007.

ANALYSIS: If demand is elastic, unit sales increase by a larger percentage than price declines. The demand for iPhones was highly elastic.

Determinants of Elasticity

Why are consumers so price-sensitive ($E > 1$) with some goods and not ($E < 1$) with others? To answer that, we must go back to the demand curve itself. The elasticity of demand is computed between points on a given demand curve. Hence *the price elasticity of demand is influenced by all the determinants of demand.* Four factors are particularly worth noting.

Necessities vs. Luxuries. Some goods are so critical to our everyday life that we regard them as "necessities." A hairbrush, toothpaste, and perhaps textbooks might fall into this category. Our "taste" for such goods is so strong that we can't imagine getting along without them. As a result, we don't change our consumption of "necessities" much when the price increases; *demand for necessities is relatively inelastic.*

A "luxury" good, by contrast, is something we'd *like* to have but aren't likely to buy unless our income jumps or the price declines sharply, such as vacation travel, new cars (that Porsche 918 Spyder!), and iPhones. We want them but can get by without them. That is, *demand for luxury goods is relatively elastic.*

Availability of Substitutes. Our notion of which goods are necessities is also influenced by the availability of substitute goods. The high elasticity of demand for fish (Table 20.1) reflects the fact that consumers can eat chicken, beef, or pork if fish prices rise. On the other hand, most bleary-eyed coffee drinkers can't imagine any other product that could substitute for a cup of coffee. As a consequence, when coffee prices rise, consumers don't reduce their purchases much at all. Likewise, the low elasticity of demand for gasoline reflects the fact that most cars can't run on alternative fuels . In general, *the greater the availability of substitutes, the higher the price elasticity of demand.*

The availability of substitutes frustrated California's attempt to both reduce smoking and increase tax revenues when it hiked the state tax on cigarettes from 87 cents a pack to $2.87 a pack in 2017 (see In the News "Californians Vote to Triple Cigarette Tax") Studies have shown conclusively that the price elasticity for cigarettes is low. But the demand for *California-taxed* cigarettes is much more elastic. Why? Because Californians can buy cigarettes in neighboring states, on Indian reservations, or even order them over the internet.

FIGURE 20.3

Elasticity and Total Revenue

Total revenue is equal to the price of the product times the quantity sold. It is illustrated by the area of the rectangle formed by $p \times q$.

The shaded rectangle illustrates total revenue ($1.60) at a price of 40 cents and a quantity demanded of 4 ounces. When price is increased to 45 cents (point *B*), the rectangle and total revenue shrink (see the dashed lines) because demand is relatively elastic in that price range. Price hikes increase total revenue only if demand is inelastic.

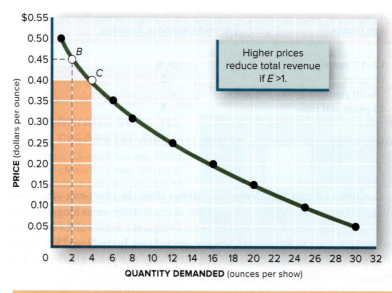

	Price	×	Quantity Demanded	=	Total Revenue
A	50¢		1		$0.50
B	45		2		0.90
C	40		4		1.60
D	35		6		2.10
E	30		8		2.40
F	25		12		3.00
G	20		16		3.20
H	15		20		3.00
I	10		25		2.50
J	5		30		1.50

quantity demanded. But what about total revenue? The change in total revenue depends on *how much* quantity demanded falls when price goes up.

Suppose we raise popcorn prices again, from 40 cents back to 45 cents. What happens to total revenue? At 40 cents per box, 4 ounces are sold (see Figure 20.3) and total revenue equals $1.60. If we increase the price to 45 cents, only 2 ounces are sold and total revenue drops to 90 cents. In this case, an *increase* in price leads to a *decrease* in total revenue. This new and smaller total revenue is illustrated by the dashed rectangle in Figure 20.3.

Price increases don't always lower total revenue. If consumer demand was relatively *inelastic* ($E < 1$), a price increase would lead to *higher* total revenue. Thus we conclude that

- *A price hike increases total revenue only if demand is inelastic ($E < 1$).*
- *A price hike reduces total revenue if demand is elastic ($E > 1$).*
- *A price hike does not change total revenue if demand is unitary elastic ($E = 1$).*

Table 20.3 summarizes these and other responses to price changes.

Changing Value of E. Once we know the price elasticity of demand, we can predict how consumers will respond to changing prices. We can also predict what will happen to the total revenue of the seller when the price is raised or reduced. Figure 20.4 shows how elasticity and total revenue change along a given demand curve. Demand for cigarettes is *elastic* ($E > 1$) at prices above $6 per pack but *inelastic* ($E < 1$) at lower prices.

The bottom half of Figure 20.4 shows how total revenue changes along the demand curve. At very high prices (e.g., $14 a pack), few cigarettes are sold and total revenue is low. As the price is reduced, however, the quantity demanded increases so much that total

Effect on Total Revenue of

If Demand is	Price Increase	Price Reduction
Elastic (E > 1)	Decrease	Increase
Inelastic (E < 1)	Increase	Decrease
Unitary elastic (E = 1)	No change	No change

TABLE 20.3

Price Elasticity of Demand and Total Revenue

The impact of higher prices on total revenue depends on the price elasticity of demand. Higher prices result in higher total revenue only if demand is inelastic. If demand is elastic, *lower* prices result in *higher* revenues.

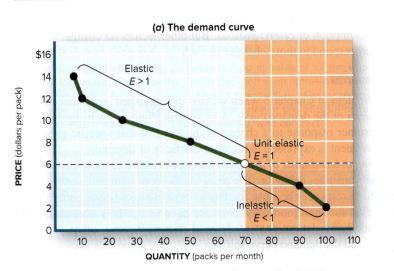

(a) The demand curve

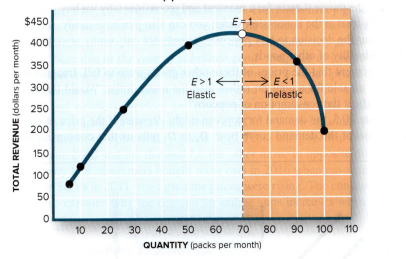

(b) Total revenue

FIGURE 20.4

Price Elasticity Changes along a Demand Curve

The concept of price elasticity can be used to determine whether people will spend more money on cigarettes when their price rises. The answer to this question is yes and no, depending on how high the price goes.

Notice in the table and the graphs that total revenue rises when the price of cigarettes increases from $2 to $4 a pack and again to $6. At low prices, the demand for cigarettes appears relatively inelastic: price and total revenue move in the same direction.

As the price of cigarettes continues to increase, however, total revenue starts to fall. As the price is increased from $6 to $8 a pack, total revenue drops. At higher prices, the demand for cigarettes is relatively elastic: price and total revenue move in *opposite directions*. Hence the price elasticity of demand depends on where one is on the demand curve.

Price of Cigarettes	×	Quantity Demanded	=	Total Revenue	
$ 2		100		$200	Low elasticity; E < 1
4		90		360	(total revenue rises
6		70		420	when price increases)
8		50		400	High elasticity; E > 1
10		25		250	(total revenue falls
12		10		120	when price increases)
14		6		84	

Think back to the impact of the iPhone price cut on Galaxy sales (see In the News "Samsung Stung by Apple Moves"). The 16GB iPhone 5s dropped in price from $199 to $99. We compute the *percentage* decline as

$$\frac{\% \text{ change}}{\text{in iPhone price}} = \frac{\text{Change in price}}{\text{Average price}} = \frac{\$199 - \$99}{\$149} = -0.67$$

Galaxy sales *declined* by 20 percent. Hence the cross-price elasticity of demand was

$$E_x = \frac{-0.20}{-0.67} = +0.30$$

Demand for Galaxys declined by 0.30 percent for every 1 percent decline in the iPhone price. A 67 percent iPhone price cut therefore caused a 20 percent decline in Galaxy demand.

Notice that the cross-price elasticity computed here is a *positive* number (+0.30). We saw earlier that the simple (same-product) price elasticity of demand is always a negative number, so we could ignore its sign. That's not the case with cross-price elasticities. In fact, the sign of the cross-price elasticity of demand is important.

If the cross-price elasticity is positive, the two goods are substitutes; if the cross-price elasticity is negative, the two goods are complements. Pepsi and popcorn are complements because a fall (−) in the price of one leads to an increase (+) in the demand for the other; in other words, the cross-price elasticity is negative.

INCOME ELASTICITY

Changes in the price of other goods aren't the only source of demand shifts. Each of the four determinants of demand is a potential shift factor. Suppose consumer incomes were to increase. How would popcorn consumption be affected? Figure 20.6 provides an answer. Before the change in income, consumers demanded 12 ounces of popcorn at a price of 25 cents per ounce. With more income to spend, the new demand curve (D_2) suggests that consumers will now purchase a greater quantity of popcorn at every price. The increase in income has caused a rightward shift in demand. If popcorn continues to sell for 25 cents per ounce, consumers will now buy 16 ounces per show (point N) rather than only 12 ounces (point F).

It appears that changes in income have a substantial impact on consumer demand for popcorn. The graph in Figure 20.6 doesn't tell us, however, how large the change in income was. Will a *small* increase in income cause such a shift, or does popcorn demand increase only when moviegoers have a *lot* more money to spend?

FIGURE 20.6

Income Elasticity

If income changes, the demand curve *shifts*. In this case, an increase in income enables consumers to buy more popcorn at every price. At a price of 25 cents, the quantity demanded increases from 12 ounces (point *F*) to 16 ounces (point *N*). The *income elasticity of demand* measures this response of demand to a change in income.

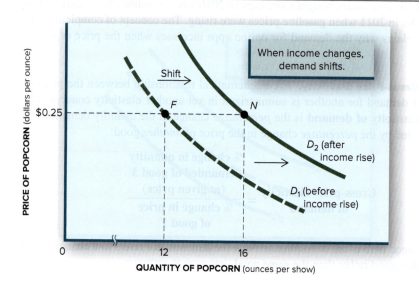

Figure 20.6 doesn't answer these questions. But a little math will. Specifically, the **income elasticity of demand** relates the *percentage* change in quantity demanded to the *percentage* change in income:

income elasticity of demand: Percentage change in quantity demanded divided by percentage change in income.

$$\text{Income elasticity of demand} = \frac{\begin{array}{c}\text{\% change in} \\ \text{quantity demanded} \\ \text{(at given price)}\end{array}}{\begin{array}{c}\text{\% change in} \\ \text{income}\end{array}}$$

The similarity to the price elasticity of demand is apparent. In this case, however, the denominator is *income* (a determinant of demand), not *price.*

Computing Income Elasticity. As was the case with price elasticity, we compute income elasticity with *average* values for the changes in quantity and income. Suppose that the shift in popcorn demand illustrated in Figure 20.6 occurred when income increased from $110 per week to $120 per week. We would then compute

$$
\begin{aligned}
\text{Income elasticity} &= \frac{\dfrac{\text{Change in quantity demanded}}{\text{Average quantity}}}{\dfrac{\text{Change in income}}{\text{Average income}}} \\[2em]
&= \frac{\dfrac{16 \text{ ounces} - 12 \text{ ounces}}{14 \text{ ounces}}}{\dfrac{\$120 - \$110}{\$115}} \\[2em]
&= \frac{4}{14} \div \frac{10}{115} \\[1em]
&= \frac{0.286}{0.087} = 3.29
\end{aligned}
$$

Popcorn purchases are very sensitive to changes in income. When incomes rise by 8.7 percent, popcorn sales increase by a whopping 28.6 percent (that is, 8.7% × 3.29). The computed elasticity of 3.29 summarizes this relationship.

Normal vs. Inferior Goods. Demand and income don't always move in the same direction. Popcorn is a **normal good** because consumers buy more of it when their incomes rise. People actually buy *less* of some goods, however, when they have more income. With low incomes, people buy discount clothes, used textbooks, and cheap beer, and they eat at home. With more money to spend, they switch to designer clothes, new books, premium beer, and restaurant meals. The former items are called **inferior goods** because the quantity demanded *falls* when income *rises.* Similarly, when incomes *decline,* people demand *more* spaghetti, pawnbrokers, and lottery tickets. *For inferior goods, the income elasticity of demand is negative; for normal goods, it is positive.*

normal good: Good for which demand increases when income rises.

inferior good: Goods for which demand decreases when income rises.

ELASTICITY OF SUPPLY

Sensitivity to changing prices is not just a consumer phenomenon. Producers, too, alter their behavior when prices change. We know from the **law of supply** (Chapter 3) that businesses will produce more output at higher prices. What we want to know is how much more they'll produce as prices go up. That is what the **price elasticity of supply** tells us. Like its counterpart on the demand side, the price elasticity of supply relates *percentage* changes in the quantity supplied to *percentage* changes in price:

law of supply: The quantity of a good supplied in a given time period increases as its price increases, *ceteris paribus.*

price elasticity of supply: The percentage change in quantity supplied divided by the percentage change in price.

$$\text{Price elasticity of supply} = \frac{\text{Percentage change in quantity supplied}}{\text{Percentage change in price}}$$

A high price elasticity of supply means that producers are very responsive to price changes; a low elasticity implies a sluggish response. As World View "Rebounding Oil Price Spurs More Rigs" reports, U.S. oil *production* responds to changes in oil *prices*.

WORLD VIEW

REBOUNDING OIL PRICE SPURS MORE RIGS

The recent spike in the price of oil has brought more rigs on line. According to the weekly Baker Hughes count, the number of active oil rigs has jumped 60 percent since last year. When oil prices were falling, the number of active U.S. rigs fell from 2,000 in 2015 to only 480 in 2016. The latest survey, for the week of March 10, 2017 put the number at 762. Higher-cost shale producers in the Permian basin are quick to respond to higher oil prices, acting as the marginal producer. Overall, economists estimate the elasticity of oil supply at around 0.1.

Source: U.S. Coast Guard photo by Petty Officer 3rd Class Patrick Kelley

Source: Media reports of March 2017.

ANALYSIS: Higher oil prices spur additional drilling and production.

THE ECONOMY TOMORROW

WILL EVS OVERTAKE GAS GUZZLERS?

Electric cars have been a hit. Sales of battery-only (BEV) and plug-in hybrid (PHEV) electric cars have risen every year. Sales in the United States hit a record of 160,000 units in 2016. Some analysts predict that EV sales will reach 400,000 a year by 2020 and surpass 500,000 a year by 2023. One EV producer, Tesla, is completing a lithium battery factory in Nevada that will produce 500,000 batteries a year by 2020.

One of the attractions of EVs is their environmental impact. The BEVs burn no gasoline and the PHEVs burn very little. They get mileage in the range of 100-120 miles per gallon, three or four times the mileage of gasoline-powered cars. Even when the pollution associated with electricity generation is factored in, EVs do less harm to the environment than do gasoline-powered autos. In view of this positive externality, both the federal government and several states offer substantial subsidies (tax credits and purchase rebates) for EV buyers.

For all their success, however, EVs are still a tiny fraction of new car sales. The record 160,000 EVs sold in 2016 pales in comparison to the 17.5 *million* gas guzzlers sold in the United States that year. EVs got less than 1 percent of the market that year and even the most optimistic forecasts of future sales envision a market share of 2.4 percent by 2023. So, EVs aren't about to overtake the gas guzzlers (a substitute good) anytime soon.

A couple of factors will materially affect future EV sales. The first, of course, is the price of the EVs themselves. Producers are hoping that advances in battery technology will bring down the cost of batteries, the most expensive ingredient in EVs. Lower battery prices (a complimentary good) will in turn lead to lower EV prices (and more sales via the price elasticity of demand).

EV producers also have to hope that the price of gasoline (another substitute good) keeps going up. The experience of the last decade shows that high gasoline prices sway consumers' decision to buy an EV. By contrast, when gasoline prices are low, consumers ignore EVs and opt to buy SUVs and bigger cars.

EV producers also have to worry about alternative technologies. Cars powered by natural gas or fuel cells may prove to be cheaper and more efficient. Then there is the prospect of more autonomous vehicles. Autonomous vehicles must be larger than EVs in order to store all the cameras, computers, and other technology embedded in self-driving cars. As these substitute goods become more popular—especially in ride-sharing services like Lyft and Uber—the demand for EVs may wane.

Last but not least, EV producers have to worry about those government subsidies. If the federal government or individual states terminate the tax credits and purchase rebates EV buyers now enjoy, the effective price of an EV will increase by a couple of thousand dollars. That could really put a dent in EV sales in the economy tomorrow.

SUMMARY

- The price elasticity of demand (E) is a numerical measure of consumer response to a change in price, *ceteris paribus*. It equals the percentage change in quantity demanded divided by the percentage change in price. **LO20-1**
- Demand for a product is *elastic* if E is greater than 1.0 or *inelastic* if E is less than 1.0. **LO20-1**
- The degree of price elasticity depends on the price of a good relative to income, the availability of substitutes, and time. **LO20-1**
- The effect of a price change on total revenue depends on price elasticity. Total revenue and price move in the *same* direction only if demand is price-inelastic ($E < 1$). **LO20-2**
- The shape and position of any particular demand curve depend on a consumer's income, tastes, expectations,

and the price and availability of other goods. Should any of these factors change, the assumption of *ceteris paribus* will no longer hold, and the demand curve will *shift*. **LO20-3, LO20-4**

- Cross-price elasticity measures the response of demand for one good to a change in the price of another. The cross-price elasticity of demand is positive for substitute goods and negative for complementary goods. **LO20-3**
- The income elasticity of demand measures the response of demand to a change in income. If demand increases (shifts right) with income, the product is a normal good. If demand declines (shifts left) when income rises, it's an inferior good. **LO20-4**
- The price elasticity of supply is the percentage change in quantity *supplied* divided by the percentage change in price. **LO20-5**

Key Terms

law of demand	substitute goods	normal good
demand curve	complementary goods	inferior good
price elasticity of demand	cross-price elasticity of demand	law of supply
total revenue	income elasticity of demand	price elasticity of supply

Questions for Discussion

1. Is the demand for enrollments in your college price-elastic? How could you find out? **LO20-1**
2. If the price of gasoline doubled, how would consumption of (*a*) cars, (*b*) public transportation, and (*c*) restaurants be affected? How quickly would these adjustments be made? **LO20-3**
3. Identify two goods each whose demand exhibits (*a*) high income elasticity, (*b*) low income elasticity, (*c*) high price elasticity, and (*d*) low price elasticity. What accounts for the differences in elasticity? **LO20-4**
4. Why does the price elasticity of demand for cigarettes differ for teenagers and adults (see Table 20.2)? **LO20-1**

5. In California, 15.7 percent of low-income households smoke but only 9.4 percent of high-income households do so. So, the burden of higher cigarette taxes (In the News "Californians Vote to Triple Cigarette Tax") falls disproportionately on the poor. Is this fair? **LO20-2**

6. If you owned a movie theater, would you want the demand for movies to be elastic or inelastic? **LO20-2**

7. How has the Internet affected the price elasticity of demand for air travel? **LO20-1**

8. If the elasticity of demand for coffee is so low (Table 20.1), why doesn't Starbucks raise the price of coffee to $10 a cup? **LO20-2**

9. Is the demand for iPhones price inelastic or elastic? Why? Is income elasticity high or low? **LO20-4**

10. In the Economy Tomorrow section, what are the substitute goods and complementary goods that will affect future EV sales? Is the price elasticity of demand for EVs likely to be high or low? **LO20-3**

11. Suppose that quantity supplied for a product falls by 10 percent. If the price elasticity of supply is 2, what should happen to the price of the product? **LO20-5**

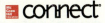

PROBLEMS FOR CHAPTER 20

LO20-1 1. What was the price elasticity of demand for iPhones in 2007 (In the News "After iPhone Price Cut, Sales Are Up by 200 Percent" and section "Computing Price Elasticity")?

LO20-1 2. According to Professor Becker (In the News "Professor Becker Rejects Clinton's Tax Math"), by how much would cigarette prices have to rise to get a 15 percent reduction in smoking in
(*a*) one year?
(*b*) three years?

LO20-1 3. What is the price elasticity of demand for cigarettes implied in In the News "Californians Vote to Triple Cigarette Tax" by
(*a*) The state's legislative analyst office?
(*b*) Anti-smoking advocates?
If the actual price elasticity of demand for California-tax cigarettes is 0.8 (In the News "Californians Vote to Triple Cigarette Tax"),
(*c*) By how much will the quantity demanded decrease with the new tax?
(*d*) How much additional revenue will the state take in?

LO20-1 4. Suppose consumers buy 50 million packs of cigarettes per month at a price of $5 per pack. If a $2 tax is added to that price,
(*a*) By what percentage does price change? (Use the midpoint formula in "Computing Price Elasticity.")
(*b*) By what percentage will cigarette sales decline in the short run? (See Table 20.1 for a clue.)
(*c*) According to Gary Becker, by how much will sales decline in the long run? (In the News "Professor Becker Rejects Clinton's Tax Math").

LO20-2 5. From Figure 20.1, compute
(*a*) The price elasticity between each of the following points
(*b*) The total revenue at each point.
(*c*) If there is a price decrease, will total revenue increase when demand is elastic or inelastic?

	Price Elasticity		Total Revenue
Point C to D	_____	At point C	_____
		D	_____
H to I	_____	H	_____
		I	_____

LO20-4 6. According to the calculation in the section "Income Elasticity," by how much will popcorn sales increase if average income goes up by 8 percent?

LO20-5 7. Using the World View "Rebounding Oil Price Spurs More Rigs," calculate the price elasticity of supply between 2016 and 2017 if the price of oil increased by 20 percent in the same time period.

LO20-3 8. If the cross-price elasticity of demand between printed textbooks and e-books is +0.50,
(*a*) Are e-books and textbooks complementary (C) or substitute (S) goods?
(*b*) If textbook prices increase by 10 percent, by how much will e-books demand change?

LO20-1 9. Suppose that in a week the price of Greek yogurt increases from $1.25 to $1.75 per container. At the same time, the quantity of Greek yogurt demanded at a typical grocery store increases from 10,000 to 18,000 containers per month. What is the price elasticity of demand for Greek yogurt?

LO20-2 10. Use the following data to illustrate the (a) demand curve and (b) total revenue curve:

Price	$10	9	8	7	6	5	4	3	2	1
Quantity	2	4	6	8	10	12	14	16	18	20

(a) At what price is total revenue maximized?

(b) At that price, what is the elasticity of demand?

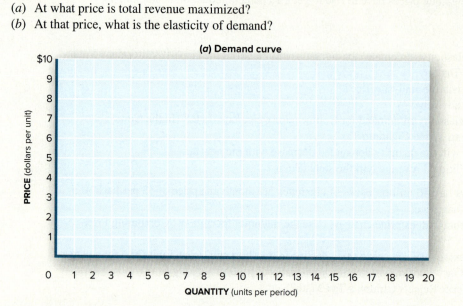

(a) Demand curve

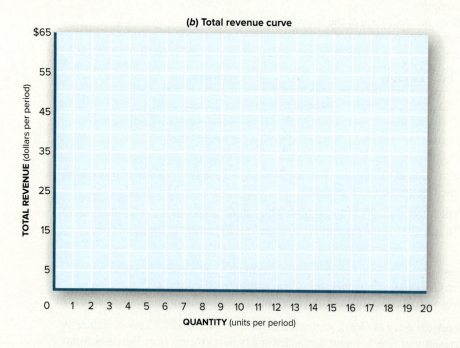

(b) Total revenue curve

LO20-3 11. On the graphs below, show the impact of the price reduction for iPhones, as described in In the News "Samsung Stung by Apple Moves."

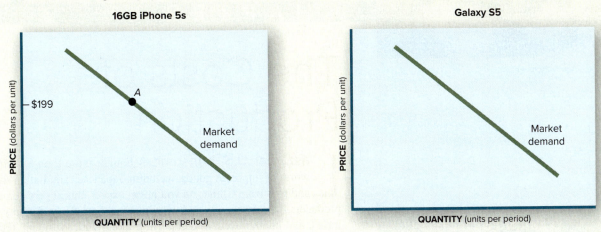

16GB iPhone 5s

Galaxy S5

12. The Economy Tomorrow: In 2016, 160,000 electric vehicles (EVs) were sold in the United States.

LO20-1   (*a*) Suppose the average price of these cars was $37,000. Calculate price elasticity of demand if a $2000 tax credit caused an increase in sales by 10,000 EVs.

LO20-3   (*b*) Calculate cross-price elasticity if a 20% increase in the price of gasoline caused an increase in sales of EVs by 3000.

©SCPhotos/Alamy Stock Photo

CHAPTER 21

The Costs of Production

Last year U.S. consumers bought more than $2 *trillion* worth of imported goods, including Japanese cars, Italian shoes, and toys from China. As you might expect, this angers domestic producers, who frequently end up with unsold goods, half-empty factories, and unemployed workers. They, along with President Trump, rage against the "unfair" competition from abroad, asserting that producers in India, Brazil, and China can undersell U.S. producers because workers in these countries are paid dirt-poor wages.

But lower wages don't necessarily imply lower costs. You could pay me $2 per hour to type and still end up paying a lot for typing. Truth is, I type only about 10 words a minute, with lots of misteakes. The cost of producing goods depends not only on the price of inputs (e.g., labor) but also on how much they produce. Paying $10 an hour to someone who types 90 words a minute is a lot cheaper than paying $2 an hour to someone who types only 10 words a minute.

In this chapter we begin looking at the costs of producing the goods and services that market participants demand. We confront the following questions:

- **How much output *can* a firm produce?**
- **How do the *costs* of production vary with the rate of output?**
- **Do larger firms have a cost advantage over smaller firms?**

The answers to these questions are important not only to producers facing foreign competition but to consumers as well. The costs of producing a good have a direct impact on the prices we pay at the grocery store, the mall, or even the campus bookstore.

THE PRODUCTION FUNCTION

No matter how large a business is or who owns it, all businesses confront one central fact: it costs something to produce goods. To produce corn, a farmer needs land, water, seeds, equipment, and labor. To produce fillings, a dentist needs a chair, a drill, some space, and labor. Even the production of educational services such as this economics class requires the use of labor (your teacher), land (on which the school is built), and capital (the building, blackboard, computers). In short, unless you're producing unrefined, unpackaged air, you need **factors of production**—that is, resources that can be used to produce a good or service. These factors of production provide the basic measure of economic cost. The costs of your economics class, for example, are

LEARNING OBJECTIVES

After reading this chapter, you should know

LO21-1 What the production function represents.

LO21-2 What the law of diminishing returns means.

LO21-3 How the various measures of cost relate to each other.

LO21-4 How economic and accounting costs differ.

LO21-5 What (dis)economies of scale are.

factors of production: Resource inputs used to produce goods and services, e.g., land, labor, capital, entrepreneurship.

measured by the amounts of land, labor, and capital it requires. These are *resource* costs of production.

To assess the costs of production, we must first determine how many resources are actually needed to produce a given product. You could use a lot of resources to produce a product or use just a few. What we really want to know is how *best* to produce. What's the *smallest* amount of resources needed to produce a specific product? Or we could ask the same question from a different perspective: what's the *maximum* amount of output attainable from a given quantity of resources?

The answers to these questions are reflected in the **production function,** which tells us the maximum amount of good *X* producible from various combinations of factor inputs. With one chair and one drill, a dentist can fill a *maximum* of 32 cavities per day. With two chairs, a drill, and an assistant, a dentist can fill up to 55 cavities per day.

A production function is a technological summary of our ability to produce a particular good.[1] Table 21.1 provides a partial glimpse of one such function. In this case, the output is designer jeans, as produced by Low-Rider Jeans Corporation. The essential inputs in the production of jeans are land, labor (garment workers), and capital (a factory and sewing machines). With these inputs, Low-Rider Jeans Corporation can produce and sell hip-hugging jeans to style-conscious consumers.

production function: A technological relationship expressing the maximum quantity of a good attainable from different combinations of factor inputs.

Varying Input Levels

As in all production endeavors, we want to know how much output we can produce with available resources. To make things easy, we'll assume that the factory is already built, with fixed space dimensions. The only inputs we can vary are labor (the number of garment workers per day) and additional capital (the number of sewing machines we lease per day).

In these circumstances, the quantity of jeans we can produce depends on the amount of labor and capital we employ. ***The purpose of a production function is to tell us just how much output we can produce with varying amounts of factor inputs.*** Table 21.1 provides such information for jeans production.

Consider the simplest option—that of employing no labor or capital (the upper left corner in Table 21.1). An empty factory can't produce any jeans; maximum output is zero per

Capital Input (Sewing Machines per Day)	Labor Input (Workers per Day)								
	0	1	2	3	4	5	6	7	8
	Jeans Output (Pairs per Day)								
0	0	0	0	0	0	0	0	0	0
1	0	15	34	44	48	50	51	51	47
2	0	20	46	64	72	78	81	82	80
3	0	21	50	73	83	92	99	103	103

TABLE 21.1

A Production Function

A production function tells us the maximum amount of output attainable from alternative combinations of factor inputs. This particular function tells us how many pairs of jeans we can produce in a day with a given factory and varying quantities of capital and labor. With one sewing machine, and one operator, we can produce a maximum of 15 pairs of jeans per day, as indicated in the second column of the second row. To produce more jeans, we need more labor or more capital.

[1] By contrast, the production possibilities curve discussed in Chapter 1 expresses our ability to produce various *combinations* of goods, given the use of *all* our resources. The production possibilities curve summarizes the output capacity of the entire economy. A production function describes the capacity of a single firm.

day. Even though land, capital (an empty factory), and even denim are available, some essential labor and capital inputs are missing, and jeans production is impossible.

Suppose now we employ some labor (a machine operator) but don't lease any sewing machines. Will output increase? Not according to the production function. The first row in Table 21.1 illustrates the consequences of employing labor without any capital equipment. Without sewing machines (or even needles, another form of capital), the operators can't make jeans. Maximum output remains at zero no matter how much labor is employed in this case.

The dilemma of machine operators without sewing machines illustrates a general principle of production: *the **productivity** of any factor of production depends on the amount of other resources available to it.* Industrious, hardworking machine operators can't make designer jeans without sewing machines.

We can increase the productivity of garment workers by providing them with machines. The production function again tells us by *how much* jeans output could increase. Suppose we leased just one machine per day. Now the second row in Table 21.1 is the relevant one. It says jeans output will remain at zero if we lease one machine but employ no labor. If we employ one machine *and* one worker, however, the jeans will start rolling out the door. Maximum output under these circumstances (row 2, column 2) is 15 pairs of jeans per day. Now we're in business!

The remaining columns in row 2 tell us how many additional jeans we can produce if we hire more workers, still leasing only one sewing machine. With one machine and two workers, maximum output rises to 34 pairs per day. If a third worker is hired, output could increase to 44 pairs.

Table 21.1 also indicates how production would increase with additional sewing machines (capital). By reading down any column of the table, you can see how more machines increase potential jeans output.

Efficiency

The production function summarized in Table 21.1 underscores the essential relationship between resource *inputs* and product *outputs*. It's also a basic introduction to economic costs. To produce 15 pairs of jeans per day, we need one sewing machine, an operator, a factory, and some denim. All these inputs make up the *resource cost* of producing jeans.

Another feature of Table 21.1 is that it conveys the *maximum* output of jeans producible from particular input combinations. The standard garment worker and sewing machine, when brought together at Low-Rider Jeans Corporation, can produce *at most* 15 pairs of jeans per day. They could also produce a lot less. Indeed, a careless cutter can waste a lot of denim. A lazy or inattentive worker won't keep the sewing machines humming. As many a producer has learned, actual output can fall far short of the limits described in the production function. Jeans output will reach the levels in Table 21.1 only if the jeans factory operates with relative **efficiency.** This requires getting maximum output from the resources used in the production process. *The production function represents maximum technical efficiency—that is, the most output attainable from any given level of factor inputs.*

We can always be inefficient, of course. This merely means getting less output than possible for the inputs we use. But this isn't a desirable situation. To a factory manager, it means less output for a given amount of input (cost). To society as a whole, inefficiency implies a waste of resources. If Low-Rider Jeans isn't producing efficiently, we're being denied some potential output. It's not only a question of having fewer jeans. We could also use the labor and capital now employed by Low-Rider Jeans to produce something else. Specifically, the **opportunity cost** of a product is measured by the most desired goods and services that could have been produced with the same resources. Hence, if jeans production isn't up to par, society is either (1) getting fewer jeans than it should for the resources devoted to jeans production or (2) giving up too many other goods and services in order to get a desired quantity of jeans.

productivity: Output per unit of input—for example, output per labor-hour.

efficiency: Maximum output of a good from the resources used in production.

opportunity cost: The most desired goods or services that are forgone in order to obtain something else.

Although we can always do worse than the production function suggests, we can't do better, at least not in the short run. The production function represents the *best* we can do with our current technological know-how. For the moment, at least, there's no better way to produce a specific good. As our technological and managerial capabilities increase, however, we'll attain higher levels of future productivity. These advances in our productive capability will be represented by new production functions.

Short-Run Constraints

Let's step back from the threshold of scientific advance for a moment and return to Low-Rider Jeans. Forget about possible technological breakthroughs in jeans production (e.g., electronic sewing machines or robot operators) and concentrate on the economic realities of our modest endeavor. For the present we're stuck with existing technology. In fact, all the output figures in Table 21.1 are based on the use of a specific factory. Once we've purchased or leased that factory, we've set a limit to current jeans production. When such commitments to fixed inputs (e.g., the factory) exist, we're dealing with a **short-run** production problem. If no land or capital were in place—if we could build or lease any sized factory—we'd be dealing with a *long-run* decision.

Our short-run objective is to make the best possible use of the factory we've acquired. This entails selecting the right combination of labor and capital inputs to produce jeans. To simplify the decision, we'll limit the number of sewing machines in use. If we lease only one sewing machine, then the second row in Table 21.1 is the only one we have to consider. In this case, the single sewing machine (capital) becomes another short-run constraint on the production of jeans. With a given factory and one sewing machine, the short-run rate of output depends entirely on how many workers are hired.

Figure 21.1 illustrates the short-run production function applicable to the factory with one sewing machine. As noted before, a factory with a sewing machine but no machine

short run: The period in which the quantity (and quality) of some inputs can't be changed.

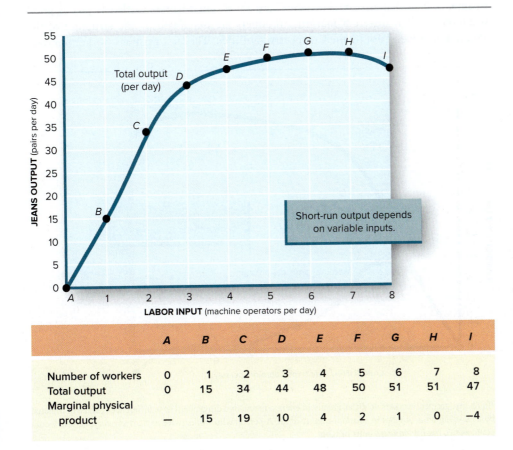

		A	**B**	**C**	**D**	**E**	**F**	**G**	**H**	**I**
Number of workers		0	1	2	3	4	5	6	7	8
Total output		0	15	34	44	48	50	51	51	47
Marginal physical product		—	15	19	10	4	2	1	0	−4

FIGURE 21.1

Short-Run Production Function

In the short run some inputs (e.g., land and capital) are fixed in quantity. Output then depends on how much of a variable input (e.g., labor) is used.

The short-run production function shows how output changes when more labor is used. This figure and the table below are based on the second (one-machine) row in Table 21.1.

operators produces no jeans. This was observed in Table 21.1 (row 1, column 0) and is now illustrated by point *A* in Figure 21.1. To get any jeans output, we need to hire some labor. In this simplified example, ***labor is the variable input that determines how much output we get from our fixed inputs (land and capital).*** By placing one worker in the factory, we can produce 15 pairs of jeans per day. This possibility is represented by point *B*. The remainder of the production function shows how jeans output changes as we employ more workers in our single-machine factory.

....

MARGINAL PRODUCTIVITY

The short-run production function not only defines the *limit* to output but also shows how much each worker contributes to that limit. Notice again that jeans output increases from zero (point *A* in Figure 21.2) to 15 pairs (point *B*) when the first machine operator is hired. In other words, total output *increases* by 15 pairs when we employ the first worker. This increase is called the **marginal physical product (MPP)** of that first worker—that is, the *change* in total output that results from employment of one more unit of (labor) input:

> **marginal physical product (MPP):** The change in total output associated with one additional unit of input.

$$\text{Marginal physical product (MPP)} = \frac{\text{Change in total output}}{\text{Change in input quantity}}$$

With zero workers, total output was zero. When that first worker is employed, total output increases to 15 pairs of jeans per day. The MPP of the first worker is 15 pairs of jeans.

If we employ a second operator, jeans output more than doubles, to 34 pairs per day (point *C*). The 19-pair *increase* in output represents the marginal physical product of the *second* worker.

The higher MPP of the second worker raises a question about the first. Why was the first's MPP lower? Laziness? Is the second worker faster, less distracted, or harder working?

The second worker's higher MPP isn't explained by superior talents or effort. We assume, in fact, that all "units of labor" are equal—that is, one worker is just as good as another.[2] Their different marginal products are explained by the structure of the production process, not by their respective abilities. The first garment worker not only

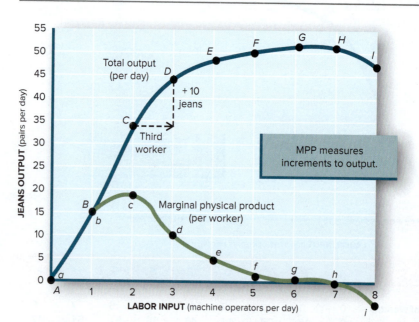

FIGURE 21.2

Marginal Physical Product (MPP)

Marginal physical product is the *change* in total output that results from employing one more unit of input. The *third* worker, for example, increases *total output* from 34 (point *C*) to 44 (point *D*). Hence the *marginal* output of the third worker is 10 pairs of jeans (point *d*).

What's the MPP of the fourth worker? What happens to *total* output when this worker is hired?

[2]In reality, garment workers do differ greatly in energy, talent, and diligence. These differences can be eliminated by measuring units of labor in *constant-quality* units. A person who works twice as hard as everyone else would count as two *quality-adjusted* units of labor.

had to sew jeans but also had to unfold bolts of denim, measure the jeans, sketch out the patterns, and cut them to approximate size. A lot of time was spent going from one task to another. Despite the worker's best efforts, this person simply couldn't do everything at once.

A second worker alleviates this situation. With two workers, less time is spent running from one task to another. While one worker is measuring and cutting, the other can continue sewing. This improved *ratio* of labor to other factors of production results in the large jump in total output. The second worker's superior MPP isn't unique to this person: it would have occurred even if we'd hired the workers in the reverse order.

Diminishing Marginal Returns

Unfortunately, total output won't keep rising so sharply as more workers are hired. Look what happens when a third worker is hired. Total jeans production continues to increase. But the increase from point C to point D in Figure 21.2 is only 10 pairs per day. Hence the third worker's MPP (10 pairs) is *less* than that of the second (19 pairs). Marginal physical product is *diminishing*. This concept is illustrated by point d in Figure 21.2.

What accounts for this decline in MPP? The answer lies in the ratio of labor to other factors of production. A third worker begins to crowd our facilities. We still have only one sewing machine. Two people can't sew at the same time. As a result, some time is wasted as the operators wait for their turns at the machine. Even if they split up the various jobs, there will still be some "downtime" because measuring and cutting aren't as time-consuming as sewing. Consequently, we can't make full use of a third worker. The relative scarcity of other inputs (capital and land) constrains the third worker's marginal physical product.

Resource constraints are even more evident when a fourth worker is hired. Total output increases again, but the increase this time is very small. With three workers, we got 44 pairs of jeans per day (point D); with four workers, we get a maximum of 48 pairs (point E). Thus the fourth worker's MPP is only 4 pairs of jeans. There simply aren't enough machines to make productive use of so much labor.

If a seventh worker is hired, the operators get in one another's way, argue, and waste denim. Notice in Figure 21.1 that total output doesn't increase at all when a seventh worker is hired (point H). The MPP of the seventh worker is zero (point h). Were an eighth worker hired, total output would actually *decline,* from 51 pairs (point H) to 47 pairs (point I). The eighth worker has a *negative* MPP (point i in Figure 21.2).

Law of Diminishing Returns. The problems of crowded facilities apply to most production processes. In the short run, a production process is characterized by a fixed amount of available land and capital. Typically, the only factor that can be varied in the short run is labor. Yet **as more labor is hired, each unit of labor has less capital and land to work with.** This is simple division: the available facilities are being shared by more and more workers. At some point, this constraint begins to pinch. When it does, marginal physical product declines. This situation is so common that it's the basis for the **law of diminishing returns,** which says that the marginal physical product of any factor of production, such as labor, will diminish at some point as more of it is used in a given production setting. Notice in Figure 21.2 how diminishing returns set in when the third worker was hired.

law of diminishing returns:
The marginal physical product of a variable input declines as more of it is employed with a given quantity of other (fixed) inputs.

RESOURCE COSTS

A production function tells us how much output a firm *can* produce with its existing plant and equipment. From Figure 21.2 we know that Low-Rider Jeans *could* produce up to 51 pairs per day, employing 6 workers. But Figure 21.2 doesn't tell us how much the firm will *want* to produce. A firm *might* want to produce at capacity if the profit picture were bright enough. On the other hand, a firm might not produce *any* output if costs always exceeded sales revenue. The most desirable rate of output is the one that maximizes total

The Total Costs of Production (Total Cost of Producing 15 Pairs of Jeans per Day)

The total cost of producing a good equals the market value of all the resources used in its production. In this case, the production of 15 pairs of jeans per day requires resources worth $245.

Resource Input	×	Unit Price of Input	=	Total Cost
1 factory		$100 per day		$100
1 sewing machine		20 per day		20
1 operator		80 per day		80
1.5 bolts of denim		30 per bolt		45
Total cost				$245

In the production of jeans, these resources included land, labor, and capital. Table 21.2 identifies these resources, their unit values, and the total dollar cost associated with their use. This table is based on an assumed output of 15 pairs of jeans per day, with the use of one worker and one sewing machine (point B in Figure 21.2). The rent on the factory is $100 per day, a sewing machine rents for $20 per day, and the wages of a garment worker are $80 per day. We'll assume Low-Rider Jeans Corporation can purchase bolts of denim for $30 apiece, with each bolt providing enough denim for 10 pairs of jeans. In other words, one-tenth of a bolt ($3 worth of material) is required for one pair of jeans. We'll ignore any other potential expenses. With these assumptions, the total cost of producing 15 pairs of jeans per day amounts to $245, as shown in Table 21.2.

Fixed Costs. Total costs will change of course as we alter the rate of production. But not *all* costs increase. In the short run, some costs don't increase at all when output is increased. These are **fixed costs** in the sense that they don't vary with the rate of output. The factory lease is an example. Once you lease a factory, you're obligated to pay for it whether or not you use it. The person who owns the factory wants $100 per day. Even if you produce no jeans, you still have to pay that rent. That's the essence of fixed costs.

fixed costs: Costs of production that don't change when the rate of output is altered, such as the cost of basic plants and equipment.

The leased sewing machine is another fixed cost. When you rent a sewing machine, you must pay the rental charge. It doesn't matter whether you use it for a few minutes or all day long—the rental charge is fixed at $20 per day.

Variable Costs. Labor costs are another story altogether. The amount of labor employed in jeans production can be varied easily. If we decide not to open the factory tomorrow, we can just tell our only worker to take the day off (without pay, of course!). We'll still have to pay rent, but we can cut back on wages. On the other hand, if we want to increase daily output, we can also hire additional workers easily and quickly. Labor is regarded as a **variable cost** in this line of work—that is, a cost that *varies* with the rate of output.

variable costs: Costs of production that change when the rate of output is altered, such as labor and material costs.

The denim itself is another variable cost. Denim not used today can be saved for tomorrow. Hence how much we spend on denim today is directly related to how many jeans we produce. In this sense, the cost of denim input varies with the rate of jeans output.

Figure 21.4 illustrates how these various costs are affected by the rate of production. On the vertical axis are the costs of production in dollars per day. Notice that the total cost of producing 15 pairs per day is still $245, as indicated by point B. This cost figure consists of

DOLLAR COST OF PRODUCING 15 PAIRS

Fixed costs:		
Factory rent	$100	
Sewing machine rent	20	
Subtotal		$120
Variable costs:		
Wages to labor	$ 80	
Denim	45	
Subtotal		$125
Total costs		$245

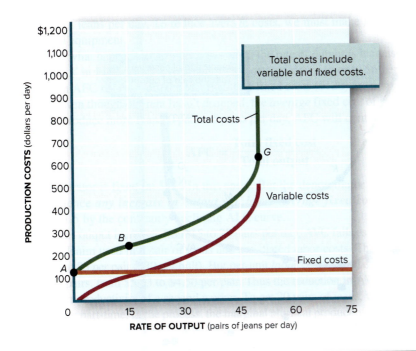

FIGURE 21.4

The Cost of Jeans Production

Total cost includes both fixed and variable costs. Fixed costs must be paid even if no output is produced (point *A*). Variable costs start at zero and increase with the rate of output. The total cost of producing 15 pairs of jeans (point *B*) includes $120 in fixed costs (rent on the factory and sewing machines) and $125 in variable costs (denim and wages). Total cost rises as output increases because additional variable costs must be incurred.

In this example, the short-run capacity is equal to 51 pairs (point *G*). If still more inputs are employed, costs will rise but not total output.

If we increase the rate of output beyond these 15 pairs, total costs will rise. *How fast total costs rise depends on variable costs only,* however, since fixed costs remain at $120 per day. (Notice the horizontal fixed cost curve in Figure 21.4.)

Capacity. With one sewing machine and one factory, there's an absolute limit to daily jeans production. According to the production function in Figure 21.1, the capacity of a factory with one machine is roughly 51 pairs of jeans per day. If we try to produce more jeans than this by hiring additional workers, our total costs will rise, but our output won't. Recall that the seventh worker had a *zero* marginal physical product (Figure 21.2). In fact, we could fill the factory with garment workers and drive total costs sky-high. But the limits of space and one sewing machine don't permit output in excess of 51 pairs per day. This limit to productive capacity is represented by point *G* on the total cost curve. Further expenditure on inputs will increase production *costs* but not *output*.

Although there's no upper limit to costs, there is a lower limit. If output is reduced to zero, costs won't completely disappear. At zero output, total costs fall only to $120 per day, the level of fixed costs, as illustrated by point *A* in Figure 21.4. As before, *there's no way to avoid fixed costs in the short run.* Indeed, those fixed costs define the short run.

Average Costs

While Figure 21.4 illustrates *total* costs of production, other measures of cost are often desired. One of the most common measures of cost is average, or per-unit, cost. **Average total cost (ATC)** is simply total cost divided by the rate of output:

$$\text{Average total cost (ATC)} = \frac{\text{Total cost}}{\text{Total output}}$$

At an output of 15 pairs of jeans per day, total costs are $245. The average cost of production is thus $16.33 per pair (= 245 ÷ 15) at this rate of output.

The average cost of production is not a constant number. On the contrary, average total cost changes with the rate of output. So, when someone cites the average cost of producing something, they must have a specific quantity of output in mind.

Figure 21.5 shows how average costs change as the rate of output varies. Row *J* of the cost schedule, for example, again indicates the fixed, variable, and total costs of producing

average total cost (ATC): Total cost divided by the quantity produced in a given time period.

economic cost: The value of all resources used to produce a good or service; opportunity cost.

The distinction between an economic cost and an accounting cost is essentially one between resource and dollar costs. *Dollar cost* refers to the explicit dollar outlays made by a producer; it's the lifeblood of accountants. **Economic cost,** in contrast, refers to the *value* of *all* resources used in the production process; it's the lifeblood of economists. In other words, economists count costs as

$$\text{Economic cost} = \text{Explicit costs} + \text{Implicit costs}$$

As this formula suggests, *economic and accounting costs will diverge whenever any factor of production is not paid an explicit wage (or rent, etc.).*

The Cost of Homework. These distinctions between economic and accounting costs apply also to the "production" of homework. You can pay people to write term papers for you or buy them off the Internet. At large schools you can often buy lecture notes as well. But most students do their own homework so they'll learn something and not just turn in required assignments.

Doing homework is expensive, however, even if you don't pay someone to do it. The time you spend reading this chapter is valuable. You could be doing something else if you weren't reading right now. What would you be doing? That forgone activity—the best alternative use of your time—represents the economic cost of doing homework. Even if you don't pay yourself for reading this chapter, you'll still incur that *economic* cost.

LONG-RUN COSTS

We've confined our discussion thus far to short-run production costs. *The short run is characterized by fixed costs*—a commitment to specific plants and equipment. A factory, an office building, or some other plants and equipment have been leased or purchased: we're stuck with *fixed costs*. In the short run, our objective is to make the best use of those fixed costs by choosing the appropriate rate of production.

long run: A period of time long enough for all inputs to be varied (no fixed costs).

The long run opens up a whole new range of options. In the **long run,** we have no lease or purchase commitments. We're free to start all over again with whatever scale of plants and equipment we desire and whatever technology is available. Quite simply, *there are no fixed costs in the long run.* Nor are there any commitments to existing technology.

That's what excited Elon Musk when he started thinking about mass-producing Tesla electric cars. Although Tesla had sold only 30,000 vehicles in its first 6 years, Musk envisioned his company selling as many as 500,000 vehicles by the year 2020. To do so, he decided he needed to get into the battery business as well. So he made plans to build a "gigafactory" of gigantic proportions to produce the lithium-ion batteries he'd need for mass production of Tesla cars (see In the News "Tesla Banks on Gigafactory"). To do so, he was willing to incur fixed costs of $4 to $5 *billion*! If and when the factory is completed, Tesla will focus on the short-run production decision of how many batteries and cars to produce from its gigafactory.

Long-Run Average Costs

The opportunities available in the long run include building a plant of any desired size, including "gigafactories." Suppose we still wanted to go into the jeans business. In the long run, we could build or lease any size factory we wanted and could lease as many sewing machines as we desired. Figure 21.8 illustrates three choices: a small factory (ATC_1), a medium-sized factory (ATC_2), and a large factory (ATC_3). All three factories have the common U-shaped average total cost curves. But there are important differences. As we observed earlier, it's very expensive to produce lots of jeans with a small factory. The ATC curve for a small factory (ATC_1) starts to head straight up at relatively low rates of output. In the long run, we'd lease or build such a factory only if we anticipated a continuing low rate of output.

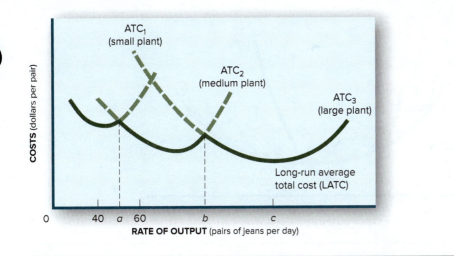

FIGURE 21.8
Long-Run Costs with Three Plant Size Options

Long-run cost possibilities are determined by all possible short-run options. In this case, there are three options of varying size (ATC₁, ATC₂, and ATC₃).

In the long run, we'd choose the plant that yielded the lowest average cost for any desired rate of output. The solid portions of the curves (LATC) represent these choices. The smallest factory (ATC₁) is best for output levels below *a;* the largest (ATC₃), for output rates in excess of *b.*

The ATC_2 curve illustrates how costs might fall if we leased or built a medium-sized factory. With a small factory, ATC becomes prohibitive at an output of 50 to 60 pairs of jeans per day. A medium-sized factory can produce these quantities at lower cost. Moreover, ATC continues to drop as jeans production increases in the medium-sized factory—at least for a while. Even a medium-sized factory must contend with resource constraints and therefore rising average costs: its ATC curve is U-shaped also.

If we expected to sell really large quantities of jeans, we'd want to build or lease a large factory. Beyond the rate of output *b,* the largest factory offers the lowest average total cost. There's a risk in leasing such a large factory, of course. If our sales don't live up to our high expectations, we'll end up with very high fixed costs and thus very expensive jeans. Look at the high average cost of producing only 60 pairs of jeans per day with the large factory (ATC_3).

In choosing an appropriate factory, then, we must decide how many jeans we expect to sell. Once we know our expected output, we can select the right-sized factory. It will be the one that offers the lowest ATC for that rate of output. If we expect to sell fewer jeans than *a,* we'll choose the small factory in Figure 21.8. If we expect to sell jeans at a rate between *a* and *b,* we'll select a medium-sized factory. Beyond rate *b,* we'll want the largest factory. These choices are reflected in the solid parts of the three ATC curves. The composite "curve" created by these three segments constitutes our long-run cost possibilities. *The long-run cost curve is just a summary of our best short-run cost possibilities, using existing technology and facilities.*

We might confront more than three choices, of course. There's really no reason we couldn't build a factory to *any* desired size. In the long run, we face an infinite number of scale choices, not just three. The effect of all these choices is to smooth out the long-run cost curve. Figure 21.9 depicts the long-run curve that results. Each rate of output is most efficiently produced by some size (scale) of plant. That sized plant indicates the minimum cost of producing a particular rate of output. Its corresponding short-run ATC curve provides one point on the long-run ATC curve.

Long-Run Marginal Costs

Like all average cost curves, the long-run (LATC) curve has its own marginal cost curve. The long-run marginal cost (LMC) curve isn't a composite of short-run marginal cost curves. Rather, it's computed on the basis of the costs reflected in the long-run ATC curve itself. We won't bother to compute those costs here. Note, however, that the long-run MC curve—like all MC curves—intersects its associated average cost curve at its lowest point.

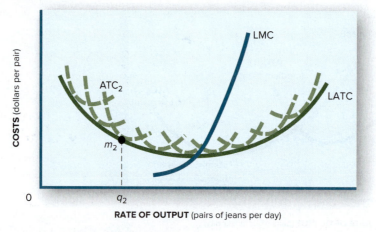

economies of scale:
Reductions in minimum average costs that come about through increases in the size (scale) of plant and equipment.

ECONOMIES OF SCALE

Figure 21.8 seems to imply that a producer must choose either a small plant or a larger one. That isn't completely true. The choice is often between one large plant or *several* small ones. Suppose the desired level of output was relatively large, as at point *c* in Figure 21.8. A single small plant (ATC$_1$) is clearly not up to the task. But what about using several small plants rather than one large one (ATC$_3$)? How would costs be affected?

Notice what happens to *minimum ATC* in Figure 21.8 when the size (scale) of the factory changes. When a medium-sized factory (ATC$_2$) replaces a small factory (ATC$_1$), minimum average cost drops (the bottom of ATC$_2$ is below the bottom of ATC$_1$). This implies that a jeans producer who wants to minimize costs should build one medium-sized factory rather than try to produce the same quantity with two small ones. **Economies of scale** exist in this situation: larger facilities reduce *minimum* average costs.

This is the kind of potential that excited Elon Musk. As he studied alternatives for building a battery factory, he saw several possibilities for bringing minimum average costs down. Innovations in manufacturing, better logistics, co-located processes, and reduced overhead could give a larger plant economies of scales that smaller plants couldn't achieve. So he decided to build a 10-million-square-foot "gigafactory" that could achieve substantial economies of scale (see In the News "Tesla Banks on Gigafactory").

IN THE NEWS

TESLA BANKS ON GIGAFACTORY

No one can say Elon Musk isn't ambitious. He wants his company, electric car maker Tesla, to get into mass production. Although Tesla sold only 200,000 cars in its first eight years, Musk wants to ramp up production to more than a million cars per year by 2020. To do so, he needs a cheap and abundant supply of lithium-ion batteries, the most expensive component in EVs. His solution? Build a "gigafactory" that will attain huge economies of scale and reduce the cost of batteries by 30 percent.

With cheaper batteries, Musk figures he can lower the price of Tesla vehicles enough to achieve a price point ($35,000) that appeals to the mass market. Tesla broke ground on its gigafactory outside Reno, Nevada in June 2014. By the beginning of 2017 it was less than 20 percent completed, with 350 workers employed. By 2020, however, Musk envisions a 1.9 million square foot factory employing 6,500 workers and producing 150 gigawatts of battery packs—enough to power 1.5 million electric vehicles. It would be the largest factory in the world, by footprint, and the second largest by volume. Now that is ambitious!

Source: News reports, January 2017.

ANALYSIS: As the size of a factory increases, it may be able to reduce the costs of doing business. Economies of scale can give a large firm a competitive advantage over smaller firms.

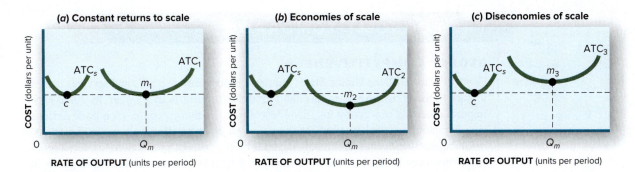

FIGURE 21.10

Economies of Scale

A lot of output (Q_m) can be produced from one large plant or many small ones. Here we contrast the average total costs associated with one small plant (ATC$_s$) and three large plants (ATC$_1$, ATC$_2$, and ATC$_3$). If a large plant attains the same *minimum* average costs (point m_1 in part *a*) as a smaller plant (point *c*), there's no advantage to large size (scale). Many small plants can produce the same output just as cheaply. However, either economies (part *b*) or diseconomies (part *c*) of scale may exist.

Larger production facilities don't always result in cost reductions. Suppose a firm has the choice of producing the quantity Q_m from several small factories or from one large, centralized facility. Centralization may have three different impacts on costs; these are illustrated in Figure 21.10. In each illustration, we see the average total cost (ATC) curve for a typical small firm or plant and the ATC curve for a much larger plant producing the same product.

Constant Returns. Figure 21.10*a* depicts a situation in which there's no economic advantage to centralization of manufacturing operations because a large plant is no more efficient than a lot of small plants. The critical focus here is on the *minimum* average costs attainable for a given rate of output. Note that the lowest point on the smaller plant's ATC curve (point *c*) is no higher or lower than the lowest point on the larger firm's ATC curve (point m_1). Hence it would be just as cheap to produce the quantity Q_m from a multitude of small plants as it would be to produce Q_m from one large plant. Thus increasing the size (or *scale*) of individual plants won't reduce minimum average costs: this is a situation of **constant returns to scale.**

constant returns to scale: Increases in plant size do not affect minimum average cost; minimum per-unit costs are identical for small plants and large plants.

Economies of Scale. Figure 21.10*b* illustrates the situation in which a larger plant can attain a lower minimum average cost than a smaller plant. That is, economies of scale (or *increasing returns to scale*) exist. This is evident from the fact that the larger firm's ATC curve falls *below* the dashed line in the graph (m_2 is less than *c*). The greater efficiency of the large factory might come from any of several sources. This is the situation Elon Musk was counting on for his proposed gigafactory (see In the News "Tesla Banks on Gigafactory").

Diseconomies of Scale. Even though large plants may be able to achieve greater efficiencies than smaller plants, there's no guaranty that they actually will. In fact, increasing the size (scale) of a plant may actually *reduce* operating efficiency, as depicted in Figure 21.10*c*. Workers may feel alienated in a plant of massive proportions and feel little commitment to productivity. Creativity may be stifled by rigid corporate structures and off-site management. A large plant may also foster a sense of anonymity that induces workers to underperform. When these things happen, *diseconomies of scale* result. Microsoft tries to avoid such diseconomies of scale by creating autonomous cells of no more than 35 employees ("small plants") within its larger corporate structure.

In evaluating long-run options, then, we must be careful to recognize that *efficiency and size don't necessarily go hand in hand.* Some firms and industries may be subject to economies of scale, but others may not. Bigger isn't always better.

THE ECONOMY TOMORROW

GLOBAL COMPETITIVENESS

From 1900 to 1970, the United States regularly exported more goods and services than it imported. Since then America has had a trade deficit nearly every year. In 2016, U.S. imports exceeded exports by roughly $500 billion. To many people, such trade deficits are a symptom that the United States can no longer compete effectively in world markets.

Global competitiveness ultimately depends on the costs of production. If international competitors can produce goods more cheaply, they'll be able to undersell U.S. goods in global markets.

Cheap Foreign Labor? Cheap labor keeps costs down in many countries. The average wage in Mexico, for example, ranges from $2 to $3 an hour, compared to more than $20 an hour in the United States. China's manufacturing workers make only $3.50 an hour. Low wages are *not,* however, a reliable measure of global competitiveness. To compete in global markets, one must produce more *output* for a given quantity of *inputs*. In other words, labor is "cheap" only if it produces a lot of output in return for the wages paid.

A worker's contribution to output is measured by *marginal physical product (MPP).* What we saw in this chapter was that *a worker's productivity (MPP) depends on the quantity and quality of other resources in the production process.* In this regard, U.S. workers have a tremendous advantage: they work with vast quantities of capital and state-of-the-art technology. They also come to the workplace with more education. Their high wages reflect this greater productivity.

Unit Labor Costs. A true measure of global competitiveness must take into account both factor costs (e.g., wages) and productivity. One such measure is **unit labor cost,** which indicates the labor cost of producing one unit of output. It's computed as

$$\text{Unit labor cost} = \frac{\text{Wage rate}}{\text{MPP}}$$

Suppose the MPP of a U.S. worker is 10 units per hour and the wage is $20 an hour. The unit labor cost would be

$$\frac{\text{Unit labor cost}}{\text{(United States)}} = \frac{\$20/\text{hour}}{10 \text{ units/hour}} = \frac{\$2/\text{unit}}{\text{of output}}$$

By contrast, assume the average worker in Mexico has an MPP of 1 unit per hour and a wage of $3 an hour. In this case, the unit labor cost would be

$$\frac{\text{Unit labor cost}}{\text{(Mexico)}} = \frac{\$3}{1} = \frac{\$3/\text{unit}}{\text{of output}}$$

According to these hypothetical examples, "cheap" Mexican labor is no bargain. Mexican labor is actually *more* costly in production despite the much lower wage rate.

Productivity Advance. What these calculations illustrate is how important productivity is for global competitiveness. If we want the United States to stay competitive in global markets, U.S. productivity must increase as fast as that in other nations.

The production function introduced in this chapter helps illustrate the essence of global competitiveness in the economy tomorrow. Until now, we've regarded a firm's production function as a technological fact of life—the *best* we could do, given our state of technological and managerial knowledge. In the real world, however, the best is always getting better. Science and technology are continuously advancing. So is our knowledge of how to organize and manage our resources. These advances keep *shifting* production functions upward: more can be produced with any given quantity of inputs. In the process, the costs of production shift downward, as illustrated in Figure 21.11 by the downward shifts of the MC and ATC curves. These downward shifts imply that we can get more of the goods and services we desire with available resources. We can also compete more effectively in global markets in the economy tomorrow.

unit labor cost: Hourly wage rate divided by output per labor-hour.

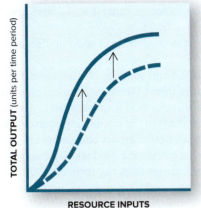

(a) When the production function shifts up . . .

TOTAL OUTPUT (units per time period)

RESOURCE INPUTS
(units per time period)

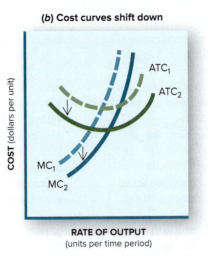

(b) Cost curves shift down

COST (dollars per unit)

ATC₁

ATC₂

MC₁

MC₂

RATE OF OUTPUT
(units per time period)

FIGURE 21.11

Improvements in Productivity Reduce Costs

Advances in technological or managerial knowledge increase our productive capability. This is reflected in upward shifts of the production function (part *a*) and downward shifts of production cost curves (part *b*).

SUMMARY

- A production function indicates the maximum amount of output that can be produced with different combinations of inputs. **LO21-1**
- In the short run, some inputs (e.g., land and capital) are fixed in quantity. Increases in (short-run) output result from more use of variable inputs (e.g., labor). **LO21-1**
- The contribution of a variable input to total output is measured by its marginal physical product (MPP). This is the amount by which *total* output increases when one more unit of the input is employed. **LO21-1**
- The MPP of a factor tends to decline as more of it is used in a given production facility. Diminishing marginal returns result from crowding more of a variable input (e.g., labor) into a production process, reducing the amount of fixed inputs *per unit* of variable input. **LO21-2**
- Marginal cost is the increase in total cost that results when output is increased by one unit. Marginal cost increases whenever marginal physical product diminishes. **LO21-3**
- Not all costs go up when the rate of output is increased. Fixed costs such as space and equipment leases don't vary with the rate of output. Only variable costs such as labor and material go up when output is increased. **LO21-3**

- Average total cost (ATC) equals total cost divided by the quantity of output produced. ATC declines when marginal cost (MC) is less than average cost and rises when MC exceeds it. The MC and ATC curves intersect at minimum ATC (the bottom of the U). That intersection represents least-cost production. **LO21-3**
- The economic costs of production include the value of *all* resources used. Accounting costs typically include only those dollar costs actually paid (explicit costs). **LO21-4**
- In the long run there are no fixed costs; the size (scale) of production can be varied. The long-run ATC curve indicates the lowest cost of producing output with facilities of appropriate size. **LO21-5**
- Economies of scale refer to reductions in *minimum* average cost attained with larger plant size (scale). If minimum ATC rises with plant size, diseconomies of scale exist. **LO21-5**
- Global competitiveness and domestic living standards depend on productivity advances. Improvements in productivity shift production functions up and push cost curves down. **LO21-1**

Key Terms

factors of production
production function
productivity
efficiency
opportunity cost
short run
marginal physical product (MPP)
law of diminishing returns

profit
marginal cost (MC)
total cost
fixed costs
variable costs
average total cost (ATC)
average fixed cost (AFC)
average variable cost (AVC)

explicit cost
implicit cost
economic cost
long run
economies of scale
constant returns to scale
unit labor cost

Questions for Discussion

1. What are the production costs of your economics class? What are the fixed costs? The variable costs? What's the marginal cost of enrolling more students?   **LO21-3**

2. Suppose all your friends offered to help wash your car. Would marginal physical product decline as more friends helped? Why or why not?   **LO21-2**

3. What will happen to Tesla if it doesn't achieve the economies of scale it anticipates from its gigafactory? (See In the News "Tesla Banks on Gigafactory.")   **LO21-5**

4. Owner/operators of small gas stations rarely pay themselves an hourly wage. How does this practice affect the economic cost of dispensing gasoline?   **LO21-4**

5. Corporate funeral giants have replaced small family-run funeral homes in many areas, in large part because of the lower costs they achieve. What kind of economies of scale exist in the funeral business? Why doesn't someone build one colossal funeral home and drive costs down further?   **LO21-5**

6. Are colleges subject to economies of scale or diseconomies?   **LO21-5**

7. Why don't more U.S. firms move to Mexico to take advantage of low wages there? Would an *identical* plant in Mexico be as productive as its U.S. counterpart?   **LO21-1**

8. How would your productivity in completing coursework be measured? Has your productivity changed since you began college? What caused the productivity changes? How could you increase productivity further?   **LO21-1**

9. What is the economic cost of doing this homework?   **LO21-4**

10. What causes unit labor costs to rise in some nations and fall in others?   **LO21-3**

PROBLEMS FOR CHAPTER 21

LO21-3 1. (*a*) Complete the following cost schedule:

Rate of Output	Total Cost	Marginal Cost	Average Fixed Cost	Average Variable Cost	Average Total Cost
0	$ 600	_____	_____	_____	_____
1	800	_____	_____	_____	_____
2	1,050	_____	_____	_____	_____
3	1,400	_____	_____	_____	_____
4	1,800	_____	_____	_____	_____
5	2,300	_____	_____	_____	_____

   (*b*) Use the cost data to plot the ATC and MC curves on the accompanying graph.
   (*c*) At what output rate is ATC minimized? (Use higher rate.)

LO21-2 2. At what level of labor input in Figure 21.2 does marginal physical product
   (*a*) First diminish?
   (*b*) Become zero?
   (*c*) Turn negative?

LO21-4 3. Suppose a company incurs the following costs: labor, $600; equipment, $300; and materials, $200. The company owns the building, so it doesn't have to pay the usual $700 in rent.
   (*a*) What is the total accounting cost?
   (*b*) What is the total economic cost?
   (*c*) If the company sold the building and then leased it back, what would be the change in
      (*i*) Accounting costs?
      (*ii*) Economic costs?

LO21-2 4. Refer to the production table for jeans (Table 21.1). Suppose a firm has two sewing machines and can vary only the amount of labor input.
   (*a*) Graph the production function for jeans given the two sewing machines.
   (*b*) Compute and graph the marginal physical product curve.
   (*c*) At what amount of labor input does the law of diminishing returns first become apparent in your graph of marginal physical product?
   (*d*) Is total output still increasing when MPP begins to diminish?
   (*e*) What is the value of MPP when output no longer increases?

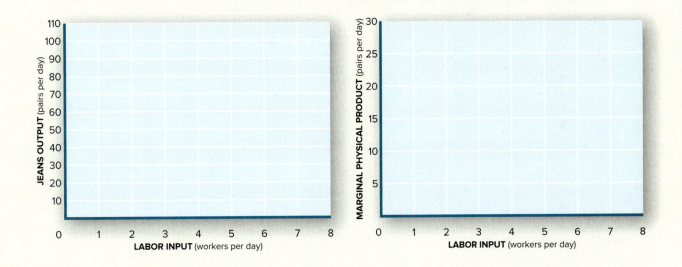

LO21-5 5. The following table indicates the average total cost of producing varying quantities of output from three different plants:

Rate of output	10	20	30	40	50	60	70	80	90	100
Average total cost										
Small firm	$ 600	$500	$400	$500	$600	$700	$800	$900	$1,000	$1,100
Medium firm	800	650	500	350	200	300	400	500	600	700
Large firm	1,000	900	800	700	600	500	400	300	400	500

    (*a*) Plot the ATC curves for all three firms on the graph.
    (*b*) Which plant(s) should be used to produce 40 units?
    (*c*) Which plant(s) should be used to produce 100 units?
    (*d*) Are there economies of scale in these plant size choices?

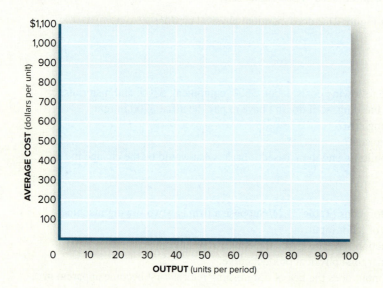

LO21-2 6. Given the following productivity information,
    (*a*) Calculate marginal physical product.
    (*b*) When does marginal productivity first diminish?

Labor	Output
0	0
1	10
2	22
3	30
4	36
5	38
6	37

LO21-3 7. Table 21.2 again shows the total cost of production for producing 15 pairs of jeans per day.

TABLE 21.2

The Total Costs of Production (Total Cost of Producing 15 Pairs of Jeans per Day)

The total cost of producing a good equals the market value of all the resources used in its production. In this case, the production of 15 pairs of jeans per day requires resources worth $245.

Resource Input	×	Unit Price of Input	=	Total Cost
1 factory		$100 per day		$100
1 sewing machine		20 per day		20
1 operator		80 per day		80
1.5 bolts of denim		30 per bolt		45
Total cost				$245

(a) Which two inputs are most likely to be fixed in the short run?
(b) Which two inputs are most likely to be variable in the short run?
To produce 15 pairs of jeans, calculate:
(c) Fixed cost
(d) Variable cost
(e) Total cost
(f) Average total cost

LO21-3 8. Complete the following table:

Quantity	Fixed cost	Variable cost	Total Cost
0			100
10		40	
20		100	
30	100		270
40		260	

LO21-3 9. Complete the following table:

Quantity	Total Cost	Marginal Cost	Average Variable Cost	Average Total Cost
0	20	—	—	—
1		10	10	
2				21
3		16		
4			14	
5	100			

LO21-4 10. Kanesha is an entrepreneur and has recently opened her first coffee shop, The Coffee Cat. Kanesha pays $5000 rent each month, $4800 for employee payroll, and $1200 for supplies. She was planning on selling several of her own tables and chairs on Craigslist for $1500, but instead she brought them to The Coffee Cat. Additionally, Kanesha quit working as an accountant where she was earning $52,000 per year to open up the shop. Based on this information identify:
(a) Explicit costs.
(b) Implicit costs.
Calculate annual:
(c) Accounting cost.
(d) Economic cost.

LO21-1 11. The Economy Tomorrow: Suppose the hourly wage rate is $24 in the United States and $3 in China, and productivity is 20 units per hour in the United States and 4 units per hour in China.

(*a*) What are per unit labor costs in the United States?

(*b*) What are per unit labor costs in China?

(*c*) If a company's goal is to minimize per unit labor costs, where would the production facility be located?

©MOF/Getty Images RF

©Lars A. Niki RF

©David A. Barnes/Alamy Stock Photo

Source: Library of Congress Prints and Photographs Division [LC-USZ62-63968]

©McGraw-Hill Education/Andrew Resek, photographer

©McGraw-Hill Education/Jill Braaten, photographer

9 PART

MARKET STRUCTURE

Market demand curves tell us what products consumers want. And production functions tell us how much it will cost producers to supply those products. What we don't yet know is how many products will actually be supplied—or at what prices. These are *behavioral decisions,* not technological facts. Chapters 22 through 26 examine these behavioral decisions. As we'll see, the *structure* of a market—the number and size of firms in it—has a profound effect on the supply of goods and services—the quantity, quality, and price of specific goods.

CHAPTER 22

The Competitive Firm

Apple Computer would love to raise the price of downloading music from its iTunes store. It isn't likely to do so, however, because too many other firms also offer digital downloads. If Apple raises its prices, customers might sign up with another company.

Your campus bookstore may be in a better position to raise prices. On most college campuses there's only one bookstore. If the campus store increases the price of books or supplies, most of its customers (you) will have little choice but to pay the higher tab.

As we discover in this and the next few chapters, the degree of competition in product markets is a major determinant of product prices, quality, and availability. Although all firms are in business to make a profit, their profit opportunities are limited by the amount of competition they face.

This chapter begins an examination of how businesses make price and production decisions. We first explore the nature of profits and how they're computed. We then observe how one type of firm—a perfectly competitive one—can *maximize* its profits by selecting the right rate of output. The following questions are at the center of this discussion:

- **What are *profits*?**
- **What are the unique characteristics of competitive firms?**
- **How much output will a competitive firm produce?**

The answers to these questions will shed more light on how the *supply* of goods and services is determined in a market economy.

THE PROFIT MOTIVE

The basic incentive for producing goods and services is the expectation of profit. Owning plants and equipment isn't enough. To generate a current flow of income, one must *use* the plants and equipment to produce and sell goods.

Profit is the difference between a firm's sales revenues and its total costs. It's the residual that the owners of a business receive. That profit residual may flow to the sole owner of a corner grocery store, or to the group of stockholders who collectively own a large corporation. In either case, it's the quest for profit that motivates people to own and operate a business (or a piece thereof).

Other Motivations

Profit isn't the only thing that motivates producers. Like the rest of us, producers also worry about social status and crave recognition. People

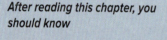

profit: The difference between total revenue and total cost.

who need to feel important, to control others, or to demonstrate achievement are likely candidates for running a business. Many small businesses are maintained by people who gave up 40-hour weeks, $50,000 incomes, and a sense of alienation in exchange for 80-hour weeks, $45,000 incomes, and a sense of identity and control.

In large corporations, the profit motive may lie even deeper below the surface. Stockholders (the owners) of large corporations rarely visit corporate headquarters. The people who manage the corporation's day-to-day business may have little or no stock in the company. Such nonowner managers may be more interested in their own jobs, salaries, and self-preservation than in the profits that accrue to the stockholding owners. If profits suffer, however, the corporation may start looking for new managers. The "bottom line" for virtually all businesses is the level of profits.

Is the Profit Motive Bad?

If it weren't possible to make a profit, few people would choose to supply goods and services. Yet the general public remains suspicious of the profit motive. As In the News "Are Profits Bad?" indicates, one out of four people thinks the profit motive is bad. An even higher percentage believes the profit motive results in *inferior* products at inflated prices. The Occupy Wall Street movement that began in September 2011 was predicated on the notion that corporate profits were a manifestation of corporate greed.

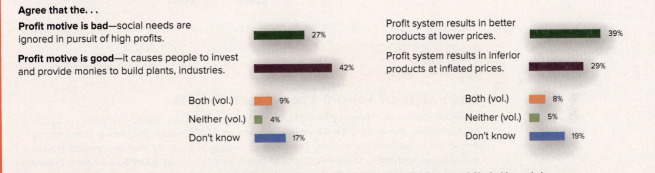

IN THE NEWS

ARE PROFITS BAD?

The following responses to a Roper survey are typical of public opinion about profits.

Agree that the. . .

Profit motive is bad—social needs are ignored in pursuit of high profits.   27%

Profit motive is good—it causes people to invest and provide monies to build plants, industries.   42%

Both (vol.)   9%
Neither (vol.)   4%
Don't know   17%

Profit system results in better products at lower prices.   39%

Profit system results in inferior products at inflated prices.   29%

Both (vol.)   8%
Neither (vol.)   5%
Don't know   19%

ANALYSIS: The profit motive is the primary incentive for supplying goods and services. Many consumers are distrustful of that motive, however.

As we'll see, the profit motive *can* induce business firms to pollute the environment, restrict competition, or maintain unsafe working conditions. However, **the profit motive also encourages businesses to produce the goods and services consumers desire, at prices they're willing to pay.** The profit motive, in fact, moves the "invisible hand" that Adam Smith said orchestrates market outcomes.

ECONOMIC VS. ACCOUNTING PROFITS

Although profits might be a necessary inducement for producers, most consumers feel that profits are too high. And that may be so in many cases. But most consumers have no idea how much profit U.S. businesses actually make. Public *perceptions* of profit are seven or eight times higher than actual profits. The typical consumer believes that 36 cents of every sales dollar goes to profits. In reality, average profit per sales dollar is closer to 5 cents.

Faulty perceptions of profits aren't confined to the general public. As surprising as it might seem, most businesses also measure their profits incorrectly.

Economic Profits

Everyone agrees that *profit represents the difference between total revenues and total costs.* Where people part ways is over the decision of what to include in total costs. Recall from Chapter 21 how economists compute costs. **Economic cost** refers to the value of *all* resources used in production, whether or not they receive an explicit payment. By contrast, most businesses count only **explicit costs**—that is, those they actually write checks for. They typically don't take into account the **implicit costs** of the labor or land and buildings they might own. As a result, they understate costs.

If businesses (and their accountants) understate true costs, they'll overstate true profits. Part of the accounting "profit" will really be compensation to unpaid land, labor, or capital used in the production process. *Whenever economic costs exceed explicit costs, observed (accounting) profits will exceed true (economic) profits.* Indeed, what appears to be an accounting profit may actually disguise an economic loss, as illustrated by the Fujishige strawberry farm once located right next to Disneyland (see In the News "The Value of Hiro's Strawberry Farm"). To determine the **economic profit** of a business, we must subtract all implicit factor costs from observed accounting profits:

$$\text{Economic profit} = \text{Total revenue} - \text{Total economic cost}$$

$$\text{OR}$$

$$= \text{Accounting profit} - \text{Implicit costs}$$

> **IN THE NEWS**
>
> ### THE VALUE OF HIRO'S STRAWBERRY FARM
>
> Anaheim, California—Hiroshi ("Hiro") Fujishige was a successful strawberry farmer in southern California. For more than 40 years, he maintained a 56-acre strawberry farm directly across the street from Disneyland. The Disney company repeatedly tried to convince Hiro to sell or lease his farm to Disney—offering to buy it for as much as $2 million an acre. Disney wanted the land to expand its theme park, but Hiro steadfastly refused to sell the farm he had bought for $3,500 in 1954 and on which he lived in a tiny house. For Hiro, the farm was precious, not for the profits it generated but for the security and freedom it provided. Having lost an earlier farm during the World War II internments of Japanese citizens, Hiro vowed not to give up another farm—at any price. "As long as I can make a profit from strawberries," he said, "I'll keep growing them." Which he did until he died in 1998.
>
> Source: News reports, September 1998.
>
> **ANALYSIS:** Mr. Fujishige's *accounting* profits were in stark contrast to his *economic* losses. The *implicit* costs of his time and land were enormous. After his death, Disney purchased the land for nearly $70 million and built the California Adventure Park.

Suppose, for example, that Table 22.1 accurately summarizes the revenues and costs associated with a local drugstore. Monthly sales revenues amount to $27,000. Explicit costs paid by the owner–manager include the cost of merchandise bought from producers for resale to consumers ($17,000), wages to the employees of the drugstore, rent and utilities

---

economic cost: The value of all resources used to produce a good or service; opportunity cost.

explicit costs: A payment made for the use of a resource.

implicit cost: The value of resources used, for which no direct payment is made.

economic profit: The difference between total revenues and total economic costs.

Total (gross) revenues per month	$27,000
less explicit costs:	
Cost of merchandise sold	$17,000
Wages to cashier, stock, and delivery help	2,500
Rent and utilities	800
Taxes	700
Total explicit costs	$21,000
Accounting profit (revenue minus explicit costs)	$ 6,000
less implicit costs:	
Wages of owner–manager, 300 hours @ $10 per hour	$ 3,000
Return on inventory investment, 10% per year on $120,000	1,000
Total implicit costs	$ 4,000
Economic profit (revenue minus *all* costs)	$ 2,000

TABLE 22.1

The Computation of Economic Profit

To calculate economic profit, we must take account of *all* costs of production. The economic costs of production include the implicit (opportunity) costs of the labor and capital a producer contributes to the production process. The accounting profits of a business take into account only explicit costs paid by the owner. Reported (accounting) profits will exceed economic profits whenever implicit costs are ignored.

paid to the landlord, and local sales and business taxes. When all these *explicit* costs are subtracted from total revenue, we're left with an *accounting profit* of $6,000 per month.

The owner–manager of the drugstore may be quite pleased with an accounting profit of $6,000 per month. He's working hard for this income, however. To keep his store running, the owner–manager is working 10 hours per day, 7 days a week. This adds up to 300 hours of labor per month. Were he to work this hard for someone else, his labor would be compensated explicitly—with a paycheck. Although he doesn't choose to pay himself this way, his labor still represents a real resource cost. To compute *economic* profit, we must subtract this implicit cost from the drugstore's accounting profits. Suppose the owner could earn $10 per hour in the best alternative job. Multiplying this wage rate ($10) by the number of hours he works in the drugstore (300), we see that the implicit cost of his labor is $3,000 per month.

The owner has also used his savings to purchase inventory for the store. He purchased the goods on his shelves for $120,000. If he had invested his savings in some other business, he could have earned a return of 10 percent per year. This forgone return represents a real cost. In this case, the implicit return (opportunity cost) on his capital investment amounts to $12,000 per year (10 percent × $120,000), or $1,000 per month.

To calculate the *economic* profit this drugstore generates, we count both explicit and implicit costs. Hence we must subtract all implicit factor payments (costs) from reported profits. The residual in this case amounts to $2,000 per month. That's the drugstore's *economic* profit.

Note that when we compute the drugstore's economic profit, we deduct the opportunity cost of the owner's capital. Specifically, we assumed that his funds would have reaped a 10 percent return somewhere else. In effect, we've assumed that a "normal" rate of return is 10 percent. This **normal profit** (the opportunity cost of capital) is an economic cost. Rather than investing in a drugstore, the owner could have earned a 10 percent return on his funds by investing in a fast-food franchise, a music store, a steel plant, or some other production activity. By choosing to invest in a drugstore instead, the owner was seeking a *higher* return on his funds—more than he could have obtained elsewhere. In other words, *economic profits represent something over and above "normal profits."*

normal profit: The opportunity cost of capital; zero economic profit.

Our treatment of "normal" returns as an economic cost leads to a startling conclusion: on average, economic profits are zero. Only firms that reap *above-average* returns can claim economic profits. This seemingly strange perspective on profits emphasizes the opportunity costs of all economic activities. *A productive activity reaps an economic profit only if it earns more than its opportunity cost.*

Entrepreneurship

Naturally, everyone in business wants to earn an economic profit. But relatively few people can stay ahead of the pack. To earn economic profits, a business must see opportunities that others have missed, discover new products, find new and better methods of production, or take above-average risks. In fact, economic profits are often regarded as a reward to entrepreneurship, the ability and willingness to take risks, to organize factors of production, and to produce something society desires.

Consider the local drugstore again. People in the neighborhood clearly want such a drugstore, as evidenced by its substantial sales revenue. But why should anyone go to the trouble and risk of starting and maintaining one? We noted that the owner–manager *could* earn $3,000 in wages by accepting a regular job plus $1,000 per month in returns on capital by investing in an "average" business. Why should he take on the added responsibilities and risk of owning and operating his own drugstore?

The inducement to take on the added responsibilities of owning and operating a business is the potential for economic profit, the extra income over and above normal factor payments. In the case of the drugstore owner, this extra income is the economic profit of $2,000 (Table 22.1). In the absence of such additional compensation, few people would want to make the extra effort required.

Risk

Don't forget, however, that the *potential* for profit is not a *guaranty* of profit. Quite the contrary. Substantial risks are attached to starting and operating a business. Tens of thousands of businesses fail every year, and still more suffer economic losses. From this perspective, profit also represents compensation for the risks incurred in owning or operating a business.

MARKET STRUCTURE

monopoly: A firm that produces the entire market supply of a particular good or service.

Not all businesses have an equal opportunity to earn an economic profit. The opportunity for profit may be limited by the *structure* of the industry in which the firm is engaged. One of the reasons Microsoft is such a profitable company is that it has long held a **monopoly** on computer operating systems. As the principal supplier of operating systems, Microsoft could raise software prices without losing many customers. T-shirt shops, by contrast, have to worry about all the other stores that sell similar products in the area (see In the News "Too Many Sellers: The Woes of T-Shirt Shops"). Faced with so much competition, the owner of a T-shirt shop doesn't have the power to raise prices or accumulate economic profits.

IN THE NEWS

TOO MANY SELLERS: THE WOES OF T-SHIRT SHOPS

Selling T-shirts is easy. People love T-shirts, especially with custom designs or logos of a special event or favorite band, product, or sports team. Consumers spend at least $15 billion a year on them. Moreover, the inventory is easy to store, doesn't spoil, and is compact. On the surface, a great business.

But there's a catch—everybody and his brother sells T-shirts. Every beach resort has dozens of T-shirt shops. And they sprout like weeds at every major sporting or concert venue. And then there are all the online sites that offer custom designs and quick delivery. So, the competition is intense. This makes it near impossible for any T-shirt shop to raise the price of its T-shirts, much less hold on to profits. The owner of a T-shirt shop in South Padre Island, Texas, lamented, "Every day you have to compete with other shops. And if you invent something new, they will copy you."

©McGraw-Hill Education

ANALYSIS: The ability to earn a profit depends on how many other firms offer similar products. A perfectly competitive firm, facing numerous rivals, has difficulty maintaining prices or profits.

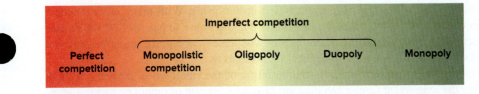

FIGURE 22.1

Market Structures

The number and relative size of firms producing a good vary across industries. Market structures range from perfect competition (a great many firms producing the same good) to monopoly (only one firm). Most real-world firms are along the continuum of *imperfect* competition. Included in that range are duopoly (two firms), oligopoly (a few firms), and monopolistic competition (many firms).

Figure 22.1 illustrates various **market structures.** At one extreme is the monopoly structure in which only one firm produces the entire supply of the good. At the other extreme is **perfect competition.** In perfect competition a great many firms supply the same good.

There are relatively few monopolies or perfectly competitive firms in the real world. Most of the 30 million businesses in the United States fall between these extremes. They're more accurately characterized by gradations of *imperfect* competition—markets in which competition exists, but individual firms still retain some discretionary power over prices. In a *duopoly,* two firms supply the entire market. In an *oligopoly,* like credit card services, a handful of firms (Visa, MasterCard, American Express) dominate. In *monopolistic competition,* like fast-food restaurants, there are enough firms to ensure some competition, but not so many as to preclude some limited monopoly-type power. We examine all these market structures in later chapters, after we establish the nature of perfect competition.

> **market structure:** The number and relative size of firms in an industry.

> **perfect competition:** A market in which no buyer or seller has market power.

THE NATURE OF PERFECT COMPETITION

Industries can be classified by their structure—the number and relative size of the firms producing a specific good. As we'll see, the structure of an industry has a profound effect on market outcomes.

Structure

A perfectly competitive industry has several distinguishing characteristics, including

- *Many firms*—lots of firms are competing for consumer purchases.
- *Identical products*—the products of the different firms are identical, or nearly so.
- *Low entry barriers*—it's relatively easy to get into the business.

The T-shirt business has all these traits, which is why store owners have a hard time maintaining profits (see In the News "Too Many Sellers: The Woes of T-Shirt Shops").

Price Takers

Because they always have to contend with a lot of competition, T-shirt shops can't increase profits by raising T-shirt prices. More than 1 billion T-shirts are sold in the United States each year by tens of thousands of retail outlets. In such a competitive industry the many individual firms that make up the industry are all *price takers:* they take the price the market sets. A competitive firm can sell all its output at the prevailing market price. If it boosts its price above that level, consumers will shop elsewhere. In this sense, a perfectly competitive firm has no **market power**—no ability to control the market price for the good it sells.

At first glance, it might appear that all firms have market power. After all, who's to stop a T-shirt shop from raising prices? The important concept here, however, is *market* price— that is, the price at which goods are actually sold. If one shop raises its price to $15 and 40 other shops sell the same T-shirts for $10, it won't sell many shirts, and maybe none at all.

You may confront the same problem if you purchase a paper copy of this book and then try to sell it at the end of the semester. You might want to resell this textbook for $80. But

> **market power:** The ability to alter the market price of a good or service.

you'll discover that the bookstore won't buy it at that price. With many other students offering to sell their books, the bookstore knows it doesn't have to pay the $80 you're asking. Because you don't have any market power, you have to accept the going price if you want to sell this book. You are a price taker in this market.

The same kind of powerlessness is characteristic of the small wheat farmer. Like any producer, the lone wheat farmer can increase or reduce his rate of output by making alternative production decisions. But his decision won't affect the market price of wheat.

Even the largest U.S. wheat farmers can't change the market price of wheat. The largest wheat farm produces nearly 100,000 bushels of wheat per year. But *2 billion* bushels of wheat are brought to market every year, so another 100,000 bushels simply won't be noticed. In other words, ***the output of the lone farmer is so small relative to the market supply that it has no significant effect on the total quantity or price in the market.***

A distinguishing characteristic of *powerless* firms is that, individually, they can sell all the output they produce at the prevailing market price. We call all such producers **competitive firms;** they have no independent influence on market prices. *A perfectly competitive firm is one whose output is so small in relation to market volume that its output decisions have no perceptible impact on price.*

competitive firm: A firm without market power, with no ability to alter the market price of the goods it produces.

Market Demand Curves vs. Firm Demand Curves

It's important to distinguish between the market demand curve and the demand curve confronting a particular firm. T-shirt shops don't contradict the law of demand. The quantity of T-shirts purchased in the market still depends on T-shirt prices. That is, the *market* demand curve for T-shirts is still downward-sloping. A single T-shirt shop faces a *horizontal* demand curve only because its share of the market is so small that changes in its output don't disturb market equilibrium.

Collectively, though, individual firms do count. If all 40 of the T-shirt shops on South Padre Island (see In the News "Too Many Sellers: The Woes of T-Shirt Shops") were to increase shirt production at the same time, the market equilibrium would be disturbed. That is, a competitive market composed of individually powerless producers still sees a lot of action. The power here resides in the collective action of all the producers, however, not in the

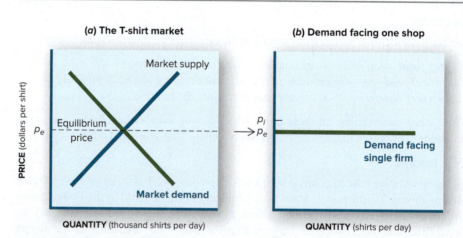

(a) The T-shirt market

(b) Demand facing one shop

FIGURE 22.2

Market vs. Firm Demand

Consumer demand for any product is downward-sloping. The equilibrium price (p_e) of T-shirts is established by the intersection of *market* demand and *market* supply, as in the graph on the left. This market-established price is the only one at which an individual shop can sell T-shirts. If the shop owner asks a higher price (e.g., p_i in the graph on the right), no one will buy his shirts because they can buy identical T-shirts from other shops at p_e. But he can sell all his shirts at the market-set equilibrium price. The shop owner thus confronts a horizontal demand curve for his own output. (Notice the difference in market and individual shop quantities on the horizontal axes of the two graphs.)

individual action of any one. Were T-shirt production to increase so abruptly, the shirts could be sold only at lower prices, in accordance with the downward-sloping nature of the *market* demand curve. Figure 22.2 illustrates the distinction between the actions of a single producer and those of the market. Notice that

- *The market demand curve for a product is always downward-sloping (law of demand).*
- *The demand curve confronting a perfectly competitive firm is horizontal.*

THE PRODUCTION DECISION

A startling implication of Figure 22.2 is that *perfectly competitive firms don't make pricing decisions;* the *market* sets the prevailing price. All competitive firms do is *respond* to that market price. As price takers, they have only one decision to make: how much to produce. Choosing a rate of output is a firm's **production decision.** Should it produce all the output it can? Or should it produce at less than capacity?

Output and Revenues

In searching for the most desirable rate of output, focus on the distinction between total *revenue* and total *profit*. **Total revenue** is the price of the good multiplied by the quantity sold:

$$\text{Total revenue} = \text{Price} \times \text{Quantity}$$

Since a competitive firm can sell all its output at the market price (p_e), total revenue is a simple multiple of p_e. The total revenue of a T-shirt shop, for example, is the price of shirts (p_e) multiplied by the quantity sold. Figure 22.3 shows the total revenue curve that results from this multiplication. Note that *the total revenue curve of a perfectly competitive firm is an upward-sloping straight line with a slope equal to* p_e.

If a competitive firm wanted to maximize its total *revenue,* its production decision would be simple: it would always produce at capacity. Life isn't that simple, however; *the firm's goal is to maximize profits, not revenues.*

Output and Costs

To maximize profits, a firm must consider how increased production will affect *costs* as well as *revenues.* How do costs vary with the rate of output?

As we observed in Chapter 21, producers are saddled with certain costs in the **short run.** A T-shirt shop has to pay the rent every month no matter how few shirts it sells. The Low-Rider Jeans Corporation in Chapter 21 had to pay the rent on its factory and lease

production decision: The selection of the short-run rate of output (with existing plants and equipment).

total revenue: The price of a product multiplied by the quantity sold in a given time period: $p \times q$.

short run: The period in which the quantity (and quality) of some inputs can't be changed.

Price (per Shirt)	×	Quantity (Shirts per Day)	=	Total Revenue
$8		1		$ 8
8		2		16
8		3		24
8		4		32
8		5		40
8		6		48
8		7		56
8		8		64
8		9		72

FIGURE 22.3

Total Revenue

Because a competitive firm can sell all its output at the prevailing price, its total revenue curve is linear. In this case, the market (equilibrium) price of T-shirts is assumed to be $8. Hence a shop's total revenue is equal to $8 multiplied by quantity sold. Total revenue is maximized at capacity output.

FIGURE 22.4

Total Cost

Total cost increases with output. The rate of increase isn't steady, however. Typically, the rate of cost increase slows initially, then speeds up. After point *z*, diminishing returns (rising marginal costs) cause accelerating costs. These accelerating costs limit the profit potential of increased output.

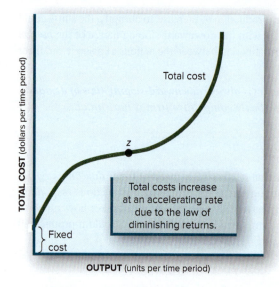

fixed costs: Costs of production that don't change when the rate of output is altered, such as the cost of basic plants and equipment.

variable costs: Costs of production that change when the rate of output is altered, such as labor and material costs.

marginal cost (MC): The increase in total cost associated with a one-unit increase in production.

payments on its sewing machine. These **fixed costs** are incurred even if no output is produced. Once a firm starts producing output, it incurs **variable costs** as well.

Since profits depend on the *difference* between revenues and costs, the costs of added output will determine how much profit a producer can make. Figure 22.4 illustrates a typical total cost curve. ***Total costs increase as output expands. But the rate of cost increase varies.*** Hence the total cost curve is *not* linear. At first total costs rise slowly (notice the gradually declining slope until point *z*), then they increase more quickly (the rising slope after point *z*). This S-shaped curve reflects the *law of diminishing returns.* As we first observed in Chapter 21, **marginal costs (MC)** often decline in the early stages of production and then increase as the available plants and equipment are used more intensively. These changes in marginal cost cause *total* costs to rise slowly at first, then to pick up speed as output increases.

You may suspect by now that the road to profits is not an easy one. It entails comparing ever-changing revenues with ever-changing costs. Figure 22.5 helps simplify the problem by bringing together typical total revenue and total cost curves. The total revenue line (in orange) is linear, since the price is constant. The total cost line, however, is sort of S-shaped, rising slowly at first, then much faster as marginal costs accelerate.

FIGURE 22.5

Total Profit

Profit is the *difference* between total revenue and total cost. It is represented as the vertical distance between the total revenue curve and the total cost curve. At output *h*, profit equals *r* minus *s*. The objective is to find the unique rate of output that *maximizes* profit.

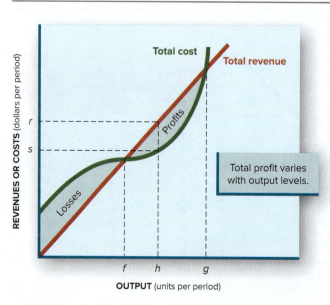

Our focus is on the *vertical distance* between the total revenue and cost curves. That vertical distance represents the *difference* between revenues and costs. Total costs in this case exceed total revenue at low rates of output (below *f*) as well as at very high rates (above *g*). The firm is profitable only at output rates between *f* and *g*.

Although all rates of output between *f* and *g* are profitable, they aren't *equally* profitable. A quick glance at Figure 22.5 confirms that the vertical distance between total revenue and total cost varies considerably within that range. ***The primary objective of the producer is to find that one particular rate of output that maximizes total profits.*** With a ruler, we could find it in Figure 22.5 by measuring the distance between the revenue and cost curves at all rates of output. In the real world, most producers need more practical guides to profit maximization.

PROFIT-MAXIMIZING RULE

The best single rule for maximizing profits in the short run is straightforward: never produce a unit of output that costs more than it brings in. By following this simple rule, a producer is likely to make the right production decision. We will see how this rule works by looking first at the revenue side of production ("what it brings in"), then at the cost side ("what it costs").

Marginal Revenue = Price

In searching for the most profitable rate of output, we need to know what an additional unit of output will bring in—that is, how much it adds to the total revenue of the firm. In general, the contribution to total revenue of an additional unit of output is called **marginal revenue (MR).** Marginal revenue is the *change* in total revenue that occurs when output is increased by one unit:

$$\text{Marginal revenue} = \frac{\text{Change in total revenue}}{\text{Change in output}}$$

marginal revenue (MR): The change in total revenue that results from a one-unit increase in the quantity sold.

To calculate marginal revenue, we compare the total revenues received before and after a one-unit increase in the rate of production; the *difference* between the two totals equals marginal revenue.

When the price of a product is constant, it's easy to compute marginal revenue. Suppose we're operating a catfish farm. Our product is catfish, sold at wholesale at the prevailing price of $13 per bushel. In this case, a one-unit increase in sales (one more bushel) increases total revenue by $13. As illustrated in Table 22.2, as long as the price of a product is constant, price and marginal revenue are the same. Hence, ***for perfectly competitive firms, price equals marginal revenue.***

Marginal Cost

Keep in mind why we're breeding and selling catfish. Our goal is not to maximize *revenues* but to maximize *profits*. To gauge profits, we need to know not only the price of fish but also how much each bushel costs to produce. As we saw in Chapter 21, the added cost of producing one more unit of a good is its *marginal cost*. Figure 22.6 summarizes the marginal costs associated with the production of catfish.

Analysis: Fish farmers want to maximize profits, not the number of fish caught.
©Brian J. Skerry/National Geographic Creative

TABLE 22.2

Total and Marginal Revenue

Marginal revenue (MR) is the *change* in total revenue associated with the sale of one more unit of output. A third bushel increases total revenue from $26 to $39; MR equals $13. If the price is constant (at $13 here), marginal revenue equals price.

Quantity Sold (Bushels per Day)	×	Price (per Bushel)	=	Total Revenue (per Day)	Marginal Revenue (per Bushel)
0	×	$13	=	$ 0	—
1	×	13	=	13	$13
2	×	13	=	26	13
3	×	13	=	39	13
4	×	13	=	52	13

FIGURE 22.6

The Costs of Catfish Production

Marginal cost is the increase in total cost associated with a one-unit increase in production. When production expands from two to three units per day, total costs increase by $9 (from $22 to $31 per day). The marginal cost of the third bushel is therefore $9, as illustrated by point *D* in the graph and row *D* in the table.

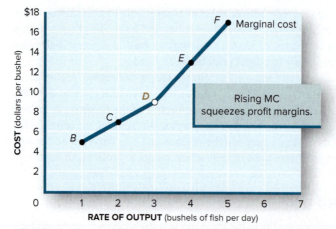

	Rate of Output (Bushels per Day)	Total Cost (per Day)	Marginal Cost (per Day)	Average Cost (per Day)
A	0	$10	—	—
B	1	15	$ 5	$15.00
C	2	22	7	11.00
D	3	31	9	10.33
E	4	44	13	11.00
F	5	61	17	12.20

The production process for catfish farming is wonderfully simple. The factory is a pond; the rate of production is the number of fish harvested from the pond per day. A farmer can alter the rate of production at will, up to the breeding capacity of the pond. As Calvin Jones, a former schoolteacher now working on a Mississippi catfish farm, says, "You raise fish. You get them out of the pond and you sell them. That's pretty much all you do. There's no genius to it."[1]

Assume that the *fixed* costs of the pond are $10 per day. The fixed costs include the rental value of the pond and the cost of electricity for keeping the pond oxygenated so the fish can breathe. These fixed costs must be paid no matter how many fish the farmer harvests.

To harvest catfish from the pond, the farmer must incur additional costs. Labor is needed to net and sort the fish. The cost of labor is *variable,* depending on how much output the farmer decides to produce. If no fish are harvested, no variable costs are incurred.

The *marginal costs* of harvesting are the additional costs incurred to harvest *one* more basket of fish. Generally, we expect marginal costs to rise as the rate of production increases. The law of diminishing returns we encountered in Chapter 21 applies to catfish farming as well. As more labor is hired, each worker has less space (pond area) and capital (access to nets, sorting trays) to work with. Accordingly, it takes a little more labor time (marginal cost) to harvest each additional fish.

Figure 22.6 illustrates these marginal costs. Notice how the MC rises as the rate of output increases. At the output rate of 4 bushels per day (point *E*), marginal cost is $13. Hence the fourth bushel *increases* total costs by $13. The fifth bushel is even more expensive, with a marginal cost of $17.

Profit-Maximizing Rate of Output

We're now in a position to make a production decision. The rule about never producing anything that adds more to cost than it brings in can now be stated in more technical terms. Since price equals marginal revenue for competitive firms, we can base the production

[1]Source: Byrd, Shelia, "Fuel, Feed Costs Crippling US Catfish Industry," *Associated Press,* June 22, 2008.

Price Level	Production Decision
Price > MC	Increase output
Price = MC	Maintain output (profits maximized)
Price < MC	Decrease output

TABLE 22.3

Short-Run Profit Maximization Rules for Competitive Firm

The relationship between price and marginal cost dictates short-run production decisions. For competitive firms, profits are maximized at that rate of output where price = MC.

decision on a comparison of *price* and marginal cost. ***There are only three possible scenarios for MC and price:***

- **MC > p.** We don't want to produce an additional unit of output if its MC exceeds its price. If MC exceeds price, we're spending more to produce that extra unit than we're getting back: total profits will decline if we produce it.
- **p > MC.** The opposite is true when price exceeds MC. If an extra unit brings in more revenue than it costs to produce, it is *adding* to total profit. Total profits must increase in this case. Hence a competitive firm wants to expand the rate of production whenever price exceeds MC.
- **p = MC.** Since we want to expand output when price exceeds MC and contract output if price is less than MC, the profit-maximizing rate of output is easily found. ***For perfectly competitive firms, profits are maximized at the rate of output where price equals marginal cost.*** The implications of this **profit maximization rule** are summarized in Table 22.3.

Figure 22.7 illustrates the application of our profit maximization rule in catfish farming. The prevailing wholesale price of catfish is $13 a bushel. At this price we can sell all the catfish we can produce, up to our short-run capacity. The catfish can't be sold at a higher

profit maximization rule:
Produce at that rate of output where marginal revenue equals marginal cost.

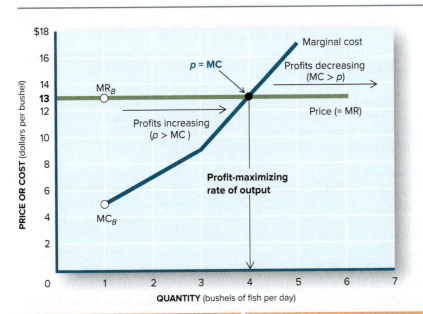

FIGURE 22.7

Maximization of Profits for a Competitive Firm

A competitive firm maximizes total profit at the output rate where MC = p. If MC is less than price, the firm can increase profits by producing more. If MC exceeds price, the firm should reduce output. In this case, profit maximization occurs at an output of 4 bushels per day.

	(1) Number of Bushels (per Day)	(2) Price	(3) Total Revenue	—	(4) Total Cost	=	(5) Total Profit	(6) Marginal Revenue	(7) Marginal Cost
A	0	$13	$ 0		$10		−$10	—	—
B	1	13	13		15		− 2	$13	$ 5
C	2	13	26		22		+ 4	13	7
D	3	13	39		31		+ 8	13	9
E	4	13	52		44		+ 8	13	13
F	5	13	65		61		+ 4	13	17

price because lots of farmers raise catfish and sell them for $13 (see In the News "The Lure of Catfish"). If we try to charge a higher price, consumers will buy their fish from other vendors. Hence we confront a horizontal demand curve at the price of $13.

IN THE NEWS

THE LURE OF CATFISH

Row-crop farmers throughout the South are taking a liking to catfish. Rising prices for catfish, combined with falling feed prices, have made the lure of catfish farming irresistible. Crop farmers are building ponds, buying aeration equipment, and breeding catfish in record numbers. Production has doubled in the last 15 years—to 340 million pounds this year—and looks to keep increasing as farmers shift from row crops to catfish.

Steve Hollingsworth, a Greensboro, Alabama farmer, now has ten ponds, each holding about 100,000 fish. He spends $18,000 a week on feed for the 1 million fish in his ponds. But he says the business is good; he takes in about $60,000 a week in sales. Crop farmers in Alabama, Mississippi, Arkansas, and Louisiana are taking the bait.

Source: Media reports, 1993.

ANALYSIS: People go into a competitive business like catfish farming to earn a profit. Once in business, they try to maximize total profits by equating price and marginal cost.

The costs of producing catfish were examined in Figure 22.6. The key concept illustrated here is marginal cost. The MC curve slopes upward in conventional fashion.

Figure 22.7 also depicts the total revenues, costs, and profits of alternative production rates. Study the table first. Notice that the firm loses $10 per day if it produces no fish (row A). At zero output, total revenue is zero ($p \times q = 0$). However, the firm must still contend with fixed costs of $10 per day. Total profit—total revenue minus total cost—is therefore *minus* $10; the firm incurs a loss.

Row B of the table shows how this loss is reduced when 1 bushel of fish is harvested per day. The production and sale of 1 bushel per day bring in $13 of total revenue (column 3). The total cost of producing 1 bushel per day is $15 (column 4). Hence the total loss at an output rate of 1 bushel per day is $2 (column 5). This may not be what we hoped for, but it's certainly better than the $10 loss incurred at zero output.

***p* > MC: Expand.** The superiority of harvesting 1 bushel per day rather than none is also evident in columns 6 and 7 of row B. The first bushel produced has a *marginal revenue* of $13. Its *marginal cost* is only $5. Hence it brings in more added revenue than it adds to costs. Under these circumstances—whenever price exceeds MC—output should definitely be expanded. That is one of the decision rules summarized earlier in Table 22.3.

The excess of price over MC for the first unit of output is also illustrated by the graph in Figure 22.7. Point MR_B ($13) lies above MC_B ($5); the *difference* between these two points measures the contribution that the first bushel makes to the total profits of the firm. In this case, that contribution equals $13 − $5 = $8, and production losses are reduced by that amount when the rate of output is increased from zero to 1 bushel per day.

As long as price exceeds MC, additional output increases total profit. Notice what happens to profits when the rate of output is increased from 1 to 2 bushels per day (row C). The price (MR) of the second bushel is $13; its MC is $7. Therefore it *adds* $6 to total profits. Instead of losing $2 per day, the firm is now making a profit of $4 per day.

The firm can make even more profits by expanding the rate of output further. The marginal revenue of the third bushel is $13; its marginal cost is $9 (row D of the table). Therefore, the third bushel makes a $4 contribution to profits.

MC = *p*: Max Profit. This firm will never make huge profits. For the fourth unit of output price and MC both equal $13. It doesn't contribute to total profits, and it doesn't subtract from them. The fourth unit of output represents the highest rate of output the

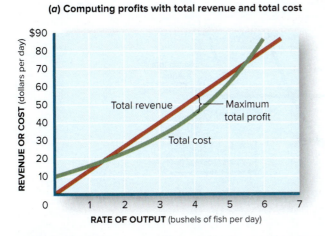

(a) Computing profits with total revenue and total cost

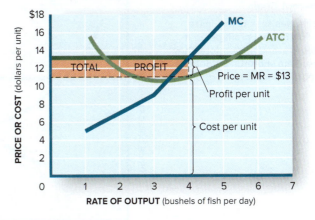

(b) Computing profits with price and average total cost

FIGURE 22.8
Alternative Views of Total Profit

Total profit can be computed as TR − TC, as in part *a*. Or it can be computed as profit *per unit* (*p* − ATC) multiplied by the quantity sold. This is illustrated in part *b* by the shaded rectangle. To find the profit-maximizing output, we could use either of these graphs or just the price and MC curves in Figure 22.7.

firm desires. *At the rate of output where price = MC, total profits of the firm are maximized.*[2]

MC > p: Contract. Notice what happens if we expand output beyond 4 bushels per day. The price of the fifth bushel is still $13 but its MC is $17. The fifth bushel adds more to costs than to revenue. If we produce that fifth bushel, total profit will decline by $4. In Figure 22.7 the MC curve lies above the price line at all output levels in excess of 4. The lesson here is clear: *output should not be increased if MC exceeds price.*

The correct production decision—the profit-maximizing decision—is shown in Figure 22.7 by the intersection of the price and MC curves. At this intersection, price equals MC and profits are maximized. If we produced less, we'd be giving up potential profits. If we produced more, total profits would also fall (review Table 22.3).

Adding Up Profits . . .

To reach the right production decision, we've relied on *marginal* revenues and costs. Having found the desired rate of output, however, we may want to take a closer look at the profits we are accumulating. Figure 22.8 provides two different ways of viewing our success.

with Total Revenue and Total Cost. The first view focuses on total revenues and total costs. Total profits are represented in Figure 22.8a by the vertical distance between the total revenue and total cost curves. This is a straightforward interpretation of our definition of total profits:

$$\text{Total profits} = \text{TR} - \text{TC}$$

The vertical distance between the TR and TC curves is maximized at the output of 4 bushels per day.

with Price and Average Cost. A second view of the same profits focuses on *average* costs and price. Total profit is equal to *average* profit per unit multiplied by the number of units produced. Profit *per unit,* in turn, is equal to price *minus* average total cost:

$$\text{Profit per unit} = p - \text{ATC}$$

[2]In this case, profits are the same at output levels of 3 and 4 bushels. Given the choice between the two levels, most firms will choose the higher level. By producing the extra unit of output, the firm increases its customer base. This not only denies rival firms an additional sale but also provides some additional cushion when the economy slumps. Also, corporate size may connote both prestige and power. In any case, the higher output level defines the *limit* to maximum profit production.

FIGURE 22.9
Different Goals

Businesses seek to maximize
total profits, not profit per unit
or total revenue. Therefore, they
pursue the short-run output rate
q_b, not the output rates q_a or q_c.

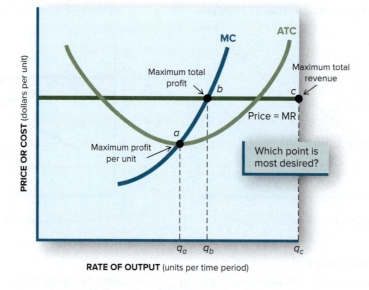

The price of catfish is illustrated in Figure 22.8b by the horizontal price line at \$13. The average total cost of producing catfish is shown by the ATC curve. Like the ATC curve we encountered in Chapter 21, this one has a U shape. The *difference* between price and average cost—profit per unit—is illustrated by the vertical distance between the price and ATC curves. At 4 bushels per day, for example, profit per unit equals \$13 − \$11 = \$2.

To compute *total* profits, we note that

$$\text{Total profits} = \text{Profit per unit} \times \text{Quantity} = (p - \text{ATC}) \times q$$

In this case, the 4 bushels generate a profit of \$2 each, for a *total* profit of \$8 per day. *Total* profits are illustrated in Figure 22.8b by the shaded rectangle. [Recall that the area of a rectangle is equal to its height (profit per unit) multiplied by its width (the quantity sold).]

Profit per unit is not only used to compute total profits but is often also of interest in its own right. Businesspeople like to cite statistics on "markups," which are a crude index to per-unit profits. However, *the profit-maximizing producer never seeks to maximize per-unit profits. What counts is* **total** *profits, not the amount of profit per unit.* This is the old \$5 ice cream problem again. You might be able to maximize profit per unit if you could sell 1 cone for \$5, but you would make a lot more money if you sold 100 cones at a per-unit profit of only 50 cents each.

Similarly, *the profit-maximizing producer has no desire to produce at that rate of output where ATC is at a minimum.* Minimum ATC does represent least-cost production. But additional units of output, even though they raise average costs, will increase total profits. This is evident in Figure 22.8; price exceeds MC for some output to the right of minimum ATC (the bottom of the U). Therefore, total profits are increasing as we increase the rate of output beyond the point of minimum average costs. Figure 22.9 illustrates the distinctions between these different markers.

THE SHUTDOWN DECISION

The rule established for short-run profit maximization doesn't guarantee any profits. By equating price and marginal cost, the competitive producer is only assured of achieving the *optimal* output. This is the best possible rate of output for the firm, given the existing market price and the (short-run) costs of production.

But what if the best possible rate of output generates a loss? What should the producer do in this case? Keep producing output? Or shut down the factory and find something else to do?

The first instinct may be to shut down the factory to stop the flow of red ink. But this isn't necessarily the wisest course of action. It may be smarter to keep operating a money-losing operation than to shut it down.

The rationale for this seemingly ill-advised course of action resides in the fixed costs of production. *Fixed costs must be paid even if all output ceases.* The firm must still pay rent on the factory and equipment even if it doesn't use these inputs. That's why we call such costs "fixed."

The persistence of fixed costs casts an entirely different light on the shutdown decision. Since fixed costs will have to be paid in any case, the question becomes: Which option creates greater losses? Does the firm lose more money by continuing to operate (and incurring a loss) or by shutting down (and incurring a loss equal to fixed costs)? In these terms, the answer becomes clear: *A firm should shut down only if the losses from continuing production exceed fixed costs.* This happens when total revenue is less than total *variable* cost.

Price vs. AVC

The shutdown decision can be made without explicit reference to fixed costs. Figure 22.10 shows how. The relationship to focus on is between the price of a good and its average *variable* cost.

The curves in Figure 22.10 represent the short-run costs and potential demand curves for catfish. As long as the price of catfish is $13 per bushel, the typical firm will produce 4 bushels a day, as determined by the intersection of the MC and MR (= price) curves (point X in part *a*). In this case, price ($13) exceeds average *total* cost ($11), and catfish farming is profitable. This is the happy situation we analyzed earlier (Figure 22.7).

The situation wouldn't look so good, however, if the market price of catfish fell to $9. Following the rule for profit maximization, the firm would be led to point Y in part *b*, where MC intersects the new demand (price) curve. At this intersection, the firm would produce 3 bushels per day. But total revenues would no longer cover total costs, as can be seen from the fact that the ATC curve now lies *above* the price line. The ATC of producing 3 bushels is $10.33 (Figure 22.6); price is $9. Hence the firm is incurring a loss of $4 per day (3 bushels at a loss of $1.33 each).

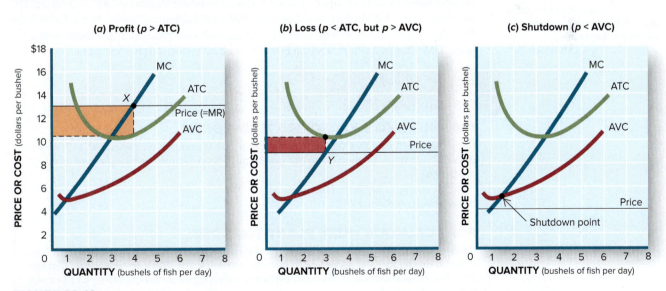

FIGURE 22.10

The Firm's Shutdown Point

A firm should cease production only if total revenue is lower than total *variable* cost. The shutdown decision may be based on a comparison of price and AVC. If the price of catfish per bushel was $13, a firm would earn a profit at point X in part *a*.

At a price of $9 (point Y in part *b*), the firm is losing money (*p* is less than ATC) but is more than covering all variable costs (*p* is greater than AVC). If the price falls to $4 per bushel, as in part *c*, output should cease (*p* is less than AVC).

Should the firm stay in business under the circumstances? The answer is yes. Recall that the catfish farmer has already dug the pond and installed equipment at a (fixed) cost of $10 per day. The producer will have to pay these fixed costs whether or not the machinery is used. Stopping production would result in a loss amounting to $10 per day. Staying in business, even when catfish prices fall to $9 each, generates a loss of only $4 a day. In this case, *where price exceeds average variable cost but not average total cost, the profit maximization rule minimizes losses.*

The Shutdown Point

If the price of catfish falls far enough, the producer may be better off ceasing production altogether. Suppose the price of catfish fell to $4 per bushel (Figure 22.10c). A price this low doesn't even cover the variable cost of producing 1 bushel per day ($5). Continued production of even 1 bushel per day would imply a total loss of $11 per day ($10 of fixed costs *plus* $1 of variable costs). Higher rates of output would lead to still greater losses. Hence the firm should shut down production, even though that action implies a loss of $10 per day. In all cases *where price doesn't cover average variable costs at any rate of output, production should cease.* Thus the **shutdown point** occurs where price is equal to minimum average *variable* cost. Any lower price will result in losses larger than fixed costs. In Figure 22.10, the shutdown point occurs at a price of $5, where the MC and AVC curves intersect.

shutdown point: The rate of output where price equals minimum AVC.

THE INVESTMENT DECISION

When a firm shuts down, it doesn't necessarily leave (exit) the industry. General Motors still produces cars even though it idled 5 of its plants in 2017 (see In the News "GM Shutting 5 Factories this Month"). *The shutdown decision is a* **short-run** *response.* It's based on the fixed costs of an established plant and the variable costs of operating it.

Ideally, a producer would never get into a money-losing business in the first place. Entry was based on an **investment decision** that the producer now regrets. *Investment decisions are* **long-run** *decisions,* however, and the firm now must pay for its bad luck or poor judgment. The investment decision entails the assumption of fixed costs (e.g., the lease of the factory); once the investment is made, the short-run production decision is designed to make the best possible use of those fixed inputs. The short-run profit maximization rule we've discussed applies only to this second decision; it assumes that a production unit exists. In the News "GM Shutting 5 Factories this Month" shows the contrast between production and investment decisions: GM *idled* its factories; Omaha Power permanently *closed* its nuclear plant.

investment decision: The decision to build, buy, or lease plants and equipment; to enter or exit an industry.

long run: A period of time long enough for all inputs to be varied (no fixed costs).

IN THE NEWS

GM SHUTTING 5 FACTORIES THIS MONTH

Detroit—GM will shut five U.S. auto assembly plants in January for periods of 1-3 weeks. Bloated inventories are the culprit: GM has 84 days of unsold new vehicles, above its target of 70 days.

Source: Media reports of January 2017.

FORT CALHOUN NUKE PLANT TO CLOSE

Omaha—The Omaha Public Power District will permanently close its nuclear plant at Fort Calhoun on October 24, according to sources inside the U.S. Nuclear Regulatory Commission. The 43-year old plant is the smallest in the United States and unable to spread its costs over enough output.

Source: Media reports of August/September 2016.

ANALYSIS: GM's decision to idle plants was a short-run *shutdown* decision; it is still in business. Omaha Power, by contrast, made a long-run decision to cease operations and *exit* a specific market.

The investment decision is of enormous importance to producers. The fixed costs that we've ignored in the production decision represent the producers' (or the stockholders') investment in the business. If they're going to avoid an economic loss, they have to generate at least enough revenue to recoup their investment—that is, the cost of (fixed) plants and equipment. Failure to do so will result in a net loss, despite allegiance to our profit-maximizing rule.

Whether fixed costs count, then, depends on the decision being made. For producers trying to decide how best to utilize the resources they've purchased or leased, fixed costs no longer enter the decision-making process. For producers deciding whether to enter business, sign a lease, or replace existing machinery and plants, fixed costs count very much. Businesspeople will proceed with an investment only if the *anticipated* profits are large enough to compensate for the effort and risk undertaken.

Long-Run Costs

When businesspeople make an investment decision, they confront not one set of cost figures but many. A plant not yet built can be designed for various rates of production and alternative technologies. In making long-run decisions, a producer isn't bound to one size of plant or to a particular mix of tools and machinery. In the long run, one can be flexible. In general, **a producer will want to build, buy, or lease a plant that's the most efficient for the anticipated rate of output.** This is the (dis)economy of scale phenomenon we discussed in the previous chapter. Once the right plant size is selected, the producer may proceed with the problem of short-run profit maximization. Once production is started, she can only hope that the investment decision was a good one and that a shutdown can be avoided.

DETERMINANTS OF SUPPLY

Whether the time frame is the short run or the long run, the central force in production decisions is the quest for profits. Producers will go into production—incur fixed costs—only if they see the potential for economic profits. Once in business, they'll expand the rate of output so long as profits are increasing. They'll shut down—cease production—when revenues don't at least cover variable costs (operating loss exceeds fixed costs).

Nearly anyone could make money with these principles if given complete information on costs and revenues. What renders the road to fortune less congested is the general absence of such complete information. In the real world, production decisions involve considerably more risk. People often don't know how much profit or loss they'll incur until it's too late to alter production decisions. Consequently, businesspeople are compelled to make a reasoned guess about prices and costs, then proceed. By way of summary, we can identify the major influences that will shape their short- and long-run decisions on how much output to supply to the market.

Short-Run Determinants

A competitive firm's short-run production decisions are dominated by marginal costs. Hence the quantity of a good supplied will be affected by all forces that alter MC. Specifically, **the determinants of a firm's supply include**

- *The price of factor inputs.*
- *Technology* (the available production function).
- *Expectations* (for costs, sales, technology).
- *Taxes and subsidies.*

Each determinant affects a producer's ability and willingness to supply output at any particular price.

The price of factor inputs determines how much the producer must pay for resources used in production. Technology determines how much output the producer will get from each unit of input. Expectations are critical because they express producers' perceptions of

FIGURE 22.11

A Competitive Firm's Short-Run Supply Curve

For competitive firms, marginal cost defines the lowest price a firm will accept for a given quantity of output. In this sense, the marginal cost curve *is* the supply curve; it tells us how quantity supplied will respond to price. At $p = \$13$, the quantity supplied is 4; at $p = \$9$, the quantity supplied is 3.

Recall, however, that the firm will shut down if price falls below minimum average variable cost. The supply curve does not exist below minimum AVC ($5 in this case).

supply curve: A curve describing the quantities of a good a producer is willing and able to sell (produce) at alternative prices in a given time period, *ceteris paribus*.

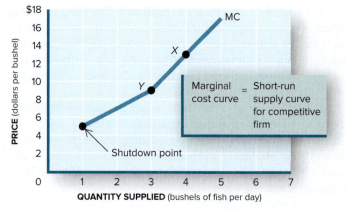

what future costs, prices, sales, and profits are likely to be. And finally, taxes and subsidies may alter costs or the amount of profit a firm gets to keep.

The Short-Run Supply Curve. By using the familiar *ceteris paribus* assumption, we can isolate the effect of price on supply decisions. In other words, we can draw a short-run **supply curve** the same way we earlier constructed consumer demand curves. In this case, the forces we assume constant are input prices, technology, expectations, and taxes. The only variable we allow to change is the price of the product itself.

Figure 22.11 illustrates the response of quantity supplied to a change in price. Notice the critical role of marginal costs: *the marginal cost curve is the short-run supply curve for a competitive firm.* Recall our basic profit maximization rule. A competitive producer wants to supply a good only if its price exceeds its marginal cost. Hence marginal cost defines the lower limit for an "acceptable" price. A catfish farmer is willing and able to produce 4 bushels per day only if the price of a bushel is $13 (point *X*). If the price of catfish dropped to $9, the *quantity* supplied would fall to 3 (point *Y*). The marginal cost curve tells us what the quantity supplied would be at all other prices as well. As long as price exceeds minimum AVC (the shutdown point), the MC curve summarizes the response of a producer to price changes: it *is* the short-run supply curve of a perfectly competitive firm.

The shape of the marginal cost curve provides a basic foundation for the *law of supply*. Because marginal costs tend to rise as output expands, an increase in output makes sense only if the price of that output rises. If the price does rise, it's profitable to increase the quantity supplied.

Supply Shifts

All the forces that shape the short-run supply curve are subject to change. Factor prices change; technology changes; expectations change; and tax laws get revised. *If any determinant of supply changes, the supply curve shifts.*

An increase in wage rates, for example, would raise the marginal cost of producing catfish. This would shift the supply curve upward, making it more expensive for producers to supply larger quantities at any given price. An increase in the price of catfish feed has the same effect. Farmed catfish are fed pellets made of corn and soybean meal. Between 2010 and 2012, feed prices rose from $350 a ton to more than $450 a ton. This cost spike squeezed profit margins and forced catfish farmers to reduce production dramatically, as Figure 22.12 illustrates.

An improvement in technology would have the opposite effect. By increasing productivity, new technology lowers the marginal cost of producing a good. The supply curve shifts downward.

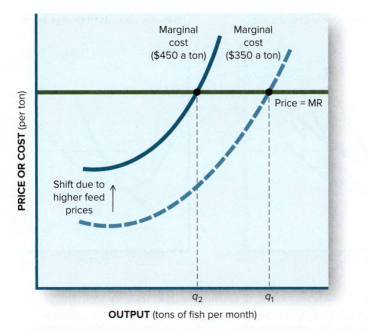

PRICE OR COST (per ton)

Marginal cost ($450 a ton)

Marginal cost ($350 a ton)

Price = MR

Shift due to higher feed prices

q_2 q_1

OUTPUT (tons of fish per month)

FIGURE 22.12

Rising MC Reduces Desired Output

An increase in feed prices (unit costs) shifts upward the marginal cost curve of a catfish farmer. That shift reduces the profit-maximizing rate of output from q_1 to q_2.

THE ECONOMY TOMORROW

TAXING BUSINESS

Changes in taxes will also alter supply behavior. But not all taxes have the same effect; some alter short-run supply behavior, whereas others affect only long-run supply decisions.

Property Taxes. Property taxes are levied by local governments on land and buildings. The tax rate is typically some small fraction (e.g., 1 percent) of total value. Hence the owner of a $10 million factory might have to pay $100,000 per year in property taxes.

Property taxes have to be paid regardless of whether the factory is used. Hence *property taxes are a fixed cost* for the firm. These additional fixed costs increase total costs and thus shift the average total cost (ATC) upward, as in Figure 22.13*a*.

Notice that the MC curve doesn't move when property taxes are imposed. Property taxes aren't based on the quantity of output produced. Accordingly, the production decision of the firm isn't affected by property taxes. The quantity q_1 in Figure 22.13*a* remains the optimal rate of output even after a property tax is introduced.

Although the optimal output remains at q_1, the profitability of the firm is reduced by the property tax. Profit per unit has been reduced by the upward shift of the ATC curve. If property taxes reduce profits too much, firms may move to a low-tax jurisdiction or another industry (investment decisions).

Payroll Taxes. Payroll taxes have very different effects on business decisions. Payroll taxes are levied on the wages paid by the firm. Employers must pay, for example, a 7.65 percent Social Security tax on the wages they pay (employees pay an identical amount). This tax is used to finance Social Security retirement benefits. Other payroll taxes are levied by federal and state governments to finance unemployment and disability benefits.

All payroll taxes add to the cost of hiring labor. In the absence of a tax, a worker might cost the firm $8 per hour. Once Social Security and other taxes are levied, the cost of labor increases to $8 plus the amount of tax. Hence $8-per-hour labor might end up costing the firm $9 or more. In other words, *payroll taxes increase marginal costs*. This is illustrated in Figure 22.13*b* by the upward shift of the MC curve.

Continued

(a) Property taxes affect fixed costs but not marginal costs.

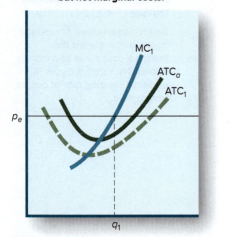

(b) Payroll taxes alter marginal costs.

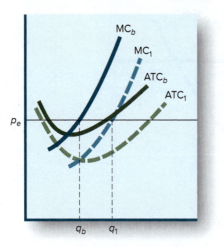

(c) Profits taxes don't change costs.

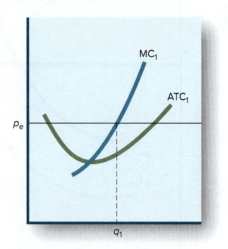

FIGURE 22.13

Impact of Taxes on Business Decisions

(a) **Property taxes** are a fixed cost for the firm. Since they don't affect marginal costs, they leave the optimal rate of output (q_1) unchanged. Property taxes raise average costs, however, and so reduce profits. Lower profits may alter investment decisions.

(b) **Payroll taxes** add directly to marginal costs and so reduce the optimal rate of output (to q_b). Payroll taxes also increase average costs and lower total and per-unit profits.

(c) **Taxes on profits** are neither a fixed cost nor a variable cost since they depend on the existence of profits. They don't affect marginal costs or price and so leave the optimal rate of output (q_1) unchanged. By reducing after-tax profits, however, such taxes lessen incentives to invest.

Notice how payroll taxes change the production decision. The new MC curve (MC_b) intersects the price line at a lower rate of output (q_b). Thus payroll taxes tend to reduce output and employment.

Profits Taxes. Taxes are also levied on the profits of a business. Such taxes are very different from either property or payroll taxes since profit taxes are paid only when profits are made. Thus they are neither a fixed cost nor a variable cost! As Figure 22.13c indicates, neither the MC nor the ATC curve moves when a profits tax is imposed. The only difference is that the firm now gets to keep less of its profits, instead "sharing" its profits with the government.

Although a profits tax has no direct effect on marginal or average costs, it does reduce the take-home (after-tax) profits of a business. This may reduce investments in new businesses. For this reason, many people urge the government to reduce corporate tax rates and so encourage increased investment. President Trump made a reduction in the corporate income tax rate a centerpiece of his economic programs.

SUMMARY

- Economic profit is the difference between total revenue and total cost. Total economic cost includes the value (opportunity cost) of *all* inputs used in production, not just those inputs for which an explicit payment is made. **LO22-1**

- A perfectly competitive firm is a *price taker*. It sells its output at the prevailing market price. It effectively confronts a horizontal demand for its output (even though the *market* demand for the product is downward-sloping). **LO22-2**

- Competitive firms don't make pricing decisions, only production decisions. **LO22-2**
- The short-run objective of a firm is to maximize profits from the operation of its existing facilities (fixed costs). For a competitive firm, the profit-maximizing output occurs at the point where marginal cost equals price (marginal revenue). **LO22-3**
- A firm may incur a loss even at the optimal rate of output. It shouldn't shut down, however, so long as price exceeds average *variable* cost. If revenues at least cover variable costs, the firm's operating loss is less than its fixed costs. **LO22-4**
- In the long run there are no fixed costs, and the firm may choose any-sized plant it wants. The decision to incur fixed costs (i.e., build, buy, or lease a plant) or to enter or exit an industry is an investment decision. **LO22-5**

- A competitive firm's supply curve is identical to its marginal cost curve (above the shutdown point at minimum average variable cost). In the short run, the quantity supplied will rise or fall with price. **LO22-6**
- The determinants of supply include the price of inputs, technology, taxes, and expectations. Should any of these determinants change, the firm's supply curve will shift. **LO22-6**
- Business taxes alter business behavior. Property taxes raise fixed costs; payroll taxes increase marginal costs. Profits taxes raise neither fixed costs nor marginal costs but diminish the take-home (after-tax) profits of a business. **LO22-6**

Key Terms

profit	perfect competition	marginal cost (MC)
economic cost	market power	marginal revenue (MR)
explicit cost	competitive firm	profit-maximization rule
implicit cost	production decision	shutdown point
economic profit	total revenue	investment decision
normal profit	short run	long run
monopoly	fixed costs	supply curve
market structure	variable costs	

Questions for Discussion

1. What economic costs will a large corporation likely overlook when computing its profits? How about the owner of a family-run business or farm? **LO22-1**
2. How can the demand curve facing a firm be horizontal if the market demand curve is downward-sloping? **LO22-2**
3. How many fish should a commercial fisher try to catch in a day? Should he catch as many as possible or return to dock before filling the boat with fish? Under what economic circumstances should he not even take the boat out? **LO22-3**
4. If a firm is incurring an economic loss, would society be better off if the firm shut down? Would the firm want to shut down? Explain. **LO22-4**
5. Why isn't the rate of output that minimizes average total cost the most profitable rate of output? **LO22-3**
6. What rate of output is appropriate for a nonprofit corporation (such as a hospital)? **LO22-3**
7. What costs did GM eliminate when it shut down its plants? (In the News "GM Shutting 5 Factories this Month") How about Omaha Power? **LO22-4**
8. What was the opportunity cost of Hiroshi Fujishige's farm? (See In the News "The Value of Hiro's Strawberry Farm") Is society better off with another Disney theme park? Explain. **LO22-1**
9. Is Apple Computer a perfectly competitive firm? **LO22-2**
10. If a perfectly competitive firm raises its price above the prevailing market rate, how much of its sales might it lose? Why? Can a competitive firm ever raise its prices? If so, when? **LO22-2**
11. Under what conditions would a firm decide to shut down in the short run but remain invested in the market in the long run? **LO22-5**
12. How does an employer-paid Social Security tax on wages affect a competitive firm's supply curve? **LO22-6**

PROBLEMS FOR CHAPTER 22

LO22-2 1. According to In the News "The Lure of Catfish,"
   (a) How many fish did farmer Hollingsworth have in inventory?
   (b) If each of his fish weighed 2 pounds, what percent of the market did he have?

LO22-1 2. If the owner of the Table 22.1 drugstore hired a manager for $10 an hour to take his place, how much of a change would show up in:
   (a) Accounting profits?   (b) Economic profits?

LO22-1 3. Kanesha is an entrepreneur and has recently opened her first coffee shop, The Coffee Cat. Kanesha pays $5000 rent each month, $4800 for employee payroll, and $1200 for supplies. She was planning on selling several of her own tables and chairs on Craigslist for $1500, but instead she brought them to The Coffee Cat. Additionally, Kanesha quit working as an accountant where she was earning $52,000 per year to open up the shop. If the shop earns $180,000 in revenue this year, calculate annual:
   (a) Accounting profit.   (b) Economic profit.

LO22-1 4. If the price of catfish fell from $13 to $7 per bushel, use Figure 22.7 to determine the
   (a) Profit-maximizing output.   (c) Total profit or loss.
   (b) Profit or loss per bushel.

LO22-2 5. Complete the following cost and revenue schedules:

Quantity	Price	Total Revenue	Total Cost	Marginal Cost
0	$50	_____	$ 50	_____
1	50	_____	60	_____
2	50	_____	90	_____
3	50	_____	140	_____
4	50	_____	200	_____
5	50	_____	280	_____

   (a) Graph MC and p.
   (b) What rate of output maximizes profit?
   (c) What is MC at that rate of output?

LO22-2 6. Complete the following cost schedules:

Quantity	0	1	2	3	4	5	6	7
Total cost	$9	$12	$16	$21	$30	$40	$52	$66
ATC	___	___	___	___	___	___	___	___
MC	–	___	___	___	___	___	___	___

Assuming the price of this product is $12, at what output rate is
   (a) Total revenue maximized?   (c) Profit per unit maximized?
   (b) ATC minimized?   (d) Total profit maximized?

LO22-3 7. Assume that the price of silk ties in a perfectly competitive market is $21 and that the typical firm confronts the following costs:

Quantity (ties per day)	0	1	2	3	4	5	6	7	8	9	10
Total cost	$10	$17	$26	$37	$50	$65	$82	$101	$122	$145	$170

   (a) What is the profit-maximizing rate of output for the firm?
   (b) How much profit does the firm earn at that rate of output?
   (c) If the price of ties fell to $15, how many ties should the firm produce?
   (d) At what price should the firm shut down?

LO22-6 8. Illustrate on the accompanying graph the changes to the cost curves due to
    (*a*) Higher feed prices.   (*c*) Higher worker productivity.
    (*b*) Lower wage rates.

    Does the profit-maximizing rate of output increase, decrease, or
    stay the same with
    (*d*) Higher feed prices?   (*f*) Higher worker productivity?
    (*e*) Lower wage rates?

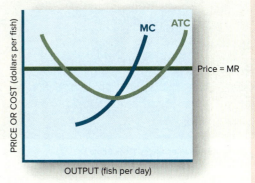

LO22-4 9. Complete the following table:

Output	Total Cost	Marginal Cost	Average Total Cost	Average Variable Cost
0	$100	_____	_____	_____
5	110	_____	_____	_____
10	130	_____	_____	_____
15	170	_____	_____	_____
20	220	_____	_____	_____
25	290	_____	_____	_____
30	380	_____	_____	_____
35	490	_____	_____	_____

    According to the table above,
    (*a*) If the price is $50, how much output will the firm supply?   (*c*) At what price will the firm shut down?
    (*b*) How much profit or loss will it make?

LO22-5 10. A firm has leased plant and equipment to produce video games, which can be sold in unlimited
    quantities at $13 each. The following figures describe the associated costs of production:

Rate of output (per day)	0	1	2	3	4	5	6	7	8
Total cost (per day)	$50	$55	$62	$75	$96	$125	$162	$203	$248

    (*a*) How much are fixed costs?
    (*b*) Draw total revenue and cost curves on the graphs.
    (*c*) Draw the average total cost (ATC), marginal cost (MC), and demand curves of the firm.
    (*d*) What is the profit-maximizing rate of output?
    (*e*) Calculate profits or losses at this profit-maximizing rate of output.
    (*f*) How much is lost if the firm shuts down?
    (*g*) Should the firm produce or shut down in the short run?

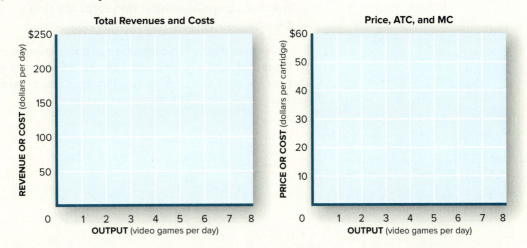

LO22-6 11. The Economy Tomorrow: Using the data from Problem 7 (at the original price of $21), determine
    how many ties the producer would supply if
    (*a*) A tax of $2 per tie were collected from the producer.   (*c*) Profits were taxed at 50 percent.
    (*b*) A property tax of $2 were levied.

©David A. Barnes/Alamy Stock Photo

23

Competitive Markets

Catfish farmers in the South are very upset. They invested millions of dollars converting cotton farms into breeding ponds for catfish. At its peak, the catfish industry employed more than 15,000 workers and produced nearly $500 million of fish per year. But those days are long gone. First catfish farmers in the South had to contend with rising competition from Vietnamese and Chinese imports. That competition put a lid on catfish prices. Then feed prices spiked in 2010–2012, raising production costs. This combination of constrained prices and rising costs killed profits. With losses mounting, a lot of farmers got out of the catfish business, filling their ponds with dirt and planting soybeans instead (see the World View "Catfish Farmers Draining Their Ponds").

The dilemma catfish farmers find themselves in is a familiar occurrence in competitive markets. When profits look good, everybody wants to get in on the act. As more and more firms start producing the good, prices and profits tumble. This helps explain why more than 200,000 new firms are formed each year and why more than 50,000 others fail.

This chapter focuses on the behavior of competitive markets. We have three principal questions:

- **How are prices determined in competitive markets?**
- **How does competition affect the profits of a firm or industry?**
- **What does society gain from market competition?**

The answers to these questions will reveal how markets work when all producers are relatively small and lack market power. In subsequent chapters we emphasize how market outcomes change when markets are less competitive.

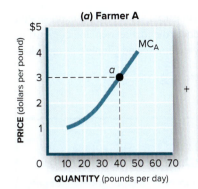
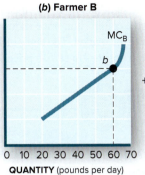
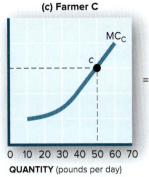
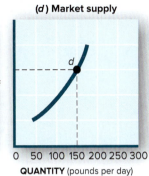

FIGURE 23.1

Competitive Market Supply

A Firm's Supply. The portion of the MC curve that lies above AVC is a competitive firm's short-run supply curve. The curve MC$_A$ tells us that Farmer A will produce 40 pounds of catfish per day if the market price is $3 per pound.

Market Supply. To determine the *market* supply, we add up the quantities supplied at each price by every farmer. The total quantity supplied to the market at the price of $3 is 150 pounds per day (*a* + *b* + *c*). Market supply depends on the number of firms and their respective marginal costs.

THE MARKET SUPPLY CURVE

In the previous chapter we examined the supply behavior of a perfectly competitive firm. The perfectly competitive firm is a price taker. It *responds* to the market price by producing that rate of output where marginal cost equals price.

But what about the *market* supply of catfish? We need a market supply curve to determine the **equilibrium price** the individual farmer will confront. In the previous chapter we simply drew a market supply curve arbitrarily to establish a market price. Now our objective is to find out where that **market supply** curve comes from.

Like the market supply curves we first encountered in Chapter 3, we can calculate the market supply of catfish by simple addition. All we have to do is add up the quantities each of America's 1,000 catfish farmers stands ready to supply at each price. Then we'll know the total quantity of fish to be supplied to the market at that price.

Remember the critical role that **marginal cost** plays in the production decision of the competitive firm. As we saw in the previous chapter, a competitive firm will produce where MC = *p*. So, the firm's MC curve is in effect its supply curve. If we know what the MC curves of the firms in an industry look like, we can compute the *market* supply. Figure 23.1 illustrates this summation. Notice that *the market supply curve is the sum of the marginal cost curves of all the firms.* Hence whatever determines the marginal cost of a typical firm will also affect industry supply. Specifically, *the market supply of a competitive industry is determined by*

- *The price of factor inputs.*
- *Technology.*
- *Expectations.*
- *Taxes and subsidies.*
- *The number of firms in the industry.*

Entry and Exit

If more firms enter an industry, the market supply curve will shift to the right. This is the problem confronting the catfish farmers in Mississippi (see World View "Catfish Farmers Draining Their Ponds"). It's fairly inexpensive to get into the catfish business: you can start with a pond, some breeding stock, and relatively little capital equipment. These **investment decisions** shift

equilibrium price: The price at which the quantity of a good demanded in a given time period equals the quantity supplied.

market supply: The total quantities of a good that sellers are willing and able to sell at alternative prices in a given time period, *ceteris paribus.*

marginal cost (MC): The increase in total cost associated with a one-unit increase in production.

investment decision: The decision to build, buy, or lease plants and equipment; to enter or exit an industry.

the market supply curve to the right and drive down catfish prices. This process is illustrated in Figure 23.2a. Notice how the equilibrium price slides down the market demand curve from E_1 to E_2 when more firms enter the market. The entry of Vietnamese and Chinese farmers into the catfish market caused steep declines in catfish prices.

WORLD VIEW

CATFISH FARMERS DRAINING THEIR PONDS

Catfish farming used to look good. So good, in fact, that hundreds of crop farmers stopped growing corn and soybeans, choosing instead to dig catfish ponds on their land. It was the "gold rush" for Southern farmers. Catfish production skyrocketed from 340 million pounds in 1989 to a peak of 662 million pounds in 2003.

Since then, it's been all bad news. A surge in imported catfish has sent prices for processed catfish spiraling down. At the same time, feed prices—primarily a mix of corn and soybeans—have jumped from $250 a ton in 2006 to $440 a ton this year. Dozens of catfish operators are draining their ponds in order to plant row crops.

Source: Media reports, Fall 2008.

ANALYSIS: When economic profits exist in an industry, more producers try to enter. As they do, prices and economic profits decline. When losses are incurred, firms begin to exit the industry.

If prices fall too far, profits will disappear. Indeed, profits will turn into losses if the market price falls below a farmer's minimum average total cost. When this happens, some farmers will drain their ponds and plant soybeans instead (see In the News "U.S. Catfish Industry Bleeding Finally Stops"). When they do so, they are *exiting* the catfish business and *entering* the soybean business. These exits will shift the market supply curve a bit to the left, helping to stabilize catfish prices and "stop the bleeding" in the industry.

(a) Market entry pushes price down and . . .

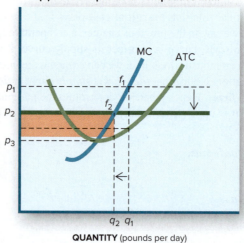

(b) Reduces profits of competitive firm.

FIGURE 23.2

Market Entry

If economic profits exist in an industry, more firms will want to enter it. As they do, the market supply curve will shift to the right and cause the market price to drop from p_1 to p_2 (part a).

The lower market price, in turn, will reduce the output and profits of the typical firm. In part b, the firm's output falls from q_1 to q_2.

U.S. CATFISH INDUSTRY BLEEDING FINALLY STOPS

Years of doom and gloom trends in the U.S. catfish industry are finally coming to an end as the industry stops losing its major companies to soybean farming.

"We've lost 50% of our farms, but I believe we've reached a point where the loss in the industry has stopped," Jack Perkins, vice president of sales and marketing for Consolidated Catfish, told *Undercurrent News*.

He estimates the industry will produce the same amount of catfish this year as it did last year, at 300 million pounds.

"Hopefully we'll see 2014 and beyond as an industry recovery time," Perkins said.

There is much to recover from, considering the past few years, [when] catfish farmers realized that converting their catfish farms to soybean farms—which is completely viable—was a better business prospect, and little by little the industry has shrunk.

Plus, staying in the industry is becoming more attractive, considering the price improvements.

Right now, prices [are] at the high level of $4 to $4.25 per pound for wholesale for fillets, which is the same price as last year at this time but a significant jump from last fall.

Stewart, Jeanine, "U.S. Catfish Industry Bleeding Finally Stops," *UnderCurrentNews,* July 3, 2013. Copyright ©2013. All rights reserved. Used with permission.

ANALYSIS: Loss-driven exits shift the market supply curve left and help stabilize prices at their long-term equilibrium, at which point net entry and exit cease.

Tendency toward Zero Profits

The profit motive drives these entry and exit decisions. Ten years ago catfish farming looked a whole lot more profitable than cotton farming. Farmers responded by flooding their cotton fields to create fish ponds; they *exited* the cotton business and *entered* the catfish industry.

The resulting shift of market supply caused the **economic profits** in catfish farming to disappear. Notice in Figure 23.2b how total profits for the typical firm shrink when price is driven down from p_1 to p_2. If price continued to fall, profits would shrink further. Indeed, if price declines to p_3, profits disappear.

When profits disappear (at the price p_3 in Figure 23.2b) there is no incentive to *enter* the industry. Were price to fall still further—below p_3—the typical catfish farmer would actually be losing money. That would motivate some farmers to *exit* the industry—planting soybeans instead of feeding fish. Eventually, price will settle at p_3, where economic profit is zero. **When economic profit disappears, entry and exit cease and the market stabilizes.** According to In the News "U.S. Catfish Industry Bleeding Finally Stops," this is exactly what has happened in the catfish industry. At this new equilibrium, catfish farmers earn only a normal (average) rate of return.

Catfish farmers would be happier, of course, if the price of catfish didn't decline to the point where economic profits disappear. But how are they going to prevent it? Keith King evidently knows all about the laws of supply and demand (see World View "Catfish Farmers Draining Their Ponds"). He would dearly like to keep all those Vietnamese and Chinese catfish out of this country. He also wishes those farmers in Maine would keep cranberries in their ponds rather than catfish. Keith would also like to get other farmers in the South to slow production a little before all the profits disappear. But King is powerless to stop the forces of a **competitive market.** He can't even afford to reduce his *own* catfish production. Even though he has 200 acres of ponds, nobody would notice the resulting drop in market supplies, and catfish prices would continue to slide. The only one affected would be King, who'd be denying himself the opportunity to share in the (dwindling) fortunes of the catfish market while they lasted.

economic profit: The difference between total revenues and total economic costs.

competitive market: A market in which no buyer or seller has market power.

King's dilemma goes a long way toward explaining why catfish farming isn't highly profitable. Whenever the profit picture looks good, everybody tries to get in on the action. This kind of pressure on prices and profits is a fundamental characteristic of competitive markets. *As long as it's easy for existing producers to expand production or for new firms to enter an industry, economic profits won't last long.*

Low Barriers to Entry

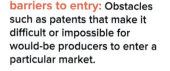

barriers to entry: Obstacles such as patents that make it difficult or impossible for would-be producers to enter a particular market.

New producers will be able to enter a profitable industry and help drive down prices and profits as long as they don't encounter significant barriers. Such **barriers to entry** may include patents, control of essential factors of production, control of distribution outlets, well-established brand loyalty, or even governmental regulation. All such barriers make it expensive, risky, or impossible for new firms to enter an industry. In the absence of such barriers, new firms can enter an industry more readily and at less risk. Not surprisingly, firms already entrenched in a profitable industry do their best to keep out newcomers by erecting barriers to entry. Unfortunately for Keith King, there are few barriers to entering the catfish business; all you need to get started is a pond and a few fish. Recall the Calvin Jones quote from Chapter 22: "You raise fish. You get them out of the pond and you sell them. There's no genius to it."

Market Characteristics of Perfect Competition

This brief review of catfish economics illustrates a few general observations about the structure, behavior, and outcomes of a competitive market:

- *Many firms.* A competitive market includes a great many firms, none of which has a significant share of total output.
- *Identical products.* Products are homogeneous. One firm's product is the same as any other firm's product.
- *Perfect information.* All buyers and sellers have complete information on available supply, demand, and prices.
- *MC = p.* All competitive firms will seek to expand output until marginal cost equals price, much as price and marginal revenue are identical for such firms.
- *Low barriers.* Barriers to enter the industry are low. If economic profits are available, more firms will enter the industry.
- *Zero economic profit.* The tendency of production and market supplies to expand when profit is high puts heavy pressures on prices and profits in competitive industries. Economic profit will approach zero in the long run as prices are driven down to the level of average production costs.

COMPETITION AT WORK: MICROCOMPUTERS

Few markets have all the characteristics just listed. That is, *few, if any, product markets are perfectly competitive.* However, many industries function much like the competitive model we sketched out. In addition to catfish farming, most other agricultural product markets are characterized by highly competitive market structures, with hundreds or even thousands of producers supplying the market. Other highly competitive, and hence not very profitable, businesses are T-shirt shops, laundromats, retail food, printing, clothing manufacturing and retailing, dry-cleaning establishments, beauty salons, and furniture. Online stockbroker services have also become highly competitive. In these markets, prices and profits are always under the threat of expanded supplies brought to market by existing or new producers.

The electronics industry offers numerous examples of how competition reduces prices and profits. Between 1972 and 1983, the price of small, handheld calculators fell from $200 to under $10. The price of digital watches fell even more dramatically, from roughly $2,000 in 1975 to under $7 in 1990. Videocassette recorders (VCRs) that sold for $2,000 in 1979 now sell for less than $30. DVD players that cost $1,500 in 1997 now sell for under $50. Cell phones that sold for $1,000 ten years ago are now given away. The same kind of competitive pressures have reduced the price of flat-screen TVs. New entrants keep bringing better TVs to market while driving prices down (see World View "Flat Panels, Thin Margins").

WORLD VIEW

FLAT PANELS, THIN MARGINS

The TVs keep getting bigger and better. Best Buy, Target, and Costco offer an almost bewildering array of TVs. The typical consumer has a difficult time deciphering the pixel counts, the varying sizes, and the myriad features of the many TV brands on display. But one thing is crystal clear: the prices keep coming down (see chart). In fact, industry experts say there is never a "right time" to buy a TV because TVs will be better and cheaper a couple of months later.

Brutal competition keeps pushing prices down and innovation up. In the last five years alone the number of LCD brands for sale in U.S. stores increased fourfold, from 26 to 102. Parts manufacturers in China, Mexico, and Taiwan make it easy to get into the industry. They will sell the needed parts to anyone—and even assemble all the pieces if asked. So, anyone with connections to big retailers can create an instant brand and get into TV retailing. At a lower price, of course.

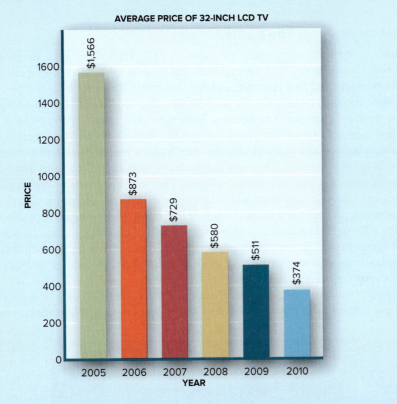

AVERAGE PRICE OF 32-INCH LCD TV

Year	Price
2005	$1,566
2006	$873
2007	$729
2008	$580
2009	$511
2010	$374

Source: Industry reports (2007–2010).

ANALYSIS: Competitive pressures compel producers of flat-panel TVs to keep improving the product and reducing prices. The lure of profits encourages firms to enter this expanding market even as prices drop.

The driving force behind all these price reductions and quality improvements is *competition*. Do you really believe the price of phone calls would be falling if only one firm supplied all telephone services? Do you think thousands of software writers would be toiling away right now if popular programs didn't generate enormous profits? Would Apple, Amazon, and Uber keep rolling out new products and services if other companies weren't always snapping at their heels?

Market Evolution

To appreciate how the process of competition works, we will examine the development of the personal computer industry. *As in other industries, the market structure of the computer industry has evolved over time. It was never a monopoly, nor was it ever perfect competition.* In its first couple of years it was dominated by only a few companies (like Apple) that were enormously successful. The high profits the early microcomputer producers obtained attracted swarms of imitators. More than 250 firms entered the microcomputer industry between 1976 and 1983 in search of high profits. The entry of so many firms transformed the industry's market structure: the industry became *more* competitive, even though not *perfectly* competitive. The increased competition pushed prices downward and improved the product. When prices and profits tumbled, scores of companies went bankrupt. They left a legacy, however, of a vastly larger market, much improved computers, and sharply lower prices.

We'll use the early experiences of the microcomputer industry to illustrate the key behavioral features of a competitive market. As we'll see, many of these competitive features are still at work in the markets for Internet services, content software, digital music, smartphones, ride sharing, cloud storage, and 4K television sets.

Initial Conditions: The Apple I

The microcomputer industry really got started in 1977. Prior to that time, microcomputers were essentially a hobby item for engineers and programmers, who bought circuits, keyboards, monitors, and tape recorders and then assembled their own basic computers. Steve Jobs, then working at Atari, and Steven Wozniak, then working at Hewlett-Packard, were among these early computer enthusiasts. They spent their days working on large systems and their nights and weekends trying to put together small computers from mail-order parts.

Eventually, Jobs and Wozniak decided they had the capability to build commercially attractive small computers. They ordered the parts necessary for building 100 computers and set up shop in the garage of Jobs's parents. Their finished product—the Apple I—was nothing more than a circuit board with a simple, built-in operating system. This first microcomputer was packaged in a wooden box (see the photo). Despite primitive characteristics, the first 100 Apple I computers sold out immediately. This quick success convinced Jobs and Wozniak to package their computers more fully—which they did by enclosing them in plastic housing—and to offer more of them for sale. Shortly thereafter, in January 1977, Apple Computer Inc. was established.

Apple revolutionized the market by offering a preassembled desktop computer with attractive features and an accessible price. The impact on the marketplace was much like

Analysis: The Apple I pictured here launched the personal computer industry in 1976. Hundreds of firms entered the industry to improve on this first preassembled microcomputer. This competition transformed the industry, the product, and prices.

©Kim Kulish/Corbis via Getty Images

that of Henry Ford's early Model T: suddenly a newfangled piece of technology came into reach of the average U.S. household, and everybody, it seemed, wanted one. The first mass-produced Apple computer—called the Apple II—was just a basic keyboard with an operating system that permitted users to write their own programs. The computer had no disk drive, no monitor, and only 4K of random access memory (RAM). Consumers had to use their TV sets as screens and audiocassettes for data storage. This primitive Apple II was priced at just under $1,300 when it debuted in June 1977. Apple was producing computers at the rate of 500 per month.

Apple didn't engineer or manufacture chips or semiconductor components. Instead it simply packaged existing components purchased from outside suppliers (much like TV brands do, see World View "Flat Panels, Thin Margins"). Hence it was easy for other companies to follow Apple's lead. Within a very brief time, other firms, such as Tandy (Radio Shack), also started to assemble computers. By the middle of 1978, the basic small computer was selling for $1,000, and industry sales were about 20,000 a month. Figure 23.3a depicts the initial (1978) equilibrium in the computer market, and Figure 23.3b illustrates the approximate costs of production for the typical computer manufacturer at that time.

The Production Decision

The short-run goal of every producer is to find the rate of output that maximizes profits. Finding this rate entails making the best possible **production decision.** In this short-run context, *each competitive firm seeks the rate of output at which marginal cost equals price.*

production decision: The selection of the short-run rate of output (with existing plants and equipment).

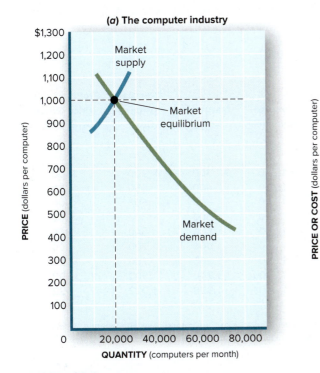
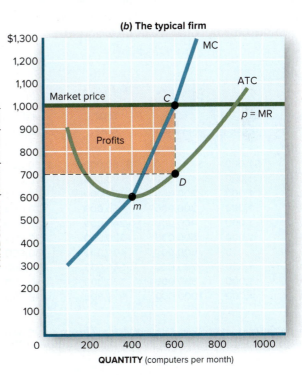

FIGURE 23.3

Initial Equilibrium in the Computer Market

(a) The Industry. In 1978 the market price of microcomputers was $1,000. This price was established by the intersection of the market supply and demand curves.

(b) A Firm. Each competitive producer in the market sought to produce computers at that rate (600 per month) where marginal cost equaled price (point C). Profit per computer was equal to price (point C) minus average total cost (point D). Total profits for the typical firm are indicated by the shaded rectangle.

Figure 23.3b illustrates the cost and price curves the typical computer producer confronted in 1978. As in most lines of production, the marginal costs of computer production increased with the rate of output. Marginal costs rose in part because output could be increased in the short run (with existing plants and equipment) only by crowding additional workers onto the assembly line. In 1978 Apple had only 10,000 square feet of manufacturing space. As more workers were hired, each worker had less capital and land to work with, and marginal physical product fell. The law of diminishing returns pushed marginal costs up.

The upward-sloping marginal cost curve intersected the price line at an output level of 600 computers per month (point C in Figure 23.3b). That was the profit-maximizing rate of output (MC = p) for the typical manufacturer. Manufacturing any more than 600 computers per month would raise marginal costs over price and reduce total profits. Manufacturing any fewer would be passing up an opportunity to make another buck.

Profit Calculations

Table 23.1 shows how much *profit* a typical computer manufacturer was making in 1978. As the "total profit" column indicates, the typical computer manufacturer could make a real killing in the computer market, reaping a monthly profit of $180,000 by producing and selling 600 microcomputers.

We could also calculate the computer manufacturers' profits by asking how much the manufacturers make on *each* computer and then multiplying that figure by total output:

average total cost (ATC):
Total cost divided by the quantity produced in a given time period.

$$\text{Total profit} = \text{Profit per unit} \times \text{Quantity sold}$$

We can compute these profits by studying the first and last columns in Table 23.1 or by using a little geometry in Figure 23.3b. In the figure, average costs (total costs divided by the rate of output) are portrayed by the **average total cost (ATC)** curve. At the output rate of

Output per Month	Price	Total Revenue	Total Cost	Total Profit	Marginal Revenue*	Marginal Cost*	Average Total Cost	Profit per Unit (Price Minus Average Cost)
0	$1,000	$ 0	$ 60,000	−$ 60,000	—	—	—	—
100	1,000	100,000	90,000	10,000	$1,000	$ 300	$ 900	$100
200	1,000	200,000	130,000	70,000	1,000	400	650	350
300	1,000	300,000	180,000	120,000	1,000	500	600	400
400	1,000	400,000	240,000	160,000	1,000	600	600	400
500	1,000	500,000	320,000	180,000	1,000	800	640	360
600	1,000	600,000	420,000	180,000	1,000	1,000	700	300
700	1,000	700,000	546,000	154,000	1,000	1,260	780	220
800	1,000	800,000	720,000	80,000	1,000	1,740	900	100
900	1,000	900,000	919,800	−19,800	1,000	1,998	1,022	−22

*Note that output levels are calibrated in hundreds in this example; that's why we have divided the *change* in total costs and revenues from one output level to another by 100 to calculate marginal revenue and marginal cost. Very few manufacturers deal in units of 1.

TABLE 23.1

Computer Revenues, Costs, and Profits

Producers seek that rate of output where total profit is maximized. This table illustrates the output choices the typical computer producer faced in 1978. The profit-maximizing rate of output occurred at 600 computers per month. At that rate of output, marginal cost was equal to price ($1,000), and profits were $180,000 per month.

600 (the row in white in Table 23.1), the distance between the price line ($1,000 at point *C*) and the ATC curve ($700 at point *D*) is $300, which represents the average **profit per unit.** Multiplying this figure by the number of units sold (600 per month) will give us *total* profit per month. Total profits are represented by the shaded rectangle in Figure 23.3*b* and are equal to our earlier profit figure of $180,000 per month.

profit per unit: Total profit divided by the quantity produced in a given time period; price minus average total cost.

The Lure of Profits

While gaping at the computer manufacturer's enormous profits, we should remind ourselves that those profits might not last long. Indeed, the more quick-witted among us already will have seen and heard enough to know they've discovered a good thing. And in fact, the kind of profits the early microcomputer manufacturers enjoyed attracted a lot of entrepreneurial interest. *In competitive markets, economic profits attract new entrants.* This is what happened in the catfish industry and also in the computer industry. Within a very short time, a whole crowd of profit maximizers entered the microcomputer industry in hot pursuit of its fabulous profits. By the end of 1980, Apple had a lot of competition, including new entrants from IBM, Xerox, Digital Equipment, Casio, Sharp, and dozens of other start-up firms.

Low Entry Barriers

A critical feature of the microcomputer market was its lack of entry barriers. A microcomputer is little more than a box containing a microprocessor "brain," which connects to a keyboard (to enter data), a memory (to store data), and a screen (to display data). Although the microprocessors that guide the computer are extremely sophisticated, they can be purchased on the open market. Thus, to enter the computer industry, all one needs is some space, some money to buy components, and some dexterity in putting parts together. Such *low entry barriers permit new firms to enter competitive markets.* This is what facilitated competition in the flat-screen TV market (see the World View "Flat Panels, Thin Margins"). The same low entry barriers existed in computers. According to Table 23.1, the typical producer needed only $60,000 of plant and equipment (fixed costs) to get started in the microcomputer market. Jobs and Wozniak had even less when they started making Apples in their garage.

A Shift of Market Supply

Figure 23.4 shows what happened to the computer market and the profits of the typical firm once the word got out. As more and more entrepreneurs heard how profitable computer manufacturing could be, they quickly got hold of a book on electronic circuitry, rushed to the bank, got a little financing, and set up shop. Before many months had passed, scores of new firms had started producing small computers. *The entry of new firms shifts the market supply curve to the right.* In Figure 23.4*a*, the supply curve shifted from S_1 to S_2. Almost as fast as a computer can calculate a profit (loss) statement, the willingness to supply increased abruptly.

But the new computer companies were in for a bit of disappointment. With so many new firms hawking microcomputers, it became increasingly difficult to make a fast buck. The downward-sloping market demand curve confirms that a greater quantity of microcomputers could be sold only if the price of computers dropped. And drop it did. The price slide began as computer manufacturers found their inventories growing and so offered price discounts to maintain sales volume. The price fell rapidly, from $1,000 in mid-1978 to $800 in early 1980.

The sliding market price squeezed the profits of each firm, causing the profit rectangle to shrink (compare Figure 23.3*b* to Figure 23.4*b*). The lower price also changed the production decision of the typical firm. The new price ($800) intersected the unchanged MC curve at the output rate of 500 computers per month (point *G* in Figure 23.4*b*). With

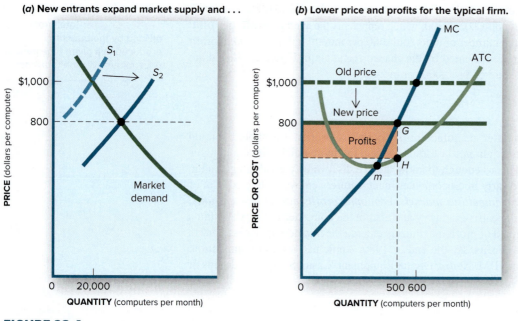

(a) New entrants expand market supply and . . .

(b) Lower price and profits for the typical firm.

FIGURE 23.4

The Competitive Price and Profit Squeeze

(a) The Industry. The economic profits in the computer industry encouraged new firms to enter the industry. As they did, the market supply curve shifted from S_1 to S_2. This rightward shift of the supply curve lowered the equilibrium price of computers.

(b) A Firm. The lower market price, in turn, forced the typical producer to reduce output to the point where MC and price were equal again (point G). At this reduced rate of output, the typical firm earned less total profit than it had earned before.

---

average production costs of $640 (Table 23.1), the firm's total profits in 1980 were only $80,000 per month [(p − ATC) × 500]. Not a paltry sum, to be sure, but nothing like the fantastic fortunes pocketed earlier.

As long as an economic profit is available, it will continue to attract new entrants. Those entrepreneurs who were a little slow in absorbing the implications of Figure 23.3 eventually woke up to what was going on and tried to get in on the action, too. Even though they were a little late, they didn't want to miss the chance to cash in on the $80,000 in monthly profits still available to the typical firm. Hence the market supply curve continued to shift, and computer prices slid further, as in Figure 23.5. This process squeezed the profits of the typical firm still more, further shrinking the profit rectangle.

short-run competitive equilibrium: $p = MC$.

As long as economic profits exist in **short-run competitive equilibrium,** that equilibrium won't last. If the rate of profit obtainable in computer production is higher than that available in other industries, new firms will enter the industry. Conversely, if the short-run equilibrium is unprofitable, firms will exit the industry. Profit-maximizing entrepreneurs have a special place in their hearts for economic profits, not computers.

long-run competitive equilibrium: $p = MC =$ minimum ATC.

Price and profit declines will cease when the price of computers equals the minimum average cost of production. At that price (point *m* in Figure 23.5b), there's no more economic profit to be squeezed out. Firms no longer have an incentive to enter the industry, and the supply curve stops shifting. This situation represents the **long-run competitive equilibrium** for the firm and for the industry. *In long-run equilibrium, entry and exit cease, and zero economic profit (that is, normal profit) prevails* (see Figure 23.6). Table 23.2 summarizes the profit-maximizing rules that bring about this long-run equilibrium.

Once a long-run equilibrium is established, it will continue until market demand shifts or technological progress reduces the cost of computer production. In fact, that's just what happened in the computer market (and in the catfish industry, per In the News "U.S. Catfish Industry Bleeding Finally Stops").

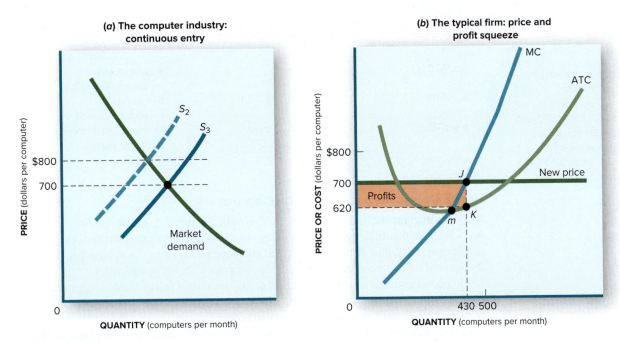

(a) The computer industry: continuous entry

(b) The typical firm: price and profit squeeze

FIGURE 23.5

The Competitive Squeeze Approaching Its Limit

(a) The Industry. Even at a price of $800 per computer, economic profits attracted still more entrepreneurs, shifting the market supply curve further (S_3). The next short-term equilibrium occurred at a price of $700 per computer.

(b) A Firm. At this reduced market price, the typical manufacturer wanted to supply only 430 computers per month (point *J*). Total profits were much lower than they had been earlier, with fewer producers and higher prices.

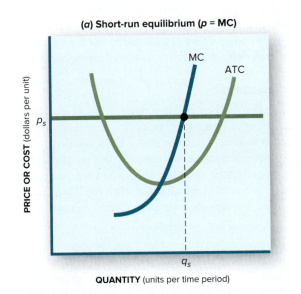

(a) Short-run equilibrium (p = MC)

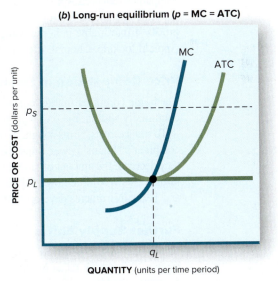

(b) Long-run equilibrium (p = MC = ATC)

FIGURE 23.6

Short- vs. Long-Run Equilibrium for the Competitive Firm

(a) Short Run. Competitive firms strive for the rate of output at which marginal cost (MC) equals price. When they achieve that rate of output, they are in *short-run equilibrium*. Whether profitable or not, there is no incentive to alter the rate of output produced with existing (fixed) plants and equipment; it is the *best* the firm can do in the short run.

(b) Long Run. If the short-run equilibrium (q_S) is profitable ($p >$ ATC), other firms will want to enter the industry. As they do, market price will fall until it reaches the level of minimum ATC. In this *long-run equilibrium* (q_L), economic profits are zero, and nobody wants to enter or exit the industry.

Price Level	Result for a Typical Firm	Market Response
$p >$ ATC	Profits	Enter industry (or expand capacity).
$p <$ ATC	Loss	Exit industry (or reduce capacity).
$p =$ ATC	Break even	Maintain existing capacity (no entry or exit).

Home Computers vs. Personal Computers

As profit margins narrowed to the levels shown in Figure 23.5, quick-thinking entrepreneurs realized that future profits would have to come from product improvements or cost reductions. By adding features to the basic microcomputer, firms could expect to increase the demand for microcomputers and fetch higher prices. On the other hand, cost reductions would permit firms to widen their profit margins at existing prices or to reduce prices and increase sales. This second strategy wouldn't require assembling more complex computers or risking consumer rejection of an upgraded product.

In late 1979 and early 1980, both product development strategies were pursued. In the process, two distinct markets were created. Microcomputers upgraded with new features came to be known as *personal* computers, or PCs. The basic unadorned computer first introduced by Apple came to be known as a *home* computer. The limited capabilities of that basic home computer greatly restricted its usefulness to simple household record keeping, games, and elementary programming.

Apple chose the personal computer route. It started enlarging the memory of the Apple II in late 1978 (from 4K to as much as 48K). It offered a monitor (produced by Sanyo) for the first time in May 1979. Shortly thereafter, Apple ceased making the basic Apple II and instead produced only upgraded versions (the Apple IIe, the IIc, and the III). Hundreds of other companies followed Apple's lead, touting increasingly sophisticated personal computers.

While one pack of entrepreneurs was chasing PC profits, another pack was going after the profits still available in home computers. This group chose to continue producing the basic Apple II lookalike, hoping to profit from greater efficiency, lower costs, and increasing sales.

Price Competition in Home Computers

The home computer market confronted the fiercest form of price competition. With prices continually sliding, the only way to make an extra buck was to push down the cost curve.

To reduce costs, firms sought to reduce the number of microprocessor chips installed in the computer's "brain." Fewer chips not only reduce direct materials costs, but more importantly, they decrease the amount of labor required for computer assembly. The key to lower manufacturing costs was more powerful chips. More powerful chips appeared when Intel, Motorola, and Texas Instruments developed 16-bit chips, doubling the computer's "brain" capabilities.

Further Supply Shifts

The impact of the improved chips on computer production costs and profits is illustrated in Figure 23.7, which takes over where Figure 23.5 left off. Recall that the market price of computers had been driven down to $700 by the beginning of 1980. At this price the typical firm maximized profits by producing 430 computers per month, as determined by the intersection of the prevailing price and MC curves (point *J* in Figure 23.7).

The only way for the firm to improve profitability at this point was to reduce costs. The new chips made such cost reductions easy. Such *technological improvements are illustrated by a downward shift of the ATC and MC curves.* Notice in Figure 23.7 how the new technology permits 430 home computers to be produced for a lower marginal cost (about $500) than previously ($700 at point *J*).

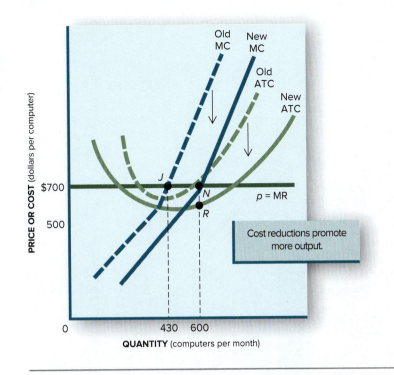

FIGURE 23.7
Lower Costs Improve Profits and Stimulate Output
The quest for profits encouraged producers to discover cheaper ways to manufacture computers. The resulting improvements lowered costs and encouraged further increases in the rate of output. The typical computer producer increased output from point *J* (where *p* = old MC) to point *N* (where *p* = new MC).

The lower cost structure increases the profitability of computer production and stimulates a further increase in production. Note in particular that the "new MC" curve intersects the price ($700) line at an output of 600 computers per month (point *N*). By contrast, the old, higher MC curve dictated a production rate of only 430 computers per month for the typical firm (point *J*) at that price. Thus existing producers suddenly had an incentive to *expand* production, and new firms had a greater incentive to *enter* the industry. The great rush into computer production was on again.

The market implications of another entrepreneurial stampede should now be obvious. As more and more firms tried to get in on the action, the market supply curve again shifted to the right. As output increased, computer prices slid further down the market demand curve.

Figure 23.8 illustrates how steeply home computer prices fell after 1980. In just over three years (December 1979 to January 1983), the price of a home computer plunged from $950 to $149. As the price plunged, so did profits. Fourth-quarter profits at Atari, for example, fell from $137 million in 1981 to only $1.2 million in 1983.

Shutdowns

That didn't stop the competitive process, however. At Texas Instruments, minimum *variable* costs were roughly $100 per computer in January 1983, so TI and other manufacturers could afford to keep producing even at lower prices. And they had little choice but to do so because if they didn't, other companies would quickly take up the slack. Industry output kept increasing despite shrinking profit margins. The increased supply pushed computer prices ever lower.

By the time computer prices reached $99 in September 1983, TI was losing $300 million per year. The company recognized then that the price would no longer even cover average variable costs. ***Once a firm is no longer able to cover variable costs, it should shut down production.*** When the price of home computers dipped below minimum average variable costs, TI had reached the **shutdown point,** and the company ceased production. At the time TI made the shutdown decision, the company had an inventory of nearly 500,000 unsold computers. To unload them, TI reduced its price to $49 (see Figure 23.8), forcing lower prices and losses on other computer firms.

shutdown point: The rate of output where price equals minimum AVC.

FIGURE 23.8

Plummeting Prices

Improved technology and fierce competition forced home computer prices down. In the span of only a few years, the price of a basic home computer fell from just under $1,000 to only $49. In the process, price fell below average variable cost, and many firms were forced to shut down.

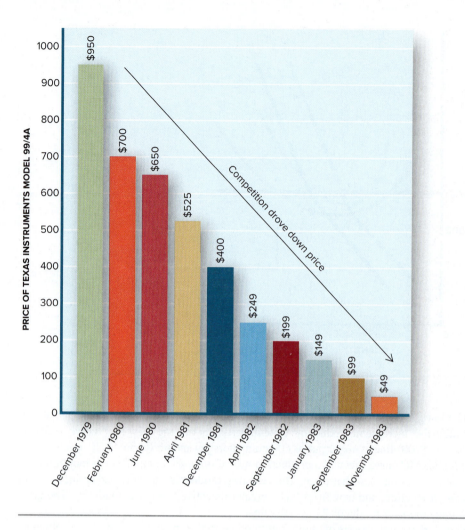

Competition drove down price

Exits

Shortly after Texas Instruments shut down its production, it got out of the home computer business altogether. Mattel, Atari, and scores of smaller companies also withdrew from the home computer market. The exit rate between 1983 and 1985 matched the entry rate of the period 1979 to 1982.

The Personal Computer Market

The same kind of price competition that characterized the home computer market eventually hit the personal computer market too. At first, competition in the PC market was largely confined to product improvements. Firms added more memory, faster microprocessors, better monitors, expanded operating systems, new applications software, and other features. New entrants into the market—Compaq in 1982; then Dell, AST, Gateway, and more—were the source of most product innovations.

The stampede of new firms and products into the PC market soon led to outright price competition too. As firms discovered that they couldn't sell all the PCs they were producing at prevailing prices, they were forced to offer price discounts. These discounts soon spread, and the slide down the demand curve accelerated.

Firms that couldn't keep up with the dual pace of improving technology and falling prices soon fell by the wayside. Scores of firms ceased production and withdrew from the industry once prices fell below minimum average variable cost. Even Apple, which had taken the "high road" to avoid price competition in home computers, was slowed by price competition.

THE COMPETITIVE PROCESS

It is now evident that consumers have reaped substantial benefits from competition in the computer market. More than 1 billion home and personal computers have been sold. Along the way, technology has made personal computers a thousand times faster than the first Apple IIs, with phenomenal increases in memory. The iMac computer introduced by Apple in 1998 made the Apple I of 1976 look prehistoric. The latest iMacs make even the 1998 model look primitive. A lot of consumers have found that computers are great for doing accounting chores, keeping records, writing papers, playing games, and accessing the Internet. Perhaps it's true that an abundance of inexpensive computers would have been produced in other market (or nonmarket) situations as well. But we can't ignore the fact that *competitive market pressures were a driving force in the spectacular growth of the computer industry.* And they still are.

Allocative Efficiency: The Right Output Mix

The squeeze on prices and profits that we've observed in the computer market is a fundamental characteristic of the competitive process. The process works as well in India (see World View "Competition Shrinks India's Phone Bills") as in the United States or elsewhere. Indeed, the **market mechanism** works best under competitive pressure. The existence of economic profits is an indication that consumers place a high value on a particular product and are willing to pay a comparatively high price to get it. The high price and profits signal this information to profit-hungry entrepreneurs, who come forward to satisfy consumer demands. Thus *high profits in a particular industry indicate that consumers want a different mix of output* (more of that industry's goods). The competitive squeeze on those same profits indicates that resources are being reallocated to produce that desired mix. In a competitive market, consumers get more of the goods they desire—and at a lower price.

iPhone 7 Plus and Apple Watch

Analysis: The evolution of personal computers from the Apple I to the latest iPhone, iPad, and Apple Watch was driven by intense competition.

market mechanism: The use of market prices and sales to signal desired outputs (or resource allocations).

WORLD VIEW

COMPETITION SHRINKS INDIA'S PHONE BILLS

Ever since the Indian government opened up its telecom industry to competition in 1999, Indian consumers have seen their phone bills shrink. In 2000, the charge for making a call with a cellular phone was 16 rupees per minute (about 27 U.S. cents). By 2011, that rate had fallen to 1 paisa per second—roughly 1 cent per minute. In the same time period, the number of mobile subscribers skyrocketed from 2 million to 584 million. Today, there are 930 million cellular subscribers, making India the world's second largest mobile phone market. How did all this come about? India opened the telecom market to new entrants, reduced license fees, and lowered tariffs, encouraging dozens of firms to compete for India's telephone customers.

Source: News reports, 2011.

ANALYSIS: Competitive pressures force companies to continually improve products and cut prices.

The ability of competitive markets to allocate resources efficiently across industries originates in the way competitive prices are set. To attain the optimal mix of output, we must know the **opportunity cost** of producing different goods. A competitive market gives us the information necessary for making such choices. Why? Because competitive firms always strive to produce at the rate of output at which price equals marginal cost. Hence *the price signal the consumer gets in a competitive market is an accurate reflection of opportunity cost.* As such, it offers a reliable basis for making choices about the mix of

opportunity cost: The most desired goods or services that are forgone in order to obtain something else.

marginal cost pricing: The offer (supply) of goods at prices equal to their marginal cost.

efficiency: Maximum output of a good from the resources used in production.

output and attendant allocation of resources. In this sense, the **marginal cost pricing** characteristic of competitive markets permits society to answer the WHAT-to-produce question efficiently. The amount consumers are willing to pay for a good (its price) equals its opportunity cost (marginal cost).

Production Efficiency: Minimum Average Cost

When the competitive pressure on prices is carried to the limit, we also get the right answer to the HOW-to-produce question. Competition drives costs down to their bare minimum—the hallmark of economic **efficiency.** This was illustrated by the tendency of computer prices to be driven down to the level of *minimum* average costs. Figure 23.9 summarizes this competitive process, showing how the industry moves from short-run equilibrium (point *a*) to long-run equilibrium (point *c*). Once the long-run equilibrium has been established, society is getting the most it can from its available (scarce) resources.

Zero Economic Profit

Competitive pressures also affect the FOR WHOM question. At the limit of long-run equilibrium, all economic profit is eliminated. This doesn't mean that producers are left empty-handed, however. The zero-profit limit is rarely, if ever, reached because new products are continually being introduced, consumer demands change, and more efficient production processes are discovered. In fact, the competitive process creates strong pressures to pursue product and technological innovation. In a competitive market, the adage about the early bird getting the worm is particularly apt. As we observed in the computer market, the first ones to perceive and respond to the potential profitability of computer production were the ones who made the greatest profits.

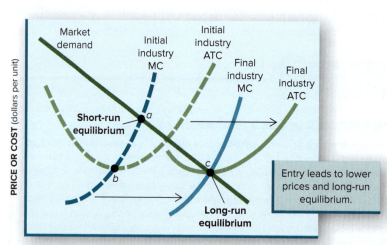

FIGURE 23.9

Summary of Competitive Process

All competitive firms seek to produce at that output where MC = *p*. Hence a competitive *industry* will produce at that rate of output where *industry* MC (the sum of all firms' MC curves) intersects market demand (point *a*).

If economic profits exist in the industry short-run equilibrium (as they do here because price exceeds ATC at point *a*), more firms will enter the industry. As they do, the *industry* MC (supply) curve will shift to the right. The shifting MC curve will pull the *industry* ATC curve along with it. As the *industry* MC curve continues to shift rightward, the intersection of MC and ATC (point *b*) eventually will reach the demand curve at point *c*. At point *c*, MC still equals price, but no economic profits exist and entry (shifts) will cease. Point *c* will be the *long-run* equilibrium of the industry.

If competitive pressures reduce costs (i.e., improve technology), the supply (MC) curve will shift further to the right and *down*, reducing long-run prices even more.

Note that MC = *p* in both short- and long-run equilibrium. Notice also that equilibrium must occur on the market demand curve.

Relentless Profit Squeeze

The sequence of events common to competitive markets evolves as follows:

- High prices and profits signal consumers' demand for more output.
- Economic profit attracts new suppliers.
- The market supply curve shifts to the right.
- Prices slide down the market demand curve.
- A new equilibrium is reached at which increased quantities of the desired product are produced and its price is lower. Average costs of production are at or near a minimum, much more of the product is supplied and consumed, and economic profit approaches zero.
- Throughout the process, producers experience great pressure to keep ahead of the profit squeeze by reducing costs, a pressure that frequently results in product and technological innovation.

What is essential to remember about the competitive process is that the *potential threat of other firms expanding production or of new firms entering the industry keeps existing firms on their toes.* Even the most successful firm can't rest on its laurels for long. To stay in the game, competitive firms must continually update technology, improve their products, and reduce costs.

THE ECONOMY TOMORROW

$99 IPADS?

Competition didn't end with computers. Steve Jobs, the guy who started the personal computer business back in 1977, knew that. He introduced another hot consumer product in November 2001—the iPod. The iPod was the first mass-produced portable digital music player. It allowed consumers to download, store, and retrieve up to 1,000 songs. Its compact size, sleek design, and simple functionality made it an instant success: Apple was selling iPods as fast as they could be produced, piling up huge profits in the process.

So what happened? Other entrepreneurs quickly got the scent of iPod's profits. Within a matter of months, competitors were designing their own digital music players. By 2003 the "attack of the iPod clones" was in full force. Major players like Sony (MusicBox), Dell (JukeBox), Samsung (Yepp), and Creative Technology (Muvo Slim) were all bringing MP3 players to the market. Competitors were adding new features, shrinking the size, and reducing prices.

Under these circumstances, Apple could not afford to sit back and admire its profits. Steve Jobs knew he'd have to keep running to stay ahead of the MP3 player pack. He kept improving the iPod. Within 2 years Apple had three generations of iPods, each substantially better than the last. Memory capacity increased tenfold (to 10,000 songs), features were added, and the size shrank further. In less than 2.5 years, the iPod's price fell by 40 percent even while quality improved dramatically.

The same kind of unrelenting competitive dynamic has hounded Apple's iPad. The iPad wasn't the first tablet computer, but it was a huge success: 300,000 iPads were sold on the first day and 15 million in the first year. Apple reaped enormous profits.

Those profits signaled a slew of companies to enter the tablet market, seeking to get a piece of the new profit pie. More than 100 companies entered the tablet market in 2011 alone, putting enormous pressure on Apple's sales, price, and profits. Apple stayed ahead of the competitive pack by reducing price, adding new features (e.g., built-in cameras, faster processor, four speakers, live video, Bluetooth keyboard), and shrinking the tablet's size and weight (the 9.7 inch iPad Pro, March 2016). With such unrelenting competitive pressure, industry analysts predict we'll see $99 iPads in the economy tomorrow.

SUMMARY

- A perfectly competitive firm has no power to alter the market price of the product it sells. The perfectly competitive firm confronts a horizontal demand curve for its own output even though the relevant *market* demand curve is negatively sloped.   **LO23-1**
- Profit maximization induces the competitive firm to produce at that rate of output where marginal costs equal price ($MC = p$). This represents the short-run equilibrium of the firm.   **LO23-2**
- If profits exist in short-run equilibrium, new firms will enter the market. The resulting shift of supply will drive market prices down the market demand curve. As prices fall, the profit of the industry and its constituent firms will be squeezed.   **LO23-3**

- The limit to the competitive price and profit squeeze is reached when price is driven down to the level of minimum average total cost ($MC = p = ATC$). At this point (long-run equilibrium) additional output and profit will be attained only if technology is improved (lowering costs) or if market demand increases.   **LO23-3**
- Firms will shut down production if price falls below average variable cost. Firms will exit the industry if they foresee continued economic losses.   **LO23-3**
- The most distinctive thing about competitive markets is the persistent pressure they exert on prices and profits. The threat of competition is a tremendous incentive for producers to respond quickly to consumer demands and to seek more efficient means of production. In this sense, competitive markets do best what markets are supposed to do—efficiently allocate resources.   **LO23-4**

Key Terms

equilibrium price	barriers to entry	shutdown point
market supply	production decision	market mechanism
marginal cost (MC)	average total cost (ATC)	opportunity cost
investment decision	profit per unit	marginal cost pricing
economic profit	short-run competitive equilibrium	efficiency
competitive market	long-run competitive equilibrium	

Questions for Discussion

1. Why would anyone want to enter a profitable industry knowing that profits would eventually be eliminated by competition?   **LO23-3**
2. Why wouldn't producers necessarily want to produce output at the lowest average cost? Under what conditions would they end up doing so?   **LO23-1**
3. What industries do you regard as being highly competitive? Can you identify any barriers to entry in those industries?   **LO23-1**
4. Why do TV prices continue to fall so much? (See World View "Flat Panels, Thin Margins.")   **LO23-2**
5. What does the "bleeding" highlighted in In the News "U.S. Catfish Industry Bleeding Finally Stops" refer to? What causes it? What cures it?   **LO23-3**

6. As the price of computers fell, what happened to their quality? How is this possible?   **LO23-4**
7. Can phone rates keep falling in India? What will cause them to rise? (See World View "Competition Shrinks India's Phone Bills.")   **LO23-4**
8. Is "long-run" equilibrium permanent? What forces might dislodge it?   **LO23-3**
9. Why don't catfish farmers raise the price of their fish and create better profits?   **LO23-2**
10. Identify two products that have either (*a*) fallen sharply in price or (*b*) gotten significantly better without price increases. How did these changes come about?   **LO23-4**
11. What happens to the factors of production that exit an industry?   **LO23-4**

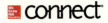

PROBLEMS FOR CHAPTER 23

LO23-3 1. According to World View "Competition Shrink India's Phone Bills," between 2000 and 2011 in India,
  (*a*) By what percentage did the price of a phone minute decline after competition emerged?
  (*b*) By what percentage did the quantity demanded increase?
  (*c*) What was the apparent price elasticity of demand?
  Note: Use the midpoint formula to compute percentage changes.

LO23-2 2. According to Table 23.1,
  (*a*) What were the fixed costs of production for the firm?
  (*b*) At what rate of output was profit per computer maximized? (Choose the highest output level.)
  (*c*) At what output rate was total profit maximized?

LO23-2 3. According to Figure 23.3*b*, if the market price for computers is $800,
  (*a*) What is the profit-maximizing quantity?
  (*b*) Calculate the profits (or losses) for this typical firm.
  (*c*) At this market price, will firms enter or exit the market?
  (*d*) Will this entry or exit cause prices to rise or fall?

LO23-1 4. Suppose the following data summarize the costs of a perfectly competitive firm:

Quantity	0	1	2	3	4	5	6	7	8
Total cost	$100	101	103	106	110	115	121	128	136

  (*a*) Draw the firm's MC curve on graph (a).
  (*b*) Draw the market supply curve on graph (b), assuming there are 8 firms identical to the one just described.
  (*c*) What is the equilibrium price in this market?

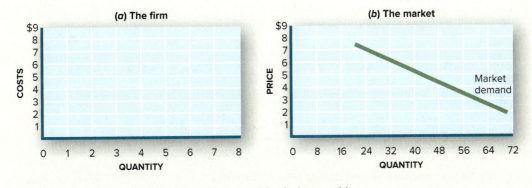

LO23-1 5. Suppose the following data describe the demand for fruit smoothies:

Price	$11	$10	$9	$8	$7	$6	$5	$4	$3	$2
Quantity demanded	7	10	13	16	19	22	25	28	31	34

Five identical, perfectly competitive firms are producing these smoothies. The cost of producing these smoothies at each firm is the following:

Quantity produced	0	1	2	3	4	5	6	7	8	9	10
Total cost	$5	$8	$10	$13	$17	$22	$28	$36	$45	$55	$67

  (*a*) What price will prevail in this market?
  (*b*) What quantity is produced?
  (*c*) How much profit (loss) does each firm make?
  (*d*) What happens to price if two more identical firms enter the market?

LO23-3 6. Suppose the typical catfish farmer was incurring an economic loss at the prevailing price p_1.

(a) Illustrate these losses on the market and firm graphs. Include the supply and demand curves on the market graph and average total cost, marginal cost, and price in the firm graph.

(b) Identify the price that would prevail in the long-run equilibrium.

(c) What supply forces would raise the price to this long run equilibrium. Illustrate your answer on the graphs.

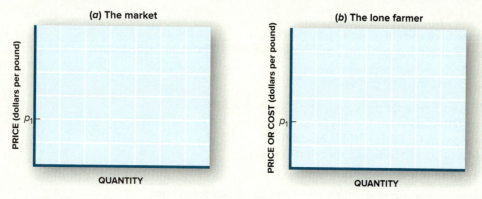

LO23-2 7. According to Table 23.1,

(a) What was the prevailing computer price in 1978?

(b) How much total profit did the typical firm earn?

(c) At what price would profits have been zero?

(d) At what price would the firm have shut down?

LO23-2 8. If a competitive firm has fixed costs of $10,000 per month and a minimum average variable cost of $28, at what price will it shutdown?

LO23-4 9. Suppose that the monthly market demand schedule for Frisbees is

Price	$8	$7	$6	$5	$4	$3	$2	$1
Quantity demanded	1,000	2,000	4,000	8,000	16,000	32,000	64,000	128,000

Suppose further that the marginal and average costs of Frisbee production for every competitive firm are

Rate of output	100	200	300	400	500	600
Marginal cost	$2.00	$3.00	$4.00	$5.00	$6.00	$7.00
Average total cost	2.00	2.50	3.00	3.50	4.00	4.50

Finally, assume that the equilibrium market price is $6 per Frisbee.

(a) Draw the cost curves of the typical firm and identify its profit-maximizing rate of output and its total profits.

(b) Draw the market demand curve and identify market equilibrium.

(c) How many Frisbees are being sold?

(d) How many (identical) firms are initially producing Frisbees?

(e) How much profit is the typical firm making?

(f) In view of the profits being made, more firms will enter into Frisbee production, shift the market supply curve to the right, and push price down. At what equilibrium price are all profits eliminated?

(g) How many firms will be producing Frisbees at this long-term price?

(a) The firm

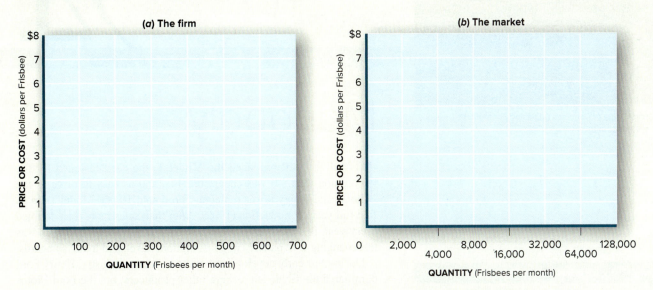

PRICE OR COST (dollars per Frisbee)

QUANTITY (Frisbees per month)

(b) The market

PRICE OR COST (dollars per Frisbee)

QUANTITY (Frisbees per month)

LO23-3 10. **The Economy Tomorrow:** Suppose the competitive tablet market is in the long run equilibrium. If at this equilibrium, the typical firm produces 10,000 per month, total costs for this production is $4,000,000, and the minimum of the average variable costs is $75, what price will,

(a) Induce entry into the market?

(b) Cause firms to shut down production in the short run?

(c) Result in firms exiting the market in the long run?

CHAPTER 24

Monopoly

In 1908 Ford produced the Model T, the car "designed for the common man." It was cheap, reliable, and as easy to drive as the horse and buggy it was replacing. Ford sold 10,000 Model Ts in its first full year of production (1909). After that, sales more than doubled every year. In 1913 nearly 200,000 Model Ts were sold; and Ford was fast changing U.S. patterns of consumption, travel, and living standards.

During this early development of the U.S. auto industry, Henry Ford dominated the field. There were other producers, but the Ford Motor Company was the only producer of an inexpensive "motorcar for the multitudes." In this situation, Henry Ford could dictate the price and the features of his cars. When he opened his new assembly line factory at Highland Park, he abruptly raised the Model T's price by $100—an increase of 12 percent—to help pay for the new plant. Then he decided to paint all Model Ts black. When told of consumer complaints about the lack of colors, Ford advised one of his executives in 1913, "Give them any color they want so long as it's black."[1]

Henry Ford had market power. He could dictate what color car Americans would buy. And he could raise the price of Model Ts without fear of losing all his customers. Such power is alien to competitive firms. Competitive firms are always under pressure to reduce costs, improve quality, and cater to consumer preferences.

In this chapter we examine how market structure influences market outcomes. Specifically, we examine how a market controlled by a single producer—a monopoly—behaves. We're particularly interested in the following questions:

- **What price will a monopolist charge?**
- **How much output will the monopolist produce?**
- **Are consumers better or worse off when only one firm controls an entire market?**

MARKET POWER

The essence of **market power** is the ability to alter the price of a product. The catfish farmers in Chapter 23 had no such power. Because 2,000 farms were producing and selling the same good, each catfish producer had to act as a *price taker*. Each producer could sell all it wanted at the prevailing price but would lose all its customers if it tried to charge a higher price.

LEARNING OBJECTIVES

After reading this chapter, you should know

LO24-1 How a monopolist sets price and output.

LO24-2 How monopoly and competitive outcomes differ.

LO24-3 The pros and cons of monopoly.

market power: The ability to alter the market price of a good or service.

---

[1]Source: Sorensen, Charles E., *My Forty Years with Ford*, New York: W. W. Norton & Co., p. 127, 1956.

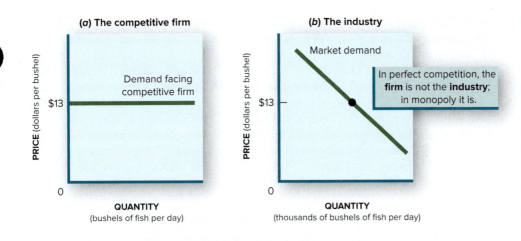

FIGURE 24.1

Firm vs. Industry Demand

A competitive firm can sell its entire output at the prevailing market price. In this sense, the firm confronts a horizontal demand curve, as in part *a*. Nevertheless, *market* demand for the product still slopes downward. The demand curve confronting the industry is illustrated in part *b*. Note the difference in the units of measurement (single bushels vs. thousands). A monopolist confronts the *industry* (market) demand curve.

The Downward-Sloping Demand Curve

Firms that have market power *can* alter the price of their output without losing all their customers. Sales volume may drop when price is increased, but the quantity demanded won't drop to zero. In other words, *firms with market power confront downward-sloping demand curves for their own output.*

The distinction between perfectly competitive (powerless) and imperfectly competitive (powerful) firms is illustrated again in Figure 24.1. Figure 24.1*a* re-creates the market situation that confronts a single catfish farmer. In Chapter 22, we assumed that the prevailing price of catfish was $13 a bushel and that a small, competitive firm could sell its entire output at this price. Hence each individual firm effectively confronted a horizontal demand curve.

We also noted earlier that catfish don't violate the law of demand. As good as catfish taste, people aren't willing to buy unlimited quantities of them at $13 a bushel. To induce consumers to buy more catfish, the market price of catfish must be reduced.

This seeming contradiction between the law of demand and the situation of the competitive firm is resolved in Figure 24.1. There are *two* relevant demand curves. The one on the left, which appears to contradict the law of demand, refers to a single competitive producer. The one on the right refers to the entire *industry,* of which the competitive producer is one very tiny part. The industry or market demand curve *does* slope downward, even though individual competitive firms are able to sell their own output at the going price.

Monopoly

An industry needn't be composed of many small firms. The entire output of catfish could be produced by a single large producer. Such a firm would be a **monopoly**—a single firm that produces the entire market supply of a good.

The emergence of a monopoly obliterates the distinction between industry demand and the demand curve facing the firm. A monopolistic firm *is* the industry. Hence there's only *one* demand curve to worry about, and that's the market (industry) demand curve, as illustrated in Figure 24.1*b*. This simplifies things: *in monopoly situations, the demand curve facing the firm is identical to the market demand curve for the product.*

monopoly: A firm that produces the entire market supply of a particular good or service.

Price and Marginal Revenue

Although monopolies simplify the geometry, they complicate the arithmetic of **profit maximization.** The basic rule for maximizing profits is unchanged—that is, produce the rate of output where marginal revenue equals marginal cost. This rule applies to *all* firms. In a competitive industry, however, this general rule was simplified. For competitive firms, marginal revenue is equal to price. Hence a competitive firm can maximize profits by producing at that rate of output where marginal cost equals *price.*

This special adaptation of the profit-maximizing rule doesn't work for a monopolist. The demand curve facing a monopolist is downward-sloping. Because of this, *marginal*

profit maximization rule: Produce at that rate of output where marginal revenue equals marginal cost.

revenue isn't equal to price for a monopolist. On the contrary, marginal revenue is always *less* than price in a monopoly, which makes it just a bit more difficult to find the profit-maximizing rate of output.

Figure 24.2 is a simple illustration of the relationship between price and marginal revenue. The monopolist can sell 1 bushel of fish per day at a price of $13. If he wants to sell a larger quantity of fish, however, he has to reduce his price. According to the demand curve shown here, the price must be lowered to $12 to sell 2 bushels per day. This reduction in price is shown by a movement along the demand curve from point *A* to point *B*.

How much additional revenue does the second bushel bring in? It's tempting to say that it brings in $12, since that's its price. **Marginal revenue (MR),** however, refers to the *change* in *total* revenue that results from a one-unit increase in output. More generally, we use the formula

$$\frac{\text{Marginal}}{\text{revenue}} = \frac{\text{Change in total revenue}}{\text{Change in quantity sold}} = \frac{\Delta \text{TR}}{\Delta q}$$

where the delta symbol Δ denotes "change in." According to this formula, the marginal revenue of the second bushel is

$$\text{MR} = \frac{\$24 - \$13}{1} = \$11.$$

Hence MR ($11) is less than price ($12) for the second bushel sold.

marginal revenue (MR): The change in total revenue that results from a one-unit increase in the quantity sold.

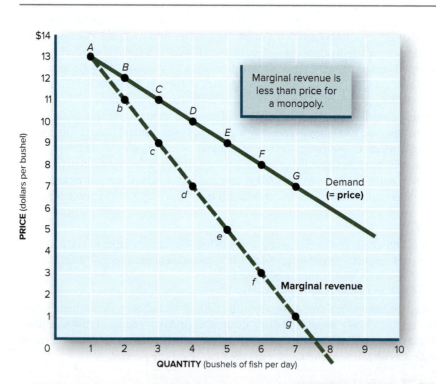

FIGURE 24.2

Price Exceeds Marginal Revenue in Monopoly

If a firm must lower its price to sell additional output, marginal revenue is less than price. If this monopoly firm wants to increase its sales from 1 to 2 bushels per day, for example, price must be reduced from $13 to $12. The marginal revenue of the second bushel is therefore only $11. This is indicated in row *B* of the table and by point *b* on the graph.

	Quantity	×	Price	=	Total Revenue	Marginal Revenue (= ΔTR ÷ Δq)
A	1		$13		$13	–
B	2		12		24	$11
C	3		11		33	9
D	4		10		40	7
E	5		9		45	5

Figure 24.2 summarizes the calculations necessary for computing MR. Row *A* of the table indicates that the total revenue resulting from one sale per day is $13. To increase sales, price must be reduced. Row *B* indicates that total revenue rises to $24 per day when fish sales double. The *increase* in total revenue resulting from the added sales is thus $11. This concept is illustrated in the last column of the table and by point *b* on the marginal revenue curve.

Notice that the MR of the second bushel ($11) is *less* than its price ($12) because both bushels are being sold for $12 apiece. In effect, the firm is giving up the opportunity to sell only 1 bushel per day at $13 to sell a larger quantity at a lower price. In this sense, the firm is sacrificing $1 of potential revenue on the first bushel to increase *total* revenue. Marginal revenue measures the change in total revenue that results.

So long as the demand curve is downward-sloping, MR will always be less than price. Compare columns 2 and 4 of the table in Figure 24.2. At each rate of output in excess of 1 bushel, marginal revenue is less than price. This is also evident in the graph: *the MR curve lies below the demand (price) curve at every point but the first.*

Profit Maximization

Although the presence of market power adds a new wrinkle, the rules of profit maximization remain the same. *Instead of looking for an intersection of marginal cost and price (as in perfect competition), we now look for the intersection of marginal cost and marginal revenue (monopoly).* This is illustrated in Figure 24.3 by the intersection of the MR and MC curves (point *d*). Looking down from that intersection, we see that the associated rate of output is 4 bushels per day. Thus 4 bushels is the profit-maximizing rate of output.

How much should the monopolist charge for these 4 bushels? Naturally, the monopolist would like to charge a very high price. But the ability to charge a high price is limited by the demand curve. If the monopolist charges $13, consumers will buy only 1 bushel, leaving 3 unsold bushels of dead fish. Not a pretty picture. As the monopolist will soon learn, *only one price is compatible with the profit-maximizing rate of output.* In this case, the price is $10. This price is found in Figure 24.3 by moving up from the quantity 4 until reaching the demand curve at point *D*. Point *D* tells us that consumers are able and willing to buy 4 bushels of fish per day only at the price of $10 each. A monopolist who tries to charge more than $10 won't be able to sell all 4 bushels.

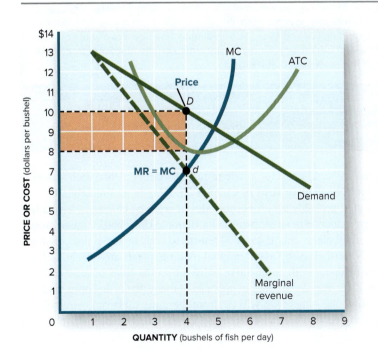

FIGURE 24.3

Profit Maximization (MR = MC)

The most profitable rate of output is indicated by the intersection of marginal revenue and marginal cost (point *d*). This intersection (MC = MR) establishes 4 bushels as the profit-maximizing rate of output. Point *D* indicates that consumers will pay $10 per bushel for this much output.

Total profits equal price ($10) minus average total cost ($8), multiplied by the quantity sold (4).

Figure 24.3 also illustrates the total profits of the catfish monopoly. To compute total profits we can first calculate profit per unit—that is, price minus *average* total cost. In this case, profit per unit is $2 at the profit-maximizing rate of output. Multiplying profit per unit by the quantity sold (4) gives us total profits of $8 per day, as illustrated by the shaded rectangle.

MARKET POWER AT WORK: THE COMPUTER MARKET REVISITED

To develop a keener appreciation for the nature of market power, we can return to the computer market of Chapter 23. The computer market wasn't perfectly competitive, but it nearly behaved as though it was. We saw how the continuing entry of new firms kept competitive pressure on computer firms to reduce costs and improve quality. In this chapter, we'll make some different assumptions about market structure. In particular, assume that a single firm, Universal Electronics, acquires an exclusive patent on the production of the microprocessors that function as the computer's "brain." This one firm is now in a position to deny potential competitors access to the basic ingredient of computers. The patent thus functions as a **barrier to entry,** to be erected or set aside at the will of Universal Electronics.

barriers to entry: Obstacles such as patents that make it difficult or impossible for would-be producers to enter a particular market.

Universal's management is familiar enough with the principles of economics (including W. C. Fields's advice about never giving a sucker an even break) to know when it's onto a good thing. It's not about to let every would-be Horatio Alger have a slice of the profit pie. Even the Russians understood this strategy during the heyday of communism. They made sure no one else could produce sable furs that could compete with their monopoly (see World View "Russia's Sable Monopoly Persists"). Let's assume that Universal Electronics is equally protective of its turf and will refuse to sell or give away any rights to its patent or the chips it produces. That is, Universal Electronics sets itself up as a computer monopoly.

WORLD VIEW

RUSSIA'S SABLE MONOPOLY PERSISTS

Ancient Greeks and Romans called the fur of the sable the "Golden Fleece." Unlike any other fur, sable is smooth in all directions, even after stroked. Living in the wilds of Siberia, the sable has always been one of Russia's most valuable exports. In 1697 Peter the Great decreed a monopoly on sable, forbidding the export of live sables or the technology of breeding them. In the 1980s Russia was selling more than 15 million sable pelts a year and reaping monopoly-type profits. Exporting live sables or the breeding technology was a crime punishable by death. The plot of the 1983 movie, *Gorky Park,* centers on the murder of three men who attempted to export live sables out of Russia.

ANALYSIS: To ward off potential competition, a monopoly must erect barriers to entry. By not letting live sables leave the country, to breed elsewhere, Russia maintained a monopoly on sable furs.

economies of scale: Reductions in minimum average costs that come about through increases in the size (scale) of plant and equipment.

Let's also assume that Universal has a multitude of manufacturing plants, each of which is identical to the typical competitive firm in Chapter 23. This is an unlikely situation because a monopolist would probably achieve **economies of scale** by closing at least a few plants and consolidating production in larger plants. Our fictional Universal company would maintain a multitude of small plants only if constant returns to scale or actual diseconomies of scale were rampant. Nevertheless, by assuming that multiple plants are maintained, we can compare monopoly behavior with competitive behavior on the basis of identical cost structures. In particular, if Universal continues to operate the many plants that once made up the competitive home computer industry, it will confront the same short-run marginal and average cost curves already encountered in Chapter 23. Later in this chapter we relax this

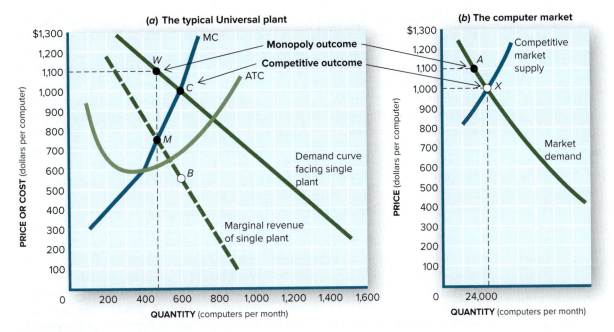

FIGURE 24.4

Initial Conditions in the Monopolized Computer Market

We assume that a monopoly firm (Universal Electronics) would confront the same costs (MC and ATC) and demand as would the competitive industry in Chapter 23. In the initial short-run equilibrium, the competitive price was $1,000 (point C), and each firm (plant) was producing 600 computers (where MC = p).

A monopolist isn't bound by the competitive market price. Instead the monopolist must contend with downward-sloping demand and marginal revenue curves. If each monopoly plant

produced where MC = $1,000 (point C in part a), marginal cost (point C) would exceed marginal revenue (point B). To maximize profits, the monopolist must find that rate of output where MC = MR (point M in part a). That rate of output (475) can be sold at the higher monopoly price of $1,100 (point W in part a).

Part b illustrates the market implications of the monopolist's production decision: a reduced quantity is sold at a higher price (point A).

---

assumption of multiplant operations to determine whether, in the long run, a monopolist may actually lower production costs below those of a competitive industry.

Figure 24.4a re-creates the marginal costs the typical competitive firm faced in the early stages of the microcomputer boom (from Figure 23.3 and Table 23.1). We now assume that this MC curve also expresses the costs of operating one of Universal's many (identical) plants. Thus the extension of monopoly control is assumed to have no immediate effect on production costs.

The market demand for computers is also assumed to be unchanged. There's no reason why people should be less willing to buy computers now than they were when the market was competitive. Most consumers have no notion of how many firms produce a product. Even if they knew, there's no reason why their demand for the product would change. Thus Figure 24.4b expresses an unchanged market demand for computers.

Our immediate concern is to determine how Universal Electronics, as a monopolist, will respond to these unchanged demand and cost curves. Will it produce exactly as many computers as the competitive industry did? Will it sell the computers at the same price that the competitive industry did? Will it improve the product as much or as fast?

The Production Decision

Like any producer, Universal Electronics will strive to produce its output at the rate that maximizes total profits. But unlike competitive firms, Universal will explicitly take account of the fact that an increase in output will put downward pressure on computer prices. This may threaten corporate profits.

The implications of Universal's market position for the **production decision** of its many plants can be seen in the new price and marginal revenue curves imposed on each of its

production decision: The selection of the short-run rate of output (with existing plants and equipment).

manufacturing plants. Universal can't afford to let each of its plants compete with the others, expanding output and driving down prices; that's the kind of folly reserved for truly competitive firms. Instead Universal will seek to *coordinate* the production decisions of its plants, instructing all plant managers to expand or contract output simultaneously, to achieve the corporate goal of profit maximization.

A simultaneous reduction of output by each Universal plant will lead to a significant reduction in the quantity of computers supplied to the market. This reduced supply will cause a move up the market demand curve to higher prices. By the same token, an expansion of output by all Universal plants will lead to an increase in the quantity supplied to the market and a slide down the market demand curve. As a consequence, each of the monopolist's plants effectively confronts a downward-sloping demand curve. These downward-sloping demand curves are illustrated in Figure 24.4a.[2]

Notice that in Figure 24.4b the *market* demand for computers is unchanged; only the demand curve confronting each plant (firm) has changed. A competitive *industry,* like a monopoly, must obey the law of demand. But the individual firms that compose a competitive industry all act independently, *as if* they could sell unlimited quantities at the prevailing price. That is, they all act as if they confronted a horizontal demand curve at the market price of $1,000. A competitive firm that doesn't behave in this fashion will simply lose sales to other firms. In contrast, *a monopolist not only foresees the impact of increased production on market price but also can prevent such production increases by its separate plants.*

Marginal Revenue. The downward-sloping demand curve now confronting each Universal plant implies that marginal revenue no longer equals price. Notice that the marginal revenue curve in Figure 24.4a lies *below* the demand curve at every rate of output. Because marginal revenue is less than price for a monopoly, Universal's plants would no longer wish to produce up to the point where marginal cost equals price. *Only firms that confront a horizontal demand curve (perfect competitors) equate marginal cost and price.* Universal's plants must stick to the generic profit-maximizing rule about equating marginal revenue and marginal cost. Should the individual plant managers forget this rule, Universal's central management will fire them.

The output and price implications of Universal's monopoly position become apparent as we examine the new revenue and cost relationships. Recall that the equilibrium price of computers in the early stages of the home computer boom was $1,000. This equilibrium price is indicated in Figure 24.4b by the intersection of the *competitive* market supply curve with the market demand curve (point X). Each competitive *firm* produced up to the point where marginal cost (MC) equaled that price (point C in Figure 24.4a). At that point, each competitive firm was producing 600 computers a month.

Reduced Output. The emergence of Universal as a monopolist alters these production decisions. Now each Universal plant *does* have an impact on market price because its behavior is imitated simultaneously by all Universal plants. In fact, the marginal revenue associated with the 600th computer is only $575, as indicated by point B in Figure 24.4a. At this rate of output, the typical Universal plant would be operating with marginal costs ($1,000) far in excess of marginal revenues ($575). Such behavior is inconsistent with profit maximization.

The enlightened Universal plant manager will soon discover that the profit-maximizing rate of output is less than 600 computers per month. In Figure 24.4a we see that the marginal revenue and marginal cost curves intersect at point *M*. This MR = MC intersection occurs at an output level of only 475 computers per month. Accordingly, the typical Universal plant will want to produce *fewer* computers (475) than were produced by the typical competitive firm (600) in the early stages of the home computer boom. Recall that

---

[2]The demand and marginal revenue curves in Figure 24.4a are illustrative; they're not derived from earlier tables. As discussed here, we're assuming that the central management of Universal determines the profit-maximizing rate of output and then instructs all individual plants to produce equal shares of that output.

individual competitive firms had no incentive to engage in such production cutbacks. They couldn't alter the market supply curve or price on their own and weren't coordinated by a central management. Thus the first consequence of Universal's monopoly position is a reduction in the rate of industry output.

The Monopoly Price

The reduction in output at each Universal plant translates automatically into a decrease in the *quantity supplied* to the market. As consumers compete for this reduced market supply, they'll bid computer prices up. We can observe the increased prices in Figure 24.4 by looking at either the typical Universal plant or the computer market. Notice that in Figure 24.4a the price is determined by moving directly up from point *M* to the demand curve confronting the typical Universal plant. The demand curve always tells how much consumers are willing to pay for any given quantity. Hence, once we've determined the quantity that's going to be supplied (475 computers per month), we can look at the demand curve to determine the price ($1,100 at point *W*) that consumers will pay for these computers. That is,

- *The intersection of the marginal revenue and marginal cost curves establishes the profit-maximizing rate of output.*
- *The demand curve tells us how much consumers are willing to pay for that specific quantity of output.*

Figure 24.4a shows how Universal's monopoly position results in both reduced output and increased prices. This result is also evident in Figure 24.4b, where we see that a smaller quantity supplied to the market will force a move up the demand curve to the higher price of $1,100 per computer (point *A*).

Monopoly Profits

Universal's objective was and remains the maximization of profits. That it has succeeded in its effort can be confirmed by scrutinizing Figure 24.5. As you can see, the typical Universal plant ends up selling 475 computers a month at a price of $1,100 each (point *W*). The **average total cost (ATC)** of production at this rate of output is only $630 (point *K*), as was detailed in Table 23.1.

As always, we can compute total profit as

$$\text{Total profit} = \text{Profit per unit} \times \text{Quantity sold}$$

average total cost (ATC): Total cost divided by the quantity produced in a given time period.

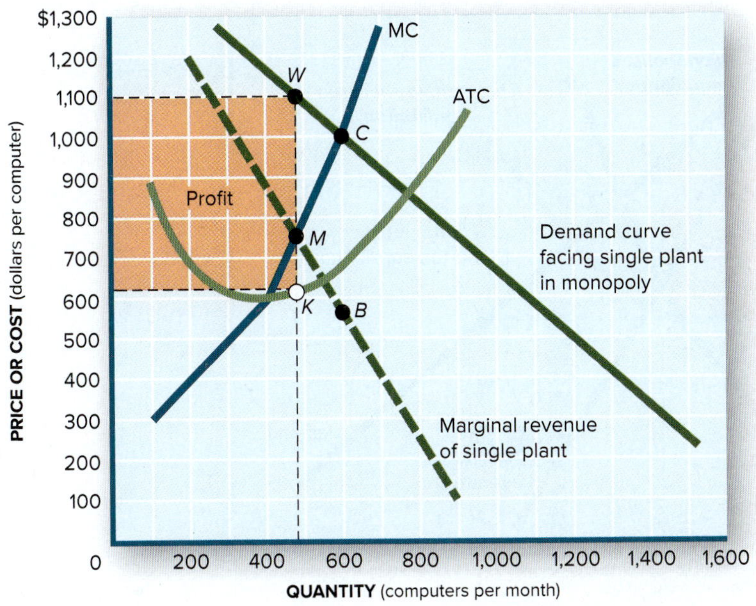

FIGURE 24.5

Monopoly Profits: The Typical Universal Plant

The profit-maximizing rate of output occurs where the marginal cost and marginal revenue curves intersect (point *M*). The demand curve indicates the price (point *W*) that consumers will pay for this much output. Total profit equals price (*W*) minus *average* total cost (*K*), multiplied by the quantity sold (475). Total profits are represented by the shaded rectangle.

In this case, we see that

$$\text{Total profit} = (\$1,100 - \$630) \times 475$$
$$= \$223,250$$

This figure significantly exceeds the monthly profit of $180,000 earned by the typical competitive firm in the early stages of the computer boom (see Table 23.1).

It's apparent from these profit figures that Universal management has learned its economic principles well. By reducing the output of each plant and raising prices a little, it has managed to increase profits. This can be seen again in Figure 24.6, which is an enlarged illustration of the *market* situation for the home computer industry. The figure translates the economics of our single-plant and competitive-firm comparison into the dimensions of the whole industry.

Figure 24.6 reaffirms that the competitive industry in Chapter 23 initially produces the quantity q_c and sells it at a price of $1,000 each. Its profits are equal to the rectangle formed by the points R, X, U, T. The monopolist, on the other hand, produces the smaller q_m and charges a higher price, $1,100. The monopoly firm's profits are indicated by the larger profit rectangle shaded in the figure. Thus, *a monopoly receives larger profits than a comparable competitive industry by reducing the quantity supplied and pushing prices up.* The larger profits make Universal very happy and make consumers a little sadder and wiser. Consumers are now paying more and getting less.

Barriers to Entry

The higher profits Universal Electronics attained as a result of its monopoly position aren't the end of the story. The existence of economic profit tends to bring profit-hungry entrepreneurs swarming like locusts. In the competitive computer industry of Chapter 23, the lure of high profits brought about an enormous expansion of computer output and a steep decline in computer prices. In Figure 24.6 the long-run equilibrium of a competitive industry is indicated by point V. What can we expect to happen in the computer market now that Universal has a monopoly position and is enjoying huge profits?

Remember that Universal is now assumed to have an exclusive patent on microprocessor chips and can use this patent as an impassable barrier to entry. Consequently, would-be competitors can swarm around Universal's profits until their wings drop off; Universal isn't about to let them in on the spoils. By locking out potential competition, Universal can prevent the surge in computer output that pushed prices down the market demand curve.

FIGURE 24.6

Monopoly Profit: The Entire Company

Total profits of the monopolist (including all plants) are illustrated by the shaded rectangle. The monopolist's total output q_m is determined by the intersection of the (industry) MR and MC curves. The price of this output is determined by the market demand curve (point A).

In contrast, a competitive industry would produce q_c computers in the short run and sell them at a lower price (X) and profit per unit (X − U). Those profits would attract new entrants until long-run equilibrium (point V) was reached. (See Figure 23.9 for a summary of competitive market equilibrium.)

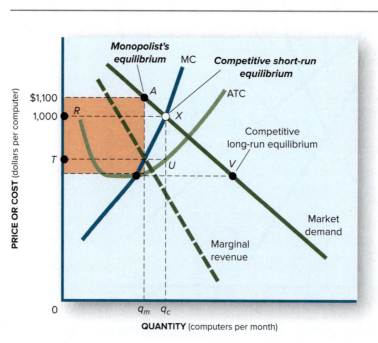

As long as Universal is able to keep out the competition, only the more affluent consumers will be able to use computers.

The same phenomenom explains why ticket prices for live concerts are so high. When Live Nation acquired Ticketmaster in 2009, it became a virtual monopolist for concert sites and ticket distribution. As In the News "Live Nation Acquires Ticketmaster" suggests, this music industry merger created a "sour note" for music fans. A monopoly has no incentive to move from point A in Figure 24.6, and there's no competitive pressure to force such a move. Universal may discover ways to reduce the costs of production and thus lower prices, but there's no *pressure* on it to do so, as there was in the competitive situation. Similarly, there's no *competitive pressure* on Live Nation to reduce concert prices.

IN THE NEWS

LIVE NATION ACQUIRES TICKETMASTER

The world's largest concert promoter, Live Nation, acquired the world's largest ticket distributor, Ticketmaster, creating a virtual monopoly on concert production and ticket sales. Bruce Springsteen warned back in 2009 that the merger of these two giants "would make the current ticket situation even worse for the fan than it is now" due to the increased monopoly power of the newly-created Live Nation Entertainment. A class action suit against the company charged it with "excessive and deceptive" fees, a suit the combined company settled in April 2016 by giving 50 million fans free or discounted tickets to select concerts. Fans continue to protest high prices, excessive fees, bloated parking fees, and outrageous prices for beer, hot dogs, and water. Nevertheless, Live Nation Entertainment sold 530 million tickets in 2015, generating over $7 billion in revenues.

Source: Media reports, 2009, 2016.

ANALYSIS: Control of concert sites and ticket distribution allows Live Nation Entertainment to charge monopoly prices for live concerts.

A COMPARATIVE PERSPECTIVE OF MARKET POWER

The different outcomes of the computer industry under competitive and monopoly conditions illustrate basic features of market structures. We may summarize the sequence of events that occurs in each type of market structure as follows:

COMPETITIVE INDUSTRY

- High prices and profits signal consumers' demand for more output.
- The high profits attract new suppliers.
- Production and supplies expand.
- Prices slide down the market demand curve.
- A new equilibrium is established wherein more of the desired product is produced, its price falls, average costs of production approach their minimum, and economic profits approach zero.
- Price equals marginal cost throughout the process.
- Throughout the process, there's great pressure to keep ahead of the profit squeeze by reducing costs or improving product quality.

MONOPOLY INDUSTRY

- High prices and profits signal consumers' demand for more output.
- Barriers to entry are erected to exclude potential competition.
- Production and supplies are constrained.
- Prices don't move down the market demand curve.
- No new equilibrium is established; average costs aren't necessarily at or near a minimum, and economic profits are at a maximum.
- Price exceeds marginal cost at all times.
- There's no squeeze on profits and thus no pressure to reduce costs or improve product quality.

In our discussion, we assumed that the competitive industry and the monopoly both started from the same position—an initial equilibrium in which the price of computers is $1,000. In reality, an industry may manifest concentrations of market power *before* such an equilibrium is established. That is, the sequence of events we've depicted may be altered (with step 3 occurring first, e.g.). Nevertheless, the basic distinctions between competitive and monopolistic behavior are evident.

Productivity Advances. To the extent that monopolies behave as we've discussed, they affect not just the price and output of a specific product but broader economic outcomes as well. Remember that competitive industries tend, in the long run, to produce at minimum average costs. Competitive industries also pursue cost reductions and product improvements relentlessly. These pressures tend to expand our production possibilities. No such forces are at work in the monopoly we've discussed here. Hence there's a basic tendency for monopolies to inhibit productivity advances and economic growth.

The Mix of Output. Another important feature of competitive markets is their observed tendency toward **marginal cost pricing.** Marginal cost pricing is important to consumers because it permits rational choices among alternative goods and services. In particular, it informs consumers of the true opportunity costs of various goods, thereby allowing them to choose the mix of output that delivers the most utility with available resources. In our monopoly example, however, consumers end up getting fewer computers than they'd like, while the economy continues to produce other, less desired goods. Thus the mix of output shifted away from computers when Universal took over the industry.

> **marginal cost pricing:** The offer (supply) of goods at prices equal to their marginal cost.

The power to influence prices and product flows may have far-reaching consequences for our economic welfare. Changes in prices and product flows directly influence the level and composition of output, employment and resource allocation, the level and distribution of income, and, of course, the level and structure of prices. Hence firms that wield significant market power affect all dimensions of economic welfare.

Political Power. Market power isn't the only kind of power wielded in society, of course. Political power, for example, is a different kind of power and important in its own right. Indeed, the power to influence an election or to sway a Senate committee vote may ultimately be more important than the power to increase the price of laundry soap. Nevertheless, market power is a force that influences the way we live, the incomes we earn, and our relationships with other countries. Moreover, market power may be the basis for political power: the individual or firm with considerable market power is likely to have the necessary resources to influence an election or sway a vote on a congressional committee.

The Limits to Power

Even though market power enables a producer to manipulate market outcomes, there's a clear limit to the exercise of power. Even a monopolist can't get everything it wants. Universal, for example, would really like to sell q_m computers at a price of $1,500 each because that kind of price would bring it even greater profits. Yet, despite its monopoly position, Universal is constrained to sell that quantity of computers at the lower price of $1,100 each. Even monopolists have their little disappointments.

The ultimate limit to a monopolist's power is evident in Figure 24.6. Universal's attainment of a monopoly position allows it only one prerogative: the ability to alter the quantity of output *supplied* to the market. This is no small prerogative, but it's far from absolute power. Universal, and every other monopolist, must still contend with the market *demand* curve. Note again that the new equilibrium in Figure 24.6 occurs at a point on the *unchanged* market demand curve. In effect, ***a monopolist has the opportunity to pick any*** *point on the market demand curve and designate it as the new market equilibrium.* The point it selects will depend on its own perceptions of effort, profit, and risk (in this case point *A,* determined by the intersection of marginal revenue and marginal cost).

The ultimate constraint on the exercise of market power, then, resides in the market demand curve. How great a constraint the demand curve imposes depends largely on the **price elasticity of demand.** The greater the price elasticity of demand, the more a monopolist will be frustrated in attempts to establish both high prices and high volume. Consumers will simply reduce their purchases if price is increased. If, however, consumer demand is highly inelastic—if consumers need or want that product badly and few viable substitutes are available—the monopolist can reap tremendous profits from market power. That was clearly the case for the monopoly that produces a life-saving drug for AIDS patients (see In the News "Drugmaker Hikes Price of AIDS Drug 5,000 Percent!").

> **price elasticity of demand:**
> The percentage change in quantity demanded divided by the percentage change in price.

IN THE NEWS

DRUGMAKER HIKES PRICE OF AIDS DRUG 5,000 PERCENT!

Turing Pharmaceuticals hiked the price of Daraprim, a critical drug for preventing infections in people with the HIV virus, from $13.50 per capsule to $750. Turing, a pharmaceutical start-up, acquired the rights to Daraprim in August. In September, it announced a price hike of 5,000 percent. The company's CEO, Martin Shkreli, defended the price hike, saying "the companies before us were actually giving it away almost." "We need to turn profit on this drug," Shkreli told Bloomberg News. Because the cost of producing the drug is only $1 a capsule, Shkreli told his board of directors that the company could earn a cool billion dollars at the higher price.

Source: Media reports of September 2016.

ANALYSIS: If demand is inelastic, a monopolist can increase price without losing many sales.

Price Discrimination

Even in situations where the *market* demand is relatively elastic, a monopolist may be able to extract high prices. A monopolist has the power not only to raise the market price of a good (by reducing the quantity supplied) but also to charge various prices for the same good. Recall that the market demand curve reflects the combined willingness of many individuals to buy. Some of those individuals are willing to buy the good at prices higher than the market price, just as other individuals will buy only at lower prices. A monopolist may be able to increase total profits by selling each unit of the good separately, at a price each *individual* consumer is willing to pay. This practice is called **price discrimination.**

> **price discrimination:** The sale of an individual good at different prices to different consumers.

The airline industry has practiced price discrimination for many years. Basically, there are two distinct groups of travelers: business and nonbusiness travelers. Business executives must fly from one city to another on a certain day and at a particular time. They typically make flight arrangements on short notice and may have no other way to get to their destination. Nonbusiness travelers, such as people on vacation and students going home during semester break, usually have more flexible schedules. They may plan their trips weeks or months in advance and often have the option of traveling by car, bus, or train.

The different travel needs of business and vacation travelers are reflected in their respective demand curves. Business demand for air travel is less price-elastic than the demand of nonbusiness travelers. Few business executives would stop flying if airfares increased. Higher airfares would, however, discourage air travel by nonbusiness travelers.

What should airlines do in this case? Should they *raise* airfares to take advantage of the relative price inelasticity of business demand, or should they *lower* airfares to attract more nonbusiness travelers?

They should do both. In fact, they *have* done both. The airlines offer a full-fare ride, available at any time, and a discount-fare ride, available only by purchasing a ticket in advance and agreeing to some restrictions on time of departure. The advance purchase and other restrictions on discount fares effectively exclude most business travelers, who end up paying full fare. The higher full fare doesn't, however, discourage most nonbusiness travelers, who can fly at a discount. Consequently, the airlines are able to sell essentially identical units of the same good (an airplane ride) at substantially different prices to different customers. This price discrimination enables the airlines to capture the highest possible *average* price for the quantity supplied.

With *perfect* price discrimination, a monopolist would sell the product to each consumer on the demand curve at the maximum price that individual was willing to pay. If that happened, the monopolist would eliminate all **consumer surplus** and capture the extra revenue that a single price misses. Doctors, lawyers, and car dealers commonly practice this type of price discrimination.

consumer surplus: The difference between the maximum price a person is willing to pay and the price paid.

Entry Barriers

It's the lack of competitors that gives monopolists such pricing power. Accordingly, ***the preservation of monopoly power depends on keeping potential competitors out of the market.*** A monopolist doesn't want anyone else to produce an *identical* product or even a *close substitute.* To do that, a monopoly must erect and maintain barriers to market entry. Some of the entry barriers used to repel would-be competitors include:

Patents. This was the critical barrier in the mythical Universal Electronics case. A government-awarded patent gives a producer 20 years of exclusive rights to produce a particular product. Turing Pharmaceuticals used those patent rights to hike the price of Daraprim by 5,000 percent overnight (see In the News "Drugmaker Hikes Price of AIDS Drug 5,000 Percent!"): No one was producing a substitute drug. The Polaroid Corporation used its patents to keep Eastman Kodak and other potential rivals out of the market for instant development cameras. In 2007 Verizon and Sprint used broad patents to curb the growth of Vonage, the leading provider of Internet phone service.

Monopoly Franchises. The government also creates and maintains monopolies by giving a single firm the exclusive right to supply a particular good or service, even though other firms could produce it. Local cable TV stations and telephone companies are examples. Congress also bestows monopoly privileges to baseball teams and the U.S. Postal Service. Your campus bookstore may have exclusive rights to sell textbooks on campus.

Control of Key Inputs. A company may lock out competition by securing exclusive access to key inputs. Airlines need landing rights and terminal gates to compete. Oil and gas producers need pipelines to supply their products. Utility companies need transmission networks to supply consumers with electricity. Software vendors need to know the features of computer operating systems. If a single company controls these critical inputs, it can lock out potential competition. Intel was accused by the Federal Trade Commission (FTC) of trying to lock out competition by enticing computer makers with hefty discounts to use Intel chips exclusively in their computers. Microsoft was accused of using similar tactics to consolidate its monopoly position in operating systems (see the Economy Tomorrow section at the end of this chapter).

Lawsuits. In the event that competitors actually surmount other entry barriers, a monopoly may sue them out of existence. Typically, start-up firms are rich in ideas but cash poor. They need to get their products to the market quickly to generate some cash. A timely lawsuit alleging patent or copyright infringement can derail such a company by absorbing critical management, cash, and time. Long before the merits of the lawsuit are adjudicated, the company may be forced to withdraw from the market.

Acquisition. When all else fails, a monopolist may simply purchase a potential competitor. Live Nation's acquisition of Ticketmaster in 2009 (see In the News "Live Nation Acquires Ticketmaster") eliminated competition in the ticket distribution system. Mergers tend to raise consumer prices.

Economies of Scale. Last but far from least, a monopoly may persist because of economies of scale. If large firms have a substantial cost advantage over smaller firms, the smaller firms may not be able to compete. We look at this entry barrier again in a moment.

PROS AND CONS OF MARKET POWER

Despite the strong case against market power, it's conceivable that monopolies could also benefit society. One argument made for concentrations of market power is that monopolies have greater ability to pursue research and development. Another argument is that the lure of market power creates a tremendous incentive for invention and innovation. A third argument in defense of monopoly is that large companies can produce goods more efficiently than smaller firms. Finally, it's argued that even monopolies have to worry about *potential* competition and will behave accordingly.

Research and Development

In principle, monopolies are well positioned to undertake valuable research and development. First, such firms are sheltered from the constant pressure of competition. Second, they have the resources (monopoly profits) with which to carry out expensive R&D functions. The manager of a perfectly competitive firm, by contrast, has to worry about day-to-day production decisions and profit margins. As a result, she is unable to take the longer view necessary for significant research and development and couldn't afford to purchase such a view even if she could see it.

The basic problem with the R&D argument is that it says nothing about *incentives*. Although monopolists have a clear financial advantage in pursuing research and development activities, they have no clear incentive to do so. Research and development aren't necessarily required for profitable survival. In fact, research and development that make existing plants and equipment technologically obsolete run counter to a monopolist's vested interest and so may actually be suppressed (see In the News "Jury Awards $26 Million for Suppressed Technology"). In contrast, a perfectly competitive firm can't continue to make significant profits unless it stays ahead of the competition. This pressure constitutes a significant incentive to discover new products or new and cheaper ways of producing existing products.

IN THE NEWS

JURY AWARDS $26 MILLION FOR SUPPRESSED TECHNOLOGY

Two Bay Area entrepreneurs won a $25.7 million judgment in Oakland's U.S. District Court yesterday for the suppression of their energy-saving technology. In 1984, C. R. Stevens and William Alling sold to Universal Manufacturing Company a new technology that reduces the energy consumption of fluorescent lighting by 70 percent. But Universal never marketed the new technology, as it had promised. Stevens and Alling claimed that Universal suppressed their invention in order to protect its existing, less-efficient technology. The jury agreed and ordered Universal to pay $25.7 million in damages.

Source: News reports, January 10–15, 1990.

ANALYSIS: A monopoly has little incentive (no competitive pressure) to pursue R&D. In fact, R&D that threatens established products or processes may be suppressed.

Entrepreneurial Incentives

The second defense of market power uses a novel incentive argument. Every business is out to make a buck, and it's the quest for profits that keeps industries running. Thus, it's argued, even greater profit prizes will stimulate more entrepreneurial activity. Little Horatio Algers will work harder and longer if they can dream of one day possessing a whole monopoly.

The incentive argument for market power is enticing but not entirely convincing. After all, an innovator can make substantial profits in a competitive market before the competition catches up. Recall that the early birds did get the worm in the competitive computer industry (see Chapter 23), even though profit margins were later squeezed. It's not evident that the profit incentives available in a competitive industry are at all inadequate.

We must also recall the arguments about research and development efforts. A monopolist has little incentive to pursue R&D. Furthermore, entrepreneurs who might pursue product innovation or technological improvements may be dissuaded by their inability to penetrate a monopolized market. The barriers to entry that surround market power may not only keep out potential competitors but also lock out promising ideas.

Economies of Scale

A third defense of market power is the most plausible. A large firm, it's argued, can produce goods at a lower unit (average) cost than a small firm. If such *economies of scale* exist, we could attain greater efficiency (higher productivity) by permitting firms to grow to market-dominating size.

We sidestepped this argument in our story about the Universal Electronics monopoly. We explicitly assumed that Universal confronted the same production costs as the competitive industry. We simply converted each typical competitive firm into a separate plant owned and operated by Universal. Universal wasn't able to produce computers any more cheaply than its competitive counterpart, and we concerned ourselves only with the different production decisions made by competitive and monopolistic firms.

A monopoly *could,* however, attain greater cost savings. By centralizing various functions it might be able to eliminate some duplicative efforts. It might also shut down some plants and concentrate production in fewer facilities. If these kinds of efficiencies are attained, a monopoly would offer attractive resource savings.

There's no guarantee, however, of such economies of scale. As we observed in Chapter 21, increasing the size (scale) of a plant may actually *reduce* operating efficiency (see Figure 21.10). In evaluating the economies-of-scale argument for market power, then, we must recognize that *efficiency and size don't necessarily go hand in hand. Some firms and industries may be subject to economies of scale, but others won't.*

Even when economies of scale are present, there is no guarantee that consumers will benefit. The 2006 merger of Boeing and Lockheed cut the costs of rocket production by $100–150 million a year (see In the News "US FTC Enables Boeing–Lockheed 'Monopoly'"). But the Defense Department ended up paying higher prices. The Justice Department initially opposed the merger of the nation's only two satellite radio companies in 2007 for the same reason. Even though there were substantial short-run economies of scale in eliminating duplicate facilities, the Justice Department concluded that even a little competition (two firms) was better than none (a monopoly) in expanding consumer choice and keeping prices low (see In the News "A Sirius Mistake? FCC Approves XM–Sirius Merger"). Both the Justice Department and the Federal Communications Commission ultimately approved the XMSatellite–Sirius Radio merger, however, in return for their promise not to raise prices for at least three years.

natural monopoly: An industry in which one firm can achieve economies of scale over the entire range of market supply.

Natural Monopolies. Industries that exhibit economies of scale over the entire range of market output are called **natural monopolies.** In these cases, one single firm can produce the entire market supply more efficiently than any large number of (smaller) firms. As the size (scale) of the one firm increases, its minimum average costs continue to fall. These economies of scale give the one large producer a decided advantage over would-be rivals. Hence *economies of scale act as a "natural" barrier to entry.*

US FTC ENABLES BOEING–LOCKHEED "MONOPOLY"

On 3 October 2006, the Federal Trade Commission (FTC) announced its tentative approval of merging Boeing and Lockheed Martin's space launch divisions to create the United Launch Alliance (ULA). . . . —this decision in essence creates a single-source supplier for putting US satellites on orbit.

In August 2006, Kenneth Krieg, head of acquisitions for the Pentagon, wrote to the FTC to support the proposed merger. He acknowledged that while it "will almost certainly have an adverse effect on competition, including higher prices over the long term, as well as a diminution in innovation and responsiveness," he still thought, "The national security advantages of ULA are paramount to the department's support of the transaction."

Apparently, the FTC took his recommendation to heart.

—**Victoria Samson for Center for Defense Information (CDI) November 30, 2006**

Source: Samson, Victoria, "US FTC Enables Boeing-Lockheed 'Monopoly,'" Center for Defense Information. ©2017 ETH Zurich.

ANALYSIS: Mergers eliminate duplicate facilities, thereby reducing total costs. But monopoly power permits the merged entity to retain the cost savings rather than pass them along to the consumer in the form of lower prices.

Local telephone and utility services are classic examples of natural monopoly. A single telephone or utility company can supply the market more efficiently than a large number of competing firms.

Although natural monopolies are economically desirable, they may be abused. We must ask whether and to what extent consumers are reaping some benefit from the efficiency a natural monopoly makes possible. Do consumers end up with lower prices, expanded output, and better service? Or does the monopoly keep most of the benefits for itself, in the form of higher prices and profits? Multiplex movie theaters, for example, achieve economies of scale by sharing operating and concession facilities among as many as 30 screens. But do moviegoers get lower prices for movies or popcorn? Not often. Because megamultiplex theaters tend to drive out competition, they don't have to reduce prices when costs drop.

A SIRIUS MISTAKE? FCC APPROVES XM–SIRIUS MERGER

The Federal Communications Commission (FCC) has approved the merger of the nation's only two satellite radio companies, XM and Sirius. The merged company, called Sirius XM, will own the entire band of spectrum allocated to satellite radio. The companies said that combining their operations would cut costs by more than $150 million. In its 3-2 decision, the FCC commissioners acknowledged that the merged company would be a monopoly provider of satellite radio. But the majority argued that concessions made by the merged company—including a three-year price freeze and the guarantee of set-asides for minority and nonprofit channels—would generate consumer benefits that outweigh potential anticompetitive effects. And they noted that terrestrial radio would always be a competitor to satellite radio. The dissenting commissioners argued that programming choices would contract and subscription prices would increase after the three-year freeze ended.

Source: News reports, July 25–31, 2008.

ANALYSIS: Monopolies may enjoy economies of scale. In the long run, however, consumers may benefit more from competitive pressures to reduce costs, improve product quality, and lower prices.

Contestable Market

Governmental regulators aren't necessarily the only force keeping monopolists in line. Even though a firm may produce the entire supply of a particular product at present, it may face *potential* competition from other firms. Potential rivals may be sitting on the sidelines, watching how well the monopoly fares. If it does too well, these rivals may enter the industry, undermining the monopoly structure and profits. In such **contestable markets,** monopoly behavior may be restrained by potential competition.

How "contestable" a market is depends not so much on its structure as on entry barriers. If entry barriers are insurmountable, would-be competitors are locked out of the market. But if entry barriers are modest, they'll be surmounted when the lure of monopoly profits is irresistible. When CNN's profits from cable news reached irresistible proportions, both domestic and foreign companies (e.g., CNBC, Fox News, Bloomberg News) decided to invade CNN's monopoly market. Since then, CNN hasn't been nearly as profitable.

Structure vs. Behavior. From the perspective of contestable markets, the whole case against monopoly is misconceived. Market *structure* per se isn't a problem; what counts is market *behavior*. If potential rivals force a monopolist to behave like a competitive firm, then monopoly imposes no cost on consumers or on society at large.

The experience with the Model T Ford illustrates the basic notion of contestable markets. At the time Henry Ford decided to increase the price of the Model T and paint them all black, the Ford Motor Company enjoyed a virtual monopoly on mass-produced cars. But potential rivals saw the profitability of offering additional colors and features such as a self-starter and left-hand drive. When rivals began producing cars in volume, Ford's market power was greatly reduced. In 1926 the Ford Motor Company tried to regain its dominant position by again supplying cars in colors other than black. By that time, however, consumers had more choices. Ford ceased production of the Model T in May 1927.

The experience with the Model T suggests that potential competition can force a monopoly to change its ways. Critics point out, however, that even contestable markets don't force a monopolist to act *exactly* like a competitive firm. There will always be a gap between competitive outcomes and those monopoly outcomes likely to entice new entry. That gap can cost consumers a lot. The absence of *existing* rivals is also likely to inhibit product and productivity improvements. From 1913 to 1926, all Model Ts were black, and consumers had few alternatives. Ford changed its behavior only after *potential* competition became *actual* competition. Even after 1927, when the Ford Motor Company could no longer act like a monopolist, it still didn't price its cars at marginal cost.

THE ECONOMY TOMORROW

MICROSOFT AND GOOGLE: BULLIES OR GENIUSES?

Ford Motor Company's experience is a useful reminder that monopolies rarely last forever. Potential competitors will always look for ways to enter a profitable market. Eventually they'll surmount entry barriers or develop substitute goods that supplant a monopolist's products.

Consumer advocates assert that we shouldn't have to wait for the invisible hand to dismantle a monopoly. They say the government should intervene to dismantle a monopoly or at least force it to change its behavior. Then consumers would get lower prices and better products a whole lot sooner.

Microsoft's dominant position in the computer industry highlights this issue. Microsoft produces the operating system (Windows) that powers 9 out of 10 personal computers. It also produces a huge share of applications software, including Internet browsers. Critics fear that this kind of monopoly power is a threat to consumers. They say Microsoft charges too much for its systems software, suppresses substitute technologies, and pushes potential competitors around. In short, Microsoft is a bully. In April 2000 a federal court accepted this argument (see In the News "Microsoft Guilty of Monopoly Abuse").

IN THE NEWS

MICROSOFT GUILTY OF MONOPOLY ABUSE

A federal judge ruled Monday that Microsoft has unfairly used its dominant position in computer operating systems to thwart competition in applications software. At the center of the case was Microsoft's practice of bundling its web browser, Internet Explorer, with its Windows operating system. Competitors charged that this practice made it difficult, if not impossible for them to sell competing web browsers (like Netscape's Navigator). They also complained that Microsoft designed its Windows operating system to render competing web browsers slow and inefficient.

Microsoft CEO Bill Gates argued that Internet Explorer and Windows were intrinsically related and should be viewed as a single product. But Microsoft sold Internet Explorer as a stand-alone product for MAC OS. Critics also charged that Microsoft forced computer manufacturers to install only Windows on new equipment, shutting the door on competing software.

U.S. District judge Thomas Penfield ruled in favor of the government, declaring that Microsoft violated the Sherman Antitrust Act by "unlawfully tying its Web browser" to its windows operating system. By "placing an oppressive thumb on the scale of competitive forces," Microsoft was guilty of abusing its dominant position in the marketplace to bully competitors, stifle competition and harm consumers.

Source: Media reports, April 4-6, 2000.

ANALYSIS: A federal court concluded that Microsoft followed the textbook script of monopoly: erecting entry barriers, suppressing innovation, and charging high prices.

To weaken Microsoft's grip on the computer market, courts in both the United States and Europe forced changes in both Microsoft's behavior and structure.

The AT&T Case. The federal government's authority to mend Microsoft's ways originates in the Sherman, the Clayton, and the Federal Trade Commission Acts. As noted in Table 24.1, these acts give the government broad **antitrust** authority to break up monopolies or compel them to change their behavior. The government used this authority in 1984 to dismantle American Telephone and Telegraph's (AT&T's) phone monopoly. AT&T then supplied 96 percent of all long-distance service and more than 80 percent of local telephone service. AT&T kept long-distance charges high and compelled consumers to purchase hardware from its own subsidiary (Western Electric). Potential competitors claimed they could supply better and cheaper services if the government ended the AT&T monopoly. After four years of antitrust litigation, AT&T agreed to (1) separate its long-distance and local services and (2) turn over the local transmission networks to new "Baby Bell" companies. Since then there has been a competitive revolution in telephone hardware, services, and pricing.

The Microsoft Case. The U.S. Department of Justice filed a similar antitrust action against Microsoft. The first accusation leveled against Microsoft was that it thwarted competitors in operating systems by erecting entry barriers such as exclusive purchase agreements with computer manufacturers. These agreements either forbade manufacturers from installing a rival operating system or made it prohibitively expensive. The second accusation against Microsoft was that it used its monopoly position in *operating* systems to gain an unfair advantage in the *applications* market. It did this by not disclosing operating features that make applications run more efficiently or by bundling software, thereby forcing consumers to accept Microsoft applications along with the operating system. When the latter occurs, consumers have little incentive to buy a

antitrust: Government intervention to alter market structure or prevent abuse of market power.

Continued

- *The Sherman Act (1890).* The Sherman Act prohibits "conspiracies in restraint of trade," including mergers, contracts, or acquisitions that threaten to monopolize an industry. Firms that violate the Sherman Act are subject to fines of up to $1 million, and their executives may be subject to imprisonment. In addition, consumers who are damaged—for example, via high prices—by a "conspiracy in restraint of trade" may recover treble damages. With this act as its principal "trustbusting" weapon, the U.S. Department of Justice has blocked attempted mergers and acquisitions, forced changes in price or output behavior, required large companies to sell some of their assets, and even sent corporate executives to jail for "conspiracies in restraint of trade."
- *The Clayton Act (1914).* The Clayton Act of 1914 was passed to outlaw specific antitrust behavior not covered by the Sherman Act. The principal aim of the act was to prevent the development of monopolies. To this end, the Clayton Act prohibited price discrimination, exclusive dealing agreements, certain types of mergers, and interlocking boards of directors among competing firms.
- *The Federal Trade Commission Act (1914).* The increased antitrust responsibilities of the federal government created the need for an agency that could study industry structures and behavior so as to identify anticompetitive practices. The Federal Trade Commission was created for this purpose in 1914.

Although the Sherman, Clayton, and FTC acts create a legal basis for government antitrust activity, they leave some basic implementation issues unanswered. What, for example, constitutes a "monopoly" in the real world? Must a company produce 100 percent of a particular good to be a threat to consumer welfare? How about 99 percent? Or even 75 percent?

And what specific monopolistic practices should be prohibited? Should we be looking for specific evidence of price gouging? Or should we focus on barriers to entry and unfair market practices?

These kinds of questions determine how and when antitrust laws will be enforced. The first question relates to the *structure* of markets, and the rest to their *behavior.*

TABLE 24.1

Antitrust Laws

The legal foundations for antitrust intervention are contained in three landmark antitrust laws.

competing product. Microsoft also prohibited computer manufacturers from displaying rival product icons on the Windows desktop. Finally, Microsoft was accused of thwarting competition by simply buying out promising rivals.

Microsoft's Defense. Bill Gates, Microsoft's chairman, scoffed at the government's charges. He contends that Microsoft dominates the computer industry only because it continues to produce the best products at attractive prices. Microsoft doesn't need to lock out potential competitors, he argues, because it can and does beat the competition with superior products. Furthermore, Gates argues, the software industry is a highly *contestable* market even if not a perfectly competitive one. So Microsoft has to behave like a competitive firm even though it supplies most of the industry's output. In short, Microsoft is a genius, not a bully. Therefore, the government should leave Microsoft alone and let the market decide who best serves consumers.

The Verdict. After nine *years* of litigation, a federal court determined that Microsoft was more of a bully than a genius. The court concluded that Microsoft not only held a monopoly position in operating systems but had abused that position in a variety of anticompetitive ways. As a result, consumers were harmed. *The real economic issue, the court asserted, was not whether Microsoft was improving its products (it was) or reducing prices (it was) but instead how much faster products would have improved and prices fallen in a more competitive market.* By limiting consumer choices and stifling competition, Microsoft had denied consumers better and cheaper information technology.

The Remedy. The trial judge suggested that Microsoft might have to be broken into two companies—an operating software company and an applications software company—to ensure enough competition. Such a *structural* remedy would have resembled the court-ordered breakup of AT&T. In November 2001, however, the U.S. Department of Justice decided to seek *behavioral* remedies only. With Windows XP about to be launched, the

Justice Department required Microsoft only to lower entry barriers for competing software applications (e.g., disclose middleware specifications, refrain from exclusive contracts, open desktops to competition). Although Microsoft reluctantly agreed to change its conduct in many ways, rivals complained that they still didn't have a fair chance of competing against the Microsoft monopoly. European regulators agreed, imposing still greater restrictions on Microsoft's business practices—particularly its continued bundling of Media Player in its operating system and confidential source code. Critics contend, however, that market *structure* is still the critical factor in determining market outcomes for the economy tomorrow.

Google a Bully? The same kind of anticompetitive concerns have been raised about Google. Google dominates the Internet search market, accounting for 87 percent of all online searches (Yahoo! has about 5 percent and Bing about 7 percent of the market). Companies pay big bucks to occupy top positions on Google search pages and to place ads in prominent locations. More than 90 percent of Google's immense profits come from paid advertising.

The core complaint against Google is that it uses its dominant search-engine position to suppress competition. Critics (including, ironically, Microsoft) say Google unfairly steers users to the company's own growing network of services (e.g., maps, travel) at the expense of rival producers. They say this harms consumers by restricting the ability of other companies to put better or cheaper products and services in front of Internet users. They contend Google reinforces its monopoly power with entry barriers such as unique key search words, long-term exclusive advertising contracts, suppression of search results for rival firms, and outright acquisitions of potential competitors. Rivals say Google is a bully. Google contends it is a genius that welcomes online competition. After a 7-year investigation (see In the News "EU Charges Google with Search Bias"), European trustbusters concluded in June 2017 that Google "denied European consumers a genuine choice of services and the full benefits of innovation." The EU imposed a record $2.7 billion fine on the company for its bullying tactics.

IN THE NEWS

EU CHARGES GOOGLE WITH SEARCH BIAS

After a five-year investigation, the European Commission has formally charged Google with "search bias." In its formal Statement of Objection, the European Union's trustbusters accuse Google of using its dominant position in Internet search to steer consumers to its own services. Google handles 90 percent of Web search in Europe. The Commission say Google "stifles competition and harms consumers" by prominently displaying ads for its own map, travel, and product services over those of rivals.

Source: Media reports, April 2015.

ANALYSIS: Does Google strengthen its dominant position in search with unfair entry barriers? Rivals say it does. Google responds that it is just a better competitor.

SUMMARY

- Market power is the ability to influence the market price of goods and services. The extreme case of market power is monopoly, a situation in which only one firm produces the entire supply of a particular product. **LO24-1**
- The distinguishing feature of any firm with market power is the fact that the demand curve it faces is downward-sloping. In the case of monopoly, the demand curve facing the firm and the market demand curve are identical. **LO24-1**
- The downward-sloping demand curve facing a monopolist creates a divergence between marginal revenue and price. To sell larger quantities of output, the monopolist must lower product prices. A firm without market power has no such problem. **LO24-1**

- Like other producers, a monopolist will produce at the rate of output at which marginal revenue equals marginal cost. Because marginal revenue is always less than price in monopoly, the monopolist will produce less output than a competitive industry confronting the same market demand and costs. That reduced rate of output will be sold at higher prices in accordance with the (downward-sloping) market demand curve. **LO24-2**
- A monopoly will attain a higher level of profit than a competitive industry because of its ability to equate industry (that is, its own) marginal revenues and costs. By contrast, a competitive industry ends up equating marginal costs and price because its individual firms have no control over market supply. **LO24-2**
- Because the higher profits attained by a monopoly will attract envious entrepreneurs, barriers to entry are needed to prohibit other firms from expanding market supplies. Patents are one such barrier to entry. **LO24-2**
- The defense of market power rests on (1) the alleged ability of large firms to pursue long-term research and development, (2) the incentives implicit in the chance to attain market power, (3) the efficiency that larger firms may attain, and (4) the contestability of even monopolized markets. The first two arguments are weakened by the fact that competitive firms are under much greater pressure to innovate and can stay ahead of the profit game only if they do so. The contestability defense at best concedes some amount of monopoly exploitation. **LO24-3**
- A natural monopoly exists when one firm can produce the output of the entire industry more efficiently than can a number of small firms. This advantage is attained from economies of scale. Large firms aren't necessarily more efficient, however, because either constant returns to scale or diseconomies of scale may prevail. **LO24-3**
- Antitrust laws restrain the acquisition and abuse of monopoly power. Where barriers to entry aren't insurmountable, market forces may ultimately overcome a monopoly. **LO24-3**

Key Terms

market power	economies of scale	price discrimination
monopoly	production decision	consumer surplus
profit maximization rule	average total cost (ATC)	natural monopoly
marginal revenue (MR)	marginal cost pricing	contestable market
barriers to entry	price elasticity of demand	antitrust

Questions for Discussion

1. The objective in the game of Monopoly is to get all the property and then raise the rents. Can this power be explained with market supply and demand curves? **LO24-1**
2. According to the Federal Trade Commission (In the News "US FTC Enables Boeing–Lockheed 'Monopoly'"), how often do monopolies lead to higher prices? Why, then, did the rocket merger get approved? **LO24-1**
3. Why don't monopolists try to establish "the highest price possible," as many people allege? What would happen to sales? To profits? **LO24-1**
4. How does individualized price discrimination by car dealers affect their total revenue and profits? **LO24-1**
5. What would have happened to iPad prices and features if Apple had not faced competition from iPad clones (Chapter 23)? **LO24-2**
6. What entry barriers helped protect the following? **LO24-2**
   (a) The Russian sable monopoly (World View "Russia's Sable Monopoly Persists").
   (b) The Live Nation monopoly (In the News "Live Nation Acquires Ticketmaster").
   (c) Turing Pharmaceutical (In the News "Drugmaker Hikes Price of AIDS Drug 5,000 Percent!").
   (d) The rocket monopoly (In the News "US FTC Enables Boeing–Lockheed 'Monopoly'").
   (e) Google's search dominance (In The News "EU Charges Google with Search Bias").
7. What similarities exist between the AT&T, Microsoft, and Google antitrust cases? **LO24-3**
8. How might consumers have benefited from the merger of XM and Sirius (In the News "A Sirius Mistake? FCC Approves XM–Sirius Merger")? How might they have lost? **LO24-3**
9. How might Google's search-engine dominance harm consumers? Help them? **LO24-3**
10. Is the demand for a life-saving drug like Daraprim (In the News "Drugmaker Hikes Price of AIDS Drug 5,000 Percent!") likely to be elastic or inelastic? How does that affect the pricing decision of a monopolist? **LO24-1**

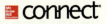

PROBLEMS FOR CHAPTER 24

LO24-1 1. Use Figure 24.3 to answer the following questions:
   (a) What is the highest price the monopolist could charge and still sell fish?
   (b) What is total revenue at that highest price?
   (c) What rate of output maximizes total revenue (partial unit okay)?
   (d) What rate of output maximizes total profit (use higher rate)?
   (e) What is MR at that rate of output?
   (f) What is the price at the profit-maximizing rate of output?

LO24-1 2. (a) Complete the following table:

Price	$24	$21	$18	$15	$12	$9	$6	$3
Quantity demanded	1	2	3	4	5	6	7	8
Marginal revenue	___	___	___	___	___	___	___	___

   (b) At what rate of output does marginal revenue turn negative?
   (c) If marginal cost is constant at $12, what is the profit-maximizing rate of output?
   (d) What price should this monopolist charge for that rate of output?

LO24-1 3. Given the following information about demand for a local utility service, graph the demand and marginal revenue curves.

Price	$ 6	5	4	3	2
Quantity demanded	20	50	90	150	210

LO24-3 Identify the barrier to entry that best matches the following news stories about monopolies:
   (a) In the News "US FTC Enables Boeing–Lockheed 'Monopoly.'"
   (b) In the News "Drugmaker Hikes Price of AIDS Drug 5,000 Percent!"
   (c) World View "Russia's Sable Monopoly Persists."

LO24-1 4. The following table indicates the prices various buyers are willing to pay for a MINI Cooper car:

Buyer	Maximum Price	Buyer	Maximum Price
Buyer A	$50,000	Buyer D	$20,000
Buyer B	40,000	Buyer E	10,000
Buyer C	30,000	Buyer F	0

The cost of producing the cars includes $40,000 of fixed costs and a constant marginal cost of $10,000.
   (a) Graph below the demand, marginal revenue, and marginal cost curves.
   (b) What is the profit-maximizing rate of output and price for a monopolist?
   (c) How much profit does the monopolist make?
   (d) If the monopolist can price discriminate, how many cars will he sell?
   (e) How much profit will he make?

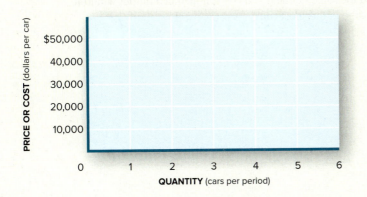

LO24-2 5. If the on-campus demand for soda is as follows:

Price (per can)	$2.00	1.75	1.50	1.25	1.00	0.75	0.50	0.25
Quantity demanded (per day)	100	90	80	70	60	50	40	30

and the marginal cost of supplying a soda is 50 cents, what price will students end up paying in
(*a*) A perfectly competitive market?
(*b*) A monopolized market?

LO24-3 6. According to the In the News "US FTC Enables Boeing–Lockheed 'Monopoly,'"
(*a*) What was the annual cost saving for the rocket monopoly (in $ millions)?
(*b*) How much of this saving did the FTC expect to be reflected in reduced rocket prices?
(*c*) According to economic theory, which is likely to be higher, A: the merged monopoly price; or B: the two-firm competitive price?

LO24-2 7. What was the profit per unit for the drug Daraprim (In the News "Drugmaker Hikes Price of AIDS Drug 5,000 Percent!"):
(*a*) Before Turing increased the price?
(*b*) After Turing increased the price?
(*c*) What barrier to entry exists in this market?

LO24-2 8. The following table summarizes the weekly sales and cost situation confronting a monopolist:

Price	Quantity Demanded	Total Revenue	Marginal Revenue	Total Cost	Marginal Cost	Average Total Cost
$22	0	_____		$ 4		_____
20	1	_____	_____	8	_____	_____
18	2	_____	_____	13	_____	_____
16	3	_____	_____	19	_____	_____
14	4	_____	_____	27	_____	_____
12	5	_____	_____	37	_____	_____
10	6	_____	_____	51	_____	_____
8	7	_____	_____	69	_____	_____

(*a*) Complete the table.
(*b*) Graph the demand, MR, and MC curves on the following graph.
(*c*) At what rate of output are profits maximized?
(*d*) What are the values of MR and MC at the profit-maximizing rate of output?
(*e*) What price will the firm charge?
(*f*) What are total profits at that output rate?
(*g*) If a competitive industry confronted the same demand and costs, how much output would it produce and what price would it charge in the short run?

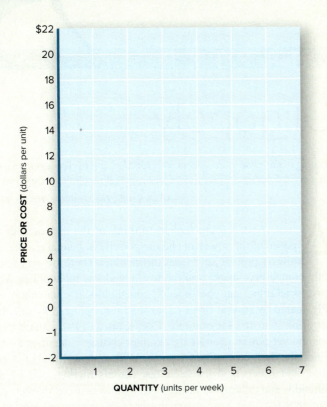

LO24-3 9. The Economy Tomorrow: Identify the market and the barrier to entry that best matches the case studies presented in The Economy Tomorrow.
  (*a*) Microsoft.
  (*b*) AT&T.
  (*c*) Google.

©McGraw-Hill Education/Andrew Resek, photographer

CHAPTER

25

Oligopoly

People of the same trade seldom meet together, but the conversation ends in a conspiracy against the public, or in some diversion to raise prices.

—Adam Smith, *The Wealth of Nations*, **1776**

Although it's convenient to think of the economy as composed of the powerful and the powerless, market realities don't always provide such clear distinctions. There are very few perfectly competitive markets in the world, and few monopolies. Market power is an important phenomenon nonetheless; it's just that it's typically shared by several firms rather than monopolized by one. In the soft drink industry, for example, Coca-Cola and Pepsi share tremendous market power, even though neither company qualifies as a pure monopoly. The same kind of power is shared by Kellogg, General Mills, and Ralcorp in the breakfast cereals market, and by Sony, Nintendo, and Microsoft in the video game console market. Apple Computer Inc., too, now shares power in the tablet computer market with Samsung, Lenovo, Huawei, Sony, LG, Microsoft, and other firms.

These market structures fall between the extremes of perfect competition and pure monopoly; they represent *imperfect competition*. They contain some elements of competitive rivalry but also exhibit traces of monopoly. In many cases, imperfect competitors behave much like a monopoly: restricting output, charging higher prices, and reaping greater profits than firms in a competitive market. But behavior in imperfectly competitive markets is more complicated than in a monopoly because it involves a number of decision makers (firms) rather than only one.

This chapter focuses on one form of imperfect competition: *oligopoly*. We examine the nature of decision making in this market structure and the likely impacts on prices, production, and profits. What we want to know is

- **What determines how much market power a firm has?**
- **How do firms in an oligopoly set prices and output?**
- **What problems does an oligopoly have in maintaining price and profit?**

MARKET STRUCTURE

As we saw in Chapter 24, Microsoft is the dominant supplier of computer operating systems and Google dominates the search-engine market. As near monopolies, those companies have tremendous market power. The corner grocery store, on the other hand, must compete with other stores and has less control over prices. But even the corner grocery isn't completely powerless. If it's the only grocery within walking distance or the only one open on Sunday, it too exerts *some* influence on prices and product flows. The amount of power it possesses depends on the availability of *substitute goods*—that is, the proximity and convenience of alternative retail outlets.

Degrees of Power

Between the extremes of monopoly and perfect competition are many gradations of market power. To sort them out, we classify firms into five specific **market structures,** based on the number and relative size of firms in an industry.

Table 25.1 summarizes the characteristics of the five major market structures. At one extreme is the structure of *perfect competition,* the subject of Chapters 22 and 23. At the other extreme of the power spectrum is perfect *monopoly.* A perfect monopoly exists when only one firm is the exclusive supplier of a particular product. Our illustration of Universal Electronics (the imaginary computer monopolist in Chapter 24) exemplifies such a firm.

Between the two extremes of perfect competition and perfect monopoly lies most of the real world, which we call *imperfectly competitive.* **In imperfect competition, individual firms have some power in a particular product market.** *Oligopoly* refers to one of these imperfectly competitive market structures. **Oligopoly** is a situation in which only a *few* firms have a great deal of power in a product market. An oligopoly may exist because only a few firms produce a particular product or because a few firms account for most, although not all, of a product's output.

market structure: The number and relative size of firms in an industry.

oligopoly: A market in which a few firms produce all or most of the market supply of a particular good or service.

Determinants of Market Power

The number of firms in an industry is a key characteristic of market structure. The amount of market power the firms possess, however, depends on several factors. *The determinants of market power include*

- *Number of producers.*
- *Size of each firm.*
- *Barriers to entry.*
- *Availability of substitute goods.*

Characteristic	Market Structure				
	Perfect Competition	Monopolistic Competition	Oligopoly	Duopoly	Monopoly
Number of firms	Very large number	Many	Few	Two	One
Barriers to entry	None	Low	High	High	High
Market power (control over price)	None	Some	Substantial	Substantial	Substantial
Type of product	Standardized	Differentiated	Standardized or differentiated	Standardized or differentiated	Unique

TABLE 25.1

Characteristics of Market Structures

Market structure varies, depending on the number of producers, their size, barriers to entry, and the availability of substitute goods. An oligopoly is an imperfectly competitive structure in which a few firms dominate the market.

When only one or a few producers or suppliers exist, market power is automatically conferred. In addition to the number of producers, however, the size of each firm is also important. More than 600 firms supply long-distance telephone service in the United States. But just four of those firms (AT&T, Verizon, T-Mobile, and Sprint) account for 98 percent of all calls. Hence it wouldn't make sense to categorize that industry on the basis of only the number of firms; relative size is also important. The same thing is true in the beer industry. There are more than 7,000 breweries in the United States, but only four produce 80 percent of industry output (see Table 22.2).

A third and critical determinant of market power is the extent of barriers to entry. A highly successful monopoly or oligopoly arouses the envy of other profit maximizers. If it's a **contestable market,** potential rivals will seek to enter the market and share in the spoils. Should they succeed, the power of the former monopolist or oligopolists would be reduced. Accordingly, ease of entry into an industry limits the ability of a powerful firm to dictate prices and product flows. In Chapter 24 we saw how monopolies erect barriers to entry (e.g., patents) to maintain their power.

A fourth determinant of market power is the availability of substitute goods. If a monopolist or other power baron sets the price of a product too high, consumers may decide to switch to close substitutes. Thus, the price of Coors is kept in check by the price of Coke, and the price of sirloin steak is restrained by the price of chicken and pork. By the same token, a lack of available substitute products keeps the prices of insulin and AZT high.

> **contestable market:** An imperfectly competitive industry subject to potential entry if prices or profits increase.

Measuring Market Power

Although there are many determinants of market power, most observers use just one yardstick to measure the extent of power in an industry.

Concentration Ratio. The standard measure of market power is the **concentration ratio.** This ratio tells the share of output (or combined market share) accounted for by the largest firms in an industry. Using this ratio one can readily distinguish between an industry composed of hundreds of small, relatively powerless firms and another industry also composed of hundreds of firms but dominated by a few that are large and powerful. Thus *the concentration ratio is a measure of market power that relates the size of firms to the size of the product market.*

> **concentration ratio:** The proportion of total industry output produced by the largest firms (usually the four largest).

Table 25.2 gives the concentration ratios for selected products in the United States. The standard measure used here depicts the proportion of domestic production accounted for by the largest firms, usually the four largest. As a rule of thumb, *an industry with a concentration ratio above 60 percent is considered an oligopoly.* As is apparent from the table, the supply sides of these product markets easily qualify as *oligopolies* because most of these industries' output is produced by just three or four firms. Indeed, in some markets, one single firm is so large that an outright monopoly is nearly attained. For example, 70 percent of all canned soup is produced by Campbell. Gerber produces 80 percent of all prepared baby food. And Google accounts for 87 percent of all web searches. All firms that have a market share of at least 40 percent are denoted by **boldface** type in Table 25.2.

Firm Size. We noted before that market power isn't necessarily associated with firm size—in other words, a small firm could possess a lot of power in a relatively small market. Table 25.2, however, should be convincing testimony that we're not talking about small product markets here. Every one of the products listed enjoys a broad-based market. Even the chewing gum market (94 percent concentration ratio) rings up annual sales of $4 billion. The three oligopolists that produce video game consoles (Sony, Microsoft, Nintendo,) have 100 percent of a $25 billion market. Accordingly, for most of the firms listed in the table, market power and firm size go hand in hand. Indeed, the largest firms enjoy sales volumes that exceed the entire output of most of the *countries* in the world (see World View "Putting

Product	Largest Firms	Concentration Ratio (%)
Video game consoles	**Sony, Microsoft, Nintendo**	100%
Instant breakfast	**Carnation**, Pillsbury, Dean Foods	100
Laser eye surgery	**VISX**, Summit Technology	100
Tennis balls	**Gen Corp (Penn)**, PepsiCo **(Wilson)**, Dunlop, Spalding	100
Credit cards	Visa, MasterCard, American Express, Discover	99
Disposable diapers	**Procter & Gamble**, Kimberly-Clark, Curity, Romar Tissue Mills	99
Wireless phone service	AT&T, Verizon, T-Mobile, Sprint	98
Razor blades	**Gillette**, Warner-Lambert (Schick; Wilkinson), Bic, American Safety Razor	98
Sports drinks	**PepsiCo (Gatorade)**, Coca-Cola (PowerAde), Monarch (All Sport)	98
Internet search engines	**Google**, Bing, Yahoo	98
Scientific calculators	**Texas Instruments**, Casio, Hewlett-Packard	97
Electric razors	**Norelco**, Remington, Warner-Lambert, Sunbeam	96
Sanitary napkins	**Johnson & Johnson**, Kimberly-Clark, Procter & Gamble	96
Cigarettes	**Altria**, Reynolds American, Imperial, Liggett	96
Baby food	**Gerber Products**, Beech-Nut, DelMonte	95
Batteries	**Duracell**, Eveready, Ray-O-Vac, Kodak	94
Web search ads	**Google**, Yahoo, Microsoft, AOL	94
Chewing gum	**Wm. Wrigley**, Mondelez, Hershey	94
Soft drinks	Coca-Cola, PepsiCo, Dr. Pepper Snapple, Cott (RC Cola)	94
Breakfast cereals	Kelloggs, General Mills, Ralcorp, PepsiCo (Quaker Oats)	92
Computer printers	**Hewlett-Packard**, Epson, Canon, Lexmark	91
Toothpaste	Colgate-Palmolive, Procter & Gamble, Church & Dwight, Beecham	91
Internet browsers	**Google**, Microsoft, Mozilla, Apple	90
Detergents	**Procter & Gamble**, Lever Bros., Dial, Colgate-Palmolive	90
Art auctions	**Sotheby's, Christie's**	90
Greeting cards	**Hallmark**, American Greetings, Gibson	88
Canned soup	**Campbell**, Progresso	85
Beer	**Anheuser-Busch**, MillerCoors, Constellation, Heineken	80

Sources: Data from Federal Trade Commission, *The Wall Street Journal, Advertising Age, Financial World, Standard & Poor's, Fortune,* and industry sources.

Note: Individual corporations with a market share of at least 40 percent are designated in **boldface**. Market shares based on selected years, 2014–2017.

TABLE 25.2

Power in U.S. Product Markets

The domestic production of many familiar products is concentrated among a few firms. These firms have substantial control over the quantity supplied to the market and thus over market price. The concentration ratio measures the share of total output produced by the largest producers in a given market.

Size in Global Perspective"). Walmart's annual revenues alone would make it the world's 23rd largest country!

Measurement Problems

A high concentration ratio or large firm size isn't the only way to achieve market power. The supply and price of a product can be altered by many firms acting in unison. Even 1,000 small producers can band together to change the quantity supplied to the market, thus exercising market power. Recall how our mythical Universal Electronics (Chapter 24) exercised market power by coordinating the production decisions of its many separate plants. Those plants could have attempted such coordination on their own even if they

WORLD VIEW

PUTTING SIZE IN GLOBAL PERSPECTIVE

The largest firms in the United States are also the dominant forces in global markets. They export products to foreign markets and produce goods abroad for sale there or to import back into the United States. In terms of size alone, these business giants rival most of the world's nations. Walmart's gross sales, for example, would make it the 23rd largest "country" in terms of national GDP.

American corporations aren't the only giants in the global markets. Volkswagen (Germany), Royal Dutch Shell (The Netherlands), and Toyota (Japan) are among the foreign giants that contest global markets.

Rank	Country or Corporation	Sales or GDP (in billions of dollars)	Rank	Country or Corporation	Sales or GDP (in billions of dollars)
1	United States	$18,036	20	Saudi Arabia	646
2	China	11,007	21	Argentina	583
3	Japan	4,383	22	Sweden	496
4	Germany	3,363	23	Walmart Stores	482
5	United Kingdom	2,858	24	Nigeria	481
6	France	2,418	25	Poland	477
7	India	2,095	26	Belgium	455
8	Italy	1,821	27	Iran	425
9	Brazil	1,774	28	Thailand	395
10	Canada	1,550	29	Norway	386
11	South Korea	1,378	30	Austria	377
12	Australia	1,339	40	Royal Dutch Shell	272
13	Russia	1,331	42	ExxonMobil	246
14	Spain	1,199	44	Volkswagon	237
15	Mexico	1,143	45	Toyota	237
16	Indonesia	862	46	Apple	234
17	The Netherlands	750	47	Finland	232
18	Turkey	718	48	Portugal	199
19	Switzerland	671			

Sources: World Bank Atlas Method, and *Fortune*'s annual ranking of the world's largest corporations, "Global 500." *Fortune* magazine, July 26, 2016.

ANALYSIS: Firm size is a determinant of market power. The size of the largest firms, as measured by total revenue, exceeds the value of total output in most of the world's 200-plus countries.

hadn't all been owned by the same corporation. Lawyers and doctors exercise this kind of power by maintaining uniform fee schedules for members of the American Bar Association (ABA) and the American Medical Association (AMA).[1] Similarly, dairy farmers act jointly through three large cooperatives (the American Milk Producers, Mid-America Dairies, and Dairymen, Inc.), which together control 50 percent of all milk production.

Finally, all the figures and corporations cited here refer to *national* markets. They don't convey the extent to which market power may be concentrated in a *local* market. In fact, many industries with low concentration ratios nationally are represented by just one or a few firms locally. Prime examples include milk, newspapers, and transportation (both public and private). For example, fewer than 60 cities in the United States have two or more independently owned daily newspapers, and nearly all those newspapers rely on only two news services (Associated Press and United Press International). Perhaps you've also noticed that most college campuses have only one bookstore. It may not be a *national* powerhouse, but it does have the power to influence what goods are available on campus and how much they cost.

[1] The courts have ruled that uniform fee schedules are illegal and that individual lawyers and doctors have the right to advertise their prices (fees). Nevertheless, a combination of inertia and self-interest has effectively maintained high fee schedules and inhibited advertising.

OLIGOPOLY BEHAVIOR

With so much market power concentrated in so few hands, it's unrealistic to expect market outcomes to resemble those of perfect competition. As we observed in Chapter 24, *market structure affects market behavior and outcomes.* In that chapter we focused on the contrast between monopoly and perfect competition. Now we focus on the behavior of a more common market structure: oligopoly.

To isolate the unique character of oligopoly, we'll return to the computer market. In Chapter 23 we observed that the computer market was highly competitive in its early stages, when entry barriers were low and hundreds of firms were producing similar products. In Chapter 24 we created an impassable barrier to entry (a patent on the electronic brain of the computer) that transformed the computer industry into a monopoly of Universal Electronics. Now we'll transform the industry again. This time we'll create an oligopoly by assuming that three separate firms (Universal, World, and International) all possess patent rights. The patent rights permit each firm to produce and sell all the computers it wants and to exclude all other would-be producers from the market. With these assumptions, we create three **oligopolists,** the firms that share an *oligopoly.* Our objective is to see how market outcomes would change in such a market structure.

oligopolist: One of the dominant firms in an oligopoly.

The Initial Equilibrium

As before, we'll assume that the initial conditions in the computer market are represented by a market price of $1,000 and market sales of 20,000 computers per month, as illustrated in Figure 25.1.

We'll also assume that the **market share** of each producer is accurately depicted in Table 25.3. Thus Universal Electronics is assumed to be producing 8,000 computers per month, or 40 percent of total market supply. World Computers has a market share of 32.5 percent, while International Semiconductor has only a 27.5 percent share. The assumed **concentration ratio** is therefore 100.

market share: The percentage of total market output produced by a single firm.

The Battle for Market Shares

The first thing to note about this computer oligopoly is that it's likely to exhibit great internal tension. Neither World Computers nor International Semiconductor is really happy playing second or third fiddle to Universal Electronics. Each company would like to be number one in this market. On the other hand, Universal would like a larger market share as well, particularly in view of the huge profits being made on computers. As we observed in Chapter 23, the initial equilibrium in the computer industry yielded an *average* profit of $300 per computer, and total *industry* profits of $6 million per month (20,000 × $300). Universal would love to acquire the market shares of its rivals, thereby grabbing all this industry profit for itself.

But how does an oligopolist acquire a larger market share? In a truly competitive market, a single producer could expand production at will, with no discernible impact on market

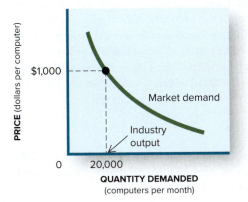

FIGURE 25.1

Initial Conditions in the Computer Market

As in Chapters 23 and 24, we assume that the initial equilibrium in the computer market occurs at a price of $1,000 and a quantity of 20,000 per month. How will an oligopoly alter these outcomes?

Producer	Output (Computers per Month)	Market Share (%)
Universal Electronics	8,000	40.0%
World Computers	6,500	32.5
International Semiconductor	5,500	27.5
Total industry output	20,000	100.0%

supply. That's not possible when there are only three firms in the market. *In an oligopoly, increased sales on the part of one firm will be noticed immediately by the other firms.*

How do we know that increased sales will be noticed so quickly? Because increased sales by one firm will have to take place either at the existing market price ($1,000) or at a lower price. Either of these two events will ring an alarm at the corporate headquarters of the other two firms.

Increased Sales at the Prevailing Market Price. Consider first the possibility of Universal Electronics increasing its sales at the going price of $1,000 per computer. We know from the demand curve in Figure 25.1 that consumers are willing to buy *only* 20,000 microcomputers per month at that price. Hence any increase in computer sales by Universal must be immediately reflected in *lower* sales by World or International. That is, *increases in the market share of one oligopolist necessarily reduce the shares of the remaining oligopolists.* If Universal were to increase its sales from 8,000 to 9,000 computers per month, the combined monthly sales of World and International would have to fall from 12,000 to 11,000 (see Table 25.3). The *quantity demanded* at $1,000 remains 20,000 computers per month (see Figure 25.1). Thus any increased sales at that price by Universal must be offset by reduced sales by its rivals.

This interaction among the market shares of the three oligopolists ensures that Universal's sales success will be noticed. It won't be necessary for World Computers or International Semiconductor to engage in industrial espionage. These firms can quickly figure out what Universal is doing simply by looking at their own (declining) sales figures.

Increased Sales at Reduced Prices. Universal could pursue a different strategy. Specifically, Universal could attempt to increase its sales by lowering the price of its computers. Reduced prices would expand total market sales, possibly enabling Universal to increase its sales without directly reducing the sales of either World or International.

But this outcome is most unlikely. If Universal lowered its price from $1,000 to, say, $900, consumers would flock to Universal Computers, and the sales of World and International would plummet. After all, we've always assumed that consumers are rational enough to want to pay the lowest possible price for any particular good. It's unlikely that consumers would continue to pay $1,000 for a World or International machine when they could get basically the same computer from Universal for only $900. If there were no difference, either perceived or real, among the computers of the three firms, a *pure* oligopoly would exist. In that case, Universal would capture the *entire* market if it lowered its price below that of its rivals.

More often, consumers perceive differences in the products of rival oligopolists, even when the products are essentially identical. These perceptions (or any real differences that may exist) create a *differentiated* oligopoly. In this case, Universal would gain many but not all customers if it reduced the price of its computers. That's the outcome we'll assume here. In either case, there simply isn't any way that Universal can increase its sales at reduced prices without causing alarms to go off at World and International.

Retaliation

So what if the alarms do go off at World Computers and International Semiconductor? As long as Universal Electronics is able to enlarge its share of the market and grab more profits, why should it care if World and International find out?

Universal *does* have something to worry about. World and International may not be content to stand by and watch their market shares and profits diminish. On the contrary, World and International are likely to take some action of their own once they discover what's going on.

There are two things World and International can do once they decide to act. In the first case, where Universal is expanding its market share at prevailing prices ($1,000), World and International can retaliate by

- Stepping up their own marketing efforts.
- Cutting prices on their computers.

Advertising. To step up their marketing efforts, World and International might increase their advertising expenditures, repackage their computers, put more sales representatives on the street, or sponsor a college homecoming week. This is the kind of behavior RC Cola used to gain market share from Coke and Pepsi (see In the News "RC Targeting Young Soda Drinkers"). Such attempts at **product differentiation** are designed to make one firm's products appear different and superior to those produced by other firms. If successful, such marketing efforts will increase RC Cola sales and market share or at least stop its rivals from grabbing larger shares.

product differentiation:
Features that make one product appear different from competing products in the same market.

IN THE NEWS

RC TARGETING YOUNG SODA DRINKERS

Tired of playing fourth fiddle to soda giants Coke, Pepsi, and Dr. Pepper, RC Cola is stepping up its advertising efforts. RC is spending $15 million to reshape the company's image as the hip alternative to "corporate colas," its characterization of Coke and Pepsi. Along with the ad blitz, RC is introducing new products, including Nehi and RC Draft, sodas designed for youthful tastes.

Some analysts are skeptical about RC's chances of success.

"Anybody in the soft drink business trying to compete with Pepsi and Coke has an uphill battle—they have huge amounts of marketing muscle, financial resources, experience and bottling agreements," said John Sicher, co-editor of *Beverage Digest,* an industry publication. "But RC's new tactics are smart. They are tossing out a bunch of beverages targeted toward younger drinkers. Against Coke and Pepsi, guerrilla warfare is the only thing that might work."

The U.S. Soda Market
Market share of soft drink makers, 2015.

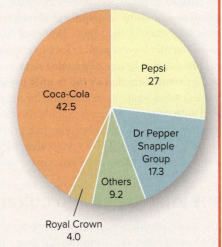

- Coca-Cola 42.5
- Pepsi 27
- Dr Pepper Snapple Group 17.3
- Others 9.2
- Royal Crown 4.0

—Anthony Faiola

Source: Faiola, Anthony, "Pop Culture: RC Goes for the Youth Market," *The Washington Post,* September 14, 1995, p. D10. Copyright ©1995.

ANALYSIS: Because price competition is typically self-defeating in an oligopoly, rival firms in an oligopoly rely on advertising and product differentiation (nonprice competition) to gain market share. RC nearly doubled its market share after it launched its new marketing.

Price Cuts. An even quicker way to stop Universal from enlarging its market share is for World and International to lower the price of *their* computers. Such price reductions will destroy Universal's hopes of increasing its market share at the old price. In fact, this is the other side of a story we've already told. If the price of World and International computers drops to, say, $900, it's preposterous to assume that Universal will be able to expand its

FIGURE 25.2

Rivalry for Market Shares Threatens an Oligopoly

If oligopolists start cutting prices to capture larger market shares, they'll be behaving much like truly competitive firms. The result will be a slide down the market demand curve to lower prices, increased output, and smaller profits. In this case, the market price and quantity would move from point *F* to point *G* if rival oligopolists cut prices to gain market shares.

market share at a price of $1,000. Universal's market share will shrink if it maintains a price of $1,000 per computer after World and International drop their prices to $900. Hence the threat to Universal's market share grab is that the other two oligopolists will retaliate by reducing *their* prices. Should they carry out this threat, Universal would be forced to cut computer prices too, or accept a greatly reduced market share.

The same kind of threat exists in the second case, where we assumed that Universal Electronics expands its sales by initiating a price reduction. World and International aren't going to just sit by and applaud Universal's marketing success. They'll have to respond with price cuts of their own. Universal would then have the highest price on the market, and computer buyers would flock to cheaper substitutes. Accordingly, it's safe to conclude that ***an attempt by one oligopolist to increase its market share by cutting prices will lead to a general reduction in the market price.*** The three oligopolists will end up using price reductions as weapons in the battle for market shares, the kind of behavior normally associated with competitive firms. Should this behavior continue, not only will oligopoly become less fun, but it will also become less profitable as prices slide down the market demand curve (Figure 25.2). This is why ***oligopolists avoid price competition and instead pursue nonprice competition*** (e.g., advertising and product differentiation).

THE KINKED DEMAND CURVE

The close interdependence of oligopolists—and the limitations it imposes on individual price and output decisions—is the principal moral of this story. We can summarize the story with the aid of the kinked demand curve in Figure 25.3.

Recall that at the beginning of this oligopoly story Universal Electronics had a market share of 40 percent and was selling 8,000 computers per month at a price of $1,000 each. This output is represented by point *A* in Figure 25.3. The rest of the demand curve illustrates what would happen to Universal's unit sales if it changed its selling price. What we have to figure out is why this particular demand curve has such a strange "kinked" shape.

Rivals' Response to Price Reductions

Consider first what would happen to Universal's sales if it lowered the price of its computers to $900. In general, we expect a price reduction to increase sales. However, ***the degree to which an oligopolist's sales increase when its price is reduced depends on the response of rival oligopolists.***

Rivals Don't Match. Suppose World and International *didn't* match Universal's price reduction. In this case, Universal would have the only low-priced computer in the market.

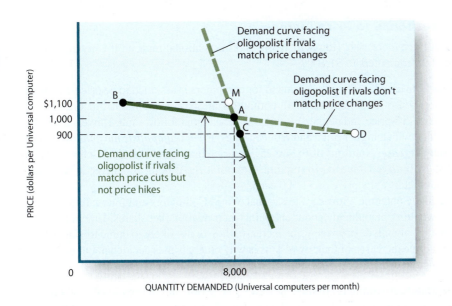

FIGURE 25.3

The Kinked Demand Curve Confronting an Oligopolist

The shape of the demand curve facing an oligopolist depends on the responses of its rivals to its price and output decisions. If rival oligopolists match price reductions but not price increases, the demand curve will be kinked.

Initially, the oligopolist is at point *A*. If it raises its price to $1,100 and its rivals don't raise their prices, it will be driven to point *B*. If its rivals match a price reduction (to $900), the oligopolist will end up at point *C*.

Consumers would flock to Universal, and sales would increase dramatically, from point *A* to point *D*.

Rivals Do Match. But point *D* is little more than a dream, as we've observed. World and International are sure to cut their prices to $900 to maintain their market shares. As a consequence, Universal's sales will expand only slightly, to point *C* rather than to point *D*. Universal's increased sales at point *C* reflect the fact that the total quantity demanded in the market has risen as the market price has fallen to $900 (see Figure 25.2). Thus, even though Universal's *market share* may not have increased, its monthly sales have.

The section of the demand curve that runs from point *A* to point *D* is unlikely to exist in an oligopolistic market. Instead *we expect rival oligopolists to match any price reductions* that Universal initiates, forcing Universal to accept the demand curve that runs from point *A* through point *C*. In the News "Rivals Match Southwest's Flash Sale" illustrates such behavior in the airline industry, where rivals were forced to match price cuts introduced by Southwest Airlines.

IN THE NEWS

RIVALS MATCH SOUTHWEST'S FLASH SALE

Rival airlines are quickly matching some—but not all—of the low fares Southwest rolled out on Tuesday as part of its 72-hour flash sale. American, United, and Jet Blue all announced fare cuts to below $100 on the short routes where Southwest is offering sale tickets. Flights between San Francisco and Los Angeles are now priced at $97, if purchased by Thursday midnight.

Source: Media reports, June 8, 2016.

DELTA ROLLS BACK FARE HIKE

Delta's fare increase didn't stick. On Tuesday Delta announced fare increases of $10–$20 per roundtrip ticket. American, United, and USAirways quickly did the same. But Southwest and Jet Blue didn't follow suit. Last night Delta started rolling back its fare hikes.

—**David Koenig**

Source: Media reports, April 19-22, 2012.

ANALYSIS: If rivals match price cuts but not price increases, the demand curve confronting an oligopolist will be kinked. Prices will increase only when all firms agree to raise them at the same time.

Rivals' Response to Price Increases

What about price increases? How will World and International respond if Universal raises the price of its computers to $1,100?

Rivals Don't Match. Recall that the demand for computers is assumed to be price-elastic in the neighborhood of $1,000 and that all computers are basically similar. Accordingly, if Universal raises its price and neither World nor International follows suit, Universal will be out there alone with a higher price and reduced sales. *Rival oligopolists may choose not to match price increases.* In terms of Figure 25.3, a price increase that isn't matched by rival oligopolists will drive Universal from point A to point B. At point B, Universal is selling very few computers at its price of $1,100 each.[2]

Is this a likely outcome? Suffice it to say that World Computers and International Semiconductor wouldn't be unhappy about enlarging their own market shares. Unless they see the desirability of an industrywide price increase, they're not likely to come to Universal's rescue with price increases of their own. This is why other airlines decided not to match the fare hikes announced by Delta (see In the News "Delta Rolls Back Fare Hike").

Rivals Do Match. Anything is possible, however, and World and International might match Universal's price increase. In this case, the *market price* would rise to $1,100 and the total quantity of computers demanded would diminish. Under such circumstances Universal's sales would diminish, too, in accordance with its (constant) share of a smaller market. This would lead us to point M in Figure 25.3.

Kinked Demand Curve. We may draw two conclusions from Figure 25.3:

- *The shape of the demand curve an oligopolist faces depends on the responses of its rivals to a change in the price of its own output.*
- *That demand curve will be kinked if rival oligopolists match price reductions but not price increases.*

GAME THEORY

The central message of the kinked demand curve is that oligopolists can't make truly independent price or output decisions. Because only a few producers participate in the market, *each oligopolist has to consider the potential responses of rivals when formulating price or output strategies.* This *strategic interaction* is the inevitable consequence of their oligopolistic position.

Uncertainty and Risk. What makes oligopoly particularly interesting is the *uncertainty* of rivals' behavior. For example, Universal *would* want to lower its prices *if* it thought its rivals wouldn't retaliate with similar price cuts. But it can't be sure of that response. Universal must instead consider the odds of its rivals not matching a price cut. If the odds are low, Universal might decide *not* to initiate a price cut. Or maybe Universal might offer price discounts to just a few select customers, hoping World and International might not notice or react to small changes in market share.

payoff matrix: A table showing the risks and rewards of alternative decision options.

The Payoff Matrix. Table 25.4 summarizes the strategic options each oligopolist confronts. In this case, let's assume that Universal is contemplating a price cut. Its rivals have only two options: either reduce their price also or not. Hence the **payoff matrix** has only four cells, each of which refers to a possible scenario. The payoff matrix in the table summarizes the various profit consequences of each scenario. One thing should be immediately clear: *The payoff to an oligopolist's price cut depends on how its rivals respond.* Indeed, the only scenario that increases Universal's profit is one in which Universal reduces its

---

[2]Notice again that we're assuming that Universal is able to sell some computers at a higher price (point B) than its rivals. The kinked demand curve applies primarily to differentiated oligopolies. As we'll discuss later, such differentiation may result from slight product variations, advertising, customer habits, location, friendly service, or any number of other factors. Most oligopolies exhibit some differentiation.

Universal's Options	Rivals' Actions	
	Reduce Price	**Don't Reduce Price**
Reduce price	Small loss for everyone	Huge gain for Universal; rivals lose
Don't reduce price	Huge loss for Universal; rivals gain	No change

TABLE 25.4

Oligopoly Payoff Matrix

The payoff to an oligopolist's price cut depends on its rivals' responses. Each oligopolist must assess the risks and rewards of each scenario before initiating a price change. Which option would you choose?

price and its rivals don't. We visualized this outcome earlier as a move from point *A* to point *D* in Figure 25.3. Note again that this scenario implies losses for Universal's two rival oligopolists.

The remaining cells in the payoff matrix show how profits change with other action/ response scenarios. One thing is evident: if Universal *doesn't* reduce prices, it can't increase profits. In fact, it might end up as the big loser if its rivals reduce *their* prices while Universal stands pat.

The option of reducing price doesn't guarantee a profit, but at least it won't ruin Universal's market share or profits. If rivals match a Universal price cut, all three oligopolists will suffer small losses.

So what should Universal do? The *collective* interests of the oligopoly are protected if no one cuts the market price. But an individual oligopolist could lose a lot if it holds the line on price when rivals reduce price. Hence each oligopolist might decide to play it safe by *initiating* a price cut.

Expected Gain (Loss). The decision to initiate a price cut boils down to an assessment of *risk*. If you thought the risk of a "first strike" was high, you'd be more inclined to reduce price. This kind of risk assessment is the foundation of game theory. You could in fact make that decision by *quantifying* the risks involved. Consider again the option of reducing price. As the first row of Table 25.4 shows, rivals can respond in one of only two ways. If they follow suit, a small loss is incurred by Universal. If they don't, there's a huge gain for Universal. To quantify the risk assessment, we need two pieces of information: (1) the size of each "payoff" and (2) the probability of its occurrence.

Suppose the "huge gain" is $1 million and the "small loss" is $20,000. What should Universal do? The huge gain looks enticing, but we now know it's not likely to h appen. But *how* unlikely is it? What if there's only a 1 percent chance of rivals not matching a price reduction? In that case, the *expected* payoff to a Universal price cut is

$$
\begin{aligned}
\text{Expected payoff of price cut} &= \left[\begin{array}{c}\text{Probability of}\\\text{rival matching}\end{array} \times \begin{array}{c}\text{Loss from}\\\text{price cut}\end{array}\right] + \left[\begin{array}{c}\text{Probability}\\\text{of rival}\\\text{not matching}\end{array} \times \begin{array}{c}\text{Gain}\\\text{from}\\\text{price cut}\end{array}\right] \\
&= [0.99 \times -\$20{,}000] + [0.01 \times \$1{,}000{,}000] \\
&= -\$19{,}800 + \$10{,}000 \\
&= -\$9{,}800
\end{aligned}
$$

Hence it's not a good idea. Once potential payoffs and probabilities are taken into account, a unilateral price cut doesn't look promising. The odds say a unilateral price cut will result in a loss (−$9,800).

These kinds of computations underlay the Cold War games that the world's one-time superpowers played. Neither side was certain of the enemy's next move but knew a nuclear first strike could trigger retaliatory destruction. As a consequence, the United States and the former Soviet Union continually probed each other's responses but were quick to retreat from the brink whenever all-out retaliation was threatened. Oligopolists play the same kind of game on a much smaller scale, using price discounts and advertising rather than nuclear warheads as their principal weapons. The reward they receive for coexistence is the oligopoly profits that they continue to share. This reward, together with the threat of mutual destruction, leads oligopolists to limit their price rivalry. This explains why analysts predict that Coke and Pepsi price wars will be brief (see In the News "Coke Reignites Price War").

IN THE NEWS

COKE REIGNITES PRICE WAR

Coke fired the first shot again in the periodic "soda wars" with rival Pepsi, cutting the price of Coke products by as much as 7.7 percent in the third quarter. Both companies have been hurt by a continuing decline in soda sales, fueled by Millennials' turn to energy drinks, juices, and bottled water. Coke's bottom line has been hit the hardest, as 100 percent of its sales come from beverages. Pepsi has an array of snack-food products to cushion declines in soda sales. Although the soda giants prefer to use packaging, new products, and advertising to compete for sales, they have used occasional price wars in the past. With loyalty rates of 90 percent, price wars are fairly ineffective in wooing consumers from a rival brand. But Coke wants to lure "fringe" consumers back from energy drinks and fruit juices. And its willing to start another price war with Pepsi to capture some of those consumers, even if it means lower profits for both Coke and Pepsi in the short run. Analysts expect the latest price war to be short-lived.

Source: Media reports, September 2015.

ANALYSIS: Price discounting can destroy oligopoly profits. When it occurs, rival oligopolists seek to end it as quickly as possible.

game theory: The study of decision making in situations where strategic interaction (moves and countermoves) occurs between rivals.

This isn't to say oligopolists won't ever cut prices or use other means to gain market share. They might, given the right circumstances and certain expectations of how rivals will behave. Indeed, there are a host of different price, output, and marketing strategies an oligopolist might want to pursue. The field of **game theory** is dedicated to the study of how decisions are made when such strategic interaction exists—for example, when the outcome of a business strategy depends on the decisions rival firms make. Just as there are dozens of different moves and countermoves in a chess game, so too are there numerous strategies oligopolists might use to gain market share.

OLIGOPOLY VS. COMPETITION

While contemplating strategies for maximizing their *individual* profits, oligopolists are also mindful of their common interest in maximizing *joint* (industry) profits. They want to avoid behavior that destroys the very profits that they're vying for. Indeed, they might want to coordinate their behavior in a way that maximizes *industry* profits. If they do, how will market outcomes be affected?

Price and Output

Thus far we've focused on a single oligopolist's decision about whether to *change* the price of its output. But how was the initial (market) price determined? In this example, we assumed that the initial price was $1,000 per computer, the price that prevailed initially in a *competitive* market. But the market is no longer competitive. As we saw in the previous chapter, a change in industry structure will affect market outcomes. A monopolist, for example, would try to maximize *industry* profits, all of which it would keep. To do this, it

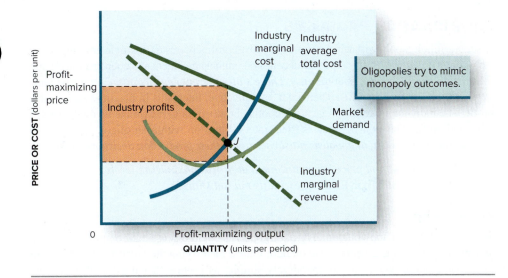

FIGURE 25.4
Maximizing Oligopoly Profits

An oligopoly strives to behave like a monopoly. Industry profits are maximized at the rate of output at which the *industry's* marginal cost equals marginal revenue (point *J*). In a monopoly, this profit all goes to one firm; in an oligopoly, it must be shared among a few firms.

In an oligopoly, the MC and ATC curves represent the combined production capabilities of several firms, rather than only one. The industry MC curve is derived by horizontally summing the MC curves of the individual firms.

would select that one rate of output where marginal revenue equals marginal cost, and it would charge whatever price consumers were willing and able to pay for that rate of output (see Figure 25.4).

An oligopoly would seek similar profits. An oligopoly is really just a *shared* monopoly. Hence **an oligopoly will want to behave like a monopoly, choosing a rate of industry output that maximizes total industry profit.**

The challenge for an oligopoly is to replicate monopoly outcomes. To do so, the firms in an oligopoly must find the monopoly price and maintain it. This is what the members of OPEC are trying to do when they meet to establish a common price for the oil they sell and agree to limit their output so as to achieve that price (see World View "Oil Spikes on OPEC Pact"). Reaching agreement requires a common view of the industry demand curve, satisfaction with respective market shares, and precise coordination.

WORLD VIEW

OIL SPIKES ON OPEC PACT

VIENNA, December 1—Oil prices spiked 14 percent, closing at a 17-month high of $51.68 a barrel on Friday. The surge in oil prices is a reaction to Wednesday's OPEC agreement to cut production for the first time since 2008. The 13 OPEC member states agreed to cut production by 1.2 million barrels a day, down from the current rate of 33.6 million barrels.

Source: Media reports, December 1–3, 2016.

ANALYSIS: An oligopoly tries to act like a shared monopoly. To maximize industry profit, the firms in an oligopoly must concur on what the monopoly price is and agree to maintain it by limiting output and allocating market shares.

Competitive industries would also like to reap monopoly-like profits. But competitive industries experience relentless pressure on profits as individual firms expand output, reduce costs, and lower prices. To maximize industry profits, competitive firms would have to band together and agree to restrict output and raise prices. If they did, though, the industry would no longer be competitive. Maximizing industry profits is easier in an oligopoly because fewer firms are involved and each is aware of its dependence on the behavior of the others.

COORDINATION PROBLEMS

A successful oligopoly will achieve monopoly-level profits by restricting industry output. As we've observed, however, this outcome depends on mutual agreement and coordination among the oligopolists. This may not come easy. ***There's an inherent conflict in the joint and individual interests of oligopolists.*** Their joint, or collective, interest is in maximizing industry profit. The individual interest of each oligopolist, however, is to maximize its own share of sales and profit. This conflict creates great internal tension within an oligopoly. To avoid self-destructive behavior, ***oligopolists must coordinate their production decisions so that***

- Industry *output and price are maintained at profit-maximizing levels.*
- *Each oligopolistic* firm *is content with its market share.*

Price-Fixing

To bring about this happy outcome, rival oligopolists could discuss their common interests and attempt to iron out an agreement on both issues. Identifying the profit-maximizing rate of industry output would be comparatively simple, as Figure 25.4 illustrated. Once the optimal rate of output was found, the associated profit-maximizing price would be evident. The only remaining issue would be the division of industry output among the oligopolists—that is, the assignment of market shares.

The most explicit form of coordination among oligopolists is called **price-fixing.** In this case, the firms in an oligopoly explicitly agree to charge a uniform (monopoly) price. This is what the 13 OPEC member-nations do when they get together to set oil prices (see World View "Oil Spikes on OPEC Pact"). Some other examples of price-fixing include the following.

Ivy League Colleges. For more than 30 years Ivy League schools worked together to offer a uniform financial aid package for individual students, eliminating price competition. The Justice Department ordered the schools to end that practice in 1992.

Electric Generators. In 1961 General Electric and Westinghouse were convicted of fixing prices on $2 billion worth of electrical generators that they'd been selling to the Tennessee Valley Authority and commercial customers. Among the corporate executives, 7 went to prison and 23 others were put on probation. In addition, the companies were fined a total of $1.8 million and compelled to pay triple damages in excess of $500 million to their victimized customers. Nevertheless, another suit was filed against General Electric and Westinghouse in 1972, charging these same companies—still the only two U.S. manufacturers of turbine generators—with continued price-fixing.

Perfume. Thirteen companies—including Chanel, Dior, and Yves Saint Laurent—paid $55 million in penalties in 2006 for fixing prices.

Auction Commissions. Sotheby's and Christie's, who together control 90 percent of the world's art auction business, admitted in 2000 to fixing commission rates throughout the 1990s. They paid a $512 million fine when they were caught.

Laser Eye Surgery. The FTC in 2006 charged the two companies that sell the lasers used for corrective eye surgery (VISX and Summit Technology) with price-fixing that inflated the retail price of surgery by $500 per eye.

Memory Chips. In 2005 the world's largest memory chip (DRAM) manufacturers (Samsung, Micron, Infineon, Hynix) admitted to fixing prices in the $16-billion-a-year DRAM market and paid nearly $700 million in criminal fines.

Elevators. In 2007 five companies were fined $1.3 billion for fixing prices on elevators and escalators in Europe for 10 years.

e-books. In June 2015 Apple was found guilty of conspiring with five book publishers to fix the price of e-books. E-book prices on Amazon went up from $9.99 to $12.99 or $14.99. Apple paid a $450 million fine.

price-fixing: Explicit agreements among producers regarding the price(s) at which a good is to be sold.

Laundry Detergent. Colgate-Palmolive was found guilty in 2016 of conspiring with its chief rival and a retailer to fix the price of laundry detergent in Australia. The company paid an $18 million fine.

Auto Parts. Bridgestone agreed to pay a $425 million criminal fine in 2016 for conspiring with other firms to fix prices, rig bids, and allocate sales of parts to auto manufacturers in the United States.

Price Leadership

Although price-fixing agreements are still a reality in many product markets, oligopolies have discovered that they don't need *explicit* agreements to arrive at uniform prices; they can achieve the same outcome in more subtle ways. **Price leadership** rather than price-fixing will suffice. If all oligopolists in a particular product market follow the lead of one firm in raising prices, the result is the same as if they had all agreed to raise prices simultaneously. Instead of conspiring in motel rooms (as in the electrical products and soft drink cases), the firms can achieve their objective simply by reading *The Wall Street Journal* or industry publications and responding appropriately. This is apparently how Coke and Pepsi communicated their desire to end their 1997 price war (see In the News "Coke Reignites Price War").

According to the U.S. Department of Justice, the major airlines developed a highly sophisticated form of price leadership. They used their shared computer reservation systems to signal *intended* price hikes. Rival oligopolists then responded with their own *intended* price changes. Only after it was clear that all the airlines would match a planned price increase was the price hike announced. The Justice Department argued that this "electronic dialogue" was equivalent to a price-fixing conspiracy that cost consumers $1.9 billion in excessive fares. In response, the major airlines agreed to stop using the reservations system to communicate *planned* fare hikes.

price leadership: An oligopolistic pricing pattern that allows one firm to establish the (market) price for all firms in the industry.

Allocation of Market Shares

Whenever oligopolists successfully raise the price of a product, the law of demand tells us that unit sales will decline. Even in markets with highly inelastic demand *some* decrease in sales always accompanies an increase in price. When this happens in a monopolistic industry, the monopolist simply cuts back the rate of output. In an oligopoly, however, no single firm will wish to incur the whole weight of that cutback. Some form of accommodation is required by all the oligopolists.

The adjustment to the reduced sales volume can take many forms. Members of OPEC, for example, assign explicit quotas for the oil output of each member country (see World View "Oil Spikes on OPEC Pact"). Such open and explicit production-sharing agreements transform an oligopoly into a **cartel.**

Because cartels openly violate U.S. antitrust laws, American oligopolies have to be more circumspect in divvying up shared markets. A particularly novel method of allocating market shares occurred in the price-fixing case involving General Electric and Westinghouse. Agreeing to establish high prices on electric generators wasn't particularly difficult. But how would the companies decide who was to get the restricted sales? Their solution was to designate one firm as the "low" bidder for a particular phase of the moon. The "low" bidder would charge the previously agreed-upon (high) price, with the other firm offering its products at even higher prices. The "low" bidder would naturally get the sale. Each time the moon entered a new phase, the order of "low" and "high" bidders changed. Each firm got a share of the business, and the price-fixing scheme hid behind a facade of "competitive" bidding.

Such intricate systems for allocating market shares are more the exception than the rule. More often the oligopolists let the sales and output reduction be divided up according to consumer demands, intervening only when market shares are thrown markedly out of balance. At such times an oligopolist may take drastic action, such as **predatory pricing.**

cartel: A group of firms with an explicit, formal agreement to fix prices and output shares in a particular market.

predatory pricing: Temporary price reductions designed to alter market shares or drive out competition.

Predatory price cuts are temporary price reductions intended to drive out new competition or reestablish market shares. The sophisticated use of price cutting can also function as a significant barrier to entry, inhibiting potential competitors from trying to gain a foothold in the price cutter's market. In the News "Eliminating the Competition with Low Prices" describes how major airlines forced Independence Air out of their market with predatory pricing in 2006.

IN THE NEWS

ELIMINATING THE COMPETITION WITH LOW PRICES

On January 5, 2006, Independence Air ceased flying. CEO Kerry Skeen, armed with $300 million in start-up capital, had positioned Independence as a low-fare entrant at the profitable Washington, DC, Dulles airport. At its launch in June 2004, Skeen observed that the Washington, DC, area was "screaming" for low fares.

The major carriers didn't agree. United Airlines, with a hub at Dulles, slashed fares as soon as Independence took flight. The rest of the "Big Six" (Delta, American, Northwest, US Airways, Continental) did the same. The fare war kept Independence from gaining enough market share to survive. As CEO Skeen concluded, "It's a brutal industry."

The week after Independence ceased flying, the "walk-up" fare between Dulles and Atlanta jumped from $118 to $478. Other fares followed suit.

Source: "Flying Monopoly Air," *McGraw-Hill News Flash*, McGraw-Hill Education, February, 2006. ©2006.

ANALYSIS: To protect their prices and profits, oligopolists must be able to eliminate potential competition. Predatory pricing can serve that purpose.

BARRIERS TO ENTRY

If oligopolies succeed in establishing monopoly prices and profits, they'll attract the envy of would-be entrants. To keep potential competitors out of their industry, oligopolists must maintain **barriers to entry.** *Above-normal profits can't be maintained over the long run unless barriers to entry exist.* The entry barriers erected include those monopolists use (Chapter 24).

barriers to entry: Obstacles such as patents that make it difficult or impossible for would-be producers to enter a particular market.

Patents

Patents are a very effective barrier to entry. Potential competitors can't set up shop until they either develop an alternative method for producing a product or receive permission from the patent holder to use the patented process. Such permission, when given, costs something, of course. In 2006 Research in Motion paid an extraordinary $612.5 million for the patent rights to produce BlackBerrys. In 2007 a federal court ordered Internet phone provider Vonage to pay $135 million and 5 percent of its future profits to its wired rivals, Verizon and Sprint. Patents and patent litigation scare off a lot of potential competition. Apple and Samsung have sued each other several times over alleged patent violations, always hoping to blunt competition.

Distribution Control

Another way of controlling the supply of a product is to take control of distribution outlets. If a firm can persuade retail outlets not to peddle anyone else's competitive wares, it will increase its market power. This control of distribution outlets can be accomplished through selective discounts, long-term supply contracts, or expensive gifts at Christmas. Recall from Chapter 24 (see In the News "Live Nation Acquires Ticketmaster") how Live Nation Entertainment locked up concert arenas and ticket distribution. According to the U.S.

Justice Department, Visa and MasterCard prevent banks that issue their credit cards from offering rival cards. Frito-Lay elbows out competing snack companies by paying high fees to "rent" shelf space in grocery stores (see In the News "Frito-Lay Eats Up Snack-Food Business"). Such up-front costs create an entry barrier for potential rivals. Even if a potential rival can come up with the up-front money, the owner of an arena or grocery store chain may not wish to anger the firm that dominates the market.

IN THE NEWS

FRITO-LAY EATS UP SNACK-FOOD BUSINESS

Anheuser-Busch is throwing in the towel on the snack-food business. The company announced it is selling off its Eagle Snacks subsidiary, after trying in vain to gain market share against Frito-Lay. Frito-Lay dominates the business, with half of all salty snack items. Competitors say Frito-Lay has secured its dominant position with shelf-space rentals in retail stores—paying as much as $40,000 a foot annually to secure prime shelf space in grocery and convenience stores. "Frito can afford it," said a regional rep for a competing company, "but we can't. It's become a real estate business." Such tactics have made Frito-Lay an invincible foe.

Source: News reports, October 1995.

ANALYSIS: Barriers to entry such as shelf-space rental and advertising enable a firm to maintain market dominance. Acquisitions also reduce competition.

New car warranties also serve as an entry barrier. The warranties typically require regular maintenance at authorized dealerships and the exclusive use of authorized parts. These provisions limit the ability of would-be competitors to provide cheaper auto parts and service. Frequent flier programs have similar effects in the airline industry.

Input Lock-Ups

Another way to deter competition is to acquire exclusive access to needed or ancillary inputs. Live Nation strengthens its power in the concert business by tying entertainers to exclusive contracts. Microsoft and Sony retain the lion's share of video console sales by contracting with developers to create games exclusively for their consoles. Apple does the same thing with applications software developers. Tesla is building a giga-factory to produce the lithium batteries that are the heart and soul of electric cars. U.S. Steel has exclusive access to coal mines it owns and operates. In all these cases, would-be competitors will find it difficult to acquire the inputs they need to produce competing products.

Mergers and Acquisition

Large and powerful firms can also limit competition by outright *acquisition*. A *merger* between two firms amounts to the same thing, although mergers often entail the creation of new corporate identities.

Perhaps the single most dramatic case of acquisition for this purpose occurred in the breakfast cereals industry. In 1946 General Foods acquired the cereal manufacturing facilities of Campbell Cereal Company, a substantial competitor. Following this acquisition, General Foods dismantled the production facilities of Campbell Cereal and shipped them off to South Africa!

Although the General Foods acquisition was more dramatic than most, acquisitions have been the most popular route to increased market power. General Motors attained a dominant share of the auto market largely by its success in merging with and acquiring two dozen independent manufacturers. In the cigarette industry, the American Tobacco

Company attained monopoly powers by absorbing 250 independent companies. Later anti-trust action (1911) split up the resultant tobacco monopoly into an oligopoly consisting of four companies, which continued to dominate the cigarette market until 2004, when R. J. Reynolds bought Brown & Williamson, leaving only three firms to dominate the cigarette industry. In 2014, Reynolds bought Lorillard, effectively creating an oligopoly (see In the News "Joe Camel Acquires Newport").

IN THE NEWS

JOE CAMEL ACQUIRES NEWPORT

In a widely anticipated move, Reynolds American, producer of best-selling brand Camel, announced yesterday that it has agreed to buy Lorillard, maker of Newport, the number 1 menthol cigarette. The $25 billion deal will combine the number 2 and number 3 cigarette manufacturers. The new company, retaining the Reynolds American name, will have 35 percent of the U.S. market, running second to Altria's 47 percent share. As part of the deal, Imperial Tobacco will purchase several of Lorillard's brands, including Blu, its popular e-cigarette, and end up with 10 percent of the market. Liggett Vector will keep 4 percent of the market. Prior to merging, Reynolds had 25 percent of the market and Lorillard had 12 percent, with Imperial at 8 percent.

Reynolds expects to cut annual costs by $800 million through eliminating overlap in sales, production, and overhead costs. Consumers worry that reduced competition will raise cigarette prices and further limit choices. The deal must win antitrust approval before it is finalized.

Source: News reports, July 15–18, 2014.

ANALYSIS: Mergers reduce competition, increase the concentration ratio, and often limit choice and raise price.

Other companies that came to dominate their product markets through mergers and acquisitions include U.S. Steel, U.S. Rubber, General Electric, United Fruit, National Biscuit Company, International Salt, and Live Nation Entertainment. Frito-Lay's 1995 acquisitions of Eagle Snacks (see In the News "Joe Camel Acquires Newport") extended its already dominant control of the chip, pretzel, and nuts markets.

Government Regulation

The government often helps companies acquire and maintain control of market supply. Patents are issued and enforced by the federal government and so represent one form of supply-restricting regulation. Barriers to international trade are another government-imposed barrier to entry. By limiting imports of everything from Chinese mushrooms to Japanese cars (see Chapter 35), the federal government reduces potential competition in U.S. product markets. Government regulation also limits *domestic* competition in many industries.

New York City also limits competition—in this case, the number of taxicabs on the streets. The maximum number of cabs was set at 11,787 in 1937 and stayed at that ceiling until 1996. The city's Taxi and Limousine Commission has since raised the ceiling to 13,605 taxis. That didn't do much to eliminate New York's perennial taxi shortage (for a population of more than 8 million people), much less reduce fares. As a result, license holders reaped monopoly-like profits for decades. A good measure of those monopoly profits was the price of the medallions that served as taxi licenses—a price that reached $1.3 million in 2014. When Uber, Lyft, and other ride-sharing services surmounted that entry barrier, the monopoly power of the medallions was shattered. In 2016, medallions were selling for as little as $250,000 and ride-sharing services had 35 percent of the market. Other states and cities are still protecting their taxi oligopolies by prohibiting Uber, Lyft, and other ride-share companies from operating.

Nonprice Competition

Producers who control market supply can enhance their power even further by establishing some influence over market demand. The primary mechanism of control is *advertising*. To the extent that a firm can convince you that its product is essential to your well-being and happiness, it has effectively shifted your demand curve. ***Advertising not only strengthens brand loyalty but also makes it expensive for new producers to enter the market.*** A new entrant must buy both production facilities and advertising outlets.

The cigarette industry is a classic case of high concentration and product differentiation. As Table 25.2 shows, the top four cigarette companies produce 96 percent of all domestic output; small, generic firms produce the rest. Together, the four cigarette companies produce well over 100 brands. To solidify brand loyalties, the cigarette industry spent more than $9 billion on advertising and promotions in 2016.

The breakfast cereal industry also uses nonprice competition to lock in consumers. Although the Federal Trade Commission has suggested that "a corn flake is a corn flake no matter who makes it," the four firms (Kellogg, General Mills, Ralcorp, and Quaker Oats) that supply more than 90 percent of all ready-to-eat breakfast cereals spend more than $500 million a year—about $1 per box!—to convince consumers otherwise.

Training

In today's technology-driven markets, early market entry can create an important barrier to later competition. Customers of computer hardware and software, for example, often become familiar with a particular system or computer package. Switching to a new product may entail significant cost, including the retraining of user staff. As a consequence, would-be competitors will find it difficult to sell their products even if they offer better quality and lower prices.

Network Economies

The widespread use of a particular product may also heighten its value to consumers, thereby making potential substitutes less viable. The utility of instant messaging—or even a telephone—depends on how many of your friends have telephones. If no one else had a phone there'd be no reason to own one. In other words, the larger the network of users, the greater the value of the product. Such network economies help explain why software developers prefer to write apps for the iPhone than applications for rival smartphones and why advertisers pay a premium to appear on Facebook.

THE ECONOMY TOMORROW

ANTITRUST ENFORCEMENT

Examples of market power at work in product markets could be extended for another 10 chapters. The few cases cited here, however, are testimony enough to the fact that market power has some influence on our lives. Market power *does* exist; market power *is* used. Although market power may result in economies of scale, the potential for abuse is evident. Market power contributes to **market failure** when it leads to resource misallocation (restricted output) or greater inequity (monopoly profits, higher prices).

What should we do about these abuses? Should we leave it to market forces to find ways of changing industry structure and behavior? Or should the government step in to curb noncompetitive practices?

Industry Behavior. Our primary concern is the *behavior* of market participants. What ultimately counts is the quantity of goods supplied to the market, their quality, and their price. Few consumers care about the underlying *structure* of markets; what we seek are good market *outcomes*.

market failure: An imperfection in the market mechanism that prevents optimal outcomes.

Continued

antitrust: Government intervention to alter market structure or prevent abuse of market power.

In principle, the government could change industry behavior without changing industry structure. We could, for example, explicitly outlaw collusive agreements and cast a wary eye on industries that regularly exhibit price leadership. We could dismantle barriers to entry and thereby promote contestable markets. We might also prohibit oligopolists from extending their market power via such mechanisms as acquisitions, excessive or deceptive advertising, and the financing of political campaigns. In fact, the existing **antitrust** laws—the Sherman Act, the Clayton Act, and the Federal Trade Commission Act (see Table 24.1)—explicitly forbid most of these practices.

There are several problems with this behavioral approach. The first limitation is scarce resources. Policing markets and penalizing noncompetitive conduct require more resources than the public sector can muster. Indeed, the firms being investigated often have more resources than the public watchdogs. The advertising expenditures of just one oligopolist, Procter & Gamble, are more than 10 times as large as the *combined* budgets of both the Justice Department's Antitrust Division and the Federal Trade Commission.

The paucity of antitrust resources is partly a reflection of public apathy. Consumers rarely think about the connection between market power and the price of the goods they buy, the wages they receive, or the way they live. As Ralph Nader discovered, "Antitrust violations are part of a phenomenon which, to the public, is too complex, too abstract, and supremely dull."[3] As a result, there's little political pressure to regulate market behavior.

The behavioral approach also suffers from the "burden-of-proof" requirement. How often will "trustbusters" catch colluding executives in the act? More often than not, the case for collusion rests on such circumstantial evidence as simultaneous price hikes, identical bids, or other market outcomes. The charge of explicit collusion is hard to prove. Even in the absence of explicit collusion, however, consumers suffer. If an oligopoly price is higher than what a competitive industry would charge, consumers get stuck with the bill whether or not the price was "rigged" by explicit collusions. The U.S. Supreme Court recognized that consumers may suffer from *tacit* collusion, even where no *explicit* collusion occurs.

Industry Structure. The concept of tacit collusion directs attention to the *structure* of an industry. It essentially says that oligopolists and monopolists will act in their own best interest. As former Supreme Court Chief Justice Earl Warren observed, "An industry which does not have a competitive structure will not have competitive behavior."[4] To expect an oligopolist to disavow profit opportunities or to ignore its interdependence with fellow oligopolists is naive. It also violates the basic motivations imputed to a market economy. As long as markets are highly concentrated, we must expect to observe oligopolistic behavior.

Judge Learned Hand used these arguments to dismantle the Aluminum Company of America (Alcoa) in 1945. Alcoa wasn't charged with any illegal *behavior*. Nevertheless, the company controlled more than 90 percent of the aluminum supplied to the market. This monopoly structure, the Supreme Court concluded, was itself a threat to the public interest.

Corporate breakups are rarely pursued today. In 2001 the Justice Department withdrew a proposal to break up Microsoft into separate systems and applications companies. The prevalent feeling today, even among antitrust practitioners, is that the powerful firms are too big and too entrenched to make deconcentration a viable policy alternative.

Objections to Antitrust. Some people think *less* antitrust enforcement is actually a good thing. The companies challenged by the public "trustbusters" protest that they're being penalized for their success. Alcoa, for example, attained a monopoly by investing heavily in a new product before anyone else recognized its value. Other firms too have captured dominant market shares by being first, best, or most efficient. Having "won" the

[3]Source: Green, Mark J., et al., *The Closed Enterprise System: The Report on Antitrust Enforcement.* New York, NY: Grossman, p. ix, 1972.
[4]Ibid., p. 7.

game fairly, why should they have to give up their prize? They contend that noncompetitive *behavior,* not industry *structure,* should be the only concern of antitrust enforcers.

Essentially the same argument is made for proposed mergers and acquisitions. The firms involved claim that the increased concentration will enhance productive efficiency (e.g., via economies of scale). They also argue that big firms are needed to maintain America's competitive position in international markets (which are themselves often dominated by foreign monopolies and oligopolies). Those same global markets, they contend, ensure that even highly concentrated domestic markets will be contested by international rivals.

Finally, critics of antitrust suggest that market forces themselves will ensure competitive behavior. Foreign firms and domestic entrepreneurs will stalk a monopolist's preserve. People will always be looking for ways to enter a profitable market. Monopoly or oligopoly power may slow entry but is unlikely to stop it forever. Eventually competitive forces will prevail.

Structural Guidelines: The Herfindahl-Hirshman Index. There are no easy answers. In theory, competition is valuable, but some mergers and acquisitions undoubtedly increase efficiency. Moreover, some international markets may require a minimum firm size not consistent with perfect competition. Finally, our regulatory resources are limited; not every acquisition or merger is worthy of public scrutiny.

Where would we draw the line? Can a firm hold a 22 percent market share, but not 30 percent? Are five firms too few, but six firms in an industry enough? Someone has to make those decisions. That is, *the broad mandates of the antitrust laws must be transformed into specific guidelines for government intervention.*

In 1982 the Antitrust Division of the U.S. Department of Justice adopted specific guidelines for intervention based on industry *structure* alone. They're based on an index that takes into account the market share of *each* firm rather than just the *combined* market share of the top four firms. Specifically, the **Herfindahl-Hirshman Index (HHI)** of market concentration is calculated as

$$\text{HHI} = \sum_{i=1}^{n} = \left(\frac{\textbf{Share of}}{\textbf{firm 1}}\right)^2 + \left(\frac{\textbf{Share of}}{\textbf{firm 2}}\right)^2 + \cdots + \left(\frac{\textbf{Share of}}{\textbf{firm } n}\right)^2$$

Thus a three-firm oligopoly like that described in Table 25.3 would have an HHI value of

$$\text{HHI} = (40.0)^2 + (32.5)^2 + (27.5)^2 = 3,412.5$$

where the numbers in parentheses indicate the market shares of the three fictional computer companies. The calculation yields an HHI value of 3,412.5.

For policy purposes, the Justice Department decided it would draw the line at 1,800. *Any merger that creates an HHI value over 1,800 will be challenged by the Justice Department.* If an industry has an HHI value between 1,000 and 1,800, the Justice Department will challenge any merger that *increases* the HHI by 100 points or more. Mergers and acquisitions in industries with an HHI value of less than 1,000 won't be challenged.

The HHI is an arbitrary but workable tool for deciding when the government should intervene to challenge mergers and acquisitions. The Justice Department reviews about 2,500 mergers a year but challenges fewer than 50.

The AT&T/T-Mobile Deal. The Justice Department's guidelines were put to the test in 2011. In March 2011 AT&T announced that it planned to purchase T-Mobile, the fourth largest wireless phone company. That acquisition would have sent the Herfindahl-Hirschmann Index through the roof. But AT&T argued that the acquisition of T-Mobile would result in economies of scale that would improve service and reduce costs. Critics said the loss of competition would raise prices and reduce phone service options. The Justice Department sided with the critics and sued in August 2011 to block the merger. AT&T abandoned the idea four months later and now competes with T-Mobile.

Herfindahl-Hirshman Index (HHI): Measure of industry concentration that accounts for number of firms and size of each.

SUMMARY

- Imperfect competition refers to markets in which individual suppliers (firms) have some independent influence on the price at which their output is sold. Examples of imperfectly competitive market structures are duopoly, oligopoly, and monopolistic competition. **LO25-1**
- The extent of market power (control over price) depends on the number of firms in an industry, their size, barriers to entry, and the availability of substitutes. **LO25-1**
- The concentration ratio is a measure of market power in a particular product market. It equals the share of total industry output accounted for by the largest firms, usually the top four. **LO25-1**
- An oligopoly is a market structure in which a few firms produce all or most of a particular good or service (a concentration ratio of 60 or higher); it's essentially a shared monopoly. **LO25-1**
- Because oligopolies involve several firms rather than only one, each firm must consider the effect of its price and output decisions on the behavior of rivals. Such firms are highly interdependent. **LO25-3**
- Game theory attempts to identify different strategies a firm might use, taking into account the consequences of rivals' moves and countermoves. **LO25-3**
- The kinked demand curve illustrates a pattern of strategic interaction in which rivals match a price cut but not a price hike. Such behavior reinforces the oligopolistic aversion to price competition. **LO25-3**
- A basic conflict exists between the desire of each individual oligopolist to expand its market share and the *mutual* interest of all the oligopolists in restricting total output so as to maximize industry profits. This conflict must be resolved in some way, via either collusion or some less explicit form of agreement (such as price leadership). **LO25-3**
- Oligopolists may use price-fixing agreements or price leadership to establish the market price. To maintain that price, the oligopolists must also agree on their respective market shares. **LO25-3**
- To maintain economic profits, an oligopoly must erect barriers to entry. Patents are one form of barrier. Other barriers include predatory price cutting (price wars), control of distribution outlets, government regulations, advertising (product differentiation), training, and network economies. Outright acquisition and merger may also eliminate competition. **LO25-2**
- Market power may cause market failure. The symptoms of that failure include increased prices, reduced output, and a transfer of income from the consuming public to a relatively few powerful corporations and the people who own them. **LO25-2**
- Government intervention may focus on either market structure or market behavior. In either case, difficult decisions must be made about when and how to intervene. **LO25-1**
- The Herfindahl-Hirshman Index is a measure of industry concentration that takes into account the number of firms and the size of each. It is used as a structural guideline to identify cases worthy of antitrust concern. **LO25-1**

Key Terms

market structure	product differentiation	predatory pricing
oligopoly	payoff matrix	barriers to entry
contestable market	game theory	market failure
concentration ratio	price-fixing	antitrust
oligopolist	price leadership	Herfindahl-Hirshman Index (HHI)
market share	cartel	

Questions for Discussion

1. How many bookstores are on or near your campus? If there were more bookstores, how would the price of new and used books be affected? **LO25-1**
2. What entry barriers exist in (*a*) the fast-food industry, (*b*) cable television, (*c*) the auto industry, (*d*) illegal drug trade, (*e*) potato chips, and (*f*) beauty parlors? **LO25-1**
3. Why does RC Cola depend on advertising to gain market share? (See In the News "RC Targeting Young Soda Drinkers.") Why not offer cheaper sodas than Coke or Pepsi? **LO25-3**
4. If an oligopolist knows rivals will match a price cut, would it ever reduce its price? **LO25-3**
5. How might the high concentration ratio in the credit card industry (Table 25.2) affect the annual fees and interest charges for credit card services? **LO25-2**
6. What evidence of economies of scale is cited in the proposed cigarette merger (In the News "Joe Camel

Acquires Newport")? Should the acquisition be approved? **LO25-2**

7. What reasons might rival airlines have for *not* matching Delta's fare increase? (See In the News "Delta Rolls Back Fare Hike.") **LO25-3**

8. The Ivy League schools defended their price-fixing arrangement (see Ivy League Colleges in Coordination Problems section) by arguing that their coordination assured a fair distribution of scholarship aid. Who was hurt or helped by this arrangement? **LO25-2**

9. Using the payoff matrix in Table 25.4, decide whether Universal should cut its price. What factors will influence the decision? **LO25-3**

10. Domino's and Pizza Hut hold 66 percent of the delivered-pizza market. Should antitrust action be taken? **LO25-1**

11. Why did the price of NYC taxi medallions decline so much when Uber started ride-sharing service in New York? Why are the medallions still worth $250,000? **LO25-2**

LO25-1 1. According to Table 25.2, in how many markets do fewer than four firms produce at least 80 percent of total output?

LO25-2 2. According to World View "Oil Spikes on OPEC Pact,"
    (*a*) By what percentage did the price of oil increase after OPEC's announcement?
    (*b*) By what percentage was the quantity supplied reduced?
    (*c*) What was the price elasticity of demand? (use the midpoint method)

LO25-2 3. According to In the News "RC Targeting Young Soda Drinkers"
    (*a*) What is the concentration ratio in the U.S. soda market?
    (*b*) If Dr Pepper Snapple split into two equal sized firms, what is the new concentration ratio?

LO25-2 4. (*a*) According to In the News "Joe Camel Acquires Newport," how many years will it take Reynolds to recoup its purchase price through cost savings?
    (*b*) If Reynolds increases cigarette prices by 10 percent and the price elasticity of demand is 0.4, by how much will its annual revenue of $11 billion increase?

LO25-2 5. If the price of a medallion is a proxy for the profits of the NYC taxi industry, by what percentage did the industry's profits decline when Uber entered the market?

LO25-3 6. Assume an oligopolist confronts *two* possible demand curves for its own output, as illustrated here. The first (*A*) prevails if other oligopolists don't match price changes. The second (*B*) prevails if rivals *do* match price changes.

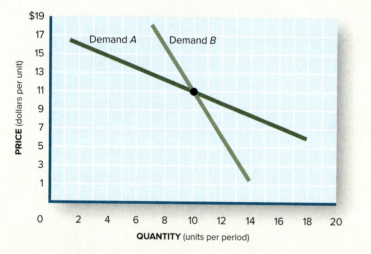

    (*a*) By how much does quantity demanded increase if the price is reduced from $11 to $9 and
      (*i*)   Rivals match the price cut?
      (*ii*) Rivals don't match the price cut?
    (*b*) By how much does quantity demanded change when the price is raised from $11 to $13 and
      (*i*)   Rivals match the price hike?
      (*ii*) Rivals don't match the price hike?

LO25-3 7. How large would the probability of a "don't match" outcome have to be to make a Universal price cut statistically worthwhile? (See expected payoff in section "Expected Gain (Loss).")

LO25-3 8. Suppose the payoff to each of four strategic interactions is as follows:

	Rival Response	
Action	Reduce Price	Don't Reduce Price
Reduce price	Loss = $800	Gain = $50,000
Don't reduce price	Loss = $6,000	No loss or gain

(*a*) If the probability of rivals matching a price reduction is 98 percent, what is the expected payoff of a price cut?

(*b*) If the probability of rivals reducing price when you don't reduce your price is 5 percent, what is the expected payoff of *not* reducing price?

(*c*) Based on your answers to (*a*) and (*b*), should the firm cut their price?

LO25-2 9. Suppose that the following schedule summarizes the sales (demand) situation confronting an oligopolist:

Price (per unit)	$20	$19	$18	$17	$16	$14	$12	$10	$ 8
Quantity demanded (units per period)	2	3	4	5	6	7	8	9	10

(*a*) Draw the demand and marginal revenue curves facing the firm.

(*b*) Identify the profit-maximizing rate of output in a situation where marginal cost is constant at $11 per unit.

LO25-2 10. What is the price elasticity of demand between points *F* and *G* in Figure 25.2 (use the midpoint method)?

LO25-1 11. The Economy Tomorrow: According to the In the News "Joe Camel Acquires Newport," what were the values of

(*a*) The concentration ratio in the cigarette industry

    (*i*) prior to the merger?

    (*ii*) after the merger?

(*b*) The *maximum* value of the Herfindahl-Hirschman Index

    (*i*) prior to the merger?

    (*ii*) after the merger?

(*c*) Which measure best reflects the increased market power?

STARBUCKS COFFEE

CHAPTER 26

Monopolistic Competition

Starbucks is already the biggest coffee bar chain in the world, with roughly 25,000 locations in 70 countries, including 13,000 in the United States. And the company is determined to keep growing by setting up coffee bars in airports, department stores, and just about anywhere consumers congregate. Even if Starbucks achieves such meteoric growth, however, it will never have great market power. There are more than 15,000 other coffee bars in the United States, not to mention a million or so other places you can buy a cup of coffee (e.g., Dunkin' Donuts, McDonald's). With so many other close substitutes, the best Starbucks can hope for is a little brand loyalty. If enough consumers think of Starbucks when they get the caffeine urge, Starbucks will at least be able to charge more for coffee than a perfectly competitive firm. It won't enjoy *monopoly* profits, or even share the kind of monopoly profits *oligopolies* sometimes achieve. It may, however, be able to maintain an economic profit for many years.

Starbucks is an example of yet another market structure—*monopolistic competition.* In this chapter we focus on how such firms make price and output decisions and the market outcomes that result. Our objective is to determine

- **The unique features of monopolistic competition.**
- **How market outcomes are affected by this market structure.**
- **The long-run consequences of different market structures.**

In this chapter we'll also see why we can't escape the relentless advertising that bombards us from every angle.

STRUCTURE

As we first noted in Table 25.1, the distinguishing structural characteristic of **monopolistic competition** is that there are *many* firms in an industry. "Many" isn't an exact specification, of course. It's best understood as lying somewhere between the few that characterize oligopoly and the hordes that characterize perfect competition.

Low Concentration

A more precise way to distinguish monopolistic competition is to examine **concentration ratios.** Oligopolies have very high four-firm concentration ratios. As we saw in Chapter 25 (Table 25.2), concentration ratios of 70 to 100 percent are common in oligopolies. By contrast, there's much less concentration in monopolistic competition. A few

monopolistic competition: A market in which many firms produce similar goods or services but each maintains some independent control of its own price.

concentration ratio: The proportion of total industry output produced by the largest firms (usually the four largest).

Product	Largest Firms (Market Share)	Concentration Ratio (%)
Auto tires (replacement)	Goodyear (16%), Michelin (8%), Firestone (7.5%), General (5%)	37
Bottled water	Coca-Cola (Dasani, 9.9%), PepsiCo (Aquafina, 9.6%), Nestle (8.3%), Glaceau (7.6%)	35
Toys	Lego (12%), Mattel (11%), Hasbro (10%), Tyco (5%)	35
Casinos	MGM, Caesars, Station, Mohegan Sun	33
Coffee bars	Starbucks (15%), Caribou (6%), Peet's (4%), Coffee Beanery (3%)	28
Pizza	Pizza Hut (8.7%), Domino's (8.2%), Little Caesars (6.8%), Papa John's (4.4%)	28
Drugs	GlaxoSmithKline (5.8%), Hoechst-Marion Merrell Dow (4.4%), Merck (4.4%), American Home Products (3.8%)	18
Fast-food restaurants	McDonald's (7.3%), Subway (2.6%), Starbucks (2.27%), Wendy's (1.8%)	14

Source: Industry sources and business publications (2014–2017 data).

TABLE 26.1

Monopolistic Competition

Monopolistically competitive industries are characterized by modest concentration ratios and low entry barriers. Contrast these four-firm concentration ratios with those of oligopoly (see Table 25.2).

firms may stand above the rest, but the combined market share of the top four firms will typically be in the range of 20 to 40 percent. Hence *low concentration ratios are common in monopolistic competition.*

Starbucks has less than 15 percent of the U.S. coffee bar business and a mere 7 percent of all coffee sales. The top four coffee bar outlets (Starbucks, Caribou, The Coffee Beanery, and Peet's) have a concentration ratio of only 28 percent (see Table 26.1). Other examples of monopolistic competition include banks, radio stations, health spas, apparel stores, convenience stores, night clubs, bars, and law firms.

Defining the Market. Concentration ratios look even lower when broader concepts of the relevant market are employed. Consider Starbucks again. Table 26.1 shows its share of the U.S. coffee bar market. But other companies also sell coffee. In fact, McDonald's sells a lot more coffee than does Starbucks. So does Dunkin' Donuts. If you include these outlets, Starbucks' market share shrinks dramatically. And on a global scale, Starbucks sells a tiny fraction of the 2.4 *billion* cups of coffee consumed daily.

The same classification problem applies to McDonald's in the fast-food market. McDonald's dwarfs Starbucks in size, with 37,000 outlets in 118 countries. In the United States, it commands close to a 50 percent share of the quickie *hamburger* market. But is that the relevant market? Or should we look at the broader *fast-food* market that includes pizzas, tacos, hot dogs, and Chinese take-out? If consumers view these other food options as close substitutes for a Big Mac, then McDonald's has a lot less market power than its share of the smaller hamburger market implies. In that larger fast-food market McDonald's has a market share of only 7.3% (Table 26.1).

The same kind of consumer choice affects how we assess market power in the pizza business. Three companies have 46 percent of the pizza *delivery* business. But they compete with more than 75,000 pizzerias in the United States, as well as all the other fast-food outlets. This reduces their market shares and power.

Market Power

Although concentration rates are low in monopolistic competition, the individual firms aren't powerless. There is a *monopoly* aspect to monopolistic competition. Each producer in monopolistic competition is large enough to have some **market power.** If a perfectly competitive firm increases the price of its product, it will lose all its customers. Recall that a perfectly competitive firm confronts a horizontal demand curve for its output. Competition is less intense in monopolistic competition. *A monopolistically competitive firm confronts a downward-sloping demand curve for its output.* When Starbucks increases the price of coffee, it loses some customers, but nowhere close to all of them (see In the News "Starbucks Ups the Price of Iced Drinks"). Starbucks, like other monopolistically competitive firms, has some control over the price of its output. This is the *monopoly* dimension of monopolistic competition.

IN THE NEWS

STARBUCKS UPS THE PRICE OF ICED DRINKS

Starbucks raised the price of iced coffee, frappuccinos, and other cold drinks by 10–30 cents, effective November 10. This is the second price hike this year, the company having raised the price of hot drinks by similar amounts last July. The average price of a venti mocha Frappuccino is now $4.95, up from $4.65 at most locations. While many customers took to Twitter to express their anger at another price hike, analysts see little risk for Starbucks, which maintains strong pricing power.

Source: Media reports, November 12–20, 2016.

ANALYSIS: A monopolistically competitive firm has the power to increase price unilaterally. The greater the brand loyalty, the less unit sales will decline in response.

Independent Production Decisions

In an oligopoly, a firm that increased its price would have to worry about how rivals might respond (like the airlines in Chapter 25, In the News "Rivals Match Southwest's Flash Sale"). In monopolistic competition, however, there are many more firms. As a result, *modest changes in the output or price of any single firm will have no perceptible influence on the sales of any other firm.* This relative independence results from the fact that the effects of any one firm's behavior will be spread over many other firms (rather than only two or three other firms, as in an oligopoly).

The relative independence of monopolistic competitors means that they don't have to worry about retaliatory responses to every price or output change. As a result, they confront more traditional demand curves with no kinks. Recall that the kink in the oligopolist's curve results from the likelihood that rival oligopolists will match price reductions (to preserve market shares) but not necessarily price increases (to increase their shares). In monopolistic competition, by contrast, the market shares of rival firms aren't perceptibly altered by another firm's price changes.

Low Entry Barriers

Another characteristic of monopolistic competition is the presence of *low* **barriers to entry**—it's relatively easy to get in and out of the industry. To become a coffee vendor, all you need is boiling water, some fresh beans, and cups. You can save on rent by using a pushcart to dispense the brew, which is how Starbucks itself got started on the streets of Seattle (see the photo). Coinstar has even replaced the pushcart with bright red Rubi kiosks in grocery stores. Such unusually low entry barriers now keep Starbucks and other coffee

Low entry barriers encourage competition.
©Chris Lawrence/Alamy Stock Photo

bars on their toes. Low entry barriers also tend to push economic profits toward zero. In the pizza business more than 4,000 firms enter and exit every year. This is the *competitive* dimension of monopolistic competition.

BEHAVIOR

Given the unique structural characteristics of monopolistic competition, we should anticipate some distinctive behavior.

Product Differentiation

One of the most notable features of monopolistically competitive behavior is **product differentiation.** A monopolistically competitive firm is distinguished from a purely competitive firm by its downward-sloping demand curve. Individual firms in a perfectly competitive market confront horizontal demand curves because consumers view their respective products as interchangeable (virtually identical). As a result, an attempt by one firm to raise its price will drive its customers to other firms.

product differentiation:
Features that make one product appear different from competing products in the same market.

Brand Image. In monopolistic competition, each firm has a distinct identity—a *brand image*. Its output is perceived by consumers as being somewhat different from the output of all other firms in the industry. Nowhere is this more evident than in the fast-growing bottled water industry. Pepsi and Coke have become the leaders in the bottled water market as a result of effective marketing (see In the News "Selling 'Pure Water': A $Billion Scam?"). Although Aquafina (Pepsi) and Dasani (Coke) are just filtered municipal water, clever advertising campaigns have convinced consumers that these branded waters are different—and better—than hundreds of other bottled waters. As a result of such product differentiation, Pepsi and Coke can raise the price of their bottled waters without losing all their customers to rival firms.

IN THE NEWS

SELLING "PURE WATER": A $BILLION SCAM?

The ads for Aquafina claim it has bottled the "purest of waters," while Dasani ads assert that what it bottles is "as pure as water can get." Visual backgrounds of glacial streams and lush woodlands reinforce the image of healthy, pure water.

The reality of bottled waters is very different, however. Every drop of water in Pepsi's Aquafina and Coca-Cola's Dasani comes out of the tap, not some mountain spring or glacial melt. Yes, the two major rivals in the bottled water business do filter the tap water, but it is still tap water. In blind tastings, most consumers either prefer simple tap water or can't tell the difference between the bottled and tap options. Further, a National Resources Defense Council found that bottled (filtered) water is no safer than tap water. The Environmental Protection Agency (EPA) tightly regulates the safety of tap water, while the Food and Drug Administration (FDA) sets less stringent requirements for bottled water and often relies on self testing.

Despite the absence of any tangible benefits, consumers spend more than $15 billion on bottled water every year. They are driven in large part by the $100 million a year that Pepsi, Coca-Cola, Nestlé and other bottlers spend on ads touting their "purest of waters."

Source: News reports, 2017.

ANALYSIS: By differentiating their products, monopolistic competitors establish brand loyalty. Brand loyalty gives producers greater control over the prices of their products.

Brand Loyalty

At first blush, the demand curve facing a monopolistically competitive firm looks like the demand curve confronting a monopolist. There's a profound difference, however. In a monopoly, there are no other firms. In monopolistic competition, *each firm has a monopoly only on its brand image; it still competes with other firms offering close substitutes.* This implies that the extent of power a monopolistically competitive firm has depends on how successfully it can differentiate its product from those of other firms. The more brand loyalty a firm can establish, the less likely consumers are to switch brands when price is increased. In other words, *brand loyalty makes the demand curve facing the firm less price-elastic.*

Brand loyalty exists even when products are virtually identical. Gasoline of a given octane rating is a very standardized product. Nevertheless, most consumers regularly buy one particular brand. Because of that brand loyalty, Exxon can raise the price of its gasoline by a penny or two a gallon without losing customers to competing companies. Brand loyalty is particularly high for cigarettes, toothpaste, and even laxatives. Consumers of those products say they'd stick with their accustomed brand even if the price of a competing brand was cut by 50 percent. In other words, *brand loyalty implies low* **cross-price elasticity of demand.** Brand loyalty is less strong (and cross-price elasticity higher) for paper towels and virtually nonexistent for tomatoes.

In the computer industry, product differentiation has been used to establish brand loyalty. Although virtually all computers use identical microprocessor "brains" and operating platforms, the particular mix of functions performed on any computer can be varied, as can its appearance (packaging). Effective advertising can convince consumers that one computer is "smarter," more efficient, or more versatile than another.

Even coffee vendors go to great length to differentiate their product. Starbucks offers not just coffee, but also WiFi hot spots, mobile payments, and powermats for cordless phone charging. These features give consumers added reason to linger at Starbucks and order more coffee. In Everett, Washington, coffee vendors differentiated themselves in 2014 with "bikini baristas"—baristas attired in skimpy bikinis. Every firm is looking to establish a unique image and greater brand loyalty. If successful in any of these efforts, *each monopolistically competitive firm will establish some consumer loyalty.* With such loyalty a firm can alter its own price somewhat without fear of great changes in unit sales (quantity demanded). In other words, the demand curve facing each firm will slope downward, as in Figure 26.1.

Repurchase Rates. One measure of brand loyalty is consumers' tendency to repurchase the same brand. Nearly 8 out of 10 Apple users stick with Apple products when they upgrade smartphones, computers, or tablets. Repurchase rates are 74 percent for Dell and 72 percent for Hewlett-Packard. Starbucks also counts heavily on return customers.

cross-price elasticity of demand: Percentage change in the quantity demanded of X divided by the percentage change in the price of Y.

FIGURE 26.1

Short-Run Equilibrium in Monopolistic Competition

Brand loyalty makes the demand curve facing a monopolistically competitive firm downward sloping. This causes MR < price.

In the short run, a monopolistically competitive firm equates marginal revenue and marginal cost (point *K*). In this case, the firm sells the resulting output at a price (point *F*) above marginal cost. Total profits are represented by the shaded rectangle.

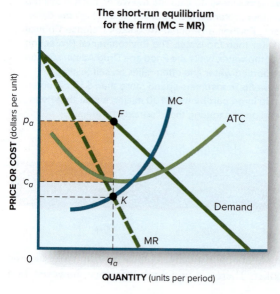

The short-run equilibrium for the firm (MC = MR)

PRICE OR COST (dollars per unit)

P_a F   MC   ATC

C_a K   Demand

MR

0   q_a

QUANTITY (units per period)

To maintain such brand loyalty, monopolistically competitive firms must often expand services or product offerings. Remember that entry barriers are low. In the coffee business, it was relatively easy for fast-food companies like McDonald's and Dunkin' Donuts to enter once they saw how profitable Starbucks was. When they did, Starbucks had to expand its menu to maintain its market dominance. Although menu expansion is costly, firms often decide that increased service is more cost-effective than price competition, given the low cross-price elasticity of demand in monopolistically competitive markets. In recent years, Starbucks has continued to pursue product differentiation with a new logo, instant coffee, new cup sizes (the 31-ounce "trenta"), single-serve machines, mobile payments, wine bars, and new food items.

Price Premiums. Another symptom of brand loyalty is the price differences between computer brands. Consumers are willing to pay more for an Apple, Lenovo, or Dell computer than a no-name computer with identical features. For the same reason, consumers are willing to pay more for Starbucks coffee, Ben and Jerry's ice cream, or Aquafina water, even when virtually identical products are available at lower prices.

Short-Run Price and Output

The monopolistically competitive firm's **production decision** is similar to that of a monopolist. Both types of firms confront downward-sloping demand and marginal revenue curves. To maximize profits, both seek the rate of output at which marginal revenue equals marginal cost. This short-run profit-maximizing outcome is illustrated by point K in Figure 26.1. That MC = MR intersection establishes q_a as the profit-maximizing rate of output. The demand curve indicates (point F) that q_a of output can be sold at the price of p_a. Hence the quantity–price combination q_a, p_a illustrates the short-run equilibrium of the monopolistically competitive firm.

> **production decision:** The selection of the short-run rate of output (with existing plants and equipment).

Entry and Exit

Figure 26.1 indicates that this monopolistically competitive firm is earning an **economic profit:** price (p_a) exceeds average total cost (c_a) at the short-run rate of output. These profits are of course a welcome discovery for the firm. They also portend increased competition, however.

> **economic profit:** The difference between total revenues and total economic costs.

Entry Effects. If firms in monopolistic competition are earning an economic profit, other firms will flock to the industry. Remember that *entry barriers are low in monopolistic competition, so new entrants can't be kept out of the market.* If they get wind of the short-run profits depicted in Figure 26.1, they'll come running.

As new firms enter the industry, supply increases and prices will be pushed down the market demand curve, just as in competitive markets. Figure 26.2a illustrates these market changes. The initial price p_1 is set by the intersection of *industry* MC and MR. Because that price generates a profit, more firms enter. This entry shifts the *industry* cost structure to the right, creating a new equilibrium price, p_2.

The impact of this entry on the firms already in the market will be different from that in competitive markets, however. As new firms enter a monopolistically competitive industry, existing firms will lose customers. This is illustrated by the leftward shift of the demand curve facing each firm, as in Figure 26.2b. Accordingly, we conclude that *when firms enter a monopolistically competitive industry,*

- *The industry cost curves shift to the right, pushing down price* (Figure 26.2a).
- *The demand curves facing individual firms shift to the left* (Figure 26.2b).

As the demand curve it faces shifts leftward, the monopolistically competitive firm will have to make a new production decision. It need not charge the same price as its rivals, however, or coordinate its output with theirs. Each monopolistically competitive firm has some independent power over its (shrinking numbers of) captive customers.

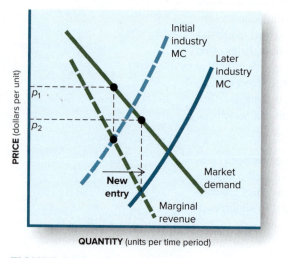

(a) Effect of entry on the industry

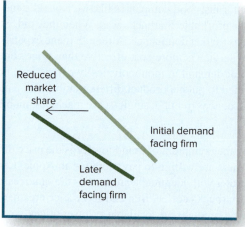

(b) Effect of entry on the monopolistically competitive firm

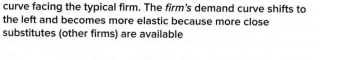

FIGURE 26.2

Market vs. Firm Effects of Entry

Barriers to entry are low in monopolistic competition. Hence new firms will enter if economic profits are available.

(a) The Market. The entry of new firms will shift the *market* cost curves to the right, as in part *a*. This pushes the average price down the *market* demand curve.

(b) The Firm. The entry of new firms also affects the demand curve facing the typical firm. The *firm's* demand curve shifts to the left and becomes more elastic because more close substitutes (other firms) are available

No Long-Run Profits

Although each firm has some control over its own pricing decisions, *entry-induced leftward shifts of the demand curve facing the firm will ultimately eliminate economic profits.*

Long-Run Equilibrium. Notice in Figure 26.3 where the firm eventually ends up. In long-run equilibrium (point *G*), marginal cost is again equal to marginal revenue (at the MR = MC intersection directly below *G*). At that rate of output (q_g), however, there are no economic profits. At that output, price (p_g) is exactly equal to average total cost.

The profit-maximizing equilibrium (point *G*) occurs where the demand curve is tangent to the ATC curve. If the demand curve shifted any farther left, price would always be less than ATC and the firm would incur losses. If the demand curve were positioned farther to the right, price would exceed ATC at some rates of output. When the demand curve is *tangent* to the ATC curve, the firm's best possible outcome is to break even. At point *G* in Figure 26.3, price equals ATC and economic profit is zero.

Will a monopolistically competitive firm end up at point *G*? As long as other firms can enter the industry, the disappearance of economic profits is inevitable. Existing firms can postpone the day of reckoning by increasing their product differentiation and advertising. But rival firms will enter as long as the demand (price) line lies above ATC at some point. Firms will exit when the demand facing the firm lies to the left of and below the ATC curve. Entry and exit cease when the firm's demand curve is *tangent* to the ATC curve. Once entry and exit cease, the long-run equilibrium has been established. *In the long run, there are no economic profits in monopolistic competition.*

Inefficiency

The zero-profit equilibrium of firms in monopolistic competition, as illustrated in Figure 26.3, differs from the perfectly competitive equilibrium. In perfect competition, long-run profits are also zero. But at that point, a competitive industry produces at the *lowest* point on the ATC curve and thus maximizes efficiency. In monopolistic competition, however, the

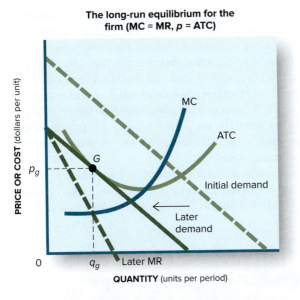

The long-run equilibrium for the firm (MC = MR, p = ATC)

PRICE OR COST (dollars per unit)

MC

ATC

G

p_g

Initial demand

Later demand

0   q_g Later MR

QUANTITY (units per period)

FIGURE 26.3

Long-Run Equilibrium in Monopolistic Competition

In the long run, more firms enter the industry. As they do so, the demand curve facing each firm *shifts* to the left as all market shares decline. Firms still equate MR and MC. Ultimately, however, the demand curve will be tangent to the ATC curve (point *G*), at which point price equals average total cost and no economic profits exist.

demand curve facing each firm slopes downward. Hence it can't be tangent to the ATC curve at its lowest point (the bottom of the U), as in perfect competition. Instead the demand curve of a monopolistically competitive firm must touch the ATC curve on the *left* side of the U.

Note in Figure 26.3 how point *G* lies above and to the left of the bottom of the ATC curve. This long-run equilibrium occurs at an output rate that is less than the minimum-cost rate of production. In long-run equilibrium, the monopolistically competitive industry isn't producing at minimum average cost. As a consequence, *monopolistic competition tends to be less efficient in the long run than a perfectly competitive industry.*

Excess Capacity. One symptom of the inefficiencies associated with monopolistic competition is industrywide excess capacity (see In the News "Coffee Shops Seeking New Identities"). Each firm tries to gain market share by building more outlets and advertising heavily. In equilibrium, however, the typical firm is producing at a rate of output that's less than its minimum-ATC output rate. This implies that the *same* level of *industry* output could be produced at lower cost with fewer firms. If that happened, the resources used to develop that excess capacity could be used for more desired purposes.

IN THE NEWS

COFFEE SHOPS SEEKING NEW IDENTITIES

ALBANY—It's easy to get a good cup of coffee on Wolf Road. And it's getting easier.

With over 35,000 specialty coffee shops in the United States, it isn't easy to brew a profit in the coffee business anymore. To buck that trend, coffee purveyors are trying to create new niches that are less competitive. In 2015 Starbucks debuted its "Starbucks Reserve Roastery and Tasting Room," located just nine blocks up the street from its very first Seattle shop. The Roastery specializes in single-source and often rare coffees, like Peru Chontali and Rwanda Maraba (for $4–$7 a cup). Consumers can observe the in-store roasting process while viewing images of the locations the beans came from. Stumptown and Microlots are pursuing the same niche, striving to preserve profits in a saturated coffee market.

Source: Media reports, 2015–2016.

ANALYSIS: Continued entry will push economic profits to zero and leave the industry with excess capacity.

marginal cost pricing: The offer (supply) of goods at prices equal to their marginal cost.

Flawed Price Signals. The misallocation of resources that occurs in monopolistic competition is a by-product of the flawed price signal that is transmitted in imperfectly competitive markets. Because the demand curve facing a firm in monopolistic competition slopes downward, such a firm will violate the principle of **marginal cost pricing.** Specifically, it will always price its output above the level of marginal costs, just like firms in an oligopoly or monopoly. Notice in Figures 26.1 and 26.3 that price lies above marginal cost in both the short- and long-run equilibrium. As a consequence, price always exceeds the opportunity cost. Consumers respond to these flawed signals by demanding fewer goods from monopolistically competitive industries than they would otherwise. We end up with the wrong (suboptimal) mix of output and misallocated resources.

Thus *monopolistic competition results in both production inefficiency (above minimum average cost) and allocative inefficiency (wrong mix of output).* This contrasts with the model of perfect competition, which delivers both minimum average total cost and efficient (MC-based) price signals.

THE ECONOMY TOMORROW

NO CEASE-FIRE IN ADVERTISING WARS

Models of oligopoly and monopolistic competition show how industry structure affects market behavior. Of particular interest is the way different kinds of firms "compete" for sales and profits. *In truly (perfectly) competitive industries, firms compete on the basis of price.* Competitive firms win by achieving greater efficiency and offering their products at the lowest possible price.

Firms in imperfectly competitive markets don't "compete" in the same way. In oligopolies, the kink commonly found in the demand curve facing each firm inhibits price reductions. In monopolistic competition, there's also a reluctance to engage in price competition. Because each firm has its own captive market—consumers who prefer its particular brand over competing brands—price reductions by one firm won't induce many consumers to switch brands. As we noted earlier, the cross-price elasticity of demand is low in monopolistically competitive markets. Thus price reductions aren't a very effective way to increase sales or market share in monopolistic competition.

If imperfectly competitive firms don't compete on the basis of price, do they really compete at all? The answer is evident to anyone who listens to the radio, watches television, reads magazines or newspapers, clicks on the Internet, or drives on the highway. *Imperfectly competitive firms engage in nonprice competition.*

The most prominent form of *nonprice competition* is advertising. An imperfectly competitive firm typically uses advertising to enhance its own product's image, thereby increasing the size of its captive market (consumers who identify with a particular brand). The Coca-Cola Company hires rock stars to create the image that Coke is superior to other soft drinks (see In the News "The Cola Wars: It's Not All Taste"), thereby creating brand loyalty. In 2015, oligopolies and monopolistically competitive firms spent more than $200 *billion* on advertising for such purposes. Procter & Gamble alone spent $4.3 billion (see Table 26.2). P&G hopes that these expenditures shift the demand for its products (e.g., Ivory Soap, Pampers, Jif peanut butter, Crest, Tide) to the right, while perhaps making it less price-elastic as well. By contrast, perfectly competitive firms have no incentive to advertise because they can individually sell their entire output at the current market price.

A company that runs a successful advertising campaign can create enormous *goodwill* value. That value is reflected in stronger brand loyalty—as expressed in greater demand and smaller price elasticity. Often a successful brand image can be used to sell related products as well. According to World View "The Best Global Brands," the most valuable brand name in the world is Apple, whose worldwide name recognition is worth $154 *billion*.

THE COLA WARS: IT'S NOT ALL TASTE

American consumers gulp nearly 40 million soft drinks per day. The Coca-Cola Company produces about 40 percent of those soft drinks, while Pepsi-Cola produces about 30 percent of the market supply. With nearly 70 percent of the market between them, Pepsi and Coke wage fierce battles for market share.

The major weapon in these "cola wars" is advertising. Coke spends $3.5 billion a year to convince consumers that its products are superior. Pepsi spends about $2.5 billion to win the hearts and taste buds of American consumers. The advertisements not only tout the superior taste of their respective products but also try to create a distinctive image for each cola.

The advertising apparently works. Half of all soft drink consumers profess loyalty to either Coke or Pepsi. Few of these loyalists can be persuaded to switch cola brands, even when offered lower prices for the "other" cola.

Ironically, few people can identify their favorite cola in blind taste tests. Seventy percent of the people who swore loyalty to either Coke or Pepsi picked the wrong cola in a taste test.

The moral of the story? That in imperfectly competitive markets, product *image* and *perceptions* may be as important as product quality and price in winning market shares.

ANALYSIS: Advertising is intended to create brand loyalty. Loyal consumers are likely to buy the same brand all the time, even if competitors offer nearly identical products.

From society's perspective, the resources used in advertising and other forms of non-price competition could be used instead to produce larger quantities of desired goods and services. Unless consumers are given the chance to *choose* between "more" service and lower prices, there's a presumption that nonprice competition leads to an undesirable use of our scarce resources. For example, marketing costs absorb more than a third of the price of breakfast cereal. As a result of such behavior, consumers end up with more advertising but less cereal than they would otherwise. They could, of course, save money by buying store brand or generic cereals. But they've never seen athletes or cartoon characters endorse such products. So consumers pay the higher price for branded cereals.

Models of imperfect competition imply that advertising wars between powerful corporations won't end anytime soon. As long as markets have the *structure* of oligopoly or monopolistic competition, we expect the *behavior* of nonprice competition. Advertising jingles will be as pervasive in the economy tomorrow as they are today.

Company	Ad Spending in 2015 ($ billions)
Proctor & Gamble	$4.3 billion
AT&T	3.9
General Motors	3.5
Comcast	3.4
Verizon	2.7
Ford	2.7
American Express	2.3
Fiat Chrysler	2.2
Amazon	2.2
Samsung	2.1

Source: Kantar Media

TABLE 26.2

Top 10 Advertisers

Firms with market power attempt to preserve and extend that power through advertising. A successful advertising campaign alters the demand curve facing the firm, thus increasing potential profits. Shown here are the advertising outlays of the biggest advertisers in 2015.

THE BEST GLOBAL BRANDS

For companies in almost every industry, brands are important in a way they never were before. Why? For one thing, customers for everything from soda pop to software now have a staggering number of choices. And the net can bring the full array to any computer screen with a click of the mouse. Without trusted brand names as touchstones, shopping for almost anything would be overwhelming. Meanwhile, in a global economy, corporations must reach customers in markets far from their home base. A strong brand acts as an ambassador when companies enter new markets or offer new products.

That's why companies that once measured their worth strictly in terms of tangibles such as factories, inventory, and cash have realized that a vibrant brand, with its implicit promise of quality, is an equally important asset. A brand has the power to command a premium price, increasing profits and sheltering a company from competition.

The World's 10 Most Valuable Brands

Rank	Brand	2016 Brand Value ($ billions)
1	Apple	154
2	Google	83
3	Microsoft	75
4	Coca-Cola	59
5	Facebook	53
6	Toyota	42
7	IBM	41
8	Disney	40
9	McDonald's	39
10	General Electric	38

Source: Forbes, May 2016.

ANALYSIS: Brand names are valuable economic assets and assist a firm in maintaining a base of loyal customers. These brands have worldwide recognition as a result of heavy advertising.

SUMMARY

- There are many (rather than few) firms in monopolistic competition. The concentration ratio in such industries tends to be low (20–40 percent). **LO26-1**
- Each monopolistically competitive firm enjoys some brand loyalty. This brand loyalty, together with its relatively small market share, gives each firm a high degree of independence in price and output decisions. **LO26-1**
- Brand loyalty is reflected in the downward-sloping demand curve facing the firm. Profits are maximized at the rate of output where MR = MC. **LO26-3**
- The amount of market share and power a monopolistically competitive firm possesses depends on how successfully it differentiates its product from similar products. Accordingly, monopolistically competitive firms tend to devote more resources to advertising. **LO26-2**

- The market power bestowed by brand loyalty is measured by low cross-price elasticities of demand, high repurchase rates, and price premiums. **LO26-1**
- Low entry barriers permit new firms to enter a monopolistically competitive industry whenever economic profits exist. Such entry eliminates long-run economic profit and reduces (shifts leftward) the demand for the output of existing firms. **LO26-4**
- Monopolistic competition results in resource misallocations (due to flawed price signals) and inefficiency (above-minimum-average cost). **LO26-3**
- Monopolistic competition encourages nonprice competition instead of price competition. Because the resources used in nonprice competition (advertising, packaging, service, etc.) may have more desirable uses, these industry structures lead to resource misallocation. **LO26-3**

Key Terms

monopolistic competition
concentration ratio
market power

barriers to entry
product differentiation
cross-price elasticity of demand

production decision
economic profit
marginal cost pricing

Questions for Discussion

1. What is the "pricing power" referred to in In the News "Starbucks Ups the Price of Iced Drinks"? **LO26-2**

2. Why do 4,000 new pizzerias open every year? Why do just as many close? **LO26-4**

3. Name three products each for which you have (*a*) high brand loyalty and (*b*) low brand loyalty. **LO26-2**

4. If one gas station reduces its prices, must other gas stations match the price reduction? Why or why not? **LO26-2**

5. In the News "The Cola Wars: It's Not All Taste" suggests that most consumers can't identify their favorite cola in blind taste tests. Why then do people stick with one brand? What accounts for brand loyalty in bottled water (In the News "Selling 'Pure Water': A $Billion Scam?")? **LO26-1**

6. Why would Starbucks invest $20 million in a new "Roastery" if the coffee-shop market is already saturated (In the News "Coffee Shops Seeking New Identities")? **LO26-4**

7. What happens to the demand curve facing a Starbucks shop when a Dunkin' Donuts store opens next to it? What can Starbucks do to maintain its business? **LO26-4**

8. How would our consumption of cereal change if cereal manufacturers stopped advertising? Would we be better or worse off? **LO26-3**

9. Why are people willing to pay more for Dreyer's ice cream when it has a Starbucks brand on it? **LO26-2**

10. According to World View "The Best Global Brands," what gives brand names their value? **LO26-2**

PROBLEMS FOR CHAPTER 26

LO26-1 1. What is the concentration ratio in an industry with the following market shares?

| Firm A | 13.2 | Firm C | 4.2 | Firm E | 2.7 | Firm G | 1.6 |
| Firm B | 11.4 | Firm D | 3.6 | Firm F | 2.2 | Other firms | 61.1 |

LO26-2 2. According to In the News "Starbucks Ups the Price of Iced Drinks,"
- (a) By what percent did Starbucks increase the price of a venti frappuccino?
- (b) If the price elasticity for frappuccinos is 0.2, by how much would unit sales drop?
- (c) After the price increase, would total revenue increase or decrease?

LO26-2 3. If Starbucks raises its price by 5 percent and McDonald's experiences a 0.4 percent increase in demand for its coffee, what is the cross-price elasticity of demand?

LO26-3 4. In Figure 26.3, at what output rate is economic profit equal to zero?

5. (a) Use the accompanying graph to illustrate the short-run equilibrium of a monopolistically competitive firm.
- (b) At that equilibrium, what is
  - (i) Price?   (ii) Output?   (iii) Total profit?
- (c) Identify the long-run equilibrium of the same firm.
- (d) In long-run equilibrium, what is (approximately)
  - (i) Price?   (ii) Output?   (iii) Total profit?

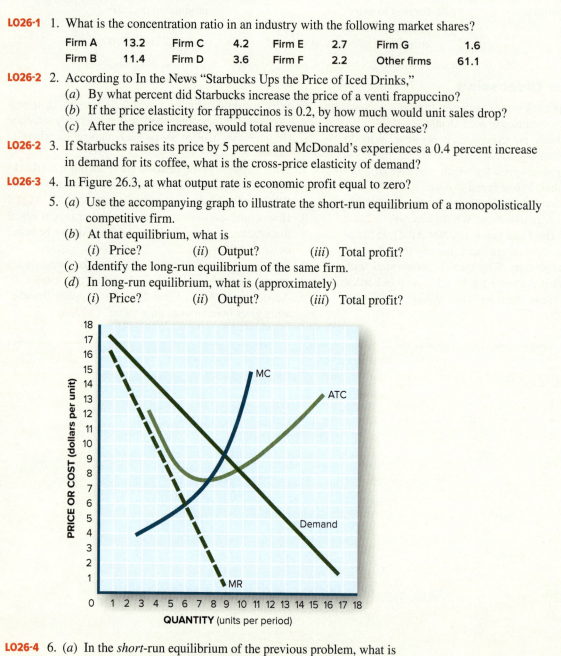

LO26-4 6. (a) In the *short*-run equilibrium of the previous problem, what is
- (i) The price of the product?
- (ii) The opportunity cost of producing the last unit?
- (b) In the *long*-run equilibrium of the previous problem, what is
- (i) The price of the product?
- (ii) The opportunity cost of producing the last unit?

LO26-4 7. On the accompanying graph, identify each of the following *market* outcomes:
   (*a*) Short-run equilibrium output in competition.
   (*b*) Long-run equilibrium output in competition.
   (*c*) Long-run equilibrium output in monopoly.
   (*d*) Long-run equilibrium output in monopolistic competition.

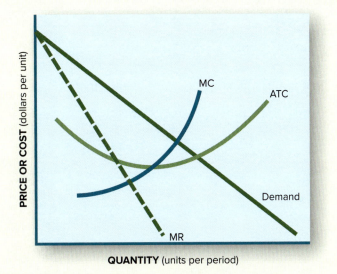

LO26-2 8. The Economy Tomorrow: On the following graph, show the effect of a successful advertising campaign on the firm's cost, demand, and marginal revenue curves.

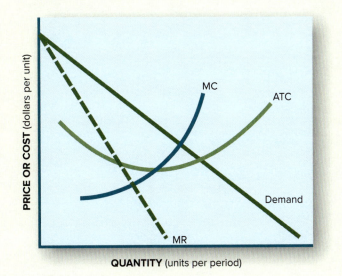

©MOF/Getty Images RF

REGULATORY ISSUES

Microeconomic theory provides insights into how prices and product flows are determined in unregulated markets. Sometimes those market outcomes are not optimal, and the government intervenes to improve them. In this section we examine government regulation of natural monopolies (Chapter 27), environmental protection (Chapter 28), and farm output and prices (Chapter 29). The goal is to determine whether and how government regulation might improve market outcomes—or possibly worsen them.

©Kevin Phillips/Stockbyte/Getty Images RF

©Alex Wong/Getty Images

©Fuse/Corbis via Getty Images RF

Natural Monopolies: (De)Regulation?

The lights went out in California in 2001—not just once but repeatedly. Offices went dark, air conditioners shut down, assembly lines stopped, and TV screens went blank. The state governor blamed power company "profiteers" for the rolling blackouts. He charged the companies with curtailing power supplies and hiking prices. He wanted *more* regulation of the power industry. Industry representatives responded that government regulation was itself responsible for throwing California into a new Dark Age. *Less* regulation, not more, would have kept the lights on, they claimed.

The battle over government regulation of the power industry quickly spread to other states. Some states that were deregulating power companies suspended the process. Other states also put (de)regulation plans on hold until they could better assess what went wrong in California. President Trump intensified the debate, asserting that excessive regulation had curbed America's energy production and eliminated thousands of jobs. He proposed a massive rollback of federal regulation.

Everyone agrees that markets sometimes fail—that unregulated markets may produce the wrong mix of output, undesirable methods of production, or an unfair distribution of income. But government intervention can fail as well. Hence we need to ask,

- **When is government regulation necessary?**
- **What form should that regulation take?**
- **When is it appropriate to deregulate an industry?**

In answering these questions we draw on economic principles as well as recent experience. This will permit us to contrast the theory of (de) regulation with reality.

ANTITRUST VS. REGULATION

A perfectly competitive market provides a model for economic efficiency. As we first observed in Chapter 3, the market mechanism can answer the basic economic questions of WHAT to produce, HOW to produce it, and FOR WHOM. Under ideal conditions, the market's answers may also be optimal—that is, the best possible outcomes. To achieve this **laissez-faire** ideal, all producers must be perfect competitors; people must have full information about tastes, costs, and prices; all costs and benefits must be reflected in market prices; and pervasive economies of scale must be absent.

LEARNING OBJECTIVES

After reading this chapter, you should know

LO27-1 The characteristics of natural monopoly.

LO27-2 The regulatory dilemmas posed by natural monopoly.

LO27-3 The costs associated with regulation.

LO27-4 How deregulation has fared in specific industries.

laissez faire: The doctrine of "leave it alone," of nonintervention by government in the market mechanism.

In reality, these conditions are rarely, if ever, fully attained. Markets may be dominated by large and powerful producers. In wielding their power, these producers may restrict output, raise prices, stifle competition, and inhibit innovation. In other words, market power may cause **market failure,** leaving us with suboptimal market outcomes.

Behavioral Focus

As we observed in Chapter 25, the government has two options for intervention where market power prevails. It may focus on the *structure* of an industry or on its *behavior.* **Antitrust** laws cover both options: they prohibit mergers and acquisitions that reduce potential competition (structures) and forbid market practices (behavior) that are anticompetitive.

Government **regulation** has a different focus. Instead of worrying about industry structure, regulation focuses almost exclusively on *behavior.* In general, regulation seeks to change market outcomes directly by imposing specific limitations on the price, output, or investment decisions of private firms.

NATURAL MONOPOLY

Regulation is almost always the policy choice when dealing with natural monopolies. A **natural monopoly** exists when a single firm has such pervasive economies of scale that it will "naturally" dominate its industry. In natural monopoly, bigger *is* always better—at least in terms of production costs. The larger the firm, the lower its costs. Because of these scale economies, a natural monopoly can produce the products consumers want at the lowest possible price. A single cable company is more efficient than a horde of cable firms developing a maze of cable networks. The same is true of local telephone service and many utilities. In all of these cases, a single company can deliver products at lower cost than a bunch of smaller firms. Dismantling such a natural monopoly would destroy that cost advantage. A natural monopoly is therefore a potentially desirable market *structure.*

But what about behavior? Do we need to regulate natural monopolies? Even though a natural monopoly might enjoy economies of scale, it might not pass those savings along to consumers. In that case, the economies of scale don't do consumers any good, and the government might have to regulate the firm's behavior.

To determine whether regulation is desirable, we first have to determine how an *unregulated* natural monopoly will behave.

Declining ATC Curve

Figure 27.1 illustrates the unique characteristics of a natural monopoly. *The distinctive characteristic of a natural monopoly is its downward-sloping average total cost (ATC)*

market failure: An imperfection in the market mechanism that prevents optimal outcomes.

antitrust: Government intervention to alter market structure or prevent abuse of market power.

regulation: Government intervention to alter the behavior of firms—for example, in pricing, output, or advertising.

natural monopoly: An industry in which one firm can achieve economies of scale over the entire range of market supply.

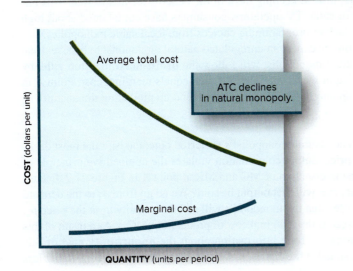

FIGURE 27.1

Declining ATC

A combination of high fixed costs and very low marginal costs generates a unique, downward-sloping ATC curve in natural monopoly. MC lies below ATC at all output levels.

curve. Because unit costs keep falling as the rate of production increases, a single large firm can underprice any smaller firm. Ultimately, it can produce all the market supply at the lowest attainable cost. In an unregulated market, such a firm will "naturally" come to dominate the industry.

High Fixed Costs. Natural monopolies typically emerge in situations where the fixed costs of production are extremely large. To supply electricity, for example, you first need to build a power source (e.g., a coal-fired plant, hydroelectric dam, or nuclear generator), then a distribution network. It's the same thing with subways and railroads: a lot of infrastructure must be constructed before anyone gets a ride. As a consequence of these high fixed costs, the *average* total cost curve starts out very high (recall that ATC = AFC + AVC).

Low Marginal Costs. Once productive capacity is built, the focus turns to *marginal costs.* In natural monopolies, marginal costs are typically low—*very low.* Supplying another kilowatt of electricity entails negligible marginal cost. Carrying one more passenger on a railroad or subway entails similarly negligible costs.

Even if marginal costs rise as production increases (the law of diminishing returns), marginal cost remains less than average total cost over the entire range of output. Notice in Figure 27.1 that *the marginal cost (MC) curve lies below the ATC curve at all rates of output for a natural monopoly.* The ATC curve never rises into its conventional U shape because marginal costs never exceed average costs. Hence there is no force to pull average total costs up, as in conventional cost structures.

The combination of high fixed costs and low (negligible) marginal costs gives the ATC curve a unique shape. The ATC curve starts out high (due to high AFC) and keeps declining as output increases (because MC < ATC at all times). *The downward-sloping ATC curve is the hallmark of a natural monopoly.*

The declining costs of a natural monopoly are of potential benefit to society. The **economies of scale** offered by a natural monopoly imply that no other market structure can supply the good as cheaply. Hence *natural monopoly is a desirable market structure.* A competitive market structure—with many smaller firms—would have higher average costs.

economies of scale: Reductions in minimum average costs that come about through increases in the size (scale) of plant and equipment.

Unregulated Behavior

Although the **structure** *of a natural monopoly may be beneficial, its* **behavior** *may leave something to be desired.* Natural monopolists have the same profit-maximizing motivations as other producers. Moreover, they have the monopoly power to achieve and maintain economic profits. Hence there's no guarantee that consumers will reap the cost-saving benefits of a natural monopoly. Critics charge that natural monopolies don't pass the cost savings along to consumers, instead keeping most of the benefits for themselves. This has been a recurrent criticism of cable TV operators: consumers have complained about high prices, poor service, and a lack of programming choices from local cable monopolies.

Figure 27.2 illustrates how we expect an unregulated natural monopolist to behave. Like all other producers, the natural monopolist will follow the **profit-maximization rule.** by producing at that rate of output where marginal revenue equals marginal cost. Point A in Figure 27.2 indicates that an unregulated monopoly will end up producing the quantity q_A and charging the price p_A.

profit-maximization rule: Produce at that rate of output where marginal revenue equals marginal cost.

marginal cost pricing: The offer (supply) of goods at prices equal to their marginal cost.

Wrong WHAT Outcome. The natural monopolist's preferred outcome isn't the most desirable one for society. This price–output combination violates the competitive principle of **marginal cost pricing.** The intersection of MC and MR at point A in Figure 27.2 dictates the output level q_A. At what price will that output be sold? We go up from q_A to the demand curve to find out. There we see that the monopolist will sell the quantity q_A at the price p_A. Hence, price (p_A) greatly exceeds the marginal cost of production (MC_A). As a result of this gap, consumers aren't getting accurate information about the **opportunity cost** of this product. This flawed price signal is the cause of market failure. We end up consuming less

opportunity cost: The most desired goods or services that are forgone in order to obtain something else.

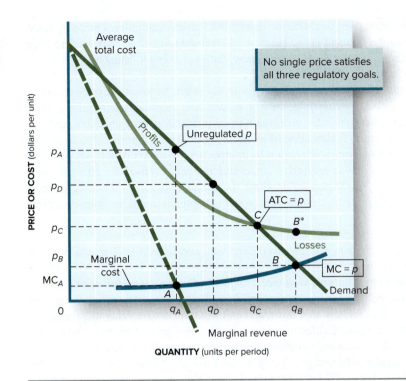

FIGURE 27.2

Natural Monopoly: Price Regulation

If unregulated, a natural monopoly will produce q_A where MR = MC (point *A*). And it will charge the price p_A, as determined by the demand curve for that rate of output.

Regulation designed to achieve efficient prices will seek point *B*, where p = MC. Still lower average costs (production efficiency) are attainable at higher rates of output (capacity), however. On the other hand, a zero-profit, zero-subsidy outcome exists only at point *C*.

Which price–output combination should be sought?

of this product (and more of other goods) than we would if charged its true opportunity cost. A suboptimal mix of output results.

Wrong HOW Outcome. The natural monopolist's profit-maximizing output (q_A) also fails to minimize average total cost. In a competitive industry, ATC is driven down to its minimum by relentless competition. In this case, however, reductions in ATC cease when the monopolist achieves the profit-maximizing rate of output (q_A). Were output to increase further, average total costs would fall.

Wrong FOR WHOM Outcome. Finally, notice that the higher price (p_A) associated with the monopolist's preferred output (q_A) ensures a fat profit (= per-unit profit of $p_A - p_D$ multiplied by the quantity q_A). This **economic profit** may violate our visions of equity. In 2001 millions of Californians were convinced that this kind of "profiteering" was the root of their electricity woes.

economic profit: The difference between total revenues and total economic costs.

REGULATORY OPTIONS

The suboptimal outcomes likely to emerge from a free-swinging natural monopoly prompt consumers to demand government intervention. The market alone can't overcome the natural advantage of pervasive economies of scale. (New, smaller firms would have higher average total costs and be unable to compete.) But the government could compel different outcomes. Which outcomes do we want? And how will we get them?

Price Regulation

For starters, we might consider price regulation. The natural monopolist's preferred price (p_A) is, after all, a basic cause of market failure. By regulating the firm, the government can compel a lower price. The California legislature did this in 1996 when it set a *maximum* retail price for electricity.

Setting a maximum price for the natural monopoly sounds like a simple solution. But what price should be set? As is apparent from Figure 27.2, there are lots of choices in setting a regulated price. We start with the conviction that the unregulated price p_A is too high. But where on the demand curve below p_A do we want to be? A price of zero (free electricity!) sounds really appealing, but we know that's not going to happen.

Price Efficiency (p = MC). A more realistic possibility might be to set the price at a level consistent with opportunity costs. As we saw earlier, a monopolist's unregulated price sends out a flawed price signal. By charging a price in excess of marginal cost, the monopolist causes a suboptimal allocation of resources (i.e., the wrong mix of output). We could improve market outcomes, therefore, by compelling the monopolist to set the price equal to marginal cost, just as perfectly competitive markets do. Such an efficient price would lead us to point B in Figure 27.2, where the demand curve and the marginal cost curve intersect. At that price (p_B), consumers would get optimal use of the good or service produced.

Subsidy. Although the price p_B will give us the right answer to the WHAT question, it will also bankrupt the producer. In a natural monopoly, MC is always less than ATC. Hence *marginal cost pricing by a natural monopolist implies a loss on every unit of output produced.* In this case, the loss per unit is equal to $B^* - B$. If confronted with the regulated price p_B, the firm will ultimately shut down and exit from the market. This was one of the many problems that plagued California. Unable to charge a price high enough to cover their costs, some of the state's utility companies were forced into bankruptcy.

If we want to require efficient pricing (p = MC), we must provide a subsidy to the natural monopoly. In Figure 27.2 the amount of the subsidy would have to equal the anticipated loss at q_B—that is, the quantity q_B multiplied by the per-unit loss ($B^* - B$). Such subsidies are provided to subway systems. With subsidies, local subway systems can charge fees below *average* cost and closer to *marginal* cost. These subsidized fares increase ridership, thus ensuring greater use of very expensive mass transportation systems.

Despite the advantages of this subsidized pricing strategy, taxpayers always complain about the cost of such subsidies. Taxpayers are particularly loath to provide subsidies for private companies. Hence political considerations typically preclude efficient (marginal cost) pricing, despite the economic benefits of this regulatory strategy.

Production Efficiency (p = min ATC). Another option is to focus on efficient *production* rather than efficient *pricing*. Production efficiency is attained at the lowest possible average total cost. At q_B we're producing a lot of output but still have some unused capacity. Since ATC falls continuously, we could achieve still lower average costs if we increased output beyond q_B. *In a natural monopoly, production efficiency is achieved at capacity production, where ATC is at a minimum.*

Increasing output beyond q_B raises the same problems we encountered at that rate of output. At production rates in excess of q_B, ATC is always higher than price. Even MC is higher than price to the right of point B. Thus *no regulated price can induce a natural monopolist to achieve minimum average cost. A subsidy would be required to offset the market losses.*

Profit Regulation

Instead of focusing on price, why don't we focus on profits instead? Simply disallow monopoly profits like those of the unregulated monopoly (at q_A and p_A in Figure 27.2). We can achieve this result by mandating a price equal to average total cost. In Figure 27.2 this regulatory objective is achieved at point C. In this case, the rate of output is q_C and the regulated price is p_C.

Profit regulation looks appealing for two reasons. First, it eliminates the need to subsidize the monopolist. Second, it allows us to focus on profits only, thus removing the need to develop demand and cost curves. In theory, all we have to do is check the firm's annual profit-and-loss statement to confirm that it's earning a normal (average) profit. If its profits are too high, we can force the firm to reduce its price; if profits are too low, we may permit a price increase.

Bloated Costs. While beautiful in principle, profit regulation can turn ugly in practice. In particular, profit regulation can lead to bloated costs and dynamic inefficiency. *If a firm is permitted a specific profit rate (or rate of return), it has no incentive to limit costs.* On the contrary, higher costs imply higher profits. If permitted to charge 10 percent over unit costs, a monopolist may be better off with average costs of $6 rather than only $5. The higher costs translate into 60 cents of profit per unit rather than only 50 cents, even though the profit *rate* is the same. Hence there's an incentive to "pad costs." If those costs actually represent improvements in the firm's wages and salaries, executive bonuses, fringe benefits, or the work environment, then cost increases are doubly attractive to the firm and its employees. Cost efficiency is as welcome as the plague under such circumstances.

Profit regulation can also motivate a firm to inflate its costs by paying above-market prices for products purchased from an unregulated subsidiary. This was the strategy AT&T used to increase its *regulated* cost base while ringing up high profits at Western Electric, its *unregulated* subsidiary (see Chapter 24). The FCC accused Nynex (the "Baby Bell" that provided phone service in New York and New England in the 1980s) of using the same strategy to pad its profits. Nynex used its *un*regulated subsidiary (Material Enterprises Co.) to sell equipment at inflated prices to its *regulated* phone company subsidiaries (New England Telephone & Telegraph and New York Telephone). Profits in all three companies increased.

Output Regulation

Given the difficulties in regulating prices and profits, regulators may choose to regulate output instead. The natural monopolist's preferred output rate is q_A, as illustrated again in Figure 27.3. We could compel this monopolist to provide a minimum level of service in excess of q_A. This regulated minimum is designated q_D in Figure 27.3. At q_D consumers get the benefit not only of more output but also of a lower price (p_D). At q_D total monopoly profit must also be less than at q_A because q_A was the profit-maximizing rate of output.

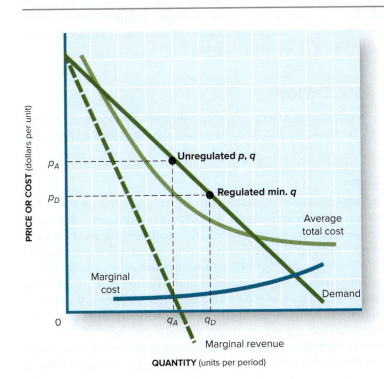

FIGURE 27.3

Minimum Service Regulation

Regulation may seek to ensure some minimal level of service. In this case, the required rate of output is arbitrarily set at q_D. Consumers are willing to pay p_D per unit for that output.

Regulated output q_D is preferable to the unregulated outcome (q_A,p_A) but may induce a decline in quality. Cost cutting is the only way to increase profits when the rate of output is fixed and price is on the demand curve.

It appears, then, that compelling any rate of output in excess of q_A can only benefit consumers. Moreover, output regulation is an easy rule to enforce.

Quality Deterioration. Unfortunately, minimum-service regulation can also cause problems. If forced to produce at the rate of q_D, the monopolist may seek to increase profits by cutting cost corners. This can be accomplished by deferring plant and equipment maintenance, reducing quality control, or otherwise lowering the quality of service. *Regulation of the quantity produced may induce a decline in quality.* Since a monopolist has no direct competition, consumers pretty much have to accept whatever quality the monopolist offers. This structural reality may explain why consumers complain so much about the services of local cable monopolies.

In addition to encouraging quality deterioration, output regulation at q_D also violates the principle of marginal cost pricing. Because an economic profit exists at q_D, equity goals may be jeopardized as well. Hence minimum service (output) regulation isn't a panacea for the regulatory dilemma. In fact, there is no panacea. *Goal conflicts are inescapable, and any regulatory rule may induce undesired producer responses.*

Imperfect Answers

The call for public regulation of natural monopolies is based on the recognition that the profit motive doesn't generate optimal outcomes in any monopoly environment. If unregulated, a natural monopolist will charge too much and produce too little. The regulatory remedy for these market failures isn't evident, however. Regulators can compel efficient prices or least-cost production only by offering a subsidy. Profit regulation is likely to induce cost-inflating responses. Output regulation is an incentive for quality deterioration. No matter which way we turn, regulatory problems result.

There's not much hope for transforming unregulated market failure into perfect regulated outcomes. In reality, regulators must choose a strategy that balances competing objectives (e.g., price efficiency and equity). A realistic goal for regulation is to *improve* market outcomes, not to *perfect* them. In the real world, *the choice isn't between imperfect markets and flawless government intervention but rather between imperfect markets and imperfect intervention.*

The argument for *deregulation* rests on the observation that government regulation sometimes worsens market outcomes. In some cases, **government failure** may be worse than market failure. Specifically, regulation may lead to price, cost, or production outcomes that are inferior to those of an unregulated market.

government failure:
Government intervention that fails to improve economic outcomes.

THE COSTS OF REGULATION

Let's *assume* that regulation actually improves market outcomes. Could we then claim regulatory success? Not quite yet. We also have to consider the *costs* incurred to change market outcomes.

Administrative Costs

As we've observed, industry regulation entails various options and a host of trade-offs. Someone must sit down and assess these trade-offs. To make a sound decision, a regulatory administration must have access to lots of information. At a minimum, the regulator must have some clue as to the actual shape and position of the demand and cost curves depicted in Figures 27.2 and 27.3. Crude illustrations won't suffice when decisions about the prices, output, or costs of a multibillion-dollar industry are being made. The regulatory commission needs volumes of details about actual costs and demand and a platoon of experts to collect and analyze the needed data. All this labor represents a real cost to society because the regulatory lawyers, accountants, and economists could be employed elsewhere.

As Table 27.1 illustrates, more than 280,000 people are employed in the more visible regulatory agencies of the federal government. That's more employees than General

Agency	Number of Employees (2018)
SOCIAL REGULATION	
Consumer Safety and Health	43,371
• Food and Drug Administration (FDA)	
• Food Safety and Inspection Service, etc.	
Homeland Security	148,152
• Transportation Security Administration (TSA)	
• Customs and Border Security	
• Immigration and Customs, etc.	
Transportation	9,300
• Federal Aviation Administration (FAA)	
• Federal Motor Carriers Safety Administration	
• Federal Railroad Administration, etc.	
Workplace	10,231
• Occupational Safety and Health Administration (OSHA)	
• Mine Safety and Health Administration	
• Employment Standards Administration, etc.	
Environment	22,554
• Environmental Protection Agency (EPA)	
• Forest and Rangeland Research	
• Fish and Wildlife Service, etc.	
ECONOMIC REGULATION	
General Business	21,668
• Patent and Trademark Office	
• Securities and Exchange Commission (SEC)	
• Federal Trade Commission (FTC), etc.	
Finance and Banking	18,234
• Federal Reserve System	
• Federal Deposit Insurance Corporation (FDIC)	
• Comptroller of the Currency, etc.	
Industry-Specific Regulation	6,482
• Agricultural Marketing Service	
• Federal Communications Commission (FCC), etc.	
Total Regulatory Employment:	**279,992**

Source: Susan Dudley and Melinda Warren, Weidenbaum Center, Washington University, July, 2017.

TABLE 27.1

Employment in Federal Regulatory Agencies

The human and capital resources the bureaucracy employs represent a real opportunity cost. The 279,992 people employed in 63 federal agencies—and tens of thousands more employed in state and local bureaucracies—could be producing other goods and services. These and other costs must be compared to the benefits of regulation.

Motors employs to build cars. On top of that, thousands more have regulatory responsibilities in smaller federal agencies and executive departments. Tens of thousands more people are employed by state and local regulatory agencies. By using all these workers to regulate private industry, we are forgoing their use in the production of desired goods and services. This is a significant economic cost.

Compliance Costs

The administrative costs of regulation focus on resources used in the public sector. By its very nature, however, regulation also changes resource use in the private sector. Regulated industries must expend resources to educate themselves about the regulations, to change their production behavior, and often to file reports with the regulatory authorities. The human and capital resources used for these purposes represent the *compliance* cost of regulation.

New rules on trucking illustrate how regulation can increase production costs. In 2013 the U.S. Department of Transportation reduced the amount of driving time permitted for interstate truckers (see In the News "Sleep Rules Raise Trucking Costs"). This rule requires freight companies to use more trucks and more labor to transport goods, thereby raising economic costs. Although the resultant gain in safety is desired, the cost of achieving that gain is not inconsequential.

IN THE NEWS

SLEEP RULES RAISE TRUCKING COSTS

The Federal Motor Carrier Safety Administration (FMCSA) now monitors the sleep hours and practices of long-haul truck drivers. As of July 1, 2013, the FMCSA insists that drivers:

- Drive no more than 11 hours a day.
- Work no more than 14 hours a day.
- Work no more than 70 hours a week.
- Take a 30-minute break in their first 8 hours of driving.
- Rest for 34 consecutive hours after completing a 70-hour week, including at least two nights between the hours of 1 and 5 a.m.

According to FMCSA, the new sleep rules will reduce chronic fatigue and related crashes, saving 19 lives per year. But the trucking industry says the new rules are too costly and even dangerous. They force drivers to sleep when they're not tired and to drive when they are tired. They also force trucks onto the road at commute times. The $700 billion industry says shipping costs will rise 2 to 6 percent, upward of $2 billion.

Source: Federal Motor Carrier Safety Administration and news reports of July 2013.

ANALYSIS: Regulations designed to improve market outcomes typically impose higher costs. The challenge is to balance benefits and costs.

Efficiency Costs

Finally, we have to consider the potential costs of changes in output. Most regulation alters the mix of output, either directly or indirectly. Ideally, regulation will always improve the mix of output. But it's possible that bad decisions, incomplete information, or faulty implementation may actually *worsen* the mix of output. If this occurs, then the loss of utility associated with an inferior mix of output imposes a further cost on society, over and above administrative and compliance costs.

Dynamic Losses. Efficiency costs may increase significantly over time. Consumer tastes change, demand and marginal revenue curves shift, costs change, and new technologies emerge. Can regulatory commissions respond to these changes as fast as the market mechanism does? If not, even optimal regulations may soon become obsolete and counterproductive. Worse still, the regulatory process itself may impede new technology, new marketing approaches, or improved production processes. These losses may be the most important. As Robert Hahn of the American Enterprise Institute observed,

> [t]he measurable costs of regulation pale against the distortions that sap the economy's dynamism. The public never sees the factories that weren't built, the new products that didn't appear, or the entrepreneurial idea that drowned in a cumbersome regulatory process.[1]

These kinds of dynamic efficiency losses are a drag on economic growth, limiting outward shifts of the production possibilities curve while perpetuating an increasingly undesired mix of output.

[1]Source: Richman, Louis S. and John Labate, "Bringing Reason to Regulation," *Fortune,* October 19, p. 94, 1992.

Balancing Benefits and Costs

The economic costs of regulation are a reminder of the "no free lunch" maxim. Although regulatory intervention may improve market outcomes, that intervention isn't without cost. The real resources used in the regulatory process could be used for other purposes. Hence, even if we could achieve perfect outcomes with enough regulation, the cost of achieving perfection might outweigh the benefits. ***Regulatory intervention must balance the anticipated improvements in market outcomes against the economic cost of regulation.*** In principle, the marginal benefit of regulation must exceed its marginal cost. If this isn't the case, then additional regulation isn't desirable, even if it would improve short-run market outcomes.

DEREGULATION IN PRACTICE

The push to *de*regulate is prompted by two concerns. The first concern focuses on the dynamic inefficiencies that regulation imposes, stifling innovation and rendering regulated industries less productive than desired. The other push for deregulation comes from advancing technology, which often destroys the structural basis for natural monopoly. A brief review of the resulting deregulation illustrates the impact of these forces.

Railroads

The railroad industry was the federal government's first broad regulatory target. Railroads are an example of natural monopoly, with high fixed costs and negligible marginal costs. Furthermore, there were no airports or interstate highways to compete with the railroads in 1887, when Congress created the Interstate Commerce Commission (ICC). The ICC was established to limit monopolistic exploitation of this situation while assuring a fair profit to railroad owners. The ICC established rates and routes for the railroads while limiting both entry to and exit from the industry.

With the advent of buses, trucks, subways, airplanes, and pipelines as alternative modes of transportation, railroad regulation became increasingly obsolete. Regulated cargoes, routes, and prices prevented railroads from adapting their prices or services to meet changing consumer demands. With regulation-protected routes, they also had little incentive to invest in new technologies or equipment. As a result, railroad traffic and profits declined while other transportation industries flourished.

The Railroad Revitalization and Regulatory Reform Act of 1976 was a response to this crisis. Its major goal was to reduce the scope of government regulation. Reinforced by the Staggers Rail Act of 1980, railroads were granted much greater freedom to adapt their prices and service to market demands.

Railroad companies used that flexibility to increase their share of total freight traffic. Fresh fruits and vegetables, for example, were exempted from ICC rate regulation in 1979. Railroads responded by *reducing* their rates and improving service. In the first year of deregulated rates, fruits and vegetable shipments increased more than 30 percent, a dramatic reversal of earlier trends. Deregulation of coal traffic (in 1980) and piggyback (trucks on railroad flatcars) traffic (in 1982) prompted similar turnarounds. The railroads prospered by reconfiguring routes and services, cutting operating costs, and offering lower rates. Between 1986 and 1993, the average cost of moving freight by rail dropped by 69 percent.

Not all rates have fallen. Indeed, one worrisome effect of deregulation is the increased concentration in the rail industry. After a series of mergers and acquisitions, the top four railroads (Burlington-Northern, Union Pacific, CSX, and Norfolk-Southern) now move nearly 90 percent of all rail freight—an extremely high **concentration ratio.** Moreover, these same firms hold monopoly positions on specific routes. Shippers in these captive markets pay rates 20 to 30 percent higher than in nonmonopoly routes.

concentration ratio: The proportion of total industry output produced by the largest firms (usually the four largest).

Telephone Service

The telephone industry has long been the classic example of a natural monopoly. Although enormous fixed costs are necessary to establish a telephone network, the marginal cost of an additional telephone call approaches zero. Hence it made economic sense to have a single network of telephone lines and switches rather than a maze of competing ones. Recognizing these economies of scale, Congress permitted AT&T to maintain a monopoly on both long-distance and most local telephone service for decades. To ensure that consumers would benefit from this natural monopoly, the Federal Communications Commission (FCC) regulated phone services and prices.

Once again, technology outpaced regulation. Communications satellites made it much easier and less costly for new firms to provide long-distance telephone service for decades. Moreover, the rate structure that AT&T and the Federal Communications Commission had established made long-distance service highly profitable. Accordingly, start-up firms clamored to get into the industry, and consumers petitioned for lower rates.

Long Distance. In 1982 the courts put an end to AT&T's monopoly, transforming long-distance telecommunications into a more competitive industry with more firms and less regulation. Soon thereafter more than 800 firms entered the industry, and long-distance telephone rates have dropped sharply. The quality of service also improved with fiber optic cable, advanced switching systems, cell phones, and myriad new phone line services such as fax transmissions, remote access, Internet access, texting, mobile computing, gaming, and payments. All these changes contributed to a quadrupling of long-distance telephone use in the United States.

Local Service. The deregulation of long-distance services was so spectacularly successful that observers wondered whether *local* telephone service might be deregulated as well. As competition in *long-distance* services increased, the monopoly nature of *local* rates became painfully apparent: local rates kept increasing after 1983 while long-distance rates were tumbling.

The Baby Bells that held monopolies on local service defended their high rates based on the high costs of building and maintaining transmission networks. But new technologies permitted wireless companies to offer local service if they could gain access to the monopoly networks. Congress responded in 1996. The Telecommunications Act of 1996 required the Baby Bells to grant rivals access to their transmission networks. The Baby Bells kept rivals at bay, however, by charging excessive access fees, imposing overly complex access codes, requiring unnecessary capital equipment, and raising other entry barriers. The battle for local access continues.

Airlines

The Civil Aeronautics Board (CAB) was created in 1938 to regulate airline routes and fares. From its inception, the primary concern of the CAB was to ensure a viable system of air transportation for both large and small communities. Such a system would be ensured, the CAB believed, only if a fair level of profits was maintained by entry and price regulations. Thus the focus of the CAB was on *profit* regulation.

P = ATC. To ensure fair profits, the CAB set fares in accordance with airline costs. This required the CAB to undertake intensive cost studies, based on accounting data provided by the airlines. Once the average cost of service and capital equipment was established, the CAB then set an average price that would ensure a fair rate of return (profit) (much like point *C* in Figure 27.2).

The CAB also wanted to ensure air service to smaller, less-traveled communities. Short hauls entail higher average costs and therefore justify higher fares. To avoid high fares on such routes, the CAB permitted airlines to charge prices well in excess of average costs on longer routes as long as they maintained service on shorter, unprofitable routes. This **cross-subsidization** was similar to that of the telephone industry, in which long-distance profits helped keep local telephone charges low.

To maintain this price and profit structure, the CAB had to regulate routes and limit entry into the airline industry. Otherwise, established carriers would abandon short, unprofitable

cross-subsidization: Use of high prices and profits on one product to subsidize low prices on another product.

routes, and new carriers would offer service only on more profitable routes. Unregulated entry thus threatened both cross-subsidization and the CAB's vision of a fair profit.

No Entry. The CAB was extremely effective in restricting entry into the industry. Would-be entrants had to demonstrate to the CAB that their proposed service was required by "public convenience and necessity" and was superior to that of established carriers. Established carriers could oppose a new application by demonstrating sufficient service, offering to expand their service, or claiming superior service. In view of the fact that new applicants had no airline experience, established carriers easily won the argument. From 1938 until 1977, the CAB *never* awarded a major route to a new entrant.

No Price Competition. The CAB also eliminated price competition between established carriers. The CAB fixed airfares on all routes. Airlines could reduce fares no more than 5 percent and couldn't increase them more than 10 percent without CAB approval.

Bloated Costs. Ironically, the established airlines failed to reap much profit from these high fares. Unable to compete on the basis of price, the established carriers had to engage in nonprice competition. The most costly form of nonprice competition was frequency of service. Once the CAB authorized service between any two cities, a regulated carrier could provide as many flights as desired. This enticed the regulated carriers to purchase huge fleets of planes and provide frequent departures. In the process, load factors (the percentage of seats filled with passengers) fell and average costs rose.

The regulated carriers also pursued **product differentiation** by offering special meals, first-run movies, free drinks, better service, and wider seats. This nonprice competition further inflated average costs and reduced profits.

product differentiation: Features that make one product appear different from competing products in the same market.

New Entrants. The Airline Deregulation Act of 1978 changed the structure and behavior of the airline industry. Entry regulation was effectively abandoned. With the elimination of this **barrier to entry,** the number of carriers increased greatly. Between 1978 and 1985, the number of airline companies increased from 37 to 174! The new entrants intensified competition on nearly all routes. The share of domestic markets with four or more carriers grew from 13 percent in May 1978 to 73 percent in May 1981. All those new entrants pushed airfares down sharply.

The CAB's authority over airfares ended January 1, 1983. Since then, airlines have been able to adapt their fares to market supply and demand. The CAB itself was eliminated in 1984.

barriers to entry: Obstacles such as patents that make it difficult or impossible for would-be producers to enter a particular market.

Increasing Concentration. Although airline deregulation is hailed as one of the greatest policy achievements of the 1980s, airline industry structure and behavior remain imperfect. In the competitive fray spawned by deregulation, lots of new entrants and even some established airlines went broke. Unable to match lower fares and increased service, scores of airline companies exited the industry in the period 1985–1995. In the process, a handful of major carriers increased their market share. The combined market share of the four largest carriers (American, Delta, Southwest, United) increased from 35 percent in 1985 to 60 percent in 2014. In many cases, firms gained near-monopoly power in specific hub airports. Not surprisingly, a study by the U.S. Government Accountability Office found that ticket prices are 45 to 85 percent higher on monopolized routes than on routes where at least two airlines compete.

The concentration ratio in the airline industry spiked even higher in 2013 when American Airlines merged with U.S. Airways. The merged airline became the largest U.S. carrier, and the concentration ratio jumped to 80 percent. Although U.S. Attorney General Eric Holder warned that the American/U.S. Air merger "would result in consumers paying the price—in higher fares, higher fees, and fewer choices," the Justice Department approved the merger three months after suing to block it.

Entry Barriers. To exploit their hub dominance, major carriers must keep out rivals. One of the most effective entry barriers is their ownership of landing slots. Air traffic is limited by the number of these slots, or authorized landing permits. In 1998 United Airlines controlled 82 percent of the slots at Chicago's O'Hare; Delta controls 83 percent of the slots at New York's Kennedy Airport. Smaller airlines complain that they can't get access to these slots, even when the slots aren't being used.

The Justice Department forced American and U.S. Airways to give up 52 slots at Washington, DC's Reagan airport; 17 at La Guardia; and 2 each at five other airports as a condition for approving their merger. Justice said it would make those slots available to low-cost carriers in order to create more competitive pricing situations.

When entry barriers (including slot access) are lowered, new competitors emerge and push down airfares as one would expect in a **contestable market.** A 2013 MIT study estimated that the entry of JetBlue into a new air travel market caused one-way air fares to drop an average of $32. More details on this "JetBlue effect" are noted in In the News "The JetBlue Effect."

contestable market: An imperfectly competitive industry subject to potential entry if prices or profits increase.

IN THE NEWS

THE JETBLUE EFFECT

When this carrier comes to town, fares go down, traffic goes up, and the airline ends up with a big chunk of the business.

	Change in Daily Passengers	Change in Average Fare	JetBlue Local Traffic Share
New York to Miami/Fort Lauderdale	+14%	−17% to $121.50	23.1%
New York to Los Angeles Basin	+2%	−26% to $219.31	18%
New York to Buffalo	+94%	−40% to $86.09	61.2%

Figures as of second quarter, 2003.

Data: Back Aviation Solutions.

—Wendy Zellner

Zellner, Wendy, "Is JetBlue's Flight Plan Flawed?" *Businessweek*, February 16, 2004. Copyright ©2004. All rights reserved. Used with permission.

ANALYSIS: If entry barriers are low enough, new entrants will contest a market, keeping pressure on prices and service.

Cable TV

The cable TV industry offers examples of both deregulation and *re*regulation. Up until 1986, city and county governments had the authority to franchise (approve) local cable TV operators and regulate their rates. In almost all cases, local governments franchised only one operator, thus establishing local monopolies. The monopoly structure was justified by pervasive economies of scale and the desire to avoid the cost and disruption of laying multiple cable systems. The rationale behind local regulation of cable prices (rates) was to ensure that consumers shared in the cost advantages of natural monopoly.

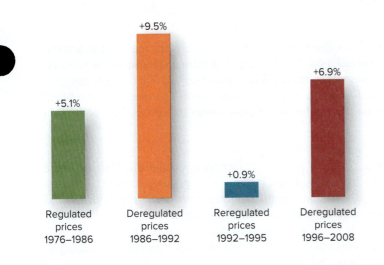

FIGURE 27.4

Annual Increase in Price of Basic Cable Service

After cable TV prices were deregulated in 1986, monthly charges moved up sharply. In 1992 Congress reregulated cable TV and prices stabilized. The Telecommunications Act of 1996 again deregulated prices and they surged, as shown in these annual averages.

Deregulation. By 1984 Congress was convinced that broadcast TV and emerging technologies (such as microwave transmissions and direct satellite broadcasts) offered sufficient competition to ensure consumers fair prices and quality service. The Cable Communications Policy Act of 1984 *de*regulated cable TV by stripping local governments of the authority to regulate prices. From 1986 to 1992, cable TV was essentially unregulated.

Soon after price regulation ended, cable companies began increasing their rates sharply. As Figure 27.4 shows, the rate of price acceleration nearly doubled after the cable industry was deregulated. Consumers also complained that local cable companies offered poor service. They demanded that Congress *re*regulate the industry.

Reregulation. In 1992 Congress responded with the Cable Television Consumer Protection and Competition Act. That act gave the Federal Communications Commission authority to reregulate cable TV rates. The FCC required cable operators to *reduce* prices by nearly 17 percent in 1993–1994. It then issued 450 pages of new rules that would limit future price increases. As Figure 27.4 illustrates, these interventions had a dramatic effect on cable prices.

While consumers applauded the new price rules, cable operators warned of unwelcome long-term effects. The rate cuts reduced cable industry revenues by nearly $4 billion between 1993 and 1995. The cable companies say they would have used that revenue to invest in improved networks and services. The cable companies also argued that increased competition from satellite transmissions and the Internet made government regulation of (wired) cable TV increasingly unnecessary.

Deregulation. Congress responded to these industry complaints by *de*regulating the cable industry again. The Telecommunications Act of 1996 mandated that rate regulation be phased out and ended completely by March 1999. Almost immediately, cable prices soared again, as Figure 27.4 shows.

Satellite Technology. The surge in cable TV prices was a boon to satellite TV providers. Satellite transmissions became a **substitute good** for cable TV—a substitute that also enjoyed pervasive economies of scale. So you suddenly had *competing* natural monopolies in a *contestable* market. Satellites won. In 1993, when cable prices were still relatively low, cable had 93 percent of the pay TV market. By 2011 the cable market share had declined to 65 percent. The high prices and profits of the cable industry ultimately spawned effective competition, first in satellite technology, then in broadband TV services (e.g., Netflix, Hulu, Blu-ray). Cable prices are still high and service below par, but at least the cable companies are now compelled by competition to improve the customer experience.

substitute goods: Goods that substitute for each other; when the price of good *x* rises, the demand for good *y* increases, *ceteris paribus.*

Electricity

The electric utility industry is the latest target for deregulation. Here again, the industry is a natural monopoly. The enormous fixed costs of a power plant and transmission network, combined with negligible marginal costs for delivering another kilowatt of electricity, give electric utilities a downward-sloping average total cost curve. The focus of government intervention was therefore on rate regulation (behavior) rather than promoting competition (structure).

Bloated Costs, High Prices. Critics of local utility monopolies complained that local rate regulation wasn't working well enough. To get higher (retail) prices, the utility companies allowed costs to rise. They also had no incentive to pursue new technologies that would reduce the costs of power generation or distribution. Big power users like steel companies complained that high electricity prices were crippling their competitive position. The only viable option for consumers was to move from a state with a high-cost power monopoly to a state with a low-cost power monopoly.

Demise of Power Plant Monopolies. Advances in transmission technology gave consumers a new choice. High-voltage transmission lines can carry power thousands of miles with negligible power loss. Utility companies used these lines to link their power grids, thereby creating backup power sources in the event of regional blackouts. In doing so, however, they created a new entry point for potential competition. Now a Kentucky power plant with surplus capacity can supply electricity to consumers in California. There's no longer any need to rely on a regional utility monopoly. At the wholesale level, utility companies have been trading electricity across state lines since 1992.

Local Distribution Monopolies. Although technology destroyed the basis for natural monopolies in power *production,* local monopolies in power *distribution* remain. Electricity reaches consumers through the wires attached to every house and business. As with TV cables, there is a natural monopoly in electricity distribution; competing wire grids would be costly and inefficient.

To deliver the benefits of competition in power *production,* rival producers must be able to access these local distribution grids. This is the same problem that has plagued competition in local telephone service. The local power companies that own the local distribution grids aren't anxious to open the wires to new competition. The central problem for electricity deregulation has been to assure wider access to local distribution grids.

California's Mistakes. The California legislature decided to resolve this problem by stripping local utility monopolies of their production capacity. By forcing utility companies to sell their power plants, California transformed its utilities into pure power *distributors.* This seemed to resolve the conflict between ownership and access to the distribution system. However, it also made California's utility companies totally dependent on third-party power producers, many of which were then out of state.

price ceiling: An upper limit imposed on the price of a good.

California also put a **price ceiling** on the *retail* price its utilities could charge. But the state had no power to control the *wholesale* price of electricity in interstate markets. When wholesale prices rose sharply in 2000, *California's utilities were trapped between rising costs and a fixed price ceiling.* Fearful of a political backlash, the governor refused to raise the retail price ceiling. As a result, some of the utility companies were forced into bankruptcy and power supplies were interrupted. The state itself entered the utility business by buying power plants and more out-of-state power supplies. In the end, Californians ended up with very expensive electricity. In Nevada, electricity prices remain high as well because the state won't allow casinos and other power users to bypass the monopoly distributor of electricity in that state unless they pay huge "exit fees" to compensate the monopoly (see In the News "Vegas Wants to Bypass Electric Monopoly").

IN THE NEWS

VEGAS WANTS TO BYPASS ELECTRIC MONOPOLY

MGM casinos in Las Vegas use more electricity to keep the neon lights bright than does the entire city of Key West, Florida. And they pay a premium price to do so. Nevada law requires residents and businesses in the state to buy their electricity from NV Energy, the monopoly power distributor in that state. Vegas casinos say they could score a jackpot by bypassing NV Energy and buying electricity directly from out-of-state power companies. With wholesale electricity priced at around 3.5 cents per kilowatt-hour and NV charging the casinos 8–9 cents per kilowatt-hour, that proposition appears to be a sure bet. In fact, MGM paid NV Energy a $86.9 million "exit fee" in 2016 for the right to stop buying electricity from that monopoly and instead buying power from a Texas power company. MGM is betting that the savings on its $600,000 per month electric bill will more than repay that fee.

Source: Media reports, October-November 2016.

ANALYSIS: A natural monopoly will want to maximize profits. If its behavior isn't regulated, consumers will end up paying the monopoly price.

THE ECONOMY TOMORROW

DEREGULATE EVERYTHING?

Deregulation of the railroad, telephone, airline, and electricity industries has yielded substantial benefits: more competition, lower prices, and improved services. Such experiences bolster the case for laissez faire. Nevertheless, we shouldn't jump to the conclusion that all regulation of business should be dismantled. All we know from experience is that the regulation of certain industries became outmoded. Changing consumer demands, new technologies, and substitute goods simply made existing regulations obsolete, even counterproductive. A combination of economic and political forces doomed them to extinction.

But were these regulations ever necessary? In the 1880s there were no viable alternatives to railroads for overland transportation. The forces of natural monopoly could easily have exploited consumers and retarded economic growth. The same was largely true for long-distance telephone service prior to the launching of communications satellites. Even the limitations on competition in trucking and banking made some sense in the depths of the Great Depression. One shouldn't conclude that regulatory intervention never made sense just because the regulations themselves later became obsolete.

Even today, most people recognize the need for regulation of many industries. The transmission networks for local telephone service and electricity delivery are still natural monopolies. The government can force owners to permit greater access. But an unregulated network owner could still extract monopoly profits through excessive prices. Hence even a deregulated industry may still require some regulation at critical entry or supply junctures. Existing regulations may not be optimal, but they probably generate better outcomes than totally unregulated monopolies.

Likewise, few people seriously propose relying on competition and the good judgment of consumers to determine the variety or quality of drugs on the market. Regulations imposed by the Food and Drug Administration restrain competition in the drug industry, raise production costs, and inhibit new technology. But they also make drugs safer. Here, as in other industries, there's a trade-off between the virtues of competition and those of regulation. ***The basic policy issue, as always, is whether the benefits of regulation exceed their administrative, compliance, and efficiency costs.*** The challenge for public policy in the economy tomorrow is to adapt regulations—or to discard them (i.e., deregulate)—as market conditions, consumer demands, or technology changes.

SUMMARY

- Antitrust and regulation are alternative options for dealing with market power. Antitrust focuses on market structure and anticompetitive practices. Regulation stipulates specific market behavior. **LO27-2**
- High fixed costs and negligible marginal costs create a downward-sloping ATC curve, the hallmark of natural monopoly. **LO27-1**
- Natural monopolies offer pervasive economies of scale. Because of this potential efficiency, a more competitive market *structure* may not be desirable. **LO27-2**
- Regulation of natural monopoly can focus on price, profit, or output *behavior*. Price regulation may require subsidies; profit regulation may induce cost escalation; and output regulation may lead to quality deterioration. These problems compel compromises and second-best solutions. **LO27-2**
- The demand for deregulation rests on the argument that the costs of regulation exceed the benefits. These costs include the opportunity costs associated with regulatory administration and compliance as well as the (dynamic) efficiency losses that result from inflexible pricing and production rules. **LO27-3**
- Deregulation of the railroad, telephone, and airline industries has been a success. In all these industries, regulation became outmoded by changing consumer demands, products, and technology. As regulation was relaxed, these industries became more competitive, output increased, and prices fell. **LO27-4**
- Recent experiences with deregulation don't imply that all regulation should end. Regulation is appropriate if market failure exists *and* if the benefits of regulation exceed the costs. As benefits and costs change, decisions about what and how to regulate must be reevaluated. **LO27-3**

Key Terms

laissez faire
market failure
antitrust
regulation
natural monopoly
economies of scale

profit-maximization rule
marginal cost pricing
opportunity cost
economic profit
government failure
concentration ratio

cross-subsidization
product differentiation
barriers to entry
contestable market
substitute goods
price ceiling

Questions for Discussion

1. Why are railroads natural monopolies? What limits their pricing power? **LO27-1**
2. New York City has limited the number of taxicabs for decades. Were taxi companies natural monopolies? What was the purpose of such regulation? Why were Uber, Lyft, and other ride-sharing companies so eager to enter the industry? **LO27-1**
3. What makes cable companies natural monopolies? How did cable profits affect the emergence of satellite transmissions? **LO27-1**
4. Given the inevitable limit on airplane landings, how should available airport slots be allocated? How would market outcomes be altered? **LO27-2**
5. Why would a profit-regulated firm want to sell itself inputs at inflated prices? Or increase wages? **LO27-3**
6. Prior to 1982, AT&T kept local phone rates low by subsidizing them from long-distance profits. Was such cross-subsidization in the public interest? Explain. **LO27-1**
7. How would you put dollar values on the benefits and costs of truck safety regulations (In the News "Sleep Rules Raise Trucking Costs")? Do benefits exceed costs? **LO27-2**
8. The Telecommunications Act of 1996 requires local phone companies to charge "reasonable" rates for transmission access. What is a "reasonable" rate? **LO27-4**
9. How could a local phone or cable company reduce service quality if forced to accept price ceilings? **LO27-2**
10. Why don't Nevada regulators allow casinos and other consumers to bypass the state's monopoly distributor of electricity? **LO27-2**

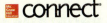

PROBLEMS FOR CHAPTER 27

LO27-1 1. Suppose a company has $400 of fixed costs and a constant marginal cost of 10 cents. What are average total costs (ATC) at
    (a) Output of 10 units?
    (b) Output of 100 units?
    (c) Output of 1,000 units?

LO27-2 2. In Figure 27.2,
    (a) How much profit does an unregulated monopolist earn?
    (b) How much profit would be earned if price efficiency ($p = MC$) were imposed?

LO27-2 3. Using the graph, identify output and price and calculate profits for
    (a) An unregulated natural monopoly.
    (b) A monopoly that is regulated according to price-efficiency ($p = MC$).
    (c) A monopoly that is required to provide a minimum service of 60.

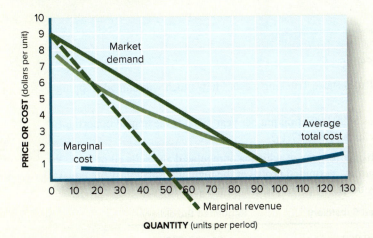

LO27-1 4. What happens to profits (or losses) when new technology reduces average total costs (shifts ATC downward in Figure 27.2) in
    (a) An unregulated natural monopoly?
    (b) A price-regulated natural monopoly without a subsidy?
    (c) A profit-regulated natural monopoly?

LO27-2 5. Suppose a natural monopolist has fixed costs of $15 and a constant marginal cost of $3. The demand for the product is as follows:

Price (per unit)	$10	$9	$8	$7	$6	$5	$4	$3	$2	$1
Quantity demanded (units per day)	0	2	4	6	8	10	12	14	16	18

Under these conditions,
    (a) What price and quantity will prevail if the monopolist isn't regulated?
    (b) What price–output combination would exist with efficient pricing ($p = MC$)?
    (c) What price–output combination would exist with profit regulation (zero economic profits)?

Illustrate your answers on the following graph:

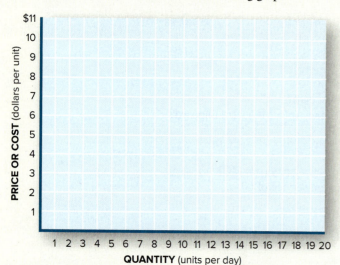

LO27-3 6. According to In the News "Sleep Rules Raise Trucking Costs," how much will annual shipping costs increase for each saved life?

LO27-3 7. If the average U.S. worker produces $120,000 of output per year, what is the annual opportunity cost of the federal regulatory workforce (Table 27.1)?

LO27-4 8. Suppose a corporation has two subsidiaries, one of which is unregulated and sells all of its output to the other, regulated subsidiary. Permitted profits at the regulated subsidiary are equal to 10 percent of total costs. Here is the initial profit picture for the subsidiaries:

	Unregulated Subsidiary	Regulated Subsidiary
Total revenue	$600,000	$1,100,000
Total costs	$400,000	$1,000,000
Total profit	$200,000	$100,000

If the unregulated subsidiary doubles its selling price and continues to sell the same quantity, what happens to profits at
(*a*) The unregulated subsidiary?   (*b*) The regulated subsidiary?

LO27-1 9. According to In the News "Vegas Wants to Bypass Electric Monopoly," if MGM's electric bill was $600,000 per month with NV Energy and its costs decrease by 60 percent in the wholesale market, how many years will it take to recoup its "exit fee"?

LO27-3 10. The Economy Tomorrow: Suppose the benefits of a regulation related to workplace safety is $10 million per year and the associated administrative costs are $200,000, compliance costs are $4 million, and efficiency costs are $5 million per year. Should deregulation occur?

©Alex Wong/Getty Images

CHAPTER 28

Environmental Protection

Progress in environmental problems is impossible without a clear understanding of how the economic system works in the environment and what alternatives are available to take away the many roadblocks to environmental quality.

—Council on Environmental Quality, First Annual Report

What good is a clean river if you've got no jobs?

—Steelworkers union official in Youngstown, Ohio

Environmental protection, what they do is a disgrace; every week they come out with new regulations

—Donald Trump, president of the United States

A hole in the ozone layer is allowing increased ultraviolet radiation to reach the earth's surface. The hole is the result of excessive release of chlorine gases (chlorofluorocarbons, or CFCs) from air conditioners, plastic foam manufacture, industrial solvents, and aerosol spray cans such as deodorants and insecticides. The resulting damage to the stratosphere is causing skin cancer, cataracts, and immune system disorders.

Skin cancer may turn out to be one of our less serious problems. As carbon dioxide is building up in the atmosphere, it is creating a gaseous blanket around the earth that is trapping radiation and heating the atmosphere. Scientists predict that this greenhouse effect will melt the polar ice caps, raise sea levels, flood coastal areas, and turn rich croplands into deserts within 60 years.

Everyone wants a cleaner and safer environment. So why don't we stop polluting the environment with CFCs, carbon dioxide, toxic chemicals, and other waste?

Economics is part of the answer. To reduce pollution, we have to change our patterns of production and consumption. This entails economic costs, in terms of restricted consumption choices, more expensive ways of producing goods, higher prices, and jobs. Thus we have to weigh the benefits of a cleaner, safer environment against the costs of environmental protection.

Instinctively, most people don't like the idea of measuring the value of a cleaner environment in dollars and cents. But most people might also agree that spending $2 trillion to avoid a few cataracts is awfully expensive. There has to be *some* balance between the benefits of a cleaner environment and the cost of cleaning it up.

This chapter assesses our environmental problems from this economic perspective, considering three primary concerns:

- **How do (unregulated) markets encourage pollution?**
- **What are the costs of greater environmental protection?**
- **How can government policy best ensure an *optimal* environment?**

To answer these questions, we first survey the major types and sources of pollution. Then we examine the benefits and costs of environmental protection, highlighting the economic incentives that shape market behavior.

THE ENVIRONMENTAL THREAT

Water, air, and solid waste pollution, and the earth's rising temperature are at the top of the list of environmental concerns. The list is much longer, however, and very old as well. As early as A.D. 61, the statesman and philosopher Seneca was complaining about the smoky air emitted from household chimneys in Rome. Lead emissions from ancient Greek and Roman silver refineries poisoned the air in Europe and the remote Arctic. And historians are quick to remind us that open sewers running down the street were once the principal mode of urban waste disposal. Typhoid epidemics were a recurrent penalty for water pollution. So we can't say that environmental damage is a new phenomenon or that it's now worse than ever before.

But we do know more about the sources of environmental damage than our ancestors did, and we can better afford to do something about it. Our understanding of the economics of pollution has increased as well. We've come to recognize that pollution impairs health, reduces life expectancy, and thus reduces labor force activity and output. Pollution also destroys capital (such as the effects of air pollution on steel structures) and diverts resources to undesired activities (like car washes, laundry, and cleaning). Not least of all, pollution directly reduces our social welfare by denying us access to clean air, water, and beaches.

Air Pollution

Air pollution is as familiar as a smoggy horizon. But smog is only one form of air pollution.

Acid Rain. Sulfur dioxide (SO_2) is an acrid, corrosive, and poisonous gas that's created by burning high-sulfur fuels such as coal. As a contributor to acid rain, it destroys vegetation and forests. Electric utilities and industrial plants that burn high-sulfur coal or fuel oil are the prime sources of SO_2. Coal burning alone accounts for about 60 percent of all emissions of sulfur oxides. As World View "Polluted Cities" illustrates, SO_2 pollution is a serious problem not only in U.S. cities but all over the world: the air is much dirtier in Beijing, Calcutta, Tokyo, and Rome than in New York City—and virtually unbreathable in coal-mining areas like Guiyang, China.

Smog. Nitrogen oxides (NO_x), another ingredient in the formation of acid rain, are also a principal ingredient in the formation of smog. Smog not only irritates the eyes and spoils the view, but it also damages plants, trees, and human lungs. Automobile emissions account for 40 percent of urban smog. Bakeries, dry cleaners, and production of other consumer goods account for an equal amount of smog. The rest comes from electric power plants and industrial boilers.

The Greenhouse Effect. The prime villain in the greenhouse effect is the otherwise harmless carbon dioxide (CO_2) that we exhale. Unfortunately, we and nature now release so much CO_2 that the earth's oceans and vegetation can no longer absorb it all. The excess CO_2 is creating a gaseous blanket around the earth that may warm the earth to disastrous

POLLUTED CITIES

The air in New York City may be unhealthful, but it's not nearly as polluted with sulfur dioxide (SO_2) as that in some other major cities.

©Steve Allen/Stockbyte/Getty Images RF

Source: The World Bank, *WDR2009 Data Set*.

SO_2 Micrograms per Cubic Meter of Air

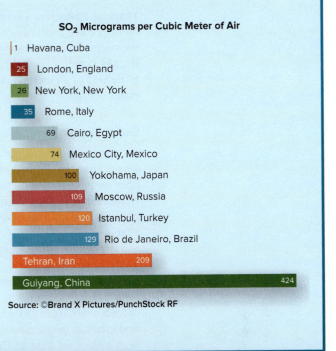

1	Havana, Cuba
25	London, England
26	New York, New York
35	Rome, Italy
69	Cairo, Egypt
74	Mexico City, Mexico
100	Yokohama, Japan
109	Moscow, Russia
120	Istanbul, Turkey
129	Rio de Janeiro, Brazil
209	Tehran, Iran
424	Guiyang, China

Source: ©Brand X Pictures/PunchStock RF

ANALYSIS: Pollution is a worldwide phenomenon with common origins and potential remedies.

levels. The burning of fossil fuels is a significant source of CO_2 buildup. The destruction of rain forests, which absorb CO_2, also contributes to the greenhouse effect.

Water Pollution

Water pollution is another environmental threat. Its effects are apparent in the contamination of drinking water, restrictions on swimming and boating, foul-smelling waterways, swarms of dead fish, and floating debris.

Organic Pollution. The most common form of water pollution occurs in the disposal of organic wastes from toilets and garbage disposals. The wastes that originate there are collected in sewer systems and ultimately discharged into the nearest waterway. The key question is whether the wastes are treated (separated and decomposed) before ultimate discharge. Sophisticated waste treatment plants can reduce organic pollution up to 99 percent. Unfortunately, only 70 percent of the U.S. population is served by a system of sewers and adequate (secondary) treatment plants. Inadequate treatment systems often result in the closure of waterways and beaches due to excessive levels of bacteria.

In addition to household wastes, our waterways must also contend with industrial wastes. More than half the volume of industrial discharge comes from just a few industries— principally paper, organic chemicals, petroleum, and steel. Finally, there are all those farm animals: the 7.5 billion chickens and 161 million cows and hogs raised each year generate 1.4 billion tons of manure (whew!). If improperly managed, that organic waste will contaminate water supplies and trigger algae blooms that can choke waterways and kill fish. Animal wastes don't cause too great a problem in Boston or New York

City, but they can wreak havoc on the water supplies of towns in California, Texas, Kansas, and Iowa.

Thermal Pollution. Thermal pollution is an increase in the temperature of waterways brought about by the discharge of steam or heated water. Heat discharges can kill fish, upset marine reproductive cycles, and accelerate biological and chemical processes in water, thereby reducing its ability to retain oxygen. Electric power plants account for more than 80 percent of all thermal discharges, with primary metal, chemical, and petroleum-refining plants accounting for nearly all the rest.

Solid Waste Pollution

Solid waste is yet another environmental threat. Solid waste pollution is apparent everywhere, from the garbage can to litter on the streets and beaches, to debris in the water, to open dumps. According to EPA estimates, we generate more than 5 billion tons of solid waste each year. This figure includes more than 30 billion bottles, 60 billion cans, 100 million tires, and millions of discarded automobiles and major appliances. Where do you think all this refuse goes?

Most solid wastes originate in agriculture (slaughter wastes, orchard prunings, harvest residues) and mining (slag heaps, mill tailings). The much smaller amount of solid waste originating in residential and commercial use is considered more dangerous, however, simply because it accumulates where people live. New York City alone generates 34,000 tons of trash a day, three times more than any other city in the world. Because it has neither the land area nor the incinerators needed for disposal, it must ship its garbage to other states. Seattle ships its trash to Oregon; Los Angeles transports its trash to the Mojave Desert; New York City sludge is dumped in west Texas; and Philadelphia ships its garbage all the way to Panama.

POLLUTION DAMAGES

Shipping garbage to Panama is an expensive answer to our waste disposal problem. But even those costs are a small fraction of the total cost of environmental damage. Much greater costs are associated with the damage to our health (labor), buildings (capital), and land. Even the little things count, like being able to enjoy a clear sunset, swim in the ocean, or just take a deep breath.

Although many people don't like to put a price on the environment, some monetary measure of environmental damage is important in decision making. Unless we value the environment above everything else, we have to establish some method of ranking the importance of environmental damage. Although it's tempting to say that clean air is priceless, *we won't get clean air, clean water, or clean beaches unless we spend resources to get them.* This economic reality suggests that we begin by determining how much cleaner air is worth to us.

Assigning Prices

In some cases, it's fairly easy to put a price on environmental damage. Scientists can measure the increase in cancer, heart attacks, and other disorders attributable to air pollution, as the EPA does for air toxins (see In the News "Air Pollution Kills"). Engineers can also measure the rate at which buildings decay or forests and lakes die. Economists can then estimate the dollar value of this damage by assessing the economic value of lives, forests, lakes, and other resources. For example, if people are willing to pay $5,000 for a cataract operation, then the avoidance of such eye damage is worth at least $5,000. Saving a tree is worth whatever the marketplace is willing to pay for the products of that tree. According to the EPA, a human life is worth $7.6 million. The EPA uses that benchmark to compute the damages due to premature deaths caused by pollution-related illnesses.

IN THE NEWS

AIR POLLUTION KILLS

Studies undertaken at Harvard's School of Public Health document how air pollution shortens life expectancies. The studies focused exclusively on airborne particulates that pollute the air—particulates that originate from vehicle traffic and smokestacks. Gaseous pollutants (sulfur and carbon dioxides, etc.) were not examined, although they, too, shorten life expectancies.

The studies' findings are dramatic: people who live in the most polluted cities (Los Angeles, Pittsburgh, St. Louis) are 15–17 percent more likely to die prematurely than those in cities with the cleanest air (Honolulu, Redding CA, Duluth MN). In the most polluted cities the decrease in life expectancy is equivalent to about one-sixth of the loss due to smoking for 25 years.

Source: National Institutes of Health.

ANALYSIS: Pollution entails real costs, as measured by impaired health, reduced life spans, and other damages.

The job of pricing environmental damage is much more difficult with intangible losses like sunsets. Nevertheless, when governmental agencies and courts are asked to assess the damages of oil spills and other accidents, they must try to inventory *all* costs, including polluted sunsets, reduced wildlife, and lost recreation opportunities. The science of computing such environmental damage is very inexact. Nevertheless, crude but reasonable procedures generate pollution-related damage estimates in the hundreds of billions of dollars per year.

Cleanup Possibilities

One of the most frustrating things about all this environmental damage is that it can be avoided. The EPA estimates that *95 percent of current air and water pollution could be eliminated by known and available technology.* Nothing very exotic is needed: just simple things like auto emission controls, smokestack cleaners, improved sewage and waste treatment facilities, and cooling towers for electric power plants. Even solid waste pollution could be reduced by comparable proportions if we used less packaging, recycled more materials, or transformed our garbage into a useful (relatively low-polluting) energy source. Why don't we do these things? Why do we continue to pollute so much?

MARKET INCENTIVES

Previous chapters emphasized how market incentives influence the behavior of individual consumers, firms, and government agencies. Incentives in the form of price reductions can be used to change consumer buying habits. Incentives in the form of high profit margins encourage production of desired goods and services. And market incentives in the form of cost differentials help allocate resources efficiently. Accordingly, we shouldn't be too surprised to learn that *market incentives play a major role in pollution behavior.*

The Production Decision

Imagine that you're the majority stockholder and manager of an electric power plant. Such plants are responsible for a significant amount of air pollution (especially sulfur dioxide and particulates) and nearly all thermal water pollution. Hence your position immediately puts you on the most-wanted list of pollution offenders. But suppose you're civic minded and would truly like to help eliminate pollution. Let's consider the alternatives.

Profit Maximization. As the owner–manager of an electric power plant, you'll strive to make a profit-maximizing **production decision.** That is, you'll seek the rate of output at which marginal revenue equals marginal cost. Let's assume that the electric power industry is still regulated by the state power commission so that the price of electricity is fixed, at least in the short run. The effect of this assumption is to render marginal revenue equal to price, thus giving us a horizontal price line, as in Figure 28.1a.

Figure 28.1a also depicts the marginal and average total costs (MC and ATC) associated with the production of electricity. By equating marginal cost (MC) to price (marginal revenue, MR), we observe (point A) that profit maximization occurs at an output of 1,000 kilowatt-hours per day. Total profits are illustrated by the shaded rectangle between the price line and the average total cost (ATC) curve.

The Efficiency Decision

The profits illustrated in Figure 28.1a are achieved in part by use of the cheapest available fuel under the boilers (which create the steam that rotates the generators). Recall that the construction of a marginal cost curve presumes some knowledge of alternative production processes. Recall too that the **efficiency decision** requires a producer to choose that production process (and its associated cost curve) that minimizes costs for any particular rate of output.

Costs of Pollution Abatement. Unfortunately, the efficiency decision in this case leads to the use of high-sulfur coal, the prime villain in SO_2 and particulate pollution. Other fuels, such as low-sulfur coal, fuel oil, natural gas, and nuclear energy, cost considerably more. Were you to switch to one of them, the ATC and MC curves would both shift upward, as in Figure 28.1b. Under these conditions, the most profitable rate of output would be lower than before (point B on the graph), and total profits would decline (note the smaller profit rectangle in Figure 28.1b). Thus *pollution abatement can be achieved, but only at significant cost to the plant.*

The same kind of cost considerations lead the plant to engage in thermal pollution. Cool water must be run through an electric utility plant to keep the turbines from overheating. Once the water has run through the plant, it's too hot to recirculate. It must be either dumped back into the adjacent river or cooled off by being circulated through cooling

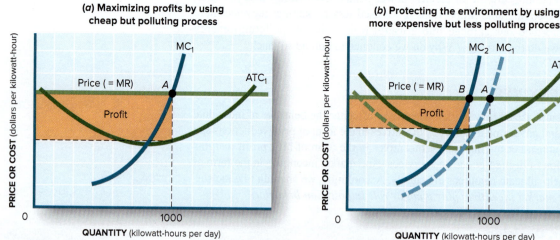

FIGURE 28.1

Profit Maximization in Electric Power Production

Production processes that control pollution may be more expensive than those that don't. If they are, the MC and ATC curves will shift upward (to MC_2 and ATC_2). At the new profit-maximizing rate of output (point B), output and total profit shrink. Hence a producer has an incentive to continue polluting, using cheaper technology.

towers. As you might expect, it's cheaper to simply dump the hot water in the river, as the Indian Point nuclear plant in New York does (see In the News "Cut the Power to Save the Fish?"). The fish don't like it, but they don't have to pay the construction costs associated with cooling towers.

IN THE NEWS

CUT THE POWER TO SAVE THE FISH?

Governor Andrew Cuomo has been trying to close the Indian Point nuclear plant since 2001. The governor and his environmentalist friends worry about the safety of nuclear plants and their impact on fish. The Indian Point plant sucks in 2.5 billion gallons of water out of the Hudson River every day to cool its generators. It also sucks up and kills millions of fish and larvae. More fish are killed when the heated water is returned to the river. The state's Department of Environmental Conservation (DEC) wants at least a temporary shutdown in the spawning and migration season (May 10—August 10). Better yet, they want Entergy Corp., the plant's owner, to reengineer a closed-circuit cooling system that will end the fish kills.

The DEC faces two problems. First, Entergy says it would be far too costly to reengineer the cooling system; no chance of that happening. Second, electricity consumers need the power Indian Point provides. The plant supplies 2,000 megawatts of electricity a day—about 25 percent of New York City's daily use. Although DEC promises to help find an alternative source of power, New Yorkers aren't willing to risk blackouts, brownouts, or higher electricity prices to save a few fish.

Source: News reports, April–June 2014.

ANALYSIS: When producers consider only *private* costs, they may select production processes that impose high *external* costs.

The big question here is whether you and your fellow stockholders would be willing to incur higher costs to cut down on pollution. Eliminating the water pollution emanating from the electric plant will cost a lot of money. And to whose benefit? To the people who live downstream? We don't expect profit-maximizing producers to take such concerns into account. *The behavior of profit maximizers is guided by comparisons of revenues and costs, not by philanthropy, aesthetic concerns, or the welfare of fish.*

MARKET FAILURE: EXTERNAL COSTS

The moral of this story—and the critical factor in pollution behavior—is that *people tend to maximize their personal welfare, balancing private benefits against private costs.* For the electric power plant, this means making production decisions on the basis of revenues received and costs incurred. The fact that the power plant imposes costs on others, in the form of air and water pollution, is irrelevant to its profit-maximizing decisions. Those costs are *external* to the firm and don't appear on its profit-and-loss statement. Those **external costs**—or *externalities*—are no less real, but they're incurred by society at large rather than by the firm.

external costs: Costs of a market activity borne by a third party; the difference between the social and private costs of a market activity.

Externalities in Production

Whenever external costs exist, a private firm won't allocate its resources and operate its plant in such a way as to maximize social welfare. In effect, society permits the power plant the free use of valued resources—clean air and clean water. The power plant has a tremendous incentive to substitute those resources for others (such as high-priced fuel or cooling towers) in the production process. The inefficiency of such an arrangement is obvious when we recall that the function of markets is to allocate scarce resources in accordance with the consumer's expressed demands. Yet here we are, proclaiming a high value for clean air and clean water and encouraging the power plant to use up both resources by offering them at zero cost to the firm.

The inefficiency of this market arrangement can be expressed in terms of a distinction between social costs and private costs. **Social costs** are the total costs of all the resources used in a particular production activity. On the other hand, **private costs** are the resource costs incurred by the specific producer.

Ideally, a producer's private costs will encompass all the attendant social costs, and production decisions will be consistent with our social welfare. Unfortunately, this happy identity doesn't always exist, as our experience with the power plant illustrates. *When social costs differ from private costs, external costs exist. In fact, external costs are equal to the difference between the social and private costs*:

External costs = Social costs − Private costs

When external costs are present, the market mechanism won't allocate resources efficiently. This is a case of **market failure.** The price signal confronting producers is flawed. By not conveying the full (social) cost of scarce resources, the market encourages excessive pollution. We end up with a suboptimal mix of output (too much electricity, too little clean air) and the wrong production processes.

The consequences of this market failure are illustrated in Figure 28.2, which again depicts the cost situation confronting the electric power plant. Notice that we use *two* different marginal cost curves this time. The lower one, the *private* MC curve, reflects the private costs incurred by the power plant when it operates on a profit maximization basis, using high-sulfur coal or without cooling towers. It's identical to the MC curve in Figure 28.1*a*. We now know, however, that such operations impose external costs on others in the form of air and water pollution. These external costs must be added to private marginal costs. When this is done, we get a *social* marginal cost curve that lies above the private MC curve.

To maximize profits, private firms seek the rate of output that equates private MC to MR (price). *To maximize social welfare, we need to equate social marginal cost to marginal revenue (price).* This social optimum occurs at point *A* in Figure 28.2 and results in output of q_s. By contrast, the firm's private profit maximization occurs at point *B*, where q_p is produced. Hence the private firm ends up producing more output than socially desired, while earning more profit and causing more pollution. As a general rule, *if pollution costs are external, firms will produce too much of a polluting good.*

---

social costs: The full resource costs of an economic activity, including externalities.

private costs: The costs of an economic activity directly borne by the immediate producer or consumer (excluding externalities).

market failure: An imperfection in the market mechanism that prevents optimal outcomes.

FIGURE 28.2

Market Failure

Social costs exceed private costs by the amount of external costs. Production decisions based on private costs alone will lead us to point *B*, where private MC = MR. At point *B*, the rate of output is q_p.

To maximize social welfare, we equate *social* MC and MR, as at point *A*. Only q_s of output is socially desirable. The failure of the market to convey the full costs of production keeps us from attaining this outcome.

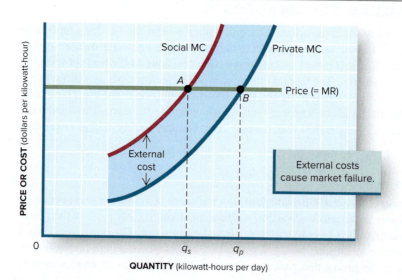

Externalities in Consumption

A divergence between private and social costs can also be observed in consumption. Consumers try to maximize their personal welfare. We buy and use more of those goods and services that yield the highest satisfaction (marginal utility) per dollar expended. By implication (and the law of demand), we tend to use more of a product if we can get it at a discount—that is, pay less than the full price. Unfortunately, the "discount" often takes the form of an external cost imposed on neighbors and friends.

Automobile driving illustrates the problem. The amount of driving one does is influenced by the price of a car and the marginal costs of driving it. People buy smaller cars and drive less when the attendant marginal costs (for instance, gasoline prices) increase substantially. But automobile use involves not only *private costs* but *external costs* as well. Auto emissions (carbon monoxide, hydrocarbons, and nitrogen oxides) are a principal cause of air pollution. In effect, automobile drivers have been able to use a valued resource, clean air, at no cost to themselves. Few motorists see any personal benefit in installing exhaust control devices because the quality of the air they breathe would be little affected by their efforts. Hence low private costs lead to excessive pollution when high social costs are dictating cleaner air.

A divergence between social and private costs can be observed even in the simplest of consumer activities, such as throwing an empty soda can out the window of your car. Hanging onto the can and later disposing of it in a trash barrel involve personal effort and thus private marginal costs. Throwing it out the window not only is more exciting but also effectively transfers the burden of disposal costs to someone else. The resulting externality ends up as roadside litter.

The same kind of divergence between private and social costs helps explain why people abandon old cars in the street rather than haul them to scrapyards. It also explains why people use vacant lots as open dumps. In all these cases, ***the polluter benefits by substituting external costs for private costs.*** In other words, market incentives encourage environmental damage.

REGULATORY OPTIONS

The failure of the market to include external costs in production and consumption decisions creates a basis for government intervention. As always, however, we confront a variety of policy options. We may define these options in terms of ***two general strategies for environmental protection:***

- ***Alter market incentives*** in such a way that they discourage pollution.
- ***Bypass market incentives*** with some form of regulatory intervention.

Market-Based Options

Insofar as market incentives are concerned, the key to environmental protection is to eliminate the divergence between private costs and social costs. The opportunity to shift some costs onto others lies at the heart of the pollution problem. If we could somehow compel producers to *internalize* all costs—pay for both private and external costs—the divergence would disappear, along with the incentive to pollute.

Emission Charges. One possibility is to establish a system of **emission charges:** direct costs attached to the act of polluting. Suppose that we let you keep your power plant and permit you to operate it according to profit-maximizing principles. The only difference is that we no longer supply you with clean air and cool water at zero cost. From now on, we'll charge you for these scarce resources. We might, say, charge 2 cents for every gram of noxious emission discharged into the air. In addition we might charge 3 cents for every gallon of water you use, heat, and discharge back into the river.

Confronted with such emission charges, you'd have to rethink your production decision. ***An emission charge increases private marginal cost and encourages lower output and***

emission charge: A fee imposed on polluters, based on the quantity of pollution.

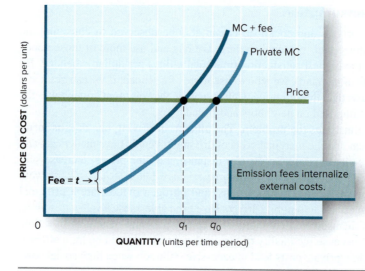

cleaner technology. Figure 28.3 illustrates this effect. Notice how the fee raises private marginal costs and induces a lower rate of (polluting) production (q_1 rather than q_0).

Once an emission fee is in place, a producer may also reevaluate the efficiency decision. Consider again the choice of fuels to be used in our fictional power plant. We earlier chose high-sulfur coal because it was the cheapest fuel available. Now, however, there's an additional cost attached to burning such fuel, in the form of an emission charge. This added cost may encourage the firm to switch to cleaner sources of energy, which would increase private marginal costs but reduce emission fees.

An emission charge might also persuade a firm to incur higher *fixed* costs. Rather than continuing to pay emission charges, it might be more economical to install scrubbers and other smokestack controls that reduce the volume of emissions. This would entail additional capital outlays for the necessary abatement equipment but might reduce variable costs (including emission charges). In this case, the fee-induced change in fixed costs might reduce pollution without any reduction in output.

The actual response of producers will depend on the relative costs involved. If emission charges are too low, it may be more profitable to continue burning and polluting with high-sulfur coal and pay a nominal fee. This is a simple pricing problem. We could set the emission price higher, prompting the behavioral responses we desire.

Economic incentives can also change consumer behavior. At one time, beverage producers imposed deposits to encourage consumers to bring bottles back so they could be used again. But producers discovered that such deposits discouraged sales and yielded little cost savings. Today returnable bottles are rarely used. One result is the inclusion of more than 30 billion glass bottles and 60 billion cans in our solid waste disposal problem. We could reverse this trend by imposing a deposit on all beverage containers. Many states do this, at least for certain cans and bottles. Such deposits internalize pollution costs for the consumer and render the throwing of a soda can out the window equivalent to throwing away money.

Some communities have also tried to reduce solid waste processing by charging a fee for each container of garbage collected. In Charlotte, Virginia, a fee of 80 cents per 32-gallon bag of garbage had a noticeable impact on consumer behavior. Economists Don Fullerton and Thomas Kinnaman observed that households reduced the weight of their garbage by 14 percent and the volume by 37 percent. As they noted, "Households somehow stomped their garbage to get more in a container and trim their garbage bill." Here again, the use of the market mechanism (higher prices) brought about the desired environmental protection.

Recycling Materials. An important bonus that emission charges offer is an increased incentive for the recycling of materials. The glass and metal in used bottles and cans can be recycled to produce new bottles and cans. Such recycling not only eliminates a lot of un-sightly litter but also diminishes the need to mine new resources from the earth, a process that often involves its own environmental problems. The critical issues are once again rela-tive costs and market incentives. *A container producer has no incentive to use recycled materials unless they offer superior cost efficiency and thus greater profits.* The largest component in the costs of recycled materials is usually the associated costs of collection and transportation. In this regard, an emission charge such as the 5-cent container deposit lowers collection costs because it motivates consumers to return all their bottles and cans to a central location.

Higher User Fees. Another market alternative is to raise the price consumers pay for scarce resources. If people used less water, we wouldn't have to build so many sewage treatment plants. In most communities, however, the price of water is so low that people use it indiscriminately. Higher water fees would encourage water conservation.

A similar logic applies to auto pollution. The cheapest way to cut down on auto pollution is to drive less. Higher gasoline prices would encourage people to use alternative transpor-tation and drive more fuel-efficient cars. Consumers would complain, of course, about higher taxes on gasoline, but at least they'd be able to breathe cleaner air.

"Green" Taxes. Automakers don't want gasoline prices to go up; neither do consumers. So the government may have to impose *green taxes* to get the desired response. A green tax on gasoline, for example, raises the price of gasoline. The taxes not only curb auto emissions (less driving) but also create a revenue source for other pollution abatement efforts. Other nations impose far more green taxes than does the United States.

Pollution Fines. Not far removed from the concept of emission and user charges is the imposition of fines or liability for cleanup costs. In some situations, such as the April 2010 BP oil spill in the Gulf of Mexico, the pollution is so sudden and concentrated that society has little choice but to clean it up quickly. The costs for such cleanup can be imposed on the polluter, however, through appropriate fines. Such fines place the cost burden where it belongs.

Although pollution fines are inevitably imposed after the damage is done, the *expecta-tion* of a fine can encourage more environmentally conscious behavior. To avoid a potential fine, oil companies may invest in double-hulled oil tankers and more efficient safety mech-anisms on offshore oil wells. When Royal Caribbean Cruises was fined $9 million in 1998 for dumping garbage and oil from its cruise ships, the firm decided to monitor waste disposal practices more closely. In the absence of such fines, firms have little incentive to invest in environmental protection.

Tradable Pollution Permits ("Cap and Trade")

Another environmental policy option makes even greater use of market incentives. Rather than penalize firms that have already polluted, let firms *purchase* the right to continue polluting. As crazy as this policy might sound, it can be effective in limiting environmental damage.

The key to the success of pollution permits is that they're bought and sold among private firms. The system starts with a government-set standard for pollution reduction. Firms that reduce pollution by more than the standard earn pollution credits. They may then sell these credits to other firms, who are thereby relieved of cleanup chores. *The principal advan-tage of pollution permits is their incentive to minimize the cost of pollution control.*

To see how the permits work, suppose the policy objective is to reduce sulfur dioxide emissions by two tons. There are only two major polluters in the community: a copper smelter and an electric utility. Should each company be required to reduce its SO_2 emis-sions by one ton? Or can the same SO_2 reduction be achieved more cheaply with market-able pollution rights?

government failure:
Government intervention that fails to improve economic outcomes.

environmental protection and discourage cost-saving innovation. There's also the risk of regulated processes becoming entrenched long after they are obsolete. When that happens we may end up with worse outcomes than a less regulated market would have generated—that is, **government failure.**

BALANCING BENEFITS AND COSTS

Protecting the environment entails costs as well as benefits. Installing smokestack scrubbers on factory chimneys and catalytic converters on cars requires the use of scarce resources. Taking the lead out of gasoline wears out engines faster and requires expensive changes in technology. Switching to clean fuels requires enormous investments in technology, plants, and equipment. The EPA estimates that a 10-year program to achieve national air and water standards would cost more than $1 trillion. Restoring the ozone layer, removing hazardous wastes, and cleaning up the rest of the environment would cost trillions more.

Opportunity Costs

opportunity cost: The most desired goods or services that are forgone in order to obtain something else.

Although cleaning up the environment is a worthwhile goal, we must remind ourselves that those resources could be used to fulfill other goals as well. The multitrillion-dollar tab would buy a lot of subways and parks or build decent homes for the poor. If we devote those resources instead to pollution abatement, we'll have to forgo other goods and services. Remember the basic principle about 'no free lunch?' Well, for the same reason there is no free environmental protection. This isn't to say that environmental goals don't deserve priority but simply to remind us that any use of our scarce resources involves an **opportunity cost.**

Fortunately, the amount of additional resources required to clean up the environment is relatively modest in comparison to our productive capacity. Over a 10-year period we'll produce more than $200 trillion of goods and services (GDP). On this basis, the environmental expenditures contemplated by present environmental policies and goals represent only 1 to 3 percent of total output.

The Optimal Rate of Pollution

optimal rate of pollution: The rate of pollution that occurs when the marginal social benefit of pollution control equals its marginal social cost.

Spending even a small percentage of GDP on environmental protection nevertheless entails value judgments. The **optimal rate of pollution** occurs at the point at which the opportunity costs of further pollution control equal the benefits of further reductions in pollution. *To determine the optimal rate of pollution, we need to compare the marginal social benefits of additional pollution abatement with the marginal social costs of additional pollution control expenditure.* The optimal rate of pollution is achieved when we've satisfied the following equality:

$$
\begin{array}{ccc}
\text{Optimal} & \text{Marginal benefit} & \text{Marginal cost} \\
\text{rate of} \quad : & \text{of pollution} \quad = & \text{of pollution} \\
\text{pollution} & \text{abatement} & \text{abatement}
\end{array}
$$

This formulation is analogous to the utility-maximizing rule in consumption. If another dollar spent on pollution control yields less than a dollar of social benefits, then additional pollution control expenditure isn't desirable. In such a situation, the goods and services that would be forsaken for additional pollution control are more valued than the environmental improvements that would result.

Cost–Benefit Analysis

A 2003 White House study concluded that past efforts to clean up the air have yielded far more benefits than costs: the benefits of a 10-year (1992–2002) air pollution abatement program were five to seven times greater than its cost. Although pollution abatement has been an economic success, that doesn't mean *all* pollution controls are desirable. The focus must still be on *marginal* benefits and costs. In that context, a surprising conclusion emerges: *a totally clean environment isn't economically desirable.* The marginal benefit of achieving zero pollution is infinitesimally small. But the marginal cost of eliminating that last particle of pollution will be very high. As we weigh the marginal benefits and costs, we'll inevitably conclude that *some* pollution is cost-effective.

Mayor Bloomberg performed the same kind of analysis for New York City's recycling program. Sure, everyone thinks recycling is a good idea. But Mayor Bloomberg started looking at the cost of the recycling program and decided it didn't make economic sense (see In the News "Recycling Wastes Money"). He figured the city could use the $57 million cost of recycling for higher-priority programs, yielding greater (marginal) benefits to NYC residents.

IN THE NEWS

RECYCLING WASTES MONEY

New York City is spending $57 million a year to recycle metal, glass, and plastic. Mayor Bloomberg says that's way too much, especially when the city is cutting police and fire budgets. The mayor says the city could save a lot of money by simply sending the waste to landfills rather than recycling it. The city spends about $240 per ton to recycle waste, while the cost of sending the waste to landfills is about $130 a ton. As he sees it, "You could do a lot better things in the world with $57 million." The mayor axed the recycling program from the city's proposed 2003 budget.

M.E. Cohen

Source: News reports, March 2002.

ANALYSIS: Recycling uses scarce resources that could be employed elsewhere. The benefits of recycling may not exceed its (opportunity) costs.

Who Will Pay?

The costs of pollution control aren't distributed equally. In New York City, the cost of the recycling program is borne by those who end up with fewer city services and amenities (opportunity costs). A national pollution abatement program would target the relatively small number of economic activities—like coal-fired power plants, paper mills, steel plants—that account for the bulk of emissions and effluents. These activities will have to bear a disproportionate share of the cleanup burden.

Higher Costs. To ascertain how the burden of environmental protection will be distributed, consider first the electric power plant discussed earlier. As we observed (Figure 28.2), the plant's output will decrease if production decisions are based on social rather than private marginal costs—that is, if environmental consequences are considered. If the plant itself is compelled to pay full social costs, in the form of either compulsory investment or emission charges, its profits will be reduced. Were no other changes to take place, the burden of environmental improvements would be borne primarily by the producer.

Higher Prices. Such a scenario is unlikely, however. Rather than absorb all the costs of pollution controls themselves, producers will pass some of this burden on to their customers in the form of higher prices. Their ability to do so will depend on the extent of competition in their industry, their relative cost position in it, and the price elasticity of consumer demand. In reality, the electric power industry isn't very competitive, and its prices are still subject to government regulation. In addition, consumer demand is relatively price-inelastic. Accordingly, the profit-maximizing producer will appeal to the state or local power commission for an increase in electricity prices based on the costs of pollution control. Electric power consumers are likely to end up footing the environmental bill.

Job Losses. Workers in the impacted industry are likely to suffer as well. All of the policy options we have looked at end up reducing the production and consumption of the polluting good. That implies job losses for the affected workers. According to the government itself, environmental regulations enacted in 2011 and 2014 eliminated thousands of coal-mining jobs across the country. Although the Obama administration claimed that the resulting decline in air pollution saved thousands of lives, those displaced coal miners argued that the economic costs of the mining regulations far outweighed the environmental benefits.

THE ECONOMY TOMORROW

THE WAR ON COAL

Forget about littered beaches, smelly landfills, eye-stinging smog, and contaminated water. The really scary problem for the economy tomorrow is much more serious: some scientists say that the carbon emissions we're now spewing into the air are warming the earth's atmosphere. If the earth's temperature rises only a few degrees, they contend, polar caps will melt, continents will flood, and weather patterns will go haywire. If things get bad enough, there may not be any economy tomorrow.

The Greenhouse Effect. The earth's climate is driven by solar radiation. The energy the sun absorbs must be balanced by outgoing radiation from the earth and the atmosphere. Scientists fear that a flow imbalance is developing. Of particular concern is a buildup of carbon dioxide (CO_2) that traps heat in the earth's atmosphere, warming the planet.

The natural release of CO_2 dwarfs the emissions from human activities. But there's a concern that the steady increase in man-made CO_2 emissions—principally from burning fossil fuels like gasoline and coal—is tipping the balance.

Scientists are still debating how much the earth's temperature is likely to rise in the economy tomorrow. But the continued buildup of carbon dioxide in the atmosphere is undeniable. A 2013 United Nations study concluded with 95 percent certainty that human activity (power generation, transportation, etc.) is increasingly responsible for the rising greenhouse gas concentrations and the climate changes that accompany them.

A Global Externality. While nearly every country recognizes the threat that CO_2 emissions pose, there is less certainty about how to reduce that threat. The core problem here is that *CO_2 emissions are a global externality.* People don't deliberately produce CO_2 emissions. Rather, they are an unintended by-product of everyday production and consumption activities. When you drive your car, you are polluting the air not just in your immediate vicinity, but the air the entire world inhales. When a Chinese coal mine spews CO_2 into the air, it increases CO_2 concentrations over Alaska and Florida.

Because CO_2 emissions are an externality, the market will produce too much of them. As we have seen, when the market fails, the government must intervene. But with a *global* externality, no single nation can resolve the problem.

The Paris Accord. In 2014 the United Nations convened a "Climate Summit" to address the problem. After two years of deliberations among nearly 200 nations, an agreement was reached in November 2016. According to the "Paris Accord," the nations of the world agreed to limit the increase in the earth's temperature over the next decade to no more than 2 degrees Celsius. To do that, each nation agreed to pledge a specific "contribution" of CO_2 reductions. President Obama committed the United States to cutting its CO_2 emissions by 26–28 percent by 2025, compared to 2005.

Focus on Coal. Global commitments to reduce greenhouse emissions inevitably look to the coal industry. Energy production accounts for one-fourth of all global greenhouse emissions, and coal is the largest contributor in that sector. In 2015 the U.S. coal industry emitted 1.4 billion tons of CO_2, more than one fifth of the total emissions. Hence, it's virtually impossible to achieve substantial emissions reductions without curbing coal.

Recognizing the critical role of coal in CO_2 emissions, President Obama essentially declared what critics called "a war on coal" (see In the News "A 'War on Coal'?"). That "war" included a ban on coal leases on federal lands (a huge issue in Wyoming), a virtual ban on new coal-mining permits, and a Stream Protection Rule that made mountain-top mining in West Virginia nearly impossible. From 2012 to 2016 nearly 40,000 coal miners lost their jobs as coal companies closed up shop. Although not all of these job losses were due to government regulation, the majority were.

Trump's Reversal. During the 2016 presidential campaign, Donald Trump said he was "committedd to reviving America's coal mining companies, which have been hurting for too long." In his first weeks as president, Trump convinced Congress to repeal President Obama's Stream Protection Rule and repealed regulations in Obama's Clean Power Plan. In June 2017 President Trump took even more dramatic action, withdrawing the United States from the Paris Accord, arguing that its pollution-reduction goals placed an "unfair" burden on American workers while subsidizing energy development in low-income nations.

How clean (and warm) the environment is in the economy tomorrow will depend on what kind of balance is ultimately struck between the benefits of environmental protection and its associated costs. The outcome of that decision will affect the level of CO_2 concentrations in the economy tomorrow.

IN THE NEWS

A "WAR ON COAL"?

Yesterday, the Environmental Protection Agency (EPA) issued its 645-page proposal for cutting America's carbon emissions. EPA's goal is to cut CO_2 emissions by 30 percent below the level of 2005 emissions by the year 2030. This would require CO_2 emissions to drop by a staggering 1.5 billion metric tons per year in only 15 years. The Obama administration views this as a necessary contribution to the fight against global warming. They also say the proposed policy is cost-effective: U.S. health care costs will drop by $55–$93 billion per year due to 100,000 fewer asthma attacks and 2,100 few heart attacks each year. EPA estimates the annual compliance cost at $7.3–$8.8 billion.

The coal industry sees it differently. Coal provides 37 percent of America's electricity. They know the Obama administration wants to faze out the 557 certified coal plants in favor of wind, solar, and other power sources. They protest that the administration's "war on coal" will increase electricity prices, devastate coal-mining communities, threaten the electricity grid, and cost thousands of jobs.

Sources: www.epa.gov; news reports, June 2–5, 2014.

ANALYSIS: Pollution abatement is not a "free good." It requires the use of real resources and creates trade-offs among competing goals.

SUMMARY

- Air, water, and solid waste pollution impose social and economic costs. The costs of pollution include the direct damages inflicted on our health and resources, the expense of cleaning up, and the general aesthetic deterioration of the environment.   **LO28-1**

- Pollution is an external cost, a cost of a market activity imposed on someone (a third party) other than the immediate producer or consumer.   **LO28-1**
- Producers and consumers generally operate on the basis of private benefits and costs. A private producer or

consumer has an incentive to minimize his own costs by transforming private costs into external costs. One way of making such a substitution is to pollute—to use "free" air and water rather than install pollution control equipment, or to leave the job of waste disposal to others. **LO28-1**

- Social costs are the total amount of resources used in a production or consumption process. When social costs are greater than private costs, the market's price signals are flawed. This market failure will induce people to harm the environment by using suboptimal processes and products. **LO28-1**

- One way to correct the market inefficiency created by externalities is to compel producers and consumers to internalize all (social) costs. This can be done by imposing emission charges and higher user fees. Such charges create an incentive to invest in pollution abatement equipment, recycle reusable materials, and conserve scarce elements of the environment. **LO28-2**

- Tradable pollution permits help minimize the cost of pollution control by (a) promoting low-cost controls to substitute for high-cost controls and (b) encouraging innovation in pollution control technology. **LO28-2**

- An alternative approach to cleaning up the environment is to require specific pollution controls or to prohibit specific kinds of activities. Direct regulation runs the risk of higher cost and discouraging innovations in environmental protection. **LO28-2**

- The opportunity costs of pollution abatement are the most desired goods and services given up when factors of production are used to control pollution. The optimal rate of pollution is reached when the marginal social benefits of further pollution control equal associated marginal social costs. **LO28-3**

- In addition to diverting resources, pollution control efforts alter relative prices, change the mix of output, and redistribute incomes. These outcomes cause losses for particular groups and may thus require special economic or political attention. **LO28-3**

- The greenhouse effect represents a global externality. Reducing global emissions requires consensus on optimal pollution levels (i.e., the optimal balance of pollution abatement costs and benefits) and the distribution of attendant costs. **LO28-2**

Key Terms

production decision	private costs	opportunity cost
efficiency decision	market failure	optimal rate of pollution
external cost	emission charge	
social costs	government failure	

Questions for Discussion

1. If "green" gasoline were sold for 20 cents per gallon more than "dirty" gasoline, would you buy it? How much of a premium per gallon do you think most people would pay? **LO28-1**

2. What are the *economic* costs of the externalities caused by air toxins (In the News "Air Pollution Kills"), beach closings, or thermal pollution (In the News "Cut the Power to Save the Fish?")? How would you measure their value? **LO28-1**

3. Should we try to eliminate *all* pollution? What economic considerations might favor permitting some pollution? **LO28-3**

4. Why would auto manufacturers resist higher fuel efficiency standards? How would their costs, sales, and profits be affected? **LO28-1**

5. Does anyone have an incentive to maintain auto exhaust control devices in good working order? How can we ensure that they will be maintained? Are there any costs associated with this policy? **LO28-1**

6. Should the Indian Point nuclear plant (In the News "Cut the Power to Save the Fish?") be closed? Who will benefit? Who will lose? **LO28-3**

7. What economic costs are imposed by mandatory sorting of trash (In the News "Recycling Wastes Money")? **LO28-2**

8. "The issuance of a pollution permit is just a license to destroy the environment." Do you agree? Explain. **LO28-2**

9. If a high per-bag fee were charged for garbage collection, how would consumers respond? **LO28-2**

10. Should coal mining be prohibited in order to reduce carbon emissions? **LO28-2**

11. Over 1 billion people in the world don't have access to electricity, relying mostly on fire for heat and cooking. Discuss the benefits and costs of carbon caps that limit the construction of new power plants in less developed countries. **LO28-2**

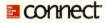

PROBLEMS FOR CHAPTER 28

LO28-2 1. (*a*) If the Indian Point nuclear plant (In the News "Recycling Wastes Money") were charged one-tenth of a mill (0.01 cent) for every gallon of water it used, how much would it pay in annual emission fees?

(*b*) If the cost of building and operating a closed-cycle cooling system was $100 million per year, would the plant prefer to reengineer the plant or pay the emission fees?

LO28-2 2. EPA says the value of a human life is $7.6 million, measured from birth to death. If life expectancy is 78 years, what is the value of the remaining life of an 18-year-old person?

LO28-2 3. How high would its pollution control costs have to be before a firm would "pay to pollute" a ton of carbon dioxide (World View "Paying to Pollute")?

LO28-1 4. Use the graph to answer the following questions:

(*a*) What is the profit maximizing quantity?
Suppose that there are external costs equal to $0.01 per kilowatt-hour.

(*b*) Calculate the social marginal cost to produce the profit maximizing quantity.

(*c*) What is the socially-optimal quantity?

(*d*) How much of an emission fee should be charged to close the gap between the private and social marginal costs?

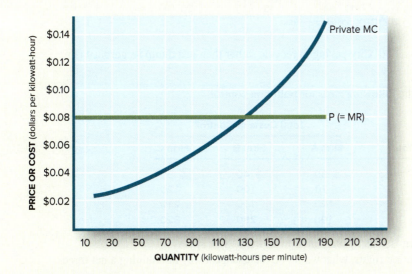

LO28-1 5. Many people pay nothing for each extra pound of garbage they create yet the garbage is a type of solid waste pollution. In view of this, we can view garbage collection as creating external benefits to society. So what's an appropriate price for garbage collection? Answer the questions based on the following graph.

(*a*) What is the quantity of (free) garbage collection now demanded?

(*b*) How much would be demanded if a fee of $4 per pound were charged?

(*c*) Draw the social demand curve when an external benefit of $2 per pound exists.

(*d*) If the marginal cost of collecting garbage were constant at $6 per pound, what would be the optimal level of garbage collection?

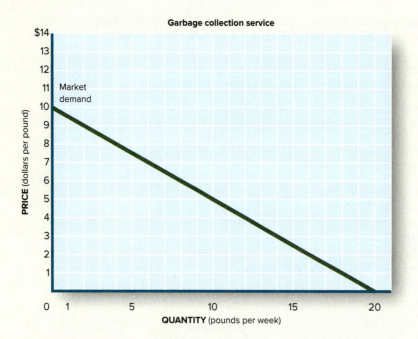

LO28-3 6. How much more per ton is New York City paying to recycle rather than just dump its garbage (In the News "Recycling Wastes Money")?

LO28-2 7. Suppose three firms confront the following costs for pollution control:

Emissions Reduction (Tons per Year)	Total Costs of Control		
	Firm A	Firm B	Firm C
1	$ 30	$ 40	$ 50
2	70	100	120
3	120	180	210
4	190	280	320

(a) If each firm must reduce emissions by one ton, how much will be spent?

(b) If the firms can trade pollution rights, what would be the cheapest way of attaining a net three-ton reduction?

(c) How much would a pollution permit trade for (price range)?

Now suppose the goal is to reduce pollution by six tons.

(d) What is the marginal cost of a second abatement ton at
   (i) Firm A?
   (ii) Firm B?
   (iii) Firm C?

(e) If each firm must reduce emissions by two tons, how much will be spent?

(f) If the firms can trade permits, what is the cheapest way of attaining a six-ton reduction?

(g) How much will a permit cost (price change)?

LO28-3 8. The table shows the total benefits and total costs to reduce solid waste pollution in in a local river.

Quantity of Pollution Abatement (Tons of Trash Removed per Week)	Benefits	Costs
0	0	0
1	60	10
2	100	30
3	130	60
4	150	100
5	160	155
6	165	220

(a) Calculate the marginal benefits of pollution abatement.
(b) Calculate the marginal costs of pollution abatement
(c) What is the optimal level of pollution abatement?

LO28-1 9. The following cost schedule depicts the private and social costs associated with the weekly use of dicamba, a strong fertilizer that can damage nearby crops that are not genetically modified to resit the fertilizer. The sales price of dicamba is $26 per ton.

Output (in tons)	0	1	2	3	4	5	6	7	8
Total private cost	$ 5	7	13	23	37	55	77	103	133
Total social cost	$45	63	85	111	141	175	213	255	301

(a) Graph the private and social marginal costs associated with dicamba production.
(b) What is the profit-maximizing rate of output for this competitive firm?
(c) How much profit is earned at that output level?
(d) What is the socially optimal rate of output?
(e) How much profit is there at that output level?
(f) How much of a "green tax" per ton would have to be levied to induce the firm to produce the socially optimal rate of output?

LO28-3 10. The Economy Tomorrow: If health care costs are evenly divided by asthma attacks and heart attacks, what dollar value does EPA put on an asthma attack or heart attack (see In the News "A War on Coal")?

©Fuse/Corbis via Getty Images RF

CHAPTER 29

The Farm Problem

In 1996 the U.S. Congress charted a new future for U.S. farmers. No longer would they look to Washington, DC, for decisions on what crops to plant or how much farmland to leave fallow. The Freedom to Farm Act would get the government out of the farm business and let "laissez faire" dictate farm outcomes. Farmers would lose their federal subsidies but could earn as much as they wanted in the marketplace. Taxpayers loved the idea. So did most farmers, who were enjoying unusually high prices and bumper profits in 1996.

The Asian crisis that began in mid-1997 dealt farmers a severe blow. U.S. farms export 25–50 percent of all the wheat, corn, soybeans, and cotton they grow. When Asia's economies plunged into recession, those export sales evaporated. With sales, prices, and profits all declining, farmers lost their enthusiasm for the "freedom to farm"; they wanted Uncle Sam to jump back into the farm business with price and income guarantees. The U.S. Congress obliged by passing the Farm Security Act of 2001. That act not only increased farm subsidies, but also extended them to peanut farmers, hog farmers, and horse breeders. The Farm Act of 2008 spread federal subsidies to still more farmers, abandoning any notion of "free-market" agriculture. The Farm Act of 2014 continued that trend, extending subsidies to hemp and organic farmers.

This chapter examines the rationale for continuing farm subsidies and their effects on farm production, prices, and exports. In particular, we confront these questions:

- **Why do farmers need any subsidies?**
- **How do government subsidies affect farm production, prices, and incomes?**
- **Who pays for farm subsidies?**

DESTABILIZING FORCES

The agriculture industry is one of the most competitive of all U.S. industries. First, there are 2 million farms in the United States. Although some of these farms are immense—with tens of thousands of acres—no single farm has the power to affect the market supply or price of farm products. That is, individual farmers have no **market power.**

Competition in Agriculture

Competition in agriculture is maintained by low **barriers to entry.** Although farmers need large acreages, expensive farm equipment, substantial credit, hard work, and hired labor, all these resources

market power: The ability to alter the market price of a good or service.

barriers to entry: Obstacles such as patents that make it difficult or impossible for would-be producers to enter a particular market.

become affordable when farming is generating **economice profits.** When farming is profitable, existing farmers expand their farms and farmers' children are able to start new farms. It would be much harder to enter the automobile industry, the airline business, or even the farm machinery market than it would be to enter farming. Because of these low barriers to entry, economic profits don't last long in agriculture.

Given the competitive structure of U.S. agriculture, *individual farmers tend to behave like perfect competitors.* Individual farmers seek to expand their rate of output until marginal cost equals price. By following this rule, each farmer makes as much profit as possible from existing resources, prices, and technology.

Like other competitive firms, U.S. farmers can maintain economic profits only if they achieve continuing cost reductions. Above-normal profits obtained from current production techniques and prices aren't likely to last. Such economic profits will entice more people into agriculture and will stimulate greater output from existing farmers. That is exactly the kind of dilemma that confronted catfish farmers in the South and the early producers of microcomputers (Chapter 23). To stay ahead, individual farms must continue to improve their productivity.

economic profit: The difference between total revenues and total economic costs.

Technological Advance

The rate of technological advance in agriculture has, in fact, been spectacular. Since 1929, the farm labor force has shrunk by two-thirds, yet farm output has increased by 80 percent. Between the early 1950s and today,

- Annual egg production has jumped from 183 to 267 eggs per laying chicken.
- Milk output has increased from 5,400 to 21,149 pounds per cow annually.
- Wheat output has increased from 17 to 56 bushels per acre.
- Corn output has jumped from 39 to 175 bushels per acre.

Farm output per labor-hour has grown even faster, having increased 10 times over in the same period. Such spectacular rates of productivity advance rival those of our most high-tech industries. These technological advances resulted from the development of higher-yielding seeds (the "green revolution"), advanced machinery (mechanical feeders and milkers), improved animal breeding (crossbreeding), improved plants (rust-resistant wheat), better land use practices (crop rotation and fertilizers), and computer-based management systems.

Inelastic Demand

In most industries, continuous increases in technology and output would be most welcome. The agricultural industry, however, confronts a long-term problem. Simply put, there's a limit to the amount of food people want to eat.

This constraint on the demand for agricultural output is reflected in the relatively inelastic demand for food. Consumers don't increase their food purchases very much when farm prices fall. The **price elasticity** of food demand is low. As a consequence, when harvests are good, farmers must reduce prices a lot to sell all that extra food. Recall the formula for the price elasticity of demand:

price elasticity of demand: The percentage change in quantity demanded divided by the percentage change in price.

$$E = \frac{\text{Percentage change in quantity demanded}}{\text{Percentage change in price}}$$

Rearranging this formula gives us a guide to how far prices must fall for farmers to unload a bumper crop:

$$\frac{\text{Required percentage}}{\text{change in price}} = \frac{\text{Percentage change in quantity (harvest)}}{\text{Price elasticity of demand}}$$

FIGURE 29.1

Short-Term Instability

Changes in weather cause abrupt shifts of the food supply curve. When combined with the relatively inelastic demand for food, these supply shifts result in wide price swings. Notice how the price of grain jumps from p_1 to p_2 when bad weather reduces the harvest. If good weather follows, prices may fall to p_3.

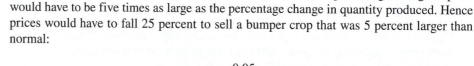

Even if the price elasticity of demand were as high as 0.2, the percentage change in price would have to be five times as large as the percentage change in quantity produced. Hence prices would have to fall 25 percent to sell a bumper crop that was 5 percent larger than normal:

$$\% \; \Delta p = \frac{0.05}{0.20} = 0.25$$

In 2016 the corn crop was 11 percent *larger* than the year before. In 2008 the corn crop *decreased* by 7 percent. As Figure 29.1 illustrates, **with low price elasticity of demand, abrupt changes in farm output have a magnified effect on market prices.** Between 2005 and 2017, corn prices ranged from a low of $1.96 a bushel to a high of $8.10 (see Figure 29.2). That's a *lot* of price instability.

income elasticity of demand: Percentage change in quantity demanded divided by percentage change in income.

The **income elasticity** of food demand is also low. The income elasticity of demand for food refers to the responsiveness of food demand to changes in income. Specifically,

$$\text{Income elasticity of demand} = \frac{\substack{\text{\% change in quantity demanded} \\ \text{(at constant price)}}}{\text{\% change in income}}$$

Since 1929, per capita income has quadrupled. But per capita food consumption has increased only 85 percent. Hence **neither lower prices nor higher incomes significantly increase the quantity of food demanded.**

In the long run, then, the increasing ability of U.S. agriculture to produce food must be reconciled with very slow growth of U.S. demand for food. Over time, this implies that farm prices will fall, relative to nonfarm prices. And they have. Between the years 1910–1914 and 2009, the ratio of farm prices to nonfarm prices fell 60 percent. In the absence of government price support programs and foreign demand for U.S. farm products, farm prices would have fallen still further.

Abrupt Shifts of Supply

The long-term downtrend in (relative) farm prices is only one of the major problems confronting U.S. agriculture. The second major problem is short run. Prices of farm products are subject to abrupt short-term swings. If the weather is good, harvests are abundant. Normally, this might be a good thing. In farming, however, abundant harvests imply a severe

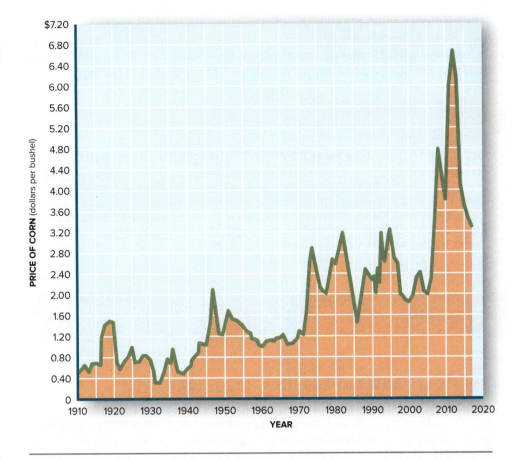

FIGURE 29.2

Unstable Corn Prices

Most agricultural prices are subject to abrupt short-term changes. Notice how corn prices rose dramatically during World Wars I and II, then fell sharply. Poor harvests in the rest of the world increased demand for U.S. food in 1973–1974. Since then prices have moved sharply in both directions.

Source: U.S. Department of Agriculture.

---

drop in prices. On the other hand, a late or early freeze, a drought, or an infestation by disease or insect pests can reduce harvests and push prices sharply higher (see Figure 29.1).

Response Lags. Time lags between the production decision and the resultant harvest also contribute to price instability. If prices are high one year, farmers have an incentive to increase their rate of output. In this sense, prices serve the same signaling function in agriculture as they do in nonfarm industries. What distinguishes the farmers' response is the lack of inventories and the fixed duration of the production process. In the computer industry, a larger quantity of output can be supplied to the market fairly quickly by drawing down inventories or stepping up the rate of production. In farming, supply can't respond so quickly. In the short run, the farmer can only till more land, plant additional seed, or breed more livestock. No additional food supplies will be available until a new crop or herd grows. Hence *the agricultural supply response to a change in prices is always one harvest (or breeding period) later.*

This lagged supply response intensifies short-term price swings. Suppose corn prices are exceptionally high at the end of a year because of a reduced harvest. High prices will make corn farming appear unusually profitable. Farmers will want to expand their rate of output—plant more corn acreage—to share in these high profits. But the corn won't appear on the market until the following year. By that time, there's likely to be an abundance of corn on the market, as a result of both better weather and increased corn acreage. Hence corn prices are likely to plummet. This is what happened in 2013–2014 and again in 2016–2017.

No single farmer can avoid these boom-or-bust movements of prices. Even a corn farmer who has mastered the principles of economics has little choice but to plant more corn when prices are high. If he doesn't plant additional corn, prices will fall anyway because his own production decisions don't affect market prices. By not planting additional corn, he only denies himself a share of corn market sales. *In a highly competitive market, each producer acts independently.*

Corn prices spiked to $4.20 per bushel after President Bush proposed expanded use of corn-based ethanol as an alternative fuel source. Farmers rushed to plant additional acreage (see In the News "Anticipated Surge in Harvest to Depress Corn Prices"). The 24 percent increase in production that followed pushed prices back down to $3.55 in 2009–2010 (see Figure 29.2).

IN THE NEWS

ANTICIPATED SURGE IN HARVEST TO DEPRESS CORN PRICES

WASHINGTON, D.C.—Corn prices are likely to fall again this year. The U.S. Department of Agriculture reported today that U.S. farmers planted 94 million acres of corn this season, up from last year's 88 million acres. That additional planting, combined with increased yields, will result in a harvest of 15,148 million bushels of corn, up from last year's 13,602 million bushels. Corn price futures on the New York Mercantile Exchange plunged in response to this forecast, hitting lows close to $3.00 a bushel.

Source: Media reports, February 9, 2017.

ANALYSIS: Price swings motivate farmers to alter their production. Abrupt changes in production may reverse the price movement in the next harvest, however.

THE FIRST FARM DEPRESSION, 1920–1940

The U.S. agricultural industry operated without substantial government intervention until the 1930s. In earlier decades, an expanding population, recurrent wars, and less advanced technology had helped maintain a favorable supply–demand relationship for farm products. There were frequent short-term swings in farm prices, but these were absorbed by a generally healthy farm sector. The period 1910–1919 was particularly prosperous for farmers, largely because of the expanded foreign demand for U.S. farm products by countries engaged in World War I.

The two basic problems of U.S. agriculture grew to crisis proportions after 1920. In 1919 most farm prices were at historical highs (see Figures 29.2 and 29.3). After World War I ended, however, European countries no longer demanded as much American food. U.S. exports of farm products fell from nearly $4 billion in 1919 to $1.9 billion in 1921. Farm exports were further reduced in the following years by increasing restrictions on international trade. At home, the end of the war implied an increased availability of factors of production and continuing improvement in farm technology.

FIGURE 29.3

**Farm Prices, 1910–1940
(1910–1914 = 100)**

Farm prices are less stable than nonfarm prices. During the 1930s, relative farm prices fell 50 percent. This experience was the catalyst for government price supports and other agricultural assistance programs.

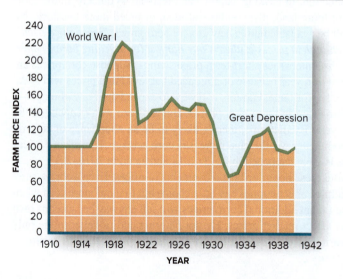

Size of Farm	Number, 1910	Percent	Number, 2002	Percent
Under 100 acres	3,691,611	58.0%	943,118	44.3%
100–499 acres	2,494,461	39.2	847,322	39.8
500–999 acres	125,295	2.0	161,552	7.6
1,000 acres and over	50,135	0.8	176,990	8.3
Total	6,361,502	100.0%	2,128,982	100.0%

Source: U.S. Department of Agriculture.

TABLE 29.1

Size Distribution of U.S. Farms, 1910 and 2002

Inelastic food demand, combined with increasing agricultural productivity, implies a declining number of farmers. Small farmers are particularly vulnerable because they don't have the resources to maintain a high rate of technological improvement. As a result, the number of small farms has declined dramatically while the number of large farms has grown.

The impact of reduced demand and increasing supply is evident in Figure 29.3. In 1919 farm prices were more than double their levels of the period 1910–1914. Prices then fell abruptly. In 1921 alone, farm prices fell nearly 40 percent.

Farm prices stabilized in the mid-1920s but resumed a steep decline in 1930. In 1932 average farm prices were 75 percent lower than they had been in 1919. At the same time, the average income per farmer from farming fell from $2,651 in 1919 to $855 in 1932.

The Great Depression hit small farmers particularly hard. They had fewer resources to withstand consecutive years of declining prices and income. Even in good times, small farmers must continually expand output and reduce costs just to maintain their incomes. Hence the Great Depression accelerated an exodus of small farmers from agriculture, a trend that continues today.

Table 29.1 shows that the number of small farms has declined dramatically. In 1910 there were 3.7 million farms under 100 acres in size. Today there are fewer than 1 million small farms. During the same period, the number of huge farms (1,000 acres or more) has more than tripled. This loss of small farmers, together with the increased mechanization of larger farms, has reduced the farm population by 23 million people since 1910.

U.S. FARM POLICY

The U.S. Congress has responded to these agricultural problems with a variety of programs. Most seek to raise and stabilize the price of farm products. Other programs seek to reduce the costs of production. When all else fails, the federal government also provides direct income support to farmers.

Price Supports

Price supports have always been the primary focus of U.S. farm policy. As early as 1926, Congress decreed that farm products should sell at a fair price. By "fair," Congress meant a price higher than the market equilibrium. The consequences of this policy are evident in Figure 29.4: *a price floor creates a* **market surplus.**

Once it set an above-equilibrium price for food, Congress had to find some way of disposing of the resultant food surplus. Initially, Congress proposed to get rid of this surplus by selling it abroad at world market prices. President Calvin Coolidge, a staunch opponent of government intervention, vetoed this legislation both times Congress passed it.

The notion of fair prices resurfaced in the Agricultural Adjustment Act of 1933. During the Great Depression farmers were going bankrupt in droves. To help them, Congress sought to restore the purchasing power of farm products to the 1909–1914 level (see Figure 29.3). The farm–nonfarm price relationships of 1909–1914 were regarded by Congress as fair and came to be known as **parity** prices. If parity prices could be restored, Congress reasoned, farm incomes would improve.

market surplus: The amount by which the quantity supplied exceeds the quantity demanded at a given price; excess supply.

parity: The relative price of farm products in the period 1910–1914.

Supply Restrictions

The goal of parity pricing couldn't be attained without altering market supply and demand in some way.

FIGURE 29.4

Fair Prices and Market Surplus

The interaction of market supply and demand establishes an equilibrium price (p_e) for any product, including food. If a higher price (p_f) is set, the quantity of food supplied (q_s) will be larger than the quantity demanded (q_d). Hence attempts to establish a "fair" (higher) price for farm products must cope with resultant market surpluses.

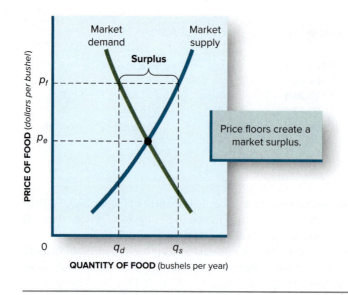

acreage set-aside: Land withdrawn from production as part of policy to increase crop prices.

Set-Asides. The easiest way to increase farm prices without creating a surplus is to reduce the production of food. Congress does this by paying farmers for voluntary reductions in crop acreage. These **acreage set-asides** shift the food supply curve to the left. In 2007 nearly 40 *million* acres of farmland—one-sixth of the nation's wheat, corn, sorghum, rice, and cotton acreage—were idled by government set-asides. If farmers didn't agree to these set-asides, they couldn't participate in the price support programs.

Dairy Termination Program. To prop up dairy prices, the federal government also started a Dairy Termination Program in 1985. This is analogous to a set-aside program. In this case, however, the government pays dairy farmers to slaughter or export dairy cattle. Between 1985 and 1987 the government paid dairy farmers more than $1 billion to "terminate" 1.6 million cows. The reduction in dairy herds boosted prices for milk and other dairy products.

Marketing Orders. The federal government also permits industry groups to limit the quantity of output brought to market. By themselves, individual farmers can't raise the market price by withholding output. If they act collectively, however, they can. If a quantity greater than authorized is actually grown, the "surplus" is disposed of by individual farmers. In the 1980s these *marketing orders* forced farmers to waste each year roughly 500 million lemons, 1 billion oranges, 70 million pounds of raisins, 70 million pounds of almonds, and millions of plums, nectarines, and other fruits. This wholesale destruction of crops gave growers market power and kept farm prices artificially high.

Import Quotas. The market supply of farm products is also limited by import restrictions. Imports of sugar, dairy products, cotton, and peanuts are severely limited by import quotas. Imports of beef are limited by "voluntary" export limits in foreign countries. Import taxes (duties) limit the foreign supply of other farm products.

Demand Distortions

While trying to limit the *supply* of farm products, the government also inflates the *demand* for selected farm products.

Government Stockpiles. An executive order signed by President Franklin Roosevelt in 1933 altered the demand for farm products. The Commodity Credit Corporation (CCC) created at that time became a buyer of last resort for selected farm products.

TABLE 29.2

2016–2017 Loan Rates

The Commodity Credit Corporation lends money to farmers at fixed "loan rates" that are implicit price floors. If the market price falls below the CCC loan rate, the government keeps the crop as full payment of the loan or *pays* farmers a "loan deficiency payment."

Commodity	Loan Rate
Corn	$1.95 per bushel
Wheat	2.94
Soybeans	5.00
Cotton (upland)	0.52 per pound
Rice	6.50 per hundredweight
Peanuts	355 per ton
Honey	0.69 per pound
Sugar (beet)	0.24 per pound

Source: U.S. Department of Agriculture (2017).

The CCC becomes a buyer of last resort through its loan programs. Farmers can borrow money from the CCC at **loan rates** set by Congress (see Table 29.2). In 2017, for example, a wheat farmer could borrow $2.94 in cash for every bushel of wheat he relinquished to the CCC. If the market price of wheat goes above $2.94, the farmer can sell the wheat in the open market, repay the CCC, and pocket the difference. If, instead, the price falls below the loan rate, the farmer can simply let the CCC keep the wheat and repay nothing. Hence, *whenever market prices are below CCC loan rates, the government ends up buying surplus crops.*

Figure 29.5 illustrates the effect of CCC price supports on individual farmers and the agricultural market. In the absence of price supports, competitive farmers would confront a horizontal demand curve at price p_e, itself determined by the intersection of market supply and demand (in part *b*). The CCC's offer to buy ("loan") unlimited quantities at a

loan rate: The implicit price paid by the government for surplus crops taken as collateral for loans to farmers.

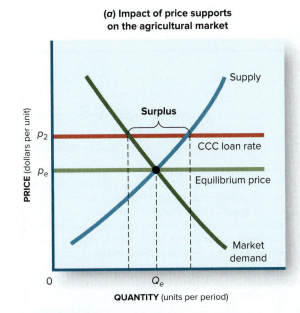

(a) Impact of price supports on the agricultural market

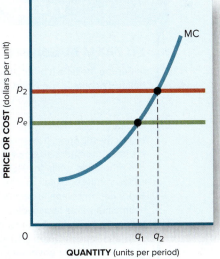

(b) Impact of price supports on the individual farmer

FIGURE 29.5

The Impact of Price Supports

In the absence of price supports, the price of farm products would be determined by the intersection of market supply and demand. In this case, the equilibrium price would be p_e, as shown in part *a*. All individual farmers would confront this price and produce up to the point where MC = p_e, as in part *b*.

Government price supports raise the price to p_2. By offering to buy (or "loan") unlimited quantities at this price, the government shifts the demand curve facing each farmer upward. Individual farmers respond by increasing their output from q_1 to q_2. As farmers increase their output, a market surplus develops.

higher price shifts the demand curve facing each farmer upward to the guaranteed price p_2. This higher price induces individual farmers to increase their rate of output from q_1 to q_2.

As farmers respond to price supports, the agriculture market is pushed out of equilibrium. At the support level p_2, more output is supplied than demanded. The market surplus created by government price supports creates an additional policy dilemma. ***The market surplus induced by price supports must be eliminated in one of three ways:***

- ***Government purchases*** and stockpiling of surplus food.
- ***Export sales.***
- ***Restrictions on supply.***

Government purchases of surplus crops have led to massive stockpiles of wheat, cotton, corn, and dairy products. At one time, the excess wheat was stored in old ammunition bunkers in Nebraska and scrubbed-out oil tanks in Texas. More than 130 million pounds of surplus nonfat dry milk is now stored in limestone caverns under Kansas City. In 2017 government stockpiles of surplus farm output included 2.3 *billion* bushels of corn, 1.1 billion bushels of wheat, and 4.8 million bales of cotton.

Deficiency Payments. To keep these stockpiles from growing further, Congress amended the CCC loan program in 2001. When market prices fall below CCC loan rates (Table 29.2), farmers don't have to turn over their crops to the government. Instead the government pays them a *loan deficiency payment* equal to the *difference* between the loan rate and the market price. The farmer can then sell his crop on the open market. By dumping excess supply on the market rather than stockpiling it, this policy tends to aggravate downward price swings.

Because farm prices are artificially high in the United States, export sales are sometimes difficult. As a result, the federal government must give away lots of food to poor nations and even subsidize exports to developed nations. The United States isn't alone in this regard: the European Union maintains even higher prices and subsidies (see World View "EU Farm Subsidies").

WORLD VIEW

EU FARM SUBSIDIES

In Europe, believe it or not, the subsidy for every cow is greater than the personal income of half the people in the world.

—**Former British Prime Minister Margaret Thatcher**

U.S. farm policy isn't unique. Most industrialized countries go to even greater lengths to protect domestic agriculture. For example, France, Germany, and Switzerland all shield their farmers from international competition while subsidizing their exports. Japan protects its inefficient rice producers, while the Netherlands subsidizes greenhouse vegetable farmers.

The motivations for farm subsidies are pretty much the same in every country in the world. Every country wants a secure source of food in the event of war. Most nations also want to maintain a viable farm sector, which is viewed as a source of social stability. Finally, politicians in every country must be responsive to a well-established and vocal political constituency.

The European Union (EU) imposes high tariffs on imported food, keeping domestic prices high. The member governments also agree to purchase any surplus production. To get rid of the surplus, the governments then subsidize exports. In 2016 direct EU farm subsidies exceeded $75 billion, triple the size of U.S. farm subsidies. All this protection costs the average EU consumer more than $150 a year.

ANALYSIS: Farm subsidies are common around the world. Such subsidies alter not only domestic output decisions but international trade patterns as well.

TABLE 29.3

2014–2018 Reference Prices

Congress sets reference prices for selected commodities. If the market price falls below the reference price, a *deficiency payment* is made directly to the farmer.

Commodity	Reference Price
Corn	$ 3.70 per bushel
Barley	4.95
Wheat	5.50
Soybeans	8.40
Rice	14.00 per hundredweight
Peanuts	$ 535 per ton

Source: U.S. Department of Agriculture (2017).

Price Supports

The government's loan program is an indirect mechanism for establishing a price floor for agricultural products. In 2014, Congress reintroduced more explicit and more generous price supports. The Farm Act of 2014 set **reference prices** for major commodities. As Table 29.3 reveals, the reference price for corn is now $3.70 per bushel. If the market price for corn falls below $3.70, the government pays farmers the difference. Thus, farmers are guaranteed to get the stipulated reference prices, regardless of how abundant the national crop may be. These reference prices serve as price floors, with the same effect on output depicted in Figure 29.5.

reference price: Government-guaranteed price floor for specific agricultural commodities.

Cost Subsidies

The market surplus induced by price supports is exacerbated by cost subsidies. Irrigation water, for example, is delivered to many farmers by federally funded reclamation projects. The price farmers pay for the water is substantially below the cost of delivering it; the difference amounts to a subsidy. This water subsidy costs taxpayers more than $500 million a year. The Department of Agriculture also distributes an additional $150 million to $200 million a year to farmers to help defray the costs of fertilizer, drainage, and other production costs.

The federal government also provides basic research, insurance, marketing, grading, and inspection services to farmers at subsidized prices. All these subsidies serve to lower fixed or variable costs. Their net impact is to stimulate additional output, as illustrated in Figure 29.6.

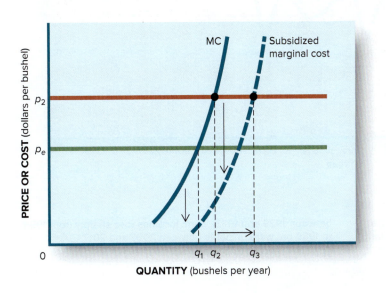

FIGURE 29.6

The Impact of Cost Subsidies

Cost subsidies lower the marginal cost of producing at any given rate of output, thereby shifting the marginal cost curve downward. The lower marginal costs make higher rates of output more profitable and thus increase output. At price p_2, lower marginal costs increase the farmer's profit-maximizing rate of output from q_2 to q_3.

CONTINUING INCOME VOLATILITY

With so many price supports, supply restrictions, cost subsidies, and income transfers, one would think that farming is a riskless and profitable business. But this hasn't been the case. Incomes remain low and unstable, especially for small farmers.

1980–1986 Depression

In fact, the entire agricultural sector experienced another setback in the 1980s. In 1980 the net income of U.S. farmers fell 42 percent. As Figure 29.7 shows, farm incomes recovered somewhat in 1981 but then resumed their steep decline in 1982. In 1983 farmers' net income was only one-third the level of 1979. This income loss was steeper than that of the Great Depression. Real farm income was actually lower in 1983 than in 1933. This second depression of farm incomes accelerated the exodus of small farmers from agriculture, severely weakened rural economies, and bankrupted many farm banks and manufacturers of farm equipment and supplies.

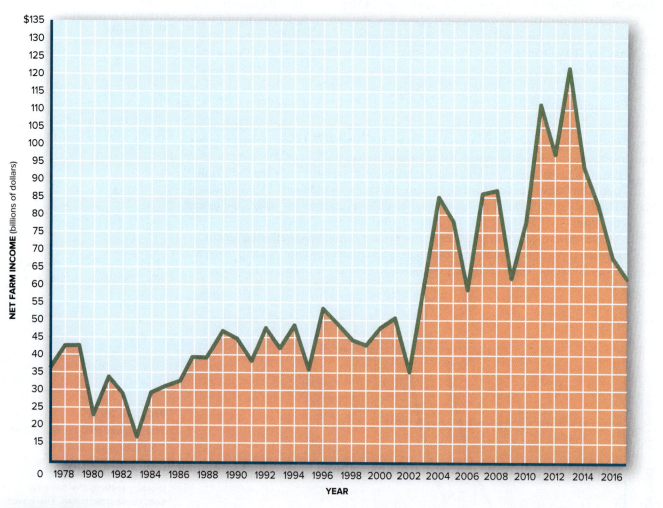

FIGURE 29.7

Net Farm Income, 1977–2017

Between 1979 and 1983 net farm income fell 64 percent. This decline was steeper than the income slide that occurred during the Great Depression (when net farm income fell 45 percent between 1929 and 1933). Farm incomes rose sharply from 1983 to 1989 but were unstable between 2007 and 2017.

Source: U.S. Department of Agriculture.

This second depression of farm incomes was not caused by abrupt price declines. Prices for farm products increased slightly between 1979 and 1983. But production costs rose much faster, led by higher fuel, fertilizer, and interest rate costs. Average farm production costs rose 30 percent between 1979 and 1983 while the average price of farm products increased only 1.5 percent. As a result, the **profit** (net income) of farmers fell abruptly.

profit: The difference between total revenue and total cost.

2008–2013 Surge

The period from 2008–2013 was a much more prosperous time for farmers. Even though the U.S. economy suffered a Great Recession in 2008–2009, American farmers did very well. A multi-year drought curtailed crop production and sent crop prices to record highs, with the price of corn exceeding $8 a bushel (see Figure 29.2). At the same time, the recession in the rest of the economy brought down the price of farm inputs. A weak dollar also helped farmers sell exports. Farm incomes peaked at $124 billion in 2013 (Figure 29.7).

Another Price Slide

As we noted earlier, high prices encourage farmers to plant more crops. That is what happened after crop prices rose to record highs in 2012–2013. Farm plantings and harvests increased significantly, driving crop prices down. The price of corn fell from over $8 a bushel in 2012 to close to $3 in 2012–2017. Weak foreign economies and a strong dollar worsened the situation further by depressing farm exports. The net result was a decline in farm incomes of roughly 50 percent between 2013 and 2017. A good thing didn't last long.

THE ECONOMY TOMORROW

FARMERS ON THE DOLE

It is apparent that farming continues to be a volatile business. Small variations in production—whether caused by the weather, global economic forces, or farmer's lagged planting responses–cause wild swings in crop prices. Furthermore, unceasing advances in agricultural technology, combined with low income and price elasticities for food, pretty much guarantee that farm prices will continue to lag behind general price inflation. Politicians also emphasize how important it is to have a secure source of food in the event of war. Given these realities, it seems certain that farmers will stay on the government dole in the economy tomorrow.

The 2018 Farm Bill. The specifics of government programs to assist farmers are spelled out in Congressional legislation. The 2014 Farm Bill eliminated direct payments to farmers and replaced them with payments based on price or revenue deficiencies. But the core system of crop subsidies was left intact.

The legal authority of the 2014 Farm Bill expires in September 2018. That will require the Congress to write a new piece of legislation, the 2018 Farm Bill. Given the recent decline in farm incomes, no one expects Congress to cut subsidy programs.

Most of the additional help farmers want lies outside the authority of the Farm Bill. Farmers are particularly angry about environmental regulations mandated by the Obama administration in 2011. Those restrictions redefine the concept of "waterways" to include ponds, creeks, and other small water accumulations, subjecting them to federal

Continued

regulation. New EPA rules also require expensive water testing, a requirement that small farmers say is very burdensome. President Trump repealed some of these regulations.

Farmers are also very concerned about immigration and trade policies. Farmers depend heavily on immigrant workers to harvest their crops. They also export as much as 30 percent of their harvests to other nations, so are hopeful that America doesn't upend international trade flows. So, the pending 2018 Farm Bill is of less concern than developments in immigration and trade.

Although farmers are sure to get continuing subsidies in the economy tomorrow, there is still a lot of opposition to these programs. Environmentalists emphasize that farming is the source of some of our worst pollution problems, especially the discharges of animal waste and other debris into waterways. They insist that if farmers are going to be subsidized, they should be required to protect the environment better. Others want stricter safeguards on food processing and safety as a condition of continuing subsidies.

Last but not least, free marketers continue to insist that the whole system of farm subsidies is inefficient and inequitable. Why do only a handful of crops (e.g., corn, wheat, sugar, honey, etc.) get subsidies while others don't? Are the prices of lemons, chickens, strawberries any less volatile than cotton or corn prices? Aren't they subject to the same internal and external forces that dictate incomes for subsidized farmers? As they see it, the current system is not only inequitable, but inefficient because it causes farmers to make uneconomical production decisions and forces the government to stockpile farm surpluses.

Despite these objections, farmers will continue on the federal dole for many years to come.

SUMMARY

- The agricultural sector has a highly competitive structure, with approximately 2 million farms. Many crops are regulated, however, by government restrictions and subsidies. **LO29-1**

- Most farm output is produced by the small percentage of large farms that enjoy economies of scale. Most small farmers rely on nonfarm employment for their income. **LO29-1**

- In a free market, farm prices tend to decline over time because of increasing productivity and low income elasticity of demand. Variations in harvests, combined with a low price elasticity of demand, make farm prices unstable. **LO29-1**

- Most of today's farm policies originated during the Great Depression in response to low farm prices and incomes. **LO29-3**

- The government uses price supports and cost subsidies to raise farm prices and profits. These policies cause resource misallocations and create market surpluses of specific commodities. **LO29-2**

- The 1996 Farm Act called for a phaseout of farm subsidies. Falling prices and incomes during 1997–2001 stalled and eventually reversed that process, as reflected in the 2008 and 2014 Farm Acts. **LO29-2**

- Farm prices and incomes continue to be highly volatile, despite government subsidy programs. **LO29-3**

- Critics demand that farmers assume more environmental responsibility in return for their subsidies. Other critics want to dismantle the whole system of farm subsidies and let farmers depend on market forces. **LO29-3**

Key Terms

market power
barriers to entry
economic profit
price elasticity of demand

income elasticity of demand
market surplus
parity
acreage set-aside

loan rate
reference price
profit

Questions for Discussion

1. Would the U.S. economy be better off without government intervention in agriculture? Who would benefit? Who would lose? **LO29-3**

2. Are large price movements inevitable in agricultural markets? What other mechanisms might be used to limit such movement? **LO29-1**

3. Why doesn't the United States just give its crop surpluses to poor countries? What problems might such an approach create? **LO29-3**

4. Farmers can eliminate the uncertainties of fluctuating crop prices by selling their crops in futures markets (agreeing to a fixed price for crops to be delivered in the future). Who gains or loses from this practice? **LO29-2**

5. How do farmers of unsubsidized crops survive and thrive? **LO29-2**

6. You need a government permit (allotment) to grow tobacco. Who gains or loses from such regulation? **LO29-2**

7. Why are the price and income elasticities for food so low? **LO29-1**

8. How have farmers increased milk production per cow so much (see section Destabilizing Forces)? How does this affect milk prices? **LO29-1**

9. What are some of the farmers' concerns beyond what is covered in the Farm Bill? How should government best help farmers? **LO29-1**

PROBLEMS FOR CHAPTER 29

LO29-1 1. According to In the News "Anticipated Surge in Harvest to Depress Corn Prices,"
  (a) By what percent did the quantity of corn supplied increase in 2016?
  (b) If the price elasticity of demand for corn is 0.15, by how much did price decline?

LO29-1 2. If this year's harvest was greater than last year's by 12%, to sell all of the crop, how much does price have to change if the price elasticity of demand is 0.2?

LO29-1 3. According to Figure 29.2, how much did corn prices change between 2000 and 2012 in percentage terms?

LO29-2 4. The following tables show the market demand and supply for soybeans.

Price ($ per Bushel)	Quantity Demanded (Bushels per Year)	Quantity Supplied (Bushels per Year)
10	0	120
9	10	110
8	20	100
7	30	90
6	40	80
5	50	70
4	60	60
3	70	50
2	80	40
1	90	30
0	100	20

  (a) What is the equilibrium price?
  (b) What is the equilibrium quantity?
  Suppose the CCC loan rate is $5.
  (c) What is the new quantity supplied?
  (d) What is the new quantity demanded?
  (e) How much is this shortage or surplus?

LO29-2 5. Suppose the market price of corn is $1.80 per bushel.
  (a) Would a farmer sell corn to the market or to the government (CCC)? (See Table 29.2.)
  (b) If the market price rose to $2, what would the farmer do with his corn?

LO29-1 6. Suppose that consumers' incomes increase 10 percent, which results in a 0.6 percent increase in consumption of farm goods at current prices. What is the income elasticity of demand for farm goods?

LO29-3 7. Assume that the unregulated supply schedule for milk is the following:

Price (per pound)	18¢	24¢	30¢	36¢	42¢
Quantity supplied (billions of pounds per year)	43	53	63	73	83

  (a) Draw the supply and demand curves for milk, assuming that the demand for milk is perfectly inelastic (vertical) and consumers will buy 53 billion pounds of it.
  (b) What is the equilibrium price?
  Now suppose the government pays milk producers to set aside production by 20 billion pounds per year.
  (c) Draw this new supply curve that reflects the government's action.
  (d) What is the equilibrium price following the government's action?
  (e) How much more money are consumers paying for the 53 billion pounds of milk because of the higher equilibrium price?

LO29-3 8. Suppose there are 100 grain farmers, each with identical cost structures as shown in the following tables:

Production Costs (per Farm)		Demand	
Output (Bushels per Day)	Total Cost (per Day)	Price (per Bushel)	Quantity Demanded (Bushels per Day)
0	$ 5	$1	600
1	7	2	500
2	10	3	400
3	14	4	300
4	19	5	200
5	25	6	100
6	33	7	50

Under these circumstances, graph the market supply and demand.

(*a*) What is the equilibrium price for grain?

(*b*) How much grain will be produced at the equilibrium price?

(*c*) How much total profit will each farmer earn at that price?

(*d*) If the government gives farmers a cost subsidy equal to $1 a bushel, what will happen to
  (*i*) Output?
  (*ii*) Price?
  (*iii*) Profit?

(*e*) What will happen to total output if the government additionally guarantees a price of $5 per bushel?

(*f*) What price is required to sell this output?

(*g*) What is the cost to the government in *d*?

(*h*) Show your answers on the accompanying graph.

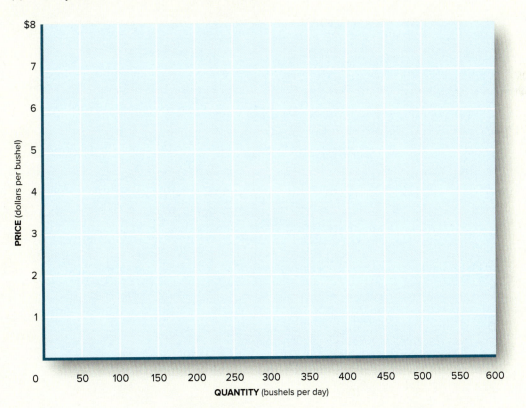

LO29-2 9. The Economy Tomorrow:

    (*a*) According to Figure 29.7, how much did farm incomes change (in percentage terms) 2008–2010?

    (*b*) If a law is passed that limits immigration, what is the predicted impact on farm incomes?

    (*c*) If subsidies are extended to agricultural products like strawberries, chickens, and lemons, what is the predicted impact on farm incomes?

©MOF/Getty Images RF

11

PART

©Chattanooga Times Free Press, John Rawlston/AP Images

©Mark Richard/PhotoEdit

©Steve Allen/Stockbyte/Getty Images RF

FACTOR MARKETS: BASIC THEORY

Factor markets operate like product markets, with supply and demand interacting to determine prices and quantities. In factor markets, however, resource inputs rather than products are exchanged. Those exchanges determine the wages paid to workers and the rent, interest, and profits paid to other inputs. The micro theories presented in Chapters 30, 31, and 32 explain how those factor payments are determined.

©Chattanooga Times Free Press, John Rawlston/AP Images

LEARNING OBJECTIVES

After reading this chapter, you should know

LO30-1 What factors shape labor supply and demand.

LO30-2 How market wage rates are established.

LO30-3 How wage floors alter labor market outcomes.

CHAPTER 30

The Labor Market

Dwayne "The Rock" Johnson was paid $6.4 million in 2016 for starring in movies like *Fast 8* and *Central Intelligence*. LeBron James received $23 million for playing basketball and another $46 million in product endorsements (see Chapter 22). Yet the president of the United States was paid only $400,000. And the administrative assistant who typed the manuscript of this book was paid just $19,000. What accounts for these tremendous disparities in earnings?

Why does the average college graduate earn close to $60,000 while the average high school graduate earns just $30,000? Are such disparities simply a reward for enduring four years of college, or do they reflect real differences in talent?

Surely we can't hope to explain these earnings disparities on the basis of the willingness to work. After all, my administrative assistant would be more than willing to work day and night for $6.4 million per year. For that matter, so would I. Accordingly, the earnings disparities can't be attributed to differences in the quantity of labor supplied. If we're going to explain why some people earn a great deal of income while others earn very little, we must consider both the *supply* and the *demand* for labor. In this regard, the following questions arise:

- **How do people decide how much time to spend working?**
- **What determines the wage rate an employer is willing to pay?**
- **Why are some workers paid so much and others so little?**

To answer these questions, we must examine the behavior of labor *markets*.

LABOR SUPPLY

The following two ads recently appeared in the campus newspaper of a well-known university:

Will do ANYTHING for money: able-bodied liberal-minded male needs money, will work to get it. Have car. Call Josh 765-3210.

Web architect. Experienced website designer. Looking for part-time or consulting position on or off campus. Please call Danielle, ext. 0872, 9–5.

Although placed by individuals of very different talents, the ads clearly expressed Josh's and Danielle's willingness to work. Although we don't know how much money they were asking for their respective talents or whether they ever found jobs, we can be sure that they were prepared to take a job at some wage rate. Otherwise they wouldn't have paid for the ads in the "Jobs Wanted" column of their campus newspaper.

The advertised willingness to work represents a **supply of labor.** These individuals are offering to sell their time and talents to anyone who's willing to pay the right price. Their explicit offers are similar to those of anyone who looks for a job. Job seekers who check the current job openings at the student employment office, tap into Monster.com, or e-mail résumés to potential employers are demonstrating a willingness to accept employment—that is, to *supply* labor. The 4,000 people who applied for jobs at a job fair in Berlin, Germany (see World View "Thousands of Refugees Attend Job Fair") were also offering to supply labor.

> **labor supply:** The willingness and ability to work specific amounts of time at alternative wage rates in a given time period, *ceteris paribus*.

WORLD VIEW

THOUSANDS OF REFUGEES ATTEND JOB FAIR

Berlin—Over 4,000 refugees showed up at the first-ever refugee-only job fair held in Germany. 211 companies sought workers in information technology, health care, tourism, and construction. One employer noted that the job seekers displayed a "huge willingness" among the refugees to find a job—any job. The mayor noted that employment would not only help fill job vacancies in Berlin but also speed the assimilation of refugees into German life.

Source: Media reports of March 1, 2016.

ANALYSIS: The quantity of labor supplied at any given wage rate depends on the value of leisure and the desire for income. These Berlin job-seekers were all willing to supply labor.

Our first concern in this chapter is to explain these labor supply decisions. How do people decide how many hours to supply at any given wage rate? Do people try to maximize their total wages? If they did, we'd all be holding three jobs and sleeping on the commuter bus. Since most of us don't behave this way, other motives must be present.

Income vs. Leisure

The reward for working comes in two forms: (1) the intrinsic satisfaction of working and (2) a paycheck. MBA grads say they care more about the intrinsic satisfaction than the pay (see In the News "Challenging Work and Corporate Responsibility Will Lure MBA Grads"). They also get huge paychecks, however. Those big paychecks are explained in part by the quantity of labor supplied: MBA grads often end up working 60 or more hours a week. The reason people are willing to work so many hours is that they want more income.

Not working obviously has some value, too. In part, we need some nonwork time just to recuperate from working. We also want some leisure time to watch television, go to a soccer game, or enjoy other goods and services we've purchased.

The Trade-Off. Since both working and *not* working are rewarding, we have a dilemma: the more time we spend working, the more income we have but also less time to enjoy it. Working, like all activities, involves an opportunity cost: *the opportunity cost of working is the amount of leisure time that must be given up in the process.*

This inevitable trade-off between labor and leisure explains the shape of individual labor supply curves. As we work more hours, our leisure time becomes more scarce—and thus more valuable. Hence **higher wage rates are required to compensate for the increasing opportunity cost of labor** (forgone leisure). We'll work more—supply a larger quantity of

CHALLENGING WORK AND CORPORATE RESPONSIBILITY WILL LURE MBA GRADS

STANFORD GRADUATE SCHOOL OF BUSINESS—A survey of 759 graduating MBAs at 11 top business schools reveals that the future business leaders rank corporate social responsibility high on their list of values, and they are willing to sacrifice a significant part of their salaries to find an employer whose thinking is in sync with their own.

The study by David Montgomery and Catherine Ramus of UC Santa Barbara examines the trade-offs students are willing to make when selecting a potential employer. They found that intellectual challenge ranked number one in desirable job attributes, while money and location were essentially tied for second, each roughly 80 percent as important as the most important factor.

The researchers found that the students expected to earn an average of $103,650 a year at their first job. Nearly all (97.3 percent) said they would be willing to make a

financial sacrifice to work for a company that exhibited all four characteristics of social responsibility. They said they would sacrifice an average of $14,902 a year, or 14.4 percent of their expected salary.

What MBAs at Some Top Schools Earn

School	Starting Salaries in 2016
University of Pennsylvania	$155,058
Harvard	153,830
Stanford	153,553
University of Virginia	150,823
Columbia	150,229
Dartmouth	148,997
Chicago	147,475
Cornell	146,252
University of Michigan	145,926

Source: Global MBA Rankings 2016, *U.S. News & World Report*, Copyright ©2016.

Source: Stanford Graduate School of Business.

ANALYSIS: The quantity of labor supplied depends on the intrinsic satisfaction of working and the wages paid. MBA grads apparently work long hours for both high wages and job satisfaction. Would they work just as hard for *less* pay?

labor—only if offered a higher wage rate. This is reflected in the upward slope of the labor supply curve in Figure 30.1.

The upward slope of the labor supply curve is reinforced with the changing value of income. Those first few dollars earned on the job are really precious, especially if you have bills to pay. As you work and earn more, however, your most urgent needs will be satisfied. You may still want more things, but the urgency of your consumption desires is likely to diminish. Another dollar of wages doesn't mean as much. In other words, *the marginal*

FIGURE 30.1

The Supply of Labor

The quantity of any good or service offered for sale typically increases as its price rises. Labor supply responds in the same way. At the wage rate w_1, the quantity of labor supplied is q_1 (point A). At the higher wage w_2, workers are willing to work more hours per week—that is, to supply a larger quantity of labor (q_2).

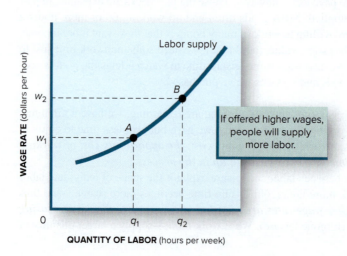

utility of income may decline as you earn more. If this happens, you may not be willing to work more hours unless offered a still higher wage rate.

The upward slope of an individual's labor supply curve is therefore explained by the fact that as hours worked increase,

- The value of leisure time increases.
- The marginal utility of income decreases.

Money isn't necessarily the only thing that motivates people to work. People *do* turn down higher-paying jobs in favor of lower-wage jobs that they like. Many parents forgo high-wage "career" jobs to have more flexible hours and time at home. Volunteers offer their services just for the sense of contributing to their communities; they don't need a paycheck. Even MBA graduates say they're motivated more by the challenge of high-paying jobs than the money (see the previous News). But money almost always makes a difference: *People do supply more labor when offered higher wages.*

A Backward Bend?

The force that drives people up the labor supply curve is the lust for more income. Higher wages enable people to buy more goods and services. To achieve higher levels of consumption, people decide to *substitute* labor for leisure. This is the **substitution effect of higher wages.**

At some point, however, higher wages may not be so persuasive. Working added hours just to accumulate a few more toys may not seem so compelling. In fact, higher wages might create the opportunity to work *less*—without giving up any toys. Muhammad Ali once announced that he wouldn't spend an hour in the ring for less than $1 million and would box *less,* not more, as the pay for his fights exceeded $3 million. For him, the added income from one championship fight was so great that he felt he didn't have to fight more to satisfy his income and consumption desires.

A low-wage worker might also respond to higher wage rates by working *less,* not more. People receiving very low wages (such as migrant workers, household help, and babysitters) have to work really long hours just to pay the rent. The increased income made possible by higher wage rates might permit them to work *fewer* hours. These *negative* labor supply responses to increased wage rates are referred to as the **income effect of higher wages.**

The conflict between income and substitution effects shapes an individual's labor supply curve. The *substitution effect* of higher wages encourages people to work more hours. The *income effect,* on the other hand, allows them to reduce work hours without losing income. If substitution effects dominate, the labor supply curve will be upward-sloping. *If income effects outweigh substitution effects, an individual will supply **less** labor at higher wages.* This kind of reaction is illustrated by the backward-bending portion of the supply curve in Figure 30.2.

substitution effect of higher wages: An increased wage rate encourages people to work more hours (to substitute labor for leisure).

income effect of higher wages: An increased wage rate allows a person to reduce hours worked without losing income.

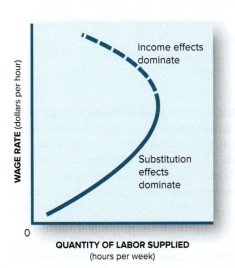

FIGURE 30.2

The Backward-Bending Supply Curve

Increases in wage rates make additional hours of work more valuable but also less necessary. Higher wage rates increase the quantity of labor supplied as long as substitution effects outweigh income effects. At the point where income effects begin to outweigh substitution effects, the labor supply curve starts to bend backward.

Backward-bending labor supply curves are more the exception than the rule. Most Americans do want more leisure. But given the choice between more leisure or more income, Americans choose added income (see World View "Your Money or Your Life"). In other words, substitution effects outweigh income effects in the U.S. labor force. This explains why Americans work such long hours despite their comparatively high incomes. Workers in Mexico and India, by contrast, appear to covet more leisure rather than more income.

WORLD VIEW

YOUR MONEY OR YOUR LIFE

Would you rather have more time or more money? Here's how people in six countries answered.

"Your Money or Your Life," *Businessweek*, May 26, 2003, p. 16. Copyright ©2011. All rights reserved. Used with permission.

ANALYSIS: Despite already high incomes, Americans are still willing to sacrifice leisure for more income; *substitution effects* outweigh *income effects*.

---

market supply of labor:
The total quantity of labor that workers are willing and able to supply at alternative wage rates in a given time period, *ceteris paribus*.

MARKET SUPPLY

The **market supply of labor** represents the sum of all individual labor supply decisions. Although some individuals have backward-bending supply curves, these negative responses to higher wages are swamped by positive responses from the 160 million individuals who participate in the U.S. labor market. As a result, the *market* supply curve is upward-sloping.

The upward slope of the labor supply curve doesn't imply that we'll all be working longer hours in the future. As time passes, the labor supply curve can *shift*. And it will whenever one of the underlying determinants of supply changes. *The determinants of labor supply include*

- *Tastes* (for leisure, income, and work).
- *Income and wealth.*
- *Expectations* (for income or consumption).
- *Prices* of consumer goods.
- *Taxes.*

These shift factors determine the position and slope of the labor supply curve at any point in time. As time passes, however, these underlying determinants change, causing the labor supply curve to shift. This has evidently happened. In 1890 the average U.S. worker was employed 60 hours a week at a wage rate of 20 cents an hour. In 2016 the average worker worked fewer than 35 hours per week at a wage rate of $22 an hour. Contributing to this long-run leftward shift has been (1) the spectacular rise in living standards (a change in income and wealth), (2) the growth of income transfer programs that provide economic security when one isn't

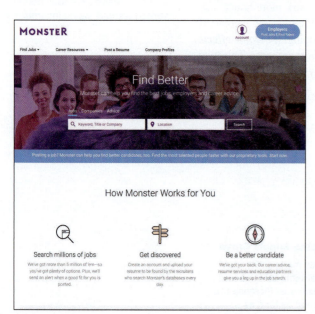

Analysis: Monster.com brings together the supply and demand for labor.

Source: www.monster.com

working (a change in income and expectations), and (3) the increased diversity and attractiveness of leisure activities (a change in tastes and other goods).

Elasticity of Labor Supply

Despite the evident *long*-run shifts of the labor supply curve, workers still respond positively to higher wage rates in the *short* run. To measure the resulting movements along the labor supply curve, we use the familiar concept of elasticity. Specifically, the **elasticity of labor supply** is the percentage change in the quantity of labor supplied divided by the percentage change in the wage rate:

$$\text{Elasticity of labor supply} = \frac{\text{\% change in quantity of labor supplied}}{\text{\% change in wage rate}}$$

elasticity of labor supply: The percentage change in the quantity of labor supplied divided by the percentage change in wage rate.

The elasticity of labor tells us how much *more* labor will be available if a higher wage is offered. If the elasticity of labor is 0.2, a 10 percent increase in wage rates will induce a 2 percent increase in the quantity of labor supplied.

The actual responsiveness of workers to a change in wage rates depends on the determinants of labor supply. Time is also important for labor supply elasticity because individuals can't always adjust their schedules or change jobs instantaneously.

Institutional Constraints

The labor supply curve and its related elasticities tell us how much time people would like to allocate to work. We must recognize, however, that people seldom have the opportunity to adjust their hours of employment at will. True, a Mark Zuckerberg or a Lady Gaga can easily choose to work more or fewer hours. Most workers, however, face more rigid choices. They must usually choose to work at a regular job for eight hours a day, five days a week, or not to work at all. Very few firms are flexible enough to accommodate a desire to work only between the hours of 11 a.m. and 3 p.m. on alternate Thursdays. Adjustments in work hours are more commonly confined to choices about overtime work or secondary jobs (moonlighting) and vacation and retirement. Families may also alter the labor supply by varying the number of family members sent into the labor force at any given time. Students, too, can often adjust their work hours. The flow of immigrants into the U.S. labor market also increases when U.S. wages rise.

LABOR DEMAND

Regardless of how many people are *willing* to work, it's up to employers to decide how many people will *actually* work. That is, there must be a **demand for labor.** What determines the number of workers employers are willing to hire at various wage rates?

demand for labor: The quantities of labor employers are willing and able to hire at alternative wage rates in a given time period, *ceteris paribus.*

Derived Demand

In earlier chapters we emphasized that employers are profit maximizers. In their quest for maximum profits, firms seek the rate of output at which marginal revenue equals marginal cost. Once they've identified the profit-maximizing rate of output, firms enter factor markets to purchase the required amounts of labor, equipment, and other resources. Thus *the quantity of resources purchased by a business depends on the firm's expected sales and output.* In this sense, the demand for factors of production, including labor, is a **derived demand;** it's derived from the demand for goods and services.

Consider the plight of strawberry pickers. Strawberry pickers are paid very low wages and are employed only part of the year. But their plight can't be blamed on the greed of the strawberry growers. Strawberry growers, like most producers, would love to sell more strawberries at higher prices. If they did, the growers would hire more pickers and might even pay them higher wages. But the growers must contend with the market demand for strawberries: consumers aren't willing to buy more strawberries at higher prices. As a

derived demand: The demand for labor and other factors of production results from (depends on) the demand for final goods and services produced by these factors.

consequence, the growers can't afford to hire more pickers or pay them higher wages. In contrast, information technology (IT) firms are always looking for more workers and offer very high wages to get them. This helps explain why college students who major in engineering, math, or computer science get paid a lot more than philosophy majors. IT specialists benefit from the growing demand for Internet services, while philosophy majors suffer because the search for the meaning of life is not a growth industry.

The principle of derived demand suggests that if consumers really want to improve the lot of strawberry pickers, they should eat more strawberries. An increase in the demand for strawberries will motivate growers to plant more berries and hire more labor to pick them. Until then, the plight of the pickers isn't likely to improve.

The Labor Demand Curve

The number of strawberry pickers hired by the growers isn't completely determined by the demand for strawberries. The number of pickers hired will also depend on the wage rate. That is, *the quantity of labor demanded depends on its price (the wage rate).* In general, we expect that strawberry growers will be *willing to hire* more pickers at low wages than at higher wages. Hence the demand for labor looks very much like the demand for any good or service (see Figure 30.3).

Marginal Physical Product

The fact that the demand curve for labor slopes downward doesn't tell us what quantity of labor will be hired. Nor does it tell us what wage rate will be paid. To answer such questions, we need to know what determines the particular shape and position of the labor demand curve.

A strawberry grower will be willing to hire another picker only if that picker contributes more to output than he or she costs. Growers, as rational businesspeople, recognize that *every* sale and *every* expenditure have some impact on total profits. Hence the truly profit-maximizing grower will evaluate each picker's job application in terms of the applicant's potential contribution to profits.

Fortunately, a strawberry picker's contribution to output is easy to measure; it's the number of boxes of strawberries he or she picks. Suppose for the moment that Marvin, a college dropout with three summers of experience as a canoe instructor, is able to pick five boxes per hour. These five boxes represent Marvin's **marginal physical product (MPP).** In other words, Marvin's MPP is the *addition* to total output that occurs when the grower hires him for an hour:

marginal physical product (MPP): The change in total output associated with one additional unit of input.

$$\text{Marginal physical product} = \frac{\text{Change in total output}}{\text{Change in quantity of labor}}$$

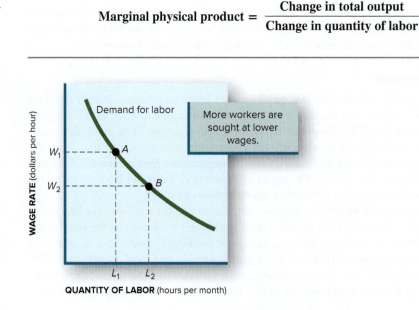

FIGURE 30.3

The Demand for Labor

The higher the wage rate, the smaller the quantity of labor demanded (*ceteris paribus*). At the wage rate W_1, only L_1 of labor is demanded. If the wage rate falls to W_2, a larger quantity of labor (L_2) will be demanded. The labor demand curve obeys the law of demand.

Marginal physical product establishes an *upper* limit to the grower's willingness to pay. Clearly the grower can't afford to pay Marvin more than five boxes of strawberries for an hour's work; the grower won't pay Marvin more than he produces.

Marginal Revenue Product

Most strawberry pickers don't want to be paid in strawberries. At the end of a day in the fields, the last thing a picker wants to see is another strawberry. Marvin, like the rest of the pickers, wants to be paid in cash. To find out how much cash he might be paid, we need to know what a box of strawberries is worth. This is easy to determine. The market value of a box of strawberries is simply the price at which the grower can sell it. Thus Marvin's contribution to output can be measured by either marginal *physical* product (five boxes per hour) or the dollar *value* of that product.

The dollar value of a worker's contribution to output is called **marginal revenue product (MRP).** Marginal revenue product is the *change* in total revenue that occurs when more labor is hired:

$$\text{Marginal revenue product} = \frac{\text{Change in total revenue}}{\text{Change in quantity of labor}}$$

In Marvin's case, the "change in quantity of labor" is one extra hour of picking strawberries. The "change in total revenue" is the *value* of the extra five boxes of berries Marvin picks in that hour. If the grower can sell strawberries for $2 a box, Marvin's marginal revenue product is simply 5 boxes per hour × $2 per box, or $10 per hour.

We could have come to the same conclusion by multiplying marginal *physical* product times *price:*

$$\text{MRP} = \text{MPP} \times \rho$$

or

$$\$10 \text{ per hour} = 5 \text{ boxes per hour} \times \$2 \text{ per box}$$

In compliance with the rule about not paying anybody more than he or she contributes, the profit-maximizing grower should be willing to pay Marvin *up to* $10 an hour. In other words, *marginal revenue product sets an upper limit to the wage rate an employer will pay.*

But what about a lower limit? Suppose the pickers aren't organized and Marvin is desperate for money. Under such circumstances, he might be willing to work—to supply labor—for only $4 an hour.

Should the grower hire Marvin for such a low wage? The profit-maximizing answer is obvious. If Marvin's marginal revenue product is $10 an hour and his wages are only $4 an hour, the grower will be eager to hire him. The difference between Marvin's marginal revenue product ($10) and his wage ($4) implies additional profits of $6 an hour. In fact, the grower will be so elated by the economics of this situation that he'll want to hire everybody he can find who's willing to work for $4 an hour. After all, if the grower can make $6 an hour by hiring Marvin, why not hire 1,000 pickers and accumulate profits at an even faster rate?

The Law of Diminishing Returns

The exploitative possibilities suggested by Marvin's picking are too good to be true. It isn't at all clear, for example, how the grower could squeeze 1,000 workers onto one acre of land and have any room left over for strawberry plants. There must be some limit to the profit-making potential of this situation.

A few moments' reflection on the absurdity of trying to employ 1,000 people to pick one acre of strawberries should be ample warning of the limits to profits here. You don't need two years of business school to recognize this. But some grasp of economics may help explain exactly why the grower's eagerness to hire additional pickers will begin to fade long before 1,000 are hired. The operative concept here is *marginal productivity.*

marginal revenue product (MRP): The change in total revenue associated with one additional unit of input.

We can measure a worker's output in *physical* terms (e.g., boxes of strawberries) or *dollar* terms (value of those boxes).

©Photodisc/Getty Images RF

Diminishing MPP. The decision to hire Marvin originated in his marginal physical product—that is, the five boxes of strawberries he can pick in an hour's time. To assess the wisdom of hiring still more pickers, we have to *consider how total output will change if additional labor is employed.* To do so, we need to keep track of marginal physical product.

Figure 30.4 shows how strawberry output changes as additional pickers are hired. Marvin picks five boxes of strawberries per hour. Total output and his marginal physical product are identical because he's initially the only picker employed. When the grower hires George, Marvin's old college roommate, we observe that the total output increases to 10 boxes per hour (point *B* in Figure 30.4). This figure represents another increase of five boxes per hour. Accordingly, we may conclude that George's *marginal physical product* is five boxes per hour, the same as Marvin's. Given such productivity, the grower will want to hire George and continue looking for more pickers.

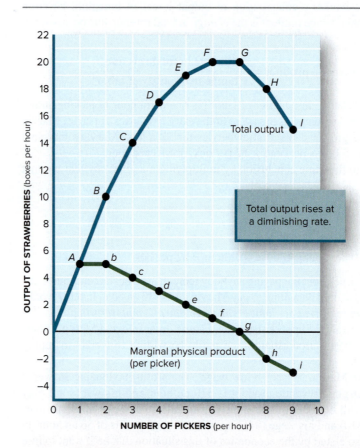

FIGURE 30.4

Diminishing Marginal Physical Product

The marginal physical product (MPP) of labor is the *increase* in total production that results when one additional worker is hired. MPP tends to fall as additional workers are hired in any given production process. This decline occurs because each worker has increasingly less of other factors (e.g., land) with which to work. When the second worker (George) is hired, total output increases from 5 to 10 boxes per hour. Hence the second worker's MPP equals 5 boxes per hour. Thereafter, capital and land constraints diminish marginal physical product.

	Number of Pickers (per Hour)	Total Strawberry Output (Boxes per Hour)	Marginal Physical Product (Boxes per Hour)
	0	0	—
A	1 (Marvin)	5	5
B	2 (George)	10	5
C	3	14	4
D	4	17	3
E	5	19	2
F	6	20	1
G	7	20	0
H	8	18	−2
I	9	15	−3

As more workers are hired, total strawberry output continues to increase but not nearly as fast. Although the later hires work just as hard, the limited availability of land and capital constrain their marginal physical product. One problem is the number of boxes. There are only a dozen boxes, and the additional pickers often have to wait for an empty box. The time spent waiting depresses marginal physical product. The worst problem is space: as additional workers are crowded onto the one-acre patch, they begin to get in one another's way. The picking process is slowed, and marginal physical product is further depressed. Note that the MPP of the fifth picker is two boxes per hour, while the MPP of the sixth picker is only one box per hour. By the time we get to the seventh picker, marginal physical product actually falls to zero because no further increases in total strawberry output take place.

Things get even worse if the grower hires still more pickers. If eight pickers are employed, total output actually *declines*. The pickers can no longer work efficiently under such crowded conditions. The MPP of the eighth worker is *negative,* no matter how ambitious or hardworking this person may be. Figure 30.4 illustrates this decline in marginal physical product, beyond point *G* on the total output curve and beyond point *g* on the MPP curve.

Our observations on strawberry production are similar to those made in most industries. In the short run, the availability of land and capital is limited by prior investment decisions. Hence additional workers must share existing facilities. As a result, *the marginal physical product of labor eventually declines as the quantity of labor employed increases.* This is the **law of diminishing returns** we first encountered in Chapter 21. It's based on the simple observation that an increasing number of workers leaves each worker with less land and capital to work with. At some point, this "crowding" causes MPP to decline.

law of diminishing returns: The marginal physical product of a variable input declines as more of it is employed with a given quantity of other (fixed) inputs.

Diminishing MRP. *As marginal physical product (MPP) diminishes, so does marginal revenue product (MRP).* As noted earlier, marginal revenue product is the increase in the *value* of total output associated with an added unit of labor (or other input). In our example, it refers to the increase in strawberry revenues associated with one additional picker and is calculated as MPP $\times p$.

The decline in marginal revenue product mirrors the drop in marginal physical product. Recall that a box of strawberries sells for \$2. With this price and the output statistics in Figure 30.4, we can readily calculate marginal revenue product, as summarized in Table 30.1. As the growth of output diminishes, so does marginal revenue product. Marvin's marginal revenue product of \$10 an hour has fallen to \$6 by the time four pickers are employed and reaches zero when seven pickers are employed.[1]

Number of Pickers (per Hour)	Total Strawberry Output (in Boxes per Hour)	×	Price of Strawberry (per Box)	=	Total Strawberry Revenue (per Hour)	Marginal Revenue Product
0	0		\$2		0	—
1 (Marvin)	5		2		\$10	\$10
2 (George)	10		2		20	10
3	14		2		28	8
4	17		2		34	6
5	19		2		38	4
6	20		2		40	2
7	20		2		40	0
8	18		2		36	-4
9	15		2		30	-6

TABLE 30.1

Diminishing Marginal Revenue Product

Marginal revenue product (MRP) measures the change in total revenue that occurs when one additional worker is hired. At constant product prices, MRP equals MPP × price. Hence MRP declines along with MPP.

[1]Marginal revenue product would fall even faster if the price of strawberries declined as increasing quantities were supplied. We're assuming that the grower's output doesn't influence the market price of strawberries and hence that the grower is a *competitive* producer.

A FIRM'S HIRING DECISION

The tendency of marginal revenue product to diminish will cool the strawberry grower's eagerness to hire 1,000 pickers. We still don't know, however, how many pickers will be hired.

The Firm's Labor Supply

Our earlier discussion of labor supply indicated that more workers are available only at higher wage rates. But that's true only for the *market* supply. A single producer may be able to hire an unlimited number of workers at the prevailing wage rate—if the firm is perfectly competitive in the labor market. This happens when the single firm (or farm) is just a bit player in a much larger labor market. Like small firms in big product markets, it has no market power. In other words, ***a firm that's a perfect competitor in the labor market can hire all the labor it wants at the prevailing market wage.***

Let's assume that the strawberry grower is so small that his hiring decisions have no effect on local wages. As far as he's concerned, there's an unlimited supply of strawberry pickers willing to work for $4 an hour. His only decision is how many of these willing pickers to hire at that wage rate.

MRP = Firm's Labor Demand

Figure 30.5 provides the answer. We already know that the grower is eager to hire pickers whose marginal revenue product exceeds their wage. He'll therefore hire at least one worker at that wage because the MRP of the first picker is $10 an hour (point *A* in Figure 30.5). A second worker will be hired as well because that picker's MRP (point *B* in Figure 30.5) also exceeds the going wage rate. In fact, ***the grower will continue hiring pickers until the MRP has declined to the level of the market wage rate.*** Figure 30.5 indicates that this intersection (point *C*) occurs when five pickers are employed. Accordingly the grower will be willing to hire—will *demand*—five pickers if wages are $4 an hour.

The folly of hiring more than five pickers is also apparent in Figure 30.5. The marginal revenue product of the sixth worker is only $2 an hour (point *D*). Hiring a sixth picker will cost more in wages ($4) than the picker brings in as revenue ($2). That makes no sense. The *maximum* number of pickers the grower will employ at prevailing wages is five (point *C*).

Equal Pay. The law of diminishing returns also implies that all five pickers will be paid the same wage. Once five pickers are employed, we can't say that any single picker is

FIGURE 30.5

The Marginal Revenue Product Curve Is the Labor Demand Curve

An employer is willing to pay a worker no more than the marginal revenue product. In this case, a grower would gladly hire a second worker because that worker's MRP (point *B*) exceeds the wage rate ($4). The sixth worker won't be hired at that wage rate, however, since the MRP (at point *D*) is less than $4. The MRP curve is the labor demand curve.

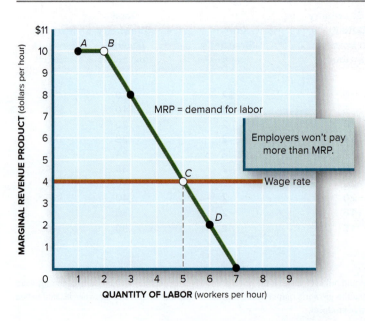

responsible for the observed decline in marginal revenue product. Marginal revenue product of labor diminishes because each worker has less capital and land to work with, not because the last worker hired is less able than the others. Accordingly, the "fifth" picker can't be identified as any particular individual. Once five pickers are hired, Marvin's MRP is no higher than any other picker's. *Each (identical) worker is worth no more than the marginal revenue product of the last worker hired, and all workers are paid the same wage rate.*

The principles of marginal revenue product apply to baseball players as well as strawberry pickers. When the Miami Marlins agreed to pay Giancarlo Stanton $325 million (see In the News "Marlins Sign Stanton to Record $325 Million Contract"), they had his MRP in mind. Not only had he led the National League in home runs and slugging, but he also caused a spike in attendance and in sales of souvenirs. If Giancarlo's bat could get the Marlins to the playoffs or World Series, total revenue would soar. The Marlins decided Giancarlo's MRP justified his extraordinary salary.

IN THE NEWS

MARLINS SIGN STANTON TO RECORD $325 MILLION CONTRACT

The Miami Marlins have signed outfielder Giancarlo Stanton to a record-breaking contract. The contract calls for Stanton to get $325 million over a 13-year period. This is the biggest amount ever paid to anyone in North American professional sports and the longest contract in baseball history. The Marlins are betting that Giancarlo (known as "Mike" prior to 2012) will propel the Marlins into National League playoffs and maybe the World Series. Last year Giancarlo led the National League with 37 home runs and a .555 slugging percentage, earning him the runner-up position in 2014's Most Valuable Player competition. He has hit some of the longest home runs in baseball history, including a 494-footer that hit the scoreboard in Coors Field.

©Jim McIsaac/Getty Images

Source: News reports, November 17–20, 2014.

ANALYSIS: Marginal revenue product measures what a worker is worth to an employer. The Miami Marlins expect a high MRP from Giancarlo Stanton.

Whatever the explanation for the disparity between the incomes of baseball players and strawberry pickers, the enormous gap between them seems awfully unfair. An obvious question then arises: Can't the number of pickers or their wages be increased?

Changes in Wage Rates

Suppose the government were to set a minimum wage for strawberry pickers at $6 an hour. At first glance this action would appear to boost the wages of pickers, who have been earning only $4 an hour. This isn't all good news for the strawberry pickers, however. *There's a trade-off between wage rates and the number of workers demanded.* If wage rates go up, growers will hire fewer pickers.

Figure 30.6*a* illustrates this trade-off. The grower's earlier decision to hire five pickers was based on a wage of $4 an hour (point *C*). If the wage jumps to $6 an hour, it no longer makes economic sense to keep five pickers employed. The MRP of the fifth worker is only

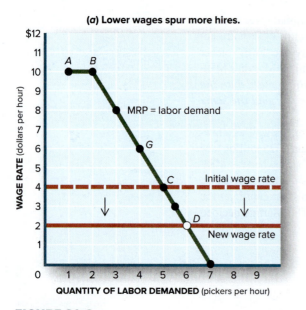

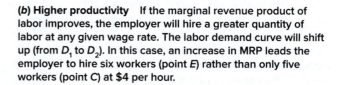

(a) Lower wages spur more hires.

(b) Higher productivity also spurs more hires.

FIGURE 30.6

Incentives to Hire

(a) Lower wage   If the wage rate drops, an employer will be willing to hire more workers, *ceteris paribus*. At $4 an hour, only five pickers per hour would be demanded (point *C*). If the wage rate dropped to $2 an hour, six pickers per hour would be demanded (point *D*).

(b) Higher productivity   If the marginal revenue product of labor improves, the employer will hire a greater quantity of labor at any given wage rate. The labor demand curve will shift up (from D_1 to D_2). In this case, an increase in MRP leads the employer to hire six workers (point *E*) rather than only five workers (point *C*) at $4 per hour.

$4 an hour. The grower will respond to higher wage rates by moving up the labor demand curve to point *G*. At point *G*, only four pickers are hired, and MRP again equals the wage rate. If more workers are to be hired, the wage rate must drop.

Changes in Productivity

The downward slope of the labor demand curve doesn't doom strawberry pickers to low wages. It does emphasize, however, the inevitable link between workers' productivity and wages. ***To get higher wages without sacrificing jobs, productivity (MRP) must increase.***

Suppose Marvin and his friends all enroll in a local agricultural extension course and learn new methods of strawberry picking. With these new methods, the marginal physical product of each picker increases by one box per hour. With the price of strawberries still at $2 a box, this productivity improvement implies an increase in marginal *revenue* product of $2 per worker. This change causes an upward *shift* of the labor demand (MRP) curve, as in Figure 30.6*b*.

Notice how the improvement in productivity has altered the value of strawberry pickers. The MRP of the fifth picker is now $6 an hour (point *F*) rather than $4 (point *C*). Hence the grower can now afford to pay higher wages. Or the grower could employ more pickers than before, moving from point *C* to point *E*. ***Increased productivity implies that workers can get higher wages without sacrificing jobs or more employment without lowering wages.*** Historically, increased productivity has been the most important source of rising wages and living standards.

Changes in Price

An increase in the price of strawberries would also help the pickers. Marginal revenue product reflects the interaction of productivity and product prices. If strawberry prices were to double, strawberry pickers would become twice as valuable, even without an increase in physical productivity. Such a change in product prices depends, however, on changes in the market supply and demand for strawberries.

MARKET EQUILIBRIUM

The principles that guide the hiring decisions of a single strawberry grower can be extended to the entire labor market. This suggests that *the market demand for labor depends on*

- *The number of employers.*
- *The marginal revenue product of labor in each firm and industry.*

Increases in either the demand for final products or the productivity of labor will tend to increase marginal revenue productivity and therewith the demand for labor.

On the supply side of the labor market we have already observed that *the market supply of labor depends on*

- *The number of available workers.*
- *Each worker's willingness to work at alternative wage rates.*

The supply decisions of workers are in turn a reflection of tastes, income, wealth, expectations, other prices, and taxes.

Equilibrium Wage

Figure 30.7 brings these market forces together. *The intersection of the market supply and demand curves establishes the* **equilibrium wage.** This is the only wage rate at which the quantity of labor supplied equals the quantity of labor demanded. Everyone who's willing and able to work for this wage will find a job.

If the labor market is perfectly competitive, all employers will be able to hire as many workers as they want at the equilibrium wage. Like our strawberry grower, every competitive firm is assumed to have no discernible effect on market wages. *Competitive employers*

equilibrium wage: The wage rate at which the quantity of labor supplied in a given time period equals the quantity of labor demanded.

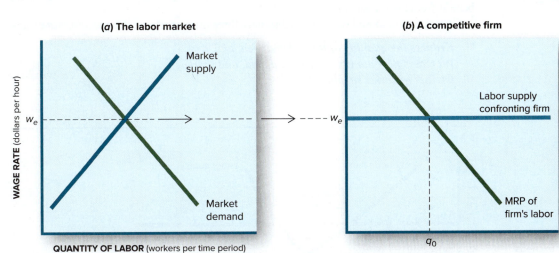

FIGURE 30.7

Equilibrium Wage

The intersection of *market* supply and demand determines the equilibrium wage in a competitive labor market. All the firms in the industry can then hire as much labor as they want at that equilibrium wage. In this case, the firm can hire all the workers it wants at the equilibrium wage, w_e. It chooses to hire q_0 workers, as determined by their marginal revenue product within the firm.

TABLE 30.2

Minimum Wage History

The federal minimum wage has been increased periodically since first set in 1938. In 2007 Congress raised the minimum to $7.25, effective July 2009.

Oct. 1938	$0.25	Jan. 1978	$2.65
Oct. 1939	0.30	Jan. 1979	2.90
Oct. 1945	0.40	Jan. 1980	3.10
Jan. 1950	0.75	Jan. 1981	3.35
Mar. 1956	1.00	Apr. 1990	3.80
Sept. 1961	1.15	Apr. 1991	4.25
Sept. 1963	1.25	Oct. 1996	4.75
Feb. 1967	1.40	Sept. 1997	5.15
Feb. 1968	1.60	July 2007	5.85
May 1974	2.00	July 2008	6.55
Jan. 1975	2.10	July 2009	7.25
Jan. 1976	2.30		

act like price takers with respect to wages as well as prices. This phenomenon is also portrayed in Figure 30.7.

Minimum Wages

Some people will be unhappy with the equilibrium wage. Employers may grumble that wages are too high. Workers may complain that wages are too low. They may seek government intervention to change market outcomes. This is the goal of Congress when it establishes a legal *minimum* wage—a **price floor** in the labor market (see Table 30.2).

> **price floor:** Lower limit set for the price of a good.

Figure 30.8 illustrates the effects of such government intervention. The market-determined equilibrium wage is W_e, and q_e workers are employed. A government-imposed minimum wage of W_M is then set, above the market equilibrium. So, what happens?

There are changes on both the supply side of the labor market and the demand side. On the supply side, the higher wage W_M encourages more low-skilled workers to seek employment; the quantity supplied *increases* from q_e to q_s. On the demand side, however, the number of available jobs *declines* from q_e to q_d. This leaves a **market surplus** at the wage W_M. As a result of the increased wage, some workers have lost jobs ($q_e - q_d$) and some new entrants fail to find employment ($q_s - q_e$). Only those workers who remain employed (q_d) benefit from the higher wage.

> **market surplus:** The amount by which the quantity supplied exceeds the quantity demanded at a given price; excess supply.

Government-imposed wage floors thus have three distinct effects: *A legal minimum wage*

- *Reduces the quantity of labor demanded, and*
- *Increases the quantity of labor supplied, and thereby*
- *Creates a market surplus.*

FIGURE 30.8

Minimum Wage Effects

If the minimum wage exceeds the equilibrium wage, a labor surplus will result: more workers will be willing to work at that wage rate than employers will be willing to hire. Some workers will end up with higher wages, but others will end up unemployed.

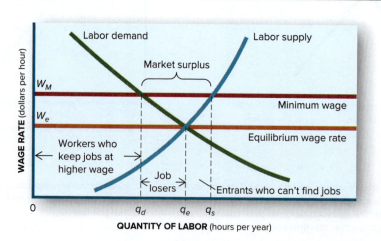

The extent of job loss resulting from a minimum wage hike is hotly debated. How many jobs are lost obviously depends on how far the minimum wage is raised above the market equilibrium.

Demand Elasticity

The elasticity of labor demand is also important. Democrats argue that labor demand is inelastic, so few jobs will be lost. Republicans assert that labor demand is elastic, so more jobs will be lost. In the early 1980s the elasticity of labor demand was found to be 0.10. Hence a 10 percent increase in the minimum wage would cause a 1 percent reduction in employment. Between 1981 and 1990, however, the minimum was stuck at $3.35 an hour while average wages increased 30 percent. By 1989 the federal minimum may have actually been *below* the equilibrium wage for low-skilled labor. When the minimum wage is below the equilibrium wage, an increase in the minimum may have little or no adverse employment effects. This appeared to be the case again in 1996. Because the federal minimum hadn't been raised for five years (see Table 30.2), the 50-cent-per-hour hike in October 1996 caused few job losses. According to Federal Reserve estimates, the 1997 wage hike may have reduced employment growth by only 100,000 to 200,000 jobs.

The same situation existed again in 2007. By then, the federal minimum of $5.15 hadn't been lifted for 10 years (Table 30.2) and had fallen below equilibrium levels (McDonald's and other fast-food outlets were paying entry wages of $6.50 and more in 2007). When Congress raised the minimum to $5.85, the legislated floor still lagged behind market wages. Further hikes, to $7.25 an hour, did cause some job losses, however. In general, *the further the minimum wage rises above the market's equilibrium wage, the greater the job loss.* That was a major source of concern when President Obama proposed raising the minimum wage again, to $10.10 an hour in 2014 (see In the News "Obama Calls for $10.10 Minimum Wage"). The Congressional Budget Office estimated that such a wage jump would eliminate 500,000 jobs, even while increasing wages for millions of workers. Since then, market wages have gone up, rendering such a hike in the minimum wage less threatening to jobs.

IN THE NEWS

OBAMA CALLS FOR $10.10 MINIMUM WAGE

Declaring that "America deserves a raise," President Obama last night called on Congress to raise the minimum wage to $10.10. The federal minimum wage has been stuck at $7.25 since 2009, and Obama said families simply can't live on such a low wage. In his State of the Union message, he urged Congress to pass a higher wage minimum this year.

Source: News reports, January 29, 2014.

ANALYSIS: A higher minimum wage encourages firms to hire fewer workers. How many jobs are lost depends on the size of the wage hike and the price elasticity of labor demand.

CHOOSING AMONG INPUTS

One of the options employers have when wage rates rise is to utilize more machinery in place of labor. In most production processes there are possibilities for substituting capital inputs for labor inputs. In the long run, there are still more possibilities for redesigning the whole production process. Given these options, how should the choice of inputs be made?

Suppose a mechanical strawberry picker can pick berries twice as fast as Marvin. Which will the grower hire, Marvin or the mechanical picker? At first it would seem that the grower would choose the mechanical picker. But the choice isn't so obvious. So far, all we know is that the mechanical picker's MPP is twice as large as Marvin's. But we haven't said anything about the *cost* of the mechanical picker.

Cost Efficiency

Suppose that a mechanical picker can be rented for $10 an hour, while Marvin is still willing to work for $4 an hour. Will this difference in hourly cost change the grower's input choice?

To determine the relative desirability of hiring Marvin or renting the mechanical picker, the grower must compare the ratio of their marginal physical products to their cost. This ratio of marginal product to cost expresses the **cost efficiency** of an input:

cost efficiency: The amount of output associated with an additional dollar spent on input; the MPP of an input divided by its price (cost).

$$\text{Cost efficiency} = \frac{\textbf{Marginal physical product of an input}}{\textbf{Cost of an input}}$$

Marvin's MPP is five boxes of strawberries per hour and his cost (wage) is $4. Thus the return on each dollar of wages paid to Marvin is

$$\text{Cost efficiency of labor} = \frac{\text{MPP}_{labor}}{\text{Cost}_{labor}} = \frac{5 \text{ boxes}}{\$4} = 1.25 \text{ boxes per \$1 of cost}$$

By contrast, the mechanical picker has an MPP of 10 boxes per hour and costs $10 per hour:

$$\text{Cost efficiency of mechanical picker} = \frac{\text{MPP}_{mechanical\ picker}}{\text{Cost}_{mechanical\ picker}} = \frac{10 \text{ boxes}}{\$10} = 1 \text{ box per \$1 of cost}$$

These calculations indicate that Marvin is more cost-effective than the mechanical picker. From this perspective, the grower is better off hiring Marvin than renting a mechanical picker.

From the perspective of cost efficiency, the cheapness of a productive input is measured not by its price but by the amount of output it delivers for that price. Thus *the most cost-efficient factor of production is the one that produces the most output per dollar.*

The concept of cost efficiency helps explain why American firms don't move en masse to Haiti, where peasants are willing to work for as little as 80 cents an hour. Although this wage rate is far below the minimum wage in the United States, the marginal physical product of Haitian peasants is even further below American standards. American workers remain more cost-efficient than the "cheap" labor available in Haiti, making it unprofitable to **outsource** U.S. jobs. So long as U.S. workers deliver more output per dollar of wages, they will remain cost-effective in global markets.

outsourcing: The relocation of production to foreign countries.

Alternative Production Processes

Typically a producer doesn't choose between individual inputs but rather between alternative production processes. General Motors, for example, can't afford to compare the cost efficiency of each job applicant with the cost efficiency of mechanical tire mounters. Instead GM compares the relative desirability of a **production process** that is labor-intensive (uses a lot of labor) with others that are less labor-intensive. GM ignores individual differences in marginal revenue product. Nevertheless, the same principles of cost efficiency guide the decision.

production process: A specific combination of resources used to produce a good or service.

The Efficiency Decision

Let's return to the strawberry patch to see how the choice of an entire production process is made. We again assume that strawberries can be picked by either human or mechanical hands. Now, however, we assume that one ton of strawberries can be produced by only one of the three production processes described in Table 30.3. Process A is most *labor-intensive;* it uses the most labor and thus keeps more human pickers employed. By contrast, process C is *capital-intensive;* it uses the most mechanical pickers and provides the least employment to human pickers. Process B falls between these two extremes.

| Input | Alternative Processes for Producing One Ton of Strawberries | | |
	Process A	Process B	Process C
Labor (hours)	400	270	220
Machinery (hours)	13	15	18
Land (acres)	1	1	1

TABLE 30.3
Alternative Production Processes

One ton of strawberries can be produced with varying input combinations. Which process is most efficient? What information is missing?

Which of these three production processes should the grower use? If he used labor-intensive process A, he'd be doing the pickers a real favor. But his goal is to maximize profits, so we assume he'll choose the production process that best serves this objective. That is, he'll choose the *least-cost* process to produce one ton of strawberries.

But which of the production processes in Table 30.3 is least expensive? We really can't tell on the basis of the information provided. To determine the relative cost of each process—and thus to understand the producer's choice—we must know something more about input costs. In particular, we have to know how much an hour of mechanical picking costs and how much an hour of human picking (labor) costs. Then we can determine which combination of inputs is least expensive in producing one ton of strawberries—that is, which is most *cost-efficient*. Note that we don't have to know how much the land costs because the same amount of land is used in all three production processes. Thus land costs won't affect our efficiency decision.

Suppose that strawberry pickers are still paid $4 an hour and that mechanical pickers can be rented for $10 an hour. The acre of land rents for $500 per year. With this information we can now calculate the total dollar cost of each production process and quickly determine the most cost-efficient. Table 30.4 summarizes the required calculations.

The calculations performed in Table 30.4 clearly identify process C as the least expensive way of producing one ton of strawberries. Process A entails a total cost of $2,230, whereas the capital-intensive process C costs only $1,560 to produce the same quantity of output. As a profit maximizer, the grower will choose process C, even though it implies less employment for strawberry pickers.

The choice of an appropriate production process—the decision about *how* to produce—is called the **efficiency decision.** As we've seen, a producer seeks to use the combination of resources that produces a given rate of output for the least cost. The efficiency decision requires the producer to find that particular least-cost combination.

efficiency decision: The choice of a production process for any given rate of output.

Input	Cost Calculation
Process A (labor-intensive)	
Labor	400 hours at $4 per hour = $1,600
Machinery	13 hours at $10 per hour = 130
Land	1 acre at $500 = 500
	Total cost $2,230
Process B (intermediate)	
Labor	270 hours at $4 per hour = $1,080
Machinery	15 hours at $10 per hour = 50
Land	1 acre at $500 = 500
	Total cost $1,730
Process C (capital-intensive)	
Labor	220 hours at $4 per hour = $ 880
Machinery	18 hours at $10 per hour = 180
Land	1 acre at $500 = 500
	Total cost $1,560

TABLE 30.4
The Least-Cost Combination

A producer wants to produce a given rate of output for the least cost. Choosing the least expensive production process is the efficiency decision. In this case, process C represents the most cost-efficient production process for producing one ton of strawberries.

THE ECONOMY TOMORROW

CAPPING CEO PAY

The CEO of Expedia, Dara Khosrowshahi, was paid $94.5 million in 2016 for his services. You might gasp at such a paycheck, but he thinks he deserves it. Expedia's sales increased 23 percent in 2016 to over $8 *billion* and its profits jumped more than 70 percent. By the end of the year, Expedia had more than 325,000 properties in its inventory and was taking reservations for 475 airlines and dozens of car rental companies and cruise lines.

Critics of CEO pay don't accept Khosrowshahi's explanation. They contend that Expedia revenues would have risen even without Khosrowshahi's leadership. Sales growth is a product of general economic growth, not just company management. They also assert that $94.5 million was way more than enough to secure Khosrowshahi's services; he probably would have worked just as hard for a mere $50 million.

Critics conclude that many CEO paychecks are out of line with realities of supply and demand. They want corporations to reduce CEO pay and revise the process used for setting CEO pay levels. President Obama moved in this direction by setting a pay cap of $500,000 for executives of corporations receiving government aid.

Unmeasured MRP. One of the difficulties in determining the appropriate level of CEO pay is the elusiveness of marginal revenue product. It's easy to measure the MRP of a strawberry picker or even a salesclerk. But a corporate CEO's contributions are less well defined. A CEO is supposed to provide strategic leadership and a sense of mission. These are critical to a corporation's success but hard to quantify.

Congress confronts the same problem in setting the president's pay. We noted earlier that the president of the United States is paid $400,000 a year. Can we argue that this salary represents the president's marginal revenue product? It has been estimated that the president's pay would be in the range of $38–58 million if he were paid on performance (MRP). The wage we actually pay a president is less a reflection of contribution to total output than a matter of custom. The salary also reflects the price voters believe is required to induce competent individuals to forsake private sector jobs and assume the responsibilities of the presidency. In this sense, the wage paid to the president and other public officials is set by their **opportunity wage**—that is, the wage they could earn in private industry.

The same kinds of considerations influence the wages of college professors. The marginal revenue product of a college professor isn't easy to measure. Is it the number of students she teaches, the amount of knowledge conveyed, or something else? Confronted with such problems, most universities tend to pay college professors according to their opportunity wage—that is, the amount the professors could earn elsewhere.

Opportunity wages also help explain the difference between the wage of the CEO of Expedia and the workers who produce its products. The call center representatives at Expedia—the people who answer your calls—get paid only $12 an hour. That works out to about $25,000 a year, more than three thousand times less than Mr. Khosrowshahi's salary. How is such an enormous wage disparity possibly justified? The answer is first and foremost marginal revenue product. The people answering the phone are essential to Expedia's business, but individually they add little to total revenue per hour. Second, they are willing to work for a much lower salary because their opportunity costs are low: they aren't trained for many other jobs. By contrast, Expedia's CEO has impressive managerial skills that are in demand by many corporations; his opportunity wages are high.

Opportunity wages help explain CEO pay but don't fully justify such high pay levels. If Expedia's CEO pay is justified by opportunity wages, that means another company would be willing to pay him that much. But what would justify such high pay at another company? Would his MRP be any easier to measure? Maybe *all* CEO paychecks have been inflated.

opportunity wage: The highest wage an individual would earn in his or her best alternative job.

Critics of CEO pay conclude that the process of setting CEO pay levels should be changed. All too often, executive pay scales are set by self-serving committees composed of executives of the same or similar corporations. Critics want a more independent assessment of pay scales, with nonaffiliated experts and stockholder representatives.

Some critics want to go a step further and set mandatory "caps" on CEO pay. President Clinton rejected legislated caps but convinced Congress to limit the tax deductibility of CEO pay. Any "unjustified" CEO pay in excess of $1 million a year can't be treated as a business expense but instead must be paid out of after-tax profits. This change put more pressure on corporations to examine the rationale for multimillion-dollar paychecks. President Obama wanted even stricter limits on CEO pay, especially for banks and other companies getting government "bailout" money.

If markets work efficiently, such government intervention shouldn't be necessary. Corporations that pay their CEOs excessively will end up with smaller profits than companies that pay market-based wages. Over time, "lean" companies will be more competitive than "fat" companies, and excessive pay packages will be eliminated. Legislated CEO pay caps imply that CEO labor markets aren't efficient or that the adjustment process is too slow. To forestall more government intervention in pay decisions, companies may tie executive pay more explicitly to performance (marginal revenue product) in the economy tomorrow.

SUMMARY

- The motivation to work arises from social, psychological, and economic forces. People need income to pay their bills, but they also need a sense of achievement. As a consequence, people are willing to work—to supply labor. **LO30-1**

- There's an opportunity cost involved in working—namely, the amount of leisure time one sacrifices. By the same token, the opportunity cost of not working (leisure) is the income and related consumption possibilities thereby forgone. Everyone confronts a trade-off between leisure and income. **LO30-1**

- Higher wage rates induce people to work more—that is, to substitute labor for leisure. But this substitution effect may be offset by an income effect. Higher wages also enable a person to work fewer hours with no loss of income. When income effects outweigh substitution effects, the labor supply curve bends backward. **LO30-2**

- A firm's demand for labor reflects labor's marginal revenue product. A profit-maximizing employer won't pay a worker more than the worker produces. **LO30-2**

- The marginal revenue product of labor diminishes as additional workers are employed on a particular job (the law of diminishing returns). This decline occurs because additional workers have to share existing land and capital, leaving each worker with less land and capital to work with. **LO30-2**

- A producer seeks to get the most output for every dollar spent on inputs. This means getting the highest ratio of marginal product to input price. A profit-maximizing producer will choose the most cost-efficient input (not necessarily the one with the cheapest price). **LO30-1**

- The efficiency decision involves the choice of the least-cost productive process and is also made on the basis of cost efficiency. A producer seeks the least expensive process to produce a given rate of output. **LO30-3**

- Differences in marginal revenue product are an important explanation of wage inequalities. But the difficulty of measuring MRP in some jobs leaves many wage rates to be determined by opportunity wages or other mechanisms. **LO30-3**

Key Terms

labor supply
substitution effect of higher wages
income effect of higher wages
market supply of labor
elasticity of labor supply
demand for labor

derived demand
marginal physical product (MPP)
marginal revenue product (MRP)
law of diminishing returns
equilibrium wage
price floor

market surplus
cost efficiency
outsourcing
production process
efficiency decision
opportunity wage

Questions for Discussion

1. Why are you doing this homework? What are you giving up? What utility do you expect to gain? **LO30-1**
2. Would you continue to work after winning a lottery prize of $100,000 a year for life? Would you change schools, jobs, or career objectives? What factors besides income influence work decisions? **LO30-1**
3. According to World View "Your Money or Your Life," does the substitution effect or the income effect dominate in Mexico? In Russia? Why might this be the case? **LO30-1**
4. Explain why marginal physical product would diminish as
   (*a*) More waiters are hired in a restaurant.
   (*b*) More professors are hired in the economics department.
   (*c*) More carpenters are hired to build a house. **LO30-2**
5. Is this course increasing your marginal productivity? If so, in what way? **LO30-2**
6. How might you measure the marginal revenue product of (*a*) a quarterback and (*b*) the team's coach? **LO30-2**
7. Who is hurt and who is helped by an increase in the legal minimum wage? Under what circumstances might a higher minimum *not* reduce employment? **LO30-3**
8. In 2016 the president of the University of Michigan was paid $750,000 and the football coach was paid $9 million. Does this make any sense? **LO30-2**
9. What is President Trump's opportunity cost for becoming president instead of running his businesses? How would you measure his marginal revenue product? **LO30-2**
10. The minimum wage in Mexico is less than $1 an hour. Does this make Mexican workers more cost-effective than U.S. workers? Explain. **LO30-3**
11. Why didn't President Obama set pay limits on baseball players who play in publicly funded stadiums? Why did he single out corporate executives? **LO30-2**

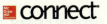

PROBLEMS FOR CHAPTER 30

LO30-1 1. (*a*) How many home runs did Giancarlo Stanton score in 2014? (See In the News "Marlins Sign Stanton to Record $325 Million Contract")
   (*b*) If his average annual salary were based on home runs alone, how much would each home run be worth?

LO30-2 2. By what percentage did
   (*a*) The federal minimum wage increase between September 1997 and July 2009? (See Table 30.2.)
   (*b*) If President Obama's wage-hike proposal (In the News "Obama Calls for $10.10 Minimum Wage") were accepted, by what percentage would the federal minimum wage increase?

LO30-1 3. According to World View "Thousands of Refugees Attend Job Fair," what was the situation in the 2016 Berlin labor market?
   A: Labor surplus   B: Labor shortage   C: Equilibrium

LO30-3 4. According to World View "Thousands of Refugees Attend Job Fair,"
   (*a*) How many people were supplying labor?
   (*b*) How many employers were demanding labor?
   (*c*) Was there a surplus or shortage in this market?

LO30-3 5. (*a*) According to Figure 30.8, how many workers are unemployed at the equilibrium wage?
   (*b*) How many workers are unemployed at the minimum wage?

LO30-1 6. Suppose a wage increase from $12 to $16 an hour for Expedia call center reps increases the number of daily job applicants from 42 to 58. What is the price elasticity of labor supply?

LO30-1 7. If the price of strawberries doubled, how many pickers would be hired at $4 an hour, according to Table 30.1?

LO30-3 8. Apples can be harvested by hand or machine. Handpicking yields 80 pounds per hour; mechanical pickers yield 120 pounds per hour.
   (*a*) If the wage rate of human pickers is $8 an hour and the rental on a mechanical picker is $15 an hour, which is more cost-effective?
   (*b*) If the wage rate increased to $12 an hour, which would be more cost-effective? _____

LO30-3 9. Assume that the following data describe labor market conditions:

Wage rate (per hour)	$3	$4	$5	$6	$7	$8	$9	$10
Labor demanded	50	45	40	35	30	25	20	15
Labor supplied	20	30	40	50	60	70	80	90

On a graph, illustrate
   (*a*) The equilibrium wage.
   (*b*) A government-set minimum wage of $6 per hour when the minimum wage is implemented.
   (*c*) How many workers lose jobs?
   (*d*) How many additional workers seek jobs?
   (*e*) How many workers end up unemployed?

LO30-2 10. The following table depicts the number of grapes that can be picked in an hour with varying amounts of labor:

Number of pickers (per hour)	1	2	3	4	5	6	7	8
Output of grapes (in flats)	20	38	53	64	71	74	74	70

(a) Illustrate the supply and demand of labor for a single farmer, assuming that the local wage rate is $6 an hour and a flat of grapes sells for $2.

(b) How many pickers will be hired?

(c) If the wage rate doubles, how many pickers will be hired?

(d) If the productivity of all workers doubles, how many pickers will be hired at a wage of $12 an hour?

(e) Illustrate your answers on the following graph.

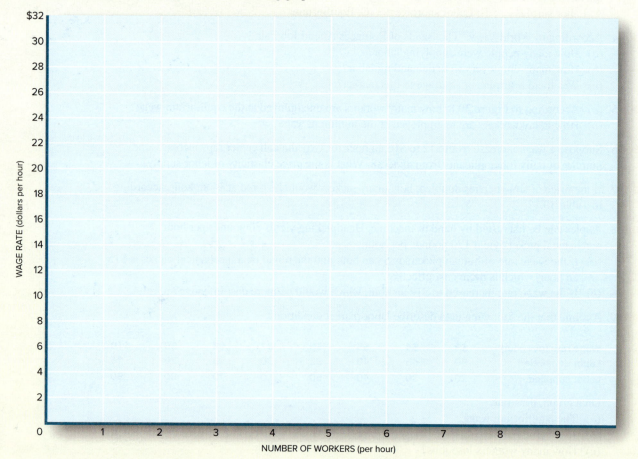

LO30-3 11. By how much would the quantity of labor demanded decrease if a minimum wage hike raised prevailing wages from $8 to $10 an hour and if the elasticity of labor demand were 0.10?

LO30-2 12. The Economy Tomorrow: If the typical Expedia call center worker is paid an annual salary of $25,000, how much higher is the CEO's annual salary in percentage terms?

©Mark Richard/PhotoEdit

Labor Unions

labor supply: The willingness and ability to work specific amounts of time at alternative wage rates in a given time period, *ceteris paribus.*

The United Auto Workers Union (UAW) launched a strike against Caterpillar, Inc., in November 1991. The union wanted the manufacturer of construction machinery to increase pay, benefits, and job security. *Four years* later, Caterpillar hadn't budged; it continued to operate with replacement workers, management crews, and union members who crossed the picket line. The union finally capitulated in December 1995, sending its 8,700 members back to work with neither higher pay nor even a new contract. The union struck again in 1996 but relented after 17 months. Seven years after their first strike, the Caterpillar workers still had no contract.

To many observers, the failed UAW strike at Caterpillar climaxed a steady decline in the power of labor unions. This impression was reinforced by the failure of *public* unions in Illinois and Ohio to safeguard benefits in early 2011. But the union movement is far from dead. Labor unions are even expanding in some sectors (especially government employment). Many unions still have considerable influence on employment, wages, and working conditions. This chapter focuses on how unions acquire and use such influence. We address the following questions:

- **How do large and powerful employers affect market wages?**
- **How do labor unions alter wages and employment?**
- **What outcomes are possible from collective bargaining between management and unions?**

In the process of answering these questions, we look at the nation's most powerful unions and their actual behavior.

THE LABOR MARKET

To gauge the impact of labor market power, we must first observe how a competitive labor market sets wages and employment. On the supply side, we have all those individuals who are willing to work—to supply labor—at various wage rates. By counting the number of individuals willing to work at each and every wage rate, we can construct a *market* **labor supply** curve, as in Figure 31.1.

FIGURE 31.1

Competitive Equilibrium in the Labor Market

The market labor supply curve includes all persons willing to work at various wage rates. The labor demand curve tells us how many workers employers are willing to hire. In a competitive market, the intersection of the labor supply and labor demand curves (point C) determines the equilibrium wage (w_e) and employment (q_e) levels.

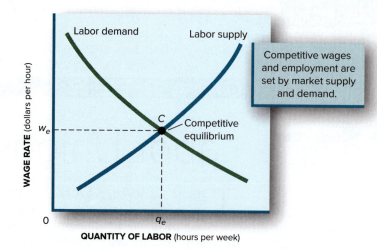

---

demand for labor: The quantities of labor employers are willing and able to hire at alternative wage rates in a given time period, *ceteris paribus*.

---

equilibrium wage: The wage rate at which the quantity of labor supplied in a given time period equals the quantity of labor demanded.

The willingness of producers (firms) to hire labor is reflected in the market labor demand curve. The curve itself is constructed by counting the number of workers each firm says it is willing and able to hire at each and every wage rate. The curve illustrates the market **demand for labor.**

Competitive Equilibrium

The intersection of the labor supply and labor demand curves (point C in Figure 31.1) reveals the **equilibrium wage** rate (w_e): the wage rate at which the quantity of labor supplied equals the quantity demanded. At this wage rate, every job seeker who's willing and able to work for the wage w_e is employed. In addition, firms are able to acquire all the labor they're willing and able to hire at that wage.

Not everyone is employed in equilibrium. Workers who demand wages in excess of w_e are unable to find jobs. By the same token, employers who refuse to pay a wage as high as w_e are unable to attract workers.

Local Labor Markets

Figure 31.1 appears to suggest that there's only *one* labor market and thus only one equilibrium wage. This is a gross oversimplification. If you were looking for a job in Tulsa, you'd have little interest in employment prospects or power configurations in New York City. You'd be more concerned about the available jobs and wages in Tulsa—that is, the condition of the *local* labor market.

Even within a particular geographical area, interest usually focuses on particular occupations and workers rather than on all the people supplying or demanding labor. If you were looking for work as a dancer, you'd have little interest in the employment situation for carpenters or dentists. Rather, you'd want to know how many nightclubs or dance troupes had job vacancies, and what wages and working conditions they offered.

The distinction among various geographical, occupational, and industrial labor markets provides a more meaningful basis for analyzing labor market power. The tremendous size of the national labor market, with more than 150 million workers, precludes anyone from acquiring control of the entire market. The largest employer in the United States (Walmart) employs less than 1 percent of the labor force. General Motors employs far fewer than that, and the top 500 industrial corporations employ less than 20 percent of all workers. The situation on the supply side is similar. The largest labor unions (National Education Association and the Service Employees International Union) each represents just 1.2 percent of all workers in the country. All unions together represent less than one out of every nine U.S. workers. This doesn't mean that particular employers or unions have no influence on our economic welfare. It does suggest, however, that **market power** *in labor markets is likely to be more effective in specific areas, occupations, and industries.*

market power: The ability to alter the market price of a good or service.

LABOR UNIONS

The immediate objective of labor unions is to alter the equilibrium wage and employment conditions in specific labor markets. ***To be successful, unions must be able to exert control over the market supply curve.***

Types of Unions

That's why workers have organized themselves along either industry or occupational craft lines. *Industrial unions* include workers in a particular industry (the United Auto Workers, for example). *Craft unions* represent workers with a particular skill (like the International Brotherhood of Electrical Workers), regardless of the industry in which they work.

The purpose of both types of labor unions is to coordinate the actions of thousands of individual workers, thereby achieving control of market supply. If a union is able to control the supply of workers in a particular industry or occupation, the union acquires a *monopoly* in that market. Like most monopolies, unions attempt to use their market power to increase their incomes.

Union Objectives

A primary objective of unions is to raise the wages of union members. In the 2012 dispute between pro hockey team owners and players, money was the sole issue. The players, who were already getting an average paycheck of $2.4 million per season, were resisting a salary cap that would restrain wages. The team owners wanted to limit total player salaries to 53–55 percent of league revenues, rather than the existing 57 percent.

An exclusive focus on wages is somewhat unusual. Union objectives also include improved working conditions, job security, and other nonwage forms of compensation, such as retirement (pension) benefits, vacation time, and health insurance. The Players Association and the National Football League have bargained about the use of artificial turf, early retirement, player fines, television revenues, game rules, the use of team doctors, drug tests, pensions, and the number of players permitted on a team. A recurring concern of the United Auto Workers is job security. Consequently, they focus on work rules that may eliminate jobs and unemployment benefits for laid-off workers.

Although union objectives tend to be as broad as the concerns of union members, we focus here on just one objective: wage rates. This isn't too great a simplification because most nonwage issues can be translated into their effective impact on wage rates. In 2016, for example, the National Basketball Association and the players' union agreed to more than a dozen different job provisions ranging from the length of time a player had to stay on the disabled list to the location of games (see In the News "NBA and Players Strike a Deal"). It was possible, however, to figure out the cost of these many provisions ($1.5 million per worker per year). Hence the "bottom line" of the compensation package could be expressed in terms of wage costs.

What we seek to determine is whether and how unions can raise effective wage rates in a specific labor market by altering the competitive equilibrium depicted in Figure 31.1. What is the source of union power and how do unions use it?

NBA AND PLAYERS STRIKE A DEAL

The games will go on. The National Basketball Association and the players' union averted a lockout by finalizing the terms of a new contract early Thursday morning. With overflowing revenues of $10 billion per year to divvy up, neither side wanted to disrupt the season schedule. The new contract will last for five years, from 2017 to 2021. Here's what the two sides got:

The players agreed

- To take a smaller share (51 percent down from 57 percent) of total basketball income, including lucrative TV deals.
- To let the league schedule games outside the United States, provided players get compensated as much as $100,000 per game for travel and inconvenience.

The owners agreed

- To increase the minimum salary from $507,500 to $555,000 by 2019, with cost of living adjustments thereafter.
- To reduce the number of exhibition games.
- To shorten the minimum time on the disabled list from 15 days to 10 days.
- To start the season a week earlier so players can get 4 more days of rest.
- To reduce the number of back-to-back games (consecutive days).
- To shorten the length of contracts so players become free agents more often.
- To raise the payroll limit on individual teams.
- To maintain the existing limits on roster size (40 players).

Despite the reduced revenue share, the players will see fatter paychecks: the average salary is projected to increase from $8.5 million in 2016 to $10 million in the 2020–2021 season.

Source: Media reports of November-December 2016.

ANALYSIS: Labor unions bargain with management over a variety of employment conditions. Most issues, however, can be expressed in terms of their impact on wage costs.

THE POTENTIAL USE OF POWER

In a competitive labor market, each worker makes a labor supply decision on the basis of his or her own perceptions of the relative values of labor and leisure (Chapter 30). Whatever decision is made won't alter the market wage. One worker simply isn't that significant in a market composed of thousands. Once a market is unionized, however, these conditions no longer hold. *A union evaluates job offers on the basis of the collective interests of its members.* In particular, it must be concerned with the effects of increased employment on the wage rate paid to its members.

The Marginal Wage

Like all monopolists, unions have to worry about the downward slope of the demand curve. In the case of labor markets, a larger quantity of labor can be "sold" only at lower wage rates. Suppose the workers in a particular labor market confront the market labor demand schedule depicted in Figure 31.2. This schedule tells us that employers aren't willing to hire any workers at a wage rate of $6 per hour (row *S*) but will hire one worker per hour if the wage rate is $5 (row *T*). At still lower rates, the quantity of labor demanded increases; five workers per hour are demanded at a wage of $1 per hour.

An individual worker offered a wage of $1 an hour would have to decide whether such wages merited the sacrifice of an hour's leisure. But a union would evaluate the offer differently. A union must consider how the hiring of one more worker will affect the wages of all the workers.

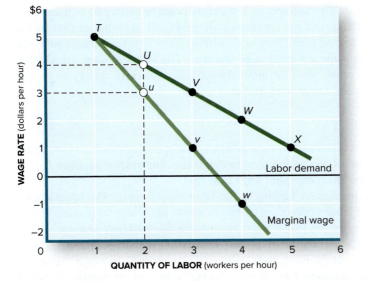

FIGURE 31.2

The Marginal Wage

The *marginal wage* is the change in *total wages* (paid to all workers) associated with the employment of an additional worker. If the wage rate is $4 per hour, only two workers will be hired (point *U*). The wage rate must fall to $3 per hour if three workers are to be hired (point *V*). In the process, *total* wages paid rise from $8 ($4 × 2 workers) to $9 ($3 × 3 workers). The *marginal* wage of the third worker is only $1 (point *v*).

The graph illustrates the relationship of the marginal wage to labor demand. The marginal wage curve lies below the labor demand curve because the marginal wage is less than the nominal wage. Compare the marginal wage (point *v*) and the nominal wage (point *V*) of the third worker.

	Wage Rate (per Hour)	×	Number of Workers Demanded (per Hour)	=	Total Wages Paid (per Hour)	Marginal Wage (per Labor-Hour)
S	$6		0		$0	
T	5		1		5	$5
U	4		2		8	3
V	3		3		9	1
W	2		4		8	−1
X	1		5		5	−3

Total Wages Paid. Notice that when four workers are hired at a wage rate of $2 an hour (row *W*), *total* wages are $8 per hour. In order for a fifth worker to be employed, the wage rate must drop to $1 an hour (row *X*). At wages of $1 per hour, the *total* wages paid to the five workers amount to only $5 per hour. Thus total wages paid to the workers actually *fall* when a fifth worker is employed. Collectively the workers would be better off sending only four people to work at the higher wage of $2 an hour and paying the fifth worker $1 an hour to stay home!

The basic mandate of a labor union is to evaluate wage and employment offers from this *collective* perspective. To do so, **a union must distinguish the marginal wage from the market wage.** The market wage is simply the current wage rate paid by the employer; it's the wage received by individual workers. The **marginal wage,** on the other hand, is the change in *total* wages paid (to all workers) when an additional worker is hired:

$$\text{Marginal wage} = \frac{\text{Change in total wages paid}}{\text{Change in quantity of labor employed}}$$

The distinction between marginal wages and market wages arises from the downward slope of the labor demand curve. It's analogous to the distinction we made between marginal revenue and price for monopolists in product markets. The distinction simply reflects the law of demand: if more workers are to be hired, wage rates must fall.

The impact of increased employment on marginal wages is also illustrated in Figure 31.2. According to the labor demand curve, one worker will be hired at a wage rate of $5 an hour (point *T*); two workers will be hired only if the market wage falls to $4 an hour

marginal wage: The change in total wages paid associated with a one-unit increase in the quantity of labor employed.

(point *U*), at which point the first and second workers will each be getting $4 an hour. Thus the increased wages of the second worker (from zero to $4) will be partially offset by the reduction in the wage rate paid to the first worker (from $5 to $4). *Total* wages paid will increase by only $3; this is the *marginal* wage (point *u*). The marginal wage actually becomes negative at some point, when the implied wage loss to workers already on the job begins to exceed the wage of a new hired worker.

The Union Wage Goal

A union never wants to accept a negative marginal wage, of course. At such a point, union members would be better off paying someone to stay home. ***The central question for the union is what level of (positive) marginal wage to accept.***

We can answer this question by looking at the labor supply curve. The labor supply curve tells us how much labor workers are *willing to supply* at various wage rates. Hence the labor supply curve depicts the lowest wage *individual* union members would accept. If the union adopts a *collective* perspective on the welfare of its members, however, it will view the wage offer differently. From their collective perspective, the wage that union members are getting for additional labor is the *marginal* wage, not the nominal (market) wage. Hence the marginal wage curve, not the labor demand curve, is decisive in the union's assessment of wage offers.

If the union wants to maximize the *total* welfare of its members, it will seek the level of employment that equates the marginal wage with the supply preferences of union members. In Figure 31.3, ***the intersection of the marginal wage curve with the labor supply curve identifies the desired level of employment for the union.*** This intersection occurs at point *u*, yielding total employment of two workers per hour.

The marginal wage at point *u* is $3. However, the union members will get paid an actual wage higher than that. Look up from point *u* on the marginal wage curve to point *U* on the employer's labor demand curve. Point *U* tells us that the employer is *willing to pay* a wage rate of $4 an hour to employ two workers. The union knows it can demand and get $4 an hour if it supplies only two workers to the firm.

What the union is doing here is choosing a point on the labor demand curve that the union regards as the optimal combination of wages and employment. In a competitive market, point *C* would represent the equilibrium combination of wages and employment. But the union forces employers to point *U*, thereby attaining a higher wage rate and reducing employment.

FIGURE 31.3

The Union Wage Objective

The intersection of the marginal wage and labor supply curves (point *u*) determines the union's desired employment. Employers are willing to pay a wage rate of $4 per hour for that many workers, as revealed by point *U* on the labor demand curve.

More workers (*H*) are willing to work at $4 per hour than employers demand (*U*). To maintain that wage rate, the union must exclude some workers from the market. In the absence of such power, wages would fall to the competitive equilibrium (point *C*).

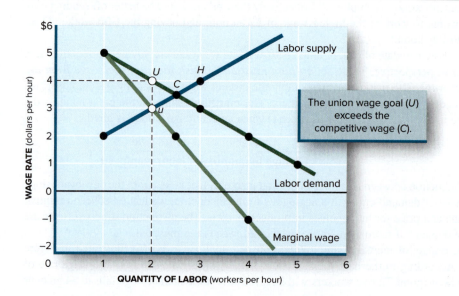

Exclusion

The union's ability to maintain a wage rate of $4 an hour depends on its ability to exclude some workers from the market. Figure 31.3 reveals that three workers are willing and able to work at the union wage of $4 an hour (point *H*), whereas only two are hired (point *U*). If the additional worker were to offer his services, the wage rate would be pushed down the labor demand curve (to $3 per hour). Hence, *to maintain a noncompetitive wage, the union must be able to exercise some control over the labor supply decisions of individual workers.* The essential force here is union solidarity. Once unionized, the individual workers must agree not to compete among themselves by offering their labor at nonunion wage rates. Instead the workers must agree to withhold labor—to strike, if necessary—if wage rates are too low, and to supply labor only at the union-set wage.

Unions can solidify their control of the labor supply by establishing **union shops:** workplaces where workers must join the union within 30 days after being employed. In this way, the unions gain control of all the workers employed in a particular company or industry, thereby reducing the number of replacement workers available for employment during a strike. Stiff penalties (such as loss of seniority or pension rights) and general union solidarity ensure that only nonunion workers will "fink" or "scab"—take the job of a worker on strike.

union shop: An employment setting in which all workers must join the union within 30 days after being employed.

Replacement Workers. Even union shops, however, are subject to potential competition from substitute labor. When the UAW struck Caterpillar in 1991, the company advertised nationally for replacement workers and set up a toll-free phone line for applicants. In the midst of a recession, the company got a huge response. The resulting flow of replacement workers crippled the UAW strike. Professional baseball players faced the same problem in 1995. When the continued strike threatened a second consecutive season, the team owners started hiring new players to replace the regulars. The huge supply of aspiring ball players forced the strikers to reconsider.

Replacement workers are even more abundant in agriculture. The United Farm Workers has been trying for decades to organize California's 20,000 strawberry pickers. But the workers know that thousands of additional workers will flock to California from Mexico if they protest wages and working conditions.

THE EXTENT OF UNION POWER

The first labor unions in America were organized in the 1780s, and the first worker protests as early as 1636. Union power wasn't a significant force in labor markets, however, until the 1900s, when heavily populated commercial centers and large-scale manufacturing became common. Only then did large numbers of workers begin to view their employment situations from a common perspective.

Early Growth

The period 1916–1920 was one of particularly fast growth for labor unions, largely because of the high demand for labor resulting from World War I. All these membership gains were lost, however, when the Great Depression threw millions of people out of work. By 1933 union membership had dwindled to the levels of 1915.

As the Depression lingered on, public attitudes and government policy changed. Too many people had learned the meaning of layoffs, wage cuts, and prolonged unemployment. In 1933 the National Industrial Recovery Act (NIRA) established the right of employees to bargain collectively with their employers. When the NIRA was declared unconstitutional by the Supreme Court in 1935, its labor provisions were incorporated into a new law, the Wagner Act. With this legislative encouragement, union membership doubled between 1933 and 1937. Unions continued to gain in strength as the production needs of World War II increased the demand for labor. Figure 31.4 reflects the tremendous spurt of union activity between the depths of the Depression and the height of World War II.

FIGURE 31.4

Changing Unionization Rates

Unions grew most rapidly during the decade 1935–1945. Since that time, the growth of unions hasn't kept pace with the growth of the U.S. labor force. Most employment growth has occurred in service industries that have traditionally been nonunion.

Source: U.S. Department of Labor.

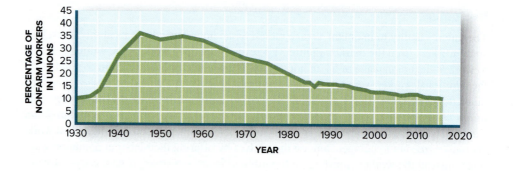

unionization rate: The percentage of the labor force belonging to a union.

Union Power Today

Union membership stopped increasing in the 1950s, even though the labor force kept growing. As a result, the unionized percentage of the labor force—the **unionization rate**—has been in steady decline for more than 40 years. The current unionization rate of 10.7 percent is less than a third of its post–World War II peak and far below unionization rates in other industrialized nations (see World View "Union Membership").

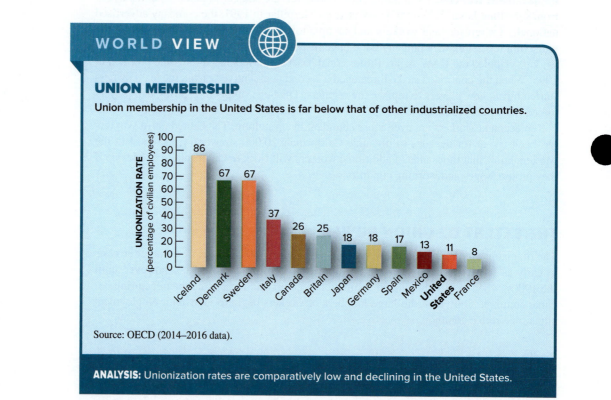

WORLD VIEW

UNION MEMBERSHIP

Union membership in the United States is far below that of other industrialized countries.

Source: OECD (2014–2016 data).

ANALYSIS: Unionization rates are comparatively low and declining in the United States.

Private vs. Public Sector Trends. The decline in the *national* unionization rate conceals two very different trends. Union representation of *private* sector workers has plunged even more sharply than Figure 31.4 suggests. In the last 10 years, the unionization rate in the private sector has fallen from 11.5 percent to only 6.4 percent. At the same time, union membership has increased sharply among teachers, government workers, and nonprofit employees. As of 2017, more than 35 percent of workers on government payrolls were union members. This concentration of unions in the public sector is evident in Figure 31.5. The trend is clear: *the old industrial unions are being supplanted by unions of service workers, especially those employed in the public sector.* Unionization is highest among public schoolteachers, including college professors.

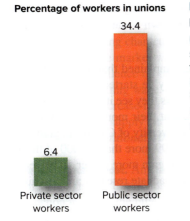

Percentage of workers in unions

Private sector workers: 6.4
Public sector workers: 34.4

FIGURE 31.5

Private vs. Public Unions

Unionization rates have declined sharply in private industry but risen in the public sector. Public sector union membership now exceeds private sector union membership.

Source: U.S. Bureau of Labor Statistics (2016 data).

Although industrial unions have been in general decline, they still possess significant pockets of market power. The Teamsters, the UAW, the United Mine Workers, the Union of Needletrades and Textile Employees, and the Food Workers all have substantial representation in their respective markets. Their strength in those specific markets, not national averages, determines their ability to alter market outcomes.

The AFL-CIO. One labor organization with a decidedly national focus is the AFL-CIO (the American Federation of Labor–Congress of Industrial Organizations). The AFL-CIO is not a separate union but a representational body of more than 50 national unions, representing 12 million workers. It doesn't represent or negotiate for any particular group of workers but focuses instead on issues of general labor interest. The AFL-CIO acts as an advocate for the labor movement and represents labor's interest in legislative areas. It's the primary vehicle for political action. In addition, the AFL-CIO may render economic assistance to member unions or to groups of workers who wish to organize.

Change to Win Coalition. The AFL-CIO's political activity upset member unions who favored more focus on traditional union interests, particularly union organizing. In September 2005 some of these unions (including teamsters, garment workers, food workers, service workers) quit the AFL-CIO and formed a new multiunion organization, the Change to Win Coalition. By 2017 the coalition included three of the largest unions, representing more than 5 million workers.

EMPLOYER POWER

The power possessed by labor unions in various occupations and industries seldom exists in a power vacuum. Power exists on the demand side of labor markets, too. The United Auto Workers confront GM, Ford, and Chrysler; the Steelworkers confront U.S. Steel and AK Steel; the Teamsters confront the Truckers' Association; the Communications Workers confront AT&T; and so on. An imbalance of power often exists on one side of the market or the other (as with, say, the Carpenters versus individual construction contractors). However, *labor markets with significant power on both sides are common.* To understand how wage rates and employment are determined in such markets, we have to assess the market power possessed by employers.

Monopsony

Power on the demand side of a market belongs to a *buyer* who can influence the market price of a good. With respect to labor markets, market power on the demand side implies the ability of a single employer to alter the market wage rate. The extreme case of such

wages also rise when the wage rate is increased to attract additional workers. If all the workers perform the same job, the first worker will demand to be paid the new (higher) wage rate. Thus *the marginal factor cost exceeds the wage rate because additional workers can be hired only if the wage rate for all workers is increased.*

The Monopsony Firm's Goal. The marginal factor cost curve confronting this monopsonist is shown in the upper half of Figure 31.6. It starts at the bottom of the labor supply curve and rises above it. The monopsonist must now decide how many workers to hire, given the impact of its hiring decision on the market wage rate.

Remember from Chapter 30 that the labor demand curve is a reflection of labor's **marginal revenue product (MRP)**—that is, the increase in total revenue attributable to the employment of one additional worker.

> **marginal revenue product (MRP):** The change in total revenue associated with one additional unit of input.

As we've emphasized, the profit-maximizing producer always seeks to equalize marginal revenue and marginal cost. Accordingly, the monopsonistic employer will seek to hire the amount of labor at which the marginal revenue product of labor equals its marginal factor cost:

$$\begin{array}{c} \text{Profit-maximizing} \\ \text{level of input use} \end{array} : \begin{array}{c} \text{Marginal revenue} \\ \text{product of input} \\ \text{(MRP)} \end{array} = \begin{array}{c} \text{Marginal factor} \\ \text{cost of input} \\ \text{(MFC)} \end{array}$$

In Figure 31.6, this objective is illustrated by the intersection of the marginal factor cost and labor demand curves at point *U*.

At point *U* the monopsonist is *willing to hire* two workers per hour at a wage rate of $4. But the firm doesn't have to pay this much. The labor supply curve informs us that two workers are *willing to work* for only $3 an hour. Hence the firm first decides how many workers it wants to hire (at point *U*) and then looks at the labor supply curve (point *G*) to see what it has to pay them. As we suspected, *a monopsonistic employer ends up hiring fewer workers at a lower wage rate than would prevail in a competitive market* (point *C*).

COLLECTIVE BARGAINING

The potential for conflict between a powerful employer and a labor union should be evident:

- *The objective of a labor union is to establish a wage rate that's* **higher** *than the competitive wage* (Figure 31.3).
- *A monopsonist employer seeks to establish a wage rate that's* **lower** *than competitive standards* (Figure 31.6).

The resultant clash generates intense bargaining that often spills over into politics, the courts, and open conflict.

The confrontation of power on both sides of the labor market is a situation referred to as **bilateral monopoly.** In such a market, wages and employment aren't determined simply by supply and demand. Rather, economic outcomes must be determined by **collective bargaining**—that is, direct negotiations between employers and labor unions for the purpose of determining wages, employment, working conditions, and related issues.

> **bilateral monopoly:** A market with only one buyer (a monopsonist) and one seller (a monopolist).

Possible Agreements

> **collective bargaining:** Direct negotiations between employers and unions to determine labor market outcomes.

In a typical labor–business confrontation, the two sides begin by stating their preferences for equilibrium wages and employment. The *demands* laid down by the union are likely to revolve around point *U* in Figure 31.7; the *offer* enunciated by management is likely to be at point *G*.[1] Thus the boundaries of a potential settlement—a negotiated final equilibrium—are

---

[1]Even though points *U* and *G* may not be identical to the initial bargaining positions, they represent the positions of maximum attainable benefit for both sides. Points outside the demand or supply curve will be rejected out of hand by one side or the other.

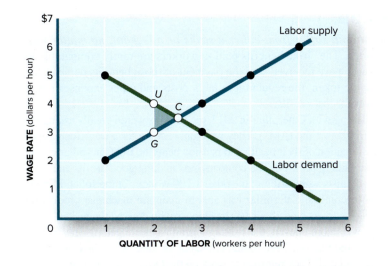

FIGURE 31.7
The Boundaries of Collective Bargaining

Firms with power in the labor market seek to establish wages and employment levels corresponding to point *G* (from Figure 31.6). Unions, on the other hand, seek to establish an equilibrium at point *U* (from Figure 31.3). The competitive equilibrium is at point *C*. The function of collective bargaining is to identify a compromise between these points—that is, to locate an equilibrium somewhere in the shaded area.

usually established at the outset of collective bargaining. In the News "Caterpillar vs. the IAM" summarizes the points of contention in the 2012 dispute between Caterpillar and the International Association of Machinists.

IN THE NEWS

CATERPILLAR VS. THE IAM
What Separates the Two Sides

	Company Proposal	Union Proposal
Wages	6-year wage freeze for 'old' employees Market-based wages for newly hired workers	Pay hike of 1.5% per year all employees
Benefits	Cut company share of health insurance premiums form 90% to 80%	Keep employee share of insurance premiums at 10%
Job security	Curtail seniority rights of individual workers	Keep seniority rights

Source: Media reports, March-April 2012.

ANALYSIS: Collective bargaining begins with a set of union demands and management offers. The outcome depends on the relative strength and tactics of the two parties.

The interesting part of collective bargaining isn't the initial bargaining positions but the negotiation of the final settlement. The speed with which a settlement is reached and the terms of the resulting compromise depend on the patience, tactics, and resources of the negotiating parties. *The fundamental source of negotiating power for either side is its ability to withhold labor or jobs.* The union can threaten to strike, thereby cutting off the flow of union labor to the employer. The employer can impose a lockout, thereby cutting off jobs and paychecks. The effectiveness of those threats depends on the availability of substitute workers or jobs.

The Pressure to Settle

Labor and management both suffer from either a strike or a lockout, no matter who initiates the work stoppage. The strike benefits paid to workers are rarely comparable to wages they would otherwise have received, and the payment of those benefits depletes the union treasury. By the same token, the reduction in labor costs and other expenses rarely compensates the employer for lost profits.

In the machinists' bargaining with Caterpillar in 2012, the workers weren't really asking for much (In the News "Caterpillar vs. the IAM"). They were only asking for a wage increase of 1.5 percent a year and the retention of their health and pension benefits. But Caterpillar was in an exceptionally strong bargaining position. The company was making good profits and sales were strong. Only 780 machinists were striking; the other 1,200 workers at the Joliet, Illinois, plant weren't joining the machinists. Caterpillar was able to maintain machinist production with supervisors, temporary workers, and about 100 machinists who crossed the picket line to work. To make the battle even more uneven, the striking machinists were getting only $150 a week in strike benefits from their union. They couldn't hold out for long. After three and a half months, the machinists capitulated. They returned to work on the terms Caterpillar set.

Collective bargaining isn't always so favorable to the employer. In 1998 the balance of power was reversed. Car sales were brisk, and inventories were lean. So when the UAW struck a key parts plant in June 1998, GM was under greater pressure to settle. Rather than continuing to lose more than $100 million a day in lost sales, GM relented after 54 days, accepting little more than a UAW promise not to strike again for a year and a half.

Collective bargaining isn't always so lopsided. In 2016 pro basketball teams were enjoying huge and growing revenues. Both the owners and the players recognized that a strike would be foolish. So they were very willing to make a deal that made both sides richer (In the News "NBA and Players Strike a Deal").

Hockey players weren't so fortunate. Bargaining between the players and the National Hockey League stalled completely in 2012. The owners expressed their frustration by cancelling the first three months of the 2012–2013 hockey season. That lockout cost the players $1 *billion* in lost pay and the team owners more than $200 million. Walmart used an extreme version of the lockout tactic to fend off union power: it simply shuttered its Canadian store and eliminated all the jobs (see World View "Walmart Shutters Quebec Store as Union Closes In").

WORLD VIEW

WALMART SHUTTERS QUEBEC STORE AS UNION CLOSES IN

Walmart decided to close its store in Jonquiere, Quebec, rather than give in to union demands. A majority of the store's 145 hourly employees had signed union cards, forcing Walmart to enter into negotiations with the United Food and Commercial Workers (UFCW) union. That was a turn of events Walmart was not prepared to accept. In preliminary negotiations, the union demanded better pay and new work rules. Walmart said the union's demands would force it to hire 30 more workers, which wasn't economically feasible. So Walmart, with a history of fending off unions, decided to close the Jonquiere store. Had the UFCW succeeded in unionizing that store, it would have been the first unionized Walmart in North America.

Walmart CEO H. Lee Scott Jr. defended his decision, saying, "You can't take a store that is a struggling store anyway and add a bunch of people and a bunch of work rules that cause you to even be in worse shape." The Canadian director of UFCW responded that, "Walmart is trying to send a message to the rest of their employees that if they join a union the same thing could happen to them . . ."

Source: News reports, February 9–12, 2005.

ANALYSIS: The power to lock out workers is the ultimate source of employer power in collective bargaining. Walmart chose an extreme use of that power.

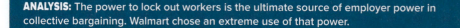

Sometimes, third parties are critical to pushing for a settlement. In October 2016 the professors at 14 Pennsylvania colleges went on strike. They had been working for more than a year without a contract and wanted the state to come to terms. The state demanded 249 changes in the work rules and pay of the professors. But the faculty resisted the changes and wanted higher wages. On October 14, 2016, they went on strike, cancelling classes for more than 100,000 students. The families of the students besieged the governor, who in turn pushed for a settlement. After a three-day strike, the professors and the state settled their differences.

Because potential income losses are usually high, both labor and management try to avoid a strike or lockout if they can. In fact, *more than 90 percent of the 20,000 collective bargaining agreements negotiated each year are concluded without recourse to a strike* and often without even the explicit threat of one.

The Final Settlement

The built-in pressures for settlement help resolve collective bargaining. They don't tell us, however, what the dimensions of that final settlement will be. All we know is that the settlement will be located within the boundaries established in Figure 31.7. The relative pressures on each side will determine whether the final equilibrium is closer to the union or the management position.

The final settlement almost always necessitates hard choices on both sides. The union usually has to choose between an increase in job security and higher pay. A union must also consider how management will react in the long run to higher wages, perhaps by introducing new technology that reduces its dependence on labor. The employer has to worry whether productivity will suffer if workers are dissatisfied with their pay package.

....

THE IMPACT OF UNIONS

We know that unions tend to raise wage rates in individual companies, industries, and occupations. But can we be equally sure that unions have raised wages in general? If the UAW is successful in raising wages in the automobile industry, what, if anything, happens to car prices? If car prices rise in step with UAW wage rates, labor and management in the auto industry will get proportionally larger slices of the economic pie. At the same time, workers in other industries will be burdened with higher car prices.

Relative Wages

One measure of union impact is *relative* wages—the wages of union members in comparison with those of nonunion workers. As we've noted, unions seek to control the supply of labor in a particular industry or occupation. This forces the excluded workers to seek work elsewhere. As a result of this labor supply imbalance, wages tend to be higher in unionized industries than in nonunionized industries. Figure 31.8 illustrates this displacement effect.

Although the theoretical impact of union exclusionism on relative wages is clear, empirical estimates of that impact are fairly rare. We do know that union wages in general are significantly higher than nonunion wages ($1,004 versus $802 per week in 2017). But part of this differential is due to the fact that unions are more common in industries that have always been more capital-intensive and paid relatively high wages. When comparisons are made within particular industries or sectors, the differential narrows considerably. Nevertheless, there's a general consensus that unions have managed to increase their relative wages by 15 to 20 percent.

Labor's Share of Total Income

Even though unions have been successful in redistributing some income from nonunion to union workers, the question still remains whether they've increased labor's share of *total* income. The *labor share* of total income is the proportion of income received by all

(a) Unionized labor market

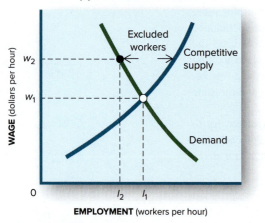

(b) Nonunionized labor market

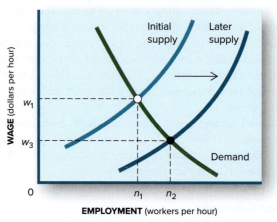

FIGURE 31.8

The Effect of Unions on Relative Wages

In the absence of unions, the average wage rate would be equal to w_1. As unions take control of the market, however, they seek to raise wage rates to w_2, in the process reducing the amount of employment in that market from l_1 to l_2. The workers displaced from the unionized market will seek work in the nonunionized market, thereby shifting the nonunion supply curve to the right. The result will be a reduction of wage rates (to w_3) in the nonunionized market. Thus union wages end up higher than nonunion wages.

workers, in contrast to the share of income received by owners of capital (the *capital share*). The labor share of total income will rise only if the gains to union workers exceed the losses to the (excluded) nonunion workers.

Evidence of unions' impact on labor's share is almost as difficult to assemble as evidence on relative wages, and for much the same reasons. Labor's share of national income has risen dramatically, from only 56 percent in 1919 to 75 percent today. But there have been tremendous changes in the mix of output during that same period. The proportion of output composed of personal services (accountants, teachers, electricians) is much larger now than it was in 1919. The labor share of income derived from personal services is and always was close to 100 percent. Accordingly, *most of the rise in labor's share of total income is due to changes in the structure of the economy rather than to unionization.*

Prices

One way firms can protect their profits in the face of rising union wages is to raise product prices. If firms raise prices along with union wages, consumers end up footing the bill. In that case, profits and the capital share of total income might not be reduced.

The ability of firms to pass along increased union wages depends on the structure of product markets as well as labor markets. If a firm has power in both markets, it's better able to protect itself in this way. There's little evidence, however, that unions have contributed significantly to general cost-push inflation.

Productivity

productivity: Output per unit of input—for example, output per labor-hour.

Unions also affect prices indirectly via changes in **productivity.** Unions bargain not only for wages but also for work rules that specify how goods should be produced. Work rules may limit the pace of production, restrict the type of jobs a particular individual can perform, or require a minimum number of workers to accomplish a certain task. A factory carpenter, for example, may not be permitted to change a lightbulb that burns out in his shop area. And the electrician who is summoned may be required to have an apprentice on all work assignments. Such restrictive work rules would make it very costly to change a burned-out lightbulb.

Not all work rules are so restrictive. In general, however, work rules are designed to protect jobs and maximize the level of employment at any given rate of output. From this perspective, work rules directly restrain productivity and thus inflate costs and prices.

Work rules may also have some beneficial effects. The added job security provided by work rules and seniority provisions tends to reduce labor turnover (quitting) and thus saves recruitment and training costs. Protective rules may also make workers more willing to learn new tasks and to train others in specific skills. Richard Freeman of Harvard asserts that unions have actually accelerated advances in productivity and economic growth.

Political Impact

Perhaps more important than any of these specific union effects is the general impact the union movement has had on our economic, social, and political institutions. Unions are a major political force in the United States. They've not only provided critical electoral and financial support for selected political candidates, but they've also fought hard for important legislation. Unions have succeeded in establishing minimum wage laws, work and safety rules, and retirement benefits. They've also actively lobbied for civil rights legislation and health and education programs. Whatever one may think of any particular union or specific union action, it's clear that our institutions and national welfare would be very different in their absence.

THE ECONOMY TOMORROW

MERGING TO SURVIVE

Unions have been in retreat for nearly a generation. As shown in Figure 31.4, the unionized share of the labor force has fallen from 35 percent in 1950 to less than 11 percent today. Even that modest share has been maintained only by the spread of unionism among public schoolteachers and other government employees. In the private sector, the unionization rate is less than 7 percent and still declining. The Teamsters, the Auto Workers, and the Steelworkers have lost more than 1 million members in the last 15 years.

The decline in unionization is explained by three phenomena. Most important is the relative decline in manufacturing, coupled with rapid growth in high-tech service industries (like computer software, accounting, and medical technology). The second force is the downsizing of major corporations and the relatively faster growth of smaller companies. These structural changes have combined to shrink the traditional employment base of labor unions.

The third cause of shrinking unionization is increased global competition. The decline of worldwide trade and investment barriers has made it easier for firms to import products from low-wage nations and even to relocate production plants. With more options, firms can more easily resist increased wage demands.

The labor union movement is fully aware of these forces and determined to resist them. To increase their power, unions are merging across craft and industry lines. In 1995 the Rubber Workers merged with the Steelworkers, the two major textile unions combined forces, and the Food Workers and Retail Clerks formed a new union. In 1999 the Grain Millers merged with the Paperworkers Union. By merging, the unions hope to increase representation, gain financial strength, and enhance their political clout. They're also seeking to broaden their appeal by organizing low-wage workers in the service industries. These efforts, together with their political strength, will help unions to play a continuing role in the economy tomorrow, even if their share of total employment continues to shrink.

SUMMARY

- Power in labor markets is the ability to alter market wage rates. Such power is most evident in local labor markets defined by geographical, occupational, or industrial boundaries. **LO31-1**
- Power on the supply side of labor markets is manifested by unions, organized along industry or craft lines. The basic function of a union is to evaluate employment offers in terms of the *collective* interest of its members. **LO31-1**
- The downward slope of the labor demand curve creates a distinction between the marginal wage and the market wage. The marginal wage is the change in *total* wages occasioned by employment of one additional worker and is less than the market wage. **LO31-1**
- Unions seek to establish that rate of employment at which the marginal wage curve intersects the labor supply curve. The desired union wage is then found on the labor demand curve at that level of employment. **LO31-1**
- Power on the demand side of labor markets is manifested in buyer concentrations such as monopsony and oligopsony. Such power is usually found among the same firms that exercise market power in product markets. **LO31-2**

- By definition, power on the demand side implies some direct influence on market wage rates; additional hiring by a monopsonist will force up the market wage rate. Hence a monopsonist must recognize a distinction between the marginal factor cost of labor and its (lower) market wage rate. **LO31-2**
- The goal of a monopsonistic employer is to hire the number of workers at which the marginal factor cost of labor equals its marginal revenue product. The employer then looks at the labor supply curve to determine the wage rate that must be paid for that number of workers. **LO31-2**
- The desire of unions to establish a wage rate that's higher than competitive wages directly opposes the desire of powerful employers to establish lower wage rates. In bilateral monopolies unions and employers engage in collective bargaining to negotiate a final settlement. **LO31-2**
- The impact of unions on the economy is difficult to measure. It appears, however, that they've increased their own relative wages and contributed to rising prices. They've also had substantial political impact. **LO31-3**

Key Terms

labor supply	union shop	bilateral monopoly
demand for labor	unionization rate	collective bargaining
equilibrium wage	monopsony	productivity
market power	marginal factor cost (MFC)	
marginal wage	marginal revenue product (MRP)	

Questions for Discussion

1. Collective bargaining sessions often start with unreasonable demands and categorical rejections. Why do unions and employers tend to begin bargaining from extreme positions? **LO31-2**
2. Does a strike for a raise of 5 cents an hour make any sense? What kinds of long-term benefits might a union gain from such a strike? **LO31-1**
3. Why do some college professors join a union? What are the advantages or disadvantages of campus unionization? **LO31-1**
4. Are large and powerful firms easier targets for union organization than small firms? Why or why not? **LO31-1**
5. Nonunionized firms tend to offer wage rates that are close to rates paid by unionized firms in the same industry. How do you explain this? **LO31-3**
6. Why are farmworkers much less successful than airplane machinists in securing higher wages? **LO31-2**

7. In 1998 teaching assistants at the University of California struck for higher wages and union recognition, something they had sought for 14 years. How might the availability of replacement workers have affected their power? **LO31-2**
8. Why did the NBA players avert a strike (In the News "NBA and Players Strike a Deal" and Collective Bargaining text) ? **LO31-2**
9. Why did Walmart choose to close its store rather than hire 30 more workers (World View "Walmart Shutters Quebec Store as Union Closes In")? **LO31-2**
10. Why do pro basketball players want team owners to limit roster size to 40 players (In the News "NBA and Players Strike a Deal")? Why would owners like larger rosters? **LO31-1**

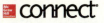

PROBLEMS FOR CHAPTER 31

LO31-1 1. Complete the following table:

Wage rate	$14	$13	$12	$11	$10	$9	$8	$7
Quantity of labor demanded	0	5	20	50	75	95	110	120
Marginal wage	—	—	—	—	—	—	—	—

    (*a*) What is the marginal wage when the nominal wage is $11?

    (*b*) At what wage rate does the marginal wage first become negative?

LO31-1 2. Complete the following table:

Wage rate	$6	$7	$8	$9	$10	$11	$12
Quantity of labor supplied	80	120	155	180	200	210	215
Marginal factor cost	—	—	—	—	—	—	—

LO31-2 3. Based on the data in Problems 1 and 2 above,

    (*a*) What is the competitive wage rate?

    (*b*) Approximately what wage will the union seek?

    (*c*) How many workers will the union have to exclude in order to get that wage?

LO31-2 4. At the time of the National Football League strike in 1987, the football owners made available the following data:

	Total Team Revenues and Costs	
Source of Revenue	**Before the Strike**	**During the Strike**
Television	$973,000	$973,000
Stadium gate	526,000	126,000
Luxury box seats	255,000	200,000
Concessions	60,000	12,000
Radio	40,000	40,000
Players' salaries and costs	854,000	230,000
Nonplayer costs (coaches' salaries)	200,000	200,000

    (*a*) Compute total revenues, total expenses, and profits both before and during the strike.

	Before Strike	**During Strike**
Total revenue	_____	_____
Total expense	_____	_____
Total profit	_____	_____

    (*b*) Who was better positioned to endure the strike? NFL owners or the players?

LO31-2 5. Suppose the following supply and demand schedules apply in a particular labor market:

Wage rate (per hour)	$4	$5	$6	$7	$8	$9	$10
Quantity of labor supplied (workers per hour)	2	3	4	5	6	7	8
Quantity of labor demanded (workers per hour)	6	5	4	3	2	1	0

Graph the relevant curves and identify the
(a) Competitive wage rate.
(b) Union wage rate.
(c) Monopsonist's wage rate.

LO31-3 6. The graphs show unionized and nonunionized labor markets.
(a) Identify a likely wage and employment outcome when the market becomes unionized on the unionized labor market graph.
(b) Show the impact of this unionization on the nonunionized labor market.

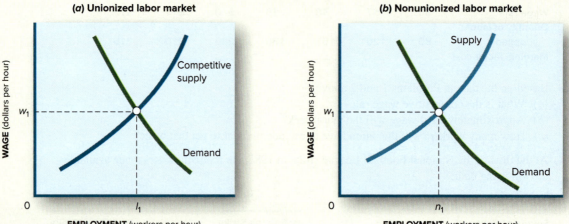

(a) Unionized labor market   **(b) Nonunionized labor market**

LO31-2 7. In the Silicon Valley hiring-conspiracy case (In the News "Judge OKs $415 Million Settlement of 'No Poaching' Charges"), attorneys for the 64,000 plaintiffs asked for $3 billion in damages.
(a) How much did this work out per worker?
(b) How much did the judge approve (per worker)?

LO31-2 8. In the 2012 Machinists'-Caterpillar confrontation, the workers' average pay was $26 per hour. If their demand for a 1.5% pay hike per year had been granted, what would their hourly wage have been
(a) In the following year?
(b) Three years later?
Caterpillar offered the machinists a one-time bonus of $5,000 if they didn't strike. Assuming the machinists worked an average of 2,000 hours per year, was this more or less than the wage demand the union made for
(c) The first year?
(d) The first three years?

LO31-2 9. The Economy Tomorrow: Identify if the following would likely strengthen or weaken a union membership in the United States.
(a) Increase in manufacturing.
(b) Faster growth of small companies.
(c) Increased global competition.

©Steve Allen/Stockbyte/Getty Images RF

CHAPTER 32

Financial Markets

LEARNING OBJECTIVES

After reading this chapter, you should know

LO32-1 How present discounted values are computed.

LO32-2 The difference between stocks and bonds.

LO32-3 Key financial parameters for stocks and bonds.

LO32-4 How risks and rewards are reflected in current values.

Christopher Columbus had a crazy entrepreneurial idea. He was certain he could find a new route to the Indies by sailing not east from Europe but west—around the world. Such a route, he surmised, would give Europe quicker access to the riches of the East Indies. Whoever discovered that western route could become very, very rich.

To find that route, Columbus needed ships, sailors, and tons of provisions. He couldn't afford to supply these resources himself. He needed financial backers who would put up the money. For several years he tried to convince King Ferdinand of Spain to provide the necessary funds. But the king didn't want to risk so much wealth on a single venture. Twice he turned Columbus down.

Fortunately, Genoese merchant bankers in Seville came to Columbus's rescue. Convinced that Columbus's "enterprise of the Indies" might bring back "pearls, precious stones, gold, silver, spiceries," and other valuable merchandise, they guaranteed repayment of any funds lent to Columbus. With that guarantee in hand, the Duke of Medina Sidonia, in April 1492, offered to lend 1,000 maravedis (about $5,000 in today's dollars) to Queen Isabella for the purpose of funding Columbus's expedition. With no personal financial risk, King Ferdinand then granted Columbus the funds and authority for a royal expedition.

Columbus's experience in raising funds for his expedition illustrates a critical function of financial markets—namely, the management of *risk*. This chapter examines how financial markets facilitate economic activities (like Columbus's expedition) by managing the risks of failure. Three central questions guide the discussion:

- **What is traded in financial markets?**
- **How do the financial markets affect the economic outcomes of WHAT, HOW, and FOR WHOM?**
- **Why do financial markets fluctuate so much?**

THE ROLE OF FINANCIAL MARKETS

A central question for every economy is WHAT to produce. In 1492 all available resources were employed in farming, fishing, food distribution, metalworking, and other basic services. For Columbus to pursue his quest, he needed some of those resources. To get them, he needed money to bid scarce resources from other pursuits and employ them on his expedition.

Financial Intermediaries

Entrepreneurs who don't have great personal wealth must get start-up funds from other people. There are two possibilities: either *borrow* the money or invite other people to *invest* in the new venture.

How might you pursue these options? You could ask your relatives for a loan or go door-to-door in your neighborhood seeking investors. But such direct fund-raising is costly, inefficient, and often unproductive. Columbus went hat in hand to the Spanish royal court twice, but each time he came back empty-handed.

The task of raising start-up funds is made much easier by the existence of **financial intermediaries**—institutions that steer the flow of savings to cash-strapped entrepreneurs and other investors. Funds flow into banks, pension funds, bond markets, stock markets, and other financial intermediaries from businesses, households, and government entities that have some unspent income. This pool of national savings is then passed on to entrepreneurs, expanding businesses, and other borrowers by these same institutions (see Figure 32.1).

Financial intermediaries provide several important services. They greatly reduce the cost of locating loanable funds. Their pool of savings offers a clear economy of scale compared to the alternative of door-to-door solicitations. They also reduce the cost to savers of finding suitable lending or investment opportunities. Few individuals have the time, resources, or *interest to do the searching on their own. With huge pools of amassed savings, how*ever, financial intermediaries have the incentive to acquire and analyze information about lending and investment opportunities. Hence *financial intermediaries reduce search and information costs* in the financial markets. In so doing, they make the allocation of resources more efficient.

Crowdfunding. Financial intermediaries come in many shapes and sizes. They are not all banks or brick-and-mortar institutions. The Internet has made door-to-door solicitations a thing of the past. Now people can disseminate their entrepreneurial ideas on a crowdfunding platform like GoFundMe, Kickstarter, or Indiegogo and hope that others like the idea enough to contribute some financing. Although **crowdfunding** has become a popular, inexpensive, and efficient method of raising start-up financing, it accounts for a tiny percentage of the funds raised by more traditional intermediaries (see In the News "Where Do Start-Ups Get Their Money?" later in the chapter).

financial intermediary: Institution (e.g., a bank or the stock market) that makes savings available to dissavers (e.g., investors).

crowdfunding: An internet-based method of raising funds from a large number of people.

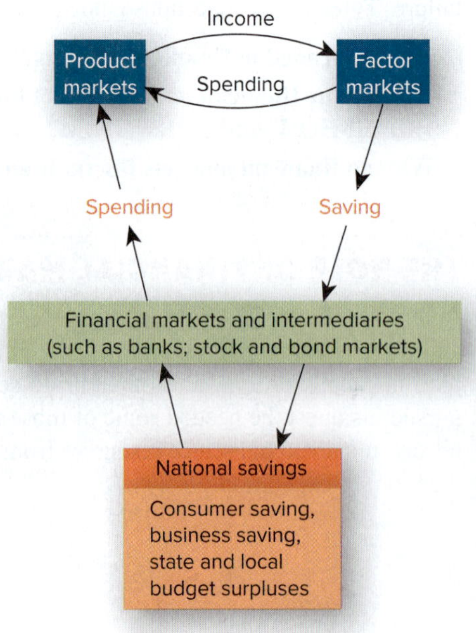

FIGURE 32.1

Mobilizing Savings

The central economic function of financial markets is to channel national savings into new investment and other desired expenditure. Financial intermediaries such as banks, insurance companies, and stockbrokers help transfer purchasing power from savers to spenders.

Although financial intermediaries make the job of acquiring start-up funds a lot easier, there's no guarantee that the funds needed will be acquired. First, there must be an adequate supply of funds available. Second, financial intermediaries must be convinced that they should allocate some of those funds to a project.

The Supply of Loanable Funds

As noted, the supply of loanable funds originates in the decisions of market participants to not spend all their current income. Those saving decisions are influenced by time preferences and interest rates.

Time Preferences. In deciding to *save* rather than *spend,* people effectively reallocate their spending over time. That is, people save *now* in order to spend more *later.* How much to save, then, depends partly on *time preference.* If a person doesn't give any thought to the future, she's likely to save little. If, by contrast, a person wants to buy a car, a vacation, or a house in the future, she's more inclined to save some income now.

Interest Rates. Interest rates also affect saving decisions. If interest rates are high, the future payoff to every dollar saved is greater. A higher return on savings translates into more future income for every dollar of current income saved. Hence **higher interest rates increase the quantity of available savings (loanable funds).**

Risk. In early 2009 banks in Zimbabwe were offering interest rates on savings accounts of more than 100,000 percent a year. Yet few people rushed to deposit their savings in Zimbabwean banks. Inflation was running at a rate of 230 *million* percent a year, making a 100,000 percent return look pitifully small. Further, people worried that political instability in Zimbabwe might cause the banks to fail, wiping out their savings in the process. In other words, there was a high *risk* attached to those phenomenal interest rates.

Anyone who contemplated lending funds to Columbus confronted a similar risk: the potential payoff was huge but so was the risk. That was the dilemma King Ferdinand confronted. He had enough funds to finance Columbus's expedition, but he didn't want to risk losing so much on a single venture.

Risk Management. This is why the Genoese bankers were so critical: these financial intermediaries could spread the risk of failure among many individuals. Each investor could put up just a fraction of the needed funds. No one had to put all his eggs in one basket. Once the consortium of bankers agreed to share the risks of Columbus's expedition, the venture had wings. The Genoese merchant bankers could afford to take portions of the expedition's risks because they also financed many less risky projects. By diversifying their portfolios, they could attain whatever degree of *average* risk they preferred. That is the essence of risk management.

Risk Premiums. Even though diversification permits greater risk management, lenders will want to be compensated for any above-average risks they take. Money lent to local merchants must have seemed a lot less risky than lending funds to Columbus. Thus no one would have stepped forward to finance Columbus unless promised an *above-average* return upon the expedition's success. The difference between the rates of return on a safe (certain) investment and a risky (uncertain) one is called the **risk premium.** Risk premiums compensate people who finance risky ventures that succeed. Because these ventures are risky, however, investors often lose their money in such ventures too.

risk premium: The difference in rates of return on risky (uncertain) and safe (certain) investments.

Risk premiums help explain why blue-chip corporations such as Microsoft can borrow money from a bank at the low "prime" rate while ordinary consumers have to pay much higher interest rates on personal loans. Corporate loans are less risky because corporations typically have plenty of revenue and assets to cover their debts. Consumers often get overextended, however, and can't pay all their bills. As a result, there's a greater risk that consumers' loans won't be paid back. Banks charge higher interest rates on consumer loans to compensate for this risk.

THE PRESENT VALUE OF FUTURE PROFITS

In deciding whether to assume the *risk* of supplying funds to a new venture, financial intermediaries assess the potential *rewards*. In Columbus's case, the rewards were the fabled treasures of the East Indies. Even if he found those treasures, however, the rewards would only come long after the expedition was financed. When Columbus proposed his East Indies expedition, he envisioned a round trip that would last at least six months. If he located the treasures he sought, he planned subsequent trips to acquire and transport his precious cargoes back home. Although King Ferdinand granted Columbus only one-tenth of any profits from the first expedition, Columbus had a claim on one-eighth of the profits of any subsequent voyages. Hence, even if Columbus succeeded in finding a shortcut to the East, he wouldn't generate any substantial profit for perhaps two years or more. That's a long time to wait.

Suppose for the moment that Columbus expected no profit from the first expedition but a profit of $1,000 at the end of two years from a second voyage. How much was that future profit worth to Columbus in 1492?

Time Value of Money

To assess the present value of *future* receipts, we have to consider the *time value* of money. A dollar received today is worth more than a dollar received two years from today. Why? Because a dollar received today can earn *interest*. If you have a dollar today and put it in an interest-bearing account, in two years you'll have your original dollar *plus* accumulated interest. *As long as interest-earning opportunities exist, present dollars are worth more than future dollars.*

In 1492 there were plenty of opportunities to earn interest. Indeed, the Genoese bankers were charging high interest rates on their loans and guarantees. If Columbus had had the cash, he too could have lent money to others and earned interest on his funds.

To calculate the present value of future dollars, this forgone interest must be taken into account. This computation is essentially interest accrual in reverse. *We "discount" future dollars by the opportunity cost of money*—that is, the market rate of interest.

Suppose the market rate of interest in 1492 was 10 percent. To compute the **present discounted value (PDV)** of future payment, we discount as follows:

$$PDV = \frac{\text{Future payment}_N}{(1 + \text{Interest rate})^N}$$

where N refers to the number of years into the future when a payment is to be made. If the future payment is to be made in one year, the N in the equation equals 1, and we have

$$PDV = \frac{\$1,000}{1.10}$$

$$= \$909.09$$

Hence the present discounted value of $1,000 to be paid one year from today is $909.09. If $909.09 were received today, it could earn interest. In a year's time, the $909.09 would grow to $1,000 with interest accrued at the rate of 10 percent per year.

Suppose it would have taken Columbus two years to complete his expeditions and collect his profits, rather than one year. In that case, the present value of the $1,000 payment would be lower. The N in the formula would be 2, and the present value would be

$$PDV = \frac{\$1,000}{(1.10)^2} = \frac{\$1,000}{1.21} = \$826.45$$

Hence *the longer one has to wait for a future payment, the less present value it has.*

Lottery winners often have to choose between present and future values. In July 2004, for example, Geraldine Williams, a 68-year-old housekeeper in Lowell, Massachusetts, won a $294 million MegaMillions lottery. The $294 million was payable in 26 annual

The success of Columbus's voyage was highly uncertain.

Source: Library of Congress Prints and Photographs Division [LC-USZ62-105062].

present discounted value (PDV): The value today of future payments, adjusted for interest accrual.

Years in the Future	Future Payment ($ millions)	Present Value ($ millions)
0	$ 11.3	$ 11.30
1	11.3	10.82
2	11.3	10.35
3	11.3	9.91
4	11.3	9.49
5	11.3	8.04
*	*	*
*	*	*
*	*	*
25	11.3	3.79
	$294.0	$168.0

Note: The general formula for computing present values is $PDV = \sum \dfrac{\text{Payment in year } N}{(1 + r)^N}$, where r is the prevailing rate.

TABLE 32.1

Computing Present Value

The present value of a future payment declines the longer one must wait for a payment. At an interest rate of 4.47 percent, $11.3 million payable in one year is worth only $10.82 million today. A payout of $11.3 million 25 years from now has a present value of only $3.79 million. A string of $11.3 million payments spread out over 25 years has a present value of $168 million (at 4.47 percent interest).

installments of $11.3 million. If the lucky winner wanted to get her prize sooner, she could accept an immediate but smaller payout rather than 25 future installments.

Table 32.1 shows how the lottery officials figured the present value of the $294 million prize. The first installment of $11.3 million would be paid immediately. Mrs. Williams would have had to wait one year for the second check, however. At the then-prevailing interest rate of 4.47 percent, the *present* value of that second $11.3 million check was only $10.82 million. The *last* payoff check had even less present value since it wasn't due to be paid for 25 years. With so much time for interest to accrue, that final $11.3 million payment had a present value of only $3.79 million. The calculations in Table 32.1 convinced lottery officials to offer an immediate (present) payout of only $168 million on the $294 million (future) prize. Mrs. Williams chose to take the immediate present-value sum—and wasn't too disappointed. Marvin and Mae Acosta made the same choice in July 2016, accepting $327.8 million in present value for their $528.8 million share of a $1.6 *billion* Powerball jackpot.

Interest Rate Effects

The winner would have received even *less* money had interest rates been higher. At the time Mrs. Williams won the lottery, the interest rate on bonds was 4.47 percent. Had the interest rate been higher, the discount for immediate payment would have been higher as well. Table 32.2 indicates that Mrs. Williams would have received only $107 million had the prevailing interest rate been 10 percent. What Tables 32.1 and 32.2 illustrate, then, is that *the present discounted value of a future payment declines with*

- *Higher interest rates.*
- *Longer delays in future payment.*

Uncertainty

The valuation of future payments must also consider the possibility of *non*payment. State governments are virtually certain to make promised lottery payouts, so there's little risk in accepting a promised payout of 25 annual installments. But what about the booty from Columbus's expeditions? There was great uncertainty that Columbus would ever return from his expeditions, much less bring back the "pearls, precious stones, gold, silver, and

TABLE 32.2

Higher Interest Rates Reduce Present Values

Higher interest rates reduce the *present* value of future payments. Shown here is the present discounted value of the July 2004 MegaMillions lottery prize of $294 million at different interest rates.

Interest Rate (%)	Present Discounted Value of $294 Million Lottery Prize ($ millions)
5.0%	$166.3
6.0	150.8
7.0	137.5
8.0	126.0
9.0	115.9
10.0	107.1

spiceries" that people coveted. Investing in those expeditions was far riskier than deferring a lottery payment.

Expected Value. Whenever an anticipated future payment is uncertain, a risk factor should be included in present value computations. This is done by calculating the **expected value** of a future payment. Suppose there was only a 50:50 chance that Columbus would bring back the goods. In that event, the expected payoff would be

expected value: The probable value of a future payment, including the risk of nonpayment.

$$\text{Expected value} = (1 - \text{Risk factor}) \times \text{Present discounted value}$$

With a 50:50 chance of failure, the expected value of Columbus's first-year profits would have been

$$\text{Expected value} = (1 - 0.5) \times \$909.09$$
$$= \$454.55$$

Expected values also explain why people buy more lottery tickets when the prize is larger. The odds of winning the multistate Powerball lottery are 80 *million*:1. That's about the same odds as getting struck by lightning *14 times* in the same year! So it makes almost no sense to buy a ticket. With a $16 million prize, the *undiscounted* expected value of a $1 lottery ticket is only 20 cents. When the lottery prize increases, however, the expected value of a ticket grows as well (there are still only 80 million possible combinations of numbers). When the grand prize reached $425 million in February 2014, the undiscounted expected value of a lone winning ticket jumped to more than $5. Millions of people decided that the expected value was high enough to justify buying a $1 lottery ticket. People took off from work, skipped classes, and drove across state lines to queue up for lottery tickets. When the prize is only $10 million, far fewer people buy tickets.

The Demand for Loanable Funds

People rarely borrow money to buy lottery tickets. But entrepreneurs and other market participants often use other people's funds to finance their ventures. *How much loanable funds are demanded depends on*

- *The expected rate of return.*
- *The cost of funds.*

The higher the expected return, or the lower the cost of funds, the greater will be the amount of loanable funds demanded.

Figure 32.2 offers a general view of the loanable funds market that emerges from these considerations. From the entrepreneur's perspective, the prevailing interest rate represents the cost of funds. From the perspective of savers, the interest rate represents the payoff to savings. When interest rates rise, the quantity of funds supplied goes up and the quantity demanded goes down. The prevailing (equilibrium) interest rate is set by the intersection of these supply and demand curves.

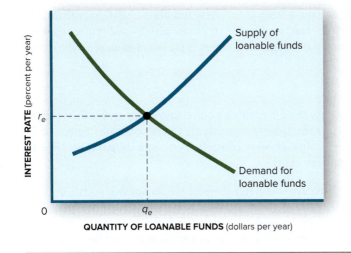

FIGURE 32.2
The Loanable Funds Market

The market rate of interest (r_e) is determined by the intersection of the curves representing supply of and demand for loanable funds. The rate of interest represents the price paid for the use of money.

THE STOCK MARKET

The concept of a loanable funds market sounds a bit alien. But the same principles of supply, demand, and risk management go a long way in explaining the action in stock markets. Suppose you had $1,000 to invest. Should you invest it all in lottery tickets that offer a multimillion-dollar payoff? Put it in a savings account that pays next to nothing? Or how about the stock market? The stock market can reward you handsomely, or it can wipe out your savings if the stocks you own tumble. Hence *stocks offer a higher average return than bank accounts but also entail greater average risk.* People who bought Amazon.com stock in May 1997 got a 1,000 percent profit on their stock in only two years. But people who bought Amazon.com stock in December 1999 lost 90 percent of their investment in even less time.

Corporate Stock

When people buy a share of stock, they're buying partial ownership of a corporation. The three legal forms of business entities are

- Corporations.
- Partnerships.
- Proprietorships.

Limited Liability. Proprietorships are businesses owned by a single individual. The owner–proprietor is entirely responsible for the business, including repayment of any debts. Members of a partnership are typically liable for all business debts and activities as well. By contrast, a **corporation** is a limited liability form of business. The corporation itself, not its individual shareholders, is responsible for all business activity and debts. As a result of this limited liability, you can own a piece of a corporation without worrying about being sued for business mishaps (like environmental damage) or nonpayment of debt. This feature significantly reduces the risk of owning corporate stock.

corporation: A business organization having a continuous existence independent of its members (owners) and power and liabilities distinct from those of its members.

Shared Ownership. The ownership of a corporation is defined in terms of stock shares. Each share of **corporate stock** represents partial ownership of the business. Apple, for example, has 5.2 *billion* shares of stock outstanding (that is, shares held by the public). Hence each share of Apple stock represents less than one-fifth of one-billionth ownership of the corporation. Potentially, this means that as many as 5.2 billion people could own the Apple Corporation. In reality, many individuals own hundreds of shares, and institutions may own thousands. Indeed, some of the largest pension funds in the United States own more than a million shares of Apple.

corporate stock: Shares of ownership in a corporation.

In principle, the owners of corporate stock collectively run the business. In practice, the shareholders select a board of directors to monitor corporate activity and protect their interests. The day-to-day business of running a corporation is the job of managers who report to the board of directors.

Stock Returns

If shareholders don't have any direct role in running a corporation, why would they want to own a piece of it? Essentially, for the same reason that the Genoese bankers agreed to finance Columbus's expedition: profits. *Owners (shareholders) of a corporation hope to share in the profits the corporation earns.*

Dividends. Shareholders rarely receive their full share of the company's profits in cash. Corporations typically use some of the profits for investment in new plants or equipment. They may also want to retain some of the profits for operational needs or unforeseen contingencies. *Corporations may choose to retain earnings or pay them out to shareholders as* **dividends.** Any profits *not* paid to shareholders are referred to as **retained earnings.** Thus

Dividends = Corporate profits − Retained earnings

In 2016 Apple paid quarterly dividends amounting to $2.28 per share for the year. But the company earned profits equal to $8.35 per share. Thus shareholders received only 27 percent of their accrued profits in dividend checks; Apple retained the remaining $6.07 per-share profit earned in 2016 for future investments.

Capital Gains. If Apple invests its retained earnings wisely, the corporation may reap even larger profits in the future. As a company grows and prospers, each share of ownership may become more valuable. This increase in value would be reflected in higher market prices for shares of Apple stock. Any increase in the value of a stock represents a **capital gain** for shareholders. Capital gains directly increase shareholder wealth.

Total Return. People who own stocks can thus get two distinct payoffs: dividends and capital gains. Together these payoffs represent the total return on stock investments. Hence *the higher the expected total return (future dividends and capital gains), the greater the desire to buy and hold stocks.* If a stock paid no dividends and had no prospects for price appreciation (capital gain), you'd probably hold your savings in a different form (such as another stock or maybe an interest-earning bank account).

Initial Public Offering

When a corporation is formed, its future sales and profits are most uncertain. When shares are first offered to the public, the seller of stock is the company itself. By *going public,* the corporation seeks to raise funds for investment and growth. A true *start-up* company may have nothing more than a good idea, a couple of dedicated employees, and big plans. To fund these plans, it sells shares of itself in an **initial public offering (IPO).** People who buy the newly issued stock are putting their savings directly into the corporation's accounts.[1] As new owners, they stand to profit from the corporation's business or take their lumps if the corporation fails.

In 2004 Google was still a relatively new company. Although the company had been in operation since 1999, search engine capacities were limited. To expand, it needed more computers, more employees, and more technology. To finance this expansion, Google needed more money. The company could have borrowed money from a bank or other financial institution, but that would have saddled the company with debt and forced it to make regular interest payments.

---

[1]In reality, some of the initial proceeds will go to stockbrokers and investment bankers as compensation for their services as financial intermediaries. The entrepreneur who starts the company, other company employees, and any venture capitalists who help fund the company before the public offering may also get some of the IPO receipts by selling shares they acquired before the company went public.

---

dividend: Amount of corporate profits paid out for each share of stock.

retained earnings: Amount of corporate profits not paid out in dividends.

capital gain: An increase in the market value of an asset.

initial public offering (IPO): The first issuance (sale) to the general public of stock in a corporation.

Rather than borrow money, Google's directors elected to sell ownership shares in the company. In August 2004 the company raised $1.7 *billion* in cash by selling 19.6 million shares for $85 per share in its initial public offering. Snap Inc., the parent company of the popular Snapchat raised even more at its initial public offering, selling 230 million shares netting the company over $3 *billion* (In the News "Snapchat IPO Nets $3 Billion").

Secondary Trading

Why were people eager to buy shares in Google? They certainly weren't buying the stock with expectations of high dividends. The company hadn't earned much profit in its first five years and didn't expect substantial profits for at least another few years.

P/E Ratio. In 2003 Google had earned only 41 cents of profit per share. In 2004 it would earn $1.46 per share. So people who were buying Google stock for $85 per share in August 2004 were paying a comparatively high price for relatively little profit. This can be seen by computing the **price/earnings (P/E) ratio:**

$$\text{P/E ratio} = \frac{\text{Price of stock share}}{\text{Earnings (profit) per share}}$$

For Google in 2004,

$$\text{P/E ratio} = \frac{\$85}{\$1.46} = 58.2$$

In other words, investors were paying $58.20 for every $1 of profits. That implies a rate of return of 1 ÷ $58.20, or only 1.7 percent. Compared to the interest rates banks were paying on deposit balances, Google shares didn't look like a very good buy.

Profit Expectation. People weren't buying Google stock just to get a piece of *current* profits. What made Google attractive was its *growth* potential. The company projected that revenues and profits would grow rapidly as its search capabilities expanded, more people used its services, and, most important, more advertisers clamored to get premium spots on the company's web pages. Given these expectations, investors projected that Google's profits would jump from $1.46 per share in 2004 to roughly $10 in four years. From that perspective, the *projected* P/E ratio looked cheap.

price/earnings (P/E) ratio: The price of a stock share divided by earnings (profit) per share.

TABLE 32.4

Stock Market Averages

More than 1,600 stocks are listed (traded) on the New York Stock Exchange, and many times that number are traded in other stock markets. To gauge changes in so many stocks, people refer to various indexes, such as the Dow Jones Industrial Average. The Dow and similar indexes help us keep track of the market's ups and downs.

Some of the most frequently quoted indexes are

Dow Jones

Industrial Average: An arithmetic average of the prices of 30 blue-chip industrial stocks traded on the New York Stock Exchange (NYSE) and by computers of the National Association of Securities Dealers (NASD).

Transportation Average: An average of 20 transportation stocks traded on the NYSE.

Utilities Average: An average of 15 utility stocks traded on the NYSE.

S&P 500: An index compiled by Standard and Poor of 500 stocks drawn from major stock exchanges as well as over-the-counter stocks. The S&P 500 is made up of 400 industrial companies, 40 utilities, 20 transportation companies, and 40 financial institutions.

NASDAQ Composite: Index of stocks traded in the over-the-counter market among securities dealers.

New York Stock Exchange composite index: The "Big Board" index, which includes all 1,600-plus stocks traded on the NYSE.

Nikkei index: An index of 225 stocks traded on the Tokyo stock market.

the same factors that determine the price of a single stock influence the broader stock market averages as well (see Table 32.4). An increase in interest rates, for example, raises the opportunity cost of holding stocks. Hence higher interest rates should cause stock prices to fall, *ceteris paribus*. Stocks might decline even further if higher interest rates are expected to curtail investment and consumption, thus reducing future sales and profits. Such a double whammy could cause the whole stock market to tumble.

Other factors also affect the relative desirability of holding stock. Congressional budget and deficit decisions, monetary policy, consumer confidence, business investment plans, international trade patterns, and new inventions are just a few of the factors that may alter present and future profits. These ***broad changes in the economic outlook tend to push all stock prices up or down at the same time.***

Broad changes in the economic outlook, however, seldom occur overnight. Moreover, these changes are rarely of a magnitude that could precipitate a stock market boom or bust. In reality, the stock market often changes more abruptly than the economic outlook. These ***exaggerated movements in the stock market are caused by sudden and widespread changes in expectations.*** Keep in mind that the value of the stock depends on anticipated *future* profits and *expectations* for interest rates and the economic outlook. No elements of the future are certain. Instead people use present clues to try to discern the likely course of future events. In other words, ***all information must be filtered through people's expectations.***

The central role of expectations implies that the economy can change more gradually than the stock market. If, for example, interest rates rise, market participants may regard the increase as temporary or inconsequential: their expectations for the future may not change. If interest rates keep rising, however, investors may have greater doubts. At some point, the market participants may revise their expectations. Stock prices may falter, triggering an adjustment in expectations. A herding instinct may surface, sending expectations for stock prices abruptly lower.

Resource Allocations

Although it's fascinating and sometimes fun to watch stock market gyrations, we shouldn't lose sight of the *economic* role of financial markets. Columbus needed *real* resources—ships, men, equipment—for his expeditions. Five centuries later, Google also needed real resources—computers, labor, technology—to expand. To find the necessary economic resources, both Columbus and Google had to convince society to reallocate resources from other activities to their new ventures.

Financial markets facilitate resource reallocations. In Columbus's case, the Genoese bankers lent the funds that Columbus used to buy scarce resources. The funds obtained from Google's 2004 initial public offering served the same purpose. In both cases, the funds obtained in the financial markets helped change the mix of output. If the financial markets hadn't supplied the necessary funding, neither Columbus nor Google would have been able to go forth. The available resources would have been used to produce other goods.

THE BOND MARKET

The bond market is another financial mechanism for transferring the pool of national savings into the hands of would-be spenders. It operates much like the stock market. The major difference is the kind of paper traded. *In the stock market, people buy and sell shares of corporate ownership. In the bond market, people buy and sell promissory notes (IOUs).* A **bond** is simply an IOU, a written promise to repay a loan. The bond itself specifies the terms of repayment, noting both the amount of interest to be paid each year and the maturity date (the date on which the borrower is to repay the entire debt). The borrower may be a corporation (corporate bonds), a local government (municipal bonds), the federal government (Treasury bonds), or some other institution.

bond: A certificate acknowledging a debt and the amount of interest to be paid each year until repayment; an IOU.

Bond Issuance

A bond is first issued when an institution wants to borrow money. Recall the situation Google faced in 2004. The company needed additional funds to expand its Internet operations. Rather than sell equity shares in itself, Google could have *borrowed* funds. The advantage of borrowing funds rather than issuing stock is that the owners can keep control of their company. *Lenders aren't owners, but shareholders are.* The disadvantage of borrowing funds is that the company gets saddled with a repayment schedule. Lenders want to be paid back—with interest. For a new company like Google, the burden of interest payments may be too great.

Ignoring these problems momentarily, let's assume that Google decided in 2004 to borrow funds rather than sell stock in itself. To do so, it would have *issued* bonds. This simply means that it would have printed formal IOUs called bonds. Typically, each bond certificate would have a **par value** (face value) of $1,000. The bond certificate would also specify the rate of interest to be paid and the promised date of repayment. A Google bond issued in 2004, for example, might specify repayment in 10 years, with annual interest payments of $100. The individual who bought the bond from Google would lend $1,000 for 10 years and receive annual interest payments of $100. Thus *the initial bond purchaser lends funds directly to the bond issuer.* The borrower (such as Google, General Motors, or the U.S. Treasury) can then use those funds to acquire real resources. Thus *the bond market also functions as a financial intermediary, transferring available savings (wealth) to those who want to acquire more resources (invest).*

par value: The face value of a bond; the amount to be repaid when the bond is due.

As in the case of IPOs of stock, the critical issue here is the *price* of the bond. How many people are willing and able to lend funds to the company? What rate of interest will they charge?

As we observed in Figure 32.2, the quantity of loanable funds supplied depends on the interest rate. At low interest rates no one is willing to lend funds to the company. Why lend your savings to a risky venture like Google when more secure bonds and even banks pay higher interest rates? Google might not succeed and later **default** on (not pay) its obligations. Potential lenders would want to be compensated for this extra risk with above-average interest rates—that is, a risk premium. Remember that lenders don't share in any

default: Failure to make scheduled payments of interest or principal on a bond.

profits Google might earn; they get only interest payments. Hence they'd want a hefty premium to compensate them for the risk of default.

Suppose that market participants will lend the desired amount of money to Google only at 16 percent interest. In this case, Google may agree to pay an interest rate—the so-called **coupon rate**—of 16 percent to secure start-up funding of $50 million. That means Google agrees to pay $160 of interest each year for every $1,000 borrowed and to repay the entire $50 million at the end of 10 years.

coupon rate: Interest rate set for a bond at time of issuance.

Bond Trading

Once a bond has been issued, the initial lenders don't have to wait 10 years to get their money back. They can't go back to the company and demand early repayment, but they can sell their bonds to someone else. This **liquidity** is an important consideration for prospective bondholders. If a person had no choice but to wait 10 years for repayment, he or she might be less willing to buy a bond (lend funds). *By facilitating resales, the bond market increases the availability of funds to new ventures and other borrowers.* As is the case with stocks, most of the action in the bond markets consists of such after-market trades— that is, the buying and selling of bonds issued at some earlier time. The company that first issued the bonds doesn't participate in these trades.

liquidity: The ability of an asset to be converted into cash.

The portfolio decision in the bond market is motivated by the same factors that influence stock purchases. The *opportunity cost* of buying and selling bonds is the best alternative rate of return—for example, the interest rate on other bonds or money market mutual funds. *Expectations* also play a role in gauging both likely changes in opportunity costs and the ability of the borrower to redeem (pay off) the bond when it's due. *Changes in expectations or opportunity costs shift the bond supply and demand curves,* thereby altering market interest rates.

Current Yields

We've assumed that Google would have had to offer 16 percent interest to induce enough people to lend the company (buy bonds worth) $50 million for its initial operations. This was far higher than the 6 percent the U.S. Treasury was paying on its bonds (borrowed funds). This large risk premium reflected the fear that Google might not succeed and end up defaulting on it loans.

Suppose that Google actually took off. The risk of a bond default would diminish, and people would be more willing to lend it funds. This change in the availability of loanable funds is illustrated in the rightward shift of the supply curve in Figure 32.4.

According to the new supply curve in Figure 32.4, Google could now borrow $50 million at 10 percent interest (point *B*) rather than paying 16 percent (point *A*). Unfortunately,

FIGURE 32.4

Shifts in Funds Supply

If lenders decide that a company's future is less risky, they will be more willing to lend it money or hold its bonds. The resulting shift of the loanable funds supply curve reduces the current yield on a bond by raising its price.

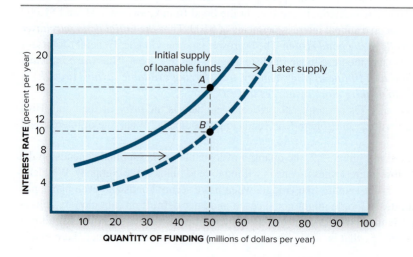

Google already borrowed the funds and is obliged to continue paying $160 per year in interest on each bond. Hence the company doesn't benefit directly from the supply shift.

The change in the equilibrium value of Google bonds must show up somewhere, however. People who hold Google bonds continue to get $160 per year in interest (16 percent of $1,000). Now there are lots of people who would be willing to lend funds to Google at that rate. These people want to hold Google bonds themselves. To get them, they'll have to buy the bonds in the market from existing bondholders. Thus the ***increased willingness to lend funds is reflected in an increased demand for bonds.*** This increased demand will push up the price of Google bonds. As bond prices rise, their implied effective interest rate **(current yield)** falls. Table 32.5 illustrates this relationship. Notice the phenomenal yield (50.5 percent) on GM bonds in February 2009. GM was teetering on bankruptcy back then, raising the prospect of a bond default. So prospective GM bondholders wanted a huge risk premium for buying GM bonds (they ended up losing when GM declared bankruptcy in June 2009).

Changing bond prices and yields are important market signals for resource allocation. In our example, the rising price of Google's bonds reflects increased optimism for the company's sales prospects. The collective assessment of the marketplace is that web search engines will be profitable. The increase in the price of Google bonds will make it easier and less costly for the company to borrow additional funds. The reverse scenario unfolded in 2008–2009. When investors concluded that the recession was sapping corporate finances, the supply of funds to dot-coms dried up. That supply shift raised interest rates and made it more difficult for firms to borrow money for new investments.

current yield: The rate of return on a bond; the annual interest payment divided by the bond's price.

Price of Bond	Coupon Rate (Annual Interest Payment)	Current Yield
$ 600	$150	25.0%
800	150	18.8
1,000	150	15.0
1,200	150	12.5

The annual interest payment on a bond—the "coupon rate"—is fixed at the time of issuance. Accordingly, only the market (resale) price of the bond itself can change. An increase in the price of the bond lowers its *effective* interest rate, or yield. The formula for computing the current yield on a bond is

$$\text{Current yield} = \frac{\text{Annual interest payment}}{\text{Market (resale) price of bond}}$$

Thus higher bond prices imply lower yields (effective interest rates), as confirmed in the table above. Bond prices and yields vary with changes in expectations and opportunity costs.

The newspaper quotation below shows how changing bond prices and yields are reported. This General Motors (GM) bond was issued with a coupon rate (nominal interest rate) of 83⁄8 percent. Hence GM promised to pay $83.75 in interest each year until it redeemed (paid off) the $1,000 bond in the year 2033. In February 2009, however, the market price of the bond was only $160.50 ("16.50"). This created a phenomenal yield of 50.5 percent!

Bond	Current Yield	Volume	Close
GM 8⅜ 33	50.5	142	16.50

TABLE 32.5

Bond Price and Yields Move in Opposite Directions

THE ECONOMY TOMORROW

VENTURE CAPITALISTS—FINANCING TOMORROW'S PRODUCTS

One of the proven paths to high incomes and wealth is entrepreneurship. Most of the great American fortunes originated in entrepreneurial ventures, such as building railroads, mass-producing automobiles, introducing new computers, perfecting mass-merchandising techniques, or pioneering social networking sites (e.g., Facebook). These successful ventures all required more than just a great idea. To convert the original idea into actual output requires the investment of real resources.

Recall that Apple Computer started in a garage with a minimum of resources (Chapter 23). The idea of packaging a personal computer was novel, and few resources were required to demonstrate that it could be done. But Steven Jobs couldn't have become a multimillionaire by building just a few dozen computers a month. To reap huge economic profits from his idea, he needed much greater production capacity. He also needed resources for marketing the new Apples to a broader customer base. In other words, Steven Jobs needed lots of economic resources—land, labor, and capital—to convert his entrepreneurial dream into a profit-making reality.

Steven Jobs and his partner, Steve Wozniak, had few resources of their own. In fact, they'd sold Jobs's Volkswagen and Wozniak's scientific calculator to raise the finances for the first computer. To go any further, they needed financial support from others. Loans were hard to obtain since the company had no assets, no financial history, and no certainty of success. Jobs needed people who were willing to share the *risks* associated with a new venture. He found one such person in A. C. Markkula, who put up $250,000 and became a partner in the new venture. Shortly thereafter, other venture capitalists provided additional financing. With this start-up financing, Jobs was able to acquire more resources and make the Apple Computer Company a reality.

Facebook. Facebook grew from equally modest origins (Mark Zuckerberg's Harvard dorm room) back in 2004. It went from a small start-up to a national phenomenon only with the help of venture capitalists. Three venture capitalists invested $40 million, giving Facebook the resources to buy its own domain name ($200,000) and build the infrastructure that allowed it to become the premier social networking site. These are classic case studies in venture capitalism.

As In the News "Where Do Start-Ups Get Their Money?" documents, most business start-ups are created with shoestring budgets, averaging less than $20,000 (Apple and Facebook started with even less). The initial seed money typically comes from an entrepreneur's own assets or credit, with a little help from family and friends. If the idea pans out, entrepreneurs need a lot more money to develop their product. This is where venture capitalists come in. Venture capitalists provide initial funding for entrepreneurial ventures. In return for their financial backing, the venture capitalists are entitled to a share of any profits that result. If the venture fails, however, they get nothing. Thus *venture capitalists provide financial support for entrepreneurial ideas and share in the risks and rewards.* Even Christopher Columbus needed venture capitalists to fund his risky expeditions to the New World.

Venture capital is as important to the economy tomorrow as it was to Columbus. For technology and entrepreneurship to continue growing, market conditions and tax provisions must be amenable to venture capitalists.

Crowdfunding is all the rage these days but start-ups get relatively little initial capital from throngs of anonymous investors. Personal savings remain the most important source of start-up capital according to a survey of 600 business owners. initial capital averages less than $20,000. Loans from banks are the second most common source of this start-up funding, as the accompanying chart shows.

WHERE DO START-UPS GET THEIR MONEY?

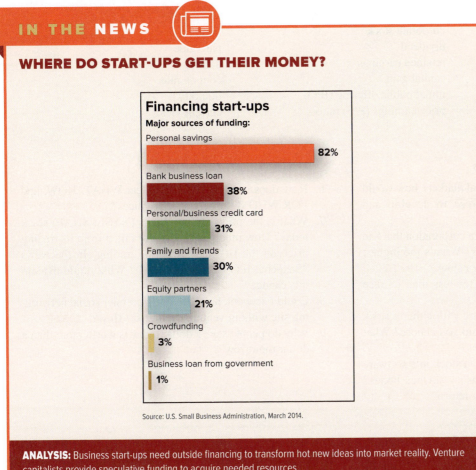

Financing start-ups

Major sources of funding:

Personal savings — **82%**

Bank business loan — **38%**

Personal/business credit card — **31%**

Family and friends — **30%**

Equity partners — **21%**

Crowdfunding — **3%**

Business loan from government — **1%**

Source: U.S. Small Business Administration, March 2014.

ANALYSIS: Business start-ups need outside financing to transform hot new ideas into market reality. Venture capitalists provide speculative funding to acquire needed resources.

SUMMARY

- The primary economic function of financial markets is to help allocate scarce resources to desired uses. They do this by providing access to the pool of national savings for entrepreneurs, investors, and other would-be spenders. **LO32-4**

- Financial markets enable individuals to manage risk by holding different kinds of assets. Financial intermediaries also reduce the costs of information and search, thereby increasing market efficiency. **LO32-4**

- Future returns on investments must be discounted to present value. The present discounted value (PDV) of a future payment adjusts for forgone interest accrual. **LO32-1**

- Future returns are also uncertain. The *expected* value of future payments must also reflect the risk of nonpayment. **LO32-1**

- Shares of stock represent ownership in a corporation. The shares are initially issued to raise funds and are then traded on the stock exchanges. **LO32-2**

- Changes in the value of a corporation's stock reflect changing expectations and opportunity costs. Share price changes, in turn, act as market signals to direct more or fewer resources to a company. **LO32-4**

- Bonds are IOUs issued when a company (or government agency) borrows funds. After issuance, bonds are traded in the after (secondary) market. **LO32-2**

- The interest (coupon) rate on a bond is fixed at the time of issuance. The price of the bond itself, however, varies with changes in expectations (perceived risk) and opportunity cost. Yields vary inversely with bond prices. **LO32-3**

Key Terms

financial intermediary	corporate stock	bond
crowdfunding	dividend	par value
risk premium	retained earnings	default
present discounted value (PDV)	capital gain	coupon rate
expected value	initial public offering (IPO)	liquidity
corporation	price/earnings (P/E) ratio	current yield

Questions for Discussion

1. If there were no organized financial markets, how would an entrepreneur acquire resources to develop and produce a new product? **LO32-2**
2. Why would anyone buy shares of a corporation that had no profits and paid no dividends? What's the highest price a person would pay for such a stock? **LO32-3**
3. Why would anyone sell a bond for less than its face (par) value? **LO32-3**
4. If you could finance a new venture with either a stock issue or bonds, which option would you choose? What are their respective (dis)advantages? **LO32-2**
5. Why is it considered riskier to own stock in a software company than to hold U.S. Treasury savings bonds? Which asset will generate a higher return? **LO32-4**
6. How does a successful IPO affect WHAT, HOW, and FOR WHOM the economy produces? **LO32-2**
7. What is the price of Snap Inc.'s (NYSE: SNAP) stock today? How much has it risen or fallen from its trading price on the first day of public trading (In the News "Snapchat IPO Nets $3 Billion")? What might explain this change? **LO32-4**
8. Could Facebook have become a premier social networking site without venture capitalists? How? **LO32-2**
9. Why do people say "a dollar today is worth more than a dollar tomorrow"? **LO32-1**

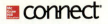

PROBLEMS FOR CHAPTER 32

LO32-3 1. If an $60 stock pays a quarterly dividend of $1, what is the implied annual rate of return?

LO32-3 2. If a $24 per share stock has a P/E ratio of 16 and pays out 40 percent of its profits in dividends,
   (*a*) How much profit is it earning per share?
   (*b*) How large is its dividend?
   (*c*) What is the implied rate of cash return?

LO32-3 3. According to the data in Table 32.3,
   (*a*) How much profit per share did Google earn?
   (*b*) How much of that profit did it pay out in dividends?

LO32-3 4. According to the data in Table 32.3,
   (*a*) How much profit per share did Intel earn?
   (*b*) How much of that profit did it pay out in dividends?

LO32-1 5. If the market rate of interest is 5 percent, what is the present discounted value of $1,000 that will be paid in
   (*a*) 1 year?
   (*b*) 5 years?
   (*c*) 10 years?

LO32-1 6. What is the present discounted value of $10,000 that is to be received in 2 years if the market rate of interest is
   (*a*) 0 percent?
   (*b*) 4 percent?
   (*c*) 8 percent?

LO32-4 7. What was the expected return on Columbus's expedition, assuming that he had a 50 percent chance of discovering valuables worth $1 million, a 25 percent chance of bringing home only $100,000, and a 25 percent chance of sinking?

LO32-3 8. Compute the market price of the GM bonds described in Table 32.5 if the yield falls to 20 percent.

LO32-3 9. What is the current yield on a $1,000 bond with a 4 percent coupon if its market price is
   (*a*) $900?
   (*b*) $1,000?
   (*c*) $1,100?

LO32-4 10. How much interest accrued each day on the immediate cash payoff of the MegaMillions jackpot? (See Table 32.1.)

LO32-4 11. Illustrate with demand and supply shifts the impact of the following events on stock prices:
   (*a*) A federal court finds Google guilty of antitrust violations. Which way (right or left) did
      (*i*) Demand shift?
      (*ii*) Supply shift?
   (*b*) Intel announces a new and faster processor. Which way did
      (*i*) Demand shift?
      (*ii*) Supply shift?

  (*c*) Corporate executives announce that they intend to sell a large block of stock.
    Which way did
    (*i*) Demand shift?
    (*ii*) Supply shift?
  (*d*) Google enhances its search capabilities. Which way did
    (*i*) Demand shift?
    (*ii*) Supply shift?

LO32-2 12. Which investment has a higher rate of annual cash return? Investment A: $1,000 bond with a coupon rate of 4 percent selling for $1,200 or Investment B: $1,000 stock with a P/E ratio of 10 that pays out half its profits in dividends.

LO32-4 13. The Economy Tomorrow: What are the three most important sources of funding for financing a start-up?

©MOF/Getty Images RF

©Jeffrey Hamilton/Digital Vision/Getty Images RF

©DreamPictures/Pam Ostrow/Blend Images LLC RF

DISTRIBUTIONAL ISSUES

Of the three core questions in economics, the FOR WHOM issue is often the most contentious. Should the market decide who gets the most output? Or should the government intervene and redistribute market incomes to achieve greater equity?

Tax and transfer systems are designed to redistribute market incomes. The next two chapters survey these systems. In the process, we assess not only how effective they are in achieving greater *equity*, but also what impacts they have on *efficiency*. High taxes and generous transfer payments may blunt work incentives and so reduce the size of the pie being resliced. This creates a fundamental conflict between the goals of equity and efficiency. Chapters 33 and 34 examine this conflict.

©Jeffrey Hamilton/Digital Vision/Getty Images RF

33.

Taxes: Equity versus Efficiency

Insistence on carving the pie into equal slices would shrink the size of the pie. That fact poses the trade-off between economic equality and economic efficiency.

—**Arthur M. Okun**

LEARNING OBJECTIVES

After reading this chapter, you should know

LO33-1 How the U.S. tax system is structured.

LO33-2 What makes taxes more or less progressive.

LO33-3 The nature of the equity–efficiency trade-off.

Eric Schmidt was rewarded handsomely for his effort in cofounding Google in 2001. When he stepped down as CEO in 2011, Schmidt had amassed 9.2 million shares of Google stock, worth nearly $6 billion. As a parting gift, Google gave him an additional $100 million bonus when he turned the CEO job over to fellow cofounder Larry Page in January 2011. That would have been enough income to lift more than 2 million poor persons out of poverty. But Schmidt didn't share his good fortune with those people, and they remained poor.

The market mechanism generated both Schmidt's extraordinary income and that of so many poor families. Is this the way we want the basic FOR WHOM question to be settled? Should some people own vast fortunes while others seek shelter in abandoned cars? Or do the inequalities that emerge in product and factor markets violate our notions of equity? If the market's answer to the FOR WHOM question isn't right, some form of government intervention to redistribute incomes may be desired.

The tax system is the government's primary lever for redistributing income. But taxing Peter to pay Paul may affect more than just income shares. If taxed too heavily, Peter may stop producing so much. Paul, too, may work less if assured of government support. The end result may be *less* total income to share. In other words, ***taxes affect production as well as distribution. This creates a potential trade-off between the goal of equity and the goal of efficiency.***

This chapter examines this equity–efficiency trade-off, with the following questions as a guide:

- **How are incomes distributed in the United States?**
- **How do taxes alter that distribution?**
- **How do taxes affect the rate and mix of output?**

After addressing these questions, we examine some proposed tax changes, including the tax cuts championed by President Trump.

WHAT IS *INCOME*?

Before examining the distribution of income in the United States, let's decide what to count as *income*. There are several possibilities.

Personal Income

The most obvious choice is **personal income (PI)**—the flow of annual income received by households before payment of personal income taxes. Personal income includes wages and salaries, corporate dividends, rent, interest, Social Security benefits, welfare payments, and any other form of money income.

Personal income isn't a complete measure of income, however. Many goods and services are distributed directly as **in-kind income** rather than through market purchases. Many poor people, for example, live in public housing and pay little or no rent. As a consequence, they receive a larger share of total output than their money incomes imply. People with low incomes also receive food stamps (now called Supplemental Nutrition Assistance Program [SNAP] vouchers) that allow them to purchase more food than their money incomes would allow.

In-kind benefits aren't limited to low-income households. Students who attend public schools and colleges consume more goods and services than they directly pay for: public education is subsidized by all taxpayers. People over age 65 also get medical services through Medicare that they don't directly pay for. Middle-class workers get noncash fringe benefits (like health insurance, paid vacations, pension contributions) that don't show up in their paychecks or on their tax returns. Even the president of the United States gets substantial in-kind benefits. President Trump doesn't pay rent at the White House and gets free food, health care, transportation, and security services. Hence his real income greatly exceeds his $400,000-a-year presidential paycheck (which he declined to take).

So long as some goods and services needn't be purchased in the marketplace, *the distribution of money income isn't synonymous with the distribution of goods and services.* This measurement problem is particularly important when comparisons are made over time. For example, the federal government officially classifies people as "poor" if their money income is below a certain threshold. By this standard, we've made no progress against poverty. The Census Bureau counted 40 million Americans as "poor" in 2016, more than it counted in 1965. In both years the Census Bureau counted only money incomes. In 1965 that approach was acceptable because little income was transferred in-kind. In 2016, however, the federal government spent $60 billion on food stamps, $50 billion on housing subsidies, and $560 billion on Medicaid. Had all this in-kind income been counted, 12 million fewer Americans would have been counted as poor in 2016. Although that would still leave a lot of people in poverty, at least more progress in eliminating poverty would be evident.

Wealth

If our ultimate concern is access to goods and services, the distribution of wealth is also important. **Wealth** refers to the market value of assets (such as houses, cars, and bank accounts) people own. Hence *wealth represents a stock of potential purchasing power; income statistics tell us only how this year's flow of purchasing power (income) is being distributed.* Accordingly, to provide a complete answer to the FOR WHOM question, we have to know how wealth, as well as income, is distributed. In general, wealth tends to be distributed much less equally than income. The Internal Revenue Service estimates that 10 percent of the adult population own 75 percent of all personal wealth in the United States but earn around 50 percent of total income.

THE SIZE DISTRIBUTION OF INCOME

Although incomes aren't a perfect measure of access to goods and services (much less happiness), they're the best single indicator of the FOR WHOM outcomes. The **size distribution of income** tells us how large a share of total personal income is received by

personal income (PI): Income received by households before payment of personal taxes.

in-kind income: Goods and services received directly, without payment, in a market transaction.

wealth: The market value of assets.

size distribution of income: The way total personal income is divided up among households or income classes.

various households, grouped by income class. Imagine for the moment that the entire population is lined up in order of income, with lowest-income recipients in front and highest-income recipients at the end of the line. We want to know how much income the people in front get in comparison with those at the back.

We first examined the size distribution of income in Chapter 2. Figure 2.3 showed that households in the lowest quintile received less than $23,000 apiece in 2015. As a group, this class received only 3.1 percent of total income, despite the fact that it included 20 percent of all households (the lowest fifth). Thus the **income share** of the people in the lowest group (3.1 percent) was much smaller than their proportion in the total population (20 percent).

Moving back to the end of the line, we observed that a household needed $117,000 to make it into the highest income class in 2015. Many families in that class made much more than $117,000—some even millions of dollars. But $117,000 was at least enough to get into the top fifth (quintile).

The top quintile ended up with half of total U.S. income and, by implication, that much of total output.

The Lorenz Curve

The size distribution of income provides the kind of information we need to determine how total income (and output) is distributed. The **Lorenz curve** is a convenient summary of that information; it is a graphic illustration of the size distribution.

Figure 33.1 is a Lorenz curve for the United States. Our lineup of individuals is on the horizontal axis, with the lowest-income earners on the left. On the vertical axis we depict the cumulative share of income received by people in our income line. Consider the lowest quintile of the distribution again. They're represented on the horizontal axis at 20 percent. If their share of income was identical to their share of population, they'd get 20 percent of total income. This would be represented by point *C* in the figure. In fact, the lowest quintile gets only 3.1 percent, as indicated by point *A*. Point *B* tells us that the *cumulative* share of income received by the lowest *three*-fifths of the population was 25.6 percent.

The really handy feature of the Lorenz curve is the way it contrasts the actual distribution of income with an absolutely equal one. If incomes were distributed equally, the first 20 percent of the people in line would be getting exactly 20 percent of all income. In that case, the Lorenz curve would run through point *C*. Indeed, the Lorenz "curve" would be a straight line along the diagonal. The actual Lorenz curve lies below the diagonal because

income share: The proportion of total income received by a particular group.

Lorenz curve: A graphic illustration of the cumulative size distribution of income; contrasts complete equality with the actual distribution of income.

FIGURE 33.1

The Lorenz Curve

The Lorenz curve illustrates the extent of income inequality. If all incomes were equal, each fifth of the population would receive one-fifth of total income. In that case, the diagonal line through point *C* would represent the cumulative size distribution of income.

In reality, incomes aren't distributed equally. Point *A*, for example, indicates that the 20 percent of the population with the lowest income receive only 3.1 percent of total income.

Source: Figure 2.3.

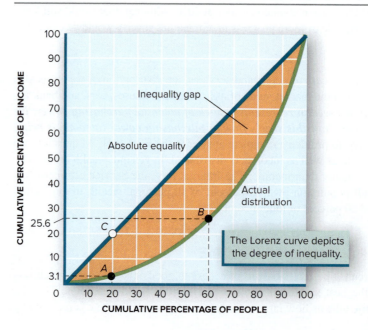

Analysis: An increase in the size of the economic pie doesn't ensure everyone a larger slice. A goal of the tax system is to attain a fairer distribution of the economic pie.

©Robert Graysmith.

our national income isn't distributed equally. In fact, the area between the diagonal and the actual Lorenz curve (the shaded area in Figure 33.1) is a convenient measure of the degree of inequality. ***The greater the area between the Lorenz curve and the diagonal, the more inequality exists.***

The visual summary of inequality the Lorenz curve provides is also expressed in a mathematical relationship. The ratio of the shaded area in Figure 33.1 to the area of the triangle formed by the diagonal is called the **Gini coefficient.** The higher the Gini coefficient, the greater the degree of inequality. Between 2000 and 2015, the Gini coefficient rose from 0.462 to 0.479. In other words, the shaded area in Figure 33.1 expanded by nearly 4 percent, indicating *increased* inequality. Although the size of the economic pie (real GDP) increased by 30 percent between 2000 and 2015, some people's slices got a lot bigger while other people saw little improvement, or even less (see the cartoon above).

> **Gini coefficient:** A mathematical summary of inequality based on the Lorenz curve.

The Call for Intervention

To many people, large and increasing inequality represents a form of **market failure:** the market is generating a suboptimal (unfair) answer to the FOR WHOM question. As in other instances of market failure, the government is called on to intervene. The policy lever in this case is taxes. **By levying taxes on the rich and providing transfer payments to the poor, the government** *redistributes* **market incomes.**

> **market failure:** An imperfection in the market mechanism that prevents optimal outcomes.

THE FEDERAL INCOME TAX

The federal income tax is designed for this redistributional purpose. Specifically, the federal income tax is designed to be **progressive**—that is, to impose higher tax *rates* on high incomes than on low ones. Progressivity is achieved by imposing increasing **marginal tax rates** on higher incomes. The *marginal* tax rate refers to the tax rate imposed on the last (marginal) dollar of income.

> **progressive tax:** A tax system in which tax rates rise as incomes rise.

Tax Brackets and Rates

In 2016, the tax code specified the seven tax brackets shown in Table 33.1. For an individual with less than $9,275 of taxable income, the tax rate was 10 percent. Any income in excess of $9,275 was taxed at a *higher* rate of 15 percent. If an individual's income rose above $91,150, the amount between $91,150 and $190,150 was taxed at 28 percent. Any income greater than $415,000 was taxed at 39.6 percent.

To understand the efficiency and equity effects of taxes, we must distinguish between the *marginal* tax rate and the *average* tax rate. A person who earned $420,000 taxable income in 2016 paid the 39.6 percent tax only on the income in excess of $415,050—that is, the last (marginal) $4,950. The first $9,275 was taxed at a marginal rate of only 10 percent.

> **marginal tax rate:** The tax rate imposed on the last (marginal) dollar of income.

TABLE 33.1

Progressive Taxes

The federal income tax is progressive because it levies higher tax rates on higher incomes. The 2016 marginal tax rate started out at 10 percent for incomes below $9,275 and rose to 39.6 percent for incomes above $415,050.

Tax Bracket	Marginal Tax Rate
$0–9,275	10%
$9,275–37,650	15
$37,650–91,150	25
$91,950–190,150	28
$190,150–413,350	33
$413,350–415,050	35
Over $415,050	39.6

Source: Internal Revenue Service (2016 tax rates for single individuals).

Here is how taxes are computed on $420,000 of income:

Marginal Tax Rate	Income		Tax
10% of	$ 9,275	=	$ 927.50
15% of	28,375	=	4,256.25
25% of	53,500	=	13,375.00
28% of	99,000	=	27,720.00
33% of	223,200	=	73,656.00
35% of	1,700	=	595.00
39.6% of	4,950	=	1,960.20
	$420,000		$122,489.95

Notice that the various marginal tax rates apply only to the income in that specific bracket. By adding up the taxes in each bracket, we get a total tax of $122,489.95. This represents only 29.2 percent of this individual's income. Hence this person had a

- *Marginal* tax rate of 39.6 percent.
- *Average* (or nominal) tax rate of 29.2 percent.

By contrast, a person with only $20,000 of taxable income would pay a *marginal* tax of only 15 percent and an *average* tax of 12.7 percent. The rationale behind this progressive system is to tax ever-larger percentages of higher incomes, thereby reducing income inequalities. **By making the *after-tax* distribution of income more equal than the *before-tax* distribution, *progressive taxes reduce inequality*.**

Efficiency Concerns

Although the redistributive intent of a progressive tax system is evident, it raises concerns about efficiency. As noted in the chapter-opening quote, attempts to reslice the pie may end up reducing the size of the pie. The central issue here is incentives. Chapter 30 emphasized that the supply of labor is motivated by the pursuit of income. If Uncle Sam takes away ever-larger chunks of income, won't that dampen the desire to work? If so, *the incentive to work more, produce more, or invest more is reduced by higher marginal tax rates.* This suggests that as marginal tax rates increase, total output shrinks, creating a basic conflict between the goals of equity (more progressive taxes) and efficiency (more output).

Tax Migration. How great the conflict is between the equity and efficiency depends on how responsive market participants are to higher tax rates. The Rolling Stones left Great Britain off their 1998–1999 world tour because the British marginal tax rate was so high. The band U2 went a step further—moving their home base from Ireland to the Netherlands to avoid paying Irish income taxes (see World View "Bono Says 'Stupid' to Pay Irish Taxes"). A 2011 study by the National Bureau of Economic Research (NBER) revealed that international soccer stars choose to live in low-tax nations even while playing for teams in high-tax nations. Many other businesses relocate to low-tax nations for the same reason.

BONO SAYS "STUPID" TO PAY IRISH TAXES

When Ireland eliminated the tax break for royalty income in 2006, the rock band U2 packed their bags and moved to the Netherlands where tax rates are much lower. The band has been subjected to criticism ever since. At the Glastonbury Festival in 2011, protesters inflated a huge banner that asked, "U pay tax 2?," which led to a violent skirmish with concert security. In interviews in 2013–2015 Bono, whose real name is Paul Hewson, has repeatedly rejected the charge that the Irish band's tax exile status is hypocritical, given its well-publicized calls for more aid to the world's poor. Bono says he doesn't have to be "stupid" about taxes; the band is just being "sensible about the way we're taxed."

Source: Media reports and interviews, 2007–2015.

ANALYSIS: High tax rates deter people from supplying resources. In this case, high taxes motivated U2 to move to another country.

Tax Elasticity of Supply. For the typical household, however, the response to higher tax rates is limited to reducing hours worked. In all cases we can summarize the response with the **tax elasticity of supply:**

$$\text{Tax elasticity of supply} = \frac{\text{\% change in quantity supplied}}{\text{\% change in tax rate}}$$

> **tax elasticity of supply:** The percentage change in quantity supplied divided by the percentage change in tax rates.

If the tax elasticity of supply were zero, there'd be no conflict between equity and efficiency. But a zero tax elasticity would also imply that people would continue to work, produce, and invest even if Uncle Sam took *all* their income in taxes. In today's range of taxes, the average household's tax elasticity of labor supply is between 0.15 and 0.30. Hence, if tax *rates* go up by 20 percent, the quantity of labor supplied would decline by 3 to 6 percent. In other words, the size of the pie being resliced would shrink by 3–6 percent. Figure 33.2 confirms that the top marginal tax rate has changed by much more than 20 percent in the past, thereby significantly altering the size of the economic pie.

Equity Concerns

As if the concern about efficiency weren't enough, critics also raise questions about how well the federal income tax promotes equity. What appears to be a fairly progressive tax in theory turns out to be a lot less progressive in practice. Hundreds of people with $1 million incomes pay no taxes. They aren't necessarily breaking any laws, just taking advantage of loopholes in the tax system.

Loopholes. The progressive *tax rates described in the tax code apply to "taxable" income, not to all income.* The so-called loopholes in the system arise from the way Congress defines taxable income. The tax laws permit one to subtract certain exemptions and deductions from gross income in computing taxable income:

$$\text{Taxable income} = \text{Gross income} - \text{Exemptions and deductions}$$

Exemptions are permitted for dependent children, spouses, old age, and disabilities. Deductions are permitted for an array of expenses, including home mortgage interest, work-related expenses, child care, depreciation of investments, interest payments, union dues, medical expenses, charitable contributions, and many other items.

The purpose of these many *itemized deductions* is to encourage specific economic activities and reduce potential hardship. The deduction for mortgage interest payments, for

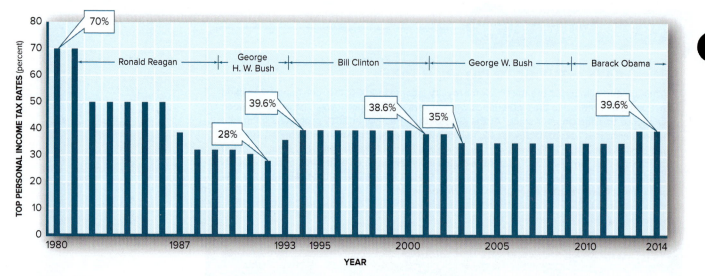

FIGURE 33.2

Changes in Marginal Tax Rates

During the past 40 years, Congress revised the federal income tax system many times. The top marginal tax rate was steadily reduced from 70 percent in 1980 to 28 percent in 1992. It was then raised in 1993–1995. The Bush tax cuts of 2001–2004 reduced marginal tax rates once more. Then President Obama increased the top marginal tax rate to 39.6 again in 2013. President Trump sought to reverse the trend again, dropping the top tax rate to 35 percent.

Source: Internal Revenue Service.

---

vertical equity: Principle that people with higher incomes should pay more taxes.

---

horizontal equity: Principle that people with equal incomes should pay equal taxes.

TABLE 33.2

Vertical Inequity

Tax exemptions and deductions create a gap between total income and *taxable* income. In this case, Mr. Jones has both a higher income and extensive deductions. He ends up with less *taxable* income than Ms. Smith and so pays less taxes. This vertical inequity is reflected in the lower effective tax rate paid by Mr. Jones (4.4 percent) than Ms. Smith (18.3 percent).

example, encourages people to buy their own homes. The deduction for medical expenses helps relieve the financial burden of illness.

Whatever the merits of specific exemptions and deductions, they create potential inequities. ***People with high incomes can avoid high taxes by claiming large exemptions and deductions.*** In fact, some people with high incomes end up paying *less* tax than people with lower incomes. This violates the principle of **vertical equity,** the progressive intent of taxing people on the basis of their ability to pay.

Table 33.2 illustrates vertical *in*equity. Mr. Jones has an income ($90,000) three times larger than Ms. Smith's ($30,000). However, Mr. Jones also has huge deductions ($70,000) that reduce his *taxable* income dramatically. In fact, Mr. Jones ends up with less *taxable* income ($20,000) than Ms. Smith ($25,000). As a result, he also ends up paying lower taxes ($4,000 vs. $5,500). How is this possible? Simply because Mr. Jones has huge itemized deductions for things like mortgage interest, charitable contributions, and the like, and Ms. Smith has nothing comparable.

The deductions that create the vertical inequity between Mr. Jones and Ms. Smith could also violate the principle of **horizontal equity**—as people with the *same* incomes end up

	Mr. Jones	Ms. Smith
1. Total income	$90,000	$30,000
2. Less exemptions and deductions	−$70,000	−$ 5,000
3. Taxable income	$20,000	$25,000
4. Tax	$ 4,000	$ 5,500
5. Nominal tax rate (= row 4 ÷ row 3)	20%	22%
6. Effective tax rate (= row 4 ÷ row 1)	4.4%	18.3%

paying different amounts of income tax. These horizontal *in*equities also contradict basic notions of fairness.

Nominal vs. Effective Tax Rates. The "loopholes" created by exemptions, deductions, and tax credits cause a distinction between gross economic income and taxable income. That distinction, in turn, requires us to distinguish between *nominal* tax rates and *effective* tax rates. The term **nominal tax rate** refers to the taxes actually paid as a percentage of *taxable* income. By contrast, the **effective tax rate** is the tax paid divided by *total* economic income without regard to exemptions, deductions, or other intricacies of the tax laws.

As Table 33.2 illustrates, someone with a gross income of $90,000 might end up with a much lower *taxable* income, thanks to various tax deductions and exemptions. Mr. Jones ended up with a taxable income of only $20,000 and a tax bill of merely $4,000. As a result, we can characterize Mr. Jones's tax burden in two ways:

$$\text{Nominal tax rate} = \frac{\text{Tax paid}}{\text{Taxable income}}$$

$$= \frac{\$4,000}{\$20,000} = 20 \text{ percent}$$

or alternatively,

$$\text{Effective tax rate} = \frac{\text{Tax paid}}{\text{Total economic income}}$$

$$= \frac{\$4,000}{\$90,000} = 4.4 \text{ percent}$$

This huge gap between the nominal tax rate (20 percent) and the effective tax rate (4.4 percent) is a reflection of loopholes in the tax code. It's also the source of the vertical and horizontal inequities discussed earlier. Notice that Ms. Smith, with much less gross income, ends up with an effective tax rate (18.3 percent) that's more than four times higher than Mr. Jones's (4.4 percent).

In the News "Taxes: The Pences vs. The Clintons" shows how the Pences and the Clintons used these many loopholes in 2015. Mike Pence had a very modest wage back in 2015, especially in comparison to Bill and Hillary Clinton, who took in over $10 million in speaking fees. Both the Pences and the Clintons took advantage of deductions for state and

> **nominal tax rate:** Taxes paid divided by taxable income.

> **effective tax rate:** Taxes paid divided by total income.

IN THE NEWS

TAXES: THE PENCES VS. THE CLINTONS

	The Pences	The Clintons
Gross Income	$115,562	$10,745,378
Deductions		
Charitable contributions	$ 8,923	$ 1,042,000
State and local taxes	6,611	1,467,501
Mortgage interest	—	41,040
Exemptions	16,000	—
Taxable Income	$ 81,492	$ 8,352,507
Income Tax	$ 8,956	$ 3,236,975

Source: Tax History.org (2015 tax returns)

ANALYSIS: Taxes are levied on *taxable* income, not total income. Various deductions and exemptions reduce taxable income and *effective* tax rates.

local taxes they paid and contributions to charity they made. Nearly all of the Clintons' $1 million charitable contributions went to their own, tax-exempt Clinton Foundation.

After all the deductions and exemptions were accounted for, the IRS recognized only a portion of their gross income as "taxable income." Only that taxable income counts for Uncle Sam. The resulting tax bills are noted in the last row of the News.

Clearly, the Clintons were among the highest income U.S. households in 2015. Their multimillion income planted them in the highest tax bracket of Table 33.1. But they didn't pay 39.6 percent of their income to Uncle Sam. Their effective tax rate was only 30.1 percent (tax paid dividend by gross income) whereas the Pences' effective tax rate was 7.7 percent. Like the Pences, the Clintons paid only a 10 percent tax on the first $9,275 of income. They then moved up the tax brackets and rates of Table 33.1 to compute their total tax bill. If there were no exemptions or deductions, the income tax bills for the Clintons would have gone up by $887,841 and the Pences would have had to pay $7,884 more.

Tax-Induced Misallocations. Tax loopholes not only foster inequity but encourage inefficiency as well. The optimal mix of output is the one that balances consumer preferences and opportunity costs. Tax loopholes, however, encourage a different mix of output. By offering preferential treatment for some activities, the tax code reduces their relative accounting cost. In so doing, *tax preferences induce resource shifts into tax-preferred activities.* The deduction for mortgage interest, for example, encourages people to purchase homes, thereby changing the mix of output.

These resource allocations are the explicit goal of tax preferences. The accumulation of exemptions, deductions, and credits has become so unwieldy and complex, however, that tax considerations often overwhelm economic considerations in many investment and consumption decisions. The resulting mix of output, many observers feel, is decidedly inferior to a *pure* market outcome. From this viewpoint, the federal income tax promotes both inequity and inefficiency.

A Shrinking Tax Base. Loopholes in the tax code create yet another problem. As the **tax base** gets smaller and smaller, it becomes increasingly difficult to sustain, much less increase, tax revenues. The tax arithmetic is simple:

tax base: The amount of income or property directly subject to nominal tax rates.

$$\text{Tax revenue} = \frac{\text{Average}}{\text{tax rate}} \times \frac{\text{Tax}}{\text{base}}$$

As deductions, exemptions, and credits accumulate, the tax base (taxable income) keeps shrinking. To keep tax rates low—or to reduce them further—Congress has to stop this erosion of the tax base.

The Bush Tax Cuts (2001–2010)

Tax reforms in 1986 and 1993 broadened the tax base but also raised tax rates (to a top rate of 39.6 percent). President Bush worried that those higher marginal tax rates would slow economic growth. He also felt that low-income households would gain more from faster economic growth than from progressive tax and transfer policies. After his 2000 election, he made tax *cuts* one of his highest priorities.

Reduced Marginal Rates. As Figure 33.2 illustrated, the 2001 Tax Relief Act reduced the highest marginal tax rate in three steps, to 35 percent from 39.6 percent. That act also reduced the marginal tax rate for the *lowest* income class to only 10 percent (from 15 percent). The goal of this rate cut was to increase the disposable income of low-wage workers (equity) while giving them more incentive to work (efficiency).

New "Loopholes." Aside from encouraging more *work,* President Bush also sought to encourage more *education.* The biggest incentive was a tuition tax deduction of $3,000 per year. This allows students, or their parents, to reduce their taxable income by the amount of tuition payments. In effect, Uncle Sam ends up paying part of the first $3,000 in tuition. In addition, the 2001 legislation allows people to save more money for college in tax-free accounts.

As welcome as these "loopholes" are to college students, they raise the same kind of efficiency and equity concerns as other tax preferences. If most of the students who take the tax deduction would have gone to college anyway, the deduction isn't very *efficient* in promoting education. Furthermore, most of the deductions go to middle-class families who itemize deductions. Hence the tuition deduction introduces new vertical *inequities*. Few students have protested this particular loophole, however.

The creation of this and other tax preferences raises all the same issues about equity and efficiency. ***The greater the number of loopholes, the wider the distinction between gross incomes and taxable incomes***, as the previous News reveals.

The Obama Tax Hikes

Despite his personal exposure to the highest tax rates, President Obama vowed to reverse the "Bush tax cuts for the rich." Within a month of his inauguration, Obama proposed to raise the highest marginal tax rate from 35 percent to its former 39.6 percent. He also proposed raising taxes on capital gains, dividends, and estates. Critics objected that the resultant gains in *equity* (Obama's avowed goal) would be more than offset by the loss of *efficiency*. In other words, the pie would shrink when Obama resliced it. When the economy fell into the 2008–2009 recession, President Obama agreed to table the proposed tax hikes. In 2011 he again pressed for higher marginal tax rates, however, and made it a pledge of his reelection campaign. In 2012, Congress agreed to increase the top marginal tax rate.

Trump Tax Cuts

The tax-rate pendulum swung back again with the election of Donald Trump. President Trump vowed to both simplify the tax code and reduce tax burdens as part of his broad "Make America Great Again" agenda. To that end, he proposed to reduce the number of tax brackets from seven to only three. He also proposed to limit sharply itemized deductions so as to shrink the gap between gross and taxable incomes. Last but not least, he proposed to reduce the top marginal tax rate on individuals to 35 percent from 39.6 percent. These changes were intended to make the personal income tax both more efficient and more fair.

President Trump proposed more dramatic changes for business taxes. He proposed to drop the tax rate on corporate incomes to 15 percent from 35 percent and to allow small, noncorporate businesses to enjoy the same low rate. The primary motivation for these proposals was *efficiency;* Trump believed such a dramatic drop in business taxes would spur a sharp increase in investment, and ultimately economic growth. Critics, though, worried about the *equity* implications of such tax cutting. The millions of businesses organized as partnerships and subchapter S corporations—disproportionately owned by higher income individuals—would get a windfall tax break. Congress had to grapple with these competing goals in deciding how to treat the Trump proposals.

PAYROLL, STATE, AND LOCAL TAXES

The federal income tax is only one of many taxes people must pay. For many families, in fact, the federal income tax is the smallest of many tax bills. Other tax bills come from the Social Security Administration and from state and local governments. These taxes also affect both efficiency and equity.

Sales and Property Taxes

Sales taxes are the major source of revenue for state governments. Many local governments also impose sales taxes, but most cities rely on *property taxes* for the bulk of their tax receipts. Both taxes are **regressive:** they impose higher tax rates on lower incomes.

regressive tax: A tax system in which tax rates fall as incomes rise.

TABLE 33.3

The Regressivity of Sales Taxes

A sales tax is imposed on consumer purchases. Although the sales tax itself is uniform (here at 5 percent), the taxes paid represent different proportions of high and low incomes. In this case, the low-income family's *sales tax* bill equals 4.75 percent of its *income*. The high-income family has a sales tax bill equal to only 2.86 percent of its income.

	High-Income Family	Low-Income Family
Income	$70,000	$20,000
Consumption	$40,000	$19,000
Saving	$30,000	$ 1,000
Sales tax paid (5% of consumption)	$ 2,000	$ 950
Effective tax rate (sales tax ÷ income)	2.86%	4.75%

At first glance, a 5 percent sales tax doesn't look very regressive. After all, the same 5 percent tax is imposed on virtually all goods. But we're interested in *people,* not goods and services, so **we gauge tax burdens in relation to people's incomes.** A tax is regressive if it imposes a proportionally *larger* burden on *lower* incomes.

This is exactly what a uniform sales tax does. To understand this concept, we have to look not only at how much tax is levied on each dollar of consumption but also at *what percentage of income* is spent on consumer goods.

Low-income families spend everything they've got (and sometimes more) on basic consumption. As a result, most of their income ends up subject to sales tax. By contrast, higher-income families save more. As a result, a smaller proportion of their income is subject to a sales tax. Table 33.3 illustrates this regressive feature of a sales tax. Notice that the low-income family ends up paying a larger fraction of its income (4.75 percent) than does the high-income family (2.86 percent).

Property taxes are regressive also and for the same reason. Low-income families spend a higher percentage of their incomes for shelter. A uniform property tax thus ends up taking a larger fraction of their income than it does of the incomes of high-income families.

Tax Incidence. It may sound strange to suggest that low-income families bear the brunt of property taxes. After all, the tax is imposed on the landlords who *own* property, not on people who *rent* apartments and houses. However, here again we have to distinguish between the apparent payee and the individual whose income is actually reduced by the tax. **Tax incidence** refers to the actual burden of a tax—that is, who really ends up paying it.

tax incidence: Distribution of the real burden of a tax.

In general, people who rent apartments pay higher rents as a result of property taxes. In other words, landlords pass along to tenants any property taxes they must pay. Thus to a large extent **the burden of property taxes is reflected in higher rents.** Tenants pay property taxes *indirectly* via these higher rents. The incidence of the property tax thus falls on renters in the form of higher rents, rather than on the landlords who write checks to the local tax authority.

Payroll Taxes

Payroll taxes also impose effective tax burdens quite different from their nominal appearance. Consider, for example, the Social Security payroll tax, the second-largest source of federal tax revenue (see Figure 4.5). Every worker sees a Social Security (FICA) tax taken out of his or her paycheck. The nominal tax rate on workers is 7.65 percent. But there's a catch: only wages below a legislated ceiling are taxable. In 2017, the taxable wage ceiling was $127,200. Hence a worker earning $200,000 paid no more tax than a worker earning $127,200. As a result, the effective tax *rate* (tax paid ÷ total wages) is lower for high-income workers than low- and middle-income workers. That's a *regressive* tax.

There is another problem in gauging the impact of the Social Security payroll tax. Nominally, the Social Security payroll tax consists of two parts: half paid by employees and half by employers. But do employers really pay their half? Or do they end up paying lower wages to compensate for their tax share? If so, employees end up paying *both* halves of the Social Security payroll tax.

Figure 33.3 illustrates how the tax incidence of the payroll tax is distributed. The supply of labor reflects the ability and willingness of people to work for various wage rates. Labor

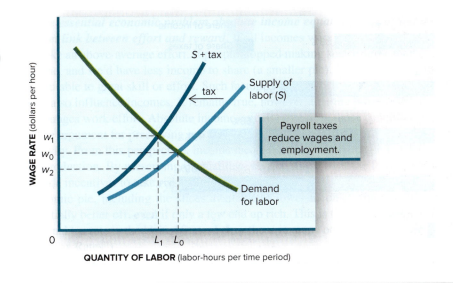

FIGURE 33.3

The Incidence of a Payroll Tax

Some portion of a payroll tax imposed on employers may actually be borne by workers. The tax raises the cost of labor and so imposes a tax-burdened supply curve (S + tax) on employers. The intersection of this tax-burdened supply curve with the labor demand curve determines a new equilibrium of employment (L_1). At that level, employers pay w_1 in wages and taxes, but workers get only w_2 in wages. The wage reduction from w_0 to w_2 is a real burden of the payroll tax, and it is borne by workers.

demand reflects the **marginal revenue product (MRP)** of labor; it sets a *limit* to the wage an employer is willing to pay.

marginal revenue product (MRP): The change in total revenue associated with one additional unit of input.

Cost of Labor. The employer's half of the payroll tax increases the nominal cost of labor. Thus the S + tax curve lies *above* the labor supply curve. It incorporates the wages that must be paid to workers *plus* the payroll tax that must be paid to the Social Security Trust Fund. This total labor cost is the one that will determine how many workers are hired. Specifically, the intersection of the S + tax curve and the labor demand curve determines the equilibrium level of employment (L_1). The employer will pay the amount w_1 for this much labor. But part of that outlay ($w_1 - w_2$) will go to the public treasury in the form of payroll taxes. Workers will receive only w_2 in wages. This is less than they'd get in the absence of the payroll tax (compare w_0 and w_2). Thus *fewer workers are employed, and the net wage is reduced when a payroll tax is imposed.*

Tax Incidence. What Figure 33.3 reveals is how the true incidence of payroll taxes is distributed. The employer share of the Social Security tax is $w_1 - w_2$. This is the amount sent to the Social Security Administration for every hour of labor. Of this amount, the employer incurs higher labor costs ($w_1 - w_0$) and workers lose ($w_0 - w_2$) in the wage rate. Hence workers end up paying *their* share (7.65 percent) of the Social Security tax *plus* a sizable part ($w_0 - w_2$) of the employer's share ($w_1 - w_2$).

These reflections on tax incidence don't imply that payroll taxes are necessarily bad. They do emphasize, however, that *the apparent taxpayer isn't necessarily the individual who bears the real burden of a tax.*

TAXES AND INEQUALITY

The regressivity of the Social Security payroll tax and of many state and local taxes offsets most of the progressivity of the federal income tax. The top 1 percent of income recipients gets 19 percent of total income and pays 38 percent of federal income tax (see Figure 33.4). Hence the federal income tax is still progressive, despite rampant loopholes. Other federal taxes (Social Security, excise), however, reduce the tax share of the rich to only 21 percent. State and local tax incidence reduces their tax share still further.

A Proportional System

The final result is that *the tax system as a whole ends up being nearly proportional.* High-income families end up paying roughly the same percentage of their income in taxes as do

The second argument is that low-income earners might actually work harder if incomes were distributed more fairly. As matters now stand, the low-income worker sees little chance of making it big. Extremely low income can also inhibit workers' ability to work by subjecting them to poor health, malnutrition, or inadequate educational opportunities. Accordingly, some redistribution of income to the poor might improve the productivity of low-income workers and compensate for reduced productivity among the rich.

Finally, we noted that the maze of loopholes that preserves inequality also distorts economic incentives. Labor and investment decisions are influenced by tax considerations, not just economic benefits and costs. If greater equality were achieved via tax simplification, a more efficient allocation of resources might result.

THE ECONOMY TOMORROW

A FLAT TAX?

flat tax: A single-rate tax system.

Widespread dissatisfaction with the present tax system has spawned numerous reform proposals. One of the most debated proposals is to replace the current federal income tax with a **flat tax.** First proposed by Nobel Prize–winner Milton Friedman in the early 1960s, the flat tax was championed in Congress by former majority leader (and former economics professor) Dick Armey.

The key features of a flat tax include

- Replacing the current system of multiple tax brackets and rates with a single (flat) tax rate that would apply to all taxable income.
- Eliminating all deductions, credits, and most exemptions.

Simplicity. A major attraction of the flat tax is its simplicity. The current 74,608-page tax code that details all the provisions of the present system would be scrapped. The 800 different IRS tax forms now in use would be replaced by a single, postcard-sized form.

Fairness. Flat tax advocates also emphasize its fairness. They point to the rampant vertical and horizontal inequities created by the current tangle of tax loopholes. By scrapping all those deductions, the flat tax would treat everyone equally.

Some progressivity could also be preserved with a flat tax. In the version proposed by Dick Armey, the flat tax rate would be 17 percent, but one personal exemption would be maintained. Every adult would get a personal exemption of $13,100 and each child an exemption of $5,300. Accordingly, a family of four would have personal exemptions of $36,800. Hence a family earning less than that amount would pay no income tax. *Effective* tax rates would increase along with rising incomes above that threshold.

Efficiency. Proponents of a flat tax claim it enhances efficiency as well as equity. Taxpayers now spend more than a billion hours a year preparing tax returns. Legions of lobbyists, accountants, and lawyers devote their energy to tax analysis and avoidance. With a simplified flat tax, all those labor resources could be put to more productive use.

A flat tax would also change the mix of output. Consumption and investment decisions would be made on the basis of economic considerations, not tax consequences.

The Critique. As alluring as a flat tax appears, it has aroused substantial opposition. As proposed by Dick Armey, the flat tax would not apply to all income. Income on savings and investments (such as interest and dividends, capital gains) wouldn't be taxed. The purpose of that exemption would be to encourage greater saving, investment, and economic growth. At the same time, however, such a broad exemption creates a whole new set of horizontal and vertical inequities. Someone receiving $1 million in interest and dividends could escape all income taxes, while a family earning $50,000 in wages would have to pay.

Critics also object to the wholesale elimination of all deductions and credits. Many of those loopholes are expressly designed to encourage desired economic activity. The Bush tax cuts were explicitly designed to encourage education, family stability, and savings. President Obama used tax deductions and credits to encourage more use of solar power. By discarding all tax preferences, the flat tax significantly reduces the government's ability to alter the mix of output.

Finally, critics point out that the transition to a flat tax would entail a wholesale reshuffling of wealth and income. Home values would fall precipitously if the tax preference for homeownership were eliminated. That would hit the middle class particularly hard. State and local governments would have greater difficulty raising their own revenues if the federal deduction for state and local taxes were eliminated. Confronted with such consequences, many people begin to have second thoughts about the desirability of adopting a flat tax in the economy tomorrow. Taxpayers seem to like the *principle* of a flat tax more than its actual provisions.

SUMMARY

- The distribution of income largely determines access to the goods and services we produce. Wealth distribution is important for the same reason. **LO33-3**
- The size distribution of income tells us how incomes are divided up among individuals. The Lorenz curve is a graphic summary of the cumulative size distribution of income. The Gini coefficient is a mathematical summary. **LO33-3**
- Personal incomes are distributed quite unevenly in the United States. At present, the highest quintile (the top 20 percent) gets half of all cash income, and the bottom quintile gets less than 4 percent. **LO33-3**
- The trade-off between equity and efficiency is rooted in supply incentives. The tax elasticity of supply measures how the quantity of available resources (labor and capital) declines when tax rates rise. **LO33-3**
- The progressivity of the federal income tax is weakened by various loopholes (exemptions, deductions, and credits) that create a distinction between nominal and effective tax rates and cause vertical and horizontal inequities. **LO33-2**
- Marginal tax rates were reduced greatly in the 1980s and have alternately risen and fallen since. **LO33-1**

- Mildly progressive federal income taxes are offset by regressive payroll, state, and local taxes. Overall, the tax system redistributes little income; most redistribution occurs through transfer payments. **LO33-2**
- Tax incidence refers to the real burden of a tax. In many cases, reductions in wages, increases in rent, or other real income changes represent the true burden of a tax. **LO33-2**
- There is a trade-off between efficiency and equality. If all incomes are equal, there's no economic reward for superior productivity. On the other hand, a more equal distribution of incomes might increase the productivity of lower-income groups and serve important non-economic goals as well. **LO33-3**
- A flat tax is a nominally proportional tax system. A personal exemption and the exclusion of capital income can render a flat tax progressive or regressive, however. A flat tax reduces the government's role in resource allocation (the WHAT and HOW questions). **LO33-1**

Key Terms

personal income (PI)	progressive tax	regressive tax
in-kind income	marginal tax rate	tax incidence
wealth	tax elasticity of supply	marginal revenue product (MRP)
size distribution of income	vertical equity	income transfers
income share	horizontal equity	government failure
Lorenz curve	nominal tax rate	flat tax
Gini coefficient	effective tax rate	
market failure	tax base	

Questions for Discussion

1. What goods or services do you and your family receive without directly paying for them? How do these goods affect the distribution of economic welfare? **LO33-2**

2. Why are incomes distributed so unevenly? Identify and explain three major causes of inequality. **LO33-3**

3. Do inequalities stimulate productivity? In what ways? Provide two specific examples. **LO33-3**

4. What loopholes reduced the Pences' and the Clintons' 2015 tax bill (see In the News "Taxes: The Pences vs. the Clintons")? What's the purpose of those loopholes? **LO33-1**

5. How might a flat tax affect efficiency? Fairness? **LO33-3**

6. If a new tax system encouraged more output but also created greater inequality, would it be desirable? **LO33-3**

7. If the tax elasticity of supply were zero, how high could the tax rate go before people reduced their work effort? How do families vary the quantity of labor supplied when tax rates change? **LO33-3**

8. Is a tax deduction for tuition likely to increase college enrollments? How will it affect horizontal and vertical equities? **LO33-3**

9. What share of taxes *should* the rich pay (see Figure 33.4)? Should the poor pay *any* taxes? **LO33-3**

10. How would President Trump's proposed changes in the tax system affect efficiency and equity? Should they have been adopted? **LO33-3**

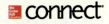

PROBLEMS FOR CHAPTER 33

LO33-1 1. How much tax did the Clintons pay in 2015 (In the News "Taxes: The Pences vs. the Clintons") on:
  (*a*) The first $9,000 of taxable income?
  (*b*) The last $9,000 of taxable income?
  How much tax did the Pences pay in 2015 on:
  (*c*) The first $9,000 of taxable income?
  (*d*) The last $9,000 of taxable income?

LO33-2 2. If there were no deduction for charitable contributions, how much more tax would the Clintons have paid in 2015 (In the News "Taxes: The Pences vs. the Clintons")?

LO33-2 3. According to In the News "Taxes: The Pences vs. the Clintons," in 2015 what was the Pences'
  (*a*) Nominal tax rate?
  (*b*) Effective tax rate?

LO33-1 4. Use Table 33.1 to compute the taxes on a taxable income of $200,000.
  (*a*) What is the marginal tax rate?
  (*b*) What is the average tax rate?

LO33-1 5. Using Table 33.1, compute the taxable income and taxes for the following taxpayers:

Taxpayer	Gross Income	Exemptions and Deductions	Taxable Income	Tax
A	$ 20,000	$ 4,000	_____	_____
B	40,000	16,000	_____	_____
C	80,000	34,000	_____	_____
D	200,000	110,000	_____	_____

  Which taxpayer has
  (*a*) The highest nominal tax rate?
  (*b*) The highest effective tax rate?
  (*c*) The highest marginal tax rate?

LO33-2 6. If the tax elasticity of supply is 0.15, by how much will the quantity supplied increase when the marginal tax rate decreases from 40 to 36 percent?

LO33-2 7. By how much might the quantity of labor supplied decrease if the tax elasticity of supply were 0.20 and the marginal tax rate increased from 35 to 45 percent?

LO33-3 8. What is the difference in the top marginal tax rate between Japan and Hong Kong (World View "Top Tax Rates")?

LO33-2 9. What percentage of income is paid in Social Security taxes by a worker with wage earnings of
  (*a*) $30,000?
  (*b*) $70,000?
  (*c*) $200,000?
  (*d*) Is this a progressive, regressive, or proportional tax?

LO33-1 10. Following are hypothetical data on the size distribution of income and wealth for each quintile (one-fifth) of a population:

Quintile	Lowest	Second	Third	Fourth	Highest
Income	5%	10%	15%	25%	45%
Wealth	2%	8%	12%	20%	58%

(a) On the a graph, draw the line of absolute equity; then draw a Lorenz curve for income, and shade the area between the two curves.

(b) In the same diagram, draw a Lorenz curve for wealth. Is the distribution of wealth more equal or less equal than the distribution of income?

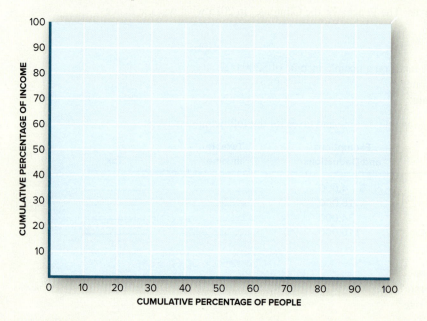

LO33-3 11. (a) On the graph shown below, draw the supply and demand for labor represented by the following data:

Wage	12	11	10	9	8	7	6	5	4	3	2	$1
Quantity of labor												
Supplied	20	17	14	12	10	8	6	5	4	3	2	1
Demanded	2	3	4	5	6	8	10	12	14	16	18	20

(b) How many workers are employed in equilibrium?

(c) What wage are they paid?

(d) Now suppose a payroll tax of $2 per worker is imposed on the employer. Draw the "supply + tax" graph that results.

(e) How many workers are now employed?

(f) Now how much is the employer paying for each worker?

(g) Now how much is each worker receiving?

For the incidence of this tax, compared to the initial equilibrium:

(h) What is the increase in the wage paid by the employer?

(i) What is the reduction in the wage received by the workers?

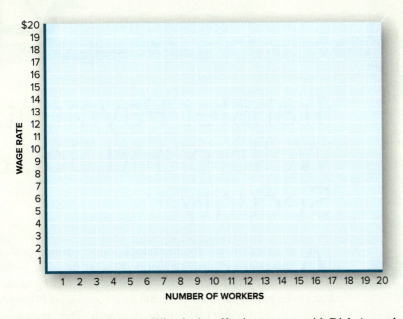

LO33-3 12. The Economy Tomorrow: What is the effective tax rate with Dick Armey's proposed flat tax for a family of four with earnings of
(a) $30,000?
(b) $50,000?
(c) $100,000?

©DreamPictures/Pam Ostrow/Blend Images LLC RF

Transfer Payments: Welfare and Social Security

income transfers: Payments to individuals for which no current goods or services are exchanged, such as Social Security, welfare, and unemployment benefits.

Americans are compassionate. Public opinion polls reveal that an overwhelming majority of the public wants to "help the needy." Most Americans say they're even willing to pay more taxes to help fund aid to the poor. But their compassion is tempered by caution: taxpayers don't want to be ripped off. They want to be sure their money is helping the "truly needy," not being squandered by deadbeats, drug addicts, shirkers, and "welfare queens."

The conflict between compassion and resentment affects not only welfare programs for the poor but also Social Security for the aged, unemployment insurance benefits for the jobless, and even disability benefits for injured workers. In every one of these programs, people are getting money without working. In effect, they're getting a "free ride."

The risk of providing a free ride is that some of the people who take it could have gotten by without it. As the humorist Dave Barry observed, if the government offers $1 million to people with six toes, a lot of people will try to grow a sixth toe or claim they have one. Income transfers create similar incentives: they encourage people to change their behavior in order to get a free ride.

This chapter focuses on how income transfer programs change not only the distribution of income but also work incentives and behavior. We address the following central questions:

- **How much income do income transfer programs redistribute?**
- **How are transfer benefits computed?**
- **How do transfer payments alter market behavior?**

MAJOR TRANSFER PROGRAMS

More than half of every dollar the federal government spends goes to **income transfers** (see Figure 4.5). That amounts to *$2.5 trillion* a year in transfer payments. Who gets all this money?

The easy answer to this question is that almost every household gets some of the transfer money. There are more than 100 federal income transfer programs. Students get tuition grants and subsidized loans. Farmers get crop assistance. Home owners get disaster relief when their homes are destroyed. Veterans get benefit checks and subsidized health care. People over age 65 get Social Security benefits and

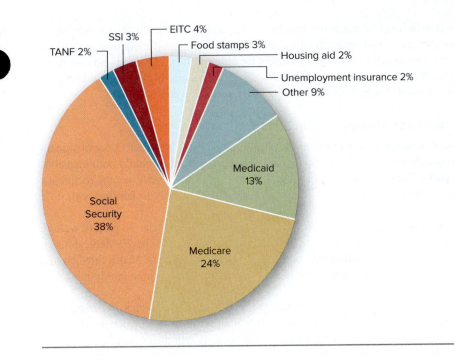

FIGURE 34.1

Income Transfer Programs

There are nearly 100 different federal income transfer programs redistributing more than $2 trillion. However, just three programs—Social Security, Medicare, and Medicaid—account for 75 percent of all transfers. Cash welfare benefits (TANF, SSI) absorb only 5 percent of all income transfers.

Source: U.S. Office of Management and Budget (FY 2016 data).

subsidized health care. And poor people get welfare checks, food stamps, and subsidized housing.

Although income transfers are widely distributed, not everyone shares equally in the tax-paid bounty. As Figure 34.1 shows, just three of the myriad transfer programs account for 75 percent of total outlays. Social Security, the largest program, alone accounts for 38 percent of the transfer budget. Medicare and Medicaid benefits absorb another 37 percent. By contrast, welfare checks account for only 4 percent of all income transfers.

Cash versus In-Kind Benefits

Income transfer doesn't always entail cash payments. The Medicare program, for example, is a health insurance subsidy program that pays hospital and doctor bills for people over age 65. The 56 million people who receive Medicare benefits don't get checks from Uncle Sam; instead Uncle Sam pays the bills for the medical *services* they receive. The same is true for the 69 million people who get Medicaid. Poor people get free health care from the Medicaid program; their benefits are paid *in-kind,* not in cash. Such programs provide **in-kind transfers**—that is, direct transfers of goods and services rather than cash. Food stamps, rent subsidies, legal aid, and subsidized school lunches are all in-kind transfer programs. By contrast, Social Security is a **cash transfer** because it mails benefit checks, not services, to recipients.

The provision of in-kind benefits rather than cash is intended to promote specific objectives. Few taxpayers object to feeding the hungry. But they bristle at the thought that welfare recipients might spend the income they receive on something potentially harmful like liquor or drugs or on nonessentials like cars or fancy clothes. To minimize that risk, taxpayers offer electronic food stamps (now called Supplemental Nutrition Assistance Program [SNAP] vouchers), not cash, thereby limiting the recipient's consumption choices. This helps reassure taxpayers that their assistance is being well spent.

Similar considerations shape the Medicare program. Taxpayers could "cash out" Medicare by simply mailing older people the $700 billion now spent on the program every year. But then some healthy older Americans would get cash they didn't need. Some sick people might not get as much money as *they* needed. Or they might choose to spend their new-found income on something other than health care. The end result would be a smaller health care gain than in-kind transfers facilitate.

in-kind transfers: Direct transfers of goods and services rather than cash, such as food stamps, Medicaid benefits, and housing subsidies.

cash transfers: Income transfers that entail direct cash payments to recipients, such as Social Security, welfare, and unemployment benefits.

target efficiency: The percentage of income transfers that go to the intended recipients and purposes.

The **target efficiency** of a transfer program refers to how well income transfers attain their intended purpose. In-kind medical transfers are more target-efficient than cash transfers because recipients can spend cash transfers for other purposes. Food stamps are more target-efficient than cash in reducing hunger for the same reason. If given cash rather than food stamps, recipients would spend less than 70 cents of each dollar on food.

Social Insurance versus Welfare

You may have noted by now that not all income transfers go to the poor. A lot of student loans go to middle-class college students. And disaster relief helps rebuild both mansions and trailer parks. Such income transfers are triggered by specific *events,* not the recipient's income. By contrast, welfare checks are *means-tested:* they go only to families with little income and few assets.

welfare programs: Means-tested income transfer programs, such as welfare and food stamps.

Welfare programs always entail some kind of income eligibility test. To receive welfare payments, a family must prove that it has too little income to fend for itself. Medicaid is an in-kind **welfare program** because only poor people are eligible for the health care benefits of that program. To get food stamps, another in-kind welfare program, a family must also pass an income test.

Social Security and Medicare aren't *welfare* programs because recipients don't have to be poor. To get Social Security or Medicare benefits you just have to be old enough. The *event* of reaching age 62 makes people eligible for Social Security retirement benefits. At age 65 everyone—whether rich or poor—gets Medicare benefits. These event-conditioned benefits are the hallmark of **social insurance programs:** they insure people against the costs of old age, illness, disability, unemployment, and other specific problems. As Figure 34.2 illustrates, *most income transfers are for social insurance programs, not welfare.*

social insurance programs: Event-conditioned income transfers intended to reduce the costs of specific problems, such as Social Security and unemployment insurance.

Transfer Goals

If the market sliced up the economic pie in a manner that society deemed fair, there would be no need for all these government-provided income transfers. Hence the mere existence of such programs implies a **market failure**—an unfair market-generated distribution of income. When the market alone slices up the pie, some people get too much and others get too little. To redress this inequity, we ask the government to play Robin Hood—taking income from the rich and giving it to the poor. Thus *the basic goal of income transfer programs is to reduce income inequalities*—to change the market's answer to the FOR WHOM question.

market failure: An imperfection in the market mechanism that prevents optimal outcomes.

Unintended Consequences

Although income transfers try to change the distribution of income in desired ways, they are not costless interventions. The Law of Unintended Consequences rears its ugly head

---

FIGURE 34.2

Social Insurance versus Welfare

Social insurance programs provide *event*-based transfers— for example, upon reaching age 65 or becoming unemployed or disabled. Welfare programs offer benefits only to those in need; they're *means-tested*. Social insurance transfers greatly outnumber welfare transfers.

Source: U.S. Office of Management and Budget (FY 2016 data).

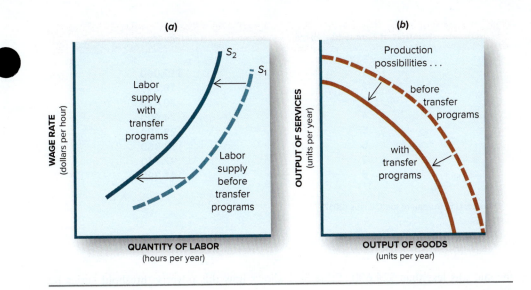

FIGURE 34.3

Reduced Labor Supply and Output

Transfer payments may induce people to supply less labor. If this happens, the supply of labor shifts to the left and the economy's production possibilities shrink. We end up with less total output.

here: *income transfers often change market behavior and outcomes in unintended (and undesired) ways.*

Reduced Output. Work incentives are a potential problem. If you can get paid for *not* working (via a transfer payment), why would you go to work? Why endure 40 hours of toil for a paycheck when you can stay home and collect a welfare check, an unemployment check, or Social Security? If the income transfers are large enough, I'll stay home too. When people reduce their **labor supply** in response to income transfers, total output will shrink. Figure 34.3 shows that *attempts to redistribute income may reduce total income.* In other words, the pie shrinks when we try to reslice it.

labor supply: The willingness and ability to work specific amounts of time at alternative wage rates in a given time period, *ceteris paribus.*

Undesirable Behavior. A reduction in labor supply isn't the only unintended consequence of income transfer programs. People may also change their *nonwork* behavior. Welfare benefits give a (small) incentive to women to have more children and to teen moms to establish their own households. Medicare and Medicaid encourage people to overuse health care services and neglect the associated costs. Unemployment benefits encourage workers to stay jobless longer. And as Dave Barry noted at the beginning of the chapter, disability payments encourage people to grow a sixth toe. Although the actual response to these incentives is hotly debated, the existence of the undesired incentives is unambiguous.

WELFARE PROGRAMS

To understand how income transfer programs change market behavior and outcomes, let's look closely at how welfare programs operate. The largest federal cash welfare program is called Temporary Aid to Needy Families (TANF). The TANF program was created by congressional welfare reforms in 1996 and replaced an earlier program (AFDC) that had operated since 1935. The new program offers states more discretion to decide who gets welfare, under what conditions, and for how long.

Benefit Determination

The first task of the TANF program is to identify potential recipients. In principle, this task is easy: find out who is poor. To do this, the federal government has established a poverty line that specifies how much cash income families of different sizes need just to buy basic necessities. In 2017, the federal government estimated that a family of four was poor if its

TABLE 34.1

Poverty Lines

The official definition of poverty relates current income to the minimal needs of a family. Poverty thresholds vary with family size. In 2017, a family of four was considered poor if it had less than $24,600 of income.

Number of Family Members	Family Income
1	$12,060
2	16,240
3	20,420
4	24,600
5	28,780
6	32,960
7	37,140
8	41,320

Source: U.S. Bureau of the Census (2017).

poverty gap: The shortfall between actual income and the poverty threshold.

income was less than $24,600. Table 34.1 shows how this poverty threshold varies by family size.

According to Table 34.1, a four-person family with $20,000 of income in 2017 would have had a **poverty gap**—the shortfall between actual income and the poverty threshold—of $4,600. The Jones family needed at least that much *additional* income to purchase what the government deems a "minimally adequate" standard of living.

So how much welfare should the government give this family? Should it give $4,600 to this family, thereby closing its poverty gap? As simple as that proposition sounds, it creates some unintended problems.

The Work Incentive Problem

Suppose we guaranteed all families enough income to reach their respective poverty line. Any family earning less than the poverty line would receive a welfare check in the amount of their poverty gap. No one would be poor.

This sounds like a simple solution to the poverty problem, but it isn't. First, people who *weren't* poor would have a strong incentive to become poor. Why try to support a family of four with a paycheck of $25,000 when you can quit and get $24,600 in welfare checks? Recall from Chapter 30 that the decision to work is a response to both the financial and psychological rewards associated with employment. People in dull, dirty, low-paying jobs get little of either. By quitting their jobs, declaring themselves poor, and accepting a guaranteed income transfer, they would gain much more leisure at little financial or psychological cost. In the process, total output would shrink (Figure 34.3).

The second potential problem affects the work behavior of people who were poor to begin with. We assumed that the Jones family was earning $20,000 before they got a welfare check. The question now is whether the welfare check will change their work behavior.

Suppose that family gets an opportunity to earn an extra $2,000 a year by working overtime. Should they seize that opportunity? Consider the effect of the higher *wages* on the family's *income*. Before working overtime, the Jones family earned

INCOME WITHOUT OVERTIME WAGES

Wages	$20,000
Welfare benefits	4,600
Total income	$24,600

If they now work overtime, their income is

INCOME WITH OVERTIME WAGES

Wages	$22,000
Welfare benefits	2,600
Total income	$24,600

Something is wrong here: although *wages* have gone up, the family's *income* hasn't. How would you like to be in this position? How would you react? Would you work overtime?

Implicit Marginal Tax Rates. The failure of income to rise with wages is the by-product of how welfare benefits were computed. *If welfare benefits are set equal to the poverty gap, every additional dollar of wages reduces welfare benefits by the same amount.* In effect, the Jones family confronts a **marginal tax rate** of 100 percent: every dollar of wages results in a lost dollar of benefits. Uncle Sam isn't literally raising the family's taxes by a dollar. By reducing benefits dollar for dollar, however, the end result is the same.

> **marginal tax rate:** The tax rate imposed on the last (marginal) dollar of income.

With a 100 percent marginal tax rate, a family can't improve its income by working more. In fact, this family might as well work *less.* As wages decline, welfare benefits increase by the same amount. Thus we end up with a conflict between compassion and work incentives. By guaranteeing a poverty-level income, we destroy the economic incentive of low-income workers to support themselves. This creates a **moral hazard** for welfare recipients; that is, we encourage undesirable behavior. The moral hazard here is the temptation not to support oneself by working—choosing welfare checks instead.

> **moral hazard:** An incentive to engage in undesirable behavior.

Less Compassion

To reduce this moral hazard, Congress and the states changed the way benefits are computed. First, they set a much lower ceiling on welfare benefits. States don't offer to close the poverty gap; instead they set a maximum benefit far below the poverty line. Hence we have this amended benefit formula:

$$\frac{\text{Welfare}}{\text{benefit}} = \frac{\text{Maximum}}{\text{benefit}} - \text{Wages}$$

In 2017, the typical state set a maximum benefit of about $9,000 for a family of four. Hence a family without any other income couldn't get enough money from welfare to stay out of poverty. As a result, *a family totally dependent on welfare is unquestionably poor.* Although the lower benefit ceiling is less compassionate, it reduces the risk of people climbing on the welfare wagon for a free ride.

More Incentives

To encourage welfare recipients to lift their own incomes above the poverty line, welfare departments made another change in the benefit formula. As we just saw, *the rate at which benefits are reduced as wages increase is the marginal tax rate.* The dollar-for-dollar benefit cuts illustrated destroyed the financial incentive to work. To give recipients more incentive to work, the marginal tax rate was cut from 100 to 67 percent. So we now have a new benefit formula:

$$\frac{\text{Welfare}}{\text{benefit}} = \frac{\text{Maximum}}{\text{benefit}} - \frac{2}{3}[\text{Wages}]$$

Figure 34.4 illustrates how this lower marginal tax rate alters the relationship of total income to wages. The black line in the figure shows the total wages Mrs. Jones could earn at $9 per hour. She could earn nothing by not working or as much as $18,000 per year by working full-time (2,000 hours per year, as depicted by point *F* in the figure).

The blue lines in the figure show what happens to her welfare benefits and total income when a 100 percent marginal tax rate is imposed. At point *A* she gets $9,000 in welfare benefits because she's not working at all. That $9,000 is also her total income because she has no wages.

Now consider what happens to the family's total income if Mrs. Jones goes to work. If she works 1,000 hours per year (essentially half-time), she could earn $9,000 (point *B*). But what would happen to her *income*? If the welfare department cuts her benefit by $1 for every dollar she earns, her benefit check slides down the blue "welfare benefits" line to point *C*, where she gets nothing from welfare. By working 1,000 hours per year, all

FIGURE 34.4

Work (Dis)incentives

If welfare benefits are reduced dollar for dollar as wages increase, the implied marginal tax rate is 100 percent. In that case, total income remains at the benefit limit of $9,000 (point *A*) as work effort increases from 0 to 1,000 hours (point *B*). There is no incentive to work in this range.

When the marginal tax rate is reduced to 67 percent, total income starts increasing as soon as the welfare recipient starts working. At 1,000 hours of work, total income is $12,000 (point *G*).

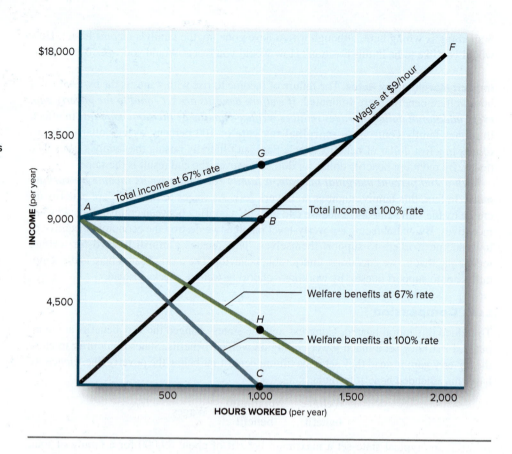

Mrs. Jones has done is replace her welfare check with a paycheck. That might make tax-payers smile, but Mrs. Jones will wonder why she bothered to go to work. With a 100 percent tax rate, her total income doesn't rise above $9,000 until she works more than 1,000 hours.

The green lines in Figure 34.4 show how work incentives improve with a lower marginal tax rate. Now welfare benefits are reduced by only 67 cents for every $1 of wages earned. As a result, total income starts rising as soon as Mrs. Jones goes to work. If she works 1,000 hours, her total income will include

Wages	$ 9,000	
Welfare benefit	3,000	= $9,000 − 2/3($9,000)
Total income	$12,000	

Point *G* on the graph illustrates this outcome.

Incentives versus Costs

It may be comforting to know that the Jones family can now increase its income from $9,000 when not working to $12,000 by working 1,000 hours per year. But they still face a higher marginal tax rate (67 percent) than rich people (the top marginal tax rate on federal income taxes is 39.6 percent). Why not lower their marginal tax rate even further, thus increasing both their work incentives and their total income?

Unfortunately, a reduction in the marginal tax rate would also increase welfare costs. Suppose we eliminated the marginal tax rate altogether. Then the Jones family could earn wages of $9,000 by working 1,000 hours *and* keep welfare benefits of $9,000. That would boost their total income to $18,000. Sounds great, doesn't it? But should we still be providing $9,000 in welfare payments to someone who earns $9,000 on her own? How about someone earning $20,000 or $30,000? Where should we draw the line? Clearly, *if we don't impose a marginal tax rate at some point, everyone will be eligible for welfare benefits.*

The thought of giving everyone a welfare check might sound like a great idea, but it would turn out to be incredibly expensive. In the end, we'd have to take those checks back, in the form of increased taxes, to pay for the vastly expanded program. We must recognize, then, a basic dilemma:

- *Low marginal tax rates encourage more work effort but make more people eligible for welfare.*
- *High marginal tax rates discourage work effort but make fewer people eligible for welfare.*

The conflict between work incentives and the desire to limit welfare costs and eligibility can be summarized in this simple equation:

$$\text{Breakeven level of income} = \frac{\text{Basic benefits}}{\text{Marginal tax rate}}$$

The **breakeven level of income** is the amount of income a person can earn before losing all welfare benefits. In the Joneses' case, the basic welfare benefit was $9,000 per year and the benefit reduction (marginal tax) rate was 0.67. Hence the family could earn as much as

breakeven level of income: The income level at which welfare eligibility ceases.

$$\text{Breakeven level of income} = \frac{\$9,000}{0.67} \text{ per year}$$

$$= \$13,500$$

before losing all welfare benefits. Thus *low marginal tax rates encourage work but make it hard to get completely off welfare.*

If the marginal tax rate were 100 percent, as under the old welfare system, the breakeven point would be $9,000 divided by 1.00. In that case, people who earned $9,000 on their own would get no assistance from welfare. Fewer people would be eligible for welfare, but those who drew benefits would have no incentive to work. If the marginal tax rate were lowered to 0, the breakeven point would rise to infinity ($9,000 divided by 0)—and we'd all be on welfare.

As this arithmetic shows, *there's a basic conflict between work incentives (low marginal tax rates) and welfare containment (smaller welfare rolls and outlays).* We can achieve a lower breakeven level of income (less welfare eligibility) only by sacrificing low marginal tax rates or higher income floors (basic benefits). Hence welfare costs can be minimized only if we sacrifice income provision or work incentives.

Tax Elasticity of Labor Supply. The terms of the trade-off between more welfare and less work depend on how responsive people are to marginal tax rates. As we first noted in Chapter 33, the **tax elasticity of labor supply** measures the response to changes in tax rates:

tax elasticity of labor supply: The percentage change in quantity of labor supplied divided by the percentage change in tax rates.

$$\text{Tax elasticity of labor supply} = \frac{\% \text{ change in quantity of labor supplied}}{\% \text{ change in tax rate}}$$

If the tax elasticity of labor supply were zero, it wouldn't matter how high the marginal tax rate was: people would work for nothing (100 percent tax rate). In reality, the tax elasticity of labor supply among low-wage workers is more in the range of 0.2 to 0.3, so marginal tax rates *do* affect work effort. *So long as the tax elasticity of labor supply is greater than zero, there is a conflict between equity (more welfare) and efficiency (more work).*

Time Limits. The 1996 welfare reforms partially sidestepped this dilemma by setting time limits on welfare eligibility. TANF recipients *must* engage in some sort of employment-related activity (e.g., a job, job search, or training) within two years of first receiving benefits. There is also a five-year *lifetime* limit on welfare eligibility. States, however, can still use their own (nonfederal) funds to extend welfare benefits beyond those time limits.

FIGURE 34.6

The Social Security Earnings Test

A worker aged 62–64 can earn up to $16,920 (point *A*) without losing any Social Security benefits. At point *C*, income includes $12,000 in benefits and $16,920 in wages.

If wages increase beyond $16,920, however, Social Security benefits decline by 50 cents for every $1 earned. After point *C*, income rises only half as fast as wages.

At the breakeven point *D*, earnings are $40,920, and there are no Social Security benefits (point *B*).

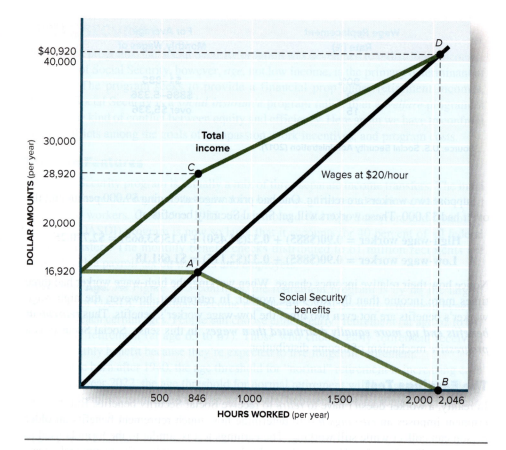

Beyond that, however, every additional hour of work brings in $20 of wages but a $10 reduction in benefits. After point *C*, his income rises *half* as fast as his wages. That's a real disincentive to work.

In reality, the marginal tax rate on Leonard's wages is even higher and the incentive to work lower. If he works, Leonard will have to pay the Social Security payroll tax (7.65 percent) as well as federal, state, and local income taxes (say, another 15 percent). These additional (explicit) taxes increase the *combined* marginal tax rate to 72.65 percent. In other words, Leonard would get to keep only 27.35 cents out of every additional dollar he earned.

Declining Labor Supply

labor force participation rate: The percentage of the working-age population working or seeking employment.

Like welfare recipients, older people are quick to realize that work no longer pays. Not surprisingly, they've exited the labor market in droves. The **labor force participation rate** measures the percentage of the population that is either employed or actively seeking a job (unemployed). Figure 34.7 shows how precipitously the labor force participation rate has declined among older Americans. This problem isn't unique to the United States. The relative size of the over-65 population is growing everywhere, and more older people are retiring earlier.

Prior to the creation of the Social Security system, most older people had to continue working until advanced age. Many "died with their boots on" because they had no other means of support. Just a generation ago, more than 75 percent of men 62 to 64 were working. Today less than 50 percent of that group is working.

Compassion, Incentives, and Cost

The primary economic cost of the Social Security program isn't the benefits it pays but the reduction in total output that occurs when workers retire early. In the absence of Social Security benefits, millions of older workers would still be on the job, contributing to the output of goods and services. When they instead retire—or simply work less—total output shrinks.

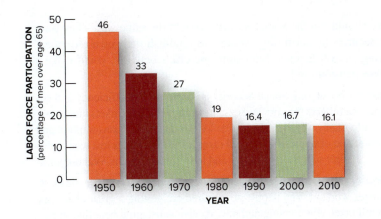

FIGURE 34.7

Declining Labor Force Participation

In the 1960s and 1970s, the eligibility age for Social Security was lowered for men and benefits were increased. This convinced an increased percentage of older men to leave the labor force and retire. In a single generation the labor force participation rate of men over age 65 was halved.

Source: U.S. Bureau of Labor Statistics.

Trade-offs. Just because the intergenerational redistribution is expensive doesn't mean we shouldn't do it. Going to college is expensive too, but you're doing it. The real economic issue is benefits versus costs. Compassion for older workers is what motivates Social Security transfers. Presumably, society gains from the more equitable distribution of income that results (a revised FOR WHOM). The economic concern is that we *balance* this gain against the implied costs.

One way of reducing the economic cost of the Social Security program would be to eliminate the earnings test. AARP (formerly known as the American Association of Retired Persons) has advocated this option for many years. If the earnings test were eliminated, the marginal tax rate on the wages of older workers would drop from 50 percent to 0. In a flash, the work disincentive would vanish, and older workers would produce more goods and services.

There's a downside to this reform, however. If the earnings test were eliminated, all older individuals would get their full retirement benefit, even if they continued to work. This would raise the budgetary cost of the program substantially. To cover that cost, payroll taxes would have to increase. Higher payroll taxes would in turn reduce supply and demand for *younger* workers. Hence the financial burden of eliminating the earnings test might actually *increase* the economic cost of Social Security.

There's also an equity issue here. Should we increase payroll taxes on younger low-income workers to give higher Social Security benefits to older workers who still command higher salaries? In 2000 Congress gave a very qualified "yes" to this question. The earnings test was eliminated for workers over age 70 and for workers who retired at "normal" age (65–67 depending on year of birth). The marginal tax rate for workers who "retire" early but continue working at ages 65–69 was also reduced to 33.3 percent. The lower earnings test and 50 percent marginal tax rate were left intact, however, for people aged 62–64, the ones for whom the retirement decision is most pressing. The *budget* cost of greater work incentives for "early retirees" (ages 62–64) was regarded as too high.

THE ECONOMY TOMORROW

PRIVATIZE SOCIAL SECURITY?

All income transfer programs entail a redistribution of income. In the case of Social Security, the redistribution is largely intergenerational: *payroll taxes levied on younger workers finance retirement benefits for older workers.* The system is financed on a pay-as-you-go basis; future benefits depend on future taxes. This is very different from private pension plans, whereby you salt away some wages while working to finance your own eventual benefits. Such private plans are *advance-funded.*

Continued

Many people say we should run the Social Security system the same way. They want to "privatize" Social Security by permitting workers to establish their own retirement plans. Instead of paying payroll taxes to fund someone else's benefits, you'd make a contribution to your *own* pension fund.

More Output. The case for privatizing Social Security is based on both efficiency and equity. The efficiency argument reflects the core laissez-faire argument that markets know best. In a privatized system, individuals would have the freedom to tailor their consumption and saving choices. The elimination of mandatory payroll taxes and the earnings test would also lessen work disincentives. People would work harder and longer, maximizing total output.

Intergenerational Equity. Advocates of privatization also note how inequitable the existing program is for younger workers. The people now retired are getting a great deal: they paid relatively low payroll taxes when young and now receive substantial benefits. In part this high payoff is due to demographics. Thirty years ago there were four workers for every retired person. As the post–World War II baby boomers retire, the ratio of workers to retirees is declining dramatically. By the year 2030, there will be only two workers for every retiree (see Figure 34.8). As a result, the tax burden on tomorrow's workers will have to be a lot higher, or the baby boomers will have to accept much lower Social Security benefits. Either way, some generation of workers will get a lot less than everyone else. If Social Security is privatized, tomorrow's workers won't have to bear such a demographic tax burden.

More Poverty. As alluring as these suggestions sound, the privatization of Social Security would foster other inequities. The primary goal of Social Security is to fend off poverty among the aged. Social Security does this in two ways: by (1) transferring income from workers to retirees and (2) redistributing income from high-wage workers to low-wage workers in retirement with progressive wage replacement rates. By contrast, a privatized system would let the market alone determine FOR WHOM goods are produced. Low-income workers and other people who saved little while working would end up poor in their golden years. In a privatized system, even some high earners and savers might end up poor if their investments turned sour. Would we turn our collective backs on these people? If not, then the government would have to intervene with *some* kind of transfer program. The real issue, therefore, may not be whether a privatized Social Security system would work but what kind of *public* transfer program we'd have to create to supplement it. Then the choice would be either (1) Social Security or (2) a privatized retirement system plus a public welfare program for the aged poor. Framed in this context, the choice for the economy tomorrow is a lot more complex.

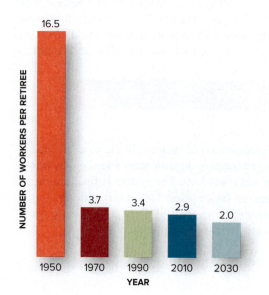

FIGURE 34.8

A Declining Tax Base

Because Social Security benefits are financed by payroll taxes, the ratio of workers to retirees is a basic measure of the program's fiscal health. That ratio has declined dramatically, and it will decline even more as the baby boomers are retiring.

Source: U.S. Social Security Administration.

SUMMARY

- Income transfers are payments for which no current goods or services are exchanged. They include both cash payments such as welfare checks and in-kind transfers such as food stamps and Medicare.   **LO34-1**
- Most transfer payments come from social insurance programs that cushion the income effects of specific events, such as aging, illness, or unemployment. Welfare programs are means-tested; they pay benefits only to the poor.   **LO34-1**
- The basic goal of transfer programs is to alter the market's FOR WHOM outcome. Attempts to redistribute income may, however, have the unintended effect of reducing total income. This is the core equity versus efficiency dilemma.   **LO34-2**
- Welfare programs reduce work incentives in two ways. They offer some income to people who don't work at all, and they also tax the wages of recipients who do work via offsetting benefit reductions.   **LO34-2**
- The benefit reduction that occurs when wages increase is an implicit marginal tax. The higher the marginal tax rate, (1) the less the incentive to work but (2) the smaller the welfare caseload.   **LO34-3**
- The Social Security retirement program creates similar work disincentives. It provides an income floor for people who don't work and imposes a high marginal tax rate on workers aged 62–64.   **LO34-2**
- The core policy dilemma is to find an optimal balance between compassion (transferring more income) and incentives (keeping people at work contributing to total output).   **LO34-3**

Key Terms

income transfers
in-kind transfers
cash transfers
target efficiency
welfare programs

social insurance programs
market failure
labor supply
poverty gap
marginal tax rate

moral hazard
breakeven level of income
tax elasticity of labor supply
wage replacement rate
labor force participation rate

Questions for Discussion

1. If we have to choose between compassion and incentives, which should we choose? Do the terms of the trade-off matter?   **LO34-3**
2. What's so hard about guaranteeing everyone a minimal level of income support? What problems arise?   **LO34-2**
3. If poor people don't want to work, should they get welfare? What about their children?   **LO34-3**
4. Once someone has received TANF welfare benefits for a total of five years, he or she is permanently ineligible for more TANF benefits. Should this person receive any further assistance? How will work incentives be affected?   **LO34-2**
5. In what ways do younger workers pay for Social Security benefits received by retired workers?   **LO34-2**
6. Should the Social Security earnings test be eliminated? What are the benefits and costs of doing so?   **LO34-2**
7. How would the distribution of income change if Social Security were privatized?   **LO34-1**
8. Who pays the economic cost of Social Security? In what ways?   **LO34-2**
9. Why don't we give poor people more cash welfare instead of in-kind transfers like food stamps, housing assistance, and Medicaid?   **LO34-3**
10. Why is the increasing ratio of older people to younger people a problem for Social Security? Is there any way to mitigate this demographic problem?   **LO34-3**

LO34-2 1. Suppose the annual welfare benefit formula is

$$\text{Benefit} = \$8000 - 0.67(\text{Wages} > \$2{,}000)$$

    (*a*) What is the marginal tax rate on
        (*i*)   The first $2,000 of wages?
        (*ii*) Wages above $2,000?
    (*b*) How large is the benefit if wages equal
        (*i*) $0?
        (*ii*) $2,000?
        (*iii*) $6,000?
    (*c*) What is the breakeven level of income in this case?

LO34-2 2. A welfare recipient can receive food stamps as well as cash welfare benefits. If the food stamp allotment is set as follows,

$$\text{Food stamps} = \$6{,}000 - 0.30(\text{Wages})$$

    (*a*) How high can wages rise before all food stamps are eliminated?
    (*b*) If the welfare benefit formula in Problem 1 applies, what is the *combined* marginal tax rate of both welfare and food stamps for wages above $2,000?

LO34-3 3. Draw a graph showing how benefits, total income, and wages change under the following conditions:

$$\text{Wage rate} = \$10 \text{ per hour}$$
$$\text{Welfare benefit} = \$5{,}000 - 0.5(\text{Wages} > \$3{,}000)$$

Identify here and label on the graph the following points:

    A—welfare benefit when wages = 0   (*a*) How much is that benefit?   _____
    B—welfare benefit when wages = $10,000   (*b*) How much is that benefit?   _____
    C—breakeven level of income   (*c*) What is that income level?   _____

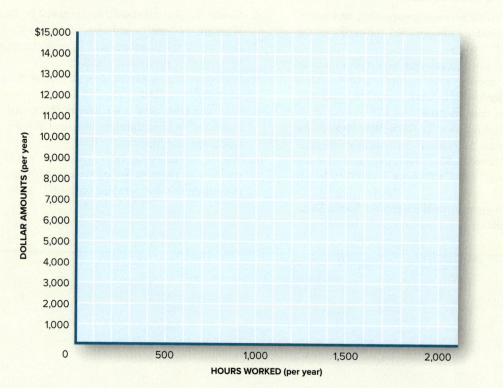

LO34-3 4. What is the breakeven level of income for Social Security as depicted in Figure 34.6?

LO34-3 5. According to the benefit formula in Table 34.2, how large will the Social Security benefit be for a worker who had prior earnings of
(*a*) $36,000 a year?
(*b*) $96,000 a year?
What is the marginal wage replacement rate for
(*c*) The $36,000-per-year worker?
(*d*) The $96,000-per-year worker?

LO34-3 6. How large a monthly Social Security check will a retiree get if her maximum benefit is $1,600 per month and she continues working for wages of $2,000 per month?

7. (*a*) On the following graph, depict the wages, income, and Social Security benefits at different hours of work for a worker aged 62–64 who earns $15 per hour and is eligible for $15,000 in Social Security benefits.
(*b*) What is the total income if the person works 1,000 hours per year?
(*c*) What is the breakeven level of income?

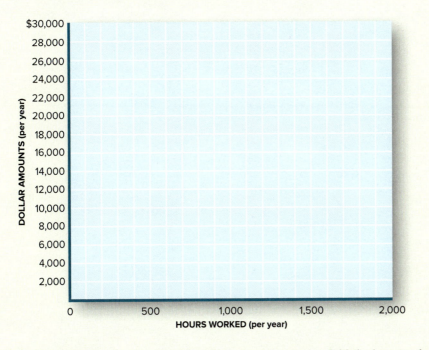

LO34-3 8. If older workers have a tax elasticity of labor supply equal to 0.20, by how much will their work activity decline when they reach the Social Security earnings test limit? (Assume *explicit* taxes of 20 percent below that limit.)

LO34-1 9. Suppose the benefit formulas for various welfare programs are

> **Food stamps: $400 per month − 0.30(Wages)**
> **Housing assistance: $1,000 per month − 0.25(Wages)**
> **Cash welfare: $400 per month − 0.67(Wages above $500)**

  (*a*) How much will someone earning $800 a month receive in
  - (*i*) Food stamps?
  - (*ii*) Housing assistance?
  - (*iii*) Cash welfare?

  (*b*) What is the cumulative marginal tax rate at
  - (*i*) Wages under $500?
  - (*ii*) Wages over $500?

LO34-1 10. The Economy Tomorrow: Social Security tax revenue comes from taxes on current workers' wages up to a cap. Social Security benefits go out to current retirees and are based on age and past earnings. In The Economy Tomorrow, it is discussed how in the near future tax revenue will be less than the benefits paid out. Identify three ways to keep this program in balance.

©MOF/Getty Images RF

©Ingram Publishing RF

©Don Tonge/Alamy Stock Photo

©William West/AFP/Getty Images

INTERNATIONAL ECONOMICS

Our interactions with the rest of the world have a profound impact on the mix of output (WHAT), the methods of production (HOW), and the distribution of income (FOR WHOM). Trade and global money flows can also affect the stability of the macro economy. Chapters 35 and 36 explore the motives, the nature, and the effects of international trade and finance.

Chapter 37 examines one of the world's most urgent problems—the deprivation that afflicts nearly 3 billion people worldwide. In this last chapter, the dimensions, causes, and potential cures for global poverty are discussed.

©Ingram Publishing RF

CHAPTER 35

International Trade

The 2016 World Series between the Cleveland Indians and the Chicago Cubs was played with Japanese gloves, baseballs made in Costa Rica, and Mexican bats. Most of the players were wearing shoes made in Korea or China. And during the regular season, many of the games throughout the major leagues were played on artificial grass made in Taiwan. Baseball, it seems, has become something less than the "all-American" game.

Imported goods have made inroads into other activities as well. All DVDs, smartphones, and video game consoles are imported, as are most televisions, fax machines, personal computers, and iPads. Most of these imported goods could have been produced in the United States. Why did we purchase them from other countries? For that matter, why does the rest of the world buy computers, tractors, chemicals, airplanes, and wheat from us rather than produce such products for themselves? Wouldn't we all be better off relying on ourselves for the goods we consume (and the jobs we need) rather than buying and selling products in international markets? Or is there some advantage to be gained from international trade?

This chapter begins with a survey of international trade patterns—what goods and services we trade, and with whom. Then we address basic issues related to such trade:

- **What benefit, if any, do we get from international trade?**
- **How much harm do imports cause, and to whom?**
- **Should we protect ourselves from "unfair" trade by limiting imports?**

After examining the arguments for and against international trade, we draw some general conclusions about trade policy. As we'll see, international trade tends to increase *average* incomes, although it may diminish the job and income opportunities for specific industries and workers.

U.S. TRADE PATTERNS

The United States is by far the largest player in global product and resource markets. In 2016 we purchased 20 percent of the world's exports and sold 15 percent of the same total.

Imports

In dollar terms, our imports in 2016 exceeded $2.7 trillion. These **imports** included the consumer items mentioned earlier as well as capital equipment, raw materials, and food. Table 35.1 represents the goods and services we purchase from foreign suppliers.

imports: Goods and services purchased from international sources.

LEARNING OBJECTIVES

After reading this chapter, you should know

LO35-1 What comparative advantage is.

LO35-2 What the gains from trade are.

LO35-3 How trade barriers affect prices, output, and incomes.

TABLE 35.1

A U.S. Trade Sampler

The United States imports and exports a staggering array of goods and services. Shown here are the top exports and imports with various countries. Notice that we export many of the same goods we import (such as cars and computers). What's the purpose of trading goods we produce ourselves?

Country	Imports from	Exports to
Australia	Beef Alumina Autos	Airplanes Computers Auto parts
Belgium	Jewelry Cars Optical glass	Cigarettes Airplanes Diamonds
Canada	Cars Trucks Paper	Auto parts Cars Computers
China	Computers Clothes Toys	Soybeans Airplanes Cars
Germany	Cars Engines Auto parts	Airplanes Computers Cars
Japan	Cars Computers Telephones	Airplanes Computers Timber
Mexico	Cars Computers Appliances	Computers Cars Chemicals
Russia	Oil Platinum Artworks	Corn Wheat Oil seeds
South Korea	Shoes Cars Computers	Airplanes Leather Iron ingots and oxides

Source: U.S. Department of Commerce.

Although imports represent only 15 percent of total GDP, they account for larger shares of specific product markets. Coffee is a familiar example. Since virtually all coffee is imported (except for a tiny amount produced in Hawaii), Americans would have a harder time staying awake without imports. Likewise, there'd be no aluminum if we didn't import bauxite, no chrome bumpers if we didn't import chromium, no tin cans without imported tin, no smartphones, and a lot fewer computers without imported components. We couldn't even play the all-American game of baseball without imports because baseballs are no longer made in the United States.

We import *services* as well as *goods*. If you fly to Europe on Virgin Airways, you're importing transportation services. If you stay in a London hotel, you're importing lodging services. When you go to Barclay's Bank to cash traveler's checks, you're importing foreign financial services. If you go to Mexico for Spring Break, you are importing tourism services. These and other services now account for one-sixth of U.S. imports.

Exports

While we're buying goods (merchandise) and services from the rest of the world, global consumers are buying our **exports.** In 2016 we exported $1.5 trillion of *goods,* including farm products (wheat, corn, soybeans), tobacco, machinery (computers), aircraft, automobiles and auto parts, raw materials (lumber, iron ore), and chemicals (see Table 35.1

exports: Goods and services sold to foreign buyers.

MOTIVATION TO TRADE

Many people wonder why we trade so much, particularly since (1) we import many of the things we also export (like computers, airplanes, cars, clothes), (2) we *could* produce many of the other things we import, and (3) we worry so much about trade imbalances. Why not just import those few things that we can't produce ourselves, and export just enough to balance that trade?

Specialization

Although it might seem strange to be importing goods we could produce ourselves, such trade is entirely rational. Our decision to trade with other countries arises from the same considerations that motivate individuals to specialize in production: satisfying their remaining needs in the marketplace. Why don't you become self-sufficient—growing all your own food, building your own shelter, and recording your own songs? Presumably because you've found that you can enjoy a much higher standard of living (and better music) by working at just one job and then buying other goods in the marketplace. When you do so, you're no longer self-sufficient. Instead you are *specializing* in production, relying on others to produce the array of goods and services you want. When countries trade goods and services, they are doing the same thing—*specializing* in production and then *trading* for other desired goods. Why do they do this? Because **specialization increases total output.**

To see how nations benefit from trade, we'll examine the production possibilities of two countries. We want to demonstrate that two countries that trade can together produce more output than they could in the absence of trade. If they can, **the gain from trade is increased world output and a higher standard of living in all trading countries.** This is the essential message of the *theory of comparative advantage.*

Production and Consumption without Trade

Consider the production and consumption possibilities of just two countries—say, the United States and France. For the sake of illustration, assume that both countries produce only two goods: bread and wine. Let's also set aside worries about the law of diminishing returns and the substitutability of resources, thus transforming the familiar **production possibilities** curve into a straight line, as in Figure 35.1.

The "curves" in Figure 35.1 suggest that the United States is capable of producing much more bread than France. With our greater abundance of labor, land, and other resources, we assume that the United States is capable of producing up to 100 zillion loaves of bread per year. To do so, we'd have to devote all our resources to that purpose. This capability is indicated by point A in Figure 35.1a and in row A of the accompanying production possibilities schedule.

France (Figure 35.1b), on the other hand, confronts a *maximum* bread production of only 15 zillion loaves per year (point G) because it has little available land, less fuel, and fewer potential workers.

The capacities of the two countries for wine production are 50 zillion barrels for us (point F) and 60 zillion for France (point L), largely reflecting France's greater experience in tending vines. Both countries are also capable of producing alternative *combinations* of bread and wine, as evidenced by their respective production possibilities curves (points A–F for the United States and G–L for France).

A nation that doesn't trade with other countries is called a **closed economy.** In the absence of contact with the outside world, the production possibilities curve for a closed economy also defines its **consumption possibilities.** Without imports, a country cannot consume more than it produces. Thus the only immediate issue in a closed economy is which mix of output to choose—*what* to produce and consume—out of the domestic choices available.

Assume that Americans choose point D on their production possibilities curve, producing and consuming 40 zillion loaves of bread and 30 zillion barrels of wine. The French, on the other hand, prefer the mix of output represented by point I on their production

production possibilities: The alternative combinations of final goods and services that could be produced in a given period with all available resources and technology.

closed economy: A nation that doesn't engage in international trade.

consumption possibilities: The alternative combinations of goods and services that a country could consume in a given time period.

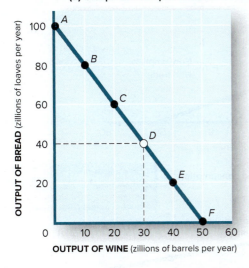

(a) U.S. production possibilities

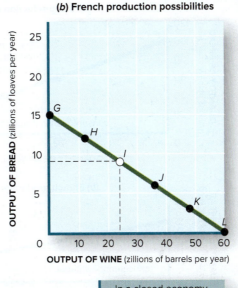

(b) French production possibilities

FIGURE 35.1

Consumption Possibilities without Trade

In the absence of trade, a country's consumption possibilities are identical to its production possibilities. The assumed production possibilities of the United States and France are illustrated in the graphs and the corresponding schedules. Before entering into trade, the United States chose to produce and consume at point *D,* with 40 zillion loaves of bread and 30 zillion barrels of wine. France chose point *I* on its own production possibilities curve. By trading, each country hopes to increase its consumption beyond these levels.

> In a closed economy, production possibilities and consumption possibilities are identical.

U.S. Production Possibilities		
Bread (Zillions of Loaves)	+	Wine (Zillions of Barrels)
A	100	+	0
B	80	+	10
C	60	+	20
D	40	+	30
E	20	+	40
F	0	+	50

French Production Possibilities		
Bread (Zillions of Loaves)	+	Wine (Zillions of Barrels)
G	15	+	0
H	12	+	12
I	9	+	24
J	6	+	36
K	3	+	48
L	0	+	60

possibilities curve. At that point they produce and consume 9 zillion loaves of bread and 24 zillion barrels of wine.

To assess the potential gain from trade, we must focus the *combined* output of the United States and France. In this case, total world output (points *D* and *I*) comes to 49 zillion loaves of bread and 54 zillion barrels of wine. What we want to know is whether world output would increase if France and the United States abandoned their isolation and started trading. Could either country, or both, consume more output by engaging in a little trade?

Production and Consumption with Trade

Because both countries are saddled with limited production possibilities, trying to eke out a little extra wine and bread from this situation might not appear very promising. Such a conclusion is unwarranted, however. Take another look at the production possibilities confronting the United States, as reproduced in Figure 35.2. Suppose the United States were to produce at point *C* rather than point *D.* At point *C* we could produce 60 zillion loaves of bread and 20 zillion barrels of wine. That combination is clearly *possible* because it lies on the production possibilities curve. We didn't choose that point earlier because we assumed the mix of output at point *D* was preferable. The mix of output at point *C could* be produced, however.

FIGURE 35.2

Consumption Possibilities with Trade

A country can increase its consumption possibilities through international trade. Each country alters its mix of domestic output to produce more of the good it produces best. As it does so, total world output increases, and each country enjoys more consumption. In this case, trade allows U.S. consumption to move from point *D* to point *N*. France moves from point *I* to point *M*.

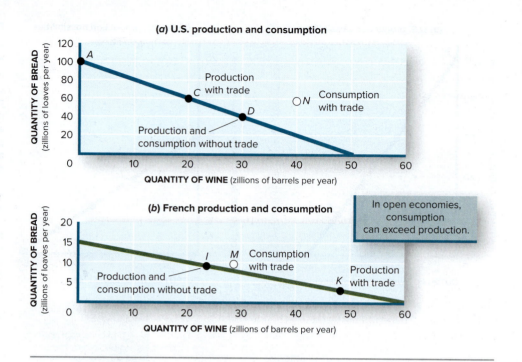

(a) U.S. production and consumption

(b) French production and consumption

In open economies, consumption can exceed production.

We could also change the mix of output in France. Assume that France moved from point *I* to point *K,* producing 48 zillion barrels of wine and only 3 zillion loaves of bread.

Two observations are now called for. The first is simply that output mixes have changed in each country. The second, and more interesting, is that total world output has *increased.* Notice how this works. When the United States and France were at points *D* and *I,* their *combined* output consisted of

A: Initial Production Choices		
	Bread **(Zillions of Loaves)**	**Wine** **(Zillions of Barrels)**
United States (at point *D*)	40	30
France (at point *I*)	9	24
Total pre-trade output	49	54

After they moved along their respective production possibilities curves to points *C* and *K,* the combined world output became

B: Revised Production Choices		
	Bread **(Zillions of Loaves)**	**Wine** **(Zillions of Barrels)**
United States (at point *C*)	60	20
France (at point *K*)	3	48
Total output with trade	63	68

Total world output has increased by 14 zillion loaves of bread and 14 zillion barrels of wine. ***Just by changing the mix of output in each country, we've increased total world output.*** This additional output creates the potential for making both countries better off than they were in the absence of trade.

This almost seems like a magic trick, but it isn't. Here's what happened. The United States and France weren't initially producing at points *C* and *K* before because they simply didn't want to *consume* those particular output combinations. Nevertheless, our discovery that points *C* and *K* allow us to produce *more* output suggests that everybody can consume more goods and services if we change the mix of output in each country. This is our first clue as to how specialization and trade can benefit an **open economy**—a nation that engages in international trade.

open economy: A nation that engages in international trade.

Suppose we Americans are the first to discover the potential benefits from trade. Using Figure 35.2 as our guide, we suggest to the French that they move their mix of output from point *I* to point *K*. As an incentive for making such a move, we promise to give them 6 zillion loaves of bread in exchange for 20 zillion barrels of wine. This would leave them at point *M*, with as much bread to consume as they used to have, plus an extra 4 zillion barrels of wine. At point *I* they had 9 zillion loaves of bread and 24 zillion barrels of wine. At point *M* they can have 9 zillion loaves of bread and 28 zillion barrels of wine. Thus by altering their mix of output (from point *I* to point *K*) and then trading (point *K* to point *M*), the French end up with more goods and services than they had in the beginning. Notice in particular that this new consumption possibility (point *M*) lies *outside* France's domestic production possibilities curve.

The French will be quite pleased with the extra output they get from trading. But where does this leave us? Does France's gain imply a loss for us? Or do we gain from trade as well?

Mutual Gains

As it turns out, *both* the United States and France gain by trading. The United States, too, ends up consuming a mix of output that lies outside our production possibilities curve.

Note that at point *C* we *produce* 60 zillion loaves of bread per year and 20 zillion barrels of wine. We then *export* 6 zillion loaves to France. This leaves us with 54 zillion loaves of bread to *consume*.

In return for our exported bread, the French give us 20 zillion barrels of wine. These imports, plus our domestic production, permit us to *consume* 40 zillion barrels of wine. Hence we end up consuming at point *N*, enjoying 54 zillion loaves of bread and 40 zillion barrels of wine. Thus by first changing our mix of output (from point *D* to point *C*), then trading (point *C* to point *N*), we end up with 14 zillion more loaves of bread and 10 zillion more barrels of wine than we started with. Time to celebrate! International trade has made us better off, too.

Table 35.4 recaps the gains from trade for both countries. Notice that U.S. imports match French exports and vice versa. Also notice how the *trade-facilitated consumption in each country exceeds no-trade levels.*

	Production and Consumption with Trade						Production and Consumption with No Trade
	Production	+ Imports	− Exports	= Consumption			
United States at	Point *C*				Point *N*		Point *D*
Bread	60	+ 0	− 6	= 54		compare	40
Wine	20	+ 20	− 0	= 40			30
France at	Point *K*				Point *M*		Point *I*
Bread	3	+ 6	− 0	= 9		compare	9
Wine	48	+ 0	− 20	= 28			24

TABLE 35.4

Gains from Trade

When nations specialize in production, they can export one good and import another and end up with *more* total goods to consume than they had without trade. In this case, the United States specializes in bread production. Notice how U.S. *consumption* of both goods increases (compare total U.S. consumption of bread and wine at point *N* [with trade] to consumption at point *D* [no trade]).

All these numbers do indeed look like some kind of magic trick, but there's no sleight of hand going on here; the gains from trade are due to specialization in production. When each country goes it alone, it's a prisoner of its own production possibilities curve; it must make production decisions on the basis of its own consumption desires. When international trade is permitted, however, each country can concentrate on the exploitation of its production capabilities. *Each country produces those goods it makes best and then trades with other countries to acquire the goods it desires to consume.*

The resultant specialization increases total world output. In the process, each country is able to escape the confines of its own production possibilities curve, to reach beyond it for a larger basket of consumption goods. *When a country engages in international trade, its consumption possibilities always exceed its production possibilities.* These enhanced consumption possibilities are emphasized by the positions of points N and M *outside* the production possibilities curves (Figure 35.2). If it weren't possible for countries to increase their consumption by trading, there'd be no incentive for trading, and thus no trade.

PURSUIT OF COMPARATIVE ADVANTAGE

Although international trade can make everyone better off, it's not so obvious which goods should be traded, or on what terms. In our previous illustration, the United States ended up trading bread for wine in terms that were decidedly favorable to us. Why did we export bread rather than wine, and how did we end up getting such a good deal?

Opportunity Costs

comparative advantage: The ability of a country to produce a specific good at a lower opportunity cost than its trading partners.

opportunity cost: The most desired goods or services that are forgone in order to obtain something else.

The decision to export bread is based on **comparative advantage**—that is, the *relative* cost of producing different goods. Recall that we can produce a maximum of 100 zillion loaves of bread per year or 50 zillion barrels of wine. Thus the domestic **opportunity cost** of producing 100 zillion loaves of bread is the 50 zillion barrels of wine we forsake in order to devote all our resources to bread production. In fact, at every point on the U.S. production possibilities curve (Figure 35.2a), the opportunity cost of a loaf of bread is ½ barrel of wine. We're effectively paying half a barrel of wine to get a loaf of bread.

Although the cost of bread production in the United States might appear outrageous, even higher opportunity costs prevail in France. According to Figure 35.2b, the opportunity cost of producing a loaf of bread in France is a staggering 4 barrels of wine. To produce a loaf of bread, the French must use factors of production that could otherwise be used to produce 4 barrels of wine.

Comparative Advantage. A comparison of the opportunity costs prevailing in each country exposes the nature of comparative advantage. The United States has a comparative advantage in bread production because less wine has to be given up to produce bread in the United States than in France. In other words, the opportunity costs of bread production are lower in the United States than in France. *Comparative advantage refers to the relative (opportunity) costs of producing particular goods.*

A country should specialize in what it's *relatively* efficient at producing—that is, goods for which it has the lowest opportunity costs. In this case, the United States should produce bread because its opportunity cost (½ barrel of wine) is less than France's (4 barrels of wine). Were you the production manager for the whole world, you'd certainly want each country to exploit its relative abilities, thus maximizing world output. Each country can arrive at that same decision itself by comparing its own opportunity costs to those prevailing elsewhere. *World output, and thus the potential gains from trade, will be maximized when each country pursues its comparative advantage. To do so, each country*

- *Exports goods with relatively low opportunity costs.*
- *Imports goods with relatively high opportunity costs.*

That's the kind of situation depicted in Table 35.4.

Absolute Costs Don't Count

In assessing the nature of comparative advantage, notice that we needn't know anything about the actual costs involved in production. Have you seen any data suggesting how much labor, land, or capital is required to produce a loaf of bread in either France or the United States? For all you and I know, the French may be able to produce both bread and wine with fewer resources than we're using. Such an **absolute advantage** in production might exist because of their much longer experience in cultivating both grapes and wheat or simply because they have more talent.

We can envy such productivity, and even try to emulate it, but it shouldn't alter our production or trade decisions. All we really care about are *opportunity costs*—what *we* have to give up in order to get more of a desired good. If we can get a barrel of wine for less bread in trade than in production, we have a comparative advantage in producing bread. As long as we have a *comparative* advantage in bread production, we should exploit it. It doesn't matter to us whether France could produce either good with fewer resources. For that matter, even if France had an absolute advantage in *both* goods, we'd still have a *comparative* advantage in bread production, as we've already confirmed. The absolute costs of production were omitted from the previous illustration because they were irrelevant.

To clarify the distinction between absolute advantage and comparative advantage, consider this example. When Charlie Osgood joined the Willamette Warriors football team, he was the fastest runner ever to play football in Willamette. He could also throw the ball farther than most people could see. In other words, he had an *absolute advantage* in both throwing and running. Charlie would have made the greatest quarterback or the greatest end ever to play football. *Would have.* The problem was that he could play only one position at a time. Thus the Willamette coach had to play Charlie either as a quarterback or as an end. He reasoned that Charlie could throw only a bit farther than some of the other top quarterbacks but could far outdistance all the other ends. In other words, Charlie had a *comparative advantage* in running and was assigned to play as an end.

> **absolute advantage:** The ability of a country to produce a specific good with fewer resources (per unit of output) than other countries.

TERMS OF TRADE

It definitely pays to pursue one's comparative advantage by specializing in production. It may not yet be clear, however, how we got such a good deal with France. We're clever traders; but beyond that, is there any way to determine the **terms of trade**—the quantity of good A that must be given up in exchange for good B? In our previous illustration, the terms of trade were very favorable to us; we exchanged only 6 zillion loaves of bread for 20 zillion barrels of wine (Table 35.4). The terms of trade were thus 6 loaves = 20 barrels.

> **terms of trade:** The rate at which goods are exchanged; the amount of good A given up for good B in trade.

Limits to the Terms of Trade

The terms of trade with France were determined by our offer and France's ready acceptance. But why did France accept those terms? France was willing to accept our offer because the terms of trade permitted France to increase its wine consumption without giving up any bread consumption. Our offer of 6 loaves for 20 barrels was an improvement over France's domestic opportunity costs. France's domestic possibilities required it to give up 24 barrels of wine in order to produce 6 loaves of bread (see Figure 35.2b). Getting bread via trade was simply cheaper for France than producing bread at home. France ended up with an extra 4 zillion barrels of wine (take another look at the last two columns in Table 35.4).

Our first clue to the terms of trade, then, lies in each country's domestic opportunity costs. *A country won't trade unless the terms of trade are superior to domestic opportunities.* In our example, the opportunity cost of 1 barrel of wine in the United States is 2 loaves of bread. Accordingly, we won't *export* bread unless we get at least 1 barrel of wine in exchange for every 2 loaves of bread we ship overseas.

All countries want to gain from trade. Hence we can predict that *the terms of trade between any two countries will lie somewhere between their respective opportunity costs in production.* That is, a loaf of bread in international trade will be worth at least ½ barrel of

WORLD VIEW

U.S. WINEMAKERS HURT BY IMPORTED WINE

American consumers are increasingly sipping imported wines. Although the domestic wine industry continues to grow at a respectable pace, imported wines are taking an increasing share of the U.S. market. Sales of domestic wines grew 5.4 percent in 2016, while sales of imports from France surged 16.1 percent, from New Zealand 15.4 percent, and Italy 6.2 percent. As the U.S. dollar continues to strengthen, domestic wine producers faced increasing price competition. They say foreign producers are also aided by unfair tax, marketing, and export subsidies that put U.S. winemakers at a disadvantage. California growers took nearly 30,000 acres out of production last year, planting almonds and avocados in the former vineyards.

Source: Media and industry reports, February 2017.

ANALYSIS: Although trade increases consumption possibilities, imports typically compete with a domestic industry. The affected industries will try to restrict imports in order to preserve their own jobs and incomes.

Import-Competing Industries. Joining with the growers will be the farmworkers and the other merchants whose livelihood depends on the New York wine industry. If they're clever enough, the growers will also get the governor of the state to join their demonstration. After all, the governor must recognize the needs of his people, and his people definitely don't include the wheat farmers in Kansas who are making a bundle from international trade, much less French vintners. New York consumers are of course benefiting from lower wine prices, but they're unlikely to demonstrate over a few cents a bottle. On the other hand, those few extra pennies translate into millions of dollars for domestic wine producers.

The wheat farmers in France are no happier about international trade than are the wine-growers in the United States. They'd dearly love to sink all those boats bringing cheap wheat from America, thereby protecting their own market position.

If we're to make sense of trade policies, then, we must recognize one central fact of life: Some producers have a vested interest in restricting international trade. In particular, *workers and producers who compete with imported products—who work in import-competing industries—have an economic interest in restricting trade.* This helps explain why GM, Ford, and Chrysler are unhappy about auto imports and why shoe workers in Massachusetts want to end the importation of Italian shoes. It also explains why textile producers in South Carolina think China is behaving irresponsibly when it sells cheap cotton shirts and dresses in the United States.

Export Industries. Although imports typically mean fewer jobs and less income for some domestic industries, exports represent increased jobs and income for other industries. Producers and workers in export industries gain from trade. Thus on a microeconomic level there are identifiable gainers and losers from international trade. *Trade not only alters the mix of output but also redistributes income from import-competing industries to export industries.* This potential redistribution is the source of political and economic friction.

Net Gain. We must be careful to note, however, that the microeconomic gains from trade are greater than the microeconomic losses. It's not simply a question of robbing Peter to enrich Paul. We must remind ourselves that consumers enjoy a higher standard of living as a result of international trade. As we saw earlier, trade increases world efficiency and total output. Accordingly, we end up slicing up a larger pie rather than just reslicing the same old smaller pie.

The gains from trade will mean little to workers who end up with a smaller slice of the (larger) pie. It's important to remember, however, that the gains from trade are large enough to make everybody better off. Whether we actually choose to distribute the gains from trade in this way is a separate question, to which we shall return shortly. Note here, however, that *trade restrictions designed to protect specific microeconomic interests reduce the total gains from trade.* Trade restrictions leave us with a smaller pie to split up.

Additional Pressures

Import-competing industries are the principal obstacle to expanded international trade. Selfish micro interests aren't the only source of trade restrictions, however. Other arguments are also used to restrict trade.

National Security. The national security argument for trade restrictions is twofold. We can't depend on foreign suppliers to provide us with essential defense-related goods, it is said, because that would leave us vulnerable in time of war. The machine tool industry used this argument to protect itself from imports. In 1991 the Pentagon again sided with the toolmakers, citing the need for the United States to "gear up military production quickly in case of war," a contingency that couldn't be assured if weapons manufacturers relied on imported lathes, milling machines, and other tools. After the September 11, 2001, terrorist attacks on the World Trade Center and Pentagon, U.S. farmers convinced Congress to safeguard the nation's food supply with additional subsidies. The steel industry emphasized the importance of not depending on foreign suppliers.

Dumping. Another argument against free trade arises from the practice of **dumping.** Foreign producers "dump" their goods when they sell them in the United States at prices lower than those prevailing in their own country, perhaps even below the costs of production.

dumping: The sale of goods in export markets at prices below domestic prices.

Dumping may be unfair to import-competing producers, but it isn't necessarily unwelcome to the rest of us. As long as foreign producers continue dumping, we're getting foreign products at low prices. How bad can that be? There's a legitimate worry, however. Foreign producers might hold prices down only until domestic producers are driven out of business. Then we might be compelled to pay the foreign producers higher prices for their products. In that case, dumping could consolidate market power and lead to monopoly-type pricing. The fear of dumping, then, is analogous to the fear of predatory pricing.

The potential costs of dumping are serious. It's not always easy to determine when dumping occurs, however. Those who compete with imports have an uncanny ability to associate any and all low prices with predatory dumping. The United States has used dumping *charges* to restrict imports of Chinese shrimp, furniture, lingerie, solar panels, and other products in which China has an evident comparative advantage. The Chinese have retaliated with dozens of their own dumping investigations, including the fiber optic cable case. As World View "U.S. Slaps China with Huge Anti-Dumping Tariffs" explains, such actions slow imports and protect domestic producers.

WORLD VIEW

U.S. SLAPS CHINA WITH HUGE ANTI-DUMPING TARIFFS

After a year-long investigation, the International Trade Administration yesterday announced a five-fold increase in tariffs on imported Chinese steel. The new tariff of 265.79 percent will make Chinese steel imports prohibitively expensive. This was good news for U.S. steel producers, who had asked the ITA for tariff relief, claiming that China was unfairly subsidizing its steel exports. The resultant dumping of Chinese steel had forced domestic steelmakers to close factories and eliminate 12,000 jobs they claimed. The new tariffs apply to cold-rolled flat steel that is used to manufacture appliances, cars, electric motors, containers, and in construction. Last year, over $270 million of that steel was imported from China. China's Commerce Ministry called the move "irrational" and said it would harm cooperation between the two countries.

Source: Media reports, March 2, 2016.

ANALYSIS: *Dumping* means that a foreign producer is selling exports at prices below cost or below prices in the home market, putting import-competing industries at a competitive disadvantage. *Accusations* of dumping are an effective trade barrier.

Infant Industries. Actual dumping threatens to damage already established domestic industries. Even normal import prices, however, may make it difficult or impossible for a new domestic industry to develop. Infant industries are often burdened with abnormally high start-up costs. These high costs may arise from the need to train a whole workforce and the expenses of establishing new marketing channels. With time to grow, however, an infant industry might experience substantial cost reductions and establish a comparative advantage. When this is the case, trade restrictions might help nurture an industry in its infancy. Trade restrictions are justified, however, only if there's tangible evidence that the industry can develop a comparative advantage reasonably quickly.

Improving the Terms of Trade. A final argument for restricting trade rests on how the gains from trade are distributed. As we observed, the distribution of the gains from trade depends on the terms of trade. If we were to buy fewer imports, foreign producers might lower their prices. If that happened, the terms of trade would move in our favor, and we'd end up with a larger share of the gains from trade.

One way to bring about this sequence of events is to put restrictions on imports, making it more difficult or expensive for Americans to buy foreign products. Such restrictions will reduce the volume of imports, thereby inducing foreign producers to lower their prices. Unfortunately, this strategy can easily backfire. Retaliatory restrictions on imports, each designed to improve the terms of trade, will ultimately eliminate all trade and therewith all the gains people were competing for in the first place.

BARRIERS TO TRADE

The microeconomic losses associated with imports give rise to a constant clamor for trade restrictions. People whose jobs and incomes are threatened by international trade tend to organize quickly and air their grievances. World View "Irish Farmers Block Barley Imports" depicts the efforts of barley farmers in Ireland to block imports of German barley. They wanted their government to impose restrictions on imports. More often than not, governments grant the wishes of these well-organized and well-financed special interests.

WORLD VIEW

IRISH FARMERS BLOCK BARLEY IMPORTS

Drogheda—Barley farmers blocked the unloading of imported barley at the port here. Joe Healy, president of the Irish Farmers Association, said "the future of grain farming in Ireland is at stake." With grain incomes at records lows, farmers see imports as a threat to their survival. Healy said barley imports—used in beer production—were "unnecessary" when there are plentiful supplies of "quality native grain" available. He pleaded for public support to restrict continuing barley imports.

Source: Media reports, August 24–26, 2016.

ANALYSIS: Import-competing industries cite lots of reasons for restricting trade. Their primary concern, however, is to protect their own jobs and profits.

Embargoes

The surefire way to restrict trade is simply to eliminate it. To do so, a country need only impose an embargo on exports or imports, or both. An **embargo** is nothing more than a prohibition against trading particular goods.

In 1951 Senator Joseph McCarthy convinced the U.S. Senate to impose an embargo on Soviet mink, fox, and five other furs. He argued that such imports helped finance world communism. Senator McCarthy also represented the state of Wisconsin, where most U.S. minks are raised. The Reagan administration tried to end the fur embargo in 1987 but met with stiff congressional opposition. By then U.S. mink ranchers had developed a $120 million per year industry.

embargo: A prohibition on exports or imports.

The United States has also maintained an embargo on Cuban goods since 1959, when Fidel Castro took power there. This embargo severely damaged Cuba's sugar industry and deprived American smokers of the famed Havana cigars. It also fostered the development of U.S. sugar beet and tobacco farmers, who now have a vested interest in maintaining the embargo.

Tariffs

A more frequent trade restriction is a **tariff,** a special tax imposed on imported goods. Tariffs, also called *customs duties,* were once the principal source of revenue for governments. In the 18th century, tariffs on tea, glass, wine, lead, and paper were imposed on the American colonies to provide extra revenue for the British government. The tariff on tea led to the Boston Tea Party in 1773 and gave added momentum to the American independence movement.

In modern times, tariffs have been used primarily as a means to protect specific industries from import competition. The current U.S. tariff code specifies tariffs on more than 9,000 different products—nearly 50 percent of all U.S. imports. Although the average tariff is less than 5 percent, individual tariffs vary widely. The tariff on cars, for example, is only 2.5 percent, while cotton sweaters confront a 17.8 percent tariff. As World View "U.S. Slaps China with Huge Anti-Dumping Tariffs" noted, the tariff on Chinese steel is a whopping 265.79 percent!

The attraction of tariffs to import-competing industries should be obvious. *A tariff on imported goods makes them more expensive to domestic consumers and thus less competitive with domestically produced goods.* Among familiar tariffs in effect in 2017 were 50 cents per gallon on Scotch whisky and 76 cents per gallon on imported champagne. These tariffs made American-produced spirits look relatively cheap and thus contributed to higher sales and profits for domestic distillers and grape growers. In the same manner, imported baby food is taxed at 34.6 percent, maple sugar at 9.4 percent, golf shoes at 8.5 percent, and imported sailboats at 1.5 percent. In 2009 President Obama imposed a 35 percent tariff on imported Chinese tires and a 26 percent tariff on Chinese solar panels in 2014. In 2017, President Trump announced a 24 percent tariff on Canadian lumber. In each case, domestic producers in import-competing industries gain. The losers are domestic consumers, who end up paying higher prices. The tariff on orange juice, for example, raises the price of drinking orange juice by $525 million a year. The tariff on Canadian lumber raises the price of a new home by $3,000. Tariffs also hurt foreign producers, who lose business, and world efficiency, as trade is reduced. These potential victims of trade protection rallied in 2017 to resist President Trump's proposal for a "border-adjustment tax," an across-the-board tariff, combined with a blanket export subsidy (see In the News "A Border-Adjustment Tax?").

tariff: A tax (duty) imposed on imported goods.

IN THE NEWS

A BORDER-ADJUSTMENT TAX?

When he first took office, President Trump expressed a lot of enthusiasm for a "border-adjustment" tax that would bring more jobs back to America. House Speaker Paul Ryan likes the idea as well and has made it part of the Republican's tax-reform plan. In the House version, a 20 percent tax would be imposed on all imports and U.S. exports would get a 20 percent tax subsidy. This would cut imports, promote exports, and create even more jobs at home.

Or, so the theory goes. U.S. retailers are horrified at the thought. Companies like Walmart import most of their inventory; raising the prices on that inventory by 20 percent would destroy Walmart's competitive position. Retailers point out that 97 percent of all the clothes sold in America are imported, as are 98 percent of the shoes. Higher import taxes would depress retail sales and force layoffs throughout the industry.

After meeting with retail executives last week, President Trump seemed to cool to the idea of a border-adjustment tax.

Source: Media and industry reports, February 2017.

ANALYSIS: A border-adjustment tax is a combined import tariff and export subsidy. it helps exporters but hurts importers and the consumers who purchase those goods.

"Beggar Thy Neighbor." Microeconomic interests aren't the only source of pressure for tariff protection. Imports represent leakage from the domestic circular flow and a potential loss of jobs at home. From this perspective, reducing imports looks like an easy solution to the problem of domestic unemployment. Just get people to "buy American" instead of buying imported products, so the argument goes, and domestic output and employment will surely expand. President Obama used this argument to include "buy American" rules in his 2009 stimulus package. President Trump was even more insistent about "bringing jobs home" by restricting imports and signing "buy American" orders.

Congressman Willis Hawley used this same argument in 1930. He assured his colleagues that higher tariffs would "bring about the growth and development in this country that has followed every other tariff bill, bringing as it does a new prosperity in which all people, in all sections, will increase their comforts, their enjoyment, and their happiness."[1] Congress responded by passing the Smoot-Hawley Tariff Act of 1930, which raised tariffs to an average of nearly 60 percent, effectively cutting off most imports.

Tariffs designed to expand domestic employment are more likely to fail than to succeed. If a tariff wall does stem the flow of imports, it effectively transfers the unemployment problem to other countries, a phenomenon often referred to as "beggar thy neighbor." The resultant loss of business in other countries leaves them less able to purchase our exports. The imported unemployment also creates intense political pressures for retaliatory action. That's exactly what happened in the 1930s. Other countries erected trade barriers to compensate for the effects of the Smoot-Hawley tariff. World trade subsequently fell from $60 billion in 1928 to a mere $25 billion in 1938. This trade contraction increased the severity of the Great Depression (see World View " 'Beggar-Thy-Neighbor' Policies in the 1930s").

WORLD VIEW

"BEGGAR-THY-NEIGHBOR" POLICIES IN THE 1930S

President Herbert Hoover signed the Smoot-Hawley Tariff Act on June 17, 1930, despite the pleas from 1,028 economists to veto it. The Act raised the effective tariff on imports by 50 percent between 1929 and 1932. Although designed to limit import competition and boost domestic employment, the Act triggered quick retaliation from America's trading partners:

- Spain passed the Wais tariff in July in reaction to U.S. tariffs on grapes, oranges, cork, and onions.
- Switzerland, objecting to new U.S. tariffs on watches, embroideries, and shoes, boycotted American exports.
- Italy retaliated against tariffs on hats and olive oil with high tariffs on U.S. and French automobiles in June 1930.
- Canada reacted to high duties on many food products, logs, and timber by raising tariffs threefold in August 1932.
- Australia, Cuba, France, Mexico, and New Zealand also joined in the tariff wars.

From 1930 to 1931 U.S. imports dropped 29 percent, but U.S. exports fell even more, 33 percent, and continued their collapse to a modern-day low of $2.4 billion in 1933. World trade contracted by similar proportions, spreading unemployment around the globe.

In 1934 the U.S. Congress passed the Reciprocal Trade Agreements Act to empower the president to reduce tariffs by half the 1930 rates in return for like cuts in foreign duties on U.S. goods. The "beggar-thy-neighbor" policy was dead. Since then, the nations of the world have been reducing tariffs and other trade barriers.

Source: " 'Beggar-Thy-Neighbor' Policies in the 1930s," *World Development Report 1987*, p. 139, Box 8.4.

ANALYSIS: Tariffs inflict harm on foreign producers. If foreign countries retaliate with tariffs of their own, world trade will shrink and unemployment will increase in all countries.

[1]*The New York Times*, June 15, 1930, p. 25.

The same kind of macroeconomic threat surfaced in 2009. The "buy American" provisions introduced by the Obama administration angered foreign nations that would lose export sales. When they threatened to retaliate with trade barriers of their own, President Obama had to offer reassurances about America's commitment to "free trade."

Quotas

Tariffs reduce the flow of imports by raising import prices. The same outcome can be attained more directly by imposing import **quotas,** numerical restrictions on the quantity of a particular good that may be imported. The United States limits the quantity of ice cream imported from Jamaica to 950 gallons a year. Only 1.4 million kilograms of Australian cheddar cheese and no more than 7,730 tons of Haitian sugar can be imported. Textile quotas are imposed on every country that wants to ship textiles to the U.S. market. According to the U.S. Department of State, approximately 12 percent of our imports are subject to import quotas.

quota: A limit on the quantity of a good that may be imported in a given time period.

Comparative Effects

Quotas, like all barriers to trade, reduce world efficiency and invite retaliatory action. Moreover, their impact can be even more damaging than tariffs. To see this, we may compare market outcomes in four different contexts: no trade, free trade, tariff-restricted trade, and quota-restricted trade.

No-Trade Equilibrium. Figure 35.4a depicts the supply-and-demand relationships that would prevail in an economy that imposed a trade *embargo* on foreign textiles. In this situation, the **equilibrium price** of textiles is completely determined by domestic demand and supply curves. The no-trade equilibrium price is p_1, and the quantity of textiles consumed is q_1.

equilibrium price: The price at which the quantity of a good demanded in a given time period equals the quantity supplied.

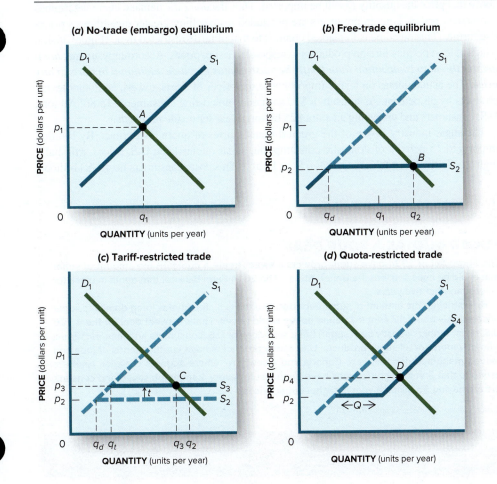

(a) No-trade (embargo) equilibrium

(b) Free-trade equilibrium

(c) Tariff-restricted trade

(d) Quota-restricted trade

FIGURE 35.4

The Impact of Trade Restrictions

In the *absence of trade,* the domestic price and sales of a good will be determined by domestic supply and demand curves (point *A* in part *a*). Once trade is permitted, the market supply curve will be altered by the availability of imports. With *free trade* and unlimited availability of imports at price p_2, a new market equilibrium will be established at world prices (point *B*).

Tariffs raise domestic prices and reduce the quantity sold (point *C*). *Quotas* put an absolute limit on imported sales and thus give domestic producers a great opportunity to raise the market price (point *D*).

Free-Trade Equilibrium. Suppose now that the embargo is lifted. The immediate effect of this decision will be a rightward shift of the market supply curve, as foreign supplies are added to domestic supplies (Figure 35.4b). If an unlimited quantity of textiles can be bought in world markets at a price of p_2, the new supply curve will look like S_2 (infinitely elastic at p_2). The new supply curve (S_2) intersects the old demand curve (D_1) at a new equilibrium price of p_2 and an expanded consumption of q_2. At this new equilibrium, domestic producers are supplying the quantity q_d while foreign producers are supplying the rest ($q_2 - q_d$). Comparing the new equilibrium to the old one, we see that *free trade results in reduced prices and increased consumption.*

Domestic textile producers are unhappy, of course, with their foreign competition. In the absence of trade, the domestic producers would sell more output (q_1) and get higher prices (p_1). Once trade is opened up, the willingness of foreign producers to sell unlimited quantities of textiles at the price p_2 puts a lid on domestic prices. Domestic producers hate this.

Tariff-Restricted Trade. Figure 35.4c illustrates what would happen to prices and sales if the United Textile Producers were successful in persuading the government to impose a tariff. Assume that the tariff raises imported textile prices from p_2 to p_3, making it more difficult for foreign producers to undersell domestic producers. Domestic production expands from q_d to q_t, imports are reduced from $q_2 - q_d$ to $q_3 - q_t$, and the market price of textiles rises. Domestic textile producers are clearly better off. So is the U.S. Treasury, which will collect increased tariff revenues. Unfortunately, domestic consumers are worse off (higher prices), as are foreign producers (reduced sales).

Quota-Restricted Trade. Now consider the impact of a textile *quota.* Suppose we eliminate tariffs but decree that imports can't exceed the quantity Q. Because the quantity of imports can never exceed Q, the supply curve is effectively shifted to the right by that amount. The new curve S_4 (Figure 35.4d) indicates that no imports will occur below the world price p_2 and above that price the quantity Q will be imported. Thus the *domestic* demand curve determines subsequent prices. Foreign producers are precluded from selling greater quantities as prices rise further. This outcome is in marked contrast to that of tariff-restricted trade (Figure 35.4c), which at least permits foreign producers to respond to rising prices. Accordingly, *quotas are a greater threat to competition than tariffs because quotas preclude additional imports at any price.* The actual quotas on textile imports raise the prices of shirts, towels, and other textile products by 58 percent. As a result, a $10 shirt ends up costing consumers $15.80. All told, U.S. consumers end up paying an extra $25 billion a year for textile products.

The sugar industry is one of the greatest beneficiaries of quota restrictions. By limiting imports to 15 percent of domestic consumption, sugar quotas keep U.S. prices artificially high (see In the News "Sugar Quotas a Sour Deal"). This costs consumers nearly $3 billion a

---

IN THE NEWS

SUGAR QUOTAS A SOUR DEAL

The Sugar Act of 1934 gave sugar growers a sweet treat—a quota on the amount of sugar that could be imported into the United States. The 2014 Farm Bill kept that quota in place for at least another five years.

By restricting the amount of sugar imported into the U.S., the quotas keep domestic sugar prices high— about 17 cent s a pound above world prices. That's a sweet deal for the 4,700 U.S. sugar farmers (mostly beet sugar) but a sour deal for U.S. consumers and manufacturers, who pay more for all sugar products. U.S. candy producers have cut thousands of jobs and moved manufacturing plants to Canada and elsewhere, where sugar is cheaper. Analysts estimate that 3 manufacturing jobs have been lost for every 1 sugar job saved and consumers are paying $3 billion a year in higher sugar prices.

Source: Industry and media reports, 2016–2017.

ANALYSIS: Import quotas preclude increased foreign competition when domestic prices rise. Protected domestic producers enjoy higher prices and profits while consumers pay higher prices.

year in higher prices. Candy and soda producers lose sales and profits. According to the U.S. Department of Commerce, more than 6,000 jobs have been lost in sugar-using industries (e.g., candy manufacturing) due to high sugar costs. Hershey alone closed plants in Pennsylvania, Colorado, and California and moved candy production to Canada. Foreign sugar producers (mainly in poor nations) also lose sales, profits, and jobs. Who gains? Domestic sugar producers—who, coincidentally, are highly concentrated in key electoral states like Florida.

Voluntary Restraint Agreements

A slight variant of quotas has been used in recent years. Rather than impose quotas on imports, the U.S. government asks foreign producers to "voluntarily" limit their exports. These so-called **voluntary restraint agreements** have been negotiated with producers in Japan, South Korea, Taiwan, China, the European Union, and other countries. Korea, for example, agreed to reduce its annual shoe exports to the United States from 44 million pairs to 33 million pairs. Taiwan reduced its shoe exports from 156 million pairs to 122 million pairs per year. In 2005 China agreed to slow its exports of clothing, limiting its sales growth to 8–17 percent a year. For their part, the Japanese agreed to reduce sales of color TV sets in the United States from 2.8 million to 1.75 million per year. In 2006 Mexico agreed to limit its cement exports to the United States to 3 million tons a year. In 2014 Mexico also agreed to curtail its sugar exports to the United States, forsaking its unique treaty rights to unrestricted exports.

> **voluntary restraint agreement (VRA):** An agreement to reduce the volume of trade in a specific good; a "voluntary" quota.

All these voluntary export restraints, as they're often called, represent an informal type of quota. The only difference is that they're negotiated rather than imposed. But these differences are lost on consumers, who end up paying higher prices for these goods. The voluntary limit on Japanese auto exports to the United States alone cost consumers $15.7 billion in only four years.

Nontariff Barriers

Tariffs and quotas are the most visible barriers to trade, but they're only the tip of the iceberg. Indeed, the variety of protectionist measures that have been devised is testimony to the ingenuity of the human mind. At the turn of the century, the Germans were committed to a most-favored-nation policy: a policy of extending equal treatment to all trading partners. The Germans, however, wanted to lower the tariff on cattle imports from Denmark without extending the same break to Switzerland. Such a preferential tariff would have violated the most-favored-nation policy. Accordingly, the Germans created a new and higher tariff on "brown and dappled cows reared at a level of at least 300 meters above sea level and passing at least one month in every summer at an altitude of at least 800 meters." The new tariff was, of course, applied equally to all countries. But Danish cows never climb that high, so they weren't burdened with the new tariff.

With the decline in tariffs over the last 20 years, nontariff barriers have increased. The United States uses product standards, licensing restrictions, restrictive procurement practices, and other nontariff barriers to restrict roughly 15 percent of imports. In 1999–2000 the European Union banned imports of U.S. beef, arguing that the use of hormones on U.S. ranches created a health hazard for European consumers. Although both the U.S. government and the World Trade Organization disputed that claim, the ban was a highly effective nontariff trade barrier. The United States responded by slapping 100 percent tariffs on dozens of European products.

Mexican Trucks. One of the more flagrant examples of nontariff barriers is the use of safety regulations to block Mexican trucking companies from using U.S. roads to deliver goods. The resulting trade barrier forces Mexican trucks to unload their cargoes at the U.S. border, and then reload them into U.S. (Teamster-driven) trucks for shipment to U.S. destinations. The U.S. agreed to lift that restriction in 1995, but didn't. In 2009 President Obama actually solidified the Mexican roadblock, despite the fact that Mexican trucks passed all 22 safety (nontariff) regulations the U.S. Department of Transportation had imposed. In so doing, President Obama secured more jobs for Teamster-union drivers, but raised costs for U.S. shippers and consumers and drove down sales and employment for Mexican trucking companies. Fed up with U.S. protectionism, Mexico retaliated by slapping tariffs on 90 U.S. export products (see World View "Mexico Retaliates for U.S. Trucking Roadblocks"). By early 2011, U.S. exports to Mexico of those products had declined by 81 percent. This prompted President Obama to offer Mexico a new round of negotiations, which ended in January 2015 with the U.S. declaring Mexican trucks to be safe enough to travel U.S. roads and Mexico repealing the tariffs on U.S. exports. Although Teamsters president Jim Hoffa declared that he was "outraged" by such a "rash decision," cross-border trade increased substantially.

WORLD VIEW

MEXICO RETALLIATES FOR U.S. TRUCKING ROADBLOCKS

The United States promised to open American roads to Mexican trucks back in 1995. But fierce resistance from the Teamsters Union and independent truckers has blocked access to American roads. Goods shipped from Mexico have to be transferred at the border to U.S. trucks, denying Mexican truckers fair access to U.S. deliveries. Two months ago President Obama effectively made that roadblock permanent.

Mexico retalliated on Monday with steep tariffs on 99 U.S. products exported to Mexico from 43 American states. The list includes hams, fresh apples, soups, cheese, beauty products, fresh pears, and pet food. In all, $2.4 billion worth of U.S. exports will feel the pain of lost sales.

Source: Media reports, March 2009.

ANALYSIS: Nontariff barriers like extraordinary safety requirements on Mexican trucks limit import competition and invite retaliation.

THE ECONOMY TOMORROW

POLICING WORLD TRADE

Proponents of free trade and import-competing industries are in constant conflict. Most of the time the trade policy deck seems stacked in favor of the special interests. Because import-competing firms and workers are highly concentrated, they're quick to mobilize politically. By contrast, the benefits of freer trade are less direct and spread over millions of consumers. As a consequence, the beneficiaries of freer trade are less likely to monitor trade policy—much less lobby actively to change it. Hence the political odds favor the spread of trade barriers.

Multilateral Trade Pacts. Despite these odds, the long-term trend is toward *lowering* trade barriers, thereby increasing global competition. Two forces encourage this trend. *The principal barrier to protectionist policies is worldwide recognition of the gains from freer trade.* Since world nations now understand that trade barriers are ultimately self-defeating, they're more willing to rise above the din of protectionist cries and dismantle trade barriers. They diffuse political opposition by creating across-the-board trade pacts that seem to spread the pain (and gain) from freer trade across a broad swath of industries. Such pacts also incorporate multiyear timetables that give affected industries time to adjust.

Trade liberalization has also been encouraged by firms that *export* products or use imported inputs in their own production. Tariffs on imported steel raise product costs for U.S.-based auto producers and construction companies. In 2007 the European Union eliminated a tariff on frozen Chinese strawberries, largely due to complaints from EU yogurt and jam producers who were incurring higher costs.

Global Pacts: GATT and WTO. The granddaddy of the multilateral, multiyear free-trade pacts was the 1947 *General Agreement on Tariffs and Trade (GATT)*. Twenty-three nations pledged to reduce trade barriers and give all GATT nations equal access to their domestic markets.

Since the first GATT pact, seven more "rounds" of negotiations have expanded the scope of GATT; 117 nations signed the 1994 pact. As a result of these GATT pacts, average tariff rates in developed countries have fallen from 40 percent in 1948 to less than 4 percent today.

WTO. The 1994 GATT pact also created the *World Trade Organization (WTO)* to enforce free-trade rules. If a nation feels its exports are being unfairly excluded from another country's market, it can file a complaint with the WTO. This is exactly what the United States did when the EU banned U.S. beef imports. The WTO ruled in favor of the United States. When the EU failed to lift its import ban, the WTO authorized the United States to impose retaliatory tariffs on European exports.

The EU turned the tables on the United States in 2003. It complained to the WTO that U.S. tariffs on imported steel violated trade rules. The WTO agreed and gave the EU permission to impose retaliatory tariffs on $2.2 billion of U.S. exports. That prompted the Bush administration to scale back the tariffs in December 2003.

In effect, the WTO is now the world's trade police force. It is empowered to cite nations that violate trade agreements and even to impose remedial action when violations persist. Why do sovereign nations give the WTO such power? Because they are all convinced that free trade is the surest route to GDP growth.

Regional Pacts. Because worldwide trade pacts are so complex, many nations have also pursued *regional* free-trade agreements.

NAFTA. In December 1992 the United States, Canada, and Mexico signed the *North American Free Trade Agreement (NAFTA),* a 1,000-page document covering more than 9,000 products. The ultimate goal of NAFTA is to eliminate all trade barriers between these three countries. At the time of signing, intraregional tariffs averaged 11 percent in Mexico, 5 percent in Canada, and 4 percent in the United States. NAFTA requires that all tariffs among the three countries be eliminated. The pact also requires the elimination of specific nontariff barriers.

The NAFTA-initiated reduction in trade barriers substantially increased trade flows between Mexico, Canada, and the United States. It also prompted a wave of foreign investment in Mexico, where both cheap labor and NAFTA access were available. Overall, NAFTA accelerated economic growth and reduced inflationary pressures in all three nations. Some industries (like construction and apparel) suffered from the freer trade, but others (like trucking, farming, and finance) reaped huge gains (see In the News "NAFTA Reallocates Labor: Comparative Advantage at Work").

TPP. The Trans-Pacific Partnership was intended to be another regional trade pact, linking 12 nations that border the Pacific Ocean in a multi-year commitment to freer trade. After eight years of negotiations, those 12 nations signed a tentative TPP agreement in February 2016. That 2,000-page agreement called not only for reductions in tariffs and nontariff trade barriers among the member nations, but also sought greater coordination of policies on environmental protection, workers' rights, and regulatory practices. To become effective, the legislatures of the 12 nations had to ratify the agreement by February 2018. By early 2017 only one nation—Japan—had ratified the agreement. The others were aware that newly-elected President Trump had campaigned heavily against TPP and all other multilateral trade agreements. He called TPP a particularly "bad deal" and vowed to kill it. He kept that vow by officially withdrawing the United States from the TPP on his very first day of office. Henceforth, he said, he only wanted bilateral deals and deals that "put America first." Critics warned that he was ignoring the benefits of freer trade and risking the perception that America was an unreliable trading partner.

IN THE NEWS

NAFTA REALLOCATES LABOR: COMPARATIVE ADVANTAGE AT WORK

More Jobs in These Industries		but . . .	Fewer Jobs in These Industries	
Agriculture	+10,600		Construction	−12,800
Metal products	+6,100		Medicine	−6,000
Electrical appliances	+5,200		Apparel	−5,900
Business services	+5,000		Lumber	−1,200
Motor vehicles	+5,000		Furniture	−400

The lowering of trade barriers between Mexico and the United States is changing the mix of output in both countries. New export opportunities create jobs in some industries while increased imports eliminate jobs in other industries. (Estimated gains and losses are during the first five years of NAFTA.)

Source: Congressional Budget Office.

ANALYSIS: The specialization encouraged by free trade creates new jobs in export but reduces employment in import-competing industries. In the process, total world output increases.

SUMMARY

- International trade permits each country to specialize in areas of relative efficiency, increasing world output. For each country, the gains from trade are reflected in consumption possibilities that exceed production possibilities. **LO35-2**
- One way to determine where comparative advantage lies is to compare the quantity of good A that must be given up in order to get a given quantity of good B from domestic production. If the same quantity of B can be obtained for less A by engaging in world trade, we have a comparative advantage in the production of good A. Comparative advantage rests on a comparison of relative opportunity costs. **LO35-1**
- The terms of trade—the rate at which goods are exchanged—are subject to the forces of international supply and demand. The terms of trade will lie somewhere between the opportunity costs of the trading partners. The terms of trade determine how the gains from trade are shared. **LO35-2**

- Resistance to trade emanates from workers and firms that must compete with imports. Even though the country as a whole stands to benefit from trade, these individuals and companies may lose jobs and incomes in the process. **LO35-3**
- Trade barriers take many forms. Embargoes are outright prohibitions against import or export of particular goods. Quotas limit the quantity of a good imported or exported. Tariffs discourage imports by making them more expensive. Other nontariff barriers make trade too costly or time-consuming. **LO35-3**
- The World Trade Organization (WTO) seeks to reduce worldwide trade barriers and enforce trade rules. Regional accords such as the North American Free Trade Agreement (NAFTA) pursue similar objectives among fewer countries. **LO35-3**

Key Terms

imports	consumption possibilities	dumping
exports	open economy	embargo
trade deficit	comparative advantage	tariff
trade surplus	opportunity cost	quota
production possibilities	absolute advantage	equilibrium price
closed economy	terms of trade	voluntary restraint agreement (VRA)

Questions for Discussion

1. Suppose a lawyer can type faster than any secretary. Should the lawyer do her own typing? Can you demonstrate the validity of your answer? **LO35-1**

2. What would be the effects of a law requiring bilateral trade balances? **LO35-2**

3. If a nation exported much of its output but imported little, would it be better or worse off? How about the reverse—that is, exporting little but importing a lot? **LO35-2**

4. How does international trade restrain the price behavior of domestic firms? **LO35-3**

5. Suppose we refused to sell goods to any country that reduced or halted its exports to us. Who would benefit and who would lose from such retaliation? **LO35-2**

6. Domestic producers often base their demands for import protection on the fact that workers in country X are paid substandard wages. Is this a valid argument for protection? **LO35-1**

7. Who, besides Chinese steel producers, was hurt by the new tariffs on Chinese imports (World View "U.S. Slaps China with Huge Anti-Dumping Tariffs")? **LO35-3**

8. According to the National Association of Home Builders, the 2017 tariff on Canadian lumber will result in the loss of 8,000 U.S. construction jobs. How does this happen? **LO35-3**

9. Who gains and who loses from nontariff barriers to Mexican trucks (World View "Mexico Retaliates for U.S. Trucking Roadblocks")? What made President Obama offer renewed negotiations? **LO35-3**

10. What are the potential benefits and risks of a border-adjustment tax? **LO35-3**

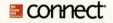

PROBLEMS FOR CHAPTER 35

LO35-2 1. Which countries are
  (a) The two largest export markets for the United States? (See Table 35.3.)
  (b) The two biggest sources of imports?

LO35-1 2. Suppose a country can produce a maximum of 12,000 jumbo airliners or 2,000 aircraft carriers.
  (a) What is the opportunity cost of an aircraft carrier?
  (b) If another country offers to trade eight planes for one aircraft carrier, should the offer be accepted?
  (c) What is the implied "price" of the carrier in trade?

LO35-1 3. If it takes 10 farmworkers to harvest 1 ton of strawberries and 3 farmworkers to harvest 1 ton of wheat, what is the opportunity cost of 4 tons of strawberries?

LO35-2 4. Alpha and Beta, two tiny islands in the Pacific, produce pearls and pineapples. The following production possibilities schedules describe their potential output in tons per year:

Alpha		Beta	
Pearls	**Pineapples**	**Pearls**	**Pineapples**
0	30	0	20
2	25	10	16
4	20	20	12
6	15	30	8
8	10	40	4
10	5	45	2
12	0	50	0

  (a) Graph the production possibilities confronting each island.
  (b) What is the opportunity cost of pineapples on each island (before trade)?
  (c) Which island has a comparative advantage in pineapple production?
  (d) Which island has a comparative advantage in pearl production?
  Now suppose Alpha and Beta specialize according to its comparative advantage and trades.
  If one pearl is traded for 1.5 pineapples,
  (e) How many pearls would have to be exported to get 15 pineapples in return?
  After this trade,
  (f) What is Alpha's consumption?
  (g) What is Beta's consumption?

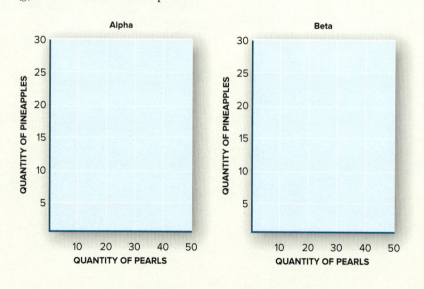

LO35-3 5. (a) How much more are U.S. consumers paying for the 12 tons of sugar they consume each year as a result of the quotas on sugar imports? (See In the News "Sugar Quotas a Sour Deal").

(b) How much sales revenue are foreign sugar producers losing as a result of those same quotas?

LO35-3 6. (a) How much was the tariff on Chinese steel imposed in 2016 (World View "U.S. Slaps China with Huge Anti-Dumping Tariffs")?

(b) If China was selling its steel for $50 a ton, what would that steel cost American automakers?

LO35-2 7. Suppose the two islands in Problem 4 agree that the terms of trade will be one for one and exchange 10 pearls for 10 pineapples.

(a) If Alpha produced 6 pearls and 15 pineapples while Beta produced 30 pearls and 8 pineapples before they decided to trade, how many pearls would each be producing after trade? Assume that the two countries specialize according to their comparative advantage.

(b) How much would the combined production of pineapples increase for the two islands due to specialization?

(c) How much would the combined production of pearls increase?

(d) What is the post trade consumption for each island?

LO35-3 8. Suppose the following table reflects the domestic supply and demand for Bluetooth headphones:

Price ($)	60	55	50	45	40	35	30	25
Quantity supplied (in millions per year)	8	7	6	5	4	3	2	1
Quantity demanded (in millions per year)	2	4	6	8	10	12	14	16

(a) Graph these market conditions and identify
 (i) The equilibrium price.
 (ii) The equilibrium quantity.

(b) Now suppose that foreigners enter the market, offering to sell an unlimited supply of Bluetooth headphones for $35 apiece. Illustrate and identify
 (i) The new market price.
 (ii) Domestic consumption.
 (iii) Domestic production.

(c) If a tariff of $5 per unit is imposed, what will be
 (i) The market price?
 (ii) Domestic consumption?
 (iii) Domestic production?

Graph your answers.

LO35-3 9. The Economy Tomorrow:

(a) Which regional trade pact is among Canada, the United States, and Mexico?

(b) Which industries have gained from this trade pact?

(c) Which industries have lost from this trade pact?

©Don Tonge/Alamy Stock Photo

International Finance

Textile, furniture, and shrimp producers in the United States want China to increase the value of the yuan. They say China's undervalued currency makes Chinese exports too cheap, undercutting American firms. President Trump agreed, claiming a higher value for the Chinese currency would "bring jobs back from China."

Walmart disagrees. Walmart thinks a cheap yuan is a good thing because it keeps prices low for the *$50 billion* of toys, tools, linens, and other goods it buys from China each year. Those low import prices help Walmart keep its own prices low and its sales volume high. Walmart is also the largest employer in the United States, providing more than 1.5 million jobs.

This chapter examines how currency values affect trade patterns and ultimately the core questions of WHAT, HOW, and FOR WHOM to produce. We focus on the following questions:

- **What determines the value of one country's money compared to the value of another's?**
- **What causes the international value of currencies to change?**
- **How and why governments intervene to alter currency values?**

EXCHANGE RATES: THE GLOBAL LINK

As we saw in Chapter 35, the United States exports and imports a staggering volume of goods and services. Although we trade with nearly 200 nations around the world, we seldom give much thought to where imports come from and how we acquire them. Most of the time, all we want to know is which products are available and at what price.

Suppose you want to buy an Apple iPad. You don't have to know that iPads are manufactured in China. And you certainly don't have to fly to China to pick it up. All you have to do is drive to the nearest electronics store; or you can just "click and buy" at the Internet's virtual mall.

But you may wonder how the purchase of an imported product was so simple. Chinese companies sell their products in yuan, the currency of China. But you purchase the iPad in dollars. How is this possible?

There's a chain of distribution between your dollar purchase in the United States and the yuan-denominated sale in China. Somewhere along that chain someone has to convert your dollars into yuan. The critical question for everybody concerned is how many yuan we can get for our dollars—that is, what the **exchange rate** is. If we can get eight yuan for every dollar, the exchange rate is 8 yuan = 1 dollar. Alternatively, we could note that the price of a yuan is 12.5 U.S. cents when the exchange rate is 8 to 1. Thus *an exchange rate is the price of one currency in terms of another.*

Which currency is most valuable? It depends on exchange rates.

©Maria Toutoudaki/Getty Images RF

FOREIGN EXCHANGE MARKETS

Most exchange rates are determined in foreign exchange markets. Stop thinking of money as some sort of magical substance, and instead view it as a useful commodity that facilitates market exchanges. From that perspective, an exchange rate—the price of money—is subject to the same influences that determine all market prices: demand and supply.

exchange rate: The price of one country's currency expressed in terms of another's; the domestic price of a foreign currency.

The Demand for Dollars

When the Japanese Toshiba Corporation bought Westinghouse Electric Co. in 2006, it paid $5.4 billion. When Belgian beer maker InBev bought Anheuser-Busch (Budweiser, etc.) in 2008, it also needed dollars—more than 50 billion of them. When Fiat acquired control of Chrysler in 2011, it also needed U.S. dollars. In all three cases, the objective of the foreign investor was to acquire an American business. To attain their objectives, however, the buyers first had to buy *dollars.* The Japanese, Belgian, and Italian buyers had to exchange their own currency for American dollars.

Canadian tourists also need American dollars. Few American restaurants or hotels accept Canadian currency as payment for goods and services; they want to be paid in U.S. dollars. Accordingly, Canadian tourists must buy American dollars if they want to warm up in Florida.

Some foreign investors also buy U.S. dollars for speculative purposes. When Argentina's peso started losing value in 2012–2013, many Argentinians feared that its value would drop further and preferred to hold U.S. dollars; they *demanded* U.S. dollars. Ukrainians clamored for U.S. dollars when Russia invaded its territory in 2014. In 2017 Venezuelans were desperately trying to sell their worthless bolivars for pennies.

All these motivations give rise to a demand for U.S. dollars. Specifically, *the market demand for U.S. dollars originates in*

- *Foreign demand for American exports* (including tourism).
- *Foreign demand for American investments.*
- *Speculation.*

Governments also create a demand for dollars when they operate embassies, undertake cultural exchanges, or engage in intergovernment financial transactions.

The Supply of Dollars

The *supply* of dollars arises from similar sources. On the supply side, however, it's Americans who initiate most of the exchanges. Suppose you take a trip to Mexico. You'll need to buy Mexican pesos at some point. When you do, you'll be offering to *buy* pesos by offering to *sell* dollars. In other words, *the* **demand** *for foreign currency represents a* **supply** *of U.S. dollars.*

When Americans buy BMW cars, they also supply U.S. dollars. American consumers pay for their BMWs in dollars. Somewhere down the road, however, those dollars will be exchanged for European euros. At that exchange, dollars are being *supplied* and euros *demanded.*

American corporations demand foreign exchange too. General Motors builds cars in Germany, Coca-Cola produces Coke in China, and Exxon produces and refines oil all over the world. In nearly every such case, the U.S. firm must first build or buy some plants and equipment, using another country's factors of production. This activity requires foreign currency and thus becomes another component of our demand for foreign currency.

We may summarize these market activities by noting that *the supply of dollars originates in*

- *American demand for imports* (including tourism).
- *American investments in foreign countries.*
- *Speculation.*

As on the demand side, government intervention can also contribute to the supply of dollars.

The Value of the Dollar

Whether American consumers will choose to buy an imported BMW depends partly on what the car costs. The price tag isn't always apparent in international transactions. Remember that the German BMW producer and workers want to be paid in their own currency, the euro. Hence the *dollar* price of an imported BMW depends on two factors: (1) the German price of a BMW and (2) the *exchange rate* between U.S. dollars and euros. Specifically, the U.S. price of a BMW is

$$\frac{\text{Dollar price}}{\text{of BMW}} = \frac{\text{Euro price}}{\text{of BMW}} \times \frac{\text{Dollar price}}{\text{of euro}}$$

Suppose the BMW company is prepared to sell a German-built BMW for 100,000 euros and that the current exchange rate is 2 euros = $1. At these rates, a BMW will cost you

$$\frac{\text{Dollar price}}{\text{of BMW}} = 100{,}000 \text{ euros} \times \frac{\$1}{2 \text{ euros}}$$

$$= \$50{,}000$$

If you're willing to pay this much for a shiny new German-built BMW, you may do so at current exchange rates.

Now suppose the exchange rate changes from 2 euros = $1 to 1 euro = $1. Now you're getting only 1 euro for your dollar rather than 2 euros. In other words, euros have become more expensive. *A higher dollar price for euros will raise the dollar costs of European goods.* In this case, the dollar price of a euro increases from $0.50 to $1. At this new exchange rate, the BMW plant in Germany is still willing to sell BMWs at 100,000 euros apiece. And German consumers continue to buy BMWs at that price. But this constant euro price now translates into a higher *dollar* price. That same BMW that you previously could buy for $50,000 now costs you $100,000—not because the cost of manufacturing the car in Germany went up, but simply because the exchange rate changed.

As the dollar price of a BMW rises, the number of BMWs sold in the United States will decline. As BMW sales decline, the quantity of euros demanded may decline as well. Thus the quantity of foreign currency demanded declines when the exchange rate rises because foreign goods become more expensive and imports decline. When the dollar price of European currencies actually increased in 1992, BMW decided to start producing cars in South Carolina. A year later Mercedes-Benz decided to produce cars in the United States as well. Sales of American-made BMWs and Mercedes no longer depend on the exchange rate of the U.S. dollar. But the dollar price of German-made Audis, French wine, and Italian shoes does.

The Supply Curve. These market responses suggest that the supply of dollars is upward-sloping. If the value of the dollar rises, Americans will be able to buy more euros. As a result, the dollar price of imported BMWs will decline. American consumers will respond by demanding more imports, thereby supplying a larger quantity of dollars. The supply curve in Figure 36.1 shows how the quantity of dollars supplied rises as the value of the dollar increases.

The Demand Curve. The demand for dollars can be explained in similar terms. Remember that the demand for dollars arises from the foreign demand for U.S. exports and investments. If the exchange rate moves from 2 euros = $1 to 1 euro = $1, the euro price of dollars falls.

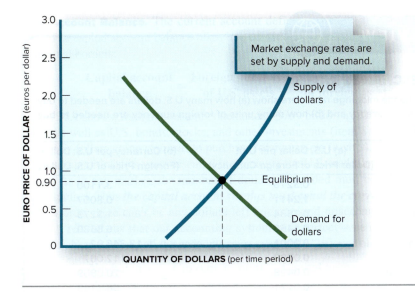

Market exchange rates are set by supply and demand.

FIGURE 36.1

The Foreign Exchange Market

The foreign exchange market operates like other markets. In this case, the "good" bought and sold is dollars (foreign exchange). The price and quantity of dollars actually exchanged are determined by the intersection of market supply and demand.

As dollars become cheaper for Germans, all American exports effectively fall in price. Germans will buy more American products (including trips to Disney World) and therefore demand a greater quantity of dollars. In addition, foreign investors will perceive in a cheaper dollar the opportunity to buy U.S. stocks, businesses, and property at fire-sale prices. Accordingly, they join foreign consumers in demanding more dollars. Not all these behavioral responses will occur overnight, but they're reasonably predictable over a brief period of time.

Equilibrium

Given market demand and supply curves, we can predict the **equilibrium price** of any commodity—that is, the price at which the quantity demanded will equal the quantity supplied. This occurs in Figure 36.1 where the two curves cross. At that equilibrium, the value of the dollar (the exchange rate) is established. In this case, the euro price of the dollar turns out to be 0.90.

The value of the dollar can also be expressed in terms of other currencies. World View "Foreign Exchange Rates" displays a sampling of dollar exchange rates in March 2017. Notice how many Indonesian rupiah you could buy for $1: a dollar was worth 13,346 rupiah. By contrast, a U.S. dollar was worth only 0.94 euro. **The *average* value of the dollar is a weighted mean of the exchange rates between the U.S. dollar and all these currencies.** The value of the dollar is "high" when its foreign exchange price is above recent levels, and it is "low" when it is below recent averages.

equilibrium price: The price at which the quantity of a good demanded in a given time period equals the quantity supplied.

The Balance of Payments

The equilibrium depicted in Figure 36.1 determines not only the *price* of the dollar, but also a specific *quantity* of international transactions. Those transactions include the exports, imports, international investments, and other sources of dollar supply and demand. A summary of all those international money flows is contained in the **balance of payments**—an accounting statement of all international money flows in a given period of time.

balance of payments: A summary record of a country's international economic transactions in a given period of time.

Trade Balance. Table 36.1 depicts the U.S. balance of payments for 2016. Notice first how the millions of separate transactions are classified into a few summary measures. The trade balance is the difference between exports and imports of goods (merchandise) and services. In 2016 the United States imported more than $2.7 trillion of goods and services but exported only $2.2 trillion. This created a **trade deficit** of $501 billion. That trade deficit represents a net outflow of dollars to the rest of the world.

trade deficit: The amount by which the value of imports exceeds the value of exports in a given time period (negative net exports).

Trade balance = Exports − Imports

EXCHANGE RATE INTERVENTION

Given the potential opposition to exchange rate movements, governments often feel compelled to intervene in foreign exchange markets. The intervention is usually intended to achieve greater exchange rate stability. But such stability may itself give rise to undesirable micro- and macroeconomic effects.

Fixed Exchange Rates

One way to eliminate fluctuations in exchange rates is to fix a currency's value. The easiest way to do this is for each country to define the worth of its currency in terms of some common standard. Under a **gold standard,** each country declares that its currency is worth so much gold. In so doing, it implicitly defines the worth of its currency in terms of all other currencies that also have a fixed gold value. In 1944 the major trading nations met at Bretton Woods, New Hampshire, and agreed that each currency was worth so much gold. The value of the U.S. dollar was defined as being equal to 0.0294 ounce of gold, while the British pound was defined as being worth 0.0823 ounce of gold. Thus the exchange rate between British pounds and U.S. dollars was effectively fixed at $1 = 0.357 pound, or 1 pound = $2.80 (or $2.80/0.0823 = $1/0.0294).

Balance-of-Payments Problems. It's one thing to proclaim the worth of a country's currency; it's quite another to *maintain* the fixed rate of exchange. As we've observed, foreign exchange rates are subject to continual and often unpredictable changes in supply and demand. Hence two countries that seek to stabilize their exchange rate at some fixed value will have to somehow neutralize such foreign exchange market pressures.

Suppose the exchange rate officially established by the United States and Great Britain is equal to e_1, as illustrated in Figure 36.4. As is apparent, that particular exchange rate is consistent with the then-prevailing demand and supply conditions in the foreign exchange market (as indicated by curves D_1 and S_1).

Now suppose that Americans suddenly acquire a greater taste for British cars and start spending more income on Jaguars, Bentleys, and Mini Coopers. This increased desire for British goods will *shift* the demand for British currency from D_1 to D_2 in Figure 36.4. Were exchange rates allowed to respond to market influences, the dollar price of a British pound would rise, in this case to the rate e_2. But we've assumed that government intervention has *fixed* the exchange rate at e_1. Unfortunately, at e_1, American consumers want to buy more pounds (q_D) than the British are willing to supply (q_S). The difference between the quantity demanded and the quantity supplied in the market at the rate e_1 represents a **market shortage** of British pounds.

gold standard: An agreement by countries to fix the price of their currencies in terms of gold; a mechanism for fixing exchange rates.

market shortage: The amount by which the quantity demanded exceeds the quantity supplied at a given price; excess demand.

FIGURE 36.4

Fixed Rates and Market Imbalance

If exchange rates are fixed, they can't adjust to changes in market supply and demand. Suppose the exchange rate is initially fixed at e_1. When the demand for British pounds increases (shifts to the right), an excess demand for pounds emerges. More pounds are demanded (q_D) at the rate e_1 than are supplied (q_S). This causes a balance-of-payments deficit for the United States.

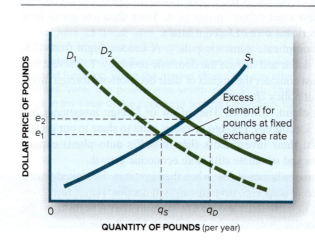

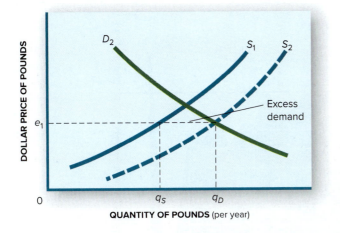

DOLLAR PRICE OF POUNDS

QUANTITY OF POUNDS (per year)

FIGURE 36.5

The Impact of Monetary Intervention

If the U.S. Treasury holds reserves of British pounds, it can use them to buy U.S. dollars in foreign exchange markets. As it does so, the supply of pounds will shift to the right, to S_2, thereby maintaining the desired exchange rate, e_1. The Bank of England could bring about the same result by offering to buy U.S. dollars with pounds (i.e., *supplying* pounds).

The excess demand for pounds implies a **balance-of-payments deficit** for the United States: more dollars are flowing out of the country than into it. The same disequilibrium represents a **balance-of-payments surplus** for Britain because its outward flow of pounds is less than its incoming flow.

Basically, there are only two solutions to balance-of-payments problems brought about by the attempt to fix exchange rates:

- Allow exchange rates to rise to e_2 (Figure 36.4), thereby eliminating the excess demand for pounds.
- Alter market supply or demand so they intersect at the fixed rate e_1.

Since fixed exchange rates were the initial objective of this intervention, only the second alternative is of immediate interest.

The Need for Reserves. One way to alter market conditions would be for someone simply to supply British pounds to American consumers. The U.S. Treasury could have accumulated a reserve of foreign currency in earlier periods. By selling some of those **foreign exchange reserves** now, the Treasury would be *supplying* British pounds, helping to offset excess demand. The rightward shift of the pound supply curve in Figure 36.5 illustrates the sale of accumulated British pounds—and related purchase of U.S. dollars—by the U.S. Treasury.

Although foreign exchange reserves can be used to fix exchange rates, such reserves may not be adequate. Indeed, Figure 36.6 should be testimony enough to the fact that today's deficit isn't always offset by tomorrow's surplus. A principal reason that fixed exchange rates didn't live up to their expectations is that the United States had balance-of-payments deficits for 22 consecutive years. This long-term deficit overwhelmed the government's stock of foreign exchange reserves.

The Role of Gold. Gold reserves are a potential substitute for foreign exchange reserves. As long as each country's money has a value defined in terms of gold, we can use gold to buy British pounds, thereby restocking our foreign exchange reserves. Or we can simply use the gold to purchase U.S. dollars in foreign exchange markets. In either case, the exchange value of the dollar will tend to rise. However, we must have **gold reserves** available for this purpose. Unfortunately, the continuing U.S. balance-of-payments deficits recorded in Figure 36.6 exceeded even the hoards of gold buried under Fort Knox. As a consequence, our gold reserves lost their credibility as a guarantor of fixed exchange rates. When it appeared that foreigners would demand more gold than the U.S. government possessed, President Nixon simply ended the link between the U.S. dollar and gold. As of August 15, 1971, the U.S. dollar had no guaranteed value.

balance-of-payments deficit: An excess demand for foreign currency at current exchange rates.

balance-of-payments surplus: An excess demand for domestic currency at current exchange rates.

foreign exchange reserves: Holdings of foreign currencies by official government agencies, usually the central bank or treasury.

gold reserves: Stocks of gold held by a government to purchase foreign exchange.

FIGURE 36.6

The U.S. Balance of Payments, 1950–1973

The United States had a balance-of-payments deficit for 22 consecutive years. During this period, the foreign exchange reserves of the U.S. Treasury were sharply reduced. Fixed exchange rates were maintained by the willingness of foreign countries to accumulate large reserves of U.S. dollars. However, neither the Treasury's reserves nor the willingness of foreigners to accumulate dollars was unlimited. In 1973 fixed exchange rates were abandoned.

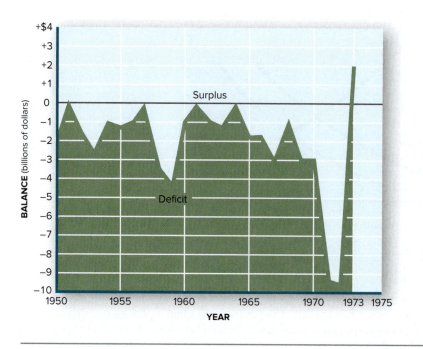

Domestic Adjustments. Government can also use fiscal, monetary, and trade policies to achieve a desired exchange rate. With respect to trade policy, *trade protection can be used to prop up fixed exchange rates.* We could eliminate the excess demand for pounds (Figure 36.4), for example, by imposing quotas and tariffs on British goods. Such trade restrictions would reduce British imports to the United States and thus the demand for British pounds. In August 1971 President Nixon imposed an emergency 10 percent surcharge on all imported goods to help reduce the payments deficit that fixed exchange rates had spawned. Such restrictions on international trade, however, violate the principle of comparative advantage and thus reduce total world output. Trade protection also invites retaliatory trade restrictions.

Fiscal policy is another way out of the imbalance. An increase in U.S. income tax rates will reduce disposable income and have a negative effect on the demand for all goods, including imports. A reduction in government spending will have similar effects. In general, *deflationary (or restrictive) policies help correct a balance-of-payments deficit by lowering domestic incomes and thus the demand for imports.*

Monetary policies in a deficit country could follow the same restrictive course. A reduction in the money supply raises interest rates. The balance of payments will benefit in two ways. The resultant slowdown in spending will reduce import demand. In addition, higher interest rates may induce international investors to move more of their funds into the deficit country. Such moves will provide immediate relief to the payments imbalance.[1] Russia tried this strategy in 1998, tripling key interest rates (to as much as 150 percent). But even that wasn't enough to restore confidence in the ruble, which kept depreciating. Within three months of the monetary policy tightening, the ruble lost half its value.

A surplus country could help solve the balance-of-payments problem. By pursuing expansionary—even inflationary—fiscal and monetary policies, a surplus country could stimulate the demand for imports. Moreover, any inflation at home will reduce the competitiveness of exports, thereby helping to restrain the inflow of foreign demand. Taken together, such efforts would help reverse an international payments imbalance.

[1]Before 1930, not only were foreign exchange rates fixed, but domestic monetary supplies were tied to gold stocks as well. Countries experiencing a balance-of-payments deficit were thus forced to contract their money supply, and countries experiencing a payments surplus were forced to expand their money supply by a set amount. Monetary authorities were powerless to control domestic money supplies except by erecting barriers to trade. The system was abandoned when the world economy collapsed into the Great Depression.

Even under the best of circumstances, domestic economic adjustments entail significant costs. In effect, ***domestic adjustments to payments imbalances require a deficit country to forsake full employment and a surplus country to forsake price stability***. China has had to grapple with these domestic consequences of fixing the value of its currency. The artificially low value of the yuan promoted Chinese exports and accelerated China's GDP growth. But it also created serious macro problems. To keep the value of the yuan low, the Chinese had to keep buying dollars. By 2011 China had more than $3 trillion of foreign currency reserves (see World View "The Risks of China's Foreign-Exchange Stockpile"). It paid for those dollars with yuan, adding to China's money supply. All that money stoked inflation in China. Ultimately, the Chinese government had to adopt restrictive monetary and fiscal policies to keep inflation in check. The Chinese government also had to be willing to keep accumulating U.S. dollars and other currencies.

WORLD VIEW

THE RISKS OF CHINA'S FOREIGN-EXCHANGE STOCKPILE

China's foreign-exchange stockpile topped $4 trillion this month, a sum equal to the entire value of China's equity markets. Some see this stockpile of U.S. dollars, euros, yen, and pounds as a testament to China's economic strength. But others warn of substantial risks to the Chinese economy of this foreign-exchange build-up.

The most obvious risk is a decline in the values of the U.S. dollar or U.S. Treasury bonds. About two-thirds of the stockpile consists of U.S. Treasury bonds. When U.S. interest rates start rising—as everyone expects—the market value of Treasury bonds will fall, cutting the value of China's holdings. Inflation poses an even greater risk. China must print more yuan every time exports exceed imports. The Bank of China says the money supply will grow 12–13 percent this year as a result. All that money threatens to accelerate domestic inflation, a problem that has already raised political concerns in China.

Critics say the problem originates in the undervalued yuan. Observers accuse China of intervening in the market to keep the value of the yuan artificially low. This helps drive exports, but adds to China's already gargantuan stockpile of foreign exchange.

Source: News reports, December 2014.

ANALYSIS: When a currency is deliberately undervalued, strong export demand may kindle inflation. The trade surplus that results also increases foreign exchange reserves.

As we noted earlier, President Trump has proposed yet another way to correct market imbalances. He blamed the huge trade deficit with China on the intentional manipulation of the value of the yuan by the Chinese government. He called China the "grand champion of currency manipulation" for its alleged role in keeping the value of the yuan low (essentially a fixed rate). To offset that "unfair" exchange rate, Trump proposed tariffs on all Chinese imports. That would reduce the flow of dollars to China and "bring jobs back from China." But China denies the charge and points to the fact that its dollar reserves have fallen since 2015. Observers also warn that unilateral tariffs can easily spark a trade war that hurts both nations.

There's no easy way out of this impasse. Market imbalances caused by fixed exchange rates can be corrected only with abundant supplies of foreign exchange reserves or deliberate changes in fiscal, monetary, or trade policies. At some point, it may become easier to let a currency adjust to market equilibrium.

The Euro Fix. The original 12 nations of the European Monetary Union (EMU) fixed their exchange rates in 1999. They went far beyond the kind of exchange rate fix we're discussing here. Members of the EMU *eliminated* their national currencies, making the euro the common currency of Euroland. They don't have to worry about reserve balances or domestic adjustments. However, they do have to reconcile their varied national interests to a single monetary authority, which has proven to be difficult politically in times of economic stress.

Flexible Exchange Rates

flexible exchange rates:
A system in which exchange rates are permitted to vary with market supply-and-demand conditions; floating exchange rates.

Balance-of-payments problems wouldn't arise in the first place if exchange rates were allowed to respond to market forces. Under a system of **flexible exchange rates** (often called floating exchange rates), the exchange rate moves up or down to choke off any excess supply of or demand for foreign exchange. Notice again in Figure 36.4 that the exchange rate move from e_1 to e_2 prevents any excess demand from emerging. *With flexible exchange rates, the quantity of foreign exchange demanded always equals the quantity supplied,* and there's no imbalance. For the same reason, there's no need for foreign exchange reserves.

Although flexible exchange rates eliminate balance-of-payments and foreign exchange reserves problems, they don't solve all of a country's international trade problems. *Exchange rate movements associated with flexible rates alter relative prices and may disrupt import and export flows.* As noted before, depreciation of the dollar raises the price of all imported goods, contributing to domestic cost-push inflation. Also, domestic businesses that sell imported goods or use them as production inputs may suffer sales losses. On the other hand, appreciation of the dollar raises the foreign price of U.S. goods and reduces the sales of American exporters. Hence *someone is always hurt, and others are helped, by exchange rate movements.* The resistance to flexible exchange rates originates in these potential losses. Such resistance creates pressure for official intervention in foreign exchange markets or increased trade barriers.

The United States and its major trading partners abandoned fixed exchange rates in 1973. Although exchange rates are now able to fluctuate freely, it shouldn't be assumed that they necessarily undergo wild gyrations. On the contrary, experience with flexible rates since 1973 suggests that some semblance of stability is possible even when exchange rates are free to change in response to market forces.

Speculation. One force that often helps maintain stability in a flexible exchange rate system is—surprisingly—speculation. Speculators often counteract short-term changes in foreign exchange supply and demand. If a currency temporarily rises above its long-term equilibrium, speculators will move in to sell it. By selling at high prices and later buying at lower prices, speculators hope to make a profit. In the process, they also help stabilize foreign exchange rates.

Speculation isn't always stabilizing, however. Speculators may not correctly gauge the long-term equilibrium. Instead they may move "with the market" and help push exchange rates far out of kilter. This kind of destabilizing speculation sharply lowered the international value of the U.S. dollar in 1987, forcing the Reagan administration to intervene in foreign exchange markets, borrowing foreign currencies to buy U.S. dollars. In 1997 the Clinton administration intervened for the opposite purpose: stemming the rise in the U.S. dollar. The Bush administration was more willing to stay on the sidelines, letting global markets set the exchange rates for the U.S. dollar.

managed exchange rates:
A system in which governments intervene in foreign exchange markets to limit but not eliminate exchange rate fluctuations; "dirty floats."

These kinds of interventions are intended to *narrow* rather than *eliminate* exchange rate movements. Such limited intervention in foreign exchange markets is often referred to as **managed exchange rates,** or, popularly, "dirty floats."

Although managed exchange rates would seem to be an ideal compromise between fixed rates and flexible rates, they can work only when some acceptable "rules of the game" and mutual trust have been established. As Sherman Maisel, a former governor of the Federal Reserve Board, put it, "Monetary systems are based on credit and faith: If these are lacking, a . . . crisis occurs."[2]

---

[2]Sherman Maisel, *Managing the Dollar* (New York: W. W. Norton, 1973), p. 196.

THE ECONOMY TOMORROW

CURRENCY BAILOUTS

The world has witnessed a string of currency crises, including the one in Asia during 1997–1998, the Brazilian crisis of 1999, the Argentine crisis of 2001–2002, the Greek and Portuguese crises of 2010–2012, and recurrent ruble crises in Russia. In every instance, the country in trouble pleads for external help. In most cases, a currency "bailout" is arranged, whereby global monetary authorities lend the troubled nation enough reserves (such as U.S. dollars) to defend its currency. Typically the International Monetary Fund (IMF) heads the rescue party, joined by the central banks of the strongest economies.

The Case for Bailouts. The argument for currency bailouts typically rests on the domino theory. Weakness in one currency can undermine another. This seemed to be the case during the 1997–1998 Asian crisis. After the **devaluation** of the Thai baht, global investors began worrying about currency values in other Asian nations. Choosing to be safe rather than sorry, they moved funds out of Korea, Malaysia, and the Philippines and invested in U.S. and European markets (notice in Figure 36.3 the 1997–1998 appreciation of the U.S. dollar).

> **devaluation:** An abrupt depreciation of a currency whose value was fixed or managed by the government.

The initial baht devaluation also weakened the competitive trade position of these same economies. Thai exports became cheaper, diverting export demand from other Asian nations. To prevent loss of export markets, Thailand's neighbors felt they had to devalue as well. Speculators who foresaw these effects accelerated the domino effect by selling the region's currencies.

When Brazil devalued its currency (the *real*) in January 1999, global investors worried that a "samba effect" might sweep across Latin America. The domino effect could reach across the ocean and damage U.S. and European exports as well. The Greek crisis of 2010 threatened the common currency (euro) of 28 nations. Hence, richer, more stable countries often offer a currency bailout as a form of self-defense.

The Case against Bailouts. Critics of bailouts argue that such interventions are ultimately self-defeating. They say that once a country knows for sure that currency bailouts are in the wings, it doesn't have to pursue the domestic policy adjustments that might stabilize its currency. A nation can avoid politically unpopular options such as high interest rates, tax hikes, or cutbacks in government spending. It can also turn a blind eye to trade barriers, monopoly power, lax lending policies, and other constraints on productive growth. Hence the expectation of readily available bailouts may foster the very conditions that cause currency crises.

Future Bailouts? The decision to bail out a depreciating currency isn't as simple as it appears. To minimize the ill effects of bailouts, the IMF and other institutions typically require the nation in crisis to pledge more prudent monetary, fiscal, and trade policies. Usually there's a lot of debate about what kinds of adjustments will be made—and how soon. As long as the nation in crisis is confident of an eventual bailout, however, it has a lot of bargaining power to resist policy changes. Only after the IMF finally said no to further bailouts in Greece did the Greek parliament pass austerity measures that reduced its fiscal imbalances.

SUMMARY

- Money serves the same purposes in international trade as it does in the domestic economy—namely, to facilitate specialization and market exchanges. The basic challenge of international finance is to create acceptable standards of value from the various currencies maintained by separate countries. **LO36-1**

- Exchange rates are the mechanism for translating the value of one national currency into the equivalent value of another. An exchange rate of $1 = 2$ euros means that one dollar is worth two euros in foreign exchange markets. **LO36-1**

- Foreign currencies have value because they can be used to acquire goods and resources from other countries. Accordingly, the supply of and demand for foreign currency reflect the demands for imports and exports, for international investment, and for overseas activities of governments. **LO36-2**

- The balance of payments summarizes a country's international transactions. Its components are the trade balance, the current account balance, and the capital account balance. The current and capital accounts must offset each other. **LO36-2**

- The equilibrium exchange rate is subject to any and all shifts of supply and demand for foreign exchange. If relative incomes, prices, or interest rates change, the demand for foreign exchange will be affected. A depreciation is a change in market exchange rates that makes one country's currency cheaper in terms of another currency. An appreciation is the opposite kind of change. **LO36-3**

- Changes in exchange rates are often resisted. Producers of export goods don't want their currencies to rise in

value (appreciate); importers and tourists dislike it when their currencies fall in value (depreciate). **LO36-4**

- Under a system of fixed exchange rates, changes in the supply and demand for a specific currency can't be expressed in exchange rate movements. Instead such shifts will be reflected in excess demand for or supply of that currency. Such market imbalances are referred to as balance-of-payments deficits or surpluses. **LO36-3**

- To maintain fixed exchange rates, monetary authorities must enter the market to buy and sell foreign exchange. To do so, deficit countries must have foreign exchange reserves. In the absence of sufficient reserves, a country can maintain fixed exchange rates only if it's willing to alter basic fiscal, monetary, or trade policies. **LO36-4**

- Flexible exchange rates eliminate balance-of-payments problems and the crises that accompany them. But complete flexibility can lead to disruptive changes. To avoid this contingency, many countries prefer to adopt managed exchange rates—that is, rates determined by the market but subject to government intervention. **LO36-4**

Key Terms

exchange rate
equilibrium price
balance of payments
trade deficit
depreciation (currency)
appreciation

foreign exchange markets
gold standard
market shortage
balance-of-payments deficit
balance-of-payments surplus
foreign exchange reserves

gold reserves
flexible exchange rates
managed exchange rates
devaluation

Questions for Discussion

1. Why would a rise in the value of the dollar prompt U.S. manufacturers to build production plants in Mexico? **LO36-4**

2. How do changes in the value of the U.S. dollar affect foreign enrollments at U.S. colleges? **LO36-4**

3. How would rapid inflation in Canada affect U.S. tourism travel to Canada? Does it make any difference whether the exchange rate between Canadian and U.S. dollars is fixed or flexible? **LO36-3**

4. Under what conditions would a country welcome a balance-of-payments deficit? When would it *not* want a deficit? **LO36-4**

5. In what sense do fixed exchange rates permit a country to "export its inflation"? **LO36-4**

6. Why did the value of the Ukrainian hryvnia depreciate so much when Russia invaded (see section Ukraine Crisis of 2014)? **LO36-3**

7. If a nation's currency depreciates, are the reduced export prices that result "unfair"? **LO36-4**

8. How would each of these events affect the supply or demand for Japanese yen? **LO36-3**
   (a) Stronger U.S. economic growth.
   (b) A decline in Japanese interest rates.
   (c) Higher inflation in the United States.
   (d) A Japanese tsunami.

9. Who in Mexico is helped or hurt by a strong U.S. dollar? Redo World View "Who Gains, Who Loses from Strong Dollar" for Mexicans. **LO36-4**

10. Why does World View "The Risks of China's Foreign-Exchange Stockpile" say the undervalued yuan is "more bane than boom"? **LO36-4**

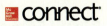

PROBLEMS FOR CHAPTER 36

LO36-1 1. According to World View "Foreign Exchange Rates," which nation had
   (*a*) The cheapest currency?
   (*b*) The most expensive currency?

LO36-1 2. If a euro is worth $1.25, what is the euro price of a dollar?

LO36-3 3. How many Ukrainian hryvnia (see section Ukraine Crisis of 2014) could you buy with one U.S. dollar
   (*a*) Before the Russian invasion?
   (*b*) After the Russian invasion?

LO36-1 4. If a McDonald's Big Mac meal sold for $6.00 in March 2017, how much would it cost in the currencies of
   (*a*) Brazil?
   (*b*) Japan?
   (*c*) Indonesia?
   (See World View "Foreign Exchange Rates.")

LO36-1 5. Between 2014 and 2017, did the U.S. dollar appreciate or depreciate (see Figure 36.3)?

LO36-1 6. If a PlayStation 4 costs 30,000 yen in Japan, how much will it cost in U.S. dollars if the exchange rate is
   (*a*) 110 yen = $1?
   (*b*) 1 yen = $0.009?
   (*c*) 100 yen = $1?

LO36-1 7. Between 1990 and 2000, by how much did the dollar appreciate (Figure 36.3)?

LO36-1 8. If inflation raises U.S. prices by 2 percent and the U.S. dollar appreciates by 5 percent, by how much does the foreign price of U.S. exports change?

LO36-1 9. According to World View "Foreign Exchange Rates," what was the peso price of a euro in March 2017?

LO36-2 10. For each of the following possible events, indicate whether the global value of the U.S. dollar will rise or fall.
   (*a*) American cars become suddenly more popular abroad.
   (*b*) Inflation in the United States accelerates.
   (*c*) The United States falls into a recession.
   (*d*) Interest rates in the United States drop.
   (*e*) The United States experiences rapid increases in productivity.
   (*f*) Anticipating a return to the gold standard, Americans suddenly rush to buy gold from the two big producers, South Africa and the Soviet Union.
   (*g*) War is declared in the Middle East.
   (*h*) The stock markets in the United States collapse.

LO36-3 11. The following schedules summarize the supply and demand for trifflings, the national currency of Tricoli:

Triffling price (U.S. dollars per triffling)	0	$4	$8	$12	$16	$20	$24
Quantity demanded (per year)	40	38	36	34	32	30	28
Quantity supplied (per year)	1	11	21	31	41	51	61

Use these schedules for the following:
   (*a*) Graph the supply and demand curves.
   (*b*) Determine the equilibrium exchange rate.

   (c) Determine the size of the excess supply or excess demand that would exist if the Tricolian government fixed the exchange rate at $22 = 1 triffling.

   (d) Which of the following events would help reduce the payments imbalance? Which would not?

      (i) Domestic inflation.

      (ii) Foreign inflation.

      (iii) Slower domestic growth.

      (iv) Faster domestic growth.

LO36-3 12. As shown in Table 36.1, in 2016 the United States was running a current account deficit. Would the following events increase or decrease the current account deficit?

   (a) U.S. companies, the largest investors in Switzerland, see even more promising investment opportunities there.

   (b) The Netherlands, one of the largest foreign investors in the United States, finds U.S. investment opportunities less attractive.

   (c) Unemployment rises and recession deepens in the United States.

LO36-3 13. The Economy Tomorrow: Show graphically the impact on the South Korean currency (won) when the Thai baht was devalued.

©William West/AFP/Getty Images

CHAPTER 37

Global Poverty

Bono, the lead singer for the rock group U2, has performed concerts around the world to raise awareness of global poverty. He doesn't have a specific agenda for eradicating poverty. He does believe, though, that greater awareness of global poverty will raise assistance levels and spawn more ideas for combating global hunger, disease, and isolation.

The dimensions of global poverty are staggering. According to the World Bank, more than a third of the world's population lacks even the barest of life's necessities. *Billions* of people are persistently malnourished, poorly sheltered, minimally clothed, and at constant risk of debilitating diseases. Life expectancies among the globally poor population still hover in the range of 40–50 years, far below the norm (70–80 years) of the rich, developed nations.

In this chapter we follow Bono's suggestion and take a closer look at global poverty. We address the following issues:

- **What income thresholds define "poverty"?**
- **How many people are poor?**
- **What actions can be taken to reduce global poverty?**

In the process of answering these questions, we get another opportunity to examine what makes economies "tick"—particularly what forces foster faster economic growth for some nations and slower economic growth for others.

AMERICAN POVERTY

Poverty, like beauty, is often in the eye of the beholder. Many Americans feel "poor" if they can't buy a new car, live in a fancy home, or take an exotic vacation. Indeed, the average American asserts that a family needs at least $58,000 a year "just to get by." With that much income, however, few people would go hungry or be forced to live in the streets.

Official Poverty Thresholds

To develop a more objective standard of poverty, the U.S. government assessed how much money a U.S. family needs to purchase a "minimally adequate" diet. Back in 1963 it concluded that $1,000 per year was needed for that purpose alone. Then it asked how much income was needed to purchase other basic necessities like housing, clothes, transportation, and so on. It figured all those *non*food necessities would cost twice as much as the food staples. So it concluded that a budget of $3,000 per year would fund a "minimally adequate" living standard for a U.S. family of four. That standard became the official **U.S. poverty threshold** in 1963.

LEARNING OBJECTIVES

After reading this chapter, you should know

LO37-1 How U.S. and global poverty are defined.

LO37-2 How many people in the world are poor.

LO37-3 What factors impede or promote poverty reduction.

poverty threshold (U.S.): Annual income of less than $24,600 for a family of four (2016).

Inflation Adjustments. Since 1963, prices have risen every year. As a result, the price of the poverty "basket" has risen as well. In 2017, it cost roughly $25,000 to purchase those same basic necessities for a family of four that cost only $3,000 in 1963.

Twenty-five thousand dollars might sound like a lot of money, especially if you're not paying your own rent or feeding a family. If you break the budget down, however, it doesn't look so generous. Only a third of the budget goes for food. And that portion has to feed four people. So the official U.S. poverty standard provides less than $6 per day for an individual's food. That just about covers a single Big Mac combo at McDonald's. There's no money in the poverty budget for dining out. And the implied rent money is only $800 a month (for the whole family). So the official U.S. poverty standard isn't that generous—certainly not by *American* standards (where the *average* family has an income of nearly $80,000 per year and eats outside their $250,000 home three times a week).

U.S. Poverty Count

poverty rate: Percentage of the population counted as poor.

The Census Bureau counted more than 40 million Americans as "poor" in 2016 according to the official U.S. thresholds (as adjusted for family size). This was one out of eight U.S. households, for a **poverty rate** of roughly 13 percent. According to the Census Bureau, the official U.S. poverty rate has been in a narrow range of 11–15 percent for the last 40 years.

How Poor Is U.S. "Poor"?

Many observers criticize these official U.S. poverty statistics. They say that far fewer Americans meet the government standard of poverty and even fewer are really destitute.

in-kind transfers: Direct transfers of goods and services rather than cash, such as food stamps, Medicaid benefits, and housing subsidies.

In-Kind Income. A major flaw in the official tally is that the government counts only *cash* income in defining poverty. Since the 1960s, however, the United States has developed an extensive system of **in-kind transfers** that augment cash incomes. Food stamps, for example, can be used just as easily as cash to purchase groceries. Medicaid and Medicare pay doctor and hospital bills, reducing the need for cash income. Government rent subsidies and public housing allow poor families to have more housing than their cash incomes would permit. These in-kind transfers allow "poor" families to enjoy a higher living standard than their cash incomes imply. Adding those transfers to cash incomes would bring the U.S. poverty count down into the 9–11 percent range.

Material Possessions. Even those families who remain "poor" after counting in-kind transfers aren't necessarily destitute. More than 40 percent of America's "poor" families own their homes, 70 percent own a car or truck, and 30 percent own at least *two* vehicles. Telephones, color TVs, dishwashers, clothes dryers, air conditioners, and microwave ovens are commonplace in America's poor households.

America's poor families themselves report few acute problems in everyday living. Fewer than 14 percent report missing a rent or mortgage payment, and fewer than 8 percent report a food deficiency. So American poverty isn't synonymous with homelessness, malnutrition, chronic illness, or even social isolation. These problems exist among America's poverty population, but they don't define American poverty.

GLOBAL POVERTY

Poverty in the rest of the world is much different from poverty in America. *American poverty is more about* relative *deprivation than* absolute *deprivation. In the rest of the world, poverty is all about* absolute *deprivation.*

Low Average Incomes

As a starting point for assessing global poverty, consider how *average* incomes in the rest of the world stack up against U.S. levels. By global standards, the United States is unquestionably a very rich nation. As we observed in Chapter 2 (see World View "GDP per Capita around the World"), U.S. GDP per capita is five times larger than the world average. More than three-fourths of the world's population lives in what the World Bank calls "low-income" or "lower-middle-income" nations. In those nations the *average* income is under $4,000 a year, less than *one-tenth* of America's per capita GDP. Average incomes are lower yet in Haiti, Nigeria, Ethiopia, and other desperately poor nations. By American standards, virtually all the people in these nations would be poor. By *their* standards, no American would be poor.

World Bank Poverty Thresholds

Because national poverty lines are so diverse and culture-bound, the World Bank decided to establish a uniform standard for assessing global poverty. And it set the bar amazingly low. In fact, the World Bank regularly uses two thresholds, namely $1.90 per day for **"extreme" poverty** and a higher $3.10 per day standard for less "severe" poverty.

The World Bank thresholds are incomprehensibly low by American standards. The $1.90 standard works out to $2,774 per year for a family of four—a mere tenth of America's poverty standard. Think about it. How much could you buy for $1.90 a day? A little rice, maybe, and perhaps some milk? Certainly not a Big Mac. Not even a grande coffee at Starbucks. And part of that $1.90 would have to go for rent. Clearly this isn't going to work. Raising the World Bank standard to $3.10 per day (**severe poverty**) doesn't reach a whole lot further.

The World Bank, of course, wasn't defining "poverty" in the context of American affluence. They were instead trying to define a rock-bottom threshold of absolute poverty—a threshold of physical deprivation that people everywhere would acknowledge as the barest "minimum"—a condition of "unacceptable deprivation."

Global Poverty Counts

On the basis of household surveys in more than 100 nations, *the World Bank classifies 800 million people as being in "extreme" poverty (<$1.90/day) and 2 billion people as being in "severe" poverty (<$3.10/day).*

Figure 37.1 shows where concentrations of extreme poverty are the greatest. Concentrations of extreme poverty are alarmingly high in dozens of smaller, less developed nations like Mali, Haiti, and Zambia, where average incomes are also shockingly low. However, the greatest *number* of extremely poor people reside in the world's largest countries. China and India alone contain a third of the world's population and 40 percent of the world's extreme poverty.

Table 37.1 reveals that the distribution of severe poverty (<$3.10/day) is similar. The incidence of this higher poverty threshold is, of course, much greater. Severe poverty afflicts more than 80 percent of the population in dozens of nations and even reaches more than 90 percent of the population in some (e.g., Burundi). By contrast, less than 15 percent of the U.S. population falls below the official *American* poverty threshold, and *virtually no American household has an income below the global poverty threshold.*

extreme poverty (world): World Bank income standard of less than $1.90 per day per person (inflation adjusted).

severe poverty (world): World Bank income standard of $3.10 per day per person (inflation adjusted).

Analysis: Global poverty is defined in terms of absolute deprivation.
©Stockbyte/Getty Images RF

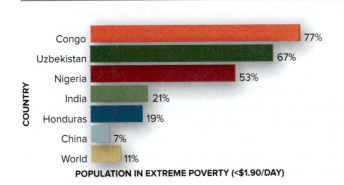

POPULATION IN EXTREME POVERTY (<$1.90/DAY)

FIGURE 37.1

Geography of Extreme Poverty

Nearly 800 million people around the world are in "extreme" poverty. In smaller, poor nations, deprivation is commonplace.

Source: The World Bank, *WDR2015-16 Data Set.*

TABLE 37.1

Population in Severe Poverty
(<$3.10/day)

More than a third of the world's
population has income of less
than $3.10 per person per day.
Such poverty is pervasive in low-
income nations.

Country	Living in Severe Poverty (Percent)
Tanzania	92%
Burundi	92
Congo	91
Uzbekistan	88
Nigeria	77
Honduras	71
Bangladesh	80
Ethiopia	71
India	58
China	11
World	**30%**

Source: The World Bank, *WDR2015 Data Set.*

Social Indicators

The levels of poverty depicted in Figure 37.1 and Table 37.1 imply levels of physical and social deprivation few Americans can comprehend. Living on less than two or three dollars a day means always being hungry, malnourished, ill-clothed, dirty, and unhealthy. The problems associated with such deprivation begin even before birth. Pregnant women often fail to get enough nutrition or medical attention. In low-income countries only a third of all births are attended by a skilled health practitioner. If something goes awry, both the mother and the baby are at fatal risk. Nearly all of the children in global poverty are in a state of chronic malnutrition. At least 1 out of 10 children in low-income nations will actually die before reaching age 5. In the poorest sectors of the population, infant and child mortality rates are often two to three times higher than that. Children often remain unimmunized to preventable diseases. And AIDS is rampant among both children and adults in the poorest nations. All of these factors contribute to a frighteningly short life expectancy—less than half that in the developed nations.

Fewer than one out of two children from extremely poor households are likely to stay in school past the eighth grade. Women and minority ethnic and religious groups are often wholly excluded from educational opportunities. As a consequence, great stocks of human capital remain undeveloped: in low-income nations only one out of two women and only two out of three men are literate.

Persistent Poverty

Global poverty is not only more desperate than American poverty, but also more permanent. In India a rigid caste system still defines differential opportunities for millions of rich and poor villagers. Studies in Brazil, South Africa, Peru, and Ecuador document barriers that block access to health care, education, and jobs for children of poor families. Hence inequalities in poor nations not only are more severe than in developed nations but also tend to be more permanent.

Economic stagnation also keeps a lid on upward mobility. President John F. Kennedy observed that "a rising tide lifts all boats," referring to the power of a growing economy to raise everyone's income. In a growing economy, one person's income *gain* is not another person's *loss*. By contrast, a stagnant economy intensifies class warfare, with everyone jealously protecting whatever gains they have made. The *haves* strive to keep the *have-nots* at bay. Unfortunately, this is the reality in many low-income nations. As we observed in Chapter 2 (Table 2.1), in some of the poorest nations in the world output grows more slowly than the population, intensifying the competition for resources.

GOALS AND STRATEGIES

Global poverty is so extensive that no policy approach offers a quick solution. Even the World Bank doesn't see an end to global poverty. The United Nations set a much more modest goal back in 2000.

The UN Millennium Goals

The UN established a Millennium Poverty Goal of cutting the incidence of extreme global poverty in half by 2015 (from 30 percent in 1990 to 15 percent in 2015). That goal was attained. But that didn't significantly decrease the *number* of people in poverty. The world's population keeps growing at upward of 80–100 million people a year. In 2017, there were close to 7.4 billion people on this planet. Fifteen percent of that population would still have left more than a *billion* people in extreme global poverty. In 2015, the World Bank set a new and more ambitious goal of *eliminating* extreme poverty by 2030.

Why should we care? After all, America has its own poverty problems and a slew of other domestic concerns. So why should an American—or, for that matter, an affluent Canadian, French, or German citizen—embrace the **UN and World Bank Poverty Goal**? For starters, one might embrace the notion that a poor child in sub-Saharan Africa or Borneo is no less worthy than a poor child elsewhere. And a child's death in Bangladesh is just as tragic as a child's death in Buffalo, New York. In other words, humanitarianism is a starting point for *global* concern for poor people. Then there are pragmatic concerns. Poverty and inequality sow the seeds of social tension both within and across national borders. Poverty in other nations also limits potential markets for international trade. Last but not least, undeveloped human capital anywhere limits human creativity. For all these reasons, the World Bank feels its Poverty Goal should be universally embraced.

> **UN and World Bank Poverty Goal:** UN goal of eliminating extreme poverty by 2030.

Policy Strategies

Eliminating severe poverty around the world won't be easy. In principle, *there are only two general approaches to global poverty reduction:*

- *Redistribution* of incomes within and across nations.
- *Economic growth* that raises average incomes.

The following sections explore the potential of these strategies for eliminating global poverty.

INCOME REDISTRIBUTION

Many people suggest that the quickest route to eliminating global poverty is simply to *redistribute* incomes and assets, both within and across countries. The potential for redistribution is often exaggerated, however, and its risks underestimated.

Within-Nation Redistribution

Take another look at those nations with the highest concentrations of extreme poverty. Nigeria is near the top of the list in Figure 37.1 and Table 37.1, with an incredible 53 percent of its population in extreme poverty and 77 percent in severe poverty. Yet the other 23 percent of the population lives fairly well, taking more than half of that nation's income. So what would happen if we somehow forced Nigeria's richest households to share that wealth? Sure, Nigeria's poorest households would be better off. But the gains wouldn't be spectacular: the *average* income in Nigeria is only $2,800 a year. Haiti, Zambia, and Madagascar also have such low *average* incomes that outright redistribution doesn't hold great hope for income gains by the poor. (See World View "Glaring Inequalities").

GLARING INEQUALITIES

Inequality tends to diminish as a country develops. In poor nations, the richest tenth of the population typically gets 40 to 50 percent of all income—sometimes even more. In developed countries, the richest tenth gets 20 to 30 percent of total income.

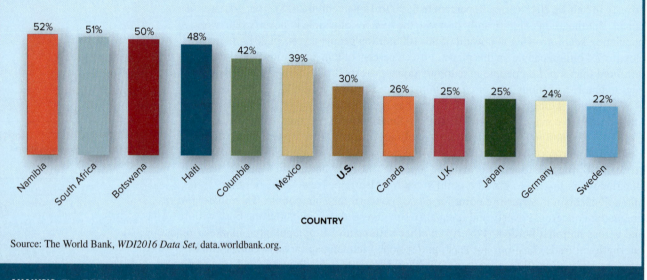

Income Share of Richest Tenth of Population

Country	Share
Namibia	52%
South Africa	51%
Botswana	50%
Haiti	48%
Columbia	42%
Mexico	39%
U.S.	30%
Canada	26%
U.K.	25%
Japan	25%
Germany	24%
Sweden	22%

COUNTRY

Source: The World Bank, *WDI2016 Data Set,* data.worldbank.org.

ANALYSIS: The FOR WHOM question is reflected in the distribution of income. Although the U.S. income distribution is very unequal, inequalities loom even larger in most poor countries.

Economic Risks. Then there's the downside to direct redistribution. How is the income pie going to be resliced? Will the incomes or assets of the rich be confiscated? How will underlying jobs, stocks, land, and businesses be distributed to the poor? How will *total* output (and income) be affected by the redistribution?

If savings are confiscated, people will no longer want to save and invest. If large, efficient farms are divided up into small parcels, who will manage them? After Zimbabwe confiscated and fragmented that nation's farms in 2000, its agricultural productivity plummeted and the economy collapsed. Cuba experienced the same kind of economic decline after the government seized and fragmented sugar and tobacco plantations. If the government expropriates factories, mills, farms, or businesses, who will run them? If the *rewards* to saving, investment, entrepreneurship, and management are expropriated, who will undertake these economic activities?

This is not to suggest that *no* redistribution of income or assets is appropriate. More progressive taxes and land reforms can reduce inequalities and poverty. But the potential of direct within-nation redistribution is often exaggerated. Historically, nations have often been forced to reverse land, tax, and property reforms that have slowed economic growth and reduced average incomes.

Expenditure Reallocation. In addition to directly redistributing private income and wealth, governments can also reduce poverty by reallocating direct government expenditures. As we observed in Chapter 1 (Figure 1.3), some poor nations devote a large share of output to the military. If more of those resources were channeled into schools, health services, and infrastructure, the poor would surely benefit. Governments in poor nations also tend to give priority to urban development (where the government and middle class reside), to the

Country	Total Aid ($ billions)	Percentage of Donor Total Income
United States	$ 32	0.19%
United Kingdom	18	0.70
Germany	14	0.42
France	11	0.37
Japan	12	0.19
Canada	5	0.24
Australia	5	0.31
Norway	6	1.00
Italy	4	0.19
24-Nation Total	$140	0.29%

Source: World Bank (2014 data).

TABLE 37.2

Foreign Aid

Rich nations give roughly $140–150 billion to poor nations every year. This is a tiny fraction of donor GDP, however.

neglect of rural development (where the poor reside). Redirecting more resources to rural development and core infrastructure (roads, electricity, and water) would accelerate poverty reduction.

Across-Nation Redistribution

Redistribution *across* national borders could make even bigger dents in global poverty. After all, the United States and other industrialized nations are so rich that they could transfer a lot of income to the globally poor if they chose to.

Foreign Aid. Currently developed nations give poorer nations $140–$150 billion a year in "official development assistance." That's a lot of money. But even if it were distributed exclusively to globally poor households, it would amount to only $50 per year per person.

Developed nations have set a goal of delivering more aid. The United Nations' **Millennium Aid Goal** is to raise foreign aid levels to 0.7 percent of donor-country GDP. That may not sound too ambitious, but it's a much larger flow than at present. As Table 37.2 reveals, few "rich" nations now come close to this goal. Although the United States is by far the world's largest aid donor, its aid equals only 0.19 percent of U.S. total output. For all developed nations, the aid ratio averages around 0.29 percent—just 40 percent of the UN goal.

Given the history of foreign aid, the UN goal is unlikely to be met anytime soon. But what if it were? What if foreign aid *tripled*? Would that cure global poverty? No. Tripling foreign aid would generate only $200 a year for each of the 2 billion people now in global poverty. Even that figure is optimistic, as it assumes all aid is distributed to the poor in a form (e.g., food, clothes, and medicine) that directly addresses their basic needs.

Millennium Aid Goal: United Nations goal of raising foreign aid levels to 0.7 percent of donor-country GDP.

Nongovernmental Aid. Official development assistance is augmented by private charities and other nongovernmental organizations (NGOs). The Gates Foundation, for example, spends upward of $1 billion a year on health care for the globally poor, focusing on treatable diseases like malaria, tuberculosis, and HIV infection (see World View "The Way We Give"). Religious organizations operate schools and health clinics in areas of extreme poverty. The International Red Cross brings medical care, shelter, and food in emergencies.

As with official development assistance, the content of NGO aid can be as important as its level. Relatively low-cost immunizations, for example, can improve health conditions more than an expensive, high-tech health clinic can. Teaching basic literacy to a community of young children can be more effective than equipping a single high school with Internet capabilities. Distributing drought-resistant seeds to farmers can be more effective than donating advanced farm equipment (which may become useless when it needs to be repaired).

WORLD VIEW

THE WAY WE GIVE

Philanthropy Can Step In Where Market Forces Don't

One day my wife Melinda and I were reading about millions of children dying from diseases in poor countries that were eliminated in this country. . . .

Malaria has been known for a long time. In 1902, in 1907, Nobel Prizes were given for advances in understanding the malaria parasite and how it was transmitted. But here we are a hundred years later and malaria is setting new records, infecting more than 400 million people every year, and killing more than a million people every year. That's a number that's increasing every year, and every day it's more than 2,000 African children. . . .

And this would extend to tuberculosis, yellow fever, AIDS vaccine, acute diarrheal illnesses, respiratory illnesses; you know, millions of children die from these things every year, and yet the advances we have in biology have not been applied because rich countries don't have these diseases. The private sector really isn't involved in developing vaccines and medicines for these diseases because the developing countries can't buy them. . . .

And so if left to themselves, these market forces create a world, which is the situation today, where more than 90 percent of the money spent on health research is spent on those who are the healthiest. An example of that is the billion a year spent on combating baldness. That's great for some people, but perhaps it should get behind malaria in terms of its priority ranking. . . .

So philanthropy can step in where market forces are not there. . . . It can get the people who have the expertise and draw them in. It can use awards, it can use novel arrangements with private companies, it can partner with the universities. . . . And every year the platform of science that we have to do this on gets better.

—**Bill Gates**

Source: Gates, Bill, "Speech at The Tech Museum," Bill & Melinda Gates Foundation, November 15, 2006. ©2006.

ANALYSIS: When markets fail to provide for basic human needs, additional institutions and incentives may be needed.

ECONOMIC GROWTH

No matter how well designed foreign aid and philanthropy might be, across-nation transfers alone cannot eliminate global poverty. As Bill Gates observed, the entire endowment of the Gates Foundation would meet the health needs of the globally poor for only one year. The World Bank concurs: "Developing nations hold the keys to their prosperity; global action cannot substitute for equitable and efficient domestic policies and institutions."[1] So as important as international assistance is, it will never fully suffice.

Increasing Total Income

The "key" to ending global poverty is, of course, **economic growth.** As we've observed, *redistributing existing incomes doesn't do the job;* **total** *income has to increase.* This is what economic growth is all about.

Unique Needs. The generic prescription for economic growth is simple: more resources and better technology. But this growth formula takes on a new meaning in the poorest nations. Rich nations can focus on research, technology, and the spread of "brain power." Poor nations need the basics—the "bricks and mortar" elements of an economy such as water systems, roads, schools, and legal systems. Bill Gates learned this firsthand in his

economic growth: An increase in output (real GDP); an expansion of production possibilities.

[1]World Bank, *World Development Report, 2006* (Washington, DC: World Bank, 2006), p. 206.

early philanthropic efforts. In 1996 Microsoft donated a computer for a community center in Soweto, one of the poorest areas in South Africa. When he visited the center in 1997 he discovered the center had no electricity. He quickly realized that growth policy priorities for poor nations are different from those for rich nations.

Growth Potential

The potential of economic growth to reduce poverty in poor nations is impressive. The 40 nations classified as "low-income" by the World Bank have a combined output of only $600 billion. That's about twice the annual sales revenue of Walmart. "Lower-middle-income" nations like China, Brazil, Egypt, and Sri Lanka produce another $5 trillion or so of annual output. Hence every percentage point of economic growth increases total income in these combined nations by nearly $60 billion. According to the World Bank, if these nations could grow their economies by just 3.8 percent a year, that would generate an extra $280 billion of output in the first year and increasing thereafter. That "growth dividend" is twice the amount of foreign aid (Table 37.2).

China has demonstrated just how effective economic growth can be in reducing poverty. Since 1990 China has been the world's fastest-growing economy, with annual GDP growth rates routinely in the 8–10 percent range. This sensational growth has not only raised *average* incomes but has also dramatically reduced the incidence of poverty. In fact, *the observed success in reducing extreme global poverty from 30 percent in 1990 to 11 percent in 2016 is almost entirely due to the decline in Chinese poverty.* By contrast, slow economic growth in Africa, Latin America, and South Asia has *increased* their respective poverty populations.

Growth of per Capita Output

The really critical factor in reducing poverty is the relationship of output growth to population growth. China has been spectacularly successful in this regard: not only does it have one of the fastest GDP growth rates, but it also has one of the world's slowest population growth rates. As a result, its per capita output has grown by a incredible 9.6 percent a year.

Notice in Table 37.3 how slow population growth rates in high-income nations allows them to achieve ever-rising living standards. Japan is the ultimate example: with zero population growth, its pretty easy to achieve an increase in per capita income.

	Average Annual Growth Rate (2000–2015) of		
	GDP	**Population**	**Per Capita GDP**
High-income countries			
Canada	1.9	1.0	0.9
United States	1.7	0.9	0.8
Japan	0.7	0.0	0.7
France	1.1	0.6	0.5
Low-income countries			
China	10.1	0.5	9.6
India	7.5	1.5	6.0
West Bank/Gaza	3.9	2.8	1.1
Burundi	3.6	3.3	0.3
Libya	1.3	1.1	0.2
Madagascar	2.8	2.9	−0.1
Haiti	1.3	1.5	−0.2
Central African Republic	−0.1	1.8	−1.9
Zimbabwe	−1.3	1.5	−2.8

Source: The World Bank, *WDR2016 Data Set.*

TABLE 37.3

Growth Rates in Selected Countries, 2000–2015

The relationship between GDP growth and population growth is very different in rich and poor countries. The populations of rich countries are growing very slowly, and gains in per capita GDP are easily achieved. In the poorest countries, population is still increasing rapidly, making it difficult to raise living standards. Notice how per capita incomes are declining in many poor countries (such as Zimbabwe and Haiti).

Zimbabwe and the Central African Republic don't fare so well. Their output shrank every year, even while their populations were increasing. As a consequence, the average citizen had less output to consume every year: extreme poverty spread.

Investing in Human Capital

human capital: The knowledge and skills possessed by the workforce.

While the math of global poverty is simple, the strategies for reducing poverty and many and diverse. A common observation, however, is the need to invest more in **human capital.**

Education. In poor nations, the need for human capital development is evident. Only 71 percent of the population in low-income nations completes even elementary school. Even fewer people are *literate*—that is, able to read and write a short, simple statement about everyday life (e.g., "We ate rice for breakfast"). Educational deficiencies are greatest for females, who are often prevented from attending school by cultural, social, or economic concerns (see World View "The Female 'Inequality Trap'"). In Chad and Liberia, fewer than one out of six girls completes primary school. Primary school completion rates for girls are in the 25–35 percent range in most of the poor nations of sub-Saharan Africa.

WORLD VIEW

THE FEMALE "INEQUALITY TRAP"

In many poor nations, women are viewed as such a financial liability that female fetuses are aborted, female infants are killed, and female children are so neglected that they have significantly higher mortality rates. The "burden" females pose results from social norms that restrict the ability of women to earn income, accumulate wealth, or even decide their own marital status. In many of the poorest nations, women

- Have restricted property rights.
- Can't inherit wealth.
- Are prohibited or discouraged from working outside the home.
- Are prohibited or discouraged from going to school.
- Are prevented from voting.
- Are denied the right to divorce.
- Are paid less than men if they do work outside the home.
- Are often expected to bring a financial dowry to the marriage.
- May be beaten if they fail to obey their husbands.

These social practices create an "inequality trap" that keeps returns on female human capital investment low. Without adequate education or training, they can't get productive jobs. Without access to good jobs, they have no incentive to get an education or training. This kind of vicious cycle creates an inequality trap that keeps women and their communities poor.

Source: The World Bank, *World Development Report 2006*, pp. 51–54.

ANALYSIS: Denying women economic rights not only is discriminatory but reduces the amount of human capital available for economic growth.

---

inequality trap: Institutional barriers that impede human and physical capital investment, particularly by the poorest segments of society.

In Niger and Mali, only one out of five *teenage* girls is literate. This lack of literacy creates an **inequality trap** that restricts the employment opportunities for young women to simple, routine, manual jobs (e.g., carpet weaving and sewing). With so few skills and little education, they are destined to remain poor.

The already low levels of *average* education are compounded by unequal access to schools. Families in extreme poverty typically live in rural areas, with primitive transportation and communication facilities. *Physical* access to school itself is problematic. On top of that, the poorest families often need their children to work, either within the family or in paid employment. In Somalia, only 8 percent of poor young children attend primary schools; in Ethiopia, Yemen, and Mali, about 50 percent attend. These forces often foreclose school attendance for the poorest children.

Health. In poor nations, basic health care is also a critical dimension of human capital development. Immunizations against measles, diphtheria, and tetanus are more the exception than the rule in Somalia, Nigeria, Afghanistan, Congo, the Central African Republic, and many other poor nations. For all low-income nations taken together, the child immunization rate is only 67 percent (versus 96 percent in the United States). Access and education—not money—are the principal barriers to greater immunizations.

Water and sanitation facilities are also in short supply. The World Bank defines "adequate water access" as a protected water source of at least 20 liters per person a day within 1 kilometer of the home dwelling. We're not limited to indoor plumbing with this definition: a public water pipe a half mile from one's home is considered adequate. Yet only three out of four households in low-income nations meet even this minimum threshold of water adequacy In Afghanistan, Ethiopia, and Somalia only one out of four households has even that much water access. Access to sanitation facilities (ranging from pit latrines to flush toilets) is less common still (on average one out of three low-income-nation households). In Ethiopia only 6 percent of the population is so privileged.

When illness strikes, professional health care is hard to find. In the United States, there is one doctor for every 180 people. In Sierra Leone, there is one doctor for every 10,000 people! For low-income nations as a group, there are 2,500 people for every available doctor.

These glaring inadequacies in health conditions breed high rates of illness and death. In the United States, only 8 out of every 1,000 children die before age 5. In Angola, 260 of every 1,000 children die that young. For all low-income nations, the under-5 mortality rate is 13.5 percent (nearly one out of seven). Those children who live are commonly so malnourished (severely underweight and/or short) that they can't develop fully (another inequality trap).

AIDS takes a huge toll as well. Only 0.6 percent of the U.S. adult population has HIV. In Botswana, Lesotho, Swaziland, and Zimbabwe, more than 25 percent of the adult population is HIV-infected. As a result of these problems, life expectancies are inordinately low. In Zambia, only 16 percent of the population lives to age 65. In Botswana, life expectancy at birth is 35 years (versus 78 years in the United States). For low-income nations as a group, life expectancy is a mere 57 years.

Analysis: Unsafe water is a common problem for the globally poor.
©Dr. Parvinder Sethi RF

Capital Investment

If they are ever going to eradicate poverty and its related social ills, poor nations need sharply increased capital investment in both the public and private sectors. Transportation and communications systems must be expanded and upgraded so markets can function. Capital equipment and upgraded technology must flow into both agricultural and industrial enterprises.

Internal Financing. Acquiring the capital resources needed to boost productivity and accelerate economic growth is not an easy task. Domestically, freeing up scarce resources for capital investment requires cutbacks in domestic consumption. In the 1920s Stalin used near-totalitarian powers to cut domestic consumption in Russia (by limiting output of consumer goods) and raise Russia's **investment rate** to as much as 30 percent of output. This elevated rate of investment accelerated capacity growth, but at a high cost in terms of consumer deprivation.

Other nations haven't had the power or the desire to make such a sacrifice. China spent two decades trying to raise consumption standards before it gave higher priority to investment. Once it did so, however, economic growth accelerated sharply. Unfortunately, low investment rates continue to plague other poor nations.

Pervasive poverty in poor nations sharply limits the potential for increased savings. Nevertheless, governments can encourage more saving with improved banking facilities,

investment rate: The percentage of total output (GDP) allocated to the production of new plants, equipment, and structures.

transparent capital markets, and education and saving incentives. And there is mounting evidence that even small dabs of financing can make a big difference. Extending a small loan that enables a poor farmer to buy improved seeds or a plow can have substantial effects on productivity. Financing small equipment or inventory for an entrepreneur can get a new business rolling. Such **microfinance** can be a critical key to escaping poverty (see World View "Muhammad Yunus: Microloans").

microfinance: The granting of small ("micro"), unsecured loans to small businesses and entrepreneurs.

WORLD VIEW

MUHAMMAD YUNUS: MICROLOANS

Teach a man to fish, and he'll eat for a lifetime. But only if he can afford the fishing rod. More than 30 years ago in Bangladesh, economics Professor Muhammad Yunus recognized that millions of his countrymen were trapped in poverty because they were unable to scrape together the tiny sums they needed to buy productive essentials such as a loom, a plow, an ox, or a rod. So he gave small loans to his poor neighbors, secured by nothing more than their promise to repay.

Microcredit, as it's now known, became a macro success in 2006, reaching two huge milestones. The number of the world's poorest people with outstanding microloans—mostly in amounts of $15 to $150—was projected to reach 100 million. And Yunus, 66, shared the Nobel Peace Prize with the Grameen Bank he founded. The Nobel Committee honored his grassroots strategy as "development from below."

You know an idea's time has come when people start yanking it in directions its originator never imagined. Some, like Citigroup, are making for-profit loans, contrary to Yunus's breakeven vision. Others, like Bangladesh's BRAC, are nonprofit but have a more holistic vision than Grameen, offering health care and social services in addition to loans.

Source: "The Best Ideas," *BusinessWeek,* December 18, 2006, pp. 96–106. Used with permission of Bloomberg L.P. Copyright © 2015. All rights reserved.

ANALYSIS: Microloans focus on tiny loans to small businesses and farmers that enable them to increase output and productivity.

Some nations have also used inflation as a tool for shifting resources from consumption to investment. By financing public works projects and private investment with an increased money supply, governments can increase the inflation rate. As prices rise faster than consumer incomes, households are forced to curtail their purchases. This "inflation tax" ultimately backfires, however, when both domestic and foreign market participants lose confidence in the nation's currency. Periodic currency collapses have destabilized many South and Central American economies and governments. Inflation financing also fails to distinguish good investment ideas from bad ones.

External Financing. Given the constraints on internal financing, poor nations have to seek external funding to lift their investment rate. In fact, Columbia University economist Jeffrey Sachs has argued that external financing is not only necessary but, if generous enough, also sufficient for *eliminating* global poverty (see World View "Jeffrey Sachs: Big Money, Big Plans"). As we've observed, however, actual foreign aid flows are far below the "Big Money" threshold that Sachs envisions. Skeptics also question whether more foreign aid would really solve the problem, given the mixed results of previous foreign aid flows. They suggest that more emphasis should be placed on increasing *private* investment flows. Private investment typically entails *direct foreign investment* in new plants, equipment, and technology, or the purchase of ownership stakes in existing enterprises.

WORLD VIEW

JEFFREY SACHS: BIG MONEY, BIG PLANS

Columbia University economics professor Jeffrey Sachs has seen the ravages of poverty around the world. As director of the UN Millennium Project, he is committed to attaining the UN's goal of reducing global poverty rates by half by 2015. In fact, Professor Sachs thinks we can do even better: the complete *elimination* of extreme poverty by 2025.

How will the world do this? First, rich nations must double their foreign aid flows now, and then double them again in 10 years. Second, poor nations must develop full-scale, comprehensive plans for poverty reduction. This "shock therapy" approach must address all dimensions of the poverty problem simultaneously and quickly, sweeping all inequality traps out of the way.

Critics have called Sachs's vision utopian. They point to the spotty history of foreign aid projects and the failure of many top-down, Big Plan development initiatives. But they still applaud Sachs for mobilizing public opinion and economic resources to fight global poverty.

Source: Sachs, Jeffrey, *The End of Poverty,* New York, NY: Penguin Random House, 2006.

ANALYSIS: World poverty can't be eliminated without committing far more resources. Jeffrey Sachs favors an externally financed, comprehensive Big Plan approach.

Agricultural Development

When we think about capital investment, we tend to picture new factories, gleaming office buildings, and computerized machinery. In discussing global poverty, however, we have to remind ourselves of how dependent poor nations are on agriculture. As Figure 37.2 illustrates, nearly 60 percent of Somalia's income originates in agriculture. Agricultural shares in the range of 35–55 percent are common in the poorest nations. By contrast, only 1 percent of America's output now comes from farms.

Low Farm Productivity. What keeps poor nations so dependent on agriculture is their incredibly low **productivity.** Subsistence farmers are often forced to plow their own fields by hand with wooden plows. Irrigation systems are primitive and farm machinery is scarce or nonexistent. While high-tech U.S. farms produce nearly $80,000 of output per worker, Ugandan

productivity: Output per unit of input—for example, output per labor-hour.

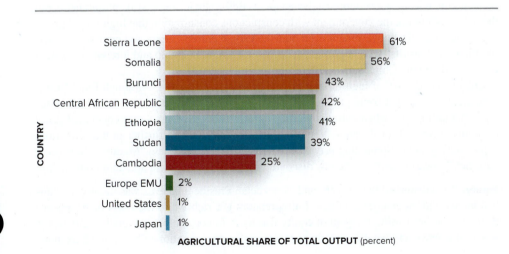

FIGURE 37.2

Agricultural Share of Output

In poor nations, agriculture accounts for a very large share of total output.

Source: The World Bank, *WDR2016 Data Set.*

FIGURE 37.3

Low Agricultural Productivity

Farmers in poor nations suffer from low productivity. They are handicapped by low education, inferior technology, primitive infrastructure, and a lack of machinery.

Source: The World Bank, *WDR2016 Data Set.*

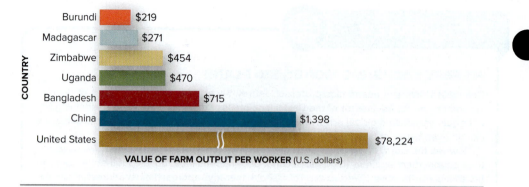

COUNTRY

Burundi	$219
Madagascar	$271
Zimbabwe	$454
Uganda	$470
Bangladesh	$715
China	$1,398
United States	$78,224

VALUE OF FARM OUTPUT PER WORKER (U.S. dollars)

farms produce a shockingly low $219 of output per worker (see Figure 37.3). Farmers in Sudan produce only 683 kilograms of cereal per hectare, compared with 7,637 kilos per hectare in the United States.

To grow their economies, poor nations have to invest in agricultural development. Farm productivity has to rise beyond subsistence levels so that workers can migrate to other industries and expand production possibilities. One of the catapults to China's growth was an exponential increase in farm productivity that freed up labor for industrial production. (China now produces nearly 5,900 kilos of cereal per hectare.) To achieve greater farm productivity, poor nations need capital investment, technological know-how, and improved infrastructure.

Institutional Reform

Clearly, poor nations need a lot more investment. But more resources alone may not suffice. To attract and keep capital, a *nation needs an institutional structure that promotes economic growth.*

Property Rights. Land, property, and contract rights have to be established before farmers will voluntarily improve their land or invest in agricultural technology. China saw how agricultural productivity jumped when it transformed government-run communal farms into local enterprises and privately managed farms, beginning in 1978. China is using the lessons of that experience to now extend ownership rights to farmers.

Entrepreneurial Incentives. Unleashing the "animal spirits" of the marketplace is also critical. People *do* respond to incentives. If farmers see the potential for profit—and the opportunity to keep that profit—they will pursue productivity gains with more vigor. To encourage that response, governments need to assure the legitimacy of profits and their fair tax treatment. In 1992 the Chinese government acknowledged the role of profits and entrepreneurship in fostering economic advancement. Before then, successful entrepreneurs ran the risk of offending the government with conspicuous consumption that highlighted growing inequalities. The government even punished some entrepreneurs and confiscated their wealth. Once "profits" were legitimized, however, entrepreneurship and foreign investment accelerated, raising China's growth rate significantly.

Cuba stopped short of legitimizing private property and profits. Although Fidel Castro periodically permitted some private enterprises (e.g., family restaurants), he always withdrew that permission when entrepreneurial ventures succeeded. As a consequence, Cuba's economy stagnated for decades. Venezuela has recently moved further in that direction, expropriating and nationalizing private enterprises (see World View "Maduro: 'Bourgeois Parasites' Thwart Growth"), thereby discouraging private investment and entrepreneurship.

Equity. What disturbed both Castro and Venezuelan President Chávez was the way capitalism intensified income inequalities. Entrepreneurs got rich while the mass of people remained poor. For Castro, the goal of equity was more important than the goal of efficiency. A nation where everyone was equally poor was preferred to a nation of haves and have-nots.

Analysis: Lack of capital, technology, and markets keeps farm productivity low.

©McGraw-Hill Education/Barry Barker, photographer

WORLD VIEW

MADURO: "BOURGEOIS PARASITES" THWART GROWTH

When he won a third presidential term in 2006, Hugo Chávez made his intentions clear. Venezuela, he said, is "heading toward socialism, and no one can prevent it." He embarked on a policy of nationalization, price controls, and a political takeover of Venezuela's central bank. Since then, the Venezuelan economy has stalled; factories, oil fields, and farms have shut down; inflation has soared; and food and energy shortages have become commonplace.

Chávez's successor, Nicolas Maduro, blames the nation's economic woes not on government policy but on the "bourgeois parasites" who have conspired to raise prices, hoard commodities, and strangle the economy. He ordered the nation's largest electronic retailer, Daka, to cut its prices in half and sent the military into its stores to enforce those price cuts. He urged Venezuelans to "leave nothing on the shelves, nothing in the warehouses" and threatened store managers with arrest if they interfered. Critics called the action "government-sanctioned looting." Maduro also levied fines and threatened jail sentences for General Motors executives who he accused of cutting back production and charging "exploitive" prices for new cars. Meanwhile, people have to wait for years to get a new car, while food, water, and energy are now being rationed because of spreading shortages.

Source: News reports, September 2014.

ANALYSIS: By restricting private ownership and market freedom, governments curb the entrepreneurship and investment that may be essential for economic development.

In many of today's poorest nations, policy interests are not so noble. A small elite often holds extraordinary political power and uses that power to protect its privileges. Greed restricts the flow of resources to the poorest segments of the population, leaving them to fend for themselves. These inequalities in power, wealth, and opportunity create inequality traps that restrain human capital development, capital investment, entrepreneurship, and ultimately economic growth.

Business Climate. To encourage capital investment and entrepreneurship, governments have to assure a secure and supportive business climate. Investors and business start-ups want to know what the rules of the game are and how they will be enforced. They also want assurances that contracts will be enforced and that debts can be collected. They want their property protected from crime and government corruption. They want minimal interference from government regulation and taxes.

As the annual surveys by the Heritage Foundation document, nations that offer a more receptive business climate grow at a faster pace. Figure 37.4 illustrates this connection. Notice that nations with the most pro-business climate (e.g., Hong Kong, Singapore, Iceland, the United States, and Denmark) enjoy living standards far superior to those in nations with hostile business climates (e.g., North Korea, Cuba, Congo, Sudan, Zimbabwe, and Myanmar). This is no accident; *pro-business climates encourage the capital investment, the entrepreneurship, and the human capital investment that drive economic growth.*

Unfortunately, some of the poorest nations still fail to provide a pro-business environment. Figure 37.5 illustrates how specific dimensions of the business climate differ across fast-growing nations (China) and perpetually poor ones (Cambodia and Kenya). A biannual survey of 26,000 international firms elicits their views of how different government policies restrain their investment decisions. Notice how China offers a more certain policy environment, less corruption, more secure property rights, and less crime. Given these business conditions, where would you invest?

The good news about the business climate is that it doesn't require huge investments to fix. It does require, however, a lot of political capital.

FIGURE 37.4

Business Climates Affect Growth

Nations that offer more secure property rights, less regulation, and lower taxes grow faster and enjoy higher per capita incomes.

Note: Business climate in 183 nations gauged by 50 measures of government tax, regulatory, and legal policy.

2011 Index of Economic Freedom, Washington, DC: The Heritage Foundation, p. 7, 2011.

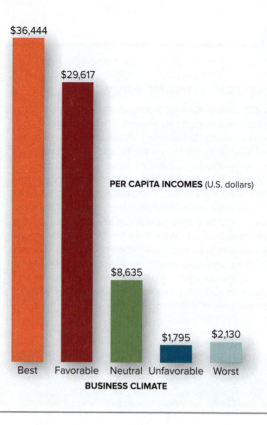

PER CAPITA INCOMES (U.S. dollars)

Best $36,444 · Favorable $29,617 · Neutral $8,635 · Unfavorable $1,795 · Worst $2,130

BUSINESS CLIMATE

FIGURE 37.5

Investment Climate

International investors gravitate toward nations with business-friendly policies. Shown here are the percentages of international firms citing specific elements of the business climate that deter their investment in the named countries.

Source: The World Bank, *World Development Indicators 2006.*

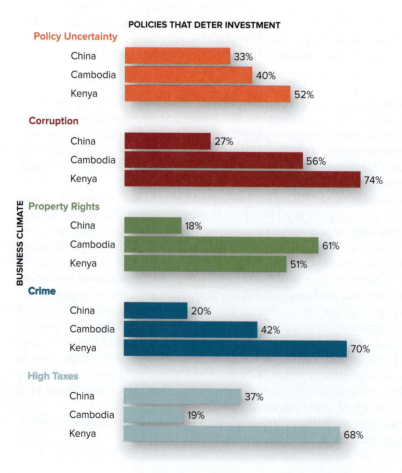

POLICIES THAT DETER INVESTMENT

BUSINESS CLIMATE

Policy Uncertainty — China 33%, Cambodia 40%, Kenya 52%

Corruption — China 27%, Cambodia 56%, Kenya 74%

Property Rights — China 18%, Cambodia 61%, Kenya 51%

Crime — China 20%, Cambodia 42%, Kenya 70%

High Taxes — China 37%, Cambodia 19%, Kenya 68%

World Trade

When it comes to political capital, poor nations have a complaint of their own. They say that rich nations lock them out of their most important markets—particularly agricultural export markets. Poor nations typically have a **comparative advantage** in the production of agricultural products. Their farm productivity may be low (see Figure 37.3), but their low labor costs keep their farm output competitive. They can't fully exploit that advantage in export markets, however. The United States, the European Union, and Japan heavily subsidize their own farmers. This keeps farm prices low in the rich nations, eliminating the cost advantage of farmers in poor nations. To further protect their own farmers from global competition, rich nations erect trade barriers to stem the inflow of Third World products. The United States, for example, enforces an **import quota** on foreign sugar. This trade barrier has fostered a high-cost, domestic beet sugar industry while denying poor nations the opportunity to sell more sugar and grow their economies faster.

Poor nations need export markets. Export sales generate the hard currency (dollars, euros, and yen) that is needed to purchase capital equipment in global markets. Export sales also allow farmers in poor nations to expand production, exploit economies of scale, and invest in improved technology. Ironically, *trade barriers in rich nations impede poor nations from pursuing the agricultural development that is a* **prerequisite** *for growth.* The latest round of multilateral trade negotiations dragged on forever because of the resistance of rich nations to opening their agricultural markets. Poor nations plead that "trade, not aid" is their surest path to economic growth.

comparative advantage: The ability of a country to produce a specific good at a lower opportunity cost than its trading partners.

import quota: A limit on the quantity of a good that may be imported in a given time period.

THE ECONOMY TOMORROW

UNLEASHING ENTREPRENEURSHIP

The traditional approach to economic development emphasizes the potential for government policy to reallocate resources and increase capital investment. External financing of capital investment was always at or near the top of the policy agenda (see World View "Jeffrey Sachs: Big Money, Big Plans"). This approach has been criticized for neglecting the power of people and markets.

One of the most influential critics is the Peruvian economist Hernando de Soto. When he returned to his native Peru after years of commercial success in Europe, he was struck by the dichot-

Analysis: Markets exist but struggle in poor nations.
©Lissa Harrison RF

omy in his country. The "official" economy was mired in bureaucratic red tape and stagnant. Most of the vitality of the Peruvian economy was contained in the unofficial "underground" economy. The underground economy included trade in drugs but was overwhelmingly oriented to meeting the everyday demands of Peruvian consumers and households. The underground economy wasn't hidden from view; it flourished on the streets, in outdoor markets, and in transport services. The only thing that forced this thriving economy underground was the failure of the government to recognize it and give it legitimate status. Government restrictions on prices, business activities, finance, and trade—a slew of inequality traps—forced entrepreneurs to operate "underground."

De Soto concluded that countries like Peru could grow more quickly if governments encouraged rather than suppressed these entrepreneurial resources. In his best-selling

Continued

book *The Other Path,* he urged poor countries to refocus their development policies. This "other path" entails improving the business climate by

- Reducing bureaucratic barriers to free enterprise.
- Spreading private ownership.
- Developing and enforcing legal safeguards for property, income, and wealth.
- Developing infrastructure that facilitates business activity.

Yunus's "microloans" (see World View "Muhammad Yunus: Microloans") would also fit comfortably on this other path.

De Soto's book has been translated into several languages and has encouraged market-oriented reforms in Peru, Argentina, Mexico, Russia, Vietnam, and elsewhere. In India the government is drastically reducing both regulation and taxes to pursue De Soto's other path. The basic message of his other path is that poor nations should exploit the one resource that is abundant in even the poorest countries—entrepreneurship.

SUMMARY

- Definitions of "poverty" are culturally based. Poverty in the United States is defined largely in *relative* terms, whereas global poverty is tied more to *absolute* levels of subsistence. **LO37-1**
- About 13 percent of the U.S. population (more than 40 million people) are officially counted as poor. Poor people in America suffer from *relative* deprivation, not *absolute* deprivation, as in global poverty. **LO37-1**
- Global poverty thresholds are about one-tenth of U.S. standards. "Extreme" poverty is defined as less than $1.90 per day per person; "severe" poverty is less than $3.10 per day (inflation adjusted). **LO37-1**
- 800 million people around the world are in extreme poverty; 2 billion are in severe poverty. In low-income nations global poverty rates are as high as 70–90 percent. **LO37-2**
- The United Nations' Millennium Poverty Goal is to eliminate severe poverty by 2030. **LO37-3**

- Redistribution of incomes *within* poor nations doesn't have much potential for reducing poverty, given their low *average* incomes. *Across*-nation redistributions (e.g., foreign aid) can make a small dent, however. **LO37-3**
- Economic growth is the key to global poverty reduction. Many poor nations are held back by undeveloped human capital, primitive infrastructure, and subsistence agriculture. To grow more quickly, they need to meet basic human needs (health and education), increase agricultural productivity, and encourage investment. **LO37-3**
- To move into sustained economic growth, poor nations need capital investment and institutional reforms that promote both equity and entrepreneurship. **LO37-3**
- Poor nations also need "trade, not aid"—that is, access to rich nation markets, particularly in farm products. **LO37-3**

Key Terms

poverty threshold (U.S.)	UN and World Bank Poverty Goal	investment rate
poverty rate	Millennium Aid Goal	microfinance
in-kind transfers	economic growth	productivity
extreme poverty (world)	human capital	comparative advantage
severe poverty (world)	inequality trap	import quota

Questions for Discussion

1. Why should Americans care about extreme poverty in Haiti, Ethiopia, or Bangladesh? **LO37-2**
2. If you had only $17 to spend per day (the U.S. poverty threshold), how would you spend it? What if you had only $1.90 a day (the World Bank "extreme poverty" threshold)? **LO37-1**
3. If a poor nation must choose between building an airport, some schools, or a steel plant, which one should it choose? Why? **LO37-3**
4. How do more children per family either restrain or expand income-earning potential? **LO37-3**

5. Are property rights a prerequisite for economic growth? Explain.   **LO37-3**

6. How do unequal rights for women affect economic growth?   **LO37-3**

7. How does microfinance alter prospects for economic growth? The distribution of political power?   **LO37-3**

8. Can poor nations develop without substantial increases in agricultural productivity? (See Figure 37.2.) How?   **LO37-3**

9. Would you invest in Cambodia or Kenya on the basis of the information in Figure 37.5?   **LO37-3**

10. Why do economists put so much emphasis on entrepreneurship? How can poor nations encourage it?   **LO37-3**

11. How do nations expect nationalization of basic industries to foster economic growth?   **LO37-3**

12. If economic growth reduced poverty but widened inequalities, would it still be desirable?   **LO37-3**

13. What market failure does Bill Gates (World View "The Way We Give") cite as the motivation for global philanthropy?   **LO37-3**

PROBLEMS FOR CHAPTER 37

LO37-1 1. The World Bank's threshold for "extreme" poverty is $1.90 per person per day.
- (*a*) How much *annual* income does this imply for a family of four?
- (*b*) What portion of the official U.S. poverty threshold (roughly $25,000 for a family of four) is met by the World Bank's measure?

LO37-2 2. There are 2 billion people in "severe" poverty with less than $3.10 of income per day.
- (*a*) What is the maximum *combined* income of this "severely" poor population?
- (*b*) What percentage of the world's *total* income (roughly $85 trillion) does this represent?

LO37-2 3. In Namibia,
- (*a*) What percentage of total output is received by the richest 10 percent of households? (See World View "Glaring Inequalities.")
- (*b*) How much output did this share amount to in 2017, when Namibia's GDP was $15 billion?
- (*c*) With a total population of 2.5 million, what was the implied per capita income of
    - (*i*) The richest 10 percent of the population?
    - (*ii*) The remaining 90 percent?

LO37-3 4. (*a*) How much foreign aid did the United States provide in 2014? (See Table 37.2.)
- (*b*) How much more is required to satisfy the UN's Millennium Aid Goal if U.S. GDP was $16.8 trillion?

LO37-3 5. If the 24 industrialized nations were to satisfy the UN's Millennium Aid Goal, how much *more* foreign aid would they give annually? (See Table 37.2.)

LO37-3 6. According to Table 37.3, how many years will it take for per capita GDP to double in
- (*a*) China?
- (*b*) Libya?
- (*c*) Zimbabwe?

LO37-3 7. According to World View "The Way We Give,"
- (*a*) How much money is spent annually to combat baldness?
- (*b*) How much medical care would that money buy for each child who dies from malaria each year?

LO37-3 8. Foreign aid to poor nations amounted to $20 per year per person. What percentage did this aid cover of
- (*a*) The extreme poverty annual budget?
- (*b*) The severe poverty annual budget?

LO37-3 9. The Economy Tomorrow: Identify the four key paths identified by De Soto to improve business climate in less developed countries.

A

absolute advantage: The ability of a country to produce a specific good with fewer resources (per unit of output) than other countries.

acreage set-aside: Land withdrawn from production as part of policy to increase crop prices.

AD excess: The amount by which aggregate demand must be reduced to achieve full-employment equilibrium after allowing for price-level changes.

AD shortfall: The amount of additional aggregate demand needed to achieve full employment after allowing for price-level changes.

adjustable-rate mortgage (ARM): A mortgage (home loan) that adjusts the nominal interest rate to changing rates of inflation.

aggregate demand (AD): The total quantity of output (real GDP) demanded at alternative price levels in a given time period, *ceteris paribus*.

aggregate expenditure: The rate of total expenditure desired at alternative levels of income, *ceteris paribus*.

aggregate supply (AS): The total quantity of output (real GDP) producers are willing and able to supply at alternative price levels in a given time period, *ceteris paribus*.

antitrust: Government intervention to alter market structure or prevent abuse of market power.

appreciation: A rise in the price of one currency relative to another.

arithmetic growth: An increase in quantity by a constant amount each year.

asset: Anything having exchange value in the marketplace; wealth.

automatic stabilizer: Federal expenditure or revenue item that automatically responds countercyclically to changes in national income, like unemployment benefits and income taxes.

autonomous consumption: Consumer spending not dependent on current income.

average fixed cost (AFC): Total fixed cost divided by the quantity produced in a given time period.

average propensity to consume (APC): Total consumption in a given period divided by total disposable income.

average total cost (ATC): Total cost divided by the quantity produced in a given time period.

B

average variable cost (AVC): Total variable cost divided by the quantity produced in a given time period.

balance of payments: A summary record of a country's international economic transactions in a given period of time.

balance-of-payments deficit: An excess demand for foreign currency at current exchange rates.

balance-of-payments surplus: An excess demand for domestic currency at current exchange rates.

bank reserves: Assets held by a bank to fulfill its deposit obligations.

barriers to entry: Obstacles such as patents that make it difficult or impossible for would-be producers to enter a particular market.

barter: The direct exchange of one good for another, without the use of money.

base year: The year used for comparative analysis; the basis for indexing price changes.

bilateral monopoly: A market with only one buyer (a monopsonist) and one seller (a monopolist).

bond: A certificate acknowledging a debt and the amount of interest to be paid each year until repayment; an IOU.

bracket creep: The movement of taxpayers into higher tax brackets (rates) as nominal incomes grow.

breakeven level of income: The income level at which welfare eligibility ceases.

budget constraint: A line depicting all combinations of goods that are affordable with a given income and given prices.

budget deficit: The amount by which government spending exceeds government revenue in a given time period.

budget surplus: An excess of government revenues over government expenditures in a given time period.

business cycle: Alternating periods of economic growth and contraction.

C

capital: Final goods produced for use in the production of other goods, such as equipment and structures.

capital gain: An increase in the market value of an asset.

capital gains tax: A tax levied on the profit from the sale of property.

capital-intensive: Production processes that use a high ratio of capital to labor inputs.

cartel: A group of firms with an explicit, formal agreement to fix prices and output shares in a particular market.

cash transfers: Income transfers that entail direct cash payments to recipients, such as Social Security, welfare, and unemployment benefits.

ceteris paribus: The assumption of nothing else changing.

closed economy: A nation that doesn't engage in international trade.

collective bargaining: Direct negotiations between employers and unions to determine labor market outcomes.

comparative advantage: The ability of a country to produce a specific good at a lower opportunity cost than its trading partners.

competitive firm: A firm without market power, with no ability to alter the market price of the goods it produces.

competitive market: A market in which no buyer or seller has market power.

complementary goods: Goods frequently consumed in combination; when the price of good *x* rises, the demand for good *y* falls, *ceteris paribus*.

concentration ratio: The proportion of total industry output produced by the largest firms (usually the four largest).

constant returns to scale: Increases in plant size do not affect minimum average cost; minimum per-unit costs are identical for small plants and large plants.

Consumer Price Index (CPI): A measure (index) of changes in the average price of consumer goods and services.

consumer surplus: The difference between the maximum price a person is willing to pay and the price paid.

consumption: Expenditure by consumers on final goods and services.

consumption function: A mathematical relationship indicating the rate of desired consumer spending at various income levels.

consumption possibilities: The alternative combinations of goods and services that a country could consume in a given time period.

contestable market: An imperfectly competitive industry subject to potential entry if prices or profits increase.

core inflation rate: Changes in the CPI, excluding food and energy prices.

corporate stock: Shares of ownership in a corporation.

corporation: A business organization having a continuous existence independent of its members (owners) and power and liabilities distinct from those of its members.

cost efficiency: The amount of output associated with an additional dollar spent on input; the MPP of an input divided by its price (cost).

cost-of-living adjustment (COLA): Automatic adjustments of nominal income to the rate of inflation.

coupon rate: Interest rate set for a bond at time of issuance.

cross-price elasticity of demand: Percentage change in the quantity demanded of *X* divided by the percentage change in the price of *Y*.

cross-subsidization: Use of high prices and profits on one product to subsidize low prices on another product.

crowdfunding: The financing of a project through individual contributions from a large number of people, typically via an Internet platform.

crowding in: An increase in private sector borrowing (and spending) caused by decreased government borrowing.

crowding out: A reduction in private sector borrowing (and spending) caused by increased government borrowing.

current yield: The rate of return on a bond; the annual interest payment divided by the bond's price.

cyclical deficit: That portion of the budget deficit attributable to unemployment or inflation.

cyclical unemployment: Unemployment attributable to a lack of job vacancies—that is, to an inadequate level of aggregate demand.

D

debt ceiling: An explicit, legislated limit on the amount of outstanding national debt.

debt service: The interest required to be paid each year on outstanding debt.

default: Failure to make scheduled payments of interest or principal on a bond.

deficit ceiling: An explicit, legislated limitation on the size of the budget deficit.

deficit spending: The use of borrowed funds to finance government expenditures that exceed tax revenues.

deflation: A decrease in the average level of prices of goods and services.

demand: The willingness and ability to buy specific quantities of a good at alternative prices in a given time period, *ceteris paribus.*

demand curve: A curve describing the quantities of a good a consumer is willing and able to buy at alternative prices in a given time period, *ceteris paribus.*

demand for labor: The quantities of labor employers are willing and able to hire at alternative wage rates in a given time period, *ceteris paribus.*

demand for money: The quantities of money people are willing and able to hold at alternative interest rates, *ceteris paribus.*

demand-pull inflation: An increase in the price level initiated by excessive aggregate demand.

demand schedule: A table showing the quantities of a good a consumer is willing and able to buy at alternative prices in a given time period, *ceteris paribus.*

deposit creation: The creation of transactions deposits by bank lending.

depreciation: The consumption of capital in the production process; the wearing out of plant and equipment.

depreciation (currency): A fall in the price of one currency relative to another.

derived demand: The demand for labor and other factors of production results from (depends on) the demand for final goods and services produced by these factors.

devaluation: An abrupt depreciation of a currency whose value was fixed or managed by the government.

discount rate: The rate of interest the Federal Reserve charges for lending reserves to private banks.

discounting: Federal Reserve lending of reserves to private banks.

discouraged worker: An individual who isn't actively seeking employment but would look for or accept a job if one were available.

discretionary fiscal spending: Those elements of the federal budget not determined by past legislative or executive commitments.

disposable income (DI): After-tax income of households; personal income less personal taxes.

dissaving: Consumption expenditure in excess of disposable income; a negative saving flow.

dividend: Amount of corporate profits paid out for each share of stock.

dumping: The sale of goods in export markets at prices below domestic prices.

E

economic cost: The value of all resources used to produce a good or service; opportunity cost.

economic growth: An increase in output (real GDP); an expansion of production possibilities.

economic profit: The difference between total revenues and total economic costs.

economics: The study of how best to allocate scarce resources among competing uses.

economies of scale: Reductions in minimum average costs that come about through increases in the size (scale) of plant and equipment.

effective tax rate: Taxes paid divided by total income.

efficiency: Maximum output of a good from the resources used in production.

efficiency decision: The choice of a production process for any given rate of output.

elasticity of labor supply: The percentage change in the quantity of labor supplied divided by the percentage change in wage rate.

embargo: A prohibition on exports or imports.

emission charge: A fee imposed on polluters, based on the quantity of pollution.

employment rate: The percentage of the adult population that is employed.

employment targeting: The use of an unemployment-rate threshold (6.5 percent) to signal the need for monetary stimulus.

entrepreneurship: The assembling of resources to produce new or improved products and technologies.

equation of exchange: Money supply (*M*) times velocity of circulation (*V*) equals level of aggregate spending (*P* × *Q*).

equilibrium (macro): The combination of price level and real output that is compatible with both aggregate demand and aggregate supply.

equilibrium GDP: The value of total output (real GDP) produced at macro equilibrium (AS = AD).

equilibrium price: The price at which the quantity of a good demanded in a given time period equals the quantity supplied.

equilibrium rate of interest: The interest rate at which the quantity of money demanded in a given time period equals the quantity of money supplied.

equilibrium wage: The wage rate at which the quantity of labor supplied in a given time period equals the quantity of labor demanded.

excess reserves: Bank reserves in excess of required reserves.

exchange rate: The price of one country's currency expressed in terms of another's; the domestic price of a foreign currency.

expected value: The probable value of a future payment, including the risk of nonpayment.

expenditure equilibrium: The rate of output at which desired spending equals the value of output.

explicit costs: A payment made for the use of a resource.

exports: Goods and services sold to foreign buyers.

external costs: Costs of a market activity borne by a third party; the difference between the social and private costs of a market activity.

external debt: U.S. government debt (Treasury bonds) held by foreign households and institutions.

externalities: Costs (or benefits) of a market activity borne by a third party; the difference between the social and private costs (benefits) of a market activity.

extreme poverty (world): World Bank income standard of less than $1.90 per day per person (inflation adjusted).

F

factor market: Any place where factors of production (e.g., land, labor, capital) are bought and sold.

factors of production: Resource inputs used to produce goods and services, e.g., land, labor, capital, entrepreneurship.

federal funds rate: The interest rate for interbank reserve loans.

financial intermediary: Institution (e.g., a bank or the stock market) that makes savings available to dissavers (e.g., investors).

fine-tuning: Adjustments in economic policy designed to counteract small changes in economic outcomes; continuous responses to changing economic conditions.

fiscal policy: The use of government taxes and spending to alter macroeconomic outcomes.

fiscal restraint: Tax hikes or spending cuts intended to reduce (shift) aggregate demand.

fiscal stimulus: Tax cuts or spending hikes intended to increase (shift) aggregate demand.

fiscal year (FY): The 12-month period used for accounting purposes; begins October 1 for the federal government.

fixed costs: Costs of production that don't change when the rate of output is altered, such as the cost of basic plants and equipment.

flat tax: A single-rate tax system.

flexible exchange rates: A system in which exchange rates are permitted to vary with market supply-and-demand conditions; floating exchange rates.

foreign exchange markets: Places where foreign currencies are bought and sold.

foreign exchange reserves: Holdings of foreign currencies by official government agencies, usually the central bank or treasury.

free rider: An individual who reaps direct benefits from someone else's purchase (consumption) of a public good.

frictional unemployment: Brief periods of unemployment experienced by people moving between jobs or into the labor market.

full employment: The lowest rate of unemployment compatible with price stability, variously estimated at between 4 percent and 6 percent unemployment.

full-employment GDP: The value of total market output (real GDP) produced at full employment.

G

game theory: The study of decision making in situations where strategic interaction (moves and countermoves) occurs between rivals.

GDP deflator: A price index that refers to all goods and services included in GDP.

GDP per capita: Total GDP divided by total population; average GDP.

geometric growth: An increase in quantity by a constant proportion each year.

Gini coefficient: A mathematical summary of inequality based on the Lorenz curve.

gold reserves: Stocks of gold held by a government to purchase foreign exchange.

gold standard: An agreement by countries to fix the price of their currencies in terms of gold; a mechanism for fixing exchange rates.

government failure: Government intervention that fails to improve economic outcomes.

gross business saving: Depreciation allowances and retained earnings.

gross domestic product (GDP): The total market value of all final goods and services produced within a nation's borders in a given time period.

gross investment: Total investment expenditure in a given time period.

growth rate: Percentage change in real output from one period to another.

growth recession: A period during which real GDP grows but at a rate below the long-term trend of 3 percent.

H

Herfindahl-Hirshman Index (HHI): Measure of industry concentration that accounts for number of firms and size of each.

horizontal equity: Principle that people with equal incomes should pay equal taxes.

human capital: The knowledge and skills possessed by the workforce.

hyperinflation: Inflation rate in excess of 200 percent, lasting at least one year.

I

implicit cost: The value of resources used, for which no direct payment is made.

import quota: A limit on the quantity of a good that may be imported in a given time period.

imports: Goods and services purchased from international sources.

income effect of higher wages: An increased wage rate allows a person to reduce hours worked without losing income.

income elasticity of demand: Percentage change in quantity demanded divided by percentage change in income.

income quintile: One-fifth of the population, rank-ordered by income (e.g., top fifth).

income share: The proportion of total income received by a particular group.

income transfers: Payments to individuals for which no current goods or services are exchanged, such as Social Security, welfare, and unemployment benefits.

indifference curve: A curve depicting alternative combinations of goods that yield equal satisfaction.

indifference map: The set of indifference curves that depicts all possible levels of utility attainable from various combinations of goods.

inequality trap: Institutional barriers that impede human and physical capital investment, particularly by the poorest segments of society.

inferior good: Goods for which demand decreases when income rises.

inflation: An increase in the average level of prices of goods and services.

inflation rate: The annual percentage rate of increase in the average price level; $(\text{Price Level}_{\text{Year 2}} - \text{Price Level}_{\text{Year 1}})/\text{Price Level}_{\text{Year 1}}$.

inflation targeting: The use of an inflation ceiling ("target") to signal the need for monetary-policy adjustments.

inflationary flashpoint: The rate of output at which inflationary pressures intensify; the point on the AS curve where slope increases sharply.

inflationary gap: The amount by which aggregate spending at full employment exceeds full-employment output.

inflationary GDP gap: The amount by which equilibrium GDP exceeds full-employment GDP.

infrastructure: The transportation, communications, education, judicial, and other institutional systems that facilitate market exchanges.

initial public offering (IPO): The first issuance (sale) to the general public of stock in a corporation.

injection: An addition of spending to the circular flow of income.

in-kind income: Goods and services received directly, without payment, in a market transaction.

in-kind transfers: Direct transfers of goods and services rather than cash, such as food stamps, Medicaid benefits, and housing subsidies.

interest rate: The price paid for the use of money.

intermediate goods: Goods or services purchased for use as input in the production of final goods or in services.

internal debt: U.S. government debt (Treasury bonds) held by U.S. households and institutions.

investment: Expenditures on (production of) new plants, equipment, and structures (capital) in a given time period, plus changes in business inventories.

investment decision: The decision to build, buy, or lease plants and equipment; to enter or exit an industry.

investment rate: The percentage of total output (GDP) allocated to the production of new plants, equipment, and structures.

item weight: The percentage of total expenditure spent on a specific product; used to compute inflation indexes.

L

labor force: All persons over age 16 who are either working for pay or actively seeking paid employment.

labor force participation rate: The percentage of the working-age population working or seeking employment.

labor productivity: Amount of output produced by a worker in a given period of time; output per hour (or day, etc.).

labor supply: The willingness and ability to work specific amounts of time at alternative wage rates in a given time period, *ceteris paribus*.

laissez faire: The doctrine of "leave it alone," of nonintervention by government in the market mechanism.

law of demand: The quantity of a good demanded in a given time period increases as its price falls, *ceteris paribus*.

law of diminishing marginal utility: The marginal utility of a good declines as more of it is consumed in a given time period.

law of diminishing returns: The marginal physical product of a variable input declines as more of it is employed with a given quantity of other (fixed) inputs.

law of supply: The quantity of a good supplied in a given time period increases as its price increases, *ceteris paribus*.

leakage: Income not spent directly on domestic output but instead diverted from the circular flow—for example, saving, imports, taxes.

liability: An obligation to make future payment; debt.

liquidity: The ability of an asset to be converted into cash.

liquidity trap: The portion of the money demand curve that is horizontal; people are willing to hold unlimited amounts of money at some (low) interest rate.

loan rate: The implicit price paid by the government for surplus crops taken as collateral for loans to farmers.

long run: A period of time long enough for all inputs to be varied (no fixed costs).

long-run competitive equilibrium: $p = MC = $ minimum ATC.

Lorenz curve: A graphic illustration of the cumulative size distribution of income; contrasts complete equality with the actual distribution of income.

M

macroeconomics: The study of aggregate economic behavior, of the economy as a whole.

managed exchange rates: A system in which governments intervene in foreign exchange markets to limit but not eliminate exchange rate fluctuations; "dirty floats."

marginal cost (MC): The increase in total cost associated with a one-unit increase in production.

marginal cost pricing: The offer (supply) of goods at prices equal to their marginal cost.

marginal factor cost (MFC): The change in total costs that results from a one-unit increase in the quantity of a factor employed.

marginal physical product (MPP): The change in total output associated with one additional unit of input.

marginal propensity to consume (MPC): The fraction of each additional (marginal) dollar of disposable income spent on consumption; the change in consumption divided by the change in disposable income.

marginal propensity to save (MPS): The fraction of each additional (marginal) dollar of disposable income not spent on consumption; 1 − MPC.

marginal rate of substitution: The rate at which a consumer is willing to exchange one good for another; the relative marginal utilities of two goods.

marginal revenue (MR): The change in total revenue that results from a one-unit increase in the quantity sold.

marginal revenue product (MRP): The change in total revenue associated with one additional unit of input.

marginal tax rate: The tax rate imposed on the last (marginal) dollar of income.

marginal utility: The change in total utility obtained by consuming one additional (marginal) unit of a good or service.

marginal wage: The change in total wages paid associated with a one-unit increase in the quantity of labor employed.

market demand: The total quantities of a good or service people are willing and able to buy at alternative prices in a given time period; the sum of individual demands.

market failure: An imperfection in the market mechanism that prevents optimal outcomes.

market mechanism: The use of market prices and sales to signal desired outputs (or resource allocations).

market power: The ability to alter the market price of a good or service.

market share: The percentage of total market output produced by a single firm.

market shortage: The amount by which the quantity demanded exceeds the quantity supplied at a given price; excess demand.

market structure: The number and relative size of firms in an industry.

market supply: The total quantities of a good that sellers are willing and able to sell at alternative prices in a given time period, *ceteris paribus*.

market supply of labor: The total quantity of labor that workers are willing and able to supply at alternative wage rates in a given time period, *ceteris paribus*.

market surplus: The amount by which the quantity supplied exceeds the quantity demanded at a given price; excess supply.

merit good: A good or service society deems everyone is entitled to some minimal quantity of.

microeconomics: The study of individual behavior in the economy, of the components of the larger economy.

microfinance: The granting of small ("micro"), unsecured loans to small businesses and entrepreneurs.

Millennium Aid Goal: United Nations goal of raising foreign aid levels to 0.7 percent of donor-country GDP.

misery index: The sum of inflation and unemployment rates.

mixed economy: An economy that uses both market signals and government directives to allocate goods and resources.

monetary policy: The use of money and credit controls to influence macroeconomic outcomes.

money: Anything generally accepted as a medium of exchange.

money illusion: The use of nominal dollars rather than real dollars to gauge changes in one's income or wealth.

money multiplier: The number of deposit (loan) dollars that the banking system can create from $1 of excess reserves; equal to 1 ÷ required reserve ratio.

money supply (M1): Currency held by the public, plus balances in transactions accounts.

money supply (M2): M1 plus balances in most savings accounts and money market funds.

monopolistic competition: A market in which many firms produce similar goods or services but each maintains some independent control of its own price.

monopoly: A firm that produces the entire market supply of a particular good or service.

monopsony: A market in which there's only one buyer.

moral hazard: An incentive to engage in undesirable behavior.

multiplier: The multiple by which an initial change in aggregate spending will alter total expenditure after an infinite number of spending cycles; 1/(1 − MPC).

N

national debt: Accumulated debt of the federal government.

national income (NI): Total income earned by current factors of production: GDP less depreciation and indirect business taxes, plus net foreign factor income.

national income accounting: The measurement of aggregate economic activity, particularly national income and its components.

natural monopoly: An industry in which one firm can achieve economies of scale over the entire range of market supply.

natural rate of unemployment: The long-term rate of unemployment determined by structural forces in labor and product markets.

net domestic product (NDP): GDP less depreciation.

net exports: The value of exports minus the value of imports: (X − M).

net investment: Gross investment less depreciation.

nominal GDP: The value of final output produced in a given period, measured in the prices of that period (current prices).

nominal income: The amount of money income received in a given time period, measured in current dollars.

nominal tax rate: Taxes paid divided by taxable income.

normal good: Good for which demand increases when income rises.

normal profit: The opportunity cost of capital; zero economic profit.

O

Okun's law: One percent more unemployment is estimated to equal 2 percent less output.

oligopolist: One of the dominant firms in an oligopoly.

oligopoly: A market in which a few firms produce all or most of the market supply of a particular good or service.

open economy: A nation that engages in international trade.

open market operations: Federal Reserve purchases and sales of government bonds for the purpose of altering bank reserves.

opportunity cost: The most desired goods or services that are forgone in order to obtain something else.

opportunity wage: The highest wage an individual would earn in his or her best alternative job.

optimal consumption: The mix of consumer purchases that maximizes the utility attainable from available income.

optimal mix of output: The most desirable combination of output attainable with existing resources, technology, and social values.

optimal rate of pollution: The rate of pollution that occurs when the marginal social benefit of pollution control equals its marginal social cost.

outsourcing: The relocation of production to foreign countries.

P

par value: The face value of a bond; the amount to be repaid when the bond is due.

parity: The relative price of farm products in the period 1910–1914.

payoff matrix: A table showing the risks and rewards of alternative decision options.

per capita GDP: The dollar value of GDP divided by total population; average GDP.

perfect competition: A market in which no buyer or seller has market power.

personal income (PI): Income received by households before payment of personal taxes.

Phillips curve: A historical (inverse) relationship between the rate of unemployment and the rate of inflation; commonly expresses a trade-off between the two.

portfolio decision: The choice of how (where) to hold idle funds.

poverty gap: The shortfall between actual income and the poverty threshold.

poverty rate: Percentage of the population counted as poor.

poverty threshold (U.S.): Annual income of less than $24,600 for a family of four (2016).

precautionary demand for money: Money held for unexpected market transactions or for emergencies.

predatory pricing: Temporary price reductions designed to alter market shares or drive out competition.

present discounted value (PDV): The value today of future payments, adjusted for interest accrual.

price ceiling: An upper limit imposed on the price of a good.

price discrimination: The sale of an individual good at different prices to different consumers.

price/earnings (P/E) ratio: The price of a stock share divided by earnings (profit) per share.

price elasticity of demand: The percentage change in quantity demanded divided by the percentage change in price.

price elasticity of supply: The percentage change in quantity supplied divided by the percentage change in price.

price-fixing: Explicit agreements among producers regarding the price(s) at which a good is to be sold.

price floor: Lower limit set for the price of a good.

price leadership: An oligopolistic pricing pattern that allows one firm to establish the (market) price for all firms in the industry.

price stability: The absence of significant changes in the average price level; officially defined as a rate of inflation of less than 3 percent.

private costs: The costs of an economic activity directly borne by the immediate producer or consumer (excluding externalities).

private good: A good or service whose consumption by one person excludes consumption by others.

product differentiation: Features that make one product appear different from competing products in the same market.

product market: Any place where finished goods and services (products) are bought and sold.

production decision: The selection of the short-run rate of output (with existing plants and equipment).

production function: A technological relationship expressing the maximum quantity of a good attainable from different combinations of factor inputs.

production possibilities: The alternative combinations of final goods and services that could be produced in a given period with all available resources and technology.

production process: A specific combination of resources used to produce a good or service.

productivity: Output per unit of input—for example, output per labor-hour.

profit: The difference between total revenue and total cost.

profit-maximization rule: Produce at that rate of output where marginal revenue equals marginal cost.

profit per unit: Total profit divided by the quantity produced in a given time period; price minus average total cost.

progressive tax: A tax system in which tax rates rise as incomes rise.

proportional tax: A tax that levies the same rate on every dollar of income.

public choice: Theory of public sector behavior emphasizing rational self-interest of decision makers and voters.

public good: A good or service whose consumption by one person does not exclude consumption by others.

Q

quota: A limit on the quantity of a good that may be imported in a given time period.

R

rational expectations: Hypothesis that people's spending decisions are based on all available information, including the anticipated effects of government intervention.

real GDP: The value of final output produced in a given period, adjusted for changing prices.

real income: Income in constant dollars; nominal income adjusted for inflation.

real interest rate: The nominal interest rate minus the anticipated inflation rate.

recession: A decline in total output (real GDP) for two or more consecutive quarters.

recessionary gap: The amount by which aggregate spending at full employment falls short of full-employment output.

recessionary GDP gap: The amount by which equilibrium GDP falls short of full-employment GDP.

reference price: Government-guaranteed price floor for specific agricultural commodities.

refinancing: The issuance of new debt in payment of debt issued earlier.

regressive tax: A tax system in which tax rates fall as incomes rise.

regulation: Government intervention to alter the behavior of firms—for example, in pricing, output, or advertising.

relative price: The price of one good in comparison with the price of other goods.

required reserves: The minimum amount of reserves a bank is required to hold; equal to required reserve ratio times transactions deposits.

reserve ratio: The ratio of a bank's reserves to its total transactions deposits.

retained earnings: Amount of corporate profits not paid out in dividends.

risk premium: The difference in rates of return on risky (uncertain) and safe (certain) investments.

S

saving: That part of disposable income not spent on current consumption; disposable income less consumption.

Say's law: Supply creates its own demand.

scarcity: Lack of enough resources to satisfy all desired uses of those resources.

seasonal unemployment: Unemployment due to seasonal changes in employment or labor supply.

severe poverty (world): World Bank income standard of $3.10 per day per person (inflation adjusted).

shift in demand: A change in the quantity demanded at any (every) price.

short run: The period in which the quantity (and quality) of some inputs can't be changed.

short-run competitive equilibrium: $p = MC$.

shutdown point: The rate of output where price equals minimum AVC.

size distribution of income: The way total personal income is divided up among households or income classes.

social costs: The full resource costs of an economic activity, including externalities.

social insurance programs: Event-conditioned income transfers intended to reduce the costs of specific problems, such as Social Security and unemployment insurance.

speculative demand for money: Money held for speculative purposes, for later financial opportunities.

stagflation: The simultaneous occurrence of substantial unemployment and inflation.

structural deficit: Federal revenues at full employment minus expenditures at full employment under prevailing fiscal policy.

structural unemployment: Unemployment caused by a mismatch between the skills (or location) of job seekers and the requirements (or location) of available jobs.

substitute goods: Goods that substitute for each other; when the price of good *x* rises,

the demand for good *y* increases, *ceteris paribus.*

substitution effect of higher wages: An increased wage rate encourages people to work more hours (to substitute labor for leisure).

supply: The ability and willingness to sell (produce) specific quantities of a good at alternative prices in a given time period, *ceteris paribus.*

supply curve: A curve describing the quantities of a good a producer is willing and able to sell (produce) at alternative prices in a given time period, *ceteris paribus.*

supply-side policy: The use of tax incentives, (de)regulation, and other mechanisms to increase the ability and willingness to produce goods and services.

T

T-accounts: The accounting ledgers used by banks to track assets and liabilities.

target efficiency: The percentage of income transfers that go to the intended recipients and purposes.

tariff: A tax (duty) imposed on imported goods.

tax base: The amount of income or property directly subject to nominal tax rates.

tax elasticity of labor supply: The percentage change in quantity of labor supplied divided by the percentage change in tax rates.

tax elasticity of supply: The percentage change in quantity supplied divided by the percentage change in tax rates.

tax incidence: Distribution of the real burden of a tax.

tax rebate: A lump-sum refund of taxes paid.

terms of trade: The rate at which goods are exchanged; the amount of good A given up for good B in trade.

total cost: The market value of all resources used to produce a good or service.

total revenue: The price of a product multiplied by the quantity sold in a given time period: $p \times q$.

total utility: The amount of satisfaction obtained from entire consumption of a product.

trade deficit: The amount by which the value of imports exceeds the value of exports in a given time period (negative net exports).

trade surplus: The amount by which the value of exports exceeds the value of imports in a given time period (positive net exports).

transactions account: A bank account that permits direct payment to a third party—for example, with a check or debit card.

transactions demand for money: Money held for the purpose of making everyday market purchases.

transfer payments: Payments to individuals for which no current goods or services are exchanged, like Social Security, welfare, and unemployment benefits.

Treasury bonds: Promissory notes (IOUs) issued by the U.S. Treasury.

U

UN and World Bank Poverty Goal: UN goal of eliminating extreme poverty by 2030.

underemployment: People seeking full-time paid employment who work only part-time or are employed at jobs below their capability.

unemployment: The inability of labor force participants to find jobs.

unemployment rate: The proportion of the labor force that is unemployed.

union shop: An employment setting in which all workers must join the union within 30 days after being employed.

unionization rate: The percentage of the labor force belonging to a union.

unit labor cost: Hourly wage rate divided by output per labor-hour.

utility: The pleasure or satisfaction obtained from a good or service.

V

value added: The increase in the market value of a product that takes place at each stage of the production process.

variable costs: Costs of production that change when the rate of output is altered, such as labor and material costs.

velocity of money (V): The number of times per year, on average, that a dollar is used to purchase final goods and services; $PQ \div M$.

vertical equity: Principle that people with higher incomes should pay more taxes.

voluntary restraint agreement (VRA): An agreement to reduce the volume of trade in a specific good; a "voluntary" quota.

W

wage replacement rate: The percentage of base wages paid out in benefits.

wealth: The market value of assets.

wealth effect: A change in consumer spending caused by a change in the value of owned assets.

welfare programs: Means-tested income transfer programs, such as welfare and food stamps.

Y

yield: The rate of return on a bond; the annual interest payment divided by the bond's price.

INDEX

Note: **Bold** page numbers indicate definitions; page numbers followed by *n* indicate material in notes.

NOMINAL GROSS DOMESTIC PRODUCT, Selected Years, 1929–2016 (billions of dollars)

| Year | GDP | Personal Consumption Expenditures Total | Gross Private Domestic Investment Total | Net Exports | | | Government Purchases | | | | State and Local | Percent Change from Prior Year GDP |
| | | | | Net | Exports | Imports | Total | Federal | | | | |
								Total	National Defense	Non-Defense		
1929	103	77	16	0	6	6	8	1	—	—	7	—
1930	90	70	10	0	4	4	9	1	—	—	7	−12.4
1931	75	60	5	0	2	2	9	1	—	—	7	−18.2
1932	58	48	1	0	2	1	8	1	—	—	6	−23.5
1933	55	45	1	0	2	1	7	2	—	—	5	−4.1
1934	65	61	3	0	2	2	9	3	—	—	6	17.1
1935	72	55	6	−2	2	3	10	3	—	—	6	11.1
1936	82	82	8	−2	3	3	12	5	—	—	6	14.4
1937	90	68	12	0	4	4	11	4	—	—	7	9.8
1938	84	64	7	1	3	2	12	5	—	—	7	−6.5
1939	90	67	9	1	3	3	13	5	1	4	8	7.0
1940	100	71	13	1	4	3	13	8	2	3	7	10.2
1941	125	81	18	1	5	4	24	17	13	3	7	25.0
1942	158	88	10	0	4	4	58	52	49	2	7	28.8
1943	192	99	6	−3	4	7	88	61	60	1	7	21.3
1944	211	108	7	−2	4	7	96	89	58	1	7	9.7
1945	213	119	10	−1	6	7	83	75	74	1	7	1.0
1946	211	144	31	7	14	7	29	19	16	2	9	−.8
1947	234	182	36	11	19	8	28	13	10	3	12	10.6
1948	260	173	48	3	13	10	31	16	10	5	14	11.1
1949	259	178	36	5	14	9	38	21	13	7	17	−.4
1980	2,795	1,762	477	−14	278	293	569	245	169	75	324	8.9
1981	3,131	1,944	570	−15	302	317	631	281	197	84	349	12.0
1982	3,259	2,079	516	−20	282	303	684	312	228	84	371	4.1
1983	3,534	2,286	564	−51	277	328	735	344	252	92	391	8.5
1984	3,932	2,498	735	−102	303	405	800	376	283	92	424	11.3
1985	4,213	2,712	736	−114	303	417	878	413	312	101	464	7.1
1986	4,452	2,895	747	−131	320	452	942	438	332	106	503	5.7
1987	4,742	3,105	781	−142	365	507	997	460	351	109	537	6.5
1988	5,108	3,356	821	−106	446	553	1,036	462	355	106	574	7.7
1989	5,489	3,596	872	−80	509	589	1,100	482	363	119	617	7.5
1990	5,803	3,839	846	−78	552	630	1,180	508	374	134	671	5.8
1991	5,995	3,986	803	−27	596	624	1,234	527	383	144	706	3.3
1992	6,337	4,235	848	−33	635	668	1,271	533	376	157	737	5.7
1993	6,657	4,477	932	−65	655	720	1,291	525	362	162	766	5.0
1994	7,072	4,743	1,033	−93	720	814	1,325	519	353	165	806	6.2
1995	7,397	4,975	1,112	−91	812	903	1,369	519	348	170	850	4.6
1996	7,816	5,256	1,209	−96	868	964	1,416	527	354	172	888	5.7
1997	8,304	5,547	1,317	−101	955	1,056	1,468	530	349	181	937	6.2
1998	8,747	5,879	1,438	−159	955	1,115	1,518	530	345	184	987	5.3
1999	9,268	6,282	1,558	−260	991	1,251	1,620	555	360	195	1,065	6.0
2000	9,817	6,739	1,679	−379	1,096	1,475	1,721	578	370	208	1,142	6.5
2001	10,128	7,055	1,646	−367	1,032	1,399	1,825	612	392	220	1,212	3.3
2002	10,469	7,350	1,570	−424	1,005	1,430	1,961	679	437	242	1,281	3.3
2003	10,960	7,703	1,649	−499	1,040	1,540	2,092	756	497	259	1,336	4.9
2004	11,685	8,196	1,889	−615	1,152	1,798	2,217	826	551	275	1,391	6.6
2005	12,422	8,694	2,086	−714	1,312	2,025	2,355	876	588	287	1,480	6.7
2006	13,178	9,207	2,220	−757	1,481	2,238	2,508	932	624	308	1,576	5.8
2007	13,808	9,710	2,130	−708	1,662	2,370	2,675	979	662	317	1,696	4.5
2008	14,291	10,035	2,087	−710	1,849	2,557	2,878	1,080	738	342	1,798	1.7
2009	13,939	9,866	1,547	−392	1,583	518	2,918	1,143	775	368	1,775	−2.0
2010	14,527	10,246	1,795	−517	1,840	562	3,000	1,223	819	404	1,780	3.8
2011	15,518	10,689	2,240	−580	2,106	2,686	3,169	1,304	837	467	1,865	3.7
2012	16,163	11,083	2,479	−568	2,194	2,763	3,169	1,291	818	473	1,878	4.2
2013	16,768	11,484	2,648	−508	2,262	2,770	3,143	1,232	770	462	1,912	3.7
2014	17,393	11,863	2,887	−509	2,375	2,884	3,152	1,219	746	473	1,933	3.7
2015	18,037	12,284	3,057	−522	2,264	2,786	3,218	1,225	732	493	1,933	3.7
2016	18,569	12,758	3,036	−501	2,232	2,734	3,277	1,245	732	512	2,032	2.9

Source: U.S. Department of Commerce.

REAL GROSS DOMESTIC PRODUCT IN CHAIN-WEIGHTED DOLLARS, Selected Decades, 1929–2016 (2009 = 100)

Year	GDP	Personal Consumption Expenditures Total	Gross Private Domestic Investment Total	Exports	Imports	Government Purchases Total	Percent Change from Prior Year GDP
1929	1,057	781	124	41	53	166	—
1930	967	739	84	34	46	183	−8.5
1931	905	716	55	29	40	190	−6.4
1932	788	652	20	22	33	184	−12.9
1933	778	638	27	22	35	178	−1.3
1934	862	683	45	24	35	200	10.8
1935	939	725	79	26	46	206	8.9
1936	1,061	798	99	27	46	239	12.9
1937	1,115	828	122	34	51	229	5.1
1938	1,078	815	84	34	40	247	−3.3
1939	1,164	860	106	36	42	268	8.0
1940	1,266	905	144	40	43	278	8.8
1941	1,490	969	176	41	53	467	17.7
1942	1,772	946	98	27	48	1,054	18.9
1943	2,074	972	61	23	61	1,626	17.0
1944	2,239	1,000	73	25	63	1,826	8.0
1945	2,218	1,061	94	35	67	1,604	−1.0
1946	1,961	1,194	225	75	56	567	−11.6
1947	1,939	1,216	217	85	53	483	−1.1
1948	2,020	1,244	273	67	62	511	4.1
1949	2,009	1,279	211	67	60	566	−0.5
1980	6,450	3,992	881	376	370	1,613	−.2
1981	6,618	4,051	759	381	379	1,628	2.6
1982	6,491	4,108	834	352	375	1,658	−1.9
1983	6,792	4,343	912	343	422	1,723	4.6
1984	7,285	4,572	1,160	370	524	1,783	7.3
1985	7,594	4,812	1,160	383	558	1,904	4.2
1986	7,861	5,014	1,161	412	606	2,008	3.5
1987	8,133	5,184	1,194	457	642	2,067	3.5
1988	8,425	5,401	1,224	531	667	2,095	4.2
1989	8,786	5,558	1,273	593	697	2,155	3.7
1990	8,755	5,673	1,241	645	722	2,224	1.9
1991	8,948	5,686	1,159	688	720	2,251	−.1
1992	9,267	5,897	1,244	735	771	2,262	3.6
1993	9,521	6,101	1,343	759	838	2,242	2.7
1994	9,905	6,338	1,502	827	938	2,246	4.0
1995	10,175	6,528	1,551	912	1,013	2,258	2.7
1996	10,561	6,756	1,687	986	1,101	2,279	3.8
1997	11,035	7,010	1,879	1,104	1,249	2,322	4.5
1998	11,526	7,385	2,058	1,129	1,395	2,371	4.5
1999	12,066	7,776	2,231	1,159	1,536	2,452	4.7
2000	12,560	8,171	2,376	1,258	1,736	2,498	4.1
2001	12,682	8,383	2,231	1,185	1,687	2,592	1.0
2002	12,909	8,599	2,218	1,165	1,749	2,705	1.8
2003	13,271	8,868	2,309	1,185	1,827	2,764	2.8
2004	13,774	9,208	2,511	1,300	2,035	2,808	3.8
2005	14,234	9,532	2,673	1,382	2,164	2,826	3.3
2006	14,614	9,822	2,730	1,507	2,301	2,869	2.7
2007	14,874	10,042	2,644	1,646	2,359	2,914	1.8
2008	14,830	10,007	2,396	1,741	2,299	2,990	−0.3
2009	14,419	9,847	1,898	1,588	1,983	3,089	−2.8
2010	14,784	10,036	2,120	1,777	2,235	3,091	2.5
2011	15,021	10,264	2,230	1,898	2,358	2,997	1.6
2012	15,369	10,450	2,436	1,960	2,413	2,954	2.3
2013	15,710	10,700	2,556	2,020	2,440	2,895	2.2
2014	15,982	10,869	2,734	2,118	2,544	2,833	2.4
2015	16,397	11,215	2,869	2,121	2,661	2,884	2.6
2016	16,662	11,522	2,825	2,128	2,691	2,907	1.6

Source: U.S. Department of Commerce.

CONSUMER PRICE INDEX, 1925–2016 (1982–84=100)

Year	Index (all items)	Percent Change
1925	17.5	3.5
1926	17.7	−1.1
1927	17.4	−2.3
1928	17.1	−1.2
1929	17.1	0.6
1930	16.7	−6.4
1931	15.2	−9.3
1932	13.7	−10.3
1933	13.0	0.8
1934	13.4	1.5
1935	13.7	3.0
1936	13.9	1.4
1937	14.4	2.9
1938	14.1	−2.8
1939	13.9	0.0
1940	14.0	0.7
1941	14.7	9.9
1942	16.3	9.0
1943	17.3	3.0
1944	17.6	2.3
1945	18.0	2.2
1946	19.5	18.1
1947	22.3	8.8
1948	24.1	3.0
1949	23.8	−2.1
1950	24.1	5.9
1951	26.0	6.0
1952	26.5	0.8
1953	26.7	0.7
1954	26.9	−0.7
1955	26.8	0.4
1956	27.2	3.0
1957	28.1	2.9
1958	28.9	1.8
1959	29.1	1.7
1960	29.6	1.4
1961	29.9	0.7
1962	30.2	1.3
1963	30.6	1.6
1964	31.0	1.0
1965	31.5	1.9
1966	32.4	3.5
1967	33.4	3.0
1968	34.8	4.7
1969	36.7	6.2
1970	38.8	5.6
1971	40.5	3.3
1972	41.8	3.4
1973	44.4	8.7
1974	49.3	12.3
1975	53.8	6.9
1976	56.9	4.9
1977	60.6	6.7
1978	65.2	9.0
1979	72.6	13.3
1980	82.4	12.5
1981	90.9	8.9
1982	96.5	3.8
1983	99.6	3.8
1984	103.9	3.9
1985	107.6	3.8
1986	109.6	1.1
1987	113.6	4.4
1988	118.3	4.6
1989	124.0	4.6
1990	130.7	6.1
1991	136.2	3.1
1992	140.3	2.9
1993	144.5	2.7
1994	148.2	2.7
1995	152.4	2.5
1996	156.9	3.3
1997	160.5	1.7
1998	163.0	1.6
1999	166.6	2.7
2000	172.2	3.4
2001	177.1	2.8
2002	179.7	1.6
2003	184.0	2.6

(continued)

Year	Index (all items)	Percent Change
2004	188.9	2.7
2005	195.3	3.4
2006	201.6	3.2
2007	207.3	2.8
2008	215.3	3.8
2009	214.5	−0.4
2010	218.1	1.6
2011	224.9	3.2
2012	229.6	2.1
2013	233.0	1.5
2014	236.7	1.6
2015	237.0	0.1
2016	240.0	1.3

Note: Data beginning 1978 are for all urban consumers: earlier data are for urban wage earners and clerical workers.

Source: U.S. Department of Labor. Bureau of Statistics.

CHAIN-WEIGHTED PRICE DEFLATORS FOR GROSS DOMESTIC PRODUCT, 1970–2016 (2009=100)

Year	Index (all items)	Percent Change
1970	22.8	5.3
1971	24.0	5.0
1972	25.0	4.3
1973	26.4	5.5
1974	28.8	9.0
1975	31.4	9.5
1976	33.2	5.7
1977	35.2	6.4
1978	37.7	7.0
1979	40.8	8.3
1980	44.5	9.1
1981	48.7	9.4
1982	51.6	6.1
1983	53.7	3.9
1984	55.6	3.8
1985	57.3	3.0
1986	58.5	2.2
1987	59.9	2.8
1988	62.0	3.4
1989	64.4	3.8
1990	66.8	3.9
1991	69.0	3.5
1992	70.6	2.4
1993	72.3	2.2
1994	73.9	2.1
1995	75.4	2.1
1996	76.8	1.9
1997	78.1	1.8
1998	78.9	1.1
1999	80.1	1.5
2000	81.9	2.2
2001	83.8	2.3
2002	85.0	1.6
2003	86.7	2.2
2004	89.1	2.8
2005	92.0	3.3
2006	94.8	3.3
2007	97.3	2.9
2008	99.2	2.2
2009	100.0	0.9
2010	101.2	1.0
2011	103.3	2.1
2012	105.2	1.8
2013	106.7	1.4
2014	108.8	2.0
2015	110.0	1.1
2016	111.4	1.3

Source: U.S. Department of Commerce, Bureau of Economic Analysis.

INTEREST RATES, 1929–2016 (percent per annum)

Year	Prime Rate Charged by Banks	Discount Rate, Federal Reserve Bank of New York
1929	5.50–6.00	5.16
1933	1.50–4.00	2.56
1939	1.50	1.00
1940	1.50	1.00
1941	1.50	1.00
1942	1.50	1.00
1943	1.50	1.00
1944	1.50	1.00
1945	1.50	1.00
1946	1.50	1.00
1947	1.50–1.75	1.00
1948	1.75–2.00	1.34
1949	2.00	1.50
1950	2.07	1.59
1951	2.56	1.75
1952	3.00	1.75
1953	3.17	1.99
1954	3.05	1.60
1955	3.16	1.89
1956	3.77	2.77
1957	4.20	3.12
1958	3.83	2.15
1959	4.48	3.36
1960	4.82	3.53
1961	4.50	3.00
1962	4.50	3.00
1963	4.50	3.23
1964	4.50	3.55
1965	4.54	4.04
1966	5.63	4.50
1967	5.61	4.19
1968	6.30	5.16
1969	7.96	5.87
1970	7.91	5.95
1971	5.72	4.88
1972	5.25	4.50
1973	8.03	6.44
1974	10.81	7.83
1975	7.86	6.25
1976	6.84	5.50
1977	6.83	5.46
1978	9.06	7.46
1979	12.67	10.28
1980	15.27	11.77
1981	18.87	13.42
1982	14.86	11.02
1983	10.79	8.50
1984	12.04	8.80
1985	9.93	7.69
1986	8.83	6.33
1987	8.21	5.66
1988	9.32	6.20
1989	10.87	6.93
1990	10.01	6.98
1991	8.46	5.45
1992	6.25	3.25
1993	6.00	3.00
1994	7.15	3.60
1995	8.83	5.21
1996	8.27	5.02
1997	8.44	5.00
1998	8.35	4.92
1999	8.00	4.62
2000	9.23	5.73
2001	6.91	3.40
2002	4.67	1.17
2003	4.12	1.15
2004	4.34	2.34
2005	6.19	4.19
2006	7.96	5.96
2007	8.05	5.86
2008	5.09	2.39
2009	3.25	0.50
2010	3.25	0.75
2011	3.25	0.75
2012	3.25	0.75
2013	3.25	0.75
2014	3.25	0.75
2015	3.26	0.76
2016	3.51	1.01

Source: Board of Governors of the Federal Reserve System.

POPULATION AND THE LABOR FORCE, 1929–2016

Year	Total Population	Civilian Noninstitutional Population	Armed Forces	Civilian Labor Force	Civilian Unemployment	Unemployment Rate	Civilian Labor-Force Participation Rate	Employment Population Ratio
							Civilian	
						Percent		
	Thousands of Persons 14 Years of Age and Over							
1929	121,767	—	—	49,180	1,550	3.2	—	—
1933	125,579	—	—	51,590	12,830	24.9	—	—
1939	130,880	—	—	55,230	9,480	17.2	—	—
1940	132,122	99,840	—	55,640	8,120	14.6	55.7	47.6
1941	133,402	99,900	—	55,910	5,560	9.9	56.0	50.4
1942	134,860	98,640	—	56,410	2,660	4.7	57.2	54.5
1943	136,739	94,640	—	55,540	1,070	1.9	58.7	57.6
1944	138,397	93,220	—	54,630	670	1.2	58.6	57.9
1945	139,928	94,090	—	53,860	1,040	1.9	57.2	56.1
1946	141,389	103,070	—	57,520	2,270	3.9	55.8	53.6
1947	144,126	106,018	—	60,168	2,356	3.9	56.8	54.5
	Thousands of Persons 16 Years of Age and Over							
1947	144,083	101,827	—	59,350	2,311	3.9	58.3	56.0
1948	146,631	103,068	—	60,621	2,276	3.8	58.8	56.6
1949	149,188	103,994	—	61,286	3,637	5.9	58.9	55.4
1950	152,271	104,995	1,169	62,208	3,288	5.3	59.2	56.1
1951	154,878	104,621	2,143	62,017	2,055	3.3	59.2	57.3
1952	157,553	105,231	2,386	62,138	1,883	3.0	59.0	57.3
1953	160,184	107,056	2,231	63,015	1,834	2.9	58.9	57.1
1954	163,026	108,321	2,142	63,643	3,532	5.5	58.8	55.5
1955	165,931	109,683	2,064	65,023	2,352	4.4	59.3	56.7
1956	168,903	110,954	1,965	66,552	2,750	4.1	60.0	57.5
1957	171,984	112,265	1,948	66,929	2,859	4.3	59.6	57.1
1958	174,882	113,727	1,847	67,639	4,602	6.8	59.5	55.4
1959	177,830	115,329	1,788	68,369	3,740	5.5	59.3	56.0
1960	180,671	117,245	1,861	69,628	3,852	5.5	59.4	56.1
1961	183,691	118,771	1,900	70,459	4,714	6.7	59.3	55.4
1962	186,538	120,153	2,061	70,614	3,911	5.5	58.8	55.5
1963	189,242	122,416	2,006	71,833	4,070	5.7	58.7	55.4
1964	191,889	124,485	2,018	73,091	3,786	5.2	58.7	55.7
1965	194,303	126,513	1,946	74,455	3,366	4.5	58.9	56.2
1966	196,560	128,058	2,122	75,770	2,875	3.8	59.2	56.9
1967	198,712	129,874	2,218	77,347	2,975	3.8	59.6	57.3
1968	200,706	132,028	2,253	78,737	2,817	3.6	59.6	57.5
1969	202,677	134,335	2,238	80,734	2,832	3.5	60.1	58.0
1970	205,052	137,085	2,118	82,771	4,093	4.9	60.4	57.4
1971	207,661	140,216	1,973	84,382	5,016	5.9	60.2	56.6
1972	209,896	144,126	1,813	87,034	4,882	5.6	60.4	57.0
1973	211,909	147,096	1,774	89,429	4,365	4.9	60.8	57.8
1974	213,854	150,120	1,721	91,949	5,156	5.6	61.3	57.8
1975	215,973	153,153	1,678	93,775	7,929	8.5	61.2	56.1
1976	218,035	156,150	1,668	96,158	7,406	7.7	61.6	56.8
1977	220,239	159,033	1,656	99,009	6,991	7.1	62.3	57.9
1978	222,585	161,910	1,631	102,251	6,202	6.1	63.2	59.3
1979	225,055	164,863	1,597	104,962	6,137	5.8	63.7	59.9
1980	227,726	167,745	1,604	106,940	7,637	7.1	63.8	59.2
1981	229,966	170,130	1,645	108,670	8,273	7.6	63.9	59.0
1982	232,188	172,271	1,668	110,204	10,678	9.7	64.0	57.8
1983	234,307	174,215	1,676	111,550	10,717	9.6	64.0	57.9
1984	236,348	176,383	1,697	113,544	8,539	7.5	64.4	59.5
1985	238,466	178,206	1,706	115,461	8,312	7.2	64.8	60.1
1986	240,651	180,587	1,706	117,834	8,237	7.0	65.3	60.7
1987	242,804	182,753	1,737	119,865	7,425	6.2	65.6	61.5
1988	245,021	184,613	1,709	121,669	6,701	5.5	65.9	62.3
1989	247,342	186,393	1,668	123,869	6,528	5.3	66.5	63.0
1990	249,924	188,049	1,637	124,787	6,874	5.5	66.4	62.7
1991	252,688	189,765	1,564	125,303	8,426	6.7	66.0	61.6
1992	255,414	191,576	1,566	126,982	9,384	7.4	66.3	61.4
1993	258,137	193,550	1,705	128,040	8,734	6.8	66.2	61.6
1994	260,660	196,814	1,610	131,056	7,996	6.1	66.6	62.5
1995	263,034	198,584	1,533	132,304	7,404	5.6	66.6	62.9
1996	265,453	200,591	1,479	133,943	7,236	5.4	66.8	63.2
1997	267,901	203,133	1,437	136,297	6,739	4.9	67.1	63.8
1998	270,290	205,220	1,401	137,673	6,210	4.5	67.1	64.1
1999	272,945	207,753	1,411	139,368	5,880	4.2	67.1	64.3
2000	282,434	212,573	1,423	142,583	5,692	4.0	67.1	64.4
2001	285,545	215,092	1,387	143,734	6,801	4.7	66.8	63.7
2002	288,600	217,570	1,416	144,863	8,378	5.8	66.6	62.7
2003	291,049	221,168	1,390	146,510	8,774	6.0	66.2	62.3
2004	293,708	223,357	1,411	149,401	8,149	5.5	66.0	62.3
2005	296,639	226,082	1,387	149,320	7,591	5.1	66.0	62.7
2006	299,801	228,815	1,414	151,428	7,001	4.6	66.2	63.1
2007	302,045	231,867	1,380	153,124	7,078	4.6	66.0	63.0
2008	304,906	233,788	1,455	154,287	8,924	5.8	66.0	62.2
2009	307,007	235,801	1,443	154,142	14,265	9.3	65.4	59.3
2010	309,438	237,830	1,430	153,889	14,825	9.6	64.7	58.5
2011	311,663	239,618	1,425	153,617	13,747	8.9	64.1	58.4
2012	313,998	243,284	1,400	154,975	12,506	8.1	63.7	58.6
2013	316,205	245,679	1,370	155,389	11,460	7.4	63.2	58.6
2014	318,563	247,947	1,354	155,922	9,617	6.2	62.9	59.0
2015	320,897	250,801	1,320	157,130	8,296	5.3	62.7	59.3
2016	323,127	253,538	1,301	159,187	7,751	4.9	62.8	59.7

Source: U.S. Department of Labor, Bureau of Labor Statistics.